The Etruscans

Edited by Mario Torelli

Rizzoli
New York

With the Patronage of
the President of the Italian Republic

The exhibition was organized by Palazzo Grassi
in collaboration with the
Ministero per i Beni e le Attività Culturali

First published in the United States of America in 2001 by
Rizzoli International Publications, Inc.
300 Park Avenue South
New York, NY 10010

1st edition Bompiani, November 2000

ISBN: 0-8478-2391-1
LC 00-111213

Printed and bound in Italy

With *The Etruscans* Venice once again hosts an exhibition dedicated to one of the key fields of archaeological research in Italy, an exhibition not only of historical importance but one that will undoubtedly fascinate today's public.

As in the case of the 1966 exhibition, which illustrated the parallel history of the Greeks on our peninsula, this event would never have been possible, given its size and scope, without the collaboration of Palazzo Grassi, one of the world's leading organizers of exhibitions, and the Ministero per i Beni e le Attività Culturali, with its long tradition of exhibition experience and its technical know-how.

Once again we are able to fully appreciate this joint effort on the part of the public and private sectors, together with the role played by the territorial agencies in their campaigns to protect and properly exploit the cultural patrimony of Italy.

It is no mere coincidence that this collaboration is bearing its fruit at the same time that an organizational reform of the Ministry, in line with the general principles established by new laws, goes into effect. Among other things, it will increase state participation in the specific field of archaeology, which, as we all well know, is not only the science which investigates past civilizations through material evidence, but also, and even more importantly, one that studies mankind's continuity and activity on the territory.

The exhibition is also the result of the collaboration of international scholars, renowned foreign institutions in possession of important Etruscan finds, and many local museums and individual collectors. The Ministero per i Beni e le Attività Culturali owes its sincere gratitude and appreciation to each and everyone of them.

Inasmuch as Venice represents an extraordinary world stage, it will be up to international public opinion to make the final judgement, but apart from the inevitable (and indispensable) diversity of opinions, the exhibition of *The Etruscans* will certainly be deemed a milestone in our knowledge of these people, by now so distant in time, but whom we still recognize as being one of the roots of Italian civilization.

Giovanna Melandri

PALAZZOGRASSI

Palazzo Grassi S.p.A.
San Samuele 3231 - Venice

The exhibition on the Etruscans at Palazzo Grassi aims to provide an exhaustive view of the different aspects of Etruscan civilization and to trace through works and documents the long history of those people prior to their integration with Rome.

This objective is being pursued together with a commitment to make sure that the exhibition communicates effectively with the visitors, while at the same time following a rigorous line of interpretation that gives significance and cultural depth to the presentation. Palazzo Grassi has been promoting a program along these lines for some time, and this exhibition is part of it, with the intent of demonstrating how the great civilizations of the past can be both intellectually and emotionally stimulating.

More than any other civilization, that of the Etruscans offers such an opportunity for it continues to provoke thoughts and raise questions, as it has from ancient times, and it is our hope that the exhibition provides answers to these.

An exhibition of this nature would not have been possible without the collaboration of the Ministero per i Beni e le Attività Culturali and its related structures who have co-operated in developing the project and seeing to it that it is of a quality and level of interest that otherwise might not have been attainable.

Essential support has once again come from FIAT which implements a significant part of its cultural projects through Palazzo Grassi.

Cesare Annibaldi

Tomba François, battle scene
ca. 340 B.C.
from Vulci, Ponte Rotto necropolis.
Rome, Eredi Torlonia

following page
Bronze statue known as
"Ombra della sera."
Volterra, Museo Guarnacci

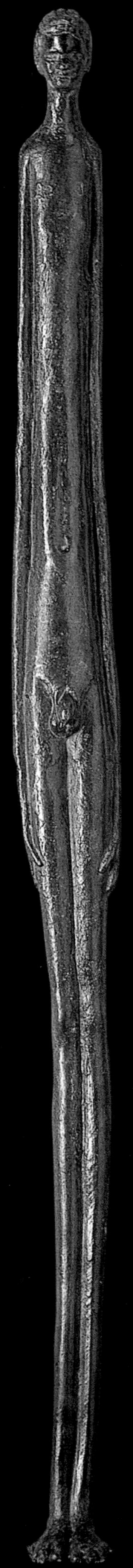

Austria
Vienna, Kunsthistorisches Museum, Antikensammlung

Belgium
Bruxelles, Musées Royaux d'Art et d'Histoire

Denmark
Copenhagen, Nationalmuseet
Copenhagen, Ny Carlsberg Glyptotek

France
Agde, Musée de l'Éphèbe
Beaulieu-sur-Mer, Villa Kérylos
Paris, Bibliothèque Nationale de France
Paris, Musée du Louvre, Département des Antiquités Grecques, Étrusques et Romaines
Paris, Musée du Louvre, Département des Antiquités Orientales
Paris, Musée Rodin, coll. Auguste Rodin
Sigean, Musée des Corbières

Germany
Hamburg, Museum für Kunst und Gewerbe
Berlin, Staatliche Museen zu Berlin, Antikensammlung
Göttingen, Archäologisches Institut der Universität
Hannover, Kestner Museum
Karlsruhe, Badisches Landesmuseum
Munich, Staatliche Antikensammlungen und Glyptothek
Tübingen, Institut für klassische Archäeologie der Eberhard-Karls-Universität
Würzburg, Takuiko Fujita collection, Martin-von-Wagner Museum der Universität

Great Britain
London, The British Museum
Much Hadham, The Henry Moore Foundation
Oxford, Ashmolean Museum

Greece
The Ministry of Culture, Hellenic Republic

Russia
St. Petersburg, The State Hermitage Museum

Switzerland
Schaffhausen, Museum zur Allerheiligen, Erbnöther collection

The Netherlands
Amsterdam, Allard Pierson Museum

United States of America
Columbia, MO, Museum of Art and Archaeology, University of Missouri
Malibu, CA, The John Paul Getty Museum
New York, The Metropolitan Museum of Art
Toledo, OH, Toledo Museum of Art

Vatican City
Vatican City, Musei Vaticani

Italy
Ancona, Museo Archeologico Nazionale delle Marche
Arezzo, Fraternita dei Laici
Arezzo, Museo Archeologico Nazionale
Bettona, Museo Civico
Cerveteri, Museo Archeologico Nazionale - Necropoli della Banditaccia
Chianciano Terme, Museo Civico Archeologico delle Acque
Chiusi, Museo Archeologico Nazionale
Cortona, Museo dell'Accademia Etrusca
Eredi Avv. Ottavio Simioneschi
Fiesole, Museo Civico Archeologico
Florence, Casa Buonarroti
Florence, Museo Archeologico Nazionale
Grosseto, Museo Archeologico e d'Arte della Maremma
Leghorn, Museo Civico Giovanni Fattori, Chiellini collection
Massa Marittima, Museo Archeologico
Milan, Civiche Raccolte Archeologiche e Numismatiche
Modena, Galleria Estense
Montopoli Valdarno, Comune
Orbetello, Museo Civico
Palermo, Museo Archeologico Regionale A. Salinas
Pesaro, Ente Olivieri, Museo Archeologico Oliveriano
Piacenza, Museo Civico Archeologico
Poggio Civitate, Museo Archeologico Etrusco, Antiquarium
Policoro, Museo Archeologico Nazionale della Siritide
Reggio Emilia, Musei Civici
Rome, Eredi Torlonia
Rome, Galleria Nazionale d'Arte Antica in Palazzo Corsini
Rome, Musei Capitolini
Rome, Museo Archeologico Nazionale di Villa Giulia
Rome, Museo Barracco
Rome, Soprintendenza Speciale per la Preistoria
Rovigo, Museo Civico
Sarteano, Museo Civico Archeologico
Siena, Museo Archeologico Nazionale
Soprintendenza Archeologica di Roma
Soprintendenza Archeologica per la Lombardia
Soprintendenza Archeologica per la Toscana
Soprintendenza Archeologica per le province di Napoli e Caserta
Soprintendenza Archeologica per l'Umbria
Soprintendenza per i Beni Archeologici dell'Emilia Romagna
Tarquinia, Museo Archeologico Nazionale
Venice, Centro Studi e Ricerche Ligabue
Viareggio, Civici Musei di Villa Paolina
Volterra, Museo Guarnacci

and all those who wish to remain anonymous

Acknowledgements

Special thanks to
Musée du Louvre, which hosted the press conference and without which the reconstitution of the Castel San Mariano chariot would not have been possible, together with Berlin Staatliche Museen, Munich Staatliche Antikensammlung and the Soprintendenza Archeologica dell'Umbria.
We also thank the Soprintendente Archeologo di Roma, Adriano La Regina, for his contribution to the restoration of the slabs from the Tomb François, the Centro di restauro, the Laboratorio Fotografico, the Ufficio Tecnico (Grazia Ugolini) and the Ufficio di Segreteria della Soprintendenza Archeologica della Toscana, Stefano Bruni, whose precious, meaningful scientific collaboration contributed to various aspects of the exhibition.

The curator expresses his heartfelt appreciation to the many friends from Italian and foreign museums who enabled the exhibition to take place, all the authors of the catalogue essays, as well as those who shared in writing the catalogue of the works on exhibit and their introductions, too numerous to be named individually. This undertaking would not have been possible without their active assistance.
Last, sincere thanks for the great contribution offered in many ways for the designing of the exhibition and the writing of the catalogue are due to a small number of colleagues and friends, and their unflagging efforts even in the occasional difficult moments, and in particular to Stefano Bruni, Fabio Colivicchi, Bruno Gialluca, Marco Giuman, Concetta Masseria, Elisabetta Setari, Fabrizio Slavazzi, Agata Villa and Cristiana Zaccagnino.

Exhibition

Concept and project
Francesco Venezia
collaborators Paolo Ambroselli
Stefano Ghiretti

Graphic design
Pier Luigi Cerri
with Dario Zannier
Caroline Bachmann

Reading of Etruscan text
Andrea Buscemi

Projections and animations
Medialogos

Coordination for illustrations
Elisabetta Setari

Lighting consultant
Piero Castiglioni

Maquettes and reproductions handled by:
Ditta Barth di Bartholomeus van der Geer
DART di Silvia Gambardella & C., S.n.c.
Franco Gizdulich
Progecor S.r.l.
Studio Romatre, Marco Travaglini
Giorgio Rossi

In preparation of the exhibition Palazzo Grassi had conservation work performed on the following items:
Campana slabs
Tyszkievicz bowl
Cerveteri *hydria*
slabs of the Bruschi Tomb of Tarquinia
larnax of the Tomb of the Duce of Vetulonia
bronze bust from Marsiliana d'Albegna
gold necklaces from Perugia, Pescia Romana and Populonia
ostrich egg from Vetulonia
ivory *pyxis* from the Tumulus della Pania
ivory *diphros* from Quinto Fiorentino
statue of the Chiusi Pluto
stone cippus with scribe from Chiusi
slabs of the Tomb François of Vulci

with the craftsmanship of the following restorers:
Ditta Albaplast di Burli Maurizio
Centro Regionale per la progettazione ed il restauro, Palermo
Consorzio l'Officina - Restauro e Conservazione Opere d'Arte
Coop. Archeologia S.c. a r.l.
Crimisos S.c. a r.l.
Areté Restauri S.n.c. di Susanna Ghilli & C
Annalisa Balsini
Adele Cecchini
DIMA S.n.c. di Gori e Manganelli
Giampaolo Nadalini
Sergio Neri
Progecor S.r.l.
Bettina Schindler-Pratesi
Under the guidance of the appropriate related Soprintendenze Archeologiche

Catalogue

Editorial Director
Mario Andreose

Chief Editor
Elisabetta Sgarbi

Coordinating Editor
Marina Rotondo

Editorial collaboration
Valérie Viscardi

Editing
Alessandra Fregolent

Graphic design
Giacomo Merli

Translations
Rhoda Billingsley
Daniela Brovedani
Jonathan Hunt
Andrew Ellis
David Lowry
Jeremy Scott
David Stanton
Susan Wise
John Young

Scientific revision of translations
Fabrizio Slavazzi

Technical staff
Eriberto Aricò
Sergio Daniotti
Carmen Garini
Valerio Gatti
Daniele Marchesi
Lorenzo Peni
Stefano Premoli
Roberto Serino
Enrico Vida

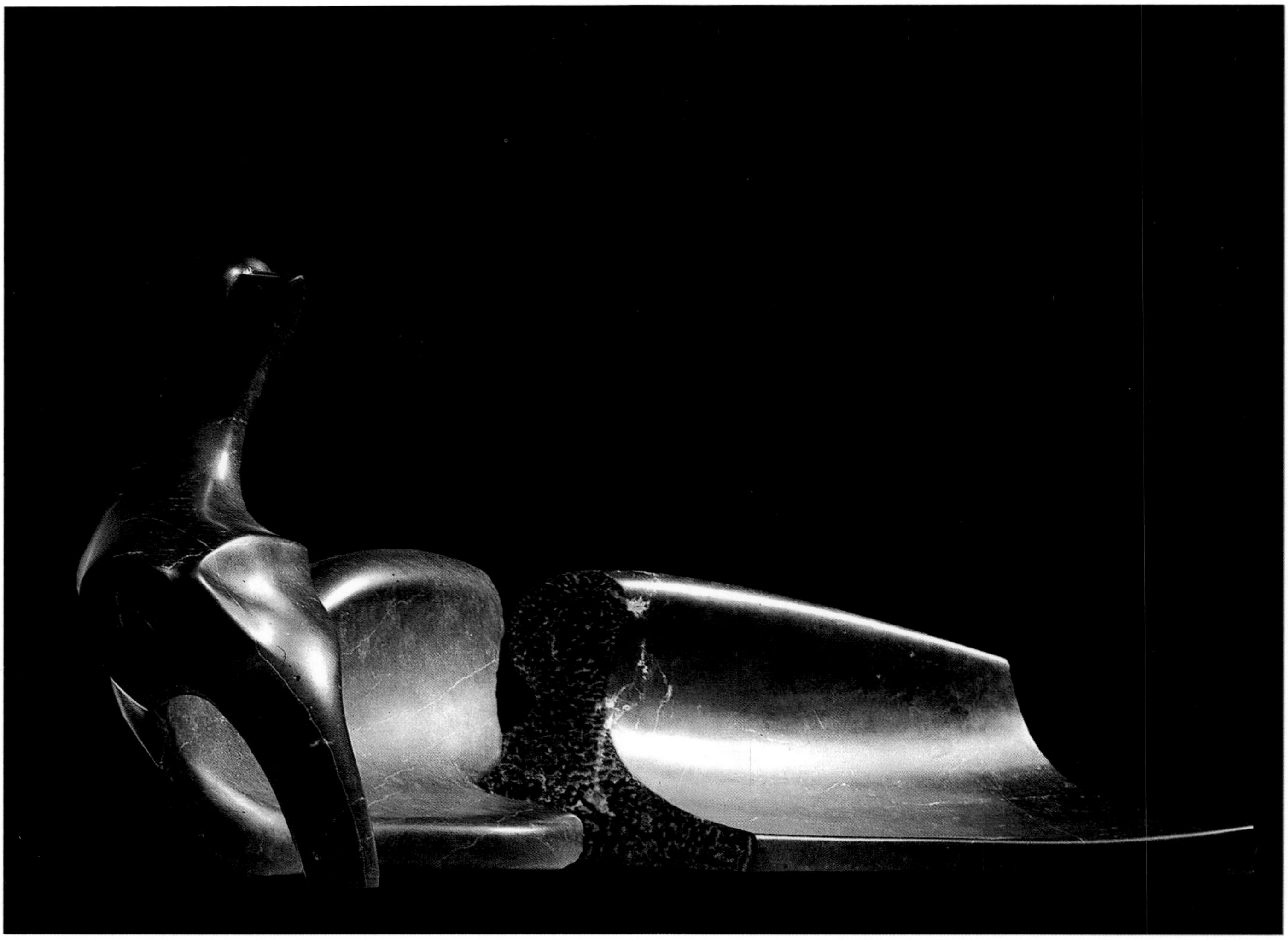

Henry Moore, Broken Figure, *marble, 1975.*
The Henry Moore Foundation, gift of the artist.
The study on fragmentation of the figure represents Moore's tribute to Etruscan art.

Contents

17 Presentation
Mario Torelli

25 The Original Features of the Etruscan Peoples
Giovanni Colonna

The Historical Context and the Economic, Social, and Political Forms

43 The Origins of the Etruscans: A Controversy Handed Down from Antiquity
Dominique Briquel

53 The Origin and Diffusion of Villanovan Culture
Gilda Bartoloni

73 Economic Structure
Marisa Bonamici

89 Coins
Fiorenzo Catalli

97 Trade
Michel Gras

111 The Etruscan Aristocracy in the Orientalizing Period: Culture, Economy, Relations
Alessandro Naso

131 The Woman's Role
Antonia Rallo

141 The Hellenization of Etruria
Mario Torelli

157 The Etruscan Expansion into Campania
Maria Bonghi Jovino

169 The Etruscan Expansion in the Po Valley
Giuseppe Sassatelli

181 Relations with Neighboring Peoples
Simonetta Stopponi

191 The Etruscans and the Veneti: Forms of Exchange and Processes of Acculturation
Loredana Capuis

197 The Etruscans and the Lands South of Campania
Angelo Bottini

205 Political Forms in the Archaic Period
Mauro Menichetti

227 Republican Political Forms
Adriano Maggiani

243 The Ideology of the Etruscan City
Luca Cerchiai

255 The Social Structure and the Serf Question
Françoise-Hélène Massa-Pairault

Culture and Forms of Art

273 Etruscan Religion
Mario Torelli

291 Etruscan Urban Planning
Stephan Steingräber

313 Civil, Religious, and Domestic Architecture
Luigi Donati

335 Tomb Architecture
Friedhelm Prayon

345 Painting
Francesco Roncalli

365 Sculpture
Stefano Bruni

393 Etruscan Bronzes
Fabio Colivicchi

405 Archaic Pottery: Impasto and Bucchero Wares
Giovannangelo Camporeale

421 Painted Pottery of the Archaic Period
Françoise Gaultier

439 Etruscan Painted Ware of the Classical and Hellenistic Period
Maurizio Harari

455 The Minor Arts
Marina Martelli, Ferdinando Gilotta

477 The Writing
Giovanna Bagnasco Gianni

485 The Language
Luciano Agostiniani

501 The Tyrrheni of Lemnos
Carlo de Simone

The Rediscovery of the Etruscans

507 Etruscan Antiquarianism
Fabio Colivicchi

511 The Vatican's Museo Gregoriano Etrusco from the Nineteenth Century and Beyond
Francesco Buranelli

515 The Museo Archeologico Nazionale of Florence
Antonella Romualdi

523 The Museo Nazionale Etrusco di Villa Giulia
Anna Maria Moretti Sgubini

Catalogue of Works

THE MAKING

533 From the Bronze Age to the Iron Age

536 The Villanovan Civilization

THE APOGEE

543 The Economy
Agriculture
The Mines
Piracy and Trade
Warfare

565 The Ideal Forms
Opulence
The Role of Women
The Cult of the Ancestors and the Continuity of the Clan
The Rituals of the Archaic Power
Hellenization
The Urban Political Forms
The Renewed Society of the Fourth Century

THE DECLINE

629 The Roman Conquest

632 The Servants

634 The Anguish of the Decline
The Role of the Past and of the Esoteric Doctrines
The Diaspora and Nostalgia

Appendix

642 Chronology

646 Bibliography

664 Topographic Index of Works

Presentation

As Giovanni Colonna so justly comments in his contribution to this catalogue, in talking about the Etruscans it is rather difficult to avoid commonplaces. Current belief—in part, supported by the ethnic stereotypes of the ancient world itself—has it that they were different from all the other peoples of ancient Italy, and sees the occupants of the Tyrrhenian regions as a dense mix of mysteries, of ethnographic, linguistic, political and cultural peculiarities. The origins of the Etruscans is seen as lost in the mists of a remote period of the history of the peninsula; their language is considered indecipherable; their political hegemony over a large part of pre-Roman Italy is argued to be as inexplicable as it was imposing—to then end in an almost abrupt collapse in the face of the nascent power of Rome. These are some of the ingredients of the modern stereotype that constitutes the "mystery" of the Etruscans. For their part, the essays in this catalogue point out that even though Etruscan script was deciphered more than two centuries ago—thanks to the fact that the Etruscans used the alphabet of the Greek colonies of Cuma (with a few changes)—the language itself continues to present numerous (essentially lexical) obscurities, in spite of the intense work carried out over the last fifty years by a handful of noted linguists; however, "indecipherable" it is not. Similarly, the origins of the Etruscans—already a subject of debate amongst the Ancients—is no more obscure than that of any of the other peoples of Eurasia, be they Indo-European or otherwise (consider the Basques, for example). The answers to such questions lie in the remote or remotest periods of the past, in the very pre-history of Europe, and therefore are bound to remain hidden or unclear. As Theodor Mommsen commented almost one hundred and fifty years ago, what should interest the modern world is the history of the Etruscans, the concrete assertion and development of their identity as a people. These are events which took place during the first half of the first millennium of Mediterranean history, and therefore can be studied through the historical sources provided by the Ancients and, above all, through archaeological research. Here again, the essays in this catalogue offer an overview of the entire extraordinary history of the Etruscans, covering such things as their appearance at the end of the Bronze–beginning of the Iron Age; the economic bases of their wealth and the forms of trade that they used; the emergence, in the period 750–650 B.C., of a rich and powerful aristocracy which in its eventful history would dominate a large part of the peninsula, establishing various forms of relations with the other Italic peoples and developing its own forms of political structure for the government of large and powerful cities; the particular structure of Etruscan society, with its subordinate semi-servile classes in the countryside (and perhaps cities) and ruling classes that tended to be oligarchic in composition; the central role of women both in the accumulation of wealth and the transmission of power (a role that is quite common in oligarchies). The catalogue also looks at the cultural aftermath of the widespread popularity of the Etruscans, discussing not only the very particular religion which the Ancients considered as one of the distinguishing features of the Etruscans, but also the various arts—from architecture (a fundamental feature of Etruscan civilization, the importance of which is indicated by the fact it gave its name to the Tuscan Order of Classical architecture) to painting (one of the rare—and therefore significant—examples of pre-Roman wall painting) and sculpture (rich in important experiments with form). Alongside these, of course, the discussion ranges over the minor "applied" arts and the manufacture of bronze objects both for ceremonial use and for everyday life—produced by a craftsman-class at the service of a demanding and wealthy aristocracy, these objects were ultimately known and appreciated throughout the Mediterranean.

These, therefore, are the topics covered by the catalogue. But the exhibition did not (could not) aim to cover such a wide range of questions. Instead, it focuses on the core problems of the whole extraordinary story of the Etruscans. What were the origins of their power, and in what forms was that power wielded? The answers to these questions offer a picture that may not be unique but is certainly remarkable in the context of ancient Mediterranean civilization as a whole. If one wanted to give a summary definition of the content of this exhibition, one could say that its subject is, above all, that of Etruscan Power. The Ancients themselves were well-aware of the profound significance of the socio-political history of the Etruscans and of the enormous influence the Etruscan world had had on the Roman (it was even the origin of all those symbols of power—the *sella curulis*, the *fasces* and the clothing and pomp adopted by magistrates and victorious generals—which were to play such a part

Cinerary statue of recumbent young man from Perugia, beginning of the fourth century B.C., *detail.*
Saint Petersburg, The State Hermitage Museum
cat. 144

in the specific forms of government and power in Rome). The layout of the exhibition reflects the two key phases in the historical process through which the particular forms of Etruscan government developed. In effect, on the first floor the visitor will follow through all the various stages in the emergence of the dominant ruling-class. This starts from the protohistory and runs through the Archaic period to describe the bases of wealth in agricultural and metallurgical productions and the ideal model of power which the Etruscan aristocracy developed in the early Archaic period (uniting indigenous traditions with their experience of Eastern opulence). The second floor, in its turn, will cover all the stages in the hellenization of the Etruscan world—reflected in everything from everyday life to urban planning—and culminate with Etruria's collapse before the inexorable might of Rome.

Looking at each part of the exhibition in closer detail, the section on the early history of the Etruscan people covers the period 1100–700 B.C. and illustrates the passage from proto-Villanovan in the Final Bronze Age (1100–900 B.C.) to the period of Villanovan culture in the Iron Age (900–700 B.C.). In the space of just a few generations, one moves from a tribal society based on clans to a society composed of family nuclei—a phase that is well-illustrated by the changes in housing types: the "long house" of the Late Bronze Age (extended huts meant to house all members of the clan) gives way to the oval or rectangular "small" hut of the Early Iron Age, which served one individual family nucleus. This transformation also reveals unmistakable evidence of the emergence of private property, owned and inherited within an individual family—a development which marked the emergence of what history recognized as a "society." During this phase the more advanced societies in the peninsula gradually emerged from the Bronze Age as distinct entities. And it was at this period that in what would be the birthplace of Etruscan civilization (modern-day Tuscany and the upper area of Latium) there was substantial settlement of land (during the Villanovan period) and, at the same time, extraordinary development in the exploitation of metal ore resources, with substantial accumulation of worked and unworked bronze. This latter feature is clear evidence of the extraordinary metallurgical abilities which the Ancients recognized in the Tyrrhenians of Lemnos and the northern Aegean (evidence that the earliest origins of the Etruscans lay in the East?), and which would be a *Leitmotiv* of Etruscan art and manufacture. It is no coincidence that the exhibition opens with the presentation of some bronze hoards—the so-called *ripostigli*—and then proceeds, over a period lasting eight centuries, to illustrate the quite amazing output of metal utensils and furnishings with an exceptional collection of masterpieces of bronze statuary. Only a very small proportion of such works have survived, yet the exhibition contains some of the very greatest, and significantly ends with the very last of them—the *Arringatore*. Thanks to the increasing opulence of grave goods in Iron-Age tombs, the visitor will also quite easily be able to follow the emergence and gradual growth of an aristocracy whose economic power was based on the ownership of land and the control of iron and, to a lesser extent, copper ore. Theoretically, the rituals of burial were the same for everyone, and yet—between the Early Villanovan period (900–800 B.C.) and the Late (800–700 B.C.)—one can note the gradual emergence of clear differences in tomb richness.

From this formative phase, one then passes to the period when the power of the Etruscan aristocracy was at its heights. As already mentioned, the economic bases for this power were colonized land (during the Villanovan period, colonization had taken place not only in Etruria but also in the Po Valley and in southern Campania) together with control over iron and copper, and these would in turn lead to the emergence of the first primitive forms of trade, via land and sea and the thalassocracy, the rule over the sea, as pirates and traders, both faces of the same activity, for which the Etruscans were famous from the earliest Antiquity. The forms of trade covered range from the ceremonial exchange of goods between chieftains—such as took place between the Etruscans and the Sardinians—to fully-fledged forms of commerce. Initially, this was carried out by the more ancient aristocratic families directly inside of their homes, but would then be handled by emporiums set up at sanctuaries (of these, Pyrgi and Gravisca—the ports of Cerveteri and Tarquinia respectively—are the most famous). Monetary commerce came only much later and was much rarer; it was not adopted by Etruscan cities until the era of reformed urban society (that is, from 350 B.C.), with the sole exception of Populonia—this port, which handled Elba's iron resources, was

Cinerary statue of recumbent young man from Perugia, beginning of the fourth century B.C.
Saint Petersburg, The State Hermitage Museum
cat. 144

already using gold and silver coins in the preceding phase.
Apart from piracy and trade, the other main source of wealth—providing land, loot and slave labor—was war. The military equipment in the rich tomb contents that date from the Iron Age onwards was more than just symbolic; as evidenced in the exhibition, the ideology of the warrior was central to that of an Etruscan aristocracy which, from its very earliest days, put great insistence on the value of marks of military distinction (exceptional finds such as the helmets of Vetulonia provide unquestionable evidence that the aristocracy participated in war followed by their dependants from the very beginning of the Archaic Age).
One then passes to the section which includes those objects that are an expression of the ideals of Etruscan culture. The most characteristic feature here is the accumulation of wealth, the exhibition of opulence and rank through rich displays of the precious materials acquired through trade with the Phoenicians or Greeks. Gold, silver, bronze, ivory, faïence, glass and precious stones were used, first of all, for personal ornaments—from clothing to jewellery and perfumes—but they also went to adorn the official manifestations of the *princeps* (the name Latin sources give to the heads of Etruscan society) and such solemn ceremonial occasions as banquets and weddings. It is in this section that one can see most clearly that, for the ruling-classes of Etruria, the display of extraordinary wealth was a political issue. All of this would, however, be incomprehensible without the other key components in the Etruscan aristocracy's ideology of dominion. First and foremost was the special—and, for the Ancients, abnormal—role of women in Etruscan society. Not only did the woman play an essential role in the process of reproduction, she was also entrusted with task of running the household and was responsible for the main product of the domestic economy, cloth (the importance of all forms of which was underlined by the dominant ideology). Women were also responsible for displaying the accumulated wealth of the family, most obviously by the jewels they wore, and themselves were an object of exchange in marriage

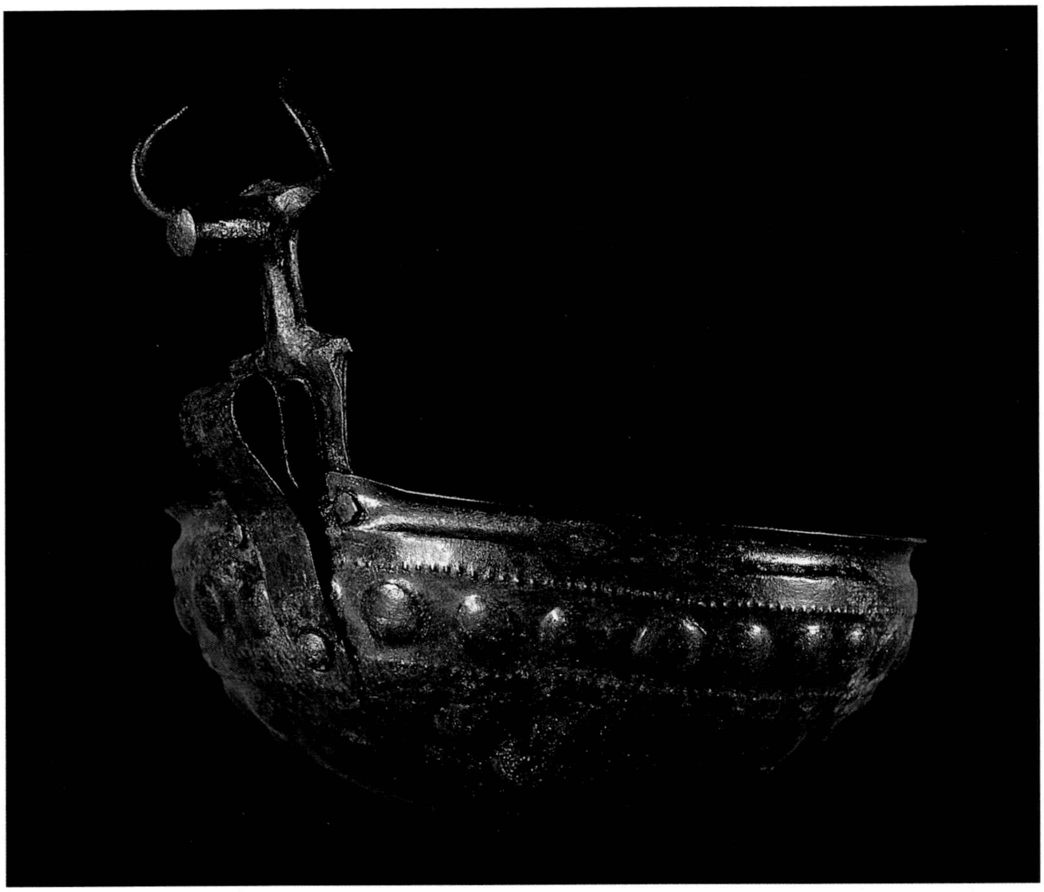

Bronze capeduncula *from the* hoard of *Coste del Marano, end of the eleventh–beginning of the tenth century* B.C.
Rome, Museo Preistorico Etnografico L. Pigorini
cat. 4.2

agreements and the pledging of alliances between different groups; the importance of such marriage alliances were emphasized not only by the gifts presented at the magnificent ceremonies but also by the use of sumptuous wedding chariots (such as that from Castel San Mariano, present in the exhibition). It therefore comes as no surprise that—as we can see from the extraordinary tomb in Sarteano, where it is the female double canopic vase that holds the axe, one of the most widespread symbols of power—women could also be the channel through which power was transmitted. This feature of Etruscan society, which in Antiquity was often the cause of amazed and moralistic comment, is to be found in all societies ruled by a restricted group of warriors, where there is always the risk of all the males branches of a family dying out.
As with all aristocracies, the central concern of the group was the preservation of the family line which, as we have seen, was one of the key tasks entrusted to women. The entire group took great care in using tombs to exalt this continuity. Undoubtedly, tombs constitute the main group of monuments that the Etruscans have left us—and that, indeed, was their aim. These grandiose sepulchres are a monumental expression of ideological concerns; often in use for centuries, they offered the group the opportunity to establish its identity through the veneration of ancestors. Archaeological evidence proves that—above all, in the Archaic period—tombs were even more than this: not only were they the site where ancestors were venerated in complex ceremonies, but they could even become the stage for veritable mise-en-scènes, recreating around the dead illustrious moments of essential—perpetual—ceremonial. Hence, the tombs often show the dead in special ceremonial attitudes—primarily, in those associated with banquets. Even in the proto-history burial goods were arranged around the cinerary urns, and then—from 700 B.C. onwards—the burial chambers of central Etruria begin to include canopic vases—a schematic representation of the bodily presence of the cremated dead—which, in generally, were actually "seated" on thrones placed before suitably-prepared tables. Gradually, increasing antropomorphism would lead

from schematic to realistic canopic vases, with a naturalistic rendering of the human head (a splendid, exceptional example in gilded wood is included in the exhibition), and ultimately to the splendid cinerary statues of the Classical age (also represented in the exhibition). The crucial social occasion of the banquet is also behind the organization of the Tomb of the Five Chairs in Cerveteri: behind the banquet table, three of the thrones carved out of the tufa are occupied by clay figures representing the ancestors (in garments that realistically depict the fashions of some fifty years earlier), whilst the two empty thrones alongside await the generations to come.

The mise-en-scène within tombs could reach high degrees of complexity. The exhibition offers the first full reconstruction of the layout of the Tomb of the Bronze Chariot in Vulci as it was when first closed. An extraordinary burial complex discovered intact some few decades ago, this tomb actually contains a simulation of the "departure on the grand journey" towards the Afterlife in a ceremonial bronze chariot. The wooden *simulacrum* of the charioteer is ready to receive aboard the second figure representing a departed lord, shown in the ritual act of boarding the vehicle (the distinction between the two figures is marked by the bronze sphere used to form the latter's head—something which can also be seen in the Marsiliana bronze cinerary, also present in the exhibition). Given that the ancestors guaranteed the continuity of the family line, they also played a role in everyday life. This can be seen, for example, in the statues placed on top of the roofs of monumental aristocratic residences, such as that in Murlo near Siena. Veritable palaces, these buildings served as a setting for the everyday ceremonial performed by the family group.

Obviously, social ceremonial was not solely concerned with the biological continuity of the family line, but also with the political continuity of its power. The main basis for this was religion, which—in the sphere of power—found its highest expression in the practices of haruspicy and auspicy. The former is the reading of the divine prognostications based essentially (but not exclusively) on an examination of the viscera—primarily, the liver—of sacrificed animals. It was the main form of divination amongst the Etruscans, and was reserved exclusively to the members of the great noble families—and from the earliest days of the Roman Republic to the very height of the Empire, the Etruscan haruspices were summoned to Rome in case of prodigies, to learn the hidden desires of the gods or the ways in which their anger might be placated. For centuries, this art guaranteed the dominant classes of Etruria a high level of social control and unparalleled prestige even outside their country; there are several points of similarity between haruspicy and divination as practiced in Mesopotamia, and so it may well have been brought into Etruria during the period of greatest Eastern influence (Orientalizing phase of 700–650 B.C.). On the other hand, the ritual of auspicy, with the associated *augurium*, dates back to pre-historic times, given that it was widespread amongst Italic peoples and therefore dates from before Etruscan hegemony over the peninsula. Like all the other Italic peoples, the Etruscans would continue to use auspicy throughout their entire existence as an independent nation—as one can see from the figure of Vel Saties in the guise of an *auspex* in the François Tomb (340 B.C.). Auspicy was a fundamental instrument in the assumption of power, given that the morning observation of heavenly portents was itself a sign of the divine investiture of the person who performed it—be that person a king (in the pre-historic and archaic periods) or a magistrate (during the time of the Republic).

At this point the visitor passes from the first to the second floor, where they will find illustrations of all the daily rituals of power. As in all archaic societies, such rituals were swathed in the veils of religion, which played an essential role not only in the solemn celebration and veneration of the gods but also in important festivities. In these latter occasions the object of celebration was the ruling aristocratic group itself: the ruling class occupied the center of the festivities, surrounded by the dependants belonging to the serf class, who were responsible for working their country estates and following the *princeps* in war. As one can see from the exhibition, whatever the period of Etruscan history, the iconography relating to these moments in the life of the aristocratic classes was imposing, revealing the importance of ceremonies which accompanied both the biological cycles of birth, marriage and death, and the social cycles of hunts, banquets, feast-days and military triumphs. Up to this point, the rituals of power were substantially based on the indigenous traditions of a society built on forms of semi-servile dependence—veneration of ancestors, the legitimization of power though the practices of auspicy and the celebration of established social rituals that played a part in the life of the collective as a whole—but the influence of the East, assimilated thanks to early-historical contacts with the world of the Near East, added a whole new dimension of opulence. However, here too, magnificence was intended to reinforce the social subjection of the dominated classes by illustrating the power of the aristocratic groups, which rested on the possession of resources (land, mines, trade), on the demonstration of traditional warrior virtues and on the scrupulous performance of ancient collective ceremonies (made prestigious by their very antiquity). Then, from the foundation of the first Greek colonies in Italy, the Etruscans were exposed to another model of civilization, and they avidly absorbed these Hellenic influences. The Greek model proposed an idea of social relations that was rather different to that embodied in Eastern despotism—which, as we have seen, was the first external model that the Etruscans had turned to—and was more consonant with the socio-political situation that was emerging in Italy. The exhibition offers wide-ranging and detailed coverage of the complex effects of this cultural influence, which made itself felt unabated over a period of at least two centuries (from 750 B.C. onwards). The rude and primitive banquet of the earlier period gave way to the more cultivated symposium, with wines produced following Greek or Eastern recipes and drunk from elegant and complex drinking vessels and accouterments (these first appeared alongside and then, around 500 B.C., replaced the traditional beverages dating from the Bronze Age with their ancestral vessels of small amphoras and *capedunculae*). The gods took on a human aspect, and thus became more benign; whilst Greek myths offered the Etruscan *principes* a perfect series of ethical-political paradigms for the celebration of their own actions and achievements, and for collective celebrations that might re-affirm the values shared by their peer group (such ceremonies—re-located in the Afterlife—are vividly depicted in the painted tombs dating from 510 B.C. onwards). Greek craftsmen—who first came to Italy in the train of the Greek aristocrats involved in trade, but later also made their own way through the bustling coastal emporiums—offered the *principes* their proverbial skill in the manufacture of luxury objects and the ever-more refined utensils required by the ruling classes. At the same time, writing—which in Etruria as in Rome was derived from the Chalcidian model of Cuma (the oldest Greek colony in Italy)—enabled the aristocracy to keep a permanent record of religious rituals, of the more or less favorable turns in events affecting both the aristocracy itself and the collectivity as a whole, and of the ceremonial presentation of gifts to the gods or the exchange of gifts between aristocrats (later, of course, writing would serve a whole range of political-social purposes in urban life).

This absorption of cultural influences also went together with the spread of a new form of urban political life throughout Etruria, the climax of which came with a general change in the institutional structure of Etruscan cities, when monarchies were replaced by republican magistrates. The exhibition covers the most archaeologically striking result of this change—that is, the rapid appearance within Etruscan cities of collective, non-gentilicial sacred buildings (the first timid traces of which date from the decades immediately before the great change to a republican constitution). One should not forget that before the final years of the sixth century B.C., non-aristocratic sacred buildings had been totally outstripped in number and richness by the frenetic building activity of the aristocratic classes, whose large residences were intended to be the site of collective celebrations and religious ceremonies (thus absorbing within themselves the entire religious and civil life of the community as a whole). The insignias and symbols of power—by now fixed and governed by severe laws—the large-scale building of urban temples and the large individual *donarii* in urban sanctuaries, all exemplify the new social context of isonomy. This new condition is well-represented by those monuments that contain a depiction of mythical or symbolic occasions of conversation between men, in which the allusion to the new equality of all before the laws of the republic is clear.

However, equality soon toughened into some form of oligarchic regime, which was responsible for a drastic and voluntary reduction in both collective and individual consumption—a fact that makes it impossible to reconstruct an archaeologically convincing picture of Etruria in the period from 470 to 350 B.C.

Shaken by the fall of the Campania, and then of the Po Valley colonies, over the period 350 to 200 B.C. Etruscan society underwent wide-ranging renewal. This started in the cities of the south, with the extension of power to new classes of citizens and an improvement in the conditions of the subordinate classes (greater or smaller sections of which were then co-opted into those categories that enjoyed civil rights). As with the emergence of the Etruscan republics in the period around 500 B.C., here too there was a new boom in both public and private building work. Alongside the old temples (many of them now rebuilt), there arose new ones; and the ethical and political content of their figurative decoration reflected the new situation and ideas. At the same time, there was a up-turn in the number of votive gifts to sanctuaries and a change in the appearance of tombs, which now had painted decoration and were furnished with urns and sarcophagi adorned with the myths that recounted the new eschatology derived from the world of Magna Graecia, or, on the other hand, illustrations of the full pomp of magistrates or the old theme of the "great journey" into the Afterlife, often recounted in a new pictorial language.
At this point one comes to the final section of the exhibition. This covers the decline of the Etruscan aristocracy, which struck the ruling classes of the reformed cities just as they were beginning to establish themselves. And elbowing its way into this new situation was Rome, which as early as 396 B.C. had already annexed one of the largest cities of Etruria, Veii (the Roman *plebs* then, following the Gauls' firing of their own city, chose Veii as their own stronghold, with the consequence that the city abounds in traces of a numerous Roman presence). Here the exhibition illustrates a fact well-known to archaeologists—that is, the contemporaneous emergence of a series of political and social phenomena within Etruscan cities. From around 150 B.C. the Late Hellenistic taste for pathos made itself felt, and figurative art became more dramatic—well expressing the intense political and social conflicts of the situation within Etruria. At the same time, esoteric doctrines—especially Dionysiac beliefs—with their heavy focus on eschatology, became widespread at all levels of society, again expressing the anxiety within an aristocracy that had for so many years dominated society. Almost as if aware of its imminent end, this class dedicated itself to contemplation of its past, evoking historical characters as legendary heroes (for example, the brothers Vibenna, the companions of the Roman king Servius Tullius) or proposing national myths which up to that moment had been almost entirely unknown. In spite of this effort to maintain its own identity—an effort that can be seen in such things as the Corsini Throne or the bilingual inscription by the *haruspex* Cafatius—the age-old aristocracy of Etruria gradually fell victim to the situation in a peninsula unified under the laws of Rome and merged with the various municipal aristocracies of Italy, forming what would be the future backbone of consensus behind Augustus.
Thus we come to the wonderful statue-portrait of Aule Meteli of Cortona. Better known as the *Arringatore*, this depicts the ancestor of a *praetor Etruriae* (one of those symbolic offices of the magistrature of the Etruscan nation, restored by Augustus) and serves as a worthy epilogue to the centuries-long history of the ruling classes of Etruria. Not only is the work dedicated to one of the divinities of Etruria, Tece Sansl, it is also made of bronze—a material which epitomizes a centuries-old craft tradition, the very earliest expressions of which are celebrated in the first room of the Venetian exhibition.

The Original Features of the Etruscan Peoples

Any attempt to condense a profile of one of the world's civilizations into a few pages without lapsing into platitudes is something of a challenge, and perhaps a non-starter. In the case of the Etruscans the task is doubtless made easier by the acknowledgment of a set of characteristics that distinguish the Etruscans from coeval peoples of antiquity, a factor that has at various levels spawned much mediocre literature on the alleged obscurity of the Etruscan people. Admittedly, the singularity of the Etruscans had already been perceived by the classicist culture of the Augustan age, when the historian of Greek origin Dionysius of Halicarnassus, resident in Rome for many years, produced a massive twenty-volume history of Rome, then the ruler of the world, tracing the city's evolution from the mythical history of its foundation up until the outbreak of the First Punic War. Despite opinion to the contrary, Dionysius nurtured a genuine admiration for the Etruscans, and had even considered devoting a separate discussion to their civilization (I, 30, 4), parallel with his work on the Romans. That task was undertaken a few decades later by the Emperor Claudius in his *Tyrrheniká*, also in twenty books, regrettably lost in its entirety in the Middle Ages. According to Dionysius (I, 30, 1), the Etruscans were of remote origin (ἀρχαῖον τε πάνυ), and comparable to no other people either for language or lifestyle (ὁμοδίαιτον). Assuming this definition as our starting point—a description widely accepted in Roman times—we can proceed to define the original characteristics of the Etruscan civilization.

"A people of remote origin." There was common accord that the formation of the Etruscan people lay in the distant past, with all the prestige such an attribution implies. Their beginnings were thought to predate even those of the Latins, whose bloodline at a certain point engendered Rome itself. Dionysius considered them autochthonous, that is, of local origin, on a par with the Umbrians, Ausones and Sicans, who predated not only Romulus, but also his progenitors Aeneas and Latinus. Even those who believed the Etruscans not to be indigenous, but instead descended from immigrants (the "Etruscan question" first arose in the commentaries of Greek authors, probably initiated by Hecataeus of Miletus), did not question their formation as an ethnic entity in the remote past; if, as was advocated, they were originally Pelasgians,

Bronze mirror with the Dioscures made in northern Etruria in 330–320 B.C.
Florence, Museo Archeologico
cat. 324

opposite
Sarcophagus of the Married Couple from Cerveteri, last decades of the sixth century B.C., detail.
Rome, Museo di Villa Giulia

Bronze crested helmet from Tomb I at Poggio dell'Impiccato (Tarquinia), eighth century B.C.
Firenze, Museo Archeologico
cat. 56

they must nevertheless have arrived prior to the Dorian "invasion" of Greece, and therefore they predated even the Hellenes; whereas if they were of Lydian stock, they dated shortly before, to the time of the foremost dynasty of that race and the era of its eponymous hero Lydos, the younger brother (?) of Tyrrhenus (otherwise held to be son or nephew of Heracles). The Hellenic idea of the Etruscans' remote genesis gained momentum when the Greeks began their navigation of the western Mediterranean, after the "dark ages" that followed the Mycenaean civilization's collapse. In contrast to the pan-Phoenician view held on the subject by Thucydides, Ephorus of Cyme (ca. 350 B.C.), whose universal history is cited by Strabo, notes that after the Trojan war Greek ships avoided for many centuries the Sicily waters owing not only to the ferocity of the natives (which was insignificant during the colonization, see Strabo VI, 2, 2, C 267), but also to the rampant piracy of the Etruscans. Unmentioned by Homer, the Etruscans first enter the Greek cultural universe with Hesiod, who, in the closing section of the *Theogony* (whose authenticity has gained increasing acceptance), has the "illustrious Tyrrhenians" inhabiting a "far-flung" (*μάλα τῆλε*) land beyond the Holy Isles, associating them with the contiguous Latins (and Sabines?), and alleging that they were ruled by Agrius and Latinus, the sons of Circe and Odysseus (vv. 1011–16), in an unusual diarchy resembling the alternating governments of Tatius and Romulus. The remarkable thing about Hesiod's version is that the eponymous rulers are posited as merely "potential" sovereigns—looking for subjects, as it were—whereas the Etruscans are an established people, however geographically remote their home was reckoned to be.
In light of these opening remarks we can only agree with Massimo Pallotino, who attributed to the Etruscans the manifestations of Villanovan culture which, from the end of the tenth

and through most of the eighth century B.C., involved an area stretching from Bologna at its northern border, to Pontecagnano and inland Eboli in the south, with scattered outposts of a limited and somewhat ephemeral nature at Fermo (Piceno) toward the Adriatic, and at Sala Consilina (Oenotria). These coordinates confirm the viability of Pallottino's working hypothesis of the Etruscans' making as a distinct ethnic group in the Final Bronze Age (twelfth–tenth century B.C.). The manifestations of this process shall be searched in the so-called proto-Villanovan civilization, whose influence involved an area far broader than historical Etruria, and whose epicenters lay not by chance in southern Etruria (Tolfa-Allumiere *facies*) and in the Po Delta (Frattesina *facies*).

"A people comparable to no other people either for language or lifestyle." In spite of Dionysius claim that the Etruscan language itself had no equivalent, attempts have repeatedly been made to decipher Etruscan texts using the "etymological" system, with the result that several disparate linguistic roots are postulated for their language. Significantly, the ancient authors were well aware of the Etruscans' being a case apart, whence the early hypothesis of their migration from afar, and that the resulting modification of ethnicity entailed a like change in language; from this it was inferred that they had undergone a *metabole*, or cultural transformation, by which they gradually evolved away from the *ethnos* of their progenitors, such that their language was also affected. Where these ancestors were presumed to be Pelasgian (an idea advanced by Hellanicus), the migrants supposedly reached Cortona, where they became Etruscan and "founded" Etruria (Dionysius of Halicarnassus, I, 28, 3). However, the diversity of Etruscan from Pelasgian had already been noted by Dionysius himself (I, 29, 2–4), following up a controversial observation whereby his precursor Herodotus—ever attentive to ethnological detail—claims that the language spoken in Cortona (written "Crestona" in the manuscripts), the city placed "on the Etruscans" overlooking the "mare Superum," was the same Pelasgian spoken in Plakía and Skyláke on the Hellespont. These were the only survivors of a terrible shipwreck, because the descendants of the Pelasgians (foremost the Athenians), were known to have changed their spoken language (I, 57, 3). Similarly, for Dionysius the difference of Etruscan from the language spoken by the Lydians was a given fact (I, 30, 1). Livy too saw a connection—which modern scholarship has since proved—between Etruscan and Raetian, while he was in agreement with the opinion held in his day (since disproved) of the Raetians' descent from the Po Valley Etruscans (V, 33, 11). The affinities between Etruscan and the language spoken on Lemnos in the Aegean—now commonly accepted—evidently went unnoticed by ancient writers, despite their calling "Tyrsenoi" the inhabitants of Lemnos and Imbros after their seizure by the Athenians under Miltiades at the end of the sixth century B.C. Gradually gaining currency now is the theory that, as Livy thought about the Raetians,

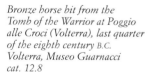

Bronze horse bit from the Tomb of the Warrior at Poggio alle Croci (Volterra), last quarter of the eighth century B.C.
Volterra, Museo Guarnacci
cat. 12.8

previous pages
View of Tuscania

opposite
Grave goods from Fontecucchiaia (Chiusi), seventh century B.C.
Copenhagen, Nationalmuseet
cat. 135

those people probably descended from Etruscan "pirates" that reached those islands in post-Homeric times, perhaps by the eighth century B.C.

As for Dionysius' comment about the Etruscans having a unique lifestyle, the term he actually used, *diaita*, obtains for the more immediate outward cultural manifestations that characterize the lifestyle of a given people or community. For Herodotus, the Lydians were basically forced to change their whole lifestyle (I, 157, 2: τῆν πᾶσαν δίαιταν τῆς ζόης) by order of Cyrus, who, following advice the vanquished Croesus had given to lessen the punishment of his former subjects, intended to transform them "from men into women," thereby inducing them to *tryphe* (I, 155, 4). Thucydides is more specific in his use of the term *diaita*: when compelled in 431 B.C. to move from their villages to Athens, the inhabitants of Attica are said to have undergone "a change of *diaita*" (II, 16, 113). The trait which perhaps distinguishes the Etruscans most from their contemporaries—and not only from the other Italic peoples on the peninsula—is precisely the singular degree of urbanization they achieved. Essentially, Etruria was a country of townships of varying dimensions; outwardly they were similar, the only substantial difference being that the larger ones were seats of political organisms of a state-wide nature. United by the federation of the *duodecim populi* (which the Greeks much more appropriately called *dodekapolis*), these cities were tantamount to a "national" entity. Similarly, in the Po Valley area and in Campania, Etruscan townships evince an analogous structuring role. This evolution toward an urban lifestyle manifested itself at a very early stage, and developed in complete autonomy from outside models (whether Greek or Semitic). The consolidation of Etruria as a "nation" during the Final Bronze and Early Iron Ages, occurred through the steady coalescence of huge agglomerations known as proto-urban settlements, a phenomenon that had practically no parallels outside Etruria, and secondly outside Latin territories. These proto-urban agglomerations with their thousands of inhabitants were doubtless what successfully thwarted the Phoenicians and later the Greeks in their relentless westward expansion, warding them off the middle Tyrrhenian coast and its related mineral resources, despite this being one of the most important objects of their expansion. The Etruscans' propensity for urban aggregation marks a profound, historical difference from most of the indigenous races of southern Italy and its islands, notably the Ausones, Oenotrians, Siculi and the western Sards, who had many of their settlements annihilated by the advance of seaborne colonization. Wherever they settled, the Etruscans established cities, or if not proper cities, then urban settlements, whose most immediately recognizable features are the orthogonal layout and associated spatial linkage—a template they also applied to their burial complexes. This layout is particularly noticeable in the Po Valley, notably Marzabotto, and has had further confirmation in recent years with the discovery of new sites at Spina (Valle di Mezzano), Forcello di Bagnolo San Vito (near Mantua), and San Basilio on the Po Delta between Adria and Spina; to these we can add sporadic cases among local populations, notably at Prestino near Como, in the valleys of Raetia, and even as far up as Santa Lucia di Tolmino.

Even historical Etruria has yielded new evidence of foundations (or "re-foundations") of urban centers, between the sixth and the fifth century B.C., starting with the port settlements—authentic *epineia* of Greek type—such as Pyrgi, Caere's port town; the port of Regae, serving Vulci; and not least a vital center at Doganella, which enabled Vulci to take possession of the entire Albegna Valley. Similar locations in Campania include the aforementioned Capua, and Fratte di Salerno; other indigenous centers evincing a high degree of acculturation include the lesser-known site at Pompeii; while new finds have come to light at Aleria in Corsica. It is no accident, therefore, that the Romans conventionally imputed the Etruscans with a complex doctrine of rituals for city foundation based on the concept of the *urbs iusta*, delimited by a *pomerium* centered on its imaginary midpoint, the *mundus*, which allowed communication with both the celestial and infernal gods. The archaeological evidence for the ritual proclamation of the city as hallowed ground is plentiful, at least as regards individual details, and its importance is borne out by the scrupulous observance and continuance of the practice by the Romans, traditionally at the hand of Romulus himself. As recent research by A. Carandini has confirmed, Romulus is reputed to have "founded" Rome using the Etruscan rite (*Etrusco ritu*) to ritually separate the Palatine and its slopes.

Various other characteristics of urban living were peculiar to the Etruscans and endorse the frequent claims that their civilization was distinct from the others around them. As a rule, the

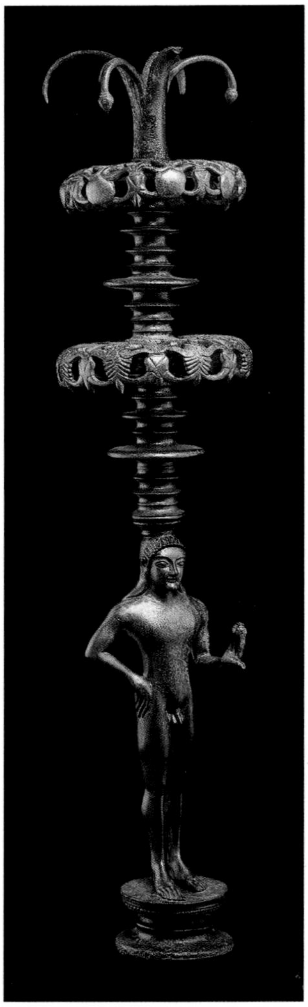

Base of bronze candelabra from Vulci, 510–480 B.C. *Munich, Staatliche Antikensammlungen cat. 232*

Aerial view of the Blera necropolis

Etruscan city had a profound effect on its surrounding territory, subsuming the area and thereby effectively overriding alternative institutional structures such as the *pagi* or *vici*, which thrived elsewhere on the peninsula. The Etruscan city successfully carried out extensive schemes for land reclamation, irrigation and drainage, all major public works that irreversibly altered the Italian landscape, from Val di Chiana to the Terra di Lavoro, from the Po Delta to the Tyrrhenian coastal plains (which neglect had reduced to malaria-ridden swampland by the Middle Ages). Such were their accomplishments that it seems only reasonable that a recent conference on the Etruscans has been entitled to "Masters of Hydraulics." In addition to their outstanding achievements in hydraulic engineering—the canal networks (much of which were navigable), man-made discharge channels, systems of *cuniculi* that drained rainwater off the outlying tufaceous catchment basins (for example, Veio)—the Etruscans built the first communications network with a proper roadbed, such as the one linking Caere to its coastal outpost, Pyrgi, not to mention the extraordinary "vie cave" (hollow-ways) with their frequent ground-leveling operations to cut roads through the tufa bedrock in the interior of southern Etruria. The growing material evidence of the Etruscans' outstanding attainments in the various fields of hydraulics, road-building, and land-surveying, such as in architectural forms (as we will discuss later) confirms beyond discussion that they were the true masters of the Romans. Moreover, they were responsible for another concept embraced by the Romans, the *termini*, or sacred border stones. According to the so-called "Prophecy of Vegoia," a Latin translation of an Etruscan text preserved in the *Gromatic Corpus*, Jupiter himself ordained the parceling out of the fields with the *termini* and their assignation to individual *domini*, as if the entrenched law of pre-urban societies—that any and all land was inalienable and undivided—was against the natural order of things.

A consequence of the land investments made by the urban aristocratic classes during the Orientalizing period was an increase in the production of olive oil and, to a greater extent, of wine. Indeed the quantity of wine produced soon exceeded the population's demand, necessitating its export to the barbarian populations of the west. To judge from the sheer quantity of trade amphoras (only recently distinguished from similar vessels), from the end of the seventh century to at least the middle of the sixth the Etruscans were perhaps the greatest exporters of wine in the western Mediterranean. Storage or trade amphoras have turned up in greater number than their coeval Phoenician and Greek counterparts in the regions of Campania, Sardinia, and especially in the Golfe du Lion and beyond to Provence, the Languedoc, and Catalonia. This aspect of Etruscan trade outside Etruria itself, anticipating a similar movement of bronze vessels in the sixth and fifth centuries toward continental Europe (again accompanied by wine and oil exports, as testified by the saga of the trader Arruns from Clusium, an authentic prototype of the Etruscan *emporos*, whose donation of these products is supposed to have brought the Celts into the Italian peninsula). During the seventh and sixth centuries, wine exports were seaborne, a factor that underscores another distinguishing feature unanimously accredited to the Etruscans by the ancient writers, namely, that they were the most capable navigators of all the western peoples.

Along with their seafaring prowess, however, the Etruscans were on the one hand inevitably equated by the Greeks with piracy, particularly as regards the waters of the Aegean, Adriatic, and above all the Tyrrhenian Sea, which by no accident took its name from *Tyrrhenoi*, the Greek word for the Etruscans; whereas on the other hand they were equated with a "thalassocracy" or sea power over the two western seas, and not only these. Piracy and thalassocracy are two notorious manifestations of a sea power and, more in general, of presence on the seas, somewhat antithetically only in terms of role, in that the second term is equatable with a sort of "dominion" exercised with implicit international consensus. As it happens, passing from a generalized acknowledgment to the hard facts, the thalassocracy over the Tyrrhenian Sea was attributed more specifically to Caere, evidently in the crucial period from the mid-sixth to the mid-fifth centuries, that is from the struggle for possession of the Corsica to the Syracusan forces' occupation of Elba; whereas thalassocratic control over the Adriatic was instead imputed to Spina, notably when at its peak of power from the start of the fifth century to the start of the fourth. Unique among all other barbarian lands, these two cities were awarded the privilege of building their own *thesauros* in the Panhellenic sanctuary of Delphi; this was perhaps also an endorsement of their claim to descend from the Pelas-

Hermes, acrotierial terra-cotta statue from the Portonaccio Temple of Veio, end of the sixth century B.C.
Rome, Museo di Villa Giulia

gians, thereby suggesting a common ancestry with the Greeks. The Etruscans' fame as pirates, active both in the Aegean and in the western seas, mainly concerned the "Tyrrhenian" branch of the Etruscan *ethnos*, relative to their claim to Lydian descent, or above all to being autochthonous, and originated either in a more recent era (fourth–third century B.C., when the Etruscan nation was already in dire disarray), or further back in time. On this score, it is worth recalling Ephorus's aforementioned caution about the perils that had long kept Greek seaborne traders shy of Sicilian waters, and together with this warning Diodorus Siculus's comment on the formidable trials the Etruscans gave the Cnidian colonizers from around 580 B.C. In terms of the Etruscan myths of origin, the archetype of Etruscan piracy is found in the figure of Tyrrhenus, the brother of Liparus, a hero of Ausonian origin and therefore autochthonous, mentioned by Servius in a passage whose importance has only recently been noted (*ad Aeneidem,* I, 52), perhaps borrowing indirectly from Philistus. After forcing Liparus to abandon Campania, his brother planned "Peloponnesum vastare," inducing Agamemnon to send Aeolus to the west to block his way out of the Straits.

A clear example of how the Greeks saw the Etruscan pirate is found in the tale of the Tyrrhenians—from the Aegean, of course—who attempt to enslave a beautiful youth, unaware that he is in fact the god Dionysus, by whom they are turned into dolphins. Although it is hard to date the Homeric hymn to the god, which focuses more on the legend, the figure's first appearances in vase painting, both Attic and Etruscan, date to the last third of the sixth century (and the Etruscan ones seem to evince a deliberate dissociation of the western Etruscans, friends of Athens, from their Aegean counterparts). More generically, the Etruscans' noted expertise in navigation accounts for their reputed invention of the rostrum (which would

Apollo, acroterial terra-cotta statue from the Portonaccio Temple of Veio, end of the sixth century B.C.
Rome, Museo di Villa Giulia

Bronze statuette of Iuno Sospita,
ca. 500–480 B.C.
Florence, Museo Archeologico
cat. 203

quickly become a standard feature on every country's warships), and of the trumpet, a military instrument used equally at sea; also attributed to the Etruscans are their attempts to sail out into the ocean, which were thwarted by the Carthaginians. Consonant with the allegation of piracy was the Etruscan notoriety for cruelty, as in the ritual sacrifice of humans, practiced as late as the siege of Lipara around 490–480 B.C., recorded with horror by Tzetzes, in the wake of Callimachus (*Historiarum Variarum Chiliades,* VIII, 889–892), and by the application of punishments of a particularly unpleasant nature, by which the condemned man was strapped to a corpse, undergoing a death as excruciating as it was slow.

The savagery imputed to the Etruscans has associations with *hybris* in its wider sense, as excess, of whatever kind—a quality the Greeks tended to attribute not just to barbarian peoples but to anyone who defied the law, such as tyrants, whether they were of Greek origin or not. A play on words in Dorian dialect—almost certainly originating in Syracuse– associated the name *tyrrhanos* with *tyrannos*), as if the Etruscans were the very personification of tyranny. Similarly, in Latin tradition we learn, especially from Vergil, that the prototype, as it were, of the tyrant was considered to be Mezentius, king of Caere (the historical veracity of whose name is now proven by an inscription on a Caeretan vase from the earlier seventh century B.C.), who was deposed for his arrogance toward men and the gods, of which the Latins had had firsthand experience in the days of Aeneas. The Caeretans responded to these defamatory accusations by adorning the front facing the town of the greater temple at the port town of Pyrgi with a representation of the impious actions of Tydeus and Capancus before the walls of Thebes, whose abysmal misdeeds were reckoned the epitome of Greek *hybris,* and probably alluded to the relentless persecution of the Etruscans at the hands of the Deinomenides (as well as a reference to tyrannical behavior on the domestic front, such as that of Thefarie Velianas, devotee of Astarte and ally of Carthage, whose biography is unfortunately still patchy). Conversely, the *pietas* of the Caeretans was significantly celebrated on the seaward façade of the same temple at Pyrgi with the representation (surviving in a mid-fourth-century remaking) of the munificent reception accorded to Leucothea and Palaemon under the patronage of Herakles. Furthermore, at the south area of the sanctuary stood the giant votive *phiale* of the Brygos Painter picturing the Mnesterophonia, a splendid votive offering cautioning newcomers to Etruria of the perils of violating the sacred rules of hospitality.

Another common idea the Greeks associated with the Etruscans was their love of luxury, termed *tryphe*, reputedly arising from excess and a general lack of moderation referring to prosperity, consumptions and good use of wealth in general; for the Greeks, an improper use of wealth inevitably led to the ruin of the city and the people affected with it. As a *topos*, the image has a moralistic and philosophical flavor, and crops up in Theopompus, Alkimos, Heraclides Ponticus, Timeaus, and in their wake reemerges in later authors, among whom the most balanced opinion is Posidonius (in Diodorus Siculus, V, 40). In all likelihood, the theme was also taken up more extensively in the few Greek writings devoted expressly to the Etruscans and their world—regrettably most of which are irretrievable—such as Aristotle's *Tyrrhenôn nómima* and the *Perì Tyrrhenôn* by his pupil Theophrastus. While such literature demonstrates a sustained interest in the Etruscans at the time, it is undoubtedly clouded by the spectacle of the progressive collapse of their nation from the end of the fifth to the mid-fourth century B.C., a decline that was heralded by their losses of Campanian territory to the Samnites, the Gaul's encroachment on their domains in the Po Valley, and not least the pruning of Etruria itself with the advance of Rome, starting with the capture of Veio and the onset of a new balance of power in central Italy. The economic basis for the accusations of *tryphe* was no doubt the great fertility of the Etruscans' land and the flourishing agriculture. According to Polybius, without considering Campania and the Po Valley one was unable to account for the former puissance and prosperity achieved by the Etruscans (II, 17, 1). From a more historically factual point of view, bolstering the agriculture were undoubtedly other important assets, namely, a robust trade network that was still intact in the fourth century, and thriving manufacturing activities whose principal market now resided in the very "barbarian" neighbors who had begun to force the borders of Etruria inward.

In Etruria's case, the roots of the Greek idea of *tryphe* lie in what is known as *habrosyne*, that is, the Etruscan aristocracy's urge to emulate the refined customs and high living standards of Ionian stamp (or, more generically, of Graeco-Oriental origin), a lifestyle they pursued from the days of the lavish Orientalizing culture of the seventh century, and with renewed vigor in the later Archaic period with the influx of Ionian refugees from Asia Minor fleeing the Persian advance. According to Timaeus, among the vectors of the high lifestyle in Italy were the Sibarites, who acted as intermediaries (and not just metaphorically) between the luxuriousness of the Milesii and that of the Etruscans. Be that as it may, the local historian Hyperocos was hardly less disparaging about the Cumaeans, whose love of luxury led them down the same path of ruin as the Milesii and Sibarites. The *tryphe* attributed to the Etruscans by the aforementioned writers of antiquity concerned details of their daily lifestyle, however, such as the sheer frequency of their meals, their dining tables laid out with delicacies of all kinds, the stylish bedcovers, and the elegance and fine attire even of their servants, who themselves owned well-furnished houses (Posidonius, in Diodorus Siculus, V, 40. 3)—a lavishness unthinkable in the Greek-Roman world. But what really struck the Greeks, particularly in the Classical period, was the fact that women were admitted to the banquets and symposium drinking parties, where wives lay beside their husbands, all in the presence of naked handmaidens, as in Greece only the heterae did. By no accident, such accounts of Etruscan behavior spawned a stream of self-perpetuating tales of sexual depravity, details of which the notoriously critical Theopompus so thoroughly related (cited in Athenaeus, XII, 517d ff.).

Actually, there is evidence that in Etruscan society women formally enjoyed a status equal to that of their menfolk. This is ostensible in the personal names system: the earliest epigraphical evidence (around 700 B.C.) shows that women were known by a combination of their given name and the family denomination, exactly as men were. Furthermore, female first names are on the whole quite distinct from those of the men. As shown by the stela of Vetulonia, from the seventh century onward, funerary inscriptions for the main clans bore both the patronymic and matronymic; and from the fourth century onward this custom filtered down to the "middle" classes and continued through into the start of the Roman Imperial age. The couple of statues linked to tombs of married couples during the early Orientalizing period actually represented two men, evidently the *pater* of the male and the female respectively, having identical status (Tomb of the Statues at Ceri; Tomb D at Casal Marittimo; Tomb of the Five Chairs, Caere, where they are accompanied by their wives). Other inscriptions, including some from the Archaic period, suggest that women not only "wrote" as much as their menfolk, in the sphere of the *instrumentum domesticum*, but were even permitted to own servants and run manufacturing outfits, such as the potteries and *figlinae*.

To return to the question of *tryphe*, other aspects of the Etruscan lifestyle might have been more deserving of this traditional allegation of lavishness, such as the complicated orchestration of the *ludi*, or "games," staged by the aristocracy to celebrate their own grandeur during the funerals of clan members; details of these games have reached us via funerary painting in Tarquinia, cippi from Clusium, and several vase paintings. Gymnastics, horse racing and theatrical performances were enacted by professional athletes and actors financed by affluent families to entertain them at their leisure. Livy informs us that such a company of performers, the most part of which were servants, was once withdrawn without notice from taking part in the *ludi* of the Fanum Voltumnae by a king of Veio, bringing the entire event to a halt (V, 1, 4–5). In truth, the Etruscan fixation with the afterlife was a blatant excuse for sprees of extravagance, basically aimed at class endorsement. And being an eminently private affair, this wanton overindulgence was beyond the establishment's control, except for the outward aspect of the tombs, which were made to conform to relatively modest standards, but only in the late Archaic period onward, notably in Caere, Orvieto and the rock-cut necropolises around Viterbo. By contrast, no restraints were imposed on what actually went into the tombs, except at Veio, and the interment of goods of all kinds—a practice abandoned by the Latins from the times of Servius Tullius (and by the Greeks some time before)—included personal effects, clothing, ornate pottery, jewelry and other finery to accompany the deceased into the afterlife.

On the contrary, the Etruscans were also lauded as *philotechnoi* (Athenaeus, XV, 700c, see also Heraclides Ponticus, *FHG* II, p. 217, fr. 16), that is, for their consummate skill in various crafts. And while these skills were openly acknowledged by the Greeks, and even more so by the Romans, the driving force behind the development of craftsmanship was their characteristic preoccupation with finery in everyday urban life, which led them first to emulate the lifestyle they admired (*habrosyne*), and thence to the love of ostentation (*tryphe*). Aeschylus, together with various Ancient Comedy authors and the sophist Critias, make clear how in the fifth century the Athenians greatly appreciated Etruscan handicrafts, particularly their toreutics and metalwork, and objects such as candle-holders, table wares, sandals, and flutes and trumpets among the musical instruments they produced. Archaeological excavations on Greek soil have yielded material evidence in quantity, mainly inside the larger sanctuaries, though the lack of epigraphical data leaves doubts as to whether the dedicants were Greek or Etruscan. Among the various bronze finds are the famous figured Vulci tripod found on the acropolis at Athens; the *thymiateria* from Olympia and Lindos; and the *infundibula* from a variety of Greek sites.

In the wake of previous Greek literature of the early Hellenistic period, the Roman author Varro among others credited the Etruscans with various unprecedented (in central Italy) achievements in the arts and crafts. The Etruscans were reportedly the first to model cult figures in clay with human features (Tertullianus, *Apologeticum*, XXV, 3); and more generally to sculpt statues from marble (Porphyrion, *Horatii Epodi,* II, 2, 180), and cast statues in bronze (Cassiodorus, Variae, VII, 15, 3). But above all, learning new skills from the many artists that came with Demaratus from Corinth around 640 B.C., the Etruscans were allegedly the first to develop the art of modeling in clay (coroplastics), wall-painting, and both residential and temple architecture. One might say that the "national" art of the Etruscans thenceforth was terra cotta modeling, largely due to the outstanding work of the Veientine master Vulca, who around 580 B.C. was summoned by the first of the Tarquins to fashion the seated Jupiter on the Capitol, and the Hercules in the Forum Boarium (Varro, in Pliny, *Naturalis historia*, XXXV, 157). Whereas Tarquinius Superbus supposedly commissioned to an anonymous artist, also from Veio, the making of the huge acroterion for the Capitoline temple representing Jupiter stand-

Terra-cotta head of an old man from the Belvedere Temple in Orvieto, late fifth–fourth century B.C.
Orvieto, Museo Archeologico
cat. 285.7

ing on a quadriga, modeled and fired in the Etruscan city (Festus 342 l). In the field of bronze-working, the name of Mamurius Veturius became legend for his replica of the original *ancile*, a shield which fell from heaven as a gift, fashioned for the twelve Salii at the time of Numa; if this name is correct, he might well be an artist from Veio (the city in which Tomb 1036 at Casale del Fosso yielded some of the earliest known shields of that type).

The material evidence gleaned from archaeological sites has corroborated the picture drawn by the Latin writers of late Republican Rome. The temple decorations and acroteria for the houses and "palaces"—at Acquarossa, at Murlo, at Castelnuovo Berardenga, and at other minor sites in northern Etruria—have revealed terracotta architectural decoration of a complexity and technical refinement hitherto unknown for such an early period, strongly suggesting the handiwork of artists who emigrated to Etruria together with Demaratus. The wall paintings in the Orientalizing tombs of Caere and Veio enable us to follow step-by-step the early formal and technical developments of painting on a large scale, in the way they were reconstructed by Greek artistic historiography of the early Hellenistic period. The same can be said for the Roman tradition, epitomized by Varro, who attributed the Etruscans with the invention of the atrium-type of house plan, now documented as early as the time of Tarquinius Superbus by new finds on the northern slopes of the Palatine Hill; also theirs was the type of temple built on a monumental scale with podium, pronaos with columns, and a back section composed either of three cellae, or of a single cella between *alae*: the temple described as "Tuscan," that is, with a label that alludes both to its Etruscan descent and to its antiquity.

View of Cerveteri necropolis

Actually, there is reason to believe that while this type of temple was conceived by Etruscan architects, it happened in Rome, where there are even earlier examples dating from the sixth century (temple of Jupiter Capitolinus, and that of the sacred area of Sant'Omobono), which served as models for many other temples of similar design built immediately afterward in Etruria and Latium. Besides receiving credit for the development of temple architecture and cult statuary, and above all for their alleged capacity to communicate with the gods, the Etruscans were also reputed by the Romans to be "more than any other dedicated to religion, the more as they excelled in practicing it" (Livy, V, 1, 6). This idea of the Etruscans was widely held in Rome from the times of Romulus, growing steadily since the disaster with the Gauls and the subsequent shelter given by the Caeretans to the *sacra* of Rome, together with the *pontifex maximus* and the vestal virgins. The Romans were indebted to the Etruscans not only for the religious rituals of the *caerimoniae*—a term derived from Caere—but for the entire business of the interpretation of omens and all other manifestations of divine will, from thunderbolts to the anomalous forms of the entrails of sacrificial victims, especially of their livers. The *Etrusca disciplina* supplied the Romans with the answers that their own system of *auspicium* and the simple *litatio* of entrails failed to offer. Hence the official recognition and accession of the haruspices to the ranks of the priesthood of the Roman state, and hence the pains the Senate took to ensure that this particular doctrine continued to be handed down within the families of the Etruscan aristocracy who traditionally cultivated it. That doctrine was steadily augmented to form a veritable corpus of sacred writings, the *libri*, the like of which did not exist for Greek and Roman religion, and whose source allegedly lay in an original "revelation" which the child-sage Tages (having appeared miraculously from out of the ground) announced to Tarchon, the mythical founder of Tarquinia and the Etruscan dodecapolis; though Clusium also had its own legend of a prophecy announced by Vegoia to Arruns Velthymnus, whose name is linked to the god known as Voltumna. This portrait of Etruscan man prevailed in Rome until the end of the

View of Norchia necropolis

pagan era, when the *Etrusca disciplina* made an unexpected comeback as part of anti-Christian doctrine related to ideas of the afterlife prompted by the theory of *dii animales*, which entailed bloody sacrifices. As such, the portrait is in stark contrast with the image of the Etruscans put forward by the Greek chroniclers—as merciless pirates or dissolute and given to excess. Nevertheless, news of Etruscan *pietas* must have circulated in the Greek world too, if only by dint of the Caeretans' visits to the Pythia at Delphi, and for the *agones* they established in memory of the slaughtered Phocaeans, as related by Herodotus (I, 167, 2); further confirmation is afforded by the evidence yielded by the aforementioned *thesauroi* built by Caere and Spina at the sanctuary of Delphi. When Plato exhorts his ideal legislator to not tamper with ceremony and ritual, "be they of local origin, Etruscan, Cypriot, or from any other land" (*Leges*, V, 9, 738), one can detect a certain deference for Etruscan religious practices. Similarly, in his eulogy of Caere (V, 2, 3), Strabo applauds the Caeretans' sense of justice for abstaining from piracy. All told, this affords a generally more plausible picture of the people that were the Etruscans.

General works: Heurgon 1961a; Cristofani 1983a; Pallottino 1984; Pugliese Carratelli 1986. *For a synthesis:* Briquel 1993a. *Noteworthy are also the exposition catalogues of 1985, the "Etruscans' year," ed. by G. Camporeale, A. Carandini, G. Colonna, M. Cristofani, A. Maggiani e S. Stopponi, as well as* Pallottino 1992. *On the mythic history of the Etruscans:* Briquel 1984; Briquel 1991; Briquel 1993b; Colonna 2000a. *On the relationship with Villanovan and proto-Villanovan culture*: Pallottino 1989, pp. 55–62. *On the relationship with Lemnos:* de Simone 1996b. *On the "proto-cities", see in* Opus, II, 1983, pp. 423–48. *On the "pomerio palatino":* Carandini, Cappelli 2000. *On Etruscan cities:* Colonna 1988, pp. 15–36. *On agriculture transformations, sea trade etc.:* Colonna 1976a, pp. 3–23; Cristofani 1983b; Gras 1985b; Colonna 1989c, pp. 361–74. *On piracy and on "tryphe"*: Musti 1989, pp. 19–39. *On Pyrgi: Enciclopedia dell'Arte Antica,* II suppl., IV, 1996, *ad vocem*. *On womens' condition:* Colonna 1993a, pp. 61–68. *On the "ludes":* Thuillier 1993. *On arts:* Mansuelli 1984, pp. 355–65; Colonna 1994, pp. 554–605. *See furthermore:* Colonna 1981c, pp. 41–59; Colonna 1984, pp. 13–59 (with Fr.-W. von Hase); Colonna 1989a, pp. 19–25; Colonna 1991a, pp. 55–122. *On the Etruscans' reputation in the Greek world:* Colonna 1993b, pp. 43–67.

The Origins of the Etruscans: a Controversy Handed Down from Antiquity

Together with the continued obscurity which surrounds their written heritage, the origins of the Etruscans provide the classic ingredients of the "Etruscan Mystery." But the simple question which is always asked, "Where did they come from?," fails to find a simple answer: the controversy rages on, and any work which deals with the civilization of the Etruscans must necessarily include a chapter on their origins.

Traditionally, scholarly opinion on the subject has been divided among three schools of thought. The first of these considers the Etruscans that we are familiar with to be the heirs of a people who migrated from the east, and who settled on Tuscan soil at the dawn of their long history, bringing with them the first rudiments of their culture and the essential characteristics of their language. This Oriental theory has long been the majority view, leading experts such as the French scholar A. Piganiol to pronounce a definitive sentence by terming the Etruscans an "Oriental people." The second school of thought also holds that the Etruscans were immigrants, but from the north, suggesting that they came down into Italy from the Alpine regions: this Northern theory was first put forward in the tendentious writings of another Frenchman, Nicolas Fréret, whose *Recherches sur l'origine et l'ancienne histoire des différents peuples d'Italie* was published in 1753. Some of the great names in German scholarship were to follow Fréret's line: B.G. Niebuhr in his *Römische Geschichte*, published in Berlin in 1811, and Th. Mommsen, in the manual of Roman history which he brought out in 1856 and which continued to appear years afterward in various revised editions and translations.

These first two schools of thought, which have in common the idea that the original ethnic group of the Etruscans was formed by immigrants to the peninsula, are both opposed to the third and final view, namely that the ancestors of the Etruscans were themselves an ancient local people, thus their historical descendants were a relict of a prehistoric substratum who continued to occupy the same territory. This Indigenous theory has been defended first and foremost—for reasons we will explain later—by linguists, particularly Italians, such as A. Trombetti, F. Ribezzo and G. Devoto.

After presenting in turn these three hypotheses, treatises on Etruscan studies will—rather in the manner of the rhetoricians of Antiquity in their *disputationes*—expound in detail their respective strengths and weaknesses, before concurring that not one of them is capable of providing a conclusive answer to all the various issues involved in the debate, and that therefore the problem must be held to be unresolved.

One certain thing is that the longstanding general acceptance gained by the foundation of the Oriental theory has now been discredited, at least in those terms according to which it has traditionally been put forward. It was long held by proponents of the eastern origins that the first Etruscans arrived around the beginning of the eighth century B.C., in the same timeframe as the establishment of the Greek colonies in Italy and the peak of Phoenician trading in the region. It was noted how, in the space of a few decades, Tuscany reached a level of wealth and development far above that of the rest of central Italy, seemingly representing a complete break with the Villanovan culture which preceded the Etruscans in the region and whose scant remains held so little attraction for excavators in the past that often they were not even collected. This sudden leap forward made it tempting to believe that Etruscan civilization did not indeed develop from the Villanovan culture, but rather that it was introduced by the Etruscans themselves when they arrived from elsewhere around the start of the eighth century B.C. That this "elsewhere" must have been in the Middle East appeared proven by evidence from the Oriental, or orientally-inspired artifacts found in large quantities in the lavish princely tombs. We may turn again to A. Piganiol for a description which neatly conveys that impression: "If one were seeking a simple phrase to sum up the Etruscan manner, one could say that it is a piece of Babylon transported to Italy."

Such a position is no longer tenable today. Given more careful research, the transition from Villanovan to Etruscan has been revealed as much more fluid and gradual than had at first been believed. Certainly there was a rapid and significant advance in prosperity, but not one which lends itself to an explanation in terms of an ethnic break. Rather it was at that period that Etruria entered the major trading circuits, while both Greeks and Phoenicians were attracted to the region by its mineral resources. The result was a kind of economic boom which drove Etruria well ahead of its relatively underdeveloped neighbors. The civilization

Golden kotyle
from the Bernardini Tomb (Palestrina), 675–650 B.C.*, detail. Rome, Museo di Villa Giulia cat. 82*

Golden kotyle *from the Bernardini Tomb (Palestrina), 675–650* B.C.
Rome, Museo di Villa Giulia
cat. 82

Gilt silver lebes *with snake protomes from the Bernardini Tomb (Palestrina), 675–650* B.C.
Rome, Museo di Villa Giulia
cat. 83

Map of the Italic proto-historic cultures

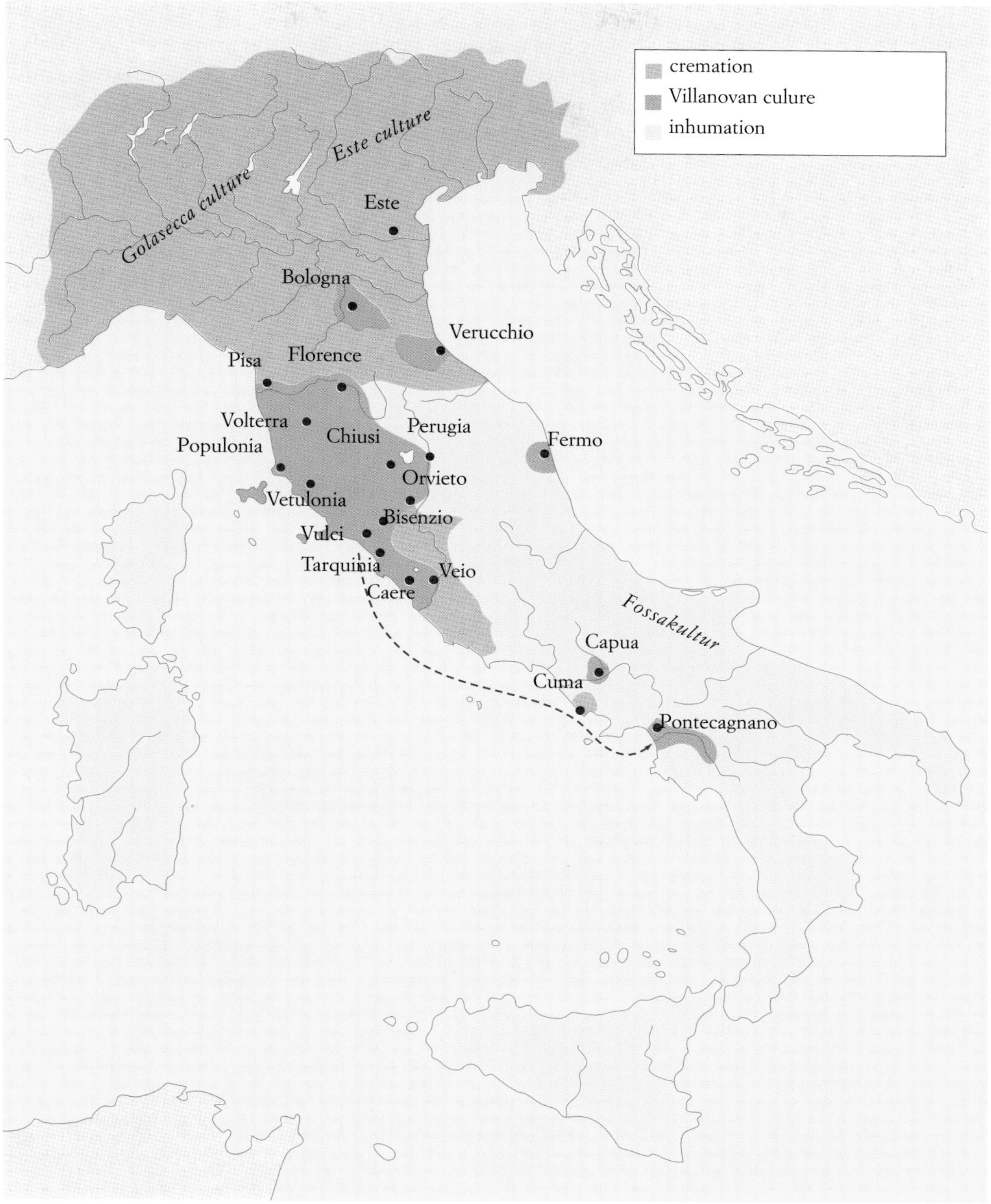

which ensued, based on exotic luxury and magnificence, was strongly influenced by eastern models. Nonetheless, what we have here is orientalizing, not Oriental: in other words, the cultural advance did not result from the arrival of allogenic populations—excepting a few merchants and craftsmen—but was instead the consequence of a conscious and deliberate shift on the part of the local inhabitants, or of their rulers at least. Moreover similar phenomena occurred in Latium, with the rich tombs of Praeneste, and in Campania at Pontecagnano. Greece also underwent its own Orientalizing phase at that period; it should be remembered that Etruscan orientalizing often developed under the intermediary influence of Greek art, rather than by direct impact with Oriental models. At all events, in none of these other regions has there ever been any attempt to explain such developments in terms of a radical transformation brought about by the settlement of an immigrant population.
Notwithstanding it remains unsupported, the Oriental theory is by no means disproved. If we allow a change of date for the supposed migration, we at once find a phenomenon which

can be more convincingly explained in such terms. We need only examine what occurred at the earliest stages of the Villanovan culture itself, at the time of the appearance of the first forms of what has been termed the proto-Villanovan, around 1200 B.C. The advent of this culture did indeed mark a complete break. Previously Tuscany was characterized by a culture called Apennine. However there are no extant signs of originality in those areas which later became Etruscan, as compared with parts of Italy which were to remain outside the Etruscan world: the Apennine culture is found at just the same stage in Umbria, in Sabina and in Latium. As the proto-Villanovan and later Villanovan cultures developed, however, this uniformity disappeared. These new cultures flourished in Tuscany, Emilia around Bologna and in certain parts of Campania, while elsewhere the old Apennine culture was protracted substantially unchanged into what is termed the sub-Apennine, and then into the *Fossakultur*.

This allows us to make a broad distinction between a part of the peninsula where the funeral rite was cremation—as introduced by the Villanovan—and another where the practice of burial continued to predominate. It is remarkable that the two territories thus defined—which can be distinguished after the end of the Bronze Age—coincide with the ethnic distribution as recorded at a later date. The regions where the Villanovan culture is found are also those where tradition has asserted an Etruscan presence and which have yielded Etruscan inscriptions. It is even more noteworthy that this correlation recurs not only in Tuscany, but also in Campania and Emilia. In contrast, in those areas which were later occupied by Italic language speakers—Sabina or Umbria, for instance—burial practices prevailed. We appear to glimpse the establishment of two groupings which were to survive into historical times in Italy, and which can be characterized in ethnic terms.

The Villanovan phenomenon must, however, be viewed in a broader context. It is, after all, no more than the manifestation in Italy of the development on a much larger scale of the so-called "urnfield" culture, characterized by the use of cremation, with the ashes placed in large, uniform cemeteries of coarse pottery urns. Such a drastic alteration in customs, alongside the rapid spread of a new rite over a vast area, may surely be explained in terms of an ethnic break.

It is not only to the north that we should look, however. The Mediterranean world also underwent a series of profound shocks during the same period. The epoch of the Mycenaean palaces drew to a close in the Greek world, while further east in Asia Minor the Hittite empire also fell. The city states along the coast of Syria and Phoenicia were devastated by raids from which some, such as Ugarit, failed to recover. Egyptian records have handed down to us an explanation for this sudden reversal in fortunes: the whole of the eastern Mediterranean was invaded by the so-called "Sea Peoples." This huge movement—which may be compared with the assault of the barbarians on the Roman Empire at the close of antiquity—was perhaps not unconnected with what went on in Italy at the same time. Among the highly diverse groups which made up the Sea Peoples were the Tursha: the name immediately recalls that of the Etruscans, called *Tyrsenói* in Greek. Italy was by no means cut off from the Greek and Oriental world; on the contrary, contacts had been established and maintained since the Mycenaean period. We may very well allow the hypothesis that these migrant peoples included a group of proto-Etruscans—and that from such a beginning, through the proto-Villanovan and later Villanovan, began the process which would lead to the emergence of the Etruscan civilization.

Thus we may expect to find traces of the Etruscans, or at least of proto-Etruscans, from the end of the Bronze Age. And in answer to the question as to the origins of the Etruscans, it is a tempting hypothesis to imagine a group of sea-faring migrants arriving from the east and bringing to Italy the rudiments of what would grow into the Etruscan world. The movements of the Sea Peoples are an indication of the state of crisis afflicting the whole of the Middle East at the time. Groups went raiding on what were often straightforward pillaging expeditions, but which could also turn into migratory journeys with the settlement of new sites. If we allow that the Tursha were a population related to the Etruscans, it is highly plausible that some of the Tursha may have preferred to venture westwards instead of heading for Egypt, or perhaps decided to turn their attention to Italy after an unsuccessful attack on the Kingdom of the Nile. One such group of people may thus have established their domi-

Drawing with the inscription of the Lemnos stela

nation in Tuscany; nor would they have had to be particularly numerous in order to do so: the proponents of this idea point to the example of the Norman conquest of England as a model.

A possible trace of their area of origin in the east has survived on the island of Lemnos: the stela and other material found there attest to the presence in the Northern Aegean of a population whose language is clearly related to Etruscan. Although the documents themselves belong to the sixth century, they are thought to record a language long spoken in the area. The Lemnians may have been a local population, the last remnant of a pre-Indo-European substratum which was then overlain by Indo-European-speaking populations, and it may have been from the island that a group which settled in Tuscany set out.

Such was the course of events according to the Oriental theory. Things may have gone quite differently, however, in keeping with the other theories which have been advanced. If we consider the sudden break which occurred in Italy around 1200 B.C. with the appearance of the cremation culture, and take that as evidence of the arrival of a new population, then it must be admitted that we would not so much look eastward for evidence of its likely origins as northwards, to the area of the initial development of the urnfield culture which, as we have seen, the Villanovan phenomenon was inseparable from. Archaeological evidence finds an extremely convincing interpretation in the shape of the northern origins theory: a group settled in Tuscany from the north, bringing with it the new funerary rite. Moreover, there is also linguistic support for this theory: the inscriptions left by the Rhaetians in the Alpine area of northern Italy reveal a language which was indisputably related to Etruscan. This would appear to point to an ancient presence of proto-Etruscans, far to the north of Tuscany.

The Northern theory is not, in any case, the only alternative to the Oriental theory: it may also be supposed that the Etruscans never dwelled outside the region with which they were associated in historical times. We have noted that the theory which sees them as an indigenous population, derived from the ancient substratum of the area, has found at least some

Male portrait in painted terra cotta from the Manganello sanctuary (Cerveteri), first quarter of the first century B.C.
Rome, Museo di Villa Giulia
cat. 304

degree of favor with linguistic experts. In linguistic terms, this is indeed the simplest hypothesis. Etruscan is a pre-Indo-European language, and may therefore have belonged to the earliest inhabitants of the place. True, the evidence of idioms related to Etruscan in Rhaetia and on Lemnos argues for the existence of "Etruscoid" elements outside the regions of Etruria proper. However, in the autochthonous perspective, both the Rhaetian and Lemnian inscriptions could be explained as substrative : the pre-Indo-European language stratum may have survived, without being overlain by Indo-European imports, in Rhaetia, Lemnos and Etruria, but without there being any contact between these groups. Rhaetian and Lemnian may have survived remote from Etruscan as scattered relicts of a preceding language, just in the same way as Romanian survived after the Romans' retirement in 271 A.D., despite being isolated from the other Latin-derived languages. Another possible explanation may be found in the phenomenon of migrations. Ancient writers identified the Rhaetians as Etruscans who had settled in the Po Valley before being forced into the Alpine regions by pressure from the Celts. As to the Lemnian documents, which as we have noted are no earlier than the sixth century, these may record the arrival in the region of Etruscans from Italy, perhaps for piracy—assuming that the Etruscans did indeed raid as far afield as the Aegean during the period.

Thus each of the three traditional theories appears capable of providing a satisfactory explanation for the first establishment, around 1200 B.C., of the elements which led to the emergence of the Etruscan civilization four centuries later. Is it only lack of information which prevents us from choosing between them? In reality, the very nature of the problem is debatable. There is now general agreement that—quite simply—we have been asking the wrong question. In 1947 a small volume by Massimo Pallottino entitled *L'origine degli Etruschi* threw into confusion the ranks of etruscologists, hitherto drawn up in good order along the three theoretical lines described above. Pallottino made what may seem to be no more than a common sense observation: the question of the origins of a people never produces a simple and unequivocal response. A people is the historical result, at a given moment, of the coalescence of various elements, and not the prolongation of a single, prior situation.

This statement of the obvious sufficed on its own to demonstrate the inadequacy of traditional theories of the origins of the Etruscans. Each of the three theories contains elements of truth. As emphasized by the Oriental theory, Etruscan civilization cannot be comprehended without reference to the external influences which it underwent. The development of Etruria must be explained by innovations received from Mediterranean sources. But this same explanation is powerless to solve the problem of how the Villanovan cremation rites came into being. These latter must certainly be connected with the spread of the urnfields. And yet the historical Etruscan civilization has little in common with such a primitive culture. On the other hand, the Indigenous theory is also open to criticism, for it seems to suppose that the Etruscan people had been always been present in Italy. But the Etruscan people and civilization only came into being as an independent entity, with its own particular character, concurrently with the Villanovan culture, and more distinctly with the opening up to outside influences of the eighth–seventh centuries. Even if we allow that the inhabitants of Tuscany spoke a proto-Etruscan idiom as early as the second millennium, the fact does not necessarily mean that they were Etruscans proper. The term Etruria only becomes appropriate with the emergence of the Etruscan civilization around the eighth century, by which time it may be said to be the historically datable result of the fusion of a multiplicity of elements. And so to ask where the Etruscans came from appears almost futile today. Instead of trying to isolate a single factor which it is hoped will provide an explanation, in the manner of the three traditional theories, we should take note of the burgeoning variety of the Etruscan world, and attempt to analyze its different components.

Once we adopt such an approach, it appears astonishing how a problem which now seems couched in completely inadequate terms should have been for so long the burning issue of Etruscan studies. Until now we have dealt only with the views of modern etruscologists, as developed since the Renaissance, when early archaeologists first began the process of digging up from the Tuscan soil the remains of a civilization which has held a constant fascination ever since. However the ensuing debate as to its origins was one that had already raged

Bronze helmet with dedication to Zeus after the naval victory off Cuma, from the Olimpia sanctuary, 474 B.C. London, British Museum

in Antiquity. The ancients, too, split into three distinct schools of thought, albeit not precisely consistent with the divisions of modern opinion. The Oriental theory had a precursor in the famous passage of Herodotus, I, 94, an account of the migration to Italy of the Lydians under the hero Tyrrhenos, from whom the Etruscans derived their Greek name of Tyrrhenians. The Indigenous theory was also well-known to the ancients, though we know of only one of its apologists, Dionysius of Halicarnassus, a Greek rhetorician who lived in Rome during the Augustan period. By contrast we have already noted that the third, Northern theory was first put forward as late as the eighteenth century; nonetheless the Ancients, too, possessed a third theory, one which predated Herodotus but which was swept aside by the very success of the work of the father of history. This earlier view saw the Etruscans as Pelasgians, the descendants of a people who the Greeks believed had inhabited the land of Hellas before their own arrival (Dionysius of Halicarnassus, I, 28).

If we refer to the chapters which Dionysius of Halicarnassus devotes to the issue, in *Roman Antiquities* I, 26–30, we find he deals with the problem of the origins in much the same fashion as our own manuals of etruscology: after an exposition of the current theories, he goes on to put them to the test of linguistic and cultural data before setting out his own personal conviction, namely that the Etruscans were an indigenous people. Unsurprisingly, then, Dionysius earned the epithet of the "first etruscologist," while later scholars have been pleased to call themselves his heirs.

Nonetheless, the impression of pure objectivity which Dionysius conveys is illusory. His manner of proceeding is the absolute opposite of disinterested scholarly impartiality! His views on the Etruscans need to be seen in the overall perspective of his work, which is quite unscientific in its approach. His intention was to convey a favorable impression of Rome to his fellow Greeks, which required him to pursue the unlikely thesis that the Romans were not in fact barbarians, and that Rome was a Greek city. To achieve this, he drew on all the legendary material handed down by tradition—the Arcadian Evander who settled on the Palatine, Heracles passing through Rome on his return from the western limits of the world, Aeneas who reached Latium after the fall of Troy. Inevitably, his view of the Etruscans was conditioned by this perspective on Rome. Not only did he attempt to prove that Rome was a Greek city, he also tried to make this an exclusive honor by depicting the other peoples of Italy as mere barbarians. And to do this he had to reject any claims from potential rivals who might also be able to boast Hellenic ancestry. The Etruscans were a people of that kind: although not thorough-going Greeks, the Pelasgians still belonged to the Hellenic universe, which was enough to induce Dionysius to refute any such tradition. He also rejected the Oriental theory as put forward by Herodotus: even the Lydians were a little too close to the Greeks and their world for such a suggestion to be acceptable. The autochthonous doctrine, on the other hand, found Dionysius fully in agreement—for obvious reasons: the Etruscans were thus indigenous Italians, quite unrelated to the Hellenes, meaning that the Romans were the sole natives of Greek descent in the peninsula.

The working methods of Dionysius of Halicarnassus are scientific, at least in appearance. However it is important to understand his approach in the context of the significance possessed by claims for the origins of peoples in Antiquity. Far from constituting a concern of scientific study, such claims were more usually an expression of the ways in which populations perceived their respective relations. When two peoples enjoyed a positive rapport, they would develop a literary basis for their common ancestry. Diplomatic custom also referred habitually to a *suggeneia*, or kinship. This is the proper perspective from which to view those theories which suggest Lydian or Pelasgian origins for the Etruscans. The core of Herodotus' argument is that the Etruscans, as descendants of Tyrrhenos, son of the Lydian king Atys, were related to the Lydians: in other words a typical *suggeneia* myth which perhaps arose in the courts of the powerful kings of Lydia during the sixth century. As for the Pelasgian theory, the supposed quasi-Hellenic origins of a people who set out from Greece, together with their legendary landfall at Spina on the Adriatic, clearly show that this was a mythical justification for the close commercial ties formed by Greeks and Etruscans at the port on the Po Delta. Conversely the view of the Etruscans as barbarians, as propounded by Dionysius in the Indigenous theory, must always have carried the same negative connotation, at least for the Greeks: it is tempting to trace it back to a hostile invention of Syracusan historiographers, at the period when Syracuse fought with the Etruscans for control of the seas around Italy.

Thus the traditions handed down by Antiquity with respect to the origins of the Etruscans were from the outset nothing but the expression of the image which their allies or enemies wished to give of them. Attributions of the kind should never be given consideration as historical documents. Naturally there has been real debate on the issue, in the course of which—for instance in the observations of Dionysius of Halicarnassus concerning the isolation of the Etruscan language—we occasionally find genuinely scientific elements and perhaps actual historical memories. Nonetheless, these were never the dominant aspects of the polemic. And it was because the Moderns did no more than take up the controversy where the Ancients left off, that the field of Etruscan studies remained for so long encumbered with this overblown question of the origins—which has finally been recognized as inapposite, in the terms in which it was put.

For an ancient introduction to the Oriental theory: Piganiol 1953, pp. 328–52. *A good introduction to this issue, displaying the modern-day theories and including a bibliography*: Heurgon 1969, pp. 363–71, Pallottino 1984, pp. 81–117. *For a detailed analysis of the three ancient theories on the Etruscans' origin*: Briquel 1984, Briquel 1991, Briquel 1993b (*for some outlines on the autochthonous theory among the Etruscans themselves:* Briquel 1986, pp. 295–313; *for the creation of the autochthonous theory by the Etruscans in the Augustan period:* Torelli 1986a, p. 42; *for autochthony as genuine Etruscan tradition*; Aigner Foresti 1992a, pp. 93–113). *For different points of view on the genesis of the Lydian tradition:* Dewes 1992, pp. 14–39 (*genesis in fifth-century Athens*); Braccesi 1998, pp. 53–61 (*genesis in Syracuse, by Hieron*). *For an analysis of Dionysius of Halicarnassus' theories:* Musti 1970. *For the traditions on the origins in classical Antiquity:* Bickerman 1985, pp. 99–117. *On the claims of "suggeneia,":* Musti 1963, pp. 225–34; Curty 1995.

The Origin and Diffusion of Villanovan Culture

The beginning of the cultural processes leading up to the First Iron Age and the concentration of settlements on the sites of the future Etruscan cities should in all probability be placed during the Late Bronze Age, that is, in the second half of the second millennium B.C. In the traditional division in ages of the stages of Italian pre-history and proto-history, the greater part of the second millennium before the Christian era is labeled Bronze Age, owing to the particular extension during that period of the use of copper and tin alloy in manufacturing utensils, weapons and ornamental articles; during the following age (called Iron Age) it is not until an advanced stage that the use of iron, especially in the production of arms and utensils, appears to have been preferred to that of bronze. The Bronze Age has been conventionally divided in three stages: Early (eighteenth-sixteenth century B.C.); Middle (sixteenth–fourteenth century B.C.); Late (thirteenth–tenth century B.C.), in turn classified in Recent (thirteenth–mid-twelfth century B.C.) and Final (mid-eleventh–tenth century B.C.). The Iron Age has been arranged in two stages, respectively the ninth and the eighth centuries. Recently, the notion of advancing these chronologies has been examined, on the grounds of dendrochronological and radiocarbon (Carbon 14) tests performed on built-up areas in central Europe and peninsular Italy (Randsborg 1996), that we have a hard time conforming with Aegean datings, which up to now have been the reference for all local seriations. Based on that new view of absolute chronology, the Orientalizing civilization in Italy would have preceded by one or two generations the same event in Greece, and Pithekoussai, for instance, would have been founded in the first half of the ninth century. Attempts to reorganize the absolute chronology, especially for advanced periods, appear for the moment to be "no more than a theoretic exercise" (Bettelli 1997).

Precedents: proto-Villanovan culture and the constitution of local cultures
In the Final Bronze Age (mid-twelfth–tenth century B.C.) the layout of built-up areas, no longer connected with cattle-tracks as during the Middle and Early Bronze, seems to be better distributed. Corroborating the intensive use of the territory and constant demographic increase, by now we have identified in southern Etruria at least seventy attested settlements, plus the same amount of traces of presence.
The typical built-up area of that chronological period usually occupies a rise or a tufaceous plateau covering five hectares at the most, secluded, at the confluence of two watercourses. An example is the site of San Giovenale, near Viterbo, bordered on the south side by the river Vesca and on the lateral ones by two of its affluents, the streams Pietrisco and Carraccio di Fammilume. These small tablelands, with natural or artificial defenses, do not appear to have been entirely built up: it is supposed that the unoccupied part of the protected areas was set aside for keeping cattle or land for cultivation, spots occupied only by specific groups, or for shelter areas in case of enemy attacks.
Castellaccio di Sorgenti della Nova, where for the last few years systematic digs have been undertaken, presents a settlement arranged on several terraces, naturally fortified, defended by steep walls and surrounded by two confluent moats. The wide terraces are carved deep into the rock walls. On the terraces there were both cave houses and huts.
The huts, always small, had foundations carved more or less deeply out of the tuff shelf, with perimetral grooves and holes for posts. The layout can be either elliptic, circular or rectangular, sometimes with traces of partitioning of the inner space; the entrance often seems to be preceded by a small portico. Next to the living structures there are rooms of like forms and constitution but mostly very small in size, probably used as storehouses and depositories; or perhaps for sheltering single domestic animals. At Sorgente della Nova there are also exceptionally well-preserved domed terra-cotta ovens and hearths for cooking food, located in small artificial caves.
In other built-up areas (at Monte Rovello near Allumiere and at Luni sul Mignone) structures of impressive dimensions have been identified, having a rectangular layout (15–17 meters long and 8–9 meters wide), the roof resting directly on a low bulwark of earth or stones. In all probability these were the houses of the leader of the respective communities, also intended for political and religious functions.
After an economy essentially based on stock-raising that had led to mainly seasonal settlements, the development of steady activities began, mostly cultivation of land and sedentary

Small bronze from Costiaccia Bambagini (Vetulonia), end of the eighth–first half of the seventh century B.C. Florence, Museo Archeologico

animal-raising. The vegetable varieties that were cultivated already feature several types of cereals, especially barley and spelt; among the animals cattle, goats and pigs prevailed. From the tests carried out on bone residues, hunting appears to have been infrequent: the inhabitants of Castellaccio di Sorgenti della Nova, for instance, ate essentially pork meat, whereas there are hardly any remains of boars, the only animal they appear to have hunted. The boosting of agricultural activity should also be connected with the increase and improvements in metal production. We are dealing with a qualitative and quantitative progression of extraordinary scope: now new categories of articles appear and others are improved, such as scythes, saws, hatchets, chisels, certainly linked to cultivation. Next to the striking increase in the volume of the production of bronze articles, local typological features are emphasized. With the last period of the Bronze Age (twelfth–tenth century B.C.), metal production appears to be a stable component of the cultural background of a region having a wealth of mines, a production that from a quantitative and economic point of view plays an increasingly important role. Of special interest in that regard is a series of casting molds for hatchets, brooches and small daggers found in one of the huts at Scarceta (hut 13), which should be considered a foundry; equally indicative are the bronze troves, particularly plentiful and differentiated precisely by the Final Bronze Age. Many of these should actually be seen as depositories belonging to casters-craftsmen-tradesmen, with everyday utensils mostly in fragments, set aside to be cast down. The bronze hoard of Coste del Marano (in the northern part of the locality of Tolfa), featuring over a hundred and forty pieces, nearly all whole and well-preserved, appears to have a different meaning: the bronzes, placed in a vase or buried in the ground, included tableware (three laminated bronze cups) and articles of personal adornment (large *fibulae*, pendants, pins, and so forth) or symbolic-ritual (miniature vane hatchets). The craftsmanship is technically excellent; the typological affinities of the materials belong to a very vast area including transalpine Europe (especially the cups) and Greece (*fibulae*, cup handles), but it now seems unquestionable that we are dealing with local products. Certainly at least part of these objects, that is the laminated bronze cups and the large *fibulae*, should be considered articles of prestige, and therefore part of a sort of "treasure."

Organized exchanges, beyond mere wide-spread transmission of technical notions and models owed to travelling craftsmen between Etruria and other areas of old Italy and perhaps indirectly with sub-Mycenaean Greece, took place by the eleventh century B.C.

As regards funerary ritual we avail of a systematic documentation by the twelfth century B.C., when cremation of corpses appears and then prevails. That rite, which coincides with the urnfield cultures (*Urnenfeldern*) of continental Europe, spreads from the Alps down to the north-eastern tip of Sicily, especially during the last stage of the Bronze Age, with necropolises usually defined as "proto-Villanovan," owing to their affinities with later Villanovan cultural aspects, that were to become manifest at the beginning of the Iron Age, yet only in one part of Italy (Etruria and connected areas).

The switch from the inhumation funerary custom to cremation is held to be attested by the dome-tombs of the Crostoletto di Lamone necropolis on the left bank of the river Fiora, not far from Castellaccio di Sorgente della Nova, with both inhumation and cremation depositions, and whose plan could be dated to the Recent Bronze Age. The tomb structures of Crostoletto di Lamone, with a diameter varying from 5 to 14 meters and a height attaining 1.5 meters, appear beyond doubt different from the more modest ones of other burial grounds, where the urn seems deposited directly in the small hollow dug in the ground or protected by tuff caskets or stone cists. The funerary urn was nearly always a biconical vase, usually covered with an overturned bowl. Occasionally the graves are for two: in a single small hollow (or casket for two) two ossuaries are deposited at the same time.

The oldest period of the use of cremation (twelfth century B.C.) is characterized by tombs nearly completely lacking in burial goods: an example is the Ponte San Pietro Valle necropolis, in the river Fiora district, ascribable at the most to the twelfth century B.C., where in the overall sparseness of the funerary furnishings, consisting exclusively in the urn and its cover, we notice two amber elements of the type "Treasure of Tiryns," having a form appearing extensively throughout several stages of the Final Italian Bronze Age (Negroni Catacchio 1999).

Bronze cart from Monterozzi (Tarquinia), first quarter of the eighth century B.C. *Tarquinia, Museo Archeologico*

As the cremation rite becomes more widespread, a few graves are also enriched, differing from other depositions; the isolated tomb of Valle del Campaccio (Allumiere) is exemplary, with articles of personal adornment (*fibula*) of an exceptional size (about 15 centimeters long), like those mentioned above of the Coste del Marano repository.

In the Poggio la Pozza (Allumiere) necropolis, where we know the absolutely greatest number of graves of this period, around fifty, ascribable for the most part to a late chronological period, the furnishings are often characterized by a remarkable number of miniaturized vases, according to a custom attested perhaps more strictly in Latium, south of the Tiber. Another likeness of this necropolis with the Latium environment consists in the use of a reduced model of a hut for the urn; this type of urn, attested in that stage at Tarquinia and Montetosto (Cerveteri) as well, must have been the prerogative of a small number, men and women, outstanding in the group they belong to: the burial goods of the Poggio la Pozza tomb, that of a woman, is remarkable by the exceptional amount of personal adornments in bronze, amber, bone, etc.

This information allows us to imagine individuals or families as leaders of several groups. It

Fragment of a tripod from Poggio la Guardia (Vetulonia), end of the eighth–first half of the seventh century B.C.
Florence, Museo Archeologico

was during the final period of the Bronze Age that must have begun the process which (at least two centuries later) was to develop the aristocratic society based on increasingly large family cells and the possession of land.

The Villanovan revolution

During the tenth century in old Italy, after an overall cultural uniformity, differences begin to appear in areas corresponding to large regions or territorial divisions, that coincide in the historical era with specific peoples: Veneti, Etruscans, Latins, Sabines.

The culture connected with the territory occupied by the Etruscans has been called Villanovan. The name comes from Giovanni Gozzadini's chance discovery in 1853, about 8 kilometers east of Bologna, of a series of tombs characterized by cremation, by the deposition of bone remains in impasto vases (that is, unrefined clay hand-worked and baked at medium temperature) commonly known as biconical, because of their form (nearly like two superimposed cone), usually covered with bowls, black impasto as well; by the more or less relevant presence of ornamental articles or at least related to the deceased (especially *fibulae*, bracelets, necklaces, arms, razors, utensils), and pottery, always impasto (beakers, bowls, dishes, and so on). Later the name was extended to exemplify like funerary manifestations of Bologna, Tarquinia, Bisenzio and other sites of Tyrrhenian Etruria and therefore of the few evidenced settlements, in connection with these necropolises.

By "Villanovan" we mean a system of customs, a typical expression of material culture of the area that will historically be Etruscan, that is the large territory that diagonally crosses Italy, from the east basin of the Po to the central Tyrrhenian down to the Tiber. There are a great number of elements of continuity linking the Villanovan with cultural features of the Final Bronze Age, which for that reason is called proto-Villanovan: the funerary ritual is identical, the use of the biconical ossuary is wide-spread, and a substantial continuity can be found in the typology and processing of the metal objects belonging to the burial goods.

This continuity of life is now ascertained in the main Etruscan cities by the last period of the Bronze Age (eleventh–tenth century B.C.). The Etruscans themselves had the origins of the Etruscan nation go back to a date coinciding with the eleventh or tenth century B.C.: Varro (in Censorino, *De die natali*, 17, 5–6, and in Servius, *ad Aeneidem,* VIII, 526) relates that the *libri rituales* gave the duration of the Etruscan *nomen* as not exceeding ten centuries; again Servius recalls (*ad Eclogas,* IX, 46) that according to Augustus the haruspices claimed that the tenth century would have begun under his empire, coinciding with the end of the Etruscan people. With the beginning of the Iron Age, at the turn of the tenth century B.C., the population left nearly all the premises of the earlier period to settle in groups of several hundreds of individuals in the areas of Veio, Tarquinia, Vulci, etc., occupying in separate complexes vast plateaus and adjoining hills.

So in the ninth century B.C. the territory appears divided in large districts presided over by very close-set groups of villages and a small number of isolated houses, dislocated in strategic positions, whereby we can assume some form of dependence. Compared to the previous period, the type of conglomeration is characterized by a greater concentration of the settlements: from an average of about 10 kilometers between one house and another in the Final Bronze Age, at the beginning of the Iron Age it is reduced to less than 1 kilometer between the settlements within a same district. The series of towns mostly located on high, rather inaccessible plateaus, their priority being defense rather than agriculture, are replaced by settlements on vast tablelands where the population is gathered in close-set villages. We can observe a sort of synectic process whereby, at Vulci for instance, the people from the district of the Fiora join with those from the Albegna.

These vast tablelands appear to have been chosen, aside from their extension and accessibility, for the availability of resources in their close vicinity (farming, grazing, metals, etc.) and for their location near landingplaces on the coast (such as Vulci, Tarquinia, Cerveteri, Vetulonia), by rivers (such as Chiusi, Orvieto and Veio), by lakes (such as Bisenzio). Populonia's position, directly on the coast, is exceptional; usually these groups prefer hillside areas where they enjoy extensive farm land with dry soil, so therefore at least 4–5 kilometers from the sea, coastal lagunas and rivers. By the early ninth century smaller groups appear on the coast line, like the settlement of Torre Valdaliga near Civitavecchia (to be held very prob-

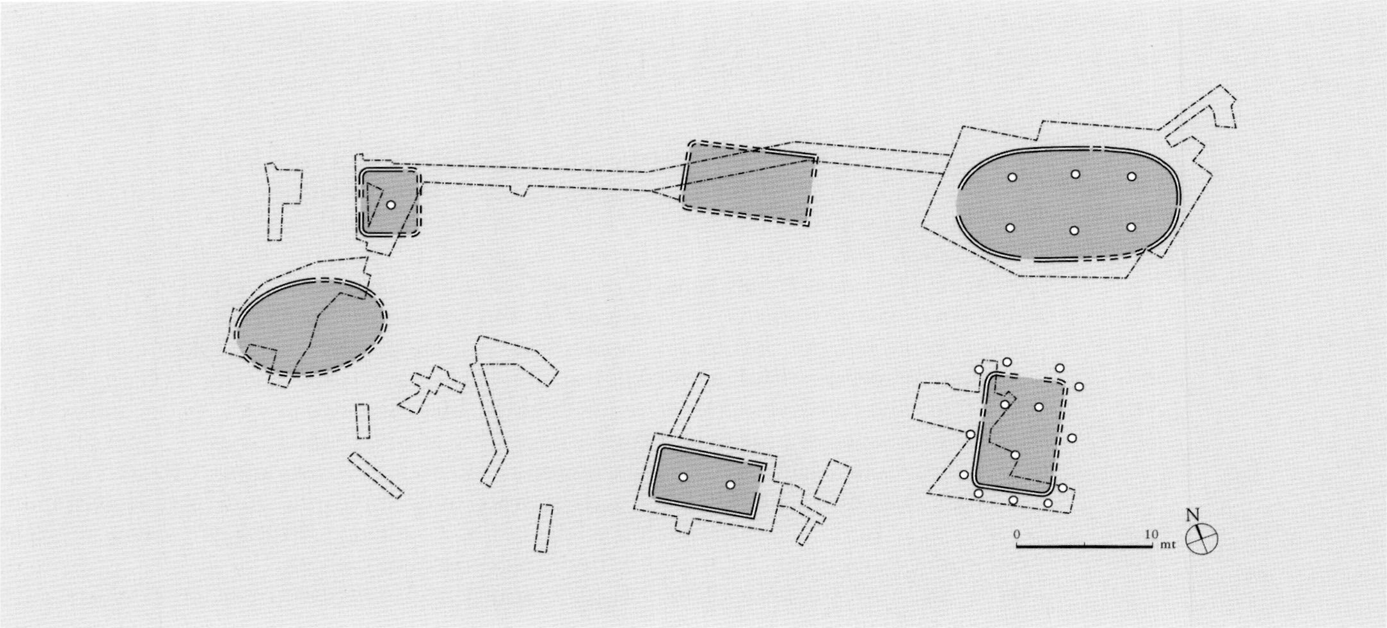

Plan of the Calvario settlement near Monterozzi (Tarquinia)

ably as a landingplace belonging to the Tarquinia group), or on lake shores, like the village of Gran Carro on the east shore of the lake of Bolsena, in all likelihood presided over by Orvieto (Volsinii). In the plain where there used to be lake Prile, a laguna overlooked by Vetulonia, a small necropolis has been discovered in which the materials present features very similar to the ones found in Vetulonia.

The process of population concentration in an area that is vast but well-delimited orographically must have taken place in a not entirely linear fashion. Aside from on the main tableland, which could reach 180 hectares like at Vulci or 190 hectares like at Veio, where we believe there was a variable number of separate villages, each one with its own necropolis, we know there were houses on the nearby tablelands as well. There are strong indications of mutations in the relationship with the territory, especially if we observe the radical change in the dislocation of the settlements and the tendency to concentrate population in tableland environments, surrounded by large cultivated areas. The cultivation of new lands on a large scale must have led to new production relationships. It is hard to imagine that the resources of several hundred square kilometers could have been exploited in a situation where the land was still prevailingly shared: so it does not seem at all unreasonable to postulate a parcelling of property at that time.

The case of Tarquinia is enlightening: the settlements of the Civita tableland, the site of the future historic city, are extended on the bordering plateaus by the Calvario settlement, undoubtedly of a certain size (it has been said about a thousand inhabitants; but demographic estimates, in the present state of our knowledge, are hard to verify), by those of the Infernaccio and modern Tarquinia (medieval Sant'Antonio district), with which coincide respectively the burial grounds of the Poggis (Poggio di Selciatello-Sopra, Poggio Selciatello, Poggio dell'Impiccato), the Arcatelle and Rose necropolises and the group recently brought to light at Villa Bruschi-Falgari (Trucco forthcoming), these last two being ascribable at the most to the ninth century B.C. We can identify as belonging to the fringes of the Tarquinia territory, with a clear strategic function, the small settlements of Barbarano Romano inland towards the Tiber area and Torre Valdaliga on the coast.

Little is known about the inner organization of the villages, owing to the scarcity of systematic excavations in built-up areas, but especially because of the type of constructions and urban works, for the most part in perishable materials.

The only sufficiently explored Villanovan settlement, yet not entirely so, is the one brought to light at Tarquinia by the Fondazione Lerici excavations in the area of the archaic Monterozzi necropolis, in the Calvario locality. Near the north ridge of the hill, in a 200 by 100 meter-area, the remains of at least twenty-five oval, oblong rectangular and quadrangular huts were found. The analysis of the marks the huts left in the ground points on the whole to the adoption of a remarkable variety of solutions. In fact, as we have seen, round, oval, square and rectangular layouts are documented, without the change in forms implying any chronological difference, as contemporary examples of hut remains and their comparison with contemporary hut urns indicate. These small funerary models, already attested in the Final Bronze Age, but in use in Etruria especially in the ninth and eighth centuries, constitute the essential documentation for the reconstruction of proto-historic houses, especially for the elevation.

We know more about necropolises than about houses, and their study has enabled us to have an idea of the cultural development.

In the course of the ninth century, the only rite of most of the Villanovan necropolises, as we have already seen, is incineration. Yet certifications of burials in graves are found not only in "colonial" areas like Pontecagnano, but in the heart of Etruria at Cerveteri as well, where since the origin of the Sorbo necropolis the two rites co-exist, and at Populonia, where graves of interred corpses, wide-spread in the following periods, appear attested at an early stage in the burial ground of Piano delle Granate (graves 7 and 8, Minto 1917 excavation). The graves dug in virgin soil are generally like wells, that is, more or less regular cylinder-shaped. In northern Etruria, in Emilia and Romagna the well or the hole can be lined with pebbles or flagstones, the latter arranged at times so as to form a lithic cist; in southern Etruria we often find a casket in tufa (Veio, Bisenzio) or *nenfro*, Tarquinia tufa, protecting the ossuary. The burial goods, extremely scanty in the oldest depositions, appear to consist mainly in the ossuary: it contains and protects with a lid the burnt bone remains, one or more *fibulae* depending on sex, spiral hairclips and spindles in female depositions, razors or brooches in male ones. Usually additional vases are rare, and arms exceptional. The typical ossuary is a biconical impasto vase, with a form elongated compared to the "proto-Villanovan" one, bearing at the most a rich engraved decoration. These vases usually have one or two horizontal handles placed at the widest point; yet in the case of two-handled vases one of the two is found broken. The decoration, obtained with a comb-shaped instrument with several teeth, appears on the body and neck of the vase and is arranged in several more or less close-set stripes; the use of decoration with affixed metal bands, previously attested in Final Bronze Age contexts (Ardea) is more unusual. That decorative technique, besides Italy, is common in French and Swiss palafitte regions, where it already appears in the Late Bronze Age, so we assume it spread from that area. The lid of the ossuary-vases nearly always consists in a bowl (or dish) also fitted with a handle. The typical Villanovan bowl-lid presents a trunco-conical container with a hollow rim and ring holders held by two pseudo-grips. Already in the oldest phase, instead of the above-mentioned bowls and dishes to close the ossuary, we find pottery knobbed-bell helmets (at Tarquinia, Veio, Cerveteri, Pontecagnano, etc.), later crested, copying bronze ones. Among ossuaries, the huts models already pointed out particularly deserve mention; hut urns are attested especially in coastal (at Vetulonia, Vulci, Tarquinia, Caere) and southern inland Etruria (Bisenzio and the Veio territory): the percentage of these funerary urns compared to the usual biconical ones is nonetheless very low and therefore special: in the various necropolises we find one hut urn for every hundred depositions. In the centers where small model houses are attested as ossuaries, the helmet-lid of the ossuary can have a top fashioned like a hut roof: even in the case of the most common type of Villanovan culture deposition, the biconical vase, beside the ideology of the armed man expressed in the helmet we have the house one molded on the top. As in Latium necropolises, especially the Osteria dell'Osa (Gabi) one, huts and weapons, symbolically miniaturized, appear combined in chief-family graves, in Villanovan Etruria as well the two functions—house-owner and warrior, that is custodian of the family within (the hut) and without (arms)—are combined and attributed to a single person.

During this first period of Villanovan culture the burial goods do not appear to reflect any difference of wealth or social status: the only distinction is between female and male depositions, and among them but a very few are connoted, by the helmet or rare arms, as belonging to warriors.

Distinctive elements such as hut urns appear indifferently to be a male or female preroga-

Impasto single-handled biconical ossuary from Tomb 59 at Poggio Selciatello (Tarquinia), first half of the ninth century B.C.
Florence, Museo Archeologico
cat. 10.1

Impasto spools from Tomb 59 at Poggio Selciatello (Tarquinia), first half of the ninth century B.C.
Florence, Museo Archeologico
cat. 10.3

Bronze and glass paste fibulae *from Tomb 59 at Poggio Selciatello (Tarquinia), first half of the ninth century* B.C.
Florence, Museo Archeologico
cat. 10.5

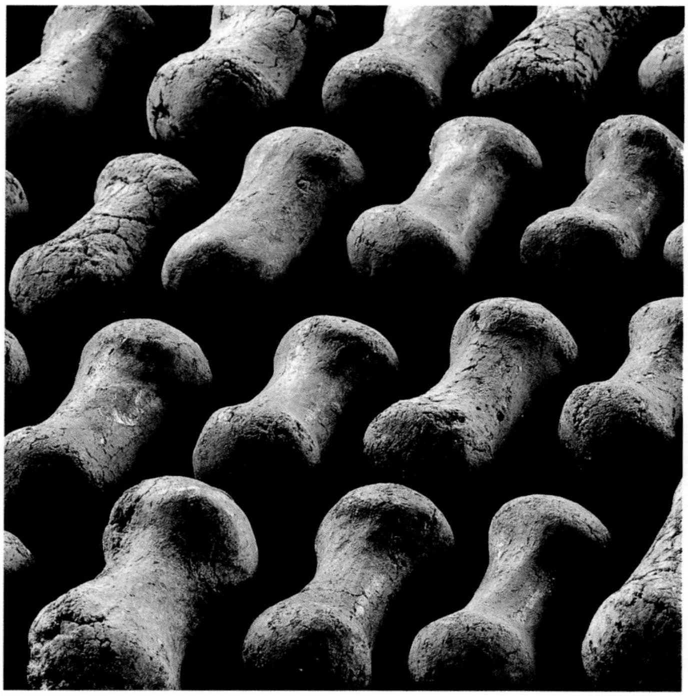

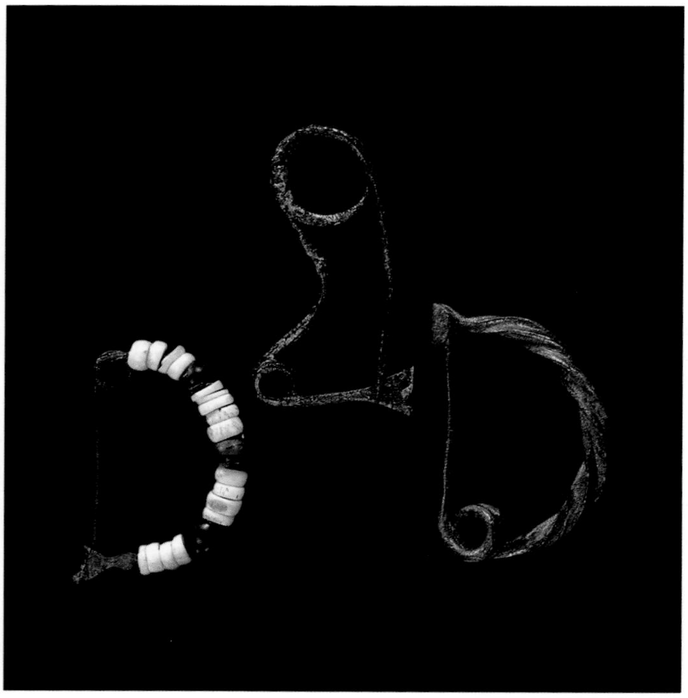

Impasto burial goods from Tomb 179 at Poggio Selciatello (Tarquinia), second half of the ninth century B.C.
Florence, Museo Archeologico
cat. 9

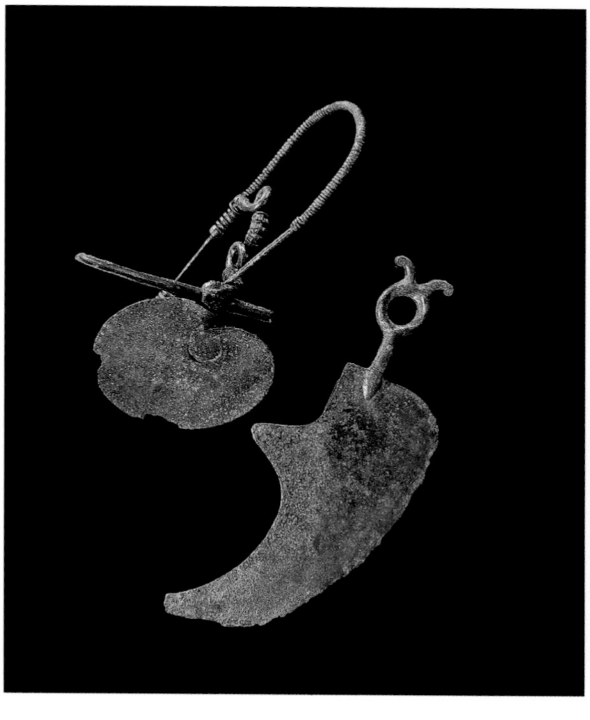

Bronze moon-shaped razor and fibula *from Tomb 179 at Poggio Selciatello (Tarquinia), second half of the ninth century* B.C.
Florence, Museo Archeologico
cats. 9.7; 9.8

Bronze spear-head and ferrule from Tomb I at Poggio dell'Impiccato (Tarquinia), first half of the eigth century B.C.
Florence, Museo Archeologico
cat. 58

tive: we should attribute to a woman some burial goods (from Vulci?) where there are two miniature impasto distaffs and a spindle. In Etruria as regards burial furnishings there is no difference between deposition in hut urns or in biconical vases.
Documentation of the necropolises therefore seems to suggest a totally equalitarian structure. Yet it is more probable that, owing to a very solid funerary ideology, members of the community were considered equal in the burial rite: there have been discussions about an isonomic intent being combined with the rigidity of the incineration rite (d'Agostino 1995).
The massive displacement of people that characterizes this period is unconceivable without political bodies capable of imposing their decisions on the single village communities: the various groups, undoubtedly each formed by people bound by family ties, displaced inside or outside the tuffaceous tablelands that are to become the sites of the later Etruscan city-states, demonstrate such close bonds among themselves, as can be seen by the examination of the artisanal production as well, that we can assume their belonging to the same political unity, and even speak of "pre-urban" human concentrations.

The diffusion of the Villanovan culture

The area in which, as soon as it appears, the Villanovan culture extends is not restricted to the territory of Etruria proper.
Besides the Tyrrhenian Villanovan we can distinguish: in the north an Emilian Villanovan, including the region south of the Po plain, Bologna being the leading town, and a Romagna Villanovan evidenced especially in the Rimini area, at Verucchio; at the center of the peninsula a nucleus at Fermo (Ascoli Piceno), entirely isolated; in the south Villanovan traits at Capua and in the Salerno area, with the necropolises of Pontecagnano, Arenosola and Capodifiume, next to Paestum, probably a bridgehead towards the other large southern Villanovan center, Sala Consilina, located inland between the Salerno territory and Lucania in the Diano vallum.
Likenesses can be observed not only in funerary practices but in settlement typologies and necropolises as well. The beginning of the formation process of Etruscan cities and "the colonial-style expansion are concomitant events" (d'Agostino 1995). Giving a certain plausibility to an eventual "colonization," that is to the presence of Etruscan people in these "Villanovan" ramifications, we are backed by historical and epigraphical sources. On the one hand we avail of information come down to us from classical authors, such as Pliny's (*Naturalis historia,* III, 70), who claims that "the territory three thousand paces long that extends from the Sorrento peninsula to the river Sele belongs to the Etruscans," information however that we do not know to what date it should be ascribed; or that of Verrius Flaccus (*Etruscarum rerum,* fr. 1 P) who held Tarchun, the eponymous hero of Tarquinia and therefore the Tarquinians, responsible for the foundation of the twelve cities of Po Valley Etruria; on the other, it is worth mentioning the evidence at Bologna of the use of Etruscan writing by the end of the eighth century B.C., a period, especially in the Emilian district, that does not appear to present a break with earlier stages, so that it is still called Villanovan; furthermore such testimonies appear more or less contemporary with the oldest inscriptions in Etruria proper.
The observation that the Villanovan expansion concerns the main and most fertile areas of central Italy has led to consider the quest for land as the mainspring for these movements (Torelli 1980).
At Bologna, a city located at the river Reno's outlet in the plain, we can ascribe to the middle of the ninth century B.C. the eastern Savena and San Vitale necropolises, with pit tombs sometimes lined with pebbles or sandstone, containing the biconical ossuary and a few bronze artifacts; large river stones marked the grave on the outside. The oldest identified and likely settlements—one beyond Porta San Vitale relative to the homonymous necropolis, another recently identified in the district of the fairground, a third connected with the Villanova di Castenaso necropolises, and last the Vigorso one on the left bank of the Idice—are even 8 kilometers away.
From the early eighth century B.C. on, although the burial grounds of Savena and San Vitale are still in use, the western necropolises beyond the Sant'Isaia gate (Benacci necropolises) began being used; extending from east to west they were to last until the historical period,

attesting the beginning of the occupation to the west of the city, the main nucleus of Villanovan Bologna, as Antonio Zannoni's investigations on "archaic housing" have proven since the last century. Bologna enjoys a fortunate geographic position: since the start of its formation it occupied the middle of a quadrivium, thus appearing to be an area of sorting of finished and unfinished products, not just local but also coming from Tuscany on the one hand, and Paleovenete or else northern on the other.
Comparison with Bologna burial grounds has allowed to attribute to the early ninth century B.C. the oldest graves of the Verucchio necropolis, near Rimini, considered "extreme north-eastern ramifications on the Adriatic for the economic and commercial interests of Villanovan Tusco-Latium centers" (Gentili 1987). The connection with Tyrrhenian areas occurred through the valley of the Marecchia, the Apennine pass of Viamaggio and the valley of the Tiber. But we should not underestimate the analogies with the Bologna area, especially in the pottery production, which preeminently represents the oldest depositions. It would make better sense to claim that analogies with the Tyrrhenian communities, such as the use of the crested helmet on the lids of the ossuaries, particularly obvious at an advanced stage of Villanovan culture, are owed to easy connections and exchanges due to the fortunate position and river ways, but that the original matrix is the same as the Bologna one; or even that the Rimini area settlement, in the Pian del Monte locality, about 15 kilometers from the sea, can be derived from Po Valley communities. The necropolises form a crown along the slopes of the hill. The Campo del Tesoro and Lavatoio one goes back to the ninth century B.C. Gino Vinicio Gentili suggested that already during the old Verucchio period (early ninth–first half of the eighth century B.C.) small groups had spread from the hegemonous center, first of all along the course of the Marecchia, "a way open to overseas trade;" besides, eastern Romagna appears to have plentiful water and woods and therefore to be very attractive for agriculture, cattle-raising and the exploitation of wood.
Fermo seems to be an island of Villanovan culture within the Picene area. Analogies, especially with the funerary burial goods of Etruria, had led to assume an interest of some community of inland Etruria (Orvieto or perhaps Chiusi) towards the Adriatic Sea and its traffic, easily accessible through the valleys of the Tiber, the Nera, and from the other side of the Apennines, of the Tenna. The localization of two burial grounds on the edge of the historic center of Fermo seems to indicate the top of the hills as the area of Villanovan housing. The well tombs are covered with one or more slabs of stone that also must have served to mark them. Numerous ossuaries feature an embossed plastic decoration between circular rings on the upper part of the neck, that has matches especially at Chiusi.
The beginning of the Iron Age, ahead of other proto-historical communities of Campania, marks the occupation of the Villanovan centers of Capua, Pontecagnano and Sala Consilina. Whereas the cultural aspects of the oldest phase of Capua appear more composite, showing a number of points of contact with communities north and south of the Tiber, the countless Pontecagnano contexts appear closely linked with southern coastal Etruria Villanovan. Not only do we observe profound differences with the neighboring communities with respect to the culture of "fossa" tombs of the Cuma-Torre Galli type in the funerary ritual, but in the organization in the territory as well: as in the large centers of Etruria the burial grounds, dense with graves, are laid out mostly in a diametrically opposite position, on the edges of the large areas meant for housing. Small, farther apart necropolises restricted to the ninth century B.C., for instance the Pagliarone one at Pontecagnano, indicate the presence in the oldest stage of small villages located outside the tableland as well. Small groups, like in the gulf of Salerno at Capodifiume, spring up in the territory with an openly strategic character. The remarkable affinities between Pontecagnano and the centers of southern coastal Etruria in personal customs, like the use of the sword with scabbards richly decorated with hunting scenes, or of spindles with disc-shaped elements in bronze foil, and in ideological and ritual choices, as documented by a hut urn or knobbed-bell helmets used as lids of the biconicals, can induce us to identify Tarquinia as the likely place of origin of the Salerno group. In the Pontecagnano terra-cotta helmets the reference to the roof of the hut is not expressed at the top, but in the engraved decoration: the lid of Tomb 6569 is of particular interest, figuring on one side a deer and boar hunt scene and on the other in all likelihood a πόθνια θηρῶν (De Natale 1996). The consideration that at Pontecagnano at first

Double flask, wheel pendant, and leech fibula from the Tomb of the Warrior at Poggio alle Croci (Volterra), last quarter of the eight century B.C.
Volterra, Museo Guarnacci
cats. 12.2; 12.11; 12.9

only men were cremated allowed us to identify in them the group of "colonizers" from Etruria (d'Agostino 1982). One might imagine a sort of *ver sacrum*, a custom that sources consistently pass down to us for the Italic world (Sabine above all), and that for most of ancient historiography sprung from the search for new lands (Martin 1973).
Whereas during the eighth century B.C., at Pontecagnano, Capua to the south and Bologna or Verucchio to the north, the Villanovan traits appear obviously present, at Fermo and Sala Consilina the respective neighboring cultures, Picene and *Fossakultur*, seem to prevail.

Relationships and exchanges with people of other cultures
Two or three generations after the advent of the so-called Villanovan revolution, burial goods, previously very plain, are enriched by accessories, signs indicating prestige, and articles attesting frequent exchanges between the various Etruscan communities and other communities with different cultures, especially with those of Nuraghic Sardinia. Next to cremation we have interments mostly in earthen graves and exceptionally, at Populonia, in chamber tombs with pseudo-vaulted roofs.
The corpse was laid out on its back entirely dressed: women with more adornments, men with arms and both sexes with vases as grave-goods. The latter consisting usually in pottery vessels appears common to all depositions, both interment and cremation. Now weapons appear to be more attested, but still connected with depositions remarkable by other elements (hut urns, scepters, etc.); more widespread among the men's depositions are burial goods with helmet and razor, exceptional ones with helmet (usually bronze), razor, sword and lance. So we observe a widespread transformation in the funerary ritual, whereby the burial goods, after being rigorously "poor" become frequently more elaborate, and the ex-

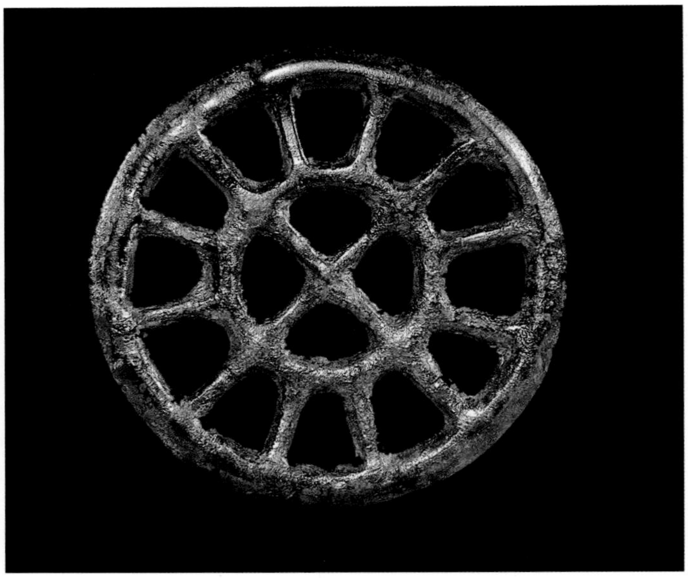

right
Bronze javelin head and spear head, from the Tomb of the Warrior at Poggio alle Croci (Volterra), last quarter of the eight century B.C.
Volterra, Museo Guarnacci
cats. 12.7; 12.6

below
Two-handled patera and hemispheric bowl from the Tomb of the Warrior at Poggio alle Croci (Volterra), last quarter of the eight century B.C.
Volterra, Museo Guarnacci
cats. 12.3; 12.4

Bronze helmet from the Tomb of the Warrior at Poggio alle Croci (Volterra), last quarter of the eight century B.C.
Volterra, Museo Guarnacci
cat. 12.1

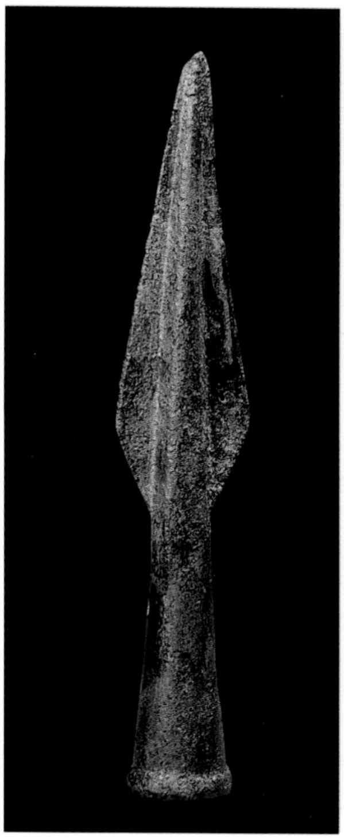

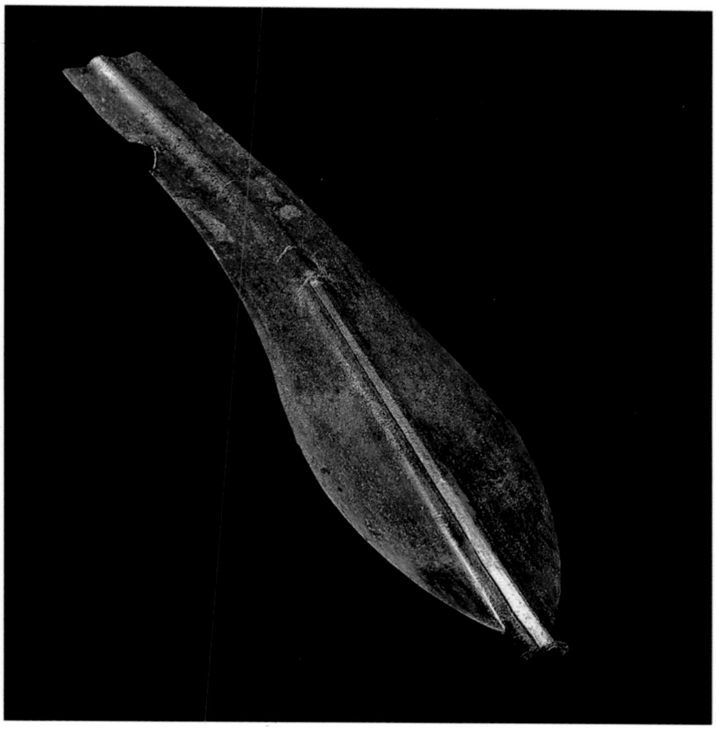

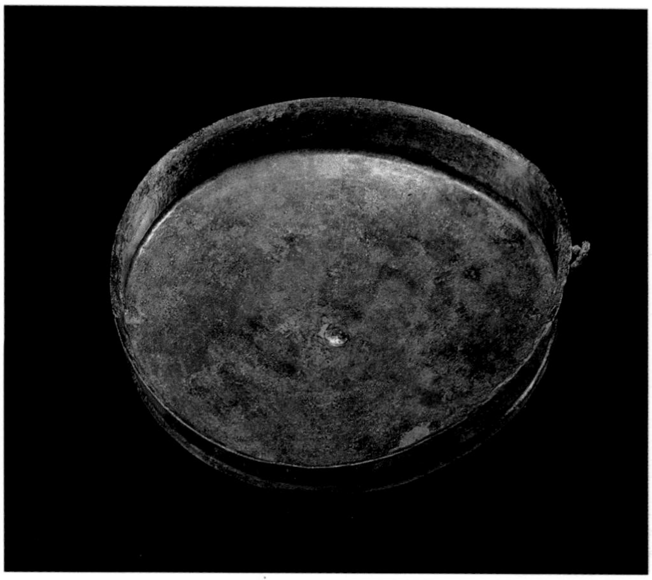

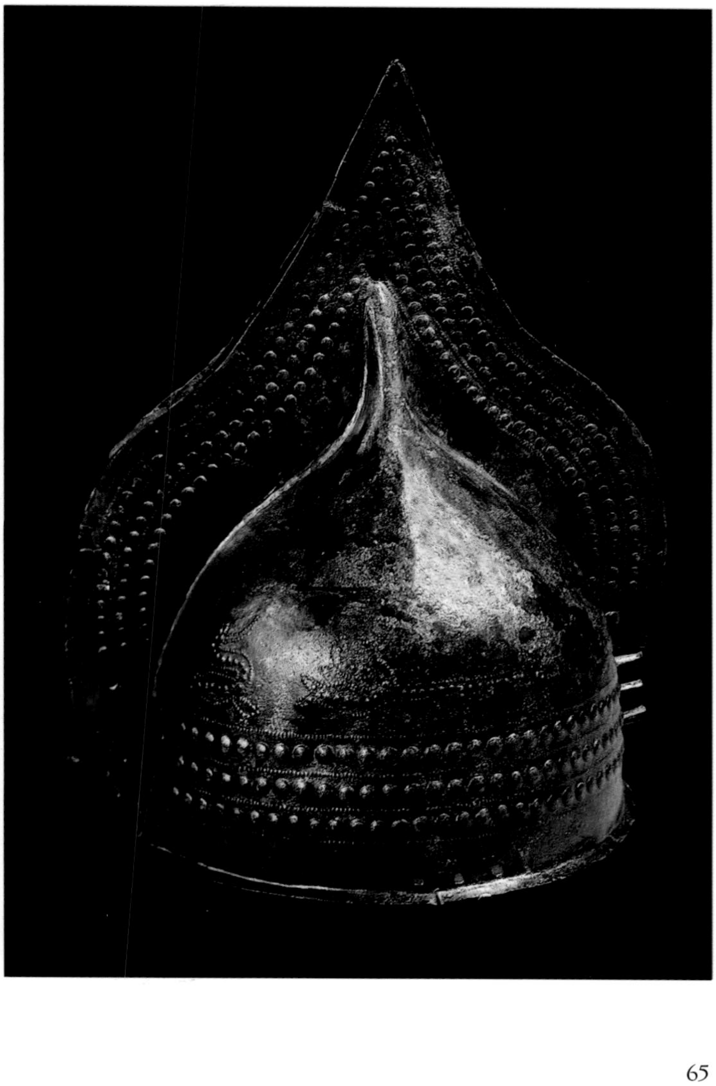

istence of a group of male and female depositions, distinguished either by the use of monumental tombs (chamber, "fossa" or well with special lids) or by the presence of articles of particular prestige, such as arms, vessels, ornamental objects in bronze or some more precious material. These remarkable changes in the funerary ideology, that indicate a process of social transformation under way and a systematic, structural character of exchange, do not present equivalent changes in the territorial organization. The examination of the necropolises allows to deduct a great demographic increase of individual towns, despite the heavy infant mortality revealed by paleontological examinations, while the study of burial goods reveals the material and ideological unity of the groups gravitating around the plateau.

By the end of the ninth century we observe in Italy a liveliness of exchanges between the various communities, within the different cultures as well as without. Contacts with the other communities of Villanovan culture in the Po Valley and the Salerno areas are highlighted mostly by the distribution of bronze products. Bologna products appear widespread in Etruria, in coastal zones, especially Populonia and Vetulonia, as well as inland (Veio), as soon as the end of the ninth century and then more frequently in the eighth century B.C.: usually they are razors and *fibulae*, bronze articles broadly represented in Villanovan burial goods of every area.

Coastal Etruria communities interested in exchanges with nuraghic populations on the one hand, and on the other in contacts with "Oenotria" communities in southern Italy, through Villanovan outposts in the Salerno area, appear at this stage to have a foremost role in the Tyrrhenian Sea. If the centers of mining Etruria are mainly interested in contacts with the islands of the Tyrrhenian, those of southern coastal Etruria (Tarquinia and perhaps Vulci) seem to control traffic along the Tyrrhenian coast.

Nuraghic Sardinia, with its metal resources and its Mycenaen-Cypriot-style bronze production, could but be a highly attractive area for the inhabitants, undoubtedly interested in metal-working, of the mining districts of Tuscany and northern Latium. Small Sardinian bronzes are very widespread in Etruria and the Salerno area in burial goods dated to the end of the ninth century B.C., such as the *appliques*-buttons (small truncated conic artifacts with the top decorated with bird and animal protomes), pendants and small votive quivers. Particularly interesting is the combination of three small nuraghic bronzes in a Vulci female tomb at the close of the ninth century B.C., attributed to a high-ranking Sardinian woman married in Etruria: a statuette of a boxer-priest, a basket (attested at Pontecagnano as well) and a miniature stool. At Populonia Sardinian material (a small boat and a sword) are attested also in a non-funerary context, in the trove of Falda della Guardiola, a deposit consisting in whole objects, that the place they were found in leads us to consider a ritual deposit (a foundation ritual?). We can attribute to Sardinian people having moved to Etruria the production of several bronzes (cups with handles with small balls) or pottery (beakers with tilted neck) found in Villanovan contexts. That rich archaeological documentation calls to mind a tradition reported by Strabo (V, 2, 7), who recalls that Sardinia was ruled by the Etruscans before the Carthaginese colonization. "In the most ancient times the name of Sards was Iolai. In fact it is said that Iolaus arrived in Sardinia with several of Heracles' sons and that he lived with the barbarians who owned the island (they were Tyrrhenians). Later the Phoenicians of Carthage took it over."

A series of considerable elements furthermore testify the existence of frequent contacts between Etruria and the Lucania-Calabria area (Oenotria), by the end of the ninth century B.C. Some vases of purified clay, with a decoration of characteristic geometric motifs (full or "tent" angles, meanders, sets of small vertical lines, radial triangles on the rim) are imported to Tarquinia and Vulci by the end of the ninth century B.C. from Ionian coastal centers (Yntema 1985), probably thanks to the mediation of the Pontecagnano people. Furthermore, there is no lack of bronze articles, found in Etruria, or bronze knives of the type diffused exclusively in Calabria, but exceptionally attested at Tarquinia as well, or razors with two cutting edges, probably originating in the *Fossakultur* background. A result of these undoubtedly not occasional contacts could be considered the biconical ossuary painted brown from the Veio-type necropolis of Valle la Fata, a vase whose form and decoration are most certainly local, but that attests absolutely in advance the manifestation of new decorative experiences that in all probability should be connected with cultural influences from the south.

Clay Oenotrian-Geometric jug from the Osteria necropolis (Vulci), first half of the eight century B.C.
Rome, Museo di Villa Giulia

Furniture decoration from Vetulonia, end of the eight–beginning of the seventh century B.C.
Florence, Museo Archeologico

The further we get from the first decades of the eighth century B.C., the more apparent the process of economic differentiation within the social body becomes: tombs contain always more and richer material and present visible signs of social differentiation. An elite appears, in which women are as privileged as men and receive an equal profusion of goods.
Men are connoted as warriors who possess chariots; essential objects of armor are the round embossed sheet-bronze shield with an inner handle, the crested helmet with small horizontal tubes at the base, the iron sword with bronze scabbard, iron and bronze lance; hatchets are rarer. At Bologna, where arms do not usually appear in graves, owing to a likely ritual prohibition, the figure of the warrior, an eminent personality in each community, is represented in the *askos* of the mostly miniaturized burial goods (ossuary, chariot) of Tomb 525 of the Benacci burial ground.
A remarkable impulse to the process of urban formation of the communities of Tyrrhenian Italy is ascribed to contact with Greek communities settled in the gulf of Naples by around

Bronze and wooden sword with sheath from Poggio dell'Impiccato (Tarquinia), eight century B.C.
Florence, Museo Archeologico
cat. 57

770 B.C. The Villanovan communities established with the first Greek immigrants, and before that with the *prospectors* who had come to reconnoiter, contacts of a certain importance: the most significant material proof of relations between native communities and Greek people is the presence in the burial goods of Tarquinia, Veio, Capua, Pontecagnano, of two-handled bowls with a painted decoration of slanting semi-circles, groups of chevrons, or with metopal schemes with birds painted on the bowl between the handles, mostly of Eubean production. First of all techniques and figurative models are assimilated, and soon more authentic cultural models (with the introduction, for instance, of writing, of a new way of banqueting, of a heroic funerary ideology, that is, a new aristocratic life style), deeply modifying the physiognomy of Etruscan society. The main cause behind these contacts should be (and has been) attributed to the interest of the Greeks in exploiting Etruscan mining hills.

Repopulation of the territory
In the middle decades of the eighth century B.C., we can perceive changes both in the organization of the various settlements and the territory, that can be attributed at least in part to the alteration in socio-economic relations. At Tarquinia for instance, the Poggi burial grounds (whose use seems to end in the last thirty years of the century) seem to loose importance by about the middle of the eighth century, whereas most of the depositions, especially the emergent ones, are concentrated in the Arcatelle-Monterozzi necropolis that, pro-

Impasto two-handled biconical ossuary with bowl lid from Badia dei Camaldolesi (Volterra), last quarter of the eight century B.C. *Volterra, Museo Guarnacci cat. 13.1*

ceeding westwards (towards modern Tarquinia), will constitute the huge necropolis of the Orientalizing, Archaic and Hellenistic eras, involving also the area occupied by the Calvario hut settlement, still occupied in the final stage of the Villanovan.

With respect to territorial organization, several rich tombs found outside the usual necropolises, out in the "country," indicate the will to display the agrarian appropriations of part of the aristocracy, and anticipate the springing up of countless settlements scattered over the territory, a phenomenon that begins in the course of the eighth century but is not fully under way until the end of the century and especially in the first decades of the seventh century: in all likelihood we are dealing with a sort of land occupation on behalf of large centers with the founding of permanent built-up areas. We should certainly not call it a spontaneous event, but instead an organized peopling. The study of the funerary ideology and the typology of pottery and metal artifacts allows us to explain several districts usually coinciding with the territories of the principal cities. The new settlements in part occupy anew those territories that seemed abandoned at the beginning of the Iron Age. Yet the hierarchical connection between major and minor centers now appears obvious.

In northern Etruria, a series of sites fanned out around Volterra, in strategic positions on primary road directrixes, delimit the vast district which from the lower Val d'Arno (Pisa) and from the Elsa basin (Casole d'Elsa) reached the mid-Tyrrhenian coast: several male tombs with nearly complete panoplies, like the ones found around the primary center (Badia Tomb, Manetti Tomb of Monte Bradoni, or the recently found Poggio alle Croci one), point to the aristocratic character of those settlements, their economy being based, aside from land properties, "on the forced levy on trade, as suits a group of warriors" (Maggiani 1997). Likenesses with Villanovan materials from the Volterra region have been discovered in the small centers found in Florence and more recently at Sesto Fiorentino, at least by the mid-years of the eighth century B.C., which seem however to offer more analogies with Felsina necropolises, offering nonetheless a picture of frontier communities between northern Etruria and Po Valley Etruria: rivers rather than mountains seem to mark the territorial limits of the large Villanovan districts.

Martin 1973, pp. 23–38; Torelli 1981a; d'Agostino 1982, pp. 203–21; Gentili 1987a, pp. 7–34; d'Agostino 1995a, pp. 315–23; d'Agostino 1996, pp. 533–40; De Natale 1996, pp. 223–30; Randsborg 1996, pp. 271–280; Bettelli 1997, p. 198; Maggiani 1997c, pp. 57–92; Negroni Catacchio 1999, pp. 241–65; Trucco forthcoming. *On proto-Villanovan culture: L'età del Bronzo finale in Italia* 1979; Di Gennaro 1986; Negroni Catacchio 1988; Negroni Catacchio 1995. *On Villanovan culture:* Fugazzola Delpino 1984; Bartoloni 1989. *On main sites. Veio:* Bartoloni, Delpino 1979; Toms, 1986, pp. 41–97; Berardinetti Insam 1990, pp. 5–28. *Cerveteri (Caere):* Pohl 1972. *Tarquinia:* Hencken 1968; Buranelli 1983; Bonghi Jovino, Chiaromonte Treré 1997; Mandolesi 1999. *Vulci:* Buranelli 1991a, pp. 5–50. *Bisenzio:* Delpino 1977a, pp. 453–93. *Orvieto (Volsinii) and territory:* Scarpignato, Di Gennaro 1988, pp. 32–42; Tamburini 1997. *Vetulonia:* Cygielmann 1994, pp. 253–92. *Populonia:* Bartoloni 1991, pp. 1–37; Bartoloni forthcoming. *Chiusi:* Bettini 2000, pp. 52–65. *Volterra:* Cateni, Maggiani 1997, pp. 43–92; Cateni, 1998. *Media val d'Arno:* Salvini 1996, pp. 117–43; De Marinis, Salvini 1999, pp. 75–78. *Bologna:* Pincelli, Morigi Govi 1975; Morigi Govi, Tovoli, Vitali, Von Eles 1979; Tovoli 1989; Taglione 1999. *Verucchio:* Gentili 1985; Tamburini Müller 1987, pp. 49–56. *Fermo:* Baldelli 1996, pp. 15–38; Baldelli 1998 pp. 57–63; Drago Troccoli 1999, pp. 62–65, 197–99 (ns. 100–106). *Capua*: Johannowsky 1983; Johannowsky 1996, pp. 59–65. *Pontecagnano:* d'Agostino, Gastaldi 1988; De Natale 1988; Bailo Modesti 1998, pp. 369–75. *Sala Consilina:* De La Genière 1968; Kilian 1970; Ruby 1995.

Economic Structure

In what follows, "the economy" is understood in a very simple and concrete sense as comprising all those activities which enabled Etruscan society to exist as such—though, of course, the methods and parameters applied in the performance of those activities changed over time, as the result of historical and cultural factors.

Before we look at the specific features of the different eras in Etruscan history, we should point out that throughout its entire existence (from the tenth–ninth to the first century B.C.) the Etruscan economy covered only a rather restricted number of activities: the cultivation of land for the production of foodstuffs and the raising of livestock; the exploitation of underground reserves for the provision of non-edible natural products (minerals, stones, etc.); the production of various types of manufactured goods; trade and commerce—to be understood as the exportation of surplus products and the acquisition of products either not available or not produced locally—and, related to these latter two activities, a certain amount of predatory raiding. A decidedly secondary role was played by that more outmoded means of guaranteeing survival which consisted in the passive exploitation of the natural resources of wild fauna and flora. Over the course of time, one might say that, whilst all these aspects were constantly present, their relative economic importance—in both qualitative and quantitative terms—would change substantially.

One could start one's description from the Final Bronze Age (twelfth–tenth century B.C.)—a period which coincides with the emergence of the Etruscans as an ethnic group and is archaeologically classified as that of proto-Villanovan culture. The population distribution patterns in the southern area of what would become Etruria are particularly well-known to us; but throughout the region there was the same pattern of a dense network of small villages a very few kilometers apart. Made up of huts, these villages generally occupied an area of less than 5 hectares in a variety of locations (highlands, plains, seacoasts, riverbanks and the shores of inland lakes); however, the most common sites were tufa plateaus that offered a natural form of fortification and stood at the junction of two watercourses.

It is of particular interest that within this substantially unchanging spread of villages and necropolises there are some significant breaks in uniformity, which suggest the emergence of a hierarchy both within individual communities and within the system of neighboring settlements. One might mention here the two large-scale houses (15–17 by 8–9 meters) which have been found at Monte Rovello in Allumiere and Luni sul Mignone, the tumulus graves at Crostoletto on the Lamone River, the single tomb of Valle del Campaccio, Allumiere (housed within tufa case and containing a large-sized *fibula*) and, finally, the prestigious furnishings of the tombs of Poggio la Pozza (some of them multiple). Most exceptional of all is the hoard unearthed at Coste del Marano (end of eleventh–beginning of tenth century B.C.), which contained three cups of embossed bronze lamina and large simple-arch *fibulae* decorated with stud-work foliation. As for the hierarchy between settlements, one might point out the unusually large ground area covered by the inhabited centers of Sorgenti della Nova and Elceto (10 hectares), as well as the relatively high number of tombs at Poggio La Pozza (forty-five as opposed to an average of around ten).

So archaeological finds seem to suggest this was a society undergoing rapid social and economic change; and—apart from the minor role played by fishing and hunting—the basis for such acceleration would seem to have been agriculture and metallurgy. Undoubtedly, the most important of those two was agriculture. Finds of plant remains indicate that this was based on various species of cereals (including the higher types) and a variety of legumes. The raising of livestock must have been a closely-linked activity; paleo-zoological remains indicate the presence of pigs (used exclusively as a source of meat) and goats used also as sources of milk, wool and hides. A relevant sign of technological progress is the presence of animal species used primarily as beasts of burden and therefore usually butchered at a much older age; these included cattle but also horses and asses.

From the ninth century onward the economic role of metallurgy became much more substantial. The working of metal was an acquired skill by the Early Bronze Age—when central Italy was involved in the circulation of bronze products between the Eastern Alps and the island of Sicily. However, it was only in the proto-Villanovan period that the communities in the mineral-rich areas of Tuscany took over direct control of all the phases of production—from the mining of local ore to the supply of raw materials to external buyers (the Aegean

Black-figure amphora.
Berlin, Staatliche Museen, Antikensammlung
cat. 165

Bronze group of the Ploughman from Arezzo, 400 B.C.
Rome, Museo di Villa Giulia
cat. 16

peoples settled in Sicily and the Gulf of Naples, or the peoples settled in north-eastern Italy and beyond) and the production of tools, whose special design shows they were well-adapted to local manufacturing activities. The finds at Limone (Montenero, Livorno) are particularly revealing here, including as they do a whole series of different chisels, whilst the finds at Pariana in Versilia include not only chisels but also a pair of spear-heads for fishing.
As is well-known, with the arrival of the Iron Age came wide-ranging alterations in the occupation of territory, which generally involved the abandonment of those upland village sites that had characterized the immediate past (and not uncommonly had been in existence since the Middle Bronze Age). Whilst the change was not sudden it did occupy only a brief period of time, and it left the territory of Etruria proper (plus its "extensions" in Campania and the Po Valley) subdivided into large areas under the rule of a single settlement located in a position of territorial domination (in the south, these sub-divisions occupied something like 1,000 square kilometers). There was at this point a clear distinction of roles between the governing settlement (located on single defended hill plateau and comprising a widely-spread network of huts) and the subordinate territory around it, which was responsible for the production of primary goods and materials.
The macroscopic transformation in the organization of territory was clearly directed by a powerful, well-organized political structure, and reveals a qualitative change in both society and economy, with the production of basic materials being the first area of activity affected. In fact, scholars agree that this new political development—which marks the emergence of the Etruscan nation as such—produced a fundamental change in the management of land: ownership now passed from the community to the individual family. Confirmation of this change in Rome comes from the story of Romulus's gift of two jugers of land to each individual family. And as for Etruria itself, the legend (Columella, X, 341 ff.) which depicts Tages and Tarchon—key figures in the myths of the Etruscan nation—whilst they are establishing the limits of their private property reveals how extraordinarily important this individual appropriation of land was in the foundation of the community.
It goes without saying that the family farming of fields led to the emergence of more intense forms of cultivation (a fact confirmed by the botanical evidence unearthed) and to a predominant role of stables and sties in the raising of livestock (the size of pig herds increased,

Drawing of the bronzes from the Pariana hoard (Massa Carrara) cat. 2

that of flocks decreased). It is also commonly held that this rigid parcelling-out of land also serves to explain the substantial uniformity to be found in burial goods of early Villanovan tombs (where differences of social status are reflected, but not differences in wealth).
As for metallurgy, the finds from this period (e.g. Gabbro, Tolfa, San Martino on the island of Elba, etc.) reveal a substantial increase in production, with a progressive stabilization both of the type of objects produced and the location of metal-working facilities (which tended to gravitate around the individual centers of settlement). A significant find here is the hoard at San Francesco in Bologna (closed towards the beginning of the seventh century B.C.), which is not to be seen as the small treasure of some itinerant artisan but rather as the reserve supply of raw materials accumulated by a smith who had set up his workshop in the city and worked predominantly for the local community.
In the middle decades of the eighth century B.C., the first Greek colonists from Euboea—who were followed shortly afterwards by Phoenician prospectors—encountered a society and economy with a certain degree of internal organization and energy, and some limited contacts with Sardinia, Latium and southern Italy. External demand further stimulated Etruscan exploitation of the mineral deposits—above all, in the Colline Metallifere of Tuscany and on Elba—and initiated intense and systematic trade, which was of great cultural, as well as economic, importance.
Archaeological and literary sources do not, unfortunately, enable us to draw up a detailed picture of the actual mechanisms of such trade. A fourth-century-B.C. Greek writer who goes under the name of the Pseudo Aristotle does—in his *De mirabilibus auscultationibus*, 93—reveal that the iron reserves of Elba were a community asset, whilst both archaeological finds

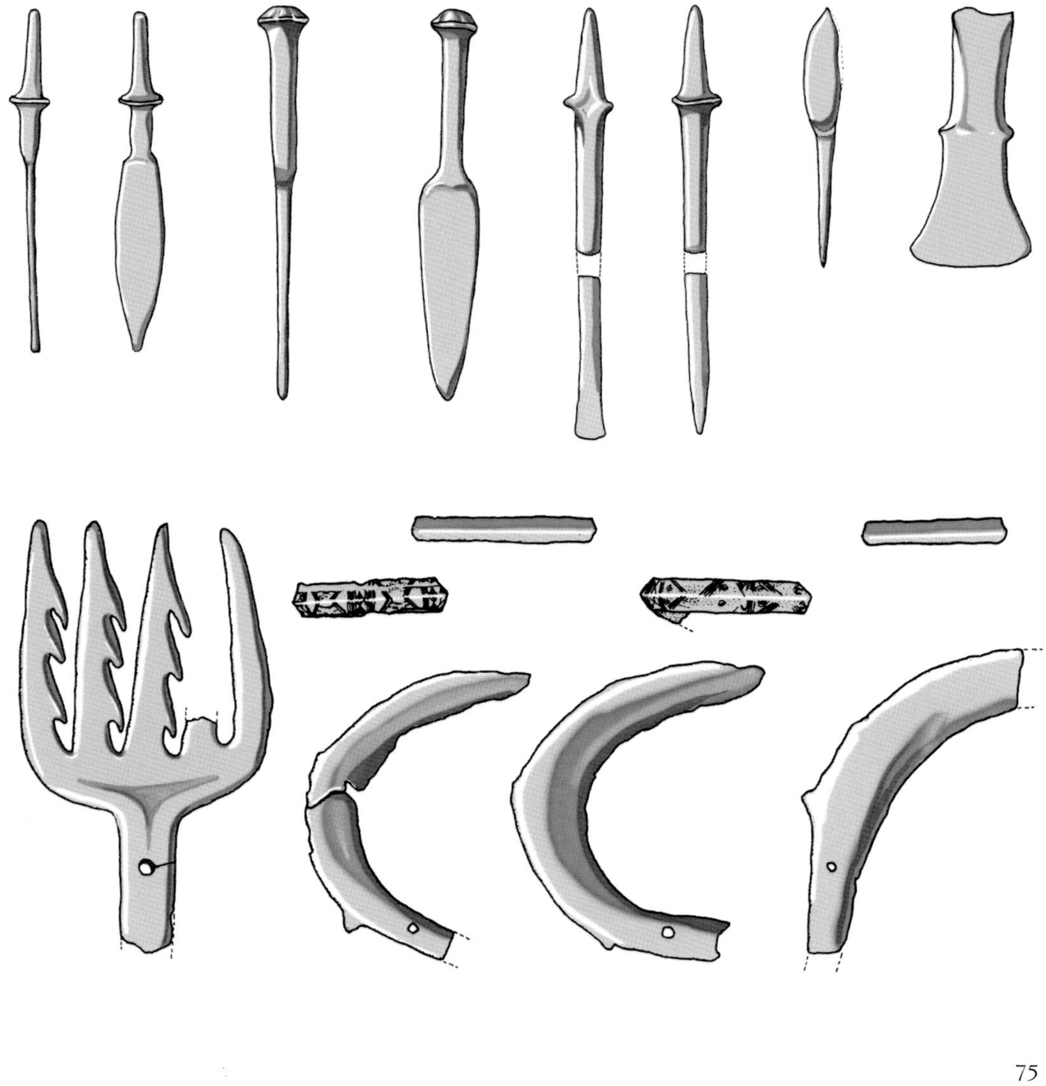

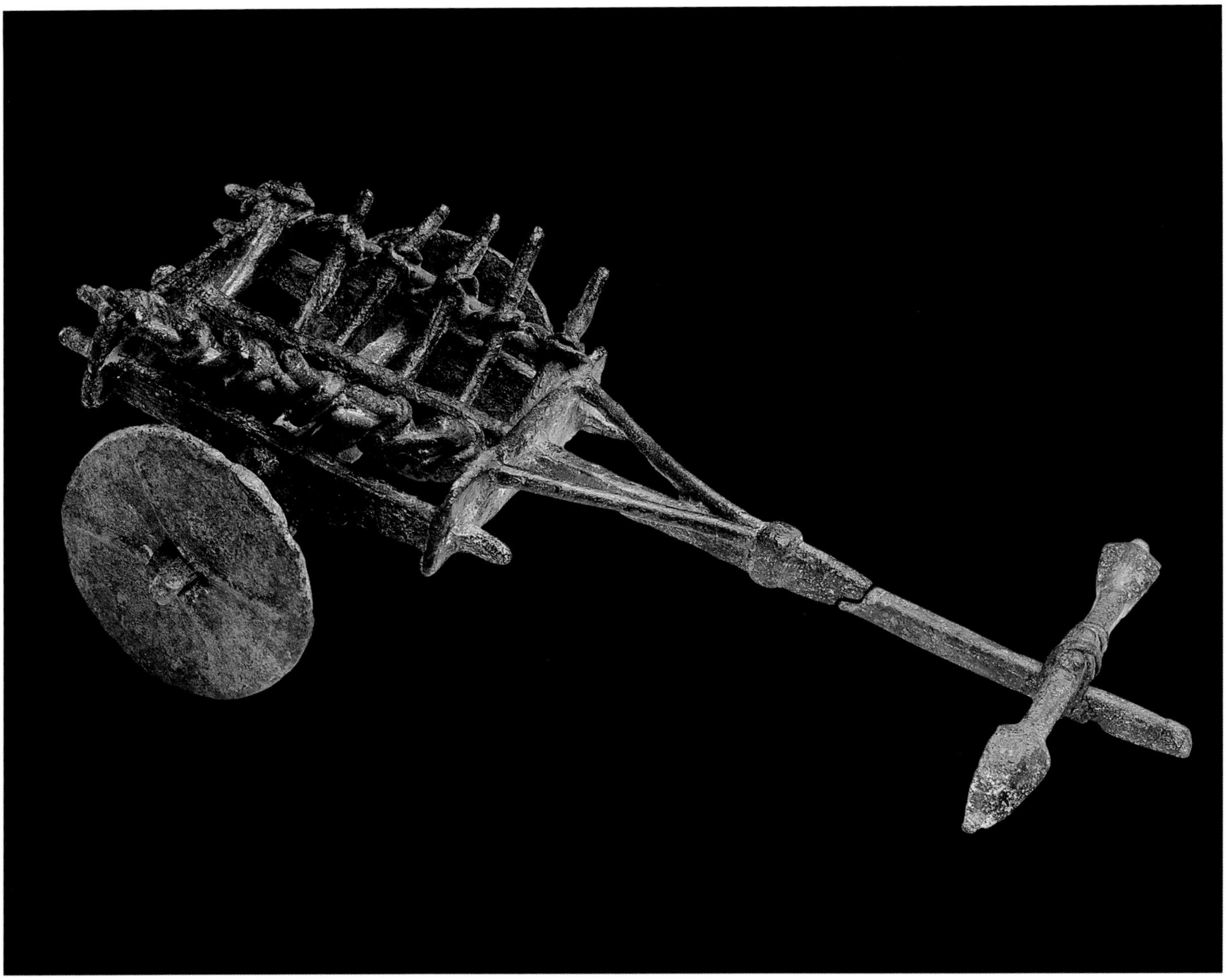

Bronze miniature cart from Bolsena. Rome, Museo di Villa Giulia

and literary sources (Diodorus Siculus, XI, 88, 4–5) suggest that those who managed (and profited from) the trade were not the communities located near the mineral deposits but those in such southern Etruscan settlements as Veio and Tarquinia, which were more socially and economically developed and in a more favorable position for establishing contacts with the Greeks.

This situation would only change in the fifth century B.C., and would have profound consequences: in fact, from the middle of the eighth century onward, the rates of cultural and economic development in the northern and southern parts of Etruria would be sharply different—due to the type of contacts the two areas maintained with the Greek world.

Looking at southern Etruria proper, one sees that as a result of a variety of factors (internal development, organized trade in metals, cultural contacts) the region underwent a positive socio-economic boom—the full extent of which is revealed by archaeology. The population spread to occupy smaller settlements around the main centers, and these latter in their turn also became more densely populated. The growth in population is similarly reflected in the necropolises, where burial goods begin to reveal a clear taste for the demonstration of wealth, with the inclusion of finely-worked precious objets that express social status (for example, weapons in male tombs and objects of adornment in female tombs). In other words, this was the period which saw the emergence of that social elite which we refer to as "the aristocracy" and which would play such a fundamental role throughout the entire future of the Etruscans.

Thanks to new technological input (often imported by foreign artisans) there was a dramatic change in the quality of manufactured goods (for example, in the fields of ceramics, metallurgy, etc.). Production was now organized in workshops, and the level—and standard—of internal consumption increased. What is more, craftsmen became skilled masters of a particular trade, and this figure of the full-time artisan would have a significant effect on the social hierarchy; in effect, this period saw the first steps taken toward the gradual creation of a social class that was in no way bound to the land—a class whose political importance would be felt time and again from the Late Archaic period onward.
However, agriculture was the area in which the technological advances imported from the Greek and Eastern worlds had the most significant influence. This was the period when crop rotation was introduced (with fields being allowed to lie fallow), when the Etruscans first started producing wine and, a few decades later, olive oil. It is also around this time that we should date the first exertion of control over the seas—if, that is, we are to believe Ephorus (mentioned in Strabo, VI, 2, 2) when he claims that the Greeks who were about to found

Map of the mineral deposits in central Italy

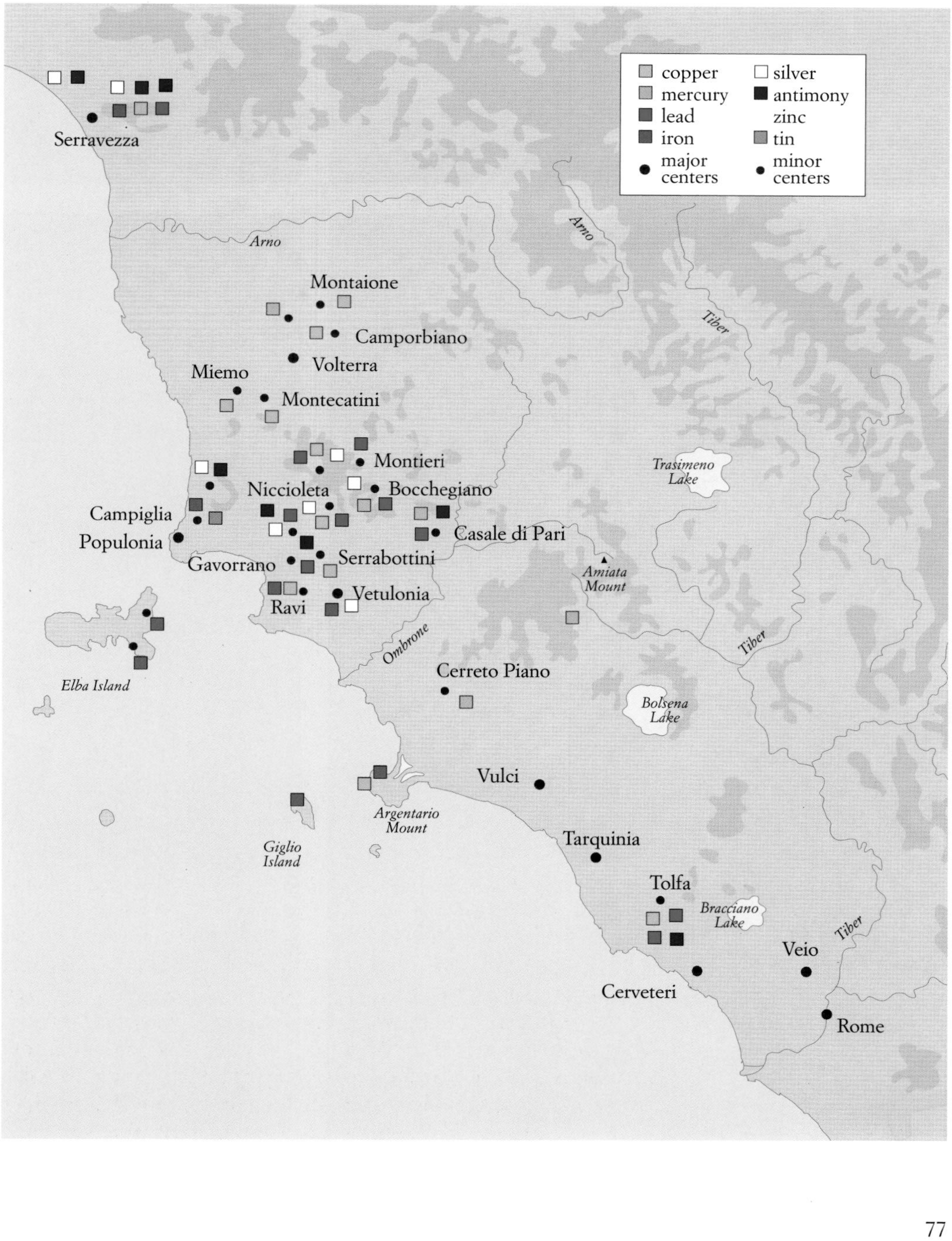

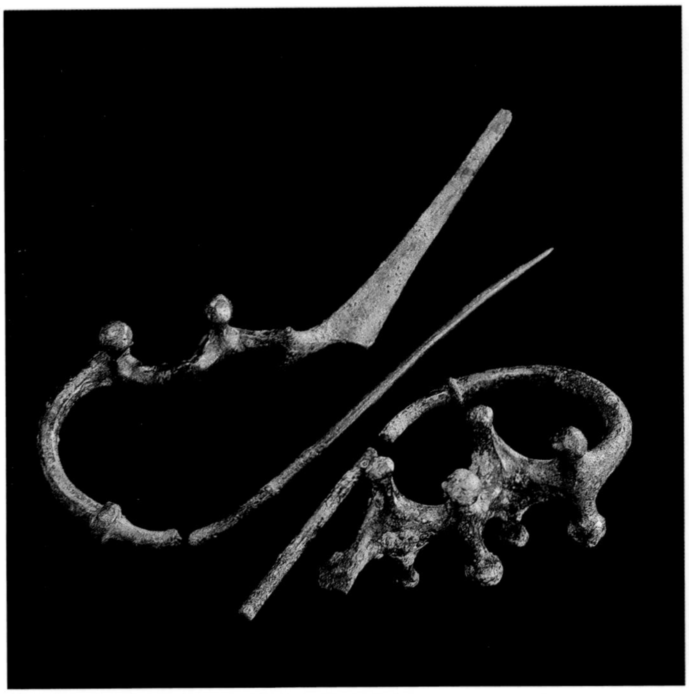

Bronze fibulae*: two leech* fibulae*, three* navicella fibulae*, one* fibula *with coated bow, from Poggio Gallinaro (Tarquinia). Florence, Museo Archeologico cats. 27.1; 27.4; 27.2; 27.3*

Naxos (in the year 734 B.C.) feared the coastal raids of the Tyrrhenians. In fact, varied archaeological evidence suggests that already by the end of the eighth century B.C. there was a route of coastal trade linking southern Etruria with the upper Tyrrhenian (Pisa, San Rocchino in Versilia) and the Ligurean coast (Chiavari, and thence the Piedmont hinterland).

Nor should one forget to mention the technique of writing, which the Etruscans learnt from the Greeks of Cuma. Not only was this an important cultural acquisition but also a powerful instrument of communication and trade (and so vastly important in purely economic terms).

The innovations that took place in this crucial period would bear their full fruit during the following century (seventh century B.C.), particularly during the first fifty years. The aristocratic class would at that point reveal itself to be the main driving-force of Etruscan society, and its influence would even be reflected in how individuals were named (with the introduction of a double name—the first individual, the second referring to a *gens*). Archaeological evidence from housing and tombs illustrates the various aspects of the life led by this social class—its banquets, its military parades, its games and its burial rites (with enormous quantities of precious objects withdrawn from use to adorn the tombs of the dead). The whole ethos of this life was one of ostentatious opulence, with ceremonies and ceremonial serving to guarantee cohesion and consensus within the *gens* and among different *gentes*—as they had done among the Greek oligarchies of the Homeric Age.

It was this elite that controlled all forms of economic production—from agriculture (organized around large estates where the workforce was made up of a patrician family's slaves and *clientes*), to crafts, which again employed people of lesser rank who were sometimes actual slaves (like that Aranth Heracanasa who painted the Tomb of the Jugglers). The patrician class was also responsible for the beginning of large-scale maritime traffic (towards the middle of the seventh century B.C.), which was closely bound up with the large surplus resulting from the vineyards of the south. We can deduce who ran this sea trade by drawing an analogy with Greek navigators (particularly those who came to Etruria). Demaratus of Corinth, for example, who after many visits to Etruria settled in Tarquinia when the tyrant Cipselus came to power (657 B.C.), was himself a member of the patrician family of the Bacchiades. Similarly, his refined lifestyle suggests that the *náukleros* of the vessel wrecked on the island of Giglio around 580 B.C. must also have been of aristocratic origin.

But, returning to sea trade, it is certain that most of it centered around Vulci and Caere, which produced the containers used in the transportation of wine; however, there is also evidence that the trade involved other cities—such as Pisa (Strabo, V, 2, 5)—and individuals from other areas—such as those who produced the graffiti found at Lattes in Languedoc (perhaps natives of the central inland areas of Etruria). Finds of amphoras and shipwrecks (for example, at Antibes and Bon Porté) reveal that Etruscan wine was not only exported along the whole of the Tyrrhenian coast down to eastern Sicily, but also to the north-eastern Mediterranean (as far as Marseilles and Ampurias). What is more, this trade was accompanied by that in all the various vessels used in the ritual of drinking; in bucchero or Etrusco-Corinthian pottery, these were soon being turned out in large numbers by the workshops of southern Etruria.

Such bucchero ware and imitation Corinthian pottery (including a number of small unguent phials) were also exported to Sardinia, western Sicily, Carthage and southern Spain—an area in which trade was carried in Punic shipping and where there was no (or very little) market for Etruscan wine. This division of territory between the two merchant navies proves that, from the third quarter of the seventh century B.C. onward (the time of the earliest known Etruscan exports to Sardinia and Carthage), Etruria and Carthage already had that alliance which very soon would become a military union against Greek power in the western Mediterranean (the Battle of Alalia) and would also have an effect at a religious level (the Lamina of Pyrgi written in the Punic language).

However, the picture of trade during the Orientalizing and Late-Archaic period must also include mention of those materials that the Etruscans had to buy abroad: from Gaul they very probably bought slaves and tin (brought to the mouth of the Rhône by the people of the area), and from Greece they acquired luxury goods—such as wine and painted pottery—as well as specialist craftsmen with their skills and know-how.

In this broadly-traced outline one should also chart some of the fundamental changes that took place in the early decades of the sixth century B.C. both within and without Etruria. The key fact at an international level, after the foundation of Marseilles (Massalia), were the repeated waves of migration from Ionian Greece to the north-eastern basin of the Mediterranean and thus disturbed the delicate political and commercial balance which had been created in the region between Massiliotes, Etruscans and Carthaginians.

The most important internal development was the culmination of a centuries-long process: Etruscan cities became established as fully-fledged civic entities with their own political institutions, and thus the community tended to take over some of the social functions that had previously been the preserve of the aristocratic class—first and foremost of which was the organization of religious life (comprising such varied activities as the use of writing, the accumulation of goods and the commissioning of craftwork, etc.). Trade traffic also came under the management of the cities themselves, with the adoption of the "Mediterranean" model of a city-emporium: groups of foreign traders were admitted, under strict supervision (Gravisca); port installations were created under civic management (Pyrgi, Regisvillae) and small trading communities of Etruscans were established in foreign cities (Genoa, Lattes, Pech Maho, Aleria, etc.).

Due to factors whose roots can be traced back to much earlier periods, this was also the time that saw the emergence of an intermediate social class; increasing archaeological evidence indicates the growing importance of that group of individuals who were engaged in trade or crafts and were characterized by an egalitarian and pro-Greek culture (a social group who is well represented by such tyrant figures as Porsenna and Thefarie Velianas). The existence of this class is also amply proved by existing inscriptions—particularly in such colonial settlements as Spina and Aleria, and in the manufacturing quarter of Populonia—as well as by the layout of certain necropolises or sections thereof (Crocifisso del Tufo at Orvieto, Banditaccia at Caere, Baratti at Populonia), where the regular lay-out of similar tombs reflects the egalitarian concepts that were characteristic of this new social body.

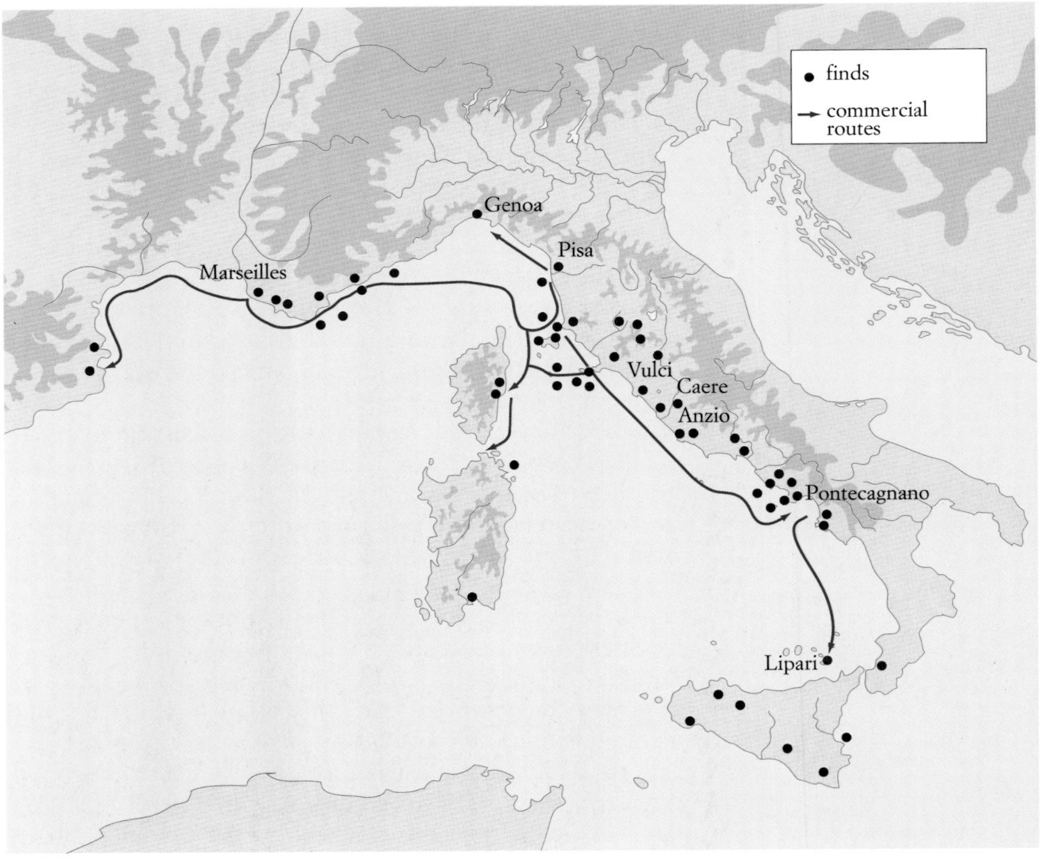

Distribution and typologies of wine amphoras from 630 to 500 B.C.

Eurytios black-figure krater,
600 B.C.
Paris, Musée du Louvre

following pages
Etruscan commercial amphora, last quarter of the seventh–first half of the sixth century B.C.
Cortona, Museo dell'Accademia Etrusca.
cat. 18

Impasto pithos *from Cerveteri, end of the seventh century* B.C.
Florence, Museo Archeologico
cat. 20

It is their influence—together with the first signs of an imminent decline in maritime power—that explains vast colonial expansion in two areas where, in fact, there had been an Etruscan presence since a much earlier period. In the Po Valley, there was not only the re-organization of the inhabited center of Felsina and participation in the lay-out of the trade city of Spina but also the foundation of Marzabotto in the valley of the Reno River, which stood on a crucial trade route. In Campania, the migratory flow came from the Veio-Caere area and tended to settle in the central-northern inland regions (Capua, Nola, Suessula).
The resultant commercial union extending over the entire peninsula would seem to be symbolized by those ferrous bronze ingots bearing the stamp of a "dried branch," which must have been a generally accepted unit of value over a substantial area.
At the same time—and following the same logic—there was also a sort of internal colonization, for which there is ample archaeological evidence. Towards the end of the sixth century B.C. various small aristocratic citadels (Acquarossa, Sovana, Bisenzio, etc.) ceased to exist, whilst a number of small colonial settlements (Doganella, Rofalco) came into existence, and various projects for the reclamation of agricultural land were put into operation—for example, that which has been identified in the territory around Veio. All the evidence points to this being part of a general program for a re-distribution of land ownership which was intended to satisfy the needs of a new social class and establish their rights of citizenship—an operation that was strongly supported by the political powers in the urban centers, who thus found themselves in open conflict with the old land-owning aristocracy.

Distribution of red-figure pottery from 350 to 270 B.C.

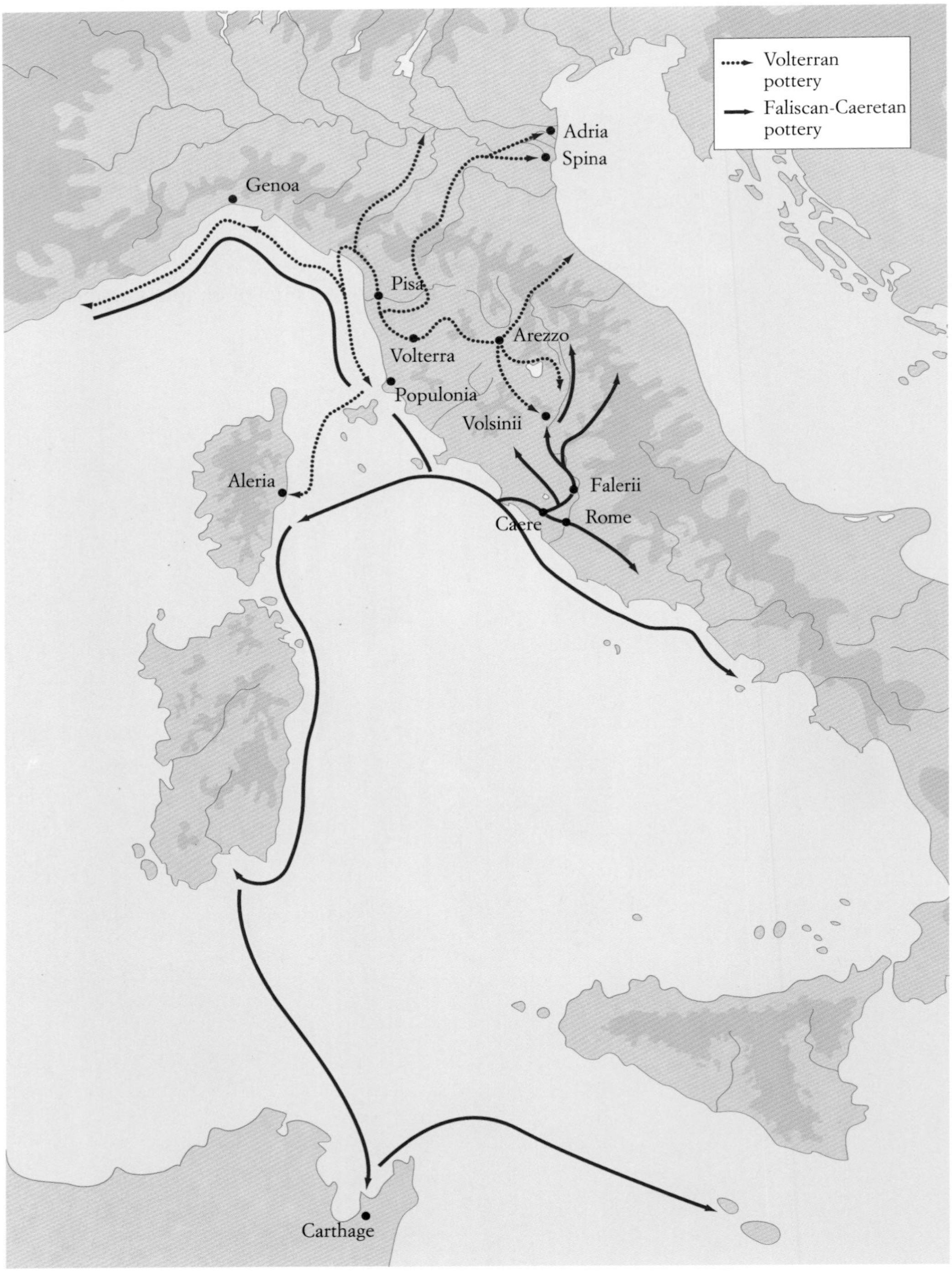

One should also point out that this phenomenon was not limited to one particular area or region. Archaeological evidence of it has been found in the south of Etruria, in the northern border areas and in internal areas of the central region (the end of the aristocratic residence of Murlo). For example, in Arena outside Pisa, a marble cippus "recycled" in a Christian church bears the inscription *lethe kakuś papnie*, which indicates someone who has only recently been included amongst those with full rights of citizenship.
Naval defeats by the Syracusans—first in the Sea of Cuma (474 B.C.), and then in the waters off Elba (453 and 452 B.C.)—necessarily placed the Etruscans in a position of inferiority, and the political-military consequences of this loss of hegemony included, amongst other things, a weakening of the control Etruria exercised over the occupied territories of Campania.

However, the economic consequences of these defeats were nowhere near as drastic or as widespread. For example, whilst it is true that the ports of the south suffered—the trade in Elba minerals was heavily affected, and there was a sharp decrease in Greek traffic (around the middle of the fifth century B.C., imports of Attic ceramics dropped dramatically)—it is also true that this region's economic losses could be counterbalanced by the intensive exploitation of agricultural resources that I have already mentioned.

As for the central-northern region, the flourishing state of agriculture in the internal area (Orvieto, Chiusi) is illustrated by the repeated evidence throughout the century (492, 440, 433, 411 B.C.) of the export of wheat to Rome (via the Tiber). Nor should it be forgotten that the most eloquent testimony to the area's economic well-bring comes from the art it produced. Orvieto here achieved levels of unchallenged excellence, not only in its temples but also in its bronze work, which involved not only such massive projects as the Mars of Todi but also a large range of tableware and other small objects (often exported north of the Apennines along the trade routes that passed through places like Marzabotto).

During this period maritime trade was also important for the Etruscan region of the Po Valley—especially for the two main emporium cities of Spina and Adria—where the wide range of Greek imports (painted pottery, amphoras and marble sculpture) reveals a high tenor of life. The basic reason for this flourishing trade was the regular number of Athenian ships calling in those ports to take on cargoes of cereals (produced in the fertile plain of Felsina) and, hopefully, metals.

On the western coast of the peninsula meanwhile, the area between Populonia and Pisa seems to have been under the protection of Syracuse; it played an active part in maritime trade and, in the second half of the century, imported large amounts of painted Attic pottery (objects which are totally absent from the centers in southern Etruria). It is no coincidence that the first Etruscan coins were minted in Populonia (the silver pieces bearing the head of a gorgon or *hyppalektrion* which were part of the treasure of Volterra), nor that that city was the first to mint regular series of coins (middle of fifth–third century B.C.): gold coins bearing a lion's head, silver coins bearing the *gorgoneion*, the head of Athena or the head of Heracles, and also series of bronze coins.

During the last decades of the fifth and the first decades of the fourth century, the crisis in Etruscan control over the lands colonized about one hundred years earlier came to a head. First, the Etruscan cities of Campania fell into the hands of the Italic populations (Sannites and Campanians), then the Po Valley region was occupied by the Celts. Attracted by the region's vines and agricultural wealth (Livy, V, 33), these latter would then push further south, ultimately burning Rome (390 B.C.) after already besieging Chiusi and establishing claims for their share of the territory it controlled. Livy (V, 36) tells us, however, that "the people of Chiusi possess more land than they cultivate." Finally, the very heartland of Etruria was sliced open by the Roman conquest and annexation of Veio (396 B.C.), a city which the plebeians of Rome then wanted to settle as their own (Livy, V, 50, 8).

All these events reveal the attractions that the well-cultivated lands of the Etruscans must have had for neighboring populations. However, at the same time, archaeological evidence reveals that from the middle of the fourth to the height of the third century B.C. there was a general recovery throughout the whole of Etruria. In the south, as in the Volsinii region and in the area comprising Chiusi, Volterra and Perugia, there was wholesale resettlement of the countryside, which led to the foundation or the restoration of the minor *oppida* scattered throughout the territory. The numerous inscriptions in the newly-founded necropolises of the major centers (Tarquinia, Caere, Vulci and Volterra) and the minor towns (Blera, Norchia, Sovana, Tuscania, Bomarzo and Monteriggioni) reveal that the leading figure in this land-based up-turn in the economy was, once more, the landed aristocracy, which implemented a policy of pan-Etruscan alliances through intermarriage between the various patrician families.

This rejuvenation of agriculture seems to have been accompanied by developments in the manufacturing crafts. Evidence for this would seem to be that, from the middle of the fourth century onward, all the major cities had workshops producing red-figure and later also overpainted and black glaze pottery; indeed, the Falisco-Caeretan and Volterran pottery seem to have had a substantial turnover and conquered sizeable markets both inland and overseas.

Bronze helmet with "eyes" decoration, sixth century B.C.
Berlin, Staatliche Museen, Antikensammlung
cat. 69

The northern ports of Pisa and Populonia were particularly busy during this period (focusing their trade in the upper Tyrrhenian), as was the southern port area of Caere, which also served Rome—friendly relations between the two cities went back a long way, and the alliance between them was probably renewed as a result of the truce of 353 B.C. (Livy, VII, 20, 8).

Nor should one underestimate the importance of the piratical activities—coastal raids, seizing of ships, imposition of tolls, etc.—in which the, by now punch-drunk, Etruscan communities of Campania and the Po Delta engaged. The economic fruits of these activities must have been quite sizeable if they were the basis for the relative up-turn in the fortunes of Spina during the second half of the fourth century B.C.

However, the picture of the Etruscan economy would not be complete if it ignored the fact that this apparently well-balanced mix of activities (agriculture, craft manufacture, maritime and overland trade) rested on a feature that, potentially, could rupture the entire system—that is, the sharp division between "lords" and "serfs"—as the two social groups were referred to by Latin writers, though we know that these "serfs" were not slaves but free citizens who had no political rights. An inscription (*Elogia Tarquiniensia*, Torelli fragments 3–4) reveals that in Arezzo around the year 350 B.C. there was an anti-patrician revolt—probably originating amongst the craftsmen of the area's smithies—which was crushed by the Tarquinian nobleman Aulus Spurinna. However in 302 B.C. a similar revolt against the Cilnii family was put down by a military force led by a Roman consul (Livy, X, 3, 2). And again it was the Roman army which stepped in to crush a serf uprising at Volsinii—significantly, when the two parties to the dispute had already reached some sort of compromise—and this military action is known to have marked the end of the city (264 B.C.).

By the middle of the third century B.C., each Etruscan city had its own individual treaty with Rome; and as federated cities they were required to pay a hefty tribute to their powerful ally each time the need presented itself. Livy's famous account (Livy, XXVIII, 45, 12–18) of the contributions made for Scipio's expedition to Africa gives a general picture of the economic and productive life of an Etruria that was by then a political vassal of Rome. What we see is an economy largely based on agriculture but also with its areas of fine craft manufacture—for example, the metal industry of Populonia and the metal-based crafts of Arezzo. However, what Livy does not tell us is that Etruria was by then a country impoverished and harried by forced tributes of not only goods but also fighting men.

During the second century B.C. social and economic conditions seem to reveal a sharp divide between the different areas of Etruria. In the south the relation city-country and the productive activities resting upon it were radically undermined—mainly as a result of mass patrician emigration to Rome. The result was a crisis not only in the management of the agricultural sector but also within the manufacturing crafts themselves (given that the landowners had been those who commissioned works). When Tiberius Gracchus passed through the Etruscan lands to the north of Rome in 133 B.C. on his way to take ship for Spain, what he found was a wasteland, with uncultivated fields now belonging to barbaric slaves (Plutarch, *Tiberius*, 8, 9).

In the north, however, things were rather different. This area was not under direct pressure from Rome—indeed, it benefited from its military importance to any push northward—and as a result enjoyed a high level of economic well-being (as we can see from urban remains and craft products). Here there was no drastic intervention by Rome in the conflicts between lords and serfs, and hence the two parties achieved some sort of—perhaps fudged—agreement. In the area around Volterra, Perugia and Chiusi we can see the division of agricultural lands, which must have accompanied some redistribution of land ownership to include the lower classes of the population. As for the social status of this group, inscriptions from the Volterra area reveal that there a rural nobility arose with family links to the equivalent social class within the city, whilst in Chiusi and Perugia we see a wide-scale process of social integration involving individuals who took on the status of freemen and made up fictitious family names for themselves on the basis of their own personal names (*Individualnamen gentilicia*).

In effect, this was a wide-ranging social and economic compromise in communities whose opposition to Roman citizenship was no accident. However, it would not be long before the full disruptive might of that citizenship made itself felt (in 90 B.C.).

For a general discussion: Peroni 1969, pp.134–60; Colonna 1976a, pp. 3–23; Cristofani 1986a, pp. 79-156; Torelli 1987a. *On agriculture:* Ampolo 1980a, pp. 15–46; Barbieri 1987; Forni 1989, pp. 1501-1515; Colonna 1985a, pp.101–31 *(wheat supplies in Rome). On metallurgy*: Bietti Sestieri 1981, pp. 225-263; Colonna 1981b, pp. 443–52; Bietti Sestieri 1998, pp. 1–67. *On maritime trade:* Gras 1985a; Gras 1985b; Bonamici 1996a, pp. 3–43; Cristofani 1998, pp. 205–32. *On coins and numismatics: Contributi introduttivi allo studio* 1976. *On the aristocracy: Aspetti delle aristocrazie* 1984, pp. 231 ff. *On the "crisis" of the fifth century B.C.: Crise et transformation* 1990. *On the situation in northern Etruria in the Hellenistic Age:* Cristofani, Martelli 1977.

Coins

As has by now been established, the use of coins in Italy first made its appearance in the Achean colonies of Magna Graecia (Sibari, Crotone, Caulonia and Metaponto) in the second half of the sixth century B.C., with the initially limited production of pieces of explicit face value and a high-value silver content. It was only much later that coins made their appearance in Etruria—and here again it was individual city-states that minted them, with the very first to do so being Populonia and Vulci.

At the height of the sixth century B.C. Populonia had an established place in the maritime trade on the Tyrrhenian coast—thanks largely to its control over the metal resources of the island of Elba and the Campiglio hinterland.

Vulci, on the other hand, played an important commercial role through the sixth and most of the fifth century B.C. as an emporium for the luxury goods which arrived in the city to then be redirected towards the cities of the central and outlying areas of Etruria.

The Vulci area is considered the origin of four different series of silver coins (base unit of weight: 5.8 grams) which bear the legends *Thezi* or *Thezle* and an image of a running winged Gorgon, a sphinx or a sea-horse. Produced in apparently limited numbers, these coins can be dated around the first half of the fifth century B.C.; the legend seems to refer not to a city but to the family name of the figures who were the representatives of authority responsible for the minting.

As for Populonia, the first known coins from there are silver pieces of small face value to a base unit of 0.69 grams; along with several bars of the same metal, these were discovered in a hoard in Volterra in 1868—which only recently has been interpreted as a collection of coins mainly produced in the Massa and Populonia areas (Martelli 1976). This interpretation has been borne out by finds of similar coins in the region of Provence (Chevillon 1999)—which thus confirms the existence of real trade between that region and Etruria and the production of Graeco-Etruscan coins in the period that goes from the end of the sixth to the early years of the fifth century B.C.

Slightly later series of silver coins from Populonia are divided between those that use the old base unit of 5.8 grams and those which use a new unit that ultimately derived from the Euboean-Attica regions whose Greek colonies in Sicily produced a stater (tetradrachm) of 17.44 grams, which was widely used in southern Italy. The first series include two of different value, bearing the head of a lion or a creature with the upper body of a lion and the lower body of a sea monster; while the second group of series consists of coins bearing a wild boar and the upper part of a lion with a serpent's tail (chimera). In each of the series the back of the coins is entirely smooth and bears no imprint.

So the common characteristics of these first series of Etruscan coins seem to be: low numbers, high face value and a restricted area of circulation. Clearly, as with the earlier pieces

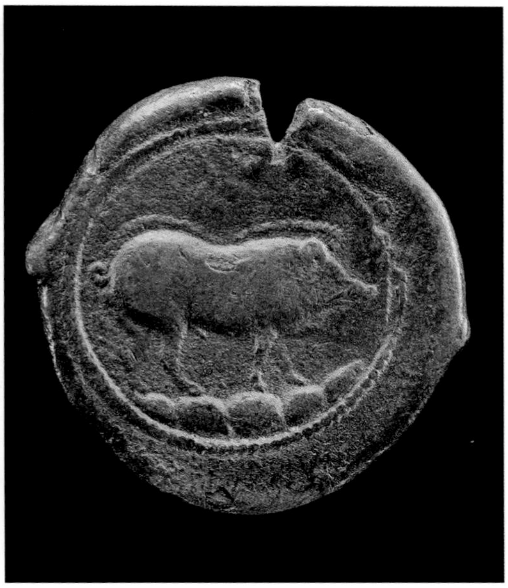

Coins with lion and wild boar, silver series, from the hoard of Populonia, beginning of the fourth century B.C.
Florence, Museo Archeologico
cat. 48

opposite
Coin with Gorgon's head, silver series from the hoard of Populonia.
Florence, Museo Archeologico
cat. 48

Coin with Gorgon's head, silver series, from the hoard of Populonia, third quarter of the fifth century B.C.
Florence, Museo Archeologico
cat. 48

Two aurei *of fifty and twenty-five face values from Populonia (?), beginning of the fourth century* B.C.
Florence, Museo Archeologico
cat. 47

minted in the southern regions of Magna Graecia, the very existence of such coins was not dictated by the internal or external trade needs of the areas where they were produced. What seems more probable is that these coins were not the result of a budgeted emission by a state authority but were produced to circulate within particular patrician groups for the payment and acquisition of services and goods (Parise 1985).
The first known publicly-minted coins are again linked with Populonia and consist of a group of pieces of different face values, amongst which the most striking is that of largest denomination bearing the head of a gorgon and the sign X to indicate its value. A piece like this has been unearthed at Prestino on Como Lake, at a level of excavation that can be dated around the third quarter of the fifth century B.C.—which further confirms the previous dating of the Populonia coin series on the basis of what we know about the history of the city. In fact, there was an intensification of activity within ore mining and metal production in Populonia during the course of the fifth and fourth century B.C., and by the middle of the fourth century the city could be said to have had a monopoly over the production and exportation of Elban iron. The development of an internal market—with its associated wages and other costs—may well have stimulated resort to monetary payments, and the coins mint-

ed were no longer restricted to high face values but also included fair numbers of much smaller denominations.
Here it is interesting to note that though the number of pieces with face value X that have so far been discovered total less than 30 (the number for all the known coins in this series is just over twice that), variations in the figure of the Gorgon indicate the existence of at least eleven different minting dies. This suggests that the overall emission was actually quite sizeable—and much larger than any previous output by this mint.
Various extreme theories have been put forward with regard to a series of gold coins bearing an image of a roaring lion and identified with face values 50, 25 and 12.5. What one can say with certainty is that they are interestingly similar—in the correspondence of weight and face value—to a series of gold coins minted in Syracuse during the time of the tyrant Dionysius I (405–367 B.C.), which therefore makes it possible to put forward a date for the Etruscan coins. Other pieces of various kinds (with male and female heads, Gorgons, sea-horses, etc.) would all seem to be part of the same monetary system of Populonia (Catalli 1998).
After an interval of time that has yet to be determined with any certainty, Populonia once again began minting coins—in larger quantities and of more varied types. The most com-

Coins with Gorgon's head, silver series, from the hoard of Populonia. Florence, Museo Archeologico cat. 48

mon (all in all, around 700 extant pieces produced by some forty different minting dies) is a silver stater bearing a Gorgon's head; this is rather similar to the previous coin of this type but is marked with a face value of XX. The backs of these coins are of various kinds and often bear a legend *Pupluna* or *Puplana*, identifying the place of origin. The correspondence of weights but change in face value suggests that between the old and new coin silver currency underwent a 50% devaluation, the reasons for which are still unknown.
Of another two series of silver coins, identified by the same face value, the first bears a fine helmeted head of Athena seen in half-profile and the legend *Pupluna* on the back, while the second bears the head of Heracles, frontal, wearing a lion-skin and the back of the coin is generally smooth (though sometimes bears an image of a club). As far as the head of Athena is concerned, there are precise chronological and design parallels with the image that appears on Syracuse tetradrachms minted under the name of Eucléidas in the last years of the fifth century B.C.
This was a period when the Populonian coins had a much wider circulation; finds in the various areas that were directly dependent upon the city reveal that the monetary system was playing a much more important role in its social and economic life. This is confirmed by the

Bronze coin with tongs and hammer, from the hoard of Populonia, third century B.C.
Florence, Museo Archeologico
cat. 48

city's minting of various bronze series bearing the legend *Pupluna* or *Pufluna*, which are characterized by the heads of different divinities (Athena, Hermes, Heracles, Hephaestus) and their respective symbols (owl, caduceus, bow, arrow and club, tongs and hammer). Though each of these series uses a different base weight unit and none are contemporary, they are all relatively close in time (around the middle of the third century B.C.).

A dozen series of bronze coins are distinguished by the presence of struck figures on the back face—which identifies then as part of a single group: however, there is no doubt that these are of Etruscan coinage and—if the information concerning their circulation is confirmed—they can be more precisely identified as originating in Populonia. Face values in this group range from 100 to 1, and on the basis of type and weight one can trace parallels between some of them and the coins being produced in Syracuse during the time of Timoleon (and thus get some idea of their date).

In line with what was a general tradition within the cast bronze coinage of Italy, various Etruscan centers produced series of cast coins using the *libra*—and twelfth divisions thereof—as the unit of measure for determining face value.

There is a series of inscriptionless coins, of which we have a few extant examples, which would seem to have been produced in the city of Tarquinia. This deduction is based not only on knowledge of the territory where the finds were made but also on a comparison between the type of designs used (head of a wild boar with the Greek letter A) and the wall paintings in the Pinie Tomb (Giglioli Tomb) which can be dated to the last decades of the fourth century B.C.—or, at least, no later than 300 B.C.; the head of that family—Vel Pinies—may well have been the magistrate responsible for the minting (the insignia of a magistrate figure in the wall paintings). All of this fits in with what we know about the history of the city itself, which after a period of unchallenged hegemony over a vast territory began—around the middle of the fourth century B.C.—to go into slow but inexorable decline, due largely to the increasingly irrepressible presence of Rome: the rivalry between the two cities erupted into armed conflict maybe twice (the wars being traditionally dated at 351 and 308 B.C.) and then just after the end of the century (281 B.C.) Tarquinia finally capitulated to Roman supremacy and had to surrender part of its territory.

The extant coins minted in Volterra seem to date from slightly later, with three different series—comprising a range from the *dupondium* to the *uncia*—and known to us through something like 600 pieces. All of the different classes of coins bear an indication of face value and an image of the two-headed divinity Culsan together with the legend *Velathri*. This output must date from the period when the craft industries of Volterra were at their height—a boom that was linked not only with population and urban growth but also with an expansion of the city's political and cultural hegemony.

Finds in tombs bear witness to the "existence" of Volterra coins throughout the whole of the third century B.C. However, given the absence of any certain information on the matter, it cannot be positively ruled out that production came to a halt during the period of the First Punic War. Similarly, the information we do have may well be an indication that Volterra coins continued to be a part of family possessions (and therefore tomb furnishings) even in a period when Roman money was already common currency in the markets of Etruria.

Other contemporary series of cast bronze coins use two different *libra* as their base weight (204.66 and 151.60 grams respectively). The latter of these is the same *libra* as that used in the Volterra series, but—on the sole basis of the area in which the coins have been found—it would appear that they originated from the inner region of northern Etruria (between Arezzo, Cortona and Chiusi).

The first five series are characterized by the same type of wheel image on the front face and various designs (two-edged axe, crater, amphora, anchor and a similar wheel) on the back face. Another two series have an archaic wheel—or, alternatively, three crescents—on both faces, while the last series has the head of an augur and various instruments of sacrifice on all the coins (irrespective of face value). Within the first group, the two series minted with the wheel and the anchor (or two-headed axe)—and clear indications of the value of the *uncia*—would seem to be complementary.

So far, attempts to use lettering and the alphabet to identify one particular place as the origin of an individual series of cast or struck coins has yet to provide precise, confirmed answers. Nor can one say with certainty whether each of the series circulated in one specific zone or whether they were all produced to circulate within the same economic area.

So far there is no justification for the idea that the presence of two different *libra* reflects the influence of the Roman *libra*. In fact, it is more probable that the two were of local origin: for example, the heavier *libra* would seem to correspond to that which is the base unit for a steelyard found at Chiusi.

The coins bearing the legend *Vatl* were minted in Vetulonia (Vatluna). The oldest series would seem to be that with a female head on the front face and a back face that might be left blank or decorated with a caduceus. Thanks to a comparison between the style of the head and that to be found on red-figured ceramics of the Clusium Volaterrae Group, the series can be dated perhaps at around the end of the fourth century B.C. The sites where the twenty-odd known pieces were found trace out what was essentially the extent of Vetulonian territory.

There are many more (almost 300) known pieces belonging to another series of two different coins (*sestante* and *uncia*) characterized by a single legend and bearing the image of a male head covered with an animal skin, paired together with an image of a trident flanked by two dolphins. The sites—and depths—at which they were found suggest they circulated within the Tyrrhenian area of Populonia and Vetulonia and must date from after the First Punic War.

All the known coins produced in Vetulonia are in bronze, and they are completed by other pieces (*quadranti* and *once*) which have come down to us in much smaller numbers. It is possible that coins were minted in Vetulonia for a limited number of years—from the end of the fourth to the early decades of the third century B.C.—and were intended to service the internal needs of an economy that had limited prospects of expansion (this was the period when after an era of cultural and economic impoverishment—due to Populonia's hege-

Bronze coins with male head (recto), trident, and dolphins (verso) from Vetulonia, third century B.C.
Florence, Museo Archeologico

mony in the fields of mining and metallurgy—the city enjoyed a brief up-turn, perhaps profiting from the Roman capture of Roselle in 294 B.C.).
Three other series of bronze coins with the legend *Peithesa* bear on their back face an owl with closed wings (the front bears the head of Hermes, Athena or Apollo). These—together with two parallel series of inscriptionless coins bearing, recto and verso, the head of a negro-elephant or male head-wolfhound—are the work of one or more mints active in northern Etruria (the distribution of the finds suggest that they circulated in an area from Val di Chiana to Chiusi and Siena). The legend does not indicate some ancient place-name but rather a patrician family name Peithe, which was common in the Chiusi area (in the legend it occurs with a morpheme that serves to identify object with possessor). The most recent analyses (Visonà 1989) confirm this area of circulation and date the coins around the years of the First Punic War.
In 1985 in Lucca eight silver coins were unearthed—three bearing the sea-horse image already associated with Etruria and five bearing the image of a backward-looking swan (probably minted in Macedonia, Ciampoltrini 1992). The level at which they were found suggests they can be dated around the early decades of the third century B.C. This find has given rise to the theory that there was a mint in Etruscan Pisa, which is credited with having produced the above-mentioned coins in a period that runs from the end of the fourth through the early decades of the third century B.C.—a period when, it is argued (and I myself agree), output at all the other Etruscan mints was at its height.

Martelli 1976, pp. 87 ff.; Parise 1985, pp. 257 ff.; Visonà 1989, pp. 17–22; Ciampoltrini 1992, pp. 27–34; Catalli 1998; Chevillon 1999.

Trade

Research into trade in the Etruscan world cannot be considered in isolation. Indeed, Etruscan studies in this field have only acquired a truly scientific dimension in the context of the overall picture of trade in the Mediterranean during the pre-Roman period. In other words, there are no uniquely Etruscan specifics in this respect, although some of the most dynamic and original practices may well have been originated by the Etruscans. Trading is only one among many functions of society, and Etruscan society was only one among many pre-Roman Mediterranean societies.

Nonetheless it would be dismissive not to underscore the fact that our knowledge of the Etruscans provides outstanding material for analyzing the development of trading procedures in the ancient world. Because of its geographical location and its history, Etruria was at the hub of movements of people and transportation of goods in the Mediterranean.

Pioneer studies: in the shadow of thalassocracy

Early etruscologists who showed interest in trading practices were initially influenced by the idea that the Etruscans were the predecessors of the Romans, struggling with Carthage for dominion of the seas. This view derived from the *Risorgimento* notion that the first Italian "empire" had been precisely that of the "Tyrrhenian-Pelasgians." It was a concept fed by a Romantic liking for the sea (the same inclination that lay behind Victor Bérard's commentaries on the homeric poems) and above all by the nationalist and imperialist forces pulsating through Europe around the mid-nineteenth century.

With such views prevailing, the Etruscan bucchero pottery found by Paolo Orsi from 1889 onward in the Archaic Greek necropolises at Megara Hyblaea and Syracuse passed virtually unheeded, as did his correspondence on the subject with Patroni, Milani and von Duhn. We need not be astonished to find the theme of "Ancient Italy on the Seas" returned to as late as the 1930s. In his preface to the book by L.A. Stella which bore just that title—*Italia antica sul mare* (Stella 1930)—P. Ducati wrote with an emphasis which appears surprising today, "it was on the seas of Italy that mankind found the way to progress." He went on to magnify the grand design of "restoring to Italy [...] the sense of Roman majesty." Rhetoric aside, the book did indeed collect the literary and archaeological data then available, and constituted the first corpus of material on the relationship between Italy and the sea.

In the post-war period, it was Pallottino who managed to convince scholars of the need to include this issue in the perspective of research on Etruscan civilization. In his manual *Etruscologia* a chapter headed "The Etruscans at Sea" was based on the notion of the thalassocracy of the "Tyrrhenians." This idea of the "dominion of the seas" was already familiar from Herodotus (III, 122) in relation to Polycrates of Samos, but in connection with earlier experiences such as that of Minos. To extend the concept to embrace the Etruscan world

Nuragic bronze incense-boat, from the sanctuary of Gravisca, end of the seventh century B.C. *Tarquinia, Museo Archeologico cat. 39*

opposite
Italo-Geometric oinochoe *with ships and fishes 700–675* B.C. *Columbia University of Missouri, Museum of Art and Archaeology cat. 50*

Main settlements of Tyrrhenian Etruria

was fairly audacious, but it allowed Pallottino to seek support from archaeological evidence among the Etruscan "bucchero nero" pottery found in the South of France. From 1949, Pallottino travelled to Marseilles, the Languedoc and Catalonia, reporting his findings in the first issue of the review *Archeologia Classica*. The interest in the subject that he aroused in his French colleagues was thus at the origins of the inventories of Etruscan material found in the stratigraphy of the *oppida* of southern France.

Pallottino quickly moved away from the study of place names, preferring pottery finds and thus archaeology as the basis of his interpretations. He was supported in the change by the work of Vallet and Villard on the links between ceramic material and economic history.

This kind of approach did, however, tend to build up an economic history from the occurrence of a particular category of finds, with the resulting risk of an unduly modernist picture of "Etruscan trade," exporting pottery ware around the Mediterranean rim. Thus one arrived again, albeit by a different route, at the notion of the Etruscans as the predecessors of Rome. Like other scholars, I myself was won over—at least initially—by this view of things, which now forms part of the history of Etruscan studies. However I was quick to point out my reasons for refusing the phrase "Etruscan commerce" and preferring instead "Tyrrhenian traf-

Attic amphora "SOS"
from Cerveteri, 675–625 B.C.
Cerveteri, Museo Archeologico
cat. 184

fic" (Gras 1985b), whereas in 1979 J.P. Morel presented a richly documented report on *Le commerce étrusque en France, en Espagne et en Afrique* (Morel 1981) and in 1983 M. Cristofani published a summary with the highly "Pallottinian" title *Gli Etruschi del mare*, and that same year organized a congress on "Il commercio etrusco arcaico" whose *Proceedings* still provide a valuable research tool today.

Over the past fifteen years there have been huge developments in our understanding of these issues; these recent changes provide the subject of this article. The publication in 1979 of Alfonso Mele's book on the commerce of Archaic Greece (Mele 1979), a volume influenced by the teachings of E. Lepore, the excavations carried out by Mario Torelli at Gravisca (in particular Torelli 1982), and the continuing field research by Giovanni Colonna at Pyrgi (Colonna in *Commercio etrusco* 1985) signalled a profound alteration in the available data. The picture obtained from archaeological finds was transformed by amphoras and shipwrecks discovered, while the theoretical possibilities were enriched by contributions from pre- and protohistorian archaeologists, historians and anthropologists. All these developments tended to place the issue of trade at the center of Etruscan studies, though far indeed from the ideological origins of the notion.

Bronze patera with movable handles from Tarquinia, seventh century B.C.
Paris, Musée du Louvre
cat. 84

The contribution from new finds

One lasting effect of Pallottino's work was the tendency to take Etruscan bucchero pottery as the guiding indicator for research into "Etruscan commerce." There were multiple finds of *kantharoi* shards in dwellings, cemeteries and sanctuaries outside Etruria, at Greek (Samos, Megara Hyblaea, Syracuse, Selinunte and Marseilles), Phoenician (Carthage, Tharros) or native sites (Saint-Blaise and other *oppida* in the Languedoc and Provence). The predominance of the *kantharos* form was marked but not exclusive.
The presence of Etruscan bucchero pottery had long been documented in Etruria, so that the Etruscan origin of such finds was not viewed as problematic, the only requirement being to distinguish ware of local manufacture. The principal difficulty was that of linking *kantharoi* to one or more of the various manufacturing centers in Etruria, and in particular to separate the products of Cerveteri, Tarquinia and Vulci. It must be said that no final and definitive consensus could be reached from fieldwork on this point.
The identification of commercial amphoras produced in Etruria was to alter this view of things considerably. In as early as 1955 such amphoras were identified as Etruscan by F. Benoit after the discovery of a wreck off Cap d'Antibes. Nonetheless the debate continued for years, inasmuch as there appeared to be no evidence for the same kind of vessel in Etruria itself. A typology was first put forward in 1974, on the basis of fragments discovered in dwellings in the Languedoc (Py 1974). The parallel research of P. Pelagatti—alerted to the theme by his finds at Camarina—was finally to put any lingering doubts at rest (Gras 1985b; Rizzo 1990). Thenceforward it was quite clear that any conclusions must be drawn on the basis of the "pairing" of bucchero and amphoras, the latter proving fundamental as pointers to a sea-go-

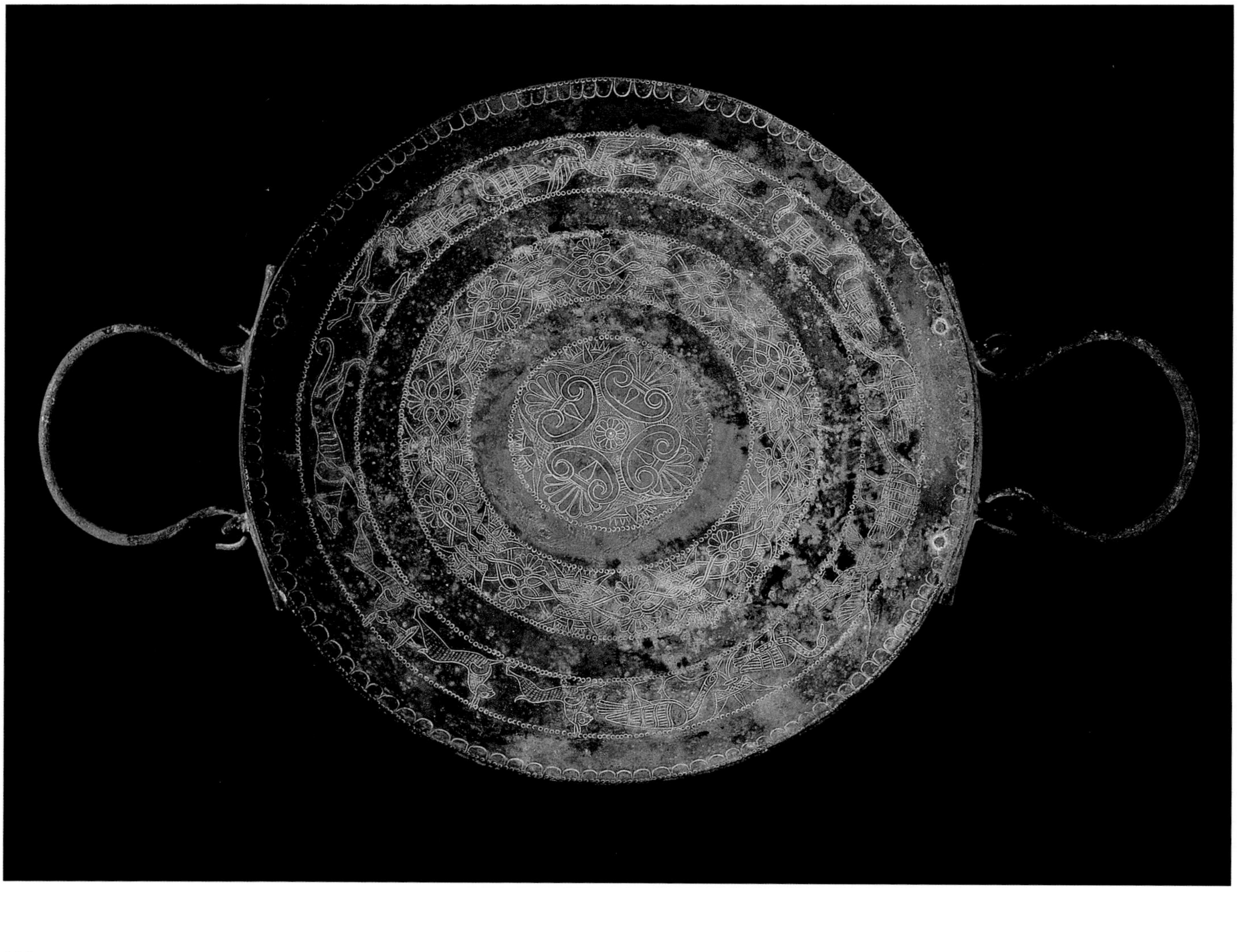

Bronze statuette of armed Aphrodite from Gravisca, 570–560 B.C.
Tarquinia, Museo Archeologico
cat. 40

Bronze statuette of armed Aphrodite from the sanctuary of Gravisca, 580–570 B.C.
Tarquinia, Museo Archeologico
cat. 41

ing trade in wine; the frequent occurrence of the *kantharos* form also gained in meaning, but the key was to enhance our understanding of the conditions of transport.

In this context, the newly-discovered shipwrecks were to prove invaluable. The first, at Antibes, was not made the subject of a proper scientific investigation, with the finds being recovered more or less haphazardly. The same could be said of the wreck at Bon Porté and even of that found off the island of Giglio (Bound 1991). There has never as yet been a thorough, scientific investigation of an archaic shipwreck (excepting the one at Pointe Lequin close to the island of Porquerolles); nonetheless, the data collected thus far have already demonstrated the complexity of the make-up of cargoes and the difficulty of identifying the place where the ship was built. The recent discoveries of archaic ships in the harbor of Marseilles (Pomey 1997) go so far as to confirm that at present we have no certain criterion for identifying a vessel built in an Etruscan port. Any conclusions must therefore await further discoveries, but it already appears that the transportation of Etruscan *kantharoi* and amphoras is not of itself sufficient to justify the notion of "Etruscan commerce." The interpretation of the Giglio wreck put forward not so long ago by M. Cristofani in one of his last works (Cristofani 1996c) reveals the extent of possible readings which can be arrived at from knowledge of cargoes, and how these can give fresh impetus to the historical debate on interpretation of archaeological data.

One last aspect of fieldwork deserves to be underlined. The latest publications of archaeological material from Gravisca (Boldrini 1994) and Tarquinia (Chiaramonte Treré 1999) contain features which go beyond a straightforward typological presentation of data: gradually a framework of material culture is being built up which makes it possible to understand

the links between the movements by sea and the craft traditions present at sites along the Etruscan coast. We thus arrive by the archaeological path at an aspect which will turn up afresh in the theoretical debate.

Trade and territorial dynamics

In the perspective of an unduly modernist vision of "Etruscan commerce," the etruscan littoral was nothing but a "long line of departure," in the words of the Belgian etruscologist Marcel Renard. By this approach the problematic issue of trade was neatly but artificially compartmentalized into two distinct and opposing categories: internal trade on the one hand and external commerce on the other. The dangers involved were exacerbated by the fact that the South of France provided data on amphoras which for a period found no supporting echo in Etruscan territory. In its most extreme form, such an approach risked formulating a notion of Etruscan commerce which omitted Etruria.

It was a risk which gradually diminished, however. First of all, the numerous publications by G. Colonna on inland Etruria provided archaeological material, backed up by copious analyses, which reinstated Etruria in the overall picture of trade issues. This shift was then broadened by the territorial interpretations developed in Etruria on the basis of analytical models typical of the English-speaking world, in this instance based on fieldwork in the area around Veii. In parallel with this, there was continued exploration of the "ager Cosanus," the coast between the mouths of the Fiora and Albegna rivers, which sadly was never properly published.

The work of F. Di Gennaro (Di Gennaro 1986) and later of M. Rendeli (Rendeli 1993) allowed a dynamic interpretation of the territories by referring in parallel to both environmental and archaeological data. The application of the model of the so-called "Thiessen polygons" made it possible to tackle the questions of borders and cultural interfaces, on a basis which might admittedly be inflexible on occasion, but which had real strategic and operational value as part of an experimental approach to territorial studies.

Further essential research enabled links to be established between this territorial approach and the information gained from the Etruscan vocabulary (Colonna 1985): there thus emerged the identity of individual communities and their links with a territory. In particular the concepts of *methlum* (cf. *urbs*) and *spura* were highlighted as the results of a lengthy

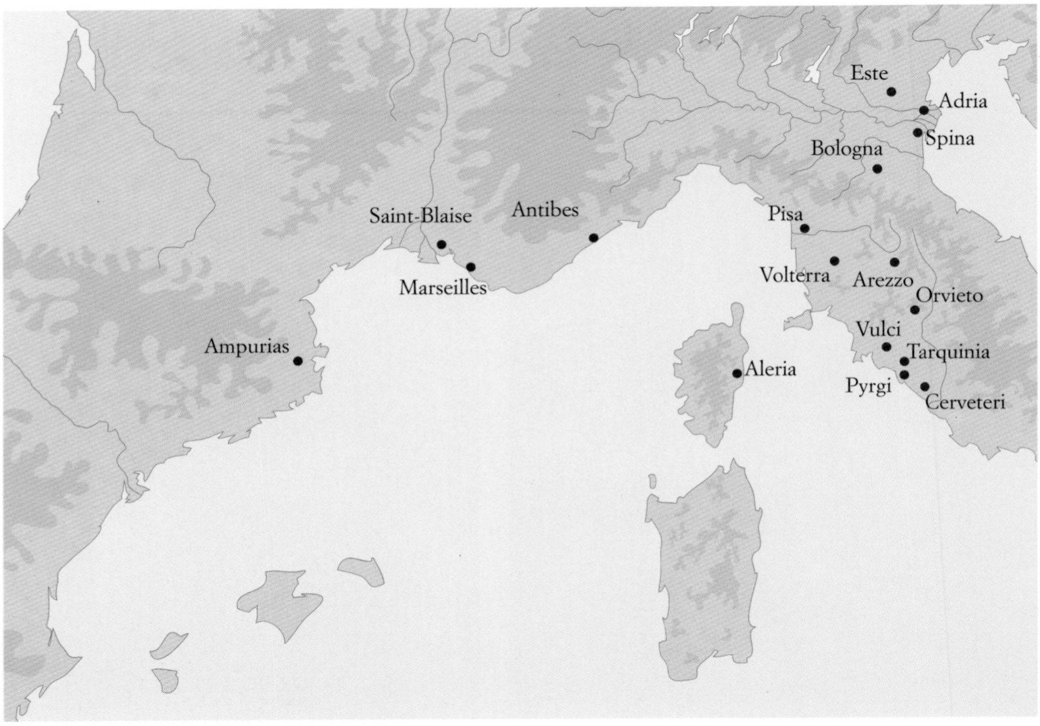

Map of western Mediterranean Sea

maturing process of Etruscan territorial organization. The dynamics of trade cannot be understood without constant reference to these kinds of study.
The question of territories is essential insofar as one thus sees the scope of a history of landscape—which, from E. Sereni to T.W. Potter and M. Rendeli has historically been one of the major strands of research in Etruria. Oddly enough, it tends to coincide with an environmental interest, conspicuous in the early issues of the review *Studi Etruschi*, but which clearly benefited from the development of such research.
In the light of all these various contributions, therefore, Etruria may no longer be seen merely as a "line of departure" from which wine was "exported." Rather it consisted of a whole series of territories controlled by communities which took on their own structures during the Early Archaic period before their later and partial reference to the organization of the Greek *poleis* in southern Italy and Sicily. Our vision of the originality of the Etruscan experience is all too easily distorted by the unduly Hellenocentric vocabulary of later written sources (and Strabo in particular).
More recently, the fieldwork carried out in the territory of Pisa (Bruni 1998a; Bruni 1999) and in Liguria (Bonamici 1996a) was able to fill in some of the gaps between the coasts of Etruria and southern France, removing the risk of an interpretation in terms of "commercial lines" which was indirectly gaining ground in some publications. The discovery at Pisa of pottery kilns of Etruscan amphoras close to the type traditionally defined as Caeretan is an instance of the advances that can be made by such research in the field. These findings brought Pisa and the mouth of the Arno fully within the scope of the issue of maritime traffic in the Tyrrhenian.
Sadly, the dynamism of Italian research has not been matched by the fieldwork in Corsica. Practically everything remains to be done on the island, so far as the study of coastal and inland territories is concerned. There are plans for fieldwork projects which I hope will come to fruition. At all events, a piece of deduction by P. Pomey has enabled a nineteenth century work to be identified as a discovery of a classical shipwreck at the mouth of the Golo, one of the two principal rivers on the eastern coastline of Corsica (Pomey 1997). M. Cristofani has also proved able to integrate the old discoveries at Aleria with the issues of traffic between Etruria and the Languedoc during the fifth century (Cristofani 1993b): the Etruscan helmets from the Aleria cemetery occur along the coasts of the Languedoc.

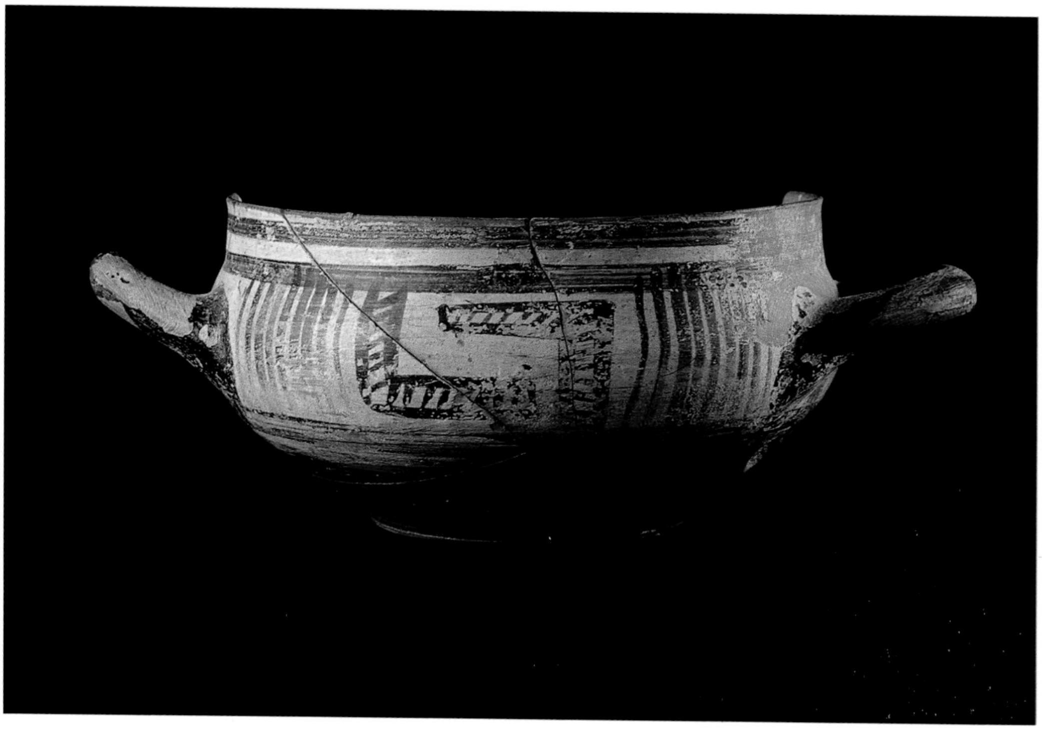

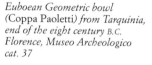

Euboean Geometric bowl (Coppa Paoletti) *from Tarquinia, end of the eight century* B.C. *Florence, Museo Archeologico cat. 37*

Aerial view of Pyrgi archaelogical site (Rome)

Circulation and traffic of artifacts

There is a cultural tradition in this respect which affects most protohistoric Mediterranean societies, and Etruria is far from being an exception. This tradition resulted from a progressively more hierarchical society and the emergence of elites which conditioned territorial organization. This question, sometimes referred to as that of the "aristocracies," the "princely phenomenon" or "prestige goods," is not introduced here for its own sake, since it is the subject of a separate exhibition in Bologna. Its establishment did, however, considerably affect the circulation of artifacts along family and political networks which were also being established at the time. The influence of sociological and anthropological studies on this point is recognized, particularly Marcel Mauss' research on gifts. It would be inappropriately reductive to speak of "commerce" in this instance. The first Greek bowls in the native communities of the western Mediterranean (including Etruria) very likely arrived in this fashion, reminding us just how much the ascertaining of the occurrence of artifacts may be misleading on its own, if not integrated within a broader historical perspective.

More clearly still, from the establishment of more organized commercial activity, notably during the sixth century, the old "gift trades" continued to be valid, though within the new commercial practices. Thus there were not two chronologically distinct phases, but a gradual pattern of practices which developed from individual and personal procedures into a more collective and more anonymous function, one which for want of a better word we might term more "modern." Only if this historical development and transformation of anthropological behavior are taken into account can the wealth of concepts surrounding trade be fully understood. It is precisely here that we grasp the significance of Polanyi's observations on how the economic dimension of trade is "embedded" in the social dimension.

"Emporian" commerce
Mele used literary sources as the basis for his sophisticated interpretation of Archaic Greek commerce as distinguished by two categories, one of *prexis* and another of *emporiè* in which the character of the travelling merchant takes on a central role in the organization of maritime movements.
This analytical model may successfully be applied to Etruria, so long as we do not forget that the "emporian" movements are routes determined by stops in the trading places, the *emporia*, that we know much more about since the analyses carried out by M. Torelli on the basis of the finds at Gravisca (Torelli 1981b; Torelli 1982).
Perhaps the most important contribution of the emporian model, however, is to lay bare the limitations of a modernist approach couched in terms of "commercial exportation." Thus the emporian traffic along the Etruscan littoral did not consist merely of exports of wine to the coast of southern Gaul. Rather that traffic was just one part of a number of routes involving the whole Mediterranean rim: the routes joining Greece to Salentum, Campania to Etruria, with halting-places along Calabria or Latium coasts, and inter-linking the various Greek *poleis*. In short, they did not necessarily link one point to another, in accordance with an unduly modernist perspective. They proceeded along the coasts, with possible changes in the make-up of cargoes at every port of call.
This emporian traffic must therefore have exerted very considerable influence on coastal societies. The arrival of goods wrought dynamic changes in the social environment. Moreover the same traffic also enhanced the mobility of people, who could travel by the same means: individuals, alone or in small groups, whose movements have often been traced by archae-

Aerial view of Gravisca archaeological site (Viterbo)

ologists studying the production of craft goods. These migrations cannot be separated from the emporian traffic; nor must we allow ourselves to imagine circuits working in parallel: in the archaic period, there was certainly no separate transportation of travellers and migrants in the Mediterranean, alongside that of merchandise and materials.

Thus we find at several sites in Etruscan territory, predominantly along the coast but also on rivers, trading stations which derive from the category of *emporia*: covering an area of average size (for instance 12 hectares at the Forcello near Mantua, 10 hectares at Prygi), these stations are planned and laid out in regular fashion. They were also to play a far more dynamic role than their physical extension would suggest, collecting together various populations, creating a linguistic melting pot and encouraging the convergence of differing stylistic models. Furthermore, they were a driving force for the development of neighboring and demographically far more significant communities.

Trade and cultural identities

Returning now to our initial model of "Etruscan commerce," it is quite clear just how far away this is. The essential matter is no longer simply to ascertain that amphoras produced in Cerveteri reached Gaul. The ships that carried them did not necessarily set out *from* Cerveteri bound *for* Marseilles. Cerveteri and Marseilles were two of many ports of call.

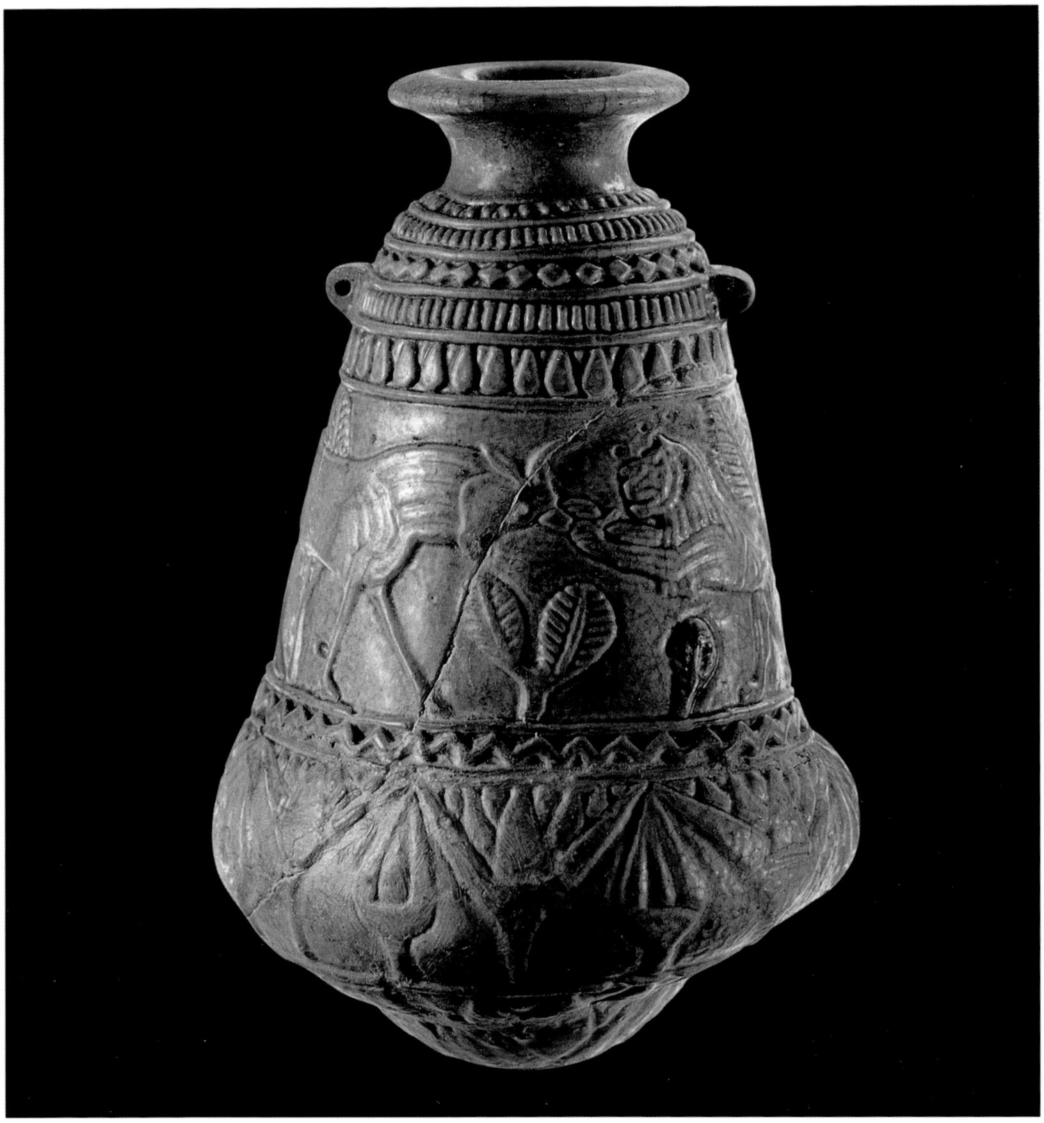

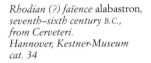

Rhodian (?) faïence alabastron, *seventh–sixth century* B.C., *from Cerveteri. Hannover, Kestner-Museum cat. 34*

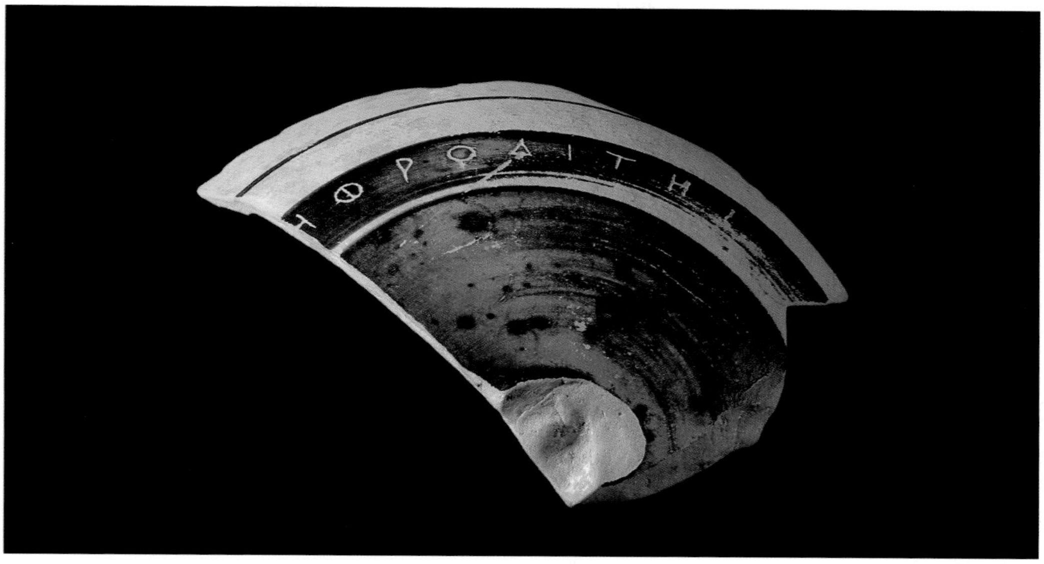

Fragment of Ionian bowl with dedicatory inscription to Aphrodite from the sanctuary of Gravisca, 550–530 B.C.
Tarquinia, Museo Archeologico
cat. 42

Fragment of Attic bowl with dedicatory inscription to Demetra from the sanctuary of Gravisca, 550–530 B.C.
Tarquinia, Museo Archeologico
cat. 43

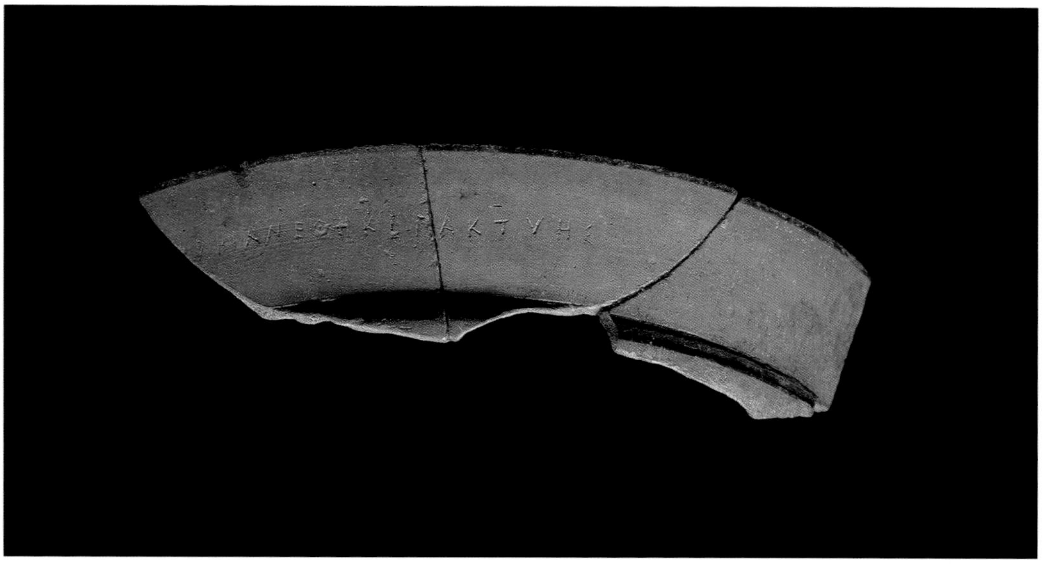

Fragment of Attic bowl with dedicatory inscription to Hera from the sanctuary of Gravisca, 550–530 B.C.
Tarquinia, Museo Archeologico
cat. 44

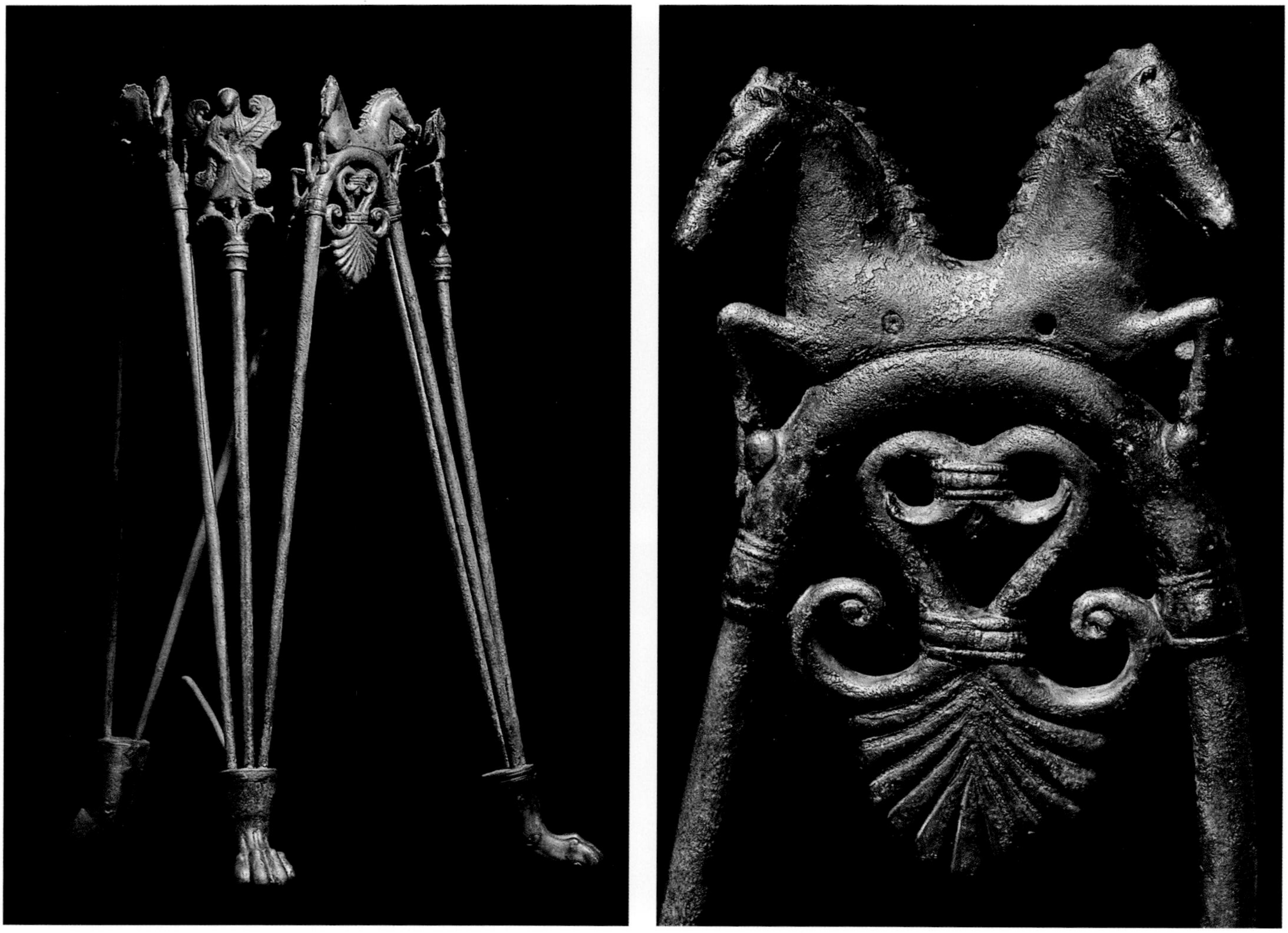

Bronze tripod from underwater excavations at Le Cap d'Agde. Agde, Musée de l'Éphèbe cat. 54

However, we must be on our guard not to fall back on outmoded primitivism. We know from recently discovered inscriptions (for instance the Pech Maho inscribed leaden plaques) that commercial practices were already highly elaborate from as early as the fifth century: the concept of earnest money was known, as were transactions before witnesses and the role of intermediaries (Pebarthe-Delrieux 1999; Decourt 2000). Such dealings cannot be dismissed lightly as mere "bartering." The value of the goods concerned (in particular, metals, wine and perfumed essences) was determined quite precisely and was probably codified to a certain extent, although the extant epigraphical evidence in the West is patchy for the centuries of the Archaic period. Commercial transactions very likely also retained some of the rituals of trade, like the "silent commerce" along the coasts of Africa, described by Herodotus (IV, 196).

Thus we have gradually shifted from a "mechanist" vision of commerce to using trade to try to outline the cultural identities of societies involved and their development. Indeed, the question we are faced with when considering the dynamism of the Etruscan territories during the Archaic period is to understand how far the contribution from emporian traffic modified the cultural make-up of the Etruscan communities. For the present we can do no more than point to some of the directions which might be taken by the great deal of work which remains to be done in this field.

We may begin with the work on the common pottery ware from Tarquinia recently presented by G. Bagnasco Gianni (in Chiaramonte Treré 1999) or that on the "Ionian" pottery from Gravisca (Boldrini 1994). It is perfectly clear that the common Tarquinian pottery was strongly influenced by models from eastern Greece, but this fact in itself is far from unique in the West during the sixth century. Rather more significant is the identification of a local variety of "grey" pottery which appeared to have been absent from Gravisca previously. This allows us once again to put the question of the impact of the craft traditions of Aeolia on western manufacture: the "grey" pottery is no longer identified as "Phocaean," but as locally produced ware which may have resulted from a specific cultural impact that in its turn was the result of emporian traffic. Moreover, observations on the type of vessels used (open or closed forms, thrown or coil-built, table or kitchen bowls, decorative patterns) enable us to distinguish traditional items from those introduced culturally. In other words, the kind of process which was so happily achieved by M. Bats for the pottery from the Provençal station at Olbia (Bats 1988) would be well worth reiterating systematically in order to define traditions, influences and the development of food practices. Going beyond the large-scale trends which have long been discerned (such as the impact of eastern Greece), more needs to be done to determine the specifics of each community, i.e. its particular response to external cultural influences.

It goes without saying that the full range of archaeological evidence should be taken into account, if possible avoiding an analytical section based exclusively on the category of material, preferring instead to address the adoption of innovative techniques (reduction firing, the potter's wheel, the use of a particular substance) or styles in the community concerned.

In this way it will be possible to obtain a valid, case-by-case assessment of the strength of impact of emporian traffic, and in so doing improve our understanding of emporian traffic itself. In my view, such an internal approach to the study of ancient commerce is more profitable at present than an approach based on the occurrence of artifacts and series. The internal view makes it possible in parallel to define cultural zones and ethno-cultural entities and to set their confines, thus making a full contribution to our understanding of how the Etruscan communities worked.

Lastly, the question of maritime and commercial "routes" seems today to belong to a view of things which has aged rather badly. Discussion is no longer focused merely on where the "traders" travelled to, but rather on gaining improved knowledge of how their itineraries worked, and to what kinds of controls particular sections of their journeys were subject. I have tried to show for instance how the pairing Antibes-Nice may have corresponded to a rupture which occurred during the last third of the sixth century, following the battle of Alalia. *Nikaia* may have been the Greek translation of an unknown Etruscan toponym signifying "victory" (we know from Diodorus Siculus V, 13 that a name of this kind was given to the site of Alalia), marking the limit of Etruscan control over the emporian route linking Etruria to Gaul, with Antibes/*Antipolis* thus termed the "opposing *polis*"—the start of the coast under the control of Marseilles. This would also afford a clearer interpretation of the passage in Skylax (*Periplous*, 5) in which the Tyrrhenian people are described as being settled "from Antipolis to Rome" (Gras forthcoming-a: *La battaglia del mare "sardonio"*).

In 1977 Mario Torelli urged us not to treat the archaic aristocracies like a Flemish bourgeoisie, and to seek instead the real economic and social structures which sustained the practices of trade (Torelli 1981b). After a quarter of a century, we may safely say that his appeal has been listened to. All those who were sceptical of the validity of using archaeological evidence to gain improved understanding of trading mechanisms must recognize today that archaeology has revised and altered the traditional vision of Etruscan "commerce" which emerged simply from a reading of Greek and Latin literary sources. There is still a long way to go, however, and many gaps in our knowledge. The study of trade in the Etruscan world is still a work in progress.

Stella 1930; Pallottino 1984; Py 1974, pp. 141–254; Mele 1979; Morel 1981, pp. 463–508; Torelli 1981b, pp. 67–82; Torelli 1982, pp. 304–25; Cristofani 1983b; Gras 1985b; Colonna 1988, pp. 15–36; *Il Commercio etrusco arcaico* 1985; Di Gennaro 1986; Bats 1988; Bouloumié 1989, pp. 813–92; Rizzo 1990; Bound 1991; Cristofani 1993b, pp. 833–45; *L'Emporion* 1993, Rendeli 1993; Ampolo 1994, pp. 29–36; Boldrini 1994; Py 1995, pp. 261–76; Zifferero, 1995a, pp. 333–50; Bonamici 1996a, pp. 3–43; Cristofani 1996c, pp. 21–48; *Confini e frontiera* 1997; Gras 1997; Pomey 1997, pp. 195–203; Bats 1998b, pp. 609–33; Bruni 1998a; Rebecchi 1998; Bagnasco Gianni 1999a, pp. 99–176; Bruni 1999, pp. 243–66; Chiaramonte Treré 1999, pp. 99–176; Decourt 1999, pp. 93–106; Pebarthe, Delrieux 1999, pp. 155–61; Gras 2000; Hérubel 2000, pp. 87–112; Gras forthcoming-a; Gras forthcoming-b.

Alessandro Naso

The Etruscan Aristocracy in the Orientalizing Period: Culture, Economy, Relations

Gilded silver drinking bowl from the Bernardini Tomb (Palestrina), detail, 675 B.C. Rome, Museo di Villa Giulia

The origins

Although the first signs of the formation of hegemonic groups on the central Tyrrhenian coast of Italy were already visible in the Late Bronze Age, in the period of the "long houses" reserved for the extended clan of Luni sul Mignone (Blera) and Monte Rovello (Allumiere), the existence of an aristocracy only became fully evident in the Iron Age. Status symbols emerged in the archaeological finds, mainly of a funerary nature, dating from the ninth century B.C., becoming more common in the eighth century: the cemeteries at Veio, which have yielded a large number of interesting finds, reveal the presence of a small male elite, clearly shown to be warriors by their complete suits of armor. A helmet with a tall crest (64 cm), a large round shield and bronze spear, an iron sword and a two-wheeled cart found in Tomb 871 of the cemetery of Grotta Gramiccia at Veio belonged to a royal or princely personage, whose renown and wealth are flaunted by the defensive weapons in thin metal sheet. The latter, that were not intended to be used in battle, but were only for ceremonial purposes—as were the bronze grave goods (tripod, wheeled incense burner, ribbed bowls, etc.)—, reflect the contacts of various kinds that Etruria and Veio had with other cultures: the crested helmet is derived from the style created by central European metalworkers in the Late Bronze Age, while the tripod is based on models that may have been introduced into the eastern Mediterranean from Cypriot workshops. Such magnificent tombs are the culmination of a long process of social articulation, which had already begun in the Late Bronze Age, when an important role was played by the acquisition of the right to possess land, which was perhaps the first type of property to become inheritable. In this respect it is enlightening to make a comparison with Roman legislation in the period of Romulus (753–716 B.C. according to traditional dating), which allowed the owner (*herus*) to leave a plot of land of two jugers (*heredium*) to his descendants (*heredes*). The historic indicator of this process is the aristocratic name, which set the seal on the bequests: its introduction to Etruria dates from, at the latest, the eighth century B.C., since inscriptions of the first half of the seventh century B.C. contain names—consisting of a personal and family name—that are already complete (Colonna 1977). Thanks to the possession of the chief source of human sustenance, land, to which, in some areas, may be added the ownership of livestock and the right to collect tolls for passage along roads or for access to certain resources—in this respect it is interesting to note the role played in relations between Veio and Rome by the salterns at the mouth of the Tiber, which eventually led to the destruction of the Etruscan city—, single kinship groups managed to emerge from the social structure of the tribal clan. The accumulation of the surplus deriving from agriculture and other economic activities consolidated the position of these elites within the community, and in the Iron Age they already comprised thousands of individuals. In south Etruria the profound social changes were emphasized by the renewal of the forms of settlement of the area: the dense network of settlements of the Final Bronze Age constructed on isolated hilltops several hectares in size was replaced in the Iron Age by a relatively small number of proto-urban centers occupying plateaus dozens of hectares in extent. The location of these proto-urban centers (Vulci, Tarquinia, Caere, etc.) in the immediate hinterland, five or six km from the coast, indicates the importance of sea trade in the economies of these settlements; protected by the sea, the Etruscan communities soon came into contact with the peoples who were attracted by the natural resources, especially metals, available in Tuscany and northern Latium (south Etruria). The propensity of the Etruscans for seafaring cannot be distinguished from the reputation as pirates that they earned in antiquity; from the practice of piracy they obtained wealth and resources, especially slaves, as is demonstrated by the significant example of the societies described in Homer's poems, in which aristocratic trade (*prexis*) was mainly based on the traffic in slaves obtained through piracy (Mele 1979). Great interest has been aroused in this respect by an account by the celebrated Greek historian Ephorus of Cyme, according to whom the Greeks did not engage in trade in Sicily for ten generations after the Trojan War because the Tyrrhenian pirates struck terror into them; it was only later that the first Greek colonies in Sicily were founded (Strabo VI, 2, 2). Calculating three generations per century and adopting the latest date that, in antiquity, was attributed to the conquest of Troy (1208, 1183, or 1136 B.C., the date preferred in F. Jacoby's day), the period of time referred to by Ephorus must be, at the latest, the beginning of the eighth century B.C.—that is, around 790–789 B.C., prior to the foundation of the oldest Greek colonies in Sicily, between 750 and 730 B.C. It has, therefore, been surmised that Tyrrhenian pirates infested the seas of eastern Sicily, at the latest, at the beginning of the eighth century B.C. (Torelli 1987). While the practice of piracy took the Etruscans far from their native soil, the exploitation of the mineral resources of Etruria attracted peoples from various regions bordering the Mediterranean Sea to the central Tyrrhenian coast. Relations with Sardinia are reflected by the imports, either isolated or concentrated in significant contexts, such as the Tomb of the Nuraghic Bronzes at Vulci, which was probably that of a woman of Sardinian origin buried in the second half of the ninth century B.C. As has been suggested on various occasions, the cremation may indicate a bond of matrimony that set the seal on an alliance between emergent Etruscan and Sardinian groups, according to a custom the frequency of which has been highlighted by anthropological studies. Relations between Sardinia and Etruria must have been linked to the diffusion of the know-how needed for the complex metallurgical techniques that developed at an early date on the island, which was noted for its rich deposits of bronze and iron. However, the metallurgists of Cyprus, the island located at the other end of the Mediterranean, had made an important contribution to the leading role assumed by the Sardinian metalworkers in the western part of the vast basin. The intensity of the contacts between Cyprus and Sardinia is indicated by a conspicuous quantity of archaeological finds dating from the Late Bronze Age or before. Leaving aside the Sardinian mediation, relations between Etruria and the regions of the eastern Mediterranean are already attested in the late ninth and early eighth centuries B.C. by the *orientalia* of central Italy, the most ancient items of which include two pendants in faience and a scarab in steatite from Egypt, found at Tarquinia, and an Aegean-Cypriot bronze patera placed in Tomb 132 at Castel di Decima, in Latium *vetus*, in the first quarter of the eighth century B.C.; to date, no similar artifact has been found in Etruria. Oriental imports were diffused in the West through a flow of trade that, in the studies, tends to be regarded as mixed, taking into account the numerous sources that have been recognized and the different origins of the goods that arrived in the central Tyrrhenian area. While, as far as the Levant is concerned, there are distinct Phoenician, Cypriot and Rhodian components (Strabo, XIV, 2, 10), it is likely that the subsequent Greek

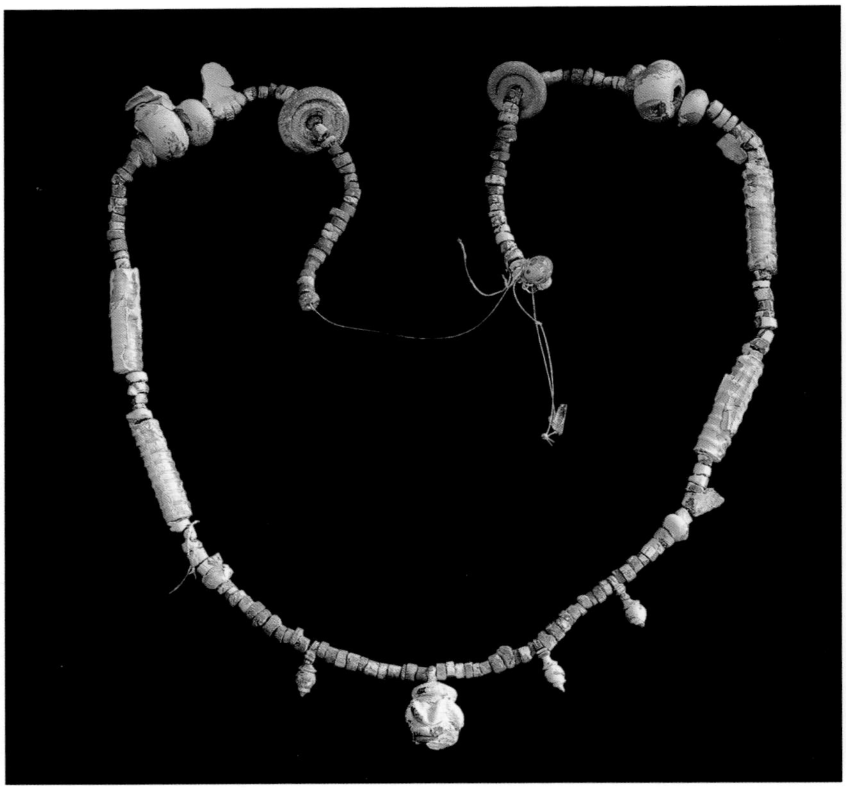

Amber and blue glass necklace from the tumulus of Castelvecchio (Vetulonia), end of the seventh century B.C.
Florence, Museo Archeologico
cat. 113

Two oinochoai *in blue glass from the tumulus of Castelvecchio (Vetulonia), end of the seventh century* B.C.
Florence, Museo Archeologico
cats. 111; 112

opposite
The Ponte della Badia (Vulci)

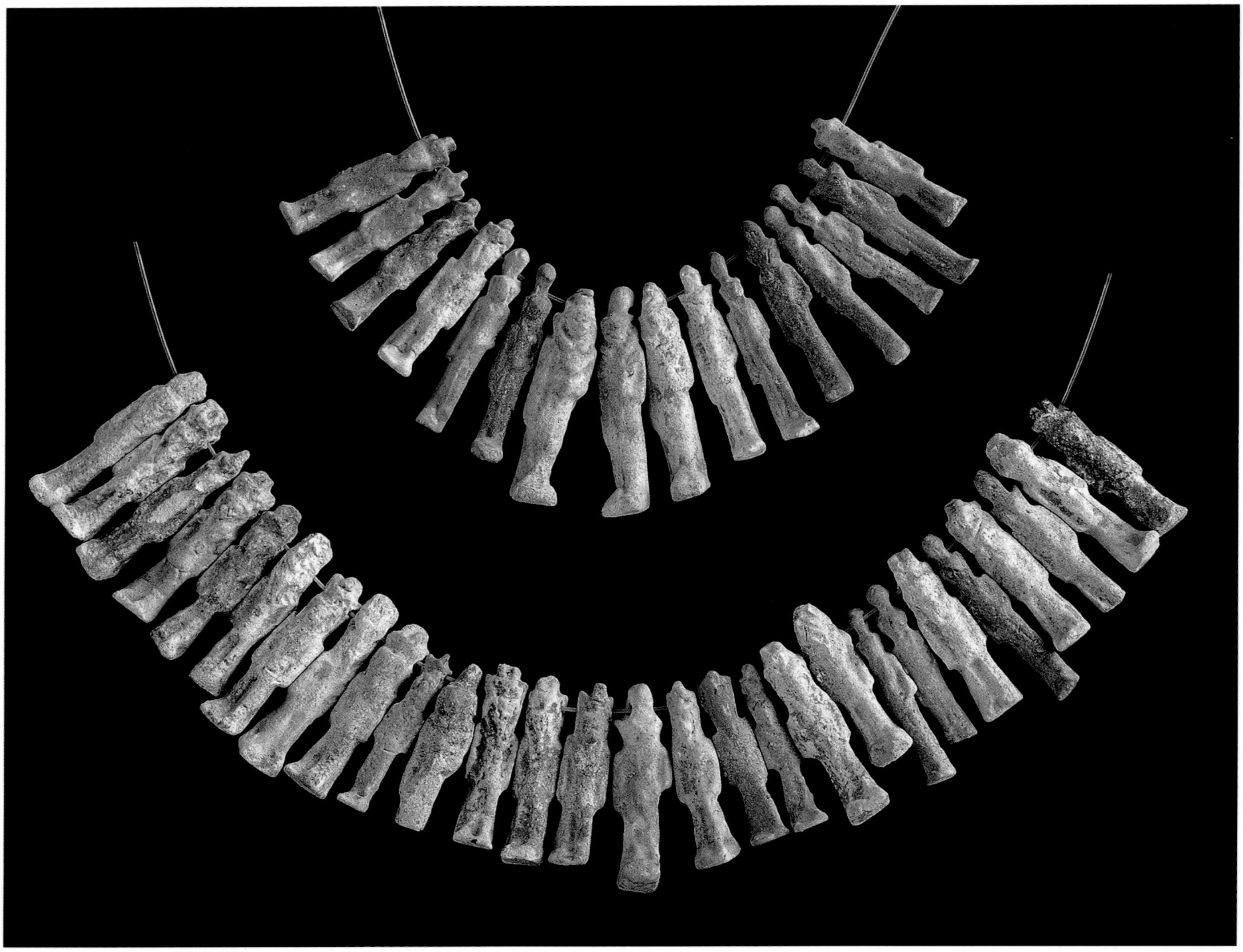

Bocchoris faïence necklace from Tarquinia, ca. 700 B.C.
Tarquinia, Museo Archeologico

Bocchoris faïence situla
from Tarquinia, ca. 700 B.C.
Tarquinia, Museo Archeologico

participation was not limited to the Euboeans, but may also have comprised the Corinthians. The wide range of products includes women's personal ornaments (seals, scarabs, necklaces, pendants) and vessels, with such precious items as the Phoenician bronze bowl found in a tomb at Vetulonia, in Tuscany, dating from the third quarter of the eighth century B.C. The presence at Tarquinia of a *fibula* with four spirals originating from Lucania or Calabria in the same context as the scarab mentioned above may indicate that the Oriental imports to the central Tyrrhenian area were distributed at a local level by native traders. The diffusion of the *fibulae* in this style, together with pottery painted with a *tenda* design of the same origin, is concentrated near the central Tyrrhenian coast, in the localities of the southern sector and the Tiber Valley, areas that were readier than the others to accept and elaborate the new developments (Martelli 1991). During the eighth century B.C., in addition to the *orientalia*, the influx of which increased, pottery of Greek origin also appeared, such as the *skyphoi* painted with pendent semicircles and the slightly later ones with chevrons, found especially among the grave goods in the tombs at Veio, the dating of which is still a cause for disagreement between scholars. While there are those who have attributed these finds to the first half of the eighth century B.C.—that is, the period preceding the establishment of the first Greek colonies in South Italy—others date them to the second half of the same century, after the stage of precolonial contacts. The debate is still far from finding a unanimous solution, but it must also take in account the results of the studies of the culture sequences of the Veientine cemeteries of Casale del Fosso and Grotta Gramiccia, yet to be completed, and the dendrochronological

analyses, which have made notable changes to the system of dates adopted hitherto for the Iron Age in Italy (Bietti Sestieri 1999). Leaving aside for the moment questions of chronology, essential as they may be, it must be stressed that the Greek vases for symposiac use are likely to have been the ceremonial gifts offered by the Greek colonists to the native elites in order to establish relations with them and have access to the resources they controlled, as is attested by the huge Euboean krater dating from the last quarter of the eighth century B.C. found at Pescia Romana (province of Grosseto). The imported pottery does not only include pieces of this importance, but also more modest items, the distribution of which often coincides with the outlets to the sea of the metalliferous basins where semi-finished metals could be obtained. Examples of these seem to comprise the fragments of Euboean pottery from the coastal settlement of Castellina (near Civitavecchia), situated at the mouth of the Marangone, the natural route leading inland to the metalliferous basin of Allumiere. This could be verified by exploring the coast near Tarquinia, which is rich in ferriferous sand, and, especially, near Populonia, the natural harbor serving the area of the Colline Metallifere. The discovery of imports in Etruria implies direct or indirect trade with the peoples who produced them: contacts

Bronze "botticella" askos *from the Tomb of the Bronze Chariot (Vulci), 680-670* B.C.
Rome, Museo di Villa Giulia
cat. 81.18

were not limited to the exchange of goods, but also comprised ideological and cultural models that left traces as evident as those of the material culture. In this regard, it has been hypothesized that the Phoenicians may have introduced the concepts of loans and interest into the West (Hudson 1992), while the diffusion of wine-drinking, which in the course of time took root in Etruria, is attested by the vases for symposiac use imported from Greece. The custom of consuming wine and meat together was transmitted to the Italian peninsula from the eastern Mediterranean, especially from the regions of the Near East and Greece, the distinctive features of which have yet to be identified with certainty (Rathje 1990; Rathje 1995). While, in the past, greater attention was paid to the role of the Greeks, more recent studies have reappraised the contribution of the Near East. In addition to wine amphoras, grave goods from Etruria and Latium *vetus* datable from the last quarter of the eighth century B.C. comprise clay tripods with a distinctive form (tripod-bowls) with signs of wear on the inside bottom, which indicates that they were used as mortars for grinding the spices that were mixed with wine to exalt its taste; the typological characteristics of these containers are to be

Bronze tripod from the Tomb of the Bronze Chariot (Vulci), 680–670 B.C.
Rome, Museo di Villa Giulia cat. 81.16

Bronze tripod from the Tomb of the Bronze Chariot (Vulci), 680–670 B.C.
Rome, Museo di Villa Giulia cat. 81.15

found in northern Syria and the Phoenician colonies of the central Mediterranean (Botto forthcoming). The representation of a ceremony widespread in the Syro-Palestinian area, called *marzeah* by Biblical sources, during which personages of high rank drank wine together, has been found in the Etruscan iconography of the seventh century B.C. (Menichetti forthcoming). On the other hand, the metal graters in bronze or, occasionally, in silver, that from, at the latest, the first half of the seventh century B.C. were included among Etruscan grave goods together with drinking vessels, demonstrate that the custom—attested in Greece from the ninth century B.C. onward—of mixing grated cheese with wine to improve its taste had spread to the Italian peninsula (Ridgway 1997). The vivacity of Etruscan society in the second half of the eighth century B.C., which is evident in its relations with the outside world, was reflected throughout the Italian peninsula, where traces of the passage of personages of Etruscan origin are attested outside Etruria itself (between the Arno and the Tiber) and the Etruscanized areas (extending from the Po to the Sele). In addition to old finds that have been interpreted in various ways, such as the crested bronze helmet dredged up from the bed of the Tanaro near Asti, recently more outstanding discoveries have been made, such as Tomb

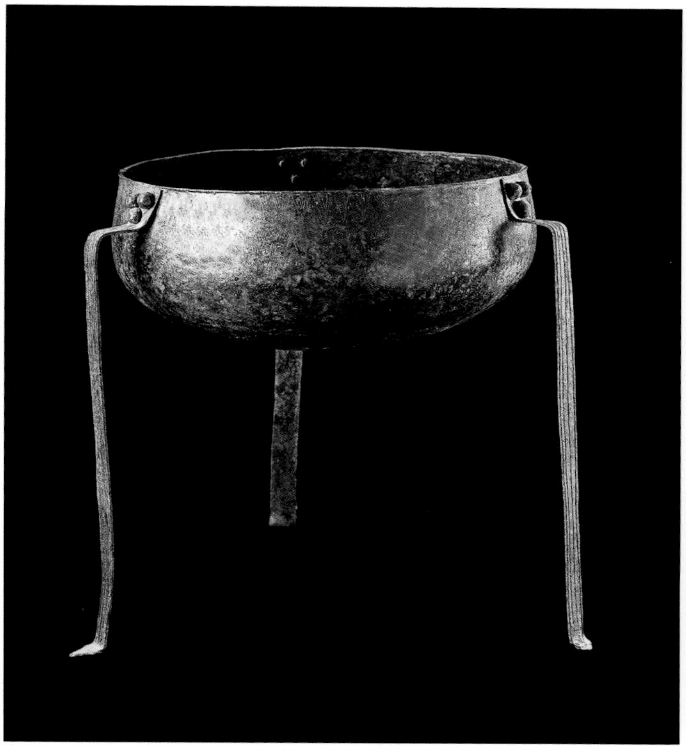

600 in the cemetery of Osteria dell'Osa, in Latium. Here, in what was later to become the territory of the city of Gabii, the remains of a tomb of the third quarter of the eighth century B.C. have been unearthed, including defensive arms (a crested helmet, two shields and a quadrangular breastplate) and offensive ones (a sword and sheath, spear, javelin and ax), as well as vessels in bronze plate (a biconical amphora, four ribbed bowls and a basin with a beaded rim). The clearly Etruscan provenance of the arms and other items suggests that these grave goods attest to a case of geographical mobility associated with an Etruscan aristocrat, possibly of Veientine origin, buried, with the insignia of his rank, together with members of the community into which he had been integrated despite the fact that his culture and language were different. The recent discovery made in a former lake at Banditella, not far from the site of Vulci, where votive objects were accumulated in the eighth—or even the ninth—century B.C., is also associated with the aristocracy. The votive deposit of Banditella, to date the oldest to be found in Etruria, confirms that, in this region, the earliest finds relating to religion are closely linked to natural phenomena. The fact that only few such sites that have been identified up

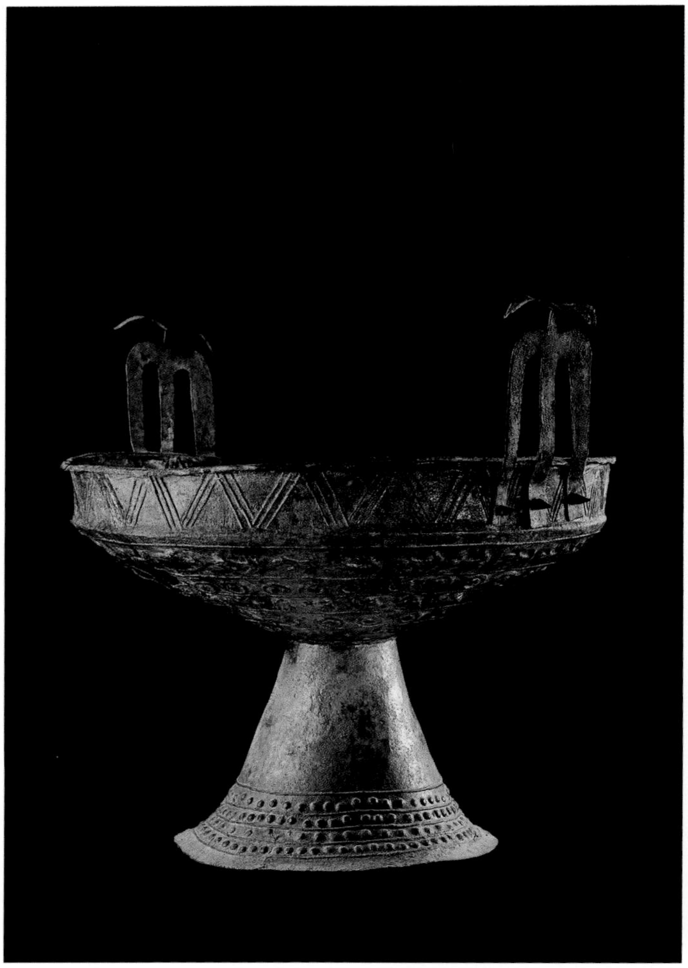

above
Bronze kantharos and biconical vase from the Tomb of the Bronze Chariot (Vulci), 680–670 B.C.
Rome, Museo di Villa Giulia
catt. 81.14; 81.13

right
Brown impasto kotyle *from the Tomb of the Bronze Chariot (Vulci), 680–670 B.C.*
Rome, Museo di Villa Giulia
cat. 81.39

opposite, above
Red impasto ollas from the Tomb of the Bronze Chariot (Vulci), 680–670 B.C.
Rome, Museo di Villa Giulia
catt. 81.33; 81.35

opposite, below
Fine-grained clay proto-Corinthian kylix *from the Tomb of the Bronze Chariot (Vulci), 680–670 B.C.*
Rome, Museo di Villa Giulia
cat. 81.40

Fine-grained clay Rhodian aryballoi
from the Tomb of the Bronze Chariot (Vulci), 680–670 B.C.
Rome, Museo di Villa Giulia
cat. 81.41

Couple of bronze bracelets
from the Tomb of the Bronze Chariot (Vulci), 680–670 B.C.
Rome, Museo di Villa Giulia
cat. 81.29

Single-handled ribbed impasto cup from the Tomb of the Bronze Chariot (Vulci), 680–670 B.C.
Rome, Museo di Villa Giulia
cat. 81.36

to now should not be interpreted as indicating that religious cults were rare, but rather that the characteristics of the rites themselves—practiced in the open air or in caves—leave only faint traces that are not easily discovered. Particularly noteworthy among the votive offerings found at Vulci—mainly consisting of miniature ceramic objects—is a problematic small solid bronze (height 9 cm) representing a harnessed horse, perhaps all that remains of a more complex group, which seems to be datable to the Late Orientalizing period, when the area ceased to be frequented. The contraction of the legs and the proportions of the animal's body, with an over-large muzzle and forequarters, indicate an early date (late eighth–early seventh century B.C.?). The choice of the animal, the possession of which conferred great social prestige, recalls the aristocratic ideals that from the ninth century B.C. onward were asserted in Greece by bronze or clay objects representing the same subject that were placed in the sanctuaries. The adhesion to this culture in the central Tyrrhenian area—at least, in the late eighth century B.C.—is marked by a pair of ceremonial horse masks (*prometopidia*) in bronze plate found in Tomb 4461 at Pontecagnano, of Etruscan production, but with evident North Syrian influence.

The Orientalizing period

The flow of men and ideas from the eastern Mediterranean, especially the successive waves of

Impasto chalices from the Tomb of the Bronze Chariot (Vulci), 680–670 B.C.
Rome, Museo di Villa Giulia
cat. 81.37

colonization undertaken by the Greek cities in the eighth century B.C. in South Italy and Sicily, introduced new, productive influences into Etruscan society, which had yet to become fully structured. The cultural level of Etruria allowed, in fact, the diffusion of stimuli and ideas that were assimilated and reworked in a way that was often quite independent, with dynamics and results that modern research has distinguished according to their chronology and geographical areas (d'Agostino 1999), and, in their turn, they were transmitted from Etruria to other parts of Italy. The natural meeting-places were the coastal ports, which, according to the excavations carried out so far, only became active after 600 B.C. (Gravisca, Pyrgi). It is likely, however, that, long before this, areas were designated for trade and the residence of merchants and foreigners on the model of the "port of trade" (Polanyi 1963). The obligations of hospitality and solidarity favored individual relationships, as the exchange of ceremonial gifts seems to indicate; this is attested by the inscriptions in the seventh century B.C. (Cristofani 1975; Cristofani 1984), or trading alliances, of which only later examples are known, in the period of the ivory *tesserae hospitales* found in Rome and Carthage. In southern Etruria and Latium *vetus* the designation through grave goods of the males as warriors, typical of the Late Iron Age, became a status symbol for the princes, heirs of the *gentes* who had emerged previously. In their culture, the ideology of the banquet became increasingly predominant, as the magnificent silver drinking-services in the Bernardini Tomb at Praeneste and the Regolini-Galassi Tomb at Caere indicate. As is well known, these contexts have a lot in common both with each other and with other princely tombs that have been identified in central Italy. The princes invested the surplus of their resources in the purchase of luxury goods in order to imitate the lifestyle in fashion at the courts of Ionia in western Asian Minor and of the Near East, based on opulence and material comfort. Deriving from the centers of the interior (Hama and Sinjirli) and the *emporia* of Syria (El Mina, Ras el Basit, Tell Sukas), these models brought to the West, via Cyprus, the ideology and the most evident attributes—the luxury goods—of the area, from which the monumental style of the palaces and tombs was also borrowed. By the mid-1970s careful comparison of various categories of luxury goods (objects of gold, bronze and ivory, ostrich eggs, glassware) and of monuments (tumuli, statues) had led numerous scholars to hypothesize that the diaspora of the Oriental craftsmen responsible for making these things—the result of the collapse of the Assyrian empire—extended as far as the West, including Etruria. The designs created in the fertile milieus of the eastern courts, especially the Egyptian and Assyrian ones, inspired the elaboration of new motifs, as B.B. Shefton demonstrated with regard to a distinctive floral trophy, the so-called paradise flower. These motifs were widely used to adorn luxury goods that reproduced the most significant moments of the aristocrats' lives, such as the Phoenician-Cypriot cups in precious metals. These and other artifacts, much sought-after in the West, were hoarded before being placed in the tombs, a practice very similar to that of the societies described in the Homeric poems (d'Agostino 1977). In fact, archaeological evidence to date indicates that, due to the different ideologies and religious customs existing in the two countries, the objects of Oriental origin, such as the cauldrons on a stand in bronze plate were included among grave goods in the central Tyrrhenian area of Italy, while in Greece they were dedicated in the large sanctuaries (Strøm 1992).

The constant progress made in Etruscan studies allows us to now comprise a greater range of artifacts in the production, which was intended not only for the princes but also for their ladies: the value of the objects for women, already evident from discoveries made long ago—such as the goods from a tomb at Tarquinia, including a Egyptian *situla* in faience with the cartouche of Pharaoh Bocchoris (720–715 B.C.), and the gold parure of the princess buried in the Regolini-Galassi Tomb at Caere—has been confirmed by recent studies. A *pyxis* in Egyptian frit (a mixture of sand, copper carbonate and other minerals), produced in the second half of the eighth century B.C. in North Syria (Rathje 1991) has been found in a grave in Vulci. Oriental craftsmen—Syrian or Phoenician—worked at Caere, where, from the second half of the seventh century B.C. onward, they produced unguent vases and implements for spinning in glass paste using the technique of the core of sand and clay, of Mesopotamian origin (Martelli 1994b). At Vulci there was a fabric for such exotic items as ostrich eggs, which, as a result of a complex process based on incision and painting, constituted the body of refined *oinochoai* made of different materials. An example, probably assembled at Vulci, which ended up in Tomb 14 in the Picene cemetery at Pitino di San Severino Marche, near Macerata, has been completed with a handle and an ivory mouth covered in gold leaf. Women were responsible for the whole cycle of the manufacture of wool, which was used to make the refined fabrics and clothes mentioned by Timaeus of Tauromenium as existing in the sixth century B.C. (*FGrH 566* F 50). However, the importance of women in the economy of the seventh century B.C. is demonstrated by finds at Etruscan sites in the Po Valley, including such precious artifacts as a bronze tintinnabulum in the Ori Tomb, near Bologna, and a carved wooden throne from Verucchio (Torelli 1997), on which there are images stressing the role of women in wool-working. Finally, women of high social rank had the honor of serving wine, as is stated in the inscriptions denoting possession scratched onto the jugs containing the precious drink. On the other hand, the social model of the high-ranking warrior established itself in northern Etruria: the grave goods of Vetulonia comprise a vast range of arms, which, unlike the armor in thin metal sheet of the eighth century B.C., were intended to be used in action as they were made of solid cast bronze. The forms, often new, remained in use for a long time. A workshop active in the first half of the seventh century B.C. was, for example, responsible for the development of the bowl-shaped helmet adorned with studs found at Vetulonia in the most significant hoards of the period (Tombs of the Warrior, of the Secondo Circolo delle Pellicce, of the Buca della Sagrona, etc.); the studs, the ends of the rivets serving to keep in place the internal padding in leather and marsh plants, were very popular in Picenum, where they stayed in fashion until the sixth century B.C. The concentration of arms in the tombs of the princes of Vetulonia of northern Etruria—which, judging by the image engraved on the funerary stela of Avele Feluske, continued for the whole of the seventh century B.C.—has yet to be fully assessed. However, it is possible they refer to the military skills required by these petty rulers to defend the resources on which their wealth was based, especially the mineral deposits. Particular importance was given to the monumental forms of the tombs. In southern Etruria, the chamber tombs were contained in huge tumuli, which, with diameters of up to 50–60 meters, form a conspicuous sign of possession of the land. Originally intended for a single individual, their use was later extended to the whole family. There is little doubt that the concept of the monumental tomb was derived from the East, perhaps from Anatolia.

Bronze and amber ring from the Tomb of the Bronze Chariot (Vulci), 680–670 B.C.
Rome, Museo di Villa Giulia
cat. 81.30

Brown impasto kantharoi *from the Tomb of the Bronze Chariot (Vulci), 680–670* B.C.
Rome, Museo di Villa Giulia
cat. 81.38

Strictly Etruscan were, however, the execution of a stone *crepidoma* (base of a building) and the external decoration of this, consisting of a series of fasciae and *torus* moldings, becoming progressively smaller towards the top. G. Colonna has attributed this to an architect working in Caere at the beginning of the seventh century B.C. who may have come from North Syria, the only area where, as far as is known at present, similar architectural elements are to be found. The funerary architecture reflects the distinct characteristics of each Etruscan city and the different solutions found in each to meet the requirements of funerary cults: for example, ramps added to the tumuli, allowing their tops to be reached are typical of Caere. Particularly frequent at Tarquinia, on the other hand, was the custom of laying out large open squares in front of the chamber tombs; in Cyprus they were used for the burial of horses, while in Etruria the funeral ceremonies took place in them. The desire for self-portrayal of the aristocracy encouraged the development of artistic genres hitherto unheard of in the West, such as the wall-paintings and the monumental statuary, widespread in the palaces of the eastern monarchs. In Caere, each monumental tomb of the first half of the seventh century B.C. (Tomb of the Sorbo, Mengarelli Tomb, Tombs of the Ship, of the Painted Animals, etc.) was embellished with wall-paintings, which were dominated by the beasts symbolizing ruinous death, stressing the funerary function of these chambers. From a technical point of view, the experimental character of these ancient works of art is evident due to the failure to use intonaco, which has been detrimental to their conservation and means it is difficult to imagine what they were like originally. The origins of the statuary are also linked to the funerary ideology and inspired by the Oriental repertoire: in the antechamber of the Tomb of the Statues at Ceri (a small *pagus* [village] in the territory of Caere) are reproduced two enthroned personages—two male dignitaries (Colonna, v. Hase 1984) or a married couple (Prayon 1998)—who, in any case, may be regarded as the ancestors of the deceased, as the two clay statuettes on the Tomb of the Five Chairs at Caere also appear to be. The statues from Ceri so closely echo the style of North Syrian art that they can be attributed to a sculptor from that area active around 680 B.C., who may also have left traces of his activity in the monumental funerary stelae of Felsina (Colonna, v. Hase 1984). Sculpture spread throughout northern Etruria in the following generation, as the discovery of a pair of freestanding statues at Casale Marittimo, in the territory of Volterra (ca. 650 B.C.) and the sculptural cycle of the tumulus of the Pietrera at Vetulonia (630–620 B.C.) demonstrate. The stone statues, which only portrayed ancestors, must be distinguished from the images of the deceased, which have been attested at an early date in the territories of Vulci and Chiusi with their series of, respectively, geometric busts in bronze sheet and clay canopic vases, now attested in contexts dating back with certainty to the seventh century B.C. thanks to the recent discoveries in the cemetery of Tolle (Paolucci forthcoming). However, the likenesses of the deceased were created not only with bronze and clay but also with relatively short-lived materials that have only rarely survived, such as a head, possibly fe-

Couples of bronze hands from the Tomb of the Bronze Chariot (Vulci), 680–670 B.C.
Rome, Museo di Villa Giulia
cats. 81.24; 81.25

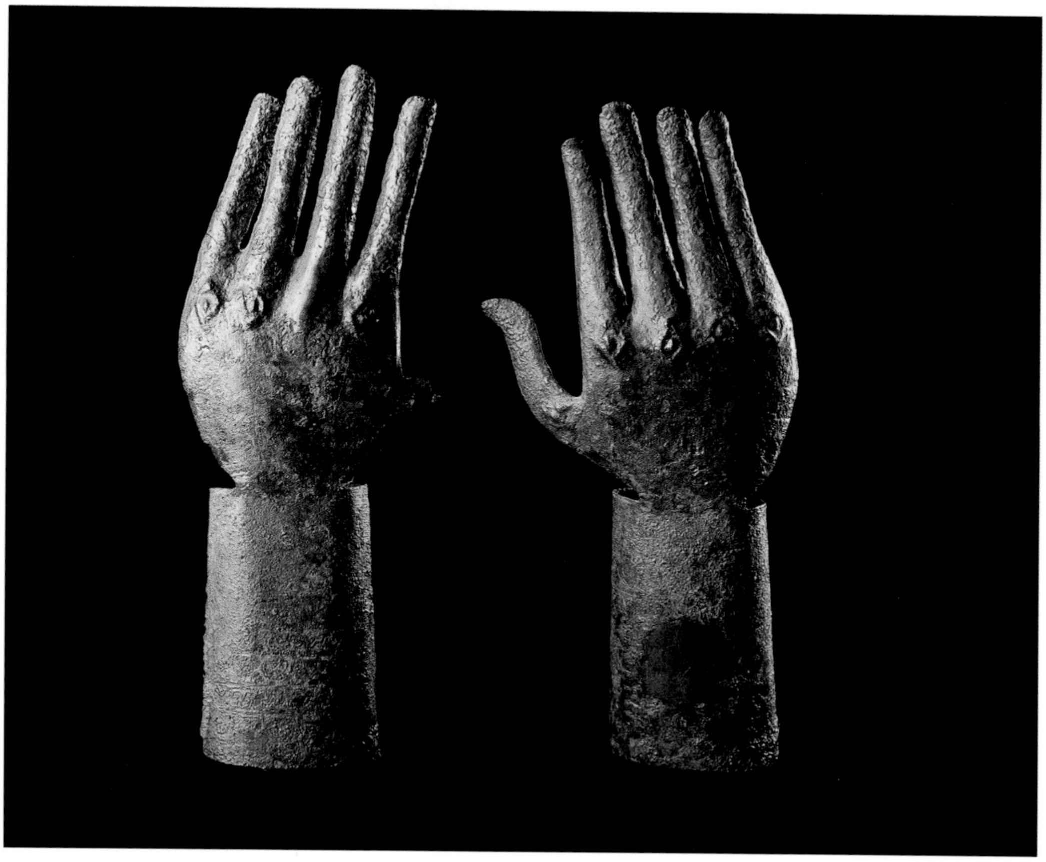

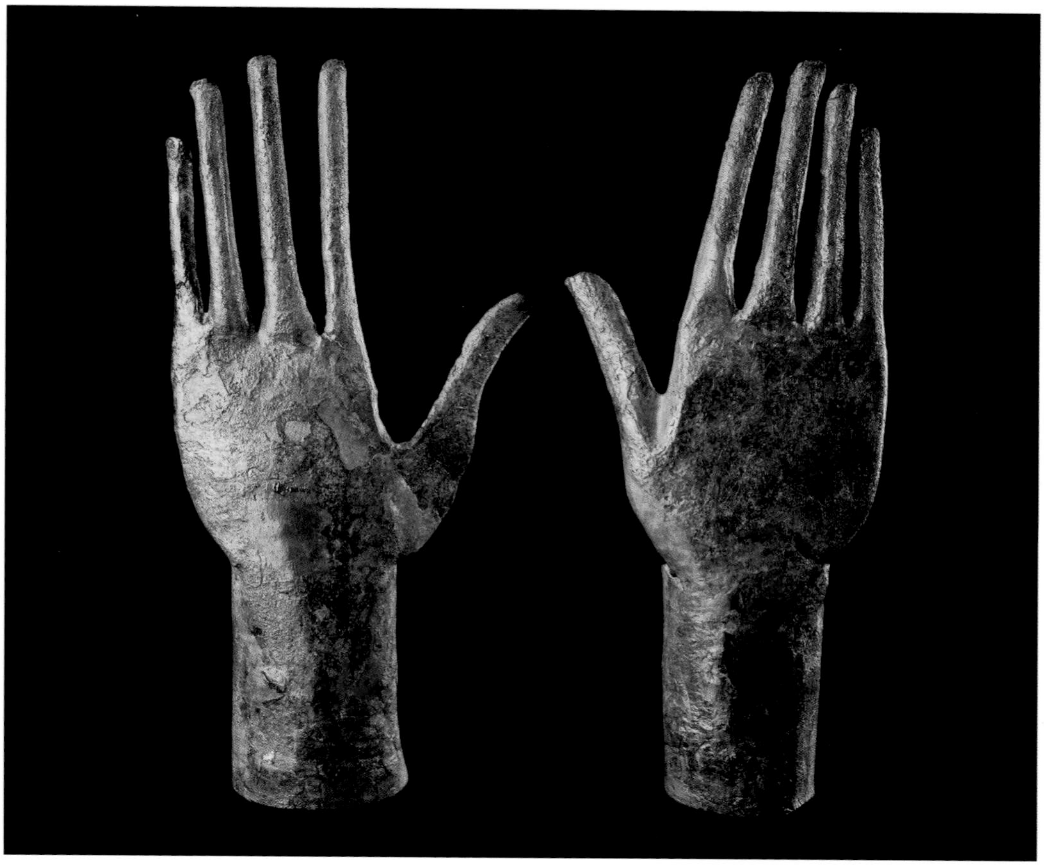

Gilt silver drinking bowl from the Bernardini Tomb (Palestrina), 675 B.C.
Rome, Museo di Villa Giulia

opposite
Terra-cotta architectonic slabs from Poggio Civitate (Murlo), first quarter of the sixth century B.C.
Murlo, Antiquarium

male, in pearwood in the Civiche Raccolte in Milan, believed to be from Vulci (Prayon 1998). These sculptures were used in the ceremonies preceding the placing of the bodies in the tombs, which were divided into numerous stages, one of the most important of which, from the seventh century B.C. onward, was the funeral banquet (*Totenmahl*), reproduced on a cinerary urn from Montescudaio (near Volterra), and the lament of the hired mourners, to which may be related the clay statuettes of the Regolini-Galassi Tomb at Caere and the later side of a tuff bed from Cortona. The rank of the aristocrats is stressed by the insignia of power: the collection of these relics, which are essential for determining their characteristics, has only just begun. The bronze *flabella*, adopted in Etruria from the East, and then transmitted to the area north of the Alps and Slovenia (Guldlager Bilde 1994) along routes followed also by the bronze cultic carts (Guggisberg 1996), reveal the high social rank of a number of female personages, who also have reproductions in glass paste of implements used for spinning. The models in bronze sheet of thrones, litui and scepters (found in the Tomb of the Statues at Ceri, while metal examples are also known) are characteristic of—but not exclusive to—men's graves. There are also numerous two-wheeled wagons among the grave goods of both men and women, clearly linked to the distinction of social class. In this period the metal and clay

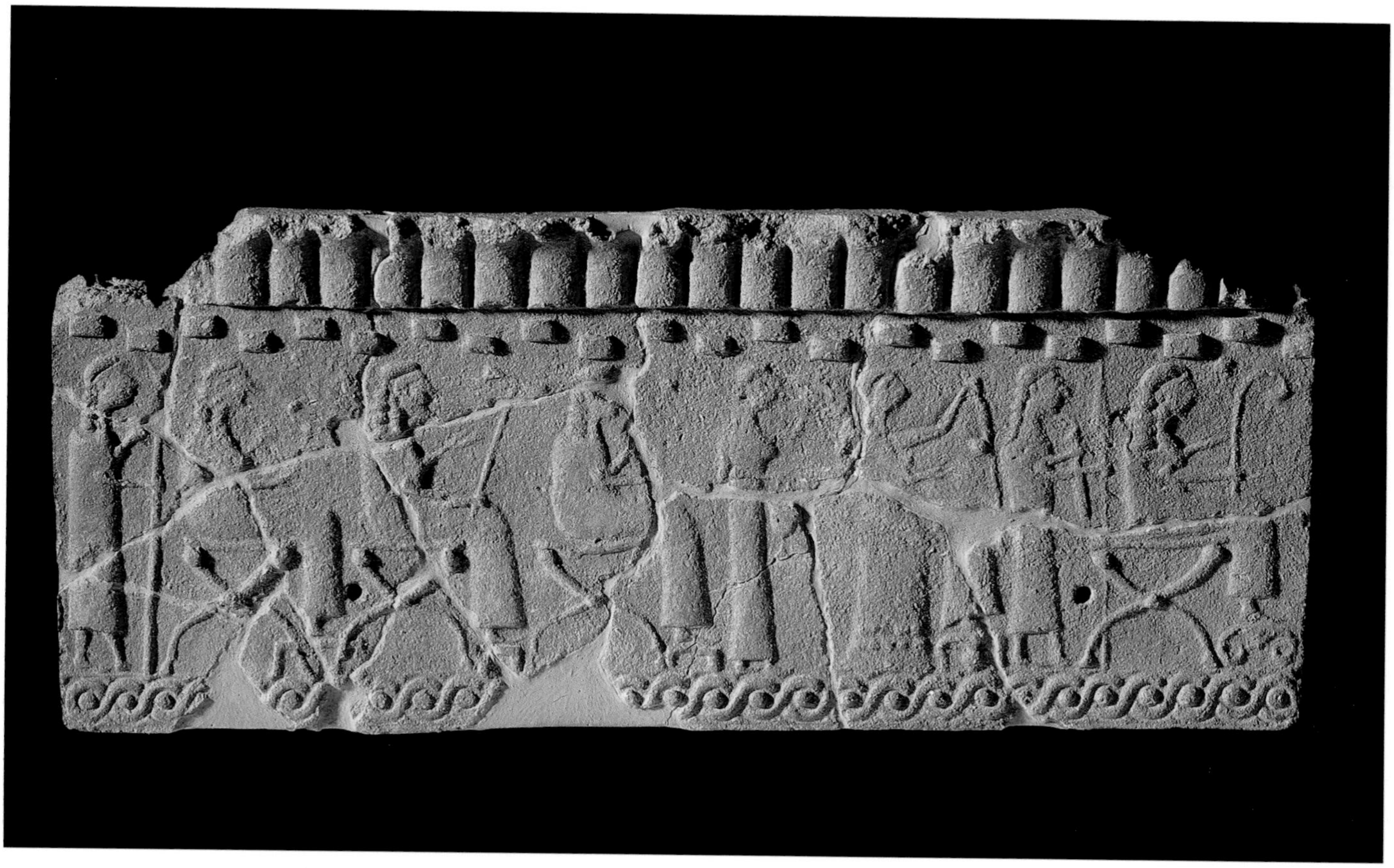

View of the Banditaccia necropolis (Cerveteri)

shields placed in the graves acquired the function, which they kept until the Hellenistic period, of indicators of social class. Axes, metal and, occasionally, clay models of which have been found in Etruria, are of Aegean derivation and are exclusively associated with men (as grave goods, votive offerings, etc.). The curved handle found on examples from northern Etruria is also characteristic of the ax held by the prince pouring a libation who is portrayed on the minute bronze in the form of a human figure dedicated in the sanctuary of Cupramarittima (Ascoli Piceno). The residences of the aristocrats are less well known, especially for the earliest period: although we have information regarding the palaces of the Late Orientalizing and Archaic periods of the lesser potentates of the interior, such as the one at Murlo in the Sienese hills, we still know nothing about the types of the palaces of the aristocrats buried in the monumental tumuli in the large coastal centers, although these buildings may be compared to the "long houses," the palaces of the Bronze Age; nor is much light shed on the matter by comparisons with Greece and Anatolia, where a very small number of residences of the society of the living and the community of the dead have been found. For the time being we cannot but imagine what the Etruscan dwellings were like on the basis of the evidence provided by funerary architecture, the reliability of which is confirmed by numerous comparisons that may be made, on the one hand, with the Caeretan tombs of the first half of the seventh century B.C. and, on the other, with the huts carved on the back of the throne from Verucchio. The large rectangular atrium—found in the Tomb della Capanna (of the Thatched Roof) at Caere or in house I of the acropolis of San Giovenale—was perhaps used to receive people of lower rank, who may be compared to the clients of Roman society. Their existence in the Orientalizing period is attested by the disposition of the tombs under tumuli in the Nuovo Recinto of the Banditaccia cemetery at Caere, which may have been the largest monumental one in the Mediterranean in the seventh and sixth centuries B.C. Dense groups of smaller tumuli, possibly reflecting the structure of Etruscan society are arranged round large tumuli, which are sometimes disposed in pairs. The links identified between the porticoed quadrangular plan of the palaces of the *bit-hilani* type, belonging to royal personages in North Syria and Anatolia in the eighth century B.C., and, on the one hand, the buildings at Murlo and Acquarossa, and, on the other, the Cancho Roano (Badajoz), in the Iberian peninsula, indicate that the eastern lifestyle was spreading to the whole Mediterranean basin. The inclusion of the Iberian aristocracy in the Mediterranean routes as early as the seventh century B.C. is confirmed by such finds as the funerary couch with bronze *appliques* in Phoenician style from Torrejón di Abajo (Cáceres). Direct or indirect contacts between the local milieu and Phoenician culture in such a remote region as the Spanish Estremadura may perhaps be explained by the iron-ore deposits in the Merida basin, accessible from the coast along the valley of the Guadiana River. Oriental models were adapted to the different needs of each cultural milieu. Thus in the Etruscan residences the sacral function is predominant—for example, in the rectangular building in the courtyard of Murlo, at Acquarossa and in the palace-cum-sanctuary at Montetosto, near Caere. The sacred aspect also played a major role in domestic architecture, as is indicated by the clay decoration on the same buildings, which, although dating from the Archaic period, is still closely linked to the figure of the dynast, who is associated with a deity in a way that is typically Oriental. The long clay friezes, on which the same subject was repeated obsessively, exalted the aristocratic figure in a strongly ideological manner (Torelli 1997), deriving from models from Asia Minor (d'Agostino 1999). The influx of goods and craftsmen from the eastern Mediterranean continued until the sixth century B.C., as is also indicated by comparison between armlets of glass paste with gold terminals from Monte Auto (Vulci) and the tumulus of Toptepe (Güre) in Lydia—but the historical climate was now very different.

The origins. The Final Bronze Age: Di Gennaro 1996, pp. 488–96. *Veio and high-ranking burials:* Bartoloni 1997, *in particular F. Delpino and A. Rathje;* Putz 1998, pp. 49–68; Cateni 1998. *Metal tripods:* Bieg 1995. *Datings gauged by dendrochronology:* Bietti Sestieri 1998. *Onomatology:* Colonna 1977a, pp. 176–92. *Thyrrenian piracy and the passage from Ephorus:* Mele, 1979; Torelli 1987b, pp. 145–60; Cristofani 1987b, pp. 51–53; Cordano 1986, pp. 28–48. *Nuragic bronzes:* Lo Schiavo, Ridgway 1987, pp. 392–400. *The Phoenician presence:* Martelli 1991a, pp. 1049–72; Botto 1993, pp. 15–27; Botto 1995, pp. 43–53; Markoe 1996, pp. 11–31. *The notion of interest:* Hudson 1992, pp. 128–43. *The banquet:* Cristofani, 1987b, pp. 123–32; Rathje 1990, pp. 279–88; Rathje 1995, pp. 167–75. *Stone and clay mortars:* Botto forthcoming. *The ceremony of "marzeah":* Menichetti forthcoming. *Metal graters:* Ridgway 1997, pp. 325–44. *In the Aegean area add at least Ephesus, Miletus (unp.) and Samos:* Brize 1991, p. 323, Abb. 3. *Geographical mobility:* De Santis 1995, pp. 365–75; Colonna 1995, pp. 325–42. *The Banditella hoard:* D'Ercole, Trucco 1995a, pp. 77–84; D'Ercole, Trucco 1995b, pp. 348–51. *Votive horses in Greece:* Zimmermann 1989. *Orientalizing period. The Etruscan aristocracies:* Polany 1963, pp. 30–45; *Aspetti delle aristocrazie* 1984; Cristofani, Martelli 1994, pp. 1147–66; v. Hase 1995b, pp. 239–85; Martelli 1995, pp. 9–26; *Interactions in the Iron Age* 1996; Winther 1997, pp. 423–46; d'Agostino 1999b, pp. 81–88. *Italic aristocracies:* Torelli 1988b, pp. 53–76; Cristofani 1995a, pp. 136–47; Bottini 1999, pp. 89–96. *Funerary ideology and ethical conceptions:* d'Agostino 1977; Spivey 1992, pp. 233–42. *Ceremonial gifts:* Cristofani 1975a, pp. 132–52; Cristofani 1984, pp. 319–24. *"Tesserae hospitales":* Messineo 1983, pp. 3–4. *Domestic architecture:* Torelli 1985b, pp. 21–32; Colonna 1986, pp. 373–530; Prayon 1995, pp. 501–19. *Funerary architecture:* Zifferero 1991, pp. 107–34; Naso 1996, pp. 69–85; Naso 1998, pp. 117–57. *Statuary:* Colonna, v. Hase 1984, pp. 13–59; Strøm 1997, pp. 245–47, fig. 1; Prayon 1998, pp. 191–207; Esposito 1999; Paolucci forthcoming. *Mural painting:* Naso 1995, pp. 439–99. *"Orientalia" in Greece:* Strøm, 1992, pp. 46–60; Martelli 1994b, pp. 1149–53; Waldbaum 1994, pp. 53–66. *"Orientalia" and Orientals in Italy*: Rathje 1979, pp. 145–85; Rathje 1984, pp. 341–54; Rathje 1986, pp. 397–404; Shefton 1989, pp. 97–117; Rathje 1991, pp. 171–75; Martelli 1994b, pp. 75–98; v. Hase 1995a, pp. 533–59; Martelli 1996, pp. 47–60; Prayon 1998b, pp. 329–41. *Flabella:* Guldlager Bilde 1994, pp. 7–34. *Cultual carts:* Guggisberg 1996, pp. 175–95; Egg 1996. *Wagons:* Emiliozzi 1997. *Shields:* Bartoloni, De Santis 1995, pp. 277–90. *The throne of Verucchio:* Torelli 1997a, pp. 52–86. *Painted potteries:* Kranz 1998, pp. 13–45. *Clay friezes:* d'Agostino 1999b, pp. 3–12; Torelli 1997c, pp. 87–121. *The Iberic paeninsula:* Almagro Gorbea 1990, pp. 251–308; Guerrero 1991, pp. 49–82; Ruiz 1996, pp. 289–300; Ruiz 1999, pp. 97–106; Jiménez Ávila 1998, pp. 67–98. *Glass armlets:* Özgen, Öztürk 1996, pp. 52, 160–61, n. 111 *(third quarter of the sixth century B.C.).*

The Woman's Role

The institutional figure of the Etruscan woman has a number of aspects, that develop between the archaic and the hellenistic periods, interwoven with the various socio-economic conditions related to the course of history. Certain behaviors are accepted in other contemporary Mediterranean cultures as well, such as that of the *domina*, although with a variety of nuances, whereas others are singular and apparently unmatched in societies of the classical world of the same period. Woman's role in Etruscan society is not easy to define because of the lack of direct, impartial evidence regarding her capacities, which are conjectured, on the basis of circumstantial evidence, from the study of data offered by historiography, iconographic sources and epigraphy. Both in antiquity and in modern times Etruscan women have been invested with qualities and roles that were actually not theirs: hearsay about their licentiousness goes back to the fourth century B.C. (Timaeus and Theopompus), apparently confirmed by several paintings in Etruscan tombs (Tomb of the Bigas of Tarquinia, where the presence of matrons at public performances clashed with social conventions of the Greek and Roman worlds), but which instead should be put back in a particular political moment and a particular Greek cultural mood, directed at stigmatizing the public image of the Etruscans. In the second half of the nineteenth century, with Bachofen, we see an attempt to overestimate the Etruscan woman's role, lending her features which in fact she did not have, precisely assumed from the singularity of a freedom of mores and attitudes substantially different from those of her Greek and Roman sisters: thus arose the myth of Etruscan matriarchy, which appears, in light of modern criticism and available information, entirely unfounded.

In the past twenty years scholars' interest in the role of women in Etruscan society has grown, following a series of studies on Greek and Roman women, mostly of Anglo-Saxon initiative, published in the wake of the 1960s' feminist movement.

The role of women within society did not remain unchanged between early Etruscan civilization and Romanization. We can identify several stages, some belonging to the archaic age, and several aspects, some remaining constant (use of the matronymic), while others, especially formal ones, are strongly influenced by Roman society, ending up, as is consistent, by conforming to it.

The leading role of the Etruscan woman was beyond a doubt that of the *domina lanifica, domiseda, univira*, in that triple name just like the Roman matron, from whom she differs by a number of collateral aspects that apparently cannot be ascribed to the Roman woman nor even less to the Greek. Above all there is the cultural aspect: some of the oldest Etruscan in-

Sarcophagus of the Married Couple from Cerveteri, 525–500 B.C. Paris, Musée du Louvre

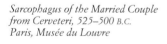

following page
Tarquinia, Tomb of the Shields, symposium scene, 350–340 B.C.

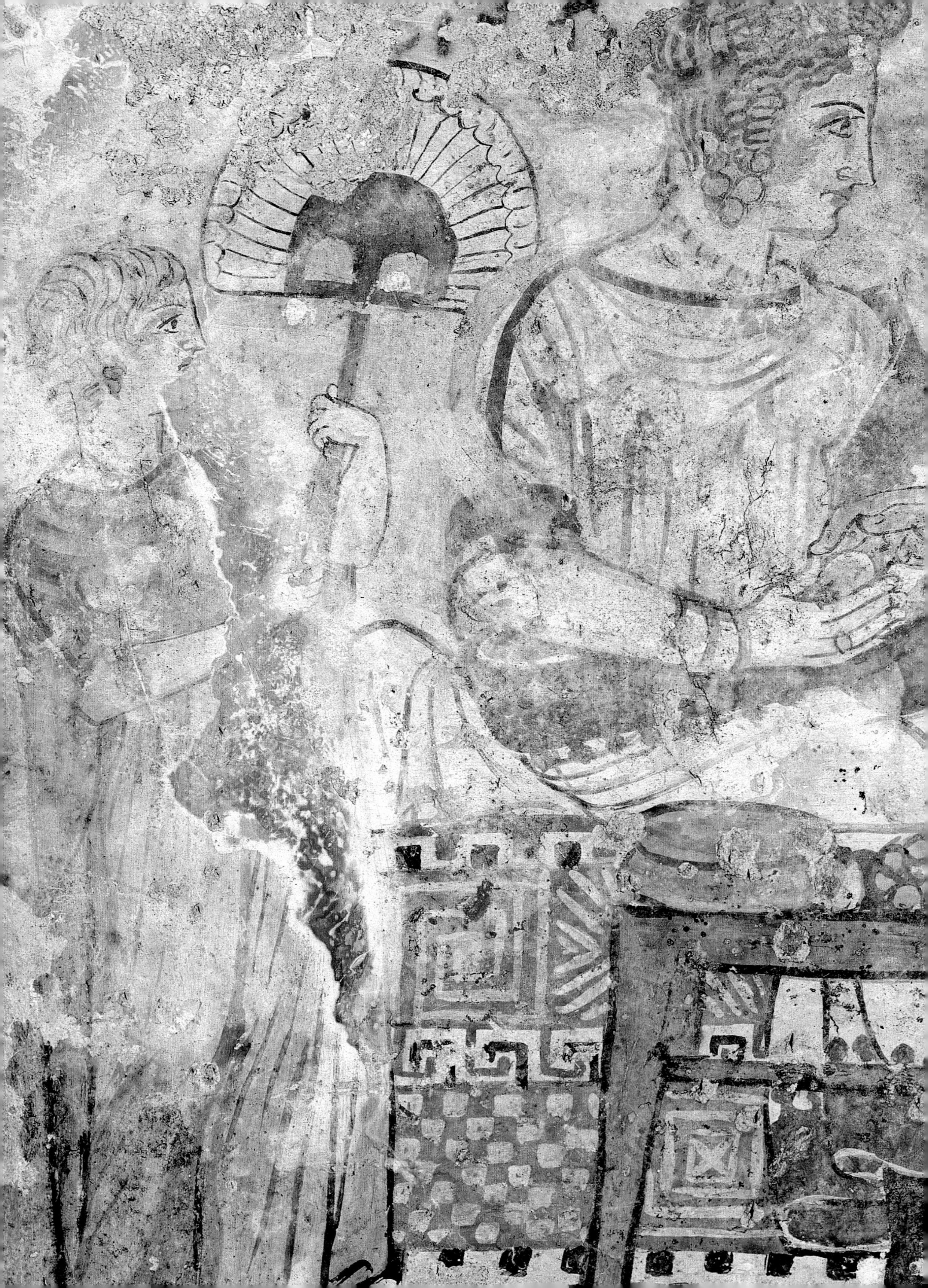

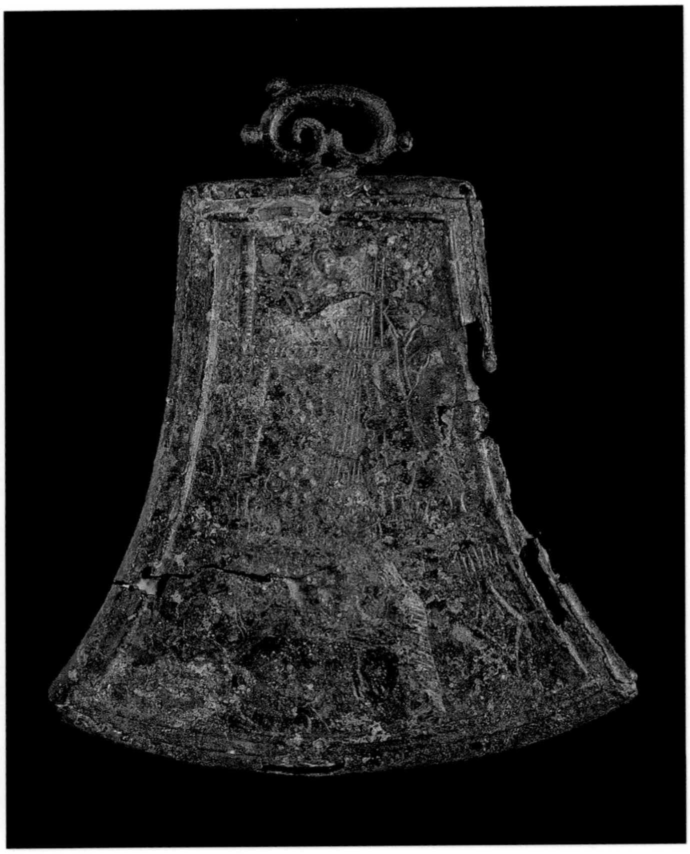

Bronze tintinnabulum from the Ori Tomb in the Arsenale necropolis (Bologna), last quarter of the seventh century B.C.,
Bologna, Museo Civico

scriptions or graphic signs are often carved on articles intended for women, and now and then present individual women's names or dedicatory formulas to female subjects, confirming women's knowledge and use of writing. More specifically we are dealing with objects that serve as supports for writing, connected with the processing of organic (wool) and vegetable (linen) fibers which, combined with the presence of implements such as bronze spindles (Veio, Quattro Fontanili, Tomb KKLL 18–19) or distaffs (Veio, Quattro Fontanili, Tomb JJ 17–18), besides the well-known and more wide-spread spools, loom weights and whorls (in some cases bearing inscriptions, like the one from Tomb 21 of the Vulci Osteria necropolis with an alphabet of the "modified" type, incised), confirm that spinning and especially weaving were prerogatives of high-ranking women. The examination of solely female burial goods from Veio reveals an intended distinction, within the community, between the status of spinners and of spinners-weavers, so that spinning-weaving seems exclusively reserved to the *mater familias-domina.* The art of weaving, to which the *mater familias* devoted herself personally, as is confirmed by both the figures of the so-called Bologna "tintinnabulum" and the Verucchio throne of Tomb 89, where the *domina* is seated on the throne, busy weaving and overseeing the servant girls, has been interpreted as the capacity to grasp and create connections which appear again in the cloth. That technique, as concerns Etruria, has been considered the basis for learning to write, which at first requires like connection patterns. The *domina,* whose function as a weaver was socially relevant (exchanges of gifts, dowries, fabrics), presumibly had an important role as well in introducing writing, a conjecture supported by the existence of sanctuaries presided by female divinities (those consacrated to Mater Matuta, Reitia), implicating the fact of writing. From that point of view we may assume that after the first appearing of alphabetical writing, whose diffusion should perhaps be attributed to the women's weaving sphere, by the second quarter of the seventh century became a male prerogative, as seems evidenced by the writing material from the Tomb of the Ivories of Marsiliana d'Albegna, belonging to a male deposition. The fact that the Etruscan woman's role was relevant and largely more involved and involving than

Impasto spools and whorls from Populonia Tomb I, seventh–sixth century B.C.
Florence, Museo Archeologico
cat. 129

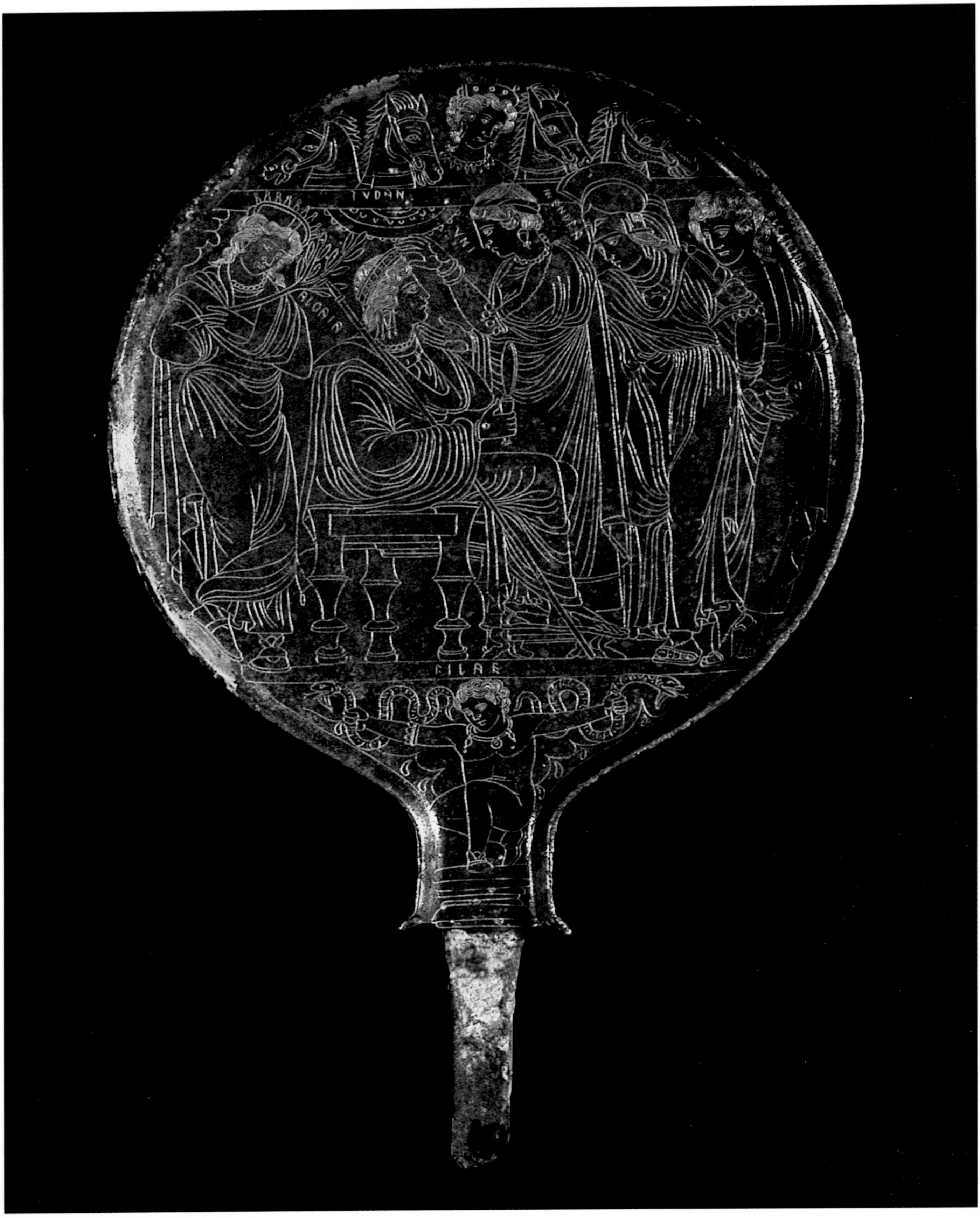

Tarquinia, Tomb of Orcus I, Velia Spurinai, beginning of the fourth century B.C.

opposite
Mirror depicting Paris Judgement with Turan (Afrodite), Uni (Hera), Menrva (Athena) e Althaia, end of the fourth century B.C.
Bloomington, Indiana University Art Museum

that of her Greek and Roman sisters is also indicated by the episode of Tanaquilla reading omens *etrusco more* (Livy, I, XXXIV, 9), on her arrival in Rome with her Lucumon husband, the future Tarquinius Priscus. The fact of referring to a woman, even of the rank of Tanaquilla, whose memory was still vivid for first-century B.C. Romans (Varro), through the veneration of the distaff she has used and which was religiously preserved in the temple of Semo Sancus, reveals the status attained by *dominae* in Etruria (and omen-reading with all the related rituals, necessarily implied a knowledge of reading as well as writing, far beyond what could be learned by oral tradition). It also indicates that it was precisely the *mater familias*, the *domina lanifica*, symbolized by Tanaquilla's distaff, that possessed the power of culture not just in the family circle but, at least in part, in those of rites as well. So here we have the concept of sacredness and of everyday life contained in the same person. And from the examination of several sarcophagi, like the one in London with the recumbent deceased and a fawn watering, we can assume that in Etruria a woman could play a part in certain religious practices too.
The importance of the role of women is also emphasized by the type of onomastic formula used in Etruria, where we constantly have, by the seventh century, the individual and gentilitial name, whereas the matronymic is introduced in a later period next to the patronymic, in all the inscriptions where filiation is given. The characteristic presence of the matronymic is so ingrained in the double onomastic formula that we still find it attested in the first imperial period, in Latin funerary inscriptions, found inside historic Etruria's boundaries, where the deceased, obviously of Etruscan origin, use the traditional onomastic formula. Besides the matronymic we should mention the use of the *praenomen* as well as the family name (gentilitian or *nomen*) to recall the woman. That element is essential as an indication of alliances and marriages between different clans, where importance is precisely due to the rank of the family with whom one is connected (and perhaps we could interpret the Verucchio

Sarcophagus lid with laying deceased from Tarquinia, 340 B.C. London, British Museum

throne and the burial goods of Tomb 89 containing them as belonging to a pre-alphabet period, but conceptually connected with the art of weaving).

The presence of the matronymic is the key for understanding the importance of the Etruscan woman's role within the family and society: a role not only explicited inside the household walls, a situation already existing and familiar in Rome or Athens, but outside too: the woman besides being recalled as wife or mother or grandmother of important figures, or by her own fecundity, assumes importance as a symbol of belonging to a high-ranking family, with the authority to pass on her own property.

Women's characteristic autonomy can also be assumed from the series of inscriptions, both archaic (*kusnailise* on pottery and *mi cusul puiunal* on a tile of the first stage) and hellenistic (of Vulsinii stamps with the inscription *vel numnal*), which we should interpret as the signature of the shop owner. They suggest a female role, within the family, that goes beyond the mere tasks of the *domina* dedicated to relatives' well-being by providing for elementary necessities such as hunger (preparation of food) and cold (weaving for clothing).

These epigraphs evidence an activity, somehow autonomous, and of handling needs inherent to the good functioning of the *oikos* and, perhaps, even of business for third parties (Pliny, *Naturalis historia*, XXXV, 151 ff.; Athenag., *Legatio pro christianis*, 17). The requirement to put one's own signature with a stamp for the recognition of materials coming from one's own workshop indicates a need to recognize and authentify that would not make much sense within a closed system (*domina*-family-workshop-*domina*); but it takes on a very different value in an open system of exchanges, where a workshop with its mistress signs its own works as a mark of recognition of its own production, guaranteeing the quality of the article.

Next to these images and their more refined representation, we have evidence of a whole series of depictions connected with the *mundus muliebris* that can represent in a more traditional manner the prevailing theme of scenes connected with nuptials or gifts for women. Compared to the gravity of some of the themes treated on other mirrors, these seem a kind of *divertissement*, in which the scene of Turan's hairdressing or of another woman gazing at herself in a mirror are not commonplace themes, but light ones suited to nuptial gifts.

Heurgon 1961a, pp. 139–60; Torelli 1965, pp. 126–29; Rix 1977, ps. 64–73; Agostiniani 1982; Pomeroy 1984, pp. 315–372; Torelli 1984; Arrigoni 1985; Gasperini 1989, pp. 181–211; Haynes 1989, pp. . 1395–405; Rallo 1989; Nielsen 1990, pp. 45–67; Schmitt Pantel 1990; Pandolfini, Prosdocimi 1990; Baurain, Bonnet, Krings 1991; Martelli 1991, pp. 337–46; Colonna 1993, pp. 61–68; d'Agostino 1993, pp. . 61–73; Bonfante 1994, pp. 243–51; Sordi 1995, pp. 159–73; Bartoloni, Berardinetti, De Santis, Drago 1997, pp. 89–100; Torelli 1997; Nielsen 1998, pp. 69–84; Peruzzi 1998; Bagnasco Gianni, Cordano 1999, pp.. 85–106.

ΛΕΑΓΡΟΣ
ΚΑΛΟ

The Hellenization of Etruria

For many years a marked bias in favor of the German "philological" approach to archaeology conditioned classical scholarship, thereby largely determining both its character and methodology from the outset, such that from the mid-nineteenth century to the World War I scholars across Europe considered Etruscan civilization a "provincial" issue, a mere offshoot of the Greek culture. Paradoxically, the negative attitude implicit in this parting vision occasioned a broadly positive view among the so-called "irrationalist" currents of thought which, making their appearance at the turn of the century, ended up taking center stage in the ensuing interwar period.

Greatly furthering the cause of contemporary art in their day, these emerging schools turned their attention on what they discerned as anti-classical, or non-classical, forms of expression from ancient civilizations, accentuating the positive values of the more supposedly crude or primitive features of the Etruscans. The Italian branch of this "irrationalist" approach, which promptly found itself being courted by the Fascist nationalists for their propaganda drive, wishfully identified Etruscan art—particularly aspects that veered from the classical canon—as the much sought-after but otherwise unspecified "Genius Italicus," whose prime qualities were touted as "innate spontaneity and expressive force," and therefore in contrast to what they considered the coldly rational aesthetics of Greek art. With the fall of Fascism after World War II, the "Etruscan question" was resumed with new vigor. Having safely cast off of the ideological trammels of the interwar years, the debate assumed a more refined working method based on philological analysis, prompting R. Bianchi Bandinelli (1973, p. 215) to assert that "without the influence of Hellenism Italic sculpture would never have developed beyond the colorful figurines of a Neapolitan crèche." In the course of the 1970s Etruscan scholarship widened its analytical tools to include the hermeneutic methods of anthropology (*Forme di Contatto* 1983), by which the Etruscan interface with Greek culture was now seen as a self-sufficient historical process of acculturation, eluding both the traditional filters of classical scholarship and neatly deflating the bloated claims of the interwar years. Boasting an extraordinary extension throughout the Mediterranean basin, Greek civilization was undoubtedly held in the utmost esteem right from the beginning of the Archaic era, and its impact was felt in all areas of culture. That influence, moreover, continued to grow in strength until the cultural supremacy of Hellenism effectively became universal (Torelli 1977). The ongoing effects this con-

Grey calcareous stone pedestal with the dedication of the Tyrrhenians to Apollo, end of the sixth–beginning of the fifth century B.C.
Delfi, Apollo sanctuary
cat. 55

opposite
Red-figure "Nolana" amphora from Vulci, detail.
Paris, Musée du Louvre
cat. 190

Marble kouros *head of Cycladic provenance from Marzabotto, ca. 500* B.C.
Marzabotto, Museo Pompeo Aria cat. 276

version to Hellenism had on the ruling classes of the "barbarian" tribes in new and ever more far-flung regions can be followed from the Archaic to the Classical era, especially in the western Mediterranean, where the Latins, Etruscans, and other Italic peoples, together with the Celts, Phoenicians and Iberians, were by no means only superficially affected by Greek civilization, each one gleaning the source's more utilitarian aspects, or those most compatible with the target culture's social fabric, its lore and customs. As we will observe in the case of Etruria, the prestige enjoyed by Greek culture as a whole derived from the inimitable Greek ability to transmit the qualities, foundations, and the technical and ideological patrimony of their civilization, and not least the political implications that this culture bore with it. The ease with which Hellenism, this intricate and multifaceted compound of diverse cultural legacies, spread through barbarian lands (Momigliano 1975) is due to two distinct though interconnected factors. The foremost vehicle of Greek culture was probably trade, in that the Greek merchants were bearers both of consumables and of ideas. They possessed, moreover, the skills necessary to penetrate deep into each country's interior, even in the most hostile of lands. The other principal vehicle of Hellenization was the extraordinary exodus of technicians and craftsmen from the Greek motherland, highly skilled people active in a wide assortment of occupations that involved the production of consumable goods, the furtherance of practical sciences and technological know-how, and intellectual activities of all kinds. Unlike their counterparts in other countries of the East, Greek craftsmen and professionals practiced their craft in relative personal freedom and possessed the basic tools of their occupation. Their birthright not only allowed them to move about unimpeded, but fostered a keen sense of enterprise, by which they equipped themselves methodically in order to serve the aristocracies of Persia, Lydia, Phrygia, Lycia, Thracia, Rome and Etruria, the Celts and Carthaginians—the ruling classes of a range of different peoples, therefore, whose societies attracted the Greek voyagers for the purposes of trade and exchange. This multifarious clientele also provided the Greeks with an excellent outlet for their innumerable skills and noted workmanship. Significantly, while these traders, artisans and technicians were all from lower classes, their constant presence on the Italian peninsula afforded a fundamental interface between Italic peoples and the Hellenic world as a whole; but their being of more humble extraction originated a patent contradiction: while there was widespread admiration for Greek culture, the class of enterprising people who actually transmitted it, the *Graeculi*, were not well regarded. Emblematic of such a prejudicial stance are the Latins, whose derogatory attitudes are well documented, their being the only Italic people whose literary tradition as been handed down to us (Torelli forthcoming-a).

Further on we shall see how these stereotypes are in truth tied to certain definable historical and social circumstances, and reflect preconceptions that did not necessarily exist when relations started. As recipients of Greek influence, however, the Etruscans were an exception. Although their acculturation proceeded substantially along parallel (though separate) lines of development, the Etruscans reacted differently from their Latin counterparts undergoing similar evolution, in that they were the only "barbarian" people caught up in this massive process of Hellenization who successfully absorbed an extremely wide range of features of the Greek culture. Their assimilation of Greek religion, politics, figurative art, literature and daily customs was such that the Etruscan world might virtually be seen as an offshoot of the Greek universe. That is not to say, of course, that the Etruscan variant did not have a distinct social makeup of its own, with respective repercussions at all levels, including artistic development and the institutional framework of the society itself. The process of acclimation has invited comparisons between the impact of Greek culture on the Romans (and by induction therefore on the Etruscans), and the rapid absorption of western culture by Japanese society today (Gallini 1973). Just why the Etruscans in particular were so stimulated to embrace the Greek world is a complex matter and not always easy to determine, though we may reasonably surmise that the principal reasons lie, first, in the frequency and sheer continuity of contacts between Etruria and Greece, an exchange prompted by the thriving markets along the Tyrrhenian coast; and second, in the presence of large and powerful Greek colonies on Italian soil which all in all enjoyed greater prosperity than those in barbarian territories elsewhere around the Mediterranean. To these likely suppositions we should add an inherent disposition toward Greek culture evinced by the Etruscan and Latin peoples, whose aristocracies evidently found common ground with the Hellenic counterparts with which they were in closest contact, particularly those of Euboea

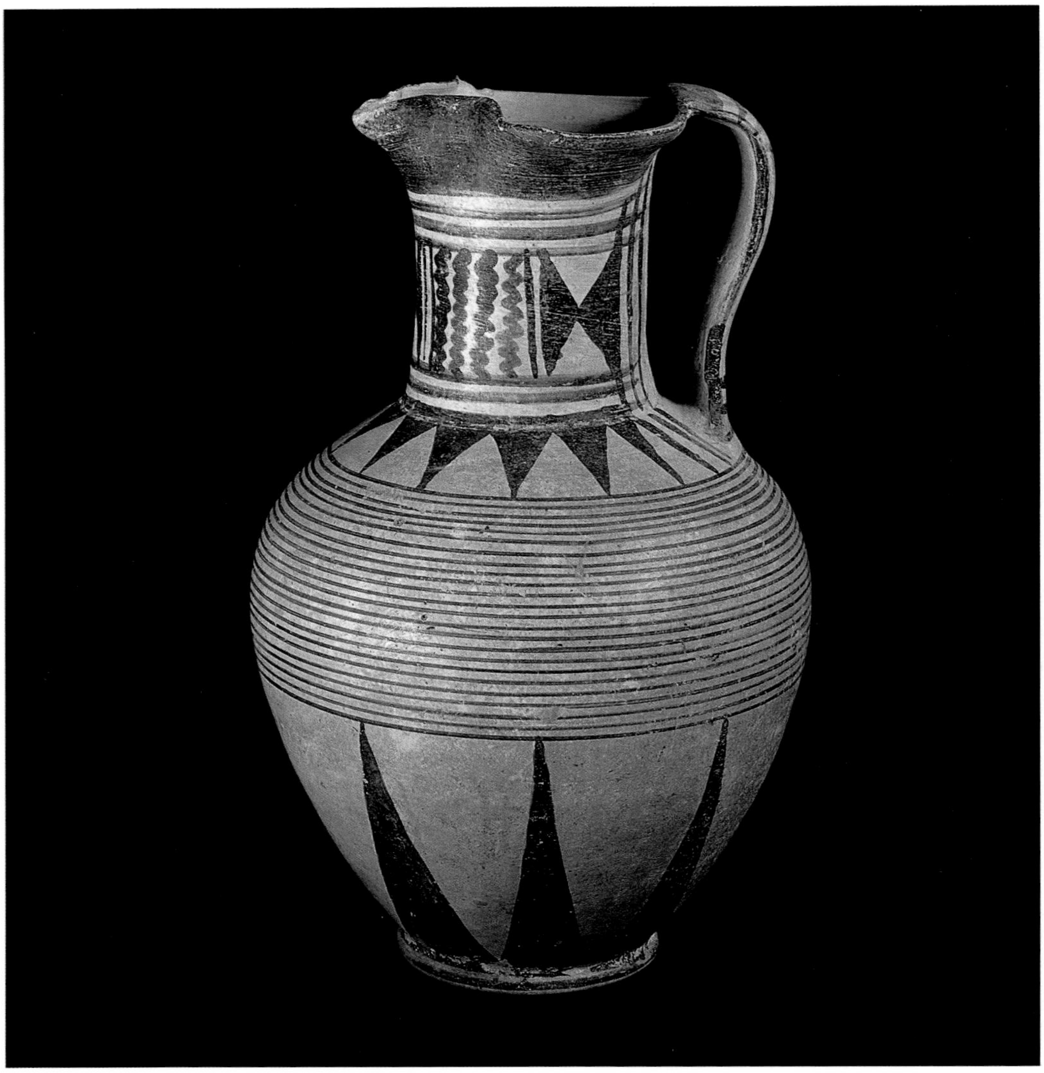

Pink clay Italo-Geometric oinochoe *first quarter of the seventh century* B.C.
Tarquinia, Museo Archeologico
cat. 185

during the early Orientalizing period, and Ionia for the age from the late Orientalizing period to the late Archaic times. The seminal event marking the onset of acculturation in Etruria took place in the distant past when the inhabitants first came into contact with Phoenician and Greek traders looking for reliable sources of metal—principally iron, but also copper and other raw materials (Torelli 1996). Occurring at the threshold of the Late Bronze and the Early Iron Ages (tenth–ninth century B.C.), just as the Etruscan *ethnos* was coming into being, the contact with a new world marked a cusp in the Etruscans' development and coincided with the height of Villanovan colonization of the more fertile areas of the Etrurian heartland and of Campania in the south and of the Po Valley in the north, marking the consolidation of what is traditionally termed the Etruscan "thalassocracy" (Torelli 1981a). The Etruscans' earliest known contact with the Orient was through the Phoenicians, to whom the Etruscans may owe their first acquaintance with a variety of new technologies. In particular, the Cypriot Phoenicians (Ridgway 1996) were responsible for the introduction of the *fibula*, long a prevalent feature of costume adornment throughout the ancient world. These early contacts must also have been the vehicle for critical crafts skills, as suggested by the preparation and crafting of precious materials such as gold, silver, glass, ivory and bone, all testified by many artifacts found among the assemblages of the proto-Villanovan site of Frattesina in the Polesine area (De Min 1984; 1986; De Min, Gerhardinger 1986). Undoubtedly of Oriental origin, perhaps dating to before a period exchanges began with the Greeks, are several Oriental features in the Etruscan culture; one of these can be discerned in vestiges of the archaic connection between kingship and hierogamic practices (Torelli 1997d, pp. 24-46); another aspect is perhaps the social connotation of the simpotic ritual (Menichetti 2000), though the latter was only in part the result of ideas transmitted to the Etruscans between the eighth and seventh centuries B.C. by the Greeks, with whom they were already familiar (Burkert 1992; 1999), or were traversing a phase of acute receptivity to such ideas, as testified by a great many other features that were current in the Orientalizing period. Archaeological evidence of previous contact with the Phoenicians' world through their products—or through artifacts originating in the Near East—occurring in aristocratic Etruscan contexts (Garbini 1996) is recorded for the grave contents of the main princely tombs in the Orientalizing period, not before the end of the eighth century B.C., though it must be said that the exquisite workmanship of such goods—witness those recovered from the Regolini-Galassi Tomb at Cerveteri, and the Bernardini, Barberini and Castellani Tombs at Praeneste—meant their use was enjoyed for some considerable time first in the hands of the intermediaries and then by the Etruscans. The estimated chronology for these goods shows that trade with the Phoenician milieu and the presence of the same may stem from long before the first contacts were made, during which the Phoenicians were alone in dealing with the Tyrrhenian area and therefore the sole vectors of ideology from diverse sources in the Orient, including Syria, Phoenicia, Egypt, Anatolia, and above all Mesopotamia. Indeed, Mesopotamian practices of divination inspired the Etruscan art of the *haruspex*, or the interpretation of omens through the inspection of the liver of sacrificial victims, which was to become a fundamental element of culture of the Etruscan ruling class. At any event, contact with the Hellenic world is undoubtedly attested by the presence in Villanovan tombs of late-Geometric pottery, largely manufactured of Euboean origin, and generally dated to the late ninth–early eighth century B.C. (Bats, d'Agostino 1998), and therefore prior to the establishment of the island emporium of Pithekoussai (ca. 770 B.C.) and the mainland colonial settlements, all founded from 740 B.C. on.

The subject of a ceaseless debate in the 1970s and '80s over the chronology and methods of Greek seafaring activity in the central Mediterranean, this type of pottery (late-Geometric, that is, almost exclusively "chevron" drinking cups), is the first securely identified Greek ceramic type present after the long gap that followed Mycenaean trade activity in the Bronze Age along the shores of Sicily, southern Italy, and southern Sardinia, with sporadic forays out to the central Tyrrhenian coasts, where documented finds include sherds of Mycenaean pottery (Vagnetti 1985; Vagnetti 1993). It should be noted that this occurrence of Mycenaean production sparked discussion over the Aegean contribution to the cultural development—and in particular the evolution of handicrafts—of the protohistoric indigenous inhabitants of the peninsula and Sicily (Jones, Vagnetti 1992); the argument however does not delve into the meaning of contacts established during the later Greek trading (*contra* Peruzzi 1973–76). As noted, in the ninth–eighth century B.C. the first wave of the Hellenization process came in the form of Euboean and Cycladic navigators (Ridgway 1990), the same trader-voyagers who plied the coastal waters off Syria and Palestine, pushing ever southward from Al-Mina on the mouth of the Orontes, and who most likely kept a keen eye on the fabled mineral resources of the Tyrrhenian coast. Tellingly, routine trading along the coasts of Campania and Sicily also strayed into Etrurian territory north of the Tiber estuary, from Caere to Vulci, in concert with the emergence of the aristocracies and spreading urbanization in southern Etruria, and contemporary with the progressive assertion of Greek presence in the lower Tyrrhenian thanks to the thriving emporial center of Pithekoussai (ca. 770 B.C.) and the expansion of the first Euboean colony of Cumae (ca. 740 B.C.). This advance phase of "experimentation," which the anthropologists have termed "chieftain trade," was managed locally by the heads of Etruscan society which, while still conforming to the clan lifestyle was accelerating toward more complex habitational system prior to full-fledged urbanism. The Euboean navigators' cargo doubtless included various coveted artifacts—witness the incense from Arabia recovered from the princely Tomb H2 at Casal Marittimo, a burial ascribed to the first half of the seventh century B.C. (Esposito 1999, pp. 90-92). These goods though quite indistinguishable from those imported earlier by the Phoenicians (except for the assorted items mentioned above), mark the dawning of customs and ways that would maturate in the next century.

In fact, the said late-Geometric cups attest the arrival in Etruria of Greek wine, probably of eastern production, and based on the spiced Syro-Phoenician kind of wine that had been a reg-

Impasto capeduncula *from Selciatello di Sopra (Tarquinia), Villanovan period, phase IIA. Florence, Museo Archeologico cat. 176*

Small two-handled impasto amphora from Selciatello di Sopra (Tarquinia), Villanovan period, phase IIA. Florence, Museo Archeologico cat. 180

ular import to Etruria in the previous period, which the Greek type substantially aimed to imitate. In this case, however, the wine was for normal religious and domestic consumption and not for ritual use in the symposium banquets, which did not enter Etrurian custom until later. In the course of the eight century B.C. the growing traffic of merchants from the Aegean began to have a lasting effect on the customs and lifestyle of an increasingly powerful Etruscan aristocratic class. With the establishment of Chalcidian colonies in Cumae, on the Messina Straits, and in eastern Sicily, the continuity of those trade links was assured. In control of Greek trade relations this time was an elite merchant class operating according to the *idie prexis* system brought to light by A. Mele (Mele 1979), which entailed meaningful exchanges between members of the elite classes on either side, by which the Hellenic social models, imbued with ostentatious *exempla* from the Near East albeit in a Greek key, found ready acceptance in the minds of the Tyrrhenian aristocracies, who from this moment on—until their absorption into the Roman system—never ceased to embrace elements of Greek culture, which percolated particularly well through Magna Graecia and Sicily, adjusted each time to the needs of the relative cultural milieu.
Another decisive factor in the virtually unrivaled affirmation of the Greek ethos as a pivotal reference point for the Etruscan elite was the steady inflow of people with technical know-how and crafts expertise, who steadily enriched Etruscan workmanship with innovative production methods and formal input of Greek origin. The pattern of behavior involved trading with an aristocratic clientele in tandem with the migration of craftsmen and technicians, which Roman writers clearly impute to the figure of Demaratus of Corinth, father of Tarquinius Priscus (Musti 1987; Torelli, Menichetti 1997). The pattern of course dovetails neatly with the ongoing transformations of Etruscan customs, given that the advances under way in agriculture, manufacturing, and handicrafts are unthinkable without adjustments to the economic well-being and lifestyle of the ruling classes. The Roman annalists are eloquent on the debt which the more civilized *gentes* of the peninsula owed to the Greeks. Indeed, the many types of Italian grapevine, the name of the *Aminaean* vine itself is a reminder of its Campanian origins (Mele 2000), the birthplace of the first trader to assume contact with the Hellenic world, Fenestella, an antiquarian of the Augustan period (fr. 7 Peter), who observed that the domesticated olive

Small Nikosthenic amphora in bucchero "sottile" from Monte Michele (Veio), 640 B.C. Florence, Museo Archeologico cat. 182

tree was not introduced to Italy or Africa until the reign of Tarquinius Priscus (Torelli 1975b, p. 23). This is either mere conjecture or has some historical basis, given that the manufacture in Etruria of large containers for foodstuffs, including those for storing olive oil, is documented in the Iron Age, drawing from experience of the previous era. From an inscription on an *aryballos*, the word used in Etruria for olive oil, *eleivana* (from **eleiva*, ἔλαιϝα in Greek; see De Simone 1968–70) is evidently a loan-word from the Greek, suggesting the likely circulation of scented oils based on their Greek counterparts and therefore, by extension, the Etruscans' emulation of the Hellenic fondness for perfumed unguents; this hypothesis finds confirmation in the fact that, in the later seventh century B.C., throughout Etruria workshops began producing *aryballoi* in bucchero or terra cotta in imitation of the Orientalizing and proto-Corinthian types, evidently made as containers for scented oils.

But the most significant case of replication is the production of wine. Recent research (Agostiniani 2000; Torelli 2000) has shown that a Latin wine (and Etruscan, one may add) existed even before imports began reaching the peninsula from Greece, known as *temetum* (Festo, p. 500 L). The product's application in ritual drinking-parties goes back into the distant past, at least to the Final Bronze Age, to the time when an important clan chief of the Tolfa Mounts area commissioned three superb bronze goblets with raised handles styled as ox-heads; the pieces were uncovered from the deposit at Coste del Marano. This particular vessel type has

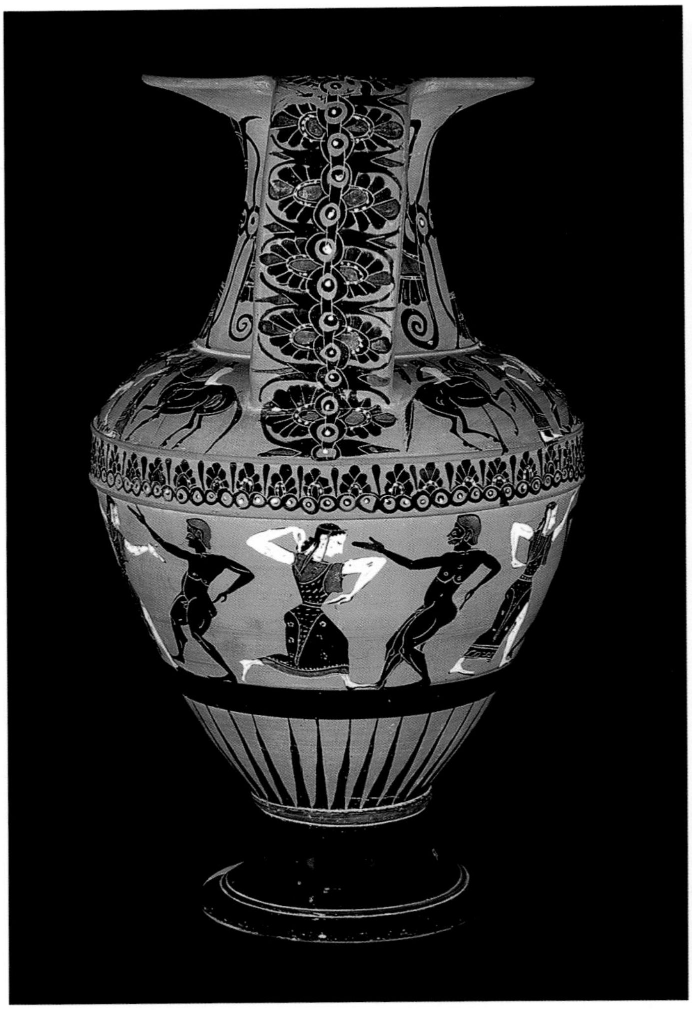

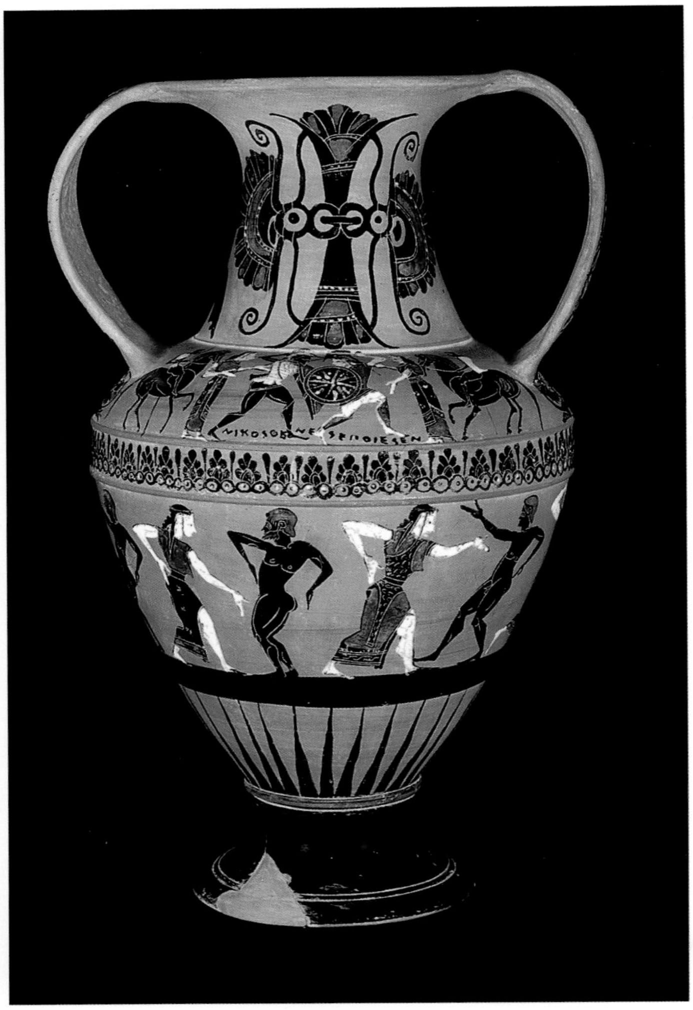

Terra-cotta Nikosthenic amphora, ca. 530 B.C.
Rome, Museo di Villa Giulia
cat. 183

distant origins in the height of the Bronze Age, with a variant vessel that was very popular even earlier in the form of a *capeduncula* (drinking cup) with raised handles, turning up with some consistency among grave groups in Latium and Etruria throughout the Iron Age. This characteristic vase used for serving wine is generally found in tombs in association with a small globular amphora for storing and transporting wine, whose hallmark double spiral decoration used through the seventh century B.C. has become a key benchmark for classifying the entire Orientalizing period of Etruscan culture. Production of these two vase-types,the capeduncula and the small globular amphora, continued throughout the sixth century B.C. and in the latter half of the century both shapes were churned out in great number by Attic pottery workshops—made expressly for shipping to Etruria—in the forms known as *kyathos* and the so-called Nikosthenic amphoras fashioned either in bucchero or Attic clay. This series of small-size vessels recurs almost obsessively over the seventh–sixth century in grave groups of southern Etruria (witness the materials from the sixth-century Maroi Tomb, Cerveteri), and embodies the "national" way of drinking ritual, so neatly dovetailed with its Greek counterpart it gave rise to the Etruscan loan-word *vinum-vinun*, by which the Etruscan mode of communal wine-consumption was increasingly adopted across Etruria (and likewise by the Latins), starting from the aforesaid exchanges with Euboean traders, right through the Orientalizing period, with manifest disparity between those areas open to Greek influence and those of a more conservative attitude. By the close of the eighth century B.C., however, a pottery workshop was set up in Vulci by immigrant Euboean craftsmen who manufactured entire sets of Greek-style vases with Geometric decoration; these sets comprised kraters, small amphoras, *oinochoai*, barrel-type *askoi*, cups, *skipoy*, and so forth; such finds are evidence of

the Etruscans' wholesale assumption at this stage of the Greek custom of *symposion*, consequently paving the way for the adoption of a new way of wine-drinking. The Greek *symposion* was ritually performed in a recumbent position, starting at least from the mid-seventh century (and hence parallel with developments in the Greek motherland: see Archilochus, fr. 2 D), as attested by a mid-seventh century vase recently recovered from a necropolis near Chianciano; the vessel carries a fully sculpted figure of the deceased in a reclining posture.
Completing this outline on the means and channels by which Greek modes of workmanship and customs reached Etruria, we can observe the progressive introduction to Etruscan and Latin military employment of hoplites (heavily armed infantry); this too was the outcome of a long and slow acceptance of battle tactics developed on Greek soil (Stary 1981), which saw the displacement of the longer sword of the Bronze Age by a short straight-edged dagger for close fighting, and the adoption of larger shields (early seventh century B.C.) for phalanx formations, a change already perceptible in the early Orientalizing phase. In this case, however, the shift in battle tactics reflects changes of an ideological nature (discussed below) affecting class issues and social changes: whereas the hoplite infantry came into being in Greece with the emergence of new small and medium landowners (Snodgrass 1993), Etruria's different social framework led to the conscription of the dependent servant class—whence the scenes of Etruscan chieftains on chariots, followed by lines of hoplites, an image repeated countless times in seventh–sixth century objects; the archaeological evidence moreover endorses this fact, with over fifty helmets recovered from a sanctuary of Vetulonia, all bearing the inscription of a single Etruscan gentilitial name commemorating a victorious battle (Maggiani 1990b, p. 48 ff.).
The principal debt to the Euboean world (and to Cumae in particular) is the art of writing—a debt owed as much by the Etruscans as by their neighbors in Latium. The introduction of the alphabetic transcription of speech, discussed elsewhere in this volume (see the article by G. Bagnasco) constitutes one of the Etruscans' most complex intellectual accomplishments, and one that cannot fail to appeal to even the shrewdest of today's observers.
That said, even more astounding is the subtle complexity with which the indigenous worldview was interleaved with carefully chosen deities from Greek pantheon and their associated mythology, all ingeniously adapted by the ruling Etruscan elite for the purpose of consoli-

Terra-cotta Laconian aryballos *from the Porcareccia necropolis (Populonia), 600–550* B.C. *Florence, Museo Archeologico cat. 125*

Red-figure "Nolana" amphora from Vulci, entire and detail. Paris, Musée du Louvre cat. 190

dating of their class self-image. On a par with processes under way within the Latin gentilitial aristocracy—and one might say that in many respects Hellenization took a parallel course in both ethnic groups—the original Etruscan pantheon was deftly reinterpreted in the upcoming Greek vein, and a work of ingenuity that shows the Etruscans' full comprehension of the Hellenic religious system. From that system the Etruscans not only derived an iconography for the representation of some of their local deities through analogies of their relative cosmic roles, but also transposed the Hellenic mode onto their religious practices and, more in general, to their forms of worship (Torelli 1986b), without forgoing distinctive features peculiar to indigenous religious ritual. The hurdles encountered were numerous, and the assimilation was not always successful, witness the goddess Uni of Pyrgi, who was there identified with the Phoenician Ishtar, who in turn is elsewhere identified with the Greeks' Aphrodite, whom the Etruscans instead usually equated with their own goddess Turan. The most striking divergence, despite the Etruscans' enthusiastic acceptance of the Greek religion and cult worship, lies in the total priority given to the divinatory practices of the auspice, a pan-Italic ritual of immense political significance. Performed all over the peninsula, divination had been in practice since the Bronze Age; the Etruscans, however, added to it an art all of their own with the institution of the *haruspices*, "professional" diviners elected exclusively from among high-ranking Etruscan families as a means of monopolizing the arcane methods of interpretation of the will of the gods. Likewise, even in their borrowings from the Greek architectural canon, the Etruscan grafted patently "national" features onto to their buildings, as exemplified by the use of the Greek temple model for housing religious statuary, albeit with a strictly native variant; this variant consisted into the construction of shrines on an inaugurated *templum* (hallowed locus) whose site is clearly marked with a podium which, while confirming the place's inauguration, is nonetheless wholly alien to Greek religious practice.
At any event, the most significant moment in the acclimation process effected in this phase of

Red-figure Attic kylix *from Cerveteri.*
Paris, Musée du Louvre

Red-figure Attic krater from Cerveteri.
Paris, Musée du Louvre
cat. 189

opposite, above
Terra-cotta amphora, second half of the fourth century B.C.
Florence, Museo Archeologico
cat. 191.8

Silvered terra-cotta amphora, second half of the fourth century B.C.
Florence, Museo Archeologico
cat. 191.9

opposite, below
Silvered terra-cotta chalice krater second half of the fourth century B.C.
Florence, Museo Archeologico
cat. 191.1

Terra-cotta situla, *second half of the fourth century* B.C.
Florence, Museo Archeologico
cat. 191.10

development was the highly selective use the Etruscan *principes* made of the corpus of Greek mythology. The earliest representations of Greek myth in Etruria, occurring in the seventh–early sixth century, focus on stories linked to Theseus, Jason, Achilles—all tales relating the conquest of sovereignty and heroic status (Menichetti 1994)—or with the Trojan cycle, which was immediately perceived (most likely upon instigation by the Greeks themselves) as a critical means of endorsement for the ethnic distinction of the Etruscans and Latins from the other barbarian peoples. Greek myths were created by a totally different civilization under unrepeatable conditions and were felt in their homeland as a moral code in a very lively and profound way. Notwithstanding, these same myths were adopted and slavishly repeated by the Latins and the Etruscans as fascinating fairy tales, which however could give the teller the same prestige that the land of origin possessed in their eyes. These same myths were most likely transmitted through Italian soil by means of epic and lyrical verses inspired on the *epos* of Homer and the cyclic poets; such verses were probably recited during *symposia* and all sort of aristocratic entertainments. The vital importance of singing and musical performances in Etruria can be inferred from the plethora of iconographical references, and from the very emphasis the Etruscans, like all other oligarchic societies of antiquity, appear to have attributed to music itself, such that an entire corpus of musical legends came into being, not least among them the myth that the Etruscans could lure boars to the catch to the sound of music (Aelian, *Historiae Animalium,* XII, 46). It is understandable that the Etruscan *principes* strove to canonize their traditional home-grown myths in a bid to counter the overwhelming cultural pressure exerted on Italy by the Greek universe in all its facets. While we know that the parallel counter-reaction taking place in the Latin world consisted in consolidating fanciful foundation stories that attributed a Trojan origin to the Romans, and in elaborating the various Alban legends (Torelli 1991a), it is still unclear what took place within the Etruscan cities, all of which continue to be insufficiently documented at archaeological level. This notwithstanding, the first returns on excavation work presently being undertaken by M. Bonghi on the sanctuary of Ara della Regina near modern Tarquinia have begun to reveal fascinating

Silvered terra-cotta patera, second half of the fourth century B.C.
Florence, Museo Archeologico
cat. 191.2

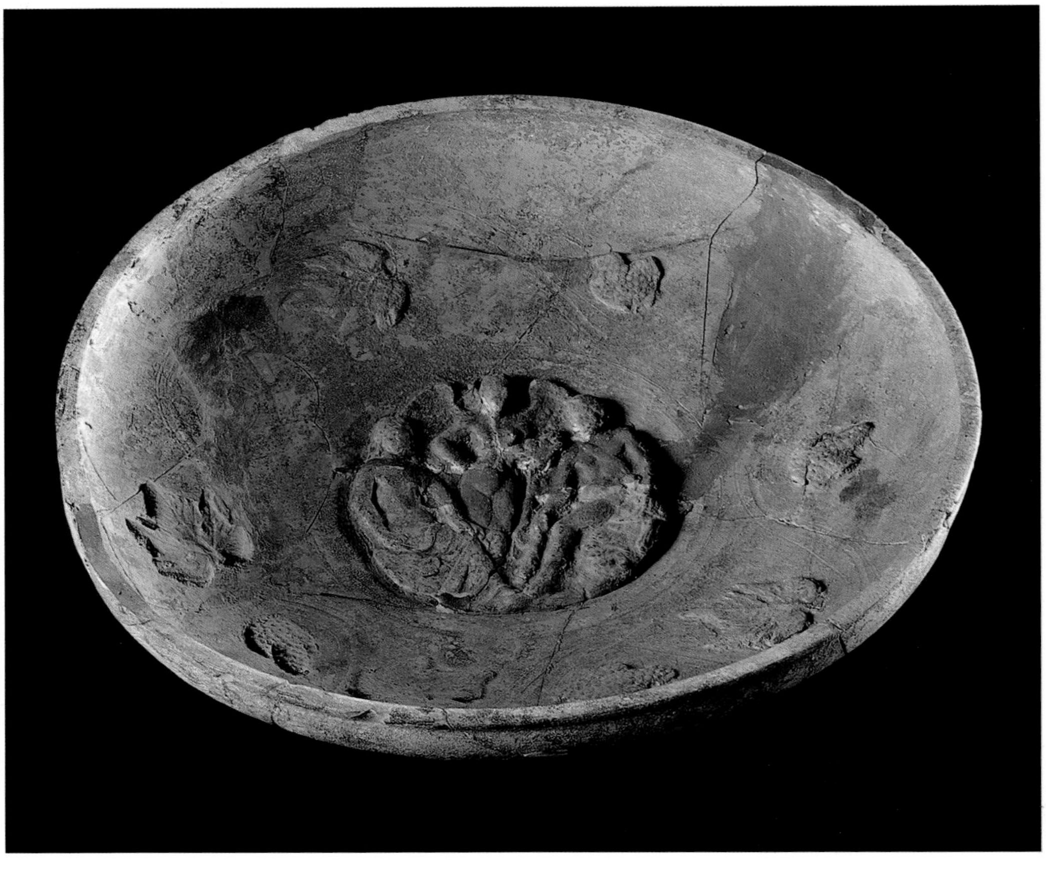

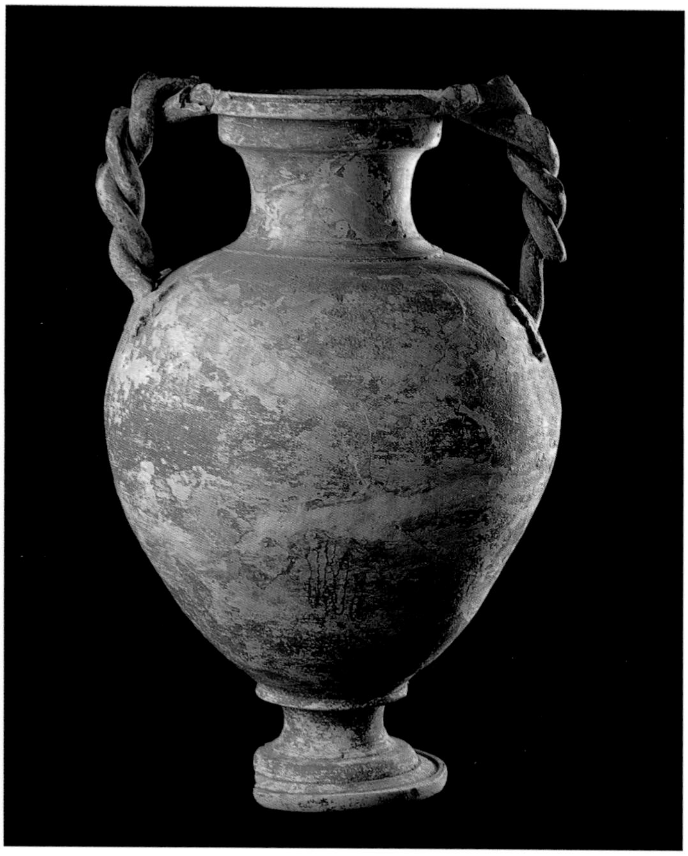

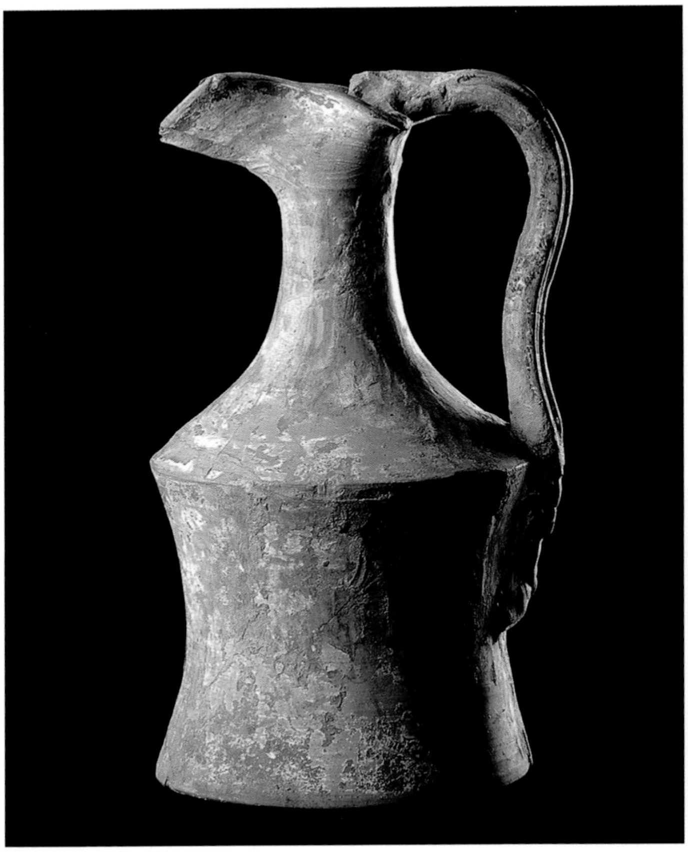

above, left
Silvered terra-cotta oinochoe, *second half of the fourth century* B.C.
Florence, Museo Archeologico
cat. 191.3

above, right
Silvered terra-cotta oinochoe, *second half of the fourth century* B.C.
Florence, Museo Archeologico
cat. 191.5

right
Silvered terra-cotta kyathoi, *second half of the fourth century* B.C.
Florence, Museo Archeologico
cat. 191.7

glimpses of the fabrication of legends around the mythical hero-founders of ancient Tarquinii. Meanwhile, the discovery of a Caeretan inscription from the first quarter of the seventh century B.C. naming one "Laucie Mezentie" (Gaultier, Briquel 1989)—a member of a *gens* whose gentilicial name, Mezentius, is not only unique but is the same *nomen* of the Caeretan tyrant allegedly slain by Ascanius—gives a vital clue on the pivotal role played by the Etruscans in the formation of "national" legends shared with the Latins. As the seventh century drew to a close, the processes of Hellenization of Etruria grew in intensity, gaining purchase both geographically and in terms of social stratification. The Greek ethos was absorbed by an increasing quota of the society, instilling the Greek values and models ever deeper into its social structure. As it entered a phase of increased social mobility, Etruscan society established the tenets and materials for a full-fledged urban lifestyle, its model conveniently borrowed from the existing Hellenic framework, which they found literally at their door—in the Greek colonies founded on Italian soil.

An ever-growing number of Etruscans began to daily utilize ceramics produced either in Greece itself, or in imitation of the Greek models and used as such, retaining however those elements of national custom deemed essential for the safe conduct of political affairs, and even of private matters. In this way, the Hellenization of Etruscan traditions—from the figurative arts to everyday customs and behavior—became to some extent universal and all-encompassing. Patterns of seaborne trade—at this stage originating largely in the main Ionian cities of Anatolia—inevitably underwent changes. Where until this moment the two systems of trade, the Greek *idie prexis* and the Etruscan "chieftain trade", had in many respects overlapped, now the evolving complexities of the Etruscan urban lifestyle entailed new forms of commerce, as it was no longer the prerogative of the aristocracies on both Greek and Etruscan sides, but was handled by trade brokers, sometimes of lower social rank (Torelli 1982), who gathered around the sanctuaries set up by the Greeks but politically and economically run by Etruscans—witness the parallel cases of Naukratis and Gravisca. The initial wave of Greek immigrants of high birth who had fostered the development of Greek culture on Tyrrhenian soil gave way to a stable immigrant population of Greek extraction that lived close to and often produced directly for the said emporial sanctuaries. This new class of metics set up many of the workshops producing goods of all kinds, including toreutics, glyptic art, bronzework, ceramics, all markedly Hellenized, replete with accents of Graeco-Oriental stamp, but repurposed to the tastes of the target, the Etruscan consumers in an unmistakable melange of "barbarian" opulence and understated Ionic workmanship. The new social category of the immigrant Greek craftsmen earned them the derogatory term *Graeculi*, a label that would stick for the centuries to come for all Greek-born outsiders living in the "barbarian" towns of the Italian peninsula. The term is of course in flagrant contradiction with the unanimous esteem for Hellenic culture, an esteem attained and consolidated through a confluence of favorable circumstances in the eighth and seventh centuries B.C. The ensuing phase of Graeco-Etruscan relations from the fifth century up until the Roman conquest of Etruria represents a swift change from the previous framework of the acculturation process, evolving instead into a dialectical exchange between the Greek motherland culture and its provincial Etruscan offshoot—the latter remaining subordinate despite its distinguishing variants—which saw the continuation of the course initiated in the Archaic period and of the setup established in the sixth century B.C. with the republics, whose political and constitutional framework brought the Tyrrhenian world ever more aligned to its Hellenic counterpart, which by this time was identified exclusively with Attic culture, and with the colonial Greek civilization.

De Simone 1968–70; Bianchi Bandinelli 1973; Gallini 1973, pp. 175–91; Peruzzi 1973–76; Torelli 1974–75, pp. 3–78; Momigliano 1975; Torelli 1975b; Torelli 1977, pp. 536–55; Mele 1979; Stary 1981; Torelli 1981a; Torelli 1981b, pp. 67–82; Torelli 1982, pp. 304–25; De Min 1984, pp. 651–60; Vagnetti 1985, pp. 127–44; De Min 1986, pp. 143–86; De Min, Gerhardinger 1986, pp. 118–41; Torelli 1986b, pp. 159–237; Musti 1987, pp. 139–53; Gaultier, Briquel 1989, pp. 41–44; Maggiani 1990b, pp. 23–49; Ridgway 1990, pp. 61–72; Torelli 1991a, pp. 47–67; Burkert 1992; Jones, Vagnetti 1992, pp. 231–35; *Forme di contatto* 1983; Snodgrass 1993, pp. 47–61; Vagnetti 1993, pp. 143–54; Menichetti 1994; Garbini 1996, pp. 73–85; Ridgway 1996, pp. 117–20; Torelli 1996, pp. 295–319; Torelli 1997d; Torelli, Menichetti 1997, pp. 625–54; Bats, d'Agostino 1998; Burkert 1999; Esposito 1999; Agostiniani 2000; Mele 2000, pp. 39–43; Menichetti 2000; Torelli 2000, pp. 89–100; Torelli forthcoming-a.

Maria Bonghi Jovino

The Etruscan Expansion into Campania

Premises

Today the expansion of the Etruscans in Campania seems to belong to the context of the appearance of their civilization on the proto-Villanovan horizon. The fact of their expansion might have already been under way during the tenth century B.C. and in the context of a complex historical process that, in Tyrrhenian Etruria, stirred entire clans to leave their small strongholds for the vast coastal plains. Although up to now, despite countless uncertainties, general opinion was that the expansion in Campania, characterized by the Villanovan culture, had occurred in the First Iron Age, especially in the early ninth century B.C., it is actually very likely that small centers from Tyrrhenian Etruria had in the previous period migrated to the fertile Campanian plain, as the tomb of Sant'Angelo in Formis seems to indicate. The great diversity of opinions in dating the oldest settlement is due to a variety of problems: the possibility of recognizing Etruscan culture through the differences in burial rites and the typology of the materials, the difficulty in interpreting the oldest sources of information, the validity of the deductions based on diachronic analyses, the significance to be attributed to archaeological and epigraphic documentation, the importance to be given to each of these elements, both as independent factors and as factors having reciprocal ties.

Funerary rituals are the first critical aspect to consider when attempting to define Etruscan culture. Cremation and inhumation are extremely "significant" phenomena, and not at all ambiguous, because, from an anthropological viewpoint, they are fundamental elements that characterize the culture of small groups of peoples. Furthermore, the significance of such rituals increases when placed in the context of a society with many, different funerary rites. For example, the indigenous peoples of Campania, who practiced inhumation, contrasted with those of Capua and Pontecagnano—restricting our example to but two of the most important centers—who practiced cremation, much like the coeval Etruscan populations of Latium and Tuscany, who were of Villanovan culture.

Various literary interpretations of classical sources agree that Etruscan colonies and settlements were founded in Campania, supporting the belief that even the *ager Picentinus*, the area between the peninsula of Sorrento and the Sele River, was owned by the Etruscans. Nonetheless, it is not imperative that historiographic sources necessarily correspond to precise archaeological findings, and vice versa, even if there remain significant convergences. Instead, the validity of diachronic interpretations is very determining in that it can provide a framework for the "before" and "after," evidencing historical processes in a consequential manner.

Looking back on the centuries, it can now be assumed that the expansion of the Etruscans, given its complexity, was likely based on a *continuum* of moves, each characterized by specific entities, some of which were more crucial than others. The move at the end of the tenth century was particularly determining, while those at the end of the seventh and in the last quarter of the sixth centuries B.C. were important.

The general picture includes a proto-historic background (the terminal phase of proto-Villanovan, at the end of the tenth century B.C.), and the Early Iron Age (ninth to eighth centuries B.C.); an Orientalizing phase, which extends from the last quarter of the eighth to the first quarter of the sixth centuries, and was characterized by an intense increase in trade, the acquisition of the written language, and by artistic and cultural models from the Aegean and the Orient; and an Archaic age, which spanned the sixth century and continued to almost the end of the fifth century B.C.

There are discrepancies in the ancient historiographic tradition as well as in epigraphic documentation and the large quantity of Etruscan materials; therefore, in studying the settlements in Campania in that last period, it is important to distinguish between a true condition of solidarity or of political dependence on the Etruscans, and close commercial and economic ties.

Early written documentation, which provides information on the Etruscan expansion in Campania, appears to find confirmation in a consistent epigraphic documentation attested in Capua, Calatia, Nola, Suessula, Pompeii, Stabiae, Vico Equense, and Pontecagnano. The distribution map renders the information from the ancient writers—which had been so greatly doubted in the past—more reliable.

Gorgon-head antefix from Santa Maria Capua Vetere. Santa Maria Capua Vetere, Museo dell'Antica Capua

The proto-Villanovan period and the Early Iron Age

The cultural differences between Capua and Pontecagnano, the two most important centers in terms of Etruscan population, are based on various conditions concerning the natural environment and the geographic location. Capua was more agriculturally inclined while commercial activities dominated in Pontecagnano.

To date, the most valid theory holds that Etruscan expansion had occurred by land and by sea. In the first instance, it is thought that the Etruscans had followed an internal route from Etruria toward the plains of Campania, where Capua was founded, while by sea they moved from Tarquinia toward the plains of the *ager Picentinus*, where Pontecagnano was founded. At the same time, the Villanovan *facies* that characterized the Early Iron Age in Campania has essentially been interpreted in two ways. The first of these interpretations is that groups of peoples migrated from central Italy in a process of colonization driven by the need to find fertile soils, while the second interpretation, which denies the correspondence between the formation of Etruscan culture and the proto-Villanovan background, suggests that the expansion was a development based on a common substratum.

In any case, it seems rather difficult to formulate the hypothesis of ethnic insurgencies on the basis of a concomitant process of socio-economic development because such development cannot fully explain the existence of similar funerary and crematory rites, which, in turn, cannot be traced back to this process. In fact, from an anthropological viewpoint, the practice of cremation is highly significant since it has always been representative of the experience of death. It involves the preparation of the cadaver, which is one of the most critical and distinguishing moments not only in the life of an individual but also in the collective life of mankind.

Until recently, dominant sources of information regarding the oldest phases of Capua included, among others: a chronological hiatus following the tomb of Sant'Angelo in Formis, dated to the late proto-Villanovan period; a consistent gap of information for the IA phase (900–800 B.C.); suitable documentation beginning with the IB phase (850–800 B.C.); the absence of the typically Villanovan biconical ossuary; and the predominance of the olla to contain the ashes. At first, the hypothesis that Capua derived from the internal Tiberine (Bisenzio) *facies* of Etruria helped explain this last element; however, the difficulty in proving such a link was exacerbated by the fact that the Villanovan *facies* of Volsinii is more structured. A more realistic hypothesis appears to be the one that promotes a connection with the Falerii-Capena area, bearing in mind that the names of the cities (Capua and Capena) seem to derive from the same root.

Knowledge on the older period (phase IA) has been altered following the discoveries in the necropolis of Capua in the eighties. These discoveries have unearthed burial goods from the first half of the ninth century, providing the following information: an evident welding with proto-Villanovan horizons; precocious Villanovan manifestations, evidenced by *fibulae* with short or spiral bows and proto-Villanovan razors; the adoption of the biconical vase with short neck and horizontal handles (Fornaci Tombs 1182 and 15–87) or with a single vertical, button-hole handle (Tombs 1–86, 23–87, 39–87), typical of proto-Villanovan cinerary urns; strong ties with the Villanovan culture of southern Tyrrhenic Etrurian centers; similarity with the coeval *facies* of Pontecagnano, evident even in the forms of certain pottery in the so-called *Fossakultur* (culture of the pit tombs), and a compact framework of "cremators" in Campania.

Essentially, this period was characterized by continual development and an amalgamation of the Etruscan population. The expansion in Campania seems to go back at least a generation in time, brought about by the same needs (substantial demographic growth and more intense use of the territory) that had stirred the other proto-Villanovan clans to establish the large Tyrrhenian cities. It does not have a "colonizing" character, in the sense of a supremacy over the Italic peoples; rather, it was more of a rapid process of integration within a context substantially marked by the continuity of its settlements. The most recent findings have evidenced how the tombs containing ollas-ossuaries, which had previously led researchers to believe that there had been a connection between Capua and internal Tiberine Etrurian centers, appear to actually have belonged to a later phase of the initial settlement period, so that the ollas must be attributed to later phases.

It seems that during the first half of the ninth century the relationship between the foreigners and the indigenous peoples became structured, and that the Etruscans from the southern coast of Etruria (Veio, Tarquinia and Vulci)—who are credited with the first migration—quickly integrated with the Italics. The integration process could have been facilitated by the practice of the same funerary rites, which, in the case of both the biconical vases and the ollas, could be related to the need to honor the deceased and to render him inoffensive, the two principal preoccupations of the burials. During this phase, the most important phenomenon is the slow diffusion of inhumation, leading to the theory that religious significance prevailed over magic.

Through an endogenous process characterized by the introduction of other cultural elements and subsequent migrations from Visenta and Veio, from the Falerii-Capena area, and from the northern Adriatic and Oenotria, the synergy between the foreigners and the locals could have created the cultural *facies*, which, amalgamated in the Iron Age, was particularly characteristic of the town of the successive phase. Given this premise, it can be assumed that the unification of several villages in the plains into a single site could have occurred in about 850 B.C. In this context, the Etruscan culture likely served as a means of amalgamation, compared with the inhabitants of the Italic villages dispersed throughout the plains.

In the outfits of the IB phase in Capua, the olla replaced the biconical ossuary. There are a number of inhumation tombs and the discovery of ollas with flat, circular handles and bowls with short vertical rims (Tombs 800/87, 805/87) indicate that contact with *Fossakultur* had increased. Specific instruments reveal that gender and social status were differentiated, as

Biconical olla from Tomb N.M. 1/86 at Santa Maria Capua Vetere, early phase IA, 900–850 B.C. Santa Maria Capua Vetere, Museo dell'Antica Capua

opposite, above
Parade bronze fibula *from the Fornaci Tomb 363 of Santa Maria Capua Vetere, early phase IIB, ca. 770 B.C. Santa Maria Capua Vetere, Museo dell'Antica Capua*

opposite, below
Parade bronze fibula *from the Fornaci Tomb 365 of Santa Maria Capua Vetere, phase IIB, 770–750 B.C. Santa Maria Capua Vetere, Museo dell'Antica Capua*

indicated by the spindle with a distaff and a "set" of iron tools found in Tomb 386. This social stratification is countered by the first relationships that these inhabitants instilled with the Greeks and with other Mediterranean peoples during the "pre-colonial" stage, which preceded the Euboean settlement in Pithekoussai.
In the successive period (phase II), while inhumation became an established rite, and sporadic incidences of cremation continued to exist, agglomerates of tombs, likely family burials, began to emerge. In a period that spanned three generations, categorized into three distinct phases known as IIA (800–770 B.C.), IIB (770–750 B.C.), and IIC (750–730 B.C.), a technological process led to various innovations that included lavish plastic decorations of vase handles, with animals'heads, and decorations with vertical grooves or helicoidal plastic ribbing. Engraved or impressed motifs also flourished, as did overpainted decorations of geometric style. Corinthian imports began to appear, such as the *skyphos* of Thapsos, with panel, and the *kotyle* Aetos 666, as well as numerous bronze objects that reveal a highly skilled artisanship, among them large ornamental *fibulae* and horse bits (Fornaci Tombs 363, 365, 917, 840, 19 Quattordici Ponti). The very rich Fornaci Tomb 365 is a typical example of the last phase.
A connection with Suessula is evidenced by the large ornamental *fibulae* with molded fig-

Silver bowl from the Fornaci Tomb 722 of Santa Maria Capua Vetere, phase IIC, 750–730 B.C. Santa Maria Capua Vetere, Museo dell'Antica Capua

urines bearing the stylized "sun boat," and the *fibulae* with very complex decorations, imported from the area around Bologna, with winding arcs and tongues decorated with birds and glass-paste beads (Fornaci Tomb 365). The fact that these artifacts were found in both Capua and in Suessula leads to the supposition that the Etruscan culture must have played an increasingly important role not only with Capua, but also in its contact with Suessula, as the Etruscans endeavored to expand into the internal plains, where the town may have functioned as an inland hinge and as an outpost for Nola.
The settlement at Pontecagnano developed along the northern outskirts of the Sele plain, on the left coast of the Picentino River, and there are indications that the urban plan of the area had been created from the onset. Evidenced by the necropolis at Pagliarone, the structure of the small settlement appears to demonstrate a unified system, aimed at a strict control of the agricultural lands.
In the initial phase (phase IA, 900–850 B.C.), the biconical ossuary placed in women's tombs was covered by a small bowl, while the helmet was for male tombs. The collection of vessels (small amphoras, *askoi*, pitchers and cups) reveals a general affinity with the coeval horizon of Capua, and with the production of *Fossakultur* in Latium and Campania. There are numerous types of *fibulae* from this period, some with disk bows, and some with twisted, but-

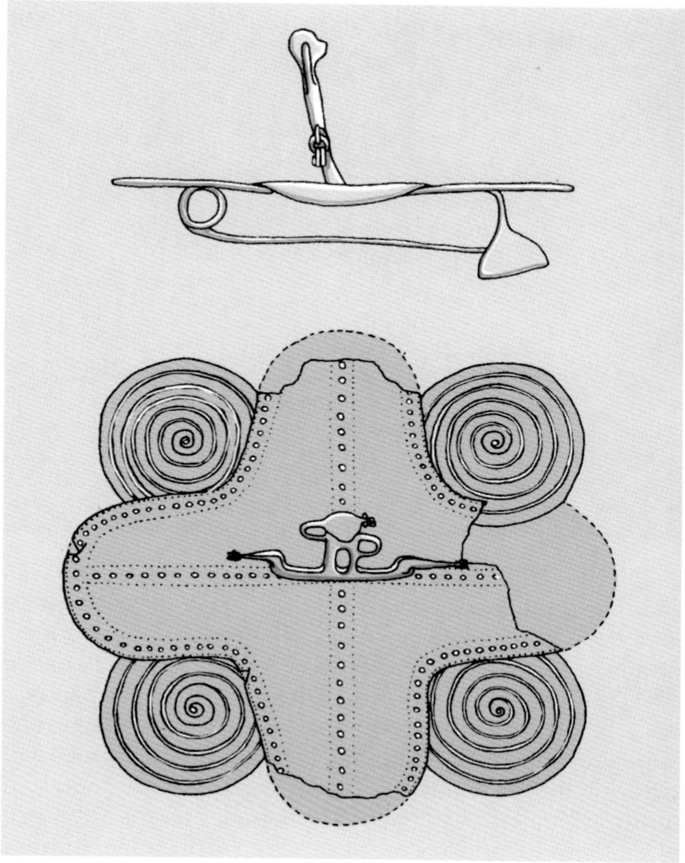

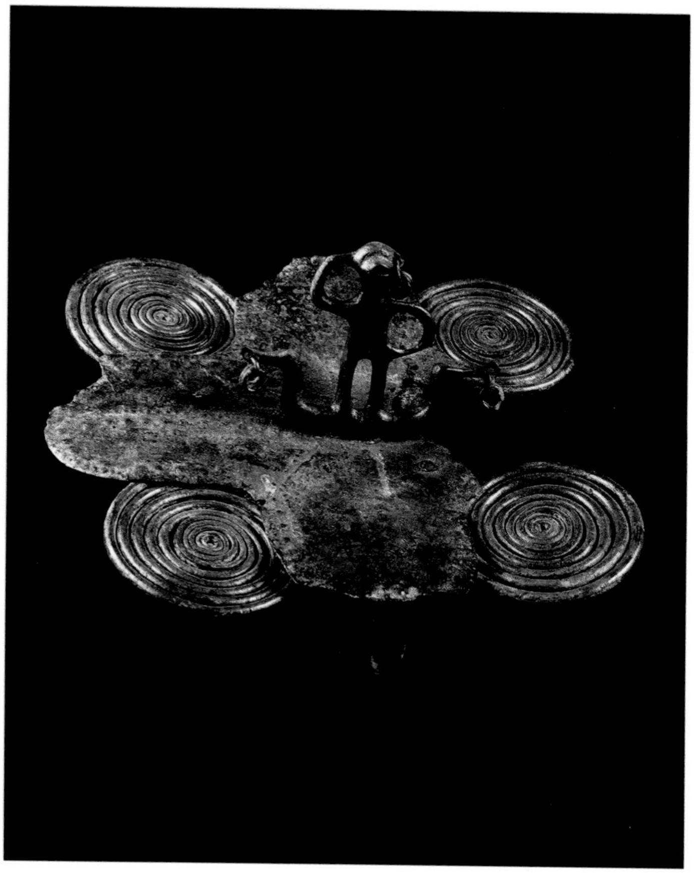

Pottery grave goods from the Fornaci Tomb 312 at Santa Maria Capua Vetere, phase IV. Santa Maria Capua Vetere, Museo dell'Antica Capua

tonhole bows, reminiscent of Umbrian artifacts. By the end of that period we can discern the organization of a hierarchy that had already begun some time before in the big centers of Tyrrhenian Etruria such as Tarquinia, and that here at Pontecagnano is evidenced by the important figure of a warrior in the grave goods of Tomb 180, with its rich bronze panoply. In the next phase (IB, 850–775 B.C.) the necropolises demonstrate very early stages of urban planning, with small funerary roads, and implantations of family cells, as well as a process of monumentalization, primarily involving the coverings, whereby the graves were contained within drums placed at their perimeter (Tomb 2145). Numerous samples of imported artifacts include bronze spades from southern Etruria, spherical censers, small molten buttons from Sardinia, and basket-like vases. Findings from more advanced periods also include some imported ceramics, painted with "tent-like" patterns, which were typical of the Vallo di Diano and Basilicata, or of "plumed" ceramics, manufactured in Sicily.

Beginning in the eighth century (phase IIA, 775–750 B.C.), there were again imports (bowls with chevrons) and new important decorative innovations in vases that included animals in relief, engravings, and imprints. On the whole, the wealth of ceramic artifacts reveals obvious similarities with those of the Tiberine, Latium and Faliscan regions, and indicates close ties with Capuan productions, resulting from a solid relationship with that area. A specialized artisanship can be intuited from the artifacts belonging to the subsequent phase (IIB, 750–720 B.C.). The artisans of this period were masters of new technological equipment, producing higher quality items intended for the market that served only the community. There is evidence of a hierarchy in social status so that there existed a true aristocracy, based on nobility, who controlled economic resources, bartering, and trade with the rest of the Greek market, both before and after the founding of Pithekoussai.

From the Orientalizing period to the first Archaic period

This long period, which marked the peak of Etruscan expansion, is subdivided into three periods: Ancient, Middle, and Recent Orientalizing. At its earliest phase, this period was characterized by a process, fundamental to ancient Italy, which included the import of goods from throughout the Mediterranean, and the migration of skilled Greek and Oriental artisans. Most important, however, it involved the diffusion of cultural techniques and models. In its later phase, the territory of Campania became more structured.

Capua (phase III, ca. 730–630 B.C.) manufactured vessels made with high-quality impasto and thin walls. Both the impasto and the pure clay pottery are characterized by certain Greek forms, particularly *oinochoai*, *skyphoi* and *kotylai*. Decorations of the impasto pottery include imprinted or engraved wolf teeth pendants with an oblique outline. Bronze was particularly popular in the manufacturing of *fibulae* shaped like small ships, dragons or leeches. Imported objects included Thapsos-type cups with a panel (Fornaci Tomb

958), and, subsequently, a rather numerous amount of proto-Corinthian ovoid *aryballoi*. In the Recent Orientalizing period (phase IV, ca. 630–575 B.C.), Capua seems to have renewed contacts with the more important cities in southern Tyrrhenic Etruria (Caere, Tarquinia, and Vulci), as well as those in inland Etruria (areas around Chiusi and Orvieto). This is attested by certain forms of impasto pottery and the precocious existence of bucchero, imported with proto-Corinthian earthenware and ceramics dating from the ancient Corinthian period. Particularly rich are some grave goods ascribable to the middle-class, among which we should mention that of the Fornaci Tomb 312. In a more advanced phase of this period, the terra cotta used for architectural purposes included, at the peak of its production, animal-shaped roofs, a typically Etruscan tradition.

In Pontecagnano the leading *gentes* controlled economic activities and mediated international relations with the Greeks and the Italic peoples. Wealth and ostentatiousness emphasized solidarity between the ruling classes, in a manner analogous to that of the great aristocracies of the Tyrrhenic regions, such as Latium and Etruria.The development of endogenous traditions was associated to the ostentation derived from the contact with the Greeks of Cuma. Burial goods contained precious objects, especially selected to form "sets." In a society in which sacred and political were not yet separate elements, objects of particular significance are those related to sacrificial rites and banquets.

During this period, the city began to develop its emporian functions through its relationship with Cuma and inland cities (Irpinian *facies* of Oliveto Citra-Cairano). Greek pottery, both imported and imitated in Pithekoussai or Cuma, abound. There as a prevalence of proto-Corinthian pottery (Thapsos-type cups without panel and with sigmated decorations, manufactured in Cuma, integrated with Corinthian *aryballoi*) or Rhodio-Cretan pottery imported by Cuma from Rhodes or Crete. Oriental artifacts from this period include scarabs and plates coated in red. Small impasto spiral amphoras were imported from Etruria (Caere), while vases decorated with engraved herons arrived from Falerii and Veio.

The male Tomb 4461 (late eighth century B.C.) contained rich metallic burial goods (two lance tips, an axe, a scalpel, and an iron knife) as well as a bronze "set" (Euboean-type *lebes*, biconical Etruscan amphora, Kurd *situla* probably from Vetulonia, and two embossed horse heads). Symbols of prestige were found in women's tombs, highlighting the importance of women as guarantors of continuity: Tomb 2465, from the early seventh century, contained a sumptuous costume, but also a "set" consisting of a vessel, an *oinochoe*, a bronze, podded *phiale*, spits, andirons, and an iron knife, smelted in bronze.

It is probable that between the end of the seventh and the first quarter of the sixth centuries B.C., groups of Etruscans from Tyrrhenic Etruria, whether aided or exhorted by the elite inhabitants of Capua, migrated to Capua for commercial purposes. The city benefited from its extensive agricultural control over the greater part of the plains. These groups of Etruscans, however, also likely moved toward Calatia, some of them settling along the internal segments of Vesuvius (Suessula and Nola) while others pushed on toward the coast, to southern Campania (Stabiae). The result of these new processes of interchange and cooperation are evident at various levels in the first half of the sixth century.

The Archaic period

Classical sources speak of an Etruscan "dodekapolis" under the protection of Capua, and they claim the origins of Nola, Calatia, Pompeii, Ercolano, and Marcina to be Tyrrhenic. Their language seems to have developed at the time of the urbanization process, begun in the Iron Age, and it can now be attributed to an aristocracy governed according to a timocracy. During this phase, settlemnts were planned, and roads projected. Residential zones were separated from industrial areas dedicated to artisanship, and public spaces as well as sacred areas began to emerge. Archaeological evidence, in its whole, seems to support the theory of the Etruscan migration in the preceding phase. Epigraphic documentation, which is reminiscent of Tarquinian and Vulcian writing, comes from Pompeii, Stabiae, Vico Equense, Fratte and Pontecagnano.

The inscriptions highlight Capua's participation in the cultural development of Etruria, with the first written testimonials appearing on bucchero vases in the first decades of the sixth century, and then increasing during the second half of the century. All of the city's sectors

Etruscan settlements in Campania

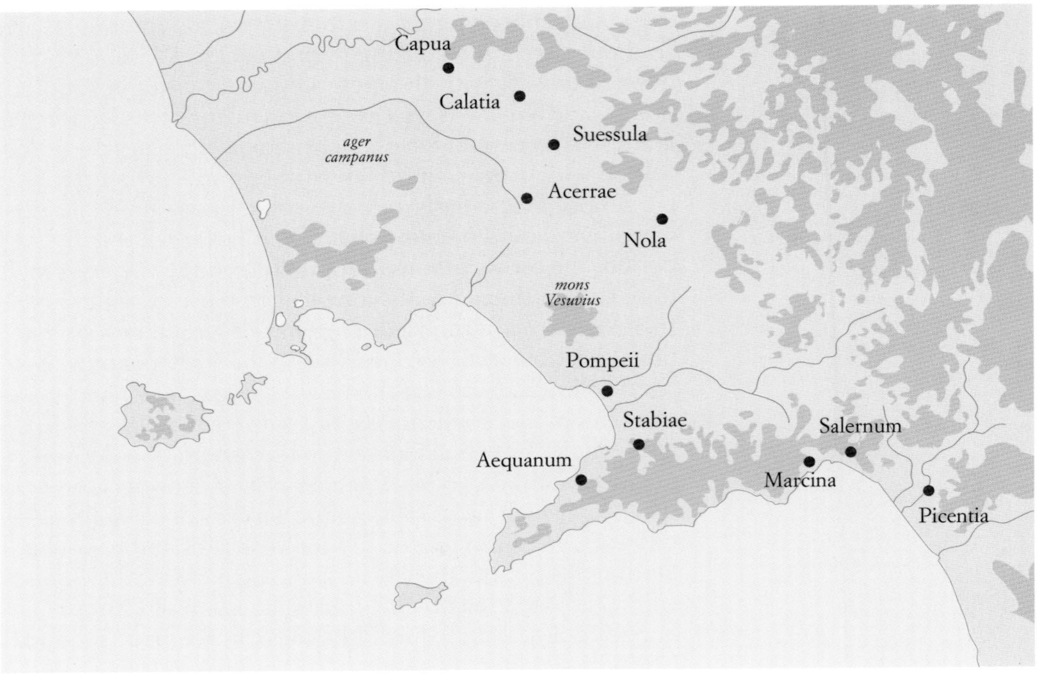

opposite
Laconian bronze krater from Tomb 1526 of Santa Maria Capua Vetere, sixth century B.C.
Santa Maria Capua Vetere, Museo dell'Antica Capua
cat. 187

appear to have been flourishing at this time: architectural manufacturing in terra cotta, grandiose and refined bronze productions, and the typical, local production of bucchero. Nor is there a lack of imported exemplars, such as the bronze cauldron and krater, of outstanding technical and artistic quality, owed to Laconic workshops. Capua established an efficient relationship with Cuma thanks to migrating artisans and technological and cultural exchanges, and it expanded its commercial contacts and its cultural influence on Vallo di Diano as well as on the internal valleys of Lucania, toward Sannio Pentro and the area of the Frentani. The antefixes with female heads found in Daunia presuppose models that were common in the towns along the Volturno.

Capua continued to be a focal point along the internal route, which, from Nola, forked into two directions: on one side it extended to the gulf of Naples through the port at Pompeii, and on the other it reached the gulf of Salerno via Nocera. The Etruscans' favorite route expressed a well-defined strategy: connecting the two gulfs with Nuceria, functioning as a solid central element, and circumventing the territory of Cuma, with the aim of controlling and maintaining the passageways toward the south. This process was based on two fundamental factors, which involved a common organizational effort. The first of these were the indigenous inhabitants of the plains, principally characterized by agricultural activities defined by an elevated cultural standard, while the second factor was the Etruscans themselves, who, with their propensity toward urbanization, possessed an unquestionable ability in projecting and managing large urban endeavors of a public nature.

Even in this phase, the Etruscans' presence in Campania must be considered an element of coagulation for economic interests and political convergences. Their settling on the coasts of Campania has been connected with their need to create a base from which to expand toward the lower Tyrrhenian area. The phenomenon of urbanization contributed to a clearer definition of the roles and position of the internal cities in relation to the coastal settlements. From what can be learned from the important but incomplete documentation, these roles included the establishment of new commercial networks and the strengthening of existing "Etruscanized" centers along the coast.

The new city-country relationship, which, at the end of the seventh and the beginning of the sixth centuries, had given rise to synechism and urbanization, is reflected along the coast of Campania, where a series of "commercial ports" (Stabiae, Vico Equense, Fratte, Vietri) was flourishing. Among these ports, Pompeii was particularly important; it was port to the Etruscans and the "Etruscanized" centers of *mesogeia*. This small city in the region of Vesuvius

was strategically selected for the purpose of incrementing and strengthening commercial activity from the very beginning. Its origins in fact reveal a great commitment on behalf of the Etruscans and, simultaneously, an active competition between the inhabitants of the plains. The Etruscans played a very important role in urbanizing, as is attested by the construction of the first delimiting wall on the slopes of the mount and the structuring of the surrounding territory, evidenced by the dislocation of the sacred urban (the *lucus* with an Etruscan votive column and the great temple of Apollo) and suburban areas (the small temple dedicated to Dionysus at Porta Nocera, built as a defence of the internal route along the Sarno River; the "sanctuary Iozzino" built to control the routes toward Stabia and Nocera, the sanctuary at Bottaro built to control the port and the coast). Archaeological findings have documented the connections between the various Etruscan centers. Capua appears to have been the governing center of these relationships, as testified by certain terra-cotta artifacts, unearthed at Pompeii, which appear to have been manufactured in Capua, as well as a number of bronze and bucchero vases, also of Capuan origin. Furthermore, the cultural *facies* of Stabiae-Nuceria indicates that there must have been some kind of activity aimed at controlling and exchanging goods with Capua, on the one hand, and with Etruscan centers in *mesogeia*, such as the commercial ports of Naples and Salerno, on the other, as well as with the Greeks of Cuma. It seems very likely that the port of Vico Equense had been created to support the abundant activity at Stabiae, which, at present, appears to have been the only settlement that was already active by the mid-seventh century. The port at Stabiae was of fundamental importance to the Sarno River district and to the inland centers, even as an access route to the Tyrrhenic trafficking, which connected the centers of Campania and Etruria. For almost the entire sixth century and a good part of the fifth century B.C., the port at Vico Equense must have functioned, initially, as an important support to the "coastal trade" that was "jointly governed" by Stabiae, Nuceria and Pompeii, though they each played a specific role. The port, however, appears to have had an even more important function as a commercial hinge between two routes, each one serving a different area and differing in intensity. In addition, Vico Equense ministered to the small centers scattered about the plains of the peninsula.
Valuable materials, relative to the necropolis and not used commercially, are indicative of a limited group belonging to a higher social class, which ruled the port. From the few tombs that have been reconstructed it is possible to discern an allusion to rituality and prestige. Tomb 39 contained a wooden plate encased in a bronze vessel, a small pitcher and a *colum*, both in bronze, as well as two glazed cups, an iron knife (with traces of a wooden handle), which had been wrapped in a cloth (probably of tightly woven linen) after the funerary rite. Tomb 67 contained lead andirons and spits, a bronze *colum*, a grater, a trilobated *oinochoe* in bucchero, an Attic *lekythos*, three black-glazed cups on a tall stand, probably manufactured in Pithekoussai, and a small chalice, likely manufactured in Cales. These artifacts seem to indicate a duplicate function. In fact, many objects relative to the *hestia* (the hearth), such as the spits, are decorated with palmettes with two valves, a sure indication that they could not have actually been used. The use of lead, used to manufacture andirons and spits, excludes the possibility that these objects could ever have come into contact with fire. So, these were the simulation of a meal rather than a real one.
In the mixed settlements in the valley of the Sarno River and on the peninsula of Sorrento, the existence of proto-Campanian inscriptions could implicate the indigenous ruling class's need to consolidate and maintain its own identity. It is important to note that, during this same period, the Etruscan alphabet and the non-alphabetic inscriptions of Nocera coexisted at Vico Equense, mirroring a linguistic dualism and documenting the concurrence of various ethnic and cultural components.
During the last quarter of the sixth century, the Etruscans were once again at the center of renewed activity. The leap in quality of manufactured products has been associated with the group of Etruscans who, along with the Umbrians and the Daunians, lay siege on Cuma in 525 B.C., but, defeated and forced to retreat, settled in the surrounding plains, in the wake of previous settlers of mixed origins. Fratte developed on the Irno River, becoming a leading commercial center in southern Campania, connecting Capua to Greek centers such as Posidonia and Elea, situated along the Tyrrhenic coast. The Greeks of Cuma continued with their Mediterranean trade.

The continued success of the Etruscans of Capua is largely based on their skilful use of the route that led them to Salerno. Testimonials of the Etruscans' flourishing commercial activity are: the abundant Attic pottery; the production and sale of black-figure pottery manufactured in their workshops; architectural and figured terra-cotta productions; finely manufactured *lebes*; and bronze strainers. All of these items were part of the trafficking along the Capua-Nola-Pompeii-Nocera-Fratte route. During this period, the materials from the sanctuary of Apollo attest to the splendor of these objects, which are in keeping with the typologies and contents that typified associated Etruscan centers.
The problem related to the co-government of the ports of Pompeii, Stabiae and Vico Equense seems to be quite evident in the congeries of Etruscan materials and in the continued blending of the two peoples, leading to the assumption that there was some degree of negotiating and amalgamation. Inhabitants of these centers also demonstrate a good capacity for absorption and acceptance of the Greek culture, as testified by the Greek inscriptions documented in the areas of Campania in which the Etruscans had settled, as well as in the Euboean (Nocera, Massalubrense) and the Achaean (Fratte, Pontecagnano) alphabets.

The end of Etruscan supremacy
Capua and Cuma appear to have entered into a conflicting relationship some time in the fifth century B.C., given that the oligarchs of Cuma, chased back by Aristodemus, sought refuge in Capua. It is just as likely that difficulties arose between the dominant Etruscans and those who, subordinate to them, spoke a different language, Oscan. Determinant events occurred within a very brief period of time. First, the Etruscans were defeated at the battle of Cuma in 474 B.C. by Hieron of Syracuse, their power diminishing and fading into the events that led to the birth of Neapolis. Uniquely Etruscan elements survived, until the fourth century B.C., only in Pontecagnano, and, according to Diodorus, the *ethnos* of the Campanians was formed in 438 B.C. At Cales, concomitant with a notable decrease in artistic production and craftsmanship, there developed a need for security that led to the erection of the first walled city. Archaic Pompeii was quickly transformed. In 421 B.C. the Samnites conquered Capua and all the cities in Campania, including Cuma. The crisis left none unscathed, acting as a prelude to new scenarios and new socio-political models that perpetuated—albeit partially—the Etruscan heritage.

The Etruscan Expansion in the Po Valley

Both the quality and the number of discoveries that have taken place in the past decade, as well as the critical comments and revisions concerning previous information, have greatly altered our knowledge of the Etruscan inhabitants of the Po Valley, and their relationship with other civilizations of northern Italy. The modifications have been so radical that they have made it possible to better understand historical sources, which, though scarce and fragmented, reveal some specific information on the subject; information that contains very important intuited data providing the essentials of certain facts and longstanding phenomena. In an essay that must so succinctly address such a complex issue, I deemed it opportune to focus on more recent findings, without neglecting some of the more consolidated ones. It must be premised that the ancient historical Latin and Greek traditions support the emphasis given to the importance and consistency of the northerly Etruscan expansion, especially the one related to the Po River Valley. According to Cato, in a testimonial provided by Servius, "in Tuscorum iure paene omnis Italia fuerat" (Servius, *ad Aeneidem*, XI, 567). That is, almost the whole of Italy was under Etruscan dominion. More specifically, Livy informs us that the Etruscans, well-known from the Alps all the way to Sicily (Livy, I, 2, 5), inhabited first the lands south of the Apennines, that is, Tyrrhenian Etruria, from which they early on moved south, reaching Campania, but also the northern territories, crossing over the Apennines, and permanently settling on a large portion of the plains of Padania. Here, they established a confederation of twelve cities, a number that echoed the amount of cities in their mother country (Livy, V, 33, 9–10), modern-day Tuscany and the section of Latium to the right of the Tiber River. Though the number twelve exceeds what archaeological research can verify, and it seems only to correspond to the desire to create a situation in the new territory that reflected the situation in the mother country, the stable presence of Etruscans in the Po Valley, as well as their perfect business, political and institutional structure, is an historical fact that even the ancients knew well. Furthermore, they had the knowledge that the Etruscan expansion to the north of the Apennines was characterized by their urban arrangement and by a political and economic structure that was strongly hinged on the cities. In addition to Livy, Plutarch and Pliny the Elder also provide important information on the issue. Plutarch recalled how the Po Valley and the Tyrrhenic regions had many trees and a wealth of pastures and rivers, but also "large, beautiful cities, well disposed for trade and with a high quality of life" (Plutarch, *Camillus*, 16). In addition to claiming the existence of a confederation of twelve cities, citing Mantua—also mentioned by Virgil (*Aeneid*, X, 102)—Pliny (*Naturalis historia*, III, 15, 115) states that there was a highly important supremacy within this confederation, centered in Felsina, modern-day Bologna. He wrote, "Bononia, Felsina vocitata tum cum princeps Etruriae esset." According to a recent interpretation (Colonna 1987), Pliny's *princeps*, understood as having a chronological more than a political-institutional significance, could have been a synonym of *metropolis*, that is, of a city having a decisive role in the genesis and development of the same Etruscan *ethnos*, like Cortona (in the Pelasgian tradition) and Pyrgi (in the Lydian tradition). Since this supremacy is recognized by Bologna, even in relation to the entire Etruscan culture, it is obvious that it derives from the acknowledgement of its ruling functions and its emphasized prominence, especially in its relationship with the expansive territory of the Po Valley. The Etruscans exerted tight control over this territory, and Bologna was in fact the "capital." Information provided by the sources relative to the founding of the confederate cities is also of prime importance. Some authors attribute the founding to Ocno, who also founded Perusia, while others credit Tarchon, the heroic, eponymous founder of Tarquinia.

This last piece of information is particularly important because it dates the Etruscans' existence to a distant, almost mythical time, establishing a synchronic relationship between the Etruscans' first contact with the Tyrrhenic area (Tarchon was also the hero of Etruscan origins) and their expansion into the Po Valley. These two traditions do not counter more established beliefs; rather, they seem to suggest a chronological sequence according to which a more recent expansion by Ocno followed an older one by Tarchon. This chronology of events seems to find confirmation in the archaeological documentation of Bologna and its territory. Such documentation essentially delineates two successive expansions; the older one, which can be dated to the Early Iron Age (ninth century), aimed at seeking new lands to cultivate, while the more recent expansion (mid-sixth century) was primarily aimed at

Aerial view of Marzabotto

Bronze kore *from Covignano (Rimini), 480* B.C.
Copenhagen, Nationalmuseet cat. 278

greatly restructuring the Po Valley for commercial purposes. Archaeological documentation asserts that the first instances of Villanovan culture north of the Apennines date to the ninth century, the same period in which this culture was forming its roots in the Tyrrhenic region. In fact, much like the events that took place in most of the Tyrrhenic cities, beginning in the late ninth century, the population of Bologna is concentrated in at least three villages, which, though still distinct, were already crowded around the area that was to become an historic city. Until about 750 B.C., the population became even denser around one of these villages (Villa Cassarini and Villa Bosi), so that it became the fulcrum of a unified center, which, extending over 200 hectares, was characterized by its early urban quality. The sepulchral grounds, located on the outskirts of the village, were arranged in a manner that already presupposed the structure of the future city, even if in this early stage the vast area designated to housing contained only groups of huts, distanced from each other by large spaces used for agricultural purposes and related activities, such as the transformation and working of products, their preservation, storage, harvesting, and livestock. Until recently, this sudden and abundant demographic growth was explained by the arrival of external groups, Tyrrhenic Etruscans, to be precise, because, in previous phases (Late and Final Bronze Age), the population of this region appeared too limited to give rise to a phenomenon of such immense proportion. Closer examination of the data, however, revealed that the population was actually much greater than had originally been assumed, and also more economically solid and structured. Consequently, a new hypothesis believes that Bologna's growth between the ninth and eighth centuries was also due to the local population that had settled there during the Bronze Age.

Etruscan elements had no doubt arrived from the Tyrrhenic region because the population alone cannot explain such a rapid and consistent demographic growth, though the inhabitants' contribution to the pre-urban development of Bologna must be reconsidered. This new theory regarding the local character of the city might also explain some of the cultural peculiarities of Villanovan Bologna, which differentiate and distinguish it from the Villanovan Tyrrhenic region. The tribal solidarity of the small Bronze Age villages in the Po Valley, which were dispersed on a large territory and lacked any internal hierarchy, were also affected by this new, emerging culture of supremacy. These villages were characterized by an elementary economy, which still lacked specialized artisanship and division of labor, so that they essentially produced only what was required for local consumption, and not the excess required for commercial purposes. The new culture rapidly assumed the qualities of an early urban center—as it was absorbed in controlling the vast surrounding territory—which was characterized by a highly structured and complex economy. The progressive conquest of this territory was inexorable, as evidenced by the chronological differences between the oldest testimonials of Bologna and those of the more distant sites, which, being the more recent, reveal a process of expansion that had not yet been completed during the seventh century. Later, this territory expanded north, almost as far as the Po River; on the south it entered the Apennine valleys; to the west it extended at least as far as the Enza Valley; and to the east it already stretched as far as the Adriatic, reaching the Mezzano Valley, toward the future city of Spina. The orographic and pedologic characteristics of this territory, a vast plain brimming with attestations of the drainage and canalization work carried out by the Etruscans—whose skills in this field were already recognized by the ancient peoples—were restructured and improved so that they could be used for agricultural purposes, especially for the cultivation of cereals. Their advanced metallurgic technologies, especially with regard to smelting bronze and working iron, also allowed the manufacturing of many tools and equipment, such as ploughs, hoes, sickles, billhooks, etc. This efficient and functional array of equipment certainly permitted high yields. Though manufacturing activities in general must not be underestimated, Bologna's economic prosperity during this phase was largely due to agriculture, and, more specifically, to the excess of agricultural products, destined for trade. Both historical documentation and archaeological finds demonstrate that such a structured and widespread expansion, especially toward the west, was not immune to conflicts and contrasts with other realities. In this regard, Livy's testimonial (V, 34, 9) of the battle of the Ticino, fought between the Gauls and the Etruscans at the time of Tarquinius Priscus, is significant. The battle is a sign of the evident and ancient conflict for control and

Po Valley Etruscan settlements

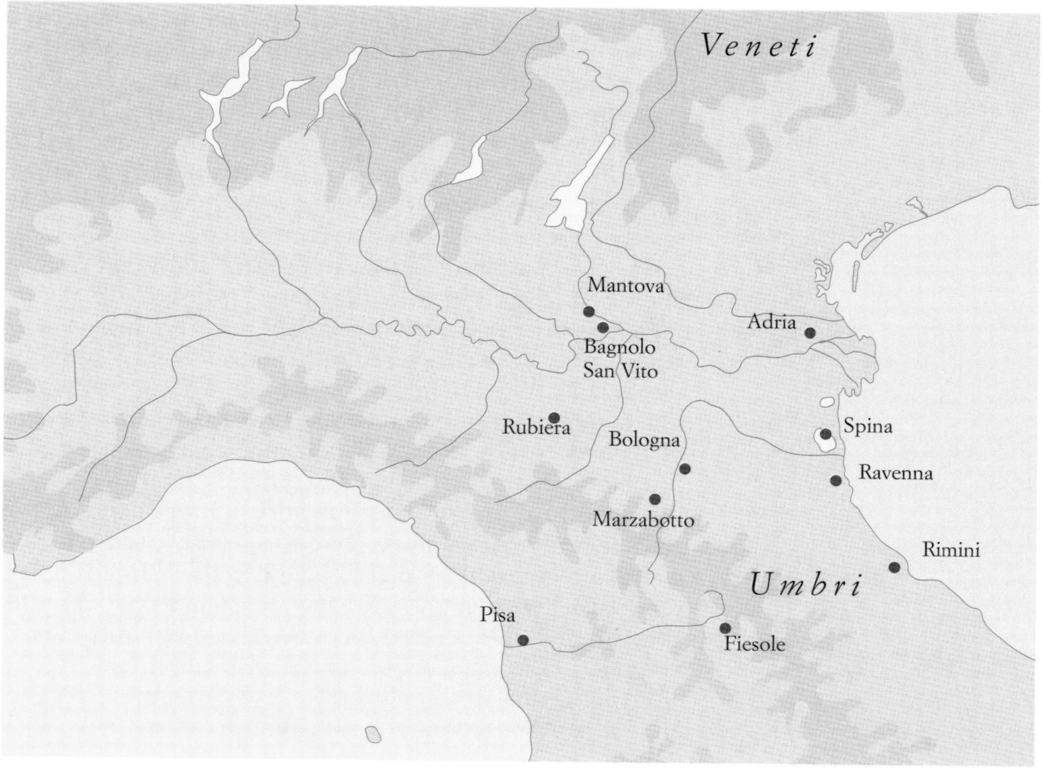

power over territories, which had long been acquired, between the groups inhabiting the other side of the Po. It is not improbable that the *zilath* on one of the two cippi of Rubiera, in western Emilia, a "military commander" by virtue of its ancient history, is the result of such a conflict. These conflicts were often caused by Bologna's interest in creating a political and military settlement that would bring an end to these minor conflicts between bordering peoples (to which Livy's "saepe pugnavere" seems to allude), and their reciprocal attempts at trespassing.

While Bologna took control of a vast territory, which extended as far as the Po and was strewn with small rural settlements, Verucchio, the Villanovan center of Romagna, appeared to be less interested in restructuring and exploiting the agricultural land surrounding it. Situated high on a hilltop, well protected, and only fifteen kilometers from the sea—like many cities of Tyrrhenic Etruria (especially the southern part)—Verucchio was more intent on controlling the route that led to Tiberine Etruria on one side, and functioning as a commercial outpost, run by a well-organized group of *aristoi*, on the side overlooking the Adriatic (toward the port of Rimini). In terms of the origin and development of Verucchio, an analogy to what was happening in Bologna can be hypothesized. In fact, the area contains a number of proto-Villanovan (twelfth to tenth centuries) attestations, some of which can be attributed to villages of some importance and to storerooms for bronze, a clear indication of flourishing economic activity in this area. Sporadic proto-Villanovan artifacts have also been found on site at Verucchio. It is true that the population of the Late Bronze Age alone insufficiently explains the genesis of Verucchio, already rapid and consistent at its beginnings (ninth century), but it certainly constituted an element of unification and of attraction for outsiders who wanted to establish an outpost in order to control the valley of Marecchia and the Adriatic coast. Such an aspiration was likely part of the same plan that foresaw controlling the Po Valley through Felsina, once again with the aim of expanding along the central Adriatic coast from the Villanovan enclave of Fermo.

In conclusion, on the basis of all these considerations, which have been made possible by both archaeological documentation and historical information, knowledge and information has greatly advanced in the past few years. This new and rich evaluation of Verucchio (and Rimini) is particularly important in understanding the important role played by the Etr-

View of the necropolis of Marzabotto

uscans in the Adriatic from very early on. In addition to information regarding the well-known expedition against Cuma, which was planned and led by the Etruscans of the Po Valley and the Adriatic as early as 524 B.C., the importance and precocity of the Etruscans and their hegemony over the Adriatic is also indirectly confirmed by another well-known testimony of Livy's (V, 33, 7–8). He very explicitly commented the powerful and widespread Etruscan dominion, which extended to both the Tyrrhenian Sea and the Adriatic Sea. He wrote, "prior to the dominion of Rome, the power of the Etruscans was vast, both on land and at sea. The names of the seas that bordered Italy both above and below, as if it were an island, can be taken as proof of this. In fact, the Italic peoples named one of these seas 'Etrusco,' after themselves; the other they called 'Adriatic,' after Adria, an Etruscan colony. For the same reasons, the Greeks called these seas 'Tyrrhenian' and 'Adriatic.'" It is of little importance that Adria was not a true "Etruscan colony," even if the ancient historic tradition and recent archaeological findings provide evidence otherwise. What is most important in Livy's statement is the awareness that the Etruscans even named the Adriatic Sea, as a consequence of their dominion over it, a dominion that was as ancient and uncontested as their supremacy over the Tyrrhenian Sea. Once again, this parallelism leads to a new evaluation of the Etruscans' presence on the Adriatic from very early in history, supporting recent archaeological findings and research, especially relative to Verucchio and Romagna. The concentration of wealth in the Po Valley, in the hands of a few, was also provoked by agricultural exploitation on the one hand and commercial structuring on the other. These few who controlled all the riches were either groups or individuals who socially and culturally behaved in a manner analogous to the aristocrats of the Tyrrhenic region. Like them, they held a very influential position from the end of the seventh to the beginning of the sixth centuries B.C. Extraordinarily important events, such as the precocious acquisition of the alphabet and the practice of writing, are proof that Po Valley Etruria, and Bologna in particular, played a very important mediating role between the Tyrrhenic area and northern Italy. The Etruscans in Bologna and the outlying areas were the first among the northern populations to learn and use the written language, eventually promoting it throughout the populations of northern

View of the acropolis of Marzabotto

Italy, both in the west, toward the Celts of the Golasecca culture, and in the east, toward the Veneti of the Este culture. Through Bologna and the Po Valley, the Etruscans furnished these environments with products manufactured by the Etruscans (bronzes as well as wine and perfume), and they provided them artisanship and cultural stimulation of great importance and influence. One need only think of the *situla*, so peculiar to Este, but perhaps originated and stimulated by the presence or influx of Tyrrhenic artisans.

Between Bologna, which on the east seems to have extended, more or less, to the Santerno Valley, and Verucchio there is a very disquieting gap in this very early phase. At least in the Apennines, it is perhaps due to the precocious and persistent presence of the Umbrians, who later wandered toward the coast.

Toward the mid-sixth century B.C., the political and economic policies of the entire Po Valley experienced a tremendous alteration caused by an agenda that presupposed the revitalization of the economic-productive system, which had begun to lag. The historical reasons of this transformation must also be sought in the Tyrrhenian region, where the Etruscans were progressively losing their uncontested supremacy over the sea as a result of competition from Greeks and Carthaginians. Consequently, they began to experience a decrease in commercial exchanges with Europe along the Rhône Valley route. To overcome this crisis and to circumvent the burdensome obstacle, the whole of Etruria located within the Po Valley had to undergo a political and economic restructuring, which concretized in the *ex novo* founding of urban centers in Marzabotto, in the Bolognese Apennines; in Spina, along the Adriatic coastline; and in Mantua, north of the Po. Bologna, which immediately became the fulcrum of this new functional system composed of a rich network of trafficking between Tyrrhenic Etruria, Greece, and transalpine Europe, also had to be refounded. A point of convergence, the Po Valley served the interests of the Greeks, via the Adriatic Sea, and of the Etruscans, through the mountain passes of the Apennines, leading to the creation of new trade routes toward central Europe, which was reached henceforth through the Alps. Splendid figured ceramics reached Spina from Athens by way of the Adriatic. Arriving from various parts of Greece there were also amphoras with oil and wine, which were sent to Man-

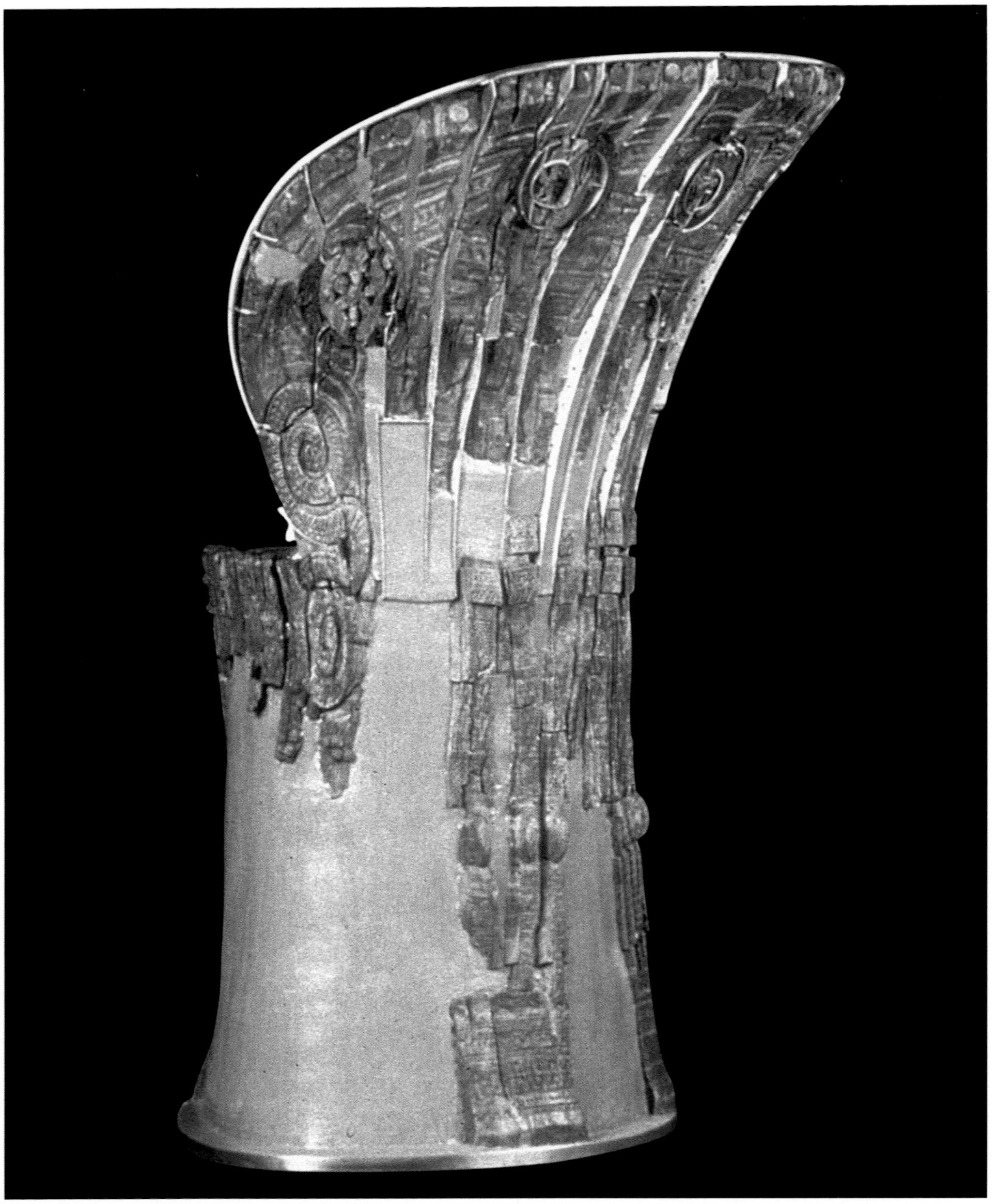

Wooden throne from Tomb 89 at Verucchio necropolis, mid-seventh century. Verucchio, Museo Archeologico

tua by river (as testified by numerous remains of small ships employed for this purpose), and then decanted into wood and leather otres before they reached the courts of the Celtic princes in the heart of Europe. Instead, handcrafts such as gold wares, ivory, and especially bronzes arrived from Tyrrhenic Etruria via the Apennines, passing perforce through Marzabotto. Bologna, which lay at the center of this system, functioned as a collection point and shunting station for the markets situated beyond the Alps. This set-up was not only perfectly structured to facilitate the trade of goods acquired elsewhere (Tyrrhenic Etruria on the one hand, and Athens and the Greek world, on the other), but it also soon become a productive organization, in the sense that many goods for export began to be manufactured here. This system in fact made it possible to receive raw materials such as copper and iron from Tyrrhenic Etruria. These were then worked in appropriate workshops with a level of production high enough to provide for the needs of a rather large market. The new structure of the Po Valley no longer has to respond to exclusively agricultural needs (although this market continued to maintain its level of importance); rather, it appears to have aimed at an "itinerant" structure with the objective of creating and strengthening safe and equipped commercial pathways. From this moment on, the directives governing the trafficking constituted the backbone of a new unification system, based primarily on the urban model. This restructuring is referred to as internal Etruria's (Clusium and Volterra) "second colonization," following a decision taken at the federal sanctuary of Volsinii (Orvieto). Nonetheless, it is important to note that noble names formed with *-alu*, typical of this northern region, prevailed in the new urban centers, especially in Marzabotto, demonstrating that a large portion of the population consisted in groups of local origin. Once again, the theory that a planned colonial movement, actuated by peoples arriving from the outside, must at the very least be attenuated. The protagonists of this radical transformation were the Etruscans of the Po Valley, and, although there was a push from the outside on the organizational and economic front, local human resources prevailed. It is inevitable to consider Bologna in particular, as it was undoubtedly involved in the transformation of the old model of production, which, centered especially on agriculture, had by then been replaced by the progression of events. The definitive urbanization process of Felsina-Bologna occurred within this very context; therefore the city had a true and proper Etruscan *arx* (stronghold), sacred pole for the entire community. It had its own monuments, constituted by at least one temple, with travertine and marble cippi used to support offerings, such as bronze *ex voto* of extremely high quality, and two images of divinities (Heracles with the golden apples from the garden of Hesperides, and Apollo, player of the lyre, very possibly referred to the cultual pantheon. Hovering about 40 meters over the houses below, the temple corresponds perfectly to the features of the *arx*, located on the fringe of the urban area, on a site that permitted a view not only of the whole city, but also of the necropolis and a great part of the surrounding area. In this manner, it was perfectly suited to its function as *auguraculum*, that is, "ritual observatory" or "sacred point," from which, overlooking the city, the augur could carry out his consecration from a four-partitioned space that transformed the city into a *templum*.

The acropolis of Marzabotto has similar characteristics. Various sources and archaeological findings have made it possible to identify and reconstruct the Apennine city's foundation rite, which took root in the acropolis. The same rite was documented in Spina, on the Adriatic coast, at the mouth of a branch of the Po's Delta. Ancient peoples claimed that it was a Greek city, perhaps because of the large quantities of Greek goods that arrived there, or perhaps simply to indicate that it was a place where Greeks could do business and feel free to come and go as they pleased. Spina, however, was undoubtedly an Etruscan city, as demonstrated by the prevalence of Etruscan inscriptions on the ceramics found there. It was a port of arrival and a shunting station for figured ceramics as well as amphoras containing wine and oil, which arrived in Spina from Greece via the Adriatic. Both the Etruscans who inhabited the city and those who lived in cities inland, especially those from Bologna, were responsible for maintaining the port's efficiency. The port had to be protected from Illyrian pirates and from the constant threats of the sea and the flooding of the delta, which compromised the port's functioning on an almost daily basis.

The perfect commercial integration of these three cities, strong points of Po Valley Etruria, indicates that there must have been a collaborative relationship, especially between Bologna and Spina, as evidenced by the stela in Bologna depicting a ship. Perhaps symbolic of an imminent war, the stela bears the name of the deceased man, Vel Kaikna, who must have held an important position of authority in marine activities carried out by the Etruscans on the Adriatic and in Spina, maritime strong point of the entire Etruscan network in the Po Valley.

After territorial and political agreements had been so arduously attained at the battle of the Ticino, they were brusquely disrupted at the beginning of the fourth century. Gaulish populations from north of the Po River, who had been living there for a long time, descended upon the Etruscans and the Umbrians in masses, moving down into Rome, which they sieged and captured. The descent of the Gauls had very disruptive effects—at least in the beginning—on the entire system that the Etruscans had created in the plains of the Po Valley. Marzabotto rapidly lost its urban identity, becoming a sort of military outpost controlling the Reno Valley, as testified by the radical reduction of the inhabited areas and the improper use of urban structures. While events in Bologna seem to not to have been so dras-

Ivory candelabra from Tomb 614 of Valle Trebba (Spina), fifth century B.C.
Ferrara, Museo archeologico
cat. 192

Bronze statue of Hercules from the sanctuary of Villa Cassarini (Bologna), ca. 400 B.C.
Bologna, Soprintendenza Archeologica dell'Emilia Romagna
cat. 205

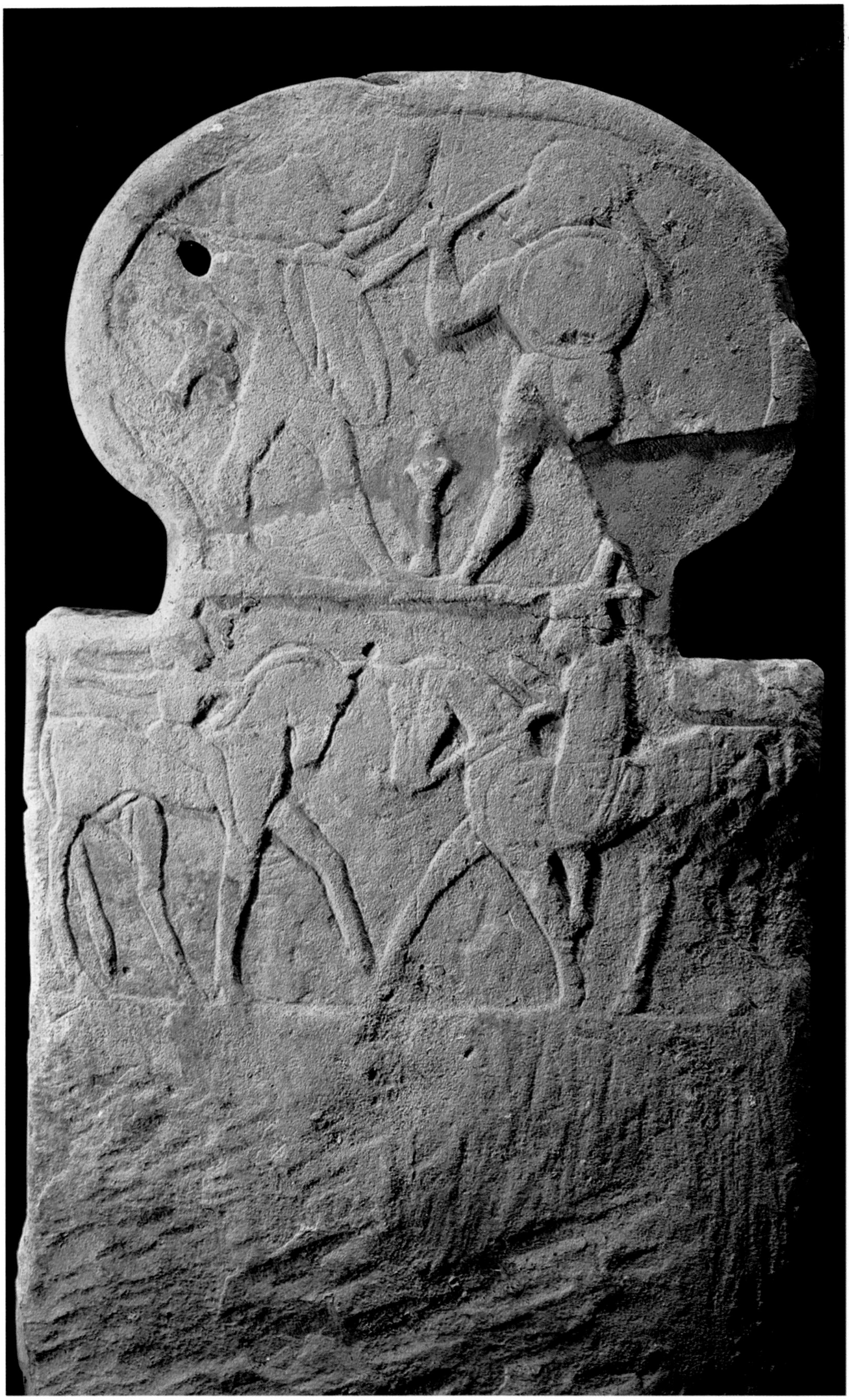

Stela from Felsina, 530–520 B.C.
Bologna, Museo Archeologico

tic, the results of the invasion were similar. The city appears to have been able to maintain its role of importance even in this new context, and it acquired a kind of political supremacy within the territory governed by the Gauls. The urban settlement, however, experienced alterations in addition to an obvious general impoverishment. These alterations involved radical novelties that undermined the foundations of the urban model created by the Etruscans in the Po Valley, consequently shattering the structure of the territory, which in turn was subjected to rapid changes in the routes, characteristics, and the distribution of the settlements. In referring to Gaulish Bologna, which he continues to refer to as Felsina, Livy (XXXIII, 37, 3–4) describes it as *urbs*, in honor of its fully urban Etruscan past, and *oppidum*, certainly as a consequence of the dismantling of the old urban contexture, not only from a topographic and urban stance, but also from an institutional and political viewpoint. The drastic changes were not attenuated even though the new ethnic groups rapidly integrated the Etruscan culture and lifestyle (the ideology of the symposium, the consumption of wine and meat, athletic games). This is demonstrated, among other things, by the different organizational structure of the territory. No longer was the area divided into "cities," but into *vici*, which is to say, plains settlements involved in agricultural production, or into *castella*, mountain settlements specifically functioning as garrisons to defend the territory and the new communication routes. This radical transformation was based on the Gauls' intent to take over the role that the Etruscans had so firmly maintained for such a long time, becoming the dominant mediators between the Mediterranean and the European continent. To this end, new trade routes connecting new mountain passes that were directed in a more easterly direction, toward Romagna, were created and strengthened, thereby depleting Etruscan itineraries and centers such as Bologna and Marzabotto of their historical role and commercial function. Only Spina and Mantua survived—albeit for a short while—the Celtic dominion by altering their position and becoming Etruscan islands. Perhaps they had even begun functioning as unification and collection points for the many Etruscans who had fled the Po Valley to escape the dangers that had taken root in the mid-fourth century B.C. It has thus been hypothesized that the well-known Athenian decree of 325–324 B.C., which called for a colony in the high Adriatic region to protect Greek trade from Tyrrhenian piracy, had actually been devised by the Po Valley Etruscans, who had foreseen a way of surviving the economic break-down of their land, caused by the arrival of the Gauls. They had therefore established settlements not only in Spina, whose thriving economy at that time was no mere circumstance, but also along the Adriatic coast, at least as far as Ravenna, and perhaps even Rimini. This late Etruscan existence along the Adriatic survived well into the third century B.C., coinciding with the first instances of the Romanization of the Po Valley, begun in Rimini, the "Adriatic door" of the Po Valley plains.

Mazzarino 1970, pp. 217–19; Martelli 1985a, pp. 90–131; Sassatelli 1986, pp. 9–56; Colonna 1987, pp. 1–36; Sassatelli 1987, pp. 197–259; Sassatelli 1990, pp. 51–100; Sassatelli 1991, pp. 693–715; Vitali 1992; Malnati 1993, pp. 145–77; Sassatelli 1993, pp. 115–28; Sassatelli 1994b, pp. 497–508; Malnati, Violante 1995, pp. 97–120; Morigi Govi, Sassatelli 1996, pp. 11–28; Sassatellia 1999, pp. 71–107; Sassatellib 1999, pp. 453–74.

Simonetta Stopponi

Relations with Neighboring Peoples

According to Cato (in Servius, *ad Aeneidem*, XI, 567), almost the whole of Italy had been under Etruscan dominion; furthermore, according to Livy (I, 2; V, 33), their power had extended from the Alps to the strait of Messina. While these affirmations do not completely correspond to facts, given that only some of the peninsula's regions were actually subjected to their direct government, they do reveal the role that ancient historiography assigned to the Etruscans in terms of their relationship with the pre-Roman peoples. In addition, the affirmations made by Cato and Livy reflect an unquestionable and substantial truth, if this hegemonic role is to be understood at a cultural level. Prior to Rome's political, linguistic, and cultural unification of Italy, there is no denying the Greek co-existence with a center of cultural diffusion in the Tyrrhenic region. Excluding the marketplaces, through which there was direct and immediate contact between indigenous peoples and individuals from the eastern Mediterranean—first the Phoenicians and then the Greeks—or from the southern coasts of the peninsula, interested in Greek colonization, the Etruscans not only diffused their own specific culture, but they also conveyed interests, inspiration and elements adopted from the East, especially from Greece. It is thanks to their precocious economic and political structure that the Etruscans were able to carry out such an incisive role in the acculturation process of pre-Roman Italian communities, influencing the dynamics of the various cultures' evolution. Naturally, the stimuli were received and re-elaborated in a variety of ways, not only according to location and time, but especially in relation to the reactive abilities of each society, which depended on their various levels of socio-economic structuring, and, therefore, of development.

In the first millennium B.C., Italy was anything but unified. While it was initially segmented into regional cultures that foreshadowed their ethnic differences, in historic time it began to experience the presence and existence of a variety of peoples, differing in origin, language, and traditions. Already by the ninth–eighth centuries B.C., however, an understanding between groups and individuals correlated these differences.

With the Iron Age, a dynamic process of evolution was instilled in Etruria. This process, so well reflected in the Villanovan "colonization" of Emilia, Romagna and Campania, led to contacts with other populations, both near and far, by land and by sea. Far from being an obstacle, the Tyrrhenian Sea was, in fact, a means of exchange between the coastal Etruscans and the nearby islanders, an exchange that reflected the same ancient trading tradition of the Tyrrhenians in Sardinia (Strabo, V, 2, 7). While the island is known for its numerous Etruscan bronzes, some of which—such as the sword with "antennae"—reveal the value given to militarism and rank, the items found in the Tomb of the Nuraghic Bronzes at the necropolis of Cavalupo provide a contrasting view. It contained the funerary goods of a Sardinian woman who had been given in marriage to a man from Vulci, likely as the seal of an alliance between two families. Relationships with Sardinia extended as far as Corsica, where, over time, a lot of Etruscans, mostly from Caere, settled. Here, too, bonds of reciprocity instilled as early as the fifth century are ascertained by the ethnic *Kursika* graffito on a bowl from Populonia.

The same type of sword mentioned above has also been found in Fermo, where certain funerary rites and goods have led to the theory that there must have existed a Villanovan enclave, not affected by the Etruscans, which was later absorbed into the Picene culture. While the community at Fermo, existent during the Iron Age, cannot, with any certainty, be defined as "Villanovan," there is no doubt that archaeological artifacts of the ninth and eighth centuries not only show affinity to Bologna and Romagna, but they also reveal a close relationship with the Tyrrhenic area (Etruria and Latium). Proof is found in the cinerary urns with their rounded decorations, which resemble some exemplars found in Clusium and Vulci, and in razors that are shaped in a manner generally attributed to southern Etruria. In addition, crested headpieces and rhomboidal women's belts are reminiscent of various Etruscan centers, where such pieces were used to denote the social position of the dead person, while the rectangular breastplate found in Tomb 78 of the Misericordia district is redolent of southern Etruscan prototypes. In the Tenna Valley, elements of Villanovan culture undoubtedly followed trade routes that had been established in the preceding era, and that were used for many years afterward. Similar elements also reached the more southern zones of eastern Italy, as testified by some of the rhomboidal belts found at Teramo, which have been traced to the "necropolis of the Salino." Tyrrhenic groups who were interested in controlling the Adriatic

Small bronze statue of an augur from the votive board of Lapis Niger (Rome), ca. 550 B.C.
Rome, Museo del Foro
cat. 146

Map of pre-Roman Italic peoples

undoubtedly employed the valleys, which opened onto the seas, and approached the territory from coastal locations, which, though not numerous, could be integrated with river routes. Toward the end of the ninth century, beginning in the more precocious, southern part of Etruria, Etruscan areas began to develop both social structures and an aristocratically-based form of power, contributing to exchanges and contacts with other members of similar elite classes, simultaneously transmitting aristocratic rituals and ceremonial traditions. Firmly established in its historic territories, supported by opulent *principes* and strong on the sea, Etruria—especially during the Orientalizing period—consolidated its presence on the peninsula by diffusing beliefs and religious practices, ideologies, and cultural models. Hence, it stimulated the social and economic structuring and development of the districts inhabited by Italic peoples. Greek and Eastern imports, controlled by Etruscan aristocrats, were redistributed internally and, along with other goods, were also received the cultural elaborations of Oriental and Greek elements produced in Etruria. This involved not only the exportation of products and technologies, or of the migration of artisans, but also the development of certain factors of acculturation that affected evolution, factors such as the acquisition of a written language and the construction of permanent, stable housing. Once they had acquired the written language of the Chalcidians of Pythecusae, the Etruscans transmitted their alphabet to all of the peninsula's inhabitants, with the exception of the southern populations and the Sicilians, who acquired it directly from the Greeks. Even the innovative method of designating an individual with a binomial (first name + gentilitial) was spread to the Faliscans, Latins and Osco-Umbrians. Adopted in Etruria during the seventh century B.C., this method replaced the original tradition of a single name, demonstrating an evolved social structure.

Relationships between the Etruscans and other ethnicities continued to be multi-directional, and, as a result of their reciprocal permeability, foreigners—so identified by their names—were accepted and assimilated within the society. This blending of peoples made it possible to share cultural experiences. Classical sources provide an example of this in the account of Demaratus, a Corinthian refugee who, with his people, sought shelter in Tarquinia. He was the father of the first king of the Etruscan dynasty, which, from the last decades of seventh century to 509 B.C., exerted control over Rome. Lucius Tarquinius Priscus, Servius Tullius, and Lucius Tarquinius Superbus enriched the city with Etruscan forms, without, however, annihilating the original Latin matrix that had been integrated with the Sabine culture. Rome owes its most important monument to the Etruscans: that temple whose construction spans the whole period, fromTarquinius Priscus' vow and the calling from Veii of the artist Vulca, up to the raising of the quadriga acroterium decided by Tarquinis Superbus. The Roman Republic laid claim to the temple built at the top of the Capitoline Hill, in the same way that the architectural model of the "Tuscan" temple, destined to endure the centuries, was transmitted to the Italic world through Rome. Etruscan forms were so deep-rooted and bountiful in the city that they were present even in the toponymy. A fine example is the *vicus tuscus*, probable venue of worship of the Etruscan god Vertumnus-Voltumna, represented in the statue attributed to Mamurio Veturio, dated to the era of King Numa Pompilius.

Rome appropriated Etruscan ceremonies, rich in allusions to royalty and to the assimilation of the extraterrestrial realm, in its triumphal depictions of parades of chariots, at times pulled by winged horses or conducted by female characters of a divine nature, reiterated in archaic clay slabs used for architectural purposes. It also adopted important Etruscan symbols such as the double-edged hatchet and the *diphros*. The hatchet was already a well-known symbol of power in Villanovan Etruria, still employed in the magisterial parades depicted on more recent Tarquinian tombs, and later adopted in Roman insignia. Instead the *diphros*, a foldable stool, was initially an attribute of kings, later adopted by the highest magistrates of Rome, where it was known as the *sella curulis*. We are aware of it in its original form through either true extant exemplars or via their representations on monuments.

Inhabitants of the right bank of the Tiber River, the Faliscans and people of Capena had a close bond of utmost importance. In addition to their common geographic location, they also had cultural affinities, which led to a substantial integration that did not, however, delete their differences, specifically their language (Faliscan has Indo-European origins and is very similar to Latin). The two communities shared the Etruscans' interest in the populations scattered between the Tiber and the Adriatic, keeping track of their historical-political events, and both communities were subjected to the same treatment at the hands of Rome.

The Tiber cut across a region that was particularly privileged in terms of exchanges between the Tyrrhenian and the Italic regions. Functioning as an axial point, the river was never a closed border; rather, it was permeable and accepting of the influences of a rather hegemonic culture. Goods and ideas floated East from the river's basin, moving beyond the Apennines, extending to the Adriatic. Middle Adriatic peoples were served well by the excellent trade routes of the Nera, Velino and Aniene Valleys, pathways resulting from the direct contact between the inhabitants along the Tiber and their neighbors at the border, the Umbrians and the Sabines.

Thanks to the direct and continuous relations with Etruria, the cultural unification process was well under way in the central part of the peninsula prior to the Roman conquest. The Umbrian example illustrates how these contacts favored the birth of an ethnic self-awareness in the Italic population, and how social differences, which gave way to the development of local warlords, developed on the crest of the diffusion that characterized the Orientalizing *facies*. In fact,

following pages
The so-called "Corsini" marble throne from San Giovanni in Laterano (Rome), first century B.C.
Roma, Galleria Corsini
cat. 330

Inscription in Etruscan and Latin from Pesaro, mid-first century B.C.
Pesaro, Museo Oliveriano
cat. 329

the Umbrian culture, which was originally a unified blend of Umbrian and Sabine *ethnos*, was segmented before the formation of the various Sabellian populations. This precocious event was undoubtedly precipitated by the Umbrians' proximity to the Tyrrhenic world, whose evolution functioned as a shuttle of acceleration for the outlying areas. It is no coincidence that the most ancient Umbrian-language document, written with an alphabet modeled after Etruscan types, dates to the mid-seventh century B.C., synchronizing with the traditionally accepted founding date of Terni, 672 B.C. (CIL XI, 4170). Two centuries later, in the Tables of Gubbio, the local community declares itself in opposition to *turskum numen*, and states that the ceremonies cannot be held in the presence of its members. Yet the relationship between the two cultures is such that the ancient tradition classifies Umbrians and Etruscans under the same common denominator, describing them as having "looseness" of morals.
Archaeological findings do, in effect, indicate the adoption of different elements. Such findings include: the hypogeum of Amelia, reminiscent of Caeretan typologies; the decorative clay protome in Bevagna; a bent tile in Terni, whose elements reflect those of the architectural style of Aquarossa; the *fibulae* with foliated bow, at the necropolis of San Pietro in Campo (Terni), created with fragments of shields decorated with embossed work imported from Etruria; and bucchero drinking vessels. Also attributed to the proximity of the Tyrrhenian region are the delimiting walls of southern Umbria, constructed in the fourth century B.C. Nonetheless, it is important to note how the formal and decorative typologies of the potteries found in the oldest Umbrian necropolises demonstrate a profound connection, besides the Etruscans, to the Falisco-Capenas and Sabine world, which is also echoed in internal Etruria and equally projected toward the Adriatic, where written documentation supports the Sabine findings.
Etruscan aristocrats welded their relationships, sanctioned by exchanges of gifts, with individuals of equal rank; consequently, these exchanges of valuable goods were coupled with the transmission of habits and models. In Latium, south of the Tiber, the furnishings of the homes in Satricum and the burial goods of the Praenestian tombs reflect the mentality and opulence of the Caeretan princes. These same sumptuary goods, the same display of wealth, and the same lifestyle are transmitted beyond the Apennines, and the lords of Fabriano, located at the entrance to a valley that led to the Adriatic, had the same meaningful objects placed in their tombs. Hence, the bronze shields and silvers, the *kotylai* and the comb *fibula* found in Tomb 3 of Santa Maria in Campo, while the andirons and spits from the same burial reveal the adopted banqueting tradition. In any case, this was still a two-way relationship since Picene materials were found in Caere, likely arriving there via Praeneste, where bronze ornaments,

typical of Picene women, were found. It is likely that these women had married local men. At Matelica, in the Marche region, the recent finding of the tomb of a warrior and local chief makes it possible to comprehend the diffusion of objects, of ideological bases, and of ritualistic traditions. Sceptres, arms, horse bits, bronze vessels, and clay *holmos* echo the coeval furnishings of aristocratic Etruscans, while the placement of grape-stones and a sacrificed pig evoke analogous ceremonial traditions and similar religious beliefs. These are new discoveries, which make it easier to identify the relationship between Etruria and the middle Adriatic Italic populations. It is safe to assume, for example, that the headpiece found in the same tomb came from Picenum. Though it still requires study, its style is very similar to a sample found in Casale Marittimo (which was presented at a recent exhibit) and invites to think about the influence of Etruscan models on mid-Adriatic productions. A similar situation envelopes the statues, which, along with the ones found at Ceri and Vetulonia years ago, contribute to an understanding of the Etruscans' influence in the great stone statues of the Marche and Abruzzo regions, best exemplified by the Warrior of Capestrano. A typical example of luxury and ostentation is the necropolis of Pitino di San Severino, while one of the most important and meaningful objects imported from Etruria is the Phoenecian-type *oinochoe*, made from an engraved ostrich egg, with an ivory beak. It is shaped in the form of a female head, and covered in gold leaf. Also from the necropolis of Pitino di San Severino is a bronze cover, which, with its rich, elegant decorations evoking funerary and magical themes, is reminiscent of eighth-century B.C. samples from Bisenzio. While accumulation of precious objects is the same in "princely" tombs of different cultures, Italic tombs reflect the somewhat more explicit aristocratic burial traditions of the Etruscans. The more important necropolises of the Orientalizing period of the Marche region are found on the eastern border of the Apennines. Here, the amount of prestigious goods is much greater than in the coeval Umbrian tombs, indicating that the economy of these local peoples was based not only on the traditional silviculture and pastures, but also on the collection of the tolls for the routes that led to the Tyrrhenic area.
Horse and chariot harnesses found in the tombs of high-ranking individuals evidence the trade of high quality objects realized in Etruscans workshops, as well as the exchange of ideas. The funerary custom, derived from Oriental, Egyptian and Greek tradition, testified in eighth century B.C., and showed by the slendid Orientalizing vehicols covered with bronze laminae, either in southern or in northern Etruria, distinguishes the tombs of the *principes*, exalting their social position and richness. Italic warlords understood and assimilated the significance of that tradition and, as the members of the Etruscan elite, were hence buried with this status symbol, which, in the tombs of extremely high-ranking women, took the form of the "calash." Numerous exemplars of this kind of have been found in central Italy, like the exemplar of the necropolis of Eretum in Tiberine Sabina or the Umbrian and Picene ones. The most revealing aspect of the diffusion of this Tyrrhenian model, and of the diversity of the Italic world, is the continuity of this tradition in non-Etruscan areas; however, during the sixth century, the decrease of attestations in Etruria is a consequence of the prevailing of towns, which led to an enlarged social foundation based on census and not on birth. Ownership of horses, chariots leading troops to war, and the celebration of parades represented aristocratic values destined to oblivion with the emergence of urban structures. Instead, in those areas where urbanization was delayed, tribal social structures endured. Consequently, a few wealthy individuals exerted their control over territories that had not yet been urbanized, so that the luxuries that had by then become obsolete in Etruria, continued to hold the same significance. This is attested by artifacts found on the outskirts of Etruria, such as the chariot and calash at Castel San Marino, near Perugia; or in Italic area, such as the laminae in Todi (Umbria); and the chariot at Montelone di Spoleto, in upper Sabine, which, besides the cerimonial function, with its depiction of Achilles' saga, also served as a model of behavior for its aristocratic owner. Many other attestations were found in the Adriatic area, and they include the tomb of the princess of Sirolo, which to date is the only female tomb that contained a biga and a calash.
It was not until Etruria became urbanized (about the mid-seventh century B.C. in some areas, and a century later in other areas) that the split amongst Etruscan and Italics groups became evident. This decisive move was shared by the Sabines, who had gravitated to the Tiber Valley, and by the peoples of Latium *vetus*. With the exception of Magna Graecia, the rest

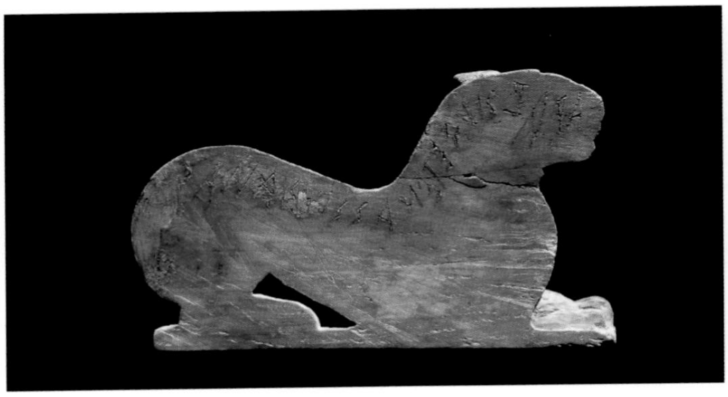
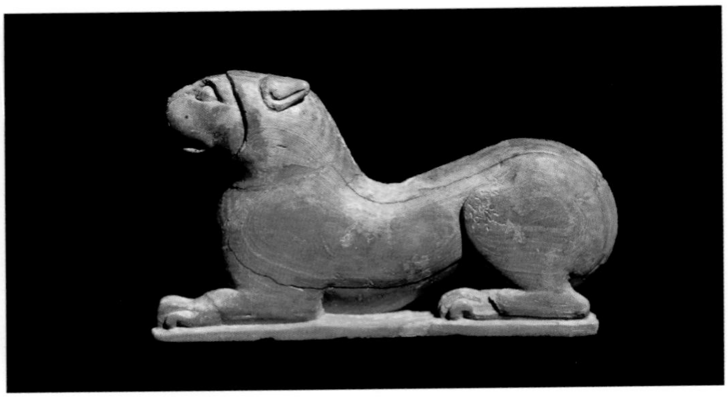

Tessera hospitalis *in engraved ivory from the sacred area of Sant'Omobono (Rome), mid-sixth century* B.C. *Rome, Musei Capitolini cat. 38*

of the peninsula continued to live according to the ancient tribal system, often becoming urbanized only through Roman intervention. Even if findings in Pesaro and Gualdo Tadino prove that by the late fifth century, huts were being replaced by a more stable, civilized, architecture, with stone foundations and roof tiles, such findings do not provide sufficient reason for considering those residential agglomerates true cities. Religious practices were also divided. In Etruria, as early as the sixth century B.C., places of worship began to assume a stable structure and they were dissociated from nobility, as evidenced by the sacred building in Piazza d'Armi in Veio. In Italic areas, however, the temple as an architectural building was essentially an adoption of Roman structures, which transformed some of those places located on mountain tops or passes, next to springs or sheets of water, into monuments. For centuries, those ancient structures had represented unified aggregates of villages scattered throughout the territory; a converging point that perpetuated a worship based on a pre- and proto-historic matrix of ethnic character, carried out by peoples bound by their tribal solidarity. Nonetheless, Etruscans and Italics had shared celebrations and forms of devotion. Auspicy was one of the most important practices, and the one for which Etruscan priests were so famous. In the Adriatic, for example, two monuments attest to this practice: the statuette of an augur with a lituus, and a bilingual epitaph. Though they originated in neighboring lands, these objects were manufactured centuries apart. The former was part of a collection of votive objects belonging to a treasure found at Isola di Fano, and it dates to the first decades of the fifth century B.C., while the epitaph commemorated an haruspex and interpreter of the lightning of Pesaro, with Perusian gentilitial, and it dates to the first century B.C. Among the faithful, the wealthiest could afford valuable offerings in bronze, which were either of local manufacture or acquired at Etruscan markets. Though only its splendid head remains, the donative of Cagli is a fine example. A discussion on important places of worship cannot exclude mention of the sanctuary dedicated to the goddess Cupra. Built by the Etruscans of the Po Valley, the temple overlooked the Adriatic (Strabo, V, 4, 2).

During the sixth and fifth centuries B.C., the Tiber reaffirmed its axial role, and relations between Etruria and the Italic peoples were essentially governed by nearest *poleis*, i.e. those of internal Etruria. By strengthening the bridgehead in Italic territories, the bordering cities assured themselves control of the centers on the other side of the riverbank. Some excellent examples are Perusia, with Arna and Bettona, and Orvieto, with Todi, whose name reveals its function as *tutere* (border). Velzna-Volsinii-Orvieto had a dominant role in the relationships with central Italy. From Romagna to Abruzzo, across the lands of the Umbrians, the diffusion of its products is evident. Orvieto has in fact been credited with the manufacturing of the greater part of the bronze utensils used by central Italic peoples for banquets and for drinking wine (spherical cauldrons or cauldrons with hemispherical covers, as well as *infundibula* and strainers, basins, *ólpai*, etc.). Both merchandise and men followed the ancient routes to the Apennines and the Adriatic, and it is easy to acknowledge the commercial and cultural influence of the Etruscan city along the obligatory pathways offered by the mountains. In Umbria, the Colfiorito route is especially important. Here, there have been discoveries of numerous, clear indications of Orvieto's presence, which later expanded to the mid-Adriatic area, from Numana to Campovalano. Workshops in Volsinii produced masterpieces such as Todi's Mars, a work that is highly indicative of the ethnic and cultural mixtures of the late fifth century. Worked in forms nearest to "classical" Greek style, donated by a Celtic woman, was found in an Umbrian sanctuary. The dedication accompanying it was written in Umbrian, but with a southern Etruscan alphabet. Over time, even the structural form of certain buildings came to resemble those of Orvieto. Though it symbolizes the Romans' expansion into the area, the sacred building of Urvinum Hortense (Collemancio di Cannara), begun in the late third century or early second century B.C., presents architectural standards similar to those of the temple of Belvedere in Orvieto. It is important to note that both structures contain references to "Vitruvian" models.

Etruscan models and structures, especially those of Volsinii, are also reflected in the attention of bordering cities. An example is the cippus with *tular larna* in nearby Bettona, dating to the same century as that of the temple of Collemancio. The Umbrian valley appears to have been tightly connected to internal Etruria, even when the latter was under Roman command. Proof of this is provided by names of Etruscan origin that have survived in epigraphic documents, or by the haruspex from Bevagna claimed to be Volsinian, or the type of worship practiced at Villa Fidelia in Spello, which continued well into the late Antiquity, as attested by the famous Constantinian *Rescript*.

Etruscan presence in the Adriatic is evident from the widespread inscriptions, probably of local origin—though this cannot be proven in all cases. The ceramics of Vasto, with their Etruscan graffiti, date from the mid-sixth century to the fourth or third century B.C. At Ostra an inscribed *dolium* mentions among the wine-producers in the *ager Gallicus* the work of someone perhaps from Perugia. These findings increase the number of testimonials offered by materials that have already been mentioned as well as many others, such as the relief mirror of Atri or of the gold wares, also from Vulci, found in the tombs of the Senones.

Relations between Etruscans and Italics, deduced from archaeological and epigraphic evidence, are supported by historical events, which also emphasize the continuity of the bond over the centuries. The Etruscan expedition of 524 B.C. against Cuma confirms an alliance with the "Umbrians, the Daunii, and many other Barbarians" (Dionysius of Halicarnassus, VII, 3, 1). At the opposite chronological pole, solidarity resurges during the conflict with Rome, when, in their final attempt to push back the Romans in the "battle of the nations," in 295 B.C., Etruscans, Umbrians, Gauls, and Samnites side against the invaders in Sentino. The consequences of the defeat and the reactions of Rome primarily affected internal Etruria.

Given the need for succinctness, in discussing relations between Etruscan districts (Tyrrhenian, Po Valley, and Campania) and the outlying Italic districts, the focus has been on the contacts between Etruria itself and the central portion of the peninsula. Nonetheless, the Etruscans equally influenced the evolution of northern Italian cultures (from the peoples of the Veneto region to those of the Alpine areas and the part of Liguria that bordered Tyrrhenic Etruria, extending to the lands of the Celts, who brought an end to the Etruscan dominion of the Po Valley) and those of Sabellian origin, who, inhabiting the more internal areas of the South, invaded the Etruscan settlements of the plains in Campania. Essentially, the multiplicity of relationships can only strengthen the claims of the ancient sources cited at the beginning, supporting Cato's opinion, which, at least on a cultural plane, in "Tuscorum iure paene omnis Italia fuerat" (that is, Italy was dominated by the Etruscans).

Among the countless works dealing in recent years with the study of Italic populations, aside from the Proceedings of the seminars of the Istituto di studi etruschi e italici on the single cultures, of great relevance are the miscellaneous books edited by G. Pugliese Carratelli in the Antica madre *series, and, for Rome, the Storia di Roma series overseen by A. Momigliano and A. Schiavone; its first volume (1988) contains M. Torelli's essay on the pre-roman populations: "Le popolazioni dell'Italia antica: società e forme di potere,": pp. 53–74. New discoveries and revised material have been dealt with in the catalogues of recent exhibitions:* Cristofani 1990b; Guzzo, Moscati, Susini 1994; Emiliozzi 1997; Pacciarelli 1997. *For documents on the center-Italic area we should point out for the Umbrians:* Roncalli 1988–91; Feruglio, Bonomi Ponzi, Manconi 1991; *the volumes devoted to archaeological finds in the series overseen by M. Montella,* Catalogo regionale dei beni culturali dell'Umbria; Bonamente e Coarelli 1996; Bonomi Ponzi 1997. *For the middle Adriatic area: La civiltà picena nella Marche* 1992; Paci 1993; Campanelli, Faustoferri 1997; Colonna 1999; D'Ercole, Cairoli 1998; Catani, Paci 2000; Naso 2000, *from the* Biblioteca di Archeologia *series, overseen by M. Torelli, containing other monographies on pre-Roman civilizations. For other studies and some specific monuments mentioned in the text, see also:* Colonna 1984b, pp. 95–105; Colonna 1992, pp. 13–45; Torelli 1992, pp. 249–74; Cristofani 1996a; Cristofani 1997b, pp. 173–89; Coen 1998, pp. 85–97; Colonna 1999b, pp. 19–29; d'Agostino 1999b, pp. 81–88; Esposito 1999; Maggiani 1999, pp. 47–71.

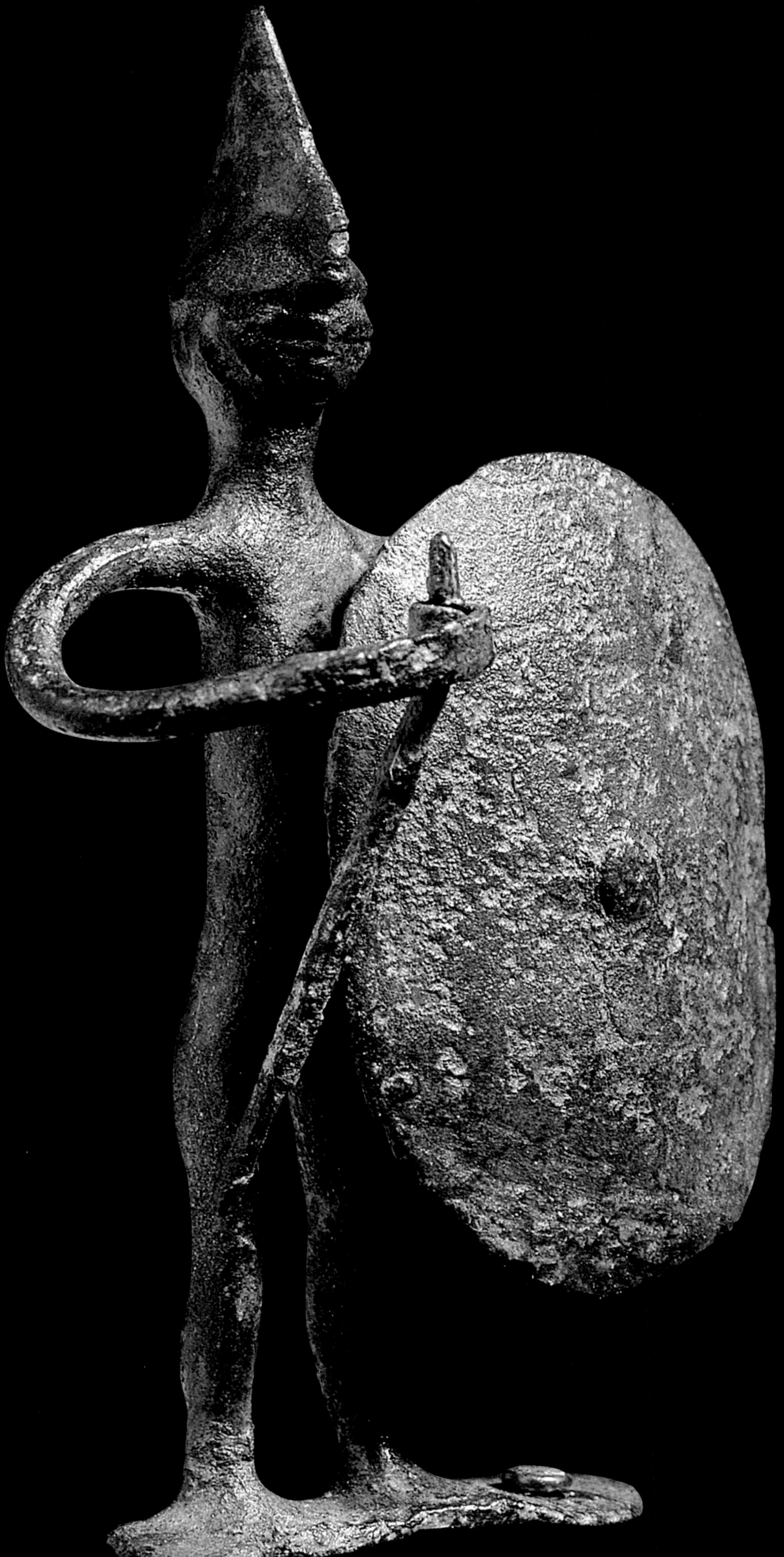

Loredana Capuis

The Etruscans and the Veneti: Forms of Exchange and Processes of Acculturation

Northern Italy, given its location, appears to have had an important role in the history of international exchanges between the Mediterranean world, the Italic peninsula and central Europe, geographic areas that appear to have been, for the most part, connected to the exploration, production and sale of metals. In particular, recent findings and more in-depth studies have contributed to an increased knowledge of the relationship between the Veneti—whose territory extended from the Adige to Tagliamento Rivers, and from the Po Valley to the Alps—and the Etruscans, undisputed protagonists of the north-south trade route.

Already by the end of the Bronze Age, between the eleventh and ninth centuries B.C., there was a systematic connection between the Tyrrhenic region and the northern Adriatic areas, evidenced by the documented diffusion of certain products that were typically Etrurian: "pani a piccone" (lingots for transportation), "palette a cannone" (perhaps used in working bronze), and "asce ad alette" (particularly prestigious objects). Such artifacts were especially numerous in Frattesina di Fratta Polesine (Rovigo), a locality on a northern branch of the Po River, at the old coastline. Frattesina was characterized by a prosperous, productive economy, and by an artisanship that was unusually specialized for its time. Such artisanship was undoubtedly born of a remarkable skill in purchasing and transforming raw materials and finished products, which were manufactured for commercial purposes: from bronze to amber, from glass paste to ivory and even ostrich eggs. A great part of the commercial-cultural factors that involved the post-Mycenaean Mediterranean region, the proto-Etruscan Tyrrhenian area, the Po Valley, and transalpine Europe were centered in Frattesina, which consequently became an Adriatic stopping point along the "new" Etruscan pathway for metals and the north European pathway for amber.

Although it is unclear whether some Etruscan people contributed to its birth, it is unquestionable that the economic-cultural system that originated in Frattesina greatly influenced the areas in which the Veneti, artificers of one of the most remarkable cultural phases of pre-Roman Italy, gradually began expanding their cultural heritage. At the beginning of the Iron Age, when, following a series of events (the worsening climate and the consequential swamping of the territory, as well as a change in the political and economic axes), the hegemony of Frattesina and the Delta area declined, Este gained control of the region. One of the leading centers of the pre-Roman Veneto region, Este also inherited supreme rule over the relationship with the Etruscan world, which by then was centered along the course of the Adige River. In fact, until the end of the eighth century, Este and the Veronese area (to which Este was connected by a coherent territorial scheme), though they had an autonomous character, appear to have gravitated toward the culture of Villanova. This is attested by the shapes of the objects, the motifs, the decorative techniques of the vases, and the types of metal objects (*fibulae*, brooches, razors, knives), which are very similar to artifacts manufactured in Tyrrhenic Etruria and Bologna. Este's close connection with the Etruscans is apparent not only in the types of materials used in its productions, but also in the funerary traditions, rituals and ideologies that characterized its culture. Examples are some richly adorned male tombs, attesting the use of bronze vases as ossuaries, the custom of wrapping the defunct person's bones in a cloth, the references to elitist activities such as hunting and carpentry, and the presence of swords, whose very limited use emphasized their quality as a status symbol. Of particular relevance to this funerary ideology of heroism is the small bronze warrior sculpture of Lozzo, a precious object that can be attributed to a northern Etruscan tradition on the basis of its linear, schematic form.

In addition, beginning in the mid-eighth century, the tombs of aristocratic males contained bronze vases used for holding liquids. A tripod and a ribbed cup, both manufactured in Vetulonia, are the most evident examples of exchanges-gifts between leaders, a custom dictated by the ceremonial canons of aristocratic reciprocity-homologation.

The imported objects selected for the tombs of female aristocrats also reveal an emerging attention to rank. In fact, it is in these very tombs that throughout the seventh century the ideal of the aristocratic life upheld by the peoples of Este reflected that society's similarity with the Etruscans. Sumptuous clothing was combined with garish breastplates-pendents adorned with glass paste pearls, bone, amber, coral, faience figurines reminiscent of Egyptian artifacts, necklaces, bronze plates and discs covered with goldleaf to be appliquéd on the

Bronze statuette of a warrior from Lozzo, mid-eighth century B.C. Este, Museo Nazionale

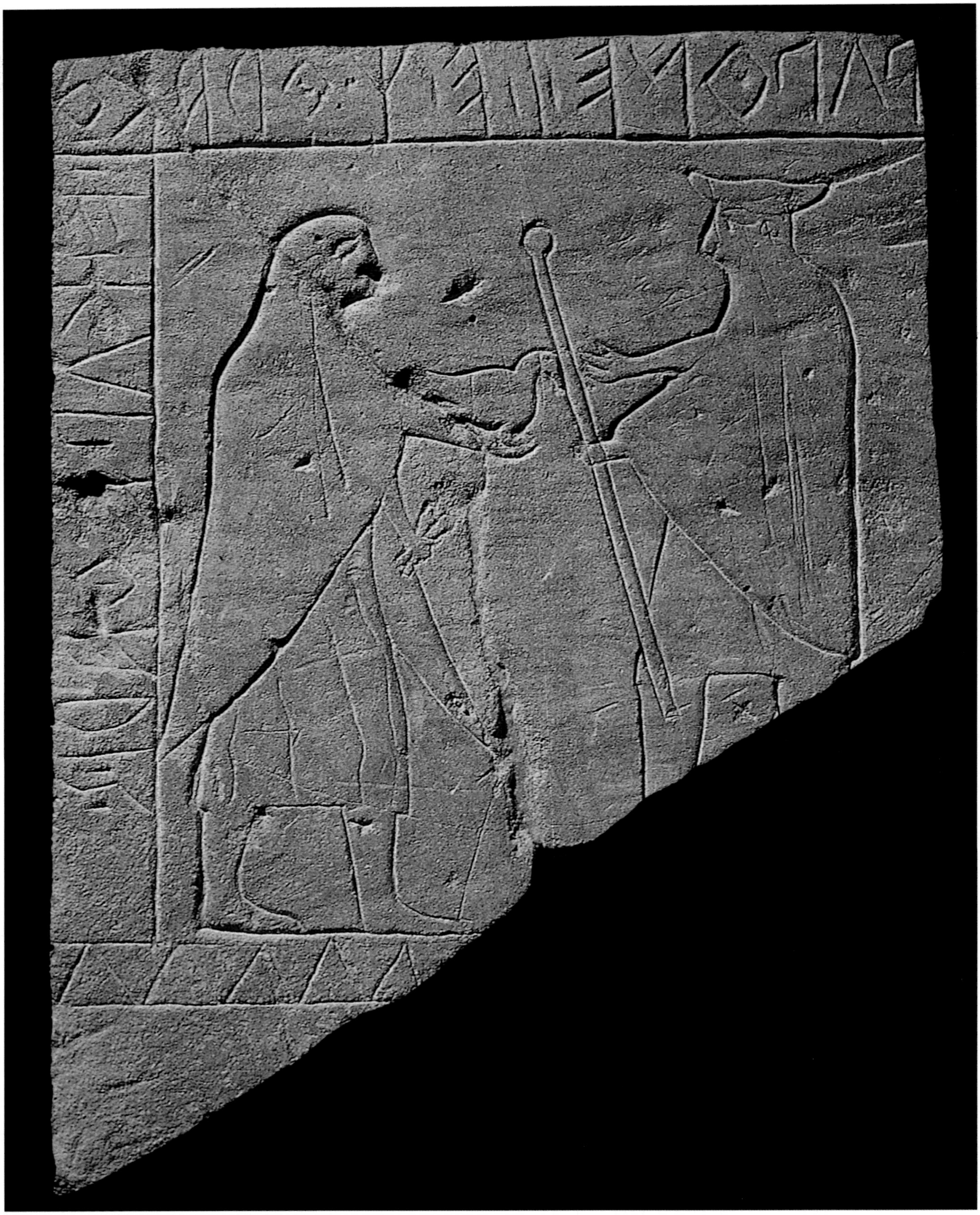

Funerary "patavina" stela in Nanto stone from Camin, sixth–fifth century B.C. *Padua, Museo Civico*

gowns. Most of these "exotic" materials indicate a relationship with Vetulonia, very likely mediated by Bologna, where similar imports have been found.

It is obvious, therefore, that the Veneto region was actively involved in the phenomenon of Tyrrhenian Orientalizing. This is evidenced by the ostentation of personal objects of luxury and by materials that not only reflect the exchange of ceremonial gifts, which was so inculcated in the relationships between north and south—along the trade route of metals, amber, salt, coral and horses—but especially the diffusion of a mentality whose tendency to homologization was a consequence of emulation, as well as, possibly, of the presence of artisans who took part in the exchanges between princely courts. The sudden and almost concomitant appearance of a common style, iconography and narrative expression, toward the end of the seventh century, in the Veneto region and elsewhere, can only be explained by the presence of common skilled workers, of itinerant artisans entrusted by a variety of commissioners. This common language was at times adapted in the production of specific objects, which, being genuine samples of a true local production, were characterized by themes that reflected the various indigenous realities of the cultures: bronzes and ivories between Chiusi and the Ombrone Valley, a tintinnabulum in Bologna, a helmet in Pitino, a wooden throne in Verucchio, and bronze vases (*situlae*) in Este.

The production of objects in bronze plate with figure decoration, the so-called "art of the *situlae*," is the most important example of art in the Veneto. Uncontested masterpiece is the *situla* found in the Benvenuti Tomb 126 in Este, dated to 600 B.C. Inside the vase was a small clay ossuary, which contained the ashes of a young child (1–3 years). Such an artifact denotes that the child was an aristocrat, in accordance with a funerary tradition that was common to Etruscan culture. Unlike previous objects, which were connected to exchanges between leaders, this artifact denotes the person's hereditary prerogatives, regardless of age. The scenes that adorn the three fasciae (a hunt, games, a banquet, war, and agriculture), evidence the identity of an elite aristocracy, which, in order to resemble Etruscan princes adopted the iconographic language of their culture, even if the innermost significance of the "local" message continues to elude us.

This method of communicating through images runs parallel to the introduction of another form of communication, writing, which followed the same route: from Etruria along the inner paths, mediated, once again, by Bologna.

In its most ancient form, this method of communication derives from northern Etruria, perhaps from Chiusi, and it is attested in Este in the first half of sixth century. Toward the end of the century, another system was introduced. Originating in a city in southern Etruria, perhaps Caere or Veii, this system is characterized by syllabic punctuation. The punctuation is connected to the teaching of writing, demonstrated by Este in the most important testimonial of all of pre-Roman Italy, the alphabetic tablets, typical votive offerings (along with styluses) of the sanctuary of the goddess Reitia. These tablets are small models in bronze lamina of the handbooks used at the time to document the consonants and vowels in a manner that makes it possible to form syllables. The first indication of the adoption of this written language is the appearance of stone funerary monuments (cippi in Este and stelae in Padua), bearing the name of the dead person. The most common inscriptions of names are composed of a single name and an appositive, derived from the father's name, according to a binomial system, which, while it is not a true gentilitial, nonetheless emulates the Etruscan model. In addition to blending an Etruscan typology with the formal language of the art of the *situlae*, the Camin stela, the oldest of the Paduan set, bears an inscription of a non-Venetus name. Furthermore, this stela bears the first example of punctuation, so that many scholars have concluded that the consignee must have been an Etruscan living in southern Etruria and who, having settled in the surroundings of Padua, "imported" a new type of funerary monuments and a new writing tradition.

By the end of the sixth century, the Etruscans undoubtedly populated the Veneto region. It was at this time that the historic re-colonization of northern Etruria took place, and one of its centers, Adria, at the Po Delta, assumed the role once played by Frattesina. While the Etruscans must be credited for their knowledge of hydraulics, with which they reclaimed their territory by opening man-made canals aimed at connecting Ravenna to Altino, the Veneti bore the task of improving river and land routes, which the Greeks and the Etruscans

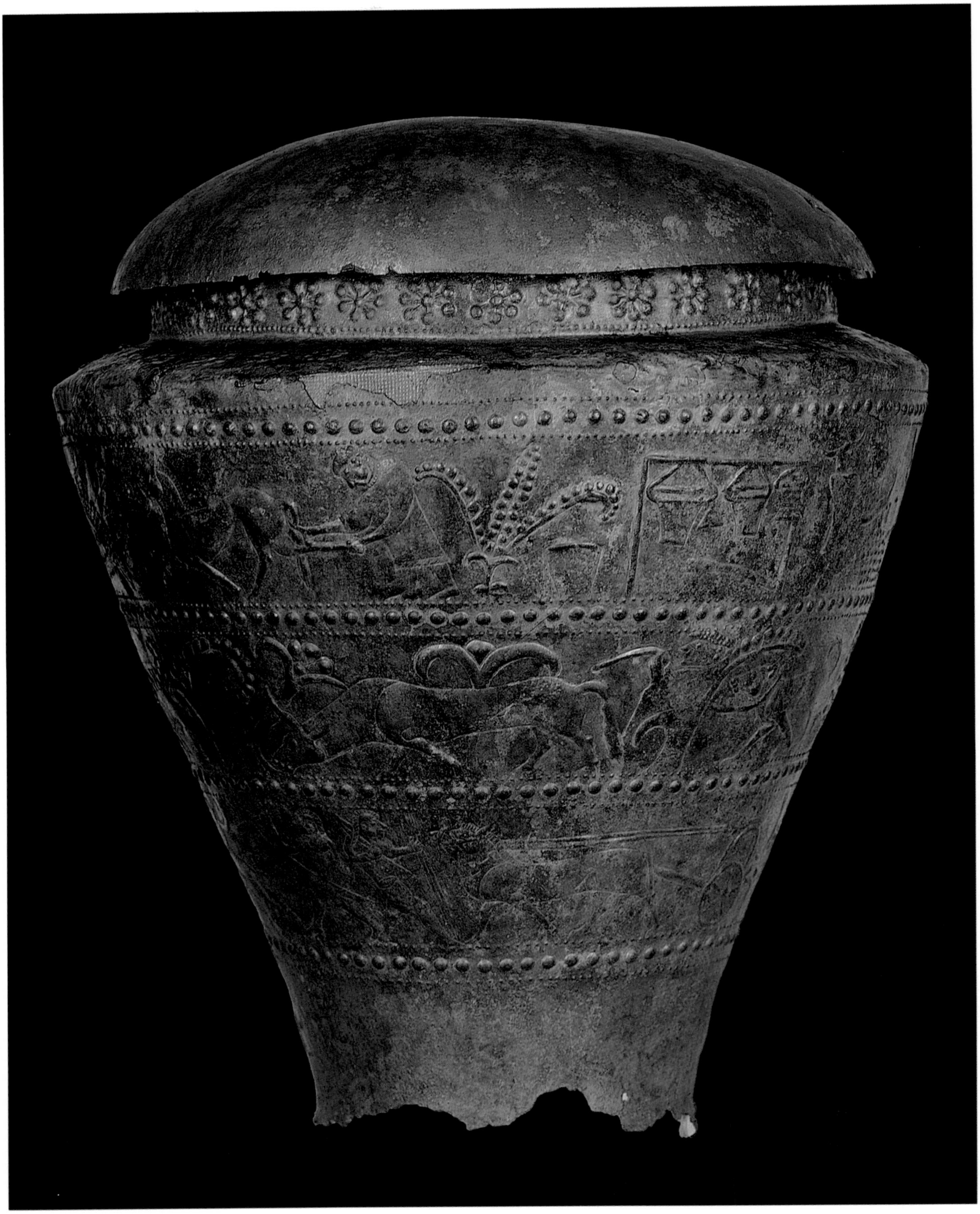

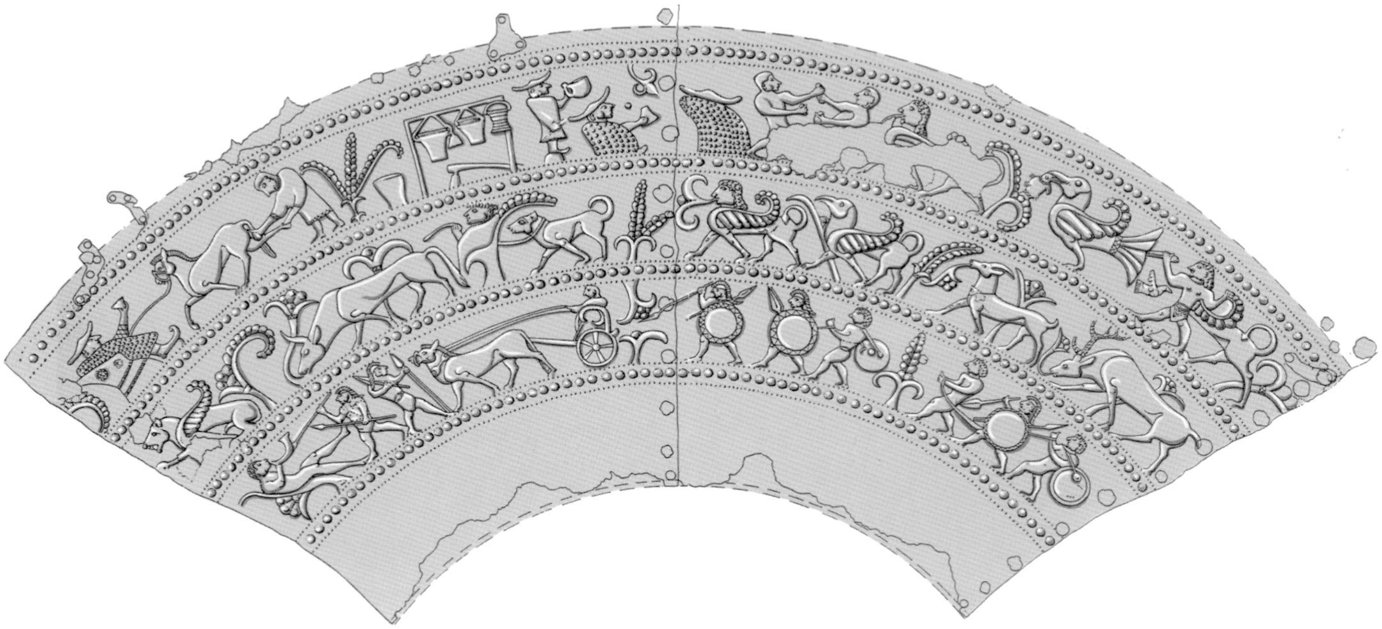

above
Graphic development of the Benvenuti situla

opposite
Bronze situla *from the Benvenuti Tomb 126, ca. 600* B.C. *Este, Museo Nazionale*

employed to transport their products to the Celtic transalpine courts. Furthermore, there is no doubt that the Veneti were present in Adria and in Spina, most likely as merchants.
The rich contents of the tombs reveal that practices and materials related to banquets/symposiums had been adopted. In the tombs there were Greek vases used for drinking (*kylikes* for men, and *skyphoi* for women), black glaze and "etrusco-padana" pottery, as well as instruments for drinking wine and roasting meat. The Veneti, however, were not passive acquirers of customs and products; rather, they adapted the ideologies through an evolved process of acculturation, which led to a modification of the productive standard of artisanship. In fact, the imports gave rise to a local production of emulated grey, semi-purified ceramics. In addition to the basic artifacts (cups, glasses, pitchers, mortars), a clay *Schnabelkanne* stands as a sample of an imitation of Etruscan bronzes, just as the small *situlae*, kraters, ladles, filters, strainers, tripods for the consumption of wine, andirons, spits, springs for cooking meat, adzes and knives for slaughtering are all examples of local manufacturing. Etruscan influence on public and community life is especially manifest in the realm of religion, which, however, was once again more than a passive adoption of products and customs. Religious influence became a model for behaviors and production, and was adapted by the Veneti to suit their purposes. Beginning in the sixth century, numerous sanctuaries and small places of worship were established in the more important centers (Este, Padua, Vicenza, etc.), and along the exchange routes. A typical ideological example of Etruscan culture is the location of the shrines outside the urban center, functioning as either a true or a symbolic border. There are many other such examples, however, like their connection to water, the prevailing use of bronze for votive offerings, the miniaturization of the offerings, the rites of passage for both boys and girls, and the practice of a written language. There are but few imported small bronzes, mostly at Adria, along the laguna and the course of the Adige, whereas local production is huge, statuettes and illustrated sheets which, while reflecting northern-Umbrian and Etruscan-Italic typologies, display a lively, expressive taste and style of their own. So the Veneto is constantly engaged in the network of trafficking between Etruscan and transalpine areas, and acculturation processes brought about by the circulation of objects, men and ideas are impressive: during a first stage connections with the mid-western area centered around Este prevailed, to which by the sixth century a more eastern directrix was added, involving Padua and the Adriatic fringe, as attested among others by archaeological excavations under way at Altino.
What did the Veneti have to offer in exchange? First of all their famed horses, but certainly freedom of transit as well, in all probability regulated by "right of way."

De Marinis 1986; Fogolari, Prosdocimi 1988; Capuis 1992; Capuis 1993; Capuis 1999; Capuis, Gambacurta forthcoming.

The Etruscans and the Lands South of Campania

Ancient literary sources, both Greek and Latin, provide only a limited amount of information regarding the relationship between the Etruscans and the part of the Italian peninsula once known as Magna Graecia. It is no coincidence that this information pertains mostly to Campania, a region deeply involved in the complex framework of Tyrrhenic relationships which were so crucial for all the Western peoples. The Greek colony of Cuma, which also belonged to Campania, in 524 B.C. was raided by an expedition in which, for the first time, was recorded the presence, near the "Adriatic" Etruscans, of Celts, Umbrians, and other "barbarians." This term presumably indicates some of the Italic peoples that inhabited almost all of Apulia and the territories of greater part of present-day Calabria and Basilicata, behind the Greek colonies (Dionysius of Halicarnassus, VIII, 3, 1).

The conflictual character of this account—together with the episode of the fortification of the Scilla promontory by Anaxilaos, ruler of Rhegion from 494 B.C., in order to block the Etruscan "pirates" from entering the strait (Strabo, VIII = C257; De Sensi Sestito 1987)—implies a climate of great political instability. Nevertheless, it must not be considered representative of all the relations between the various protagonists, nor must it give rise to the thought that they were strictly juxtaposed in homogeneous and stable ethnic groups.

As was often the case, civilian relationships were not the same as political-military relations. Therefore, though we are aware that the Athenians appealed to the Etruscans to help them in their battle against Syracuse in 415–413 B.C. (Torelli 1975b), we cannot ignore the tradition that places Sybaris near them. Certainly not an anachronistic commercial axis that extended as far as their allied city, Miletus (Will 1972), it was nonetheless a relationship centered on goods of luxury.

If, therefore, we can be certain the Greeks colonies blocked the southern expansion of the Etruscans before it could even take root (Bonghi Jovino 1986b), archaeological findings confirm the existence of an exchange network that, during the Archaic period, involved processes of socio-anthropological rather than explicitly "commercial" nature (Schnapp 1995). This network implies a connection between the Greeks and the Etruscans, largely mediated by the Italics, given the latter's geographical location. Nonetheless, there exists proof that hand-made products (Delpino 1984) were circulating on a large part of the peninsula in the proto-historic period, and, therefore, long before the Greeks settled there (Peroni 1989; Peroni 1993).

The consequences of this migration, which occurred between the eighth and seventh centuries B.C. (certainly the first crucial incident in the history of Italy for which we have a complete historical account), were as deep as they were varied and long-lasting. As far as Italics are concerned, the complete demise of the communities along the coasts, where the colonists had arrived, is counterbalanced by the growth, first of all in population, of the more internal settlements, which were important in terms of both production, and mid-range and long-range communication. This process was undoubtedly favored by the *poleis* themselves, as evidenced by the case of Sybaris, which, according to Strabo (VI, 1, 13 = C263) controlled four *ethne* (tribal clans) and twenty-five *poleis*, evidently inserted within a single and organic political system.

From a socio-cultural perspective, this phenomenon primarily corresponds to the development of dominant individuals and groups (the true governors of the relations with various, external partners), which underwent an intense process of cultural assimilation. "With the adoption of specific customs such as the convivial of the sacred and the profane, based on meat and wine, came the acquisition of kitchen tools and utensils used at banquets. With the adoption of methods of self-representation and of mythical projection came the construction of living spaces (and perhaps of sacred venues, at times decorated with illustrated friezes), subverting the entire 'urban layout' of the habitations, as well as the ulterior elaboration and enrichment of both the ornamental female parures, and the regal and sacral emblems of the atavistic Italic tradition. The same can be said for the solely exhibitory acquisition of the defensive hoplitic panoplies" (Bottini forthcoming).

Research has revealed that the hand-made articles found in the valleys of the Sinni, Agri and Basento Rivers, overlooking the Ionian Sea—which later became the region of Lucania—were often made by the Etruscans (Bottini, Tagliente 1993; Bottini, Setari 1996). Such artifacts were often found in the most significant tombs, provided with grave goods that demon-

Paestum, Tomb of the Diver, detail, 500–450 B.C.

Bronze candelabra with dancer from Vulci, ca. 500 B.C.
Karlsruhe, Badisches Landesmuseum
cat. 231

strate a long lasting structural affinity with their Tyrrhenian homologous. The true "fossil-guide" is the metallic ware that was both very diffused and precocious in its manufacture. In particular, there were many containers, both medium- and large-sized, characterized by their wide body, but there were also drinking vessels (including some *phialai*, whose ceremonial function is of particular relevance) and jugs for pouring wine, including *oinochoai*, especially those traditionally referred to as "Rhodian." In general, these artifacts were part of serial production (according to an archaic notion of "serial"), including some single Greek specimens of particularly high quality. Nonetheless, there were also some unique, and equally important artifacts, evidence of a skilled Tyrrhenian artisan tradition that was commissioned—either directly or mediated by the usual methods of social exchange—by locals (Bottini 1996). At the same time, certain types of typical fine-grained clay ceramic, adorned with "sub-Geometric" decorations, offer evidence of contacts with Tyrrhenian models.

A large number of Tyrrhenian bronzes, including some fifth-century specimens, such as the candelabras from Vulci, can be traced to northeastern Basilicata. This was a "frontier territory" (Lepore 1970) inhabited by different peoples, including those Daunians mentioned previously relative to the attack on Cuma. These peoples gravitated toward Canusium (modern Canosa), almost at the mouth of the Ofanto River, which penetrated the entire area, descending on to the Apennines behind it.

It is probably no coincidence that a similar situation is found along the Adriatic coast, in the bordering district of Peucetia, which main center was Ruvo di Puglia. Although recent studies tend to disagree with the hypothesis that black-figure pottery found *in loco* was produced by Etruscan craftsmen who had migrated to the area (Ciancio 1995), the presence of single, precious artifacts (for goldsmiths, see Guzzo 1993b) among the remains of the necropolises of Ruvo is highly significant, as is the funerary painting style reminiscent of the Tyrrhenian region (Todisco 1994–95; Todisco 1996).

The Daunian area of the Apulian Tavoliere was instead connected to Campania by the more northern Apennine routes, which led to the introduction of not only bucchero wares (not as widespread in any other areas), but also some architectural elements such as the "haloed" antefixes. At the opposite extreme, the peninsula of Salento appears to have had a very small role in this system of land trade (Tarditi 1996). Nonetheless, it cannot be excluded that sin-

Bronze barrel with protomes from Chiaromonte, end of the seventh–beginning of the sixth century B.C.
Policoro, Museo Archeologico
cat. 224

gle Etruscan artifacts arrived on the Apulian coast as a consequence of a sea trade route along the Adriatic, extending to Spina and Adria (De Juliis 1993).

The emphasis of a relationship with at least one part of the Italic community must not diminish the fact that the Greek city-states were fundamental interlocutors for the Etruscans. In part due to the nature of the exchanged merchandise itself (metals and other raw material as well as food products), and in part due to the different destination of such merchandise (except in very rare circumstances, the Greeks very early abandoned the tradition of burying precious objects in tombs), there are very few direct archaeological evidences of Hellenic origin that could provide us with information. The problem becomes even more acute when the commercial aspect of the issue is enlarged by the cultural aspect—augmented in the more advanced stages. It becomes crucial, therefore, to be able to define with some degree of accuracy the conditions of exchange and the contracting parties.

To this end, architecture has been one of the disciplines that have aroused the most interest, considering the relative geographical proximity between many of these cities. The intense exchanges of artistic patterns and designs between the Campanian area, from Cuma to Capua, and the more southern areas, from Hyele (Velia) and Poseidonia (Paestum), has been emphasized since a long time. Paestum, for example, appears to have been the recipient of some northern traditions, especially in monuments such as the hypogean sacellum and the Tomb of the Diver, with its famous mural paintings. On a more general level, however, modern research has adopted a more prudent approach (Prayon 1993; Mertens 1993), preferring to speak in terms of a multiplicity of influences by several Hellenic centers, and of a convergence of phenomena, even those resulting from factual situations (such as the scarcity of suitable stone), as opposed to claiming the existence of a real dependence of the

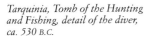

Tarquinia, Tomb of the Hunting and Fishing, detail of the diver, ca. 530 B.C.

Etruscan from the Greeks. A particularly debated issue concerns the decorated clay friezes, as there appears to be a concrete possibility of establishing a connection between them on the basis of the existence of a pathway that allowed communication between Metaponto and the indigenous territory under its influence, centered around Serra and Braida di Vaglio, close to present-day Potenza (d'Agostino, Cerchiai 1999).
Beginning in the mid-fifth century, within an ethnic framework that was very different both politically and culturally from that of the Archaic period—when the changing of the protagonists, Greeks and Italics, involves the weakening of the afore mentioned relations and consequently the diffusion of "good of luxury"—a more direct syntony settles in the field of arts. Thus, in Etruria and Latium, depending on the areas and centers, there was a flow of men as well as of schemes and motifs, in part thanks to the "sketchbooks" that scholars are now beginning to know.
This new phenomenon affected above all painting, in terms of red-figure pottery—developing in a parallel manner in the South and in Etruria, where Athenian artisans began to move (Cristofani 1987d)—as well as in more complicated productions. Some examples are the Tarquinian sarcophagus of the Amazons (now the subject of archaeometric studies), and especially the megalographies that were discovered in Vulci from the François Tomb (Cristofani 1967; Cristofani 1987e). These same schemes are also found in engravings on metal household items such as mirrors and cists, which reveal contacts with Magna Graecia even in plastic ornamentation (Denoyelle 1993; Bordenache Battaglia, Emiliozzi 1986–90). A connection between Greek sculpture has been established (also due to the lack of stone, as mentioned previously), especially given the abundant use of terra cotta throughout the Italian peninsula well after the Archaic age. This can be attested especially in late fourth-cen-

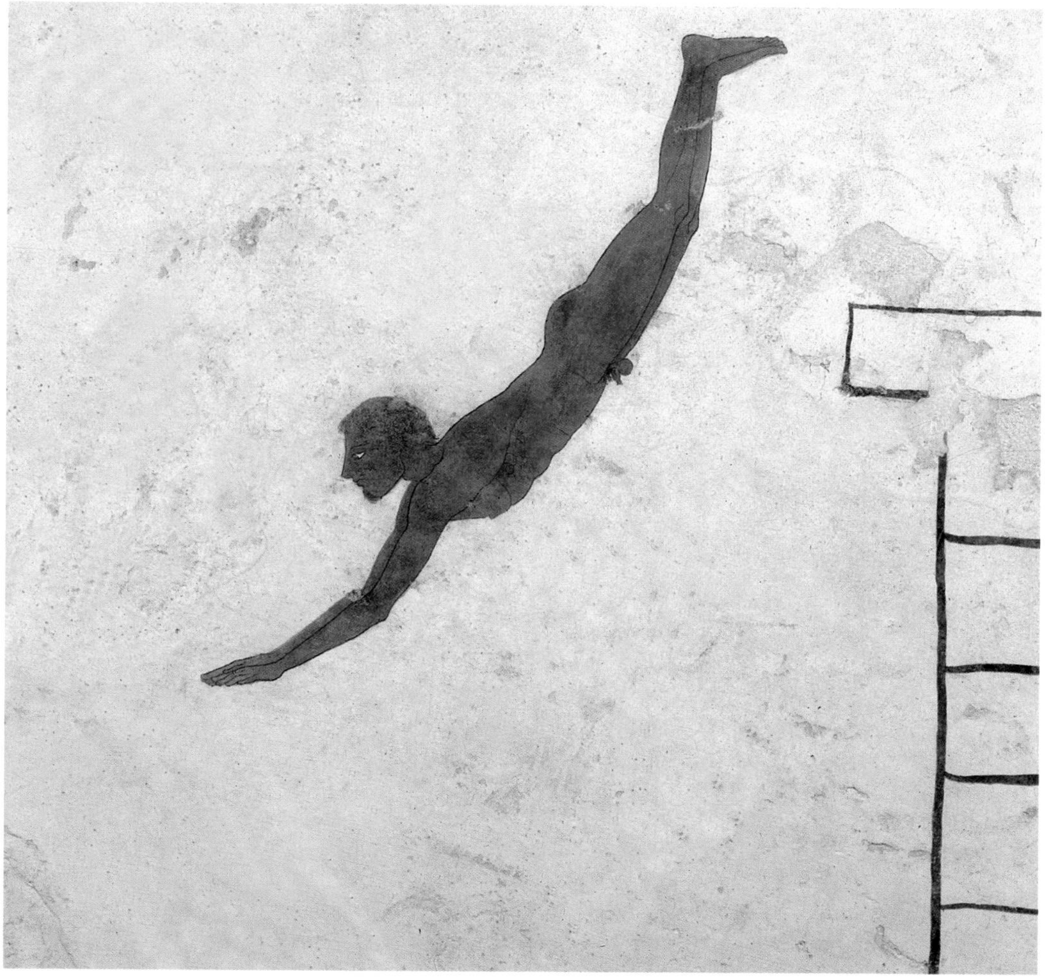

Paestum, Tomb of the Diver, detail, 500–450 B.C.

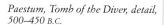

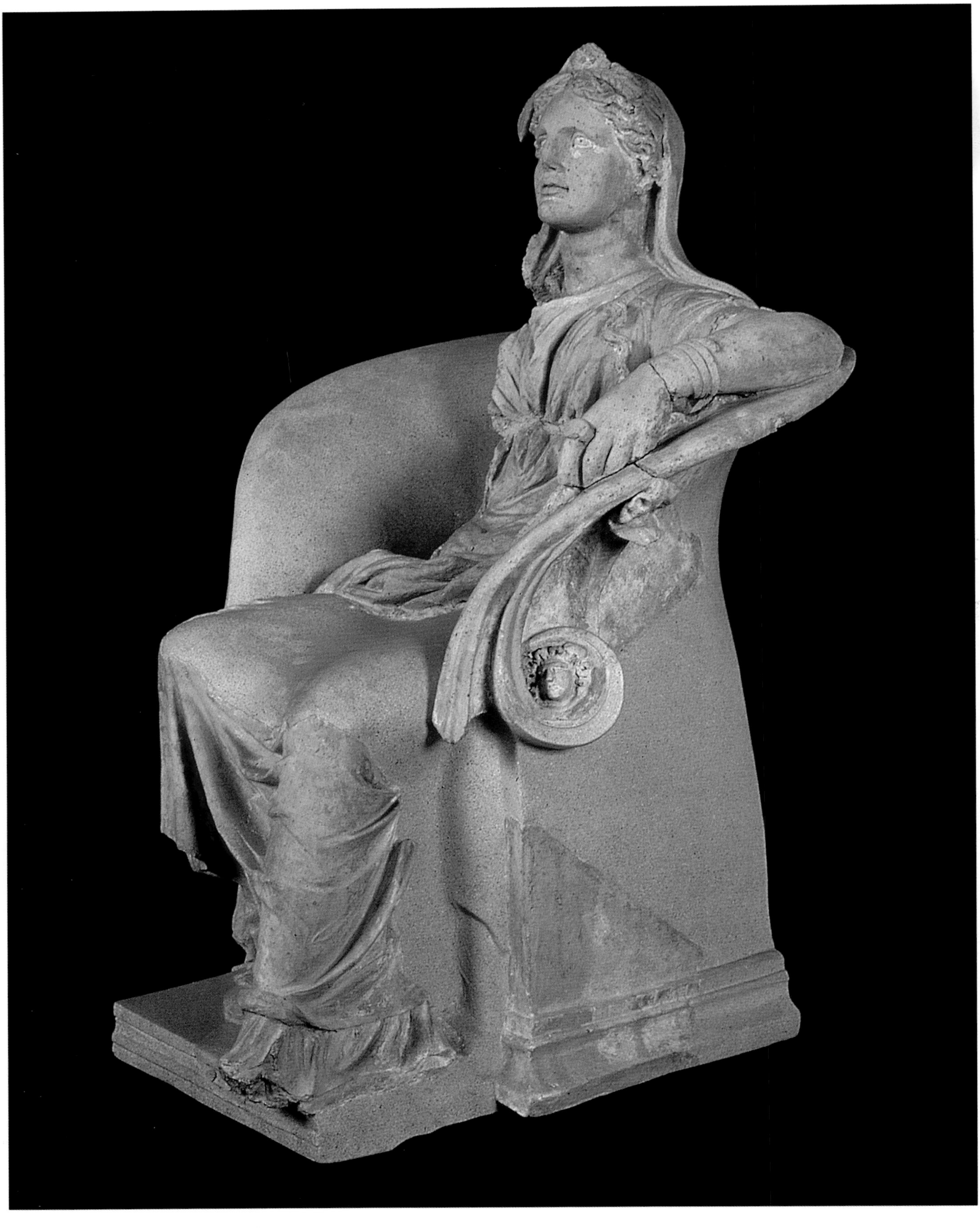

right
Terra-cotta female bust from Ariccia, fourth century B.C.
Rome, Museo Nazionale Romano

left
Terra-cotta female figure from Ariccia, fourth century B.C.
Rome, Museo Nazionale Romano

tury Latium, thanks to the large number of statues and busts that were found in Ariccia (Orlandini 1983). In the Faliscan territory, instead, the sanctuary of Scasato demonstrates typically Italiot qualities (Comella 1993).

All of these discoveries have led to recognizing Taranto as a center of irradiation. This function—real though not exclusive (Guzzo 1987)—takes its place in the larger context of the phenomena of cultural exchanges between the Etruscans, the Greeks and the Italic *ethne* (whether they had already been active for long time, like the Apulians, or more recently, like the Lucanians). This function is also evident in the area of religious-philosophical beliefs, as attested by the diffusion of eschatological views, in which Dionysian salvific beliefs play a rather significant role. Such views were transmitted by the images principally found on the ceramics (Massa-Pairault 1992).

Cristofani 1967, pp. 186–221; Will 1973, pp. 21–67; Lepore 1975, pp. 43–58; Torelli 1975a; Orlandini 1983, pp. 331–554; Delpino 1984, pp. 257–71; Bonghi Jovino 1986, pp. 717–23; Bordenache Battaglia, Emiliozzi 1986–90; De Sensi Sestito 1987, pp. 229–304; Guzzo 1987, pp. 35–39; Cristofani 1987d, pp. 43–53; Cristofani 1987e, pp. 199–203; Pailler 1988; Peroni 1989; Comella 1993; Guzzo 1993b; Peroni 1993; Bottini, Tagliente 1994, pp. 487–528; De Juliis 1994, pp. 529–60; Denoyelle 1994, pp. 281–93; Mertens 1994, pp. 195–219; Prayon 1994, pp. 183–93; Todisco 1994–95, pp. 119–42; Ciancio 1995, pp. 71–86; Bottini 1996, p. 97 ff.; Bottini, Setari 1996, p. 57 ff.; Tarditi 1996; Massa-Pairault 1997, pp. 325–53; d'Agostino, Cerchiai 1999; Schnapp 1999, pp. 63–69; Todisco 1999, pp. 435–65; Bottini forthcoming.

Mauro Menichetti

Political Forms in the Archaic Period

For sailors of the Mediterranean between the ninth and the eighth centuries B.C., Phoenicians, Levantines, Greeks from Euboea, the western limits of the world were at the level of Campania, where tradition located the Avernus, the entrance to Hell. This was Hesperia, the remote West bounded by Ocean (Mele 1991). The isle of Ischia, the ancient Pithekoussa, already by name matches the island of monkeys (Greek *pithecos*), meaning the dwelling-place of creatures midway between men and animals, those who inhabit deserted areas (Torelli 1994a, Cerchiai 1996). In this very ancient ethnography, Pithekoussa is placed at the end of the world, where the realm of Hades begins, on a horizon felt to be marginal compared to the well-known courses and countries inhabited by bread-eating men.

The poet Hesiod (*Theogonia*, vv. 1011–1016) recalls that the sons of Odysseus and Circe, Latinus and Agrius, ruled the Tyrrhenians: the kingdom of the Tyrrhenians is located in the "blessed isles." These lie beyond the limits of the world and of Ocean, fantastic places full of wonders but fraught with danger too, and for that very reason befitting places for heroes' feats, like the islands of the Sirens and of Circe, located also on the Tyrrhenian shores. Herakles, to gain the island of Erytheia where Geryon's immortal oxen pasture, must sail westward aboard the bowl of the Sun (d'Agostino 1995b). On Achilles' shield described by Homer (*Iliad*, XVIII, 483–607), the boundaries of the inhabited world are marked out by Ocean's currents.

In the "blessed isles," so it was said, Latinus and Agrius rule over the Tyrrhenians. So in one of the oldest available sources, datable between the seventh and the sixth centuries B.C.—the verses mentioned are held to come after the rest of Hesiod's work—, the Tyrrhenian area is shown as being ruled by kings.

The successive literary tradition is unanimous in qualifying the most ancient history of Etruria and Latium as a royal age: the kings of Alba Longa, Romulus and his successors, the dynasty of the Etruscan kings of Rome, the tale of Mastarna-Servius Tullius, Porsenna, king of Chiusi. Archaeology, on the other hand, adds to the record with a pottery fragment bearing the inscription *rex* coming from the *regia* of Rome datable to the late sixth century B.C. (Cristofani 1990b), or with the royal figure of Thefarie Velianas attested by the Pyrgi plaques (*Göttin von Pyrgi* 1981) but, above all, with a henceforth vast, capillary documentation that attests the existence in the archaic Tyrrhenian world of a marked social differentiation, henceforth lasting, that puts at the head of the communities leaders we can define as *principes* or *reges* (Torelli 1988b; d'Agostino 1999b; Carandini, Cappelli 2000).

Elsewhere this catalogue (in particular the essays by L. Cerchiai and A. Naso) explicits later aspects of the political, social, economic and cultural forms pertaining to the formation of the Etruscan world and closely connected with the themes dealt with here. Our contribution aims at establishing the principal stages of the constitution and the related symbologies of archaic royalty in the Tyrrhenian area, which was to disappear at the end of the sixth century B.C. in connection with the isonomic trends under way in the various *poleis* at the time.

Tyrrhenian royalty of the Archaic age is a part of the processes leading to a lasting social differentiation within the First Iron Age communities. To define it univocally is impossible and would not reflect reality: we can attempt to define it through a multitude of incentives and references that vary in time depending on the communities involved. We should in turn consider different contexts, traditions, monuments, taking into account the complexity of archaic thought, deeply influenced by religion. The particular lifestyle that qualifies the Tyrrhenian lords retains several essential, recurrent elements: the display of insignias of political-religious power and of wealth involving exotic objects and ceremonies, the elevation of genealogy, a privileged relationship with death and with the gods and, as of the seventh century B.C., the identification of their own conduct with that of the heroes of Greek myths. These *principes* in fact tend to present themselves each one as a *rex* within his own social background, whether that be the *familia* or the more or less enlarged *gens*, the *curia* or the *populus*.

In order to present coherently the outstanding evidence of a rather complicated material, involving space and time, we shall refer to four main phases that seem likely to illustrate the changes and developments under way: the original stages of the passage from Bronze Age to Iron Age; the stabilizing of social differentiation in the course of the eighth century B.C.; the

Stamped terra-cotta wall-facing slab from Velletri, detail, ca. 530 B.C. Neaples, Museo Archeologico cat. 168

Terra-cotta helmeted head from Poggio Civitate (Murlo), 580-570 B.C.
Murlo, Antiquarium
cat. 140

Terra-cotta bearded head from Poggio Civitate (Murlo), 580–570 B.C.
Murlo, Antiquarium
cat. 138

heightening of an idiom of power thanks to the seventh-century B.C. Orientalizing contribution and, last, the arising during the sixth century B.C. of a royalty that, by then in the midst of a dialectic with the urban structures, wraps itself in more complex, sophisticated symbologies and ceremonies which, however, have their roots in the preceding stages.

A first piece of evidence: the relationship with the gods

At Ceri, near the ancient Caere, there is the Tomb of the Statues that owes its name to two sculptures carved in the tufa, damaged by time but extremely important. The tomb features an access *dromos*, an entrance hall and a chamber with beds for the deceased. The statues are placed in the second room, appearing solemnly seated on thrones, slight variations revealing the attempt to differentiate the two figures (Colonna, von Hase 1984).

The placing of the statues in the entrance hall or in a room preceding the deposition room, as usually occurs in the tombs of Etruria (Prayon 1975a), and the comparison with the passage in Virgil (*Aeneid*, VII, 177–191) referring to the royal palace of the Latin king Picus, allow us to understand that these are statues of forefathers, the *imagines maiorum* displayed in the atrium of the Roman house and borne in procession at the solemn funerals of Roman patricians. The stylistic and iconographic analysis has revealed for the two statues the influence of Oriental models, specifically from northern Syria, and a chronology between 690 and 670 B.C. At the beginning of the seventh century B.C. an Etruscan *gens* displays its forefathers, placed in a context recalling the Etrusco-Roman house, like Oriental sovereigns seated on a throne and holding the attributes of their power.

The latter reveal the same combination of elements. The statue on the left carries a scepter or a fan, very ancient symbols of Oriental royalty, while the other holds a lituus. This coincides with one of the original attributes of archaic royal figures in the Tyrrhenian area, then passed on to the augur, which reminds us of the possession of the *imperium* based on the correct interpretation of the gods' will. In other words, the translation of the Oriental attribute of power, present on the other statue and yet not without connections with the divine, corresponds to the lituus, symbol of the archaic kings' divinatory capacities.

That aspect, associating political and religious power, should always be kept in mind in the following analysis.

following pages
Stamped terra-cotta wall-facing slabs from Velletri, ca. 530 B.C.
Neaples, Museo Archeologico
cats. 168; 167; 169; 166

The origins of power

The premises of Tyrrhenian royalty, however, go back even farther than the context of the Tomb of the Statues. For the sake of clarity, we can schematically claim that three elements contribute in varying degrees to the formation of Tyrrhenian royalty: the tradition of outstanding, regal-type figures inherited from the proto-historical stage; the diffusion of models belonging to the *tryphe* and Oriental royalty, owed mostly to Phoenician and Levantine navigation, but also to Euboean and Cycladic circuits; last, the early, lasting contact with the Greek world, which means absorbing Homeric royalty onto which is then grafted the strain of myth.

At the time of the passage to the Iron Age, around 1000 B.C., the Etruscan area, especially the southern part, undergoes a redefinition of housing, creating settlements of about 100–150 hectares, far vaster than the previous dispersed villages, and characterized by an equally significant demographic concentration, as in the cases of Veio, Tarquinia, Vulci, Orvieto-Volsinii, Bisenzio and Cerveteri.

These transformations, although rapid, are preceded by a prolonged phase during the Bronze Age in which there is a succession of modalities of accumulation of wealth, especially metal, and the arising of leaders qualified by the display of symbologies, by their larger residences and, above all, by tombs of extraordinary complexity and wealth compared to usual standards (Guidi 2000). With the affirmation of the Villanovan civilization, the first stage of Etruscan history, that world appears to disappear behind a facade of egalitarianism often mentioned with respect to necropolises between the tenth and the ninth centuries B.C.

This entire process seems to be best explained by a new, radically different way of cultivating the land, now divided in private property (Peroni 1996). Hence the progressive consolidation of an unbalance between social groups capable of taking over ever greater parts of the territory, to the disadvantage of the rest of the population, and resulting in the rising of an aristocratic class, clearly evidenced in the course of the eight century B.C., featuring wealth and military strength.

Actually there is no lack of signs of an early social differentiation, in light of new evidence showing that during the formation of the Villanovan large populated centers, several individuals immediately display authentic insignia of a power that is certainly hard to define but rooted in the family and larger kinship groups. The fact, for instance, is easy to see at Pontecagnano (d'Agostino 1995b) as well as in the Tarquinii area (Zifferero 1995; Delpino 1998). At Pontecagnano part of the male burial goods is connoted by a biconical vase covered with the impasto helmet, a symbolic element in view of the material which, concurrently for instance with the miniaturization of arms in the Latium area but also that of Veii and Tarquinii, recalls the status of the free, warrior adult.

Furthermore the top of the helmet has the shape of a hut roof, beside which appear other like figurations always found on helmets: we are at the start of a long process that emphasizes the claim of ancestry, the importance of genealogies connected with the family group, the promotion in that context of myths and local legends (Carandini 1997). The importance of that ideological principle is reinforced by the diffusion, first in the Latium area then in the Etruscan one, of burials in small hut-shaped urns (Bartoloni, Buranelli, d'Atri 1987).

We should mention in particular the urn with the small modeled figure placed over the door, the incunabulum of the one appearing in monumental dimensions in the forefathers' statues of the *regia* of Murlo placed, during the sixth century B.C., to protect the *princeps*' household (Menichetti 1988). With the small urn we are at the origin of that right of ownership of the *imagines maiorum* that later appears as the prerogative of gentilitial groups. The hut urns and the connected symbology that we find on the helmets covering the depositions represent the nucleus around which develops the most ancient royal ideology in the Tyrrhenian area and, in time, other motifs are formed that work occasionally as a strengthening of the original idiom of power, associated with the growing complexity of social and urban structures.

Ever since the most ancient times a significant role in this situation should be attributed to the Phoenicians. Accustomed to exchanges and connections with various populations, the Phoenicians adapt to the society they come in contact with, founding emporiums, attending sanctuaries that guarantee immunity and order of exchanges, creating actual colonies. The

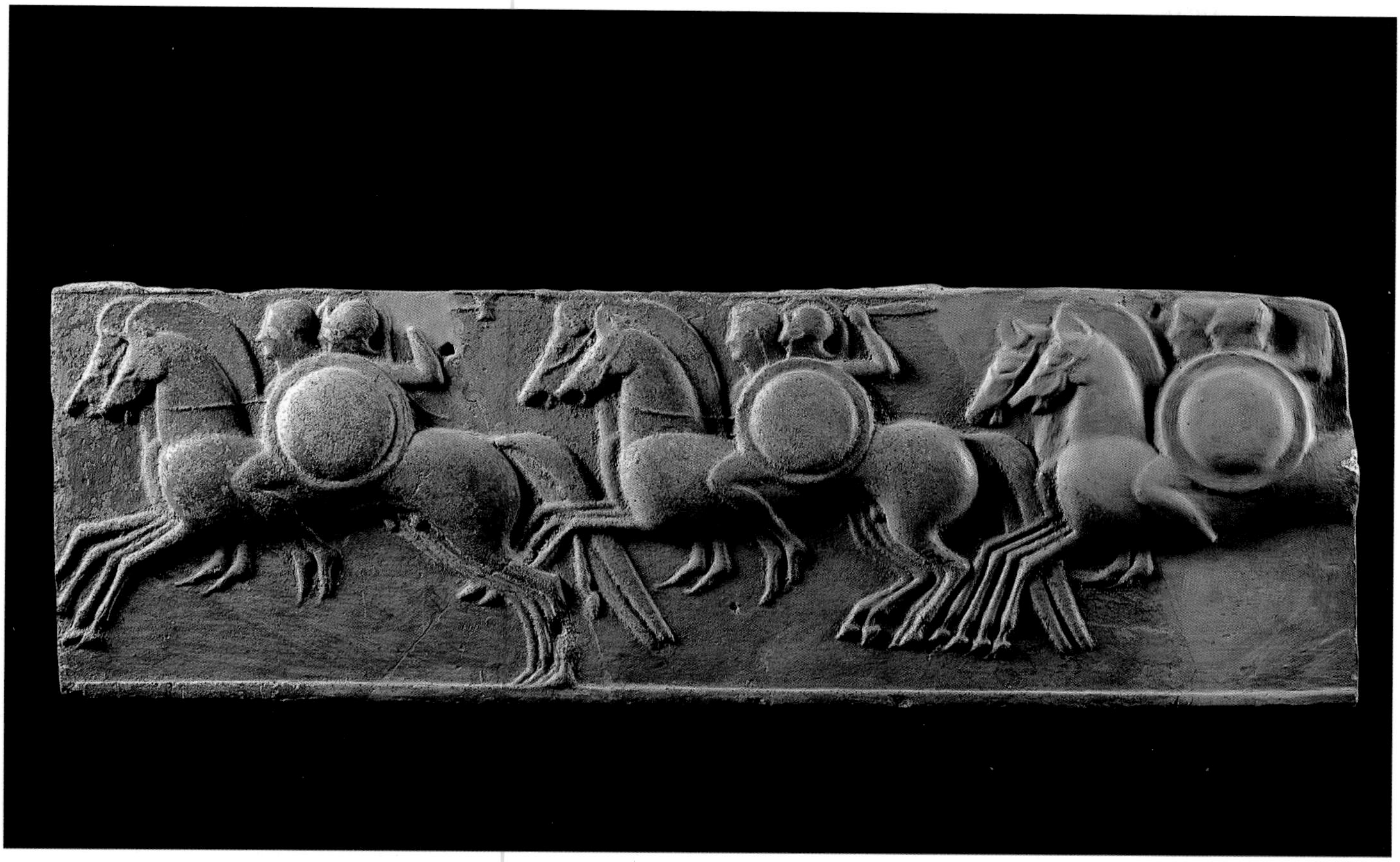

Ceremonial bronze cart from the Olmo Bello necropolis (Bisenzio), second half of the eighth century B.C.
Roma, Museo di Villa Giulia
cat. 14

varied and multiple goods they transport share a particular trait: they are often precious wares, both in material and in processing. And since the transit of goods equally means passing technologies and craftsmanship, ideas, customs, through the Phoenicians the forms of a lifestyle marked by *tryphe*, by luxury, spread throughout the Mediterranean (*Aspetti delle aristocrazie* 1984; Cristofani, Martelli 1994; Torelli 1994b). That lifestyle is first of all the expression of that world with which the Phoenician bases—Tyre, Sidon, Byblos, Arvad—and the other Oriental stations had set up daily connections and exchanges, meaning the kingdoms of the Syrian-Palestinian areas and especially the great Assyrian and Pharaonic empires.

In other words, the *tryphe* of Phoenician goods is the final expression of the forms of ceremony and display of riches, connected with royal power, that availed of a long-standing tradition in the Orient. In particular, we should at least mention the exceptional repertory of images and symbols gathered from the historical Assyrian relief between the ninth and seventh centuries B.C. (Matthiae 1996). Here there are themes, re-visited and re-elaborated with new meanings, such as the king presented as invincible warrior and skillful hunter, processions of captives and wares seized from the vanquished, the warring king on his chariot

Bronze cinerary urn from the Olmo Bello necropolis (Bisenzio), 730–700 B.C. *Rome, Museo di Villa Giulia cat. 15*

following pages
Tumuli of the Banditaccia necropolis (Cerveteri)

or crushing the enemy underfoot, the lion-hunt as metaphor of royal control over the order of nature, and in which the hereditary prince also takes part, the banquet celebration after victory.
These and other like ones are well-known themes in the West, as we see in the remarkable repertory of metal cups of Phoenician make, or in any case Oriental, datable between the eighth and the seventh centuries B.C. (Markoe 1985; Moscati 1988; Amadasi 1991). The greatest number of these pieces was precisely unearthed in the Tyrrhenian area: six from Praeneste, four from Caere, one each from Pontecagnano and Vetulonia and, last, one from Macchiabate in the vicinity of Sybaris in Magna Graecia. The scenes represented are arranged in concentric bands, for example, in two cases we have in the center the pharaoh crushing his enemies, in another the so-called "day of the hunter" with the sovereign leaving the city, overlooking the hunt and the sacrifices, fighting victoriously against a monstrous figure, and then going back to the city.
The other foreign component that was to have a lasting success coincides with the contact with the Greek world, represented first of all by the Euboean connections, responsible among other things for the diffusion of the Homeric *epos*, as we see in the famous Nestor's

bowl from Pithekoussa (Cassio 1994; Murray 1994; Ridgway 1997) datable to the last quarter of the eighth century B.C., and for the westernizing of myths (Mele 1991) that smoothes the way for the reception of Greek mythology in the Tyrrhenian area.
In short, Greek contacts insure the passage and re-elaboration in the Etruscan-Latium-Campania world of a heroic life style, centered on the rituals of consumption of wine, of war and the "beautiful death" of Homeric origin. An extraordinary expression of that world is the famous Homeric description of the shield of Achilles (*Iliad*, XVIII, 483–607), the paradigmatic hero of Homer's world, whose shield displays at center the king surrounded by the fixed stars and, on concentric bands that recall the arrangement of the scenes represented on the above-mentioned Phoenician material, as on the Cretan shields from Mount Ida, the typical institutions of the human community: seasonal work, administering justice, nuptials, war, the initiatory *chorós* of boys and girls placed in the border band next to Ocean.

The structuring of royal power in the course of the eighth century B.C.
The Tyrrhenian *principes'* power already appears firmly established by the eighth century B.C. (Herring, Whitehouse, Wilkins 1991). On the renowned bronze chariot from Bisenzio (Torelli 1997a), there is the description of the life cycle that assembles the family group and nature, the representation of man's valor in war and woman's activity of accumulating wealth, the duel between heroes wielding prestigious arms for the designation of a leader, you might say the *rex* of a *curia* including the gentilitial groups, that we will see acting in the ambit of rites performed around the votive trench of the Tarquinii acropolis, the provenance, among others, of several remarkable bronze insignias of power such as a hatchet, a shield and a trumpet-lituus (Bonghi Jovino 1986a; Bonghi Jovino, Chiaramonte Treré 1997).
On one side of the Bisenzio chariot the family group is represented by the armed man and the woman with the vase, symbol of abundance of grain, hidden underground and felt as similar to the "concealing" of human reproduction, as shown by the archaic calendarial structure of Rome (Torelli 1984), where a sexual gestuality is performed whose consequences are revealed by the presence of the small son, equally figured as armed.
If we have here an iconographic representation of descendance and the valor of ancestry, warrants of the wealth of the *gens*, the need to expand this idiom of power in the decades spanning the eighth and seventh centuries B.C. leads to the building of an exceptional monumental ensemble such as the one recently discovered at Casale Marittimo. There, surrounding the deposition of the *pater familias* according to the most typical Homeric ritual, with the *princeps'* bones gathered after cremation and wrapped in a linen cloth placed in a bronze cinerary urn, the other family members are placed, until the great monumental tomb with *dromos* is installed, marking the moment of the ulterior boosting of the family fortune and the acquisition of the manners of the Orientalizing culture, including raising a palatial residence. Keep in mind among other things, aside from the wealth of bronze and pottery materials, the presence in those tombs' burial goods of elements having a highly exotic and prestigious character, such as the pomegranate, the honeycomb, incense of quality produced only in a small area of Somalia and Arabia, wood of various types and value for the handles of arms and instruments (Esposito 1999; Torelli 1999b).
It was precisely at that time, between the eighth and seventh centuries, that is outlined that "image of power" represented by the dislocation of the funerary tumuli and the first manifestations of those complex residential architectures later identifiable in the archaic *regiae* marking eternal possession of land and its related resources such as metals, grazing, wood.
The tumuli embody an extraordinarily swift qualitative leap, more complex than during the previous stage. The royal power of the Tyrrhenian *principes* now projects outwards, ratifying its own spectacular presence in the territory and producing inevitable conflicts and clashes owing to the affirmation of social and political supremacy. As the Greek-style consumption of wine contains a ceremonial element involving exclusively the aristocratic group, the raising of the funerary tumulus multiplies that value, spreading it over the surrounding territory by means of a real strategy of the image.
The grandiose tumuli having a diameter of 40 to 50 meters that invade the territory of Cerveteri, Tarquinii, Vulci, Vetulonia, Pontecagnano as well as the Latium areas of Castel di Decima, Praeneste, Acqua Acetosa Laurentina, represent above all the power of the gentili-

following pages
Ivory pyxis *from the Pania Tomb (Chiusi), third quarter of the seventh century* B.C.
Florence, Museo Archeologico cat. 170

Gilt silver bowl of the Pharaoh from the Bernardini Tomb (Palestrina), second quarter of the seventh century B.C.
Rome, Museo di Villa Giulia

tial group that is expressed in the various chamber tombs contained inside the structure (Bedini, Cordano 1977; d'Agostino 1977; Bedini 1984; Bedini 1985; Cerchiai 1985; Arietti, Martellotta, Ghini 1987; Zifferero 1990; Naso 1996a; d'Agostino 1999). The concurrent spreading of the bi-member structure of the onomastics (Colonna 1977a) only confirms the evolution under way. An essential part of that power lies in the display of a *tryphe* already apparent in the cost of materials and labor necessary for its execution, echoed by the wealth of the burial goods that include metal and pottery vessels of Oriental and Greek provenance, ivories, jewellery, perfumes, insignias of power, ceremonial structures. The overall layout of these tumuli reveals great, striking likenesses with Anatolian models from Lydia and Phrygia as well as from Salamina of Cyprus, outfits characterized by an extremely eloquent *tryphe* that significantly led to speak of "Midas' tomb" (Prayon 1990; Naso 1998). Even the architectural external decorations of the tumuli go back to North-Syrian models, perhaps brought by Oriental craftsmen, while pictorial decoration appears also, inside as well as outside those structures (Naso 1996b).
Around these prestigious constructions authentic rituals of power must have been performed, as can be assumed from the slopes that must have led to the top of the tumuli, or from the theatrical-style outfitting found in the area in front of the entrance *dromos*, meant to contain the spectators invited to attend the *ludi funebri* (Colonna 1993).
Structures and ceremonies of that kind give us the measure of a hierarchization of the communities, managed by the most influential groups and that results in figures of royal rank who wrap themselves in prestigious, exotic symbols, in special relationships with the gods and with the world of death. The distance spanned since the early stages of the rise of an aristocratic, warring power can also be seen in the process of symbolic relocating of elements previously connected with the military sphere and now passed on to mark a particular status of ownership. That is the case for instance of the shields found among the arms of the Etruscan-Latium depositions of the Final Bronze Age. By the end of the eighth century B.C. the bronze shield seems to have a value exceeding the indication of the warring function of the deceased, and to be invested with themes associated with the celebration of gentilitial continuity (Bartoloni, De Santis 1995). The diffusion in funerary rituals of terra-cotta shields, therefore not functional, that concerns the Etruscan, Latium and Faliscan areas, combined with the procession chariot, indicates the evolution under way. This is also confirmed in iconography by the scenes of the warrior's departure, accompanied by two or three shield-bearers, so the shield seems to refer to a triumph-style celebration as well.
The same process has also been pointed out in the case of the *hasta* in Latium period III, by about the eighth century B.C., echoed by concurrent developments in the Etruscan area. So the *hasta*, that *summa armorum et imperii*, shifts to no longer qualifying the warrior in the narrow sense, but the original unifying power, the *manus*, held by the *pater familias*, and that qualifies him as sovereign (Scarano 1996). The link between *manus* and *hasta*, symbol of the *rex*, moves from the family circle to broader forms of social solidarities, as witnessed by the connection with Mars and Quirinus in Rome's archaic tradition: "Per ea tempora adhuc reges hastas pro diademata habebant, quas Graeci 'sceptra' dixere" (At those times, instead of diadems, kings used to show staffs, which were called sceptres by the Greeks; Justin, *Epitome Trogi Pompei* 43, 3, 3). The above-mentioned Bisenzio chariot may offer one of its oldest iconographic reflections.

"Principes" and heroes of myth

By the seventh century B.C., if not earlier, Tyrrhenian royalty acquired another impressive instrument, that was to prove highly successful. The probable use of local myths in forming the oldest idiom of power has already been pointed out. That is now completed by the figurative and narrative dynamism of mythological tales elaborated in the Greek world.
The advent of the Greek myth (Torelli 1986; Massa-Pairault 1992; Menichetti 1994; Torelli 1997a; d'Agostino, Cerchiai 1999) allows the identification of the Tyrrhenian lords with the great heroic models of the epic poem and its countless reformulations—just think of the work by Stesichorus—enforced even by the oral nature of circulation. Odysseus, Achilles, Herakles, Theseus appear in the scenes illustrated, initiating an entire re-elaboration of the iconographies and related meanings, which is justified by the aspirations of the Tyrrhenian

Drawing of the Castelvetro mirror

Beige terra-cotta olla from Bisenzio, early seventh century B.C.
Florence, Museo Archeologico
cat. 164

principes to elevate their rank to the level of mythical heroes. This idiom of power is new, immensely more suggestive than the preceding one, but at the same time it must flow and enter a pre-disposed channel coinciding with the themes of the oldest idiom of power prepared by the Tyrrhenian aristocracies.

In order to explain such a phenomenon, it is worthwhile referring to at least two pieces, the first Pania *pyxis* from Chiusi and the *oinochoe* of Tragliatella, near Cerveteri, which are a good illustration of the process under way. The two works are also a good example of that stage wherein, faced with the prevailing pressure of the Greek world, the elements of the indigenous world and the renewed ones of Oriental origin remain nonetheless active. In the Pania *pyxis*, datable to the last quarter of the seventh century B.C. (Torelli 1986b; Menichetti 1994; Cristofani 1996b; Minetti 1998), the scenes represented are arranged in superimposed registers allowing a coherent reading from bottom up. The lower band displays the representation, in initiatory terms, of the forest inhabited by real and imaginary animals through which a horseman is riding; in the band above, the *princeps*, preceded and followed by a procession of hoplites equipped with helmet, round shield and spear, climbs on the chariot flanked by the protective rites of the female *threnos* and a dance by warriors in arms suggesting heroic valor and the success of the military undertaking (Menichetti 1998). This symbolic journey ends in the frieze higher up with the representation of a dual scene belonging to the Homeric *epos*: the monstrous figure of Scylla, and Odysseus' and his companions' flight from Polyphemus' cave hanging onto the rams' fleece. Odysseus' victorious exploits warrant an equal success to the exploits of the *princeps*, all contained in a sort of funerary background created by the landscape and the animals in the bands below, by the female *threnos* above, by the obvious references to Odysseus' exploits. Victory concurrently takes on heroic tones strongly associated with overcoming death: the victories of Odysseus coincide with the "beautiful death" of the *principes* attested archaeologically as well by ritual depositions (d'Agostino 1977; Bartoloni, Cataldi Dini, Zevi 1982; Boitani 1983b; Bartoloni 1984; Cerchiai 1984; Esposito 1999).

Power and the victorious outcome of the undertaking whose protagonist is the *princeps* climbing on the chariot are also warranted by another theme. The ivory *pyxis*, already by the material and the metal prototypes inspiring it, like the one we can see in the burial goods of the Regolini-Galassi Tomb (Pareti 1947), refers to the world of the Oriental *tryphe*. If we can discern, outlined behind the departure of the *princeps*, the influence of iconographies connected with the departures of Achilles or Amphiaraüs, the connections with iconographies belonging to

Oriental sovereignty are even more obvious. Compare for instance the analogous scenes present on the decorated ostrich eggs (Rathje 1986) or on the wonderful Orientalizing goldwork like the *lebes* from the Bernardini Tomb of Palestrina (Canciani, von Hase 1979), whose burial goods also contain the patera with the above-mentioned "day of the hunter," or on the bowls of the Regolini-Galassi Tomb of Cerveteri with processions of horsemen, warriors on their chariot and foot-soldiers with round shields, spears, helmets or headwear (Cristofani, Martelli 1983). The difference of rank we can see between the sovereign on the chariot and the horseman recalls, on the model of Assyrian reliefs, the representation of the king and his successor, just as we also see in the next-to-last band of the Pania *pyxis*. All this is confirmed by the countless chariots unearthed in the princes' tombs of Latium (Emiliozzi 1998).

On the Tragliatella *oinochoe*, concurrent with the *pyxis*, the figured decoration is distributed over the neck and the body of the vase, and tells of Theseus' labyrinthian exploit, that has a clear relevance as a royal initiation (Bouke van der Meer 1986; Menichetti 1992; Capdeveille 1993; *contra* Martinez Pinna 1994), translated in terms of rite (frieze on the neck) and myth (frieze on the body). In the latter instance we again have the representation of Arianna's magic gift to Theseus in the nurse's presence, the dance of the *ghèranos* expressed in the style of the *pyrriche*, the exit and rescue from the labyrinth, an infernal place, experienced from the point of view of two horsemen, in all probability the king and his successor who identify their heroic conduct with the titulary of the myth, Theseus. The two kings also take part in the double hierogamy significantly represented on the opposite side of the labyrinth, and the two thrones of slightly different sizes over which a female figure comparable to Arianna-Aphrodite extends her protection belong to them.

Thus the reception of a theme central to Oriental royal tradition is very openly expressed—the sacred union with the goddess—, probably begun long before (Saeflund 1986). The Oriental components of hierogamy on the Tragliatella *oinochoe* are well-exemplified by the Castelvetro mirror, with ceremonial scenes climaxing in a union similar to the one on the *oinochoe* that takes place on a *kline* in the form of a ship, and by the double *protome* of a bird in a space marked by pillars. But the Tragliatella *oinochoe* also provides us with one of the clearest testimonies of an archaic social structure including the age groups of the *juvenes* and of the *equites*, all culminating in the royal figure whose exploits are identified and readapted in the perspective of the Greek myth.

The diffusion of like motifs is confirmed by the recent re-interpretation of the Regolini-Galassi Tomb of Cerveteri, already mentioned for its bowls with processions of warriors (Colonna, Di Paolo 1997). The tomb consists in two basic elements, the entrance hall and the *thalamos*. In the first there are two niches, the one on the right pertaining to a deceased and the one on the left reserved for part of the burial goods. The back opens onto the cell that contains a woman's grave. The new reconstruction proves the existence of two graves and the connection of the burial goods of the left niche to the deceased woman in the cell. In the entrance hall-*dromos* the last part of the funerary ceremony took place, so the woman's corpse, borne in a chariot, was deposited upon a bed present during the sacrificial ceremonies, banquet and ritual acts attested by the various elements belonging to the burial goods. On the walls eight bronze shields were hung, a tangible mark of the deceased's rank, henceforth detached from the original male military role. Later the deceased was deposited in the cell, among her precious personal *keimelia*, the place from which the public part of the funerary ceremony is banned. The structure of the tomb coincides with the heart of the Etruscan-Roman house, which can be identified with the role of *penus* pertaining to the left-side niche that opens onto the entrance hall.

The right niche, pertaining to a deceased, is closed, whereas the cell behind must have appeared closed at mid-height, nearly forming a triangular window interpreted as an element of the *thalamos*, precisely belonging to a queen or a goddess, serving as a sort of epiphany during the rites performed in the entrance hall. The "goddess at the window" coincides with a well-known Oriental mythical structure—present for instance in the decoration of the *kline* of the famous relief of Assurbanipal from Niniveh—related to the accession to royalty on behalf of a hero or a god, on the model of the now well-known rites of Adonis at Gravisca (Torelli 1997e) in the saga of the royal descendence of the Tarquinii in Rome as well (Coarelli 1988; Carandini 1997).

following pages
Wooden male head with traces of golden leaf from Vulci (?), half of the seventh century B.C.
Milan, Civiche Raccolte Archeologiche e Numismatiche
cat. 137

It is interesting to point out that in the case of the Regolini-Galassi Tomb the mythical structure of the "woman at the window" appears in an architectural context entirely identifiable with the fundamental structure of the Etruscan-Roman house, and confirms that the ideology of royalty in the Tyrrhenian world springs from the original cell of the *oikos.*

The sixth century: from "regiae" to "polis"

All the elements mentioned up to now in defining Tyrrhenian royalty since the oldest stages fit and are given a new monumental interpretation in the context of the sixth-century B.C. Etruscan-Latium *regiae*, to which the iconographical cycles of the so-called stage I terra cottas refer (Andrén 1940; Rystedt, Wikander, Wikander 1993). Here again we have the dialectic between myth and rite; the ceremonial moments that mark the ideology of the *principes*; the identification between Herakles' feats and those of the *principes*, exemplary model of the archaic apotheosis; the representation of the rituals of hierogamy (Torelli 1992).

In the extraordinary palatial ensemble of Murlo (Phillips 1993; De Puma Small 1994), toward the second quarter of the sixth century B.C. we again have the three components with which we started off our investigation: the original heart of the *oikos* is now expressed in the monumental forms of a palatial architectural structure, intended to contain an enlarged family under the *manus* of a *princeps* who appears warranted by forefathers placed on the roof (Edlund Berry 1992), on the model of the Villanovan small urn seen above, statues similar to a fragment from the *regia* of Rome (Cristofani 1990b, n. 3. 2. 4) or to the ones recently published by F. Gaultier (Gaultier 1990). In the second place, the atmosphere drawn from the iconographies and the materials unearthed blends with the borrowing of Oriental models in the architectural structure of the palace (Torelli 1985a; Prayon 1990), where we can also see the probable reference that transpires from the plaques with banqueters at the Oriental *marzeah* ceremony, based on consumption of wine and worship of ancestral heroes, the *rapiuma* (Rathje 1988; Rathje 1995; Menichetti forthcoming).

These *regiae* that, by the seventh century and especially in the course of the next, shape a new image of power, are completed by the continuous diffusion of the *princeps*' victorious exploits copied on Herakles' exploits, such as the one against the Nemean lion or the Cretan bull. Beside the latter a female figure appears, a goddess like the one we saw on the Tragliatella *oinochoe*, responsible for helping the hero: a theme tempered by Tyrrhenian references, in the manner of Herakles and Athena used in the Athens of Pisistratus, and that put a goddess-maker-of-kings in the foreground, as in the cases of the remarkable acroterion from Veii (Colonna 1987), the recent rendering of the *regia* of Satricum (Lulof 1997), the Herakles of Sant'Omobono in Rome, the instances of Thefarie Velianas at Pyrgi (see also Verzàr 1980) and the cult of Adonis at Gravisca we already mentioned, occasionally hesitating between a Greek *interpretatio*—Herakles-Athena—or a more openly Oriental one—Herakles-Aphrodite—(Coarelli 1988).

In the course of the seventh century B.C., after the beginning of the processes of urban structuring, we can observe a decisive structuring and canonizing of rituals associated with royal power. We have a very clear example of this process in the triumph ritual in Rome. As we know, the Roman triumph's roots lie in the oldest Salian religion, in turn connected with juvenile rites of passage (Torelli 1990a; Torelli 1999a).

The final ceremonial disposition and affirmation of the triumph takes place under the Etruscan tyranny of the Tarquinii where, in connection with meanings associated with the world of wine and with certain aspects of Dionysiac worship (Coarelli 1995), a man, the king and victor, is identified with the highest divinity, Jupiter Capitoline, albeit for a given time. On a tablet from Praeneste, found in connection with a probable triumphal itinerary, the *rex* leaves the chariot to mount on a biga with winged horses, symbolizing his new condition as triumphant hero (Torelli 1989; Colonna 1992b). Associated with the triumph celebration we find the connection with the *Regia*, where the sacella of Mars and Ops are preserved, meaning the transposition of the original family nucleus in monumental terms within an already established urban structure, seen for instance in the couple of the Bisenzio chariot. Furthermore, in the framework of the triumphal ceremony we see the structuring of those *ludi* (*October equus, Equirria, ludi saeculares*), recalling the ones that originally surrounded the

Bucchero olpe *from San Paolo (Cerveteri), ca. 630 b.c.*
Rome, Museo di Villa Giulia
cat. 212

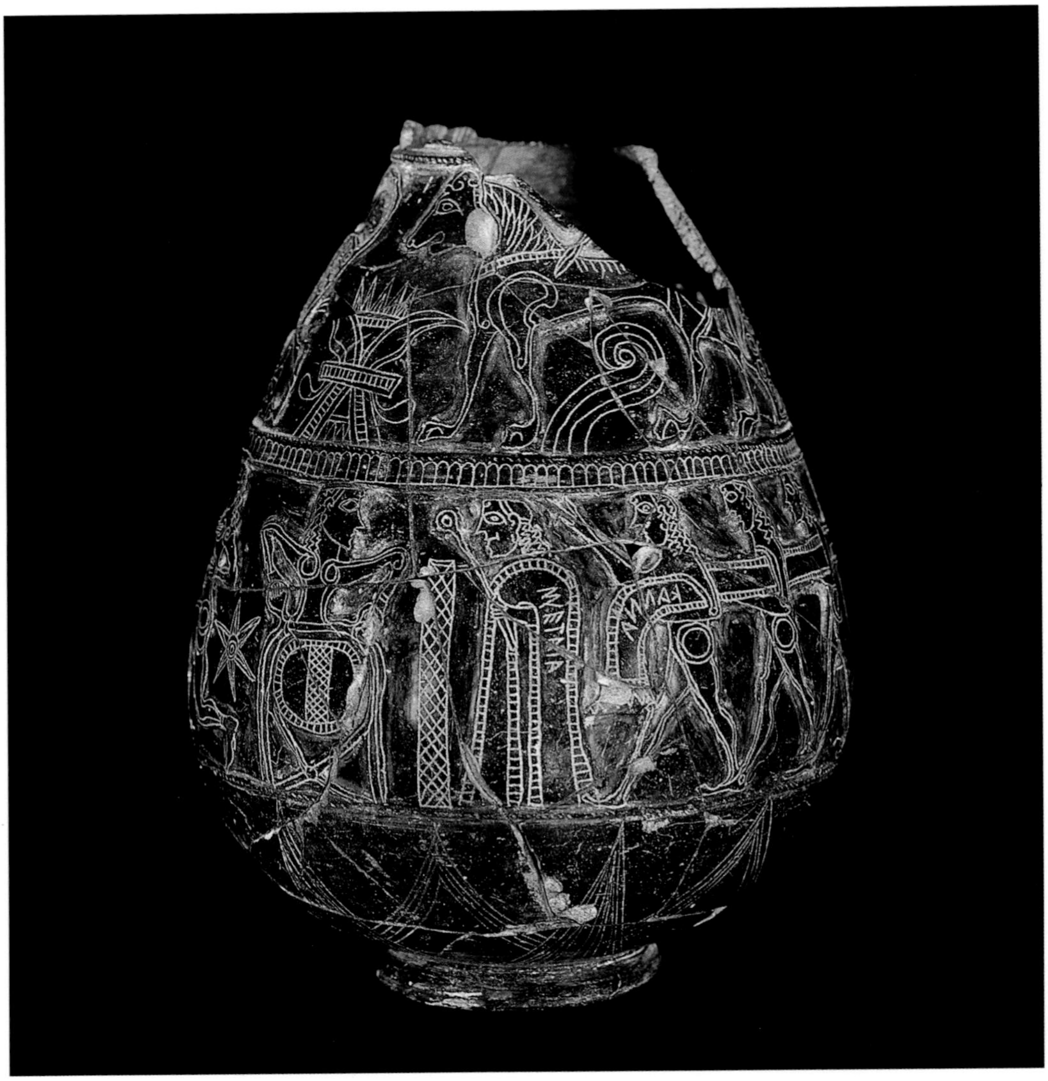

great funerary preparations on the occasion of *ludi* in honor of the Tyrrhenian *principes* (Colonna 1993; Coarelli 1993).

But the sixth century marks also the decline of the princely culture. At the end of the century the myth appears the exclusive prerogative of the temple structures of the communities, thus removed from princely hegemony, still dominant however in areas less caught up in processes of urban formation, as we see, for instance, in the case of the culture reflected in the chariot of Monteleone di Spoleto (Emiliozzi 1998). In reference to the Greek world, I. Morris (Morris 1999) recalled the difference between princes and heroes: the latter act and extend their benefits to a vaster community compared to the princes' gentilitial structures. In a like perpective, the Servian *regia* with the frieze of Theseus (Coarelli 1983; Torelli 1983; Massa-Pairault 1992; Menichetti 1994; *contra* Cristofani 1995b) that alludes to the king who promoted Athenian synecticity, is placed on the same level as the tradition that tells of the disappearance of Romulus at the *comitium* and his transformation in Quirinus, the god of the community united in *curiae* (Coarelli 1983; Carandini 1997; Carafa 1998).

That appropriation by the *polis* of the themes of the *principes*' culture irremediably marks its end, as we can see from the macroscopic process of disappearance of the archaic *tryphe*, so that at the turn of the sixth century B.C. the iconographies belonging to the princely culture disappear from public embellishments, withdrawing to the private sphere of the tomb. Myth also now shifts to designate the collective destinies of political communities rather than the *principes*' individual exploits. Concurrently we have the affirmation of sumptuary laws (Colonna 1997b; Ampolo 1984; Bartoloni 1987) tending to limit funerary luxury, clearly felt to be the main vehicle of the celebration of the princely rank, and therefore challenged by the isonomic tendencies under way.

Yet that extraordinary world of religious, political and cultural traditions, of monumental structures, of iconographies, does not definitively disappear, but seems to form a subterranean flux, ready to surface in the successive history in the role of personalities connoted in a negative sense for an *adfectatio regni*. The great revival of these themes, reviewed and readapted, coincides with the forming and legitimizing by the first century B.C. of an imperial power in Rome, which, besides the hellenistic models of the *imitatio Alexandri*, takes up trends of very ancient traditions, in the wake of great antiquarianism as well. The imperial iconographies of the *profectio* and of the *reditus* plunge their very roots in the princely rank of the Archaic Age.

Andrén 1940; Pareti 1947; Prayon 1975a; Bedini, Cordano 1977, pp. 274 ff.; Colonna 1977a, pp. 175 ff.; Colonna 1977b, pp. 131 ff.; d'Agostino 1977; Canciani, von Hase 1979; Verzàr 1980, pp. 35 ff.; *Göttin von Pyrgi* 1981; Bartoloni, Cataldi Dini, Zevi 1982, pp. 257 ff.; Boitani 1983b; pp. 535 ff.; Coarelli 1983; Cristofani, Martelli 1983; Torelli 1983, pp. 471 ff.; Ampolo 1984, pp. 71 ff.; *Aspetti delle aristocrazie* 1984; Bartoloni 1984, pp. 13 ff.; Bedini 1984, pp. 377 ff.; Cerchiai 1984, pp. 39 ff.; Colonna, von Hase 1984, pp. 13 ff.; Torelli 1984; Bedini 1985, pp. 44 ff.; Cerchiai 1985; Markoe 1985; Torelli 1985, pp. 21 ff.; Bartoloni 1986, pp. 143 ff.; Bonghi Jovino 1986; Bouke van der Meer 1986, pp. 169 ff.; Rathje 1986, pp. 397 ff.; Saeflund 1986; Torelli 1986, pp. 159 ff.; Arietti, Martellotta, Ghini 1987, pp. 208 ff.; Bartoloni, Buranelli, d'Atri 1987; Colonna 1987b, pp. 7 ff.; Coarelli 1988; Menichetti 1988, pp. 75 ff.; Moscati 1988, pp. 436 ff.; Torelli 1988, pp. 53 ff. Torelli 1989, pp. 15 ff.; Cristofani 1990b, pp. 22 ff.; Gaultier 1990, pp. 271 ff.; Prayon 1990, pp. 501 ff.; Torelli 1990, pp. 93 ff.; Zifferero 1990, pp. 107 ff.; Amadasi 1991, pp. 409 ff.; Herring, Whitehouse, Wilkins 1991; Mele 1991, pp. 237 ff.; Colonna 1992b, pp. 13 ff.; Edlund Berry 1992; Massa-Pairault 1992; Menichetti 1992, pp. 1 ff.; Torelli 1992, pp. 295 ff.; Capdeville 1993, pp. 191 ff.; Coarelli 1993, pp. 211 ff.; Colonna 1993d, pp. 321 ff.; Phillips 1993; Rystedt, Wikander, Wikander 1993; Cassio 1994, pp. 55 ff.; Cristofani, Martelli 1994, pp. 1147 ff.; De Puma, Small 1994; Martinez Pinna 1994, pp. 79 ff.; Menichetti 1994; Murray 1994, pp. 47 ff.; Torelli 1994a, pp. 117 ff.; Torelli 1994b, pp. 295 ff.; Bartoloni, De Santis 1995, pp. 277 ff.; Coarelli 1995, pp. 196 ff.; Cristofani 1995b, pp. 63 ff.; d'Agostino 1995a, pp. 7 ff.; d'Agostino 1995b, pp. 315 ff; Rathje 1995, pp. 167 ff.; Zifferero 1995, pp. 257 ff.; Cerchiai 1996; Cristofani 1996b, pp. 2 ff.; Matthiae 1996; Naso 1996a; Naso 1996b, pp. 69 ff.; Peroni 1996; Scarano 1996, pp. 321 ff.; Bonghi Jovino, Chiaramonte Treré 1997; Carandini 1997; Colonna, Di Paolo 1997, pp. 131 ff.; Lulof 1997; Ridgway 1997, pp. 325 ff.; Torelli 1997d; Torelli 1997e, pp. 233 ff.; Torelli 1999a, pp. 227 ff.; Carafa 1998; Delpino 1998, pp. 475 ff.; Emiliozzi 1998; Menichetti 1998, pp. 71 ff.; Minetti 1998; Naso 1998, pp. 117 ff.; d'Agostino 1999b, pp. 81 ff.; Esposito 1999; Morris 1999, pp. 57 ff.; Torelli 1999; Carandini, Capelli 2000; Guidi 2000; Menichetti forthcoming.

From monarchies to republics

In classical historiographical reconstruction, the tyrannical monarchies that were concurrently consolidated in Athens and Rome, in the mid-sixth century, fell simultaneously at the beginning of the last decade of that century. Some indications lead us to believe that the same model applied to Etruria as well. A tradition of that sort is hinted at in the story Dionysius of Halicarnassus (V, 3, 2) tells, recalling for the year 509 B.C. in Tarquinii a popular assembly (*ekklesia*), and mentioning magisterial offices (*tà télé tòn Tarkunietón*). This passage, generally viewed with some scepticism since it is thought to apply to the Archaic period more recent events, is nonetheless important insofar as, while retaining a tradition that might even be late but seems aimed at creating a parallel between the political affairs of Etruria and those of Rome, it is substantially corroborated by Livy's text (V, 1, 6), recalling that in 404 B.C. the "populi Etruriae" refused their assistance to the population of Veii "donec sub rege essent": that seems to presuppose a rather solid, even if not long-lived, familiarity with the republican form of government.

The situation must have differed in the different city states. The monarchical institution is explicitly attested for 432 B.C. at Veii; it was not until after Lar Tolumnius' defeat that a republican government was set up, soon abandoned anyway if in 404 B.C. the inhabitants of Veii "taedio annuae ambitionis [...] regem creavere." And it does not appear that the new institutional organization underwent further transformations before the city was taken by Furius Camillus.

It is now nearly common knowledge that in the middle of the fourth century Cerveteri was still ruled by a *rex*: we have an explicit testimony in Aulus Spurinna's *elogium* in the forum of Tarquinii during the age of Claudius: the *elogium* recalls that in his role as *praetor*, he removed from power a certain "Orgolnius, Caeritum rex." Archaeological sources also pro-

opposite
Tarquinia, Tomb of the Augurs, detail with priest, 530 B.C.

Sarcophagus of a magistrate who performed the entire cursus, *from Tuscania. Città del Vaticano, Museo Gregoriano Etrusco*

vide us with some information. In remote Felsina the supreme magistrates mentioned in the illustrated stelae of the fifth and perhaps also the fourth century B.C. should probably be identified as *reges*, on the grounds of the explicitly "regal" ideology that surfaces from the figurative programs displayed on the most important funerary monuments of the city, which frequently show the apotheosis of the deceased. At Chiusi, the great southward thrust Porsenna undertook which would lead to a substantial expansion of the Chiusi state, even absorbing Volsinii, and succeed in bowing Rome, seems to be arrested at the end of the century with the disaster of Ariccia. Investigation into the Chiusi archaeological situation indicates instead that the political circumstances at Chiusi did not change until the second quarter of the fifth century B.C., when only with the collapse of the production of cippi and illustrated urns does the class that had furthered the rise to power of the tyrannical figure of Porsenna seem to really disappear, and the return of the typology of the anthropomorphic

Bronze helmet from the Tomb of the Warrior in the Osteria necropolis (Vulci), ca. 520 B.C.
Rome, Museo di Villa Giulia
cat. 61

cinerary statue allow us to identify the reconquest of the aristocracy that based its power on the possession of land.

This being acknowledged, processes unquestionably sprung up between the sixth and fifth century in the different city states that led them to try out new forms of government.

Archaeological evidence and epigraphic records are quite balanced: the republican order is the one to which texts and monuments the most frequently refer. For the preceding period, the one in which sources recall the existence of *reges*, available data, although slight, allows a few simple considerations.

In literary tradition there is a trend, converging in Servius, whereby Etruscan kings were called Lucumons; as M. Cristofani convincingly demonstrated, that tradition was formed in the late period, being the reconversion into an institutional term of a surname, Lucumone

Pair of embossed plaques from the Tomb of the Warrior in the Osteria necropolis (Vulci), ca. 520 B.C. Rome, Museo di Villa Giulia cat. 62

(Etruscan: *lauchume*), known by sources as the Etruscan name of the one who would become king in Rome under the name of Tarquinius Priscus. For the Archaic period, Etruscan epigraphic records recall (on a cippus found at Rubiera-Modena) a personage who was *zilath* at Misala, at the beginning of the sixth century B.C. The elimination of the confusing evidence regarding *lucumones* gives us leave to translate the term by *rex*. But in the Archaic age, beside the regal figure a second public office is attested as well, the *marunuch*, mentioned on an important, still partly unpublished cippus from Tragliatella (Cerveteri) from the mid-sixth century B.C.

Republican institutions

Tradition in full shows the rule, after the expulsion of kings, of oligarchies of *principes*; as Jacques Heurgon claimed in his day, the word *principes* in latin means "en général les

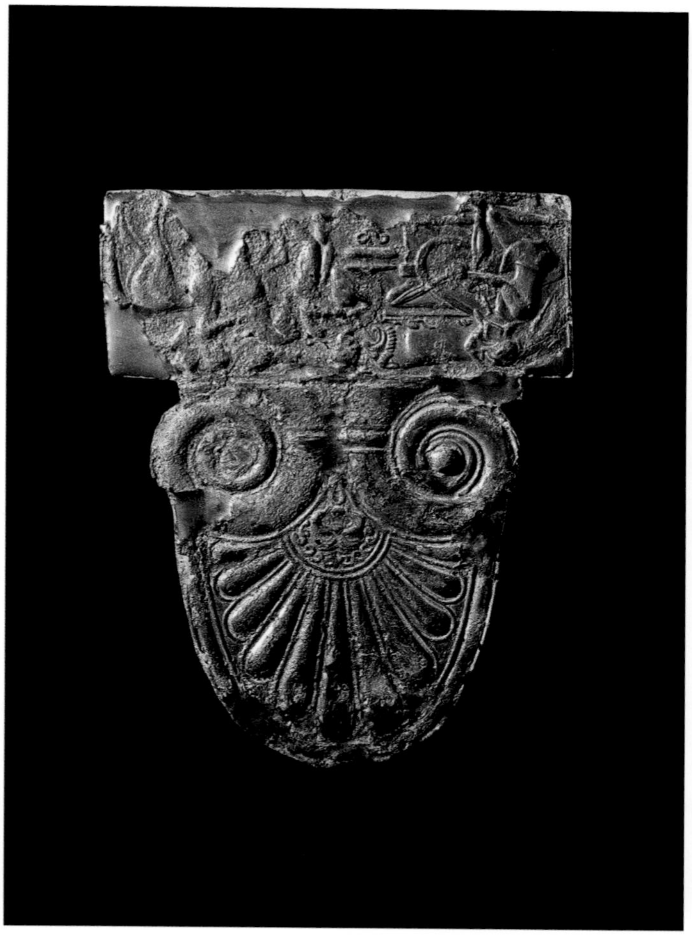

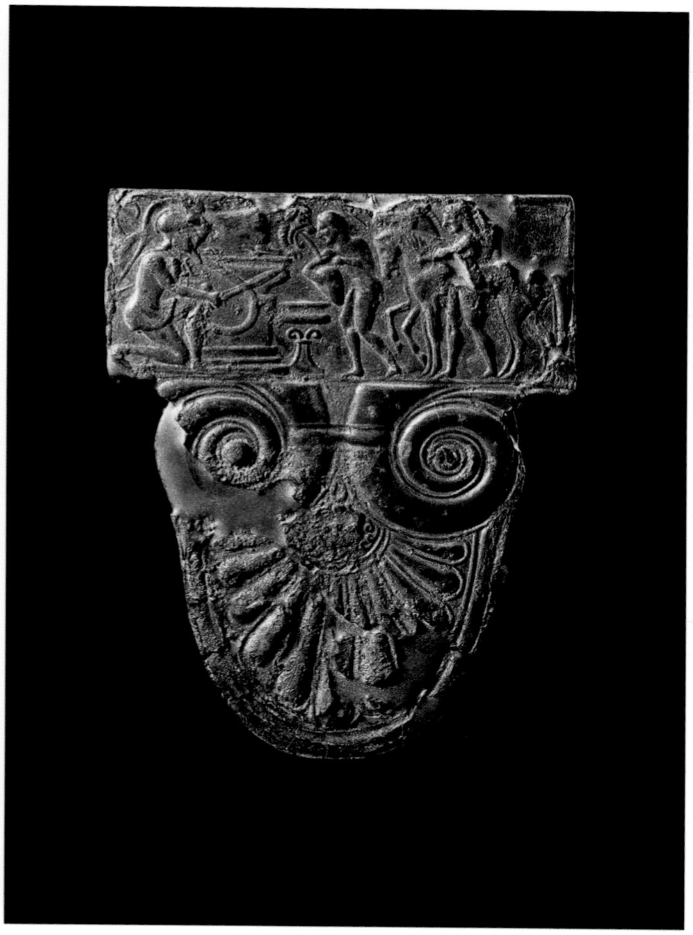

'grands' de toutes les cités italiques" (in general the "prominent persons" of all the Italic cities). On the other hand, that term is often used in sources as synonym of the highest magistrature in Etruria, especially in the formula *princeps civitatis*. Heurgon also pointed out the passage in Servius, *ad Aeneidem* II, 649 (completed by Macrobius, *Saturnalia*, III, 7, 2), recording the exceptional fate reserved to the one who, struck by lightning in his role as *rex* or *princeps civitatis*, had survived. The clear reference to an Etruscan source relative to *fulguratura* gives extraordinary weight to the assimilation, suggested by the passage, between *rex* and *princeps civitatis*, an identity justified only if the latter were the institutional successor of the former.

This solid background enabled the French scholar to sketch a sufficiently convincing picture of the late-classical and Hellenistic socio-political situation in Etruria, conjecturing on

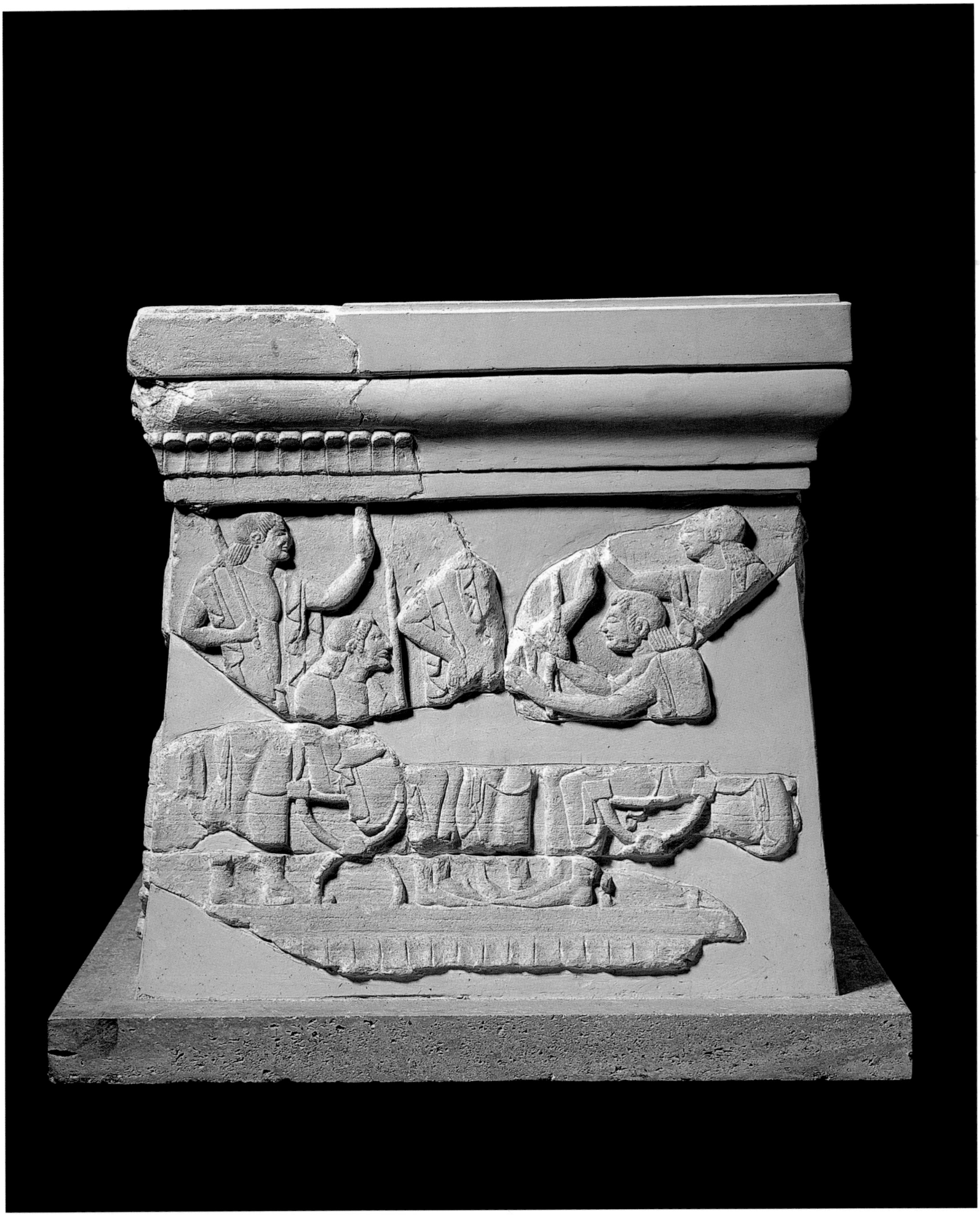

previous pages
Fragments of a cippus in limestone from Chiusi (?), 490–480 B.C.
Monaco, Glyptothek
cat. 260

the one hand an *ordo principum*, that is, substantially an oligarchy managing all public powers, and on the other a rural, semi-servile plebe, without civic rights; an opposition the sources express in the highly opposed terms of *domini* and *servi*, *dynatotatoi* and *oiketai* or *penéstai*. However, the picture implies a certain dynamism, and dialectics between the various components of Etruscan society must have developed in time and in the various regional situations in quite different ways, as shown by the fourth-century "servile" conflicts. Indeed in Arezzo the opposition between the oligarchy run by the *genus praepotens* of the Cilnii and the *plebs* (*servi*) was easily resolved by the interventions, towards the middle of the fourth century, of Aulus Spurinna acting, as M. Torelli suggests, in the name of the Etruscan League, and at the end of the century by the Roman consul M. Valerius Maximus. Yet the social advancement of the lower classes at Volsinii was far more disruptive, according to the narration in sources (Zonaras, VIII, 7, 4, ff.; Orosius; *Auct. De vir. ill.*, 36); as the authors recall, the process unfolded in the successive stages of the concession of political rights (including the right of *conubium*) to the *servi*, their gradual entry in the ranks of the senate ("libertini in partem potestatis recepti," as recalled in Orosius, IV, 5, 4), and finally the total occupation of public offices to the prejudice of the old ruling class.
On the other hand, the opposition *domini-servi* in Arezzo must also have been resolved by a broadening of the power base if, a century after the events Livy told, it was again the Paduan historian who informed us of a senate in Arezzo formed by a number of persons, with a clear differentiation of rank within it, where *septem principes senatus* were distinguished from the other senators, who must have been numerous since they were able to provide Rome with a good hundred and twenty sons as hostages.
Archaeological and epigraphic evidence confirms that the process continued until in northern Etruria (Chiusi and Perugia) in the second century B.C. it led to a broad and perhaps overall concession of civic rights to masses of individuals who had previously been subaltern.

Structures of the republican city-state: institutions and magistratures
Records of the political institutions of Etruria pertaining to the period between the fifth and the second centuries are remarkably modest as regards literary sources, but relatively plentiful as regards archaeological and epigraphic evidence. It has been observed on more than one occasion that the ancient authors are extremely reserved on the subject, and well-defined public offices are practically never mentioned: in sources pertaining to the Etruscans we find nothing comparable, Heurgon remarked, to Rome's consuls and praetors, or Capua's *meddices*…
The only institutional term brought down to us by literary tradition is precisely the word designating magistrature, which the late lexicographer Hesychius transcribes in Greek as δρου̃να, "the magistrature for the Tyrrhenians." The equivalent Etruscan word, that M. Pallottino reconstrued as *truna* or better said *θruna* , is not to be found in texts; however it might go back to the conspicuous nucleus of Greek loanwords in Etruscan, identifying its model in the Greek *θρόνος* (Etruscan *θruna* from Greek *ϑρόνος* as *aska* from *ασκός, paχa* from ***Bάκχος***), in the sense of seat for kings or gods, whose meaning translated as "royal dignity" is already attested in Sophocles (*Oedipus Coloneus*, 425). If this assumption, based on a sheer possibility, is correct, we are probably dealing with a loanword of the royal period, perhaps passed on later to generically indicate the highest magisterial dignity of the republican regime.

Territorial structures
The political-territorial structures involved are certainly those mentioned in the *Liber Linteus*, in the descriptions of rituals and sacrifices, that is, *cilth, spura, methlum*, to which we should add the terms *rasna* and *tuthina*. The interpretive pattern of the terms established by G. Colonna offers the following matches with Italic-Latin institutional vocabulary: *cilth = arx = okri; spura = civitas = tota; methlum = urbs; tuthina = vicus; rasna = populus* (in the oldest stage the people in arms; the people in possession of civic rights in a more recent age, according to the formulation by H. Rix).
It is highly probable that each of these political-territorial institutional situations matched a

Sarcophagus of the Priest, mid-fourth century B.C., *detail. Tarquinia, Museo archeologico cat. 293*

well-defined framework of political-administrative offices, which for the most part eludes us, especially as regards diachrony. The main referential structures can be substantially identified in the couple consisting in the city state, *populus* (Etruscan *rasna*), and by the city as a more circumscribed civic and territorial situation, a part of the *rasna*, the *civitas* (Etruscan *spura*).

Magistratures and pseudo-magistratures

As for the epigraphic documentation of the different magisterial offices and titles, we can only point out the great unevenness in the distribution of texts according to the area: six epigraphs come from Cerveteri and Orvieto (Volsinii Veteres), four from Vulci and Chiusi, one each from Vetulonia, Cortona and Volterra, a good forty from Tarquinii and its territory.

The first step to take in the rather confused area of epigraphic testimonies is distinguishing between authentic magistatures and pseudo-magistratures. It has been proven that some titles, traditionally connected with political institutions, should actually be attributed to other ambits. The title *camthi eterau* as exclusive prerogative—it would seem—of young boys and girls, should be removed from the dossier and put back in the ambit of activities connected with the cult, the term *camillus* being the one best suited to be associated with it. The instance of the title *zilath eterau* is more complicated. Insofar as that qualification uses an undoubtedly magisterial term (*zilath*, see below), it also seems to apply exclusively to youngsters. It might, as has been recently suggested, be an office connected with the youth orga-

Bronze statuette of offerer from Mount Falterona, 500 B.C.
Paris, Musée du Louvre
cat. 206

nizations of the city or even a preparatory office, in a certain sense, to higher magistatures of the young members of the most important families. The title *pr(aetor) iuv(entutis)* of several latin inscriptions could offer a good opportunity for comparison. The passage from the *Commentaria Bernensia* (*ad Lucanum*, I, 636) appears particularly enlightening as to the central role played by the young members of the *gens* ruling the cities: it recalls that the founding precepts of the *disciplina etrusca*—the group of norms forming the gist of aristocratic ideology in Etruria, until the end of its independence and even much later—had been dictated by Tages (the miraculous creature with the appearance of a boy and the wisdom of an elder) to the "duodecim principum pueris," that is, it would seem, to the offspring of the rulers of the twelve city states.

Institutional onomatology
In the framework of authentic magistratures, the first task is distinguishing between names of the magistratures and names of the officials. It has been recently proved that

Bronze statuette of offerer, second half of the third century B.C.
Florence, Museo Archeologico
cat. 288

Bronze male statuette, third century B.C.
Florence, Museo Archeologico
cat. 289

names of magistratures are all characterized, with but one possible exception, by the suffix *-uch*, *-uc* of abstract names, whereas names of officials present a greater variability in form.
The pairs deriving from it are: *zilath* = *zilach*, *maru* = *marunuch*, *eisne* = *eisnevc*, *purth* = *eprnevc*, *macstre* = *macstrevc*; *purtśvana* = *purtśvavc*.
Most of the records, although very reticent, seem to confirm the remarkable diversity of the organization of the different cities. Whereas at Volterra and Vetulonia we know of only a single magistrature, the highest (*zilach*), on the other hand two offices are attested at Chiusi (*zilach*, *eprthnevch*) and at Cerveteri (*zilach, marunuch*), three at Volsinii (*zilach, eprthnevch, marunuch*); at Tarquinii instead the picture is rather more articulated. The inscriptions, in this last case, come from the main center but also from the main inhabited centers of the territory, Tuscania, Musarna, Norchia.

The levels of the "cursus"
The wealth of documentation pertaining to the *polis* of Tarquinii allows us to draw up for that city a hypothesis of a *cursus honorum*, which from the lowest office to the highest outlines the following functions: *marunuch, eisnevc-cepen*, *eprthnevc, macstrevc*, *zilach*.
The first level was the office of *marunuch* (the name of the official *maru*). That is a *munus* known in Umbrian ambits as well, where it is usually believed to be an Etruscan wordloan, but without that being fully demonstrated. It is a collegial magistrature with a broad range of mandates. The term, when it appears in the singular, is always specified by an attribution that clarifies the ambit of its duties; when the term appears without attributions it is always plural; there are no exceptions. We can mention various specifications of the office: in the first place the one connected with the *spura, marunuch spurana*, the "civic *marunuch*." The one expressed by the genitive of the term *hil* (*hils marnuch* at Volsinii in the fourth century and probably at Cerveteri in the mid-sixth century) appears to be a particularly important determination: a word of uncertain meaning, it seems to have something to do with the semantic

Bronze statuette of offerer bearing a pig from Campetti sanctuary (Veio), fourth century B.C.
Rome, Museo di Villa Giulia
cat. 297.1

ambit of the *limitatio* (given its frequent association with the term *tular* = boundary)...
A sacral function of the office is—as has always been observed—the one indicated by the terms *marunuch pachathura, marunuch pachanati, maru pachathuras cathsc*, that connect the function with the college of the *bacchiads,* with the *Bachanal*, with the college of the *bacchiads* and of Catha (a female divinity). If, in a Tarquinii epigraph, the rendering of an office of *marunuch thunca* is correct, and if *thunca* means unique (and not, for instance, first), it raises a contradiction, at least in appearance, with the apparently certain collegial nature of the institution.
The re-interpretation of a Caeretan mural inscription, where a figure, whose name we cannot elucidate, performed "under the marunuch of L. Lapicane, son of Vel" an unprecised operation (perhaps the opening of a side road, on the wall of which the inscription is carved), constitutes a good element of comparison with the inscriptions of Umbrian *marones*, who often oversee the execution of buildings and public monuments. We can consider that the *marunuch* had responsibilities in building and religious ambits, probably through the control of colleges and cults and in the definition of the sacrality of public

spaces, maybe offering partial comparisons with the spheres of jurisdictions of the Roman *quaestor* and *aedilis*.

For the time being, most of the *cursus* place after the *marunuch* the name *cepen*, to which we usually attribute the meaning "priest." That name raises a problem, as it introduces a dissymmetry in the typological model of names of offices suggested above. In fact the texts in which the term appears allow to translate it either as the name of an official ("in the quality of priest"), or as the name of the office ("priesthood"). The difficulty can be partly overcome by recalling the like instance of the Latin *magistratus*, which can name both office and official. Whatever may be the case, unquestionably this early stage of the *cursus* implies a strong link with religious practices: on an inscription of Norchia, a city where the term *cepen* is not used, we have instead, exactly in the same position occupied by that last term (and depending on the same verbal voice *ten-*, a technical term with the meaning of "occupying an office"), the word *eisnevc*, certainly the name of a magistrature, formed on an official's name *eisne*, not attested but obviously associated with *esina*, which means sacred deed, sacrifice.

The name *purth* is widely documented at Tarquinii, but also appears at Volsinii and Chiusi. Its rank would seem to be quite eminent. While the conjecture of its identification with the Greek *prytanos* or its connection with the historic name *Porsina*, expressed many times in the past, are still not particularly confirmed, it may be more worthwhile to emphasize the circumstances, which in this instance we can do by glancing at the scope of its activity.

The inscription of a member of the *gens [m] urinas*, the owner of the Tomb of Orcus I at Tarquinii, recalls that the personage, who had been "zilath mechl rasnal...s purth ziace ucntm hecce," probably meaning "in his quality of *purth* decided (? *ziace* ?) and he himself had performed" an operation the name of which we only have the last letter "[...]*s*."

At Vulci the office does not appear; instead the pair *purtśvana* = *purtśvavc* is attested, certainly once again an office and an official. The nominal base might be, though it is not certain, the same as the name *purth*. We could then have an epichoric variant of the magistrature seen above, with its own characteristics. However, the very special circumstance wherein *śethre tutes*, named in one of the two Vulci inscriptions, died while holding the *zilath* and the office of *purtśvavc*, implies that the latter could not be a normal level of the *cursus*, which obviously could not have been occupied at another level by the same person, but an exceptional nomination, having nothing to do with the *cursus*, like censorship in Rome.

There have been endless discussions about the magistrature of *macstrevc*, and its obvious connection with the historical name *Macstrna* (Servius Tullius' Etruscan name) and the Latin term *magister populi* (identifiable with dictator). Its position in the *cursus* is quite high; its pomp could suggest a connection with military circles.

As supreme magistrature, the *zilath* presents a series of specific traits, perhaps bound to a multiplicity of offices, expressed by genitives (*zilath parchis*, a completely obscure title; *zilath scuntnues*, attested once only at Chiusi, to be connected perhaps with the root *scun-* which expresses the notion of building (?); *zilach mechl rasnal*, see below), by adjectives (*zilath selaita*, attested in the Archaic period at Cerveteri; *zilath eterau, etereaia* "that has to do with the *etera*," the latter being perhaps a particular age group, the *iuvenes*, see above); by a dative of interest (*zilach cechaneri*, the *zilach* for the *cechana*, see below).

But the name *zilath* (magistrature *zilach*) often appears also without further attributions. The widespread opinion that *zilath* without further attributions should be identified with *zilach mechl rasnal* should probably be reconsidered. Yet one of the main functions of the *zilath* is certainly that of eponomy, which is usually expressed by the locative of the office, *zilci*, followed by the genitive (or by the "pertinentive") of the name (or the names) of the magistrate (for instance: "zilci velusi hulchniesi" = during the *zilach* of *Vel Hulchnies*). In many ambits of the ancient world eponomy is the prerogative of the supreme office, but not everywhere; for instance in Athens the situation is different. The new text on the Cortona bronze tablet, datable between the end of the third and the second century B.C., presents in two places the magisterial term in speech; the first time it is attributed to the leader of a long series of persons who can be identified as witnesses: "art cucrina zilath mechl rasnal;" the second time it appears in a dating formula: "zilci larthal cusus [...] larthal salinis." The evidence is relevant insofar as it might indicate that the offices mentioned were

Votive male head from the sanctuary of Diana (Nemi), third century B.C.
Florence, Museo Archeologico
cat. 291

different. Of particular relevance appears the distribution of these two titles in centers of the Tarquinii state. It is widely held that each territorial reality of any substance could boast, as *spura*, its own magistrates, municipal compared to those of the principal center. Tuscania, Musarna, Norchia count rich, articulated *cursus honorem*, graduated from the *marunuch* to the *zilach*, formed on the image and in the likeness of those practiced in the capital Tarquinii. If the names of public offices are identical in Tarquinii and its outlying centers, can we identify a term characterizing the specific authority of the capital over the whole extent of the territory of the city-state? In other words, what was the name of the supreme magistrate of the *populus tarquiniensis*, as of the *volcentanus* or the *clusinus*? The distribution of the term *zilath mechl rasnal*, which never appears in minor centers of the Tarquinii territory, but only (twice) at Tarquinii itself, is decisive. It leads us to assume that the function underlying that title differed from that of the normal *zilath*. Whereas the latter has competency, as the epitaphs claim explicitly, over the *spura*, the *zilath mechl rasnal* has competency over the *populus*, and its related territorial entity, that is over the entire extent and entire free people of the city-state.
Whereas probably the "normal" *zilath* occupies his office for a year (hence the eponymy), it is not at all certain that is the case for the office of *zilath mechl rasnal*.

Votive female head from the sanctuary of Diana (Nemi), third century B.C.
Florence, Museo Archeologico
cat. 290

The pomp of the "zilath"

The various offices and functions of the republican city state must certainly have counted on their own pomp, consisting in a specific presence of bodyguards and a particular display of insignias and symbols. The available iconographic documentation however is limited to the *zilath* represented at the highest moment of his magisterial dignity: the *profectio* in the biga (Tarquinii, Vulci, Orvieto) or on foot (Volterra, Tarquinii?), accompanied by lictors, various *apparitores* and musicians. The number of lictors and other participants in the procession was not fixed in time nor was it identical from one city to the next. In the late fourth century, at Tuscania, the *zilath* is accompanied by two lictors with fasces and by a third with a spear (*hasta summa imperi*, witnessed by Festus, at Rome). Between the end of that century and the beginning of the third, at Tarquinii (but at Volterra too), the *zilath* is accompanied by three lictors with fasces and staffs, as well as other *apparitores* (bearing *sella* and *tabellae*); but at Vulci, it would seem, there are only two lictors. During the third century, and towards 200 B.C., both at Tarquinii and at Vulci they reach at least four. Later the number is set at two, both at Tarquinii and Volterra; in the latter city, in the late second century B.C., undoubtedly under the influence of the Roman triumph, the type of the *profectio* of the magistrate in a quadriga is introduced for the first time.

Terra-cotta mask of Silenus from Tarquinia, end of the fourth–beginning of the third century B.C.
Tarquinia, Museo Archeologico cat. 296.1

Terra-cotta mask of Dionysius from Tarquinia, end of the fourth–beginning of the third century B.C.
Tarquinia, Museo Archeologico cat. 296.3

A federal magistrature?

We still should consider the possibility that among the terms epigraphic tradition has handed down to us there might be some we could link up with the Etruscans' federal institutions, to which historiographical sources allude many times. At Tarquinii, in the Tomb of the Meeting (Tomba del Convegno), decorated at the beginning of the third century B.C. with an important pictorial cycle, a very high-ranking personage is qualified as holding the magistrature of *zilch cechaneri*. The title is mentioned again twice at Tarquinii: always attributed to very high-ranking persons, it is never alongside other magisterial titles.

The symbolism and pomp accompanying this magistrate in the Tomb of the Meeting is quite significant: beside the lictors with fasces, and an attendant with what may be a travelling bag, there are others carrying two different types of spears and two big iron two-edged hatchets, which certainly refer to the *summa potestas* of the magistrate himself.

Since we know, by Dionysius of Halicarnassus, that the Etruscan *populi* (that is, the city states), when forming a military alliance, on the occasion of campaigns carried out together, chose a common leader, and, confering on him the *autokratora archen*, also attributed to him a number of lictors with shields matching the number of members of the league, we can plausibly recognize in the anonymous personage of the Tomb of the Meeting the leader of an alliance between two cities.

This being the case, the office *zilath cechaneri* (that literally ought to mean "*zilath* for higher things" or "for the higher institution") might represent a supra-city office.

All in all, the institutional structure of the Etruscan city states evolved with a differentiated passage from one region to another, from the Archaic age, where it was qualified by the pair *zilath:maru*, meaning by the *rex* and the *maro,* until the Hellenistic age, ruled by a republican institutional form with a generally rather complex inner organization.

In the Hellenistic age, the remarkable number of offices recorded at Tarquinii may indicate

Terra-cotta mask of a satyr from Tarquinia, end of the fourth–beginning of the third century B.C.
Tarquinia, Museo Archeologico cat. 296.2

the greater complexity of the state organization of that city: at the top of the *cursus honorem* there is the collegial authority (two members?) of the *zilach*, with defined duties and the right to eponymy, exercised alone or in pairs. Above the *zilath*s (*spurana*) we might imagine another magistrate, the *zilath mechl rasnal* having competency over the entire city state, with perhaps a plurennial duration of the office. There are indications that in the instance of alliances between *populi* an exceptional magistrature could be created, characterized by very great prestige and extraordinary symbolic pomp, perhaps called *zilch cechaneri.*
Should the hypothesis expressed here prove correct, Rosemberg's old notion (moreover based on absolutely untenable elements) of a political structure of republican Etruria with lots of correspondences between the various institutional ambits, might somehow be revived on the basis of other assumptions: two (or more?) *zilath*s would be at the head of the various city situations, the *civitates* (*spura*), one *zilath* would be the leader of the various *populi* (*rasna),* one *zilath*, with exceptional powers and particular prowess in the military field, would lead the eventual coalition of *populi*, leading those *concilia* of the Etruscan *principes* mentioned in the sources (with whom the term *cechana* might then be identified?); it might be the figure that Livy, in a particular historical context, calls "sacerdos," but that Diodorus and Dionysius specifically name "strategos egoumenos" and "autokrator," emphasizing particular competency in the military ambit.

Rosemberg 1913; Mazzarino 1945; Heurgon 1957, pp. 63 ff.; Camporeale 1958, pp. 6 ff.; Frankfort 1959, pp. 3 ff.; Lambrechts 1959; Cristofani 1975, pp. 53 ff.; Torelli 1975; Rix 1984, pp. 451 ff.; Colonna 1988, pp. 15–44; Maggiani 1996, 1998, pp. 95 ff.; Maggiani 1999; Maggiani forthcoming.

The Ideology of the Etruscan City

One of the most stimulating effects of the mutual relation between anthropology and marxism is the broadening of the concept of ideology. Beyond a reductive view of the ideological function as an illusory product of historical alienation, its active role, essential for the rendering of production connections, has been confirmed. M. Godelier expressed that interpretative model in clear terms: "Unlike marxism as it is usually exercised, soon lapsing into commonplace materialism, we claim that Marx, by distinguishing between structure and superstructure, and assuming that, when all is said, the profound logic of societies and their history depend on the transformation of structure, plainly brought to light for the first time a hierarchy of functional distinctions, without in the least presuming the nature of the structures assuming these functions (kinship, religion, politics, etc.), nor the number of functions such a structure can sustain." The formulation of the active role of ideology implies focusing on the organized, segmentary character of its pertinence: at the heart of the construction of a collective identity, ideology is equally so in the representation of dialectics and social conflict. The concept of ideology is not the exclusive prerogative of the ruling class—even if it is an impressive instrument for its affirmation and conservation—, but is materialized in organized strategies of knowledge and display performed by members who, within a same group, co-exist and compete for the control of the process of social reproduction. From this it ensues that ideological production constitutes the expression of a "social arbitrariness." It does not describe reality, but endeavors to put it into practice: it consists in an autonomous communication strategy that builds, selects and manipulates social meanings. In light of these principles, our contribution proposes a few remarks on some quandaries regarding the ideology of the Etruscan city as has been recently investigated.

"What do we mean by city? The city materialized in its physically visible structures or the city as institution and political subject? The city of houses and temples or the city of citizens?" Thus, in 1988, G. Colonna summed up with exemplary clarity the problem of the definition of the Etruscan city: an elusive definition because caught between conflicting documentary elements. On the one hand, in fact, archaeological evidence shows that, during the late Orientalizing period, an overall process of urbanization of settlements took place in the Etruscan world. Certainly the most significant aspect of such an event consists in the planification within the city of monumental spaces having a public character, of a religious and political type, the result of a process of objectification of the two functions wherein a broader-based political community than the aristocratic one is formed. On the other hand, classical historical tradition emphasized, as a structuring feature in Etruscan society, the polarity between *domini* and *servi*, preventing the formation of an intermediate civic class of free men and, as a result, the growth of an idea of the city as a political construction, similar to that of the Greeks and the Romans.

The lack of such an evolutionary process has been pointed out by B. d'Agostino who, on the subject, formulated the definition of a "non-*polis*" of the Etruscans. Yet we should examine the value of such a contradiction. In the first place, it is based on two non-homogeneous terms: on the one hand, the monumentalization of the urban plan that involves the public image of the community, stressing its identity and political cohesion; on the other, the representation of the class struggle within it, founded on the structural opposition between a small component enjoying full political rights and a "social body," diversely extended and organized, that on the contrary is deprived of them. Then we should mention that the contradiction between a tendency to consolidation of the urban institution and the conservative resistances of a ruling oligarchy is not specific to archaic Etruscan society, but at the same period typifies Magna Graecia and Rome, proving the non-linear character of the formative process of the political community. These comments lead us to reconsider the Etruscan case. G. Colonna pointed out, although drawn from a late document like the *Liber Linteus*, the existence in the Etruscan lexicon of institutional terms such as *spura* = *civitas, meθlum* = *urbs* and *cilθ* = acropolis: however later on M. Cristofani challenged that last identification.

The institutional picture is provided by the *corpus* of the magisterial inscriptions, recently the object of A. Maggiani's thorough re-examination. In particular, the mention of the title *zilath* in the Rubiera cippus is particularly significant, enabling us to date the institution of the highest magisterial charge to the end of the seventh century B.C., at the same time as the rise of the phenomenon of urban consolidation mentioned above.

Terra-cotta acroterion with Ajax from the sanctuary of Cannicella (Orvieto), 490–480 B.C., detail.
Orvieto, Museo Archeologico
cat. 268

Bronze statuette of a warrior from Brolio (Arezzo), ca. 550 B.C. Florence, Museo Archeologico cat. 272

Bronze statuette of an armed man. Florence, Museo Archeologico cat. 196

What image of such a process of political structuring, especially at its oldest institutional level, does historical tradition reflect? The accounts of classical historians like Livy and Dionysius of Halicarnassus offer the coherent image of cities governed by a small oligarchy: by the group of *principes*, according to Livy's definition, or by the *dynatotatoi* according to that of Dionysius. That privileged segment expresses the figure of the king, whose power seems to be represented as the emanation of aristocratic authority: Dionysius' testimony is especially significant, wherein the term *dynatoi-dynatotatoi* extended to designate the representatives of the Etruscan cities in the League of the Twelve Peoples, at the time of the war against Tarquinius Priscus (Dionysius of Halicarnassus, III, 59, 1 and 4) again declared against Servius Tullius. It is worthwhile mentioning that both kings, at the conclusion of their victorious campaigns, grant the defeated Etruscan cities the autonomy of their *politéia* in exchange for their recognition of Rome's *hegemonia* (Dionysius of Halicarnassus, III, 60–61; IV, 27).
The same denotation logic of regal authority is perhaps reflected in the correspondence that can be established between the definitions, in Livy and in Dionysius, designating the supreme representative of the League: he is, according to the first author (I, 8, 3), the *com-*

Bronze statuette of Ajax killing himself from Populonia, 480–460 B.C.
Florence, Museo Archeologico
cat. 79

muniter creatus rex; according to the other (III, 61, 2), he who "receives the supreme office" (λαβὼν τὴν αὐτοκράτορα ἀρχήν; on the concept of *arché* see also III, 59, 4). Further confirmation can be found in the correspondence established in the Pyrgi plaques between the Phoenician *mlkj* (reign) and the office of the **zilac selaita*, which A. Maggiani suggests matches that of the Roman *praetor maximus*.

If most of these associations are correct, by its elevation of the magisterial character of the regal office, the situation of the Etruscan world presents remarkable likenesses with that of Rome, where—as we know—at the sovereign's death *auspicia ad patres redeunt*.

In Livy (V, 27, 5) the *principes* are defined *capita rerum*; in Dionysius, the requisites of their *auctoritas*—those, for instance, underlying the choice of ambassadors sent by the *Concilium* to negotiate peace with Rome at the time of Tarquinius Priscus (III, 59, 4)—are the prestige owed to age (*oi presbytatoi*) and the notion of *timé* (*oi timiótatoi*) that, from a negative propaganda point of view, is overturned in the deprecative binomial *tryphé* and *hybris* (behind, for instance, the popular etymology *tyrrhenoi*), *opes* and *superbia* (Alcimus in *FGrHist* 560 F 3; Aristotle, *Tyrrhenon Nomima*, fr. 607 Rose; ; Theopompus in *FGrHist* 115 F 204; Her-

Painted terra-cotta torso from the temple in Via San Leonardo at Orvieto, beginning of the fourth century B.C.
Orvieto, Museo Archeologico
cat. 284

acleides Ponticus in *FHG ii*, p. 217 fr. 16; Timeus in *FGrHist 566 F 1*, *F 50*; Livy, v, 1, 4 but also I, 50, 3; 53, 4 and 9 regarding Tarquinius Superbus).
The aristocracy's power rests on the economic and social structure of the *gens*, whose economic base consists in the possession of a large, undivided *ager*. The gentilitial structure is organized around kinship, relations of private solidarity and clientele, according to a series of components faithfully recorded by historical tradition: in Livy, the *gens* is formed by *cognati, sodales, clientes*; likewise Dionysius mentions the *suggheneia*, the *philoi* or the *hetairoi*, the *pelatai* (more infrequently, the *oikeioi*). The same association of *suggheneia* with *hetaireia* recurs in Theopompus (in Athenaeus, XII 517 f and *FGrHist* 115, F 204).
In Dionysius, *pelatai* tend to be different from serfs (*therapontes*, *therapeia*): their designation—as J. Heurgon remarked—matches the Latin *propinqui*, enhancing the positive relationship of assistance and reciprocal *fides*, binding client to patron.
In this perspective, we can then reconsider the value of the famous definition of Etruscan clients as *penestai* (the "poor," liable to *ponos*) besides expressed by Dionysius in just one

Fragment of a male head from the temple in Via San Leonardo at Orvieto, beginning of the fourth century B.C.
Orvieto, Museo Archeologico
cat. 283

following pages
Sarcophagus of the "Magnate" from the Partunus Tomb (Tarquinia), third quarter of the fourth century B.C.
Tarquinia, Museo Archeologico
cat. 294

passage (IX, 5, 4–5 to compare with II, 9, 2): the comparaison with Thessalian serfs whose condition was semi-slavery—rather than pointing to a specific statute of subordination of Etruscan clients—seems, in the context it is set in, to act as a rhetorical device opposing the militias of dependents serving the Tyrrhenian *dynatotai* (still equipped with splendid arms, and above all able to fight with *homonoia*), to Rome's army composed of free citizens. As M. Torelli pointed out, historical tradition corroborates the intermediary statute of clients, placed in a condition of μεταξύ ἐλευθέρων καί δούλων (Pollux, *Onomasticon*, III, 83). Such a statute does not belong to Etruscan society alone: L. Capogrossi Colognesi has in fact validated in the case of Rome too the existence of a number of judicial conditions of subordination that are relics of a greater organization of archaic law: an organized subordination placed between *libertas* and *servitus*.
So we can then wonder if the opposition *domini-servi*, emphasized in the case of the Etruscans—beyond a logic of controversial propaganda—does not coincide, on the level of relationships within Etruscan society, with an ideological opposition aiming at "naturalizing"

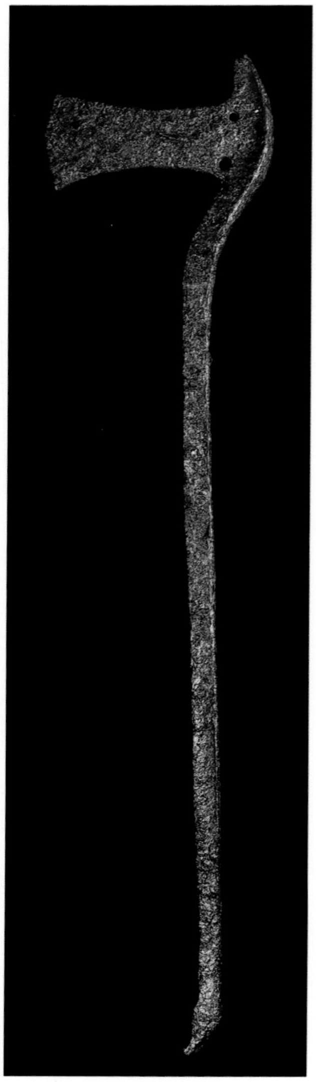

Iron ax from the sacred area at Fucoli (Chianciano Terme), second century B.C.
Chianciano Terme, Museo Archeologico
cat. 265

the privileges of an aristocratic class, thereby legitimising the exploitation and repression of the lower classes. In that sense the closed character of the society of *principes* and the conflictual nature of class relationships is suggested in the tradition of the uprising of *servi* at Volsinii in 265–264 B.C.: the rebellious *oiketai* are accused of the crime of claiming rights which the plebe at Rome has already long won: *conubium* with patrician women and access to public offices.

In the definition of gentilitial organization, the correspondence that can be established in historical tradition between the designation of the group of *poiloi* and of *hetairoi* and that of *sodales* is particularly enlightening: a term that the remarkable *Lapis Satricanus* inscription allows to refer to the military sphere. From that point of view, we should mention J. Heurgon's hypothesis recognising a copy of the Greek *etairos* in the Etruscan word *etera*, combined, among other things, with two magisterial titles attested in epigraphic records, the *zilaθ* and the *camθi eterau.*

H. Rix, acknowledging a conjecture by C. Olzscha, has suggested attributing to the term *etera* the meaning of "member of the *iuventus*;" A. Maggiani follows the same interpretative trend when he identifies in the *zilaθ* a *praetor iuventutis*. That reading does not appear necessarily in contradiction with Heurgon's suggestion, if we consider that the semantic pertainance of the Greek *hetairos* embraces both meanings of "companion-in-arms" and "young." A possible confirmation of such a hypothesis might come from the analogous extension whereby Livy uses the term *iuventus*: in V, 17, 9–10 (to which add V, 18, 10) the League of the Twelve Peoples—accepting only in part the request, expressed by the Faliscans and the people of Capena in 397 B.C., to intervene against Rome in support of Veii—does not prevent "qui iuventutis suae voluntate ad id bellum eant."

The theme of military organization leads us to examine the issue of the claim of hoplitic tactics, and the incidence of that phenomenon on the consolidation of the Etruscan city.

The question has been discussed in countless contributions, among which we should especially recall those by M. Torelli and B. d'Agostino. Historical tradition (Diodorus Siculus, XXIII, 2, 1; *Inedita Vaticana,* 3; Athenaeus, VI, 273) refers to the existence in Etruria of armies of the hoplitic type, even attributing to the region primacy over Rome in introducing phalanx military tactics. At the same time, archaeological records show that, by the second half of the seventh century, the acceptation of hoplitic models constitutes one of the expressions displaying aristocratic rank. It appears, either by the introduction, in particularly eminent burial goods, of elements of the panoply, or by the choice of the image of the armed man on funerary monuments and, above all, on the architectural friezes of phase I where processions of warriors with heavy armor, behind a "leader" climbing on a war chariot, acquire a specific significance. Although with divergences, M. Torelli and B. d'Agostino have observed that, in the Late Archaic period, the organization of the aristocratic army along hoplitic lines could play an active part in the transformation dynamics of a social body appearing to be reorganized along timocratic lines. Torelli for instance has suggested seeing in a significant funerary context like the Tomb of the Warrior at Vulci the expression of the existence of "hoplites not belonging to the aristocratic class." Instead d'Agostino has remarked that, compared to a more conservative southern district, the hoplitic image is validated especially in northern Etruria: "In that part of Etruria, the figure of the hoplite seems to coincide henceforth with a social standard, and therefore with an important presence within the political community [...] which however maintains its elitary character."

Undoubtedly—compared to more advanced political situations like those of the Greek *polis* and centurial Rome—in Etruria the introduction of phalanx military tactics never leads to a hoplitic city: it does not bear the affirmation of an autonomous class of *homoioi* able to wield its political weight within the aristocratic city. The capacity to control the process of social reproduction exercised by the aristocratic organization, which—as we saw in the case of the Volsinii—successfully resists attempts to extend civic and political rights, is still too powerful.

Nonetheless, too marked an opposition between Etruria and the Greek and Roman world of the Archaic age is not entirely satisfactory since, on the one hand, it does not allow to corroborate the existence of common, at least at first, structural elements and evolutionary leanings; on the other hand, it tends to neglect the uncertainties and contradictions whereby,

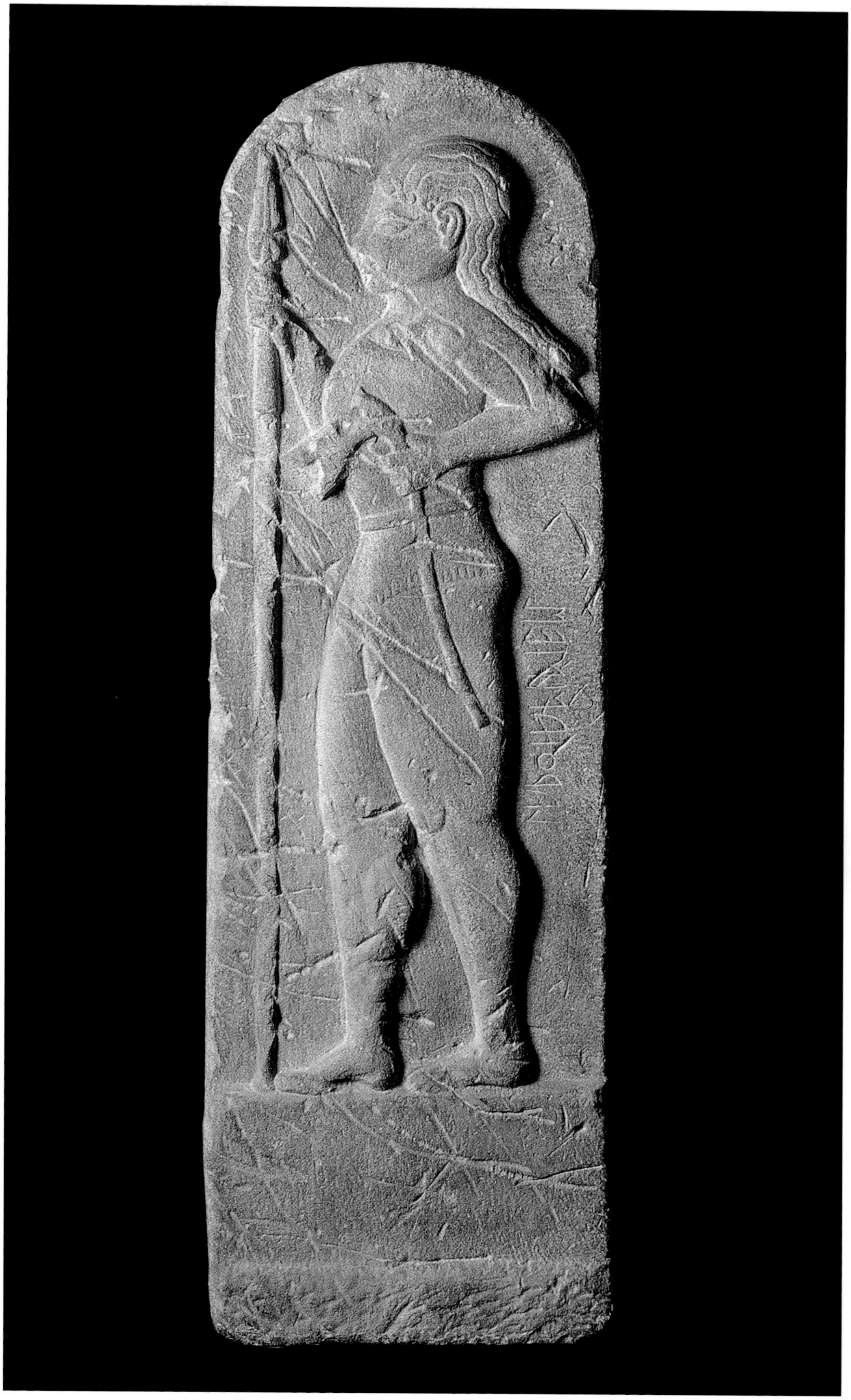

Stela of Larth Ninie from Fiesole,
520–510 B.C.
Firenze, Casa Buonarroti
cat. 76

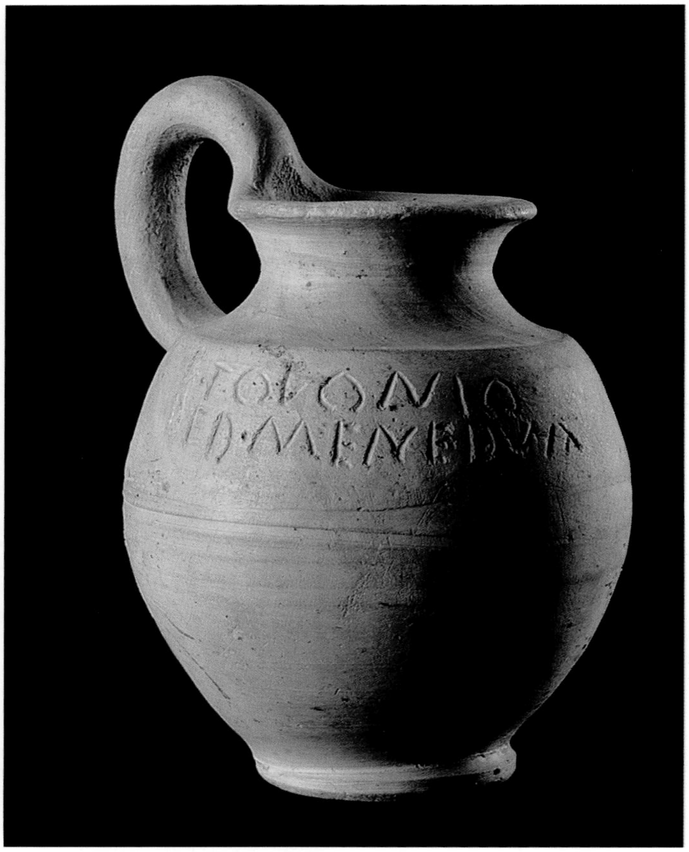

Poculum *with inscription from the sanctuary of Campetti (Veio). Rome, Museo di Villa Giulia cat. 297.2*

Small jug with dedicatory inscription from the sanctuary of Portonaccio (Veio), mid-fourth century B.C. *Rome, Museo di Villa Giulia cat. 298.2*

even in "reformed" contexts, the extension of the right to citizenship came about.
Let us consider first of all the relationship with Rome.
The ensemble of the Servian reforms represents a remarkable attempt to limit aristocratic power to the benefit of a process of objectification of the authority of the *civitas* and the creation of a political identity founded on censual grounds.
As G. Colonna proved in an authoritative study, the same tendency towards a timocratic evolution of social structures occurs concurrently in the Etruscan world where, as we know, it is emblematically displayed on the funerary level: in the planification of the blocks of cube tombs in the necropolises of Caere and Volsinii, or Tarquinii, in "the decline of the dome tomb, the monumental expression of the gentilitial group, which is replaced by the chamber tomb with painted decoration, intended for the married couple and, therefore, the expression of the family and new economic fortunes" (d'Agostino).
Concurrently in Rome the new centurial and tribal organization does not eliminate the traditional privileges of the ruling aristocracy which, soon after the foundation of the Republic, reaffirms its own primacy in the form of a patrician "dike."
An indication of the strength of these resistances is given—as we know—by the voting mechanism in the *comitia centuriata* and the persistence of gentilitian militias alongside the citizen army, exemplified by the famous episode of the private *bellum* of the Fabii in 477 B.C. (Livy, IX, 15, 2). But we should particularly point out the slowness with which, according to L. Capogrossi Colognesi's convincing rendering, land ownership is transferred from "factual" possession of the *gens* to that of the *familia proprio iure*, that is, through the role of the *pater familias*, to the *civis sui iuris*. Even if individual possession of land was a central element in civic organization probably already since the Servian era, it is actually not until the course of the fifth century, under plebeaian pressure, that the principle of the quiritary subdivision of the *ager publicus* is affirmed. That principle is fully applied with the massive program of agrarian distribution following the conquest of Veii in 396 B.C., later juridically sanctioned by the Licinian-Sestian reform laws of 367 B.C.

Comparison with Magna Graecia offers a like situation. For the Archaic period Greek colonies, M. Lombardo drew a picture of the hoplitic phenomenon that largely resembles the Etruscan one. In a political structure tensed by "ideological requirements towards *isomoiria* and institutional and private procedures of differentiation and accumulation," the diffusion of the *hopla* is already documented by the seventh century; the phalanx of foot soldiers seems however, in the course of the sixth century, to play a secondary role to cavalry, traditional expression of the aristocratic order.
"The hoplitic experience occurs, probably at first, within structures centered around the aristocratic-landed *oikoi* ": which explains "the delay with which [it] introduces novelty and transformations in the political sphere [...] from the point of view of the dynamics in political-institutional structures, with the persistence of oligarchic structures and the slowness and difficulty with which crises and internal transformations occur [...]." It is not until the end of the sixth and during the fifth century B.C. that the military organization of infantry becomes an instrument of assertion on behalf of the *demos* in the well-known cases of Cumae, Taranto, Reggio. The hoplitic phenomenon crosses various formations of ancient Italy that, separated on the ethnic level, have a common socio-economic base: patrician oligarchies use the introduction of new military tactics to consolidate their control at the crucial stage of the urban transformation of settlements, when some of their prerogatives are handed over to the authority of the civic *nomos*.
In this highly delicate transition process where the city in formation is reinforced while preserving the guarantees of aristocratic privileges, the model of military organization assumes a relevant political significance: it is no coincidence if the iconography of the warrior climbing onto the war chariot is celebrated, both in the Achaean colonies and the Tyrrhenian area, in the architectural decoration of public monuments such as sanctuary and palace, combined with the introduction of the new casting technique.
As B. d'Agostino suggested, the adoption of such a technique allowing serial reproduction should actually be read in connection with the need to insure the "stability and visibility" of an iconographic repertory which, being linked "with the solemn moments of social communication, is laden with a particularly intense political content."
So we can question whether, in the Etruscan area, in architectural decoration the choice of the scene of the military leader followed by his hoplitic formation does not have a dual role: elevating the ideal of the aristocratic hero, accompanied by the *hetairoi* and, at the same time, suggesting the collective image of a community representing its own socio-institutional identity by the military designation *rasna/populus*. From that point of view, the hoplitic organization model can actually suggest the assertion of a new political *kosmos*, ruled by the rational, regulating action of the *nomos*.
A like paradigmatic role transpires in Virgil's description of King Caeculus' *legio agrestis* (*Aeneid*, VII, 681–90), in the opposition between the troups equipped with *arma, clipei* (hoplitic shields covering the entire body: Servius, *ad Aeneidem,* VII, 686) *currusve* and the main element of the army, marked by a savagery that makes it comparable to a pack of wolves: "most of them shower pellets/ of livid lead; some wield twin javelins,/ with tawny caps of wolfskins as their headgear./ They wear their left foot naked as they march/ the other foot is shod in a rawhide boot."

On the notion of ideology: Godelier 1977, pp. 43–107; Godelier 1999, pp. 19–30, 174–79. *On the ideology of the city:* Colonna 1985c, pp. 242–44; d'Agostino 1998, pp. 125–31. *On the institutional lexicon of the city in Etruria:* Colonna 1988, pp. 15–36; Cristofani 1997a, pp. 109–12. *On the magistratures*: Maggiani 1996, 1998, pp. 95–138. *On the inscription of the Rubiera cippus:* de Simone 1992. *On the model of a collegial designation of sovereignty:* Mazzarino 1992. *On the gentilitial structure and forms of dependence*: Heurgon 1970, pp. 29–41; Torelli 1987d, pp. 35–73; Torelli 1990b, pp. 71–83; Capogrossi Bolognesi 1994. *On the "servitus"*: Heurgon 1959, pp. 713 ff. Torelli 1987c, pp. 87–95; Benelli 1996, pp. 335–44. *On the value of "etera"*: Heurgon 1957, pp. 63–97. *On the "Lapis Satricanus":* de Waele 1996, pp. 231–42, *mentioned also for the bibliography*. *On hoplitism in Etruria*: d'Agostino 1990, pp. 59–84, with bibliography; d'Agostino 1998. *On the development of a timocratic society*: Colonna 1976a, pp. 3 ff. *On the organization of the "comitia centuriata"*: Coarelli 1998, pp. 133–43. *On the hoplitic phenomenon in Magna Graecia*: Lombardo 1997, pp. 225–58. *On architectural friezes*: Cristofani 1987a, pp. 95–120; Torellic 1997, pp. 87–121; d'Agostino 1999a, pp. 3–12. *On the notion of "rasna":* Rix 1984, pp. 451 ff.

Françoise-Hélène Massa-Pairault

The Social Structure and the Serf Question

Young serf from the Golini Tomb I (Orvieto), fourth century B.C.
Orvieto, Museo Archeologico

Our knowledge of Etruscan society has developed notably over the last thirty years: the study of the necropolises and the cities and their territories, and the analysis of inscriptions have provided new information allowing us to have a more concrete idea of the social groups and classes that were protagonists of almost a thousand years of history (ninth–first centuries B.C.). Thus a picture of a society has been constructed that is more complex as regards its historical development and is richer in nuances according to the region—Etruria between the Tiber and the Arno, Etruscan settlements in the Po Valley, Etruscan Campania—or cities considered. A new approach has been taken to the problems relating to its structure and social dynamics, although it is still difficult to provide a brief answer to the main questions emerged in the most recent studies: what is the originality of Etruscan society with regard to the other peoples living in the Italian peninsula—Latins, Romans, Umbrians, Sabines, etc.? What are the signs, contributing factors, and agents of the transformations? What is the structure of this society and the particular type of dominion (possession of property) at the basis of this development?

The originality of the Etruscans with regard to the other peoples of antiquity was first perceived—and carefully analyzed—by the Greek historians and philosophers. They stressed the existence of an evident dichotomy in their society between those they called lords (*despotai*) and those they generally called "serfs" (*oiketai*) or domestics (*therapontes*), describing the dominance of the former and the subservience of the latter to the family group (*oikos*). Most of the information we have about Etruscan society—mainly gleaned from the work of Athenaeus of Naucratis (third century A.D.) *The Learned Banquet*—is, however, generally submerged by moralistic reflections on Etruscan customs. In fact, quoting Aristotle (I, 23), Theopompus (XII, 517 ff.), Heraclides Ponticus or Timaeus of Tauromenium (IV, 153r. ff. and XII, 517r.), Athenaeus's learned banqueters expatiate, during the conversation, on the extravagant luxury (τρυφή) of the Etruscans, the excesses to which they abandon themselves in the banquet, the fact—inconceivable in Greece—that married women and the ladies of the house take part in them, the promiscuity between masters and their serfs, the cult of corporeal beauty, the style of the clothes worn by masters and serfs, and the free practice of love in all its forms. In other words, Etruscan society was seen through the distorting lens of moral censure or was regarded as the land of Cockaigne. But, although they were partisan, the Greek thinkers must have had a much more complex point of view. In the work of the Stoic Posidonius of Apamea, summarized by the historian Diodorus (V, 40 ff.), it may be noted that the reasons for the Etruscan dominion over Italy prior to that of the Romans was seen in relation to their economic resources and social equilibria. Thus, in some cases, starting from a reflection on customs, an explanation was given for the peculiarity of the religious practices, laws, and constitutions. Seen from this point of view, the anomalous status of the serfs with regard to Greek customs could almost appear to be the hidden key to the wealth and productive capacity, allowing us to view τρυφή in a more positive light. Thus Posidonius informs us about the prosperity of the serfs, who were well dressed, "better than is becoming for subordinate people," and possessed, if not land, at least buildings of every type—workshops, and town and country houses. The promiscuity of the banquets is transformed into industrious promiscuity: the masters' large houses were noisy hives of activity swarming with serfs. The masters, however, found a remedy by creating a space surrounded by a peristyle, thus allowing the serfs to be kept at a suitable distance, while, at the same time, they could direct their work. The "atrium," to which Posidonius was probably referring and which he believed to have been invented by the Etruscans, is, therefore, a space adapted to a certain mode of production. But exactly what type of atrium is the one mentioned here? With regard to this term, must we conclude that the condition of the Etruscan serfs was similar to that of the Roman clients that Late-Republican sources describe as waiting for favors in their masters' *atria*? The reply to this question cannot but be negative. The Roman clients—in Latin, *clientes*, in other words, those who listen (*cluunt*)—are described by Greek authors (Dionysius of Halicarnassus, II, 9, 2) as "relatives, members of the family" (*pelatai*) and not serfs (*oiketai*). From a legal point of view, although the clients abandoned their domestic cults in order to embrace those of their patrons—renouncing a considerable part of their legal rights in exchange for the protection of the more powerful individual—they did not, as a result, lose their citizenship or right to vote. It is a situation that our sources do not seem to associate with the Etruscan serfs, whose subjection seems, in fact, to be reflected by the internal layout of the house with an atrium. Indeed, the oldest form of the atrium, the testudinate (vaulted) space in which the roof was supported by columns (as in the Tomb of the Capitals or that of the Shields and Chairs at Cerveteri), appeared between the last quarter of the seventh and the beginning of the sixth centuries B.C., just as public spaces in the city were being given a monumental character, almost as if this were a sign for the introduction of a social order that relegated the serfs and not the citizens to the only public space in which they have a function, the hall of state and government in their masters' houses. There, seated on a throne, the *pater familias* and *mater familias* received their serfs according to a ritual that we must imagine as being similar to the one described by Macrobius (*Saturnalia*, I, 16, 32) and other authors with regard to the "Etruscan kings" who, every nine days (the day on which the markets were held), received their peasants, who brought them the produce of their land, explained the reasons for quarrels, and renewed their pledges of loyalty. Another illustration of the condition of the serfs, from the same period (ca. 630 B.C.) is provided by the scenes carved on the back of the wooden throne found in Tomb 89 at Verucchio: these depict the most prestigious domestic activity, associated with the rites of matrimony and triumph of a gens, the production of textiles and woolen clothes. Numerous serfs take part, grazing the flocks of sheep, taking the shorn wool to be carded, then bringing it to the mistress, who before the large pedimented house, dies and spins it with her daughters and maids. A number of armed men (the master and his relatives) protect these domestic activities, heralding the triumph.

But what dynamics and social models can explain the nature of the Etruscan ruling class, what were its origins and how did it come to dominate the whole society? A preliminary answer is provided by an examination of the phenomena that occur in the Final Bronze Age and Early Iron Age: in the ninth and eighth centuries B.C., the Villanovan—then Etruscan—world was affected by short-, medium-, and long-range migratory movements, comparable to internal colonization, which had the aim of occupying land suitable for agriculture. In the north, the Bologna area, part of Romagna (Verucchio) and the Marches (Fermo), and, in the south, Campania, the Vallo di Diano and the upper valley of the Sele, are the furthest limits of these movements, the center of which may be located in the area that was later to be occupied by Tarquinia and Veio. This expansion, perhaps originally led by institutions governed by egalitarian rules (probably *curiae*, that is, groups of families gathered in political communities), must have been accompanied by conflicts in order to gain possession of the land at the expense of the weaker communities and the peoples who already occupied it. Thus the Umbrians arrived in Romagna and the Po Delta, the proto-Sabines in the Marches, and the Ausonians, Oenotrians, and Iapygians in Campania and the Vallo di Diano. The dense distribution along rivers (*per pagos*) of the Villanovan settlements seems, therefore, to relate to a division—for the appropriation of the agricultural surplus—between subject and tributary communities (either of the same origin or belonging to other peoples) and dominant ones. This colonizing process then proved to be the cause of inequality that favored some communities and was detrimental to others. The emergence around the mid-eighth century B.C. of important cities (known to the Romans as *capita Etruriae*), formed by the synoecism of smaller communities, produced two phenomena that were apparently related: a growing social differentiation—attested by the increasing quantities of luxury and prestige items among the grave goods—and a growing influx of people into the newly created cities. This increase in population, as is demonstrated by the case of the Quattro Fontanili necropolis at Veio, cannot be explained only by the logic of demography, but must also reflect the arrival in the cities of families employed by the most affluent members of the community. This suggests that there was a reorganization of property and a redistribution of products and people that was now no longer in favor only of the dominant community, as had previously been the case, but also of a number of individuals. Thus the Etruscan aristocracy emerged by exploiting the new legal system of the city and its territory in order to bring the poorest members of the community (Latin *tenuiores*) into its service. The institution of the patronage system (linked to the *heredium*, the minimum area of land that could be inherited) that Romulus had created in Rome at about the same time attempted to address the problems of social organization resulting from the extension of and changes to the forms of property. The Etruscans seem to have found other solutions to these problems: the level of wealth reached by a number of lords—frequently thanks to the practice of piracy—allowing them to have immense political power and military prestige, and the fact that they could turn the last migratory movements in the direction of Campania to their advantage (as in the case of Veio),

Volterran cinerary urn , ca. 120 B.C.
Florence, Museo Archeologico
cat. 317

resulted in even more drastic appropriation of land, men, and implements by individuals and more marked forms of subjection, leading, in some cases, to the poorest people being deprived of their citizenship. During the whole of the Orientalizing period (from the end of the eighth to the beginning of the sixth centuries B.C.), in fact, what the Romans called *caput gentis* (leader of the gens) exercized his uncontested power over the smaller villages (Latin *vici*) scattered in the countryside, where they often built sumptuous residences—for instance, the palace of Murlo and the great houses of Acquarossa—and monumental tombs (often tumuli) that both publicized and celebrated the cult of his ancestors with stepped altars, such as in the Melone del Sodo II tumulus at Cortona, or unique cultic objects, such as those in the Tomb of the Five Chairs at Cerveteri or in the Cima tumulus at San Giuliano. This dominion was also exercized over the large centers, and was indicated by imposing residences in the cities and remarkable tombs in the urban necropolises—such as those at Cerveteri, Tarquinia, Vetulonia, Vulci and Cortona—but, in this context, the *caput gentis* was faced with the economic and political competition of his peers, including the king and leader of the army (*zilath*), who was probably elected, as in Rome, his power being limited by public institutions and the growing complexity of Etruscan society, with the development of the economic activities providing sources of wealth. One of the signs of the order existing in the property in the more competitive situation in the cities was the generalization of an onomastic system that formalized, in a stable manner, the continuity of descent on the basis of inheritance and citizenship. The *nomen gentilicium* (name of the *gens*), an adjectival form—generally in *-na*, transmittable from one generation to another—of an older patronymic, thus extended from a small nucleus of important families (ca. mid-seventh century) to include the majority of free citizens. This phenomenon foreshadowed another one—that is, the progressive stratification of the aristocracy, the result of horizontal social mobility at a high and medium level from the countryside to the town, and from the Italic areas of the interior towards Etruria—as is indicated at Cerveteri by the name Vestirikinai (from the Oscan Vestirikis), a woman of Sabellian origin, or Kalatur Phapena (also Caeretan and probably associated with the Fabia, a Romano-Sabine *gens*), or, more rarely, from Greek cities, such as, in Capua, the Cumaean (?) Mamarce Asklaie or, in Tarquinia, the Corinthian Demaratus, who settled in the city and married an aristocratic woman; his descendant, Tarquinius

Priscus, became the first Etruscan king of Rome. The standardization of the titles to property as the result of a common legal system did not, however, solve the problem of the lower classes in the rural areas. The history of Volsinii (Orvieto) in the sixth and fifth centuries B.C. provides an excellent illustration of the reasons for this, with an insight into the social dynamics of the period: considerable social mobility, with a migratory influx of *gentes* of a high and medium level from the adjacent region of Umbria and the Sabine and Faliscan territories (for ex. the Fescennine Hescanas), and from even further afield, such as the Celt Katacina; the equality of its citizens before the law, reflected by the existence of modular units in the city's cemeteries; its economic growth, stimulated by its position on the border and the existence of trade routes leading mainly to the Tiber, where there was an emporium. Thus there was a trend toward the parceling out of the land (with medium-sized estates run by freemen), which came into competition with the system of the large aristocratic estates, run on a semi-servile basis. However, this was probably avoided, or reduced, in various ways. Firstly by involving the surplus population in distant colonial ventures, in the Po Valley, as in the case of Thucer Hermanas, whose name appears on a votive bronze at Ravenna, or in Campania, as the story of Porsenna, whose son may have attempted to found a colony there, demonstrates. Secondly, by regenerating the large estates around the villages and smaller centers in the area, slowly absorbing the weakest of these middle-rank landowners and their serfs, as is indicated by the presence of serfs of other families in the house of the Leinie, near Volsinii. Finally, by establishing the great religious, political, and economic institution of the Fanum Voltumnae—the temple of Voltumna, where the general assemblies of the Etruscan Confederation were held—to guarantee social order. Although this did not resolve the problem of the subordinate peasant class, the growth of the cities provided Etruscan society with a number of new experiences deriving from both the development of trade and the expansion towards the Po Valley and Campania. The emporia, trading settlements that were somewhat marginal with regard to the cities, comprised ports, warehouses, and dwellings that were now necessary because of the increase in trade with the Greek and Oriental world. Places where Corinthian, Ionian, Attic, and Punic products were exchanged, they seem to have been administered in different ways: by the local rulers at Pyrgi, the port of Cerveteri; granted as a concession, at least in part, to Greeks of various origins, who, as in Naucratis in the Nile Delta, were allowed to worship their own gods, at Gravisca, the port of Tarquinia; governed in ways unknown to us at Regisvillae, one of the ports of Vulci, or in the mining district located between Elba, Populonia, and Pisa. The activity in these emporiums was carried on by people of various origins and social classes: Greeks, Etruscans and other peoples, Orientals, metics and serfs, craftsmen, free or otherwise, such as the potter from Vulci Kape Mukathesa (Kape, the employee of Mucathe), or the painter Arath Heracanasa (Arath, the employee of Heracana), who signed the frescoes of the Tomb of the Jugglers at Tarquinia; local traders and foreigners working on their own account, or on behalf of their aristocratic masters resident in the Etruscan cities, or in their cities of origin, either Greek or Oriental. The emporiums constituted a safety valve for the cities because they allowed the integration of many members of the lower classes into the socio-economic system, while they supplied the city with products that were constantly being renewed and the wealth deriving from the profits of trade. This wealth was the cause of the emergence of new figures in the traditional aristocracy, or outside it: at Tarquinia, Arath Spuriana, the owner of the Tomb of the Bulls, sent his commercial representatives to Rome and areas (Asia Minor) of the Greek world; at Cerveteri, because of its architecture and location, Marce Ursus' Tomb illustrates a new form of self-assertion with regard to the older ones covered by a tumulus. Moreover, the wealth represented by personal property brought about social development on different levels; first of all among the aristocracy, then in the poorer classes. Once again, it is the study of the cemeteries, especially those at Vulci, Cerveteri, and Tarquinia, that suggests that the objects serving as status symbols—for instance, drinking-services and the social norms relating to their use—were widespread because they were found not only in the tombs of a number of emergent personages. The southern coastal cities responded to the economic stimuli, therefore, with a marked and extensively diffused social structure comprising various levels of wealth, with the possibility of progressing from one level to another (vertical social mobility) and a larger variety of obligations and social types, not all based on the gentilitial model of servitude: crafts or commercial guilds and societies with religious, military, nautical, and trading objectives were able to express themselves with greater freedom. The phenomenon of the painted tombs of Tarquinia in the last quarter of the sixth and the first quarter of the fifth centuries B.C. may be regarded as reflecting this social development. Relationships within the societies seem to be stressed, in particular, by the frescoes in the Tomb of the Inscriptions at Tarquinia; in a huge building, perhaps the seat of a *Collegium Mercatorum* (corporation of merchants), a festival is being celebrated with joyous freedom—and games—bringing together the serfs (*oiketai*) Tetiie and Pumpu (both of Sabellian origin) and members, all male, of various families, such as the Matue, the Recieniie, and the Vinacna, whose names were not found, so it seems, among those of the subsequent, more limited, oligarchy of the city in the fourth century. The growth of the middle and lower classes is also attested in the context of the various "colonial" societies of the Etruscan world, in the Po Valley and Campania. The influx of *gentes* into the Bologna area from central and northern Etruria from ca. 520 onward—at the same time as the development of Spina as a port, the foundation of Mantua, and the growth of Marzabotto as a town laid out as a rectangular grid—injected new blood into the old Etruscan stock. The adoption of isonomic models seems to have gone hand in hand with the emergence of a small group of magistrates, suggesting that the state controlled the growth of wealth, perhaps through the primitive currency system of ingots stamped with a "bare-branch" sign. At Marzabotto the complex social fabric of the town comprised many craftsmen, especially bronze workers, and numerous owners of workshops belonging to the middle class. The difference in the names suggests the existence of a hierarchical relationship between those having gentilitial names ending in *-alu*, who were often owners of workshops (thus [...] *śvalu* was the owner of one of the town's principal foundries), and those who were only called by personal names (fAkiu), sometimes of Greek origin (Śinu), which seem to indicate a subordinate origin or position. In this context, one Lautunie, whose gentilitial name, meaning "the freedman," appears on a weight, may have held a public position (perhaps that of the controller of the "bare-branch" ingots), as was also the above-mentioned *Śinu*, whose name is accompanied by a graffito in the form of a bare branch. Also in the port of Spina there were many people having local gentilitial names in *-alu* and some with names originating from central and northern Etruria (Volsinii, Cortona, Arezzo), including those of some of the rich merchants and middlemen engaged in the Attic trade with Bologna. These names are not necessarily those typical of the higher echelons of the aristocracy, but they certainly had business relations links with this more restricted Bolognese social class. The same may be said of shipowners, such as Kutikluna, buried together with his ship's anchor, and, in general, of the vitality of the Etruscan fleet of Spina, the voyages of which were

Plan of the Crocifisso del Tufo necropolis (Orvieto)

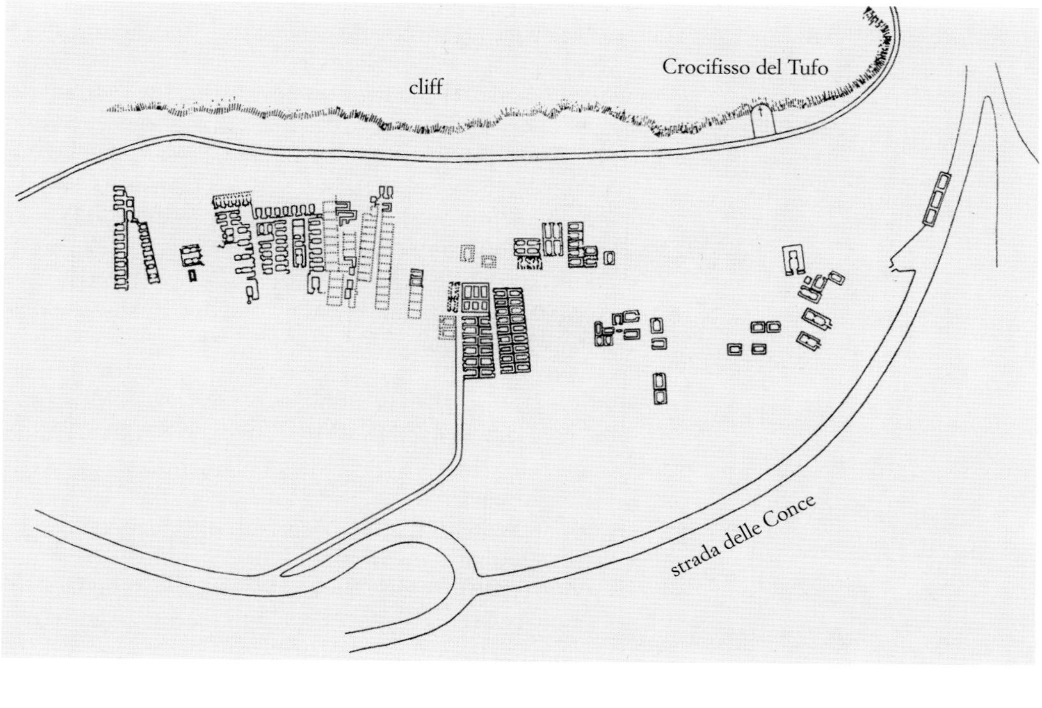

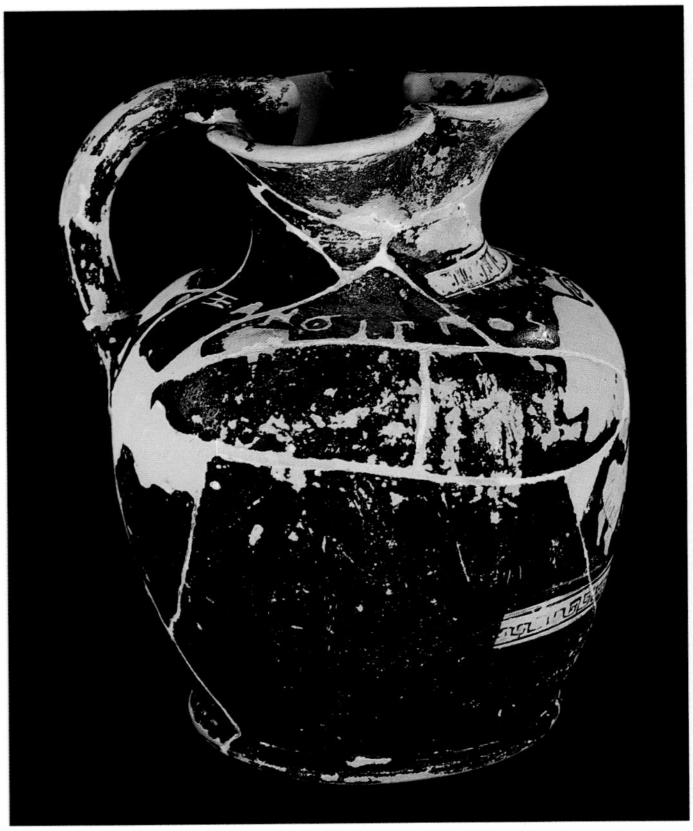

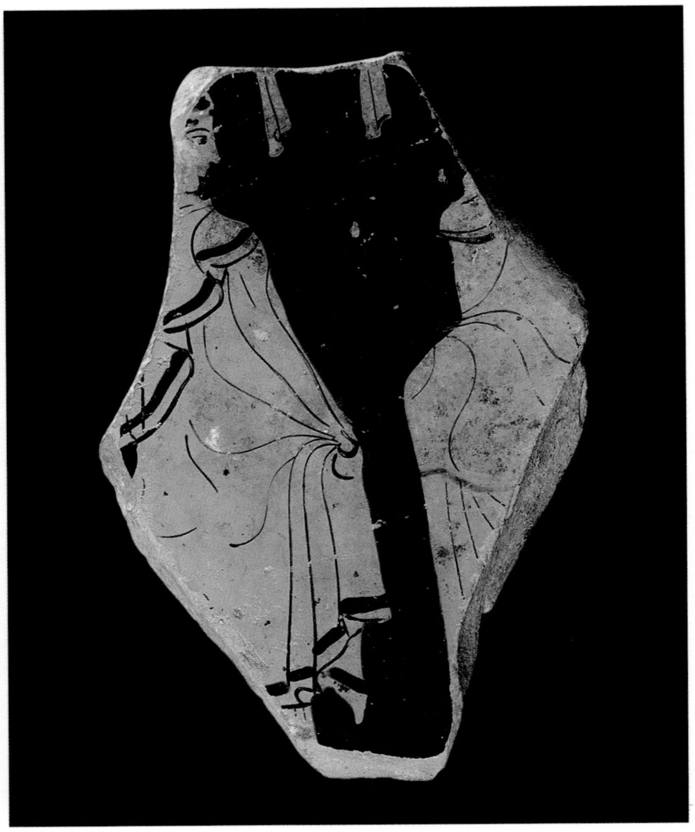

Black glaze oinochoe *with "Xanthippos" graffito from Tomb 709 at Valle Trebba (Spina), fifth century* B.C.
Ferrara, Museo Nazionale

Signature of the Greek artisan Metru from Populonia, second half of the fifth century B.C.
Florence, Museo Archeologico

often financed and controlled by the Bolognese, as demonstrated by the stela, found in Bologna, showing Vel Kaikna in his ship, leading a sea expedition. The cosmopolitan character of the town is attested by the presence of foreigners integrated into Etruscan society, especially Veneti and Greeks, the latter perhaps partially deriving from Attic servile classes who worked and traded on the spot for their masters in Athens. With just a few variations, this social structure was to be found in the other large Etruscan port, Populonia on the Tyrrhenian, which served the mining district. Here, in the Classical period, the signatures of Greek artisans, such as Metru and Karmy, who were among the metics who had settled there, have been identified. And perhaps also in the ports serving Vulci and Tarquinia in the same period the complex organization of the workshops producing the *spurinas* pottery with the labor of metics and serfs, may reflect the way the craftsmen's workshops were run in Athens. In Campania the multiplicity and complexity of the social models relating to each geopolitical area hinders a unified vision of this large region that then became Etruscan. At Capua the system of semi-servile tenancy of land, mainly on the part of Italic peoples called Opici ("those who work"), must have been in effect until the pressure, towards the middle of the fifth century, of a new Italic state that had formed on the eastern border of Capuan territory in the Matese massif, obliged the small group of Etruscan landowners to divide the ownership of the land (and also of the Opici) and the government of the city with the leaders of those who were known henceforth as Campanians; in fact, a term in the treaty between the Etruscans of Capua and the Italic peoples who had settled in the city and its territory specified, in the Latin translation, *societas urbis agrorumque*. However, although this ended in 421 B.C. with the liquidation of the Etruscan oligarchy, this outcome to a contradictory situation was preceded, from ca. 530 to 490 B.C., by a notable development of trade and industry in the city, and the growth of the middle and lower classes parallel with the establishment of Aristodemos's tyranny in Cumae. Social relationships were stimulated by the tradition of hospitality that held sway particularly in the upper classes, both as regards the Greeks of Cumae and the Italic peoples, as is demonstrated by the relations between the Etruscan Racu and the Etruscanized Oscans Vinuchs Peracis and Venel Vinicius. The relationship of Nola, half the population of which was Italic, with its port of Herculaneum—together with its social system and the role of the stakeholders in the economic growth, which was notable thanks to the Athenian domination of Neapolis—was probably very similar to that of Tarquinia and Gravisca (the political system, has yet to be investigated). In the last quarter of the sixth and the early fifth centuries Pompeii was very much in the hands of the Etruscan aristocracy, which promoted the foundation of sanctuaries—dedicated to Apollo and Heracles—in order to regulate the trade in the emporium and the influx of foreign traders. The episode, depicted in the frieze of the Barone *lebes*, of Heracles, Cacus and the cattle of Geryon, a theme that regarded the safety of trade on the road to Herculaneum, demonstrates that—like Marce Ursus in Cerveteri and Arath Spuriana in Tarquinia—the Capuan aristocracy of the day invested in commercial ventures. It is perhaps in the southernmost area of Campania that the most original social innovations were introduced; these were based on the model of the peoples of the "empire" of Sybaris, inherited—after Croton had destroyed the Achaean city in 510 B.C.—by the colony of Poseidonia. At Pontecagnano, in the second half of the sixth century B.C., there was a partial renewal of the local aristocracy—the name of the Amina stands out—and the town was reorganized around new market and religious areas. True colonization (with a new influx of population), probably due to an initiative of Vulci, appears, from around 530 B.C. onward, to have affected Fratte di Salerno (the Etruscan Marcina), while Buccino (the Etruscan Volcei) seems to have been founded by the Velcha from Tarquinia. The inclusion of other Italic peoples in the social structure (such as the Nunie, whose name reappears as Nonia, an important *gens* in Roman Herculaneum) and also the Greeks from Poseidonia, illustrates notable social mobility at a high and medium level. This is confirmed by the study of the cemetery, where, in addition to relatively few tombs that practically monopolize the possession of Attic pottery, there are also numerous tombs—in which wine amphoras have been found—belonging to the medium level of the aristocracy or the better-off lower classes earning a living with trade or acting as middlemen for the upper classes; and, finally, there are more modest tombs. In this context, Etruscans (such as Volcha from Tarquinia, attested at Fratte by a graffito having an erotic meaning) and the Greeks of Poseidonia created trading relations and religious societies—as the famous Tomb of the Diver at Poseidonia probably indicates, as does the settlement at Vulci of Greek artisans, such as Arnthe Praxias, from areas using Achaean script. At the end of the Archaic period (ca. 480 B.C.), Etruscan society overcame the most marked inequality of the Orientalizing period between gentes of the upper class and the lower classes, or, at least, it managed to find room for new participants and models within the older, well-tried social organization. A series of events that had a disastrous outcome for the nation that had hitherto been hegemonic in Italy then followed: a naval defeat off Cumae at the hands of the Syracusans and Campanian Greeks in 474 B.C.; the end, due to the Italic peoples of Campania, of Etruscan domination of the cities in that region in 435 B.C.; the end, due to the attacks of the Gauls, of the Etruscan cities in the Po Valley at the beginning of the fourth century; and the conquest of Veio by the Romans in 396 B.C. However, aside from these setbacks, the social equilibrium achieved thus far could only have been maintained on two conditions. Firstly, if the exploitation of Celtic and Italic social mobility as a source of manpower had lasted; but this was reduced everywhere at the same time as the political structures of the other Italic peoples were strengthened and the Celts settled in the Po Valley on a large scale. Secondly, if the advancement of the urban middle classes had had a more logical outcome, with greater opportunities for access to property ownership and government; but this was hindered everywhere by the failure to strengthen—or even the removal of—the currency system, which was confined to port areas, such as that of Populonia. The failure, albeit spread out in time and space, to satisfy these two conditions caused a crisis to which Etruria proper (between the Tiber and the Arno) and—as long as it was governed by Etruscan magistrates—Capua gave a political response aiming at social conservation rather than innovation. This is the attitude that is to be found, for example, in the scenes on the sarcophagus from the Sperandio cemetery at Perugia, where the possessions (in Latin, *familia*, family property) of the deceased are paraded before us: flocks of sheep driven by a serf, and prisoners, possibly of war, or else *nexi*, debt-slaves. Just as in Rome, where the re-establishment of the archaic client system was one of the series of legislative and religious measures intended to restore their coercive powers taken by the aristocracy in the fifth century, in Etruria, too, the restoration of the power of the oligarchy led to the revival of the system of domination over the countryside on which Etruscan society was based in the Orientalizing period, with the large estates being run on a semi-servile basis. But times had changed and it was the cities that had the legal tools adapted to this policy; these ranged from the creation (generally around local sanctuaries) of rustic tribes (local electoral districts), in which members of *gentes* having property and employees in the district could enroll, to the granting of the right to found, or refound, towns (*oppida*) on the land belonging to them. The "recolonization" of the cities' territories—due to the increased demand for food supplies from the main centers—was intended to exercise political control over the urban lower and middle classes, to whom marriage alliances were eventually proposed. It was also indispensable for the containment of Roman expansion; in fact, it was evident as early as 480 B.C., when, during a war between Rome and Veio, the latter obtained reinforcements from all over Etruria. Dionysius of Halicarnassus (who lived in Augustus's reign), recalls the episode in his *Roman Antiquities* (II, 44, 7), mentioning the presence among the troops of Veio's allies, of numerous "Penests" (*Penestai*) under the command of the most powerful leaders (*dunatotatoi*). In Greece, the term Penests referred to a people that had been conquered by the Thessalians (Archemacus, Athenaeus, VI, 264 c–b) and worked the large estates of their masters, dividing—on an unfair basis, no doubt—the produce of the land with them; they were also required to do military service as foot-soldiers alongside the cavalry of the landowners. This status, which was certainly not that of free citizens, did not prevent them, nevertheless, from enjoying a degree of affluence and having the right to own certain forms of property—for instance, houses. According to classifications that date from the Hellenistic age and are repeated in Pollux's *Onomasticon* (III, 83), the condition of the Penests was in-between that of freedom and slavery (*μεταξὺ ἐλευθερῶ καὶ δοῦλων*). The appearance of the term "Penests" cannot, therefore, be considered to be a coincidence in the writings of Dionysius of Halicarnassus; he had read Aristotle, who wrote a work on the customs of the Etruscans (*Tyrrhenon Nomima*), and also works by Theophrastus, who, according to Cicero (*De fin*ibus, V, 4), not only described the customs, institutes, and learning of the barbarian peoples, but also collected their laws. Although very little of Theophrastus' vast output has survived, there is perhaps an echo of these works in the writings of the Byzantine historian Johannes Zonaras where he stresses the equilibrium of the constitution of Volsinii (*πόλις εὐνομουμήνη*) before it was overthrown by those he called "serfs." Dionysius's text also gives an extremely accurate picture of southern Etruria after 480 B.C. It is sufficient to mention the recent discovery at Vetulonia of the helmets of the *gens* Haspna (fifth century B.C.), who must have led their freemen and "Penests" to war in much the same way as the *gentes* allied with Veio described by Dionysius. Or else a comparison may be made with the information given by Dionysius with

Helmet with the inscription "haspnas" from Vetulonia, fifth century B.C.
Florence, Museo Archeologico cat. 70

Tarquinia, Tomb of the Shields, scene of banquet with the Velcha family and their serfs, second half of the fourth century B.C.

that provided by Livy (IX, 37, 12) with regard to a later period (late fourth century), when he describes the cohorts of peasants mobilized by their masters to defend the lands that the Roman troops had invaded, in order to plunder them, from the Monti Cimini. This seems to suggest that, in the countryside, there was a network of large estates located near the owners' residences and cultivated by a subordinate peasant class. This system hindered the formation and growth of a free middle or lower peasant class resident in towns and cultivating its fields in the form of farms—as was the case in the fifth century in the Po Valley near Modena, or at Veio of the Casale Pian Roseto farm, managed by Larth Patara, a freeman, although not necessarily of a high social class. Both inscriptions and paintings help our understanding of the contradictions arising in the fourth century from the social system described above. The frescoes (ca. 380 B.C.) in the Golini Tomb I at Orvieto are enlightening, in particular, with regard to the economic condition of a large family of magistrates living in Volsinii, the Leinie, whose land was located close to the town, near Sette Camini. The imaginary room where the owners' banquet takes place is quite distinct from the kitchens, where a large number of serfs are busy preparing the food. Judging by the names with which they are designated, in which no gentilitial name appears, the majority of them have grown up in the owners' house. Some of them are well dressed, like the woman who seems to be a stewardess; others are perhaps also members of city corporations, such as the *tesinth tamiaturas* (apparently head of the corporation of cooks, who were always present at the sacrifices of animals in the sanctuaries). Others, like the young Pazu Mu[...]lane who is pounding the spelt of the rich Volsinian countryside in a mortar, remind us of the origin of the wealth produced by the estate. Yet others, such as Thresu Penznas (that is, Thresu, an employee of Penzna) or Runchlvis Papnas (that is, Runchlvis, an employee of Papna), seem to be serfs acquired from other families apparently not depicted in the banquet of the Leinie, although their role as *familiares* (close friends) or obligees of this large gens is stressed, as is the fact that their serfs are now in the service of the Leinie. Despite the difficulties involved in interpreting these badly damaged frescoes, the Golini Tomb I offers a very complete picture of the social order that was considered to form the basis of a city well-governed by an oligarchy. Other evidence, such as that of the serfs of the Velcha family, in the Tomb of

Drawing of the pediment of the Talamone temple

the Shields at Tarquinia, or of the Hescanas family (Petinate Hescanas, Pethnace Hescanas) in the eponymous tomb at Porano (near Orvieto) enlighten us with regard to the condition of the domestic serfs, while the inscription of Petru Alethnas near Bolsena throws further light on this semi-servile peasant class. However, it is only rarely that the names of the lower, semi-servile classes are visible and, when they are, this is simply in order to promote their masters' public image. These classes associated with the exploitation of the large estates—or, in the cities, with the output of the major workshops, such as Murila Hercnas at Tarquinia—do not, however, seem to be the only social groups in the countryside and smaller centers. Throughout the fourth century many Etruscan cities, especially Tarquinia, Vulci, and Volsinii created new secondary centers, such as Musarna (between Tuscania and Viterbo), or the development of others, such as Tuscania, Blera, San Giuliano, Norchia, Bomarzo, Ferento, Sorrina, and Sovana, in all of which the society was stratified. Both the necropolises, with a series of isonomic cube tombs and, as at Musarna, the layout of the cities on a grid plan indicate that land was parceled out into equal plots for a considerable number of free families. Socially comparable to colonists, they lived in these centers that were often governed by small oligarchies comprising members—perhaps belonging to secondary branches—of the leading families of their respective metropolises: thus the Alethna, an important family of Tarquinia, are among the magistrates of Musarna. It is possible that this "colonial" model—in which, on a political level, there could have been concessions relating to citizenship and self-government—served, like that of the Roman colonies for the plebeians, to satisfy the demand for land on the part of the urban middle classes, but under the supervision of the aristocrats, who continued to lead these ventures. A magistrate—although not all scholars agree on this interpretation—known as the *zilath eterav* or *zileteraia* and found principally at Tarquinia and in its colony of Musarna (an office held by one of the Alethna), at Vulci (Tomb of the Inscriptions), and perhaps also at Volsinii, could designate the judicial guarantors of these free colonists, who may be compared socially to the Roman clients. The rare title of *zilath eterav* does not appear to have been in use after the third century B.C.; but in the cities of Chiusi and Perugia, in the third and, above all, in the second centuries B.C., a number of individuals were described as *etera* or *lautn eteri*, two terms that seem to be fossils of the social vocabulary in a world that increasingly conformed to Roman models. There is disagreement over the meaning of these expressions: due to the humble nature of the inscriptions (all of them are in modest tombs) and the appearance of the word *lautn*—that is, former serf (?), equivalent to the Latin *libertus*, freedman (in reference to his

following pages
Fragments of the pediment of the Talamone temple (Orbetello), second century B.C.
Florence, Museo Archeologico
cat.307

manumitter), or *libertinus*, freedman (in reference to his status in society or the state) or the son of a freedman—the term *lautn eteri* appears to designate freed families of the serfs of the important landowners. For instance, near Perugia there is the inscription (CIE 4549) of an individual described as the *lautn eteri* of a Precu (the latter was perhaps a member of one of the families named in the hypogeum of San Manno, the Precuthura). With regard to the term *etera*, which is found both in simple tombs and ones belonging to the aristocracy, such as the Perugian Venete or Tite Petruni, it may have referred to a client with the right to share in the inheritance of a number of families. Inheritance, in fact, must have been of fundamental importance in public law (*tesna*? *rasna*), as is clearly attested by the stipulations made between the Velthina and Afuna families, which are inscribed on the cippus of Perugia.
The discovery of a bronze tablet at Cortona (dating from before the war with Hannibal?) provides further evidence with regard to the ownership of property that formed the basis of the social structure. The inscription on the tablet refers to land (with vineyards and olive groves) situated on the plain and in the hills near Lake Trasimene (Tarśmina). Two groups of people are listed: the members of two or three large *gentes* with their wives, allies, and descendants, and the members (fifteen names) of families forming the other party, designated with the collective name of *nuthanathur*. The inscription, which probably concerns a contract (originally deposited in a sanctuary) between landowners and the tenants of their lands, reveals the existence in the Etruscan countryside of two economically distinct groups of large and small landowners (or perhaps just tenants), comprised of freeman. A study of the typology of the tombs and the structure of the names at Chiusi in the third and second centuries confirms this analysis, allowing us to identify a limited number of important *gentes* with their allies and lesser branches in both the city of Chiusi and the towns (*oppida*) in its territory (Chianciano, Sarteano), and a larger number—but having more humble social origins—of families engaged in the cultivation of the vineyards between the lakes of Chiusi and Trasimene. It is possible that the transformation of many former "Penests" and other members of the lower orders who worked on the land, especially tenants, was the outcome of older forms of production based on the semi-servile peasant class. And it was this class of tenants, now free, of the large estates between Chiusi and Cortona that seems to have produced the remarkable Etruscan colonists—"the Dardan (colonists)," as they style themselves on the boundary markers of their fields consecrated to Jupiter—who sought their fortune in Tunisia, in the valley of the Wadi Miliane, perhaps in the Gracchan period. One of the causes of this emigration may be due to the fact that the new generation of servile manpower was of a more modern type because it was purchased on the markets of the East controlled by the Romans, thus competing with the small-scale free tenants, partially deprived the latter of their function in order to serve the interests of the leading gentes. In fact, the presence of these new serfs—in reality, slaves—"purchased abroad and barbarians" (**οἰκέται ἐπείσακτοι καὶ βάρβαροι**), whom Tiberius Gracchus (Plutarch, *Tiberius Gracchus*, 8, 9) had already glimpsed on the Etruscan coast when he was traveling to Spain, is attested, especially towards the end of the second century, by the inscriptions of many *lautni* (freedmen) with Etruscanized Greek names. Bearing in mind the evolution of the systems of production and what appears to be the state of affairs in Etruscan society on the eve of its complete Romanization (in 90 B.C. all Etruscans became Roman citizens), we are in a better position to assess the crises and conflicts that shook the Etruscan world between the fourth and the beginning of the second centuries B.C. It is worthwhile focusing our attention on the events that affected two cities: Arretium (Arezzo) and Volsinii. The Latin inscriptions (*elogia*) of the Spurinna family adorning the forum of Tarquinia in the Julio-Claudian age (part of the *Elogia Tarquiniensia*) recalled a certain Aulus Spurinna who repressed a serf revolt in Arezzo. This event should be seen in the context of the relations between the Etruscan states, regularly sealed by hospitality and marriages between members of the important families—a recently discovered inscription attests, in fact, to the marriage of a Spurinna of Tarquinia to a Cilnia of Arezzo—and may be dated to the fourth century B.C. This serf revolt should probably not be confused with the one, recorded by Livy (X, 3, 2) in 302 B.C., of the urban plebeians of Arretium against the excessive power and the enormous wealth of the family holding sway over the city, the Cilnii (the ancestors of Maecenas), for the pacification of which Roman mediation was necessary. The backbone of these uprisings was formed by artisans, especially those who wrought the bronze artifacts—on the "patera Cospiana," a mirror found in Arezzo and datable to

View of the Anina Tomb (Tarquinia), third–second century B.C.

around the mid-fourth century, Sethlanś, the god of the artisans, is wearing a *bulla*, an amulet in a nonprecious material, round his neck, like the serfs—and other subordinate classes who worked on the lands of the Cilnii, perhaps supported by the free social classes who aspired to more equitable access to property and to the government of the city, and for whom it was necessary to create a currency system that was absent here, as it was in most of Etruria. It must, however, be pointed out that, perhaps in order to avoid events like those in Arezzo, probably to meet the requirements of the middle and upper urban classes, and certainly to oppose the monetary expansion of Rome, Tarquinia—probably thanks to the Pinie, owners of the Giglioli Tomb—put into circulation a new bronze coin at the end of the fourth century. At almost the same time, Volsinii issued the oval series. In the case of Volsinii it is possible to follow the development of a crisis lasting from the late fourth to the early third centuries. It seems that the oligarchs of Volsinii first shared various military duties with their serfs (the wars against Rome from the late fourth century B.C. to the battle of Sentinum of 295 B.C. and the battle of Lake Vadimonis of 283 B.C. are the probable context for these events). The serfs were apparently then required by their masters to participate (perhaps when they became free citizens) in the government of the city (*διοίκησυς πόλεωσ*), perhaps with regard to the administration of the enormous riches of its sanctuaries, including those of the sanctuary of the Etruscan Confederation, the Fanum Voltumnae. From then onwards there were more specifically political demands, such as the right to become members of the senate and hold government posts; this was, in fact, obtained in a violent manner by eliminating the majority of the members of the old ruling class and marrying their wives. This is the account of the Byzantine historian Johannes Zonaras (and of Johannes Antiochensis, fr. 50 Müller), which tallies with the Roman sources (especially Paulus Orosius, I, 5, 3, 5), in which reference is made to wills made under threat, and property taken by force from the natural heirs. Instigated by a number of Volsinian oligarchs who had survived the violence, Rome put an end to this situation in 264 B.C. by storming Volsinii after a difficult campaign, crushing the rebels, laying waste to the city, sacking it and resettling the survivors —masters and the serfs loyal to them alike—on the site of what is now Bolsena. The rebellion of Volsinii took place, as in Arezzo, in a city in which the importance of the urban artisan class had grown, and even more so that of the plebeian and lower classes eager to obtain citizenship and own property. Other echoes of the events in Volsinii are to be found in the so-called prophecy of Vegoia (*Gromatici Veteres*), a document of a socio-political polemic known to us in the transcription contained in the texts written by Roman land-surveyors, although it was probably originally written at the time of what seems to be an agrarian reform at Volsinii. The nymph Vegoia, a semi-divine seer, warns the Volsinian Arruns Velthymnus against the moving of boundary markers of the estates which would be liable to cause the subversion of the institutions and the creation of unlawful dominion. However, since a number of properties are the object of Vegoia's attacks, it may be deduced that not all the owners were unfavorable to the land reform. Moreover, Pseudo-Aristotle's *De mirabilibus ascultationibus* (94)—which gather information regarding good government in a Utopian spirit reflecting the Hellenistic interest in ethnography typical of the Ptolemaic court—refer to a city in Etruria, isolated on the top of a hill surrounded by springs and forests, called Oinarea: this is, in other words, the city of Wine, Abundance, and Liberty, or Oina, resembling Vina (vineyard in Etruscan) o Velzna (Volsinii in Etruscan). The landowners in Oinarea, to avoid the excessive power of one of their number—it appears that the lesson of the revolt at Arezzo against the Cilnii had been learnt—entrusted the government of the city to their manumitted serfs, who, like Roman consuls, held office for a year. This throws further light on the events at Volsinii, and before their dramatic outcome, no trace of which has remained. Could it be, therefore, that it was learnt at the court of Ptolemy II Philadelphus on the occasion of the Roman diplomatic mission of 273 B.C., one of the members of which was Quintus Gallus Ogulnius (whose family's origins were in Chiusi and Volsinii)? The fall of Volsinii marked the end of hopes for social advancement within the Etruscan political system, although these events may have driven the aristocracy to make a number of concessions, spread out in time, evidence of which may be found in the countryside—and also in central and northern Etruria—with the numerous *lautni* (freedmen), and in the cities. It is possible, for example, that the employees of the Anina *gens* of Tarquinia—whose tombs flanked the avenue leading to the square (resembling a forum?) laid out in front of the tomb of their masters—were free, their status being comparable to that of Roman clients. It is probable, however, that the fact that their aspirations were disregarded prompted both the urban and the rural plebeians to revolt. Thus, after the war with Hannibal there was the phenomenon of the band recruited in the Val di Chiana (coins with the legend of Peithesa, with the head of a black man, etc.) until the serf revolt of 196 B.C.—it is not known where this took place, but the main sanctuary of Bolsena, the Pozzarello, has a dedication to Selvans, the guardian of the faith—but it ended with a battle against a Roman legion, with a huge death toll and the crucifixion of many prisoners, and the repression, in 186 B.C., of the Dionysian societies, which were well represented in the same region.

Heurgon 1957, pp. 63–97; Mazzarino 1957, pp. 111–16; Frankfort 1959, pp. 3–22; Heurgon 1959, pp. 713–723; Rix 1963, pp. 356 ff.; Capozza 1965; Colonna 1967, pp. 3–30; Heurgon 1970, pp. 29–41; Lambrechts 1970; Colonna 1973, pp. 45–72; Colonna 1975, pp. 181–92; Colonna 1977a, pp. 175–92; Cristofani, Martelli 1977; De Simone 1978; Torelli 1981a; Cristofani 1983b; Colonna 1985a, pp. 101–31; Cristofani 1985; Roncalli 1985; De Marinis 1986; Pugliese Carratelli 1986; Bermond Montanari 1987; Torelli 1987a; Momigliano Schiavone 1988; Greco, Pontrandolfo 1990; Massa-Pairault 1990; Romualdi 1992; Berti, Guzzo 1993; Menichetti 1994; Sassatelli 1994a; Cerchiai 1995; Massa-Pairault 1996; Maggiani 1998, pp. 95–132; Agostiniani, Nicosia 2000.

Mario Torelli

Etruscan Religion

Our current knowledge of the religious practices of the Etruscans essentially derives from two forms of documentation, the first being archaeological evidence related to actual rites and practices, the second the Roman written sources concerning the *Etrusca disciplina*, the term the Romans used to describe the practices of the Etruscan haruspices, who were summoned to Rome to provide a *procuratio*, i.e. to "find remedies," to unusual phenomena that indicated a disturbance in the *pax deorum*, or harmony between the gods and humankind. Many writers of antiquity, among them Livy, held the Etruscans to be "more than any other dedicated to religion," an opinion endorsed by the Greek pseudo-etymology of the name given to the Etruscans, *Thyrrenoi*, derived from *thyein*, meaning "sacrifice." From the copious evidence available it is reasonable to infer that practically every action performed by the Etruscans was prompted by religious necessity, or unfolded within some form of ritualistic framework—a fact borne out by the abundant material they produced in the performance of their convoluted religious practices. Indeed, archaeologists have been able to piece together extensive knowledge of Etruscan religious practices by systematically cross-referencing the philological, epigraphical and linguistic data afforded by the mass of archaeological material unearthed during excavation work carried out in sanctuaries, dwellings and tombs, submitting these finds to an iconographical analysis of the figurative content of temple decorations, frescoes, pottery, candelabres, mirrors and cists, plus inscriptions and antiquities related to votive objects and material for religious or daily household use. The Roman literary sources (or Greek ones dating from the Roman period) have meanwhile passed on vital information on religious practices that would otherwise have been hard to retrieve, including some texts with the haruspices' responses.

It is worth noting that, amid all this material so fortunately salvaged are two outstanding documents whose contents are of unparalleled significance for the study of Etruscan religious practices, despite the hermeneutic difficulties in deciphering the language. These documents are the *Liber Linteus* of Zagreb, a liturgical calendar complied in the second century B.C. in the area of Cortona or Perugia, cut into strips and reused as wrappings for a mummy in Egypt; and the Piacenza Liver, a small bronze model of a sheep's liver for use in divination, also dating to the second century B.C. bearing epigraphical indications regarding the identification of specific ar-

opposite
Bronze mirror from Tuscania with haruspicy scenes, mid-fourth century B.C. Florence, Museo Archeologico cat. 319

Liber Linteus, *second century B.C. Zagreb, National Museum*

Fragment of bronze lituus from Sant'Ilario d'Enza (Reggio Emilia), sixth century B.C. *Reggio Emilia, Musei Civici cat. 149*

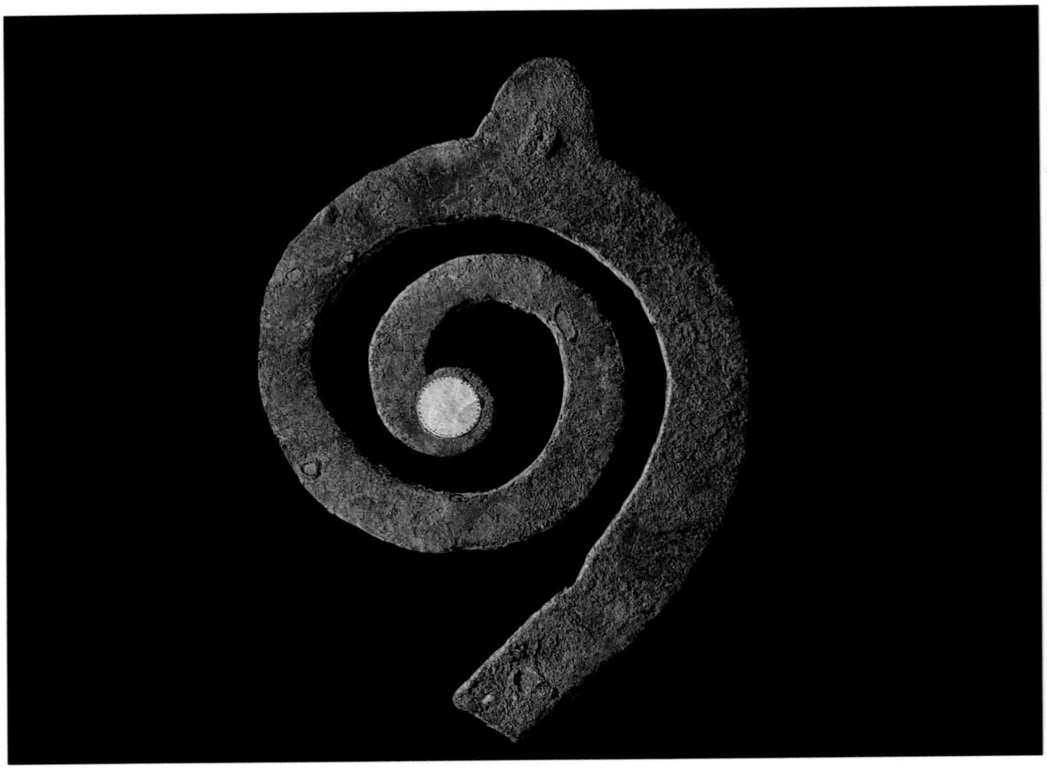

eas of the liver with individual deities, based on a set of alleged supernatural links between the areas of sheep's organ and the divisions of the heavenly spheres (and of the underworld). These documents are complemented by other Etruscan finds of varying difficulty of interpretation, though of undoubted religious significance, namely the large Capua Tile bearing details of funerary rites conducted from March to October, unearthed in the Etruscan capital of Campania (sixth century B.C.); the lead lamina from Santa Marinella, thought to be an oracular text from the Ceri area (end sixth century B.C.), both confirming the fact that the longest extant inscriptions in the Etruscan language are of a religious nature.

This brief summary soon makes it clear that attempts at reconstructing the religious practices are conditioned by a highly fragmentary overall picture and by serious gaps in our knowledge of the complex scientific procedures themselves, the outcome being a historical and "systematic" vision of Etruscan religion; by the same token, many religious phenomena have perforce been reconstructed by analogy, comparing them against similar phenomena of the "neighboring" religions, a method which, while providing a generally plausible picture, must remain conjecture. Etruscan religion is the outcome of a complex series of events that progressively modified the foundations of a much earlier system of worship, whose basic features can be glimpsed through successive layers deposited by strong outside influences from diverse sources, some of prehistoric origin deriving from the Latin and Italic world, together with those from the Near East and from Greece in the Orientalizing, Archaic and Classical epochs. The earliest secure evidence documenting prehistorical Etruscan religious ritual comes from an excavation made during the past few years, when there was the discovery of a place of worship with undoubted "political" connotations, dating to between the Later Bronze Age (tenth century B.C.) and the Hellenistic Age (third century B.C.) in the heart of ancient Tarquinia. This find has brought to light significant new information on Etruscan religious developments prior to the onset of Hellenization in the eighth–seventh centuries B.C.. Results of the find include the identification of what looks like a *curia*, a political and religious body characteristic of the Roman Archaic period whose existence in Etruria is known through a Latin inscription dating from the time of Tiberius that mentions a *curia Asernia* at Cerveteri. The original locus of this cult is a deep cavity in the ground where various kinds of sacrifices were made; the pit has yielded unprecedented evidence suggesting sacrificial rites involving infants, a practice to which our sources attribute the origin of the Roman festival of the *Compitalia* performed for the cult of the domestic goods known as *Lares* (Macrobius, *Saturnalia*, I, 7, 35). Subsequently, in the seventh century B.C. a cult building was erected, complete with altars linked to the mouth of the shaft, and a large trapezoidal precinct, probably the site of collective rituals and gatherings: the deposits of bronze parade weaponry, ceremonially rendered unserviceable, suggest observances similar to those of the Roman rites of Iuppiter Feretrius. This primitive Tarquinian sanctuary has shed important light on a previous discovery that had long been the subject of debate, namely, certain material dating from the Iron Age (ninth–seventh century B.C.) uncovered in other Etruscan sanctuaries of historical times, including extra-urban sites, at Veii and Tarquinia.

Providing clues as to the Etruscans' conception of religion during the protohistoric period are teratomorphic or nonetheless non-anthropomorphic representations of deities found on cinerary urn lids, such as the famous lid from Pontecagnano (ninth century B.C.), on which appears a couple from the underworld with elongated extremities and faces, caught in a sacred conjugal embrace; or the one from Bisenzio (eighth century B.C.), depicting a pyrrhic around a gigantic figure with monstrous features (more a deity than a bear-figure as suggested). Before the beginning of the Hellenization process it seems that deities were believed to be horrendous, animalesque figures (at least those connected with death). This tradition arose in historical times in the guise of the monster Olta, who emerged from the land of Volsinii and was struck down by a thunderbolt summoned by Porsenna (Pliny, *Naturalis historia,* XI, 140), a feature that survived in the underworld *larvae* and the subterranean *dei indigetes-pisciculi* (gods in form of fishes) of Roman tradition. There can be little doubt that in this early phase of Etruscan religion a fundamental role was entrusted to the elements of nature, housed in the sky, earth, and the underworld; not endowed with anthropomorphic features they were of terrifying appearance, and often of ambiguous sexual connotation: ever since the remote past, this ambiguity attributed to the gods applied not only to the retinue of "demons" of historical Etruscan deities, but even to Velthumna-Vertumnus himself, *deus Etruriae princeps* and lord of the federal sanctuary of Volsinii (Varro, *De lingua latina*, V, 46), whose features are described in Propertius (IV, 2) as protean and sexually ambiguous, despite the inevitable Hellenistic euhemerisms.

To this same period we owe the development of one of the principal features of Etruscan religious practice (shared with its Latin counterpart), namely, the cult of the regenerative power of male and female, and thence the constitution of the dominant forms of domestic worship aimed at favoring the aristocracy's growth in number and power. Texts of later date, as widely known as they are controversial, betray lingering traces of Etruscan beliefs filtered through the haruspices, and lay emphasis on the inexplicability (*involuti*) and unpredictability (*opertanei*) of the supernal powers, on their multiplicity (*complices* and *consentes*) in either male or female form, and lastly on the presence of "lesser" deities, the *Genii*, *Favores*, or *Lares*. In much the same way as happens with the vague attribution of "groups of deities" and the presence of "demons" of the underworld or entourage of Turan-Aphrodite termed *lasa* (perhaps linked to the Latin *lar*) and often coupled with a qualifier, such as Lasa Vecuvia (Latinized to Nympha Begoe, as we shall see), so the deities of this latter category all betray remote vestiges of collective religion, such as domestic ritual, in which pride of place is given to heroized ancestors and the deification of the ancestry of the Etruscan *pater familias*, as seen in the Latin counterparts *lares* and *genii*. Indeed, the identification of the Etruscan equivalent of Genius, Farthan—referring to the generative capacity of the head of the clan and the *pater familias*—has been convincingly linked to the root **farth-*, i.e., "to generate," known by its passive perfect form *farthnache*, meaning "it has been generated."

This curious and widespread phenomenon of religious interchange between Etruscan spheres and Latin, Faliscan and Umbrian ones, mainly involves ceremonies of religious power, marriage rituals, and rites of passage, and primitive religious practices originating deep in the past; this heritage enabled the Etruscan pantheon to absorb a fair quantity of fairly important Latin and Italic gods, whose actual assimilation dates to before the onset of strong Hellenic influences, and before the spread of Etruscan cultural and political hegemony over most of the peninsula (eighth–seventh century B.C.). Of evident Latin extraction are the gods linked to man's reproductive power and to nature, and hence to the primordial landscape and the earliest notions of agricultural cycles: Menerva-Minerva, Maris-Mars, Nethuns-Neptunus, Uni-Juno, Vetis/Veive-Vediovis, Satre-Saturnus, Selvanus-Silvanus, Ana-Anna

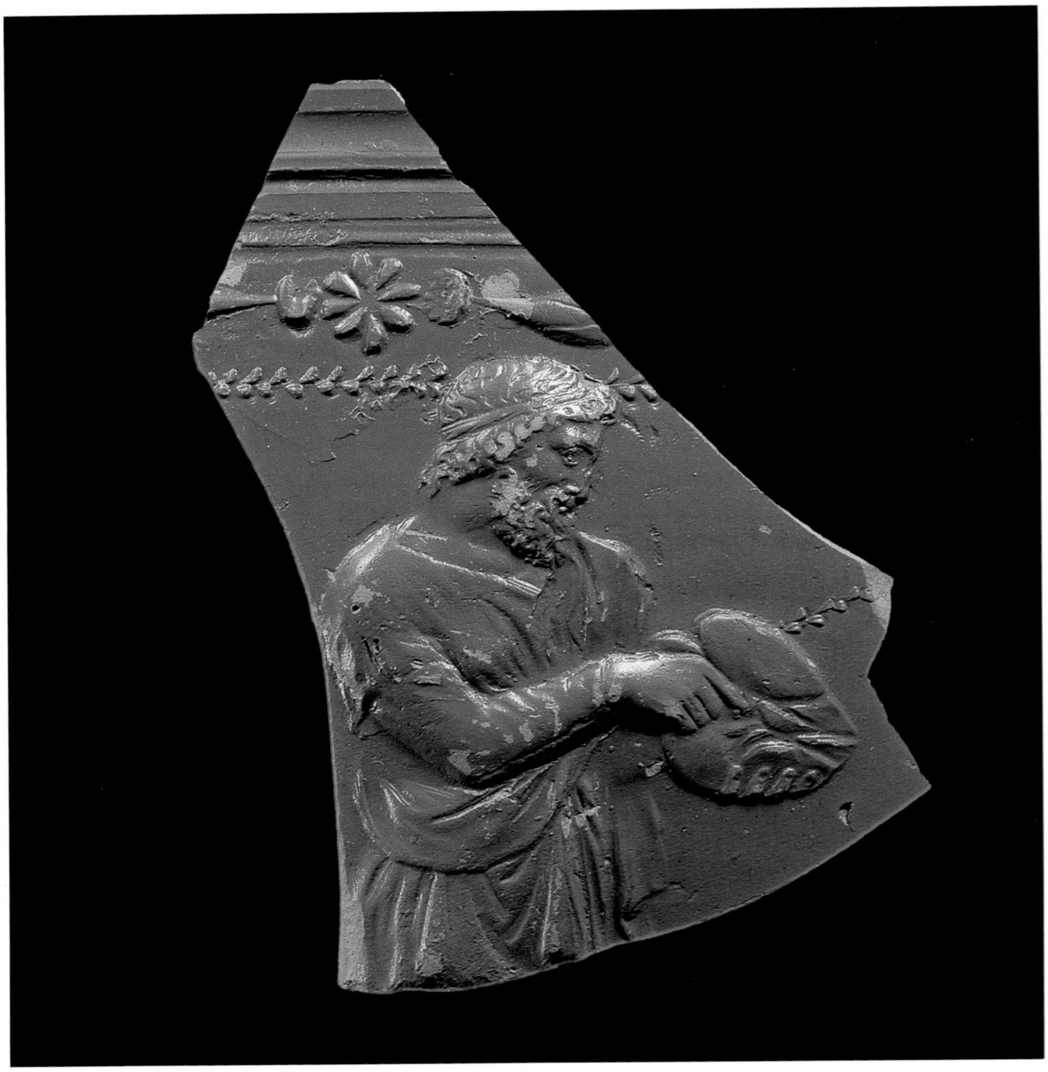

Arretine "sigillata" fragment from Rasinius' workshop,
ca. 15 B.C.
Tübingen, Institut für Klassische Archäologie
cat. 158

Perenna, among others. Whereas of Faliscan origin are Suris-Soranus; and of Umbrian influence the less significant Vesuna. Another feature of Etruscan religion shared with these three source areas includes the long tradition of attributing double names to their gods, akin to the Latin forms Ianus Qurinus and Panda Cela; to the Umbrian Torsa Iovia; or to the Oscan Anaceta Cerria. This coupling of appellatives was employed to denote a sort of functional specialization for the deity concerned or to designate spheres of opposing forces, whence come Tinia Calusna to signify Tinia of Calu, i.e., the force Tinia-Zeus whose sphere of influence thereby extended to the realm of the catachthonic deity Calu.
The puzzle is made more complex by the extensive framework of beliefs shared by Etruria, Latium and the Umbro-Sabine region regarding omens and auguries. This was brought to light very recently with the discovery of what seems to be an augural *templum* in a sanctuary at Este, proving that auspices was practiced in a vast area in ancient Italy and is a vestige of prehistoric religious practices common to diverse Italic peoples. Throughout Etruria divination in its broadest sense was in widespread use, providing man's closest link with the world of the gods, legitimizing power, and organizing space and primitive technical knowledge; to this end, an elect of specifically Etruscan "theoreticians" of divinatory practices emerged, the haruspices.
As a whole, these factors indicate that back in the deepest past, in the late second and early first millennium, the ancestors of the Etruscans had already established an elaborate groundwork of ritual: in this phase these ancestors appear to have been in close contact at both social and cultural levels—most likely through intermarriage and "political" interaction—with neighbor-

Bronze model of a sheep's leaver from Settima (Piacenza), end of the second–beginning of the first century B.C.
Piacenza, Museo Civico
cat. 160

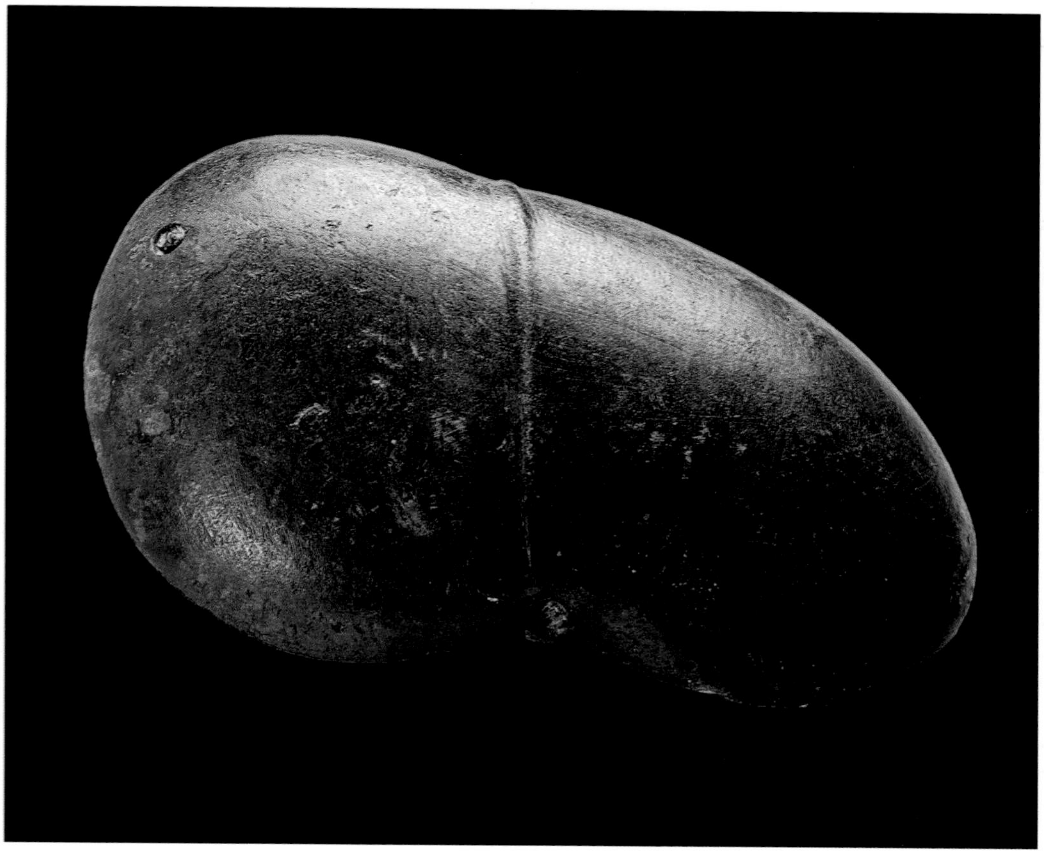

right and opposite
Bronze statuettes of haruspices.
Göttingen, Archäologisches Institut der Universität
cats. 154; 153; 155; 152 (side and front)

Small bronze plaque with haruspex, 400–375 B.C.
Amsterdam, Allard Pierson Museum
cat. 151

Small bronze plaque of a Schnabelkanne,
end of the fourth century B.C.
Arezzo, Museo C. Cilnio Mecenate
cat. 150

ing peoples on the peninsula, an exchange that applied particularly in the case of the Latins, to whom they were marginal if not subordinate, given that Etruscan worship was an offshoot of the formers' system of beliefs. Collective and domestic practices which developed amid the incipient Etruscan aristocracy in early historic times seem to have emerged from this framework of beliefs, founded on notions of the forces of nature and reproduction—a worldview shared by other peoples of ancient Italy, with whom the Etruscans were in contact from the remotest of times. From the beginnings of class stratification in the eighth century B.C., and the consequent cohesion into increasingly evolved complex settlements (eighth–sixth century), Etruscan society found its ideal counterpart in Greek civilization, which was soon adopted as a model for an emerging aristocratic social setup styled on the Greek *poleis*. This process of cultural induction, whose byproduct was the Hellenization of the Etruscan pantheon and religious ritual, generated a combination of Greek models forged with characteristics of traditional pre-protohistorical cult practices, with a sprinkling of eastern elements introduced into Etruria by Phoenician trade dating to before the first significant impact of contact with the Greeks, at the start of the eighth century B.C. This interchange was responsible for the Orientalizing features of Etruscan religion, epitomized by the Etrusco-Punic goddess Uni-Astarte in the sanctuary at Pyrgi; other manifestations are the emergence of the haruspex, which thenceforth rapidly became a standard Etruscan means of divination in historical times, having undoubted roots in the Mesopotamian science of hepatoscopy. All these influences reached the Etruscans by means of the peninsula's varied contacts with the East in the early stages of the first millennium B.C. This notwithstanding, it was primarily the Greek civilization in all its cultural complexity—literature, visual arts, lifestyle, production techniques, military science, and hence the very material and cultural identity of both the individual and society—that offered the pivotal reference point for the emerging Etruscan elites, which as early as the eighth century B.C. sifted through the vast legacy of Hellenic culture for aspects that were not only compatible with the existing local power setup but would ultimately afford endorsement and ensure its continuing development.

One of the most crucial aspects of this assimilation process—and one that guaranteed the Etruscan political future—was the Greek religious legacy, whose absorption wrought a sweeping revolution of beliefs following by the Hellenization of a large quota of the Etruscan pantheon and the assumption of a great many Greek myths; this fostered a manifest alignment of religious practices with the Greek system, and brought with it the Hellenization of the rituals and conceptions involved in indigenous worship, such that on the surface the Etruscan religion began to look like a provincial variant of its Greek counterpart. Many were the channels of this Hellenization: while the transfer of the Greek mythical apparatus and the process of *interpretatio graeca* of Etruscan deities largely concerned the ruling classes and priesthood, the effects of the more mundane business of daily commerce—which from late seventh to early fifth century thrived among the trading centers (of which Gravisca and Pyrgi are outstanding examples)—trickled down to the lower classes, favoring the spread of religious integration. However, this ongoing process of ideological accommodation was not exclusive to the Tyrrhenian basin. Fortunately, most of the data available for Rome show that Roman culture was likewise being affected, with the piecemeal Hellenization of its gods and forms of worship in a manner similar to the process then under way in Etruria. Thus the Etruscan deities adopted a Greek slant, with Tinia aligned with Zeus, Uni with Hera, Menerva with Athena, and so forth. Turan becomes Aphrodite, Turms Hermes, Maris Ares, Nethuns Poseidon, Sethlans Hephaestus, Fufluns Dionysos, Usil Helios, Vei Demeter, and Thesan Eos. Along with the reinterpretation of the local deities are significant "borrowings" that induced a sort of Etruscan version of the Greek *dodekatheon* consisting of a handful of the more salient figures of the world of Hellenic heroes, whence Apulu-Apollo, Aritimi-Artemis, Letun-Latona, Aita-Hades, Phersipnei-

Relief of a mirror with the inscription "Vesuna" from Castel Giorgio

Relief of a mirror with Usil

Persephone, Charun-Charun, Hercle-Heracles, Castur-Castor, Pultuce-Pollux, and Atunis-Adonis. Thanks to these conversions and loans, integrated with the divinities of Italic origin noted above (Selvans, Satre, Suris, Veive, Ana...), the Etruscan pantheon took shape. By cross-referencing the iconography with Latin epigraphical documentation and archaeological finds, we obtain a plausible picture of the functions and physiognomy of the other components that escaped the process of Hellenization. Thus we have Culsans, which appears to stem from the word **culs* ("gate" or "doorway") representing a two-headed deity comparable to Janus, it too linked to the Latin word for gate, *ianua*. Meanwhile Laran is a war-like figure who features in many local myths and perhaps corresponds with Quirinus; Calu inhabits the underworld, and Pethan might be his *paredra*; Catha (or Cautha) is a sun-god with underworld connotations similar to the Latin (Sol) Indiges, though the Latin pantheon has no equivalent of *Cathas sech* (Daughter of Catha) but may be the "Celeritas Solis filia" mentioned in a famous passage of an Etruscan oracular literature handed down somewhat confusedly in the *De nuptiis Mercuri et Philologiae* (I, 45 ff.) by the erudite Marziano Capella (sixth century A.D.); Tiv corresponds with Luna; Cel is the Etruscan of Tellus-Ghê; while *Manth- (or Manthurna) has linguistic affinities with the lower Latin deity Mania, its association with Dispater may be more tenable; Mlacuch is almost certainly equivalent to the Latin Bona Dea and to the Sabine Cupra; Rath appears to be a young god linked to the art of divination; the goddess Alpan belongs to the circle of Aphrodite, but inscriptional dedications assign her a cult of her own; Cilen may be linked to the god of Fate; in its Latinized form Velchumna becomes Vortumnus (perhaps linked to the Etruscan god Tevere-Volturnus?) and rather than represent an independent deity could be one of the (Tinia)Velchumna, i.e., a kind of youthful Zeus, protector of vegetation; Apa and Ati, respectively Mother and Father, have recently been revealed as the titular deities of the temple in the acropolis of Volterra, and therefore hypostases of the supreme couple of the heavens, or more likely of the underworld.

Despite some reservations regarding the attributes of each deity, many of these non-Hellenized gods are indubitably allocated to the underworld, a relevant sphere in the Etruscan worldview, and one that found scant material for assimilation in the Greek pantheon. On the other hand, the very abundance of loans from the Greek to the Etruscan set of underworld deities would indicate that the latter's pantheon was far less populated than its Hellenic counterpart. At any event, there are critical gaps in our knowledge of the gods featured in the Piacenza Liver, and their very inclusion in the haruspical system means their importance cannot be denied, so much so that several are even known through other sources: foremost Thuflthas, often thought to be equivalent to the Latin Penati; Letham, a deity hovering between the realms of life and afterlife, is present on the Capua Tile; Mae, perhaps Maius, related to the Latin Maia, *paredra* of Vulcan and eponymous with the month of May according to a passage of doubtful interpretation in Macrobius (*Saturnalia*, I, 12, 17 ff.); Tece or Tecvm, a benign force, whose cult based around Lake Trasimene is referred to the bronze statue of the *Arringatore*; Cvlalp, a chthonic deity, perhaps a variant of Cul(su) Alp(an), i.e., Alpan in the sphere of Culsu/Culsans-Janus; Lvsl, a theonym linked to the noble line of Luvisu; Velch, another theonym from which the family name Velch derives; and finally Tlusc, a deity from whose position on the model liver one can surmise is far from benign. Similar difficulties in establishing precise connotations arise with the impenetrable retinue of *daimones*, nymphs and retinue of *Turan*-Aphrodite, whose erotic imagery is common on late Classical and Hellenistic mirrors, and includes male such genii as Aminch, Svutaf, and Pulchisf, together with the female *lasa* figures, each with its affix Lasa Sitmica, Lasa Racuneta, Lasa Achunanu and Lasa Vecu, and others iconographically similar such as Ach(a)vis(e)r, Zipna, Leinth, Snenath, Reschual (Recial), Evan, Mean, Hinthia, and Munthuch. Some of these function as "messengers of fate," moving thus between worlds bearing individual or collective *fata* written on *rotuli*; during the Hellenistic period their presence in the Etruscan Hades and in Greek mystical contexts is conspicuous (for example, with Aeacus and Amphiaraus); others (Thalna, Thanr, and Ethausva) are assigned the function similar to that of the Latin attendants of childbirth, the Carmentae, who "sing the fate" of the newborn like their Latin counterparts, whose etymological roots is the noun *carmen*, meaning "singing."

By the end of this fervid phase of *interpretatio Graeca* of a number of the local deities—a

Relief of a mirror with Minerva

process that ended in the seventh century B.C.—the Etruscan pantheon had established its definitive state. In parallel, the absorption into the Etruscan political and religious canon of a large quantity of myths of Greek origin is a great help in understanding the renewal of ideology that this Hellenization of the pantheon entailed, and sheds much light on the actual forms of worship involved. From the seventh to the end of the fourth century B.C. the repertoire for decoration of whatever articles with intrinsic ideological significance—from the parade items and luxury goods to the sculpted ornamentation of the large sanctuaries—is dominated without exception by Greek mythology, the medium chosen by the ruling class to transmit its political and cultural message to the public at large. The mythical themes of Hellenic stamp adorning the monuments in the early Antique period (seventh century B.C.) are unequivocally of a political nature, celebrating the sovereignty and *aristeia* of the noble families, declaring the mythical origins of their *ghenos* and the conquest of power. As a result, considerable space was given over to the myths of Theseus and Heracles, to the Theban and Trojan cycles, in which the thematic material mentioned above found easy correspondence; whereas representations of such myths as battles against giants, titans and amazons—at the time very popular in contemporary Greece to portray the triumph of cosmic order over the chaos and barbarity of mankind—are surprisingly few and far between. From this distinguishing fact one can reasonably surmise inherent differences in the Etruscan view of celestial and cosmic order from that of the Greeks.

It is not until the fourth century B.C. and thereafter, with the massive upheavals in Etruscan society, that representations of local legend enter the canon. The new imagery takes the form of "historical" sagas, similar to the legends of the historical myths of the Latins and Romans. Prime examples are the tales of the brothers Vibenna-Vipinas (their attack on a Cacu-Cacus in the guise of *mantis*), some briefly cited in Roman written sources. Among the exceedingly rare Etruscan legends known to us through written literature is that of the remarkable unearthing of the childlike sage Tages, the legendary founder of the science of divination. Other legends have reached us through iconographical media alone, of which two are relevant here: the battle of the armed god Laran and Cels *clan* ("Son of Cel-Tellus," probably an Etruscan version of the Battle of the Giants); and above all the one portraying Menerva in the act of immersing the boy Maris *husrnana* ("Mars infantilis"?) in a vase in the presence of Turan and two other youths known as Leinth and Maris *thalna* ("Mars iuvenilis"?). One can only guess the meaning underlying such myths, though generally this type of narrative appear to stem from the legendary *origo* of the *ethnos*, of the *poleis*, of the *gentes*, or to myths about the foundation of given institutions and rites. Here too the Hellenization of worship is no less profound. Certain discernible similarities between cult practices—the distinction between underworld and celestial sacrifice; the belief in a mystical "sympathy" between the deities' attributes and the nature of their victims; the use of *escharai* and *bothroi*—may have instead developed along separate parallel paths. Be that as it may, the overall system of cult shrines in historical times seems largely borrowed from the Greek, comprising a *temenos*, altar, and temple complete with cella and peristyle. To these the Etruscans added other formal features of their own devising, the most significant being the podium: the theoretical basis of this distinct departure from the Greek format is to be found in the pan-Italic augural doctrine by which the site of the *templum*, once identified as the *locus effatus*, was ritually "purged of spirits" and marked with the creation of the podium. This difference in level of the "house of god" was both a material and a symbolic means of distinguishing it from the surrounding world, thereby establishing a sacred locus purified through the science of divination.

As we have seen, the triad of outside cultures—Italic, Phoenician, and Greek—wrought profound changes on the Etruscan pantheon. And yet it was the Greek influence, notably in terms of the iconography it provided, which gave the indigenous deities a "second skin," as it were, a sort of veneer beneath which their original connotations remained substantially unaltered. The most obvious cases of this veneer are the Etruscan deity *Tinia*, whose nature was at once infernal and celestial, of both darkness and light, yet only superficially coincides with the Greek Zeus; the Etruscan *Menerva*, goddess of fate and oracles, was far from identical to the Greek goddess Athena, despite having the same apparel; *Uni* can be identified both with the more common Hera and with the Phoenician goddess Ishtar-Aphrodite. While the *interpretatio Graeca* that took place in the Archaic period—favored by successive outside philosophical and religious influences upon Etruscan religion (particularly Orphism and Pythagoreanism spreading from Magna Graecia)—helped establish a theological framework explaining the balance of powers, spheres of influence, and divinities, it never entirely obscured the original and often ambiguous nature intrinsic to the Etruscan gods, whose distinguishing feature was their uncanny ability to shift from heaven to earth, to switch from one type of power to another, to trespass between domains and, not least, their sexual ambivalence.

Thanks to this peculiarity of the Etruscan religious mentality, the ambiguity of the indigenous gods allowed them to transit from one sphere to another and therefore assimilate the corresponding powers of wherever they went. The result was the development of a concept essential to Etruscan and Italic culture, known to us through the art of divining: the mystical correspondence between *templa*, *in caelo*, *in terris*, and *sub terra*, that is, the coexistence of supernal forces in the celestial spheres, on the earth, and in the underworld. This analogy was transferred to the haruspicy, by which the subdivisions of heaven and earth were identified on the surface of the liver of the victim. Arising at source from the pan-Italic branch of the practice of interpreting omens and portents—probably influenced by Mesapotamian concepts during the Orientalizing period of the eighth and seventh centuries B.C—haruspicy was a political and religious peculiarity refined by the Etruscan priesthood, which systematically developed three distinct kinds of divining in parallel: the scrutiny of entrails or livers (hepatoscopy), of lightning (*fulguratoria*), and thunder (brontoscopy). The class of priests developed within the larger clans and soon saw the emergence of an oligarchy, a characteristic of Etruscan society from the fifth century B.C. onward, which developed the esoteric science of reading omens reputed unintelligible to the common man, and whose interpretation was reserved to the priestly members of the ruling class. As a consequence, to ensure the correct interpretation and determine the subsequent *procuratio* to perform, the Romans would summon the Etruscan haruspices to the capital to provide a remedy for the *ostenta* that had manifested themselves. In the Hellenistic period this elite of expert consultants, composed of heirs of the aristocracy of the Etruscan dodecapolis, established a *collegium lx haruspicum* based in Tarquinii, the sacred town where Tages was born. Providing vital information of the procedure followed by the haruspices are the *Etrusca disciplina* and the Piacenza Liver, which surface is divided into two parts designated as *usils* and *tivs* ("of the sun" and "of the moon") denoting a primary opposition/correspondence between the day sky and night sky; a similar dualistic pair is provided by *pul* and *metlvmth* ("cosmic" and "terrestrial"); just beyond the *incisura umbilicalis* near the *vesica fellea* lies a third dichotomy ("Olympus" vs. "Hades"?) by which a certain favorable force identified as Maris (celestial?) accompanied by Hercle, is counterpoised by an unfavorable embodiment of the same Maris accompanied by the obscure (and underworld ?) force Tluscv; a suggested water-fire polarity may be implied by the model's placing of the overtly propitious water-spirit Neth(uns) opposite its fiery and negative counterpart Maris. These polarities clarify the more deeply rooted opposition contained in the Piacenza Liver between two sets of deities capable of issuing the *ostenta*—perhaps indicating two opposing *templa*, one celestial, the other infernal. The names of these deities are repeated in two sequences, one comprising sixteen names along the outer band, and another internal set comprising twelve names (in turn subdivided into two groups of six), such that the right lobe of the model, starting from the *processus pyramidalis* (the *caput iecinoris* in the Latin sources), contains the eight and six propitious deities (as far as the liver's *incisura umbilicalis*, or *fissum* in the written sources), and on the left lobe the eight (plus six) negative forces. In this way, the contrast between the celestial and chthonic spheres, and between the positive and negative forces exerted by the various gods, are little more than an update of a belief of far earlier date, by which the same gods can have both a celestial *sedes* and an infernal one. The gods interfere in the life of mankind by means of portents; they interact among themselves, just as they can join together (witness *Tinia calusna*), or "cohabit" in the same *sedes*, as we learn from that other Etruscan specialization, the *fulguratoria* together with the *haruspicina*. According to the former practice (Pliny, *Naturalis historia*, II, 138; Seneca, *Naturales quaestiones*, II, 4), the Etruscans' Jupiter, Tinia, has three different *manubiae* or ways of releasing thunderbolts, depending on whether he hurls them alone, or together with his counsel of *dei consentes* or *dei involuti*; it is no surprise, therefore, that in hepatoscopy the three favorable *sedes* of the outer band of the Piacenza Liver, corresponding to the northeast sector of the celestial *templum*, show Tin(ia) with two other gods, namely Cilen, Thvf (or Thuflchas) and most likely Nech(uns); even the somewhat confused lists of Marziano Capella record the triple presence of Jupiter (I, 45 ff.).

Together with the aforementioned magical-religious synergy created through the coupling of theonyms—very common among early Mediterranean religions—this characteristic "cohabitation" of gods in both celestial and infernal *sedes* sheds light on yet another peculiarity of Etruscan religion, namely the grouping of gods in threes. Only occasionally occurring in the Greek world (witness the Delphic triad), this association of deities is considered to have originated with the Etruscans: after the foundation of the Capitol with its three gods and the dedication of the temple of the plebeian triad carried out subsequently on the Aventine, the idea was passed down to the Romans, who celebrated it all across the Mediterranean in the course of Romanization. This notwithstanding, the Etruscans cannot be credited with the introduction of the divine triad, nor with its exclusive usage: the *Tabulae Iguvinae*, a set of liturgical texts written in Umbrian, relate the existence of more than one triad composed on a purely functional basis, rather than on a family-based system comprising a celestial couple with a son, suggesting that this feature shared by Etruria and Umbria most certainly has its origins in prehistory.

At any event, the progressive "normalization" of Etruscan religious culture as it succumbed to the influence of the Hellenic world resulted in a more clearly defined, less protean and ambiguous pantheon. Thus prompted to conform with their Greek counterparts, the Etruscan gods gradually acquired more stable theological attributes, compatible with the prevailing characteristics of the original deities—whether hostile or benign, chthonic or celestial—according to their appointed *sedes* and to the ability of the haruspices to deliver interpretations of prodigious natural events requested of them. Thanks again to Greek influence during the late Classical and above all Hellenistic periods, these doctrines steadily absorbed input from the Orphic-Pythagorean tradition and from astrological practices of varying nature and significance, a process that gradually saw the *Etrusca disciplina* evolve into a complex corpus of religious knowledge. That science was managed by professional haruspices based in each town of the Dodecapolis, gathered into a corporation of sixty priests, the *collegium lx haruspicum*, with its headquarters in Tarquinii, the birthplace of the fabled child-like seer Tages. The resulting corpus of doctrines was systematically enhanced with the college's collective *responsa* together with the specific prognostications made each time by individual diviners (generally a member of the *collegium*) and compiled in volumes.

For obvious political reasons, Rome exercised a control over these publications through the *ii*

Bronze statuette of Selvans from Cortona, first half of the third century B.C.
Cortona, Museo dell'Accademia Etrusca
cat. 201

Bronze statuette of Culsans from Cortona, first half of the third century B.C.
Cortona, Museo dell'Accademia Etrusca
cat. 200

viri sacris faciundis (later *x viri* and finally *xv viri*), appointed to keep watch over "foreign" forms of cult worship. Though not always organized to precise criteria, the volumes nonetheless provided a calendar of sorts, cataloguing by type the *ostentaria* or lists of prodigious phenomena, which served as an almanac of rites (*libri rituales*) for public or private performance, together with ceremonial guidelines for deaths and the afterlife (*libri Acherontici*), treatises on haruspicy (*libri haruspicina*) and for interpreting lightning (*libri fulgurales*). Of particular interest are the *libri fatales*, a compendium of rules covering the mysterious workings of fate. All these records testify to a predominant tendency toward the art of prophecy among the ruling classes, whence the discipline originated, a tendency particularly manifest in the Hellenistic period, as borne out by the fragment of a declaration made by the Etruscan *lasa* Vecu (her name later Romanized to Nympha Vegoia or Begoe; *Gromatici Veteres,* p. 350 Lachmann). Transcribed by the haruspex Arruns Velthymnus (perhaps of Perugian origin), the seer's prophecy involves a series of dramatic punishments, to be meted variously among the *domini* and their *servi*, should they usurp certain lands, and worse penalties for similar actions committed by *servi* with the complicity of their *domini*.

What we are witnessing is a logical extension of the oligarchic system of the priesthood which, still tied to the logic of the ritual books of the *Etrusca disciplina*, is totally oriented toward divinatory practices involving the close scrutiny of messages from the goods and the scrupulous observance of rituals, of which the haruspices were deemed the only legitimate interpreters.

Though scarce, what fragments survive of the written sources provide vital insights into the fundamental features of the Etruscan spiritual ethos. The gods themselves are distant, their *sedes* remote, whence, either alone or concomitant with others in a group or divine compound, they make their will manifest to mankind. However, whereas the Greek and Roman religions of this same period theorized on the *pax deorum*, the peaceful balance between the divine and human spheres and the need to reestablish harmony whenever man's actions upset the balance, the Etruscans' idea of order—attested by their disregard for such cosmogonic myths as Giants and Titans—answers to criteria whose theoretical basis is still largely obscure, but at all events obeys a different logic to Greek thought in the Classical and Hellenistic ages. Etruscan mentality has been effectively described by Seneca in a famous passage from the *Naturales quaestiones* (II, 32, 2): "We believe that thunderbolts are the outcome of a collision of clouds; instead, [the Etruscans] believe that the clouds collide in order to produce thunderbolts: since they attribute all phenomena to the will of the gods, they are convinced that things have meaning not because they happen, but because they are bearers of portents." Divine will is by nature occult, inexplicable, hidden from the eyes of the common man, and manifests itself in complex signs or omens that could not be recognized without the haruspices, who were able to interpret these omens on the basis of an exacting set of classifications that assigned positive and negative values to people, animals, and natural or prodigious natural phenomena. The portent, or to use the technical word the *ostentum* or "sign," was analyzed in minute detail; subsequently, an equally intricate *procuratio* was devised to redress the imbalance the phenomenon portended—first, by comprehending its meaning, then by trying to eliminate the abnorm physical product of the god's will, the *ostentum*, if such were possible. It is easy to imagine, given the highly individual and archaic social composition of Etruria, that considerable emphasis was laid on the phenomenology of signs from the spheres of power, by dint of which the Etruscan haruspices guaranteed themselves an official role in the political and religious affairs of Rome, where they were empowered to explain *ostenta*, and hence the reasons for the gods' hostility. The long lists reported in annals and early written sources concerning occurrences of *prodigia* in Rome—and the *procurationes prodigiorum* devised by the Etruscan haruspices consisting of magical practices usually based on the "sympaty" of opposites—constitute the most substantial corpus of intelligence on the Etruscan religion known to us.

The singular groundwork of Etruscan society, based on an extensive aristocracy headed by *principes*, reemerges in their acute attention to the disposal of their dead, right from the early Archaic period. This preoccupation transpires not only in their construction of imposing funerary complexes for the aristocracy—among the most monumental and lasting documents left by the ruling classes of Etruria—but also in the minutely elaborate rituals dedicated to the dead, and to the importance of ensuring both material and ideal ties between the living and their deceased ancestors. Forebears were attributed the status of gods or demi-gods and imputed with special powers for the conservation and continuance of the group, as shown by the funerary imagery that repeats itself obsessively from the Archaic period through to Classical and Hellenistic. Though there is no literature on the matter, the epigraphic material concords with the iconography and archaeological finds in defining a complex framework of beliefs comparable to the Roman practices of domestic worship. Despite the lack of precise written testimony, we can deduce that even after the darkest prehistoric times in which these figures must have had vaster and greater significance, the Etruscans were already familiar—albeit in different outward guises—the Lares, Manes and Genii, having roles and functions similar to those ascribed to them by the Romans. And just as, at a linguistic level, we might educe an Etruscan root behind the Latin noun Lares (witness the Etruscan *lasa*, meaning "female demon," and the derivative given names Laris and Larth); in this way we might even identify the lance-bearing Etruscan god Laran mentioned earlier with the corresponding Latin god Quirinus, a

Incised bronze mirror with the breast-feading of Heracles. Florence, Museo Archeologico cat. 320

collective ancestor (in Rome known as the "deified Romulus") and god of the *curiae* whose name the ancient writers associate with the lance and had manifest underworld connotations. And thus the *lapis manalis* and the *mundus* of Roman religion, the *foramina* (holes or thresholds) that allow communication between the underworld and the realm of mankind, undoubtedly share very remote roots with their Etruscan counterparts, even at linguistic level.
Once again the Hellenization process played a seminal role, fostered by the Orphic and Pythagorean religious doctrines that had begun to spread through Etruria in the fifth century B.C., with the result that the Etruscan concept of Hades—known through abundant iconographic data—developed connotations of a marked Greek savor. But we should not be misled, this veneer is very thin: in the mid-fifth century B.C. among their gods the Etruscans worshipped a plural form of Charun that was utterly unprecedented in the Hellenic world. As borne out by some of the main painted tombs in Tarquinia (of the Charuns, Blue Demons and Cardinal), these spirits possess variant names (*charun*, *charun chunchulis*, *Charun huths*) and visual forms (some are winged, others not) and certainly performed different functions in Hades. One striking case is the object formerly recognized as a "hammer," wielded by the chief of the Etruscan Charun figures, is in fact none other than the huge mallet used to board up the city gates. From this it is clear that for the Etruscans, Charun was not just the "ferryman" (though he also appears as such in Etruscan tomb paintings), but also the inexorable demon who barred forever the deceased's escape from Hades. These Charun figures are accompanied by a host of minor infernal forces of local invention, including *lase* and the like, among which the most notable are *Vanth* (allegedly an "angel of death"), keeper of the prescribed

Bronze statuette of Heracles from Fiesole, fifth century B.C.
Fiesole, Museo Civico Archeologico
cat. 204

Bronze statuette of Hermes,
480 B.C.
Paris, Musée du Louvre
cat. 199

destiny of each individual; and *Tuchulcha*, a monster with serpent's wings and a hooked beak, whose task was to watch over a special set of the damned. Bearing some resemblance to the ideas related in the Orphic texts, for the Etruscans, the journey into the bowels of the earth was plagued with such demons and myriad dangers and traps. Be that as it may, the scrupulous observance of the rites contained in the *libri fatales* and *libri Acherontici* was reputed to make the journey less hazardous. At the end of the journey, however, the traveler's final reward was admission to the circle of the Blessed at their eternal banquet table in Elysium. The more perilous their descent into the underworld, the greater the joy of arrival for the lords of Etruria, who through paintings on their sarcophagi and the walls of their tombs, have granted posterity a vision of unshakable faith in their doctrines of life and afterlife, their rites and privileges.

Müller, Deecke 1877, II, pp. 1 ff.; Thulin 1909; Herbig 1922; Taylor 1923; Van Essen 1927; Rose 1928, pp. 161 ff.; Bayet 1929; Messerschmidt 1929, pp. 21 ff.; De Ruyt 1934; Clemen 1936; Koch 1939; Olzscha 1939; Hermansen 1940; Olzscha 1955, pp. 71 ff.; Herbig 1957, pp. 123 ff.; Pfiffig 1963; Hampe, Simon 1964; Olzscha 1964, pp. 229 ff.; Herbig 1965; Catalano 1966; Pfiffig 1968; Fauth 1974, pp. 105 ff.; Pfiffig 1975; Torelli 1975; Bloch 1976; Colonna 1976–77, pp. 45 ff.; Comella 1978; Radke 1979; Van der Meer 1979, pp. 49 ff.; *Die Göttin von Pyrgi* 1981; Penny Small 1982; Maggiani 1982b, p. 53 ff.; Torelli 1984; Rix 1985, p. 21 ff.; Meyer 1985, pp. 105 ff.; *La divination* 1985; *Santuari d'Etruria* 1985; Maggiani, Simon 1985, pp. 136 ff.; Torelli 1986b, pp. 159 ff.; Krauskopf 1987; Van der Meer 1987; Valvo 1988; Torelli 1988a, pp. 109 ff.; Prosdocimi 1989, pp. 477 ff.; Torelli 1991b, pp. 19 ff.; Rix 1991, I, pp. 665 ff.; Cristofani 1995c; Torelli 1997a; Torelli 1997b, pp. 575 ff.; Briquel, Gaultier 1997.

Etruscan Urban Planning

That we know far more about the world of the dead in Etruria than we do about that of the living can be explained by a number of causes: history, culture, geology and building techniques, as also the history of research itself. Etruscan tombs, whether constructed or hollowed out from the rock, are generally more massive and lasting in form than other buildings, which were mostly constructed from more precarious materials. The Etruscans were conspicuous among ancient peoples for the working effort and financial resources they invested in their tombs and cemeteries and thus—so to speak—in what lay beyond. Another significant factor is that many Etruscan settlements—above all in northern and inland Etruria—were later overlain by Roman, mediaeval and/or modern towns and cities, making systematic excavation and research a practical impossibility. Conditions are better in southern Etruria, where many of the former settled plains have since been built over only partially or not at all. From the eighteenth century onward, moreover, the Etruscans' cities of the dead exerted so great a fascination on scholars, Grand Tourists, writers, artists and draftsmen—not to mention the *tombaroli*—that interest in the remains of ordinary Etruscan settlements almost inevitably remained restricted until a matter of forty or fifty years ago. Despite all the new finds and the progress made over the past decades and in very recent times, it nonetheless remains the case that the present state of our knowledge of Etruscan urban planning fails even to come close to our awareness of Greek and Roman practice in the field.

History

The Etruscan cities of the historical period are known to have been in the nature of *poleis* with pronounced regional characteristics. They presided over territories or areas of influence which were of course subject to alterations through the centuries and whose exact confines can barely be traced today, although we can gain an approximate idea from certain ancient sources, as also from the distribution of the respective cultural and artistic traits and from later diocesan boundaries. In the eighteenth and nineteenth centuries the names and exact locations of various Etruscan cities were still a matter of dispute which has continued to the present day for some, mostly minor, centers. At all events the most prominent cities in terms of size and significance were the *XII populi Etruriae* whose representatives met annually in the Fanum Voltumnae near Volsinii. By the late sixth century the members of this league of 12 cities, whose legendary founder was Tarchon, but whose real inspiration no doubt derived principally from the Ionian Dodecapolis, were certainly to be found among such centers as Veio, Caere, Tarquinia, Vulci, Vetulonia, Roselle, Populonia, Volterra, Volsinii, Chiusi, Cortona, Arezzo and Perugia. Changes to the league's make-up perhaps came about following the destruction of Veio in 396 B.C. Most of the principal centers listed above were founded as early as the Villanovan period and then developed continuously. In contrast, most of the smaller settlements were established only later and were not always permanently inhabited. In particular toward the end of the Archaic period there was a crucial turning point, as many smaller and medium-sized towns such as Marsiliana and Acquarossa were destroyed and abandoned or at least much reduced in importance: in other words, there was an enforced *synoikismos* of smaller centers to create larger ones. These latter underwent corresponding demographic growth, founding new "satellite towns" and expanding their influence. Partly in response to conflicts with the ever more powerful Romans, during the late fifth and above all the fourth century many Etruscan cities erected walls, while in the inland areas of southern Etruria several smaller towns and *oppida* were founded or else re-occupied and fortified, as at Luni, San Giovenale, Musarna, Norchia and Castel d'Asso. Lastly, after the military conquest of the whole of Etruria in the early decades of the third century, from around 273, many walled Latin colonies were founded to secure Roman supremacy, especially in coastal areas. Precisely during the late period, however, when Rome's political dominance had already been established, many towns and cities in northern Etruria enjoyed great prosperity and were often provided with major public buildings under the first Emperors.

Dimensions and demographics

Whether they enjoyed a natural defensive advantage or were surrounded by walls, the sites of towns or cities naturally varied greatly in extent, with some of the southern Etruscan cities reaching a considerable size. Chief among these was Veio with 190 ha, followed by Caere, Tarquinia and Vulci with ca. 150, 120 and 90 ha respectively. The inland cities of Volsinii-Orvieto

Walls of Santa Maria di Falerii (Viterbo)

Aerial view of Vulci archaeological site

Aerial view of Cortona

and Chiusi were built on sites measuring respectively 80 and 26 ha. In the north-west, Populonia at 150 ha and Vetulonia at 100 ha were outstandingly large, while Roselle was significantly smaller at 41 ha. In the inland part of northern Etruria, only Volterra had a site of over 100 ha. The north-eastern Etruscan towns Fiesole (30 ha), Arezzo (32 ha), Cortona (30 ha) and Perugia (32 ha) were much smaller. It may be assumed that the larger city sites were never fully built on and populated. Population figures can hardly be proved in absolute terms, and were in any case subject to fluctuation over the centuries in accordance with historical developments and the varying importance of individual centers. We may however gain some interesting indications as to population from the dimension of settlement, extent and density of cemeteries, certain literary sources (and also the capacity of theaters and amphitheaters of some Etruscan cities in the early Roman imperial period). The remarkable population density of Cerveteri is stressed in sources, and J. Heurgon has estimated some 25,000 inhabitants for the city at the peak of its prosperity. That figure makes Cerveteri into a metropolis by ancient standards, at least in the pre-Hellenistic era, with a population density of 160 to 170 inhabitants per ha. On the basis of these various indices the following projections have been made for the most important Etruscan cities at the height of their power: Veio 32,000; Cerveteri and Populonia 25,000 each; Tarquinia 20,000; Vetulonia and Volterra 17,000 each; Vulci 15,000; Volsinii 13,000; Roselle 12,500; Perugia, Cortona and Arezzo 6,000 each; Chiusi 5,000. A decline in population can definitely be noted during the fifth century B.C., due to the emigration of sizeable population groups that moved south to Campania or north to settle in the Po Valley. This was not a phenomenon which affected all Etruscan centers equally, but its effects are particularly striking at Chiusi. The "wave of emigration" petered out completely in Campania during the fifth century B.C. and in the Po Valley in the early fourth century B.C., and a revitalization and in part also an increase in population ensued in many towns and cities in the Etruscan heartland. From deductions based on literary reports of the troop strengths of certain Etruscan armies, the total population for the whole of Etruria has been estimated at some 274,000 inhabitants, of whom a good 60% were urban dwellers while the rest lived in the countryside. The clashes with Rome in the late fourth century B.C. and above all in the first half of the third century B.C. doubtless led to a decrease in population to about 200,000, roughly equivalent to 15 inhabitants per sqkm.

Foundation and planning

In theory the foundation and planning of a new Etruscan city followed strictly enjoined religious and ritual rules, which have come down to us thanks to the Roman records of the Etruscan *Libri Rituales* and *Libri Tagetici*. Cities were to be laid out on axes determined by the augurs after observing the flight of birds, a practice we are also familiar with from Etruscan temple building and orientation. A furrow—the *sulcus primigenius*—was ploughed in the soil to mark the confines of the site, and interrupted at the places where the city gates were to stand. The ideological and religious purpose derived from the Etruscan belief that the heavens were divided into sectors following the points of the compass, and that the same division was reflected on earth, in other words that the geometrically ordered heavenly macrocosmos was reflected in the earthly microcosmos. Emblematic of this order—based on religion but also entirely rational—was the sacred and inviolable character of all boundaries, including those between properties, which were marked by cippi. Special stones, marked with a cross (*decussis*) to indicate the cardinal points, were buried under all the main crossroads of a city. It must be noted that such "ideal" towns, laid out on a grid plan with rectangular *insulae* according to what the Greeks recognized as Hippodamos' principle, were built only at newly founded sites and "colonial" settlements as Marzabotto, Spina and Capua. The strict application of the system, which the Etruscans probably took from Magna Graecia, was in any case possible only if certain conditions were fulfilled by the proposed site. Excavations such as those at San Giovenale, Acquarossa and Veio have shown that the towns and cities of the Etruscan motherland, largely arosen through replacement or absorption of earlier Villanovan settlements around the eighth–seventh centuries B.C., tended to follow the typical early Mediterranean plan with streets that were not laid out at right angles. Especially from the second quarter and the middle of the sixth century, however, new urban planning trends can be identified: in building complex F at Acquarossa and above all in the great suburban cemeteries at Cerveteri and Orvieto, as also—to a lesser extent—in the rock cemeteries of Blera, San Giuliano and San Giovenale.

Boundary cippus, end of the third–beginning of the second century B.C.
Bettona, Museo Civico
cat. 22

These innovations took the form of more rational utilization of space, stricter regulation and a grid plan street layout. However, the necropolises at Cerveteri and Orvieto predate by at least half a century the foundation of the new town at Marzabotto, which provides a virtually perfect expression of the new urbanistic principles. Since the cities in the Etruscan heartland mostly tended to undergo continuous development in the Archaic period, the new principles no doubt were applied only to the layout of single districts or individual complexes. Even districts from the Hellenistic period such as the one in Vetulonia (with *tabernae* along a street) are not uniformly laid out in the manner of Hippodamos.

History of the development of Etruscan urban planning
So far as the proto-urban phase is concerned, the Early Iron Age and Villanovan settlements do not generally occupy the same sites as those of the Late Bronze Age, of which so far some seventy have been identified in southern Etruria. Typical among the latter are Vignale di Civita Castellana, Sorgenti della Nova, Pontone di Barbarano, Monte Rovello, San Giovenale and Luni sul Mignone, with a surface area of up to 15 ha and consisting mostly of oval huts. On the other hand, the most important settlements and population concentrations of the transitional phase from proto-Villanovan to Villanovan (tenth–mid-ninth centuries), such as those at Veio, Orvieto, Cerveteri, Tarquinia, Vulci, Chiusi, Pisa, Volterra, Vetulonia and Populonia, already occupied the sites of the later Etruscan *poleis*. From as early as the commencement of the Iron

Partial plan of Acquarossa complex F

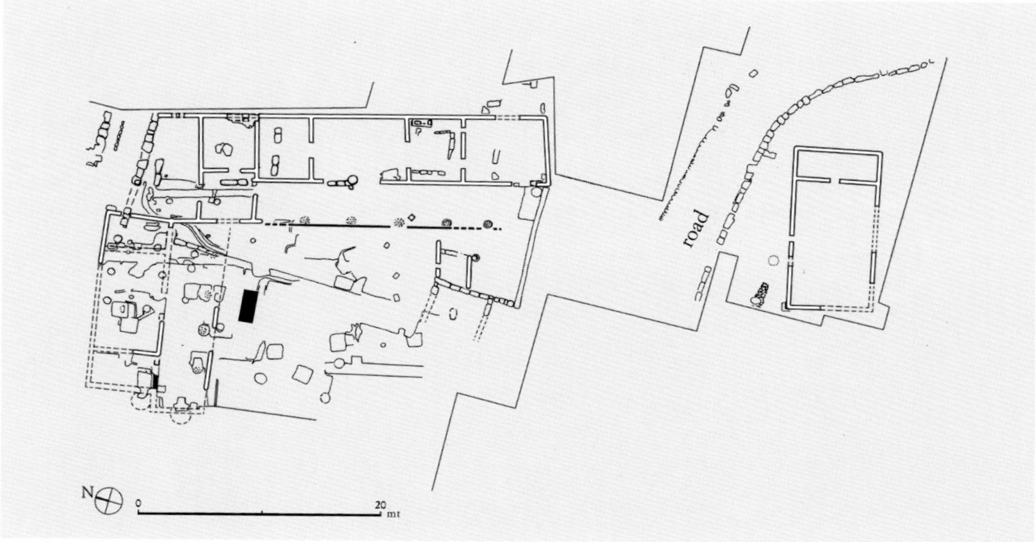

Age there are signs of a first process of *synoikismos*, which revolutionized the population structure of Etruria from Veio to Felsina (Bologna). Among the Villanovan settlements which can be classified as proto-urban and which have already been excavated, a particularly interesting site is the one at the Calvario locality on the Monterozzi hill at Tarquinia. This was investigated (in part by uncovering later tumuli) by R.E. Linington in 1975–78. It had an area of around 2 ha with 25 huts of various sizes but built mostly on a rectangular plan. The largest huts have an oval plan but still cover some 80 sqm, no doubt attesting to a social hierarchy that was already in place. We also have a familiar "sculptural" model of such Villanovan huts with various details and decorations, in the shape of the hut-urns—mostly molded in impasto, but sometimes made of bronze—found in Etruria and southern Latium (the Alban Hills). Similar huts are also shown on a Villanovan stela from Bologna and on the back of the wooden throne from Verucchio. Remains of Early Iron Age or Villanovan hut settlements have also been excavated at Luni sul Mignone, San Giovenale, Narce, Veio and Rome. Villanovan villages were originally scattered in layouts with no regard to any regular plan and quite clearly no strict functional distinction between public, sacred and secular-private buildings, while the *oikos* was the primary status symbol of the head of the family. From the mid-eighth century B.C., however, a

Plan of the Tarquinia area

Plan of the Borgo at San Giovenale (Viterbo)

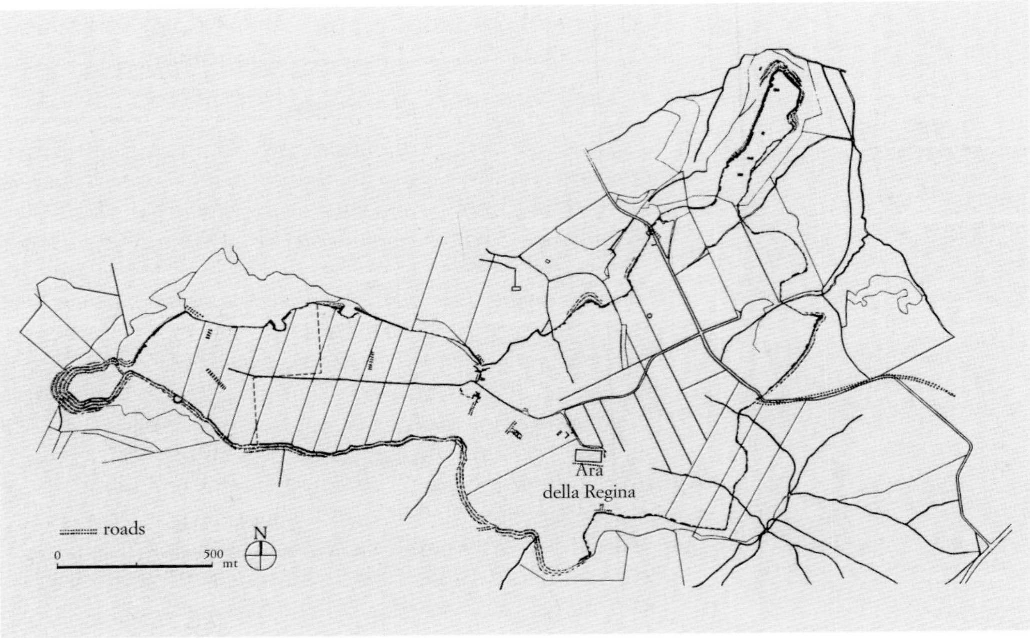

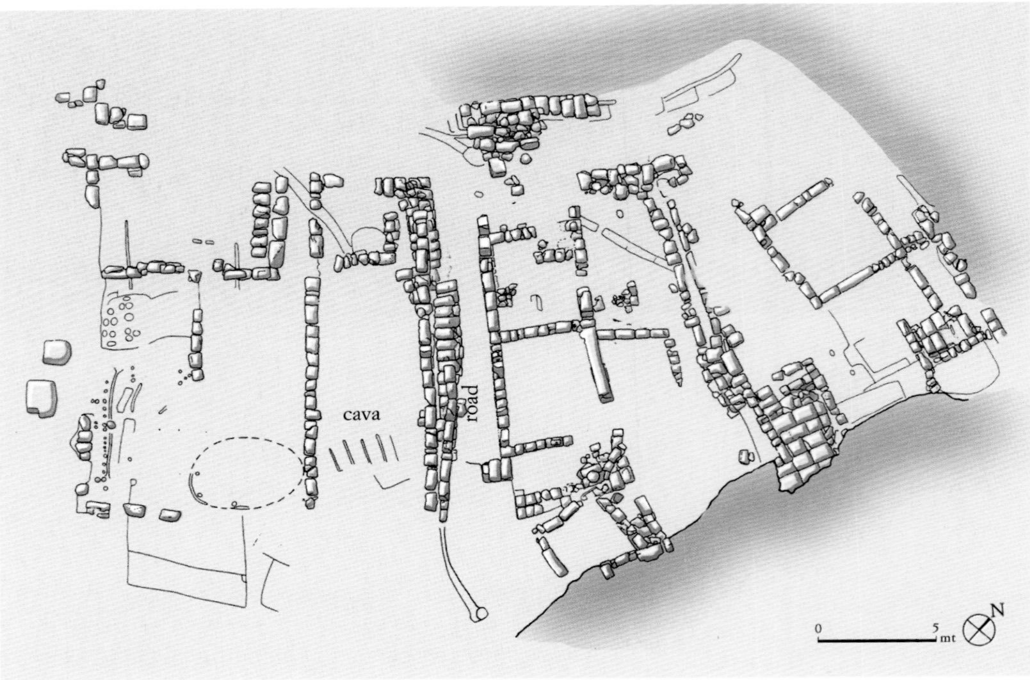

second phase of *synoikismos* led to the formation of larger settlements in what was to be a typical pattern for the area of Etruria and Latium. The process can be traced very clearly at Tarquinia and Veio, where there were originally ten Villanovan villages on a surface area of 190 ha. The main necropolises became equally concentrated at the same time, typically on the Monterozzi hill in the case of Tarquinia and on the Banditaccia and Monte Abatone plain in the case of Cerveteri. A monumentalization of tomb architecture—as compared to the simple wells (*pozzi*) and pits (*fossae*) of the Villanovan—had obviously been introduced already in the late Villanovan, especially at Populonia. In southern Etruria tomb architecture became more monumental a bit later, in the first decades of the seventh century B.C., with the introduction of chamber tombs and large tumuli, as can clearly be seen at Cerveteri. During the seventh and sixth centuries B.C. the process of urbanization was completed, with the functions of public-po-

Remains of houses in the Borgo at San Giovenale

litical, religious and private domains clearly distinguished, the urban area demarcated by a wall or earthen rampart (*agger*) and the replacement of huts by mostly right-angled, more massive structures. The most recent excavation of Pian di Civita carried out at Tarquinia by M. Bonghi Jovino has shown that massive timber-framed buildings were constructed along a 3 meter-broad street as early as the first half of the seventh century B.C. Prominent among these structures was a *megaron* with a clear political and perhaps also sacred function, attested to by the "buried" bronze implements and their powerful symbolism. The same process of urbanization can also be traced in Archaic Rome under the Tarquinian Kings around the turn of the seventh and sixth centuries B.C., again associated with an increasingly monumental building style. The Swedish excavations of the 1960s and 70s in San Giovenale brought to light the massive remains of houses built in blocks of tufa and dating to the late seventh and sixth centuries B.C. Two "urban districts" could also be distinguished by urbanistic, typological and social criteria: one, zone B, was an aristocratic quarter on a grid plan with three impressive, multi-roomed houses including a banqueting room and a courtyard; the other, termed as *Borgo*, was a more popular district laid out on a terraced slope with simpler, more tightly-packed houses, narrow streets and sewer drains. Generally speaking, the Etruscan cities of the seventh and sixth centuries B.C. were not as yet organized on the "Hippodamos" plan, as is indicated by the more or less haphazard distribution of buildings in several groups at such centers as Acquarossa and San Giovenale. Only in certain more monumental districts which may clearly be interpreted as seats of political and religious power, such as zone F at Acquarossa and the aristocratic quarter of San Giovenale, can innovative and more progressive tendencies in urban planning be made out. The Swedish excavations of the 1960s and 70s in the medium-sized center of Acquarossa—barely 1 ha of the total site area of 32 ha was examined during the dig—revealed several such groups of buildings, totalling some 70 "longhouses" and "broadhouses." These had surface areas of up to 120 sqm at ground level and were built either of tufa blocks in *opus*

quadratum, or else timber-framed using clay bricks or *opus craticium*. Their roofs were often adorned with terra-cotta tiles. Since the 1980s G. Camporeale has led an archaeological excavation at the so-called "mining settlement" on Lake Accesa below Massa Marittima in the hinterland of Vetulonia, rich in mineral deposits. The site, which flourished in the first half of the sixth century B.C., sloped down to the lake with several groups of ten or so houses each. The houses themselves had two or three rooms, preceded by a *vestibulum* of clay bricks. Each group of dwellings possessed its own small necropolis. Although no uniform urban planning can be detected there are the first signs of regulation. Interestingly, in contrast to most centers in southern Etruria, there were no marked social distinctions among the inhabitants of this settlement, as is made clear by the relatively uniform dwellings without terra-cotta roof ornaments. In Roselle, one of the few towns in northern Etruria with favorable conditions for excavation, archaeological researches carried out since the 1960s have brought to light the remains of Etruscan buildings dating from the mid-seventh century B.C., including one with a circular plan that no doubt served some public or religious purpose. Together with the building of a first circuit of walls, using clay bricks on a masonry base, these remains point to urbanization at Roselle already in the Orientalizing period. The site of Murlo-Poggio Civitate south-west of Siena has been excavated by American archaeologists since the 1960s. In this instance there is not an urban organism as such, but what has been described as a *potentato signorile*: it possessed an aristocratic palace measuring some 60 × 60 m and laid out around a rectangular courtyard with porticos, probably rising to two storeys in height and with rich roof decorations in terra cotta, some of unusual design. Dating from the first quarter of the sixth century B.C., it occupied the site of an earlier building from the second half of the seventh century B.C. and was surrounded by other simpler buildings including workshops. Another *palazzo* has come to light in Acquarossa (the Regia, in complex F): built from scratch shortly before the mid-sixth century, this was also distinguished by a courtyard partly surrounded by porticos, and by rich terra-cotta roof ornaments; its rooms include one which can clearly be identified as a space for banquet-

View of Lake Accesa

Remains of houses at Accesa

ing. These *palazzi* point unequivocally to the existence of a still extremely hierarchically structured aristocratic social order; such indications are reflected in some of the more or less contemporary rock tomb facades found in southern Etruria, notably in the house-formed three-chambered tomb preceded by a portico and with rich stone roof sculptures at Pian di Mola near Tuscania. On the plateau of the so-called Acropolis area at Piazza d'Armi in Veio, abandoned toward the end of the sixth century B.C., the buildings were laid out on an approximate grid plan, with one main and several intersecting side streets centered on an open square (ca. 25 × 35–40 sqm). At the center of the square was a massive oval cistern, open to the sky. However the first thorough-going applications of the so-called Hippodamos system, with intersecting streets on a grid plan and regular *insulae* of housing, date from no earlier than the Late Archaic period: typical instances are newly-founded towns such as Marzabotto, Spina and Forcello di Bagnolo San Vito (near Mantua) in north-east Italy, harbor towns such as Pyrgi, Regisvilla-Regae and probably also Gravisca on the southern coast of Etruria, as also Doganella, sited inland from the mouth of the Albegna and identified by M. Michelucci with Kalousion. The prerequisite condition for these new developments, as for the new definition of the urban organism in itself during the sixth century B.C., was undoubtedly the formation and rise of a politically independent middle class. The new social stratum, probably founded on a census system and isonomy, had its own, quite different requirements which found clear expression in the egalitarian and levelling tendencies that can be seen in the building of both towns and cemeteries. Most of the old aristocratic sanctuaries on the acropolis, which largely consisted of extremely simply, *oikos*-like temple structures with no fixed typology, were now given up, while the new urban sanctuaries were often situated within the area of the town itself. The maximum architectural effort was now devoted to the construction of new temples and public buildings, which are distinguished during the Late Archaic phase by particularly rich terra-cotta roof decoration. Examples of such new monumental temples, generally—in accordance with Vitruvius and Varro—of the Tuscan Order, can be found at Veio (Portonaccio), Cerveteri (Temple of

Altar on the area of the Portonaccio temple, Veio

The sanctuary of Pyrgi

Hera), Pyrgi (Temple A), Vulci (locality Legnisina), Orvieto (Belvedere Temple), Marzabotto (Temple C) and also in the "grande Roma dei Tarquini" (Temple of Capitoline Jupiter). The three-*cellae* ground plan (or featuring a central *cella* flanked by two *alae*) was also taken up in domestic (Acquarossa) and tomb architecture (Cerveteri and hinterland). Marzabotto, whose ancient name (Melpum ?) has remained a mystery, was founded in part by "colonists" from northern Etruria, but certainly also by elements from the local Po Valley Etruscan population. Built *ex novo* at the beginning of the fifth century B.C. on an important through route from Etruria into the Po Valley in the Apennine hills of Emilia south of Bologna, it overlays the site of an earlier, pre-urban hut settlement of the sixth century B.C. (Marzabotto I) on the Pian di Misano and provides a fine—and to date the most carefully investigated—example of a progressive "Hippodamian" urban plan, despite the fact that a third of the city has fallen prey to the erosion of the nearby Reno River. Three large *plateiai* on an E–W axis and one on a N–S axis and a series of smaller *stenopoi* in N–S direction make up the town, which measures some

Aerial view of Marzabotto archaeological site

25 ha and was protected partly by an *agger* and partly by the steep bank of the Reno. There were eight main districts, each with five oblong *insulae*, which in turn included generally seven or eight very large houses of the so-called "courtyard" type, covering an area of 600–800 sqm. The houses were built of river pebbles, timber-framing and also of partly baked clay bricks, and roofed with undecorated tiles. For the most part shops and workshops opened on to the road. As at Pompei, large stepping stones were placed in the street to allow citizens to cross, especially in rainy weather. Narrow culverts separated the houses, flowing into larger covered drains which followed the line of the main streets. The water supply was provided by public and private wells. The streets are strictly laid out in accordance with the cardinal points. Beneath the main crossing of the two *plateiai* A and C, a cippus was found buried with a *decussis* scratched on the upper side. This was the practical starting point for the layout, but doubtless carried ritual, symbolic and commemorative significance as well. There is no certain evidence of a large-scale square at Marzabotto, but the town did possess an acropolis, conceived at the same time

opposite
The settlement at Monte Bibele, near Monterenzio

and built on distinctly higher ground, again with temples and altars that are mostly laid out strictly on N–S or E–W axes. There were also two cemeteries to the north and east of the town, reached by gates that were only symbolic in function, probably with a total of 295 stone cist tombs, often crowned with cippi. The present state of research indicates that the urban plan was certainly not only the result of the *disciplina Etrusca*, but was also influenced above all by the innovative Greek planning models. As G.A. Mansuelli put it: "The plan of Marzabotto may well have been a compromise between the Etruscan doctrine which prescribed the intersection of cardinally orientated axes, and the experience of Greek urban planning." The relative uniformity of both dwellings and tombs points to a similar level of uniformity in social terms, i.e. a broad middle class or else a young "colonial society," distributed among specific districts by trade or profession. This medium-sized urban center which flourished principally in the fifth century B.C. probably depended for its prosperity on domestic trade, metalworking and pottery before it was finally conquered by the Celts around the mid-fourth century B.C., when its population declined rapidly. The nearby fifth-century B.C. Etruscan site at Casalecchio di Reno also revealed a grid plan, but with much simpler houses than at Marzabotto. Another city founded *ex novo* in the late sixth century B.C. and active until the fourth–third centuries was Spina, sited between the old course of the Po River and the Lake of Comacchio and inhabited by a population which included a large proportion of Greeks and Veneti. In this instance the regular grid of streets was replaced to a large extent by navigable canals, as was to be done later in Venice. The main settlement in Valle di Mezzano—there were other settled nuclei besides this—covered an area of some 6 ha and was surrounded by an *agger* 10-meter broad and fortified by a palisade. It was laid out on a grid plan. Stones with the groma cross were also found here at important roads. One stone with the inscription "mi tular" may possibly have marked off a public domain. The houses were built mainly from wood and *opus craticium* with lightly baked clay bricks; the same techniques were used for dwellings at Forcello di Bagnolo San Vito on the Mincio River near Mantua, where there was a 16-hectare settlement of the fifth century B.C. structured in much the same way as Spina. The type of settlement, as also the necropolises, with tombs made from simple wooden boxes but with lavish grave goods, point to a prosperous society of merchants and seafarers. Hoewer, at Verucchio, in the Apennines inland from Rimini, the settlement at Pian del Monte della Baldissera consisted of stone-built houses. The aristocratic tombs found there had very rich, sometimes almost unique grave goods such as ornamented wooden furniture, and attest to a process of urbanization which can be detected from as early as the seventh century B.C. In the most important center of Po Valley Etruria, namely Felsina, the *princeps Etruria* of the Po Valley, the conditions for excavation and research are less favorable than elsewhere because of the many later strata of occupation. Nonetheless, it has been possible to trace initially a four-part Villanovan phase with scattered hut settlements (remains of some 500 huts), followed as early as the advanced Orientalizing and Archaic periods by unequivocal signs of *synoikismos,* a hierarchically-structured social order with magistrates or municipal officers and urbanization. Clear pointers to this are the monumental additions and alterations to important streets of necropolises, remains of houses and streets, kilns and votive offerings, proto-Felsina stelae and the ritual complex uncovered in Via Fondazza. The latter has two large profiled stone cylinders which were perhaps more likely votive monuments than altars and whose decorations in relief with plant motifs in late Orientalizing style testify to a considerable level of architectural culture. Two further cippi from Rubiera near Reggio Emilia, with relief decorations from the late Orientalizing period and inscriptions referring to the magistrature, attest to a similar process of urbanization in western Emilia too, and a socio-political system that M. Torelli in defined as a "repubblica aristocratica." Another site worthy of note among further Etruscan settlements in western Emilia is Sant'Ilario d'Enza. There were also obviously significant changes in urban planning around the turn of the sixth and fifth centuries B.C. in major Etruscan centers such as Cerveteri. Here a large temple of the Tuscan Order and a building with an oval structure of at least 35 m in length were built around 480–470 B.C. over older structures (houses and cisterns). The new building, similar to the Greek *ekklesiasterion,* was probably used for assemblies and performances. In many centers of southern Etruria there are clear signs of upswing in prosperity during the fourth century B.C. Typical instances are the monumental temple complexes at Tarquinia (Ara della Regina), Vulci and Falerii (Celle and Scasato), new or rebuilt defensive walls and a renewed ostentation in tomb ar-

Plan of the Ghiaccio Forte settlement (Scansano)

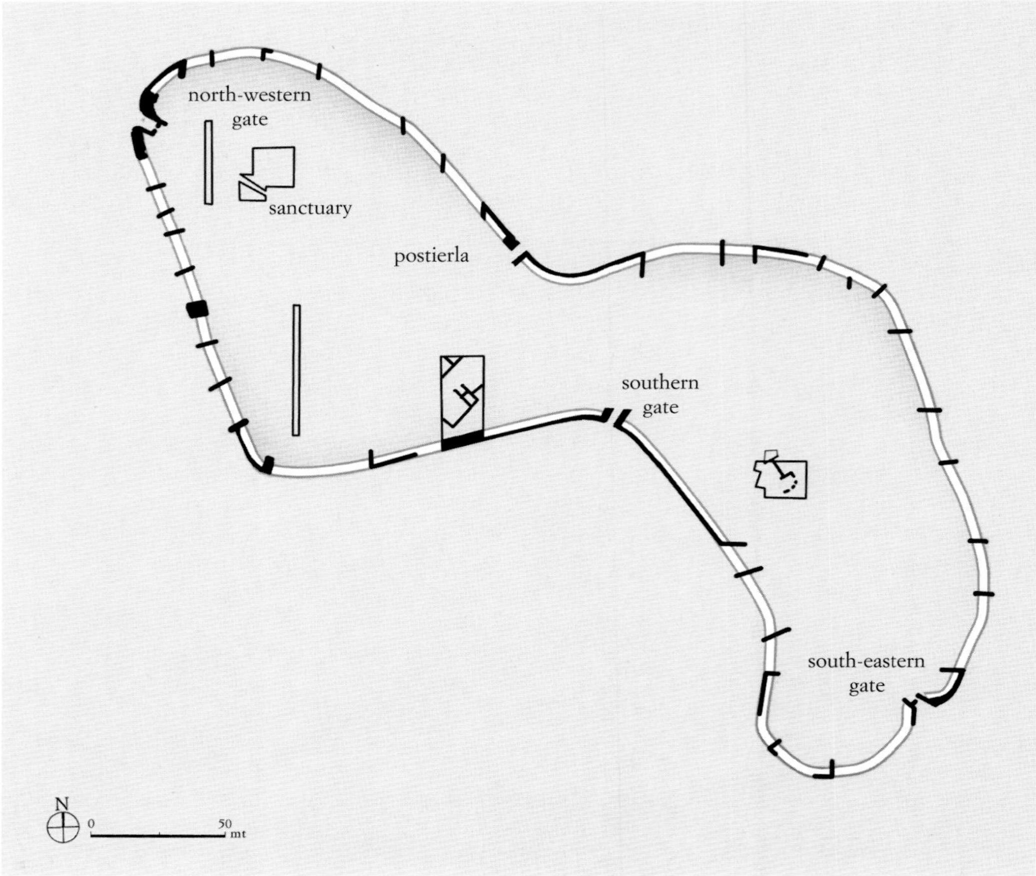

chitecture, often with more stress laid on the outward facade. New towns that were founded later all had a regular urban plan, as in the case of several smaller towns of the late fourth century B.C. in the hinterland of Vulci (Ghiaccio Forte) and Tarquinia (Musarna). At Ghiaccio Forte M. Del Chiaro has shown that in addition to a late Archaic sanctuary there was a settlement with streets on a grid plan, remains of right-angled buildings and a town wall with gates (with inner chambers), spread over an area of some 4 ha on a hilltop. The town flourished from ca. 350–280 B.C. and was then destroyed and abandoned. The terraced settlement above Bolsena, again on a grid plan and with a circuit of double-shelled walls, was also abandoned around 280 B.C. At Musarna, excavations found a town plan with a 6.70 m wide N–S axis and about 4 m wide intersecting streets enclosing twelve *insulae*. The main street broadened out at one point to form a square measuring 80 × 18 m, with a public building along one side transformed during the Late Hellenistic period into baths with mosaic decorations. The settlement at Monte Bibele near Monterenzio in the Bolognese Apennines was occupied from ca. 350–200 B.C. by a mixed Etruscan and Celtic population. It had simple, one-roomed "row houses" with dry stone walls, distributed on ten terraces and pointing to a relatively egalitarian population structure. Made necessary by the devastation caused by the Romans, the new foundations of the third century B.C. such as Volsinii Novi near Bolsena (after 264 B.C.), Ferentium-Ferento near Acquarossa and Falerii Novi (after 241 B.C.) had a grid plan with *insulae* and defensive walls in *opus quadratum*, well-preserved in part. Among the sanctuaries and temples of Hellenistic Etruria, one particularly striking site is the unusual second-century terraced complex at Poggio di Castelsecco near Arezzo. Influenced by sanctuaries in Latium, the site had extensive substructures, a temple and a theater. Latin colonies were founded on the Etruscan-Tyrrhenian coast during the third and second centuries B.C. to secure the Romans' hold on the territory. All of these *coloniae maritimae*—of which the first was Cosa in 273 B.C.—were characterized by a "geometric" distribution and functional subdivision of the urban surface, as also by often in part well-preserved defensive walls in *opus polygonalis*. Large, lavishly furnished villa complexes such as those at

Mosaic of Musarna (now in Viterbo, Museo Archeologico)

Plan of Volsinii Novi

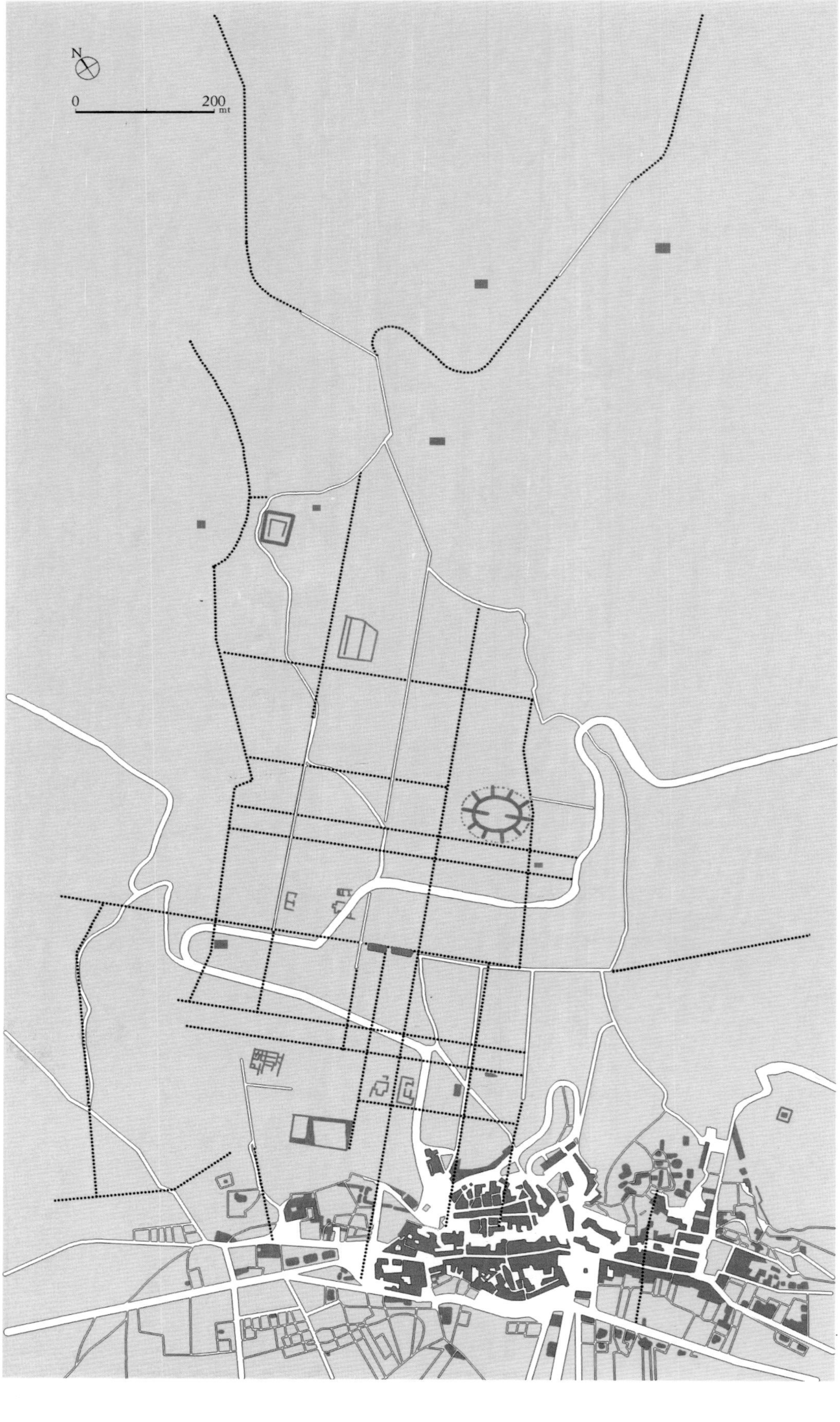

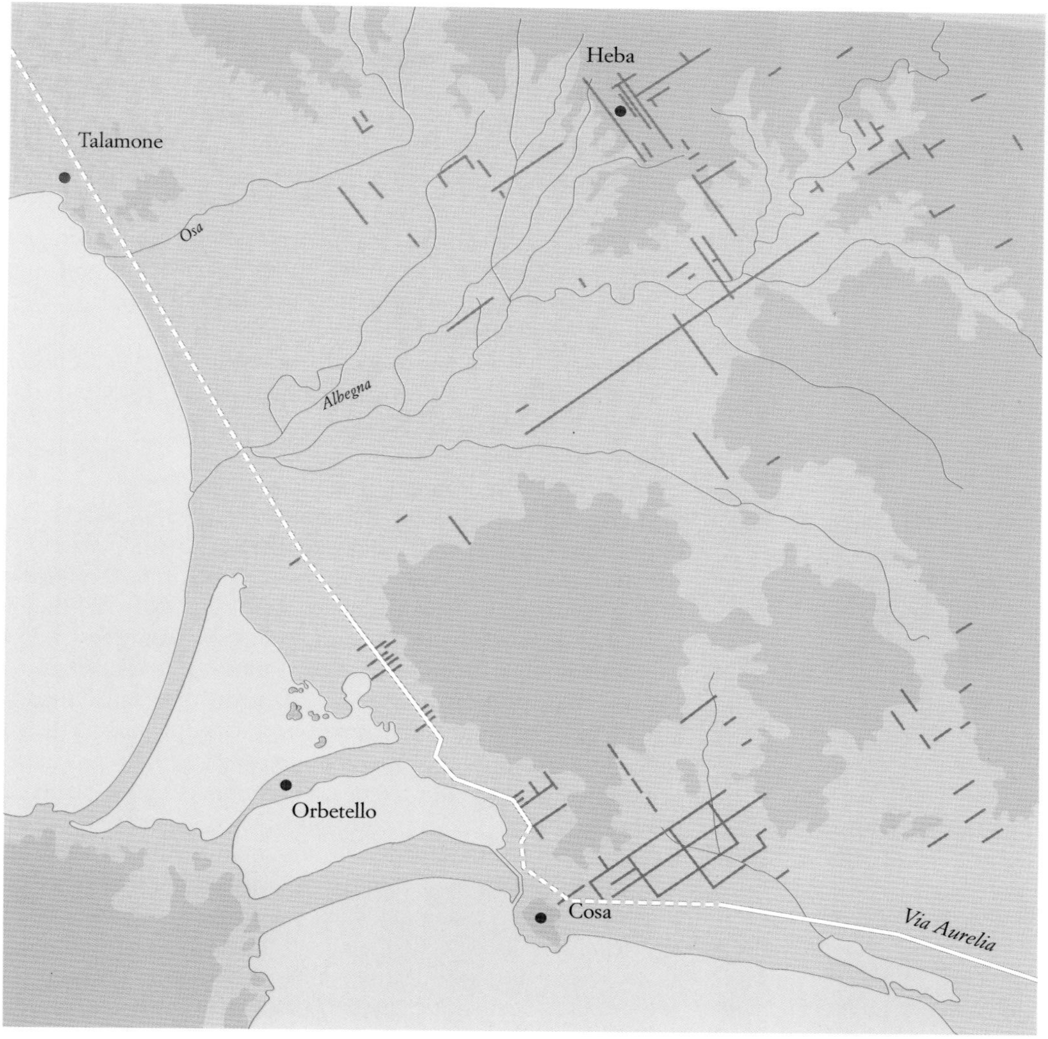

The Roman centuriatio *in the area of Cosa and Heba*

Roselle, Vulci and Bolsena appeared only in the second–first centuries B.C., already characterized by late Republican Roman architecture and attesting to the establishment of a completely new social system, partly based on latifundia. Large, multi-storeyed tenement houses, such as those built at Ostia under Imperial Rome, are a building type which is absent from Etruria.

Greek influences

The advanced, so-called Hippodamian principles of urbanistics—applied above all in new towns and cities founded by the Etruscans—were the result of Greek influence, derived mainly from the Greek colonies of southern Italy and Sicily. Although these were at least to some extent political and military rivals of the Etruscan *polis* states, there was a fruitful level of economic and cultural exchange. Moreover, from the sixth century B.C. onward the Greek model of the *polis* exerted an ever greater attraction in Etruria, too. Thus an orthogonal layout of the urban area (with five main districts) has been shown to have existed at Megara Hyblaea in eastern Sicily as early as the seventh century B.C. A decisive factor was the advent of new techniques for *agrimensura* (land measurement). In this context we have also to see the adoption of the Greek word *groma* into Etruscan (and later into Latin). Earlier researchers tended to distinguish rather simplistically between two urban types with regard to Greek urbanistics—although the term "urbanistics" itself had neither a Greek nor a Latin equivalent—namely "regular" and "irregular" cities. Even with regard to Athens a distinction was made between the irregular old city and the regular new city, i.e. the Piraeus, designed by Hippodamos of Miletus in the mid-fifth century B.C. During the fifth and fourth centuries B.C. this "geometrical" urban system reached its zenith in the Greek world, too: we need only think of such instances as Piraeus, Halieis, Olynthos, Kassope, Megalopolis, Priene and lastly Alexandria. Credit for the so-called Hippodamian principles was, however, by no means all due to the architect who gave the system his name: there were many precedents in the world of the Greek colonies, especially in Asia Minor from Smyrna to Miletus, in Sicily and Magna Graecia. New foundations in colonized areas provided fertile ground for experimentation and the application of new ideas and models of urban planning, particularly since at most sites there were no older settlements of previous occupiers to condition development. Moreover a majority of Greek colonists settled in towns and cities rather than villages. From the seventh and especially in the sixth century B.C., the regular urban layout of *strigae* predominated. The broader *plateiai* (10–18 m wide) intersected perpendicularly at regular intervals with narrower *stenopoi* (4–5 m wide), thus forming right-angled *insulae*. Already during the Archaic period it was customary to reserve large open spaces for *agorai* and public functions: at Poseidonia an area of some 10 ha was set aside. In addition to Megara Hyblaea, interesting insights are provided in Sicily by Colle Manuzza at Selinus, Agrigento (with 6 *plateiai* on an E–W axis and numerous *stenopoi* running N–S), Syracuse (Ortigia) and Himera, while in mainland southern Italy the most rewarding sites are Poseidonia, Metapontum and Tarentum. At Metapontum the rectangular *temenos* which encloses the most significant temples is marked off by special cippi, the *argoi lithoi*. The same kind of urban planning based on *strigae* is found also in new foundations of the fifth century B.C. such as Naxos in eastern Sicily, Heraklea and Neapolis (with three *plateiai* on an E–W axis and some twenty *stenopoi* running N–S, enclosing *insulae* of 180 × 35 m). Fundamental innovations in urban planning may only be noted from the mid-fifth century B.C., due in large measure to the genius of Hippodamos, who not only wrote theoretical treatises on the ideal form of the Greek city and society—handed down to posterity only indirectly and in fragmentary fashion by Aristotle—but also put his principles into practice in the design of Piraeus, Rhodos and Thurii. The last-named of these three cities was founded by the Athenians in 444 B.C. as a pan-Hellenic colony to replace the destroyed Sybaris. As described by Diodorus Siculus (XII, 10, 7), the urban plan of Thurii was especially instructive, with its perfect chequer-board pattern, 4 particularly broad *plateiai* and subdivision of the individual quarters by smaller *stenopoi*. The suggestion which has occasionally been put forward equating this kind of rational urban plan with democracy, i.e. a city for equals, as also the labeling of Hippodamos as the Architect of Democracy, are certainly both far too simplistic, if only because there were clear precedents in absolutely non-democratic cities and societies. Lastly the foundation of Alexandria in 331 B.C. set a benchmark in the history of Greek urban planning. Our scant knowledge of the city's broad streets and magnificent palaces, libraries, sanctuaries, gardens, arsenals and harbors has depended largely on literary sources, while we have barely any detailed record of its urban plan.

Walls

Most of the cities in southern Etruria occupied sites on high-lying plateaus, given a large measure of natural protection by deep tufa canyons, and therefore had need only of short stretches of defensive walls. On the other hand, the hill towns of northern and inland Etruria were

Groma *used for the* centuriatio

Porta Diana at Volterra

mostly ringed by a circuit of walls, built from materials determined by local resources. In the north, limestone, travertine, sandstone and clay bricks were used, while tufa was practically the sole material employed in the south. Techniques for wall construction included Cyclopean-Pelasgic masonry, *opus incertum, opus quadratum, opus pseudo-polygonalis* and *polygonalis*. The earliest walls date back to the seventh century B.C. (clay brick walls on a masonry base at Roselle); in the sixth century B.C., notable defensive systems included the mighty circuits at Vetulonia and Roselle (3.270 km-long limestone walls in *opus pseudo-polygonalis* with at least seven city gates and one postern), as also the acropolis walls of Populonia and Veio (Piazza d'Armi), while the fifth century saw building at Tarquinia, Veio (over 6 km in length with at least ten gates and a broad earthen rampart in the north-west sector, isodomic masonry in *opus quadratum*), Falerii Veteres and Capena. In Genoa, too, in the district of San Silvestro, remains of the fortifications of an Etruscan *oppidum* with a double masonry shell have come to light, while remains of a clay brick wall have been found on the site of the Etruscan-dominated town of Aleria on the eastern coast of Corsica. In the fourth century B.C., during the period when the Etruscan cities were increasingly threatened by Rome, and in part during the third century B.C., too, defensive walls were rebuilt and strengthened at Tarquinia (some 8 km long in *opus quadratum*), Roselle, Vetulonia, Populonia and Volterra (7.283 km in length, gates with inner chambers) while entirely new circuits were erected at Caere, Vulci, Orbetello, Cortona, Fiesole, Perugia (almost 3 km long with at least eleven gates), Bolsena and Falerii Novi. From the point of view of construction technique, Arezzo provided an exception with its early Hellenistic city wall in clay bricks. Only in exceptional cases were the walls equipped with towers, as in one sector at Populonia and at Falerii Novi (third century B.C.). Especially in southern Etruria, some sections were fortified by ditches and earthen ramparts (*agger*). The walls of the Latin colonies such as Cosa, Pyrgi and Saturnia were mostly built in the characteristic *opus polygonalis*. Monumental stone-built gate complexes with arches built using dressed wedge-

The cavone *of Sovana*

shaped stones and sculptural decorations were only introduced in the Hellenistic period, as at Volterra (Porta all'Arco), Perugia (Porta Marzia, Arco d'Augusto) and Falerii Novi (Porta Giove), and were certainly influenced by Greek and Magna Graecian models, such as the famous fourth-century B.C. Porta Rosa in Velia. In the pre-Hellenistic period gates were very likely often built from timber and sometimes provided with inner chambers.

Drainage and water supply

Etruscan cities usually possessed paved streets and sewers, as has been documented by the particularly well-preserved network at Marzabotto, but also by the earlier remains found in the Borgo at San Giovenale. On the hilltop plateaus of many towns and cities, mostly in southern Etruria, underground *cuniculi* have survived which functioned as drains. An enormous, uncovered cistern is known to have existed in the center of the so-called acropolis area at Veio. The Etruscans' reputation as excellent hydraulic engineers is attested to both by the frequent mentions of ancient writers and by impressive works such as the Pozzo Sorbello in Perugia, the Ponte Sodo at Veio and the *emissarium* or outlet built at Lake Albano.

Roads, "cavoni" and bridges

Especially in the inland areas of southern Etruria, in the modern province of Viterbo, impressive remains have survived of the *cavoni*, the Etruscan roads which were hewn out from the tufa, overcoming the often considerable difference in height between the hilltop sites and the valleys below, and which in many cases can still be walked or even driven along today. Excellent examples are found at San Giuliano, Norchia (Cava Buia) and above all at Sovana, all well reported by M. Cristofani in his 1985 book *Strade degli Etruschi*. The monumental, 10.40 meters-wide road equipped with a drainage conduit which ran generally in a straight line between Cerveteri and its most important port at Pyrgi was built as early as the Archaic period. It was flanked by tombs for part of its length. Construction of solid bridges was certainly undertaken in Etruria from at least the Late Archaic period, as is shown by the remains of a viaduct/bridge, originally a wooden structure supported on masonry piers in *opus quadratum*, at Fosso Pietrisco near San Giovenale. Examples from the late Hellenistic period have been better preserved, such as the Ponte della Rocca and the Ponte del Diavolo in the Fosso Biedano below Blera, and the monumental, some 30 m-high and enormously picturesque Ponte dell'Abbadia above the gorge cut by the Fiora River at Vulci, which originally also functioned as an aqueduct.

Castagnoli 1956; D'Ambrosio 1956; Ward-Perkins 1961, pp. 1–123; Bizzarri, Costa 1962, pp. 1–154; Mansuelli 1962, pp. 14–27; Castagnoli 1963, pp. 180–90; Judson, Kahane 1963, pp. 74–99; Mansuelli 1963, pp. 44–62; Boethius 1964, pp. 3–16; Mansuelli 1965, pp. 314–25; Bizzarri 1966, pp. 3–109; Giuliano 1966; Mansuelli 1967, pp. 5–36; Staccioli 1968, pp. 141–50; Bloch 1970, pp. 1114–120; Boethius, Ward Perkins 1978; Gentili, Mansuelli, Gualandi at ali 1970, pp. 215–49; Mansuelli 1970a, pp. 215–49; Mansuelli 1970b; Schmiedt 1970a; Schmiedt 1970b, pp. 91–107; *Studi sulla città antica* 1970; Pallottino 1970–71, pp. 11–14; Castagnoli 1971; Tripponi, Manino, Schiffone 1971, pp. 217–99; Klakowicz 1972; Mansuelli 1972, pp. 111–44; Colonna 1974, pp. 253–65; Gentili, Mansuelli 1974, pp. 221–33; Mansuelli 1974, pp. 289–300; Östenberg 1974, pp. 75–87; Asheri 1975, pp. 5ff.; Östenberg 1975; Prayon 1975; *Roselle, gli scavi e la mostra* 1975; Staccioli 1976, pp. 961–69; Zanker 1976; Cristofani 1977c, pp. 74–80; Boethius 1978; Colonna di Paolo 1978; *Le città di fondazione romana* 1978; Torelli, Boitani, Cataldi et al. 1978; Mansuelli 1979, pp. 353–71; Potter 1979; Ampolo 1980b; Torelli 1980; Castagnoli 1981, pp. 133–42; Drews 1981, pp. 133–65; Gros 1981; Judson, Hemphill 1981, pp. 193–202; Morselli, Tortorici 1981, pp. 151–64; Steingräber 1981; *Guida alla città etrusca* 1982; Oleson 1982; Greco, Torelli 1983; Gullini 1983, pp. 205–328; Sassatelli 1983, pp. 65–127; *Studi sulla città antica* 1983; Torelli 1983, pp. 471–92; Cristofani 1983a; Gentili 1984, pp. 16–20; Berti 1985, pp. 189–96; Cristofani, Boitani, Moscati et al. 1985; Di Vita 1985, pp. 359–414; Moscati 1985, pp. 45–74; Pohl 1985, pp. 43–63; Steingräber 1985, pp. 19–40; Stopponi 1985; Bartoloni 1986, pp. 7–17; Bouloumié 1986, pp. 385–88; Broise, Jolivet, Musarna 1986, pp. 365 ff.; Colonna 1986, pp. 369–530; Cristofani 1986c, pp. 1–24; De Marinis 1986, pp. 140–63; Mantino 1986; Prayon 1986, pp. 174–201; Romanelli 1986; Bermond Montanari 1987; Stopponi 1987, pp. 61–82; Gros, Torelli 1988; *La formazione della città preromana* 1988; Sommella 1988; Forte 1988–89, pp. 81–193; Levi 1989; Mansuelli 1989, pp. 407–40; Prayon 1989, pp. 41–49; Quilici 1989, pp. 451–506; Sassatelli 1989; Strandberg 1989, pp. 163–83; *I nuovi scavi dell'Università di Bologna* 1990; Wikander, Wikander 1990, pp. 189–205; Bergamini 1991; Potter 1991, pp. 191–209; Rendeli 1991, pp. 9–45; Sgubini Moretti 1991, pp. 23–38; Cristofani et al. 1992; Sassatelli, Govi 1992, pp. 125–39; Steingräber 1992, pp. 221–23; Rendeli 1993; Zapicchi 1993; Colonna 1994, pp. 554–65; Fontaine 1994, pp. 73–86; Verger, Kermorvant 1994, pp. 1077–94; Brocato 1995, pp. 57–93; Malnati, Violante 1995, pp. 97–123; Miller 1995; Di Vita 1996, pp. 263 ff.; Greco 1996, pp. 233 ff.; Izzet 1996, pp. 55–72; Mertens, Greco 1996, pp. 243 ff.; Steingräber 1996, pp. 75–104; Adam, Briquel, Massa–Pairault 1997; Broise, Jolivet 1997, pp. 1327–50; Damgaard Andersen 1997, pp. 343–82; Greco, Sommella 1997, pp. 894–904; Bruni 1998; Warden, Thomas, Galloway 1999, pp. 231–46.

Luigi Donati

Civil, Religious, and Domestic Architecture

The approach in present-day research

From its very beginning the study of Etruscan society tended to focus on the excavation of necropolises; however, in recent decades there has been a gradual shift of interest toward the study of inhabited centers. Noteworthy advances have been made in our knowledge of the layout of built-up spaces and the evolution of architectural types—all of which bring out the variations resulting from economic, environmental and cultural factors.

Thanks to the use of advanced methods of excavation and an increasingly interdisciplinary approach—which has enabled archaeology to draw on the assistance of other sciences—it has been possible to throw some light on Etruscan crafts and industries, on daily and domestic life. Here, an important contribution may come from research involving submerged settlements, in which underwater archaeology plays a leading role (think, for example, of the information gleaned from the discovery of the lakeside Villanovan village of Gran Carro in Bolsena, whose exceptional state of conservation is due not only to environmental conditions but also to the very absence of subsequent archaeological sedimentation above the original village). The advances in research have borne out the original belief that in both their public and private buildings the Etruscans made large use not only of clay but also of timber, which was available in plentiful supply. However, it is also true that where stone was readily available, they gradually began to make use of it in the construction of walls, without abandoning the more traditional techniques (which might well figure together in the same building).

Alongside the study of inhabited centers, another fruitful line of inquiry has focused on rural settlements, which resulted from a desire to exploit natural resources and/or to exercise some control over territorial borders. Even more than urban archaeology, these studies rely on the information supplied by other scientific disciplines (e.g. geography and the natural sciences) and on the use of modern surveying techniques (e.g. aerial photography and satellite "remote sensing", geophisical prospections and geomorphical study of landscape). With regard to the archaeology of landscape, the British School in Rome has always played a leading role; its investigations of the farms that formed the base unit for territorial settlement have produced important information—one might mention here the farms of Casale Pian Roseto (Veio), of San Pietro (Tuscania), of Podere Tartuchino (Valle dell'Albegna), Pian d'Alma (Vetulonia) and numerous others that have been located in the Po Valley area.

The study of these socio-economic micro-systems, when accompanied by adequate sampling techniques and analyses of animal remains, provides information on the type of livestock bred and how it was employed; at the same time, the study of plant remains reveals what crops were cultivated and whether there was any system of crop rotation. Studies of industrial sites are of equal importance—especially when they concern metallurgical facilities (e.g. Populonia, Rondelli near Follonica, L'Accesa near Massa Marittima and Marzabotto). The wholesale accumulation of the data these sites provide complements the study of material artifacts and thus extends our knowledge of the economic interaction between these early communities, enabling us to understand the hierarchy established between central and peripheral settlements and the overall dynamics of the relationship between city and outlying territory.

Important information on that relationship is also emerging from the recent research into upland fortresses. Be they *oppida* (fortified towns) such as Ghiaccio Forte, Trequanda, Poggio La Croce, Cetamura, Monte Castello di Procchio, or *castella* (fortresses) such as Castiglione di San Martino and Poggio Civitella, these were structures which during the course of the fourth century B.C. served to impose and defend the control urban centers exercised over territory (or, in the case of Elba, over shipping routes). Of particular importance are the excavations at Poggio Civitella (Montalcino), which are gradually bringing to light our first complete example of an upland fortress with a complex defensive system of three barriers: one irregular circle of walls over four meters thick enclosing the summit, and two elliptical rings lower down the sides of the hill. Given its imposing position (at a height of 650 meters) and the complexity of its military engineering, the fort seems to have been a crucial component in a whole series of similar facilities set up at key points to provide comprehensive protective cover for the borders of the Chiusi territory.

Hut cinerary urn with terra-cotta lid from Vetulonia, ninth century B.C. Florence, Museo Archeologico

Plan and axonometric drawing of the farm of Podere Tartuchino, in the Albegna Valley

opposite
Walls of the Poggio Civitella fortress, near Montalcino

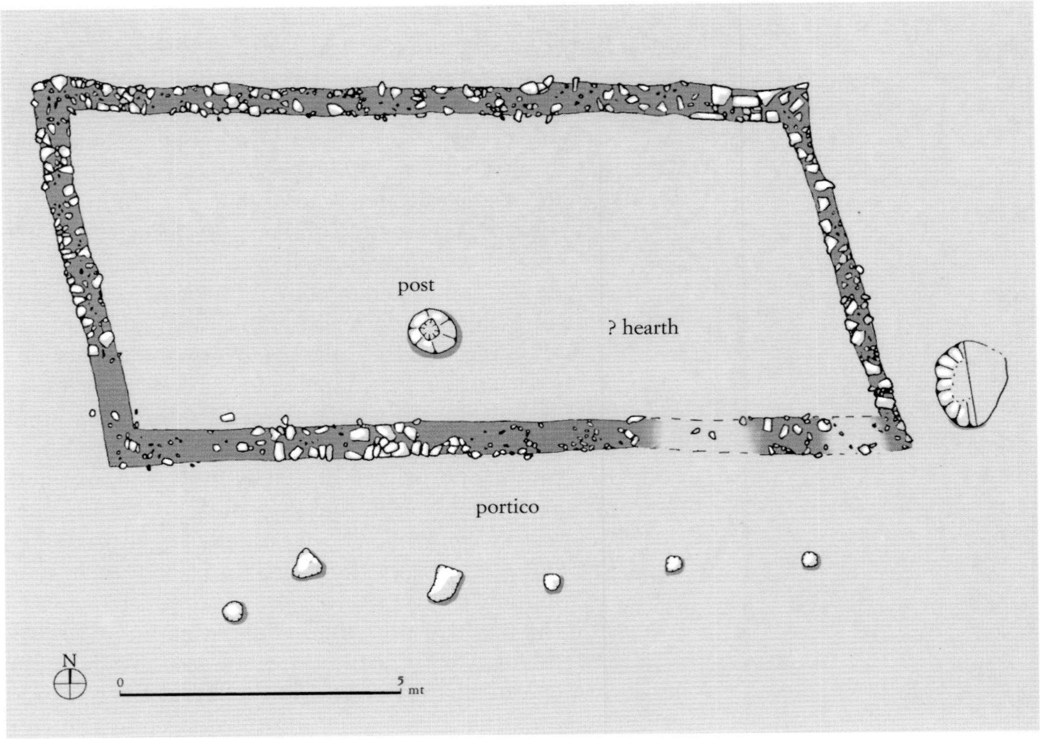

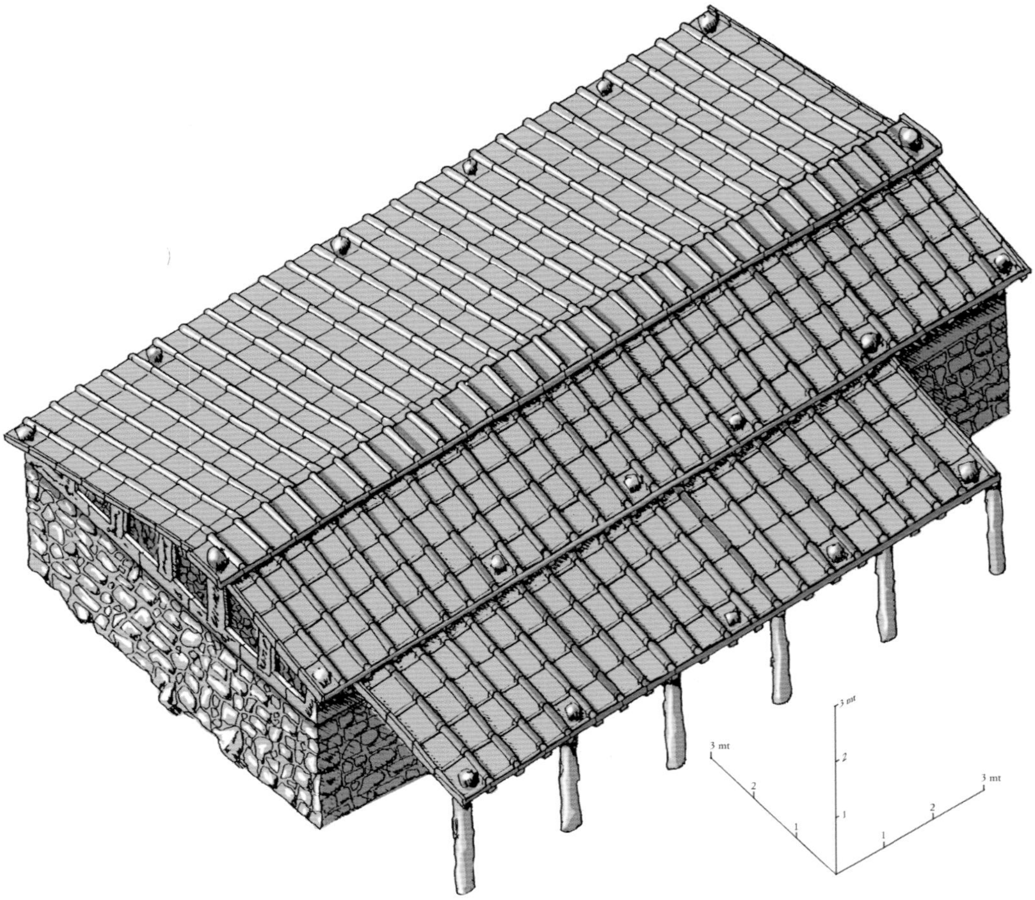

The early villages

The initial emergence of Etruscan civilization was accompanied by the establishment of stable, fixed activities such as the raising of livestock and the planting of crops. As a result, there was a general shift in the pattern of settlement away from the upland sites, often connected with the routes of transhumance, which had been a characteristic feature of the last phase of the Bronze Age (toward the end of the second millennium B.C.). People now chose to settle at strategic territorial points which made it possible to satisfy the need for security but also offered more opportunities for the rational exploitation of environmental resources—as well as allowing for easier communications (made essential by the growing mobility of persons and goods). So, depending on the geographical features of terrain, settlements would tend to be sited either on rocky plateaus—veritable islands at the foot of whose steep faces ran available water supplies—or on the summit of hills (as long as they were in ready proximity to plain lands).

The appearance and organization of these settlements are still largely unknown—not only because of the absence of any systematic program of excavation in these areas, but also because the building techniques of the day favored materials that have since perished, leaving very little trace of themselves behind. In effect, the absence of any extensive project of research means that the discovery of these structures is generally a matter of good luck. In broad outline, one can say that these villages were a whole made up of distinct conglomerations of huts separated by areas of relatively open ground, with a distinct burial area nearby. Only later, due to the increase in population, would these conglomerates expand and melt together, giving rise to the inhabited centers that we know. In some cases there is evidence of an even more sparsely-scattered pattern of settlement, with distinct villages occupying an area that was even more extensive than that which would be occupied by the future city. This is the case, for example, with Tarquinia, where the area of the original pattern of settlement has been estimated thanks to the identification of a village of huts on the Monterozzi uplands and the spread of the necropolises (Poggio Gallinaro, Poggio Selciatello, Poggio dell'Impiccato, Poggio Quarto degli Archi and the burial-grounds of Ar-

The territory of Tarquinia

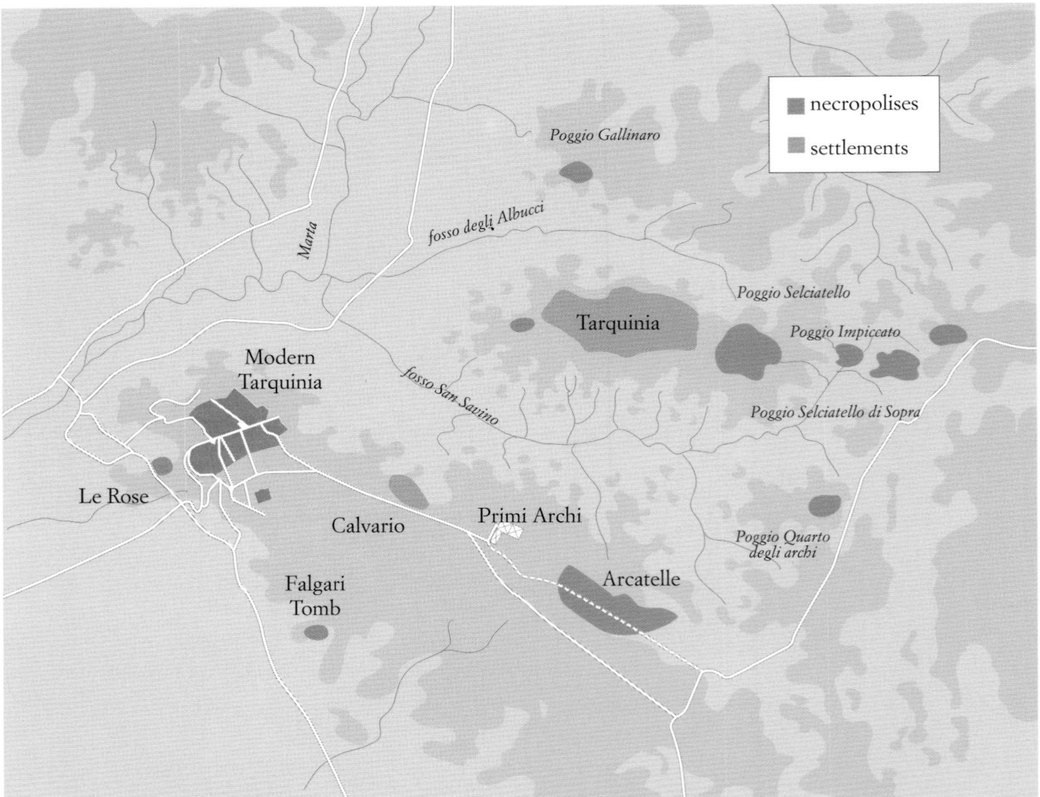

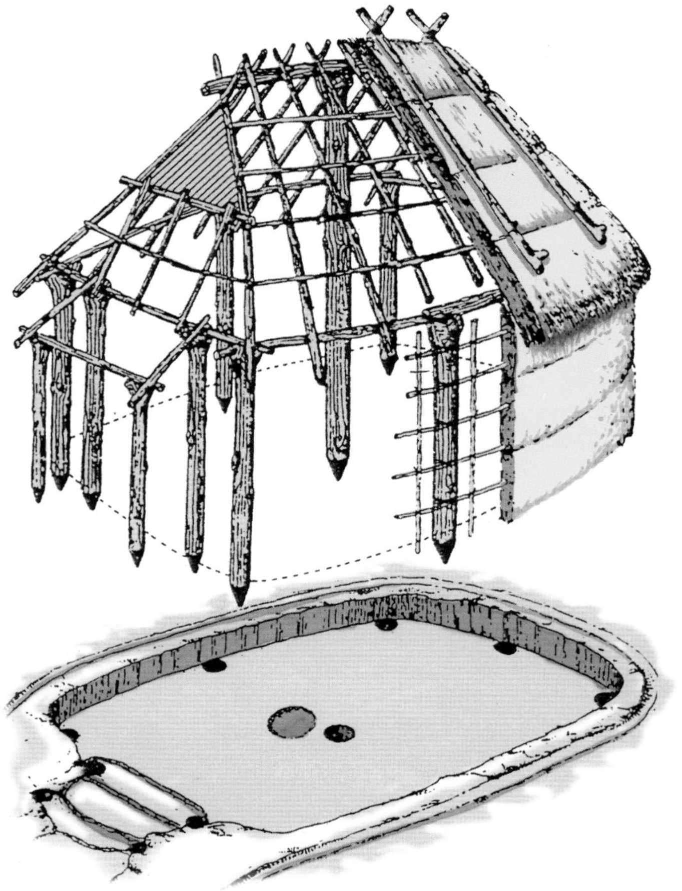

Reconstruction of hut A on the Palatine

catelle and Le Rose on the outskirts of modern-day Tarquinia) occupying a number of hills around the Civita flatland which was the site of the historic city.
Initially, the building materials consisted almost exclusively of timber, brushwood, straw and clay—the latter being used mainly for wall-plaster. Hence, these were structures made of materials which, in normal conditions, rot away almost without trace; at most, one might come across a fragment of wall-plaster bearing the markers of the scraper used to apply it (preserved because it accidentally dried out or was actually baked by the heat of a fire). All of this makes it very difficult to "read" these buildings, unless, that is, they were cut directly into rock or else sited on particularly homogeneous terrain—in which case it is fairly easy to make out the floor area (often trodden lower than the surrounding land), the fireplaces, the holes for the structure poles and the perimeter groove for the walls. From these features we can see that the huts were generally oval or circular and thus continued to follow the model of more ancient dwellings; straight-lines make their appearance in floor-plans only later—and then not everywhere. Even though nothing is left of the walls, one can reconstruct their appearance thanks to the fact that the impsto or bronze urns for the ashes of the dead were often made in the form of huts and so—for all their simplification and standardization—offer us an image of contemporary dwelling-places. From a comparison of these models and actual remains we can see that the walls usually consisted of a horizontal weave of branches, brushwood or reeds reinforced by vertical poles and subsequently strengthened by a thick coating of clay mixed with straw. There do not seem to have been any buildings of dry-stone walls—a technique which was however also rare in the Greece of the Geometric Age. The weight-bearing structure consisted of a series of larger poles set up within these walls; the number could vary from one—a single central pole— to six, which were organized in two rows and thus made the larger huts into structures with a central nave and two side aisles. There might also be internal dividing walls, set into special grooves dug in the floor. The entrance, which in oval or rectangular huts was always aligned on the main axis, was sometimes protected by a small porch (though this feature was most common in the

Remains of dwellings at San Giovenale

Latium area). There might also be a second smaller doorway or, more often the case, a square window. The fact that one urn model shows a second window in the roof suggests that there could also have been a sort of raised loft (as has also been claimed might have been the case with contemporary structures in Metaponto and Pithekoussai, present-day Ischia). The roof itself consisted of a thick thatch of vegetation held in place by a frame of small beams which criss-crossed above the ridge beam forming a "sun boat" that ended with decorations in the form of aquatic birds or a pair of horns (intended as both adornment and an apotropaic talisman). Given that thatched roofs had to be sharply pitched to prevent rainwater collecting (and thus rotting the wooden structures), they were held in place by a second series of small beams tied to the underlying frame. The covering was shaped rather like a tortoise shell; below the ridge beam there were two open tympana which served as skylights and ventilation openings to release the smoke from the fire (generally located at the centre of the hut).

A valuable source of information was the excavation carried out at Castellaccio di Sorgenti della Nova, on the edges of the Selva del Lamone in the middle Fiora Valley. Still under way, these excavations are bringing to light a village sited on a defended spur of tufa and pumice stone which, between the eleventh and ninth century B.C., dominated the surrounding area and nearby villages. The settlement housed more than 1,500 inhabitants in a number of huts, some of them built on artificial terraces dug into the side of the rock; other openings dug into the rock served as storerooms for the huts themselves (or for the larger grottoes that were used as dwelling-places). It is possible that the arrangement of the huts on different levels was due not only to growing population numbers but also to some internal hierarchy within the community; in fact, the large elliptical huts on the sides of the spur must have housed extended groups of families, while the smaller circular huts on the summit were probably reserved for the families that exercised power over the community and the surrounding territory.

Roselle, the Foro Romano area

The formation of cities. Public building

As early as the middle of the eighth century B.C., Etruscan society had come into contact with the reality of a Greek *polis*—thanks to the colonists from the island of Euboea who had settled in Campania. Then, as a patrician class gradually established itself, the social equilibrium that had reigned in earlier communities was broken, resulting—among other things—in the radical innovations within settlements that took place during the course of the seventh century B.C. The most striking change came in the organization of inhabited areas, with the transformation of villages into cities; thanks to its centralized power and its ability to co-ordinate a large labor force, the latter was able to equip itself with imposing defensive walls (in order to supplement natural defences, if these were insufficient). We have an example of this at Roselle, where the absence of stone that could be easily worked with the tools available at the time led to the use of unbaked bricks (in line with a tried and trusted tradition of the Near East). The remains that have come to light at the base of the irregular sixth-century defence structure on the north and western slopes of the northern hill reveal that a mix of techniques was used: the brick wall stood on a platform of rough-hewn stone which was probably mixed together with clay. This was a technique that was not infrequent in the West in this and following centuries (there are examples at Kaulonia, Siris-Metaponto and Aleria during the Archaic Age, in Gela in the fourth century B.C. and Arezzo during the Hellenistic period). From the present research we cannot say if, at that stage, the Roselle defence structure was continued to include the southern upland—as it certainly was during the Archaic Age—or if it was limited to the northern hill, which in effect contains the greatest evidence of the settlements of the Orientalizing period.

Another feature of the shift from village to city was the attempt made to rationalize the layout of urban spaces, to meet collective needs in ways that were compatible with the morphology of terrain and the previous organization of the inhabited area. For example, at San Giovenale, the population growth in the first Orientalizing period led to the occupation of the entire plain area, with the construction of massive terrace walls to level out the sloping terrain on the northern side of the town and on the southern side of the acropolis—thus making it possible to use them for the construction of housing. At Veio too, a re-examination of the plans drawn up after the 1944 excavations of the acropolis in Piazza d'Armi reveals a regular layout of inhabited zones along a main road intersecting with other minor roads (the center of the urban space being occupied by a large open-topped oval cistern). Another result of this attempt to organize buildings so as to make best use of available land was that the former curved ground-plan for individual huts was replaced by rectangular or square models. Clearly this ground-plan made it possible to align the structures better and also meant that the internal space could be exploited more efficiently (as well as making it possible to extend buildings—where necessary—by the simple addition of further external walls). Clear examples of the full exploitation of this type of structure would not come until the sixth century; however, even though the model took some time establishing itself, it would gradually become the norm in areas of urban expansion. In the "historic" inhabited zones one continues to find buildings with curved sides—though mixed-line ground-plans are not uncommon.

One, so far unique, example of this mix is the *tholos* of Roselle (mid seventh century B.C.), sited at the back of a rectangular enclosure, with another similar enclosure behind it. This construction was buried beneath the area of the Roman forum together with the remains of some oval huts (contemporary or earlier); but what is significant is that no further building work had been carried out over it. Unlike the huts, the *tholos* is in unbaked bricks, with an oval internal layout (perhaps with a false cupola) enclosed within a square. Given that this design involves a series of technical complications, it is clear that this choice was dictated by a certain religious conservatism—similar to that one can see in the contemporary burial chambers of Cerveteri (the Mengarelli Tomb, the Tomb of the Painted Animals and the Tomb of the Ship), in which there is a circular vestibule enclosed within a series of rectangular spaces. The fact that this Roselle building has a similar plan, which explicitly echoes the layout of the primitive huts of the ancestors and thus is rich in symbolic associations, would suggest that this was a special building with a clear, religious purpose. This, therefore, is perhaps a "sacred house" like those in Tourkovounia (Greece) or on the acropolis of Satricum (Latium). Its very positioning at the back of the enclosure is also significant—think, for example, of the similar position of the "Building Beta" of Tarquinia, and of the later temple in the Belvedere sanctuary of Orvieto.

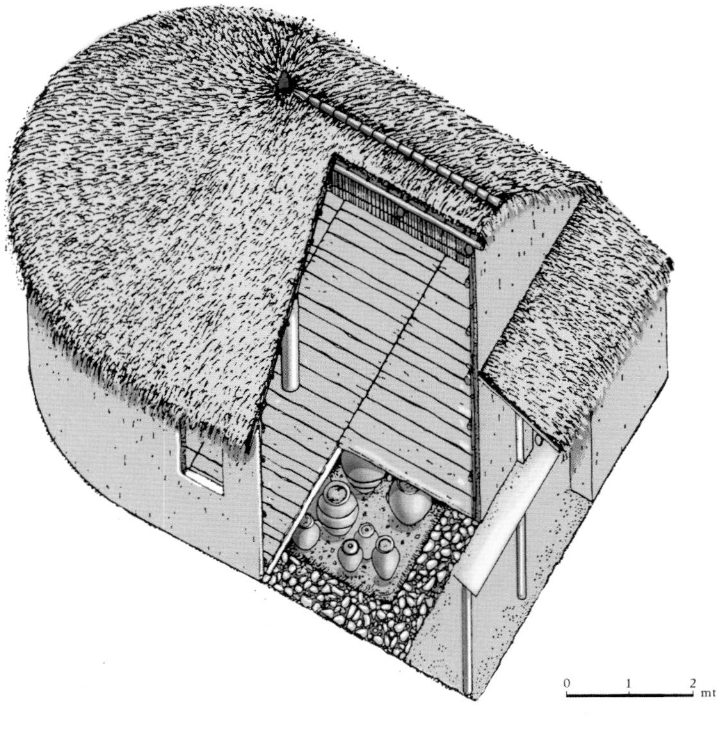

Recontruction of Baggiovara hut (Modena)

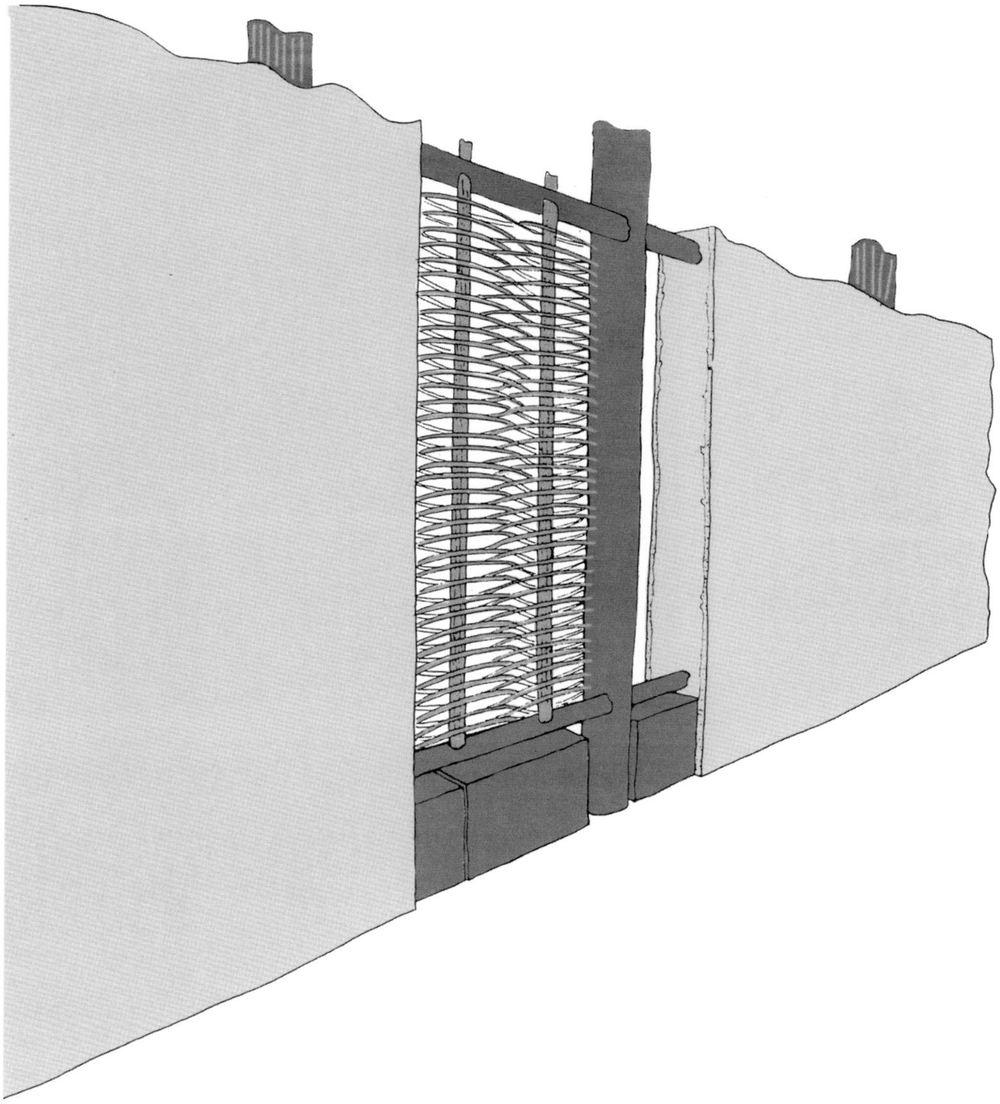

Example of the building technique of fencing wall

Housing

In the Etruscan areas of the Po Valley the basic building materials and structure remained largely influenced by those of earlier huts. However, quite apart from the images carved on the back of the wooden throne found in a tomb at Verucchio, the excavated foundations of numerous huts reveal a general shift from the curved to the right-angled ground-plan within settlements (where there was a greater tendency to regular organization of land use), while in rural constructions there was greater freedom of choice in ground-plans. An example of such rural constructions is the late-archaic hut excavated at Baggiovara (Modena), which has a rectangular ground-plan ending in an apse, within which was a deep cavity where jugs and various other containers were discovered. This latter feature is also to be found in a number of other huts in the region, and would have served as an underground storeroom covered by planks of wood.

In Etruscan Latium the traditional fencing or woven wall continued to be used; however, in its traditional form it was restricted to secondary structures, while for the main walls a developed version was used, with the support poles being fixed into a stone base. There were also other techniques in use: walls of unbaked bricks (as in the *tholos* of Roselle); walls of hewn stone laid out in regular horizontal rows; walls of irregular stones held together with mud; and *pisé* (with mud being mixed together with gravel and/or branches and "poured" into a wood mold, which was dismounted when the clay dried, then reassembled for a second coating, and so on). The choice was in part dictated by the materials available, given that in the ancient world such materials had to come from the immediate neighborhood.

The fairly extensive information we now have has revealed that there was never a standardized house type: the choice of one model as opposed to another depended not only on the degree of the builder's attachment to traditions but also on economic and logistical factors. Hence, it should come as no surprise that different types of housing may co-exist in the same

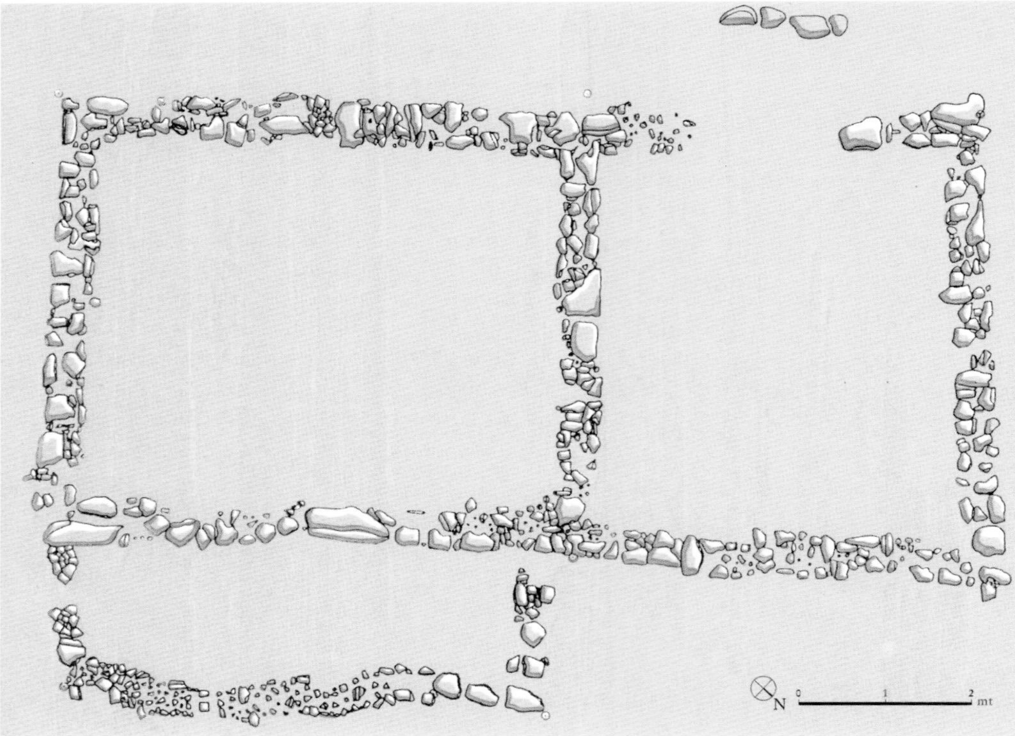

Plan of a house in the Etruscan settlement of Accesa (Massa Marittima)

place. However, in broad terms, one can say that the first shift away from the early models was toward a lengthways model of hut—in which the door was in one of the long sides and the internal space consisted of a single rectangular room (*oikos*-style) or, more commonly, of two or three rooms next to each other (sometimes these might have led off a long rectangular atrium or portico giving onto the street). This layout is faithfully reproduced in tombs and was probably derived from the models to be seen in Greek colonies (for example, the late-seventh-century houses to be seen at Cospito-Caserta in Policoro, which had three rooms giving onto an area that may have been porticoed). While the actual size of the structures is probably a reflection of social status (as is the size of tombs and the richness of their burial goods), the internal division of the living space—which occasionally occurs even in the huts of the Villanovan period—would seem to indicate that, at certain levels of society, there was now a generally-felt need for the domestic space to be divided according to function. The evidence from the tombs of the day which were dug direct into tufa suggests that it was beginning to be common for houses to have flat, coffered or beamed ceilings covered by a weave of reeds. As with the Villanovan huts, air and light for the internal spaces—and, above all, for those without any external access—may have been provided by windows. This is borne out by a small urn of the Archaic period from the Chiusi area, which shows the facade of a building with a door alongside a barred window. However, it must be said that windows cannot have become a standard feature, given that no direct evidence of their existence has ever been found (even in those structures where the extant walls reached up to a certain height). Hence, it cannot be ruled out that in many cases, air and light came through simple openings placed high up in the structure (as was the case with the earlier huts).

Initially, roofs continued to be in the traditional thatch (the houses in Borgo di San Giovenale), which had the advantage of being cheap but did not last long. Then, in the second half of the seventh century B.C., there was a move toward roofs of terra-cotta tiles, which obviously required much more substantial carpentry, were much more expensive, but in the long term were more economical because more solid and long-lasting. The system used was a mixed Spartan-Corinthian system—that is, with flat rectangular tiles joined by semi-circular curved tiles (double slant roofs would also have had curved tiles along the ridge, making them rather similar in appearance to modern roofs). The stability of these structures must have been guaranteed by the weight of the tiles themselves (much bigger and thicker than modern tiles; each flat tile weighed somewhere between 10 and 15 kilograms). However, the fact that some tiles had holes for nails fixing them to the wooden roof frame reveals that weight was not always enough.

The social status of the house owner was also reflected by the use of painted or molded terra cotta. This might take the form of acroteria on the ridge tiles (similar to the decoration of Villanovan huts); antefixes decorated with human heads or palms, placed at the edge of the gutter tiles; overflows in the form of a cat; facing panels decorated with scenes of banquets, games, processions, etc.; lacunars or simple tiles decorated with plant motifs or images of real or imaginary animals. Some of these features were merely intended as decoration or to enhance protection against natural wear and tear, others were celebratory or even apotropaic. With the introduction of such features, building work became the province of specialized and trained craftsmen, and we get a hint of this in Pliny (*Naturalis historia*, XXXV, 152), when he tells us of the arrival of three Greek artists, experts in the plastic arts, who accompanied the rich Corinthian merchant Demaratus when he was exiled to Etruria (where he would father Tarquinius Priscus, the future king of Rome). The three *fictores* bore the very significant names of Eucheir (he of the good hand), Eugrammos (he of the fine drawing) and Diopos (he who looks stealthily)—all of which are clear references to the molding of clay to form architectural decorations, to the paintings of panels and walls, and to the use of optical instruments in such work. While admitting that the Greek colonies in the West played a key role in passing on such traditions (Magna Graecia had veritable teams of skilled craftsmen working on the construction and decoration of buildings—one of whom actually identifies himself as "Diopos" on an antefix in sixth-century Camarina), one must underline the essential truth of Pliny's tale: it was the specialized craftsmen of direct Greek extraction who first introduced these revolutionary innovations into the architecture of Etruscan Latium.

Public building: city walls

As already mentioned, the most imposing element of a city was its defensive walls. However, the construction of the walls varied from the northern to southern areas of Etruria, given that in the latter the terrain is largely tufa and therefore offers more naturally secure plateaus. This meant that the walls generally came after the city had achieved its full splendor (that is, during the Archaic period), and often played little role in the built-up zones of dwellings, which covered too vast an area to be entirely enclosed within walls. Indeed, the 190 hectares of Veio, the 150 of Cerveteri and the 120 of Tarquinia suggest that semi-rural zones for crops and herds survived within the sprawling urban area. Given the ready availability of easily-cut stone, the walls were generally made of regular-sized hewn blocks aligned in horizontal rows. At Veio the encircling walls—still extant up to a height of six meters—ran round the whole of the plateau (covering a distance of more than 6 kilometers). Elsewhere, however, they were limited to those areas where natural obstacles did not guarantee adequate defence. The introduction of chamber gateways—such as the North Gateway of Tarquinia—may well have been due to the developments in Greek siege technology, which during the course of the fourth century B.C. saw the introduction of the first siege artillery.

The situation in northern Etruria was different, given that the construction of city walls which physically delimited the area of urban settlement was a key initial phase, and naturally imposed the planned use of the space enclosed. The walls were of various types—partly because they were built on the slopes of hills and their circuit necessarily followed the most tactically feasible route, partly because of the nature of the stone available (at times, this might lead builders to opt for the use of square-hewn blocks arranged in more or less regular rows, at others lead them to choose more irregular stonework, where the stability of the walls was guaranteed by a mass of more or less unworked rocks). One of the best-known examples of this latter type is again provided by the walls of Roselle, built toward the middle of the sixth century B.C. to replace the earlier defences in eastern-style unbaked brick. A total length of 3,270 meters, the walls run mid-slope around both of the hills on which the city is built, and at many points their extant height is 5 meters. Formed of rough-hewn rocks from quarries that can still be seen further uphill, the walls had seven gateways, the preferred design for which was the so-called *sceo* type (this was the simplest of all, and consisted of an

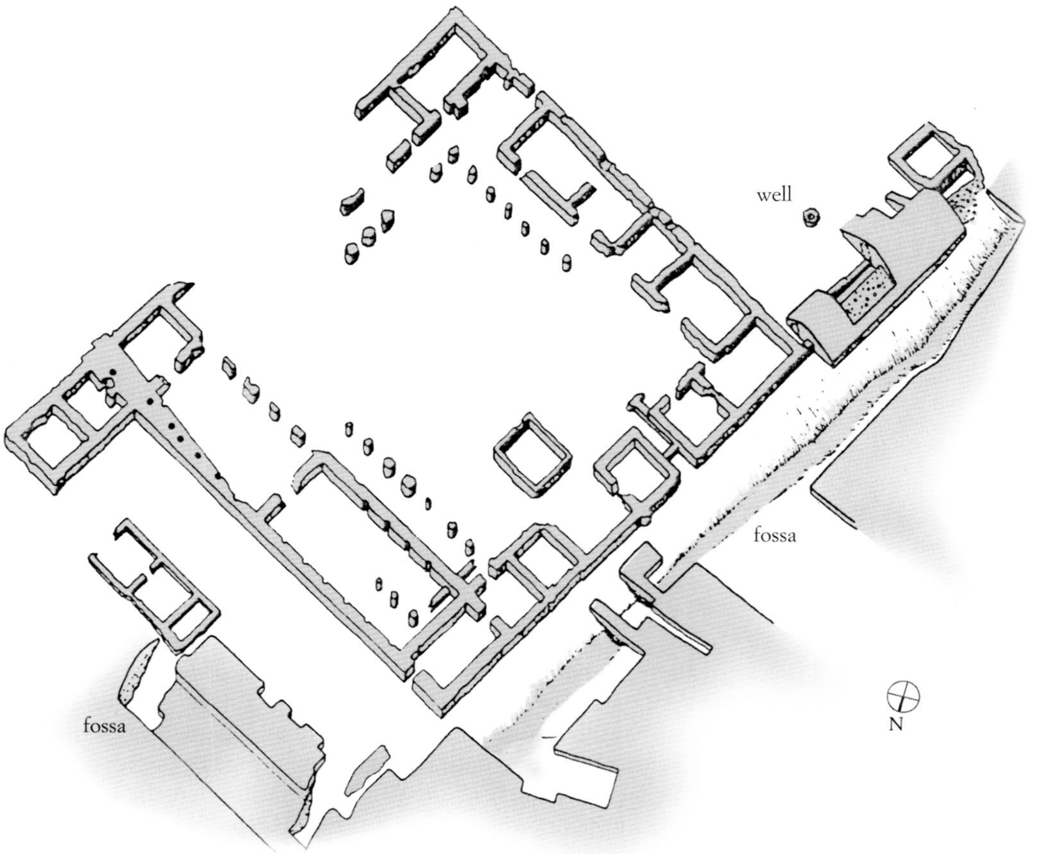

Plan of the arcaic princely residence of Poggio Civitate, near Murlo (Siena)

obliquely placed entrance approached by a long salient, which meant that the right side of besiegers—unprotected by their shields—was exposed to the weapons of the besieged).

Patrician houses

During the course of the sixth century B.C. a new type of house plan emerged: a square, with all the rooms arranged around a central atrium. The most immediate predecessor for this type is to be found in the palaces of the inland regions of Etruria, which—longer than other areas—tended to maintain a social structure centering around a patrician leader; examples of this type of princely residence can be found at Poggio Civitate (Murlo-Siena) and Acquarossa (Viterbo).

On the border between central Tuscany and the Tyrrhenian coastal region, the Poggio Civitate residence (still under excavation) stands on a wide plateau on the top of a ridge of hills that provides no natural protection. The structure is actually a rebuilding—carried out in the early decades of the sixth century B.C.—on the site of the ruins of a previous construction destroyed by fire. The foundations of the large complex are in stone with the walls in perishable material (unbaked bricks or *pisé*), and the ground-plan consists of a large central square (60 by 60 meters) with an addition to the north and a courtyard and well to the south. The sides of this central unit are occupied by eighteen rooms; four identical rooms occupy the corners (as was the case in certain eastern places built around a large courtyard with well). Three sides of the court were enclosed by a portico of wood columns or pilasters raised on stone bases, and access was via two main gateways (on the east and west sides), with a secondary entrance point in the north-west corner. The rooms along the porticoed sides were probably living space (perhaps including some workshops and storerooms), and the most striking among them are two large neighboring halls which together occupy the entire length of the northern side of courtyard. Evidence gleaned from the colonnade within these rooms and from their walls reinforced with poles suggests that these halls were not only larger than the others but were also higher—so it is fair to assume they had some public function. As in Villanovan huts, the ridge of the roof was protected with tiles; but here the richly-decorated terra cottas probably served a propaganda function as well, and it is likely that this wing of the building was the site of a series of life-size sculptures depicting ancestors and other characters (perhaps attendants) together with sphinxes. The other smaller-scale animal sculptures of horses, cats, rams and boars may have stood on the other sides of the portico. However, the central focus of the enclosed courtyard is to be found on the side without a portico, where there is a series of three rooms—two symmetrical spaces flanking a sort of rectangular exedra which was probably intended as a public area (rather like the *tablinum* in a Roman *domus*). The exedra enclosed a small sacellum—perhaps open to the sky or with a thatch-covering (like the Roselle *tholos*)—which served to invoke divine protection over the place itself (and divine legitimation of the power exercised by the dynasty occupying it).

Houses

The widespread adoption of the Poggio Civitate model in ordinary houses—creating a sort of miniature geometric universe turned-in upon itself—reveals a new concept of the relation between private and social life. Previously, houses had been designed so that—when weather permitted—certain domestic activities could be performed outside (for example, there were moveable stoves for the preparation of food). The new type of houses meant that these activities could now be performed in the semi-covered space of the atrium, thus guaranteeing the inhabitants a greater degree of privacy. It is significant here to note that—as we can see from Etruscan tombs—all windows in these houses opened onto the courtyard and not outward (the outer walls presumably having only the same infrequent narrow openings as Greek houses). Judging by the House of the Impluvium in Roselle—an almost square struc-

Roselle, House of the Impluvium, *plan of the excavation*

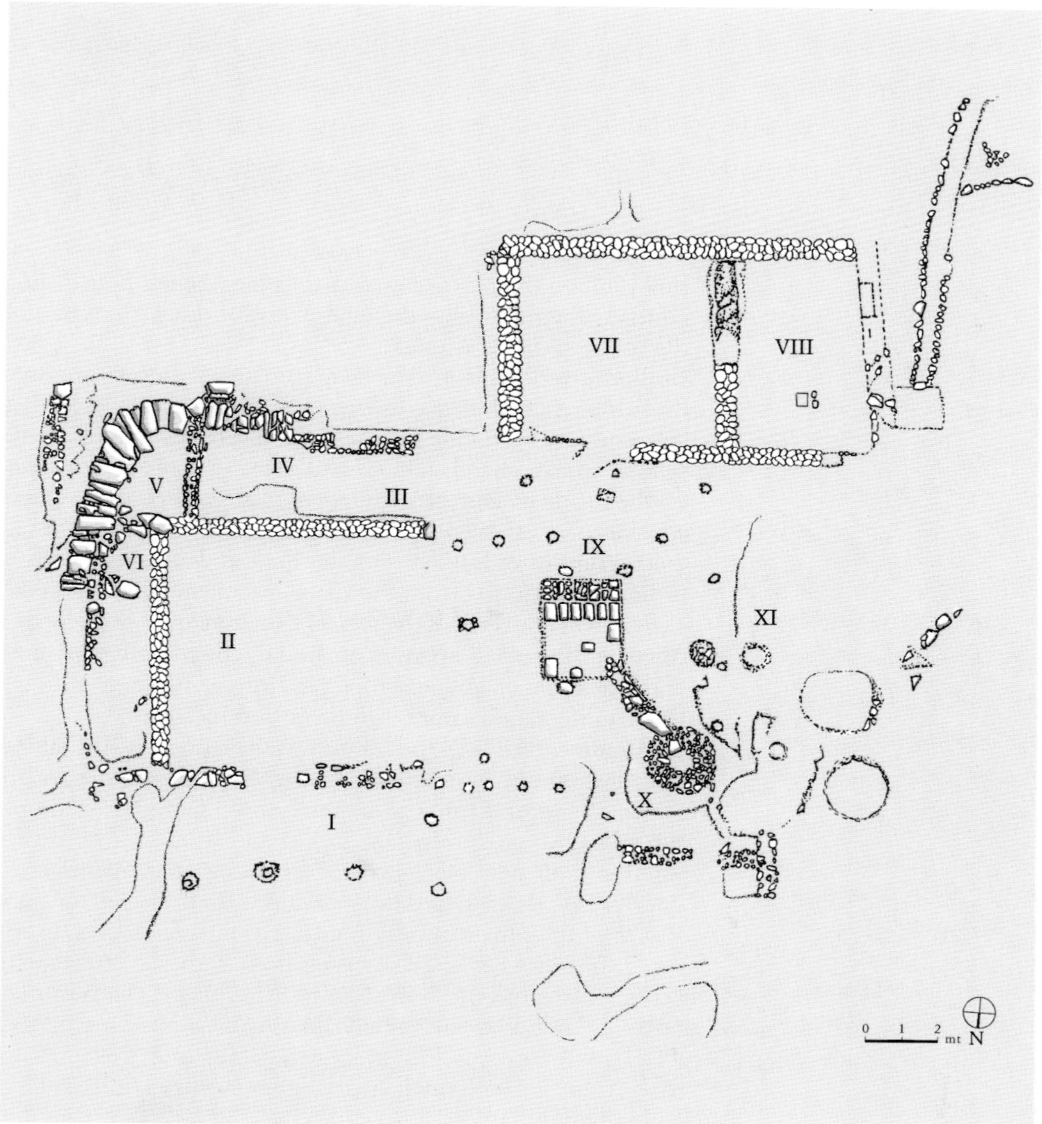

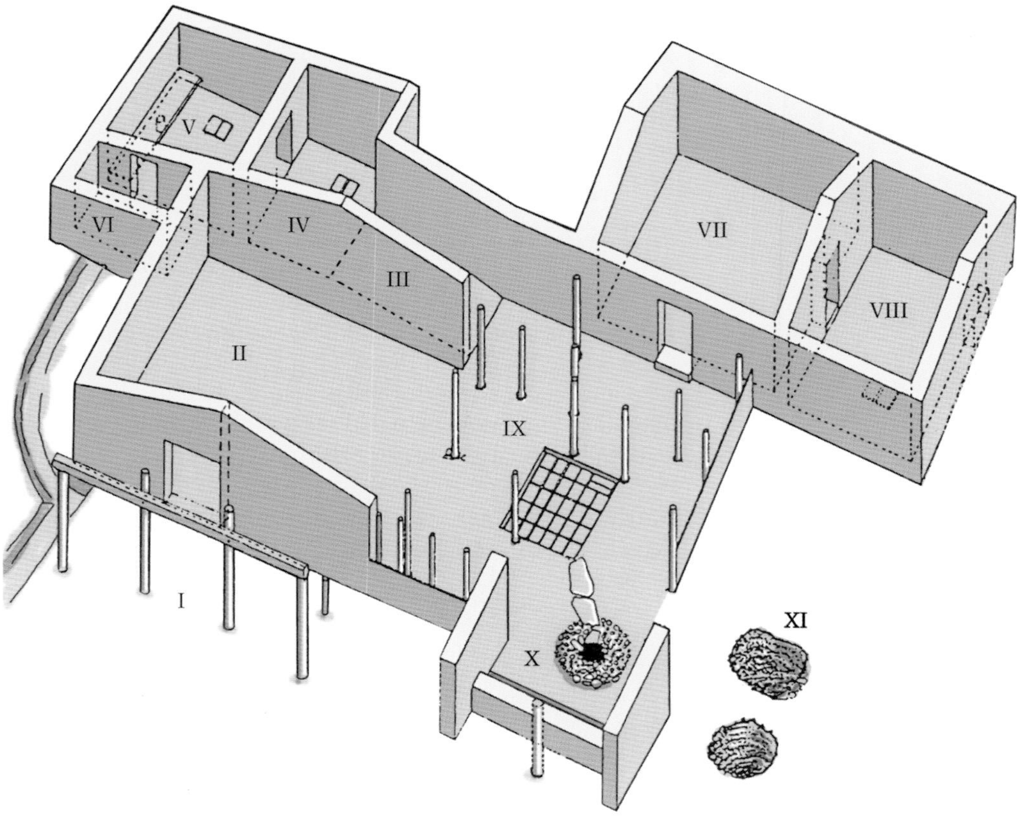

Reconstruction of the House of the Impluvium *at Roselle*

ture built on the ruins of an old-style lengthways house of two adjacent rooms giving onto a courtyard with a well—the emergence of this atrium-model can be dated around the middle of the sixth century B.C.

Built in stone like its predecessor, the new structure not only incorporates the two rooms in its southern side but also incorporates the entire courtyard of some 300 square meters—thus substantially predating the layout and architecture of the Roman-style house. The groundplan is approximately square and shows a series of rooms around an atrium (IX) enclosed on the inside by a portico (Vitruvius's *atrium tetrastilum*) with a roof that slopes inward and special corner tiles (*compluvium*). This roof structure not only provides an ingenious way to collect rainwater but also enables light and air to enter the rooms arranged around it (even if the term atrium—from the Latin *ater* meaning "dark" and "smoky"—suggests that, as far as light was concerned, the results were not always totally satisfactory). Rain water would fall through the central opening created by the *compluvium* into a large basin (*impluvium*) lined with terra-cotta slabs, and then pass into an underground cistern (X) which, once full, overflowed into an adjacent basin protected by a roof.

The main entrance to the house was via a portico (I) that led into an ample space (II) fitted out for domestic worship and giving directly onto the atrium (like the exedra in the Poggio Civitate palace). From the atrium a stone ramp (III) led up to three small rooms that functioned as the penetralia (IV, V, VI) and were clearly reserved for the couple of the house (light and air here were provided by a circular opening in a tile equipped with a rotating cover, *opaion*, that could be operated from below by means of a pole). The larger of the two rooms of the previous buildings (VII) must have been used for symposiums; at this period these were held in the Greek fashion, with the participants reclining upon beds (*klinai*) arranged around the walls (the benched-lined room in the Acquarossa palace and that in house I, zone F at San Giovenale must also have served for banquets). The adjacent room (VIII), with its central fireplace and grindstone, was used for the preparation and storing of food (there is also a small larder dug out of the wall), while corn itself was stored in the well from the old house (partially filled in by the rubble from that previous structure) and in another adjacent cavity (XI). It should be underlined that though it stood in the heart of the urban area, the house itself was surrounded by agricultural land, and hence functioned as both a residence and a center of agricultural production. Clearly, during the Archaic period certain sectors of Roselle maintained that mix which has been found in earlier settlements, where the space around houses was left free for the cultivation of crops and the raising of livestock.

Urban planning in newly-founded cities

As we have seen with Roselle, in those "historical" cities which had grown up over time, the attempt to rationalize the use and layout of urban space encountered severe difficulties. However, such projects could be applied much more thoroughly in newly founded—that is, colonial—cities, such as Marzabotto and, perhaps, Capua. In such places urban development followed isonomic principles which reflected the "egalitarian" organization of Etruscan society in the Late Archaic period (after the waning of patrician power). Similar characteristics can be found in the cities of Adria and Spina in the Po Delta—a marshy environment where there had to be substantial resort to the use of wooden piles to create an ordered series of platforms for the, entirely wooden, constructions.

What is more, one can find this attempt to impose a planned layout also in newly-founded settlements of much smaller size, such as that currently being excavated on the uplands of Poggio Civitella (which would later be occupied by a fortress): there the houses are distributed over large artificial terraces on the gentler and less exposed sides of the hill (a layout similar to that followed in the later settlement of Monte Bibele, near Bologna).

However, even those cities with a planned layout do not bear out Servius' claim that "for the Etruscans, those were not considered *iustae urbes* (true cities) which did not have three gateways, three streets and three temples dedicated to Jupiter, Juno and Minerva" (*ad Aeneidem*, I, 422). Nevertheless, this claim does indicate the importance of the divine in urban planning: the benevolence of the gods was a major concern and the *Libri Rituales* laid down the prescriptions to be followed in foundation rituals and in the allocation and use of space within the city.

In fact, Marzabotto, the best known example of Etruscan urban-planning, was really an "extension" of the sacred town that stands some dozen meters or so above it on an upland. In that small town all the sacred buildings have the same astronomical alignment as those in the city, and the very highest point was occupied by a small structure (discovered last century) which must have served as the *auguraculum*, a sort of observatory from which to observe the flight of birds and thence draw auspices—in short, the place at which the augur exercised his office while dominating the entire city by his gaze. In fact, Marzabotto imitates a model that arose in both mainland Greece and the colonies of Greek Italy toward the end of the sixth century B.C. and would then be theoretically outlined by Hippodamus of Miletus during the age of Pericles. Sited on an alluvial terrace that overlooks the Reno River, the city has a network of streets organized around the orthogonal alignment of three equidistant arteries of equal width all running east-west. Between these run a number of parallel alleys of irregular interval, forming long rectangular "city blocks." The arteries comprised a central part reserved for wheeled traffic which was flanked by two 5-meter-wide pavements. Perhaps under porticos, these latter in their turn contained cobbled channels for the liquid waste from the houses. As at Pompeii, there were large stepping-stones which facilitated the passage from one side of the street to the other (particularly in bad weather).

The houses had tile roofs—something totally unknown anywhere else north of the Apennines—and were built using wicker panels or unbaked bricks. It is, therefore, natural that all that remains are the foundations, of unbroken cobble walls—which may not make it possible to identify the location of doors but do make it possible to understand the ground-plan of the houses (which was, in fact, strikingly uniform). On average, the dwellings were very spacious—the largest are up to 800 square meters in floor area—and consisted of an entrance corridor (with a waste channel set under the flooring) flanked by what were probably workshops and leading into a central cross-shaped courtyard with a well. All the various rooms gave onto this courtyard, with those along the end wall being particularly worthy of note. While these three rooms echo the tripartite division known to us from Ac-

quarossa, the fact that the central room is open directly onto the courtyard again anticipates the *tablinum* of the Roman *domus* (as we also saw was the case with the Poggio Civitate palace and the House of the Impluvium at Roselle). Indeed, recent discoveries on the Palatine hill, would seem to bear out that this model was much older than was previously thought on the basis of the evidence gathered from Pompeii. Again as with the House of the Impluvium, the courtyard here had its own roof system for gathering rainwater—though here the sloping roofs were supported solely by horizontal beams running into the perimeter walls. This was the model of atrium that Vitruvius described as *tuscanico*, believing it to be the invention of the Etruscans, and which marked a substantial step forward because it eliminated the pilasters that in the *tetrastylum* stood at the corners of the *impluvium* (and, which, being wooden, were inclined to rot). Some evidence also suggests that the houses here had spaces dedicated to toilet facilities; these were small rooms with a small sloping channel running into the sewers and a terra-cotta tube that passes through the wall to then form a bend on the inside (these probably had a function comparable to that of the "close-stools" of Olinto, which were an early precursor of the modern toilet).
The discovery of numerous loom weights in the houses reveals that fabrics—along with other everyday articles—were produced at home. At the same time, evidence from Populonia and Roselle shows that in Etruscan—as in Greek—cities there were distinct areas of workshops, usually located on the edge of the inhabited center to reduce the annoyance of smoke and the risk of fire, even if it is not unusual to find fully-fledged workshops within

Plan of the city of Marzabotto

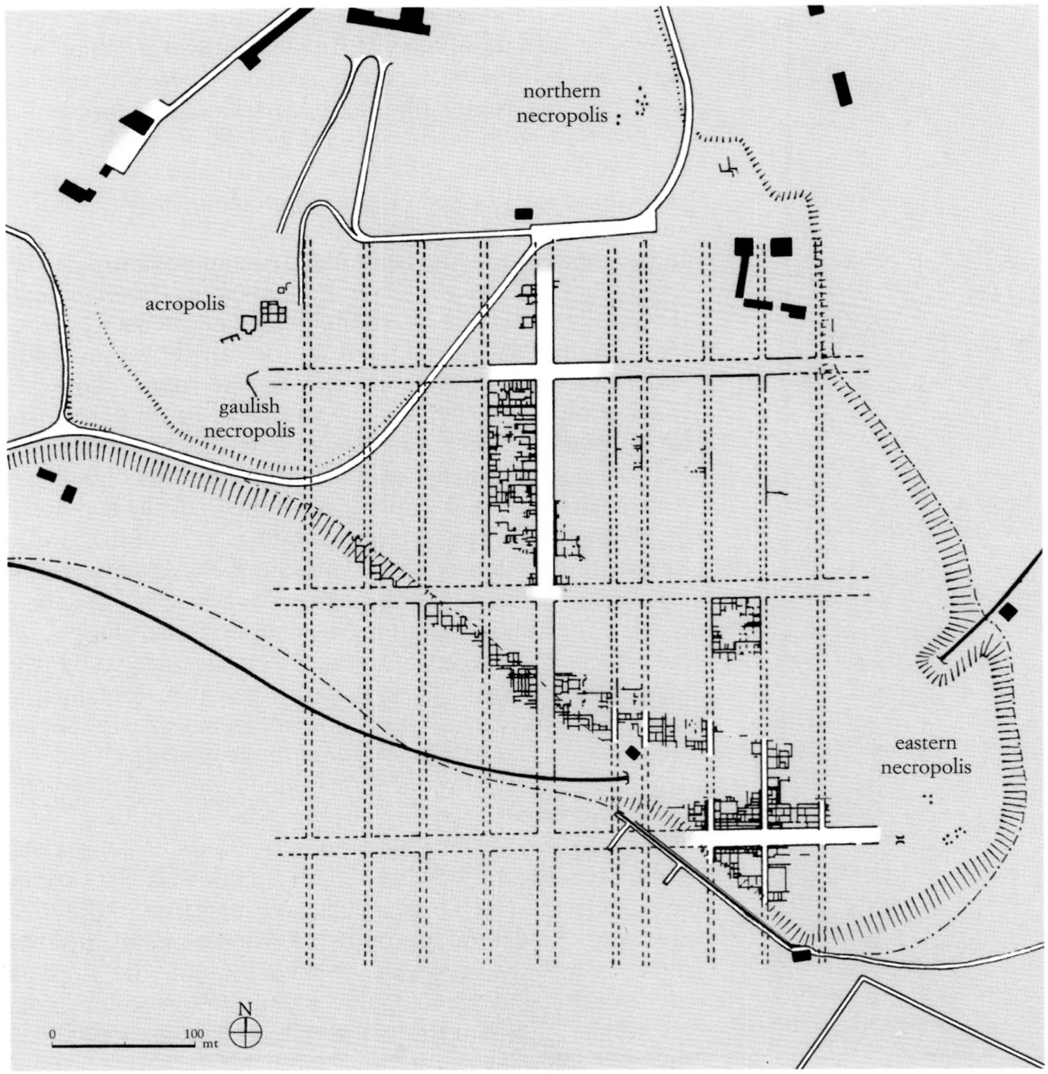

Plan of a dwelling in Marzabotto, end of the sixth–beginning of the fifth century B.C.

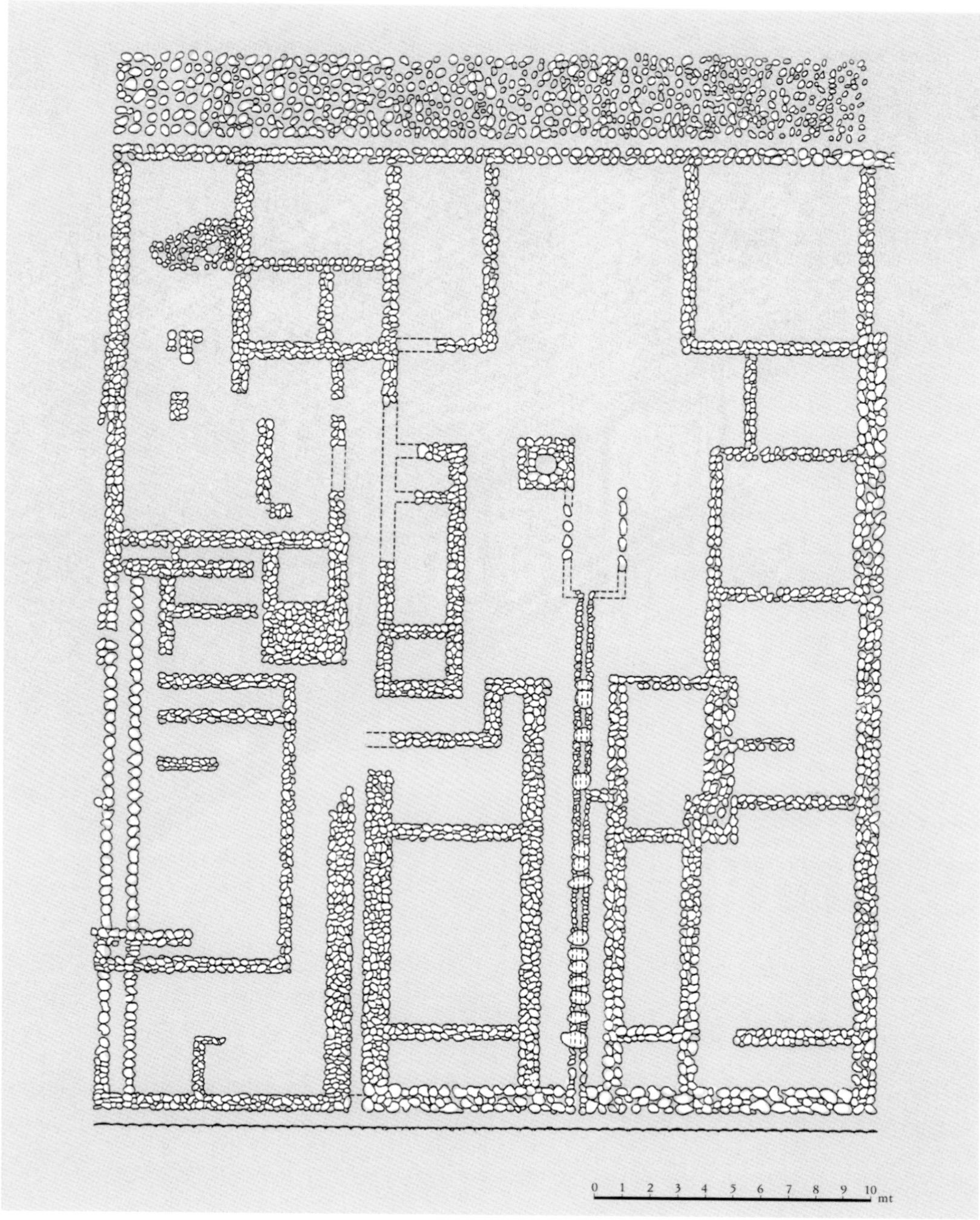

inhabited areas. All of which suggests there was a certain freedom of choice when it came to the location of such facilities.

At Poggio Civitate, for example, beneath the archaic complex archaeologists have found a long roofed structure used for drying out the tiles used in the Orientalizing building (tiles which must, therefore, have been produced nearby). And in Marzabotto one does not only find large clay kilns, ceramic furnaces and smithies within the residential areas, but also houses themselves which contained smithies—and, perhaps, shops for the sale of related products—in the facade spaces (which may have had their own entrance). This type of arrangement is also known to us elsewhere in Italy (for example, the Pithekoussai "blacksmith's workshop" of the eighth century B.C. and the Elea "Casa ad Ante" of the second half of the sixth century B.C.); here perhaps it indicates the importance of the craftsman classes in these new colonial cities.

Reconstruction of the Temple B of Pyrgi

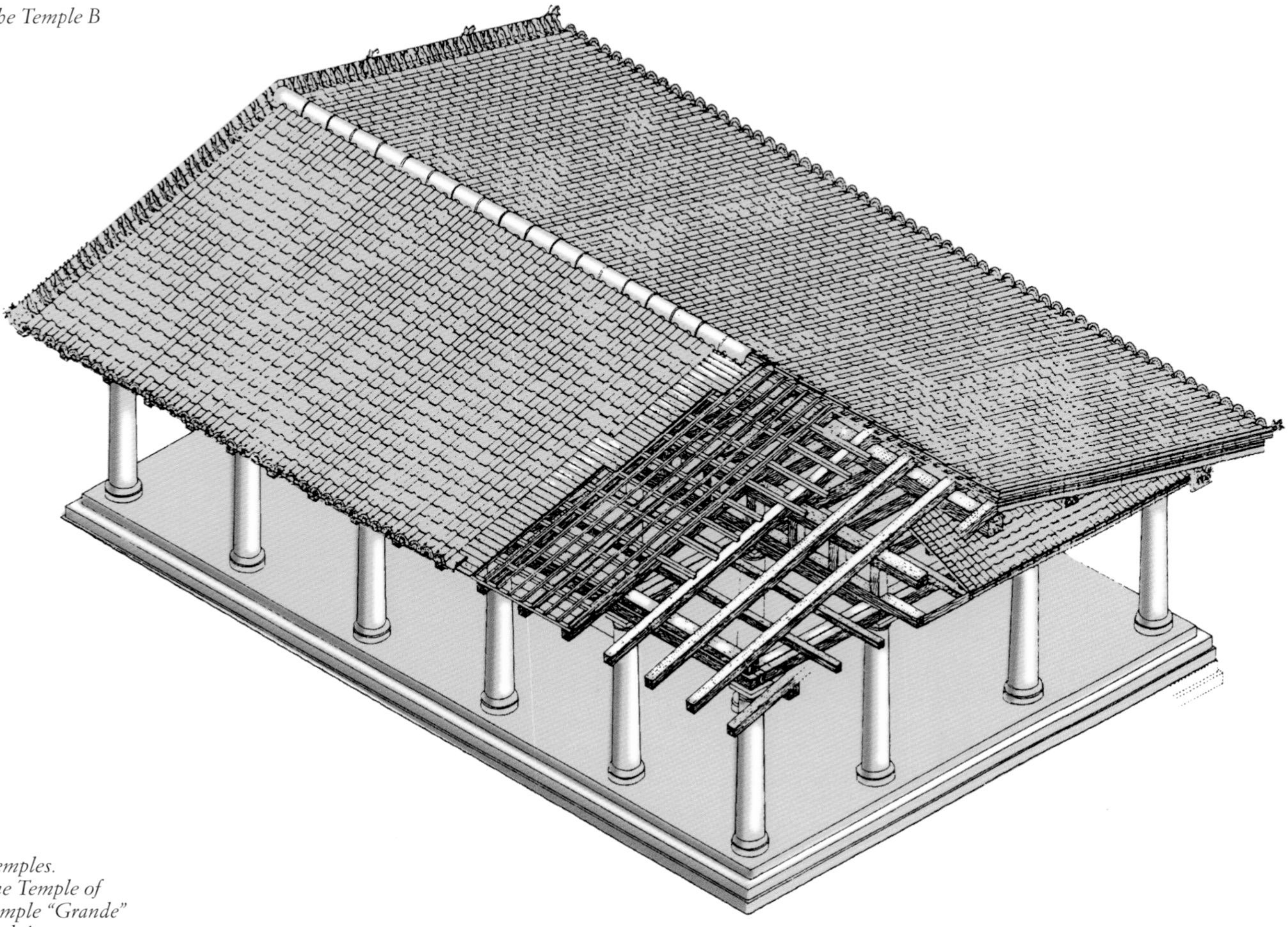

Plans of Etruscan temples. From left, Capitoline Temple of Jupiter in Rome; Temple "Grande" in Vulci; the so-called Ara della Regina in Tarquinia

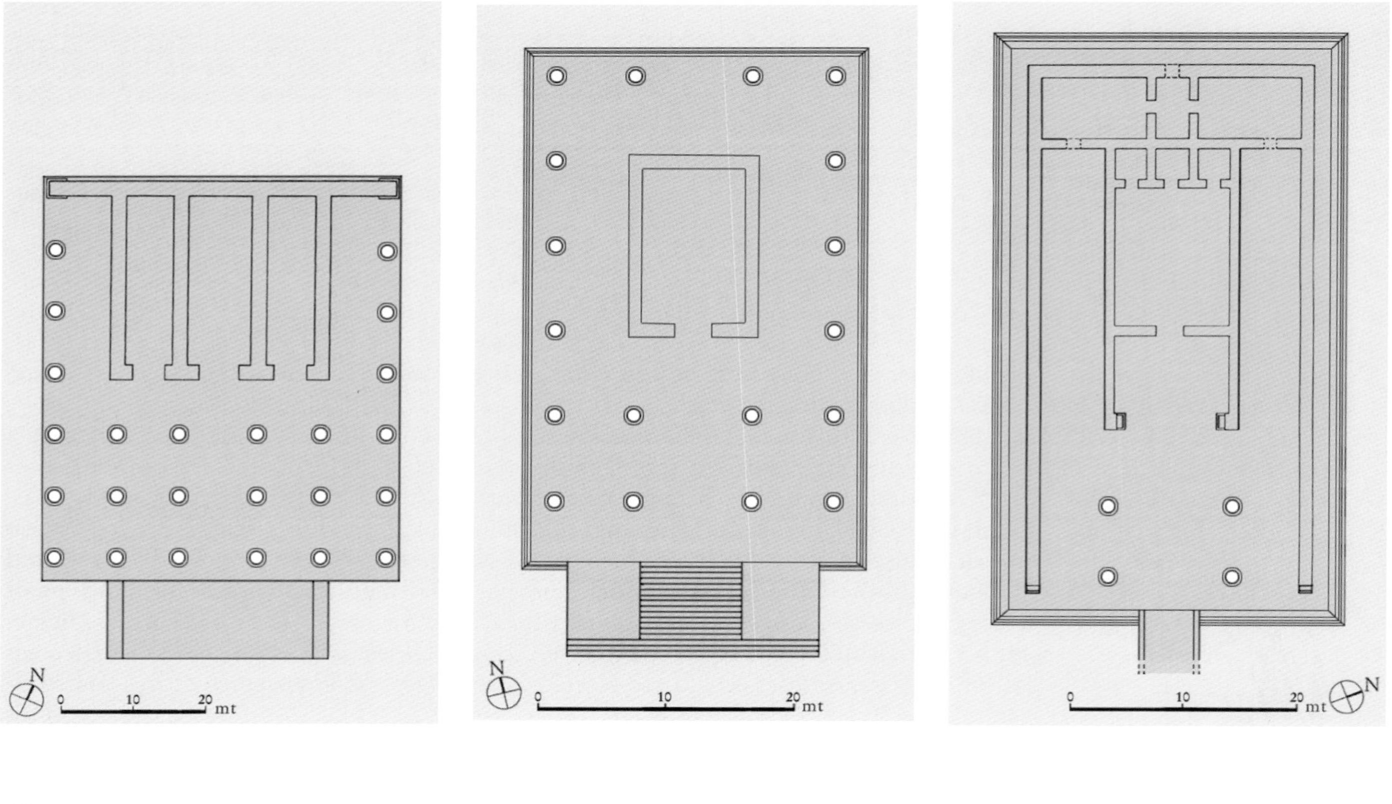

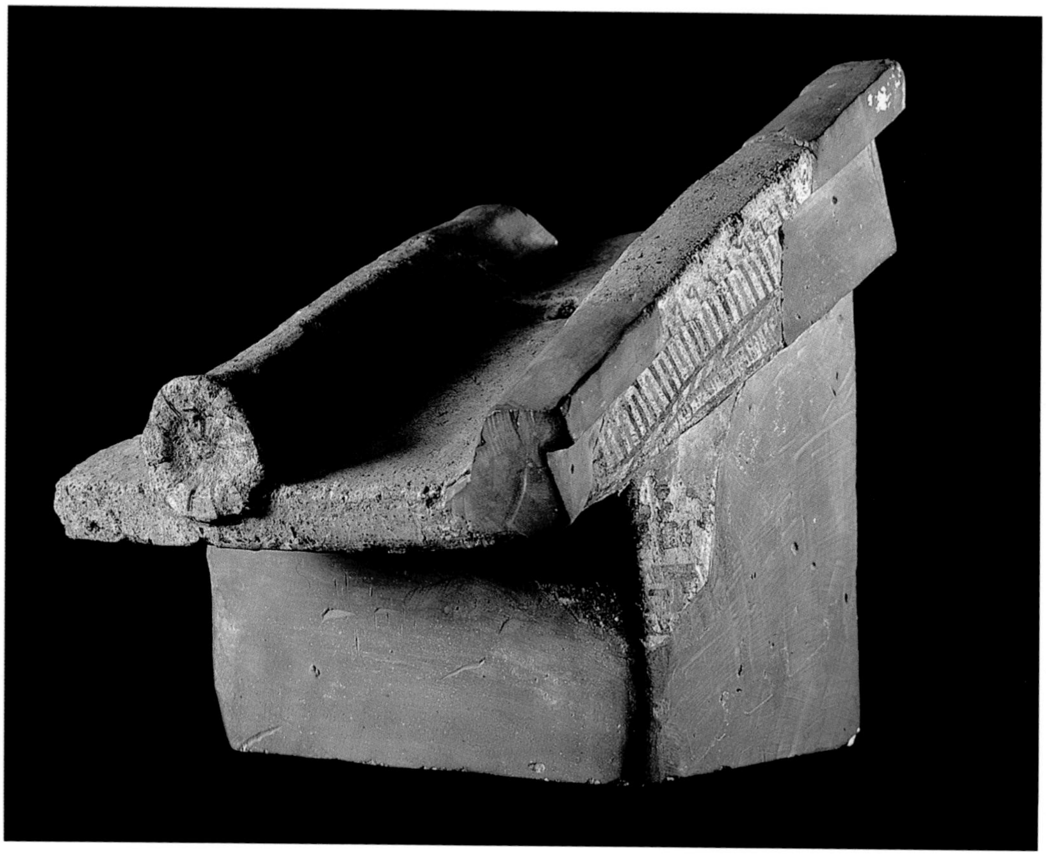

Votive model of temple from Orvieto, fifth century B.C.
Florence, Museo Archeologico
cat. 267

Temples

The Roselle *tholos* reveals that already by the middle of the seventh century B.C. religious architecture was characterized by the conservatism which would remain one of its constant features. However, the temple as an entity as such would only make its real appearance toward the end of the century, as the layout of Etruscan cities became defined by a clear-cut urban plan. Like other public buildings, the temple would be adorned with terra-cotta decorations; however, its specifically religious purpose would be reflected in its location, which set it apart from the areas of housing.

As in the Greek world, the initial basic type was the *megaron*—a rectangular-shaped structure that developed lengthways and was clearly derived from the patrician residences known to us from tombs. The oldest known example is on the acropolis of Veio (dating from the end of the seventh century), while the most monumental is the temple of the city's patron deities in Tarquinia, which is known as the Ara della Regina (Altar of the Queen) and measures 27 meters by 12. Dating from toward the middle of the sixth century B.C., this building has all the main features that will be characteristic of Etruscan temples: a high podium and a sole means of access via a central staircase leading up to the front, which makes that part of the structure the key focus. The model of housing with a lengthways atrium giving access to a number of rooms would provide the basis for the "Tuscan-order temple," which tends to meet Vitruvius's rule that the ratio between width and length should be 5 : 6 (*De architectura*, IV, 7, 1 ff.). This almost square building was divided crossways into an open front half (*pars antica*) with an ample colonnade, and an enclosed rear half (*pars postica*), which in its turn was divided into three separate adjacent rooms. Along the front walls of these rooms were placed the columns of the pronaos, the position of which corresponds to that of the atrium in a house. Presumably, it was the requirements of religious worship and of a rational use of space which led to the *pars postica* being divided up in various different ways. There might be one central cell, three cells (with those at the sides slightly smaller), or a single cell flanked by *alae* (that is, spaces giving directly onto the pronaos

View of the sanctuary of Pyrgi

and defined by the side walls, which extended unbroken to the facade). Then within these various models there were different types, depending upon how the cells were divided internally and on the extent of the end wall. Look, for example at the Tarquinia Ara della Regina, which after its restructuring in the fourth century B.C. had *alae* with side walls reaching to the facade, a pronaos with a double row of columns, and a vestibule preceding a central cell—the back of which was further divided into three small spaces (there were also a further three rooms beyond the end wall delimiting the cell and *alae*). As examples of the single cell type one might mention the Temple B of Pyrgi (ca. 510 B.C.), with a peristyle and a double front colonnade after the Greek model, or the monumental temple of Vulci, the first version of which perhaps dates from the same period. However, the oldest and most monumental evidence of the Tuscan-order temple is still to be found in the Rome of the Tarquins, where it was part of an imposing city-planning project that also envisaged the construction of city walls in massive blocks of stone. The oldest example is that *in antis* of Sant'Omobono (ca. 580 B.C.), with a central cell flanked by two *alae* and two front columns in stone. The most colossal is the Capitoline Temple of Jupiter (62 meters by 53.5). Commissioned by the Tarquinii but finally completed in 501 B.C., the building was decorated with terra-cotta acroteria—similar to those of the Poggio Civitate palace—produced by Etruscan artists brought in from Veio (Pliny, *Naturalis historia*, XXXV, 157), and brings together the model of the "Tuscan temple" with a Greek-style peristyle of columns, which become three-deep across the facade. Generally, the ground-plan of the "Tuscan" temple was much simpler, and the structure had no peristyle at all. Examples of this can be seen in the Belvedere Temple of Orvieto, the Temple C in Marzabotto and the Portonaccio Temple in Veio (though the latter is adorned with terra-cotta acroteria, like the Capitoline Temple of Jupiter). A similar ground-plan can also be seen in the Pyrgi Temple A, dating from the second quarter of the fifth century B.C., which also intro-

Votive model of temple from Vulci, third century B.C.
Rome, Museo di Villa Giulia

duces the functional idea of setting up a division toward the back of the two side cells.
In part due its being dug into rock, the Fiesole temple is in a particularly well-preserved state. It was built on the site of a late-archaic temple some time between the end of the fourth and beginning of the third century B.C. (perhaps as part of a building project linked with the construction of the city walls). An *alae*-plan structure with a row of Tuscan base columns between *antae*, its walls were made of small blocks of stone that were then plastered and painted red (the extant walls now stand up to a height of about 2 meters).
In conclusion, therefore, one might say that the principal model of the Tuscan-order temple was that with a triple partition of the *pars postica*. From the end of the third century onward, this was the model that would be adopted in Roman *municipia* and in the *capitolia* of the colonies, and can be seen at Segni (in the Capitoline version with the triple row of columns across the front), just as at Minturno, Cosa, Volterra and Luni. The elevation of this latter temple, what is more, was in full agreement with prevailing Roman tastes, and seems to have envisaged the use of local marble to create two rows of four columns each.

For town-planning and architecture, aside from the articles of the "Enciclopedia dell'Arte Antica Classica e Orientale" (in particular the supplements), those of the "Dizionario della Civiltà Etrusca," Firenze 1985, *and the plates (only for town-planning) in G. Schmiedt "Atlante aerofotografico delle sedi umane in Italia,"* Firenze 1970, *see in general:* Boëthius, Ward Perkins 1978; Steingräber 1981; Pianu 1985, pp. 269–335; Cristofani n.d., pp. 14–28; Colonna 1986b, pp. 369–530; De Marinis 1986; Gros, Torelli, 1988. *On city walls:* Lugli 1957; Fontaine 1997, pp. 121–46 (with bibliography for each city). *On dwellings:* Östenberg 1975; Stopponi 1985; Colonna 1986b, pp. 369–530; *Architettura etrusca nel viterbese* 1986; Camporeale 1985b, pp. 127–30; Phillips 1993; Donati 1994; Camporeale 1997. *On household furnishings:* Steingraber 1979. *On temples:* Castagnoli 1966–67, pp. 10–14; Staccioli 1968; Cristofani 1978, pp. 92–102; Colonna 1985b; Colonna 1986b, pp. 369–530.

Tomb Architecture

Studies into various other areas of Etruscan life have in recent years made great progress, and yet tomb architecture remains one of our fundamental sources of information on the civilization of Etruria. Hollowed out of volcanic tufa—which, in part, explains their good state of preservation—the tombs of southern Etruria provide us with invaluable insight into how graves developed as architectural forms, revealing burial customs, funeral rites and specific aspects of the Etruscan idea of the afterlife. What is more, these graves also tell us a lot about everyday life: some necropolises reflect the urban layout of cities, with tombs emulating not only the architecture but also the furnishings and wall-paintings of houses. Etruscan tomb paintings themselves are of a cultural and artistic importance unrivaled anywhere in the western Mediterranean; and typical tomb furnishings included not only high-quality ceramics, jewels and weapons, but also works of sculpture and portraiture, whose place in the funeral art of Etruria reveals that civilization's special interest in the underworld and afterlife.

Necropolises

Etruscan necropolises are the most extensive of the ancient world. As in Greece and other areas of Italy, the tombs were placed outside the area inhabited by the living community but within a certain proximity—on neighboring hills or plains—with roads linking the two communities. In the period before the seventh century B.C., the necropolises were located in isolation from each other (Veio and Tarquinia), then, during the seventh and sixth centuries, these individual nuclei would extend until they entirely surrounded the inhabited center and even outstripped it in ground area—as is well-illustrated in Cerveteri. The most famous necropolises at this latter site are Banditaccia, Monte Abetone and Sorbo, while at Tarquinia one should mention the necropolis of Monterozzi, at Vulci the Osteria and Polledrara necropolises and at Veio the Quattro Fontanili necropolis. The seventh century B.C. saw monumental tumuli replacing the small "archaic tumuli"; a development that reveals a desire among the ruling classes for this high-placed monument to be both visible and distinguishable from the area of habitation. Visual contact between inhabited centers and necropolises would seem to have remained a key

opposite and below
The Banditaccia necropolis (Cerveteri)

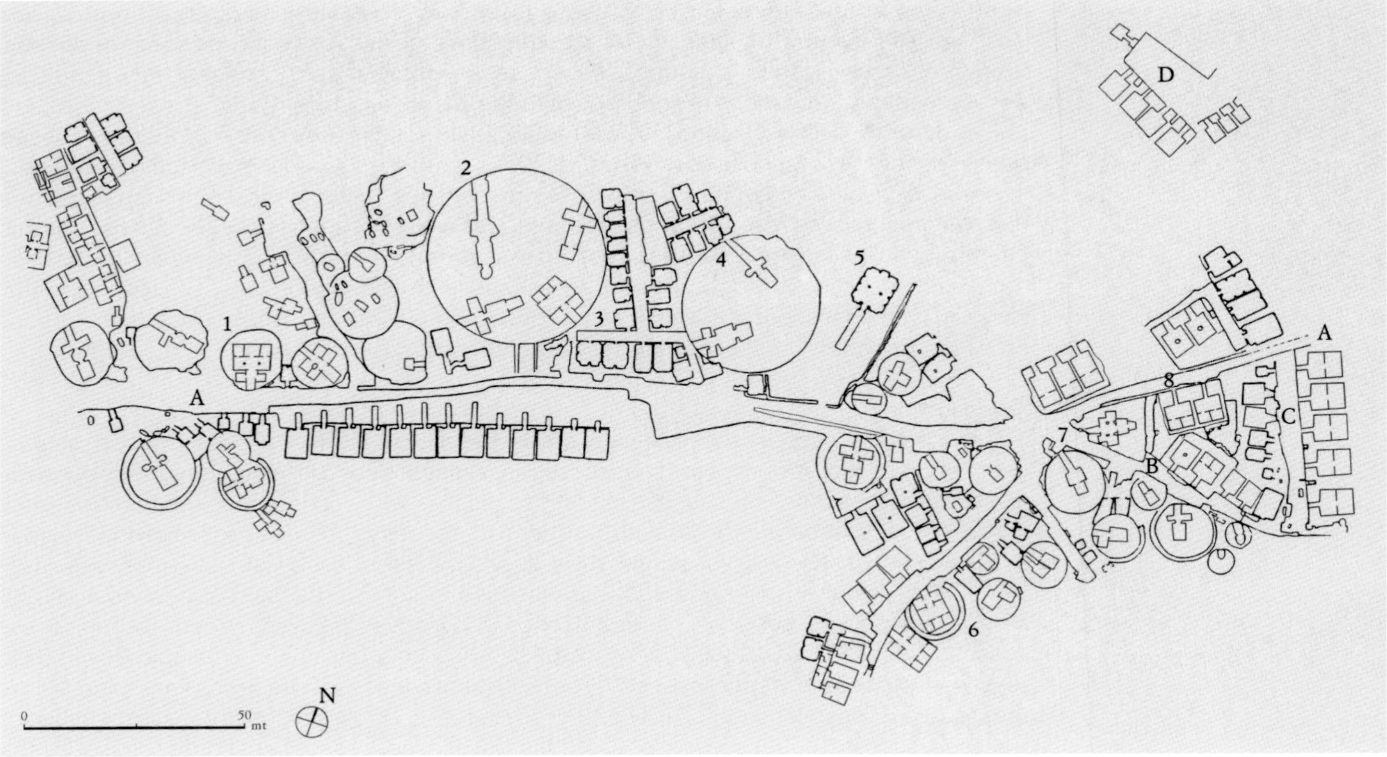

Plan of the Banditaccia necropolis.
(area of the Vecchio Recinto)
1 Tomb of the Capitals
2 Tomb of the Capanna
3 Tomb of the Attic Vases
4 Tomb 2 of tumulus I
5 Tomb of the Reliefs
6 Tombs of the Frame
7 Tomb of the Casetta
8 Tomb of Marce Ursus
A Via Sepolcrale
B Via delle Serpi
C Via dei Vasi Attici
D Small square

concern thereafter (until at least the second century B.C.): to see this one need only look at the necropolises of Norchia, Blera and San Giuliano, where the tombs dug into the steep slopes of the surrounding hills all tend to be turned toward the inhabited area. A first examination of the internal road systems and the location of individual tombs would suggest that there were no clear rules governing the layout of necropolises. However, if one looks more closely, one sees certain differences both between the various necropolises and within one individual necropolis, reflecting changes in social structure and external influences upon the layout of Etruscan cities. On the one hand, we can identify periods when tombs were more or less uniform—for example, from the ninth to eighth century B.C. there were the so-called well or pit tombs, then in the fifth century single-chamber tombs—and, on the other, there are periods when there might be sharp differences between tombs (in the seventh and beginning of sixth, or in the fourth–second centuries one finds both standard forms of tomb and imposing and well-appointed graves). During the second half of the sixth century B.C. there was a reorganization of necropolises and tombs, with the orthogonal road system used in cities being introduced into burial palaces—a development that, in its turn, was linked with the creation of uniform tombs. Probably this change was no merely formal adjustment, intended to modernize and rationalize the appearance of necropolises, but was dictated by new norms governing burials (the result of social changes or, perhaps, of laws intended to limit the opulence of tombs).

Types of tombs

Like other aspects of Etruscan civilization, tomb architecture was continually developing, due not only to religious changes but also to social needs and technical advances. Whatever regional variations there might be, however, one can identify one constant feature of such burial places throughout their entire history (from the ninth to the second century B.C.): the Etruscan tomb was intended to resemble a dwelling-place, the home of the living. Even in the Villanovan period (ninth–eighth century B.C.) one can find in Latium and Etruria not only the prevalent form of biconical ossuary dug into the ground (well tombs) but also urns for the ashes of the dead which were modeled in the form of a small hut—with the four pitched segments of roof, a door, window and outlet for smoke. A less evident echo of living domesticity are the so-called pit tombs, the main form of burial in a large part of Italy during the eighth and early seventh cen-

opposite
Ildebranda Tomb at Sovana, end of fourth–third century B.C.

below
Aerial view of the Ildebranda Tomb

ter 550 B.C., the internal layout of the tombs in Cerveteri was determined not so much by the design of contemporary domestic interiors as by the function performed by places of burial. The number of chambers was reduced, so that around 500 B.C. tombs consisted of a single chamber, and the sculptured beds were replaced by a single undecorated bench running around the walls. In other necropolises (Vulci) one finds tombs with numerous burial chambers laid out symmetrically and decorated with features of domestic architecture (for example, a coffered ceiling—for which there are some parallels in the painted tombs of Chiusi). What is more, the tomb itself, which had previously been a tumulus formed from earth piled on a tufa base, would during the course of the sixth century become cubic (the so-called cube tomb)—again in response to the (external) appearance of contemporary housing—and aligned according to the road plan of the necropolis. This can be seen in other necropolises throughout Etruria, but with local variations: the aedicula tombs of Populonia, or the house tombs of Tuscania, complete with single gable roof and animal-form acroteria on the ridge. During the Hellenistic period (end of fourth–second century B.C.), one finds two different types of tomb. The first type, favored by the aristocrats of the large cities such as Perugia, Vulci, Tarquinia and Cerveteri, looks toward archaic tradition and reproduces the interior of a patrician home, with the atrium being decorated with objects that indicate the family's prestige and power. In one of the most impressive and best-preserved of Late Etruscan patrician tombs—the Matunas Tomb (or Tomb of Reliefs) dating from around 300 B.C.—the architrave is decorated with a frieze consisting of the *gens'* weapons (shields, greaves, and helmets). A ground-plan of the tomb reveals a long stepped *dromos*, a monumental chamber with two central pilasters, thirteen wall niches and a whole series of simple beds in the hall. Thanks to an inscribed cippus found near the entrance, we know that the name of this *gens* was Matunas, and the

Tomb of the Five Chairs at Cerveteri, interior

painted inscriptions at the back of the niches enable us to partially reconstruct the genealogy of this family. The second type of Etruscan tomb during the Hellenistic period shows more attention being paid to external appearance: great care and imagination is lavished on the exterior of the monument, while the interior becomes more simplified as a stark space for the burial of the dead. One can trace the beginnings of this development back to the Late Archaic Age, with the above-mentioned cube, aedicula and house tombs. Examples of the later development can be seen in the so-called "crag necropolises" (to be found in the Archaic Era at Blera and San Giuliano, and later at Sovana, Norchia and Castel d'Asso). Given the nature of the terrain around the settlements (sheer gullies of tufa), it would seem that from the sixth century onward there was a tendency to focus on the facade of the tomb carved right into the vertical rock face. The result was the cube—or rather, semi-cube—tomb, with the nature of the rock then inspiring both sculptor and patron to try for refinements upon a basic model. One variation was the so-called cube tomb with under-facade—in effect, a system of different structures superimposed upon one another. Above stood the tomb proper with its *dromos* and burial chamber, below was the "under-facade," a structure with a jutting roof resting on pilasters enclosing a space furnished with benches and a small fake door. Derived from archaic architecture, the upper facade of the "cube" had a more monumental fake door and a system of coping that (from bottom to top) incorporated the motifs of hawksbeak, *torus*, sash, bell, *torus*, and sash. The whole culminated in a large platform that could be reached by steps that ran alongside the monument, linking that upper space with the area of the under-facade. Other innovations in the Hellenistic period are the "temple" facade tombs (third–second century B.C.). At Sovana, in the Vulci hinterland, there is the imposing Ildebranda Tomb, recently restored. Here again, the burial chamber, reached by a long staircase carved out of the rock, contained a series of sarcophagi. The "facade" is transformed into a temple, with a shaped podium complete with six front and four lateral columns—all of them fluted and crowned with composite capitals of acanthus leaves, human heads and Ionic volutes. The architrave too—though little of it survives—was richly decorated with animal and plant motifs, all carved in high relief. Other "temple" tombs are the twin pair of monuments in Norchia; now in a poor state of conservation, these can be understood better from an old drawing made by Luigi Canina in 1849. One tomb is a temple with six columns or pilasters, flanked by a second of four pilasters—most of which no longer survive. The two richly sculpted pediments have also suffered severe damage.The Museo Archeologico of Florence now houses the part missing from the pediment of the temple on the left, which includes a scene of warriors carrying a dead man and seems to recount some story from Greek mythology (no longer decipherable), while the temple on the right has a less crowded pediment of two people flanking a winged figure. In both, the dominant motif is death, with the corners decorated with gorgon's heads (an apotropaic symbol here, as in the Greek world). One exceptional feature is the relief of a funeral procession which decorated the wall of the portico. Now almost totally destroyed, one can still make out the traces of certain cloaked figures facing toward the left, together with the details of a demon's wing, a shield and a greave.

Tombs as places of religious worship

Etruscan tombs served not only as a burial place but also as the site for funeral rites and for the worship of the dead. Certain tumuli in north Etruria had jutting platforms or terraces whose function in religious worship is not very clear. Did they serve as the *prothesis* of the dead? Other tomb complexes were served by ramps—as was the case with tumuli—or by steps—as was the case with cube or under-facade tombs. At first (end of eighth–beginning of sixth century B.C.) the *dromos* was aligned toward the north-east (the direction of the afterlife) and the doorways were arched, just like the gateway to the Underworld. The *dromos*—or an open space before the burial chamber—could be used to deposit offerings or make libations, as we can see from the altars at Bolsena, or from the antechambers of certain tombs at Cerveteri which contain altars and tables carved out of the tufa. One unique space is that in the lateral cell to the left of the Tomb of Five Chairs in Cerveteri (seventh century B.C.): it is furnished with five chairs placed behind two tables, with two thrones raised on a rectangular podium, a basket and an altar with three hemispherical cavities for libations. All the furnishings—on a smaller scale than normal—are carved out of the tufa. On the five chairs there were small terra-cotta statuettes depicting the ancestors in the act of pouring libations and eating together with the two people buried in the tomb (who may be symbolically linked with the two empty thrones). In other tombs—such as that of the Shields and Chairs, the empty thrones may be interpreted as a symbol of the *potestas* and social position of the *pater* and *mater familias*; and it seems very likely that their position in the vestibule corresponds to the position of the so-called *solium* in a contemporary patrician house. But whereas in the Roman world, the *solium* was the seat of the *pater familias* alone (Cicero, *De oratore*, II, 143; III, 133), Etruscan tombs reveal that in Etruria the *mater familias* also had her *solium*—further evidence of the important role of patrician women in Etruscan society (an importance that was already being commented on by Roman writers).

Boethius-Ward Perkins 1978; Minto 1922; Prayon 1975a; Prayon 1975b; Colonna di Paolo 1978; Oleson 1982; Colonna 1986; Prayon 1986; Zamarchi Grassi 1992; Naso 1996a.

Painting

The Greeks used the word *graphe* to describe a drawing or painting and *graphike* (*techne*) for the art of painting. The same words described a written text, writing and the art of the scribe in general. This was probably also the case in Etruria. Words expressing the notion of writing, which also derived from the original gesture of scratching an inscription (**zich-*) appear in all extant Etruscan texts (inscribed or otherwise), from the *Liber Linteus* of Zagreb to the "new" *Tabula Cortonensis*, as well as in the signatures of vase painters from the seventh century B.C. But it would be something of an over-simplification to trace the lexical affinity and contiguity of meaning back to the common derivation of the gesture and instruments of "early" drawing or writing with a sharp point, on stone, metal or ceramic. The art of reproducing reality through images and that of recording the spoken word by means of written symbols, that is to say of making mute substance "speak" by one or the other means, remained always conceptually and functionally realted and interlaced: the palette and the alphabet were often the complementary tools of the art of signifying and of symbolizing.

An excellent example of this is found in the words with which Aeschylus evokes through the chorus the last moments Iphigenia being led away for sacrifice in *Agamemnon* (vv. 238–241): "As her saffron-colored robe slipped to the ground/she sought out with her eyes, one by one, her executioners/and endeavored with her imploring gaze to speak to them *as in paintings ὡς ἐν γραφαῖς.*" To express the intensity of the admonition, for which the vehicle of words is denied, the poet inverts the logical relationship between reality and representation and sees the former modeling itself on the latter; Iphigenia speaks the same language as the friezes in the epic paintings in which she will be celebrated: the color of her robe, her gesture, and her gaze, which seeks out each onlooker in turn, silently beseeching them and casting onto them the weight of the presence, the assent and the name, just like the captions to those friezes, which the poet would certainly have been familiar with. It is reasonable to assume that in Etruria, too, where the figurative idiom involved a similar connection between written word and image that was no less intense than in Greece, the notion of drawing and painting would have had the same connotations.

Earliest examples

Only few traces of painting on wall or on panels, in temples, or for "civil" or funerary use from Greece preceding sixth century B.C. survive, and what little we do know of the art of this period comes to us indirectly through vase painting. By contrast, the Etruscan custom (unknown tin Greece) of digging burial chambers out of the soft rock and painting their walls, has resulted in a collection of art covering a broad time span (from seventh to second century B.C.), the richness and continuity of which is matched by no other ancient civilization in the western world.

Before embarking upon an examination of this legacy, however, we should remember that there is limited historical legitimacy in the distinction that is typically made between "great pictorial art" and other forms of monumental Etruscan figurative art (e.g. sculpture) or "lesser" artistic applications (e.g. ceramics). It is a tenuous distinction indeed—and dependent on precise historical and social variables—whether we consider the status of the artist (his expertise and manual skills) or the function of the product he was required to produce. With regard to the former, we see from the beginning of the seventh century B.C., painted clay slab roof coverings, tiles and antefixes or acroteria with their sculpted extensions, fashioned in all probability by the same hands that decorated urns and vases made of the same clay compound; and the frescoing of the walls of noble hypogea would not have been the only activity of artists, whose cultural and stylistic contiguity is seen also in the more common ceramic vases or, in a few rare cases, in examples of entire walls painted for non-funerary purposes. This also fits in naturally with the notion—popular with ancient writers—of painting and sculpture being linked in their origin in an almost genealogical way: born one of the other and uniting to give substance through line, color and volume to an empty profile, the shadow (*skia*) of the real. And the description Pliny gave of Damophilus and Gorgasus, well-known artists from Magna Graecia who decorated with paintings and statues the temple of Ceres in Rome in the early fifth century B.C. (*Naturalis historia*, XXXV, 154: "plastae laudatissimi [...] iidem pictores"), probably applied to many, if not to all painters up to that time. As for the capability of painting to evoke and fix messages and symbols, it should be pointed out that in the funerary context, of which the richest legacy sur-

Battle scene from the Sarcophagus of the Amazons, second half of the fourth century B.C.
Firenze, Museo Archeologico

Fragment of a terra-cotta slab with female figure from Cerveteri, 530–520 B.C. Berlin, Staatliche Museen, Antikensammlung cat. 270

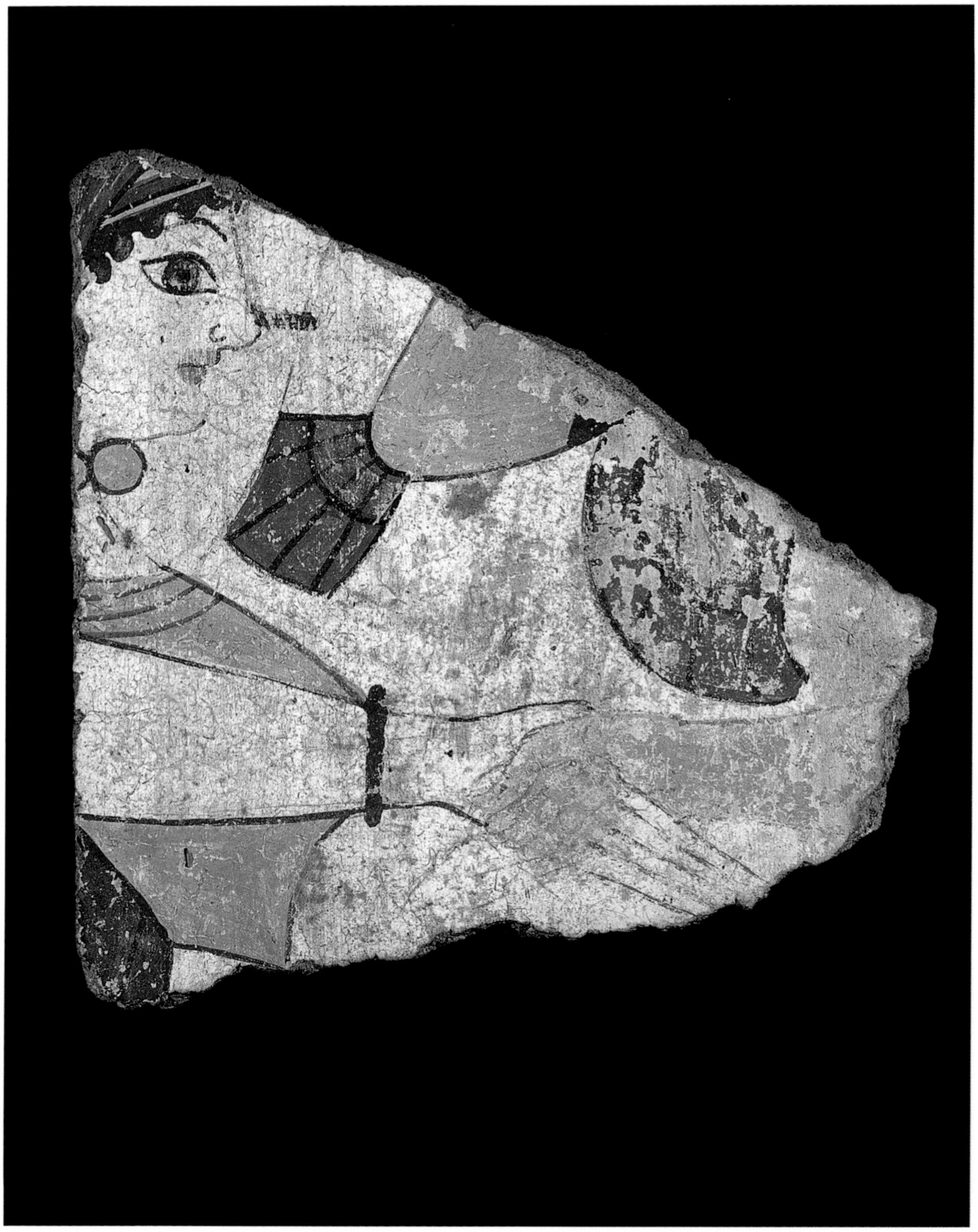

vives, Etruscan painting seems in the initial period to have remained a complementary instrument, on a par with others (architecture, furnishing, ornamentation in general), for the expression of selected messages. Not until well into the seventh century B.C. (and with greater enthusiasm in the eighth) was there any awareness of its unmatched ability to tell stories, evoke events and personalities and more importantly still to create "other" spaces, opening up, altering or annulling the physical spaces on which the works were painted.
It is customary to consider the beginning of painting in Etruria as coinciding with the Orientalizing period to which the earliest finds of such products as terra-cotta roof elements, large vases, urns and tomb walls date back, when (around the end of the sixth century B.C.) Etruscan communities were gradually settling in the areas around which their history is centered. However, the indisputable continuity that links the people, places, culture and history of this phase with those of the previous generations of Villanovan culture legitimizes our

curiosity as to the specific extent of the legacy of that recent past, and not only in the more obvious area of ornamental patterns, but in the function of painting, the possible meanings attached to different colors, the borderline between "ornamentation" and "meaning" etc. In the geometric idiom that took shape on cinerarium walls during the Iron Age there was quite frequently an intention to do something to enliven the dark surface with chromatic touches, filler compounds or little metal plates, while in thematic terms there are signs of a hierarchical organization that subordinated themes-frames to themes-content, ornamental motifs to symbolic motifs or figurative abstractions: the hooked cross or sun boat, the string of winged creatures or the human figure, which in turn were bearers of almost indecipherable attributes: "blazons" of family clans, or evocations of more complex contents. So we can reasonably imagine that the first "great" paintings were applied directly to the mud finish or to the plaster screed applied to walls and ceilings of the village huts, in combinations of symbols and colors that were no less charged with significance than the many solid excrescences, which were also reproduced in miniature versions for funerary uses (a geographically though not culturally distant example is a cinerary urn found in Sala Consilina). This type of painting probably had more to do with domestic ritual than with art: and the actual painting activity itself is also likely to have been a domestic task, possibly executed by the women (as happens to this day in tribal communities, such as the Ndebele in South Africa), thus suggesting an interesting ideological basis for women's acknowledged role in the organization of craft workshops in subsequent periods.

The seventh century

In the seventh century B.C. painting became more "professional," within the limitations described. This is revealed by written sources, such as those collected by Pliny concerning the entourage of artists who fled to Etruria with Corinthian "prince" Demaratus, toward the middle of the century. It is confirmed by the first appearance of artist's signatures, such as the one that appears on a Caeretan impasto *pyxis*, now in the Louvre, by the Painter of the Birth of Menerva, whose hand has also been recognized in examples of wall painting in the necropolis of the same town. But the geometric legacy in all its hieratic, repetitive rigor persisted (albeit less and less incisively) throughout the new period. With old rows of colored-in, hatched or reticulated triangles, zigzags and broken meanders, it continued to supply the familiar background—almost as the guarantee of tradition—to the new themes received.

This was the figurative culture that displayed itself from the second half of the century, in the clay decoration (also, and in some cases exclusively, painted) used both on the first "palace" of Murlo and even more clearly on the one in Acquarossa, and in the Caeretan "a casetta" (house-shaped) urns. And though nothing remains of the actual wall paintings of the time, because of the weak plasterwork, or the perishable wooden panels attached to equally fragile walls, it is precisely the lavish decoration of the exteriors in the first case, and the care taken to recreate the domestic environment in the second, that makes the idea that the ceremonial spaces of the interior walls were completely devoid of painting a fairly implausible one.

The geometric tradition permeates the oldest extant painted Etruscan tomb: the Tomb of the Ducks in Veio (680–670 B.C.). It is seen in the sequence of aquatic birds that crosses the rear wall, their bodies alternately fully colored-in or with criss-cross or zigzag hatching; but even before that in the definition of space within the tomb, which would seem to be organized and oriented not so much by its unusual architecture (a hut?), as by the heraldic arrangement of the red and yellow fields of the walls and four ceiling surfaces. These fields are crossed by the waterfowl, and the manner in which they fly unimpeded across the confines of the inhabited world is seen in ceramic products from the same period (such as the vases found in the same tomb) in which they advance in an inverted sequence—an unusual and undoubtedly significant feature—below other upright land animals. Remains from this phase are spread over a vast area from Quinto Fiorentino to Chiusi and Cerveteri, from the coast (Magliano, Cosa, Vulci) inland (Veio, Trevignano), and the painting of walls was possibly also customary in the nearby Faliscan and Sabine urbanized communities (the rich Tomb XI of Colle del Forno/Eretum has plastered walls). The palette is dominated by red (often the only color, as in the Tomb of the Flabella at Trevignano or the Vaccareccia Tomb in Veio), followed by yellow, black/brown and white. The soft stone is cut and smoothed, while the presence or absence of a priming surface is almost an autograph clue to the greater or lesser importance attached to painting in the or-

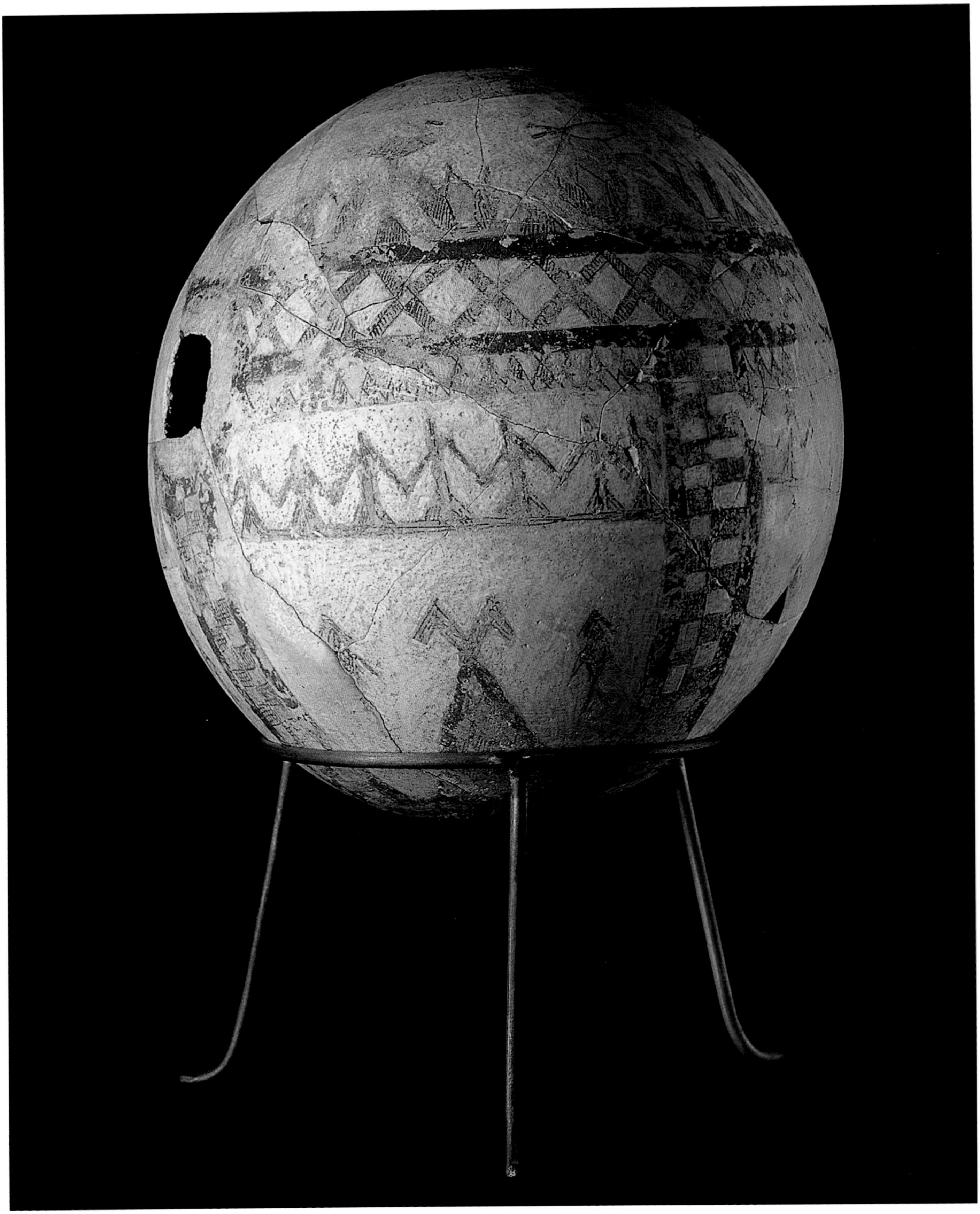

Glazed ostrich egg from Montalto di Castro (?), mid-seventh century B.C. *Tarquinia, Museo Archeologico cat. 118*

ganization of the tomb as a whole: it is present in the Veio tradition and absent at Caere.
Caere (Cerveteri), by far the most "literate" seventh-century B.C. city, has the largest group of painted tombs: but the color was applied directly onto the rough, carbon-spotted tufa surface and only survives in the less exposed crannies of the interior architecture. In Caeretan tombs, in fact, the aim was the construction of full-fledged hypogea, determined by their layout, their furnishings and even in the occasional "animation" of the interiors with the inclusion of sculptures or models of human figures (see for example the Tomb of the Statues and of the Five Chairs). Painting appears to play a subordinate role, be it the almost omnipresent coloring of entablatures and wooden frames (as in the Wolf's Teeth and Campana I Tombs), or the inclusion of elaborate figured friezes: like the "Lord of the Beasts," prominently placed in the pediment of the right-hand side cell of the Tomb of the Painted Lions, or the sequence of exotic or fantastic beasts, either rampant (the Sorbo and Mengarelli Tombs) or in attack (the Tomb of the Painted Animals), arranged in friezes, sometimes overlapping, along the walls of the rooms and accompanied by floral inserts in the smaller spaces left free by the furnishings.
The aristocracy of this opulent Tyrrhenian city depicted itself in the models, conveyed by immigrant craftsmen or by the exchange of luxury items (silver, ivories etc.), of the oriental dynasties, and the ancient polychrome bands and colored-in triangles continue, mixed in with new strings of palmettes and lotus flowers, framing and separating friezes of the new repertoire in the Syro-Phoenician style. It is certainly difficult to discern to what extent, in this architecture, painting dedicates space to themes that were more in tune with funerary ideology: the "Oriental-style bestiary" extensively found on products of all kinds and uses, and an episode of life at sea such as the one depicted in the Tomb of the Ship could well have been intended to evoke similar epics (mythical or real) celebrated in paintings or tapestries on the walls of the residence of the *princeps*. And yet the obsessive, intriguing presence of wild beasts and monstrous creatures (often supplemented with stone sculptures), and the success that all the themes now introduced—the killing of the animal/victim by the wild beast, or by man the hunter; the sea—would continue to enjoy in Etruscan funerary painting for centuries (quite apart from any architectural or imitative suggestion) suggests that while the architecture and sculpture modeled the interior spaces of the tombs in a realistic way, painting was used to evoke other places and tell stories set elsewhere: of wild, hostile powers to be countered, of heroic tasks to be carried out on the journey to the final resting place. It was certainly not for the exclusive benefit of those who would later visit the tombs that most of the paintings in Caere are found mainly near the entrance or in the middle areas (including side cells where depositions were made) and not in the chamber at the back of the tomb. Nor is it a coincidence that in more peripheral areas (such as Magliano in Tuscany), or where tomb architecture follows other models (such as the "partition" tomb in Poggio Renzo), the sequence of monsters seems to leave behind their ornamental purposes and proceeds realistically on the ground, sometimes even ignoring the architectural partitions of the chamber.
The most important monument in Etruscan painting of the seventh century B.C., the Campana Tomb, dated around 620 B.C., takes us to Veio. Once again the relationship between architecture and painting seems to be inverted, and it is this that gives meaning to the structural partitions. There was no taboo that might have prevented the painter from reproducing on the rear wall of the second room bronze shields (of an earlier type?) which used to hang from the walls of hypogea of equal rank, while the rear wall of the first room, almost deconstructed by the paintings crowded into it, is detached from the others, which are totally bare, and hangs like a curtain from the amorphous ceiling. The impression that the "expedition" described in the upper right-hand panel depicts the journey of the deceased to the Afterlife (or that it is a metaphor for it) is strengthened by this, and the tamed feline curled up on the back of its mount gives a similar message to the one conveyed by the rigid scheme of the δεσπότης θηρῶν in the Tomb of the Painted Lions. The painting is now distressingly illegible, unlike the version that appears in the nineteenth-century water-color by L. Canina. The careful preparation, the elegant artwork, the exuberant and controlled use of color, the lively composition that distributes the figures on three planes, the narrative verve that exudes from the contrasting processions and bestows credibility and naturalness on felines, sphinxes and conventional inflorescences, tell of a master whose Oriental style is now tempered by the Greek teachings of the Corinthian school.
The Etruscan ceramic output of this period is discussed elsewhere in the volume: here we

see that while the repeatedly asserted relationship with "great painting" is undebatable, the fondness of emerging artists for large or even monumental vases (the Painter of the Birth of Menerva in Cerveteri, the Painter of the Bearded Sphinx in Vulci, the creator of the Trevignano amphora in Veio) must persuade us to leave prudently unresolved the void left by the lost megalographs that decorated the residences and public buildings of the day.

The Archaic period

The changes seen in painting and elsewhere toward the end of the Orientalizing period, in the late seventh century and on into the sixth century B.C., while not constituting a real break, can neither be explained as being the result of a straightforward, linear evolution. The ways in which each individual town's arts and crafts developed were too distinct, and to a certain extent too "closed-off," to allow us to interpret the evolution in any other way than as being the result both of a new ranking and organization of artists and workshops in the new social and urban environment, and of the arrival en masse of new, specific products and skilled artists, who, in the presence of well-established traditions, or particularly favorable conditions, were called upon to work in the various districts of ancient Etruria. This is the context in which we should see on the one hand the legacy left by Caere in the field of temple and/or "civil" art, and on the other the imperious emergence of Tarquinia in funerary wall painting. Out of a total of some 190 painted tombs known to exist in the whole of Etruria, no fewer than 140 are in Tarquinia: it was indeed in this period that this massive proliferation came about.

Pliny (*Naturalis historia* XXXV, 17) tells us that ancient paintings (*antiquiores Urbe*) of excellent quality and technical execution existed in his day in Caere, as well as in the sacred buildings of Ardea and Lanuvio. It is unlikely that Pliny dated these paintings back to pre-Romulean times: he more likely thought of them as older than anything else in Rome at that time (he speaks in fact of "ruins"!). It was certainly archaic painting, applied directly onto the plasterwork of the walls, nothing of which, of course, survives. A slightly better fate, meanwhile, was suffered by another genre of painting: that onto terra-cotta slabs, aligned in rows to form continuous friezes along the walls. The use of wooden boards is possibly older and more ancient, if it is true that the wooden support panel was, in many of the series that have come down to us from town buildings and tombs, a typical ornamental feature. *Πίνακες λελευκώμενοι*, or plastered panels, were a cross between wall painting (the purpose they also served) and "easel" painting (the method of manufacture they also involved).

Pliny's writings are confirmed in Caere. The oldest series comes from the oldest area of the city: heavy terra-cotta panels onto which the overlapping friezes are painted, the central one with a mythological theme (Perseus and the Gorgons, the Judgement of Paris, an enthroned figure), while the upper order represents the themes of the banquet, the armed horse race, the hunt (?). The old preference for a reddish-brown background and sober palette (black, white and a shade of red only slightly lighter than that of the background) demonstrate the power of the archaist dictates to which the painter—a temple, perhaps, in this context—is faithful, while the compositional balance and the monumentality of the rhythmical procession of the figures, the faces with the large eyes brought forward to the bridge of the nose, suggest they belong to the Corinthian school, as reflected in the changeover in painted pottery style from mid- to late Corinthian: and the comparisons that can be made for the lesser friezes—especially that of the banquet—with the relief slabs of the second building of Murlo narrow down the date to within the second quarter of the sixth century B.C.

The Caeretan legacy did not, though, end with the waning of the Corinthian influence. Indeed from around 540 B.C. to well into the fifth century, it demonstrates, albeit in sporadic "samples," how the main artistic schools that had appeared on the Etruscan scene—first the Ionic, then the Attic—were represented by painters and ateliers working on the town's temples and aristocratic residences (with occasional applications also in tombs) of the highest order. These were probably Pliny's "plastae [...] iidem pictores" mentioned earlier, as is confirmed by the frequent use of painting only also for external clay decorations of temples in Caere. Two interesting factors come into play here: the close stylistic affinity that links a series of fragments undoubtedly from one of the city's temples with the group of Caeretan *hydriai*, created by a workshop of artists of the northern Ionic school active in Caere between 540 and 520 B.C.; and the deep-rooted familiarity with wall painting these artists brought with them, as documented with

increasing certainty by new finds in Phrygia and Lycia. In Tarquinia, this same school and these same artists would be the vehicle and instrument of profound changes in the role of painting in the conceptual organization of the tomb. But at this point we must take a step back in time. The series begins with the Tomb of the Panthers, which can still be dated back to the end of the seventh century B.C. The "bestiary," which forms the only theme, and the stylistic conventions it involves can be ascribed to the Orientalizing legacy (even older examples of which would certainly have existed also at Tarquinia): two felines flanking the door, another two on the rear wall, with a front paw held out over the head of a third, lying on the floor in the center, severed and bandaged. What is surprising here, however, is the already mature signs of an interpretation of the burial chamber itself which, both in the tectonic layout and in the arrangement of paintings and the themes they contained, prefigures specific later developments. Not until well into the fourth century B.C. would there be any substantial change to the structure of the rectangular chamber with pitched roof whose two slopes converged at the center toward a flat longitudinal strip forming a kind of support beam, and the pairs of animals located at the two crucial points of the tomb, one pair positioned menacingly at the entranceway, the other perpetuating the cruel sacrifice with its obvious funerary associations, held sway for over a century, and did not move higher up the opposing walls until the arrival of a narrative vein to which painting contributed its own very special evocative capabilities to funerary ideology.
At this stage, strangely, there is an apparent void in Tarquinian documentation that extended throughout the first half of the sixth century B.C. and was interrupted by just a few tombs (including the Tomb of the Hut), though these are dated more by the idea of the "simplicity" of their decoration than on the basis of their funerary gift content, which was either lost or of uncertain relevance. In these tombs (which were possibly more numerous originally, but eventually sank into oblivion precisely because of the paucity of their decorative paintwork!) the interiors are plastered white, while black brushstrokes denote a door at the center of the rear wall, connected—in the most notable case—to others, suggesting a dividing up of the room. The painting-on of "faux" architectural details is also seen elsewhere (such as at Caere where occasional use of this is made), and yet the ideological significance of this introduction of a theme as powerful and successful as that of the false door, which alludes to the inaccessibility of the more intimate resting place of the deceased, prompts us to discard any over-simplistic judgements of archaism or "poverty." Indeed, parallel at least to the first period of more richly decorated tombs, is the persistent habit of leaving the walls of the chamber white, with any painting limited, on the facing tympana, to confronted pairs of felines, separated from the field below by polychrome bands (the Tomb of the Lions, the Tomb of the Red Lions, etc.). The link between this and the previous group is rendered explicit by the cases in which the new decorative system incorporates the theme of the false door (as in the splendid Tomb of the Jade Lions). In this case too, the idea of attributing sobriety to the humble intentions, or means, of the patrons of the tombs appears banal, and inappropriate in a class of monuments that was always elitist. It is perhaps preferable to think of it as the sound, conservative ideological resistance of part of Tarquinian aristocracy to the new stylistic taste then being introduced by Ionic masters to "relate the passing" (with ritual, ceremony, myth); revealing in this connection is perhaps the fact that the pictorial and symbolic efforts in those tombs are still concentrated on the old entrance walls and at the rear, selecting from the new repertoire elements that did not conflict with traditional orthodoxy, and merely stylistically modernizing choices that we have already seen used in the Tomb of the Panthers. Indeed between the last quarter of the sixth and the first quarter of the fifth century B.C., Tarquinia itself would content itself with the same traditional thematic choice in the parallel experience of the chamber tombs, decorated with the so-called bronze "studs," which would have only protomes of lions and rams, on one side, and masks of monsters on the other ("Acheloos" or the Minotaur?). In Caere too, when the predilection for "architectural" hypogea resulted in the same paintings that decorated the houses being copied there, we see the same polarization of the tomb space: hence the continued arrangement of the Boccanera slabs (ca. 540 B.C.) at the sides of the entrance way, in the ancient style, two heraldically opposed sphinxes, and the concentration on the rear wall of two themes—the Judgement of Paris and the taking of the veil by the bride (Helen?)—certainly intended to signify, at least in this latter position, the process of death as the election/initiation of the deceased.

Tarquinia, Tomb of the Bulls, rear wall of the eastern chamber with the ambush of Troilus by Achille, 540 B.C.

In around 530 B.C., Tarquinia was the setting for one of the most extraordinary moments in ancient western painting that began with the arrival in an already well-established tradition of a surprising variety of new cultural, ideological and artistic contributions. And while these new aspects illustrate to begin with the unmistakable prevalence of the eastern Greek influence and later on, from the end of the century, the Attic influence, when it came to the content conveyed painting paved the way for an intermingling and polysymbolical superimposing of themes in the hypogeum, through which the new Hellenized urban patrician order arranged for death to be depicted: how it is overcome by the deceased, and of its exorcization by the group to which it belonged. The layout of the burial chamber retains the traditional pattern: an access corridor with steps leads down to a medium-sized, quadrangular space (the short side measuring 2 to 4 meters, the long side 4 to 5), covered by a pitched roof whose two slopes converge toward a flat central strip. With various degrees of precision, the painting accentuates the architecture: it nearly always concerns the upper truss and the opposing tympana, to which are added, especially in the fifth century B.C., ornamental variations on the theme of the sloping roof beams. However, this basic procedure never has any cogent force, ready as it is to give way to contamination, as the chosen messages require. The palette is enhanced with white, pale blue and green, in a greater number of shades; the wall priming technique becomes established, using a thin layer of plaster made from a mixture of lime and the same soft compound (*macco*) below. The main decorative panels are marked out by "snapping" lines of string on the fresh plaster, while the figures are roughly traced using a sharp point and/or paintbrush.

Through this extremely rich gallery we shall try to identify the main patterns of development, both stylistic and thematic. It was, as we have already seen, in the hands of masters of the Gre-

co-Ionic school that painting unleashed all its narrative and symbolic potential. Until recent years, this explosive re-evocation of open spaces, seascapes, banquets, dances and games seemed to constitute an ideologically self-sufficient "theme," a "support" almost, with a magical potency for the survival of the deceased: latest studies suggest there were more complex and refined messages, on the level both of the self-representation of the deceased, his class and his expectations, and on the representation of the trauma of death and of the idea of "passage."
The Tomb of the Bulls and the Bartoccini Tomb—the most complex architecturally—occupy an enlightening intermediate position, between the bare and the decorated tombs. In the former, the careful pictorial decoration "silently" surrounds three of the four walls of the chamber—where the walkway for the living is located—while the tympanum of the entrance wall "speaks" and, closed in by the crowded rear wall (a reminder of the Campana Tomb in Veio!), bursts into life with the evocation of the landscapes, places, and events of the legend. In the Bartoccini Tomb too the chamber is decorated with a double polychrome frieze (as in the Tomb of the Jade Lions), and the pictorial efforts are concentrated on the opposing tympana (as in the smaller cells), linking together their content and enhancing the rear wall.
But important new features are woven into the traditional ones in this scheme: while the clash between monsters and wild beasts (winged and unwinged lions, panthers, sphinxes) and victims (ibex, bulls) harks back to familiar themes, there is now on the entrance wall tympanum the theme of the sea crossing to the Island of the Blessed, alluded to by the seahorse rider heading toward the cliff in the Tomb of the Bulls, and more concisely in the Bartoccini Tomb in the pair of seahorses. The ambush of Troilus by Achilles, the only explicit reference to the Greek legend in archaic Etruscan tomb painting, reveals perhaps precisely because of its use here, one of the reasons for its popularity in Etruria: the ambush at the fountain and the killing of the young son of Priam in the wood sacred to Apollo Timbreus are superimposed in a message in which the celebration of heroic virtues and, perhaps even more so, the sacrificial killing of the young prince (it is he who is going to his death) express the rank and "election" of the Spuriana, who owned the tomb. Another connection here, though harder to understand, is the dual contraposition, certainly not "apotropaic," of the erotic scenes concentrated above the doors of the cells. The painter, close to the Pontic Group of vase painters, worked (ca. 530 B.C.) spontaneously and made repeated corrections to the drawing, but it is lively and pleasing nonetheless. The composition of the central picture, though well thought out, is labored and overladen; the lesser friezes are more relaxed and more attractive: this contrast gives the full measure of a new trend that did not depend on the size of the surface being painted. The painter of the Bartoccini Tomb, working in the same tradition, had similar problems to tackle. With the symposium on the tympanum at the back of the central chamber he introduces a successful theme. And the heroic sense of the event, which takes place "elsewhere," is made explicit by the contrast between the unruliness of the animal figures painted in the other pediments and the solemn composure of this theme, accentuated by the archaic-effect dark background, evocative of ancient clay friezes on palaces and temples (we are reminded of the Caeretan slabs with the Gorgons). The inventive variety in the last three decades of the century is truly striking, and is a sign of the cultivated nature of the tomb's patrons, in which tradition and "ideology of status" broaden out, in an almost eclectic way, to embrace such Hellenic philosophical and religious elements as the cult of Dionysus and of the Dioscuri. Pictorial representations make implicit reference to the customs of the new aristocracy, and there is a conspicuous resistance to explicit representations of death; but equally apparent is the unexpressed presence of the deceased: the real focus is, as it were, "off stage" and the space of the tomb expands to weave in the "Beforelife" of the living and the "Afterlife" of the dead, with eschatological passages that are for this period surprisingly clearly defined.
The theme of the symposium dominates in the Tomb of the Lionesses (530–520 B.C.). In one of the most complete and successful expressions of the Ionic-Etruscan style ever seen, the master passes from the solemn feebleness and sumptuous coloring of the symposiasts to the agile depiction and the levity and colorful luminosity and transparency of the dancers frolicking around the sides of the krater. But the dolphin-crowded sea, which in the frieze extends beyond the columns of the pavilion, shifts the event onto a more ambiguous plane, which as the centrality of the ivy-draped krater (the focus of the therapeutic action of the musicians) suggests, involves both the Dyonisiac *ekstasis* of the elected company and (as

opposite
Tarquinia, Tomb of the Lionesses, female dancer on the rear wall, 530–520 B.C.

right
Tarquinia, Tomb of the Lionesses, rear wall, 530–520 B.C.

Tarquinia, Tomb of the Lionesses, dancers on the rear wall, 530–520 B.C.

Tarquinia, Tomba of the Augurs, rear wall, 530 B.C.

seen also in the cruel fight above it) the participation of the deceased. In the Tomb of the Augurs, the "closed door" on the rear wall returns: but all reticence is gone, and the theme is for the first time commented on, so to speak, by the presence and gestures of those present. The evidently expert painter—possibly an eastern Greek—is an uncontainable narrator with a sure, flowing hand who uses rich colors and complex compositions. We feel a closeness here not so much with the style as with the verve that pervaded the Caeretan *hydriai* workshop. What now appears, among the stories told on the opposing walls, is a new correspondence, pre-announced by the (partly-lost) "tug-of-war" on the entrance wall: and if the explanations give a realistic quality to the figures, contests and battles depicted, the duel repeated, with opposite outcomes, between the demoniac mask of Phersu and the naked man "blinded" by a sack covering his head clearly has explicit funerary connotations.

An even clearer contrast is seen in the Tomb of the Jugglers, which though close to the previous tomb, teaches us the extent to which in this art, as elsewhere (for example in literature or in music), different "styles" are to be attributed not to the unmistakable manner of the painter, but to the choice of theme: had they been in different tombs we would never have attributed to the same artist the solemn calligraphic quality, the ecstatic mood of the large figures dancing to the sound of the *syrinx* on the right-hand wall, and the subdued "realism" of the small figures on the left, which respectively represent the symbolic depiction of the initiation of the *coetus* of the elect and the vision, already expressed, of the journey to Hades and the fears such an event arouses in mere mortals. This also tempers the "different" quality of the Tomb of the

Tarquinia, Tomb of the Jugglers, rear wall, 530 B.C.

Hunting and Fishing, where the two chambers, aligned along the same axis, fully develop the seascape theme, with orgiastic ceremonial in the first (rather awkwardly set in a conventional "abstract" landscape) and the remote, intimate symposium of the second, with the mild eroticism of an affectionate couple. The sea, the place of flight and catharsis, is depicted by the painter in one of the most charming scenes to be found anywhere in ancient Western painting. A new spirit, rather than a new style, marked by the influence of Athens, began to make its presence felt in Etruscan painting, one that would soon bring about new stylistic and thematic codes, though not before a further period of experimentation. One example is the Tomb of the Baron, where a master still displaying a clear Ionic influence portrays in four separate, balanced paintings with an Attic flavor, the passage of the deceased to the symposium that awaits him, guided by two riding figures which have been interpreted as an explicit reference to the Dioscuri. Or in the Tomb of the Hunter, in which the hunt and the presence/alienation of the deceased are rendered in a daring reverse perspective: the deceased is enclosed within his pavilion with its ancient embroiderywork while through the transparent material, a grazing deer that could have been painted by an Attic master of the first decade of the new century, touches on—and sanctions—his isolation.

The fifth century

A good example of the midway stage between the old and the new is the slightly more recent Tomb of the Bigas. While the main frieze faithfully adopts the scheme that would last

previous pages
Tarquinia, Tomb of Hunting and Fishing, rear wall of the second chamber, 530–520 B.C.

below
Interior of the Tomb of the Triclinium, 480–470 B.C.
Tarquinia, Museo Archeologico

for over a century (music and dance among the trees, and a symposium that overflows from the rear wall onto the side walls, incorporating into the representation the physical presence of deathbeds) we see a return, compressed into the tympanum at the rear, to the theme of the "other" symposium, which the krater at the center of the shelf-altar and the larger-than-life symposiasts indicate as pertaining exclusively to the deceased. And although the drawings here show Ionic inflections, as if part of a now-ritualized style, the new feature of the lesser frieze makes unrestrained use of the new influence (seen now also in temple painting, as certain *pinakes* in Veio and a few works in Caere demonstrate): adults and ephebes, athletes and spectators, profiles, partial views, front and side views, hairstyles and costumes all seem to have come out of the pattern book of an Attic vase painter of the first decades of the fifth century: from the Painter of Kleophrades to Makron, to the Berlin Painter and the Brygos Painter. The elite patrons were indeed now modeling themselves on the ideals of the Greek *aristoi*, and there is no doubt that the entire ritual function was almost totally encapsulated in this self-portrait, based on symposium, hunt and *athla* without undermining the traditional eschatological code (fights between wild beasts persist in the pediments, "updated" by the appearance of cocks toward the end of the century). This is the context into which nearly all the tombs of the century fit: and it is precisely the power of the model now defined, together with the withdrawal of the patron class (for ideological reasons among others), that has made the dating of many of them one of the thorniest etruscological issues of all. Let us look at few examples. The Tomb of the Triclinium (480–470 B.C.) marked the high point of the new style. Above sea waves that appear for the first time in stylized form, in a Dionysiac atmosphere marked by sprays of ivy and corymbs, a graceful dance takes place around the symposium, traced with delicacy and elasticity: the concentration of the musicians and animation of the dancers are tempered and linked by reciprocal glances (the eye is still not rendered in

Tarquinia, Tomb of the Triclinium, left wall, lyre player, 480–470 B.C. *Tarquinia, Museo Archeologico*

Tarquinia, Tomb of the Triclinium, right wall, dancer, 480–470 B.C. *Tarquinia, Museo Archeologico*

profile, but is foreshortened, as in the Brygos Painter, and "looks") that remove all motionlessness from the cadence of the trees. On the entrance wall, the opening flanked by the archaic felines now includes new elements: two horsemen, the pictorial or "theatrical" representation of the Dioscuri. If we think of the like-dated Tomb of the Leopards, where the theme and the same patterns are treated with a gesticulatory ardor that harks back to the Late Archaic style; of the calligraphic and rather cold elegance with which they are represented in the Tomb of the Black Sow; of the clumsy iconographical and stylistic collage of the Francesca Giustiniani Tomb; of the weary repetition of elements from the same repertoire in later tombs, such as those of the Warrior and of the Cockerel (suggested datings range between the fifth and fourth centuries B.C.!), we understand how delicate the business of achieving such balance, though standardized, was, and in the "crisis age," unrepeatable. Thematic and stylistic breaks do, however, emerge here and there, and it is no surprising that they coincide with the best works. In the Tomb of the Funerary Bed, the ancient sea theme is enriched and enhanced, and the dual presence signified by the catafalque around which the symposium takes place, allows for the inclusion in the self-referential theme of ritual and eschatological attributes, inspired by the salvific presence of the Dioscuri. In the Tomb of the Ship we see what is a highly significant return to contrasting styles: the stiff ritual style of the symposium, and the freer style—freer to archaize and innovate—of the uninhibited landscape scene, in which the clearly defined self-celebration of the deceased seems to be grafted onto the theme of the sea, and perhaps also onto that of "passage." Between the late fifth and early fourth centuries the breaks widen, while the figurative idiom seems to relax into a new-found, more consistent mode, doubtless under the influence of the Italiot world: almost as a point of arrival we see, in the Tomb of the Gorgoneion, the rarefied "garden" in which, beneath the tympanum of a *naiskos* in which lightweight volute patterns have supplanted the hitherto omnipresent felines; the only activity is the meeting between the deceased and a relative. More explicit allusions to the journey to the af-

Tarquinia, Tomb of the Ship, detail of the left wall

terlife begin to appear, for example in the Tomb of the Pygmies, where a group of riders moves toward a banquet positioned beyond the Land of the Pygmies; or in the Tomb of the Blue Demons, the first which actually begins to describe the feared journey: the demons showing their opposition, Charun the ferryman who will complete the journey; improbable dances and other residual movement give way to the solemn departure of the deceased and the cortege accompanying the body: a theme frequently used on the new sarcophagi production.

From the fourth to the second century B.C.

It was not, as was long believed, the arrival from the Hellenistic world in Etruria of a new, anguished view of the hereafter, but a whole new tomb concept which dictated, from the fourth century B.C. onward, the pictorial style of its ultimate phase: this concept was, in turn, encouraged by changes in the socio-political context of the Etruscan cities—turbulent within and menacing without—that prompted the elites ancient and modern to join together in proud association with the *gens*. And the great hypogea, in which dozens of burials took place over several generations, once again became final resting-places: the hall of a princely palace or the royal house of Hades and Persephone. Before them, banquets were held and preparations made—an excellent example of genre painting with still life in the Golini I Tomb in Volsinii, possibly prior to the mid-fourth century, in which the identification in writing of the personalities, even of menial rank, was on the one hand part of the solid "literate" culture of the city, and on the other gives us a clue as to the social ferment of the day: meanwhile the style reveals the power of a pure late-Classical legacy, brought up to date, especially in the "realist" part of the frieze, by scenes enhanced through chiaroscuro effects and shading. This same climate also comes across in the fine male head that survives from a fragment of a *pinax* in the

Temple of Celle in Falerii Veteres: it comes as no surprise, given their influence, the styles of Classical Greece and Magna Graecia should feature so prominently in the public buildings of both cities. The same presence is evoqued in the Tomb of the Reliefs in Cerveteri, in the Tomb of Orcus II in Tarquinia, and in the François Tomb in Vulci: and while in the second it is explicit, in the former there is the self-identification of the couple at the head of the family with the Hades couple (Cerberus and Scylla scratch about under the *trapeza*), while in the third it is the liminal nature of the chosen themes for the entrance wall that reveals where the rear cell is, and with whom the person resting there is identified. The celebration of prestige and the metaphorical representation of the idea of passage are the ideological, often intertwined tracks along which tomb painting moved from this stage on: the former is seen in the display of sumptuous arms rooms or halls decked with festoons with ceilings sculpted and decorated with historical scenes or embroidered drapes; the latter in the depiction of processions and pomp or more realistic journeys to the Afterlife, or encounters in the Hereafter. The rank, wealth and culture of the patrons of the tombs varied, as did the quality of the decorative scheme and the artists, though the results were not always of the same standard; likewise styles differed, producing different results in the monuments of the fourth century, sometimes in the same tomb, as the formal late-Classical heritage came together with new experiences of "tonal" painting.
Exceptions here, of the former and latter styles, are the François Tomb of Vulci (ca. 330 B.C.) and the Orcus II Tomb of Tarquinia (only slighter older). In the first, a carefully controlled programme extols the tomb's occupant for a military exploit (possibly at the head of an Etruscan alliance) in an exemplary comparison between the figures and stories of the Troy and Theban cycles and events in the ancient conflicts between Etruscans whose protagonists were the Vulci brothers Vipinas and Macstarna-Servius Tullius. Drawing from the celebrated Hellenistic repertoire whose well-established compositions he reworks, the painter is more confident in the former, but calligraphic and cold, more uncertain yet vigorous in the second: it is enough to compare the portrait of Vel Saties, with his intent expression and lined face, with its dense light effects, shades of color and shading, and the figures of Nestor and Phoenix face to face, flat and motionless in a scheme that was about one hundred years out of date.
In the Tomb of Orcus II the spectator, like a latter-day Ulysses, is presented with a complete descent to the underworld: on the left-hand wall he encounters Tiresias, Agamemnon and Geryon, while on the opposite side the worst demon ever dreamed up by the Etruscan imagination, Tuchulcha, watches menacingly over those (Sisyphus, Tantalus, Theseus) impiously wishing to challenge the threshold of death. Craggy rocks, swirling mists and levitating *animulae* offer suitable terrain for the spread of "new" painting, made of splashes and shades of color, shaded areas, sculptural effects created with thick outlines and chiaroscuro effect, while the painter allows himself a masterstroke in the shiny vases on the *kylikeion* to the left of the entrance.
Often in third century B.C. tombs (Tomb of the Charuns, Tomb of the Aninas), the painting is limited to certain sections only, or contents itself with the representation of the demon guardians: and the result is frequently a testimony to the successful union between Etruscan imagery and the Hellenistic pictorial idiom. An important though scanty example of this idiom, firmly dated around 270 B.C., is the underground "nymphaeum" decorated with palms, of C. Genucios Clousinos, which emerged in Caere, this time in the urban area.
In the same period, a new style of painting began to emerge that took the form of bare line drawing. In the smaller compositions and in its monochrome tendencies, especially in the small square composition above the loculi/sarcophagus dug out of the passageways (Querciola II Tomb, Tomb 4912), but also in the longer friezes (Tomb of the Cardinal and Tomb 5512), this style seems to be influenced by the relief work on the more elaborate sarcophagi.
To conclude this examination of Etruscan tomb painting we return to the idea with which we began: that of the link between image and written word. Intense portraits and long epitaphs, complementary in their evocation of ancestors, now begin to appear in the tombs (for example in the Tomb of the Shields and the Tomb of Orcus I in the fourth century, and in the Tomb of the Meeting for the third): it was this same link between *imagines maiorum* and *elogia* that so astounded the Greek historian Polybius in the solemn funeral of the Roman patricians. A link which smaller purses, in many of these hypogea, had to somehow fulfil: as for example the case of the ultra-centenarian veteran of Hannibal's wars, Larth Felsnas, whose changing fortunes and whose longevity are remembered in a simple painted epitaph

Sculpture

With the exception of a few rare examples of bronze furnishings, such as the wheeled incense-burner from the well tomb in the Monterozzi necropolis in Tarquinia (which would seem to take up motifs and forms from the Danube area), the first examples we have of Etruscan plastic arts are connected with the art of molding clay and relative to furnishings intended for rituals that were intimately connected with the social structure of the various communities of Etruria. As an example of these one might take the small plate from Tomb XLVIII of Le Rose necropolis in Tarquinia, which depicts the ceremonial epiphany of the patron who commissioned it, complete with all the attributes indicating his social status. Within this collection of pieces intended to celebrate the social standing or role of the deceased, one should also include the rare impasto statuettes of carts drawn by two or more horses, which appear in Tarquinia some time rather late in the ninth century B.C., in tombs of persons of rank; occasional examples of the same type of statue are also recorded at San Giuliano, Bisenzio and perhaps Vulci and Vetulonia.

The evidence available at the moment all seems to suggest that the earliest expressions of the plastic arts were limited almost exclusively to Tarquinia, where—again dating from some time during the ninth century B.C.—we also encounter the first examples of what one might describe as monumental sculpture in stone: two *nenfro* stelae in the form of hut roofs which were found between the Tombs 189 and 190 of the burial ground of Selciatello di Sopra (along with which one should also mention a sporadic example from the Polledrara necropolis in Bisenzio). With the arrival of the eighth century such works spread to other areas of Etruria, as one can see from a well-known lid for a cinerary urn found in Poggio Renzo near Chiusi; the top of this cover depicts a *symplegma* with two rather crudely modeled figures, in which only the heads are characterized in more detail (a deliberate attempt to indicate some distinction between the two).

In the Villanovan period the plastic arts were slow in breaking away from the traditions in which they were rooted; and only around the third quarter of the eighth century does one begin to see—alongside the persisting tradition of rather massive, non-individualised forms—a new trend, the first examples of which are to be found in the small bronzes of Veio and the area around Vulci. These bronzes reveal the influence of the Greek Geometric style, most probably from the Euboic and Crete areas; and it is certainly is no accident that this new trend coincides with the arrival of new Greek-inspired techniques and styles in the working of ceramics and in the production of vessels for the more up-to-date Hellenic rituals in the consumption of wine (Euboea, in fact, was the region largely responsible for a veritable revolution in the production of ceramics). Though faithful to the previous simplified formulas applied in the plastic arts, the molding of these figures is much more three-dimensional, with clearly articulated forms and compositions that sometimes achieve effects of surprising realism. The animals figures too—for example, the horses that decorate the feet of a series of small tripods from the Veio area—are markedly geometric, with a clear emphasis on the modeling of the head (unlike the rather lumpy Villanovan forms that were hardly distinguishable from each other). With the exception of the problematic figure of a fully-cast horse—the oldest *anathema* to have been found in recent years (at a place of worship associated with a pond at Banditella near Vulci)—these bronze works seem to have been purely decorative and, most of them, are toreutic works of particularly high quality (for example, the well-known Vulci sword from the Massimo Collection, now in the Villa Giulia collection). However, there were also narrative works. Sometimes rather complex, these embodied the ideology of the nascent aristocracies—see, for example, the figurative compositions from a ceremonial cart found in Tomb II of the Olmo Bello necropolis in Bisenzio, or the lid to a cinerary urn found in Tomb XXII of the same necropolis. Yet it does not seem to be accidental that alongside these representations—connected with highly developed expressions of ideology—there were older forms (significantly produced in ceramic work) for use in more traditional rituals: evidence of this in Bisenzio itself is provided by the cup with the shaped handle found in Tomb 2 of the Polledrara burial ground and datable just after the beginning of the second half of the eighth century B.C. A few decades later, similar works are also to be found in Tarquinia—as one can see from a series of *fibulae* with shaped arches—and in northern Etruria (Vetulonia), where there developed a flourishing sector involved in the production of furnishings decorated with "Subgeometric" figures (works which show a gradual move beyond the limits and restrictions imposed by the formal language of the Geo-

Female head and bust from the Pietrera tumulus at Vetulonia. Firenze, Museo Archeologico

Sandstone stela from the Antella (Florence).
Florence, Museo Archeologico

Limestone statue from the necropolis of Casa Nocera, near Casale Marittimo (Pisa).
Florence, Soprintendenza archeologica della Toscana

metric to achieve a more restrained and alert style). However, although one can begin to note differences between the works produced in different places, the distinctions are not yet such that one can identify origin with any comfortable margin of certainty.

The breakdown in the formal language of the Geometric tradition and the emergence of figurative tendencies characterized by a greater degree of naturalism cannot be seen in isolation from the deep changes that occurred in the main centers of Tyrrhenian Etruria at the end of the eighth century B.C., changes which clearly had their effect on artistic activity. However, the experimentation with new expressive forms was not only a response to internal factors but also to stimuli from more distant regions (the Hellenic world and that of the Phoenicians, as well as the East in general). The forms of self-representation adopted by the new aristocracies are characterized by ostentation of the symbols of prestige and status which had been adopted from amongst the repertoire of regal symbols and iconography made available by the East. The effect of such borrowings on local crafts and arts (which is what interests us here) was that the development of a monumental architecture was accompanied by the emergence of large-scale sculptures in stone (the creation of which presupposes the learning of craft techniques and skills from foreign experts and craftsman). It is no accident that the earliest known example of such work—the fragment of an anthropomorphic statue found in the *dromos* of the so-called Hut Tomb inside tumulus II of the Banditaccia necropolis in Cerveteri—dates from around 700 B.C. and goes together with one of the most noteworthy and earliest of the new examples of architectural forms inspired by eastern magnificence. This sculpture is only known to us through a rather scanty description, so we have very little to go on when forming a judgement on it; however, the discovery in the 1970s of a couple of figures (ca. 680 B.C.) in the vestibule of a chamber tomb in Ceri, a satellite town a few kilometres from Cerveteri, enables one to attribute the introduction of monumental sculpture into Etruria to artists trained in the North Syria area (the obvious crudity of the Ceri works is due, above all, to the poor quality of the local tufa). Carved in extreme high-relief, the works depict two seated bearded male figures—both solemnly robed; with one carrying a sceptre,the other a lituus—which were probably the *imagines maiorum* of those buried in the tomb (a clear visual and ideological parallel with the simulacra of the ancestors which ancient sources tell us were kept in the atria of aristocratic residences). It would seem that the master-craftsman who produced the Ceri statues—or else a fellow-craftsmen with the same cultural background—is also to be credited with a similar statue found in Veio. However, it is only in Cerveteri that one can see the development of a sculptural tradition proper, which ranges from figure statues associated with ancestor worship (and therefore serving as an expression of social structure) to statues of animals and monsters largely drawn from the Orientalizing bestiary, which would very soon become an important part of tomb decorations (see, for example, the sphinx in red tufa found near the socle of the monumental Montetosto tumulus and dating from the first half of the seventh century B.C.). As future traditions would confirm, these figures were generally placed near the entrance to the tombs; however they should not be read as apotropaic guardians of burial (a notion that is largely anachronistic if applied to the Archaic Age), but rather as being symbolic representations of the sphere of death, thanks to their liminal status as creatures of fable.

During the course of the seventh and the first half of the sixth century B.C., the tradition of sculpture in stone also made itself felt in the minor centers of the southern inland areas of Etruria. However, from the middle of the seventh century onwards this tradition was joined—and probably replaced—by a tradition of work in terra cotta, which is to be seen as originating with the arrival of Greek *fictores* as part of the retinue of the Corinthian Demaratus just before 650 B.C. (it is Pliny who tells us that is was these craftsmen who introduced clay modeling into Italy). Nevertheless, the formal and semantic repertoire was the same whether works were in stone or clay, the end purpose remaining the self-celebration of the aristocracy (for example, the statues of ancestors from the Tomb of the Five Chairs, which date from around 640 B.C.). Similarly, the introduction of clay marked no change in the furnishings required for the rites of burials—as one can see from the male sphinx found near the entrance to the *dromos* of the Tomb of the Dolii and Alari, or the sarcophagus from Procoio di Ceri.

Cortona, tumulus II of Melone del Sodo, monumental staircase to the altar

Those two works were both produced in the second half of the seventh century B.C. using a technique—assembly from separate parts—that echoes that used in the more complex works of architecture (a pale reflection of this method is also be found in the series of small house-shaped cinerary urns that are characteristic of the Cerveteri area and in the roof adornments in the oldest complex in Murlo near Siena). Monumental statuary seems to have made a late and only occasional appearance in Tarquinia—the only extant example being the Poggio Gallinaro lion dating from the end of the seventh century. This absence was due to the local preference for alto-relievo work in *nenfro* (a local kind of tufa), which is documented as early as the first half of the seventh century B.C. and would subsequently develop to produce series of decorative stepped slabs that can be dated as Late-Orientalizing and Early-Archaic. Similarly, stone sculpture only appears in Vulci in the last quarter of the century, with a female figure and a sphinx—both carved in tufa and now in the Berlin Museum. However, from the very beginning of the century Vulci was producing monumental forms, created using beaten panels of bronze that were then joined together to form anthropomorphic figures. The beating of bronze lamina was known in the mid-Tyrrhenian area from the Final Bronze Age onwards, but the move from the creation of practical everyday objects to the forming of human figures is a cultural phenomenon of extraordinary importance, which cannot be seen in isolation from the new input of eastern craft traditions which probably arrived via the Greek world. These large statues were in beaten metal lamina, with only certain parts being made in bronze (the head and the hands), while the rest was made of wood. The oldest extant example, that in the Tomb of the Chariot identified by Anna Maria Moretti, actually provides an example of a powerfully-atmospheric group consisting of two figures, one of which is mounted on the parade chariot. Another work connected with this tradition is the bust from the Marsiliana d'Albegna Circolo della Fibula, which dates from the second quarter of the seventh century and is entirely in bronze, like a veritable Greek *sphyrelaton*. A rapid glance at the current data available might suggest that such works were not widespread. However, the

very opposite must have been the case: the series of hands cut out of bronze lamina for which we have no clear provenance (with the exception of a hand from Pescia Romana) would seem to confirm the existence of quite a number of these *sphyrelata*, of varying quality and manufacture, even though we have no records of or other fragments from them. The actual significance of these statues seems to be different to that of the contemporary work being produced in Cerveteri. The site provenance (when known) indicates the composite *sphyrelata* from the Vulci area figured in the burial of the ashes of persons of rank, so that they seem to recompose the image of the deceased, which is "de-structured" as a result of the particular treatment to which the body itself was submitted. They give monumental expression to the same ideology as that expressed by the sealed cinerary urns with lids in the form of the human body, which were typical of this area from the last quarter of the eighth century to the middle of the seventh century B.C. (the very style of the bronze sculptures, with their abstract geometric handling of volumes, suggests further parallels). The fact that so few of the *sphyrelata* have survived means that we cannot trace how this particular craft tradition developed; though in Vulci by the end of the century it was achieving forms of a severe and accomplished realism, as one can see from the image of a goddess from the Tomb of Isis, to which one must also add the wooden head recently donated by a private collector to the Civiche Raccolte Archeologiche in Milan—which is now claimed to have come from the Vulci area. The striking formal similarities between the two works go well beyond a shared stylistic background (the prominent cheekbones and strong chin suggest the influence of the Peloponnese) and are, at one and the same time, counter-balanced and confirmed by a whole series of technical similarities. In both works the eyes are created using glass paste or bone/ivory, the hair is rendered in bronze (lost in the Milan piece, but clear from the discoloration of the wood) and there was an original covering in gold leaf (also to be seen on the bird held in the left hand of the goddess from the Tomb of Isis). The use of gold may well explain the choice of wood for the Milan statue, as it was too soft a metal to hold up such a monumental work; nevertheless, it should not be forgotten that practise of carving figures in wood and then using metal lamina to cover them is closely bound up with the Greek tradition of *sphyrelata*.

One can see the same evolution from geometric forms to a more accomplished realism in the works of sculpture from the Chiusi area, whose cultural significance is in some ways similar to that of the composite *sphyrelata* produced in Vulci. In the former area, where the dead were always cremated, the use of canopic urns continued throughout the whole of the seventh century B.C. and, contrary to what was formerly supposed on the basis of stylistic evidence alone, would seem to have died out in the first decades of the following century—a claim confirmed by recent discoveries. With significant predecessors in the Villanova cinerary urns which used outline breasts, a necklace or even a fabric draping to suggest the form of a human body, these later canopic urns were intended for the burial of eminent figures and social status was indicated by various eloquent features—for example, the setting of the urn on a throne or the inclusion of insignia held in the hand of the urn figure. The oldest examples are abstractly geometric in their handling of volume; but already by the second quarter of the seventh century B.C., there are works that render traits of physiognomy, even if the influence of geometric stereometry is still clear. At their highest point of development, the increasingly natural handling of volumes produces work that achieves noteworthy rendering of form. In these urns the language of the local tradition is blended with elements of Orientalizing influence—for example, some details in the handling of hair—and of the Daedalic figurative tradition, which becomes all the stronger in such later works as the Dolciano canopic urn. The dating of this piece is a matter of debate, but it seems likely to be of around the same period as the *sphyrelaton* from Tomb of Isis—as is borne out by stylistic features of the face and the antique fashioning of the hair (in spite of some odd and misleading parallels drawn with Attic works dating from the Late Archaic period, there is, within the Chiusi area itself, a clear echo of the style of this piece in the animation and chiaroscuro of the work produced by the sculptors employed on the Archaic complex of Murlo, dating from around 590 B.C.).

In the North, the formal language and iconography of the Villanovan funerary monumens—characterized by a taste for purely linear forms and by an *imagerie* intended to exalt the status of the deceased (for example, the stela from the San Vitale necropolis)—received a new input of energy around this time, probably thanks to the arrival, in the first decades of the

Head and part of the bust of a warrior from the Portonaccio sanctuary at Veio.
Rome, Museo di Villa Giulia
cat. 246

seventh century B.C., of craftsmen from a Levantine background. These men not only brought with them all the ideologically-charged imagery of the eastern repertoire but also a new way of sculpting, which combined monumentality with a sure sense of plastic values. This can be seen in the Malvasia stela or the, slightly later, stela from Via Tofane. The result was a tradition that was able to grow and develop right up to threshold of the fourth century B.C., continually absorbing figurative modes and themes that might best reflect and express the changes within the society of Felsina.

The appearance of monumental sculpture in the area of northern Etruria can be dated around the third quarter of the seventh century, thanks to the recent discovery at Casale Marittimo (on the coast between Populonia and Volterra) of two statues carved in fine yellowish limestone. These are fully-rounded figures which are rather limited in the handling of volumes and show limited plastic rendition of anatomy (although the reliance on simple inscribed lines becomes slightly less rigid in the modeling of the back of the headless statue); however, they are undoubtedly the work of a craftsman of no small ability. The formal language of these statues is noteworthy because of the effort made at large solid forms and the conjunction of rounded masses (there is a more decorative touch in the slight engraving used to render the belt and the woven locks of hair). While available data does not allow us to establish the original provenance of the statues—probably they come from Tomb C in the small necropolis—it does seem clear that they were intended as *imagines maiorum* present at the celebration of funeral rites. What is rather more difficult is fitting them into the context of the rest of the sculpture being produced in the region, where most works of the same period remained faithful to the Subgeometric tradition (though with some borrowings of motifs from the aristocratic ideology of the Orientalizing period). The two statues are undoubtedly a new departure; and possible links with the sculpture of North Etruria are limited to their antique fashions of clothing and hairstyle. However, some parallel with the Casale Marittimo figures—particularly with the more complete of the two—can be seen in the handling of arm and hand and the rendering

Statue of Latona bearing the infant Apollo from the Portonaccio temple at Veio. Rome, Museo di Villa Giulia cat. 219

above
Bronze statuette of Turms from Uffingham (Berkshire). Oxford, Ashmolean Museum cat. 202

Statuette of fighting Menerva. Modena, Galleria Estense cat. 198

opposite
Bronze statuette of Tinia (?) from Populonia. Malibu, J. Paul Getty Museum cat. 195

of rounded surfaces in the various works of sculpture that have been found in the Pietrera tumulus in Vetulonia (a well-known collection which requires complete re-examination if we are to have a less disjointed and impressionistic reading of the find as a whole). A head and a female bust found in the upper levels of the Pietrera tumulus do, however, reveal a different figurative language. More works of high-relief than fully-rounded statues, these are characterized by a weakness of structure and composition, scanty rendition of anatomy, abrupt articulation and rather fragile, cramped form (above all, in the head). All of this reveals not so much the influence of models taken from the decorative work of contemporary ceramics and minor arts, but rather the eastern influence which can also be seen in the small contemporary votive bronzes of North Etruria. Although contradictory and inconclusive, the data we have as to where the pieces were found suggests that the sculpture was located in the *dromos* and served as *imagines maiorum* engaged in the ritual of the *ploratio* (the same ideology and iconography of burial as behind the two Casale Marittimo figures).
In this period the sculpture of Tyrrhenian Etruria appears to have been heavily influenced by Daedalic forms—probably due to those *fictores* who Pliny has it came to Etruria as part of the retinue of the Corinthian Demaratus and whom one can imagine as being among the *clientes* of the rather more historically-solid figures of Rutile Hipukrates of Tarquinia or the Corinthian Kleikles or Kleiklos (buried in a rich chamber tomb in the Esquiline necropolis, Rome). Wonderful examples of such Tyrrhenian work—which also help us to understand local variations in sculptural language—are the statue of a donor in alabastrine gypsum from the Vulci Tomb of Isis (probably part of a group with the above-mentioned *sphyrelaton* of a goddess), the famous Vulci Centaur (often compared to the Delphi *kouroi* by [Poly]medes of Argos for

its solid, compact structure and its clear handling of volumes), the series of cinerary statues produced by workshops in the Chiusi area of inland northern Etruria (characteristic features of which are the clear Daedalic handling of the facial mask and the *Etangenperücke* hairstyles), the series of female figures unearthed in the Chiusi necropolis (markedly xoanon-like in appearance), and some of the more ancient sphinx statues (probably all produced by the same workshops). The uncertain data with regard to the finds of Chiusi sculpture suggests there was a complex and systematic organization of these statues in monumental compositions within the tumulus tombs, while the recognized fact that the statues of Asciano served as cinerary urns (presumably within burial chambers where, thanks to their clothing and insignia, they represented high-ranking personages) raises some problem with regard to their supposed collocation in the *dromos* of chamber tombs and to their function as *imagines maiorum*.

In the sculpture produced for architecture—which, just like contemporary ceramic-work, used recurrent molds—one can see a mixture of Corinth-inspired tastes and Daedalic stylistic features, slightly diluted by the presence of an Ionian influence. Such sculpture was mainly concerned with the production of antefixes in the form of female heads and plates of bas-relief freizes—all intended to decorate the roofs of Etruscan or Latin *regiae*. The inspiration here came from the work of itinerant craftsmen, and was probably ultimately derived from the Greek colonies of the Ionian, which may also be responsible for the influence of Corcyra that can be seen in the pediment dating from the first phase of the temple of Sant'Omobono in Rome (where the figurative work carried out during the reign of the Tarquins is fully Etruscan). The themes and narrative content of the frieze panels are all expressions of the dominant ideology of the aristocracy, with a self-celebration of the continuity of the patricians line; an ideology that is also expressed by the terra-cotta statuary, largely the work of the same craftsmen as those who produced the architectural fixtures. The collection of statues of monsters and ancestors from the second palace of Murlo (dating from around 580–570 B.C.) is the most significant example we have of this work in the Early Archaic period, while the larger-than-life-size torso of a *kouros* discovered at the Portonaccio sanctuary in Veio may be an echo of the work of Vulca, the sculptor whom Tarquinius Priscus called to Rome to produce the image of the Capitoline Jupiter.

As for stone sculpture, finds have been so haphazard that the only real example we have in Vulci of a continuity in the use of Daedalic forms comes from a few statues of sphinxes and winged lions. However, it does seem to be the case that already by the first decades of the sixth century B.C. there was a change in the forms and types of stone sculpture produced in Vulci; this was largely due to a fresh input of Ionian influence and a marked concentration on the most significant funerary themes. Unearthed at the end of last century, these statues are now known to us without any precise context and still dated rather generally as sixth century B.C. or (on the evidence of style only) the second half of the sixth century. However, a useful point of reference in determining the chronology of these works is the sphinx from the so-called Tomb of the Painter of the Bearded Sphinx, a rich burial complex in the Osteria necropolis in Vulci, which was used for various burials between 630 and 580 B.C. This master's work is characterized by a very fluid and clear Ionian language, and he may also be considered responsible for the famous Rider on a Pistrix in the Villa Giulia Museum; the two fragments of male torsos found in the Camposcala estate (Vulci) in 1828; a headless sphinx that first appeared on the London antiques market; and perhaps even the two horsemen in the Ortiz collection and the Ny Carlsberg collection in Copenhagen. Along with the usual funeral bestiary, this repertoire of work also includes themes associated with the journey into the afterlife—the man mounted on a sea-monster or a horse—and other motifs closely bound up with the new aristocratic ideology (for example, the armed horsemen with helmet and hoplite shield).

A similar pattern can be seen in the inland areas of northern Etruria, where the Daedalian features in both bronze and stone sculpture seem to last into the second quarter of the sixth century—as one can see from the terse structure of the warriors and female figure which were part of a wide range of furnishings from the deposit of Brolio in Val di Chiana. In the Chiusi area too one can see how fully statues adhered to the new ideals of the patrician class (for example, the Munich Warrior dating from around 580 B.C.). However, here, a clearly Ionian language was making itself felt during this period. As regards sculpture in stone, this language also occurs in the building of such imposing structures hosting funerary ceremonies, as the recently discovered one at Melone del Sodo II in Cortona. The same taste, although more directly influenced by North Ionian forms (from the Chios area) can be seen in a well-known bucchero *oinochoe* with a spout in the form of a bull's head and richly-molded decoration highlighted with engraving, and in the extant fragments of a second such vessel with a ram's-head spout (unpublished). Both of these were the work of a potter active in Chiusi between the first and second quarter of the sixth century B.C., and they show how early the artistic language of the central-northern regions of Greek Asia Minor was known in this area of Italy. These phenomena should be read and understood in the general context of the interest the Tyrrhenian area was showing in Greek Asia, an interest which around 600 B.C. took on more concrete form with the foundation of Marseilles and the sanctuary-emporium of Tarquinia Gravisca. At the same time, there was a consolidation of urban settlements in the whole of Etruria (though the rate of such consolidation varied from the coastal/southern centers to those in the inland/north); and this was accompanied by a development in trade, the adoption of new forms of intensive agriculture (for example, the cultivation of olive-trees and vines) and, last but not least, the establishment of a timocratric social structure. It is easy to imagine how deeply Etruria on its whole attracted the Greek world. Take for instance a talented vase painter known as the Painter of the Swallows, who already by the last quarter of the seventh century had set up his workshop in Vulci, having moved there from a center in Asia Minor and whose influence must not have been confined to the pottery production.

It is only by positing the arrival of architects and sculptors from the Asia Minor areas that one can understand the extraordinary terrace-altar of Melone del Sodo II in Cortona or the series of above-mentioned sculptural works from Vulci. Undoubtedly, the arrival of craftsmen from the Ionian area was neither occasional nor limited to a certain brief period: around 550 B.C. the sculptures from Vulci belonging to the Amsterdam and Hamburg groups, likely due to the same workshop tradition, were made by craftsmen trained in the northern Ionian area. Moreover, the change in international equilibria following the foundation of Alalia, the diaspora to the West as a result of the Persian advances into Asia Minor, and the outcome of the Battle of the Sardinian Sea (ca. 540 B.C.) led to a new influx of skilled craftsmen, who had a significant effect upon the development of the local figurative arts.

In the south, around 530–520 B.C. Vulci, which had been the source of such works for inland Etruria, abruptly abandoned the production of sculpture in stone, at the same time as Tarquinia just as brusquely ceased to produce relief carvings. This latter fact coincides with the development of tomb paintings and is probably due to the emergence of an oligarchic social structure within the city (which led to more "concealed" ways of exhibiting status and wealth). This process seems to occur only later in northern/inland Etruria, where there was, in effect, a positive outburst in the production of Ionian-inspired sculpture, with regional differences depending to some extent on the availability and quality of the necessary raw materials. In Orvieto, the Ionian forms can be seen in both small-scale devotional objects in bronze and in the larger tomb sculptures, and there was even importation of Greek works themselves (the so-called Cannicella Venus, the simulacrum of a goddess sculpted in a block of Naxos marble by an artist of Eastern-Greek training). In the Chiusi area, on the other hand, there was an adaptation of the local tradition of cinerary statues: for example, in the so-called Palermo Pluto, the archaic iconography of the seated male figure is enlivened with touches that reveal the influence of Miletus. Similarly, urns and cippi in *pietra fetida* or travertine with relief decoration, which would continue to enjoy popularity right up to the second quarter of the fifth century B.C., replaced the more ancient repertoire based on an eastern-inspired bestiary with depictions of banquets, dances, battles and *prothesis* (only at the beginning of the fifth century B.C. would these be organized into complete systems that were different for men and women). The formal language of such works is generally that of a rather flat and fluid bas-relief, sometimes enlivened with details obtained by skilful play on different planes of depth, while works such as urn 5501 in the Florence Museum or the H 204 cippus in Copenhagen reveal more reliance on chiaroscuro and greater skill with the chisel. However, it is in isolated pieces of clear importance—for example, cippus 2255 in the Chiusi Museum (probably from the tomb of a priestess of an agrarian cult)—that one can most clearly see the influences of work from Asia Minor. In the coastal areas, Pisa already had a long tradition of marble work, dating from the beginning of the century; but the new forms also made themselves felt—as one can see from

the bases with ram's-head destined to hold bulbous or lion corners cippi (both derived from North Ionian influences). And in Populonia, the same craftsmen who worked on the sandstone decoration of aedicula and cist tombs also used the marble from the Campigliese quarries for some *louteria* with exuberant bas-relief decoration. The atmosphere in this work—and in the Pisan work in particular—would make itself felt in a series of relief sculptures produced in the Volterra area and in the tradition of the so-called "Fiesole Stones," which contained large fully-sculpted figures. It is likely that the influence of the artistic languages developed in the Ionian area—from Miletus to Phocaea—was largely due to the trade between that region and Marseilles; and such influence would continue to be important in Etruria until the end of the century, when local craftsmen produced such formally-demanding works as the so-called Lorenzini Head (probably from a more-than-life-size religious statue in marble) and the head of a limestone *kouros* unearthed at Castellina in Chianti which echoes the very highest achievements of the Miletus school.
Something more than a series of Eastern-Greek influences are evident in the bronze work being produced in the central/northern regions. These significant pieces range from fully-rounded figures created using the traditional technique of full casting (for votive but also domestic/decorative use) to the particularly important series of lamina in alto rilievo intended to decorate furnishings and parade chariots. The distinction between the various schools working in this field is still rather uncertain, and the insistent attribution of almost all the Late Archaic bronzes to Vulci is misleading, if not false. Undoubtedly, Vulci played a key role in the production both of refined furnishings and of devotional pieces—two traditions that were closely bound up with each other (the furnishings served as *anathemata* in the sanctuaries of northern Etruria—and even in the Acropolis of Athens—or were stockpiled for generations in the various cities of the Po Valley). The full, solid modeling in the votive bronzes, the balance between clarity of structure and refined modulation of surfaces—see, for example, the *kouros* from Talamone of 540–530 B.C.—appear to be strongly influenced by the sculptural language

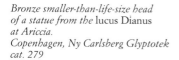

Bronze smaller-than-life-size head of a statue from the lucus Dianus *at Ariccia.*
Copenhagen, Ny Carlsberg Glyptotek cat. 279

Cinerary statue known as "Mater Matuta" from the Pedata necropolis (Chianciano).
Florence, Museo Archeologico
cat. 145

of the Samos-Miletus area. Obviously drawn from the Greek world, the figure of the *kouros*—an abstract expression of the devotee, as well as an ideal embodiment of perfection—constituted a significant novelty in the field of devotional images (and was clearly in step with the radical new anthropomorphism in the representation of the gods). New questions about the development of plastic forms in the area have been raised by the recent presentation of a full-cast statue, two feet in height, found near Orbetello, which can be dated around the third quarter of the sixth century B.C. and reveals the clear influence of the Samos-Miletus school, but has no parallel amongst the known work produced in Etruria during that period. Partly on the basis of the toreutic work produced there during the first half of the century (for example, the *carpentum* of Castel San Mariano), the Chiusi—rather than the Orvieto or Cerveteri—area must probably be credited with the laminate coverings of the chariots in the tomb of Castel San Mariano, together with a whole series of furnishings, of which the most important pieces are: the so-called Loeb Tripods (recovered from a richly-appointed tomb in San Valentino di Marsciano near Perugia), the remains of a piece of furniture unearthed at Ostra Vetere in the

Cinerary statue from the necropolis of the Pedata (Chianciano). Florence, Museo Archeologico cat. 145bis

middle of the nineteenth century, and the identical pieces to be found in the Louvre and the Bibliothèque Nationale. All influenced by the Samos school, these pieces are characterized by soft and swelling forms, whose fullness is not disturbed by finely-inscribed ornamental details. If one excludes the relief lamina for the covering of the chariot from Ischia di Castro (530–520 B.C.), the first real traces one has of the bronze work produced by Cerveteri and Veio date from the end of the century. Given the rather incomplete and discontinuous picture we have of the toreutics of southern Etruria, the Cerveteri school has been credited with a tripod statue from the *lucus Dianus* in Ariccia (a provenance which has led to the statue being seen as somehow related to the history of the second Tarquinius, after his expulsion from Rome). Like the statue of a Javelin Thrower now in the Louvre (which may be slightly later), this is a hollow-cast work made using alost wax technique which, ancient tradition had it, was invented by Theodoros of Samos; though characterized by incisively-defined forms, its smooth, flowing modeling recalls that of contemporary work being produced in Cerveteri. Similar formal parallels with the work of the Master of the Apollo characterize the work of the Veio sculptor who around 500 B.C. produced the well-known Capitoline Wolf, distinguished by the same excessive attention to anatomical details that one can find in the deer in the Portonaccio acroters, and by the use of fine lines to render the ordered locks of the animals coat (similar to, but slightly less abstract than, the touch to be found in the embossed bronze lamina coverings for the chariot from the Tenuta di Roma Vecchia on the Appia Antica, which probably dates from the third quarter of the sixth century B.C.).
The links in these two centers of production between bronze work and terra-cotta modeling come as no surprise when one thinks of what, Pasiteles, a master of sculpture and toreutics, would write at the beginning of the first century B.C. in his five books on the *nobilia*

Cinerary statue from the necropolis of the Pedata (Chianciano), detail of the heads.
Florence, Museo Archeologico
cat. 145bis

opera—in which he describes the art of modeling as "matrem caelaturae et statuariae scalpturaeque" (Pliny, *Nauralis historia*, XXXV, 45.156). However, perhaps more to the point is that, around 530 B.C., both cities experienced an extraordinary boom in the production of terra-cotta sculpture. In Cerveteri there were not only a number of different craftsmen and workshops producing the traditional decorative fixtures for the roofs of the main urban buildings (fittings that now included refined groups of acroters, such as the Thesan and Tinthun group), but also one specific workshop that was responsible for the large cinerary urns known as the Sarcophagi of the Married Couples. These latter two works—with their Ionian features skilfully highlighted by soft modeling and large volumes, and details rendered by a vivid use of surface color—are the undoubted masterpieces of a artist who was capable of translating into clay the ideals of the aristocratic *tryphe*, expressed (as in the contemporary painting in Tarquinia) by the composition of the married couple in a *symposium* seen not as a social function within a society of equals (as it would be a few decades later) but rather as an exaltation of the *oikos*. Alongside these works commissioned by private patrons who inclined toward "concealed" forms of self-celebration, there is the work on various large public buildings, which—together with the decoration of various sanctuaries (places of both devotion and propaganda)—offered the main area for the development of this craft tradition; and parallel shifts toward anthropomorphic gods and the adoption of the temple as a definite building meant that mythological figures and scenes now became a part of this terra-cotta repertoire.

The evidence relating to Cerveteri here is still rather fragmentary at the end of the sixth century, so it is difficult to read the scale of this new development. However, things are much clearer in Veio, thanks to the material recovered from the sanctuary of Portonaccio. Already

The so-called Mars of Todi, a bronze statue dedicated by Ahal Trutilis from Monte Santo (Todi). Città del Vaticano, Museo Gregoriano Etrusco

Fragment of a warrior from the pediment of the Belvedere Temple in Orvieto.
Orvieto, Museo Claudio Faina cat. 285.5

in 530 B.C., the sanctuary received a small (and now rather damaged) votive offering which in reduced form reveals an accomplished Eastern-Greek language in its depiction of the apotheosis of Hercle and Menerva—a theme dear to the "tyrannical" ideology of the second half of the sixth century and destined to reappear in more complete form in the Rome complex of Sant'Omobono attributed to Tarquinius Superbus. The vitality and reputation of the Veio school must have been substantial if, in the last years of his reign, the second Tarquinius commissioned craftsmen from the city to create the four-horse chariot set as an acroter on the roof of the temple of Capitoline Jupiter in Rome; and the level of work achieved is perfectly illustrated by the decoration of the main temple of the Portonaccio sanctuary (ca. 510 B.C.). The acroters there recount the history of Apollo, and though undoubtedly by various artists reveal an extraordinary unity of imagination and style; the main characteristic being a language in which the effort to create dynamic forms has not yet achieved perfect equilibrium, and at the same time goes together with excessive attention to anatomical detail and a surprising harshness of line. However, the Veio school is not limited to the Master of the Apollo and his circle; a few years later, around 500 B.C., another artist, the so-called Master of the Hercules and Minerva, began to impose much greater formal elegance on terra cotta, with works in which the subtle and skilful modulations of surface seem to echo the influence of the Ionian-Caeretan traditions. In fact, in those very years in Cerveteri we know there was a particularly dynamic workshop, whose work—characterized by a plastic language of clearly-structured volumes—was also to be seen in Rome. As well as non-figurative architectural fixtures in terra cotta, the workshop produced half-life-size panels in high-relief to decorate

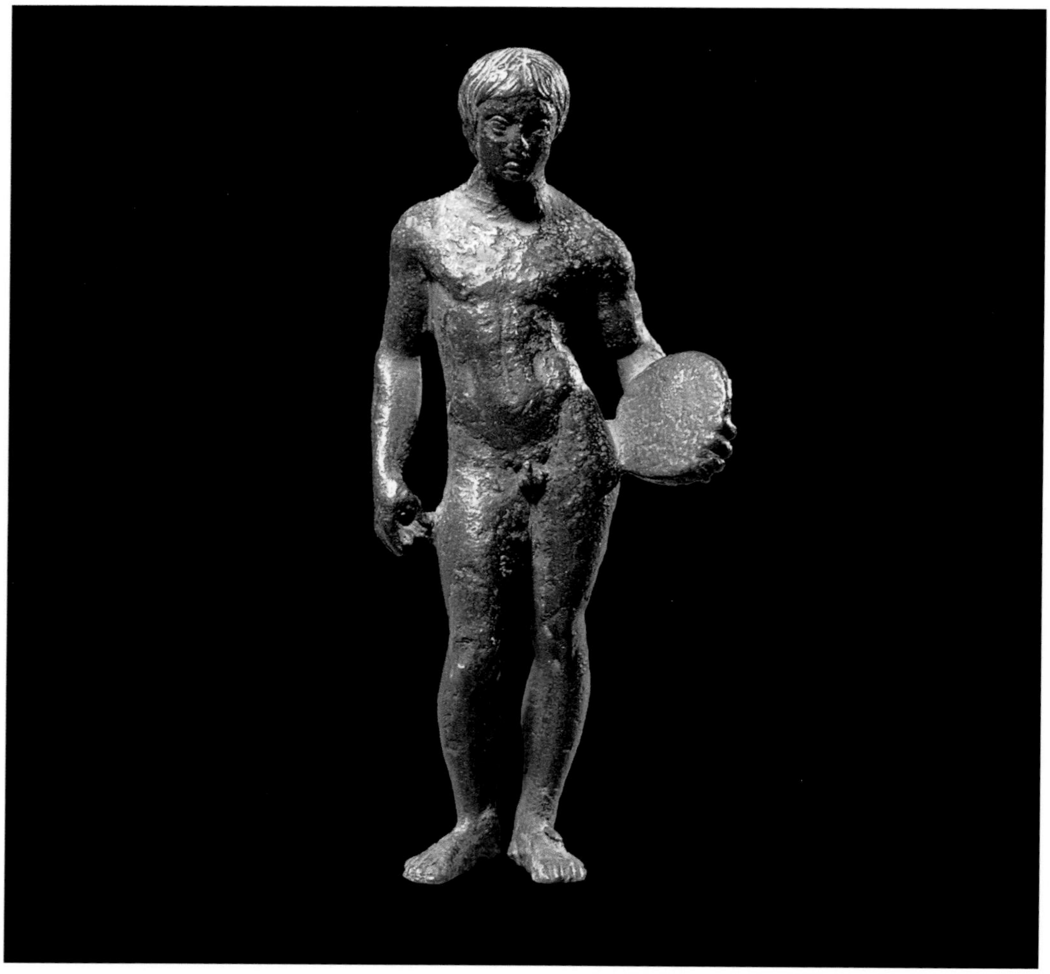

Bronze statuette of discophoros. Florence, Museo Archeologico

the heads of the *columen* and *mutuli* of Temple B in Pyrgi, thus introducing into Etruria new types of terra-cotta fixtures: the so-called "second phase", most probably filtered through from the Campania region in a "Chalcidian" circuit that involved Sicily (Himera), Cuma, Cerveteri and Rome. From Pisistratus to the second Tarquinius, the myth of Herakles offered the perfect model for the "tyrant" ideology, and such legends also fitted in perfectly with the ideology of Thefarie Velianas, "king" of Caere, who had the Pyrgi temple built in the third year of his reign.

The formal characteristics of the above work maintained echoes of the North Ionian tradition, but there would be a profound change in the language of plastic form around 500 B.C. The influence of the figurative tradition of the Ionian school would fade away, replaced by the, more or less directly exerted, influence of Aegina—a change which is probably due to the shift of trade away from the former area to the latter (which is clearly indicated by the well-known cippus of Sostratos from Gravisca and by the various pieces of Attic pottery carried in his ships). In fact, it is no coincidence that the first real expressions of this new style are to be found in the work produced in those coastal centers that most attracted the trade of Sostratos and his fellow Aeginians: look, for example, at the lofty and haughty character of the bronze statues produced in the first quarter of the fifth century B.C. in Populonia, Vulci and (perhaps) Tarquinia, or such Caeretan clay-work as the terra-cotta figure on the lid of a cinerary urn from Tomb 92 in the Bufolareccia necropolis and the decoration of the back facade of Temple A in Pyrgi (470 B.C.). In this latter work the scenes of the Seven Against Thebes are orchestrated with a skilful superimposing of surfaces and planes, and the sharply-marked modeling of the figures is more concerned with the rendering of line than the plastic molding of drapery, beards and hair. This almost mannered style can also be

Head of bronze statue from Fiesole. Paris, Musée du Louvre cat. 303

found in the terra-cotta architectural fixtures of the Satricum sanctuary in Latium, probably a fruit of the same craft tradition. Similar, but slightly less severe, handling of form can also be seen in the terra-cotta architectural fixtures of Volsinii (the acroters of Cannicella, Campo alla Fiera and Piazza Buzi), as well as in the terra-cotta work in the Temple of Piazza San Jacopo in Arezzo.

The defeat of Cuma in 474 B.C. and the Syracusan incursions into Etruscan territory—together with the gradual emergence of a close-knit oligarchic social structure in all the various centers of Etruria—provide the inauspicious framework within which to read the lingering influence of the Archaic, which—in all the various schools of sculpture in the main cities of the Tyrrhenian (and the southern Tyrrhenian, in particular)—went together with a certain severity of execution. In Veio, however, one can see echoes of that profound development which in Greece would lead to the emergence of a "classical" language in sculpture. Though there are no extant large bronzes from this period, some devotional statues in terra cotta do reveal how the craftsman in this city were moving from the extreme formal clarity to be seen in some severely-executed heads to much more gently-modeled forms—such as the so-called Malavolta Head of the end of the fifth century—where the use of chiaroscuro has something of the work of Polyclitus.

From both their bronze and terra-cotta work, one can see that the sculptors of Volsinii were moving in the same direction. Around 420 B.C., a group of such craftsmen worked on the alto-relievo pediments of the temple in Via San Leonardo, and though their sculptural language has some echoes of the Late Archaic (particularly in the handling of the heads), there are traces of a fully-classical style in the sober but robust modeling of the bodies and the striking chiaroscuro in the draftsmanship of the decoration. However, the solid structure of

Statue of Aule Meteli, known as the "Arringatore", from Pila (?), Perugia. Florence, Museo Archeologico cat. 306

the figurative language seems to fade into rather less intense modeling in the alto-relievo work for the Temple of Belvedere (end of the century) and for what is supposed to have been the main building at the Cannicella sanctuary (of about the same date), as well as in such contemporary bronze sculpture as the so-called Mars of Todi (attributed to the same tradition of craftsmanship). It clearly would be improper here to speak of a Phidian model of sculptural language; and yet the head of a bearded god (now in the British Museum) does present forms of extraordinary classical coherence (close to that to be found in the San Leonardo high-relief work).

In the Chiusi area there does not seem to have been any public commissioning of work. However, the local school of sculptors were at work of a whole series of fully-carved cinerary urns in *pietra fetida*, which—after the hiatus of the period of Porsenna—returned to the traditional representation of the deceased seated solemnly on a throne. The heavy-handed restoration to which no small number of these monuments were subjected during the nineteenth century makes it rather difficult to really evaluate these works; what we can say is that the sculpture suggests a school which passed from a rather Late Archaic style (the Marcianella cinerary urn in Palermo, of around 475 B.C.), though a more severe handling of form (the female head, Chiusi 2234) to a mix of severe stylistic mannerisms and classical motifs reminiscent of Polyclitus (the so-called Mater Matuta from Chianciano, dating from around the end of the third quarter of the century) and finally achieved, rather impoverished echoes of the Parthenon tradition by the turn of the century (see, for example, the solid volumes and heavy use of chiaroscuro in the rendering of the drapery of the statue from Marciano in Val di Chiana).

This evolution in the language of sculptural form ran parallel to the development and subsequent break-down in the Archaic patrician ideology which lay behind the iconographic schemes employed in this series of monuments. From the enthroned female and reclining male figure, which were typical of the more ancient repertoire characterized by exalted Hellenic forms, one passes (around 430 B.C.) to another type (Chiusi 2611) with the deceased semi-reclining and the figure of a *Vanth* (sometimes accompanied by an ephebe shown in the funeral ritual of pouring wine onto the ground from a small *oinochoe*—a ritual that may be that described in the *Liber Linteus*). At the end of the fifth or beginning of the fourth century B.C., the markedly funereal themes in this sculpture—still well evident in the famous cinerary urn of Chianciano (in which the deceased's fate was probably described in the *volumen* held in the right hand of the *Vanth*)—gave way to a new motif: the representation of husband and wife engaged in the ceremony of the symposium, which might be depicted with them both naked from the waist up as they tenderly embraced, or else with the woman seated near the knees of her reclining husband and depicted in the ceremonial act of unveiling. The positioning of the figures—which so clearly reveal the desire of the Chiusi patrician class to celebrate their rank—has perhaps less to do with the increasing dignity of the role of women within that society than with the fact that around the end of the fifth–beginning of the fourth century B.C. there was a new emphasis on the patrician values of the *oikos*. This new focus did make use of motifs and schema that were already present in the area (thanks to the influx of Southern Etruscan models during the Late Archaic age—for example, the Asciano urn); but precisely because those sculptural types were the expressions of a different ideology, they had, at the time, made only occasional appearances in the Chiusi area and had never become widespread. The reasons for the change are to be found in the new economic relations resulting from changes in land ownership and in the structures of the dominant groups within the Chiusi area: from being a strictly urban aristocracy (see the evidence provided by Late Archaic cippi), these groups developed into conservative oligarchies with substantial landed interests in a interregional context that was characterized by the growing importance of Volsinii in the Tiber area and the crisis of the northern territories (as revealed by the legend of Arrunte Chiusino).

It is no accident that this classical language in the arts was well-established in the area around the Tiber, and its development seems to have been partly due to the influence of the western Greeks; studies have often underlined the parallels with works in Magna Graecia and Sicily—which are solidly demonstrated at the beginning of the century by the fragment of alto rilievo from the Esquiline and the Roman episode of Damophilos and Gorgasos.

Thus we find a more coherent explanation for certain formal aspects of the bronze sculpture produced at the end of the fifth–beginning of the fourth century B.C.—for example, the large votive offering of the Chimera of Arezzo or the lid of the cinerary urn from Perugia (both produced in Chiusi-area workshops in the last decades of the fifth century B.C.) or the Bolsena head (now in London), which dates from around 380 B.C. and clearly reveals the influence of Polyclitus in the handling of the hair (though that influence is less clear in the restrained modeling of the facial mask). More diluted forms of the same inspiration—gradually mixed with motifs that echo Praxiteles—can also be seen in the small devotional statues and the decorative ceremonial objects and vessels produced by the workshops of Orvieto, Chiusi, Vulci, Populonia and (at least up until 380 B.C.) Felsina.

With the return of large public commissions around 400 B.C., it was the Orvieto tradition in the handling of terra cotta that made itself felt in numerous cities of Etruria (including those in the coastal area). This influence—probably, in part, due to the prestige of the Volsinii within the league of the *XII Populi*—rested not just on the borrowing of models and motifs but, presumably, on the circulation of the craftsmen themselves (as would seem to be confirmed by the case of Vulci). In contrast to this tradition stands the style of a high-relief produced in the third quarter of the fourth century B.C. and set on the *columen* in front of Temple A in Pyrgi. This work recounts an episode in the legend of Leucotea and its accomplished style is marked by a tension between the dynamic molding and heavy chiaroscuro of the goddess's hair and the fluid elegance and supple modeling of the figure of Hercules (which seems to indicate the influence of Praxiteles).

In the south of Etruria the social and political picture changed when the old and the more recent elites proudly banded together behind the ideology of the *gens* and its continuity through time. This ideology naturally involved a new concept of the tomb, which remained the last resting-place of the dead but also became a place of congregation for the peer group. It was in this context that sculpted stone sarcophagi made their appearance. In Cerveteri, the examples from the so-called Tomb of the Sarcophagi appear to be isolated works of modest quality. However, in Vulci and the Tarquinia areas output was both sizeable and continuous from the fourth to the beginning of the second century. Two works from Vulci—the two sarcophagi with conjugal *symplegma* found in the Tomb of the Tenies and datable around the middle of the fourth century, reveal a virtuoso handling of relief carving in clear and synthetic forms; in effect, these are works that do not appear to fit in with the Etruscan tradition, and may have been the work of a highly-skilled sculptor influenced by the school of the Taranto area. Similar influences can also be seen in the best examples of full-figure tomb sculpture in tufa and in the carvings intended as architectural fixtures within tombs, where the language seems to owe something to the traditions of sculpture in Sovana. However, the tradition of tufa sculpture in Vulci seems to have been closely dependent on that in Tarquinia, which from the middle of the fourth century produced a rich series of tufa sarcophagi. The sculpted lids depict a banqueting figure, at first shown reclining and then, from the end of the century, recumbent; while the relief panels of the body of the sarcophagus employ both strictly funeral motifs (which might include some mythological episodes) and powerfully evocative scenes (such as the journey into the afterlife or the pomp and majesty of a magistrate) that are intended to highlight the public role of the deceased and focus on the symbols and insignia of the power conferred by the *polis*. As with votive terracotta work, the figures depicted on the lids are generic representations of age and sex. The emphasis is on those aspects that can highlight wealth and opulence—for example, female hairstyles or the obesity of certain male figures (the cause of much irony amongst Greek writers). The figures make no attempt to render physiognomy, and the heads reveal the direct influence of the heroic model of pathos of early Hellenism inspired by the portraits of Alexander and the Diadochoi (for example, in the Sarcophagus of the Obese Man from the Partunu Tomb). Sometimes, however, one can see the influence of mid-Italic stylemes in the heavy molding of the face and the attempt toward the characterization of physiognomy (as in the Magnate Sarcophagus, again in the Parunu Tomb).

The same craftsmen also produced the full statues or alto-relievo work that were now used to adorn tombs. These included relief friezes, figures of roaring beasts and *naiskos* cippi or those reproducing a head or a fully-sculpted figure. The influence of the Taranto school here

Head perhaps from a terra-cotta statue from the Ara della Regina sanctuary at Tarquinia.
Tarquinia, Museo Nazionale
cat. 305

is very clear; not only in the types of figures, but also in the handling of form (sometimes indicative of an early response to the influence of Lysippus). The strength of Tarquinia's socio-economic structure meant that schools of sculptors also became established in the area around it; those at Ferento and Tuscania developed a tradition of a certain standing, giving a more vernacular reading of the formal language and motifs employed in the workshops of Tarquinia itself.

From the final decades of the fourth century onwards, the family links between the various local aristocracies in Etruria were such that there was a certain mobility of artisans from one center to another, with the end result that a homogeneous Etruscan language in the plastic arts emerged. The move of craftsmen from the southern area around Tarquinia to the north of Etruria is very significant here, even if it is only a marginal indication of the political standing of the city not only its relations with Rome but also within the Etruscan nation as a whole (as one can see from the resolute role played by Aulo Spurinna in squashing the attempted revolt by the serfs of Arezzo in the central decades of the fourth century B.C.—an action that is recalled in the *elogium* of Spurinna in the forum of Tarquinia). This homogeneity of artistic language meant that from the last third of the fourth century, the Chiusi area would begin to produce sarcophagi, as well as its traditional cinerary urns (and would continue to do so until the second century). Connected with a returned to burial as opposed to cremation funeral rites, these sarcophagi were initially strongly influenced by south-Etruscan models (perhaps exerted via Volsinii and Sovana). This is particularly clear in the lids, the development of which follows the same pattern as that described for Tarquinia (from a reclining or semi-reclined figure to a recumbent one). On the contrary, the body of the sarcophagus, at least the oldest examples of them, reproduced the *kline* (a coffin with wooden panels). It was only well into the third quarter of the third century that narrative friezes made their appearance (significantly in the same period as they do in the tufa or travertine urns being produced by the same workshops). And only at the end of the century would the themes drawn

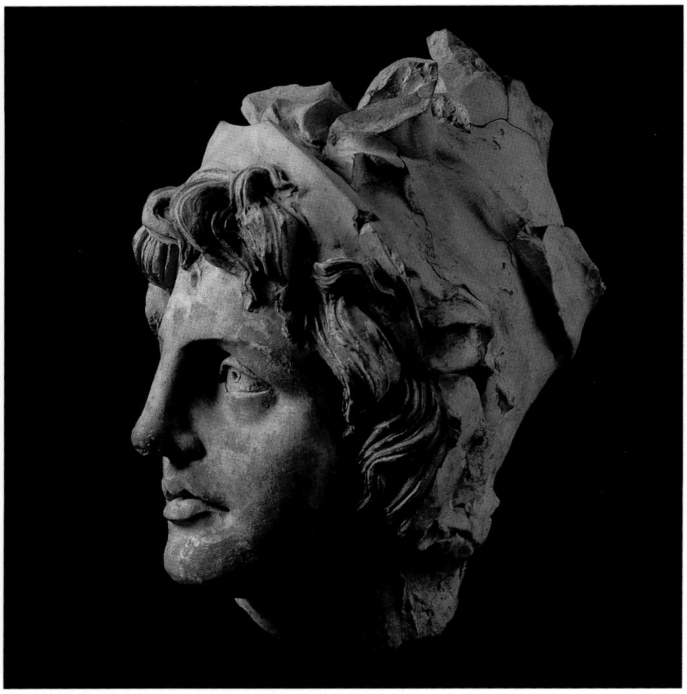

Terra-cotta heads from Catona (Arezzo), first quarter of the second century B.C.
Arezzo, Museo C. Cilnio Mecenate cats. 318.1; 318.2

from mythology or strongly evocative of contemporary history (for example, the *Galatomachia*) be replaced by scenes more directly associated with the world of death—for example scenes of leave-taking or the journey into the afterlife. The fact that the sudden drop in the quality of work produced in Tarquinia coincides with a marked development in the formal language of the Chiusi works (with the adoption of the Late Classicism characteristic of Early Hellenism) is probably to be explained by an exodus of craftsmen northwards in the years 283–280 B.C., when commissions in Volsinii and Vulci became scarce due to the aggressive policy of Rome in the south.

Rectangular urns with ridged lids had been known in the Volterra area since the Archaic Age, but the input of southern models also had an effect here, with the production of a series of tufa urns with figured lids. The use of alabaster only came in the second quarter of the third century B.C. (in parallel with increased demand from patrons), and it was not until the last third of the century that the decoration of the body of the urn began to include narrative scenes (either mythological or related directly to the world of death and the afterlife). This renewal of repertoire was accompanied by a qualitative improvement in sculptural form; around the year 200 one passes from the rather rough and rigid execution of earlier works to a skilful use of Hellenistic modeling, which is to be explained by the presence in Etruria of new, skilled craftsmen familiar with Greek culture. During the course of the third century, these works were joined by fully-rounded marble figures of female figures intended for tomb adornment and similar to those produced in the Tarquinia area. These must have had something to do with the Pisan workshops which had been experienced in the working of marble for centuries and during this period were themselves renewing their repertoire (up until then limit to club-shaped cippi) with the production of iconic *semata* (probably exemplified by the unpublished female figure unearthed at Fauglia in the Pisan hills). For its part, the bronze sculpture produced in the north at the end of the fourth century reveals clear links with the Volsinii schools, and is characterized by a Polyclitus-style classicism tempered slightly by a more flamboyant modeling which is closer to the tastes of Early Hellenism. A rather special version of the same features turns up in the second third of the following century in the famous *Evening Shadow*, the creator of which would also seem to have worked in the field of votive terra-cotta works, as one can see from the female head in Berne (usually attributed to the Caeretan school, this presents clear analogies of form and iconography with the Volterra bronze, and so must be attributed to at least the same tradition).

Again, influxes of migrating southern craftsmen would seem to be the explanation for the development of a lively school of sculpture in Populonia from the second half on the fourth century onwards. Using the local sandstone, these craftsmen produced sarcophagi with recumbent figures, cippi, architectural fixtures and lions. Even if only known to us from fragmentary pieces, this work would seem to bear a number of iconographic and formal parallels with that produced by the Volterra school.
If we now look at the extreme north of Etruria, we see that from the last third of the fourth century B.C. foundries were producing such important bronze works as the Head of an Ephebe now in the Florence Museum (dating from 330–320 B.C., this reveals the influence of Praxiteles' classicism in its fluid elegance of modeling) or the Head from Fiesole (dating from a few decades later, and revealing some echoes of the so-called Mid-Italic portrait sculpture). The lack of further examples of votive offerings and the thin scattering of small, high-quality bronzes through the course of the third century means we cannot chart the process which in the first quarter of the second century led, in Arezzo, to the production of the votive offering of Aule Meteli and, in Cortona, to such sculptures as the so-called Graziani Putto, the two lost Ansidei boys from the votive offering deposit of Mandoleto (on the Perugia side of Lake Trasimeno) and the, slightly later, Boy with a Goose from the Montecchio deposit (which already reveals traces of the baroque style of the second quarter of the second).
Different trends can be seen in the bronze sculpture of the south, where iconography and style tended more and more to originate in the Latium area (via Volsinii, this influence would also make itself felt in the north). The female figure from a large votive offering which the Campanari discovered at Vulci in 1835 is not easy to date, and seems to be a linguistically faithful copy of a Praxiteles original of the mid fourth century; while the so-called Carrara Pluto (first half of the second century) brings out how one cannot consider these bronzes in isolation from contemporary devotional statues in terra cotta, which have the same rigidity of structure and sharp, linear rendition of details.
In the decades from the end of the war against Hannibal to the conquest of Macedonia (167 B.C.), the arts in Rome went through a profound change, with the emergence of an elitist culture that drew directly on models taken from the Greek East; and this phenomenon could not but have repercussions on a Etruria now drawn—with some regional variations—into the orbit of Rome. The return of large public commissions in the cities of the north saw a new burst of life in the working of terra cotta, with craftsmen engaged on the alto-rilievo pediments and roof fixtures for the sanctuaries of Populonia, Talamone, Sovana, Vulci, Fiesole, Volterra, Arezzo and Chianciano. Though such work is clearly by different hands, it reveals an substantially homogeneous formal language, characterized by a dynamism and pathos typical of Asia Minor (sometimes mixed together with more classical motifs). This style would seem to be due to the arrival in this part of Etruria of Greek craftsmen, who were soon an integrated part of the local social structure; this is confirmed, for example, by the terra cotta craftsman Cnei Urste, who was a native of the Greek world and signed his name to an alto-relievo panel produced in Arezzo (*C.I.I.* 469). Although most of the extant evidence enables us to offer only a conjectural reading of iconography and themes, it does seem that—as at Talamone—the works alluded to the universal values of *concordia ordinum*. As for private commissions, it seems that the standard of the bronze work created sank to a uniformly low standard , while the vitality in the tradition of stone sculpture seems to have faded, with that material being replaced by the cheaper terra cotta—for example, in the Tarquinia and Chiusi areas. In the former of the two, terra-cotta works were also supplied by workshops in Tuscania, which produced terra-cotta sarcophagi of no high standard; in the latter, it seems that the oligarchy responded to the social tensions of the early part of the second century B.C. by allowing political rights to at least part of the servile classes, and thus created a rather extended middle class (particularly evident in the countryside around the city) which formed a distinct market for terra-cotta works. In fact, while the urns created for the aristocracy were hand-made spatula works in which the handling of form reveals a clear Hellenic-inspired taste, the new middle classes were supplied with standardised mold-produced urns with rather summary figurative decoration. This difference in style and technique is also echoed in the subject-matter of the decoration: those intended for the aristoc-

Terra-cotta sarcophagus of Larthia Seianti from the Marcianella necropolis at Chiusi.
Florence, Museo Archeologico

racy used scenes from the Greek myths, while those intended for the new middle class of artisans and small landowners made clear allusions to the resolution of social tensions and the ethical basis for the new *concordia* (with such scenes as the Fratricide of Thebes or the *monomachia* of the Hero with the Plough). The different socio-economic situation in Volterra can be seen in the works of sculpture it produced. The protomes included amidst the quoins of the vault of the so-called Gateway of the Arch (previous dated in the period of Early Hellenism, but now—on the basis of recent excavations—to be considered as rather later) are too worn and damaged for us to give a clear reading of their characteristics. However, even if its attribution is not certain, a full bust of a warrior's head carved in rather fine-quality tufa is useful in defining the key points in the tradition of stone sculpture of the Volterra school, the language of which is substantially the same as that to be seen in the major terracotta works produced around the same time. Nevertheless, it is the series of cinerary urns that provides the information most useful to an understanding of the dynamics of contemporary culture in Volterra. The sudden appearance in this region of the so-called Master of Enomao, a craftsman of undoubtedly Hellenic inspiration, transformed the local style characterized by a certain pathos in the rendering of faces and an accentuation of anatomical details (the man most probably reached Etruria as a result of Roman campaigns in Asia Minor and then from inland Etruria moved to Volterra in the retinue of an aristocrat from that area—such as the Perugian Arnth Fethiu who was adopted in this period by the Ceicna). The teachings of the Master of Enomao would find fertile ground in the local tradition—first in the works of the Master of the Small Paterae, then in those of the Master of Mirtilo (ca. 160 B.C.), which give fullest expression to his baroque style. In these latter pieces, the liveliness of the relief decoration on the body of the urns, enliven by the use of color (which has now almost completely disappeared), contrasts with the more restrained chiaroscuro in the modeling of the lids (where the touches of realism in the handling of the heads gives way to a tendency to idealised portraits). This tradition would have an effect on terra-cotta work produced throughout the territory, and would continue up to 130–120 B.C. thanks to the Workshop of the Rosettes and Palmettes; while within the Volterra tradition proper there was a tendency to a standardised product intended to satisfy the demands of the aristocracy that was moving into the city from the countryside. The figure types depicted on the urns reflected the traditional forms of "self image" chosen by patrician groups, with the only change being that of costume (the deceased was shown as a recumbent figure in a tunic and then, toward the end of the century, as veiled). There is however a clear difference in the relief decoration on the body of the urns: on those in alabaster, the iconography is drawn from mythology, while on those in tufa there are scenes relating to the world of death and the afterlife or an exaltation of the worldly rank of the deceased (a distinction which would seem to suggests the two materials and iconographies were used for different groups of patrons). During the first half of the first century B.C., the vitality of Volterra workshops seems to have been largely undiminished, with the development of various tendencies that range from an extreme form of the baroque idealisations of the Master of Mirtilo, to forms characterized by a rather cold pathos or else greater realism. In the late second century B.C., the vitality of these workshops also made itself felt in the Fiesole area (where it is very likely that a little-studied group of sarcophagi in *pietra serena* were the work of a sculptor from Volterra); and there is no doubt that their continuing fortunes are to be seen in the context of the contemporary history of the area (the failure of the Silla colony). Even in the third quarter of the first century B.C., when most of the work being produced was of poor, standardised form, there were still some gleams of energy and vitality: and the last expressions of the Volterra tradition are to be seen a small group of urns (of which only the lid remains) dating from the early days of the Roman Empire—a fine example of the antiquarian nostalgia felt by some members of the aristocracy of the *VII Regio.*

Ducati 1911, c. 357; Cultrera 1921, po. 37 ff.; Andren 1939; Riis 1941; Ducati 1943 c. 373 ff.; Pallottino 1945; Pallottino 1950; Herbig 1952; Hus 1961; Hus 1966, pp. 665 ff.; Nicosia 1967, pp. 267 ff.; Hencken 1968; Tuerr 1969; Colonna 1970a; Cristofani 1971b, pp. 12 ff.; Martelli 1971, pp. 268 ff.; Vagnetti 1971; Sprenger 1972; Roncalli 1973; Gempeler 1974; Cristofani 1975c; Martelli 1975, pp. 87 ff.; Prayon 1975c, pp. 165 ff.; Colonna 1977b, pp. 131 ff.; Delpino 1977b, pp. 173 ff.; Hus 1977, pp. 31 ff.; Cristofani 1977b, pp. 2 ff.; Brendel 1978; Cristofani 1979b, pp. 85 ff.; Cristofani 1979a; Martelli 1979, pp. 33 ff.; Aigner Foresti 1980; Hus 1980, pp. 117 ff.; Martelli 1980, pp. 35 n. 44; Paribeni 1980, pp. 55 ff.; Spadea 1980, pp. 210 ff.; Colonna 1980–81, pp. 157 ff.; Ampolo 1981, pp. 32 ff.; Colonna 1981a, pp. 13 ff.; Riis 1981; StaryRimpau 1981, pp. 75 ff.; Comella A. 1982; Dohrn 1982; Jannot 1982, pp. 261 ff.; Buranelli 1983; Della Fina 1983; Martelli 1983, pp. 25 ff.; Colonna, von Hase 1984, pp. 13 ff.; Donati 1984, pp. 273 ff.; Jannot 1984; Sassatelli 1984b, pp.107 ff.; *Artigianato artistico* 1985; Bonamici 1985a, pp. 123 ff.; Bonamici 1985b, pp. 157 ff.; Buranelli 1985; *Case e palazzi d'Etruria* 1985; Colonna 1985a, pp. 101 ff.; Colonna 1986, pp. 371 ff.; Cristofani 1985c; Esposito 1985, pp. 138 ff.; Haynes 1985; Hofter 1985; Rastrelli 1985, pp. 100 ff.; Bruni 1986a, pp. 59 ff.; Bruni 1986b; Cristofani 1986b, pp. 56 ff.; Hostetter 1986; Micheli 1986, pp. 58 ff.; von Freytag 1986; Bartoloni, Baglione 1987, pp. 233 ff.; Buranelli 1987, pp. 214 ff.; Colonna 1987a, PP. 55 ff.; Colonna 1987b, pp. 7 ff.; Colonna 1987c, pp. 11 ff.; Cristofani 1987e, pp. 199 ff.; Cristofani 1987c, pp. 27 ff.; Delpino 1987, pp. 152 ff.; Gentili 1987b, pp. 207 ff.; Ducci 1987–88, pp. 131 ff.; Buranelli 1988, pp. 143 ff.; Cataldi 1988; Cerchiai 1988, pp. 227 ff.; Cygielmann 1988, pp. 281 ff.; D'Agostino 1988, pp. 217 ff.; *Die Welt der Etrusker* 1988; Maggiani 1988, pp. 253 ff.; Martelli 1988, pp. 22 ff.; Nagy 1988; Romualdi 1988, pp. 273 ff.; Briguet 1989; Bruni 1989a, pp. 267 ff.; Colonna 1989b, pp. 303 ff.; F. Donati 1989, pp. 44 ff.; Gilotta 1989, pp. 69 ff.; Haynes 1989, pp. 1395 ff.; Maggiani 1989a, pp. 1557 ff.; Maggiani 1989b, pp. 995 ff.; Sassatelli 1989, pp. 927 ff.; Colonna 1989–90, pp. 99 ff.; Mangani 1989–90, pp. 57 ff.; Comella, Stefani 1990; Cristofani 1990a, pp. 67 ff.; Gaultier 1990, pp. 271 ff.; Rhode 1990; Stopponi 1990a, pp. 204 ff. n. 3.3; Bonamici 1991, pp. 2 ff.; Bruni 1991, pp. 41 ff.; Buranelli 1991b; Cohen 1991; Colonna 1991b, pp. 117 ff.; Cristofani 1991a, pp. 2 ff.; Egg 1991, pp. 202 ff.; Emiliozzi 1991, pp. 943 ff.; Lulof 1991; Maggiani 1991, pp. 985 ff.; Stopponi 1991, pp. 1103 ff.; Torelli 1991c; Bentz 1992; Colonna 1992, pp. 92 ff.; D'Ercole, Trucco 1992, pp. 77 ff.; Edlund 1992; Girardon 1992, pp. 225 ff.; Zamarchi Grassi 1992; Blumhofer 1993; Colonna 1993c, pp. 337 ff.; Cygielmann 1993, pp. 369 ff.; Maetzke 1993, pp. 133 ff.; Maggiani 1993b, pp. 149 ff.; Maggiani 1993a, pp. 35 ff.; Micozzi 1993, pp. 2 ff.; Morigi Govi, Sassatelli 1993, pp. 103 ff.; Rastrelli 1993, pp. 351 ff.; Romualdi 1993, pp. 102 ff.; Szilagyi, 1993, pp. 271 ff.; Torelli 1993, pp. 269 ff.; Bruni 1994, pp. 47 ff.; Colonna 1994, pp. 548 ff.; Gentili 1994; Hillgruber 1994, pp. 17 ff.; Pautasso 1994; Sannibale 1994; Maggiani 1995, pp. 75 ff.; Mertens Horn 1995, pp. 257 ff.; Cagianelli 1995–96, pp. 11 ff.; Bonamici 1996b, pp. 2 ff.; Bruni 1996, pp. 139 ff.; Colonna 1996; Lulof 1996; Micozzi 1996, pp. 2 ff.; Bruni 1997, pp. 129 ff.; Iozzo 1997, pp. 33 ff.; Jannot 1997, pp. 139 ff.; Maggiani 1997c, pp. 57 ff.; Maggiani 1997a, pp. 123 ff.; Maggiani 1997b, pp. 149 ff.; Riis 1997, pp. 179 ff.; Spivey 1997; Strøm 1997, pp. 245 ff.; Torelli 1997d; Boitani 1998, pp. 203 ff.; Bruni 1998a; Bruni 1998b, pp. 67 ff.; Feruglio 1998, pp. 207 ff.; Paolucci 1998, pp. 11 ff.; Prayon 1998a, pp. 191 ff.; Romualdi 1998, pp. 371 ff.; Roncalli 1998, pp. 15 ff.; Cagianelli 1999a; Cateni 1999; Esposito 1999; Colonna 2000, pp. 104 ff.; Minetti 2000, pp. 84 ff.; Paisi Presicce 2000; Cagianelli forthcoming.

Etruscan Bronzes

Right from the formative period of the Etruscan culture, metallurgy, especially bronze-working, was a significant element in the process of economic, social and cultural organization. In fact, the presence in what was to become Etruria of important mining districts favored the early development of metallurgy in the area and it appears that from the Bronze Age onward this attracted the attention of the more advanced peoples of the eastern Mediterranean, on the lookout for metals for their growing needs.

In the Final Bronze Age innovatory phenomena were clearly evident in the field of bronze-working, linking Etruria with the central European area and with the Aegean and the eastern Mediterranean, allowing us to intuit the formation of a vast and complex network of relations between the most highly developed metalworking areas and those having the greatest consumption of metal artifacts. This must have involved the diffusion of techniques and repertoires of forms, which was favored by the status of bronze-workers, who were highly specialized and well respected craftsmen. The demand for their products was, however, frequently discontinuous, so they tended to be mobile and not fully integrated into the community. The output of bronzes in this period attests, on the one hand, the development of agriculture, a necessary precondition for the sustenance of a growing population, through the notable production of tools and, on the other hand, the formation of social stratification due to the link that was established between ownership of bronze and social class.

With the advent of the Iron Age and the Villanovan culture these tendencies became more marked and there was a considerable increase in the production of bronzes, the result of a growing demand determined by economic and social development. Bronze personal ornaments (*fibulae*, pins, bracelets, necklaces, belts), and also spindles, razors, horse-bits, arms (swords, spears, and axes, the latter having an important ceremonial function), elements of defensive armor (helmets, breastplates, shields), and more complex objects, such as flasks, carts, and biconical or hut funerary urns, in sheet and cast bronze, embossed and incised with motifs deriving from central European bronzes, have all been found in the most important tombs, depending on the sex and social class of the deceased, especially those of the eighth century B.C., which marked the culmination of a long process of social differentiation. Significantly, the areas of greatest socio-economic development were linked to the mining districts, which offered returns supplementing those from agriculture, with greater opportunities for accumulation. This allowed them to participate in trade over long distances, as

Bronze oinochoe *with trilobate mouth from the Tomb of the Flabelli at Poggio della Porcareccia (Populonia), 600–550* B.C.
Florence, Museo Archeologico
cat. 226

Bronze lamina kardiophylax *from the necropolis of Prato Rosello (Artimino), end of the eighth–beginning of the seventh century* B.C.
Carmignano (Prato), deposits of the Soprintendenza ai Beni Archeologici della Toscana
cat. 59

opposite
Bronze chalice from Cerveteri, seventh century B.C.
Florence, Museo Archeologico
cat. 222

right
Bronze single-handle semispherical bowl from the dolium *Tomb M7 at Monterozzi (Tarquinia), mid-eighth century* B.C.
Tarquinia, Museo Archeologico
cat. 177

Bronze kantharos, *635–600* B.C.
Amsterdam, Allard Pierson Museum
cat. 223

is attested by the imports: Greek geometric pottery, personal ornaments from the East (especially the Levant), and also small bronzes from Sardinia, another leading mining region having a bronze-working tradition with which it appears relations were particularly well developed. One of the most important of these areas was that of Tarquinia, with its hinterland of the Tolfa Mounts, which certainly played a major role in the development of the Villanovan culture and to which is attributed a rich output of sheet bronze objects decorated with geometric motifs. But, although as a result of processes differing in their modes and time, similar phenomena also occurred at Veii and Vulci, then, in the eighth and seventh centuries B.C., at Vetulonia and Caere, and, finally, at Populonia and Volterra. Flourishing bronze-works developed in these centers, often having their own characteristics, a sign of an activity that, thanks to a strong and constant local demand, took root in the area, giving rise to a long-lasting tradition.

The network of relations determined by the presence of metals is also evident in the repertoire of these bronze-workers—for example, the adoption of the forms of the "pilgrim's flask" and the tripod, probably the result of contacts with the Phoenicians, to whom the eastern world delegated its trade in the Mediterranean. The metals of Etruria did not attract only the Phoenicians, however, but also the Greeks, who, after an earlier period of contacts, had begun their colonization of the West by settling at Pithekoussai (present-day Ischia)—relatively close to southern Etruria—where, as we know from archaeological finds, iron ore from Elba was smelted.

With the assimilation by the Etruscan aristocracies of Orientalizing modes around 730 B.C., Etruscan bronze-working was renewed, especially by the adoption—in addition to or as a substitute for the previous status symbols—of the utensils required for the sacrificial banquet, a ceremonial occasion of fundamental importance for the reproduction of the social structure through the emphasis laid on social rank. In particular, these included bronze cauldrons, often on high stands, intended, according to a custom of Oriental origin, for boiling meat. They were, however, also used for wine; the services for this comprised silver and bronze *phialai*, cups and *oinochoai*. These vessels, as well as the other objects having a symbolic function, such as scepters, fans and ceremonial chariots made in the East or in Greece, were sometimes imported whole. More often, only the most significant parts arrived in Etruria, rapidly giving rise to development of an Etruscan production that reproduced and reworked the prototypes according to local sensibility, as is well attested especially at Vetulonia and Vulci, and also at Caerveteri, Veio, and Tarquinia. The importance of the large bronze services used at banquets is attested, moreover, from the mid-seventh century B.C. onward, by bucchero vases, which, above all in the "heavy" version, appear to be a substitute for the precious metal prototypes, the rich embossed and incised decoration of which they reproduce. On the other hand, the large shields and thrones in embossed bronze sheet derive from the local tradition; they are well attested, for example, in the Chiusi area, where they are associated with the typical canopic vases, of which metal versions exist.

In the same period, the process—which had already begun in the eighth century B.C.—of the adoption of hoplitic weaponry was completed, with the consequent change in the types of arms used.

In addition to the introduction of new models, however, the Orientalizing period was characterized by the new organization of production in general, in the context of a complex but very successful system allowing the exchange of goods, technologies, and people, and involving, first and foremost, the Greeks, from both mainland Greece and the colonies, as well as the Phoenicians, Sardinians (especially at Vetulonia), and central Europe. Etruria played an active role in this system with its presence on the seas, where there were conflicts with the initiatives of the Greeks, and it began the massive exportation of Etruscan artifacts. Bronzes took pride of place among these, not only in the Italic world but also in the Greek one, where some Villanovan objects had already arrived. This popularity is attested by the Etruscan bronzes found in the sanctuaries of Dodona, Delphi, Samos, and Olympia. Pausanias (V, 12, 5) mentioned a throne donated to the latter sanctuary by an Etruscan king, Arimnestus, the first barbarian to make a dedication to the Zeus of Olympia.

During the sixth century B.C., with the new social and economic order resulting from the process of urbanization, Etruscan bronzes started to be produced on a large scale, partic-

Bronze base of thymaterion *from Castel San Mariano (Perugia), 575–550* B.C.
Monaco, Staatliche Antikensammlungen
cat. 234

ularly in a number of cities with a long-standing tradition of craftsmanship and availability of raw materials, especially Vulci and Populonia, and probably in others in southern Etruria, such as Cerveteri, and also in Capua. In these centers classes of objects of good—or even excellent—technical and aesthetic quality were made that were closely related to the contemporary output of Greece (especially Corinth and Ionia) and Magna Graecia. They tended, however, to be made in a series and repetitive, although, at times, in an unsystematic manner, composing sets: tripods, candelabras, and *thymiateria*, adorned with statuettes in the round in Ionian style; vase stands; vases and equipment for symposiums, at times also having parts, such as the handles, stands and feet, modeled in the form of human or animal figures in the round; *lebetes* with a brim embellished with a plait motif and *lebetes* with a beaded brim (their export by sea is also attested by the shipwreck containing *lebetes* with beaded brim found at Capo Enfola, on the Elba Island); bucchero ware; and Etruscan amphoras for transport. These products had a notable capacity to penetrate the markets of central and southern Italy, the Po Valley, and Gaul, spreading as far as central and northern Europe, while even the Greek world was very receptive, as the tripod from Vulci found on the Acropolis of Athens demonstrates.

The restoration of the power of the oligarchy in the fifth century B.C. and the social tensions, with the related fall in public and private consumption, that occurred in southern Etruria did not have serious consequences for the manufactures of bronze artifacts at Vulci, which exported its products, especially candelabras surmounted by statuettes, to the Etruscan settlements in the Po Valley. This area was flourishing at this time and was the center of an economic system extending toward the Adriatic and northern Europe, which also benefited the cities of northern and central Etruria directly linked to it, such as Volsinii and Arezzo. In these two cities—the former the site of the sanctuary of the Etruscan Confederation, the Fanum Voltumnae, and closely associated with Vulci, on which it appears to have depended artistically in the previous century, the latter controlling the mining district of the Monti Rognosi—a local production of bronzes developed, reaching its climax with such great sculptures as the Mars found at Todi and, in the late fifth or early fourth centuries, the Chimera.

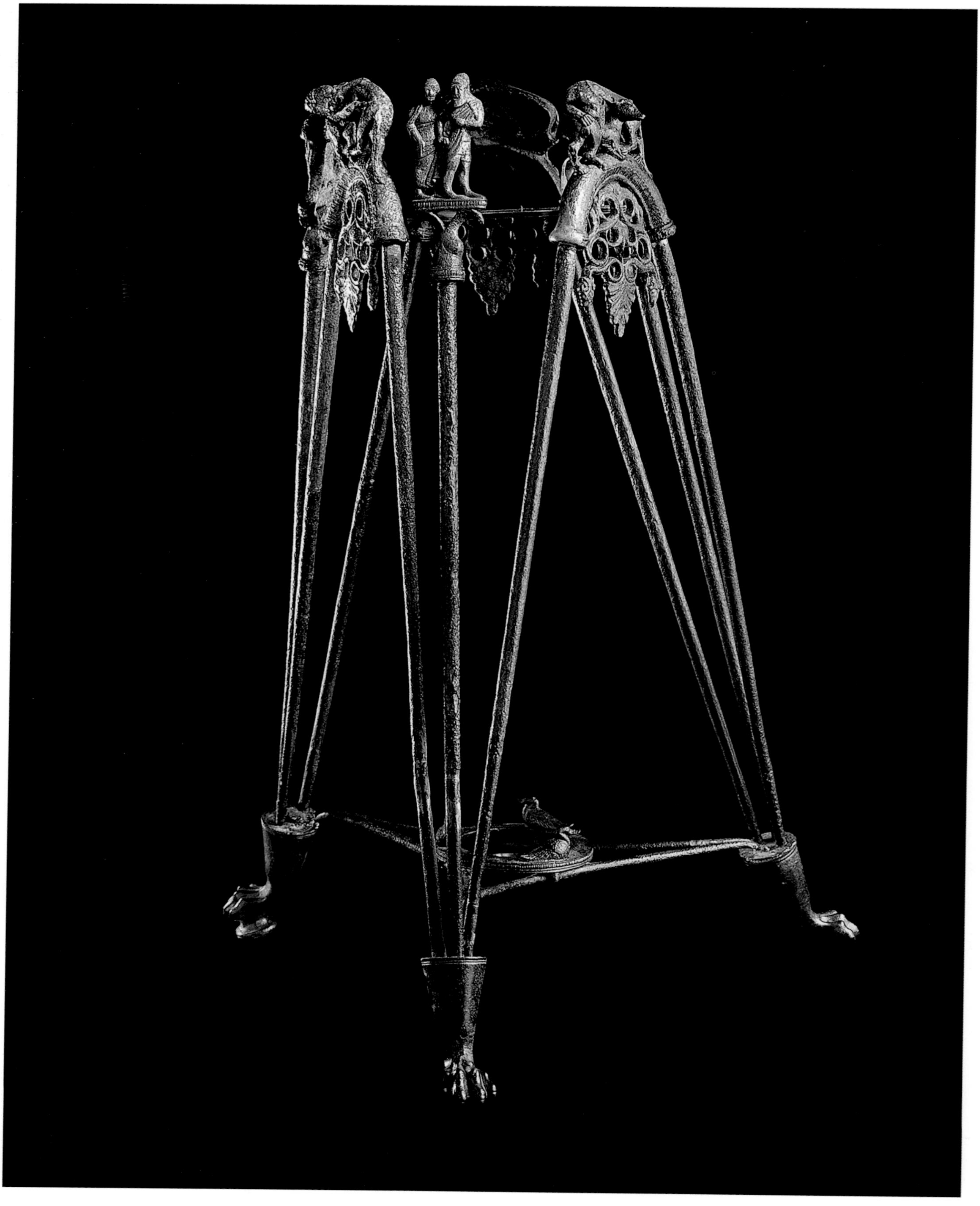

Bronze tripod from Vulci, from Tomb 128 at Valle Trebba (Spina), beginning of the fifth century B.C.
Ferrara, Museo Archeologico
cat. 233

Feet of bronze tripod, 480–460 B.C.
Florence, Museo Archeologico
cat. 281

Furthermore, Etruscan products must have had a good reputation in Greece in the fifth century B.C. because Critias, a leading intellectual, poet, and politician in Athens at that time, famous for being one of the Thirty Tyrants, praised the quality of the Etruscan bronze goods, while a line of the Attic comedy writer Pherecrates (second half of the fifth century), states: "Of what origin are the candelabras? Etruscan." (in Athenaeus, *Deipnosophistai*, I, 50, 286; XV, 60, 700c).
The fourth century witnessed the rise of the interior of central Etruria, as well as the north, areas which were less involved in the turbulent social transformations of the cities on the southern coast and were favored by their links with the Etruscan settlements in the Po Valley; this not only allowed them to expand their trade but also provided an outlet for internal tensions, permitting the maintenance of the traditional social order. Thus the leading center of production became Arezzo, while Volsinii and then Falerii also had a central role and Populonia continued to be an important metallurgical center.
From the middle of the fourth century onward, especially in the last quarter, there was an increasing output of high quality products that were, however, repetitive, and were intended for the middle classes. The latter now formed part of the urban society—although with modalities that varied from one city to another—and wanted to possess the traditional status symbols: bronze vases; candelabras, with the statuettes now an integral part of the shaft; strigils and women's toilet articles, especially mirrors, decorated with engravings on the rear, sometimes with complex subjects alluding to national or family traditions. The techniques used to make metal vessels and their types resembled those of the Hellenic and Hellenized world, especially those of the Magna Graecia; this is attested by finds in a large part of the peripheral areas where there were aristocracies that accumulated these goods—which were made in the centers with an old-established metalworking tradition—and used them as grave goods. As the century progressed, however, the decline of the institution of

Bronze olpe, oinochoe *and* situla *from Tomb 13/1908 at Populonia. Florence, Museo Archeologico cats. 229.1; 229.2; 229.5*

Bronze patera and colum *from Tomb 13/1908 at Populonia. Florence, Museo Archeologico cats. 229.6; 229.7*

the symposium caused a notable decrease in the repertoire of forms and, in the following century, this was further reduced, so that it comprised, above all, vases that were used not for wine but to contain food.

Mirrors were made by workshops exporting to northern Etruria, but the type of alphabet used in the inscriptions suggests these were made especially in the interior of central Etruria (probably Volsinii) and southern Etruria (Vulci, perhaps also Cerveteri and other cities), while the output of northern Etruria, which has also been attested, seems to have been more limited. In addition to the high quality and more easily recognizable bronze objects, there was, however, a considerable output of standardized products, for which it is difficult to give a precise provenance; probably the result of a relatively widespread metalworking tradition, they were commissioned by members of the middle or lower classes.

In bronze-working, as in the other types of production, there was an artistic *koine* that was also in use in Latium and Campania; of particular importance in this process was the new stimulus given to the mobility of the craftsmen by the opening up of the social groups of the Etruscan cities with the arrival of the Greeks, probably mainly from Magna Graecia, that is attested by the inscriptions. The assimilation of this culture on the part of Rome then led to its diffusion in Italy until the late Republican period.

In the first quarter of the third century B.C., as a result of a series of campaigns following the battle of Sentinum, Rome established its dominion over Etruria, and the subsequent rebellions of Volsinii and Falerii were unable to cast this off. The new order affected, above all, the middle classes, who lost their social cohesion and were reduced to poverty and expelled from the confiscated land, thus determining a drastic reduction in the demand for the ordinary bronzes that had been so widespread previously, while the aristocrats maintained their former privileged position, even taking advantage of it in order to get their lands back, possibly as favored tenants, and were protected by Rome against attempts to subvert the social system. It was for this limited group of landowners that the few refined products—more likely to be made of silver than of bronze—were produced, while the ordinary objects declined in quality and their execution became increasingly perfunctory, as may be seen in the series of mirrors engraved with figures of the *lase* or the Dioscuri.

Detail of a bronze round shield from Poggio del Roccolo at Settecamini (Porano), third quarter of the fourth century B.C.
Orvieto, Museo Archeologico
cat. 74

However, rather than the decline in quality of the artifacts, what counted was economic stagnation and the isolation of Etruria from the more dynamic regions of Roman Italy, especially Latium and Campania, so that there was resort to agriculture, which was anything but dynamic, and commercial initiative was abandoned. Economic innovations were only to be found in the coastal areas, where the Romans intervened directly—for example, at Populonia, where the traditional smelting of iron ore from Elba was reorganized to make use of slave labor, in the areas where colonies were founded, such as the *ager Cosanus*, and in crafts sectors in which Rome had a direct interest, such as the production of arms, defensive armor, and metal tools, which was concentrated in a few cities with a metallurgical tradition and assumed industrial characteristics. The production of arms was a traditional activity of the Etruscan bronze-workers, who were probably responsible for the development of the type of helmet known as "Gallic." In use from the fourth century B.C. onward, this became part of the equipment of the Roman legions and was made on a large scale in the third century B.C., a period in which, according to Livy's account of Scipio's African expedition in 205 B.C. (XXVIII, 45, 13–20), Arezzo dominated the production.

The belated appearance of middle classes in the northern areas (Volterra, Chiusi, Perugia) in the second century B.C., the result of a process that in the more advanced cities had taken place much earlier, did not substantially change the situation. It did, however, lead to the limited production of objects—almost exclusively for funerary use—for local consumption, very few of which were metal artifacts. The last traces of the ancient tradition of Etruscan bronzes regard the late production of simple vases for everyday use, bottles for

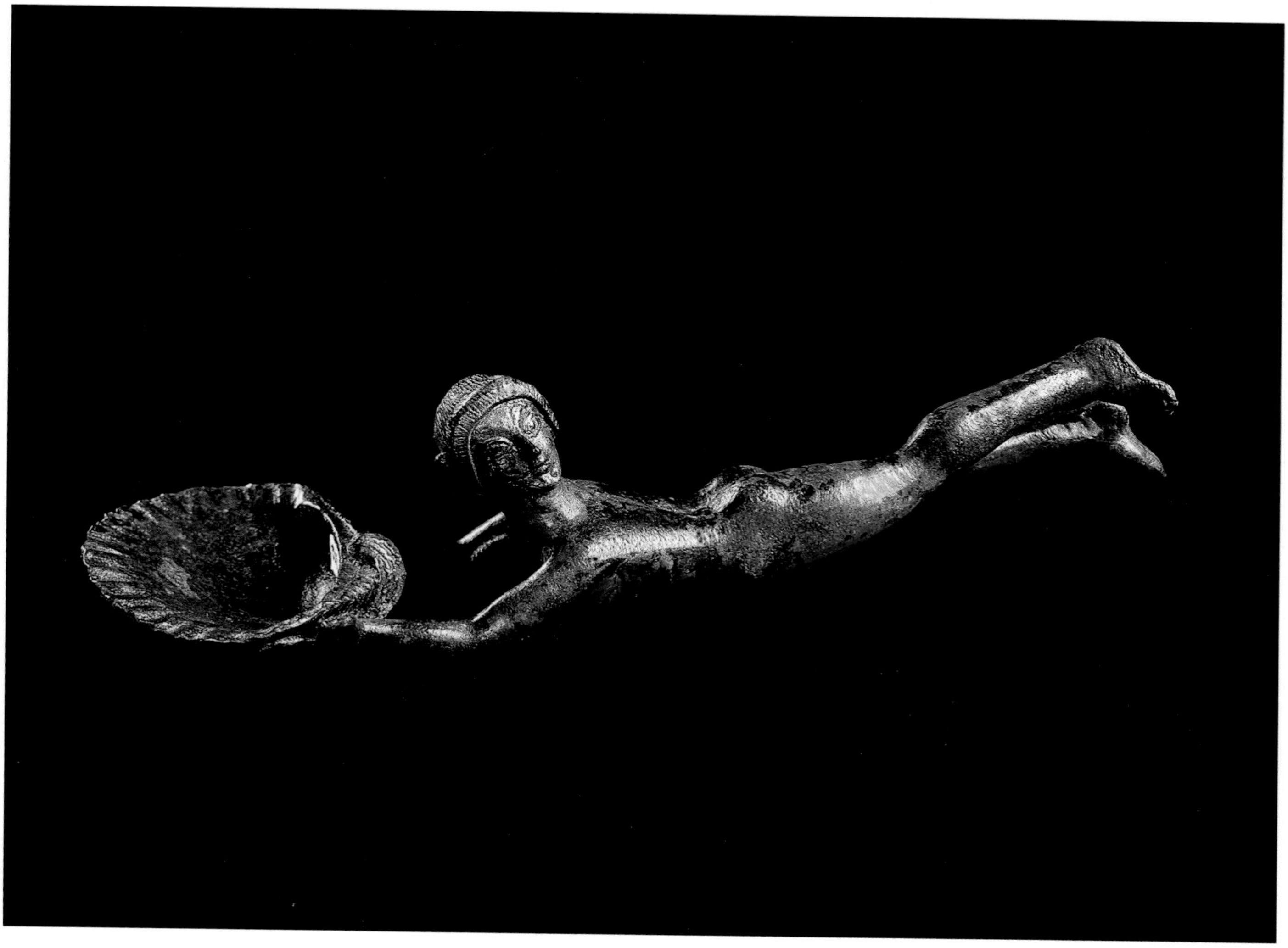

Bronze spoon from the Tomb of the Boncia (Chiusi), 480–470 B.C.
Florence, Museo Archeologico
cat. 86

perfumed oil, paterae, and other objects of this kind, which, in the second half of the second century B.C., were sent to the Picenum, Samnium, and Daunia, along trade routes that were already functioning in the Archaic period. These were, however, the last manifestations of an old commercial tradition before the production of Etruscan bronzes having recognizable characteristics finally came to an end as a result of the competition of Campanian workshops—especially at Pozzuoli and Capua—and the triumph of manufacture based on slave labor in the former Etruscan territory.
The Roman aristocrats of the early Empire had not, however, forgotten the excellence of *Tyrrhena sigilla*, Etruscan bronzes (Horace, *Epistulae*, II, 2, 180 ff.), partly as a result of a tendency to nostalgia and an interest in collecting works of art typical of the Augustan and Julio-Claudian ages, the most famous exponent of which was the "Etruscologist" emperor, Claudius.

Gerhard 1840–97; Riis 1938, p. 22 ff.; Neugebauer 1943, p. 206 ff.; Kunze 1951, pp. 736–46; Marunti 1959, pp. 65–77; Haynes 1965; Maxwell-Hyslop 1965, pp. 150–67; Johansen 1971; Hencken 1971; Bouloumié 1973; Hus 1975; Wells 1980, pp. 144–66; Herrmann 1984, pp. 271–91; Howes Smith 1984, pp. 73–107; Albanese Procelli 1985, pp. 179–206; Bouloumié 1985, pp. 167–78; Camporeale 1985a, pp. 21–36; Cianferoni 1985, p. 148; Cristofani 1985a, pp. 29 ff., 46, 80 ff., 146 ff., 234 ff., 341 ff.; Mangani 1985a, pp. 21–40; Mangani 1985b, pp. 166–67; Moustaka 1985, pp. 353–64; Torelli 1985b, pp. 7 ff., 13 ff., 34 ff., 102 ff., 131 ff., 179 ff., 228; Adam, Briquel, Gran-Aymerich et al. 1992, pp. 166–83; Aigner Foresti 1992b, pp. 120–53; Bottini, Tagliente 1994, pp. 487–528; De Juliis 1994, pp. 529–60; Mangani 1995, pp. 387–91, 422–30; Riis 1997.

Archaic Pottery: Impasto and Bucchero Wares

Manufacturing techniques

Impasto and bucchero are two characteristically Etruscan types of pottery whose production phases run almost in parallel (seventh–sixth century B.C.), and have certain features of design and manufacture in common.

Impasto is an amalgam of clay and chips ("inclusions") of tiny particles of mica and stone that vary in size (from less than one to several millimeters in diameter) and vary in density.In earlier production the medium itself (*impasto grezzo*) was coarse-grained, vessels were still made by hand, the firing was irregular, vessel walls were thick, and the hue could vary from gray to russet or brown; the clay's surface was either left rough or smooth, and the vessel was often finished off with a variety of applied ornament (knops, ribbing, etc.), or decorated with grooves, graffito, and occasionally applied metal strips. The earliest known pottery dates from prehistoric times and, as regards the Etruscan world, production was plentiful in the Final Bronze and Iron Ages (tenth–eighth century B.C.); the manufacture of domestic wares continued steadily through to the Romanization of Etruria. By the eighth century the clay used (*impasto depurato*) had ostensibly been purged of its main impurities, the inclusions were barely visible to the naked eye (or only through the microscope), and vessels were now made on the wheel (an innovation almost certainly brought to Etruria by Greek ceramists); vessel walls were meanwhile thinner and the techniques of firing the clay had been perfected. This second phase of manufacture complemented the first, and involved the production of both household and ceremonial wares. Whereas during the previous period most pottery had been fashioned at home by women, the introduction of the potter's wheel led to increasing specialization and the establishment of full-fledged pottery workshops.

Bucchero wares represent a more advanced stage of development: the clay used (*bucchero fine*) was smoother, the little chips or inclusions were of exceptionally fine grain, vessel were at this stage all turned on the wheel and their walls notably thinner; the firing was perfect, surfaces were smooth and shiny and often completed with graffito, incisions, or relief decoration; the finished color was black, both inside and out.Various explanations for the color of Etruscan pottery have been advanced over the years. Some have suggested that the readied pieces were put into a smoke-filled chamber prior to the final firing; others propose that the clay was mixed with powdered carbon or special black clay (a great rarity, found only in a small area between Arezzo, Chiusi, and Siena). Neither idea has proved to be tenable. A much more likely hypothesis, now universally accepted, is that the prepared pieces were placed in a reducing kiln to cause the production of iron oxide of a characteristic dark hue—a possibility corroborated by rejects from defective firing, in which the clay's original reddish tone has remained unaltered due to an insufficient reduction of oxygen in the kiln. On occasion the pieces are deliberately given an ash-gray finish, as with production from Roselle and Volsinii-Orvieto. Some exemplars dating from the seventh century B.C. are decorated with gold or silver plating, though few such cases have survived. In late-seventh- and early-sixth-century Etruscan production the vessel walls are noticeably thicker (*bucchero pesante*) and their surfaces duller with relief and plastic decoration. There is also another kind of ware, that is the so-called "impasto buccheroide," because it is comparable to bucchero for the fine-grained clay and dark finish surface, even if it doesn't achieve the latter's technical perfection. Impasto buccheroide wares are prior or contemporary with the bucchero ones.

Terminology

The term "impasto"—in use in Italy since the sixteenth century—refers to the material that results from mixing the aforementioned primary materials of clay and inclusions with water; the Italian term has entered the terminology of ceramics in other languages.

Bucchero is a hybrid Italianization of the Spanish *búcaro* or Portuguese *pocaro*, used in reference to a pungent, strongly colored matter (red, black or pallid) known in America and employed in the production of plasters (*pastiglie*) and vases. Vessels of this kind were imitated in Portugal in the seventeenth century and exported to Italy, where their popularity even occasioned a literary sub-genre, notable examples of which are either the *Lettere sopra i buccheri* by Lorenzo Magalotti, or the *Bucchereide* by Lorenzo Bellini, that is a trivial writing composed for the Florentine Accademia della Crusca meeting of September 13th, 1699. Owing to their striking resemblance to the shiny black *pocaro* pottery of Portuguese make,

Impasto lebes *with weeping figures and horse men from Valle Rodeta near Pitigliano (Grosseto), second half of the seventh century* B.C. *Florence, Museo Archeologico cat. 173*

the many vases that began to turn up during excavation work carried out on Etruscan soil—particularly in northern Etruria—from the fifteenth century onward were ascribed the collective term "bucchero." Like its complement, impasto, this term is also used internationally to describe wares fashioned with this technique.

Research evolution

The more or less random occurrence of archaeological evidence that turned up in the subsoil of Etruria from the fifteen century onward, were gradually collated and used as illustrations (drawn by hand) for the first tentative surveys of the Etruscan civilization, published in the eighteenth century. The earliest such comprehensive overview, edited by Filippo Buonarroti, was Thomas Dempster's *De Etruria regali*, published in Florence in 1723. Buonarroti's focus fell largely on the representational evidence which, as noted by himself, supplied "an enormous quantity of elements on Etruscan religion and customs, features that are missing from the descriptions of the ancient writers." He was referring to the yields of statues, bronzes, gems, coinage, steles, and urns, embellished with relief decorations, painted vases (actually Greek, but at the time thought to be Etruscan), tomb paintings, and mirrors with designs in graffito. Two of the illustrated plates of Dempster's volume show sets of bucchero vases, which suggests that conoisseurs of the period did not exclude this type of pottery from their collections, despite the latter rarely having decorative features that admitted hermeneutic analysis. Evidently the workmanship of such vessels was not held in much regard, as suggested by the episode recounted in the 1840s by G. Dennis while preparing his book *Cities and Cemeteries of Etruria*: during a visit to the necropolis at Vulci he witnessed the opening of a tomb that contained a fair quantity of bucchero wares; considered of scant material value, these were summarily smashed by the digging crew. When Dennis protested, the crew's foreman shrugged off the pieces as totally worthless. At any event, bucchero wares soon began to comprise the bulk of the collections being assembled in the mid-nineteenth century, for the most part unearthed in Etruscan tombs—witness the Louvre and Hermitage collections, formed from the dismemberment of the Campana collection early in the second half of the nineteenth century. In the catalogues compiled during this period for the major museums' collections of ceramics—like the L. Stephani's Hermitage (1869), the A. Furtwängler's Berlin Antiquarium (1885), and the E. Pottier's Louvre (1897, 1901, 1922) ones—bucchero wares were treated on a par with the painted Greek vases. An earlier ground-breaking appraisal was made by S. Gsell in his *Fouilles dans la nécropole de Vulci* (1891), which published the contextual data for the Vulcian necropolises then being excavated under the direction of the École Française in Rome. For once, the bucchero vases were not merely described but classified by type and shape, with an itemization of associated material uncovered in the same context, especially where these were Greek vases, thereby finally providing the necessary information for assigning dates to the wares found.

Further major advances in that field came with the publication of the Castellani collection by P. Mingazzini (1930), and Benedetto Guglielmi collection by F. Magi (1940). In both cases the bucchero vessels were compared with their Greek counterparts in terms of shape and decoration, and an effort was made at establishing their chronology. As excavations progressed, a clearer map of production centers began to emerge according to context and to technical specifics of manufacture, shape, and decoration. On this basis, bucchero wares decorated with relief friezes impressed with a roller were sorted and assigned to separate centers of production: Chiusi (Scalia 1968); Volsinii-Orvieto (Camporeale 1972a); and Tarquinia (Camporeale 1972b). Other vital contributions are those of N. Hirschland Ramage (1970) and T.B. Rasmussen (1979). By associating data by context and vase typology, they shed new light on the diffusion of types through the Etruscan heartland, and concluded that production originated in the second quarter of the seventh century B.C. from the workshops of Caere (Cerveteri), and subsequently spread to other centers in southern Etruria (Veio, Tarquinia) and then northward. Today there is general consensus regarding the existence of workshops specializing in bucchero wares in various regions of Italy, formed either under the direct influence of models or set up by itinerant master potters from Etruria. The literature produced in the last few decades on this subject is considerable, and largely focuses on the importance of bucchero as a means of reconstructing the socioeconomic framework of Etruria.

Impasto bull-shaped askos *from Poggio Selciatello di Sopra (Tarquinia), second half of the ninth century* B.C.
Florence, Museo Archeologico
cat. 9.5

Impasto knobbed-bell helmet from Poggio Selciatello di Sopra (Tarquinia), second half of the ninth century B.C.
Florence, Museo Archeologico
cat. 9.2

Usage

Most of the wares fashioned in impasto and bucchero were used in the kitchen or as tablewares, for storing foodstuffs, for ceremonies, or for body care (unguents, oils). Other varied items in the same material, such as braziers, kitchenware, stands, lamps, and candleholders were part of the equipment for general daily use in the household. Before proceeding further, however, we should note that for centuries archaeological exploration in Etruria focused on necropolises and sanctuaries; it is only in recent years that this research has begun to include dwellings and urban structures, and at any event in limited areas due to the high costs involved. As a consequence, our present knowledge of finds, including impasto and bucchero wares, are restricted to specific sectors. Some vases, typically the biconical Villanovan type, appear to have been used exclusively in funerary contexts to contain the ashes of the person cremated; those equipped with a single handle were clearly of no practical utility; those with two, which may have had some daily use, had one handle broken before their deposition in the tomb. The frequent signs of repair to vessels found among the grave goods would suggest that many—or most—were previously used for everyday practical purposes. Furthermore, excavations in inhabited areas have disclosed wares similar to those found in the tombs, though for obvious reasons all in fragments. Domestic finds also apply to bucchero, which was previously long thought to be exclusive to funerary functions. The use of such vessels depends of course on their shape and size.

Impasto wares

In addition to the aforementioned biconical cinerary urns, the most common impasto wares produced from the tenth to eighth centuries B.C. were hut-urns, bowls, cups, plats, jugs, ollas, and animal *askoi*, all of which were created for use in banqueting and symposiums, and therefore each one freighted with a specific ideological significance. The decoration, usually scored into the surface with a comb-like tool, comprises such geometric devices as stippling, horizontal or wavy lines, corners, squares, lozenges, swastikas, meanders, and so forth. The only narrative features are the very common heraldic arrangement of schematic figures seated facing each other at the top of the handles of the biconical vases, probably enacting a scene of farewell. On bronzework for this same period—razors, sword sheaths, wheeled incense-burners, cinerary urns, whether in graffito or in the round—the rare narrative scenes that occur have an undeniable ideological function, such as the "sun boat," hunting, plowing, duels, aristocratic gatherings. As one might imagine, being designed for funerary purposes, the so-called biconi-

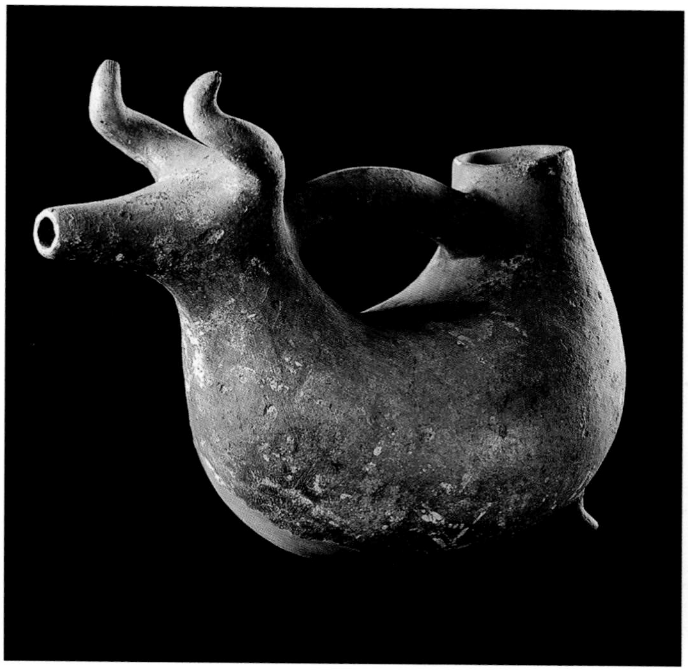

cal vases have an appropriate figurative decoration, while the bronze pieces, even where occurring in a burial context, appear to have been among the deceased's belongings prior to entombment, and were therefore presumably status symbols. Though rare, the molded decorations to the impasto vessels are limited to animal heads, mainly rams and bulls, applied to the handles or included in the mouths of the *askoi*. Exceptions to this rule are the human figure on the door of a hut-urn, perhaps from Bisenzio, probably representing the deceased or an ancestor positioned at a threshold (as a guard?); and two embracing figures on the lid of a cinerary urn from Chiusi, once again presumably engaged in farewell. Indeed, such urns for burial invariably have decoration relating to funeral rites. To complete the picture it is worth noting the practice of adding surface relief by applying strands around the vessel to form ridges, sometimes in place of graffito; or impressing the surface with designs (geometrical motifs, swastikas, rosettes, etc.). Both techniques came into use in the eighth century B.C. and survived into the next. The closing decades of the eighth century saw the introduction of narrative scenes to impasto pottery, examples of which are the stylized horse-tamers (*despotes hippon*) or images of horses feeding, as seen on the border of cups with a tall stem from Narce in the Faliscan district; such imagery suggests the vases were made for a wealthy patron. The same period witnessed an evolution of form, continuing through the seventh century B.C., that engendered the vessel on a conical stand, probably developed by induction from production originating in Latium and filtering through the Faliscan-Capenate area and to other workshops in southern Etruria; and other drinking vessels such as goblets and *kantharoi*. Deserving a special mention is the spiral amphora, so-called for its spiral decoration on both sides, a vase that would be repeated into metalwork and in widespread application into bucchero wares until the mid-sixth century B.C. As stated above, the Etruscan potteries continued producing impasto wares

Lid of impasto cinerary urn featuring a farwell, eighth century B.C., from Chiusi.
Chiusi, Museo Archeologico

Impasto pitcher with double horse protomes neck from the Falerii area, second half of the seventh century B.C.
Tübingen, Institut für Klassische Archäologie

through into the seventh century and beyond, overlapping with the production of bucchero. Consequently, as many vase forms of both types were produced in parallel, what has been said for impasto largely applies to bucchero also. Where bucchero production is absent or poor, for instance in Chiusi or in the Faliscan-Capenate area during the seventh century, impasto wares become more refined. Engraved friezes depicting animals or narrative motifs, which usually decorated seventh-century bucchero wares produced in Veio and Caere, recur in Falisco-Capenas impasto wares as well. Certain impasto vases styled on metalwork from the Near East recur in specific areas alone, notably the ribbed bowls and the large *lebetes* with griffin protomes; unearthed in centers dotted across the Faliscan district and almost certainly produced in local workshops, these types derive from Syrian imports to Etruria. Due most likely to their daily use such in cooking or storage, other vase types were made in impasto rather than bucchero, and this category are the small ollas, made for storing salt or substances like honey or fat.

Bucchero wares

The earliest known tomb that has yielded bucchero wares is Tomb 2 of Casaletti di Ceri, near Caere. On the basis of the contextual associations of the material discovered (the grave goods include a *kotyle* and various proto-Corinthian *skyphoi* with black glazed ground; a Rhodian-Cretan *aryballos*; a globular *aryballos* of the early proto-Corinthian type; a Subgeometric *oinochoe* of Cumaean manufacture), the tomb has been tenably dated around the second quarter of the seventh century B.C. The vases include a *situla*, a cup, a spiral amphora, which, together with others in the aforementioned proto-Corinthian style and local impasto artifacts (goblets, cups, plates, *oinochoai*, ollas)—all part of a service for use in banqueting and symposium ritual. Vases of similar shape, or to put to the same use, become common in the grave goods of Caere around the mid-seventh century (Regolini-Galassi Tomb, Tomb 4 of Monte Abatone, among others). The bucchero vases among these tomb-groups are slightly greater

Bucchero amphora with spiral decoration from Tomb 2 at Casaletti di Ceri, second quarter of the seventh century B.C. Cerveteri, Museo Cerite

Bucchero kotyle *from Cerveteri, mid-seventh century* B.C.
Rome, Museo di Villa Giulia

in number than the Greek vases, and less than samples of local production. This seems to suggest that bucchero wares were particularly appreciated for their elegance of form as their shiny surface, decorative workmanship and more delicate fabric.

While bucchero may be considered a sort of emulation of metal prototypes, its resemblance is not limited merely to the outward aspects mentioned above. Other comparable features are the crisp outline, the ribbed body, the long handles with bosses reminiscent to riveting. Although bucchero pottery may bear a striking resemblance to certain metal vessel types, cases of direct borrowing are nonetheless rare; for instance the bucchero *oinochoe* styled on Cypriot- or on Rhodian-type metalwork. On this point it is useful to discuss each type in turn.

While certain bucchero wares are styled on the local impasto forms established in the later eighth century, they generally evince greater evolution and refinement than their impasto counterparts. Take, for instance, the so-called spiral amphoras: the impasto specimens dating from the eighth century vary in height from 9 to 15 centimeters, the body is wider than it is tall, the neck very short, the coils are scarce; those dating to the early seventh century are less stout and have more coils; the bucchero spiral amphoras of the second and third quarters of the seventh century have affinities with their impasto contemporary equivalents, being taller than wide, a narrow neck, and densely coiled spirals with vertical striations over the entire body; those in the last decades of the seventh and early sixth centuries are more elongated, their decoration distributed in horizontal bands, and the foot forming an inverted echinus; those from the second quarter of the sixth century exemplify the so-called Nikosthenic type, with its characteristic ring round the body delimited by two strips. A silver replica from the Regolini-Galassi Tomb (Caere) dates to no earlier than the second quarter of the seventh century, which suggests it merely reproduces a model that had already been established for several decades.

Similar arguments apply to other vase types: for instance, the *kantharos*, the goblet and the jug; all have precedents in eighth-century impasto production, and enjoyed wide popularity in their

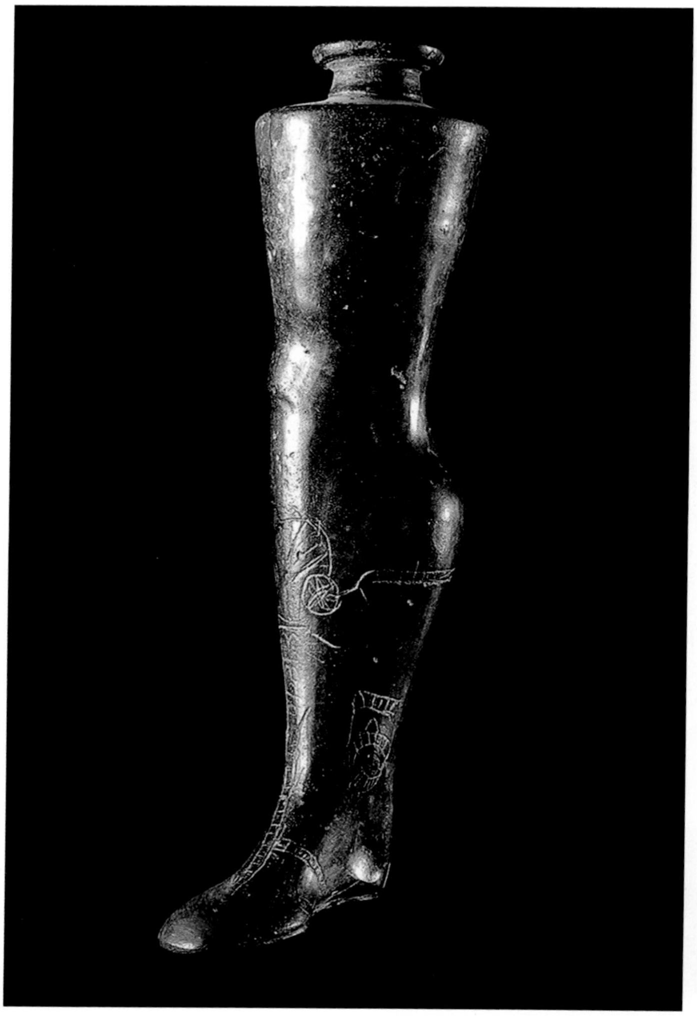

Bucchero leg-shaped balsam from Tarquinia, first half of the seventh century B.C.
Tarquinia, Museo Archeologico

Bucchero zoomorphic oinochoe, *first half of the sixth century* B.C.
Florence, Museo Archeologico
cat. 242

bucchero versions through the seventh and sixth centuries. The first two evolved in parallel: the foot, originally low and annular, gradually elongated into a trumpet shape, the bowl yielded its curviness to a more rigid and oblique outline; the base and attachment of the lip went from plain to decorated with ribbing and impressed diamond patterns. All three forms have their acknowledged versions in metal—the silver *kantharos* from Camiro and two bronze ones respectively from Lozzo Atestino and Ascoli Piceno; two couples of bronze goblets from two tombs at Castro and Casaglia; three goblets on figured supports from Caere; three jugs from Narce—in each case the artifact is of later date than its impasto or bucchero counterpart, and once again probably a replica in a more expensive material of an established ceramic product. Elegant and highly original are the set of globular *oinochoai* with twin horse-protome necks (the only exemplar that has survived virtually intact is the guttus from the Calabresi Tomb at Caere) and several cups with spouts terminating in animal protomes that served for sipping special liquids (perhaps during certain rituals), both these Caeretan wares had forerunners in impasto production from the Faliscan-Capenate district.

Among the fine bucchero (*sottile*) vases produced during the mid-seventh century B.C. in Caere are the *pyxides* decorated with applied animal protomes, the cylindrical *situlae* with animal friezes either engraved or in relief in horizontal bands (see silver replicas from the Regolini-Galassi Tomb at Caere and from the Castellani Tomb at Praeneste-Palestrina), and a group of *kotylai*, *kantharoi* and *kyathoi* with decorated relief or incized friezes of hunting or animal scenes, these too in many cases indebted to metalwork: the heraldic lion patterns that appear on the inside of the *kyathoi* bowls derive from their bronze counterparts—also found at Caere. Moreover, bucchero wares of this class were exported outside the district to Chiusi, Roselle,

Bucchero kantharos *with "cilindretto" frieze, first half of the sixth century* B.C. *Florence, Museo Archeologico cat. 243*

Vetulonia, and Monteriggioni—perhaps even to Populonia, where they became standard production; it is likely that a Caeretan potter moved to Populonia and set up a workshop. A similar movement of potters may explain the presence of certain types of vase (*kantharos*, ollas with pierced tenons) in Massa Marittima, items with no prior models of local manufacture, and yet in wide circulation in Caere. This is an important factor for understanding phenomena of social mobility and integration. Several other vase types prevalent among early bucchero production instead took their cue from external sources, such as Near-Eastern, Corinthian, and Ionic imports. One such type—the small elongated *oinochoai* with conical neck, low disc or annular foot, and rod- or strip-handle—draws directly from silverware of Cypriot or Syrian origin found in the princely tombs of the second and third quarter of the seventh century B.C. (Regolini-Galassi, Bernardini and Barberini at Praeneste, Tomb 104 of the "Fondo Artiaco" at Cumae, Tomb 928 at Pontecagnano, the Tomb of the Duce at Vetulonia. The later replicas have protracted curved necks and ovaloid bodies, the handle is uppermost; such evolution heralds a shift in emphasis from metal prototypes toward a ceramic art in its own right. Meanwhile Syro-Phoenician silverware seems to have inspired a certain kind of Caeretan bowl trimmed with small human heads, of which only two specimens are known (Villa Giulia, Rome; Sammlung Archäologisches Institut, Zurich), suggesting that local potters were familiar with such products from the Near East. Owing to intensive trade with Corinth from the early seventh century B.C. onward, Corinthian vase types were soon adopted for bucchero production, primarily for the entire range of items used in the symposium drinking ritual, which included cups, *skyphoi*, *kotylai*, *olpai*, and the small elongated *oinochoai* with cylindrical neck, these last often unearthed in close association with specimens of their Corinthian counterparts. By the same token, bucchero imitations often emulated the painted designs on the originals; being an incised decoration, however, the effect was sometimes quite different: in the case of the so-called tall *kotyle*, in the Corinthian originals—with their sunburst decoration on the base, horizontal stripes running around the body and vertical nicks around the rim—the pattern harmonizes with the shapes, whereas on the early bucchero versions the vertical grooves on the rim become

little fan-shaped patterns; while from ca. 650 B.C. on the fan patterns overrun the horizontal lines, causing a loss of harmony between shape and decoration. Whereas the cups, *skyphos* and *kotyle* had their counterparts in silver and gold—produced after the appearance of imported Corinthian models and of their bucchero versions—we can note that some silver *kotylai* carry the dotted fan pattern characteristic of seventh-century bucchero, used here to decorate the space between the handles (e.g. the specimen from the Circolo degli Avori, Marsiliana d'Albegna), or on the strip dividing the friezes (Tomb of the Duce, Vetulonia). Moreover, the original Corinthian types are repeated in local production of impasto and clay wares. One can therefore logically surmise that the drinking ritual of the symposium—which involved the consumption of wine imported to Etruria from either Corinth or other areas of Greece and therefore through the same channels as the symposium "kit" itself—was sufficiently widespread in Etruria to prompt local potteries to start catering to the growing demand; that demand was furthermore catalyzed by the start of wine production in Etruria itself in the eighth century B.C., probably introduced by Euboean vine-growers. Other regular types of Corinthian make imported to Etruria throughout the seventh and earlier sixth century B.C. include several classes of oil flasks and jars, such as *aryballoi* (spheroid, ovoid, elongated, globular), *alabastra*, and *pyxides*. Reaching Etruria principally through the trade of their contents of perfumed oils, balsams, and cosmetics, these particular container types were subsequently copied in terracotta, glass, and in bucchero, though in limited quantities; this indigenous production suggests the local manufacture of perfumes, implying by extension the possession of the proper ingredients for concocting aromatic distillations, such as oil and vinegar, together with the requisite herbs and essences. It is noteworthy, moreover, that the fashion for cosmetics reached Etruria from Corinth (through its relative imports) in the seventh century B.C., and soon became a common luxury fostered by the flourishing economy during the period. After Corinth, Ionia was another source of imported symposium and toiletry wares in the seventh century, once more reaching Etruria through the trade of the vessels' contents: bird-cups, painted lines below the rim cups, Rhodian-type *oinochoai*, *aryballoi* of Rhodian-Cretan type, tapered and plastic balsams; both the cups and Rhodian *oinochoai*—the latter made of bronze—entered the local repertoire of bucchero and pottery production. Also the plastic perfume-flasks were imitated in the bucchero production, a fine specimen of which in the museum in Tarquinia features a human leg. The decoration of the earliest bucchero wares offers further insights into the development of the potter's art: besides the aforementioned fan-shaped patterns, recurring spirals, striations, and impressed designs, we also find some fascinating friezes obtained through incision representing files of animals, both real and imaginary, sometimes also in descriptive scenes (boxing, hunting); such designs evolve along similar lines to the vase-painting on coeval Etruscan production. In each case, the animal imagery shifts from the Phoenician or Cycladic repertoire, to the Corinthian or Ionic, or even to iconography of local inspiration; for this reason, the frieze decorations allow an assessment of the state of the art as it is beginning to establish its identity. The narrative scenes meanwhile shed light on the substance and puissance of their future owners. While Caere is credited with being both the source and the seedbed of bucchero's early development, by the second half of the seventh century production had burgeoned in other centers across southern Etruria (Veio, Tarquinia, Vulci) and Campania (Capua, Pontecagnano). Wherever they were produced, however, the workmanship, shapes, and decorative patterns or figures on the vases betray undeniable links with Caere, and strongly suggest not only the circulation of Caeretan products, but the migration of practiced craftsmen from Caere to address the thriving demand for a product that had become increasingly popular all over Etruria. To summarize the cardinal points of development in the seventh century: bucchero production borrows alternately from indigenous and outside styles for both metal and ceramic wares, occasionally blending the two in a single work; the shape and decoration of bucchero vases are influenced by both local and outside sources, from the Near East and the Hellenic world, adapting these in reference to the current stage of development of Etruscan art; the metal equivalents of bucchero wares (except for the Cypriot and Rhodian *oinochoai*) are posterior replicas fashioned from more expensive material for a wealthy clientele; bucchero wares in general can be considered a luxury item, given that such vases are associable with elite customs such as the symposium or body care, and because they carry inscriptions declaring their ownership, or the

Bucchero kyathos *with "cilindretto" frieze, first quarter of the sixth century* B.C.
Florence, Museo Archeologico
cat. 237

Bucchero drinking glass with "cilindretto" frieze and bull heads, first half of the sixth century B.C.
Florence, Museo Archeologico
cat. 244

name of the donor (effectively, the same thing) or even that of the craftsman. The end of the seventh century and early sixth witnessed the mass exportation of bucchero wares from the production centers of southern Etruria, spreading through the peninsula, but also across to central Europe, to Provence, Languedoc and Catalonia; to southern Iberia, also beyond the Straits of Gibraltar; to ancient Carthage and Utica on the north African coast; to Corsica, Sardinia, and Sicily; to Vis on the Dalmatian coast; to Corfu, Ithaca, Amyclae, Corinth, Perachora, Athens and the Aegean Islands (Delos, Naxos, Chios, Samos, Rhodes); to Naucratis and as far as Ras el-Bassit at the mouth of the Orontes. Such wares served as dippers and pitchers for drinking purposes, especially the *kantharoi*. Distribution varied considerably: in the countries around the western Mediterranean basin the distribution of bucchero is extensive (thousands have been uncovered) and occurs both in dwellings and in funerary contexts and are often found in association with amphoras for transporting wine. Put simply, the diffusion of bucchero vases was intimately linked to wine in all its aspects: to its transportation, to the ritual drinking parties (*symposia*) during which it was consumed in quantity, and not least to the ideological significance attributed to it by the Etruscan aristocracy. Sites around the eastern coast of the Mediterranean have yielded few specimens of bucchero, and these occurred in sacred areas and tombs; the importance placed on such wares in their places of destination is affirmed by a *kantharos* discovered at the sanctuary in Perachora bearing an inscription in Greek (*Near[chos an]etheke*, meaning "Nearchus offered [me]"). Furthermore, a dozen or so (fragments of) bucchero *kantharoi* were unearthed in the so-called "trader's complex," a warehouse situated on the road leading from Corinth to its seaport Lechaion, together with vases from Chios, Rhodes, and Corinth itself, proving that Etruscan bucchero wares were traded internationally and, once they reached their destination were available for purchase by local people for votive use. From the end of the seventh century to well into the sixth bucchero production spread to various sites in Etruria. Decoration was generally applied on the surface while the clay was still soft, that is, after it had been exposed to the air, but before firing. Such process was carried on in some ways like rolling a small cylinder with designs recessed in intaglio on the soft clay, applying decorative inclusions on the outer surface, pressing the vase wall from the inside against a mold, and finally impressing a die directly onto the surface. The repertoire of patterns comprised animal and plant motifs, human heads, and narrative scenes (particularly the friezes impressed with a cylinder). Several distinct production units have been identified on the basis of the various designs of the dies, applied heads, and frieze figures: Roselle, Vulci, Poggio Buco, Volsinii-Orvieto, and Chiusi. In nearly all cases the vases produced were made for symposium use. Now and then a bronze equivalent has turned up, as in the case of the *infundibula* (funnel-strainers), or the

Bucchero chalice with "cilindretto" frieze, first half of the sixth century B.C.
Florence, Museo Archeologico
cat. 238

squat or tapered *oinochoai*, but here again, metal versions are merely replicas in more precious material of established everyday vase forms. During this phase of development, vessels increased in size and their decoration was likewise emphasized, sometimes making the vessel less practical—witness the goblets produced around Vulci, Volsinii-Orvieto, and Chiusi, in which the vessel wall is either undulating or its rim even crested, making it awkward to drink from. The target of these wares was the new middle class, which had emerged from the socioeconomic system in Etruria with the advent of the new town-based society that gradually came into being in the later seventh and early sixth centuries. Curiously, while the cylinder-frieze patterns for certain wares produced in Chiusi show scenes of gift-bearing to enthroned dignitaries, perhaps denoting their use by an aristocratic class, the large number of identical specimens suggests a more "democratic" use of this kind of vessel, perhaps by a larger middle class that had subsumed the ways and manners of its superiors. The so-called "heavy" bucchero of the sixth century was produced more or less in the same areas. Exports decreased sharply, though not beyond a radius of several dozen miles from the centers of production: cases of wares that traveled short distances include a goblet and two jugs with cylinder-impressed decoration from Tarquinia uncovered in Vulci; vases with cylinder decoration from Volsinii-Orvieto found in the Fiora Valley (Sovana, Poggio Buco, Pitigliano, Grotte di Castro) and Albegna Valley (Saturnia); two braziers made in Chiusi found in Roselle and Florence respectively. Conversely, sixth-century bucchero shapes were resumed by both Etruscan and Attic black-figure and red-figure pottery (trumpet-stem goblets from Vulci; braziers from Chiusi). Such Attic vessels were

Bucchero amphora with "cilindretto" frieze, mid-seventh century B.C.
Florence, Museo Archeologico
cat. 240

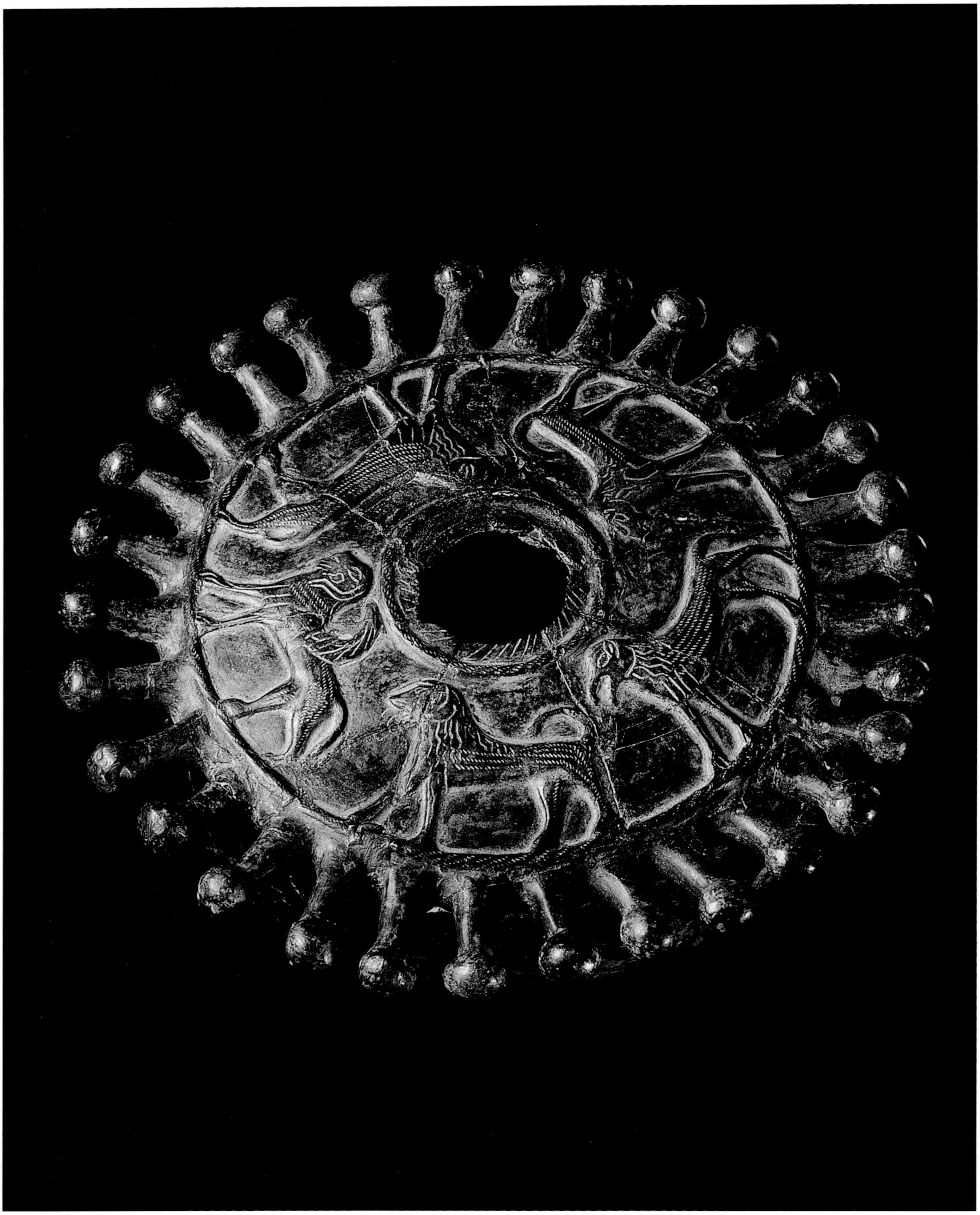

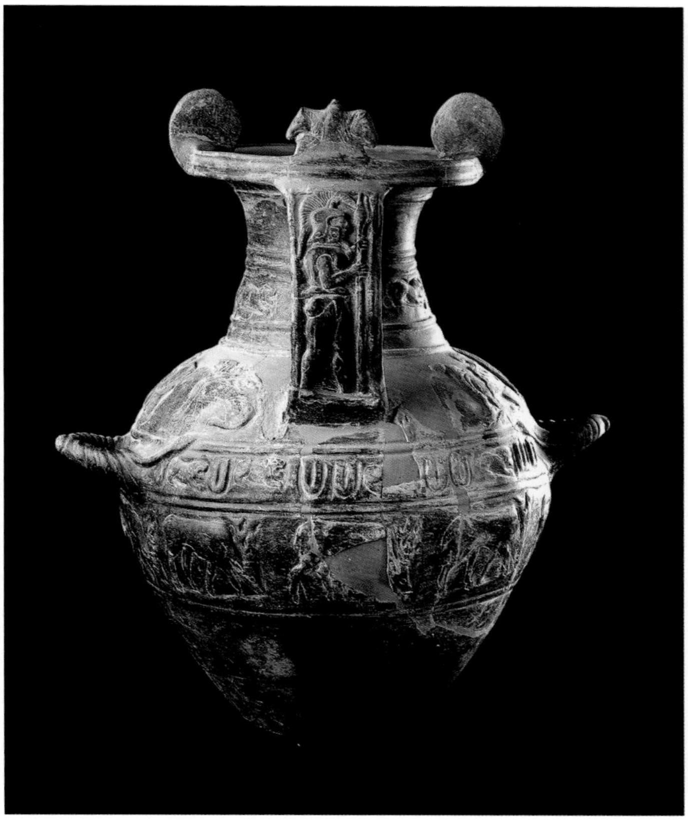

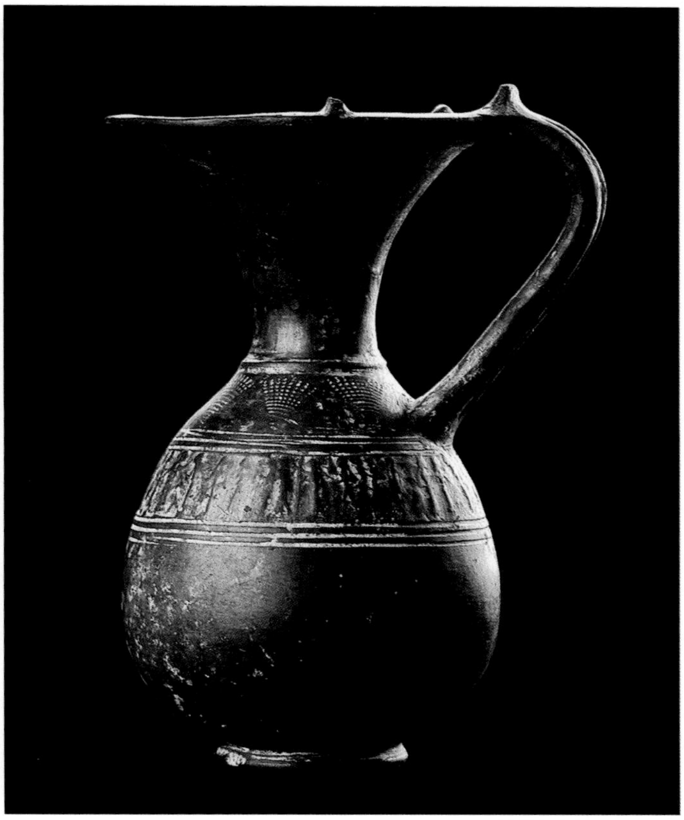

opposite
Bucchero lid of pyxis *from Cerveteri, mid-seventh century* B.C.
Roma, Museo di Villa Giulia
cat. 235

above
Bucchero hydria *with "cilindretto" frieze, first half of the sixth century* B.C.
Florence, Museo Archeologico
cat. 236

Bucchero olpe *with "cilindretto" frieze, mid-sixth century* B.C.
Florence, Museo Archeologico
cat. 239

made for exportation to Etruria: amphoras crafted by the potter Nikosthenes; conical *kyathoi*, long strip-handle *kantharoi*; semi-cylindrical vase stands; and stamnoi. Their affirmation in the Attic workshops was prompted by a surge in demand, and by the popularity their bucchero equivalents had enjoyed in Etruria. Throughout the sixth century, other regions of Italy—Liguria, Picenum, Campania, Samnium, and Lucania—produced their own bucchero in parallel with Etruria. However, differences can be detected in the quality of the clay, the uneven black finish, and the variations or innovations of the shapes. The products of manufacturing centers in Campania (Pompeii, Vico Equense, Nocera, Capua and Pontecagnano) were the ones with the closest resemblance to their Etruscan counterparts. Some strayed from the canon, however, such as the squat goblets with trumpet or ring foot and handles attached horizontally to the bowl; or the *situla* with a fixed handle and heart-shaped body. The activity of the potters who migrated to Campania in the second half of the seventh century B.C., continued through into the sixth century. Campanian bucchero production—particularly those of Capua—were exported to southern Italy in various directions, including Samnium (Alfedena, Pozzilli); the Frente area (Termoli, Larino); Daunia (Arpi, San Severo); various sites in the Vallo di Diano, Ofanto Valley, through ancient Lucania and down as far as Tarentum. Around the end of the sixth century bucchero production petered out; in Campania it was superseded by a form of black glazed ceramics of both Attic and local origin, while Etruria itself saw the arrival of the *bucchero grigio*, a gray impasto that would endure for several centuries.

Mingazzini 1930; Magi 1940; Poupé 1963, pp. 227 ff.; Hiller 1966, pp. 16 ff.; Donati 1967, pp. 619 ff.; Donati 1968, pp. 319 ff.; Donati 1969, pp. 443 ff.; Hirschland Ramage 1970, pp. 12 ff.; Camporeale 1972a; Camporeale 1972b, pp. 115 ff.; Cristofani Martelli, Cristofani, Bonamici 1972, pp. 75 ff.; Gran Aymerich 1972, pp. 7 ff.; Camporeale 1973–74, pp. 103 ff.; Gran Aymerich 1973, pp. 217 ff.; Verzár 1973, pp. 45 ff.; Bonamici 1974; Macintosh 1974, pp. 34 ff.; Paribeni 1974, pp. 131 ff.; Capecchi, Gunnella 1975, pp. 33 ff.; Isler Kerényi 1976, pp. 33 ff.; Donati 1977, pp. 85 ff.; Beijer 1978, pp. 7 ff.; *Le "bucchero nero" et sa diffusion* 1979; Rasmussen 1979; Colonna 1982, pp. 33 ff.; Gran Aymerich 1982; Regter 1988, pp. 486 ff.; Bruni 1989a, pp. 121 ff.; Hase 1989, pp. 327 ff.; Camporeale 1991; Donati 1991, pp. 82 ff.; Gran Aymerich 1992; Bonghi Jovino 1993; Camporeale 1995, pp. 69 ff.; Gilotta 1997, pp. 113 ff.; Minoja 2000.

Françoise Gaultier

Painted Pottery of the Archaic Period

It should be remembered at the outset that interest in Etruscan painted pottery was initially founded on a persistent eighteenth century misconception with regard to Etruria, namely that the vast numbers of ancient red- and black-figure vases then being unearthed in Italy were of Etruscan manufacture. In reality, the majority of such vases were Greek. Nonetheless, supported by such apologists for the superiority of the arts in ancient Tuscany as Passeri (*Picturae Etruscorum in Vasculis*, Rome 1767) and Piranesi (*Ragionamento apologetico in difesa dell'architettura egizia e toscana*, Rome 1769), the misunderstanding was the catalyst for a veritable bout of "Etruscomania" throughout Europe, and a lasting craze for decoration in the Etruscan style. Despite being contested by Pierre-François Hughes d'Hancarville (*Antiquités étrusques, grecques et romaines...*, Neaples 1766–67) and Luigi Lanzi (*Dissertazione de' vasi antichi dipinti volgarmente chiamati etruschi,* Rome 1806) and then finally exposed by Eduard Gerhard ("Rapporto intorno i Vasi Volcenti" in *Annali dell'Istituto di Corrispondenza archeologica*, 1831) after studying the thousands of vases found at Vulci in the 1820s by Luciano Bonaparte, the misconception—deliberately sustained by patriotic interests—lived on outside academic circles for some time. It continued to serve as an example for the entry "Etruscan" in the *Dictionnaire des Idées reçues* compiled by Flaubert after 1850 and published shortly after his death in 1880.

Set aside by the victorious notion of Greek pottery finds in Italy, Etruscan painted pottery was almost ignored by the first two major comprehensive studies of Etruscan art, those of J. Martha in France (*L'art étrusque*, Paris 1889) and of P. Ducati in Italy (*Storia dell'arte etrusca*, Florence 1927).The following observations by Martha on the various types of painted pottery found in Etruria (pp. 478 ff.) will serve to show the attitudes then prevailing with regard to this area of ancient pottery: "Black pottery [the name then given to bucchero ware] is entirely Etrurian in origin... Painted vases are Greek and belong to the history of Hellenic art... they are certainly Greek works [...], whether made in Greece or originating [...] from Greek workshops established in Etruria. The other kind appear mere imitations [...]. Since pottery of the kind was much sought after in Italy and doubtless fetched high prices, the same thing happened as always in such circumstances: fakes came on the market [...]. Such temptation is irresistible to any people in any era. The Etruscans were all the less likely to resist, given that fakes—or imitations, if one prefers—had been characteristic of their craft industries for centuries. They were quick to attempt painted decorations on vases, copying the models imported by traders, but their efforts were unimpressive [...] and I doubt that they ever succeeded in producing artifacts which could be compared even with the feeblest creations of Greek potters."

With such ideas in circulation, it is easy to see why Etruscan vases attracted very little interest, as also why the more attractive pieces were often initially attributed to Greek potters and why, more recently, false Greek vases could be identified as Etruscan. Current terminology still bears the signs of past confusions, since the expression Pontic vases designates a category of Etruscan black-figure vases once attributed to Pontus Euxinus workshops on the basis of the Scythian archers they depict, while certain recent monographic or comprehensive studies exclude vases such as the Caere *hydriai* from the history of Etruscan ceramics, thus revealing an approach which in my view is still over-influenced by the Greek focus.

Early attempts at classification were often encouraged by the process of compiling the catalogues of major museums. Only in the 1930s and 40s did a few pioneers such as Åkerström, Payne, Beazley, Dohrn, Blakeway lay the foundations for pottery studies and define the goals for modern scholarship: identification of schools, workshops, individual craftsmen, and understanding of the relations between them, not with the sterile objective of classification and the blinkered vision of an art historian—as the partisans of New Archaeology could rightly complain until not so many years ago—but because such an approach was the condition *sine qua non* for using pottery as a historical record.

The method of attributing painted vases used with such well-known and happy results by John Beazley is still valid for us today: developed by Giovanni Morelli in the second half of the nineteenth century studying Italian picture, later taken up again and made more systematic by Bernard Berenson, the method is based on the identification of motifs which recur in the work of a painter and can thus be taken as characteristic of his hand. These "signature motifs" are defined by both formal and technical examination: the analysis of a draw-

Amsterdam Painter, terra-cotta amphora, 660–640 B.C.
Amsterdam, Allard Pierson Museum cat. 211

ing, like that of handwriting, must take into account at one and the same time both the form and how it is traced, the pressure exerted by the hand on the brush or point, its assured or hesitant strokes, its pauses...

The rigorously exact and prudent application of these methods of attribution—which must also pay attention to secondary decoration, the shape of the vase and the idiosyncrasies of the potter—is the foundation of our knowledge of an art and craft which is not only one of the best represented in terms of materials and distribution but also, by reason of its figurative decoration, everyday use and constant evolution, undoubtedly the surest guide to the development of Etruscan art and civilization and to the essential ties which these had with Greece.

The adoption of painted pottery in Etruria towards the mid-eighth century B.C. is in itself emblematic of the impact of Greek colonization in the West.

Before that date pottery made in Etruria was hand-crafted on a household scale in coarse-grained clay (impasto), decorated with simple incised or stamped geometric motifs. The very rare painted vases are only isolated examples, perhaps explained by the very early links established between Etruria and southern Italy, where painted pottery flourished at an early date.

Etrusco-Geometric pottery

Painted pottery only established a genuine presence in Etruria with the imitation of Greek Geometric pottery, which was imported into Italy from the close of the ninth century B.C. even before the foundation of the first Greek settlements in the West. The label Etrusco-Geometric is thus applied to the first Etruscan pottery with painted decorations.

The first Greek Geometric pottery imported into Etruria took the shape of cups with decorations of pendent semi-circles, chevrons or a silhouette of a bird enclosed within metope borders. Of various origins, but mostly of Euboean or Cycladic manufacture, the greater part of such finds were made at Tarquinia or Veii, cities which, sited respectively on the coast and a ford of the Tiber, controlled much of the trade between Etruria and southern Italy in the first half of the eighth century.

Contacts between the two regions were intensified when the Euboeans, rivals to the Phoenicians for domination of the Mediterranean trade routes and already present on the coast of Syria, were attracted westward by the mineral wealth of central Italy and settled in Campania, initially at Pithekoussai around 770 B.C. and later in Cumae around 550 B.C.

It is thus clear that immigrant Greek craftsmen were behind the first Etruscan workshops producing fine painted pottery. Sometimes their work can be distinguished from imported ware by the use of a local clay, as well as their personal style can be told by the application, to a Villanovan shape, of decorations which attest to firsthand knowledge and perfect mastery of Greek Geometric designs.

Judging by the places where finds are known to have been made, the earliest Etrusco-Geometric pottery, dating from the second and third quarter of the eighth century B.C., was produced for the most part at Veii, but also in the other major centers of southern Etruria: the most common artifacts were vases of local shape, stands or fragments of stands, decorated with motifs from the Euboean repertoire.

At the start of the Orientalizing period, during the last quarter of the eighth century B.C., pottery production enjoyed rapid economic and cultural growth and gradually came to be concentrated at Vulci, which controlled the sea and land routes along the littoral that joined the towns and cities of southern Etruria with those in northern parts. Characterized from the outset by its close ties with the Greek model, painted pottery at this stage showed no real changes despite the arrival of artifacts, designs and forms imported from the Near East. The Geometric and linear decorations (concentric circles, cross-hatched diamonds, reticulated triangles, wavy lines, checker and meanders) and more rarely figured motifs (birds, four-footed animals, human figures) continued to borrow from the repertoire of Euboean pottery proper, or from the ware of Euboean workshops in Campania, which themselves bore the marks of other influences (Cyclades, Argos, Corinth) carried by the various ethnic populations which had contacts with the first Greek colonies. The shapes, whether of local (biconical urns, ollas, *holmoi*) or Greek origin (amphoras, *lebetes, dinoi,* cups and above all kraters) were often dictated by the serving of wine: Etruria not only learned from Greece the techniques of the potter's wheel and painting pottery made from fine-grained slip clay, but also imported improvements in wine-growing, raising the drinking of wine to a significant place in daily life and funerary rites and making the *symposion* into the symbol of a new aristocratic lifestyle.

Among the more remarkable items—often of considerable size—found in the territory of Vulci, one of the best-known is the lidded krater found at Pescia Romana. Generally attributed to the Cesnola Painter, one of the best exponents of Late Geometric Euboean pottery, the krater has sometimes been thought to be local rather than imported work, so strong seems to have been the influence of the Cesnola Painter and his workshop on local manufacture, including that of the Argive Painter, whose name is derived from the presence in his work of certain motifs typical of Argive pottery (such as the rectangular panel which often appears over the rump of his animals), but who also borrows extensively from the Euboean repertoire. One of the most gifted and original personalities active in Vulci at the time, the Argos Painter also gave considerable scope to figured designs, sometimes already creating compositions that crossed over the subdividing metopes, with narrative scenes such as the stag hunting scene featured on a *holmos* in the Villa Giulia Museum.

A biconical vase from the Osteria necropolis, again attributed to the Vulci workshops, has a composite form which demands particular attention. Decorated in the Euboean canon, this vase has lower parts (foot and body) in the Greek fashion, but upper parts (neck and lip) like those of a Villanovan impasto funerary urn, while its handle was deliberately broken, as was usual with the latter kind of vase.

In Bisenzio there were lesser workshops, more or less dependent on those of Vulci, which at the same time specialized in the production of fine-grained clay or clear-glazed impasto vases, sometimes of rare form (kraters, ollas, bird-shaped *askoi*, cask-shaped jars) decorated with simple motifs. Outstanding among these is an olla found in a tomb datable to around 700 B.C. at the Buccace necropolis, whose technique and decoration are both remarkable: it is bi-chromatic (black and red) in a fashion which has been recorded for Cyprus, the Cyclades and at Al Mina, but which was only occasionally adopted in Etruria; the decoration depicts a ritual dance scene probably inspired by the funeral lamentation scenes found on Late Greek Geometric pottery.

Subgeometric and Orientalizing pottery

Around the turn of the eighth and seventh centuries B.C., the Euboeans lost their leadership in the West to the growing domination of their rival Corinth. The models of Corinthian Orientalizing pottery—still termed proto-Corinthian—exerted a growing influence on Etruscan painted pottery workshops, either directly or by the intermediary of Cumae; nonetheless pottery in the Geometric tradition after the fashion of the Euboeans did not disappear altogether but continued in the shape of the abundant Subgeometric pottery produced as late as the second half of the seventh century B.C. in major centers of the Faliscan region, southern and central Etruria.

One early Subgeometric ware with decoration still inspired by Euboean patterns but with shapes often in the local tradition is referred to as the *Metopengattung* because of the metope borders decorated with diamonds and simple geometric designs that form the leitmotifs of its decoration. This ware was produced until the mid-seventh century at Tarquinia, Vulci and in the towns that had cultural ties with the two cities: Castro, Pitigliano, Poggio Buco, Sovana.

The Subgeometric ware of Tarquinia, although more innovative than that of Vulci, nonetheless admitted certain influences from proto-Corinthian ware and more extensively still from Greek Orientalizing pottery. From the start of the Middle Orientalizing period at the outset of the seventh century B.C., the ovoid *oinochoe* typical of the Early proto-Corinthian (720–690 B.C.) made its appearance. Examples were found in the rich burial goods of the Tomb of Bocchoris, so-called because of the Egyptian faience vase found there bearing the name of the Pharaoh who ruled between 720 and 712 B.C. together with a *kotyle*, also of proto-Corinthian inspiration, decorated with figures of four-footed animals with birds' feet and heads, attributable to the same painter, known as the Bocchoris

Painter. This was also a motif much used by the Palm-tree Painter, active in the early decades of the seventh century, who owes his name to a plant motif for which precedents must be sought in the Late Geometric ware of Kos and Rhodes and in proto-Attic ware. Together with his name-piece, another vase which may be attributed to his hand is an *oinochoe* at Columbia University. It is decorated on the shoulder with fish silhouettes, a motif of proto-Corinthian origin that occurs frequently in Subgeometric ware, and on the body with a line of ships that evokes the seafaring ventures of the Etruscans, who were thus far from being passive subjects of Greek trade...

Among the ware produced by the workshops of Tarquinia during the Orientalizing period, however, one item that is even more worthy of attention is an *oinochoe*, now in the British Museum, dating from the first quarter of the seventh century B.C. and attributed to the Long Horse Painter, whose background was Cumaean-Euboean, although the decoration is still largely based on geometric motifs. The neck carries a scene which has been interpreted—over-audaciously in the opinion of some scholars—as an illustration of the crane dance performed on their arrival at Delos by Theseus, Arianna and the young Athenians who had escaped from the Minotaur. Whatever the action depicted, the scene is one of the earliest representations in Etruscan art of what was very probably a mythological subject. Moreover this vase features a highly personal interpretation of human and animal figures, especially of the bird figure conventionally termed a "heron" which also—in a more abstract form, mixing the Villanovan legacy with various Greek traditions—became a characteristic figure of the Subgeometric ware made by workshops in Caere, Veii and the Faliscan-Capena area, territories which at the time had cultural ties.

"Heron" figures were also the decorative motifs in the earliest known wall painting that in the Tomb of the Ducks, dated around 675 B.C. They appeared not only on fine-grained clay ware but also on a category of red impasto ware decorated in white, produced principally by the Caere workshops and those of the Faliscan-Capena area, but also later at Vulci and several other smaller centers of southern Etruria. The appearance at the turn of the eighth and seventh centuries of this white-on-red technique, also used in architectural decoration, was undoubtedly prompted by the example of Phoenician red clay ware. It was used until the first quarter of the seventh century B.C.

With the development of Corinthian commerce Caere became a key site in trade with the East and Greece, as well as a distribution channel for imports towards the north. In the course of the seventh century the city also established itself as the most innovative center, rapidly tiring of traditional formulas and mass production. One of the first artists to break free from the Subgeometric repertoire was the Crane Painter, who was bilingual and active in the first quarter of the seventh century. He introduced into the Subgeometric patterns large amphoras in fine-grained clay and large *pithoi* in white-on-red impasto with broad zoomorphic friezes sometimes interrupted by several human or monstrous figures.

Only a little later, in the period 680–660 B.C., the narrative scenes and monumental figures which appear in the works of the Heptachord Painter, whose style recalls alternately that of Attic or Cycladic Orientalizing ware, are equally evocative of the ferment of creativity in the Caere workshops of the time. Marking a decisive break with the rows of fish and herons, the monotonous formulae and repetitive motifs of Subgeometric pottery, the decoration of the Heptachord Painter's vase reproduces a curious acrobatic dance which unfolds in a frieze around the body and shoulder. On another major work by the same artist, a large biconical vase whose general shape is still that of the Villanovan cinerary urn but whose twin handles and foot are those of a Greek krater, a couple is depicted in an attitude often recorded in Greek literature and pottery, with the woman holding her hand to the man's chin in a gesture of supplication. It is beyond doubt that some Greek picture was the model for the scene, but at the same time its adaptation to an entirely different taste is an equally inescapable fact: the scene occupies the whole height of the body and neck, quite ignoring the structure of the vase and the constraints of order and harmony which typified Greek pottery at all times, while certain details of clothing may find counterparts more easily in the Etruscan than in the Hellenic world. Whether this iconographical scheme had the same semantic value in Etruria as in Greece, or whether it was adapted locally to pre-existing myths or legends, this vase—like the *oinochoe* of the Long Horse Painter at Tarquinia—marks the

Civitavecchia Painter,
olla with boxing scene.
Bruxelles, Musées Royaux d'Art et d'Histoire
cat. 51

Terra-cotta black-figure amphora, ca. 670 B.C.
Würzburg, Martin-von-Wagner Museum der Universität
cat. 207

Bearded Sphinx Painter, terra-cotta black-figure oinochoe *with* Ilioupersis, *630* B.C.
Paris Bibliothèque Nationale cat. 209

introduction of mythological subjects into Etruscan painting. It is thus possible to fill what appeared to be a continuity gap in the first half of the seventh century B.C. and to gain a fuller understanding of the situation of the Aristonothos krater, an outstanding piece which was quickly dated to the mid-seventh century but which long remained isolated.

Written in Greek letters, the name of Aristonothos is the oldest craftsman's signature yet found in Etruria, and it gives us some indication of the value which the artist himself attributed to this vase. One side bears a scene depicting the battle between a war galley and a merchant ship, while the other carries a motif this time clearly borrowed from Greek epic: an episode of the *Odyssey* in which Ulysses and his companions blind the Cyclops Polyphemus, a realistic and an allegorical representation of the conflicts which were then rife in the Mediterranean. The composite form and style of the vase, in which scholars have detected proto-Attic, Cycladic, Sicilian and Italiot alongside Etruscan elements, indicate that the work was made *in situ* by a craftsman of Greek origin whose precise background and career must necessarily remain a mystery. Nonetheless it does provide yet another illustration of the direct role played by immigrant Greek craftsmen in the introduction of Greek myth into Etruria, as in the development not only of pottery but of Etruscan arts and crafts in general, at a time indicated by ancient writers (Pliny, *Naturalis historia*, 152 ff.) as the period when the tyrant Demaratus fled to Etruria after Corinth had fallen into the hands of the rival family of the Cypselidae, reaching Tarquinia in the company of artists with such evocative names as Eucheir, Diopos and Eugrammos...

During the second half of the seventh century, however, vase painters were no longer susceptible only to Greek Orientalizing models, but also to those from the Orient proper, introduced by artifacts imported from the Syrian and Phoenician coasts. These Oriental designs not only inspired the patterns of large, fine-grained clay amphoras decorated with line-drawn animal figures amid exuberant plant motifs, but also extensively influenced the decoration of white-on-red impasto ware, whose impetuous and monumental compositions are echoed by the first megalographs in the tombs at Cerveteri, doubtless carried out by the same workshops as the painted vases.

At the beginning of the Late Orientalizing period, towards 630 B.C., the influx of Corinthian ware combined with the immigration of craftsmen from various Corinthian and Greek-Oriental backgrounds to anchor Etruscan pottery firmly and permanently to the Greek model.

In Vulci, a burgeoning center at the time, two strong personalities dominated the decade of the 630s B.C.: the Swallow Painter and the Bearded Sphinx Painter. The Swallow Painter, brought up in the "wild goat" style typical of workshops in eastern Greece, was unquestionably an immigrant. His first creations in Etruria would not look out of place beside those of his country of origin, but he soon moved on to new forms and motifs, often of Corinthian origin, such as the *aryballos* or *olpe*, and the dotted rosette. His mode of expression became more barbaric in the process: one of his last works, a large amphora now in the Louvre, expands to a monumental scale the characteristic motifs of this decorative and miniaturist style, transforming them completely and giving them an entirely local feel. The work of the Swallow Painter found no followers, however, quite unlike that of the Bearded Sphinx Painter.

Etrusco-Corinthian pottery

Despite a number of borrowings from Eastern Greek ware, whose outline contour technique he occasionally used, and from the local Orientalizing repertoire, notably the Bearded Sphinx motif from which he took his name, this painter must in effect be credited with the introduction of the black-figure technique (in which details are incised through the black glaze within the outline of the figure, and then further enhanced by white and red) and with initiating Etrusco-Corinthian ware, whose prolific manufacture only ceased in around 540 B.C. The *olpe* fragment from Ischia di Castro, decorated with a row of chariots, horsemen and infantry, and the *oinochoe* of the Cabinet des Médailles of the Bibliothèque Nationale, decorated on the shoulder with a frieze showing a siege scene and perhaps recounting an episode in the *Ilioupesis*, constitute exceptional pieces in the output of the artist and his workshop, commissioned by an aristocratic clientele that wished to assimilate the legacy

Eagle Painter, Caeretan hydria *and support of a* dinos, *520–510* B.C. *Amsterdam, Allard Pierson Museum cat. 162*

of the great mythological subjects and epic poems of the Hellenic world. Schooled in the transitional Corinthian style (650–620 B.C.), the Bearded Sphinx Painter was above all responsible for a vast output of vases in various shapes (amphoras, *oinochoai, olpai, alabastoi*) decorated with friezes of real and imaginary animals. These vases are generally divided into two groups. The first includes all the works of high quality, closer to the transitional Corinthian model, and the earliest pieces, decorated with the dotted rosettes typical of transitional Corinthian style; the second includes later and less perfectly finished pieces, decorated with full rosettes borrowed from the late Corinthian style. Since finds of the first kind were made mostly in the territory of Vulci and those of the second principally in the area around Cerveteri, it has been deduced that the painter may have moved to the second city late in his career. And indeed his hand can be detected in some pieces of the Caere Fish-Scale Amphoras Group, so-called because of the many large amphoras with decorations dominated by bands of overlapping fish-scales, alternating around the shoulder with zoomorphic friezes whose miniaturist style grows progressively more relaxed.
The black-figure technique was not the only one to be practiced first by Etrusco-Corinthian potters. The first polychrome vases were produced at Caere from as early as 630 B.C. They were decorated almost exclusively with zoomorphic figures, incised on a black ground and heavily highlighted in brown, white or purple. The application of the colors suggests that chromatic and ornamental effects were paramount and anatomical accuracy only a secondary consideration.
Polychrome technique, borrowed from Corinthian ware—in which however it was used only for limited areas of the surface—was used at Caere to decorate the whole surface of the large amphoras of the Monte Abatone Group. The decoration of these vases sometimes has the attractive simplicity of children's or primitive designs, but continues in general to be tied to the experience of Orientalizing painted pottery or bucchero ware... This may again be said—though in this instance a stronger influence from transitional Corinthian style is ap-

parent—of the works brought together in the Castellani cycle, a contemporary cycle dominated by the personality of the Castellani Painter and localized by tenuous hypothesis to Veii… Characterized by a rather miniaturist style, the cycle includes *olpai* and *oinochoai* but is dominated by small-scale pieces, notably *aryballoi.*

Polychrome technique was only rarely used in Vulci before 600–590 B.C. It is well represented, apart from several series with non-figured decoration (Phoenician palmette and Lotus flower groups), by the work of the Pescia Romana Painter, who however soon abandoned it in favor of the black-figure technique. Even in black-figure he continued to make liberal use of incision and polychrome effects, thus appearing to play a pivotal role between the first and second generation of Etrusco-Corinthian painters. Within this second generation, active in the decades 600–580 B.C., he occupied a key position alongside the Feoli Painter, so-called after the owner of his name-piece. Once again a bilingual artist, the Feoli Painter is however essentially known to us by his black-figure vases. Attached to the Corinthian model at the outset of his career, he was happy to adopt its vase shapes such as the *olpe, alabastos* and *aryballos*, but for the *oinochoe* he chose a shape which has virtually no known antecedents in Greek pottery; in the same way he took over from Corinthian ware his unusually varied iconographical repertoire in which gorgons and centaurs sometimes interrupt the rows of animals that he imaginatively assembled, often accentuating their ornamental qualities. Among artists active at Vulci in the same period, another figure worth mentioning is the Boehlau Painter, named after the German scholar who identified his hand. This painter kept no more of the Etrusco-Corinthian model than the shape of its *olpai* and certain decorative motifs. Using black-figure technique, albeit in a highly idiosyncratic version which owed more to the tradition of polychrome pieces, he painted misshapen animal figures like images seen in a distorting mirror, whose anatomical details are either a pretext for creating decorative motifs, or else purely the fruit of his fantastic imagination, which amused itself by placing a cross of Saint Andrew on a lion's muzzle or covering a panther's body in scales.

Imitators and followers of the Boehlau Painter can be traced at Tarquinia, while the direct influence of the Feoli and Pescia Romana Painters is recognizable at Vulci even on artists of their own, as well as on the next generation. Foremost among these is the Painter of the Fallen, whose few identifiable works, datable to 590–580 B.C., only rarely feature human figures, generally isolated amid friezes of real or imaginary animals. His most striking feature, however, is the depiction of "battlefield scenes" in which a fallen warrior is left as carrion for birds and beasts, or finished off by his enemies. Although less talented than the Feoli Painter, the Pescia Romana Painter paradoxically exerted greater influence on mass production in the years 580–560 B.C., a period in which pottery tended towards greater standardization and diminished quality as the most cost-effective response to the demand of a middle class that aped the tastes and lifestyle of the elite. Produced in greater quantities and distributed more widely, but at the same time less carefully made, this kind of pottery is more difficult to attribute to individual artists and is mostly shared out among the Cycle of the *Olpai* and the catalogues of the Rosette Painter and the Knotted Tails Painter.

In the Cycle of the *Olpai,* most pieces are *olpai* of the Corinthian type, but there are also *oinochoai,* amphoras and plates of local or Oriental origin, all decorated with monotonous friezes of walking animals. Among the five or six artists responsible for their decoration, the Herclé Painter and the Castro Painter are the best-known and the most representative. The Herclé Painter—whose name is derived from the company that financed the excavations in the 1960s—decorated his pieces with lines of animals walking in the same direction, mostly lions and birds. The second artist takes his name from Castro, the place where his name-piece—now in the Grosseto Museum—was discovered. His hand may easily be recognized by the two wavy lines which he joins to represent the outlines of birds that constantly occur in his work, as also by the line which he uses to draw the backs of his four-legged animals, spiralling to the join of the neck, or again by the exaggerated lengthening of a back leg, the crudely-drawn hooves of equine figures. Less prolific than the Herclé Painter, his work is also more original and of higher quality.

The Rosette Painter preferred to decorate the smaller shapes (cups, *phialai* and plates), but his output also included *olpai* and kraters, a form not previously recorded in Etrusco-

Corinthian ware. His favorite decorative motifs were panthers and bird figures, frequently crowded amid the large rosettes which gave him his name. Among the many pieces attributed to him, a column krater now in the Louvre collection is outstanding: the main band of decoration features narrative scenes that are difficult to interpret but which may relate to the legend of Heracles or to unknown episodes from local mythology.

The masterpiece in the catalogue of the Knotted Tails Painter, whose name derives from the curly tails he drew on his four-legged animals, is the Hunchback krater, so-called because of the characteristic silhouette of its human figures. Undoubtedly commissioned by a patron from Caere, the site where it was found and a city where the krater form was especially popular, the piece brings together some remarkable motifs: mythological scenes inspired by Greek art, representations of local rites, a monstrous figure of oriental origin…

If Vulci enjoyed uncontested leadership of the manufacture of Etrusco-Corinthian ware during the first half of the sixth century, it was by no means the only center of production. The first ware made by the workshops of Tarquinia, around 590 B.C., and by those of Vulci, the Vitelleschi Group and the so-called Wolf's Head Painter, display numerous ties with pottery by the Feoli, Boehlau and Pescia Romana Painters and the Painter of the Fallen, but later work rapidly moved away in style. Active in the years 580–565 B.C., the Senza Graffito Painter, who worked mostly on *omphalos*, *phialai* and bowls, stopped using incision and instead made simple line drawings detailed with highlighting colors, multiplying the motifs of uncertain shape which were used to fill in the outlines; in the Grashmere Group, so-called after the place where the name-piece *olpe* is kept, the crudely drawn animal figures show the same tendency to dissolve forms.

The final phase of Etrusco-Corinthian ware (560–540 B.C.) was generally characterized by a marked decline and increasing remoteness from Corinthian models. Large vases were replaced by *alabastoi*, globe-shaped *aryballoi, pyxides*. These smaller pieces are divided among three major groups: the Maschera Umana Group, whose decoration is not unconnected with the work of the Rosette Painter from Vulci, takes its name from a type of cup modeled in the form of a human face and also includes a large number of vases molded into the shapes of birds, monkeys or four-legged creatures; the Bird Cycle, dominated by the figure of the Tree Painter, groups together mostly *aryballoi, alabastoi* and *pyxides* decorated with a frieze of three or four birds; the Facing Cockerels Group includes *aryballoi* and *alabastoi* decorated with the motif that gives the group its name, but also with facing winged or apterous panthers, sometimes separated by a tree or by one or two bird figures.

Of mediocre quality and mostly destined for export, these vases were produced in large numbers and widely distributed by workshops which it is difficult to determine with any certainty. They may have been located in smaller towns at a time when the workshops of Caere and Vulci, stimulated by the growing imports of Attic ware and the arrival of Ionian craftsmen fleeing before the Persian menace, were developing an entirely different kind of black-figure pottery.

Black-figure pottery

From the decade of the 560s B.C., a number of Attic ware workshops adapted their output to suit demand from Etruria and began producing almost exclusively for Western custom. One instance is the Tyrrhenian amphoras workshop, specialized in the manufacture of vases for the elite classes of the great Etruscan cities along the Tyrrhenian coast, Caere, Vulci… Decorated with mythological scenes on the shoulder, but with animal friezes circling the body, the Tyrrhenian amphoras are somewhat archaic in feel in comparison with other Attic ware of the time, which no longer featured rows of animals of that kind. Animal figures were very probably retained in deference to the tastes of a clientele that was used to the zoomorphic friezes of Corinthian and Etrusco-Corinthian vases.

The fall of the tyrannical regime and subsequent decline of Corinth led to a shortfall in production and imports of Corinthian ware. But the opportunity which this created was not exploited solely by Attic imports. Craftsmen from Ionia, such as the painters of the *hydriai* workshop at Caere and the Campana *dinoi* workshop in Vulci, settled in Etruria around the mid sixth century. Adapting to the requirements of their new customers, they contributed to the renewal of local pottery and fine painting. Two masters stand out among the *hydriai*

Busiris Painter, black-figure Caeretan hydria *with Heracles and Busiris, ca. 510* B.C.
Vienna, Kunsthistorisches Museum cat. 213

painters of Caere: the Eagle Painter, with a more calligraphic drawing style, and the Busiris Painter, whose drawing is more rapid. Both came from the northern part of Ionia. Together with two assistants from markedly local backgrounds, they specialized in the manufacture of a particular form of vase, perhaps in order to enable them to establish a bridgehead in a market where there was stiff competition from Attic ware, producing brightly-colored, rather stocky *hydriai*, often decorated with hunting scenes or mythological episodes. The overall effect is lively enough, and their muscle-bound figures have often been compared with those of the Tomb of the Augurs.

The Campana *Dinoi* Painters, the Louvre Painters E 736 and E 737–739 (or Ribbon Painter), doubtless also originated from northern Ionia and specialised in the same way in a particular form of vase used for serving wine and decorated for the most part with Dionysiac motifs.

Eastern Greek by culture if not by origin, the Paris Painter, active between 550/40 and 520 B.C. and regarded as the founder of the Pontic vases workshop in Vulci, also had a typically Ionian style and frequently made use of the decorative repertoire of eastern Greece. Despite the preponderance of Ionian models in his work, influence from Corinth and Athens can by no means be excluded. The form and ornamental grammar of his *hydriai*, for instance, he borrowed from Corinthian ware, while he turned to Athenian models for those of his amphoras, close to the Tyrrhenian amphoras and like them often decorated with mythological scenes in which Heracles was the main protagonist. Open to influences from any source, the

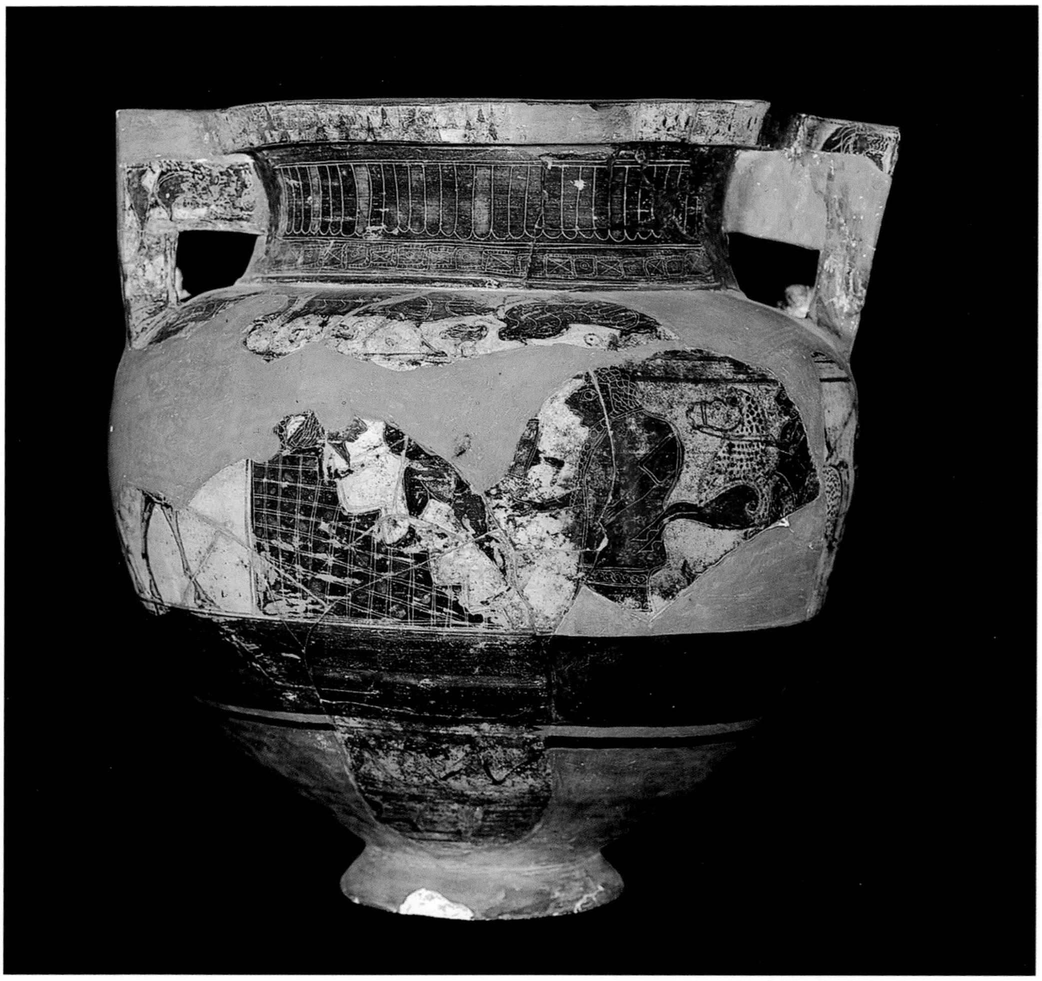

Terra-cotta Etrusco-Corinthian column krater from the Banditaccia necropolis (Cerveteri), 570–560 B.C.
Cerveteri, Museo Archeologico
cat. 210

Paris Painter created a highly original style backed up by a sure hand and a cheerful temperament which led him to make generous use of polychromy.
The Pontic Group currently brings together more than two hundred and fifty pieces. Apart from the fifty or so attributed to the Paris Painter, the remainder are divided among four attributions: the Silenus Painter, a figure close to the Paris Painter who preferred Dionysiac motifs, the Tityos and Amphiaraos Painters and Bibliothèque Nationale No. 178. The latter three typically painted local shapes, such as the *kyathos* and *kylix*, in an increasingly eclectic style which became gradually more relaxed and—in the strict sense—barbaric.
During the same period 550/40–520, the Ionian style is again characteristic of the Tolfa Group. Named after the place where one of the vases first identified was found, this group now includes more than seventy pieces attributable to the same workshop, located in Caere. Most of these are amphoras, decorated with figures of animals both real (lions, panthers, swans) and imaginary (chimeras, hippocampi, sometimes ridden by young men), large running human figures (Scythian archers, divine or anonymous figures), hunting scenes or mythological episodes such as Achilles ambushing Troilus and the Rape of Europa. Attribution of these vases to one or more hands is still a matter of debate. In my view, they were probably the work of a number of painters, dominated by two figures: the Boston Hunting Painter whose style is very close to that of the Caere *Hydriai* Painter; and the Angular Faces Painter, who can be recognized by the tense and nervous outline of figures that often take on a monumental dimension while retaining all their calligraphic qualities. The founder of the workshop, a vase painter and no doubt also a potter, the Angular Faces Painter may also have worked in fresco: more than the Pontic Group itself, it is this

following pages
Terra-cotta hydria, *520–510* B.C.
Toledo, Museum of Art
cat. 52

Terra-cotta black-figure amphora, first quarter of the fifth century B.C.
Paris, Musée du Louvre
cat. 215

painter's work and the Tolfa Group vases which share stylistic and iconographical features with the wall paintings of the Tomb of the Bulls at Tarquinia.

Attic influence was discreet in the Tolfa Group, being traceable chiefly in the way the treatment of draperies developed, but it is a dominant presence in the vases of the Ivy Leaf Group, probably produced at Vulci in the same period. These pieces echo the works of the Amasis, Nikosthenes and Affected Painters. The group, mainly composed of large picture amphoras, decorated with rare mythological scenes that are Dionysiac in tone, or with figures of real and imaginary animals, owes its name to the large male or female figures holding large ivy leaves in their hands which decorate a dozen or more of the pieces. Some fifty pieces make up the group; they have been variously attributed to a single or to two separate painters (albeit without any precise distinction), so that certain attribution must await further research. My own view is that the Ivy Leaf Painter may already be joined by a second painter, recognizable by his more rigid hand and sharper sense of line and decorative composition, whom I suggest naming as the Arezzo Wrestlers Painter after the most original motif in his repertoire. Some time ago—rightly so, in my opinion—the vases of the Munich No. 833 Painter were withdrawn from the Ivy Leaf Group. This painter was a complex figure, close in style and certain iconographical details to the Caere *hydriai* workshop, but was also linked with the Ivy Leaf Group, whose decorative language he took over, and the early pottery of the Micali Painter, from which he adopted certain graphic conventions.

The protean figure of the Micali Painter dominated the scene at Vulci in the final quarter of the sixth century B.C. He decorated various shapes: amphoras, *hydriai, stamnoi, kyathoi* and *kylikes*. Initially close to Pontic ware in style, he gradually opened up to Attic influences, from the black-figure pottery of the Leagros group of painters and from the red-figure ware of the Andokides Painter. He was, however, ignorant of red-figure technique—perfected in Greece around 530 B.C. and introduced into Etruria only several decades later—adapting all the various Greek models to his own imagination. His favorite subjects were monstrous and fantastic creatures, winged horses, sirens, sphinxes and centaurs, setting a joyous tonality throughout his scenes, whether drawn from mythology or from daily life.

The style of the Micali Painter was followed by numerous painters, and its echo can be traced as late as in Capuan ware. In Vulci itself, one of the closest and most gifted followers of the Micali Painter was the Vatican No. 238 Painter, active around 510–500 B.C. He showed a distinct preference for mythological scenes, sometimes on rare subjects, and illustrated a two-handled *hydria* in the Toledo Museum with Tyrrhenian pirates being turned into dolphins, an episode narrated in the seventh Homeric *Hymn to Dionysos*.

From the first quarter of the fifth century B.C., the quality of Etruscan black-figure pottery appears to have declined rapidly. Most of the painted pottery workshops, sited no longer only in Vulci and Caere, but also in Chiusi, Orvieto and perhaps also in Tarquinia, were reduced to monotonous repetition of formula borrowed from the last Attic black-figure designs. They also increasingly gave up incision altogether, using instead simple outline drawings highlighted in white, or else limiting themselves to the manufacture of vases decorated just with bands, plant motifs, even a straightforward inscription, such as the "dotted garland" or Spurinas plates at Vulci.

The tradition established by the Micali Painter and his school nonetheless survived in a number of exceptional pieces which in around 480 B.C. transposed into the black-figure technique the innovations which were associated with the adoption of red-figure in Athens: they display increased interest in the treatment of anatomical features and the rendering of space and demonstrate accurate knowledge of Greek mythology and epos. Typical instances are the Berlin amphora No. 2154 and the Würzburg amphora L 799, which some years ago I attributed to the Dancing Girl with Rattles Painter, along with a number of other vases with more current decoration. These artists proved capable of bringing together in their own style various elements from the figurative culture of the great southern Etruscan cities, and produced works which bear comparison with the best pieces painted during the period.

Lastly, other works of fairly high quality were produced by the Lotus Buds workshop, dominated by the figure of the Dancing Satyrs Painter, a fine draughtsman with a quick, sure hand, skilled at representing space and foreshortening. The ware attributable to this workshop has been expanded considerably by the work of Tobias Dohrn in identifying the Lotus

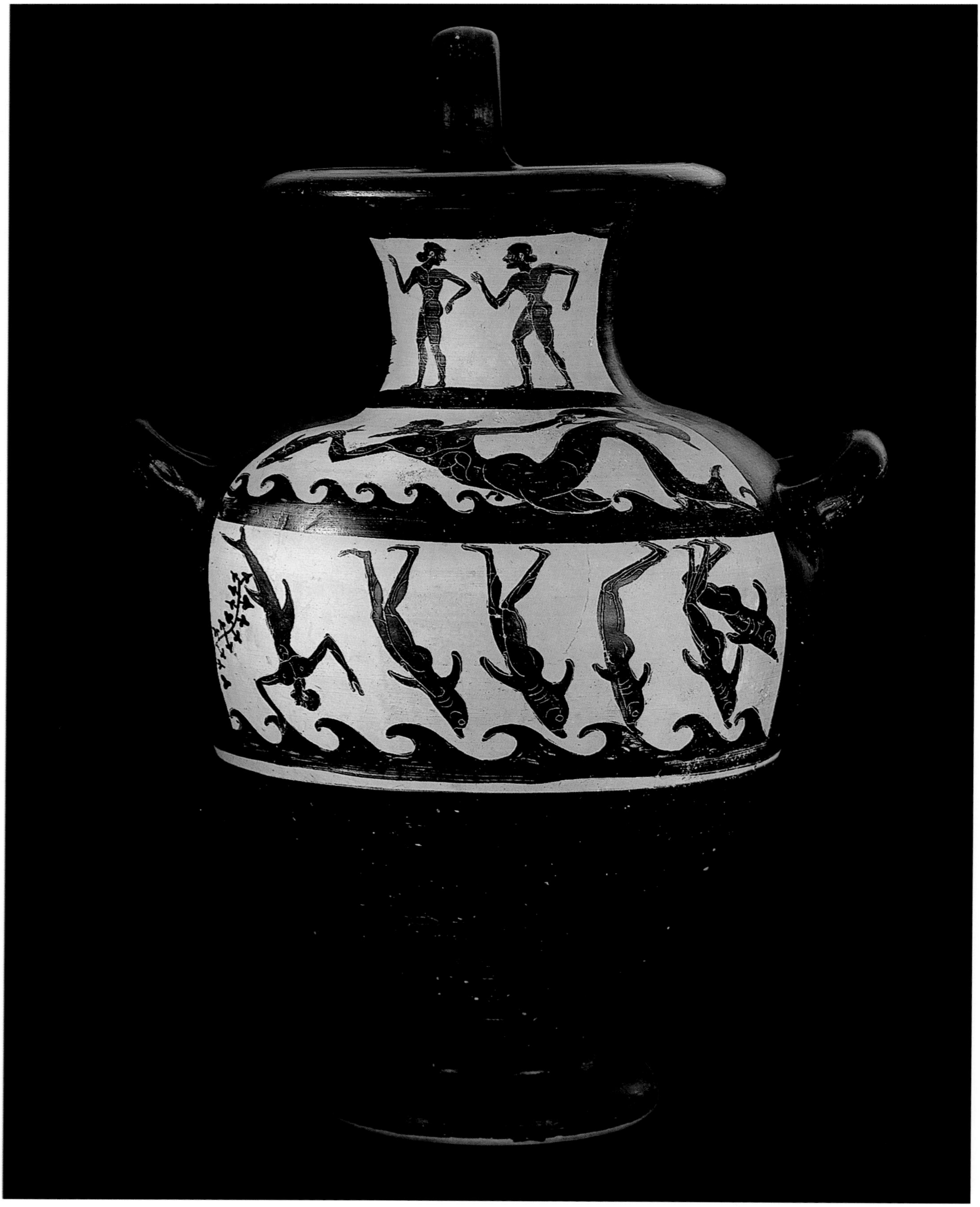

Terra-cotta black-figure stamnos, *ca. 500* B.C.
Florence, Museo Archeologico
cat. 217

Buds Group. It includes vases of various shapes already attested to in the work of the Micali Painter (amphoras, two-handled *hydriai,* kraters, *oinochoai, olpai*) featuring a variety of decorative schemes (gymnasium and arming scenes, mythological episodes, including a remarkable depiction of Epeios, identified by a caption in Greek, working on the Trojan Horses. To judge by the proven or supposed provenance of the new pieces attributed, the center of this kind of manufacture may perhaps have been located at Caere. While production of painted pottery seems to have been abruptly broken off there some time around 520–510 B.C. with the last works of the Tolfa Group, this kind of ware suggests continued production of quality pottery until late in the first half of the fifth century.

However this may be, when the over-painted red-figure appeared in around 480 B.C., there was no unbridgeable gap between declining black-figure and over-painted red-figure work of superior quality; rather a gap existed between contemporary ware which might be made by a servile hand (if the inscription *kapé mukathesa* on a vase attributed to the Micali Painter's school is correctly interpreted as *kape*, slave to *mukathe*) and pottery of superior quality which might be made by craftsmen from Sicily or Magna Graecia, as is perhaps indicated by a Greek text inscribed on a vase in the Lotus Buds Group whose writing type has been referred to that of Rhegion, or by the signature of Arnth Praxias, the maker of a celebrated amphora in the Cabinet des Médailles of the Bibliothèque Nationale in Paris decorated in over-painted red-figure technique, an innovation which in the final analysis was closer to black-figure than to the true red-figure which was its model. Pseudo-red-figure replaced black-figure seamlessly, following the same tradition and retaining in its repertoire the forms preferred by the Micali Painter, maintaining the same graphic con-

Terra-cotta black-figure stamnos, *ca. first quarter of the fifth century* B.C.
Florence, Museo Archeologico
cat. 217

ventions and like black-figure taking inspiration from Attic black- or red-figure ware of the end of the Archaic period.

It was only towards the mid-fifth century that the Archaic phase of Etruscan painted pottery drew to a close, with the adoption of true red-figure and an entirely Attic language of expression. The phase was sufficiently long for us to be able to trace both its fidelity to Greek models, sustained by the constant and varied imports of Greek vases and by the immigration of craftsmen of many different origins, and the liberty with which these models were imitated. This very free play with Greek influences was due only in part to politico-economic reasons (the vagaries of commercial traffic and immigration flows) or structural factors (workshop organization, social status of craftsmen, the role of foreigners). At least so far as ware of higher quality is concerned, Etruscan potters chose to adopt one technique rather than another, to mix motifs and shapes from different periods and elaborate upon them, to make a drastic selection of scenes and patterns as and when required, in a creative process that was an adaptation, not a banalization of Greek iconographical schemes.

Volumes and articles of general interest: Martelli 1987; Szilagyi 1989. *Etruscan Geometric and Subgeometric pottery*: Åkerström 1943; Canciani 1974; Isler 1983, pp. 9–48; Williams 1986, pp. 295–304; Leach, pp. 305–08. *"White on red" pottery*: Micozzi 1994. *Etrusco-Corinthian pottery*: Payne 1931; Szilagyi 1992–98 (with previous bibliography). *Black-figure Etruscan pottery*: Dohrn 1937; Beazley 1947; Hemelrijk 1984; Schwarz 1984, pp. 47–77; Gaultier 1987, pp. 63–93; Spivey 1987; Ginge 1987; Ginge 1988–89, pp. 61 ff.; *Un artista e il suo mondo* 1988; Gaultier 1995 (with previous bibliography).

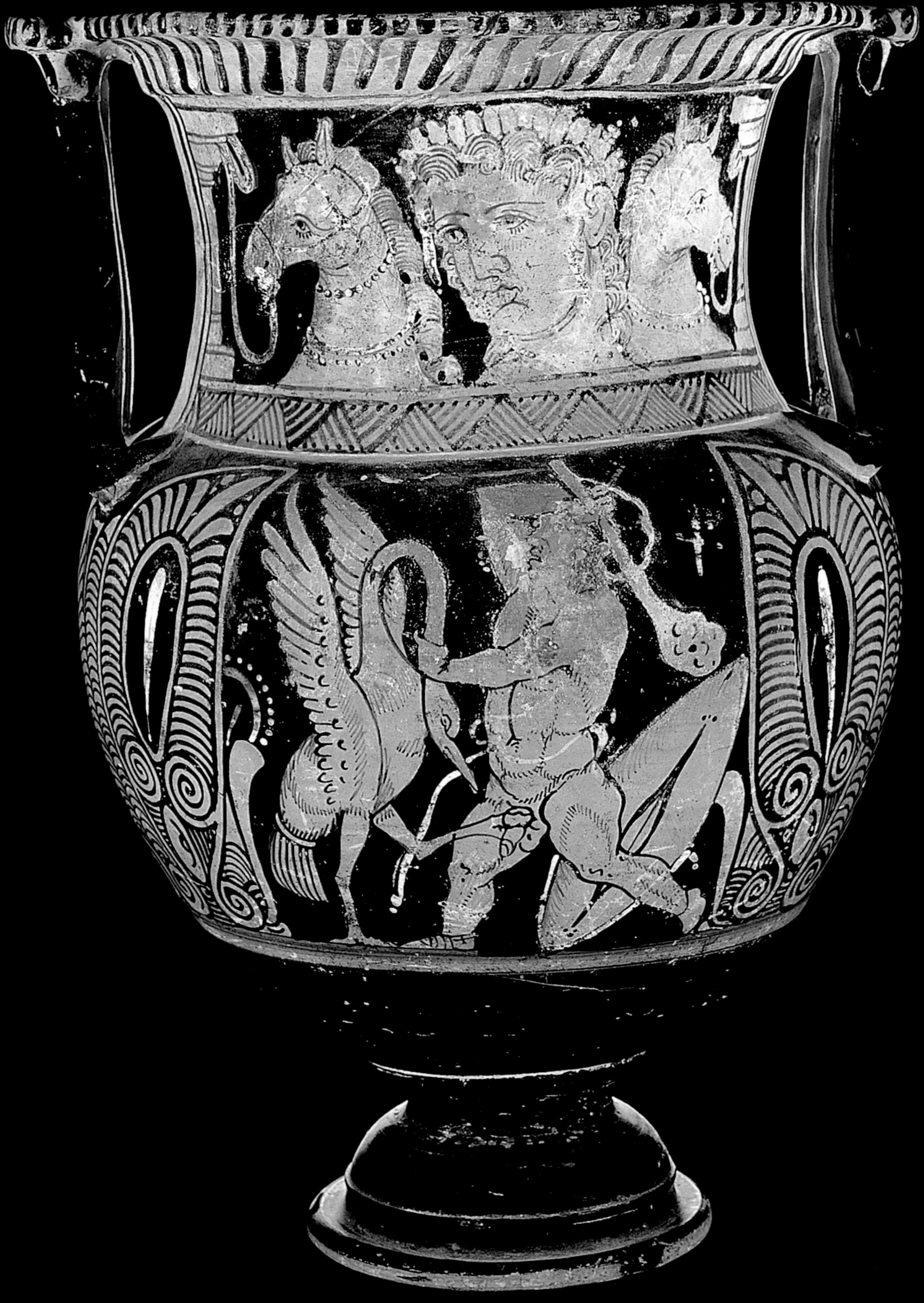

Etruscan Painted Ware of the Classical and Hellenistic Period

Introduction

Despite the significant contribution of major early twentieth-century scholars in the field of classical archaeology—notably Sir John Beazley whose groundbreaking efforts were first followed up by the long and virtually single-handed militancy of Mario A. Del Chiaro, and subsequently by the wave of research effected in the 1980s and 1990s, the study of Etruscan red-figure ware continues to be fraught with pressing issues, many as yet unresolved, not least those concerning the very basics of method, a question that calls for some preliminary considerations.

The first and most critical problem concerns the chronological framework, not only in terms of the overall period of Etruscan painted pottery production, but also regarding the sequences within each of the established typological and stylistic groupings, that is, their seriation within a framework of evolution of the kind that has long obtained for the analogous study of Attic ceramics.

In this respect, a definitive chronology for painted wares crafted in Etruscan workshops is no more forthcoming than it was for experts studying Attic pottery back in the early 1900s. The reasons for this difficulty are plain, and as usual derive from an insufficient contextualization of the material uncovered in two centuries of unmonitored excavation in the Etruscan necropolises, particularly the more southern sites (witness the heinous plunder of Vulci and Caere, modern Cerveteri), principally no doubt at the hands of bounty-hunters and dealers, but also through the questionable policies of the archaeological authorities themselves. The only assemblages that offer proper association data come from a handful of necropolises in the Etruscan interior, from Agro Falisco, Volterra, and various emporiums. As for Spina, while at first sight the substantial finds have proved very promising, they are only partly published, and the presence of figured Etruscan wares is nonetheless scant. Furthermore, in the case of burial goods dating from the late Classical period, those that have included Etruscan red-figure ware lack other secure yardsticks for establishing dates—a role usually played by pottery—resulting inevitably in circular arguments. One notable exception is offered by the tombs found at Volterra, which benefited from the rare emergence of coins of both local and Roman mintage; it is most regrettable that the relative research work—including the archiving— undertaken by Enrico Fiumi in the late 1950s has not been adequately followed up.

As commonly occurs with historical art-research work, this dearth of documentation has led to an over-reliance in a logical evolution of style that is effectively only an impression, and not a proven sequence; this has entailed the formulation of more or less organic evolutionary models based on presupposed concepts (yet again) of the Plinian kind, namely, that Etruscan figure ware can be arranged in order, starting with those stylistically close to their supposed Attic models, and evolving progressively away from these in the local potters' drive for originality, up until the wholesale (and irreversible) rejection of the grammatical baggage of its allegedly "noble" forebear, culminating in what has aptly been dubbed the "dying gasp" of Etruscan red-figure decoration.

This picture of evolution was necessarily based on the notion that Attic ceramic production "passed the baton" to the Etruscans, so to speak, the latter's production only tenable after the crisis in maritime trade in the Tyrrhenian (a crisis generally equated with the victory of Syracuse off the shores of Cumae in 474 B.C., and subsequently aggravated by Athenian commitments in the Peloponnesian War in the latter decades of the century), which entailed a sharp decline in imports to Etruria. While exceptions to this process are allowed for the so-called "port" *facies* and for the ample colonial areas of the Po Valley and Adriatic, the overall picture is that Etruscan red-figure ware was a surrogate for the increasingly unobtainable Athenian product, appearing in the interval of the fourth century just before the advent in both Italy and Greece of the new Hellenistic preference for vessels with an even, uniform glazed surface design inspired by toreutics. The most productive period for Etruscan red-figure pottery is therefore assumed to run from the late fifth century, tailing off in the early third, passing through the early "primitive" and intermittent phases classified by Beazley as "earlier red-figure" production, and gaining a certain consistency in Falerii and inland Etruria, with a final decline in quality and workmanship in the more standardized versions from southern Etruria.

Florence Painter 4035, column Krater with episode of geranomachy, from Volterra, last quarter of the fourth century B.C. Florence, Museo Archeologico

Bargagli Painter, overpainted column krater with scene of divination, from the Paccianese Tomb (Chiusi), mid-fifth century B.C.
Chiusi, Museo Archeologico
cat. 159

This said, recent research has shed light on the structural eclecticism of Etruscan production, an eclecticism that could in itself be considered the distinguishing feature of Etruscan art as a whole, enabling the inhabitants of Etruria to choose from among the established historical styles for Greek art the form of expression most apt for conveying native subject matter or, where originally Greek, retarget it to the specific needs of the local area in question. By "eclecticism" here we mean a phenomenon typical of "peripheral" yet creative spheres having a marked cultural receptivity that results in a commingling of stylistic features extrapolated from a visual language that was held exemplary and authoritative: thus Etruscan red-figure vases evince a carefree and frequent admixture of individual formal modes that may be defined, in Greek terms, respectively as Archaic, Severe or Classical in style—a fact that effectively annuls any attempt at dividing Etruscan production into the same periods of stylistic evolution that are applied to their Greek counterparts in comparable categories.

Above all the revision of Beazley's definition of "earlier red-figure" undertaken so meticulously by Fernando Gilotta, has shown up the weaknesses in using the Greek pattern, and posited a new chronology that dates production considerably forward. The result is a further reduction of the timespan of red-figure vase production in Etruria, which some scholars now date to between the second quarter of the fourth century (or shortly before) and around 300 B.C. (or soon thereafter), as if the aforementioned eclecticism—involving a slight or total variance from the Greek stylistic evolutionary sequence—eludes periodization and instead involves applying a synchronic, Saussurian-style framework.

At any event, today it is unthinkable to propose an overall chronology for painted Etruscan pottery without taking the coeval output of the Greek workshops on Italian soil as primary points of reference, especially those of Lucania and, more so, of Campania, an area that had freshly get out of Etruscan environment in the fourth century, and the area of all the south that was closest geographically and culturally to the Etruscan and Latin milieus.

Despite the considerable advances in the relative fieldwork, the highly specialized field of Italiot pottery suffers from the same lack of valid archaeological association data that hampers inquiry into Etruscan vases; and Italiot production was equally influenced by its corresponding Athenian models. Once again there is a risk of setting up preconstituted chronological timeframes that largely elude verification and merely become reciprocally self-referential.

Luckily, the reappraisal (and publication) of pottery finds from the painted-chest tombs at Paestum (Pontrandolfo and Rouveret) has cast new light on Lucanian and Paestan workshop production, which influenced the "Campanizing" style of some Etruscan manufactures. For this reason, as far as red-figure vases are concerned, a coherent (and tenable) timeframe cannot exclude regular occurrences of stylistic synchronism, with late Attic groups and especially with the Lucanian so-called "proto-Italiot" vases and the more or less standardized workshops of Cumae, Capua, and Paestum.

If, as will be discussed later on, one can reasonably distinguish within the category of so-called "earlier red-figure" vases an initial phase that was in keeping with the said "proto-Italiot" style, and hence a Campanizing and Paestanizing tendency, then whatever chronology is proposed must take account of the timeframe established for parallel production in Magna Graecia.

A second question of fundamental relevance involves issues of topography, that is, the differentiation and distribution of the main production centers in the "historical" Etruria. Here again, the task of establishing a map is hindered by the paucity of reliable hard data, I mean the archaeological evidence from the sites themselves. One of the "topographical" criteria established in Beazley's day was based on statistical data of provenance, with the assumption that the distribution of a given type was prevalently contained within a restricted radius; thus, a relative concentration around a particular site logically indicated a center of production. The work of Albizzati and Beazley both rely significantly on the provenance approach, but as a criterion it can be misleading inasmuch as, on its own, it omits making a distinction between actual production and mere consumption. Added to this is the intrinsic vagueness of the term "center of production," which fails to specify whether the workshops were located within the town proper, or scattered about the hin-

terland (a problem compounded by irksome imprecisions regarding the real boundaries of the Etruscan city-states). If this were not enough, further confusion may arise when scholars frequently picture migrant artisans and peripheral workshops.

On its own, the use of statistical data based on provenance has failed to dispel the outstanding doubts and queries, such as the rapport between the so-called Clusium and Volaterrae Groups; or the purported existence of a self-reliant workshop in Tarquinii, albeit related to that of Vulci; or the extent of production in Orvieto and Perugia. Not even testing with neutron activation analyses—proposed by the author some fifteen years ago—was decisive, owing to the fact that Tuscan clay is variable to the eye but chemically almost indistinguishable.

Another feature which to my mind sets the production of Etruscan red-figure vases apart from its Attic counterparts is the way in which workshops tended to specialize in particular shapes of vase, a phenomenon that becomes increasingly noticeable in the late and industrial series—the so-called *Genucilia* plates and the *Torcop* (Toronto-Copenhagen) jugs (see below, *Standardization...*)—, but anticipated to some degree by the potters (and purchasers) of the Etrurian interior for the special symposium cups, and in some cases induced—as in Volterra—by binding rules of ritual (notice the cinerary column-kraters, which are somewhat improperly called *kelebai*).

This mention of ritual brings us straight to the heart of another issue concerning method that likewise involves Greek vases, and not only the red-figure category, and that is the old question of *function*. Given that the exemplars that lend themselves best for exegetic study are those still intact (or almost intact) uncovered in funerary contexts—and less frequently in votive contexts—while in the (rare in Etruria) excavations within the urban area one seldom unearths more than a few shards, our impression is that vessels were made prevalently for funerary practices. Whence the ever-pending question of whether the such vessels may have served for symposium prior to being deposited in the tomb, or a quota of production was devoted expressly to funerary practices, that is, newly made vessels were destined for immediate deposition in the tomb.

Such questions have generated highly differing opinions, from the point of view (as one might expect) of exegesis, but also in terms of chronology: the furnishing contex dates the "new" vase (and vice versa), but not the "old" vase, which is naturally of earlier manufacture—possibly prior by several decades, even. As for the relation of function to exegesis, from the days of antiquaries such as Passeri and Inghirami up until the latest inquiries into iconology, the bibliography on vase production shows how scholarly interpretation of vase imagery as symbolizing the Dionysiac mysteries and the afterlife alternates regularly (depending on the method currently in vogue) with the more literarl, non-religious attribution of the imagery to *eros*, or to the symposium. Regrettably, only one secure testimony able to dispel doubt has survived—the famous inscription on two Faliscan *kylikes* "foied.vino.pipafo.cra.carefo" (today wine, tomorrow no more), which Mauro Cristofani was fond of quoting to ward off what he considered an overemphasis on the otherworldly connotations of the Dionysiac cult. There still remains the question of what purpose exactly the symposium itself served, or more precisely, what significance this ritual and conceptual space of Greek origin (more specifically from Athens) obtained within the Hellenized Etruscan world (and at what levels of the social strata). For the time being, these questions must remain unanswered.

Incunabula and earlier red-figure vases: the problem of origins

Scholars are generally unanimous in assigning the origin of Etruscan red-figure pottery, starting around 480 B.C., to a sizable series of products finished with decoration in superposed color, whose correspondent Attic technique—introduced by certain potters in the last quarter of the sixth century—is known as the "Six." This technique involves filling in red painting the silhouettes on the black glazed surface of the vase, adding details by scoring the surface or applying other colors, instead of outlining the shapes in black to save the slip, which would turn red during the firing—the technique adopted by "authentic" red-figure ware. This technique of applying the color must have been quicker (and far easier when it came to firing) like the parallel black-figure technique, despite the inversion of the contrasts, and hence more economical; nor did it require any additional training for craftsmen already familiar with the black-figure technique. It is no surprise, therefore, that Vulci, the capital of black-figure vase production in Etruria noted for the sizable output of the so-called Micali Painter, appears to have spawned the first workshops specializing added color vase production.

The proprietor of the largest production outfit in Vulci may be the craftsman who signed himself Arnthe Praxias before the firing on an amphora now kept in the Cabinet des Médailles, Paris. This coupling of names—one Etruscan (albeit with the Greek affix "e" and one Greek—suggests a *metoikos* (outsider), either from Cumae or Chalcidian Sicily, to judge from the alphabet used, or an Etruscan son of a Greek immigrant. Certainly, the handling of figures on the eponymous vase and on most of the workshop's creations is at most modest, even naive, with vestiges of the Micali Painter's style. And yet a very small group of vessels stands apart from the routine pieces in terms of quality; these are attributed to the Jahn Painter, who evinces a more refined aesthetic and a sometimes surprising penchant for epic narrative—particular the Trojan epic. The scholar Prag has inferred close links between this artist and the Copenhagen Painter (an Athenian vase-painter active from 480 to around 460 B.C.), probably the fruit of a special trading relationship that fostered the transmission of certain iconograpihic devices—the Jahn Painter acting as his associate at Vulci—or even through personal trips to Athens, where he may have apprenticed or perfected his craft at the Cerameicus (Potters' Quarter). This prompts one to wonder why he chose added color given that his "colleague" the Copenhagen Painter was accomplished in the more elaborate red-figure method, and whether the Jahn Painter really did study at the Cerameicus. But here one must take note of another technical factor, which may explain the greater and more lasting success of added color in Etruria with respect to Greece, and that is the quality of Tuscan clay. As anyone can see from museum exhibits, Tuscan clay oxidizes less easily, and even when fired at length fails to achieve the intense red-ocher coloring of the slip that makes the finer Attic vases so appealing; whereas, though opaque and less durable, the red pigment immediately gave the desired effect, thereby reducing the number of items rejected for excessive reduction or oxidation.

These considerations on the technical aspects of production immediately bring to mind another well-known signature, *metru.menece* on a fragment of red-figure vessel found in Populonia, showing two clothed figures in conversation. There is no doubt that the Etruscan word *menece* is equivalent to the Greek *epoiese*, and the name Metru is the Etruscanized version of the Greek name Metron, giving us the motto "Metron made me." Be that as it may, the shard is decidedly Attic both in technique and style, and appears to derive from the well-known workshop of the Penthesilea Painter (ca. mid-fifth century). Two explanations are possible: either the potter from the Cerameicus in Athens, working exclusively on Etruscan commission, signed his work in Etruscan—the only such case, without proof but nevertheless possible; alternatively, we are dealing with another *metoikos* (like Praxias), who ran a workshop in Etruria, once again presumably at Vulci. However, we run up once more against the question of technique: if it is possible that a branch of the Penthesilea Painter's workshop existed in Vulci, this implies a flow of Attic clay into Etruria (a point lucidly explained by David Gill), which may have served as ballast for vessels sailing from Greece to Italy. It is hard to assess how economically viable such transport would have been, but most certainly the case of Metru stands alone, and is as more eloquent about the organization of Attic trade than about the origins of Etruscan red-figure vase production.

On this point, it is more useful to stress the existence of a class of vases with decoration in superposed color deriving from the Jahn Painter, which, as recently pointed out by Stefano Bruni, developed around Chiusi with a certain consistency in the course of the fifth century, paving the way for the refined red-figure wares that followed in the ensuing century.

Vulci stands out once more as the wellspring of all the early experiments in true red-figure technique on Etruscan soil; there are also certain large vases, kraters, and amphoras datable to the fifth century of a marked Attic stamp, though of modest workmanship which are now assigned to Orvieto and Chiusi (i.e., inland Etruria), thereby confirming a hitherto unsuspected autonomy and precocity of development in these areas. But especially Vulci was the original and enduring driving force behind development.

Rodin Painter, so-called Vibenna kylix *portraying two satyrs, from Vulci (?), ca. 400* B.C.
Paris, Musée Rodin
cat. 323

An interpretative model of exemplary clarity and cogency that still holds today was proposed by Brian B. Shefton over thirty years ago, when he discussed the Rodin Painter *kylix* in Paris and a remarkable *stamnos* at the Museo Episcopal in Vich, Spain, attributed to the London Painter F 484. In both our cases we have the Attic model from which they derive: on the outside of the cup, the satyr scenes are clearly copies which, while slightly simplified, faithfully conform to the original motif on the so-called Œdipus Painter cup in the Vatican (or its possible twin).

The *thiasos* of the London Painter F 484 proposes a clumsy reduction of the renowned frieze known from the Paris amphora of the Achilles Painter (Cabinet des Médailles). In the case of the former, the Etruscan artifact establishes a faithful rapport with the Attic model, complying in both imagery and style; the latter, instead, borrows only the imagery—probably indirectly—implying a different "distance" of the London Painter F 484 vase from its respective original work in terms of both of style and time, and therefore it may fall outside the traditional earlier red-figure timeframe and belong to the fourth century, leaving the said Paris Rodin *kylix* dating around 400 B.C., when I do not believe entirely untenable the double syncopation in the tondo inscription "avles vpinas," however premature it may seem.

Undoubtedly, chronological revisions will arise from the publication of the finds made at the excavations in Civita di Tarquinia, where a fragment of a kylix deriving from earlier Vulci production was found in association with material dating to the first half of the fifth century.

Dating to the dawn of the fourth century is a masterpiece of Etruscan artistry, the so-called Casuccini *stamnos* (Museo Archeologico, Palermo), which bears a running frieze representing the putative motherhood of Leda (nursing the egg of Nemesis) and the suicide of Ajax Telamonius: the eerie juxtaposition of birth and death as a laconic summary of the entire Trojan epic, which opens with the abduction of Helen, Nemesis' daughter, and endswith the suicide of the most noble of Greek heroes. Upon close examination the imagery and style betray hints of the post-Parthenon late-fifth-century Attic models championed by Polion, the Kadmos Painter, the Chrysis Painter, whose art must have been transmitted through branches active in Lucania in the decades immediately following the foundation of Thurii. Similar echoes of Italiot manufacture can be discerned in the eponimous krater of the so-called Argonauts Painter (Florence, Museo Archeologico), found at Chiusi, in which the male nude types are allowed a varied and liberally chiastic arrangement, with large heads full of hair reminiscent of the proto-Lucanian Amykos Painter, dated by Trendall and Cambitoglou to the last quarter of the fifth century.

At this point in our historical overview of Etruscan production it may be useful to note the markedly different output of the so-called Settecamini Painter, formerly considered to be of Vulci but assigned to northern Etruria by Cristofani. This artist—doubtless active at a later date—also turned to major epic and mythological subjects, recasting the intense story of Le-

Argonauts Painter, bell krater with conversation scene, from Chiusi. Florence, Museo Archeologico

da's motherhood and the suicide of Ajax. This artist's work heralds the start of a "Campanizing" ("Paestanizing") stylistic trend, particularly in the handling of the drapery. Pontrandolfo's redating of the start of Assteas' workshop production toward 380 B.C. (instead of 360) should put us on our guard against contraction on the chronology of developments in Etruria. This does not prevent us from observing a notable gap between the two final phases of earlier red-figure painting, namely, between the "Lucanizing" manner exemplified by the painter of the Casuccini *stamnos*, or the Argonauts Painter, around the first quarter of the fourth century; and the "Paestanizing" vein of the Settecamini Painter in the second quarter, or shortly thereafter.

The Faliscan workshop

Owing to the consistency and sheer quantity of its output, the pottery manufactured at Falerii Veteres (modern Civita Castellana) affords one of the clearest patterns of the evolution of styles; this impressive production was fueled by the sustained demand of a clientele concentrated in the Tiber area and environs. Notably, Faliscan pottery offers a rich repertoire of keenly Hellenized mythological figuration that in turn provides insights into its local *interpretatio*; together with the incised mirrors, Faliscan red-figure vases are quite frequent in the catalogue of *Lexicon Iconographicum Mytologiae Classicae*: despite the fact that the Faliscans were, paradoxically, not properly Etruscan in either the ethnic or the linguistic sense, their output remains one of the most representative of Etruscan visual culture.

As a means of identifying features developing in synchrony or parallel with those of Italiot painting, it is worth making use of the category Arturo Stenico coined as "proto-Faliscan" (on the lines of "proto-Italiot"), into which he slotted items of earlier manufacture, e.g., large symposium vessels (kraters and *stamnoi*) nobly decorated in late-fifth-century style by workshop masters of Athenian origin or by their immediate descendants. It was here, during the tumultuous years of the Peloponnese War, that the popularity of the dominant Attic aesthetic gave rise to the so-called "Tiburtine Classicism," which many scholars consider a sort of *interim* period.

In her PhD dissertation Benedetta Adembri punctually revised the timeframe of the said proto-Faliscan phase, relocating it to 380 B.C., tracing an arc of development from the Del Chiaro Painter (ostensibly a painter of Attic birth active in the circle of the Jena Painter), progressing through the Nepi, Nazzano, and Diespater Group painters; meanwhile the painter of the Aurora krater (Villa Giulia) is allied with the Diespater Group's production and allegedly attests to stylistic influences of Apulian stamp dating to shortly before mid-century; such an "Apulian" characterization is questionable, however, given Apulia's marked reliance on entrenched late-Classical Attic models, and the scarcity of archaeological evidence of direct trade links between Etruria and Apulia in the fourth century B.C. As a result, the earlier phase of Faliscan kylikes is datable to 350 B.C., followed by the so-called "fluid" phase (Beazley) from 340 or 330 B.C. This entails a certain telescoping of the production chronology, with the first spell of the largest Etruscan workshop's stylistic evolution condensed into forty years of the fourth century.

It is significant that in mid-century ended the first of the Falisco-Etruscan wars against Rome, followed by long truce before hostilities resumed in 311 B.C. At this point we can fairly reasonably fix the emergence of Attic-style Faliscan production and its rich mythological contents in parallel with the first prewar period, in the first half of the fourth century, that is. The ensuing phase toward Beazley's "fluid" production belongs to the forty-year period of the *indutiae*, when moreover one can assume considerable mobility among craftsmen, as proven by the clearly Faliscans origin of the workshops at Cerveteri and Tarquinia in the second half of the fourth century (see below *Vulci and Tarquinia* and *Standardization...*), and the Vanth Painter, a master craftsman of manifest Faliscan training, who is known to have opened a workshop in Orvieto, specializing in funerary vases of somewhat redundant monumentality. This shift away from elite products toward items of everyday consumption is confirmed by the return to the technique of added color in a workshop that takes its name from the signatory, "Sokra," meaning Socrates, in all likelihood the name of another foreigner of Greek nationality.

The northern workshop

In the present case, "northern" means the Clusium and Volaterrae Groups combined, whose topography and classification have long been the topic of weary and unfruitful controversy. This said, it is widely agreed that the earliest workshops (those dating to the third quarter of the fourth century) served a relatively wealthy clientele concentrated in Chiusi and today's Val di Chiana, who dictated precise requirements for vessel shapes—*kylikes*, plastic vases, tiny *skyphoi*; later, around 320 B.C., the transfer of a couple of craftsmen to Volterra fostered new specializations in funerary kraters and *stamnoi* production—vessels required for rituals specific to the district—which continued with increasing standardization up until around 270 B.C.

Doubts remain as to the background and training of the foremost vase-painters of Chiusi—the Sarteano and Montediano Painters—with their highly personal calligraphic hand that combines strands of the Severe style with late Classical, and employs largely Dionysiac scenes inserted in the tondos of the *kylikes*, accompanied by the progressive stylization of outside painted figures. While there is enough evidence to trace out the earliest phases of vase-painting in inland and northern Etruria (see above, *Incunabula...*), and the links with the Faliscan cups group (whose work doubtless made its way to Clusium), theultimate link between the two sets is still missing; furthermore, and particularly in light of Adembri's redefinition of production chronology, the *kylikes* of the Clusium Group cannot be imitations of their Faliscan counterparts, not even of those immediately preceding them, but were of contemporary production.

Moreover, the usual semantic ambiguity of the Dionysiac and erotic imagery are apposite for both symposium and tomb milieus; this applies to the peculiar figures on the outsides of the cups, and for the likely symbolism of certain epico-mythological themes (once again Leda's alleged motherhood, the apotheosis of Heracles, Menelaus's assault of Helen); but are

Montediano Painter or Montebrandoni Painter, satyr-head-shaped jug, ca. 320 B.C. Paris, Musée du Petit Palais

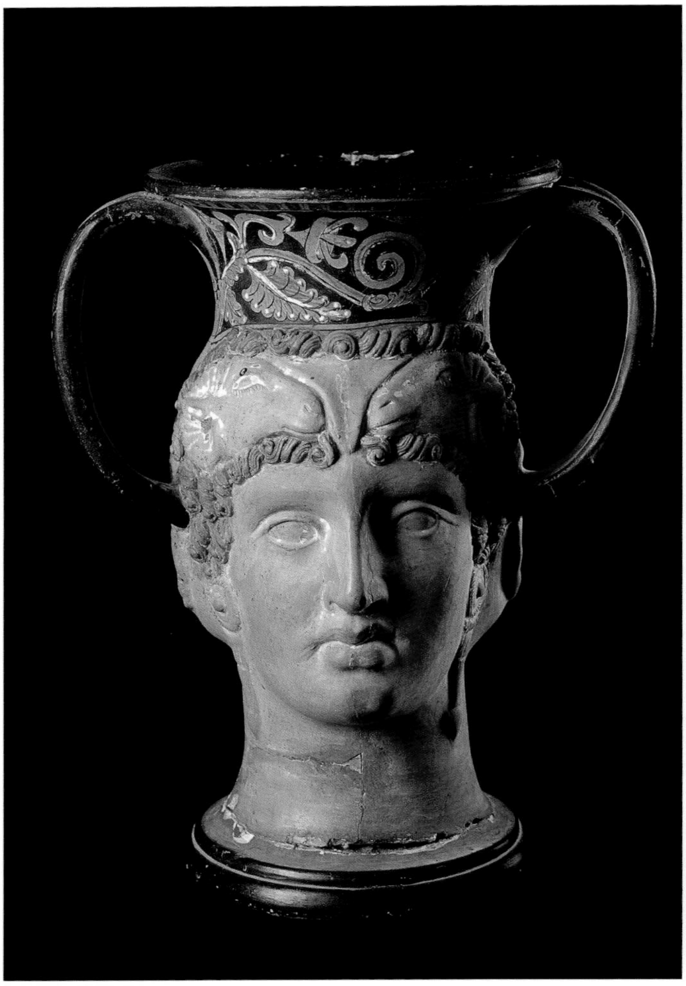

Two-headed kantharos *with Heracles and Omphale from Cerveteri (?), ca. 320* B.C. *Rome, Museo di Villa Giulia*

sure the funerary implications of the (winged) Nereids displaying the arms of Achilles on several duck-*askoi* ointment jars. An exceptional instance is afforded by the frieze on the *calyx*-krater decorated by the Montebradoni Painter, an artist who moved from Chiusi to Volaterra, in which a Greek "cartoon" of early fourth-century style was sapiently crammed with figures of Lysippian stamp and therefore assignable stylistically to fifty years later, aiming at Etruscanizing the *kathodos* (in the manner of Vergil *ante litteram*) of a hero (Agamemnon?) in an Underworld overruled by Achilles.

For the more specifically Volterran pottery, I have divided production into two distinct phases based on the English terminology used for Italiot painting, the first being Early Volterran (320–300 B.C.), with the "plain" manner typical of the so-called Transitional Group, and the "ornate" or "monumental" embodied by the Hesione Painter and his circle; and the second, the Fully Developed Volterran style of the first quarter of the third century, typified by the painters known by the names of the Pygmy Trumpeter (or Monteriggioni), the Tuscan Column, and the Nun. While Early Volterran evinces close ties with the imagery and style of the Clusium Group, the Fully Developed phase shows a greater fluidity, moving radically and irreversibly away from the Hesione Painter's pictorial manner.

Of particular interest is the repertoire of images which, in the case of Volterra, have an indisputable funerary meaning, and capture the latest developments in Greek mythological painting (foremost the Liberation of Hesione, whence the name attached to that painter), and especially remarkable is the outstanding series of *excerpta* of a late-Classical geranomachy which portrays the Pygmies as acting in a liminal and otherworldly context, and connotes them nonetheless as amicable "buffers" against the anguish of loss.

Florence Painter 4035, bowl with volutes and female head,
ca. 310 B.C.
Sydney, Nicholson Museum

Montediano Painter, duck-shaped askos *with flying female demons,*
ca. 320 B.C.
Paris, Musée du Louvre

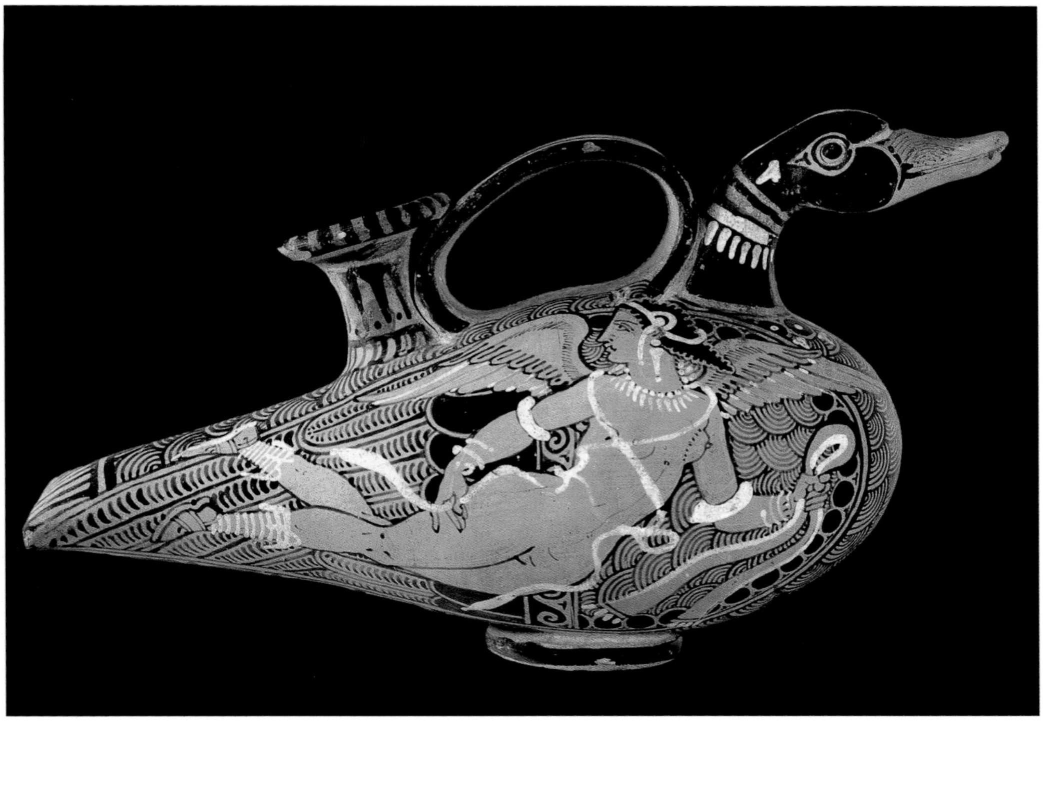

Vulci and Tarquinia

The study of southern production in mid- and late-fourth-century Etruria has suffered from a rather loose taxonomic definition: the whole production was referred by Beazley to the Funnel Group , based on the recurrence of an accessory detail that is not in itself a discriminating feature of the decoration. As a result, the Funnel Group classification more or less directly covered nearly all the red-figure vases produced and distributed through southern Etruria, except of course the distinctive Caeretan ones, which will be discussed later. The ensuing debate—involving those who assigned the production to Vulci, and Del Chiaro's somewhat isolated assignation to Tarquinia—came unstuck because of an overly rigid adherence to ideas that relied on evidence of lesser consistency than was being claimed.

Upon closer examination, the available evidence shows the need to distinguish pottery of Faliscan style—albeit with linguistic features of Paestan extraction—which issues from Vulci from the hands of the Alcestis Painter (or Group) around 350 B.C. and develops (as observed by Cristofani) in the brutally naive manner of the so-called Turmuca (or Aturmuca) Group at the close of the century; then the so-called Vatican workshop, which is considered Vulcian and lies behind the authentic Funnel Group, comprising of the Würzburg Painter and the so-called Frontal workshop; furthermore, the Berlin Funnel Painter (with his Berkeley "brother") who, after an apprenticeship in Tarquinia, appears to have moved to Vulci to work in the Vatican-Würzburg workshop.

A highly curious feature of the Vulcian and Tarquinian vase-painting that goes against the prevailing trend is its preference for symbolic and religious meaning, something one notes in more recent works executed in the twenty-year period of late fourth–early third century B.C.

A superb example is the Hague Painter, whose work marks the acme of the Frontal style and of the Funnel Group's production, which, in the pair of Fould *stamnoi* (Paris, Louvre), provides a skillful juxtaposition of gallant and jocose motifs (the rows of amorini, a *thiasos* on the lines of the Lysippian krater from Derveni, Macedonia), and tragic myth (Troilus killed by Achilles, Achilles in turn victim of Paris' treacherous arrow), all borrowing with astounding awareness from the late Classical style of painting, with apprenticeships most likely in northern Etruria. The reason for this semantic intensity, which successfully achieves the right means of expression, may stem from the heightened ideological awareness of the Vulci elites prior to the Roman conquest of 280 B.C., as had already transpired in the pictorial works in the François Tomb.

Standardization in Caere and elsewhere

The first signs of standardization in the second half of the fourth century variously implicated all levels of craftsmanship in central Italy, and while it affected mirror carving, coroplastic art, architectural terra cottas, and sarcophagi, its repercussions on ceramics are particularly evident. Giampiero Pianu summed up the process as an ongoing reduction "in variation, objects and imagery, leading to the banalization and repetition of a handful of prototypes in series that often exceeded the hundred mark."

This all points to a growing tendency for the Etruscan workshops to turn out a preset range of vessel types—for example, exclusively *oinochoai*, cups, or dishes—denoting a lapse into routine that drastically impaired thematic inventive and replaced narrative figuration with increasingly stereotyped figures, which were mainly stand-alone and often anatomically simplified (female heads in profile were prolific); or with sketchy floral and geometric patterns. On occasion the increasingly slipshod execution affected the technical aspects too, by which the red figures were reduced to a mere outline, with the return of that most telling of decorative shortcuts, added color.

Contrary to what it might seem, the new mode of production does not denote a decline in aesthetic sensibility—nor is it a by-product of cultural or ethnic assimilation. It signals the escalation of mass-production to address the emerging Etruscan "middle classes" who, having shed the traditional ritual and funerary practices, were increasingly interested in the quantity of objects—however repetitive— rather than the individual message they contained.

As mentioned earlier, a case in point is the production of the workshops in Falerii (Civita

Castellana), where one notes a standardization of vase-painting in the work of the Fluid Group and the Sokra Group, and in Caere espite an earlier phase (of equally unvarying standard) that has earned the somewhat generous label of "figured" ware.
Though Caere itself has yielded no earlier instances of "earlier red-figure" production, it nonetheless managed to consolidate and extend its standardized lines of production in the second half of the fourth century (the so-called *Torcop* jugs, and the *Genucilia*-type plates), supplying wares to an expanding catchment area that covered most of the territory of Latium and Etruria, with the occasional outlets in Corsica, Sardinia, the Iberian peninsula, and northern Africa.
As Pianu has aptly observed, the "neutral," characterless (and industrial) nature imputed to Caeretan ceramics and their efficient circulation are both cause and effect of a close dovetailing their distribution with that of the Roman trade network, taking advantage of the unique privileges accorded to Caere in the mid-fourth century within the frame of Roman citizenship. Exemplary of the process under way is how the typical stammed plate decorated with a female head in profile framed by a wavy border—a kind of artifact doubtless "invented" in Falerii—was introduced in Caere by immigrant Faliscan potters, among which

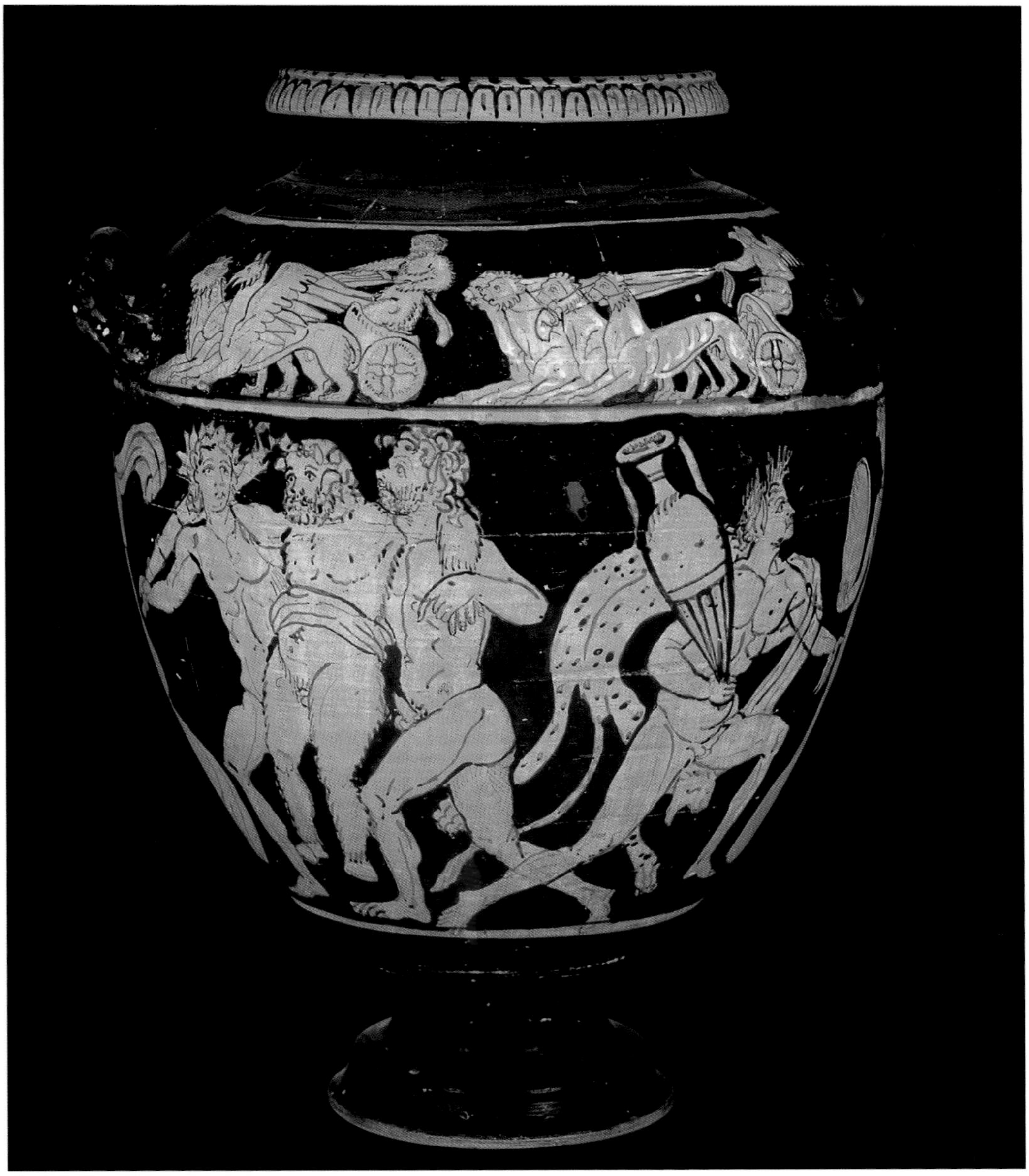

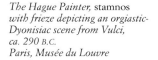

The Hague Painter, stamnos *with frieze depicting an orgiastic-Dyonisiac scene from Vulci, ca. 290 B.C. Paris, Musée du Louvre*

perhaps the woman who signed herself "P. Cenucilia" under the foot of the eponymous plate, now in the Providence Museum: historically, the period sees Caere in marked expansion, while Falerii is at the dawn of the aforementioned forty-year truce.
At any event, as an ongoing phenomenon, standardization of workshop production was widespread and not only affected Etruscan and Italic goods. Indeed, it may be considered a characteristic of the Hellenistic age in general. The process shows up in a similar guise in the art of vase-painting—with a narrowing of variety resulting in the ostensible prevalence of certain shapes; a predilection for female protomes with an unnaturalistic, almost "abstract" manner; the reduction of black painted fields—all over Magna Graecia, Sicily, and Picenum. For the latter region, recent research has established the background to the so-called *Altoadriatica* (upper Adriatic) pottery workshop, tracing its early Atticizing phase, strongly influenced by the models of the Filottrano Painter and the Fat Boy Group; dating soon afterward is the boom in Spina and Adria, where production of these "barbarian" and anti-classical wares continued through until well into the third century.

Alcestis Painter, krater with volutes portraying Alcestis' leave, from Vulci, 350 B.C. Paris, Cabinet des Médailles

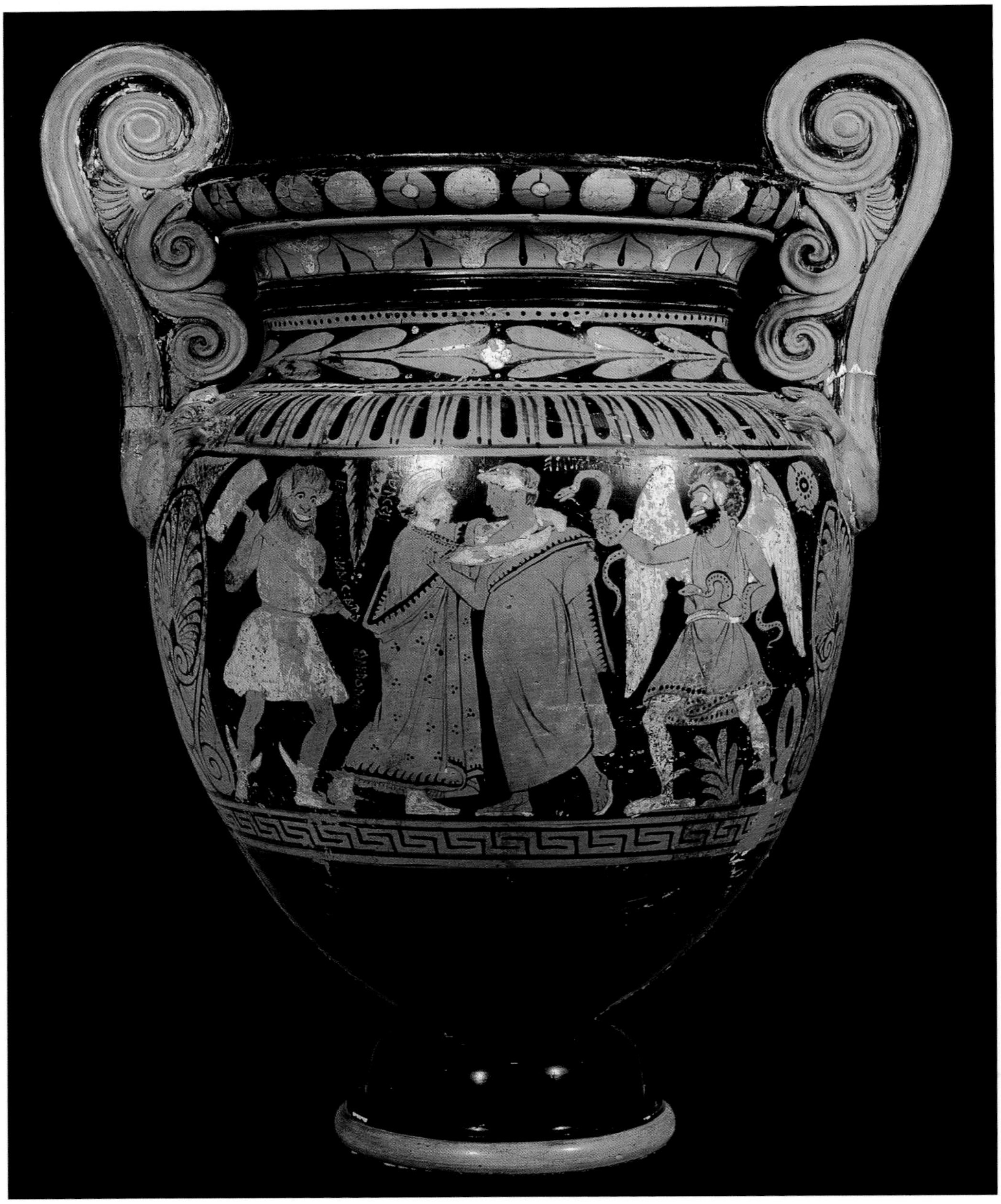

Overpainted oinochoe *from the Group of the Phantom, Tarquinia, late fourth century* B.C.
Tarquinia, Museo Archeologico

Genucilia-*type plate, late fourth century* B.C.
Bassano del Grappa, Museo Civico

This peculiar Altoadriatic style, recently imaginatively dubbed "Picassian" (no less!), absorbed influences from southern Etruria and Campania, evidently filtered and mediated by the Picenum milieu.

Beazley 1947; Del Chiaro 1957; Stenico 1958, pp. 286–306; Shefton 1967, pp. 529–37; Montagna Pasquinucci 1968; Del Chiaro 1974a; Del Chiaro 1974b; Harari 1980; Pianu 1980; Jolivet 1982; Pianu 1982; Cristofani 1985b; Prag 1985, pp. 21–23, 98–101; Gilotta 1986, pp. 2–18; Cristofani 1987d, pp. 43–53, 313–31; Gill 1987, pp. 82–7; Harari 1988, pp. 169–93; Cavagnaro Vanoni, Serra Ridgway 1989; Pianu 1989, pp. 1095–99; Adembri 1990, pp. 233–44; Harari 1990, pp. 33–48; Cristofani 1992, pp. 89–114; Mangani 1992, pp. 115–43; Romualdi 1992b; Bruni 1993, pp. 271–95; Berti, Bonomi, Landolfi 1996; Harari 1996, pp. 127–63; Harari 1997, pp. 193–205.

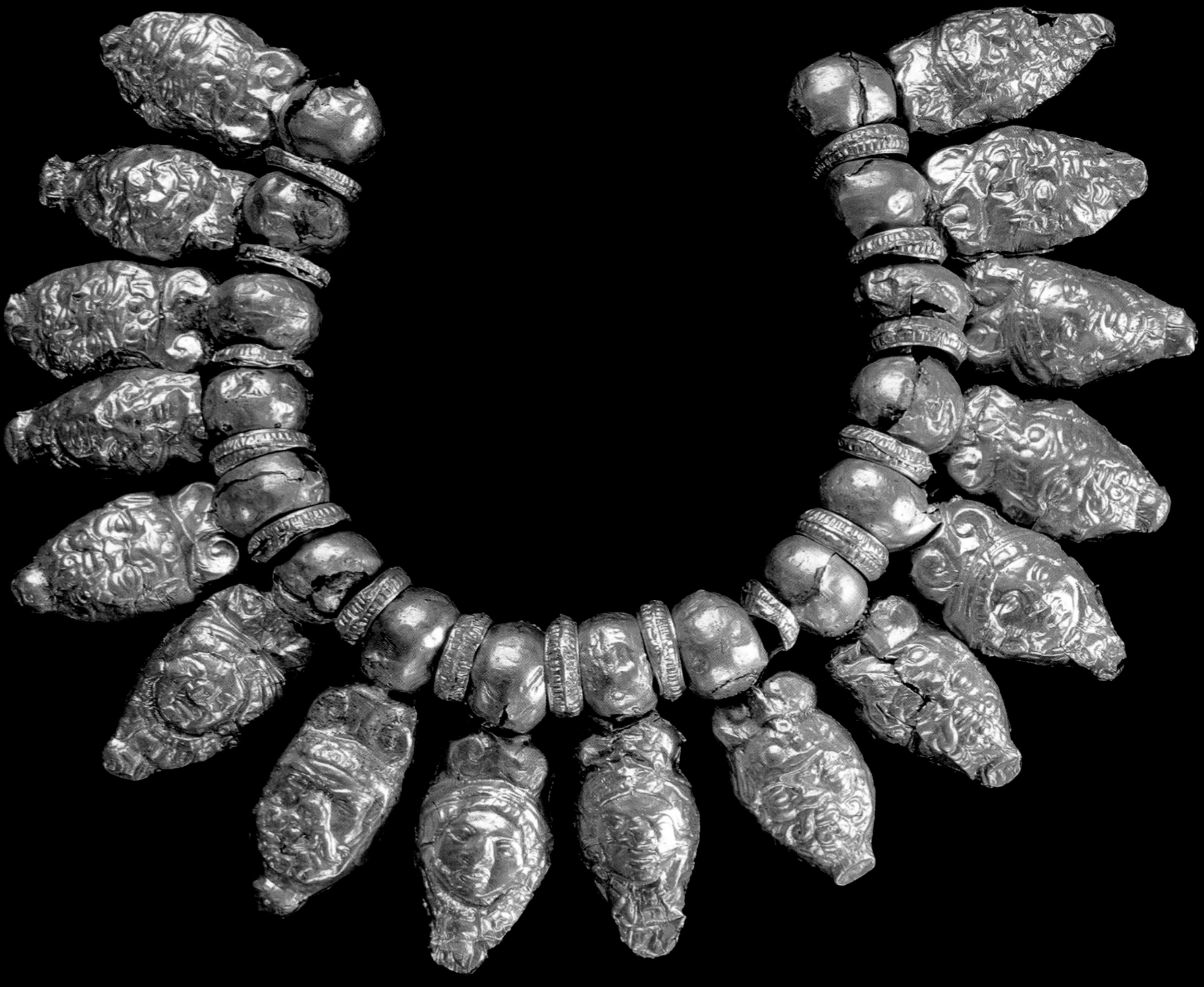

Marina Martelli
Fernando Gilotta

The Minor Arts

Sphragistics and glyptics
Of the considerable flow of *athyrmata* that poured into Etruria and the neighboring Faliscan region and Latium from the end of the ninth century and throughout the eighth century B.C., as well as onto the Tyrrhenian coast where it intensified from the mid-eighth century circa and during the following century after the foundation of the colonies of Pithekoussai and Cuma, a substantial amount was made up of Egyptian and imitation Egyptian scarabs and scaraboids (produced in the Syrian-Phoenician region, on Cyprus, and in the Aegean area on Rhodes). In addition to faïence, blue paste, glass paste, and bone etc., these were also made in semi-precious stones of varying hardness ranging from steatite to quartz, onyx and jasper. Mounted in swivel pendant settings of precious metals, usually silver, which the Etruscan goldsmiths were quick to imitate during the Orientalizing period, these amuletic devices—by means of the magical or religious significance expressed in hieroglyphs with the names of divinities or royalty, sacred symbols, and augural formulas which must have been suggestive if not puzzling for the Etruscan receptors—appear in the Villanovan burial sites of the elite that was emerging in the ongoing process of social stratification not only in the North (Vetulonia, Populonia), but more often and even earlier in the South (Veii, Cerveteri, Tarquinii, Bisenzio, Vulci, Marsiliana d'Albegna).
Noteworthy among these are the five sealstones in red serpentine or jasper of the Lyre Player Group (of Cilician manufacture or, better, Levantine engravers active in Rhodes) from the third quarter of the eighth century B.C. Of widespread diffusion, sealstones reached Tarquinii, Vetulonia, Montalcino and Falerii and were recognized, together with the *Vogelperlen* and tricuspid necklace pieces, as eloquent indicators of the shifting flow from the eastern Aegean. Their value has been assured by the fact that the only two assemblages known, the Vetulonian one of Castelvecchio and that of Montarano, which are datable to the beginning of the seventh century B.C., belonged to women of an elevated social rank.
Simultaneously, contributions from the same Aegean maritime area include the six rare ivory seals found in three tombs, also female, in the necropolis of San Pietro in Campo near Ter-

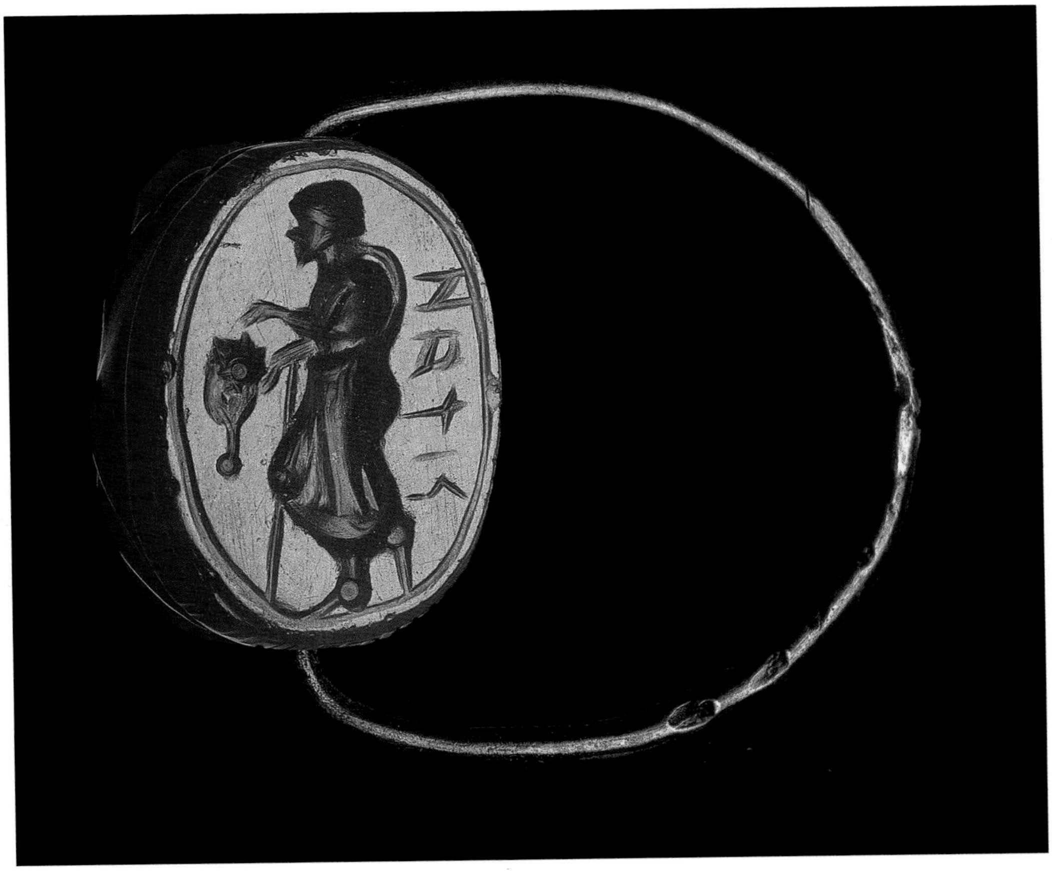

Carnelian scarab with haruspex from Volterra, fourth century B.C.
Berlin, Staatliche Museen, Antikensammlung
cat. 156

opposite
Necklace with protomes of satyrs and maenads, second half of the fourth century B.C.
Florence, Museo Archeologico
cat. 95

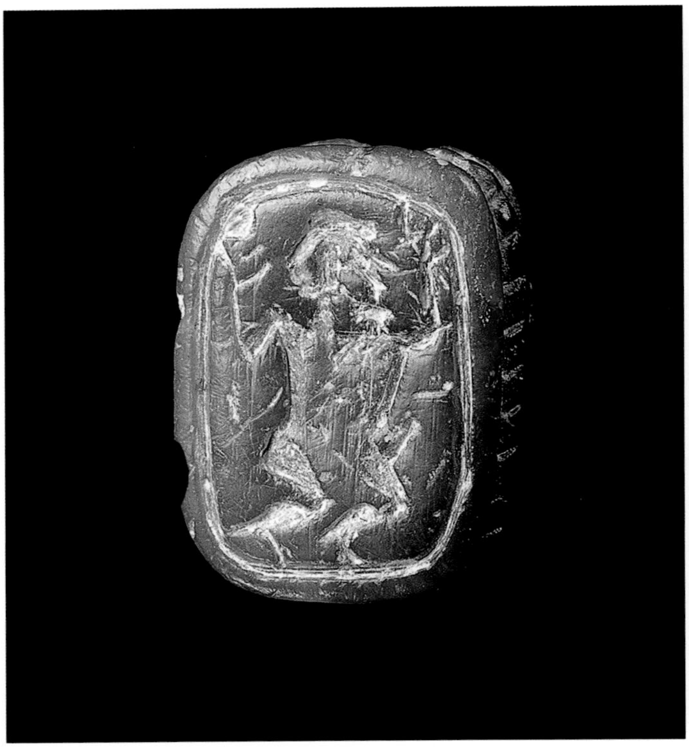

Green serpentine seal, recto *and* verso, *from Poggio Civitate (Murlo), third quarter of the seventh century* B.C.
Murlo, Antiquarium

ni, belonging to a sub-Geometric group, related to Near Eastern prototypes, and most probably produced in Rhodes early in the seventh century B.C. from whence they most likely came through Etruscan mediation.

These trinkets are an indication of the increasing trade and traffic between Villanovan Etruria and the Levantine and Greek agents employed not only in the Syrian emporium of Al-Mina, but also on Cyprus and Rhodes. Starting at the end of the eighth century B.C. and throughout the seventh century B.C., luxury objects began to be imported from the Asia Minor in bronze, precious metals, ivory, glass, etc., the appanage of a by-then consolidated aristocracy that was employing in the meantime workers highly specialized in different crafts who had emigrated from the Near East and were active in Etruria. One of these artists was responsible for the exceptional ivory seal, unfortunately damaged, of the Levantine typology of the *Tiersiegeln* (animal seals), which was also repeated in Cyprus and Peloponnesian Greece during the Geometric and Orientalizing periods. It belonged to a high-ranking male who had been placed with a magnificent parure on an iron funerary couch in one of the richest tombs of Marsiliana d'Albegna, the Circolo di Perazzeta, in the second quarter of the seventh century B.C. While the subject incised on the base, a male figure seated on a throne furnished with a footstool, is faithful to Near Eastern sources in its workmanship and representation of royal or divine entities, and was explicitly chosen by the Etruscan "prince" because of its reference and self-celebratory quality, the exotic little monkey in stamped relief departs from those archetypes and is a more familiar figure in the culture of the seal owner, for the pithecomorphic imagery is indeed found again on an ivory ring, a gold buckle, and a small bronze pendant.

Among the more ancient testimony of semi-precious intaglios in Etruria known to date are two pendant seals in green serpentine that do not come from a funerary complex but, more significantly, from a palatial one, that of Poggio Civitate (Murlo) which confirms their sphragistic use, which was related to their owner's exercise of his prerogatives, and whose configuration is the result of a direct commission on the part of the dynasty installed there. One, opisthographal, with an androphagous lion on one side (a common motif in the Orientalizing repertoire, especially in metalwork, incised bucchero, ivories, Etrusco-Corinthian pottery) and a dancing male figure on the other, was found with other precious objects in the layer of destruction of the first palace which was destroyed by a fire at the end of the seventh century B.C., and thus has a *terminus post quem*; the second, connected typologically to the above-

mentioned animal seals with two lions attacking a boar decorating the back, reveals on its oval bezel, with its partitions and series of zoomorphic figures, numerous syntactic and stylistic correspondences with a more ancient series of gold finger rings with cartouche-like settings, datable within the third quarter of the sixth century B.C., which will be discussed later.
Confirmation that the members of the upper class of Archaic Etruria were used to marking seals with symbols together with their own name, clan or position is to be seen from another pendant-seal, formerly in Göttingen, in the shape of a leveret, with the inscription *mi larθia* xuḷnas, "I (I am the sign) of Larθ Xulna," which, although of unknown provenance, is to be situated paleographically in the Chiusi territory, the same location of the clan residence of Murlo.
At the end of the Orientalizing period and during the sixth century B.C., the progressive transformations of the socio-economic structure and the parallel conclusion of the process of urbanization brought about substantial modifications and innovations—principally and primarily in the coastal centers in southern Etruria, which were organizing and equipping their port installations at the same time for the developing emporium activities and increased import-export trading, in particular with the Greek cities of Asia. The arts and crafts, including glyptics, were also affected by these changes which occurred under the banner of that global "Ionic" character that dominated the entire Archaic period. Within these co-ordinates the intaglio of semi-precious stones reached its own specific and autonomous physiognomy from about 540 B.C. due to the initiative of the East Greek engravers who in the thick of the diaspora following the great Persian king's subjection of Ionia, and later of Egypt and the closing of the pan-Ionic *emporion* of Naukratis, set up their workshops in the southern part of Etruria, as did their colleagues who were specialized in megalography (Tarquinii), ceramography (painters of the Caeretan *hydriai* and the Campanian *dinoi* at Caere, the "Pontic" group at Vulci), and gold work (Vulci), putting their own tried and tested technical abilities and new categories of luxury objects at the disposition of a dominating elite that was much greater in numbers than the exclusive, rigid aristocracy of the previous century.
Gemstones were being produced in Etruria (at Vulci, Chiusi, Marzabotto, but above all at Tarquinii whose port of Gravisca was a busy hub of Ionian *emporoi*) just about the same time or a short time after exemplars were being imported from the East Greek area or the islands, between the mid-sixth century and the first decades of the fifth century B.C. The Etruscan production was primarily in cornelian, less frequently in agate, sardonyx, and banded agate, and only occasionally in chalcedony, onyx, hyacinth, or emerald plasma. The gemstones, like the Greeks ones (which probably originated through Cypriot mediation from the Phoenicians who in turn took them from the Egyptians) were in the form of a scarab (and very rarely scaraboid), the border usually decorated and carefully worked, a form introduced by the first generation of immigrant engravers and maintained uninterruptedly, unlike in Greece, until the Hellenistic age, at which time the Etruscan glyptic production ceased.
Their function as seals, combined with that as status symbols enhanced by a wealth of significant images, was made possible by the setting that allowed for their insertion—with or more often without a bezel—in gold rings with a hoop that could be full, smooth, twisted, flattened or tubular with wire often wrapped around the extremities so that the stones were free to rotate if necessary. Their function as ornaments is also confirmed by their more limited use as pendants set onto necklaces with different beads or elements.
One of the pioneers responsible for introducing new glyptic techniques, morphologies, styles and motifs in Etruria was the Master of Dionysus of Boston who was active around 530–520 B.C. In the ten-odd examples attributed to him, where the most popular motif is the armour of Achilles, the formal stylistic features, in particular the broad faces, massive bodies and compact drapery, reveal, in my opinion, a South Ionian origin, genetically related to that governing the more exacting, ambitious creations of the coeval toreutics. This is all the more evident in the Dionysus with a *keras* represented on the upper side of the eponymous scarab, while Hercules and Nereus struggle in the presence of Athena and Thetis (or Dorís) on the underside.
The Boston gem in discussion is the first of a less common but also thematically notable series of pseudo-scarabs, concentrated for the most part in the first half of the fifth century B.C., in which, in substitution for the usual anatomical divisions of the coleopteran on the upper side, divinities were carved in low relief, such as Fufluns, components of his *thíasos* (satyric proto-

me), a winged female figure, and still others personifying death in war and fear (Ker, Phobos), a hoplite, a Negro slave and, more often, sirens, whereas the heroes associated with the Trojan and Theban cycles (Achilles, Capaneus, perhaps Tydeus), other warriors, the Trojan horse, a hunter, a cithara player, etc, were depicted on the underside.
Like other categories of the *Kleinkunst,* glyptics, although marked by a certain conservatism, also followed the stylistic evolution of the *Grosskunst*. With respect to its periodization, however, it is divided into broader periods and chronological times: the Archaic style (530–480 B.C.), the Severe style (480–430 B.C.), the Free style (430–320 B.C.), of which the last stage is called Transition or Late Free style (350–100 B.C.), and while maintaining a substantial dependence, particularly iconographically, on Hellenic models, it began to develop its own character at the beginning of the fifth century B.C.
The microcosm that was enclosed on the base of the scarabs, often set in an outlined or beaded frame, was divided into a multitude of single figures or groups, generally *excerpta* from more complicated compositions, which were usually placed vertically. Magnified, it was a reflection of the macrocosm of Etruscan culture and society, contributing in its entirety to a close-up view and reconstruction not only of the mentality, ideal models, and social customs of the consumers, but also of their pantheon and religious beliefs, mythology, figurative manifestations, ritual aspects, craft categories, and still more.
Various divinities are depicted in fact, with the greatest percentile held by *menerva* /Athena (in this case as in all the following ones, the name in Italics is the Etruscan one as documented on the gemstone), followed by Hermes and, in reduced numbers, by *nethunus*/Poseidon, Apollo, Artemis, *turan*/Aphrodite, Dionysus, Zeus, *seϑlanś*/Hephaestus, Culsans/Janus, as well as the gigantomachy or the single Giants (one of whom with the caption *me[m]as*/Mimas), and the Dioscuri (*castur*/Castor; Pollux who, as on the Ficoroni cist, ties *amuχe*/Amykos to a tree).
But the undisputed protagonist of the entire Etruscan glyptic production is *herc/kle*, *her(c/k)le*, Hercules, once designated by the epithet *calanic(e)*, employed in several of his typical labors or struggling with Achelous, Antæus, *kukne*/Cycnus or wresting with Apollo for the tripod or bearing the heavens while *aril*/Atlas gathers the apples of Hesperides. He is also depicted in his apotheosis or while making a sacrifice or in actions that are generally less common in ancient imagery, like the devastation of the vineyard of Syleus or drawing off wine from the *pithos* of Pholus. On the other hand, his fundamental connection in the Etruscan world, where he was widely venerated from the early Archaic age, and considered a divinity *pleno iure,* to the realm of water, as lord of the *fontes* and sources, his power as the provoker and protector of springs, is illustrated by the numerous gemstones on which he is represented as he is about to make water gush forth, or filling an amphora at a fountain, resting his foot on it in some cases, or sailing on a raft of amphoras, alluding thus to his journeys beyond the known world and his course toward immortality.
This very limited number of scarabs does present, however, a substantial group of heroes, both Greek (first of all, *aχa/e/ile*, *aχle*/Achilles, followed by *aivas*/Ajax son of Telamon, *uθ/tuz/ṣe*/Ulysses, Philoctetes, *antilχe*/Antilochus and his father Nestor, Diomedes, Ajax son of Oileus with Cassandra and the palladium, *talmiθ/te*/Palamedes, a proverbial *polyheuretes*) and, to a lesser extent, Trojan (*paris*/Paris, Memnon, Aeneas with Anchises, *truile, tru(ile)*/Troilus, as well as Sarpedon, identifiable as the dead person designated as *tinias*, or (son) of Tinia, whose body is transported by a winged *turan* on a sardonyx from Chiusi from the first quarter of the fifth century B.C.), together with exponents from the Theban saga, from Œdipus and his sons to the Seven against Thebes (*amφiare*/Amphiaraus, *aθreste,* [*atr*]*śte*/Adrastus, *capne*/Capaneus, *parθanapaes, partinipe*/Parthenopœus, *tute*/Tydeus, *φulnice*/Polynices), five of whom, identified by name, are united in assembly on a famous cornelian, 500–480 B.C., from Perugia and now at the Staatliche Museen of Berlin. Previously in the collection of Baron Philipp von Stosch, and studied in depth by scholars in the seventeenth and eighteenth centuries, J.J. Wincklemann had commented "of all the engraved stones that one is the Homer of the poets." Other leading characters from the Greek myths, such as Bellerophon, Cadmus, Chiron, *easun*/Jason, *pele*/Peleus and Thetis, Prometheus, Sisyphus, *θese*/Theseus, *φerse*/Perseus, *atalanta*/Atalanta, *elina, eḷe[n]a*/Helen, and Penthesilea alternate with less familiar minor figures who are rarely depicted in ancient imagery, su-

ch as Glaucus and Polyidus, Minos and Pasiphae, i*χsiun*/Ixion, lunχe/Lynceus, *ṃenụçi*/Menœceus, *puce*/Phocus, *stenule*/Sthenelus, *ṣχuθe*/Skythes. This selection is a further indication of the ramification and penetration of Hellenic culture among the Etruscan ruling classes.

Nor is the sphere of artisan activities to be ignored, for it was represented, in addition to the above-mentioned Seϑlanś and a series of forgers of weapons who could be his anonymous peers, by mythical craftsmen like Argos and, above all, by *taitle*/Dedalus (recurring three times with his name and other times without it; the precocious penetration of the latter into Etruria is for that matter attested to by the by-now famous bucchero jug from a Cerveteri tomb from the third quarter of the seventh century B.C.), as well as by a gem cutter, busily working with a drill driven by a bow, which is obviously self-referential, and underlines the high level and importance of that profession.

In addition to those figures identified by name, in which the Greek alphabet was adapted to Etruscan phonetics, or by established schemes and attributes corresponding to Hellenic models, a crowd of anonymous warriors and athletes made its appearance starting with the late Archaic style, and more pronouncedly with the Severe style. The warriors are represented either singly or in man-to-man combat, while the athletes are in various poses, their bodies arched, flexed or caracoling, all suitable for insertion in the oval bezel of the scarab, the iconographic *clichés* of which were absolutely homologous and interchangeable with those identified by name. This certainly does not mean, as has been asserted—and not only with respect to glyptics—that the Etruscan jewellers and their clients were unable to interpret the images of Greek derivation so that they frequently incurred misunderstandings, incomprehension, errors, or still worse, banalities. On the contrary, the deliberate, conscious selection of Hellenic themes and subjects—even minor ones, as mentioned before—was a deliberate response to the cultural parameters and interests of its receivers, who were quick to adapt them when required to their own traditions, ideological canons, and social needs, imparting new meanings to them. On the other hand, there are figurations based on native legends, such as Tages, the *puer senex* who was attributed with the revelation of the *Etrusca disciplina* (found, for example, on a sardonyx in Boston that comes *pour cause* from Tarquinii), or on the Latin tradition, like that of the dancing priest-warriors found in Veii on a well

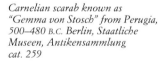

Carnelian scarab known as "Gemma von Stosch" from Perugia, 500–480 B.C. Berlin, Staatliche Museen, Antikensammlung cat. 259

Carnelian scarab with Glaukos, Pasiphae, Minos, and Polyeidos, fourth century B.C.
Paris, Cabinet des Médailles

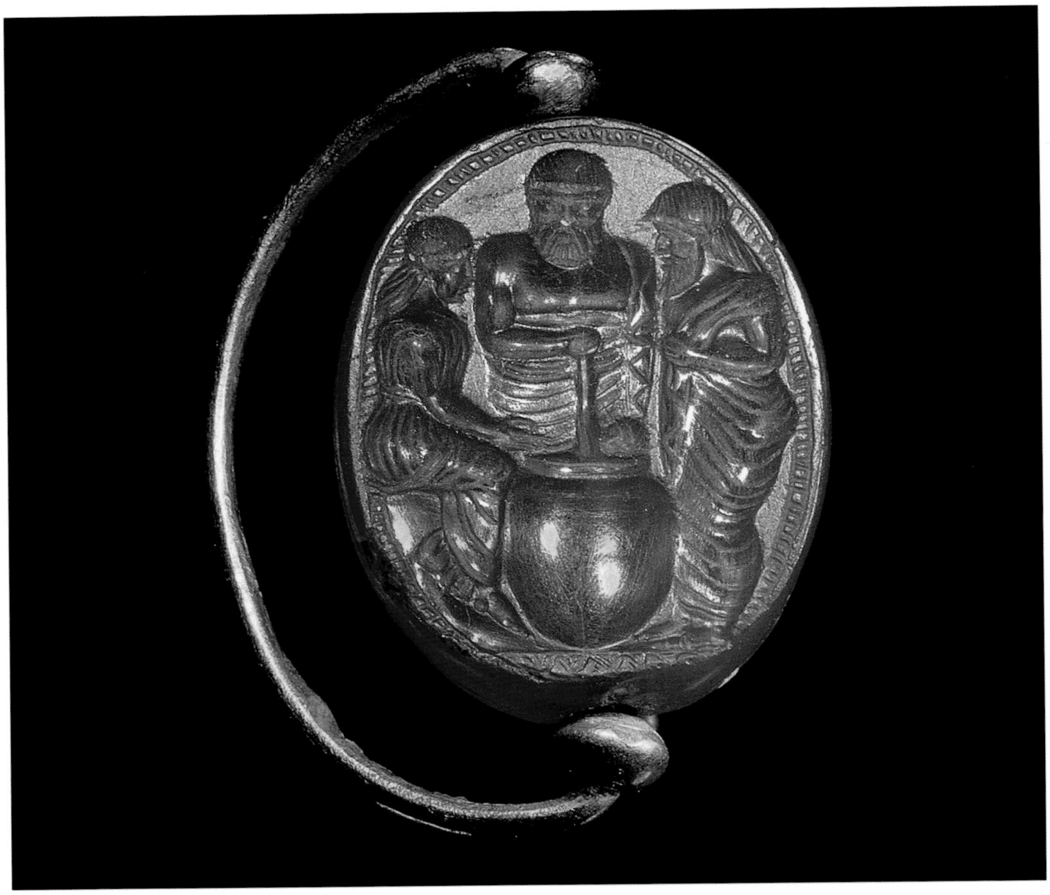

known banded agate of unknown provenance, now in the Archaeological Museum of Florence, with two *Salii*, bearers of *ancilia* hanging on a rod, and the donor's inscription and forename *Appius* in Etruscan characters and the Etruscan preterit *alce*. Others concern the realm of the sacred, like the haruspices (worthy of note is one on a cornelian from Volterra in Berlin designated with the appellation *natis*, correlative to *netś/sviś /s*) or prophesying witnesses, as well as scenes of offering or sacrifice. There is also no lack of winged demons or *Fabelwesen* who have a funerary significance in monuments and contexts of a different nature, but on the gems have an apotropaic purpose; nor of animals, some of which are recognizable as a clan or personal blazon especially in the later series.
Assessed in its entirety, the figural iconography of the Etruscan gemstones, with its Gotha of heroes, warriors, athletes and other emblematic figures, offers an articulated collection of *paradeigmata* appropriated from the ideology of the *aristoi*, who demanded that their values be expressed by an elaborate iconic system. The purchaser-patrons, in an interactive relationship with the engravers centered on the significance of the images, identified with these elected models, and used them as an ideal reference and representation of themselves in order to sanction and strengthen their own social statuses, lifestyles, customs, age groups, authority and professions, genealogies, and local mythical and historical traditions.
The fact that the engravers' workshops were located in southern Etruria (Cerveteri or Vulci according to Zazoff, although I personally maintain that Tarquinii is an equally valid and more plausible candidate) is documented not only by the general stylistic inflections and indications suggested by the distribution of the scarabs based on geographic-linguistic variations, but also by the palaeographic characteristics of the inscriptions (at the moment about 130), almost exclusively onomastic, that accompany the figurations. However, the very few texts with northern orthographic signs ([*atr*]*śte, herkle, kukne, seϑlanś*) could hypothetically refer to Chiusi where a considerable amount of testimony exists.
In concomitance with the flourishing of the Free and Late Free styles, between the end of

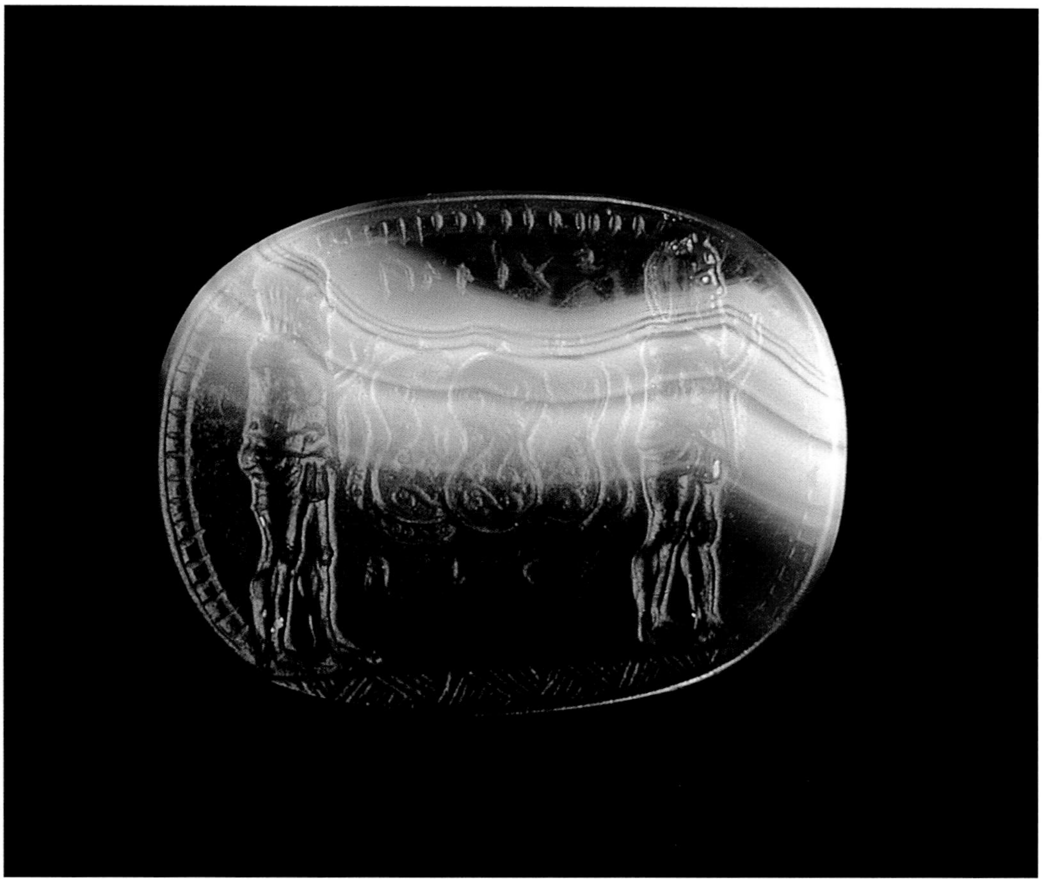

Agate scarab, end of the fourth century B.C.
Florence, Museo Archeologico
cat. 36

the fifth century (for example, in some tombs in Aleria) and the second century B.C., the so-called "a globolo" type work made its appearance and developed. It was characterised by disjointed, plain figures, and a lack of inner details, anatomical notations and particulars, emphasized by the "globetti" or small globes which were obtained using a drill with a rounded tip. There is still no general agreement as to whether this work was manufactured in the Etruscan or the central Italic area, although the mature stage of this glyptic style does seem to refer to the latter.

In the "globular" series, which is quantitatively consistent and accompanied at times by Latin inscriptions, the sphragistic function gives way to the ornamental. In addition to Etruria, its widespread distribution reached central and southern Italy, Aleria (Corsica) and Tharros, and it was present sporadically in the areas of Greece (Athens, Eretria, Melos), Asia Minor (Smyrne), Illyria (Pharos), and as far as the remote Panticapeum (Kerch) in the Cimmerian Bosporos.

While the stones that were used the most continued to be cornelian, agate and sardonyx, and occasionally onyx, jasper, glass, nicolo, and amber, the motifs repeat in part familiar figures from the Severe period, such as some of the Seven against Thebes or Capaneus struck by lightning, the suicide of Ajax, winged demons with a warrior's body (Hypnos and Thanatos, Eos and Memnon ?), falling warriors or ones sitting in pensive poses, archers, riders, athletes, and satyrs. Hercules takes pride of place, appearing in some of his *áthla*, or on a raft of amphoras (at times substituted by a satyr), at a fountain, or standing along with his usual attributes.

In addition to divinities such as Zeus, Janus, Eros, Apollo on a swan-drawn chariot, and his beloved Hyacinthus on the swan, there are also representations of Phalantos (or Taras) on a dolphin, some gigantomachy or single Giants, the fall of Phaeton, and the front views of chariots with a charioteer or horses. However, with respect to the epic-mythological themes that prevailed in the previous centuries and in the contemporary Etruscan ones, the iconography

Golden disc fibula *from Ponte Sodo (Vulci), ca. 650* B.C. *Monaco, Staatliche Antikensammlungen cat. 89*

now includes centaurs and mythical animals (Cerberus, Chimera, Pegasus), *Mischwesen* (griffin, siren, sphinx, Scylla, Triton, hippocampus), fighting animals and real ones (dogs, horses, deer, goats, birds, fish, insects) which probably had some heraldic significance.
The decline and eventual cessation of the activity of the Etruscan glyptic workshops was connected inevitably to the progressive conquest of the country by Rome and her political expansion across the peninsula. This, together with changes in patronage, which now included the less wealthy, was also instrumental in the development of new centers of manufacture in this sector—from Campania to Latium and from the city of Rome itself to Aquileia—which in turn introduced new iconographic motifs that were no longer influenced by the repertoire of their Hellenic ancestors, and stylistic formulas that were an eclectic combination of the late Etruscan style, South Italian and Italic contributions, and Hellenistic tendencies.

Jewellery

The working of precious metals—gold, electrum, silver—dates back to the first half of the ninth century B.C., and therefore to the earliest period of the Iron Age. These were employed in rather limited amounts for objects of personal ornament for funerary deposits in which the quantity and quality of the assemblage was indicative of the elitist nature of the tomb and constituted the first limited but explicit signs of an incipient process of socio-economic differentiation.
The most consistent type of ornaments in precious metals from the Villanovan period is represented by *fibulae* in various forms and of diverse typologies usually according to the gender of the wearer. Corresponding perfectly to much more common examples in bronze or iron, they were created entirely in gold or silver, or more frequently in bronze decorated with gold wire wound around the bow or the acus, or by gold beads inserted on the bow or by silver (or amber) rings strung on the pin. These are found in the tombs of the ruling class *in statu nascendi,* both male, where the warrior role of the deceased is indicated by combinations of different weapons up to the complete panoply, and female, in which besides forming parures with other *fibulae* and pendants in a variety of precious materials (amber, glass paste, faïence), they were often used to hold head-dresses, veils or other articles in perishable material of the funerary costume, as well as children, where they often occurred in miniature form.
The tombs of women and children of rank in the Veii and Bisenzio necropolises, and those of Latium (Castel di Decima, and Palestrina), which date between the second half of the eighth century and the early Orientalizing period, have produced elaborate *fibulae*, generally in pairs, in several materials, with the leech-shaped bow made up of graduated segments of amber that alternate with embossed sheet gold or with bone and/or wooden discs also covered in gold foil.
Other simple types of jewels in precious metals in use during the Iron Age are the spiral *armillae* or armlets and hair rings in wire, sometimes with undulating ends, or in flat strips which held and adorned locks of hair or parts of a hairdo. In the Late Iron Age and the early Orientalizing period, necklaces started to appear in the tomb depositions of women and children. These were generally made of multiform elements which alternated with beads and pendants in other materials, including disc pendants in sheet gold which sometimes covered a bronze core and whose decoration of embossed bands was indicative of the gradual transition, similarly to what was happening in the coeval bronze work, from an exclusively Geometric style to the more varied and complex motifs that were typical of the Orientalizing repertoire such as Phoenician palmettes and rosettes, and zoomorphic and anthropomorphic figures.
Exclusive to women and children, these disc medallions most likely had a talismanic or protective function judging from their vast territorial diffusion—from the area of Salerno (Sala Consilina, San Marzano, Pontecagnano) to Cuma, from Latium (Castel di Decima, Tivoli) to Narce, from Etruria proper (Veii, Tarquinii, Trevignano, Bisenzio, Vetulonia) to Bologna—and reveal morphological and decorative correspondences that are hardly casual with examples from tombs of the Late Geometric period of the principal centers of the island of Rhodes, to which they probably refer or at least share the same derivation from Near Eastern prototypes of remote antiquity which were recovered on Cyprus and in the Phoenician colonies in the West.

Necklace from the Circolo dei Leoncini d'Argento, Vetulonia, third quarter of the seventh century B.C. *Florence, Museo Archeologico*

Another eloquent category of ornaments of both men and women of rank, documented from the first half of the eighth century B.C. and throughout the Orientalizing phase, is made up of a series of gold or gilded bronze *appliqués* in the shape of a swastika, fret or triangle, etc., that were applied to the head-dresses, belts, and clothes worn by the deceased in the funeral ceremony, but most likely not only on the occasion of funeral rites.
During the Villanovan age therefore there was a sparing but gradually increased use of precious metals, which were shaped prevalently in wire, strips or sheets and decorated with *repoussé* geometric motifs, using techniques and decorations of local tradition, which were substantially identical to those employed by the bronzesmiths. Their use, which was limited because of their scarcity (gold was undoubtedly imported from abroad given that Etruria, although rich in mineral resources, did not have any goldmines) and high cost, determined by their intrinsic value, was reserved for individuals or family groups who were emerging within the community just as these villages were turning into urban centers.
Substantial innovations also started to appear in the sector of jewellery, in the last decades of the eighth century B.C., and even more in the seventh century at the time of the grandiose, multiform cultural phenomenon of the Orientalizing period. These were stimulated and fuelled primarily by the intensification and diversification of maritime traffic and mercantile relations with two worlds which in turn had been interactive for centuries; on the one hand, Greece with its *apoikiai* and, on the other, that of the Near East, whose wide range of luxury products were transported principally although not exclusively by the Phoenician *nausiklytoi*.
In Etruria in particular, but also in Latium and Campania, there was an authentic explosion of jewellery production especially during the first half of the seventh century B.C., one that reached unequalled levels of excellence. It was one of the most effective and clamorous expressions of the enormous accumulation of wealth by the consolidated aristocratic classes: a result of the acceleration of those changes in the social structure which, as has been pointed out, had been ongoing for some time and of the social hierarchy that had been created. The

profusion of manufacture in precious metals was the tangible result of a sudden prosperity that created new needs, accentuating and multiplying the requirements of a lifestyle cadenced by solemn ceremonial events and moments and marked by an exhibition of opulence and power, as evidenced by a systematic set of "status symbols": the monumentality and grandeur of the sepulchres, parade and transport carts, weapons like the two-edged axes, sceptres, fans, thrones and footstools, andirons and spits, as well as imported food delicacies (oil, wine), inlaid furnishings and sumptuous tableware.

Together with the sumptuary goods and wares brought from the Levant (Assyria, northern Syria, the hinterland of Anatolia, the territories of Urartu and Caucasia, Egypt, Phoenicia, Cyprus) and from Greece, there were valuable raw materials (for example, ivory) and advanced technologies that stimulated the sudden production or imitation *in loco* of allogeneous products, in the same way as the transfer of experts with different specializations, metalworkers, glassworkers, engravers—of ivory, wood, semi-precious stones (see above), amber, ostrich eggs, etc.—, and goldsmiths.

It was the goldsmiths from the Levant who brought to Etruria the new, advanced ornamental techniques based on the age-old traditions of the Near East, granulation and filigree, which was first documented as being used in jewellery in the third quarter of the eighth century B.C. Together with these techniques, they were also responsible for innovations in iconography and stylistic formulas which came from the eclectic reservoir of experiences of their regions of origin, and so assumed leading roles in the elaboration and propagation of the composite cultural mosaic of the Orientalizing phase.

Adapting themselves to the customs and needs of the Tyrrhenian hegemonic classes, their innovations affected objects of personal use primarily. These were more varied for the women's costumes, and included brooches, hair rings, earrings, necklaces, *fibulae* and bracelets which were organized in parures of variable composition, while men's ornaments were more limited in number and categories and usually included *fibulae* and buckles. Whereas on the one hand, many of these jewels represented an evolution of those in fashion during the Villanovan age, of which the greatest majority were in bronze, on the other hand, a broader typological spectrum now appeared together with an insistent search for decorative effects through the use of granulation, filigree *à jour,* knurling, sequences of small buttons, terminals with plaques of human, leonine or serpentine heads. At the same time, the tried-and-true technique of embossing, integrated with newer ones, continued its own development—simultaneously to that of bronze—conforming to a repertoire now dominated by the nume-

Gold ring from the Tomb of the Flabelli, Poggio della Porcareccia, Populonia, ca. 575 B.C.
Florence, Museo Archeologico

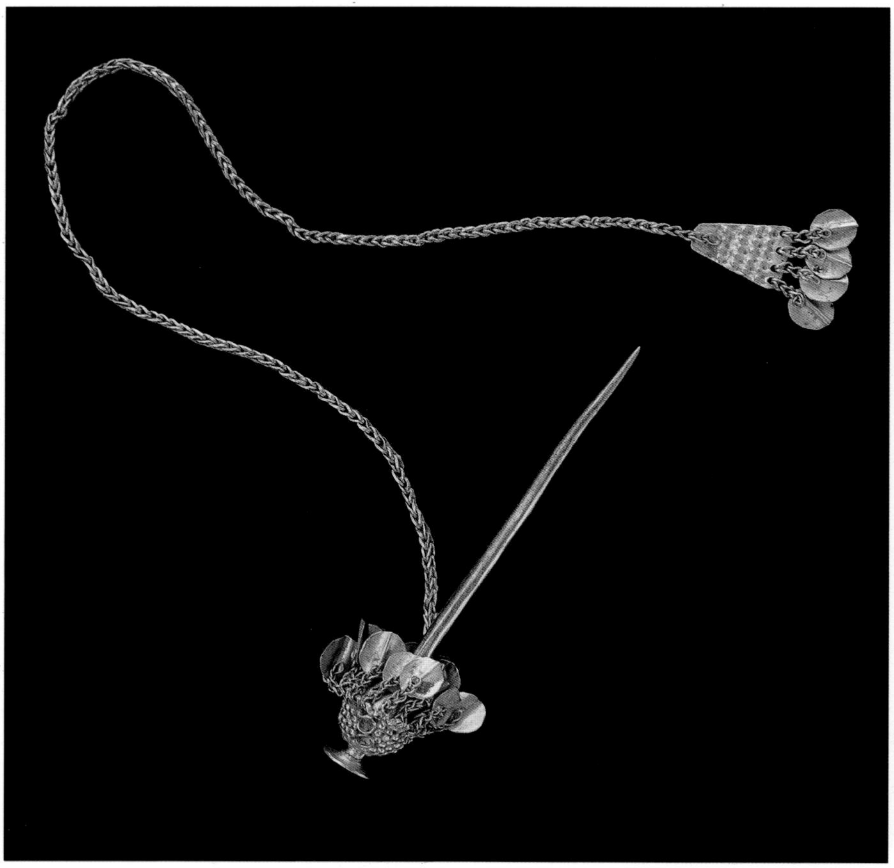

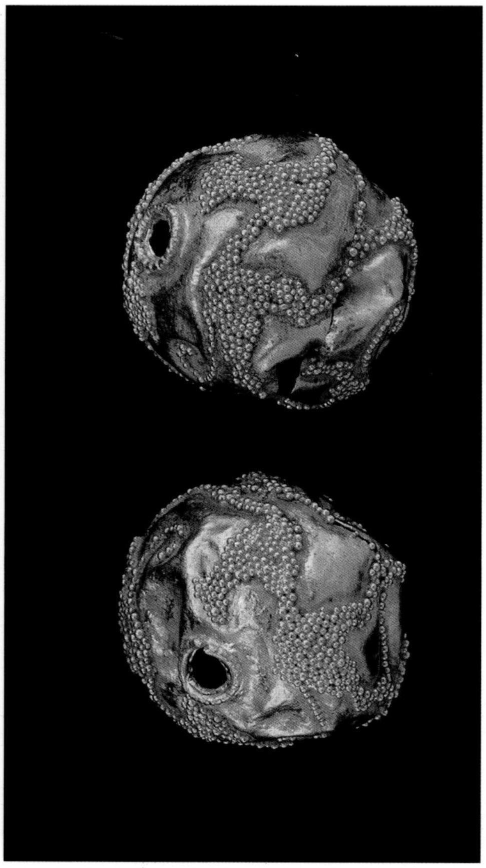

Gold brooch, third quarter of the seventh century B.C.
Chianciano Terme, Museo Archeologico
cat. 105

Two gold brooch heads, third quarter of the seventh century B.C.
Chianciano Terme, Museo Archeologico
cat. 104

Silver and gold dragon-shaped fibula *known as "Fibula Corsini," from Marsiliana d'Albegna (Grosseto) 675–650* B.C.
Florence, Museo Archeologico
cat. 87

Gold leech-type fibula *from Vulci, second half of the sixth century* B.C.
Chianciano Terme, Museo Archeologico
cat. 109

rous formulations of the *potnia* and the *despotes theron*, that is, female figures with sceptres or fans, real or fantastic animals in heraldic patterns or in processions in the same or opposite directions, crescent moons, palmettes, lotus flowers, loop in loop chains, *guilloches*, etc. Besides the bulla medallions considered above, which now also bear astral symbols, there also appear, based on Eastern models, some series of necklace pendants in the shape of an anchor, a "U," a small amphora, a female protome with Hathoric braids set on a palmette, or a nude female figure (an iconographic copy of Ishtar). On the other hand, the oval rings with scarabs and scaraboids in swivel settings (see above) are of Syrian-Phoenician origin. Imported since the second half of the eighth century B.C. and widespread—from Pithekoussai to Cuma, Veii, Caere, Tarquinii, Bisenzio, Vulci, Marsiliana and Vetulonia—they were soon copied in Etruria where they substituted the *aegyptiaca* with scaraboids in amber or rock crystal, or freely re-elaborated ones, as in the case of a noteworthy example in gold from Vulci, now in Munich, from the mid-seventh century B.C. circa, on which lively hunting scenes, a subject perfectly suitable for its eminent owner, are depicted in very fine granulation on the sheet gold bezel.
Other reproductions of strictly Phoenician models, referable to a workshop active in Caere around 630 B.C. are found on plaques that probably served as belt fasteners since they have hooks and occur in pairs, and are decorated with granulation and embossed with the torsos of winged females with Hathoric hairdos surrounded by lush plant forms, which suggest one of the many variations on the theme of the *potnia*.
One definite must for the "princely" male depositions in Etruria, as well as in Latium and Campania, were the buckles and the *fibulae* with serpentine bow, of which some thirty variations exist. The bow may or may not have a lateral apophysis or transversal tube or *antennae*, small spheres, buttons or discs, etc. These reached their aesthetic peak with the long bow and catch-plate decorated with granulated gold and zoomorphic figures in the round in examples such as those from the Barberini Tomb in Vulci (at the British Museum) and from Marsiliana (the so-called Corsini *fibula*). Another shape of *fibulae*, the flat bow with a

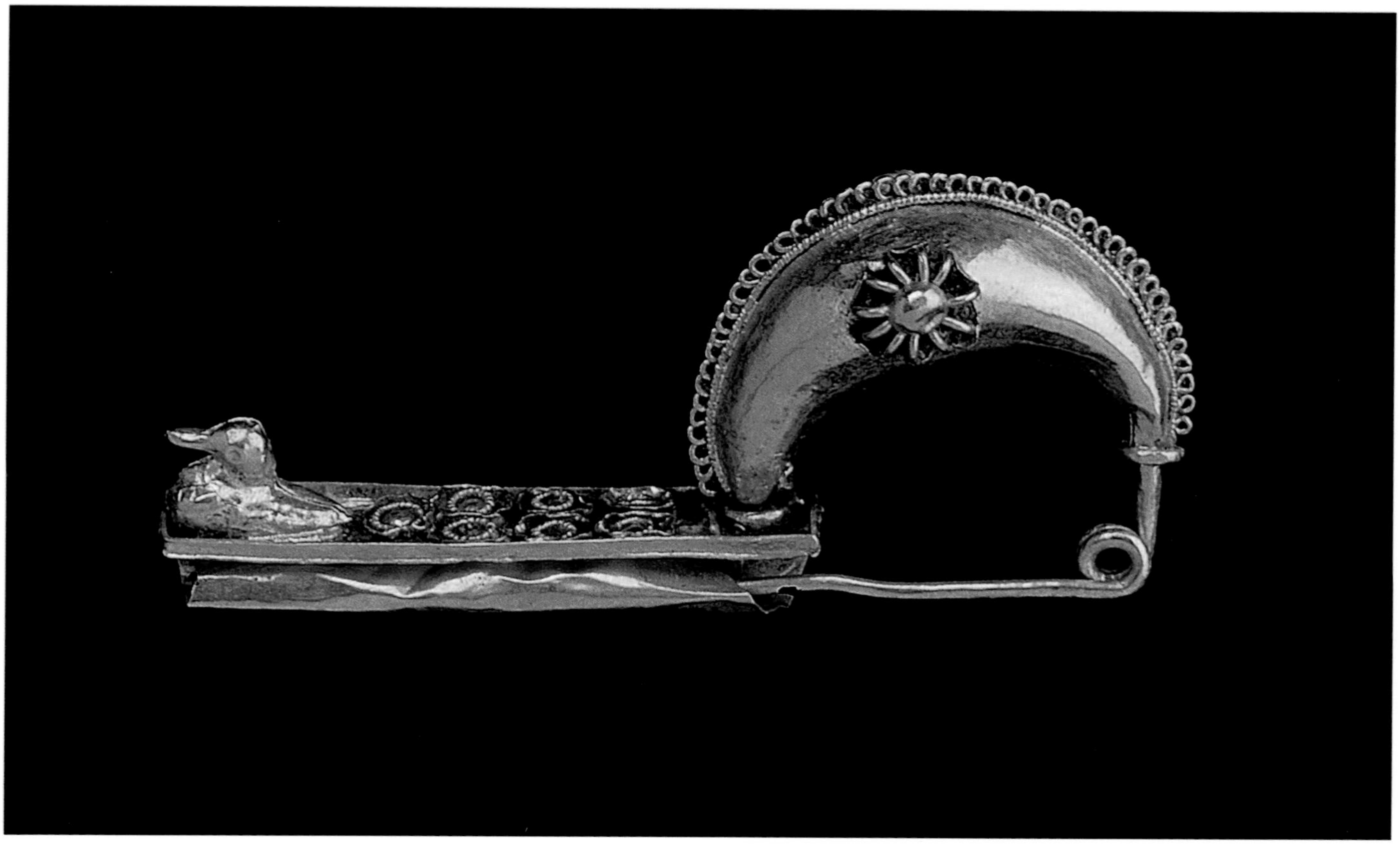

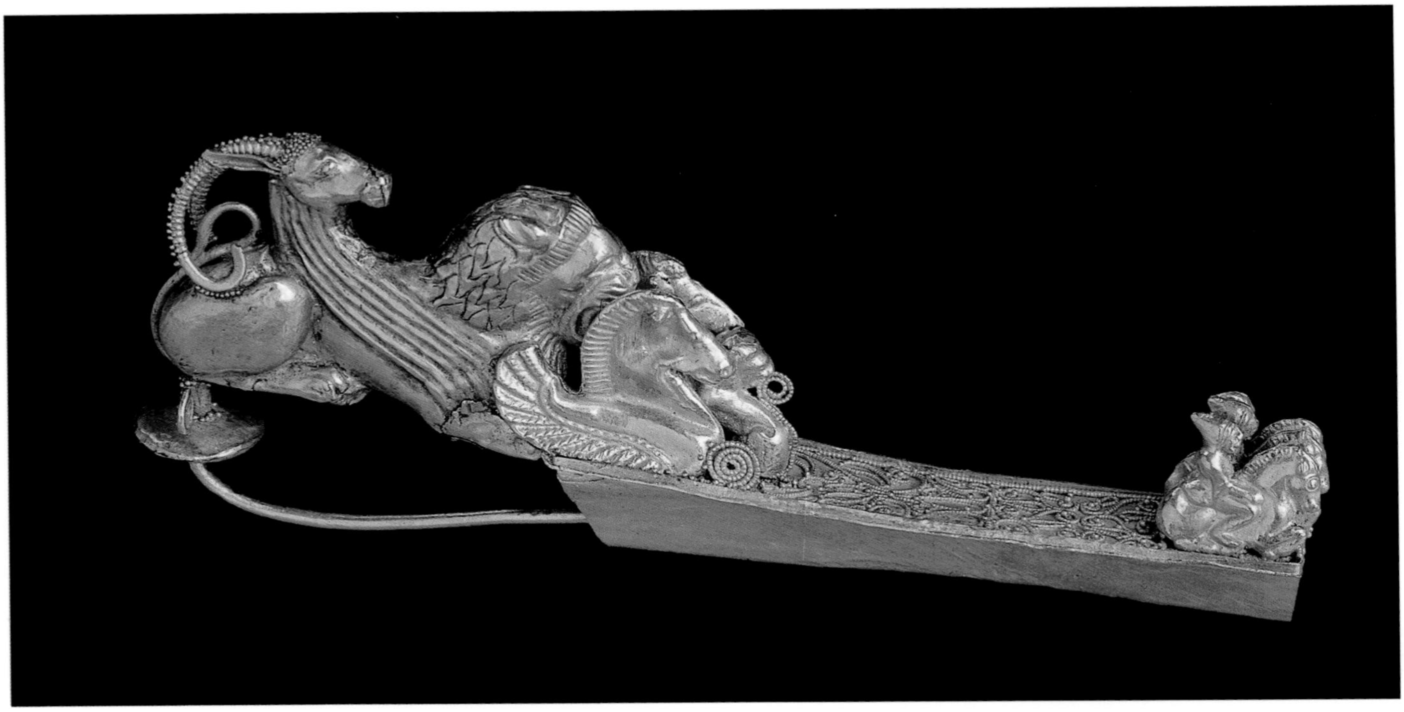

Gold fibula *with plastic decoration from Vulci (?), 525–500* B.C.
Schaffhausen, Museum zu Allerheiligen, Sammlung Ebnöther cat. 90

trim similar to that of the armlets edged in filigree, exemplifies a more ancient stage of the *Dragofibeln* in precious metals, which appeared in the final decades of the eighth century B.C. in the Tomb of the Warrior in Tarquinii and was later re-elaborated in the territory of the north and center as far as Bologna and Verucchio.

A still more select category of "princely" if not royal depositions that emerged in particular between the last decades of the eighth and the middle of the seventh centuries B.C., especially in female tombs, was constituted by the laminated gold pectorals decorated in *repoussé*, the most ancient group of which includes, in addition to the examples with amber inlay of Caeretan origin (Tomb 2 of the Montetosto tumulus), and from Latium (Praeneste, Castel di Decima), the *kardiophylax* from the Tomb of the Warrior in Tarquinii, which was followed a few decades later by two others of Tarquinian origin, all of which were of local manufacture. The most famous example of all of the group is that which was sewn on a magnificent gown worn by a high-ranking woman occupying the innermost chamber of the renowned Regolini-Galassi Tomb in Cerveteri. The gown, like others a generation or two older at Tarquinii (Bocchoris Tomb) and Marsiliana (Banditella, Tombs 2 and 34), was also embellished with gold sheet *appliqués* with *repoussé* motifs which, as we have mentioned, first appeared in the second stage of the Iron Age. The pectoral in question, whose form (at the moment a *hapax*) is Eastern in origin as is its decoration which is made up of eight different *repoussé* registers of Syrian-Phoenician mark, was created in the second quarter of the seventh century B.C., as was the entire set of jewels of the princess (among which stand out a pair of broad armlets, trapezoidal pendants, and the large disc *fibula*, a "modern" version of the ancient Villanovan one), from a local workshop that also produced the pair of armlets in the Galeassi Tomb of Praeneste and the exceptional silver-covered urn from the Tomb of the Duce at Vetulonia.

The deceased person in the Regolini-Galassi Tomb provides us with the most representative artistic projection of the aristocratic ideology according to which a woman was considered an *agalma* in whom were concentrated and reflected the accumulation and treasure of the goods of the clan, which was manifested by the display of luxurious parures and furnishings.

Related to high-ranking personages and at the virtuosic heights that the art of the southern Etruscan goldsmiths reached in the second quarter of the seventh century B.C. are the two superb plaques filled with a swarm of some 130 animals, both real and fantastic, in the round

and covered with granulation which were recovered in two of the richest tomb complexes of the Orientalizing period, the Bernardini and Barberini Tombs of Praeneste, whose occupants had commissioned them from a Cerveteri workshop, the same one that produced the bolt and comb buckles found in the same sepulchres in Praeneste and in the Caeretan Tomb of the Five Chairs, the gold *kotyle* in the Bernardini Tomb, the above-mentioned Corsini *fibula*, and another magnificent dragon *fibula* from Vulci (now in the British Museum).
The ostentatious propensities and the ceremonial rituals of the Tyrrhenian aristocracy from Pontecagnano to Vetulonia was expressed not only by the profusion of personal dress jewellery and exotic objects and by the various already-mentioned status symbols, but also by the sumptuous banquet sets that usually included drinking cups and bowls of Greek, principally Corinthian, manufacture and tableware in silver or gilded silver (only exceptionally in gold) which were of Near Eastern import—among which the so-called Phoenician-Cypriot paterae and cups, and related to them, the small *lebés* from the Bernardini Tomb, and the pyriform *oenochoae*, also called conventionally Phoenician-Cypriot although they are more likely of northern Syrian provenance—or of southern Etruscan production. The latter, often occurring in multiples, were divided basically into *skýphoi* and *kotylai*, and scale-decorated cups whose morphology was borrowed, respectively, from proto-Corinthian clay and metal prototypes or Near Eastern glassware. Those in the innermost chamber of the Regolini-Galassi Tomb (where some of them bear the inscription *larθia* or *mi larθia*, the possessive genitive of the male name *larθ*, presumably a relative of the "princess" whose grave furniture they are part of) have Etruscan forms added to them like the small amphora with spirals and the cup with "pinched" handles.
The earliest and most important centers of gold-work were those of southern Etruria, with Cerveteri in the lead. The latter also played a vital role supplying sumptuary goods to the magnates of Vetulonia as well as to the Latin *principes* of Praeneste and the other cities of Latium and Campania. However, the northern Etruscan school of gold-work, located at Vetulonia where it was presumably set up by craftsmen from the southern district who had been attracted there by the economic potential of the dynamic capital of the most important mining area of Etruria and by its wealthy clientele, also flourished in the middle and late Orientalizing period and was distinguished by its own characteristics of a technical, iconographic and formal order.
In the numerous sheet-gold, broad-band armlets and leech *fibulae*, prevalently of female usage, and in general in the stamped series of jewellery— the extremely rare electrum frontal from a peripheral tomb of the Pietrera tumulus is of prime importance as is the *fibula* from the Poggio Pelliccia tumulus with its parade of riders—the exuberance of the conventional repertoire is handled with indulgence as it alternates the "Lady" and the "Lord of the animals," customarily with female heads and Hathoric hairstyles, stereotyped zoomorphic images occurring either singly, in heraldic groups or in paratactic alignment, lunate shapes, Phoenician palmettes, etc.
The real speciality of the Vetulonian workshops was in any case the very fine gold granulation, which, while it originated from southern Etruscan antecedents, attained its own particular forms and was appreciated in a wide territorial area, considering that ornaments executed with this technique have been found, not only in neighboring Roselle, but also in Chiusi and Bologna. It expressed meticulous stylistic features in *fibulae*, bracelets and brooches, privileging motifs and figurations that were curvilinear and sinuously elongated, and lacking in a certain organicity given the difficult technical process, which points to a substantial unity among the workshops, and it showed that it could adopt even less repetitious and elaborated subjects, like single combat and hunting scenes, which presented ideological paradigms of a heroic-warlike mark and the prestigious activities practised by the upper class of society. *(M.M.)*

After the flourishing of the Orientalizing period, the urban transformation of Etruscan society left rather limited space to the accumulation of private wealth and consequently the diffusion and luxury of jewellery production also underwent a drastic reorganization. A new period of splendor for this branch of artisan artistry commenced in the middle decades of the sixth century B.C. when the "Asian Minor model of life" was introduced to all the strata

Pair of gold "bauletto" earrings from Pescia Romana, second half of the sixth century B.C.
Chianciano Terme, Museo Archeologico
cat. 108

Gold "bauletto" earrings from Poggio della Porcareccia (Populonia), second half of the sixth century B.C.
Florence, Museo Archeologico
cats. 91; 92; 93

Gold disc earrings worked with granulation and filgree technique from Pescia Romana, second half of the sixth century B.C.
Florence, Museo Archeologico
cat. 99

Gold lamina and quartz boss with embossed decoration from the Cupa necropolis (Vignanello), ca. 480 B.C.
Rome, Museo di Villa Giulia
cat. 98

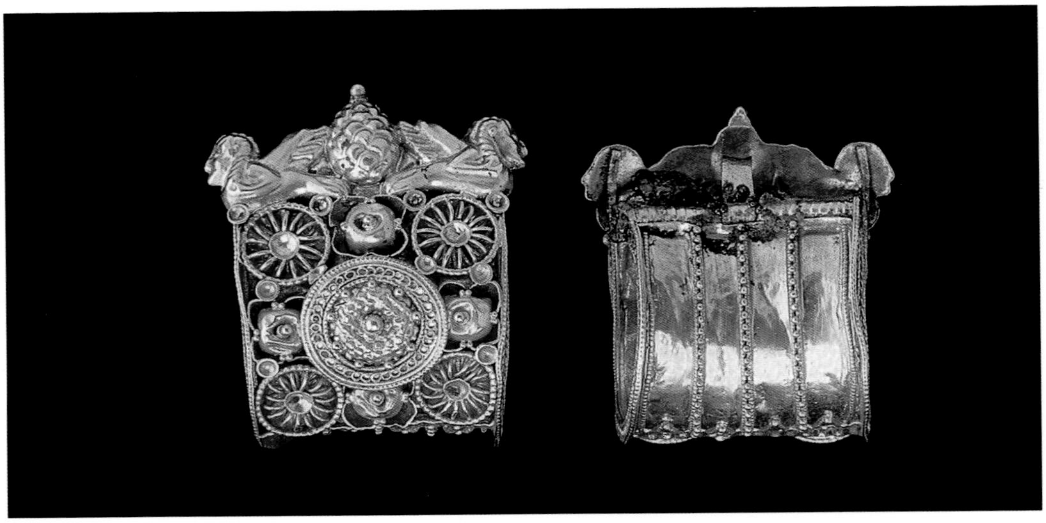

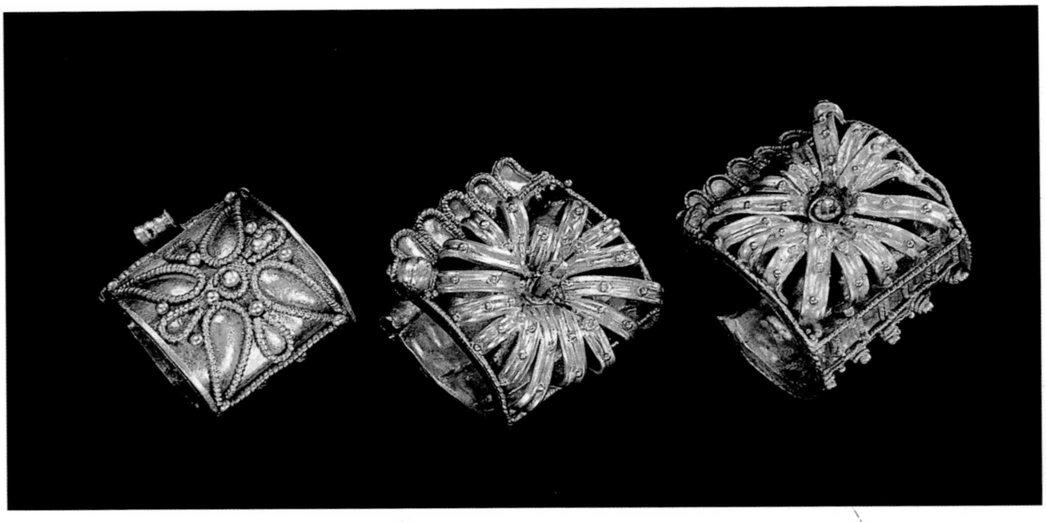

Gold ring with almond-shaped setting featuring a warrior and a female figure, from Populonia, end of the fifth century B.C. *Florence, Museo Archeologico cat. 96*

of Etruscan society, conditioning and inspiring even the most specialized and qualified sectors of production such as those dedicated to the working of precious metals. In a technical field that had not witnessed substantial changes with respect to the previous period, new types of jewellery now became very popular: the "bauletto" earrings, made of a strip of gold leaf bent into the shape of a cylinder and decorated in various techniques (filigree, granulation, embossing, etc.), were probably produced in different workshops, and not only in northern Etruria, starting at least in the first half of the sixth century B.C.; the disc earrings, reminiscent of the Lydian models found in the East Greek cities and mainland Greece (attested to by the representations on the Anatolian frescoes and the korai of the Acropolis) and perhaps produced in southern Etruria; a variegated series of necklaces with acorn-shaped pendants or ones with the head of a satyr or the river god Achelous, the latter precious documents of the late Archaic plastic arts, which referred stylistically to the bronzes and terracotta production from southern Etruria and Campania. Together with the *fibulae*—at times with zoomorphic figures in the round at the end of the catch-plate—and the brooches, the use of finger rings became popular with a prevalently female clientele starting in the middle decades of the sixth century B.C. Decorated in various techniques, the oval settings had representations of animals or complex figural scenes (sacrifices, women at fountains, Hercules and the three-bodied monster, etc.). The style of these decorations is so coherently Hellenic in its formal qualities and so perfectly aligned to the East Greek character that prevailed in the principal Etruscan cities in the South that it has led some scholars to attribute its paternity to artisans who had immigrated there from the East Greek cities, as has also been postulated for some well-known groups of coeval painted pottery.

The architectonic terra-cotta work, votive statues (first and foremost, the statues from the sanctuary at Lavinio) and funerary sculptures, along with the precious jewellery that has been recovered, are to be considered sources of information about the gold-work in vogue in the Etruscan area during the Classical and Hellenistic periods. The majority of these are diadems terminating in decorated plaques; hoop earrings, which substituted the "bauletto" and discs ones during the first half of the fifth century B.C. and were popular in northern Etruria and the Po Valley; earrings with a cluster of globules mounted on an oval shield; necklaces with pendants: on the whole, they were forms which reflected strictly local decorative tastes and traditions. But the materials that perhaps illustrate most vividly the nature of the Classical period production are the round *bullae* and the semicircular pendants. Destined both for young men and for women, the *bullae* and the bosses or studs with stamped decorations constitute a very important series for the study of late fifth century B.C. Etruscan gold-work. Examples with the heads of young men in profile which repeat the more severe types of the *Interimszeit* (Vulci, Filottrano) were followed in the fourth century B.C. by others whose images were closer to the repertoire of the late Classical *koine* (Todi, Vulci). Toward the middle of the fourth century B.C., there is evidence of a growing popularity of *bullae* with a die-formed decoration usually depicting complex narrative scenes. Those representations, based on stories of the gods and heroes of Greek myth, would seem to indicate an ethical-genealogical reference related to the owner, analogous to those that governed the choice of subjects in the glyptic production. The large embossed pectorals and plaques worn by some of the female statues from Lavinio (representations of the Alcestis myth, winged female divinities and so on), on the other hand, also seem to correspond to similar examples. Another important group is made up of gold wreaths which were used at funerals and cult ceremonies, and which refer, according to the type of leaves mounted on the support, to different divinities (although in some cases they may have been of an initiatory nature). The terminals are decorated with stamped figural motifs that were used for the previously mentioned *bullae* and pectorals of the same Etrusco-Latin tradition.

In the final decades of the fourth century and during the third century B.C., the formal, decorative repertoire of Etruscan gold-work departed from the Greek one of Macedon-Pontic imprint which flourished at the courts of Philip and Alexander and then spread across the eastern Mediterranean to southern Italy. Nonetheless, Etruria also adopted different typologies of Greek-style jewels, such as the necklace with lance-shaped pendants and the disc or pelta earrings with pendants (in the shape of a pyramid, amphora, etc.). Numbering among the real Greek imports (from North Greece?) are the splendid boat-shaped earrings

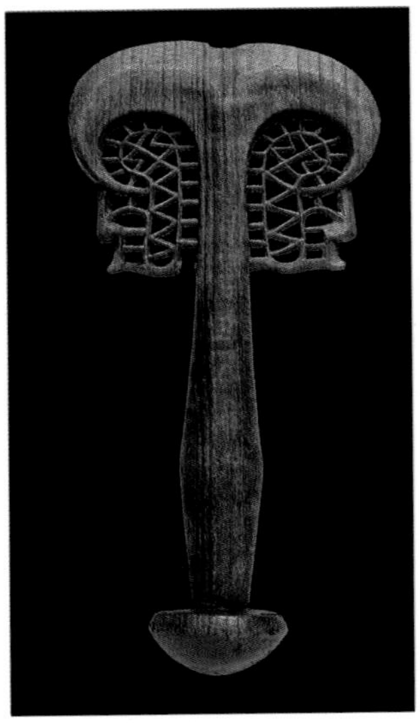

from Bolsena with Nike driving a chariot. Relations between South Italy and Macedonia must have been sufficiently articulated at that time since the entire sector of Etruscan metal production and the related one of terracotta relief work, among the most refined and Hellenized in the Mediterranean area, show noteworthy typological and stylistic similarities with the area of Macedonia and Magna Graecia.

Ivories

Ivory work, together with the more modest one of bone, enjoyed a certain popularity in Etruscan society. Its great value and elaborate workmanship (of Near Eastern origin, as was the raw material) limited its possession to a wealthy elite. It is therefore not surprising that the precious objects created in this material—vases, caskets, bracelets, pendants, small carved objects, as well as fan handles, sword hilts, etc.—constitute a noteworthy part of the richest princely depositions during the Orientalizing phase in Etruria and Latium. It was already possible in the first half of the seventh century B.C. to distinguish imported objects imitating the Near Eastern models from those produced locally, even after the arrival of foreign engravers. Among the former, which were not numerous, were those of Phoenician manufacture, such as the open-work panel from Praeneste (Barberini Tomb) with a heraldic group of animals, which was of significance because of the use of the *cloisonné* technique and the gold sheet backing, or others of (South) Syrian imprint, like the carved groups depicting a lion and its human victim from Caere (Montetosto) and Praeneste (Barberini Tomb). The local production was quantitatively more substantial, like the panels, again from Praeneste, with ritual and hunting scenes, the fan handles in the shape of forearms, and the caryatid chalices from Praeneste (Barberini Tomb), in that it re-proposed Syrian-Phoenician motifs in a more succinct fashion, which were presumably elaborated in workshops set up in Caere itself. Ivory work was

Wooden handle of flabellum *from Tomb 89 at Verucchio, mid-seventh century* B.C. *Verucchio, Museo Archeologico*

Ivory handles of flabella *from the Barberini Tomb at Palestrina, second quarter of the seventh century* B.C. *Rome, Museo di Villa Giulia*

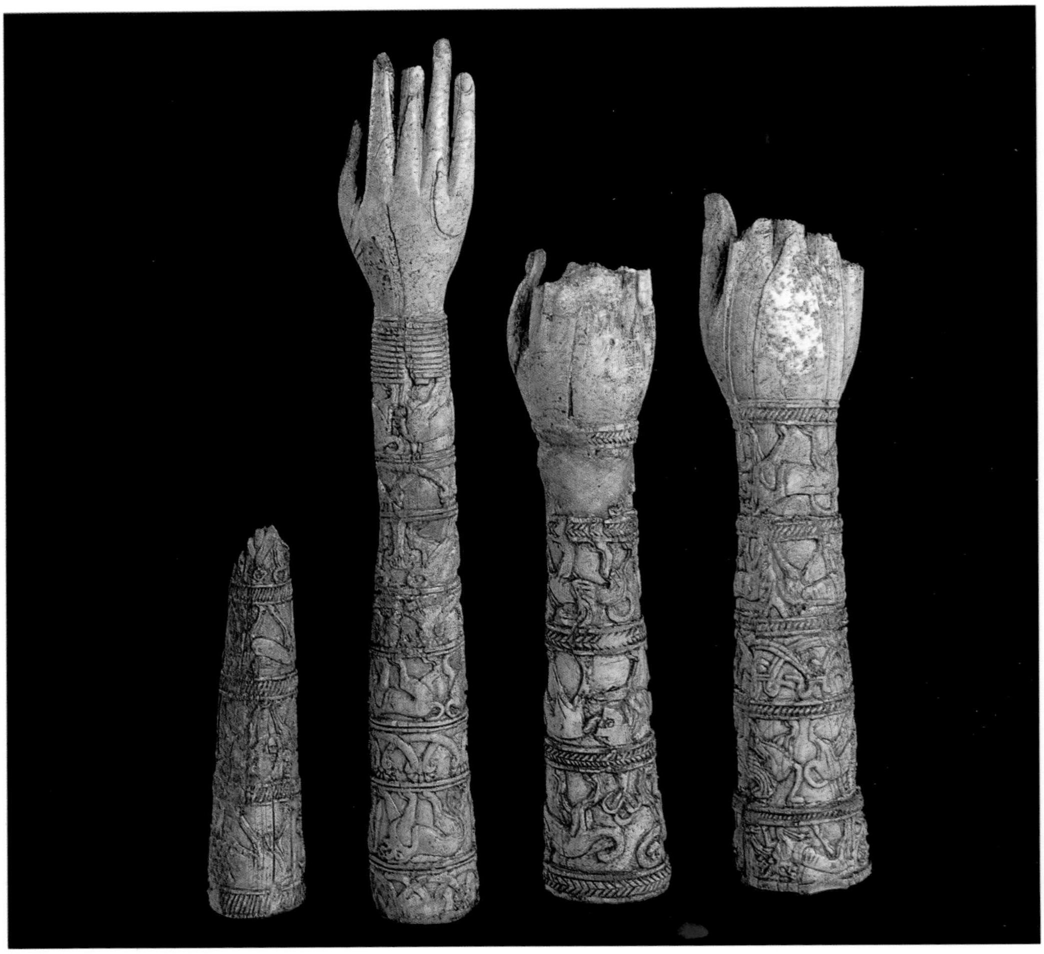

Ivory chalice with caryatids from the Barberini Tomb at Palestrina, second quarter of the seventh century B.C. *Rome, Museo di Villa Giulia*

not restricted to the important coastal centers of southern Etruria; important testimony, at times similar in typology to those of the Caere-Praeneste area, has been found at Marsiliana d'Albegna which can still be dated before the mid-seventh century B.C. Particularly significant are a comb decorated with sphinxes and winged lions, a handle with two warriors wounding a lion, a cylindrical *pyxís* with groups of fighting animals, all of which are referable for their general characteristics and style to workshops in Vetulonia, the center of the mining district in the north where blocks of raw material have also been recovered: that is ivory that had not been worked, sure evidence of a flourishing local production.

The development of inhabited areas and residences of princely character in northern Etruria along the valleys of the Tiber, Arno and Ombrone Rivers favored, particularly in the second half of the seventh century and the first decades of the sixth century B.C., the multiplication in this area of local workshops for the working of ivory, bone and horn. Chiusi—whose production was in a developmental stage at that time, and instrumental in the increased exchanges between that city and the important center of Vulci—has furnished important evidence relative to this kind of production: the *pyxís* from Fonte Rotella and, even more important, the two *pyxídes* from Pania, whose complex figuration abounds in mythological references (the departure of the warrior, the labors of Hercules and Ulysses), are indicative of the cultural models of the local aristocracy between the late Orientalizing and the early Ar-

chaic periods. Equally important are the materials that have been recovered in Cortona, Murlo, Castelnuovo Berardenga, Comeana, and Quinto Fiorentino: the female statuettes and, above all, the *pyxides*, combs, and panels are here characterized by a method of intaglio that is sometimes very similar to wood-carving, and by a decoration which refers, on the one hand, to the above-mentioned Chiusi production and, on the other, shares some characteristics of the Bologna Orientalizing style, whose roots are most probably to be found in the cultural milieu of Chiusi and the northern Etruscan interior.
Ties with the Chiusi ivory work and bucchero are also evident in a group of panels decorated with cloaked female figures, with Hellenic stylistic features of Corinthian origin, which can be dated between the first and second quarters of the sixth century B.C. A richer series

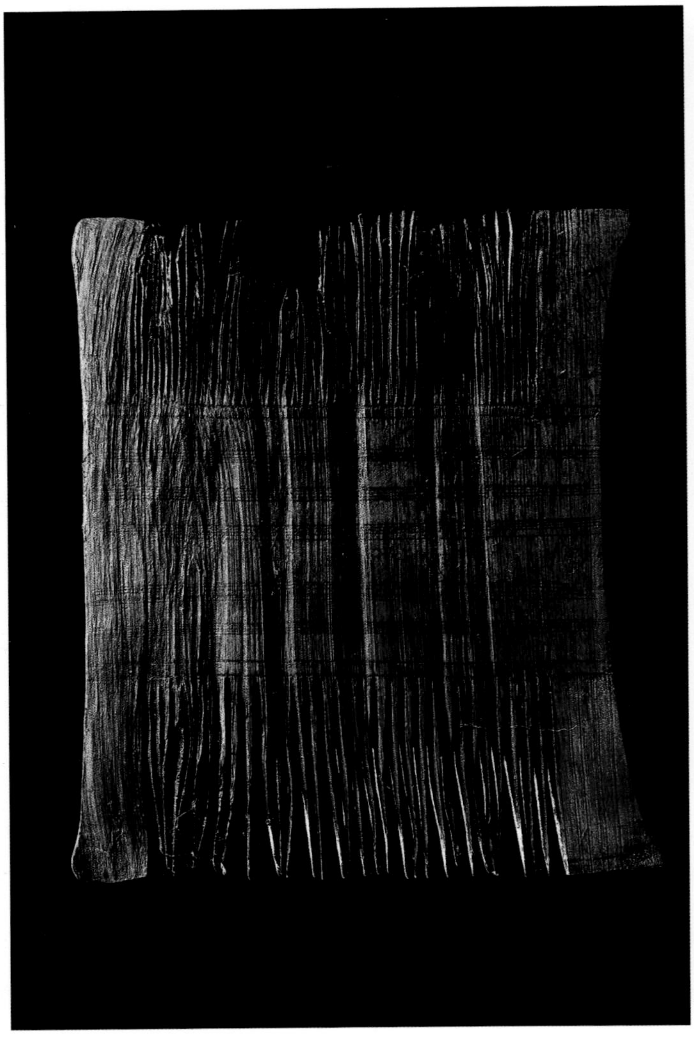

Wooden comb from Valle Trebba (Spina), fifth century B.C.
Ferrara, Museo Archeologico
cat. 122

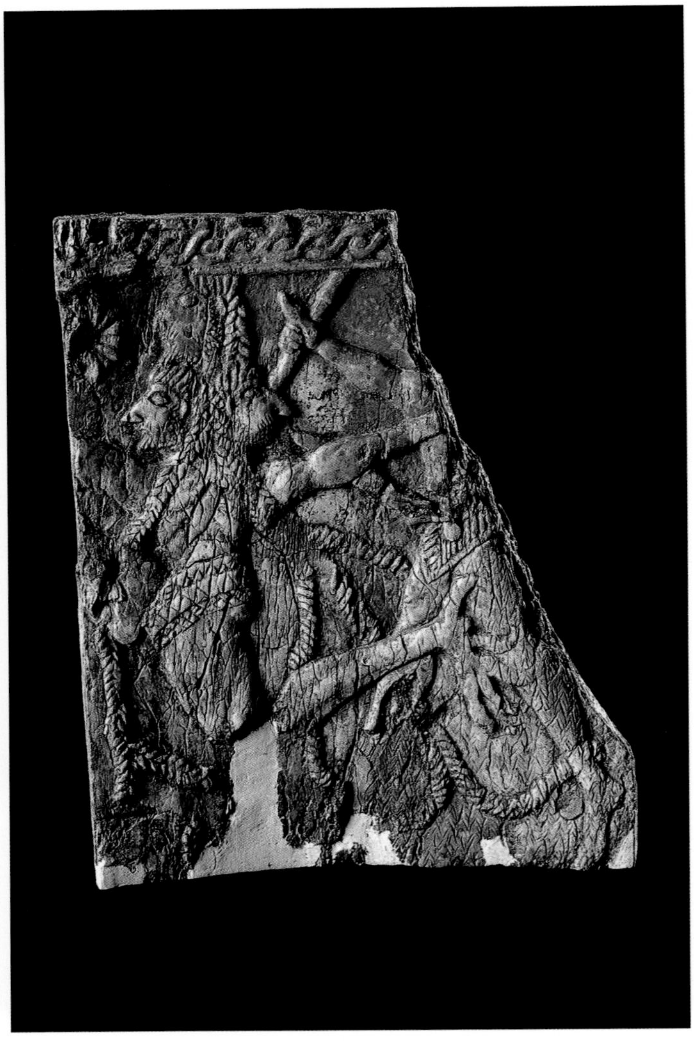

Small ivory plaque with Geryon, from Comeana, tumulus of Montefortini, second half of the seventh century B.C.
Florence, Museo Archeologico
cat. 119

of plaques, clearly of East Greek imprint, can instead be dated to the height of the Archaic period. Probably produced in Vulci between the third quarter of the sixth century and the early decades of the fifth century B.C., the latter substituted the richer, more varied typology of the Orientalizing ivories in the tastes of the new aristocratic clientele, and seem to illustrate their lifestyles and ambitions through a general repertoire of status symbols (symposiums, dancing or hunting scenes) which only rarely leave space for any mythological or ritual content (winged figures, sphinxes, tritons, satyrs). In addition to Etruria proper, these were diffused in the Po Valley and Campania, and given the widespread commercial relations and intense mobility throughout the entire Mediterranean in the Archaic period, reached as far as Apulia, Sardinia, Malta, Athens, Delos, Rhodes, Cyprus and the Balkan interior.

Between the Orientalizing and the Archaic periods, ivory and bone work was not exclusive to the Etruscan area, for important testimony exists even in the neighboring Italic districts like that of the Picenum. In this area, primarily in centers situated along the routes leading to the Tyrrhenian coast (Belmonte, Pitino di San Severino, Matelica, Fabriano), numerous nuclei of materials have been recovered, datable between the middle decades of the seventh and sixth centuries B.C. Among these are to be distinguished Orientalizing style objects of possible Rhodian matrix (e.g. the sphinx and panel from Belmonte); certain Etruscan imports, which can be associated to some degree to the above-mentioned Caere-Praeneste materials (e.g. the rider and centaur from Pianello di Castelbellino); and also a local eclectic production which seemed to combine, between the end of the seventh and the first half of the sixth centuries B.C., Peloponnesian, East Greek and Levantine styles (e.g. statuettes from Castelbellino and Belmonte; cf. also the *kouroi* and the *korai* from Numana which are stylistically quite close to examples from the Forum Boarium in Rome and obviously the work of craftsmen of East Greek formation). Information of this type indicates an extremely composite cultural picture, one that reflects the multiple relations that the region was carrying on not only with the neighboring Etruscans but also with the more distant cultures of the Hellenic and Near Eastern worlds.

A definition of the characteristics of the intaglios of the fifth century B.C. seems more problematic due to the profound changes that affected the Etruscan productive structures after the battle of Cuma when a general contraction of the economic potential occurred. At this time there is little documentation of importance: notable are the casket panels from the Chiusi area with a sequence of female figures that is stylistically reminiscent of the Greek reliefs and pottery from the first third of the fifth century B.C.; and some examples of small carved decorations from the Po River area (the statuette of a warrior from Felsina, a candelabra finial from Spina with a Peleus and Thetis group): both of which are evidence of the long-lasting vitality of this type of workshop tradition in the northern Etruscan interior. Between the fourth and third centuries B.C. new objects appeared, like the bone mirror handles with relief decoration, while various types of boxes continued to be decorated with panels (there are examples primarily from Praeneste which seems to have been an important center for the production of this kind of terra-cotta and bone *appliqués*). The subjects represented thereon, tritons, divinities, winged youths, are rendered in a rather flat, rigid style that is somewhat archaizing in the handling of the faces and anatomy. It is closely related to a certain "Tiber" sculptural style, as seen in the reliefs of the sarcophagi and the funerary sculpture of late Classical period tombs (like the Caeretan one of Greppe Sant'Angelo). However, other panels (also from Praeneste) with their vivid plastic rendering and choice of Dionysian subjects (e.g. the dancing maenad) are reminiscent of an analogous production in the Hellenic area. Lastly, the casket panels with telamons from Vulci, dating from the third century B.C., resemble typologically those from Magna Graecia; however, their actual relationship to South Italy can be fully evaluated only after a re-examination of materials from the extra-Etruscan area that are still not very well known or unknown. Often belonging to a female clientele of the middle to upper classes, these intaglios were the product of the new economic and cultural prosperity that the Etrusco-Italic area enjoyed between the fourth and third centuries B.C. The importance of Praeneste in this sector comes as no surprise for that city held a key position between the Greek-dominated area in the southern part of the peninsula, Latium and interior Etruria along the Tiber River. *(F.G.)*

Sphragistics and glyptics: Furtwängler 1900, pp. 170 ff.; Boardman 1968, *passim*; Zazoff 1968; Boardman 1970, in particular pp. 152–53, 186–87, pls. 406–13, p. 403; Martini 1971; Boardman 1975, pp. 37–45, 102–10; Zazoff 1983, pp. 214–59; *Die Welt der Etrusker* 1988, pp. 373–80; Zazoff 1990, pp. 287–90; Krauskopf 1995. *Jewellery*: Becatti 1955; Coche de la Ferté 1956, pp. 72–86; Higgins 1980, pp. 135–52; Cristofani, Martelli 1983; Markoe 1985; Coen 1999. *Ivories*: Huls 1957; Brown 1960, pp. 2 ff., 30 ff., 134 ff.; Aubet 1971; Cristofani 1971a, pp. 63 ff.; Martelli 1985b, pp. 207 ff. Martelli 1991a, pp. 1049 ff.; Gilotta 1995, pp. 51 ff.; Rocco 1999.

Writing appeared in southern Etruria in the area between the cities of Veio and Vulci and at Bologna sometime between the end of the eighth century B.C. and the first decades of the seventh century B.C. The first Etruscan epigraphic evidence, datable within the first quarter of the seventh century B.C., is rather homogeneous from the point of view of where it was found, for the most part in the tombs of women of rank, and the typology of the objects—all of which is pottery—on which the writing appears. However, the shapes of the objects and the texts they bear are different, although the latter fall within distinguishable and recognizable categories, even at first sight, by the way they are written and their layout. These features suggest that the diffusion of writing, at the beginning of its history, came about because of the indissoluble bond that had formed between the function of the objects chosen to support the texts and the texts themselves.

Probably the written word was initially perceived as being different from the pronounced word and considered to be the result of a system of signs that was to be received and assimilated differently with respect to tradition. This is not to say, however, that the introduction of writing constituted a total caesura with respect to previous customs. According to documents, in fact, it seems that the Etruscans had planned to introduce writing into their social fabric, when they found that by accepting a new system or convention, it was possible to join the isolated signs that had been imported from other Mediterranean alphabets, and thus produce connections that could express the sounds of their own language. This new system presumably had to be accepted alongside the other fundamental one of the Etruscan religion which recognized the presence of the divine in every sign. The importance of this phenomenon is evident from the most ancient testimony to the most recent, and demonstrates that during the course of its history Etruscan writing was profoundly tied to divine revelation, and to the sacred books of the *Etrusca disciplina*, as can be seen for example in the funerary monuments. We are unable, however, to calculate the entity of the possible destruction of documents and consequently the lacunas in the documentation. Notwithstanding this, the question arises as to whether the writing was initially considered as an instrument of communication, as it is today. Indeed the way that writing appeared demonstrates that it was never meant to be subordinate to the signs of religion. Therefore it comes as no surprise that the acceptance of writing had been prompted by a contemplation of the Etruscan language and at the same time of the alphabetic writings, in particular archaic Greek, that had started to circulate in the Mediterranean during the eighth century B.C. Confirmation of this can be seen by the attention paid to the writing of certain combinations of letters, such as those that render the gutturals, where the initial intention was to establish precise norms whereby letters were joined together to form the sounds proper to the Etruscan language.

The importance of the phenomenon initially can be grasped, however, by the many features that make up the evidence constituting the inscription: from the archaeological site to the epigraphic support, the execution of the text, and its content. With regard to the sites of the most ancient inscriptions, two were from inhabited areas. First among these is the "sacro-institutional" complex that dates back to the origins of the city of Tarquinia, which was of extraordinary importance in the religion and daily life of the Etruscans and dedicated to the Etruscan female divinity Uni. One of the most ancient Etruscan inscriptions was found here, and was obviously connected to the constructions of the first quarter of the seventh century B.C. Almost coeval, moreover, is the so-called San Francesco deposit at Bologna where an exceptional deposit of bronze fragments from about 680 B.C. was found inside a closed earthen jar under the floor of a hut. Secondly, there are the funerary tombs. Out of the ten that have been preserved, eight are the tombs of women, the other two are of uncertain attribution. It was not until the second quarter of the seventh century B.C. that women's grave goods containing inscribed objects were found alongside those of men, which were obviously of a "princely" order. Although it may be risky to presume that the evidence found in the female tombs reflected the reality of the ancient society—because those aspects of the world of the dead were governed by precise ideological choices that could have filtered such a reality so much as to transform it radically—it is legitimate to believe that as the situations were modified a corresponding change may have occurred within the society, albeit of a different mark. Therefore the evidence in the tombs containing inscribed objects, female at first and only later male, certainly furnishes important information for an evaluation of the

Cockerel-shaped impasto vase with letters of the Etruscan alphabet, from Viterbo, mid-seventh century B.C. New York, Metropolitan Museum of Art cat. 250

Bucchero foot with Aule Vipienna's inscription from the Portonaccio sanctuary (Veio), sixth century B.C.
Rome, Museo di Villa Giulia
cat. 32.2

Impasto spools from Tomb 870 at Casale del Fosso necropolis (Veio), end of the eighth century B.C.
Rome, Museo di Villa Giulia

introduction of writing into early Etruscan society. On removing such evidence from its context, however, there is risk of associating writing with the sphere of women, in opposition perhaps even to that of men, whereas the effective means by which the male and female roles were expressed in Etruscan society are still not clear. Other indications in such a sense nevertheless come from the objects found in these tombs and the texts they bear.

North and south of the axis formed by the course of the Tiber River, at Veio and in Bologna, weaving implements have been found on which the association between the first letter of the alphabet, *a*, with a sign in the form of a cross is repeated. In the case of a group of spools from Veio, the cross is inscribed in the circle represented by the terminal part of the spool and occupies one of the quadrants. Five ritual plates that are identical in shape were found in the area of Cerveteri where the same term *spanti* appears in the text of each inscription. Assimilated into the Etruscan language as a cultural borrowing, the term also refers to the sphere of the ritual and is included in the lexical family of Indo-European verbs that indicate libation. On one of these plates, in addition to the inscription, there is a cross inscribed within a circle, a sign that also appears on other plates and objects from the same period. Therefore, many signs and countersigns also appear together with writing on objects whose use seems to have determined the character of the signs and texts as in the case of the ritual plates. The same thing happens in the rest of southern Etruria where the objects are of various types. Cups, small amphoras, jugs and vases bear different texts, which are always introduced by the personal pronoun *mi* or *mini* because the object presents itself in first person. One of these texts, the longest and most ancient, comes from Tarquinia and is scratched on a cup imported from Corinth and dated before the end of the eighth century B.C. Although the text is obscure for the most part, it contains the sequence *ka-cri-qu* which constitutes a kind of primer. Three combinations can be read in the sequence, each formed by the letter corresponding to the slight guttural /k/ followed by the letter corresponding to a vowel. The letter that serves to render the consonant varies therefore depending on the letter that follows: the *kappa* with *a*, the *gamma semilunato* (half-mooned gamma) with *i*, the *qoppa* with *u*. These specific graphic variants constitute one of the most obvious features of the Etruscan application of the alphabetic writing, which do not influence the pronunciation of the consonant which remains */k/*. In the occlusive series of consonants in fact, based on the information that has come to us regarding Etruscan adaptations of Greek words, we know that voiced stops did not exist in Etruscan. In addition to this primer, the same inscription furnishes precious information about the origin of the Etruscan letters. Here the so-called *gamma semilunato* was taken from the Corinthian alphabet where, however, it produced the sound */g/*, while the *lambda con il vertice in basso* (with the vertex below) was imported from the Euboean Greek alphabet.

The presence of the *ka-cri-qu* sequence provides direct information about the functioning of the Etruscan alphabetic writing, which in a certain way enlivens our knowledge of the surviving alphabet tablets. If in fact the question of the provenance of the letters employed by the Etruscans indicates their cultural contacts and the situations existing prior to the creation of their alphabet, the question of how it worked, autonomously with respect to other writings, throws light on the ways in which the writing was formed.

The tomb of a person who knew how to write was found in the exceptional Circolo degli Avori of Marsiliana d'Albegna. Together with styli and scrapers is an ivory tablet on which the most ancient Etruscan alphabet is inscribed; it is made up of a series of letters, taken for the most part from the Euboean Greek alphabet, such as the *gamma a uncino* (hooked), the *lambda con il vertice in basso* and the *chi a tridente* (trident). However, there are also letters that have no relationship to the Euboean series, namely the sibilant M (Corinthian alphabet) and the sign ⊞, which appear neither in Greek nor in Phoenician. The information provided by this alphabet, although it is dated at least thirty years later than the *ka-cri-qu* cup, concurs with the latter in showing that the Euboean series was not the only reference for the formation of the Etruscan alphabet.

The concept of sequence returns on other ancient evidence, such as that of the single letters and pairs of letters incised on the bronzes of the San Francesco deposit of Bologna. These allow for a reconstruction of an alphabetic series which lacks the Greek letters that were never employed in the Etruscan application of writing, although they were documented in co-

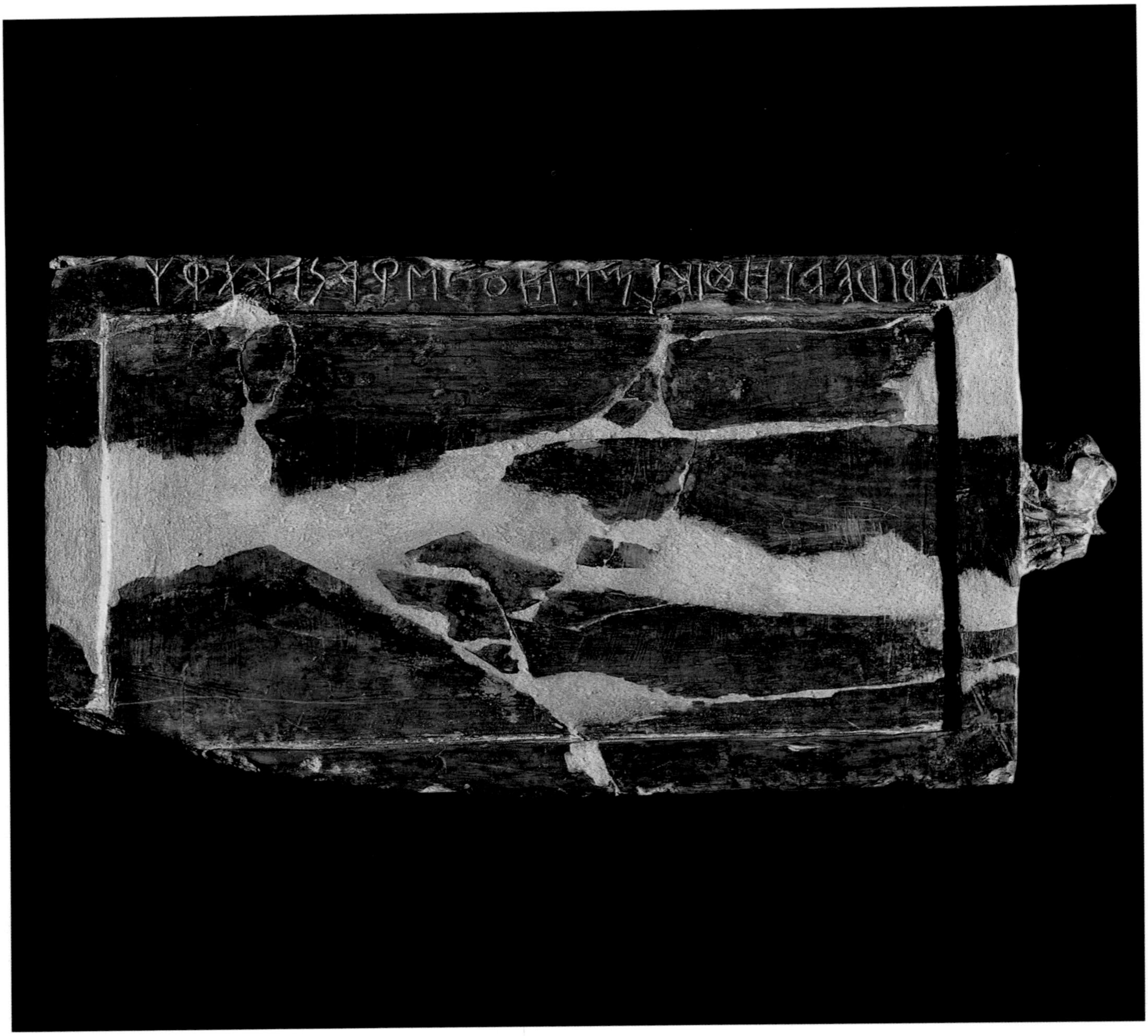

Ivory tablet with incised alphabet from the Banditella Circolo degli Avori (Marsiliana d'Albegna), mid-seventh century B.C.
Florence, Museo Archeologico

eval alphabets. The closing in ancient times of the so-called deposit guarantees that these letters were not missing by chance. It can therefore be affirmed indirectly that at Bologna, quite early in time, the letters of the alphabet followed the order of the Etruscan series in its effective use and were presumably used with a numeral value, hence in sequence.
This same evidence underlines the importance of the introduction of writing and its methods. The nature of some of the objects, in particular the weaving implements, are a reference themselves to an art that pre-eminently translates what is separate and single into combinations. In fact, in both ancient and modern anthropology weaving refers to the concept of linkage and construction in all cultures. The reference to this art of female appanage is set alongside the evidence of the prevalently female funerary contexts and that of the sacred contexts in which writing is involved, like the "sacro-institutional" complex of Tarquinia dedicated to Uni. Subsequently, writing continued to appear primarily in sanctuaries dedicated to female divinities. The question arises whether writing may have in some way come into the sphere of female competence, inasmuch as weaving was a model of the mechanism

Nenfro *stone Sarcophagus of Laris Pulena from Monterozzi (Tarquinia), second half of the third century* B.C.
Tarquinia, Museo archeologico

of combinations, links and sequences and represented the earlier function of all alphabetic writing. Once again in fact, with the information that comes from the series of the so-called San Francesco deposit, we return to the concept of the linkage between different objects, united by an alphabetic sequence employed with a numeral value. Indeed, in the most ancient text found to date, the reference is to the correct linkage of the letters according to the Etruscan convention of *ka-cri-qu*.

If the most ancient documents that have reached us present the fascinating dimension of the formation of an alphabet, the subsequent history of Etruscan writing can only confirm such evidence. Starting in the middle of the seventh century B.C., two principal writing areas emerged in Etruria. The southern area, whose centers adopted the same system of rendering the gutturals with differentiated graphic variants, but different sibilants (ϟ and ⟨), and the northern area, extending from Vulci northward, whose centers instead adopted the same system of rendering the gutturals with the single sign *kappa* and the sibilants with the single sign M. At Vetulonia at the end of the seventh century B.C., the sound for */f/*—previously rendered in all the Etruscan centers with the combination of the letters 𐌅 and 𐌇, which could invert their position—was united in the single sign 8. Following the process that started during the second half of the seventh century B.C., which only seemed to be completed at the beginning of the following century, the Etruscans carried out a real graphic reform of their own: the question of the rendering of the sibilants—which in Etruscan were two (*/s/* and */š/*)—was resolved definitively. In fact, in the sixth century B.C., the use of the sibilants was established differently in different areas. In the area south of Vulci the sound */s/* was rendered with the sign 𐌔, of the Euboean series of the Greek alphabets, and */š/* with the sign M of the Corinthian series; in the area north of Vulci the situation was inverted. There was also a restricted area south of Vulci where the sign + was used to render */s/* and 𐌔 to render */š/*. The phenomenon, introduced in a relatively significant way at Tarquinia, was of short duration and was immediately resolved. There were no substantial changes in the graphic systems in the subsequent history of Etruscan writing, apart from the simplification in southern Etruria of the signs for the guttural in the single *gamma semilunato,* and the introduction of some special sign in the northern area, particularly during the Hellenistic period.

Impasto plate with red slip from Tomb 2 at Casaletti di Ceri, seventh century B.C.
Cerveteri, Museo Nazionale

Flint sors cleromantica
from Arezzo, second century B.C.
Arezzo, Museo C. Cilnio Mecenate

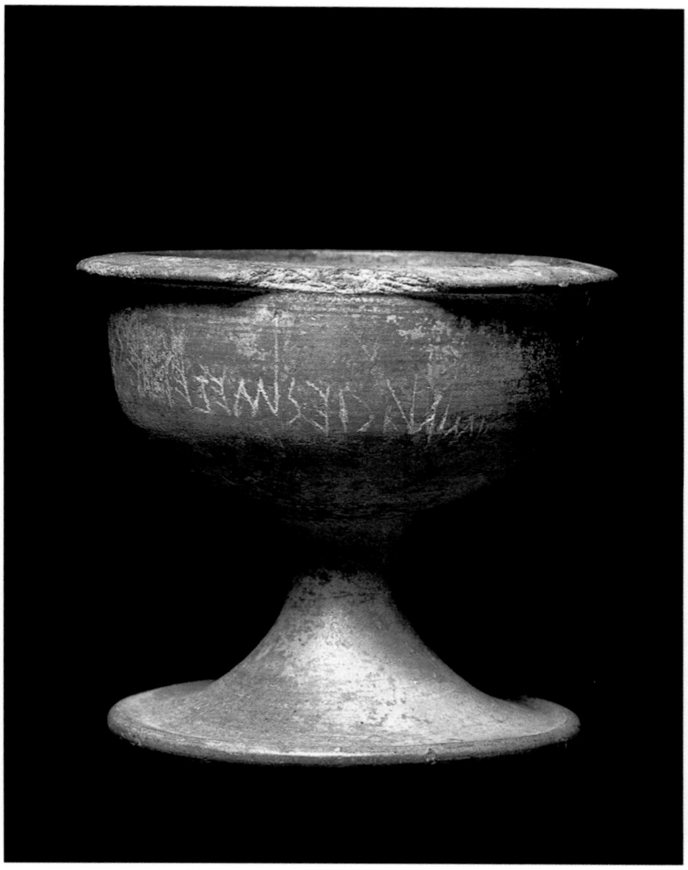

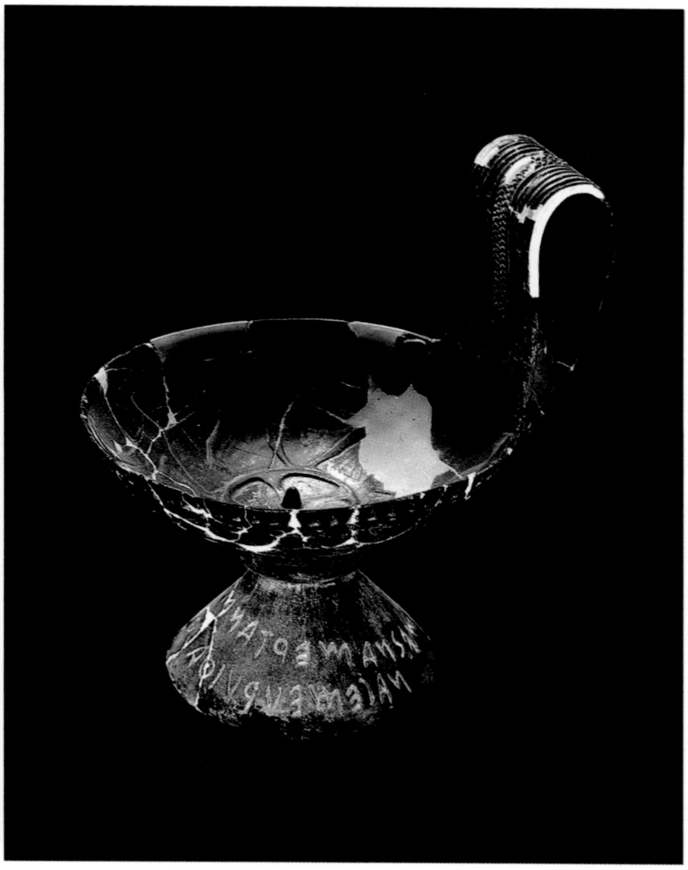

Dark gray impasto chalice with brown slip, 675–650 B.C.
Paris, Musée du Louvre

Impasto buccheroide kyathos *from the Tomb of the Duce at Poggio al Bello (Vetulonia), seventh century B.C.*
Florence, Museo Archeologico

The process for the construction of Etruscan writing certainly occupied the entire seventh century B.C. but it was not until the end of the century that it really took shape as an instrument that was available to everyone and used to write texts that were destined to everyone. Such a result does not fail to reflect that aspect of the choice to write, the transformation of which marked the passage from a limited diffusion, in which the writing was totally autonomous and strictly related to the objects on which it appeared, to one in which it became a purely conventional sign. It is likely that the use of materials other than pottery, stone and metal was not extraneous to such an evolution for they could offer a variety of applications and perhaps satisfy the need to transmit messages with quite different destinations. Such information may be obtained from a find like the lead blade from Pech Mao in southern France, datable to the first half of the fifth century B.C. On one side there is an inscription in the Ionic Greek alphabet and on the other a more ancient Etruscan inscription. There are six lines of some hundred letters in which the personal name *Venelus* appears twice. The blade may be associated with the intense maritime traffic between the Greek settlements in southern France and Etruria.

General works: Pallottino 1986, pp. 311–67; Cristofani 1991b. *The making of Etuscan writing in comparison with Mediterranean ones:: Phoinikeia Grammata* 1991; *Scritture Mediterranee* 1999. *The development of writing in comparison with language*: Durante 1969, pp. 295–305; Cristofani 1969a, pp. 99–113; Colonna 1970b, pp. 637–72; Cristofani 1973–74, pp. 151–65; Colonna 1976b, pp. 7–26; Cristofani 1977a, pp. 193–204; Rix 1984, in particular pp. 210–22; Cristofani 1987f, pp. 25–37; Pandolfini, Prosdocimi 1990; Agostiniani 1992, pp. 37–74. *The development of writing in comparison with society*: Torelli 1965, pp. 126–29; Colonna 1973-1974, pp. 132–50; Colonna 1975, pp. 186–92; Colonna 1977a, pp. 175–92; Cristofani 1981b, pp. 47–78; Colonna 1983, pp. 49–64; Colonna 1984c, pp. 311–18; Cristofani 1984, pp. 319–24; Colonna 1993a, pp. 61–68; Bagnasco Gianni 1996a, pp. 307–18; Bagnasco Gianni 1996b. *Writing in more recent periods*: Cristofani 1996, pp. 103–09; Maggiani 1982, pp. 147–65; Maggiani 1990a, pp. 177–217; Stopponi 1990b, pp. 1–32; Agostiniani 2000, pp. 46–52.

The Language

The documentation *

Etruscan is a dead language. Unlike other dead languages such as ancient Greek and Latin, all knowledge of it has been lost, so that our only access to it is through the evidence and testimonies that remain: the written documents and the so-called "Etruscan glosses." We must note immediately that the contributions of the latter are minimal. It regards some sixty words or so, the majority of which are to be found in the *Lexicon* of Hesychius and in the *Liber Glossarum,* while the rest are in works by Varro, Verrius Flaccus, Dioscorides, Strabo and others in which those ancient writers handed down Etruscan words with a translation in Greek or Latin. The number of words, already small, diminishes even more when we consider that some of them such as *κάπρα* or *δέα* quoted by Hesychius are obviously not Etruscan words. Moreover, the words often appear in Graecized or Latinized form which means they are hardly reliable testimony of the Etruscan sounds or forms.

Our knowledge of the Etruscan language therefore lies basically in written documents which, except for one case which we shall examine, consist of inscriptions. Now, if for "inscriptions" we include, in a general sense, any manifestation of writing, even alphabetic monograms, abbreviations and so forth, then about 11,000 Etruscan inscriptions exist, which bear witness to a widely developed use of writing (there are no more than 3,000 Latin inscriptions for the same corresponding period). The earliest inscriptions date from the beginning of the seventh century B.C. (the oldest Etruscan inscription appears to be a graffito known as the "antiquissimum of Tarquinia," Ta 3.1), while the latest inscription dates from the first century A.D. as seen in the bilingual inscription on a cinerary urn from Arezzo, Ar 1.8 (in agreement with Dionysius of Halicarnassus, I, 30, who states that Etruscan was still spoken at the time of Augustus). Geographically speaking, the inscriptions are distributed throughout a territory which includes Etruria proper and the areas of Etruscan expansion: Campania (Capua, Suessula, Nola), Emilia-Romagna (Piacenza, Bologna, Ravenna, Adria, Spina), Lombardy, and Corsica (Aleria). To these are to be added three other inscriptions which are eccentric and out of place in terms of geographical expansion. Two of them are presumably the result of the sporadic and chance presence of the Etruscans: the funerary stela from the end of the sixth century B.C. discovered at Brusca in Piedmont, Li 1.1, and the *tessera hospitalis*, again from the sixth century B.C., found at Carthage (Af 3.1). As for the third example, the funerary inscription from the sixth century B.C. found at Kaminia on the island of Lemnos, the issue at hand is quite different. The inscription is in the local Greek alphabet and is dedicated to a warrior, Holaie Phokias, and mentions his age and some events of his life. The language of the Lemnos stela is nothing other than a variety of Etruscan and is not a generic "Etruscoid" language as has been asserted in the past. It is characterized by sections that are more archaic in respect to what one would expect, considering its dating. Concerning the historical significance of the presence of an Etruscan inscription on Lemnos, the debate is wide open: Etruscans coming from Italy, perhaps in the role of pirates? Or is it not a question rather of a group linked with a "migration" from East to West as maintained by those who accept the hypothesis of the Etruscans as originating in Asia Minor?

Taken all together the Etruscan inscriptions seem to reflect the same language and this would presuppose the existence of a standardized version, at least as far as concerns the written language. Yet this written standard is not entirely homogeneous; indeed this is to be expected since the inscriptions are spread over a wide geographical area and over a stretch of time of at least seven centuries. Thus, the existence of two chronological types has long been ascertained, one called "archaic Etruscan," which includes the inscriptions of the seventh, sixth, and fifth centuries B.C., the other called "recent Etruscan" or "neo-Etruscan" which includes the inscriptions from the fourth to the first century B.C. In respect to archaic Etruscan, the more recent Etruscan is characterized by the presence of protosyllabic stress with the consequential weakening and elimination of post tonic vowels; by the replacement of the archaic diphthong *ai* with an *e*, and lastly by replacing, in some cases, the original *i* with an *e* (we shall come back to these phenomena later when discussing sounds). Concerning the existence of geographical diversities, a recent discovery points to at least one feature which seems to distinguish, linguistically, the two varieties of Etruscan, "northern" and "southern," which is already evident in the field of writing (see Bagnasco). This regards the presence, in northern inscriptions, of the palatal *s* /š/ which in the same context is present-

Bucchero aryballos *with dedicatory inscription to Turan, from Cerveteri (?), second half–end of the seventh century* B.C.
Rome, Museo di Villa Giulia
cat. 126

Lead slab from the oppidum *of Pech Maho, fifth century* B.C.
Sigean, Musée des Corbières
cat. 257

ed as a dental *s* /s/ in southern inscriptions (we shall return to this matter as well when discussing sounds). If we take into consideration the kinds of texts that make up the corpus of Etruscan epigraphy, it is easy to note that all documents quite predictably pertaining to the "normal" use of writing in the Etruscan world have been lost: papyri, parchments, wax tablets, all *books* on linen except one, the greater part of the lead laminae, or plaques. Their loss is to be ascribed for the most part to the perishability of the materials as well as to their re-use in the case of bronze and lead. The result is an almost total absence of representative texts of certain types of writing such as literary texts, documents from archives (juridical extracts, annals, and historical texts), letters, dictionaries, grammars. In fact the so-called "long texts" of the Etruscan corpus, of which less than ten have more than 30 or 40 words, which have furnished us with most of what we know about the language, belong to one of the above-mentioned categories, principally from archives. But their survival is due for the most part to exceptional and fortuitous circumstances. We are not referring so much to the accidental preservation of texts for which materials typically subject to recovery were used, such as lead or gold (as in the case of the Piombo di Magliano, the Santa Marinella Plaque, and the Pyrgi Plaques), but rather to the occasional use of non-perishable materials such as the clay used in the Capua Tile, and to the fact that the document was transcribed onto a non-perishable, durable surface, such as stone in the case of the Perugia Cippus, or bronze for the *Tabula Cortonensis*, not to mention the preservation of the script of the *Liber Linteus* which is due to "recycling" (see the following).

The longest Etruscan test of all is the *Manuscript of Zagreb*, the only non-epigraphic document in the Etruscan corpus. It is a *Liber Linteus*, that is a manuscript written on linen with a brush, datable to the third–second century B.C. It ended up, for reasons unknown, in Egypt where it was "recycled" by cutting it into long horizontal strips which were used to wrap a mummy. Originally it had been divided into twelve rectangular sections, each one with 34 written lines, and the cloth had been folded like "an accordion," following the vertical lines which divided the sections like the pages of a book. Only some of the strips were saved so that large parts of the text are missing. The text is made up of about 400 basic words or lexemes, some of which are repeated several times so that the total number of words comes to about 1350. It is a ritual calendar describing what ceremonies are to be performed on what days in honor of which divinities. Here is an example (LL VIII 3):

celi	*huθiś*	*zaθrumiś*	*flerχva*	*Neθunsl*	*śucri...*
September	six	twenty	offerings	to Neptune	are dedicated (?)

The second largest text is the so-called Capua Tile inscribed on a terra-cotta tile found at Santa Maria Capua Vetere in Campania. It is divided into ten sections by horizontal lines and in its present state is made up of 62 lines, some with gaps, and of about 200 lexemes which through repetition makes a total of 390 words, not all of them preserved in their entirety. The lettering is the one in use in Campania about the middle of the fifth century B.C., and it too is a ritual calendar as in the case of the Zagreb Mummy. Ceremonies are prescribed to be performed on certain dates (and in certain places) in favor of certain divinities. Here is an example from Section I, lines 2–3:

leθamsul	*ci*	*tartiria*	*ci-m*	*cleva*	*acasri...*
at Lethams	three	*tartiria*	and three	*cleva*	are offered (?)

The recently acquired *Tabula Cortonensis*, is a bronze tablet with a text of 32 lines on one side and eight on the other, comprising a total of 206 words which puts it in third place among the "long texts" of the Etruscan corpus. It is a document of juridical nature, datable between the end of the third and the beginning of the second century B.C., and records a transaction involving land (presumably the subdivision of a large landed estate—*latifundium*—for which, given the period involved, there are indications of a historico-archaeological nature). Half of the words are made up of the names of people. The true and proper lexemes are 60 in number, some of which are used more than once so that the total number of words is 90. We give as an example the incipit of the test:

et	*pêtruiś*	*scêvêś*	*êliun-tś*	*vinac*	*restm-c*	*cenu*
thus	from Petru	Scevas	the *eliun*	the vineyard	and the *restm*	are -ated

A document of the same juridical nature is the so-called Perugia Cippus, a rectangular *cippus* or boundary stone found near Perugia. The inscription, datable between the third and second century B.C., runs for 24 lines on its front and continues on one of the sides for 22 lines for a total of 128 words. It is a transcription on stone of a sentence or judgement relating to questions of property between the Perugian families of the Velthina and the Afuna.

The other "long texts" are still smaller. These are four inscriptions which we shall describe briefly. The Santa Marinella Plaque (Cr 4.10) is a small lead plate found in the sanctuary at Punta della Vipera (Rome). Two non-fitting fragments have come down to us. The text, all told of about 80 words, of which only 40 are legible, is written on both sides. It can be dated between the end of the sixth and the beginning of the fifth century B.C. and is believed to be the response of an oracle. The Piombo di Magliano (Av 4.1) is also a lead plaque, more or less round in shape. The inscription runs along both faces in a spiral manner and it dates from the middle of fifth century B.C. It contains about 60 words and is believed to be a description of rituals. The Inscription of Laris Pulenas (Ta 1.17) is inscribed on the *volumen* or scroll held in the hand of the figure of the deceased sculpted on the cover of a sarcophagus found at Tarquinia. The text contains 59 words , dates from the first half of the second century B.C., and deals with the genealogy and events in the life of the deceased. Lastly, there are the two gold Pyrgi Plaques (Cr 4.4–4.5) bearing texts respectively of 36 and 15 words.

Nenfro *stone Sarcophagus of Laris Pulena, from Monterozzi (Tarquinia), second half of the third century* B.C., *detail.*
Tarquinia, Museo Archeologico

They were found inside a sanctuary together with a third gold plaque written in Phoenician and they register, along with the Phoenician one, the dedication of a temple to Uni/Astarte by a local Etruscan sovereign about 500 B.C. Generally speaking, the "long texts" are linguistic compositions where the creative aspect prevails; nevertheless they do often contain various repeated or stereotyped phrases. This occurs, for example, in the descriptions of the various rituals in the *Liber Linteus*. A typical example is the expression *cisum pute tul θans hatec repinec*, which we find on pages III (lines 22–23), IV (lines 3–4 and 16), IX (lines 4–5, 11–12 and 20), and the same is valid for the Capua Tile where, for example, *iśvei tule ilucve apirase* appears in section II, line 8 and in section III, line 17.

The greater part of the shorter inscriptions is altogether another matter. Some are totally lacking in any articulated structure since they are made up either of initials and abbreviations—presumably of proper names or words from formularies—or of proper names placed on objects to betoken (without expressing it linguistically) the relationship between the object and the person designated by a proper name. It may have to do with simple names or with more or less complex name-bearing, or onomastic, formulas. This type of inscription is very common on tombs, urns and sarcophagi. Some examples:

Cm 2.44 (Capua, vase, 500–450 B.C.): *cupe veliesa* "Cupe (son) of Velie"; Cl 1.393 (Chiusi, cinerary urn cover, second century B.C.): *peθna larceś remznal* "Pethna (son) of Larce and of Remznei."

Other brief inscriptions do present some sort of linguistic framework, but they are marked by a strictly formula-regulated system. The text, that is, is based on pre-existing models—which we define as "formulary outlines"—which linguistically designate the ownership of a certain object by a certain person, or the dedication of the object (by a particular person; to a particular person) by speaking in terms such as "of So-and-So," "this object belongs to (is of) So-and-So," "I belong to So-and-So," "So-and-So gave me (to So-and-So)," etc. The object can be a tomb, the dedicatee a divinity. Some examples:

Vs 2.8 (Orvieto, vase, fifth century B.C.): *uχus* "of Uchu"
Cr 4.8 (Pyrgi, vase, fifth century B.C.): *unial* "of Uni"
Cr 2.51 (Caere, vase, 575–550 B.C.): *uχus θafna* "cup of (belonging to) Uchu"
Cr 2.13 (Caere, silver vase, 650–600 B.C.): *mei larθia* "I (am) of (belong to) Larth"

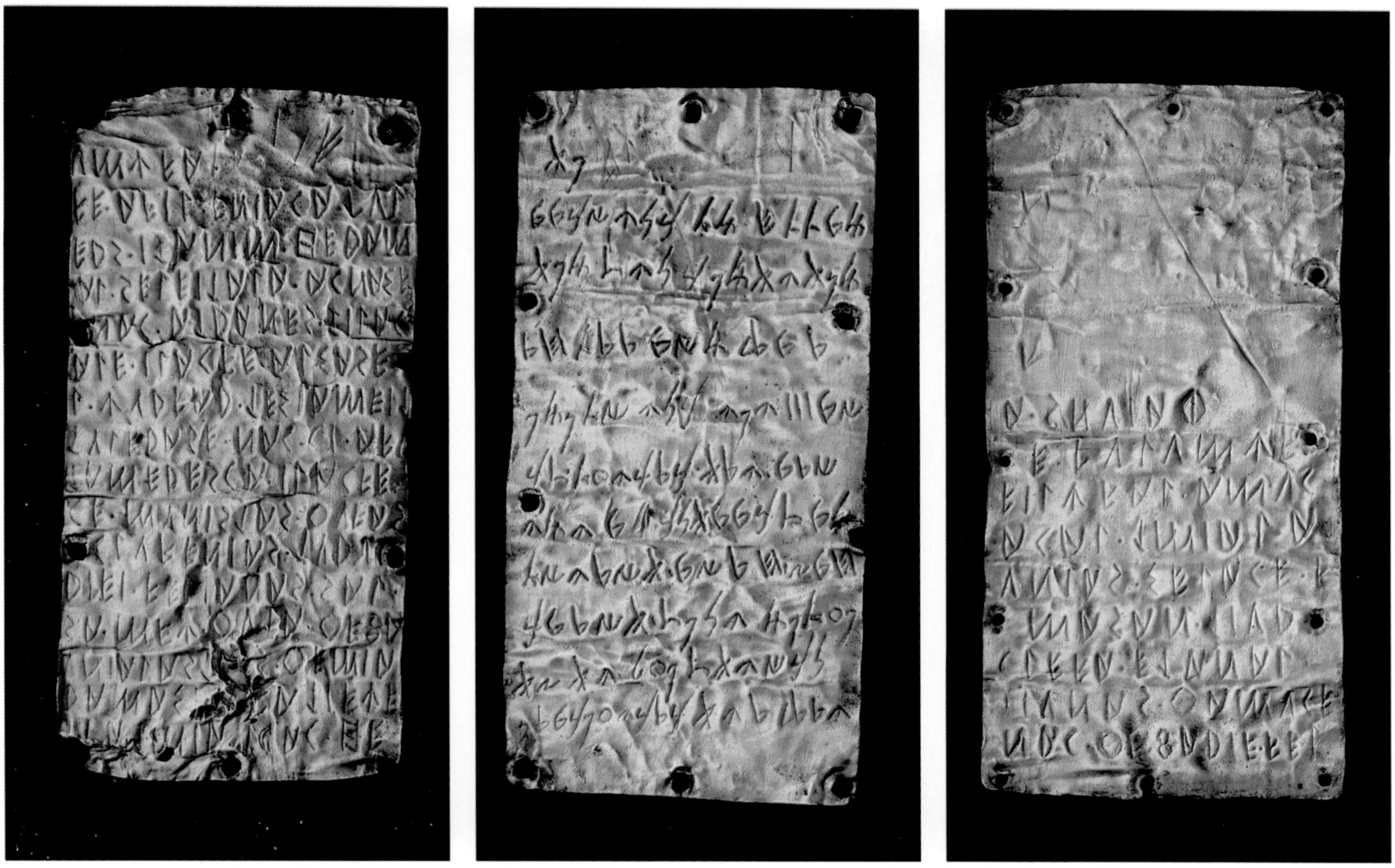

Gold laminae with inscriptions from Pyrgi, near Santa Severa (Rome), fifth century B.C.
Rome, Museo di Villa Giulia
cat. 255

Cm 2.8 (Capua, vase, 550–500 B.C.): *mi numisiies vhelmus* "I am of (belong to) Numesie Felmus"
Cr 2.20 (Caere, vase, 700–650 B.C.): *mi qutum karkanas* "I am the jug of Karkana"
Cr 2.33 (Caere, vase, 650–625 B.C.): *mi squrias θina mlaχ mlakas* "I (am) the jar of Squria, the beautiful (object) of a beautiful (person)"
Ve 3.6 (Veii, vase, ca. 600 B.C.): *mini mulvanice karcuna tulumnes* "Karcuna Tulumnes donated me"
AT 3.1 (Blera, 650–600 B.C.): *mi mulu kaviiesi* "I given by/to Kavie"
Ta 3.2 (Tarquinia, vase, end of sixth century B.C.*): itun turuce venel atelinas tinas cliniiaras* "Venel Atelinas dedicated this to the sons of Tinia" (the Dioscuri)
Cm 2.13 (Suessula, 500–450 B.C.): *mi χulinχa qupes alθrnas ei minipi capi* "I (am) the cup of Cupe Althrna; do not take me"

It is to be noted that above all during the Archaic period these inscriptions indicating possession or gift/dedication followed the model of the so-called "talking inscriptions," based on the stylistic pretence that it is the object itself that bears the inscription declaring to whom it belongs or to which given person or personage it is destined. Also worthy of note is the fact that the model for the "talking inscriptions," like others such as "it is forbidden to appropriate" ("do not steal") or the stylistic usage "beautiful object of/for a beautiful person" used to supplement forms of possession and gift/dedication, extends beyond the Etruscan linguistic borders and corresponds to uses in Greek, Latin and other languages of ancient Italy. Thus the above-cited *mi larθia* "I (am) of Larth (belong to Larth)" corresponds to formulas such as the Latin *Marci sum* "(I) am of Marcus," the Oscan *kanuties sim* "(I) am of Kanutie," and the Greek *Σοταίρο εἰμί* "(I) am of Sotarios;" the above-cited *mi squrias θina mlaχ mlakas* "(I) am the jar of Squria, beauty of a beauty" corresponds to the provincial Latin (Faliscan) *eco quton* [...] *titias duenom duenas* "(I) am the *koton* [...] of Tizia, beauty of a beauty" and the Greek *'Αριστοκλεῖας ἐμὶ τᾶς καλᾶς καλά* "[I] am the beautiful kylix of the beautiful Aristokleia;" and to the above-cited *ei minipi capi* correspond the Latin ex-

Terra-cotta leg-shaped votive offering, second century B.C.
Tarquinia, Museo Archeologico
cat. 308

pressions such as *ne atigas me, noli me tangere, noli me tollere*, and the like, and to the Greek expressions *με̃ θίγες* "do not touch me," *με̃ με ἄνοιγε* "do not take me away" and the like. Recurring formulas appear as well in more complex inscriptions, especially to supplement inscriptions of tombs, or on urns. Here, the name of the person is followed by information about his or her personality, deeds, offices held—if any, age at time of death, etc. For example:

Ta 7.59 (Tarquinia, Tomb of the Orcus, 325–300 B.C.):

spur]inas	*an*	*zilaθ*	*amce*	*meχl*	*rasnal*
Spurinas	who	zilath	was	*rei*	*populi*

Ta 1.167 (Tarquinia, third–first century B.C.):

metli arnθi	*puia*	*amce*	*spitus larθal*	*svalce*	*avil LXIII*	*ci clenar anacnas arce*
Arnthi Metli	wife	was	of Larth Spitu	lived	years 63	three sons generated

Cr 5.3 (Caere, end of fourth century B.C.):

vel	*matunas*	*larisalisa*	*an*	*cn*	*śuθi*	*ceriχunce*
Vel	Matunas	of Laris	who	this	tomb	built

Last of all, let us take into consideration, as a case apart, the captions written in relation to scenes or representations which were, for the most part, painted on the walls of tombs or incised onto the backs of mirrors. In practically all these cases the captions bear the name of the person represented; thus, for example, in the Tomb of the Orcus in Tarquinia, datable 325–300 B.C., we find *φersipnei* "Persephone," *eivas* "Ajax (Aias)," *θese* "Theseus," *uθuste* "Odysseus," and on the back of a mirror, again from Tarquinia, datable from the fourth century B.C. (Tarquinia, S.3), one reads *apulu* "Apollo," *menrva* "Minerva" and *hercle* "Hercules." In a few cases, the captions relate not to a single personage, but to the entire scene and become thereby an explanation or description. The scene of Hercules nursed by Hera on the back of a mirror from the fourth-third century B.C. from Volterra (ET Vt S.2) bears the following statement: *eca sren tva iχnac hercle unial clan θrasce*, that is "this image shows how Hercules became (?) the son of Uni." And there appears to be a similar arrangement in the sentence *eca ersce nac aχrum flerθrce* which comments the scene of Alcestis taking leave of Admetus, painted on a vase dating from the end of the fourth century B.C. from Vulci (Vc 7.38).

The structure of the language

Due to the fact that the Etruscan language was not transmitted uninterruptedly down to us, all that we know today about that language, its sounds, forms, word meanings, and syntax, is the result of a process of reconstruction based on the interpretation of written texts which, as we have seen, are practically our only documentation of the language. We cannot reasonably use, as a way of understanding the texts, what is called the "etymological method," that is the comparative procedure which, by hypothesizing a genealogical link between Etruscan and other known languages, alleges to infer (unknown) meanings for the Etruscan words from those of other known languages which are similar in form. The method is correct as such, but incorrect when applied to Etruscan for the obvious reason that Etruscan is a genealogically isolated language and any supposed correlation with any other language (Hebrew, Basque, Armenian, Ugro-Finnic languages, Ural-Altaic languages, Caucasian, Berber languages, Tuareg, the languages of Asia Minor, Sanskrit, Latin, Italic languages, Greek) is plainly an illusion. That which is traditionally defined as the "combinatory method" is another matter. It was originally intended to be based exclusively on the identification, confrontation and cataloguing of the words and forms present in a text: in disagreement with those who were partisans of the "etymological method." Obviously a procedure of this kind is indispensable, indeed it is an a priori requisite for the analysis of an unknown language or for the reconstruction of its morphological and syntactical characteristics. Yet it must be admitted that since it deals with the type of analysis that works exclusively with forms, it would not be capable, by itself, of furnishing information about the overall sense of the text, the meaning of the words, or the value of the grammatical forms. To obtain this kind of data one must integrate different kinds of information with formal analysis by examining, for example, the contexts of the inscriptions, the typology of the object bearing the inscription, the relevance of the proper names used and so forth. The third "method" that is traditionally recognized is the so-called "bilingual" or "parallel texts" method which quite naturally becomes integrated with formal analysis by furnishing clues to the meanings and structures of the texts. Its premise is based on the well known fact that the populations of ancient Italy had many cultural factors and values in common which led, among other things, to the use of analogous textual patterns or canons so that the structure or sense of a text in a known language, say Umbrian, will give us indications of the sense and structure of an Etruscan text. In fact, even our partial knowledge of the contents of the rituals in the *liber linteus* and the Capua Tile lies in good measure on a comparison of these texts with those of another lengthy ritual text of ancient Italy, the Gubbio Tables. By way of confirmation we are reminded of the converging factors seen earlier regarding the "talking inscriptions," the admonition "it is forbidden," or the formula "beautiful object of/for the beautiful person."

To these three traditionally recognized "methods," a fourth can be added which can be defined as the "typological method." This refers to aspects of the typology of languages, above all, but not only, the fact that some of the characteristics of a language are conditioned by the presence of other characteristics. For example, if a language places the direct object before the verb, it will then tend to place the genitive before the noun/name (substantive) and it will use postpositions, not prepositions. This method can be used to "reveal," in Etruscan, the presence of certain characteristics and to check upon the possible presence of others based on other methods, for example, the combinatory one (later we shall deal with the morphology and syntax of Etruscan).

Our present knowledge of Etruscan is actually quite ample when measured against the scarcity of written documentation on which, after all, our reconstruction of the language is based to date. It is a bit of a paradox, since we are dealing with a dead language, that the feature we know most about is phonetics. Thanks to a series of indications supplied principally by the phonetic value of the signs in the model Greek alphabet (the Chalcidian alphabet) on which Etruscan writing is based, as well as through the phonetic use of loan words in Etruscan, the

Tabula Cortonensis,
end of the third–first half of the second century B.C.
Florence, Museo Archeologico
cat. 263

Graphic reconstruction of the Tabula Cortonensis

evolution of the writing, the general principles of phonologic typology, and some (a few) explicit statements made by ancient writers, it has been possible to reconstruct the series of functional voice sounds or phonemes in Etruscan, be they vowels or consonants.

The Etruscan vocalic system, at least during its archaic stage, had four vowels indicated as *iota, alpha, ypsilon* and *epsilon*, meaning that it was made up of the three base vowels /i a u/ plus /e/. Similar systems are widely certified throughout the world. We argue that, during the Archaic period, the /a/ was a velar (back) vowel (as in the French *pâte*) and in recent or neo-Etruscan it became a central (mixed) vowel (the /a/ is a central vowel in Italian, Spanish and in many other languages). This is shown by the diverse use in the Archaic and Recent periods of the diphthong /ou/ of Italic loan words in Etruscan, by which the Italic personal name *Loucios* is rendered in archaic Etruscan as *Laucie* or *Lavcie*, and in recent Etruscan as *Luvcie*. It is also shown by the different genitive endings or inflexions of stems rendered in dental consonants as in the proper names *laris* and *larθ,* which during the archaic period were not pronounced *larisal* and *larθial* (as instead they were in neo-Etruscan, and as required by the forms of the "pertinentive" case: see later on), but rather *larθia* where the final velar /l/ was assimilated into and substituted by the velar /a/. This type of assimilation was no longer possible during the Recent era when the /a/ lost its velar character. Therefore, during the Archaic period the Etruscan vowel system was symmetric quadrangular, in the Recent period it was asymmetric triangular as in this outline:

Archaic Etruscan *Recent Etruscan*

i u i u
e
e a a

The acquisition of the *Tabula Cortonensis* has, however, shown with certainty as far as the variety of Etruscan used in Cortona is concerned, but perhaps also for other varieties as well, if not all of them, that the situation is even more complex. In the Cortona text there are two different /e/ letters, one marked by an epsilon which follows the right to left direction of the writing, and another using the same sign but retrograde (left to right). The regularity of their use shows that it had to be a matter of different sounds, phonetically distinct due to their length and/or due to their different openings. In these conditions, the vowel system in recent Etruscan makes its asymmetry worse: no longer two palatal (central) vowels, but three palatal vowels against one velar (back) vowel.

Before going on to an analysis of the consonants, two facts must be remembered which characterize the use of vowels in recent Etruscan in respect to the archaic phase. The first consists of /e/ substituting /i/: *etan* "this" for *itan* , *peθe,* a personal name, for *piθe,* and so on. This opening from /i/ to /e/ appears to be blocked by the presence, in the succeeding syllable, of a closed (front) vowel for which *vipina* does not become **vepina* and *cicu* does not become **cecu.* The second phenomenon typical of neo-Etruscan is the changing of the diphthong /ai/ into /e/ by which the Etruscan name for Ajax (Aias) is *Aivas* in the archaic inscriptions, and *Evas* in more recent ones. When dealing with female clan, or family *(gens)* names, and sometimes elsewhere, *ei* appears instead of *e* as an evolution of *ai*. For example, one reads *velimnei* and not **velimne* in respect to the archaic *velmnai* and its masculine form *velimna*. This is due to restructuring for morphological reasons since *-i* indicates the female gender (as we shall see later) and a term such as *velimnai* is immediately identifiable as the name of a woman, as opposed to the masculine *velimna*, but once /ai/ changes from a diphthong to the single vowel /e/ the gender sign is no longer "visible" and must be reintroduced.

As far as the sounds of consonants are concerned, there are not many differences between the archaic and recent phases of the language (except for the sibilants as we shall see shortly). The consonants consist of a double series of occlusives, aspirated and not aspirated /p t k p^h t^h k^h /, one affricate /ts/, two liquids /l r/, two nasals /m n/, four fricatives /f s š h/, two semi-vowels /j w/. This system seems highly plausible from a typological point of view. All the phonemes that make it up are, in fact, part of the 20 most frequent consonants in the languages of the world, and, what is more, the foreseeable relationships of implications established by the typology are complied with. For example, the presence of /f s š h/ in the series of fricatives respects the typological principle whereby if there is only one fricative, then

Bronze tablet with inscriptions end of the third–beginning of the second century B.C.
Tarquinia, Museo Archeologico cat. 262

it is /s/; if two, then /f s/; if three, then /f s š /; if four, then /f s š h/. The absence of the occlusive voiced consonants /b d g/ is evidenced by the fact that *beta* and *delta* are not used and *gamma* is used for the voiceless velar, tongue back stop /k/. This is confirmed by Varro's testimony in which he states that *itus* is the Etruscan word for the Ides *(Idus)*, and by the manner in which Greek loan words are used. Note the series *paχa-, tiφile, creice* for **Βάκχος**, *Δίφιλος, Γραικός*, in which the Greek /b d g/ have been changed to /p t k/ which are phonetically the closest.

Regarding the sibilants, the signs (see Bagnasco) show that the Etruscan system used two: one apical (dental) /s/, the other palatal /š/ (arguments used in the past to maintain that the difference was a matter of length/intensity, or /s ~ ss/, are by all means to be rejected). The / š / occurs much more frequently in the North than in the South. The northern usage shows palatization of the sibilant when placed before a consonant or when in contact with /i/ or /j/. Therefore, one of the words for "city" is [š]*pur* in the northern usage, whereas in the South is appears as [s]*pur*. The proper name Pesna is *pe*[š]*na* in the North, *pe*[s]*na* in the South; the proper name Laris is *lari*[š] in the North, *lari*[s] in the South; the clan name Keisi is *kei*[š]*i*- in the North, *kei*[s]*i*- in the South; and so on.

Other aspects regarding consonants are more marginal. It will be worth our while to examine briefly the use of syllables and accents. In archaic Etruscan the fundamental kind of syllable is the open syllable, or at most one ending in /m n r l/. Concerning accents, it must have been, for the most part, melodic and not dynamic as can be seen by the fact that this syllabic structure was maintained for a long time, from the seventh to the fifth century B.C. In neo-Etruscan, during the first half of the fifth century B.C., a stress on the first syllable of the word developed. This led, in the end, to the loss of non-accented vowels, especially those that followed the accented syllable so that there consequentially developed a reduction in the number of syllables in a word and the appearance of more or less complex closed syllables (ending in a consonant). For example the archaic tri-syllable *turuce* ("he dedicated") corresponds in recent Etruscan to the bi-syllable *turce,* to *avile*, a masculine proper name, corre-

Bronze and lead Aequipondium *from Sant'Antonio (Cerveteri), third century* B.C.
Roma, Museo di Villa Giulia cat. 287

sponds *avle*, to *ramuθa*, a female proper name, corresponds *ramθa,* to *venel*, a male proper name, corresponds *vel* (from **venl*), to *clutumusta*, the local version of Clytemnestra, corresponds *clutmsta.* Vowel loss was preceded by a phase of vowel weakening with consequent graphic variations. Note the series *aχile – aχele – aχale* (later *aχl*e), the proper name as either *avile – avele – avale* (later *avle*).

Our information on Etruscan morphology and syntax is far less extensive. It has been ascertained that it was an agglutinative language in which each grammatical category was expressed by a morphemic unit, or segment, placed right after the basic lexical root. The succession of building units of the word is what one would expect: root (+ derivative morphology) + number + case. In nouns there is the "absolutive" case, without distinctive forms, sign 0, plus a series of sign-bearing cases. If we take the word "son" as an example and confront it with a corresponding structure in Turkish (another agglutinative language) and contrast it with Latin (which uses fusional affixation) we obtain:

clan	*clen-ar*	*clen-si*	*clen-ar(a)-si*
oğul	*oğul-lar*	*oğul-a*	*oğul-lar-a*
fili-us	*fili-i*	*fili-ō*	*fili-is*
"son"	"sons"	"to the son"	"to the sons"

Apart from the absolutive, the known sign-bearing cases in Etruscan are the ablative, the locative, and the "pertinentive." Formally the pertinentive is close to the genitive; as one can observe, for example, in inflexions in proper names such as *larθ* (gen. *larθ-ia larθ-ial,* pert. *larθ-ia-le*), *venel* (gen. *venel-us*, pert. *venel-us-i*), *marce* (gen. *marce-s,* pert. *marce-s-i*). The genitive however, in spite of what was believed in the past, is functionally different. The genitive expresses belonging while the pertinentive expresses the destination, so that *turuce* "(he) dedicated" is construed with the genitive, *muluvanice* "(he) gave" is construed with the pertinentive, and so forth. The ablative is also formally close to the genitive as is shown, once again, by the inflexions of proper names such as *larθ* (gen. *larθ-al*, abl. *larθ-al-s*), *tute* (gen. *tute-s*, abl. *tute-i-s*), *vel* (gen. *vel-u-s*, abl. *vel-u-i-s*), *tarna* (gen. *tarna-s*, abl. *tarn-e-s* from

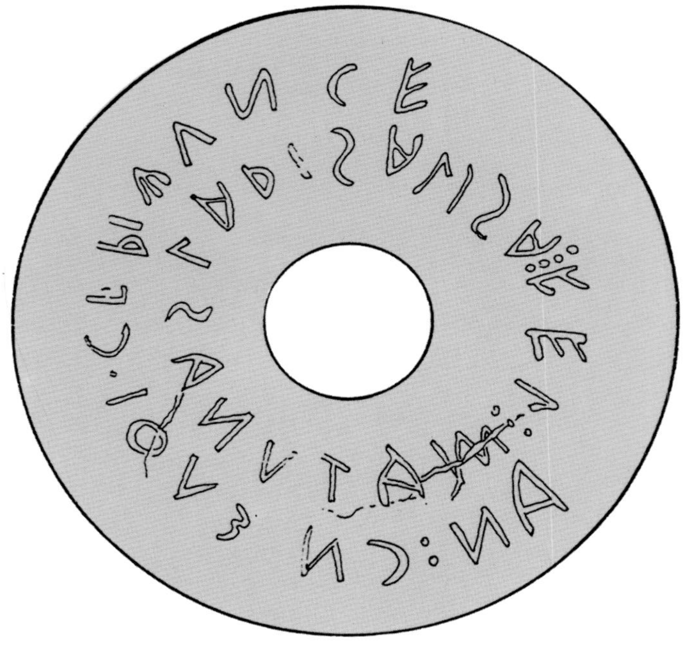

Graphic reconstruction of the cippus of Cerveteri, end of the fourth century B.C.

**tarna-i-s*). It is quite evident that both the pertinentive and ablative are complex cases derived from the genitive through the addition of suffixes.

The noun inflections are made up of a noteworthy variety of endings which belies the agglutinative character of the language and could indicate, along with other traits, that Etruscan was originally an agglutinative language which was evolving into another type.

As far as syntax is concerned, we shall limit our observations to three important points. The first concerns the reciprocal position of the element which has the function of determining and the element which is determined. As we can see already in the structure of compound words such as *θana-cvil* (proper name of a woman) or *tins-cvil* ("votive offering," from a preceding meaning of *"gift of Tins") in Etruscan, the determinant stands to the left of the determined (unlike a language such as Italian, for example). In the same manner, the direct object precedes the verb (as in formulas such as *ci clenar* [...] *arce* "three sons [...] generated" or *cn ziχ ... acasce* "this writing [he] made," respectively in Ta 1.167 and Ta 1.17), and the genitive precedes the noun (as in the formula *larθal clan* "son of Larth"). The morphemes, be they derivatives or inflected, are made up exclusively of suffixes; there are no prepositions, only postpositions, (see expressions such as *aritimi-pi* and *turan-pi* "for Aritmi," "for Turan" in Ve 3.34, or the formula *clen ceχa* "to the son's advantage"). Vice versa, the adjective seems to follow the noun to which it refers, as in syntagmata like **caper zamθic* "vase of gold"—vase golden—(LL VIII 10) or *ziχ neθsrac* "writing of a haruspex"—writing haruspical—(At 1.105), but it is known that in many languages the adjective, in this respect, is used in unexpected ways.

The second point to be taken up is that there is no distinction in grammatical gender in Etruscan of the type, let us say, that in Latin distinguishes a masculine *mons* from a feminine *vallis* from a neuter *flumen,* and relies exclusively on gender agreement whereby we have *magnus mons, magna vallis* and *magnum flumen.* Phenomena of this type are totally missing in Etruscan. There exists instead the arranging of nouns into two semantically motivated classes: the animate nouns, and the inanimate nouns. Only the nouns with an animate referent show a need for a plural sign when accompanied by a number (obviously more than one) for which we have *clen-ar ci* "three sons" (*clan* "son"), but *ci avil* "three years." Moreover, the plural sign is indicated through the use of two different morphemes for animate and inanimate nouns, with *ais-er* "gods," *clen-ar* "sons," *husur* "boys" for one type, and *anvilχ-va* "years," *cilθcva* "fortresses," *culscva* "doors" (or "gates") for the other type. The first of these two phenomena is typologically normal. In the presence of numbers greater than one, the plural signs are favored with animated nouns, for example, in languages such as Amhar-

ic or in Pashto. A plural sign (different) for both classes of nouns is less easily found, but examples do exist.
Only the vocabulary remains to be dealt with—briefly. In the beginning we noted a lack of the most obvious aspects of writing in written Etruscan documentation: from literature to written correspondence. One of the most unpleasant aspects of this situation is that the few hundreds of words the texts have handed down to us, already numerically trivial for a language of such cultural depth as Etruscan, are plainly only those words needed by the kind of Etruscan texts that have survived. The result is that we are quite well informed about certain sectors of Etruscan vocabulary, even many specialized and technical ones. We have, for example, the names of vases from *spanti* "plate" to *qutum* "jug," *aska* "askos," *leχtum* "lekythos;" and from *θina* "jar" to *χuliχna* "cup," and others. Many basic words, however, involving vast areas of the vocabulary, escape us. For example, for the terms of ordinary meaning, we know that "to be" is signified by *am-* (*amce* "was," *ame* "is/be," etc.), "gold" by *zam(a)θi,* that *mlaχ* is "beautiful," *cel* is "earth," *avil* is "year," *tiur* is "moon/month," and, after the acquisition of the *Tabula Cortonensis*, that *val* equals "look" (or "see") and "plain" was called *span,* but we are completely in the dark about which words express simple concepts such as "to place," "to stay, stand, live," "go," "come," "see," "say," "eyes," "hand," "head." In fact, those areas of the basic Etruscan vocabulary we know most about are the terms for kinship and the words for numbers. For kinship a list will suffice: *apa* "father," *ati* "mother," *clan* "son," *sec* "daughter," *husur* "boys," *papals* and *tetals* "grandchild," *nefts* "grandson," and *prumts* "great grandchild" (by lateral descendants?), *apa nacna* and *ati nacna* "grandfather" and "grandmother."
Regarding the words for the numbers from 1 to 10, we are certain about those from 1 to 6 which in numerical order are: *θu(n), zal, ci, sa, maχ, huθ,* we are certain about the number 10 which is *sar*. The words for "7," "8," and "9" are without doubt **cezp, *nurφ* and **semφ* but we are unable to say which word corresponds to which number. For multiples of ten there is, on the one hand, *zaθrum* "20," which is not etymologicaly definable, and on the other hand, the series formed with the suffix *–alχ*, which is a multiplier: *cialχ* "30," *sealχ* "40;" *muvalχ* "50" (?), **huθalχ* "60," *cezpalχ, semφalχ, nurφalχ,* "70-90." Neither the word for "100" nor the word for "1000" can be attested. The rest of the numbers are formed by a process of addition and subtraction. Addition is used for the first six numbers between ten and one multiple of ten and another; for example: *ci sar* "13," *huθzar* "16," *ci zaθrum* "23," *maχ zaθrum* "24," and so on. For the last three numbers subtraction is used. Thus "19" is *θun-em zaθrum* "one-without // twenty," that is, "twenty // without one," as in the Latin *undeviginti;* "18" is *esl-em zaθrum,* as in the Latin *duodeviginti,* but the use of the subtraction system is more extensive than in Latin since "17" is *ci-em zaθrum* whereas in Latin the additive form *septemdecim* is used. It may very well be that, as the Roman graphic system for numbering is of Etruscan origin, so might the numbers formed by subtraction (which in fact is not to be found in the Indo-European matrix of which Latin is one).
By way of a general conclusion, we can state that all the examples of words listed above confirm what already appears clear from the morphological and syntactical structure of the language; to wit, Etruscan is a genealogically isolated language. This does not at all imply that single morphological and syntactical elements or words that refer to Latin or Italic languages are missing in Etruscan. This is certified by words such as *nefts* (Latin *nepos*) "grandson," or by *prumts* (Latin *pronepos*) "great grandson," by the enclitic conjunction *-c* (Latin *-que*), or the preterit past tense morpheme *-ke* (Latin *fe-ced*). But the lack of a systematic correspondence of basic words (see words for kinship or numbers) demonstrates that it is a question of homologies due to the long contact between the Etruscans and other populations of ancient Italy, as is most evident in the similarities of place names as well.

The initials and numbers by which the inscriptions are identified refer to the collection in the Etruskische Texte (H. Rix et al., edited by, Tübigen 1991). Other abbreviations are standard usage.

De Simone 1968; Pallottino 1968; Pfiffig 1969; de Simone 1970; Colonna 1973–74, pp. 132–50; Torelli 1976, pp. 1001–1008; Pallottino 1978; Agostiniani 1982; Agostiniani 1984, pp. 84–117; Pallottino 1984; Rix 1983, pp. 210–38; Roncalli 1985; Agostiniani 1986, pp.15–46; Cristofani 1991b; Rix 1991; Agostiniani 1992, pp. 37–74; Agostiniani 1993, pp. 23–24; Agostiniani 1995a, pp. 21–65; Agostiniani 1995b, pp. 9–23; Cristofani 1995c.

The Tyrrheni of Lemnos

The "Tyrrhenian" presence on the island of Lemnos (as well as on nearby Imbros) represents the crux of a problem regarding a rather complicated set of linguistic questions as well as the analysis and critical evaluation of ancient sources relative to the presence of the "Pelasgians" or "Tyrrheni" on the island itself and in the upper Aegean. The problem which is fundamentally an historical one, that is based on reconstructed or hypothesized "events" relative to this set of data, is particularly incisive and important as far as the question of the historical origin or the ethnogenesis of the Etruscan people is concerned. Some scholars (H. Rix, G. Meiser: de Simone 1998, *passim*) continue to argue that the Tyrrhenian presence in the upper Aegean goes back to ancient times (and disappears in the protohistory of the region) and, in particular, that the Tyrrhenian language of Lemnos (as seen on the epigraph of a stela and in some other epigraphic fragments, cf. *infra*) is related in a genealogical sense to a presumed pre- or para-Greek linguistic substratum, one that is rather extensive but not duly defined or describable in methodologically valid terms (for a history of the problem, de Simone 1996a, pp. 91-96; de Simone 1996b, pp. 62-65), which must have been widespread in a "primitive" (non-datable) era in the Aegean area and/or Asia Minor (a geographic area that is not precisely defined). It is the thesis of Rix-Meiser therefore that the ethnogenesis of the Etruscan people in Italy is related to a phenomenon of massive and epochal "Tyrrheni" immigration from the northern Aegean-micro Asian area toward Italy which probably took place some time during the second millennium B.C. In this sense, the origin and the historical formation of a people like the Etruscans, considered as an abstract, pre-constituted entity (or "block") and thus not a real one (therefore decidedly metahistorical), are resolved in a rather simplistic and strikingly invasionistic fashion based on an "arrival-invasion" turn or event following the classic model of the *Völkerwanderungen* (migrations of peoples). It must be pointed out *in primis* that no evidence of this "language" exists, nor can it be reconstructed as an *explicative model* (in any case, not as a real "language") on the classic base of comparative reconstruction that is traditionally used for the Indo-European languages. Moreover, the search for the "primitive" (*Ur-*) also constitutes an effective "ideological" instance in fact operating on (and subject to) the basis of these (and similar) reconstructed imaginations of ethnic and linguistic stages of a pre- or proto-historical level (for a clarification and a criticism, de Simone 1997, p. 41; de Simone 1998, p. 404).

It is pointless to discuss here all the theories (with their relative variations), let alone the relative historical explanations that have been formulated to date regarding the Tyrrhenian presence on Lemnos (and Imbros); however, it is opportune and useful to provide a synthesis of the objective data at our disposition. Constituting the *princeps* document of the Tyrrhenian presence on Lemnos is the engraved stela, now in the Archaeological Museum of Athens, found at Kaminia, on the eastern part of the island, in 1884. This is a block of local sandstone which has an inconspicuous piece of undetermined size broken off on the lower part; the block was previously smoothed with pumice to prepare it for the subsequent engraving of the figured relief and the epigraph. Roughly sculpted on the front of the stela is the profile of a warrior armed with a lance and a large round shield which covers the lower part of his body, while he seems to have a kind of cap on his head. The monument can be dated around the end of the sixth century B.C. The Lemnos stela has two distinct texts, traditionally indicated as A and B (de Simone 1986, p. 724). Text A is on the front part of the stela and fills the remaining space around the warrior. Text B is on the minor right side of the stela instead and consists of three regularly placed lines, given that no figuration blocks the epigraph. While the alphabet of the two texts is essentially identical, the latter are probably the work of different hands and were executed at different (yet not distant) times. What is debatable is the exact succession of the different lines that make up inscription A. This problem cannot be resolved with certainty since it is impossible to translate the entire text, which would of course allow for a syntactic order of the single constituents to be established, as well as the concatenation of the subject matter. The alphabet of the Lemnos stela, which is also repeated in the few inscribed fragments from Kabeirion (Hephaistia), is of the western Greek ("red") type, and from this point of view represents an *unicum* or significant exception among northern Aegean epigraphy, in which there has only been evidence of alphabets of the eastern type ("blue", see de Simone 1995; Malzahn 1999, for a highly debatable

Stela of Lemnos, end of the sixth century B.C. Athens, Archaeological Museum cat. 1

contribution; de Simone forthcoming). The close relationship between the Lemnos stela alphabet and the actual Etruscan one is also (and not in the end) due to the sporadic presence (by now in a stage of depletion) in text A of cases of punctuation by syllables (a well known phenomenon of southern Etruscan epigraphy that started in 600 B.C. circa; cf. de Simone 1986, p. 723) which coexists (co-functions) with the inter-verbal punctuation, and also occurs in some archaic Etruscan inscriptions (Chiai, de Simone forthcoming).

The following considerations are of fundamental importance in dealing with the basic historico-linguistic problem. The strict relationship between the "Tyrrhene" of Lemnos and the Etruscan of Italy can be demonstrated in the first place by the fact that the alphabets used in the two linguistic areas in question responded to a need to establish phonological systems that coincided in their essential and qualifying points at a graphemic level (de Simone 1986). This regards the following phenomena: the systems of occlusive consonants, the opposition between two types of sibilants (*s* : *ś*), and the lack of a vowel of a velar timbre. In addition to these phonological data, there are a series of striking coincidences at a morphological as well as a properly lexical level (de Simone 1996a, p. 105). One obvious case is the exact coincidence of the terms used to indicate age: the formula of text B: *sivai avis šialXvis* ("he lived 40 years"), in which *sivai* (Lemnos) is a verbal form in *-ai*, is immediately comparable to parallel expressions (lexically coincident) in Etruria such as *zivas avils lxxvi* (Tarquinia; "having lived 76 years"), in which *zivas* is the participial form; and can furthermore be compared to the Etruscan expression *lupu-m avils maXs šealXls* (Tarquinia; "he died at 45 years"), as well as to *avils cealXls lupu* (again Tarquinia; "at 30 years he died"). A comparison of the Lemnian numbers with the corresponding Etruscan ones reveals, apart from the substantial lexical identity of the numbers themselves in question, an important and unequivocal *morphological* coincidence (formative principle) that unites the two documents: the tens are formed (starting from 20) by the suffix *-alX-* (Agostiniani 1995a, pp. 105); this structural coincidence is specific and cannot be incidental (as well as fully coherent with a rather significant series of arguments of another order). The onomastic formula also takes on particular importance: (A) *Aker Tavarsio Vanalašial*, constituted by the elements of the forename + *gens* name + matronymic, exactly as in the Etruscan (note that the *gens* name with *–io* = the Etruscan *–iu* comes within a particular category of Etruscan *gens* names deriving directly from individual names, cf. de Simone 1996b, pp. 24–25).

This significant and characteristic linguistic-institutional aspect can in no way be dated to the second half of the second millennium B.C. (according to the Rix-Meiser theory), by hypothesizing as a consequence that it had been transferred to Italy from Lemnos. We know very well that the creation of the onomastic system within the framework of the Etrusco-Italic *koine* was a very precise historical phenomenon, socio-structurally and thus chronologically determined, and tied in Etruria to the economic emergence and political affirmation of an aristocratic class (power of the *gentes*), an event that took place during the eighth century B.C. It is both absurd and factually impossible to try to backdate this complex sociological phenomenon at will. The Tyrrhene of Lemnos could not have had (nor transfer to Italy) the matronymic category at the time argued by Rix-Meiser, let alone a two-element onomastic system. The same type of argumentation holds true regarding the mention of the eponymous magistrates, which are documented in the same way on the stela (B) with the formula *Holaiesi Φokašiale seronaiθ*, "in the magistracy *serona-* of Holaie of Phocis."

It is by now apparent that the eponymous mention of the magistrates was not only Roman, but also an institutionalized and codified norm at the linguistic level throughout the Etrusco-Italic world (cf. for now de Simone 1998, p. 404) in which it had its historical *fieri*. A direct comparison for the eponymous dating formula of Lemnos is offered for example by the Etruscan inscription of the Tomb of the Orcus in which we can read *Larθiale HulXniesi* (cf. also for the morphology *Larθiale Melacinasi* in an archaic Vulci inscription): the distribution of the two allomorphs *-si* and *-iale* (only in an inverted order in the two linguistic traditions) is immediate and cogent (the syntagma is expressed formally by the same categories), as H. Rix himself has demonstrated for some time. The morphological coincidences existing between the Lemnian and the Etruscan are synthesized in the following outline (de Simone 1996a, p. 105):

Lemnian	Etruscan
a) Nominative case represented by zero (-Ø): *Aker*	*Ø: Θuker, Avile etc.*
b) Genitive I (*-s*): *Holaies*	*-s* (*Aviles etc.*)
c) "Pertinentive" *-si*(*: -iale*): *Holaiesi Φokasiale*	*-si* (*: -iale*): *Larθiale HulXniesi*
d) Locative in *-i: seronai*	*-i: fulinusnai* (arc.); cf. rec. Etruscan *-e*(< *-ai*): *zusleve, zaθrumsne*
d) Locative "re-determined" *-i-θ(i)*: *seronaiθ*	*-a-i-θ(i)*: *vinaiθ, hamaiθi*; rec. Etruscan *-neθi< -na-i-θi: hupnineθi* etc.
e) Verbal forms ("perfect tense"?) in *-ai: aomai, arai, sivai*	*-ai: akarai* (arc.)
f) Enclitic conjunction *-m: maras-m*	*-*(*u*)*m*

Lastly, there is a rule of inter-linguistic correspondence which does not seem to me to have been observed and used to advantage in the corresponding Lemnian-Etruscan framework. Within the framework of the cultural Etrusco-Italic *koine*, but also with respect to the Greek language, from which the Etruscan language borrows, a reciprocal, absolutely systematic (and historically determined) rule applies in which the stems in *-o-* are rendered in Etruscan with *-e*, and—with full coherence and structural solidarity—the stems in *-io-* with those in *ie*. This is also, and not by chance, the situation in Lemnos, as demonstrated by Holaies (gen.) which corresponds to the Greek ‛Yλαῖος.

The few fragments that come from Hephaistia (Della Seta 1937; Beschi 1998a, p. 76; Beschi 1998b) are not of particular importance. However, the archaic fragment [...]*aries* does merit special attention. Scratched on a rose-colored clay handle, it was found in 1960 at Myrina (Beschi 1998b, p. 269): the best comparison, taking into account the consistence of the lacuna (two or three letters) is offered by the (already archaic) Etruscan names, for example, *θefarie*(s) (and variations), and possibly *Aparie*.

What do the sources tell us? Of prime importance is a fact which is often not given due consideration: the most ancient periods of tradition on Lemnos were not at all "Tyrrhenian." There is no reference whatsoever to the Tyrrheni in Homer, who did, however, know about the (Thracian) people of the Sinti and the (Hellenic) descendants of the Argonauts on Lemnos (de Simone 1996b, pp. 41–44; de Simone 1998, pp. 397–98). A Mycenaean period (or presence) at Lemnos is now considered likely due to recent archaeological finds (fragments of Mycenaean pottery, IIIA and IIIB of the late Helladic period; Messineo 1997; de Simone 1998, p. 398). It was not until much later that reference was made to the fact that the Pelasgians may have been at Lemnos (Hecataeus), while Thucydides mentioned the presence of the Tyrrheni at Lemnos (de Simone 1996b, pp. 66–84). That a "Tyrrhenian" people were already practicing piracy in the Aegean during the Archaic period can be demonstrated ("illustrated") incontestably by the Homeric hymn to Dionysus (de Simone 1996a, pp. 100, 117).

It must be recognized objectively that the "Tyrrhene" dialect of Lemnos does not represent a distantly related language with a pre- or para-Greek substratum (cf. above), but is merely archaic Etruscan which does, however, present some autonomous phenomena. These, which are also present in Etruscan, are simply dialectic variants that exist for that matter in all the historical languages (the phenomenon in question seems normal): languages without variants (at a different level) do not exist. The theory that the Etruscans arrived at Lemnos (and Imbros) in a period notably anterior to the stela (around 700 B.C.?) does not hold up as L. Beschi has rightly pointed out several times (Beschi 1996; Beschi 1998a), since there is no archaeological evidence of the Etruscans ever having been on the island. The argument in itself is valid, and I recognize it as such. However, the "arrival" of the Etruscans in Lemnos is not to be considered, in our opinion, as a phenomenon corresponding to a "colonization" in the Hellenic sense; as an hypothesis it constitutes an improper historical inference. In any case, a general consideration has to be made in principle regarding the actual

Terra-cotta mermaid from Lemnos, second half of the sixth century B.C. Lemnos, Myrina Museum

state of our systematic knowledge of Lemnian archaeology for the period of time under consideration (ca. eighth–seventh century B.C.). The second argument is more general in character. Ethno-linguistic studies have demonstrated that there does not necessarily exist a bi-unique correspondence between a "material culture" and a certain language, because rather different concrete conditions are constituted (socio-linguistically) within which a language (or even more languages simultaneously) is actually formed within a certain society or organized group of speakers; moreover the identity of an *ethnos* seems strongly subject to change in time as ethno-linguistics studies have proven and illustrated (de Simone 1997, pp. 48–49, with bibliography). Furthermore, the concept of "culture" ("the Etruscan culture") represents a rather sensitive and improper approximate abstraction, and can no longer be accepted as such, because the necessary, organically interdependent relationship between the single factors making it up does not exist (social realities are much more complex and differentiated). While remaining within the debatable framework of the lack of an Etruscan (material and/or spiritual) "culture" at Lemnos, it should be pointed out that incineration was practiced on the island during the pre-Hellenic period, and this was later substituted by inhumation at the time of the Attic conquest around the end of the sixth century B.C. (cf. lastly Salomon 1997, p. 34). Why is incineration as such not to be considered "Etruscan" (funerary ideology)? Are not the language and the alphabet (partial) aspects of the (no longer essentially material) culture of an organized community?

Della Seta 1937, pp. 119–46; de Simone 1986, pp. 723–25; Agostiniani 1995, pp. 21–65; de Simone 1995, pp. 145–63; Beschi 1996, pp. 132–36; de Simone 1996a, pp. 89–121; de Simone 1996b; de Simone 1997, pp. 35–50; Messineo 1997, pp. 241–52; Salomon 1997; de Simone 1998, pp. 392–411; Beschi 1998, pp. 48–76; Beschi 1998a, pp. 259–74; Malzahn 1999, pp. 259–79; Chiai, de Simone forthcoming; de Simone forthcoming.

IACOBVS·VITERBE
EX·ORD·PRÆDICAT
EPS·FIRENTINVS
FHESVLA
BISENTIO
ARIN IANVM
LVNA
ARRETIVM
OGYGIANVM
VOLATERRA
ROSELLÆ
VOLSI NIVM
ETVR SIA
VOLCEN
ARYNIANVM
PHEREGE NÆ
IANI CVLVM
GENERE·ANIMANTIVM·OMNI
POST·AQVARVM·ELVVIEM·ADAVCTO
NOA·QVI·P·I·IANVS·DVODENAS·HASCE·COLO
NIAS·HANCQ·REGIAM·TETRAPOLIM·VOLPVR
NÆ·FANVM·ARBANVM·VETVLONIAM·LONGVIA
QVE·PRIMVM·ETVRSIAM·ETVRRIAM·VE·DEIN
DE·ETRVRIAM·A·QVA·ETRVRIÆ·REGIO·PO
STREMO·VITERBIVM·NVNCVPATAM·ANNO
CENTENO·OCTONOQVE·AB·IPSA·AQVAR
SALVTE·HAC·EA·REGIONE·TVM·TEMPO
RE·TVM·AVCTORIS·ORIGINE·SPLENDI
DISSIMA·CONSTITVIT
EX·QVO·VETVS·VRBIS·HVIVS·NOMEN
ET·SPLENDOR·VNDIQVE·MAXI
MVS·ILLVCESCIT

Etruscan Antiquarianism

Fabio Colivicchi

In Italian and European culture, the birth of the "Etruscan myth" is mostly owed to the Dominican friar Annio da Viterbo (1432–1502). His grandiose project sought a connection between Etruscan history—which had already been investigated from a minicipal perspective, fostered by archaeological finds—, and Biblical history. Relying on apocrypha and on epigraphic and archaeological documents, including some fantastical, invented texts whose "discovery" was an arranged pretext, Annio claimed that Etruscan society had very ancient roots, connecting it to the Scriptures through the figures of Janus and Noah. In this way, the Etruscans were considered even more ancient than the Romans, a claim that was not without rivalry, much like the classical historiographic tradition, considered a falsity, countered by a very ancient and uncorrupted veracity and knowledge.

Word of Annio's work echoed far and wide, but he remained rather unpopular in Florence until the history of the Etruscans became an important element in the ideology of power of the Medici family. Cosimo I favored the theories of Giovan Battista Gelli and Pierfrancesco Giambullari, who, drawing on the theories of Annio, attributed the founding of Florence to Noah-Janus, claiming that Aramaic was the original language of the first inhabitants of the peninsula. In their view, Etruscan and Hebrew derived from this first language. On one hand, this erudite construction of the origins of the culture provided the developing Medicean state with an ideological basis, founded on a connection with the Etruscans rather than on the disputed acceptance of Florentine supremacy. On the other hand, it provided the opportunity to develop an expansionist program based on the totality of the ancient territory of Etruria. In this way, Cosimo's official title of *Magnus Dux Etruriae* was well justified, and the discovery of the Chimera from Arezzo could be immediately employed by the central power.

The cultural-political project also attracted Guillaume Postel, French author of *De Etruriae regionibus, quae prima in orbe europeo habitata est, originibus, institutis, religione et moribus*, which he dedicated to Cosimo. In his work, Postel readopted the theory of the Aramaic origin in an anti-Roman spirit, applaying it also to explain the origin of the Gauls.

Nonetheless, Annio's theses did not meet with unanimous support in Florence. In fact, it would appear that his theory was not the sole, specific source of support for the Medici ideology, except within linguistic-scholarly circles and the encomiastic literature of the age. Moreover, this myth soon lost its fervor, as evidenced by the character of Cosimo's subsequent collections and the prevalent return to the Roman tradition. It was not until the 1720s that the myth was revived, in a moment of delicate transition from the Medici dynasty to that of the Lorena family. A fundamental event was the publication of Thomas Dempster's *De Etruria regali*, one of the last achievements of the Medici rule. Cosimo II had commissioned the Scottish writer some time between 1616 and 1619, but the book had never been published because of the grand duke's fading interest in Etruscan origins. Thomas Coke, a young English aristocrat, was responsible for the publication of the manuscript, which he purchased during his Grand Tour. In his work, Dempster connected the splendor of the ancient "Etruria of the Kings" with that of the Tuscany of the Medici, who had returned splendor to the region through the "traditional" monarchical statute. The text was based on the often-personal interpretation and compilation of information drawn from ancient, medieval and humanistic sources, including much apocrypha. Though it was written in a typical scholarly style, it required some revision to make it suitable to the needs of eighteenth-century society. Filippo Buonarroti, a scholarly man of politics, took on this responsibility. Perhaps influenced by Montfaucon's *Antiquité expliquée et représentée en figures*, a set of engravings of monuments were added to the text, including explanatory notes authored by Buonarroti, which served not only as a commentary, but also as an attempt to provide an overview of Etruscan culture, revealing its habits and customs through inscriptions as well as images. The classical sources, instead, which formed the core of Dempster's work, were used only as an occasional support. Particularly noteworthy are the linguistic considerations, which for the first time confronted the issues of language and of the alphabet, considered to be a derivative of the Greek alphabet.

While Dempster's manuscript was being edited in Florence, the issue of the Etruscans began to capture the attention of Scipione Maffei, whose "reasoning" in *Degl'Itali primitivi* of 1727 began with the Gubbio Tables to support the theory that the Etruscans had originated in Canaan. Later, in his *Trattato sopra la nazione etrusca e sopra gl'Itali primitivi*, published in 1739, he developed a vaster and more functional plan. The revived interest in the Etruscans, however, found

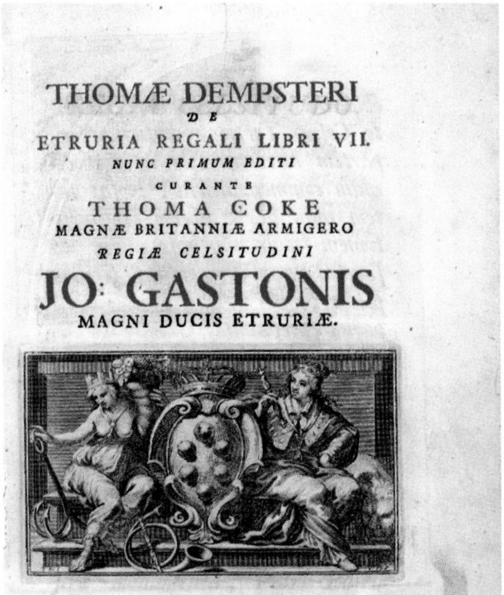
THOMÆ DEMPSTERI
DE
ETRURIA REGALI LIBRI VII.
NUNC PRIMUM EDITI
CURANTE
THOMA COKE
MAGNÆ BRITANNIÆ ARMIGERO
REGIÆ CELSITUDINI
JO: GASTONIS
MAGNI DUCIS ETRURIÆ.
FLORENTIÆ. M.DCC.XXIV.

Frontispiece of De Etruria regali *by Thomas Dempster, Florence, 1727. Florence, Biblioteca Nazionale Centrale*

opposite
Noah Showing to His Sons the Twelve Colonies of the *Etruria Regio* and the Etruscan Tetrapolis. *Viterbo, Palazzo Comunale, Sala Regia*

great support in Tuscany among the members of the small patrician class and the local clergy, who, in the midst of a great transition, saw in this theory an affirmation of the citizens' identity and of their own cultural and political role. The most important result of this phenomenon was the Accademia Etrusca of Cortona, founded on 29 December 1726, on the initiative of the Venuti brothers, Ridolfino and Marcello, who were soon joined by their younger brother, Filippo. Ridolfino continued his career in Rome, where he came into contact with the most erudite people and the most important personalities of the foreign colonies, contributing to the Accademia's success and to its opening toward foreign lands. Marcello instead, who had moved to Naples, where he had also became librarian and curator of the Museum, was forced to return to Cortona to take care of the family's properties. Just as *De Etruria regali* served the purposes of the Medici family, the activities of the Accademia also paid homage to the Medici and, subsequently to Francesco di Lorena, destined to further the annals of the "Etruria of the Kings." Such effective propaganda brought the institution immediate fame; consequently, both Italian and foreign intellectuals, including Montesquieu and Voltaire, whom Filippo had met during his long sojourn in France, adhered to its policies.

In Florence, Anton Francesco Gori, founder of the Accademia Colombaria in 1735, and curator of the Museum Florentium, which contained a graet amount of Florentine collections, assumed the leading role in the field of aantiquarian studies. His main interest, however, was Etruscan antiquaries, and he published a number of books on the subject, including *Museum Etruscum*, introducing a large variety of objects, most of them belonging to the collections of the local patrician class, who made of them objects of public and private prestige.

Gori's interest in the Etruscans, as well as that of erudite individuals in general, encouraged and augmented this tendency, giving rise to projects of public collections in the more vibrant localities, especially in Volterra. This was in part due to the discoveries of tombs containing small urns, a privileged object of the exegetic work of scholars. Soon, there were enough artifacts to develop a communal collection, enriched by the private collections of the wealthier families of Volterra, such as that of Mario Guarnacci, who opened their doors to visitors.

In Florence, instead, Etruscan antiquities did not assume the same autonomous role and the strong "patriotic" connotations that prevailed in Tuscany. With the exception of some small objects, especially the large bronzes, which were so valued at the time of Cosimo, these antiquities tended to be categorized in the rather undistinguished category of "ancient" objects. The collections of the grand duke in particular reflected the truly scarce interest in Etruscan objects, and even the private collections rarely echoed a conscious and specific interest in Etruscan themes. Etruscan "antiques"—among others—were the object of the often creative and overly elaborate exegetic efforts of antiquarians, among whom Gori held a place of honor, excercized in the living rooms and in the Accademia Colombaria.

Scipione Maffei was very much against these environments, and he disagreed with Gori in particular. His polemic was motivated by personal resentment, caused by the scarce attention given to his contributions as well as by the cultural distance between the artificial and religious interpretations of Gori and the tendency to date the Etruscan civilization to the most ancient eras.

After Gori died, the most important exponents of Etruscan antiquaria became Giovan Battista Passeri and Mario Guarnacci. Passeri contributed abundantly to the study of the language. He proposed an inductive methodology, putting aside the hypothesis concerning provenance, and focusing instead on more "archaeological" issues related to language. Published in 1767, Passeri's three-volume work entitled *Picturae Etruscorum in vasculis* illustrated a wide variety of decorated ceramics, which belonged to collections from all over Italy, The

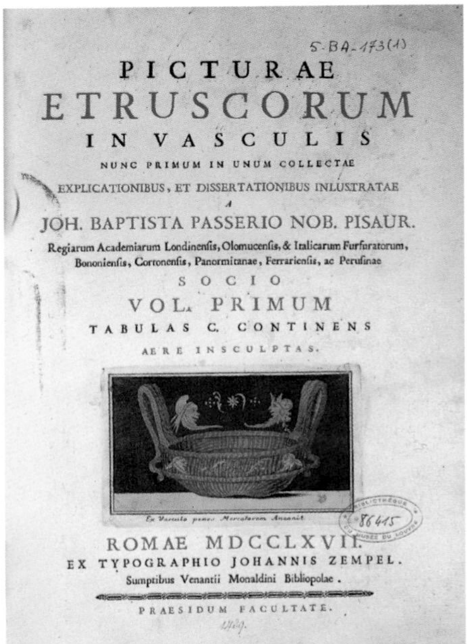

PICTURAE
ETRUSCORUM
IN VASCULIS
NUNC PRIMUM IN UNUM COLLECTAE
EXPLICATIONIBUS, ET DISSERTATIONIBUS INLUSTRATAE
A
JOH. BAPTISTA PASSERIO NOB. PISAUR.
Regiarum Academiarum Londinensis, Olomucensis, & Italicarum Furfuratorum, Bononiensis, Cortonensis, Panormitanae, Ferrariensis, ac Perusinae
SOCIO
VOL. PRIMUM
TABULAS C. CONTINENS
AERE INSCULPTAS.
ROMAE MDCCLXVII.
EX TYPOGRAPHIO JOHANNIS ZEMPEL.
Sumptibus Venantii Monaldini Bibliopolae.
PRAESIDUM FACULTATE.

Illustration and frontispiece of Picturae Etruscorum in vasculis *by G.B. Passeri, 1767–75. Paris, Bibliothèque Nationale*

Etruscan provenance of these artifacts was asserted on the basis of the typical antiquarian methods. Guarnacci, instead, embodies the typical expounder of the local features of Etruscan antiquarianism. A member of one of the most important families of Volterra, he had pursued an ecclesiastic career in Rome before retiring to his natal city, devoting his time to writing *Origini italiche*, which was published between 1767 and 1772. This work represented the ultimate synthesis of Etruscan antiquarian tradition in which he reproposed Annio's theories on the Hebrew origins and on the Etruscan supremacy of the European culture. By then, however, Guarnacci represented an anachronistic position, which had very few followers. In fact, the study of the Etruscans had been plagued by scepticism and boredom, and was considered an arduous and inconclusive research.

If Etruria continued to be a topic of interest, it was only to serve as an example of the region's once prosperous period, and as a model for the present in terms of "reformist" policies. Giovanni Targioni Tozzetti defended such interests. In his view, the pre-Roman period had been one of efficiency and of the development of Tuscany's structures of production within a regime of peaceful independent cities. Similarly, Giovanni Maria Lampredi was the supporter of the "federalist" regime of the Etruscan cities, which fought against the regal government, and Carlo Denina, from Piedmont, who had frequented the Florentine environment, wrote *Delle rivoluzioni d'Italia*, a history of Italy from its origins to modern times, in which he described the pre-Roman age as a harmonious society, first governed by kings elected by the people and later run according to a "federative" republican system.

Although involved less directly and enduringly, Rome also participated in the study of the Etruscans, especially thanks to the discovery of the painted tombs in Tarquinia, which drew the attention of Scipione Maffei who visited them in 1739. It was not until the 1760s, however, that scholars as well as artists and antique dealers became interested in these discoveries. Among the visitors was Giovan Battista Piranesi, who devoted two texts in particular to the Etruscans: *Magnificenza ed architettura dei Romani* was published in 1761, while *Ragionamento apologetico in difesa dell'architettura egizia e toscana* was published in 1769, in conjunction with *Camini*. Supporting his thesis with abbot Barthélemy's theory concerning the Etruscans' role in the development of Roman culture as well as the antiquarian tradition, Piranesi fervently confirmed the supremacy of the Etruscan "nation" and its "taste" for collective expression, evident also in its artisan artifacts, particularly in its decorated pottery. Piranesi, heavily influenced by Caylus and his *Recueil d'antiquités*, considered the pottery to be exemplary of a typically Etruscan tradition. Piranesi's view was very similar to that of Montesquieu's "spirit of the nations," contrasting with *Greek Revival*, and possibly directly counterpoising Winckelmann, whose *Geschichte der Kunst des Altertums* was published in 1764.

In his chapter on Etruscan art, the German scholar described Etruscan art as evolutionarily imperfect. Due to their passionate character, in fact, he claimed that the Etruscans would never have been able to attain the "noble simplicity and quiet grandeur" of the Greeks. Instead, he considered them indelibly affected by an exaggerated search for effect, characterized by an even harsher and uncalculated style, qualities that he evidenced especially in gems, statues and ornaments that were, whether directly or indirectly, reminiscent of the pre-classic stages of Greek art.

The languishing Florentine environment returned to assuming a central role with its arrangement of the Uffizi and the work of Luigi Lanzi, a former Jesuit who had studied antiquity in Rome, and who had been selected as assistant to the Director of the Galleriea Giuseppe Pelli Bencivenni.

The great project of rearranging the Galleries, which had then recently received a great number of Etruscan objects, caused Pelli to confront his more traditional tendencies in view of the need to create a more modern and systematic display, as Lanzi saw fit and as the grand duke Pietro Leopoldo had requested. The grand duke intended to open the exhibit to the public and, therefore, he wanted to make the collection more enjoyable. This project made it possible for Lanzi to confront the issue of language, which he approached in a clear and rational manner, applying the basic rules of philology. The study of the alphabet proved to be the most successful. In *Saggio di lingua etrusca e di altre antiche d'Italia*, published in 1789, Lanzi recognized the similarity between the Etruscan alphabet and the Greek alphabet, especially in its more ancient phases, thereby arriving at an initial deciphering that was substantially correct. The linguistic research proved more difficult. He proposed that Etruscan and other pre-Roman languages derived from a single common root, Greek. His *Saggio*, however was not merely a linguistic treatise. Making great use of the epigraphic and archaeological sources available to him, Lanzi was able to provide a summary of Etruscan history and civilization, which he formulated without the prejudices and influences of antiquarianism, to which he was completely extraneous, but, rather, by employing an empirical method based on his knowledge of Greek culture, which was by then quite widespread. It is no coincidence, then, that Lanzi is credited with being the first to attribute to a Greek manifacture the decorated vases found in Italy in his *De' vasi antichi dipinti volgarmente chiamati etruschi*, published in 1806.

With Lanzi, the study of Etruria ceased to be a study of antiquarianism, by then in decline, and began instead to employ more scientific methods, though not always in a linear fashion, at the dawn of the commencement of the great eighteenth-century excavations and research.

Cipriani 1980; *Annali della Facoltà di Lettere e Filosofia dell'Università di Siena, II,* 1981; Pallottino 1981; Cristofani 1983c; Barocchi, Gallo 1985; Borsi 1985; Camporeale 1992.

The Vatican's Museo Gregoriano Etrusco from the Nineteenth Century and Beyond

Francesco Buranelli

In Italy, strong political tension characterized the beginning of the nineteenth century. The 1797 Treaty of Tolentino had forced heavy sanctions on the pope, and many of the masterpieces belonging to the Vatican collections were transferred to the Louvre, which had been renamed the Musée Napoléon.
It was not until 1815, with the victory over France and the Congress of Vienna, that all of the artwork that had been taken from the pontificate during the occupation was returned. This, thanks to the allies and their subtle diplomatic activities, which also guaranteed a "restoration of governments." Only a small number of Etruscan antiquities were actually involved in this turbulent state of affairs because only a handful of Attic vases had been brought to France. Unfortunately, however, these were not returned.
The Museo Gregoriano Etrusco's current collection was not begun until the eighteenth century, with a few single exemplars and some more substantial groups of Etruscan, Italiot and Italic artifacts (especially vases, bronzes, and some terra-cotta pieces), which were neatly arranged at the top of some closets in the Vatican Library's Galleria Clementina. Other pieces, inserted as marginal additions, included the famous bronze votive statue of the seated boy, which was found near Tarquinia in 1770 and presented as a gift to Pope Clement XIV by Monsignor Francesco Carrara, as well as the other bronze statue (known as the *Graziani Putto*), found near Lake Trasimeno in 1587. The latter statue was subsequently included in various Perugian collections before Clement XIV finally had it brought to the Vatican. Even the Museo Pio-Clementino had a collection of some inscribed Perugian urns in addition to "other ancient Etruscan artifacts." They were unearthed in 1782 and brought to the museum so that—as Lanzi stated—"such an imposing collection will not lack even this kind of antiquity." A great number of Etruscan artifacts were discovered as a result of the intense archaeological studies of the eighteenth century, most of which were carried out in Tuscany. Consequently, many aristocrats established private collections, which, however, very rarely became prefigurations of public or museum collections. The Museo dell'Accademia Etrusca in Cortona, founded in 1726, and the Museo Guarnacci in Volterra, founded in 1732, are exceptions. In 1812, the first museum of antiquity belonging to the Papal States was established in Perugia. It is no coincidence that the famous vases from Cardinal F.A. Gualtiero's collection in Orvieto ended up in the display cases of the Vatican Library in those very years, under Pope Clement XII Corsini (1730–40). Originally donated to Gualtiero by Monsignor Bargagli, Bishop of Chiusi, most of those Etruscan vases had been unearthed at Chiusi. Few years later, in 1741, Pope Benedict XIV purchased the collection of antiquities that had belonged to the Museo Carpegna, founded by Cardinal G. di Carpegna between the end of seventeenth and the beginning of the eighteenth centuries. Toward the end of the eighteenth and the beginning of the nineteenth centuries, this "passion" for archaeological findings became even more widespread, and the necropolises of Chiusi, Tarquinia, Vulci, Cerveteri, Veio, Orvieto and Perugia were assaulted. Carried out impetuously by land owners, antiquarian collectors or, at times, even by merely enterprising individuals, excavations were conducted with a methodology deemed censurable even from the point of view of the archaeological techniques of the time. In an attempt to attenuate the situation, the Papal States declared the famous "Editto Pacca" on 7 April 1820. Issued by Cardinal Pacca, the edict constituted the first law for the protection of archaeological finds. Governmental assistants were sent to oversee excavations, while the General Advisory Committee for Antiquity and Fine Arts was responsible for determining which of the pieces were to be sent to the Vatican Museums. Purchases were made by using the 10,000 scudi that were part of the annual fund. Simply put, the Museo Gregoriano Etrusco can be considered the outgrowth of this legislation.
In 1815, Pope Pius VII decided that the residential chambers formerly housing Cardinal Francesco Saverio de Zelada, Pope Pius VI's librarian, should be used to house the museum. These rooms were located around Pirro Ligorio's Nicchione, on the first floor of the building that had been erected near Pope Innocent VIII's Palazzetto di Belvedere, as per Pope Pius IV's orders. Also known as the Tor de' Venti retreat or the Belvedere retreat, this apartment was used by the popes as a sanctum or as a temporary residence for illustrious guests, such as Cosimo I, the Duke of Florence, and his wife, Leonora. Decorated with scenes from the Bible, the walls of the apartment had been frescoed by Barocci as well as Federico and Taddeo Zuccari. This is where all of the materials purchased by the General Advisory Committee for Antiquity and Fine Arts, were collected. In 1829, the Candelori collection, consisting almost entirely of vases from Vulci, was purchased.
In 1834, influenced by this intense wave of archaeological findings, the Vatican formed a partnership with Vincenzo Campanari, helping to support his excavations at the Camposcala estate in Vulci. The findings were very

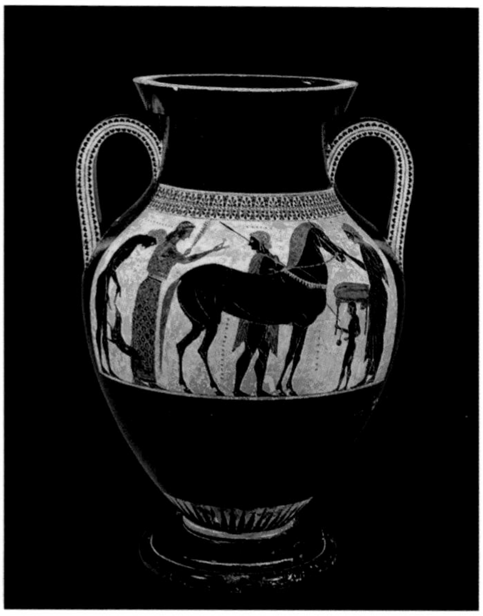

Exekias' Attic amphora, ca. 540 B.C.
Città del Vaticano, Museo Gregoriano Etrusco

Museo Gregoriano Etrusco, Room of the Bronzes and Room of the Italiot Vases, historical settings

important, numerous and rich. They were kept at Monte di Pietà until 1837, when the partnership terminated and they were shared between the Vatican and Campanari.

On 6 June 1835, the papal delegate sent a letter to the Camerlengo informing him of the discovery of the so-called *Mars* of Todi, in Monte Santo, close to Todi. About a year later, on 22 April 1836, two enterprising diggers from Cerveteri penetrated the extremely rich Orientalizing sepulchre, which was subsequently named Regolini-Galassi after Galassi, the owner of the excavation permit, and his partner, don Alessandro Regolini, archpriest of Cerveteri. Finally, in August of that year, the purchase was finalized for a part of the archaeological furnishings that had been unearthed about twenty years earlier, in a Latin Iron Age necropolis of Castelgandolfo. On 20 November 1836, after so many years of waiting, Monsignor A. Fieschi, prefect of the Sacri Palazzi Apostolici, communicated to Cardinal Galeffi, Camerlengo, the Vatican's intention—supported by many scholars—to found the Museo Etrusco in the former Appartamento Zelada. This announcement was made less than three months from inauguration day, after the Advisory Committee had made its final deliberation in those very rooms on the fifteenth of November. Those days were characterized by a frantic amount of purchases. On 18 January 1837 (two weeks from the date of the inauguration) a purchase was finalized for nine vases belonging to the Roman antiquarian, Basseggio. Among them was the famous Attic amphora of the Achilles Painter. Despite the many attempts to inaugurate it sooner, the museum was officially opened on February 2, 1837, on the sixth anniversary of Pope Gregory XVI's ascension to the throne. In any case, the collection was far from being complete in terms of both the objects to be exposed and the rooms where they were to be displayed. In the entry dated 11 February 1837, the Rome *Diario* mentions seven rooms, while the *Album* dated 24 March 1838 lists eleven. Unequal in size, lighting conditions and architectural quality, the

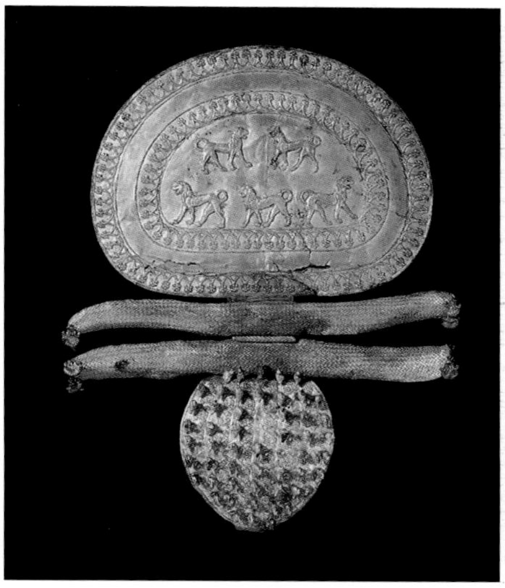

Disc fibula *from the Regolini Galassi Tomb, seventh century* B.C. *Città del Vaticano, Museo Gregoriano Etrusco*

Gold bracelets from the Regolini Galassi Tomb, seventh century B.C. *Città del Vaticano, Museo Gregoriano Etrusco*

rooms were all arranged within halls I, II, and III of the building's north wing and within the halls facing the Pigna courtyard. Facing south—like the medial hemicycle—the elegant and spacious rooms were equipped with a set of large windows, which allowed natural light to permeate the environments. The rooms were perfectly suited to the exposition of the vases collection and these artifacts which were more familiar to the taste and culture of the period.
Enormous and austere (like the entertainment halls) or small and subdivided by partitions (as the current Room I), the other rooms of the same wing were also characterized by a penumbral light that proved a most suitable medium, conferring a rather generic character to the displayed objects. The large room containing the bronzes was a blend of artifacts, from Mars of Todi to old Etruscan bronzes and Roman bronzes as well as reconstructed panoplies, which were arranged along the walls. Jewellery, exposed in display cases, was also included in this room. Instead, Greek urns and votive Caeretan vases were housed in the smaller, semi-lit hallways, while the Hellenistic sarcophagus from Tarquinia, with the myth of Atrus' descendants was surrounded by hut-urns from Castelgandolfo, which date to the Iron Age. A small room, reconstructed to look like an Etruscan tomb, marked the end of the visit. Two *nenfro* lions from Vulci guarded its entrance.
This last room had been constructed at the end of Vincenzo Campanari's excavations made in partnership with the papal government at Vulci and on the basis of the experience provided by the Etruscan exhibit that Campanari himself had presented in London. His reconstructions in London had been based on integral reproductions of tombs found at Vulci, Tarquinia, and Tuscania. Unfortunately, his remained an isolated, unique sample of the Museo Gregoriano's exhibit. In fact, the rich grave goods belonging to the Regolini-Galassi Tomb of Cerveteri, which the Vatican purchased soon after to embellish the "public museums," was separated and rearranged in the various exposition halls, according to typology (bronzes in the bronze room, gold with the gold, vases with vases, etc.).
Located at the entrance to the museum, a plaque read: "Museum Gregorianum ex monumentis Hetruscis," reflecting the strangeness of this museum, warning the visitor that the contents of the exhibit were not at all what the term "museum" in itself might infer. The plaque also referred to what the visitor might find in the Museum Pium in general, without providing any further specifications.
After 1840, the Museo Gregoriano Etrusco purchased only a few isolated objects, some of which, however, are noteworthy. For example, there was the polychrome sarcophagus found in the Tomb of the Sarcophagi in Cerveteri, discovered by Marquis Campana in the winter of 1845–46, and the bronze outfit of a tomb in Bolsena, purchased in 1857.
In 1870, even the Pope's archaeological "temporal power" over southern and central Etruria ceased to exist. Findings were delivered to the Italian government, who in 1889 opened the Museo Nazionale di Villa Giulia, the natural heir of the Museo Gregoriano. It was not until the end of the nineteenth and early twentieth centuries that the museum's scientific activities were taken up again, thanks to the Vatican Museums' first etruscologist, Bartolomeo Nogara. Nominated Special Director of the Museo Etrusco, he favored the purchase of the Falcioni collection, which consisted in Etruscan, Faliscan and Roman objects discovered around Viterbo. Though conspicuous, the museum's current acquisitions are primarily limited to donations, such as those of the Marquis Benedetto Guglielmi, who donated his collection of primarily Vulcian objects to Pope Pius XI in 1935. More recently, in 1967–68, Mario Astarita donated a very rich collection of Greek and Etruscan pottery, Italiot antiquities, and Roman glassware to Pope Paul VI.
Finally, the purchase for part of the Guglielmi collection was finalized in 1988. It was rejoined to the part that Benedetto Guglielmi had previously donated, thereby reintegrating in the Museo Gregoriano Etrusco one of the most famous nineteenth-century private collections.
These new donations almost always lead to new phases of study and scientific assertions, such as the study that I carried out between 1990 and 1995. My investigations coincided with a total restructuring of the museum and were included in the new series of systematically published scientific catalogues.

The Museo Archeologico Nazionale of Florence

Antonella Romualdi

The years immediately following the middle of the nineteenth century, with the political unification of Italy and its proclamation as a kingdom in 1861, were of a fundamental importance for the organization of the nation's museums. During that period not only a number of local museums came into being, for there was a renewed interest on the part of the individual communities in their own pasts and in the results of scientific research, but also national museums were instituted in order to meet the demands of a policy of centralization which for the most part has remained unaltered still today. In Florence, the capital of the kingdom from 1865 to 1871, the majority of the museums were established when the immense patrimony conserved in the Uffizi Galleries was divided up. On March 17, 1870, the Museo Etrusco in Florence was founded by a decree of King Vittorio Emanuele II, that was based on a proposal of the Minister of Education Cesare Correnti, and this was followed in May 1871 by the creation of a Deputazione per la conservazione e l'ordinamento dei Musei e delle Antichità Etrusche (Deputation for the conservation and organization of the museums and of the Etruscan antiquities). The motivations stated in the decree are of interest in order to reconstruct the history and the climate of those years: it was emphasized in fact that there was a need "to collect and organize scientifically" the considerable number of Etruscan objects that already existed in the Uffizi Galleries and elsewhere; furthermore "the museum will expand with the new excavations, bequests and temporary deposits of objects belonging to private collections as has occurred in many cities in Tuscany and Umbria which have their own Etruscan Museums whereas Florence lacks one." The last point mentioned in the decree, that is the fact that the transfer of the Etruscan objects to another place would provide the Uffizi Galleries with space to exhibit its prints and drawings, almost seemed to be an attempt to justify a possible impoverishment of the Galleries, although it must have been quite clear that the former convent of the so called Cenacolo of Foligno where the Museo Egizio was housed would be inadequate for a museum that was bound to grow. In addition to Aurelio Gotti, the Director of the Galleries; Gianfrancesco Gamurrini, the Conservator; and the Marquess Carlo Strozzi; the other members of the Supervisory Commission of the Museo Etrusco in Florence were eminent scholars in the field of archaeology such as Giancarlo Conestabile della Staffa of the University of Perugia and Ariodante Fabretti of the University of Turin. The presence of Achille Gennarelli was of particular significance for he taught Archaeology at the Istituto di Studi Superiori Pratici e di Perfezionamento (Institute of Superior Studies and Specialization) which was behind the most innovative initiatives in Florentine culture between the second half of the nineteenth century and the beginning of the twentieth century. In the heated debate among the members of the Supervisory Commission regarding what criteria were to be adopted in the organization of the Museo Etrusco, Gennarelli argued for a system "that would be in perfect harmony with the progress of archaeological studies and with the new ideas that prevail today regarding the way monuments should be considered in their relationship to the history of peoples... the most useful and rational organization of a museum is that in which the monuments are arranged geographically and already divided into general series..." However, what prevailed at that time was the theory of Gamurrini and Fabretti, through the mediation of Conestabile: "to leave the monuments in single series but arrange them on a geographical and topographical basis."
The Museo Etrusco in Florence was thus established on the basis of scientific criteria which in a certain sense were already old-fashioned. On the one hand, what Alessandro François, the first really active archaeologist in Tuscany, had hoped for was being fulfilled, on the other hand, his idea of a new topographically organized museum that was to be established as a consequence of the excavations conducted by the state authorities was not. In 1871, when the Museo Etrusco, located since 1853 in "the corridor that connected the Galleries to the Pitti Palace," was moved to the location of the Cenacolo di Foligno in Via Faenza, the short period in which Florence was the head of the unified kingdom had come to an end: the capital was transferred to Rome thus causing an immediate collapse in the economy of the city, which was followed in 1873 by a world economic crisis.
The historical account of the Regio Museo Egizio ed Etrusco written by Gamurrini, in his role as antiquarian and conservator, outlines the history of the museum that originated from those "three marvelous monuments of Etruscan sculpture in bronze that appeared during the time of the first Cosimo and that now figure as its most important works: the Pallas, the Chimera and the Orator." There were in fact few Etruscan artifacts and vases in the Medici collections and it was not until the Lorena period that the archaeological collection of the Grand Duchy was enriched through the acquisition of some private collections: from that of the Galluzzi of Volterra in 1771 to that which Giusto Cinci of the same city had amassed in 1828 thanks to a series of excavations carried out in Volterra during the 1820s in the necropolis of Portone.
With the unification of Italy numerous other materials came to enhance the nucleus of antiquities of the Florentine museum, first and foremost those that the Colombaria Society of Florence had recovered in a series of excavation campaigns in Chiusi, Sovana, Cosa, and Roselle after it had taken over some projects of A. François. These were followed by the gems and valuables that an English gentleman, William Currie, bequeathed to the Florence gallery, and in 1870 by the materials that Count Pietro Bucelli had collected during the eighteenth century in the territory between Chiusi and Montepulciano.
The plaque above the entrance to Room IX of the Etruscan Antiquarium is the original one, recalling the transfer in 1870 of the Museo Etrusco to the

page 514
View of the ground floor great room of the Spedale degli Innocenti in the 1960s

View of the room dedicated to Tarquinia in the Museo Topografico dell'Etruria before the flood of 1966

former convent of Sant'Onofrio of the Franciscan Sisters of Foligno where the Museo Egizio was already located. The initial words "to compare with the relics of the ancient Orient," clearly expresses the reason why the two collections were united in the same building. It was a choice that strongly conditioned and still does the exploitation and very survival of both institutions.
In the convent of Foligno the first five rooms contained the collections of pottery and terra cottas including the impasto vases, antefixes, votive objects and Hellenistic pottery. In the second room, the François Vase "triumphed" together with other Attic and Corinthian vases. The tribune of the Ori also housed the collection of glass acquired those same years by Fanelli of Sarteano and Bruschi of Tarquinia, followed by the epigraphic collection, the tribune of bronzes with the statue of Minerva and various statuettes, mirrors and some bronzeware. The *Chimera* was in the second tribune together with burial goods containing a rich bronze armor that were discovered in 1863 during the excavations in the necropolis of Settecamini at Orvieto conducted by Domenico Golini, a professional digger. In the same tribune, above the "precious trunk of an Oriental alabaster column", hung the situla of Bolsena, acquired in 1871, while the *Arringatore* and the sarcophagus of the Amazons, found at Tarquinia in 1869, were in the room of the urns. According to the calculation that Gamurrini made at the end of his report, there were about 2400 objects in the Museo Etrusco in 1873, and it shared with the Museo Egizio three custodians and 6000 Lire per year for acquisitions.
The decade that immediately followed the political unification of the country was a particularly fertile period in the field of archaeology as well, thanks to the local communities' renewed interest in their own pasts. The case of Chiusi was emblematic in Tuscany since the excavations that the Archaeological Commission carried out after more than fifty years of widespread destruction of the necropolises made it possible to constitute the first nucleus of a Civic Museum in 1870. During those same years, the Civic Museum of Grosseto was also established with a small group of objects in the Library of the Canon Giovanni Chelli of Siena, and it later developed, thanks also to Gamurrini's intervention, into a city museum in which the artifacts were organized topographically.
The ever-increasing need for more and larger space, primarily because of the intensity of the excavations, seemed to have been resolved at first when the Council of Ministers decided to move the Museo Archeologico of Florence to the Palazzo della Crocetta. The proposal had been made by a technical commission that included Luigi Pigorini, Commissioner for the Direction of the Museums and Galleries of Italy, the sculptor Giovanni Dupré, Ruggero Bonghi, Giuseppe Fiorelli and Domenico Comparetti, Professor of Greek language and literature at the Institute of Superior Studies. According to this new ambitious project, the Museo Etrusco was to become the Museo Archeologico, and in addition to the Etruscan and numismatic collections, and Greek and Roman bronzes, it would also include all the ancient marbles conserved in the Uffizi Galleries, the Pitti Palace, the Boboli Gardens, and the Villa of Poggio Imperiale so as to constitute a huge museum of sculpture and of the collectiosn of antiquities in Florence. The project was the result of a specific cultural and political agreement between Giuseppe Fiorelli, who was in charge of the General Direction of the Museums and Excavations of Antiquity, which had been instituted in 1875 notwithstanding the great difficulties raised by the students of antiquities in Rome, and the Florentine Institute of Superior Studies, where the area of classical studies was dominated by the figure of Domenico Comparetti to whom the archaeological research of those years owed a great deal.
After the death of Giancarlo Conestabile, the Director of the Museo Etrusco who in 1876 became Professor of the first Chair of Etruscan Archaeology in Italy at the Institute of Superior Studies, and in keeping with the wishes of Fiorelli, Comparetti and Pigorini, a general inventory of the material in the Egyptian-Etruscan Museum was made. Antonio Sogliano was responsi-

ble for the Etruscan section, Ernesto Schiaparelli for the Egyptian collection, and Luigi Adriano Milani, a student of Comparetti and known to be a competent numismatist, for the grand ducal numismatic collection. Throughout 1879 Pigorini and Fiorelli intensified their efforts to move the museum to the Palazzo della Crocetta, particularly since the latter was aspired to by many others in the city. In order to hasten the transfer of materials, it seemed opportune to them to accept the offers of collaboration made by Vittorio Poggi, who was already known for having published the first edition of the bronze "liver of Piacenza." Therefore in 1880 while the structural work intensified inside the Palazzo della Crocetta, Poggi was entrusted with the classification of the works that were to be transferred there and with the drawing up a preliminary idea of the entire installation and the distribution of the pieces in the rooms. According to Poggi's project, the Greek-Roman section, containing the approximately 1500 marble works that were coming from different places in the city, and an equal number of small and large bronzes, gems and gold work, would be on the ground floor. It also foresaw the creation of two long galleries on the sides of the garden, interrupted by two hemicycles containing the masterpieces, while the great salon of the Nicchio in the building of the Innocenti, was destined for the group of the children of Niobe. The Etruscan section was to occupy the entire first floor and be subdivided according to typological classes, while space would also be made available for the copies of important works in other museums. The Museo Egizio would be located on the second floor together with the grand ducal numismatic collection and the offices.
The history of the activity of the Museum Commission, which Gamurrini headed and which included many who were prominent in the field of Italian archaeology at that time, throughout the tense period of 1880-1881 and the different alliances and pacts that were later periodically established remains to be reconstructed more fully with the aid of the still partially unpublished documentation conserved in the State Archives in Rome. In 1880, Vittorio Poggi had already drawn up 5226 entries for the catalogue, and Luigi Adriano Milani had become one of the members of the Museum Commission. In 1881, the Commission, ignoring the project that Poggi had presented, decided to concentrate the Egyptian-Etruscan Museum on the first floor of the Palazzo della Crocetta and use the second floor for a Museum of Plaster Casts, according to a project that Milani, who enjoyed the support and approval of the Ministry, had proposed.
At the same time, as a result of the controversies between Gennarelli and Pigorini, Giuseppe Fiorelli and Domenico Comparetti combined forces to support Milani's work and exclude Vittorio Poggi from the museum. Milani not only saw to it that Poggi's catalogue was never published but that his colleague's name was eliminated forever from the history of the Museo Archeologico in Florence. That same year, Gamurrini, whose history as a scholar and archaeologist is yet to be written, left Tuscany because of his disagreements with Fiorelli, and took on the job of preparing an official archaeological map of Italy.
The new Museo Archeologico was inaugurated at the Palazzo della Crocetta in 1883. By then Isidoro Falchi, an outstanding patriot and "amateur archaeologist" who played a leading role in late nineteenth century archaeological research, had already written a report to the Minister of Education in 1882 about the ruins of the ancient city of Vetulonia, after having found the Etruscan walls, which he identified as the small village of Poggio Colonna in the Maremma territory of Grosseto. From 1884 to 1913, thanks to the excavations that Falchi was making, albeit with extremely limited methods, more and more was being discovered at Vetulonia amidst the more or less declared hostility of the Director of the Museo Archeologico of Florence and local controversies regarding the identification of ancient Vetulonia. Not even Milani himself was extraneous to these controversies, and at a certain moment, as a result of Inspector Giuseppe Sordini's finds at Poggio Castiglione in Massa Marittima, he confuted Falchi's theory regarding the location of Vetulonia. The extraordinary discoveries of Vetulonia during those years went on to form the topographical section that Milani inaugurated in 1897, when he also returned to the scientific criterion of organization that Gennarelli had favored in 1870. The decree emanated in 1888 by King Umberto I that sanctioned the city of Florence's right to possess a Central Museum of Etruscan Civilization momentarily calmed the anxieties of the director who feared that his territory of competence risked being re-dimensioned by the General Direction in Rome which was then headed by Felice Barnabei. The following year, a decree establishing the Museo di Villa Giulia proved his fears to be well-founded. What ensued was what Barnabei referred to as "the war of Etruria against the Museum of Villa Giulia fought by the Florentine lords who raised their shields in the name of Florence's regional rights and the advantage of its studies." In order to set up a Museo Topografico, Milani tried to secure the antiquities that were coming to light in the ongoing excavations in Etruria or which were in the palaces of the nobility, although he continued to run into difficulty in his attempt to unite all the Florentine collections of antiquities as much as possible for the Museo Archeologico as well as to assemble a great collection of classical sculpture. In 1883, the numerous marbles stored in the Uffizi were transferred, in 1890 it was the turn of the *Idolino* and the Greek and Roman bronzes, and finally, in 1895, of the numismatic collection. Milani's attitude and perseverance in breaking up the grand ducal collections is to be explained on the one hand by Milani's formation for he was basically insensitive to the ways of collectors and antiquarians, and on the other hand by his at times furious quarrel with the Uffizi Galleries. The new additions accentu-

ated the already chaotic situation of the exposition space—the second floor which had been designated for the plaster casts had been occupied in 1883 by the Gallery of the Tapestries which remained there until 1925—creating enormous inconvenience, and revealing at the same time what would prove to be throughout time the worst feature of the Museo Archeologico of Florence, and that is the total inadequacy of its exposition space. This factor, which still today conditions the future of the museum, together with the lack of a general plan, the desire to create a great museum, and the inflexibility in maintaining one section, the so-called Antiquarium, which was meant to be a manual almost of the history of Etruscan crafts, has led in time to the diaspora of materials from one section to another and the development of some parts of the museum to the detriment of others.
Milani's policy of centralization, notwithstanding repeated assertions that he intended to safeguard the local museums, appears emblematically manifest in the case of the Talamone pediment which had initially been deposited in the Civic Museum of Grosseto and later removed with the consent of the state authority in 1891 in anticipation of the Museo Topografico. When the latter was inaugurated on May 5, 1897 on the ground floor of the Palazzo della Crocetta, the new institute had 17 rooms that were arranged rather chaotically and without any respect for a precise geographic order given the lack of space. While three rooms had already been dedicated to Vetulonia and the Villanovan material of Poggio alla Guardia with the deposits from the Tombs of the Duce, Pietrera and Littore, Populonia was represented only by a collection of coins, even though Isidoro Falchi had already started the excavations in the necropolis of St. Cerbone that very year. One of the rooms destined to Chiusi, the second one, housed the Etruscan collection that the Baron Foucques de Vagnonville had left to the city of Florence which Milani had managed to secure for the museum. On view with the Luni pediments, exhibited together with the other antiquities from Luni in the gallery facing the garden—today reduced to a passageway and filled with the Superintendent's office files—were the remains of the structures and marble entablatures that had been found in the excavations carried out in the centre of Florence during the last two decades of the nineteenth century. Apropos of the difficulties that the limited space imposed on the scientific installation of the museum, it may be of some interest to point out that the bronzes found at Acquasanta near Chianciano had been temporarily placed on the first floor and not in the rooms of the topographical section dedicated to Chiusi. In 1898, the most ancient part of the Medici glyptic collection was transferred from the Uffizi Galleries to the Museo Archeologico. And in the early years of the twentieth century, Milani transformed the Palazzo Crocetta garden into the architectural section which was annexed to the Museo Topografico with the reconstruction, using original pieces, of some tombs from Orvieto, Vetulonia, Casale Marittimo and Chianciano, and the execution of copies of the Inghirami Tomb of Volterra and that of the Velii of Orvieto. The collection of classical sculptures already in the museum was installed in the arcades of the garden and along its paths, while vitrines filled with objects were placed next to the Etruscan monuments, and cippi, steles, sarcophagi and urns from different parts of Etruria were set up in the garden. Three small rooms were built on the Via della Colonna side of the garden which was isolated by a high wall and these contained artifacts from Perugia, Fabbrecce and Trestina which had come to light during the last twenty years of the nineteenth century and the early part of the twentieth century, the prehistoric and the Italic sections, as well as the gallery of facsimiles of Etruscan painting that Antonio Minto set up in the 1930s and which reflected the typical nineteenth century archaeological installations that had already been used in the Museo Etrusco of the Vatican and the Civic Museum of Bologna.
The last decade of the nineteenth century and the first of the twentieth were particularly fertile years for archaeological research in Italy: Milani managed to acquire some burial goods for the Florence museum from the excavations conducted at Falerii by the antiquarian Benedetti and at Narce by Adolfo Cozza, Angiolo Pasqui and Felice Barnabei. Between 1895 and 1903, the excavations carried out at Saturnia by the painter Riccardo Mancinelli of Orvieto in the necropolises of Pian di Palma, Pancotta and Sterpeti brought many depositions to light, part of which were acquired between 1902 and 1903. Others discovered by the brothers Benedetti in 1900 and 1901 in the necropolises of Monte Michele near Veio also become part of the Museo Topografico collection. From 1893 to 1916 Prince Tommaso Corsini, with Milani's authorization, undertook a systemic research campaign, one marked by great scientific rigor, on his estate at Marsiliana d'Albenga, which brought to light the wealthy Banditella and Perazzeta necropolises whose depositions, studied by Antonio Minto, provided valuable information about the Orientalizing period of Etruscan culture. It could almost be said that the most outstanding figures in Tuscan archaeology at the turn of the century were in a certain sense two amateur archaeologists, Isidoro Falchi and Prince Tommaso Corsini, both men who in different ways due to their formation and origin conducted their work with passion and a social and political commitment. Once the problems and misunderstandings that had arisen between Falchi and the representatives of official archaeology had been resolved, and after the first national law of protection had been enacted, state sponsored excavations started in the necropolis of St. Cerbone at Populonia in 1908, while numerous objects were acquired from Vulci in the years between the end of the eighteenth and the beginning of the nineteenth centuries.
A reading of the inventories and historical archives of the museum, and

ARCANA ETRVSCORVM RESERENTVR

Entrance to the Museo Archeologico of Florence from Piazza Santissima Annunziata nel 1964

the testimonies of leading figures like Felice Barnabei, demonstrate how frenzied Milani's activity was during that period as he attempted to make sure that the museum would have at least a part of the most significant discoveries from the numerous excavations in Etruria. Milani's interests lay primarily in the museum's numismatic and medal collections, but also in that of gems for which he was to write the catalogue. His studies which almost exclusively privileged significance and religious symbols as he tried to find a unity of origin in language and religion according to the dictates of anthropological science that he considered so similar to archaeology, had a strong negative influence on the physiognomy of the museum. An obvious example is the pre-Etruscan and pre-Hellenic section that he set up in order to demonstrate the relationship in origin between Etruria, Asia Minor and Eastern Greece which was also a clear reflection of his teachings at the university. This combination of factors, plus his controversial attitude about the ancient marbles of Florence, and the fact that he was backed by the authorities, tended to isolate Milani in a certain sense from the world of Italian archaeology of those years, and prevented the Museo Archeologico from ever taking root in the life of the city, something that still holds true today.

It was up to Antonio Minto, Milani's successor as the head of the museum and the Sovrintendenza after the brief interval of Luigi Pernier, to implement Milani's project for the Museo Archeologico more fully.

The presentation and approval of a new project in 1925 which would enlarge the museum space included the opening of a new entrance on Piazza Santissima Annunziata, the establishment of the International Institute of Etruscan and Italic Studies and the Museo della Scultura Classica, and the construction of a series of rooms along the Via Laura side. On the occasion of the First International Etruscan Congress which was held in 1928, Minto published a short guide to the museum in the review *Studi Etruschi* which is invaluable when confronted with the report drawn up in 1945 for a reconstruction and examination of the different stages of the installation project. These reflected the course of the new discoveries that followed one another in rapid succession, thanks above all to Minto's research work which affected the entire territory in the regions of Tuscany and Umbria.

The Museo Topografico had 26 rooms on the ground floor, while two rooms were used for storage, one for the prehistoric materials from Etruria and the other for the inscriptions of the ancient collection of Strozzi di Montughi. Milani's installation was maintained in the garden although Minto complained of the risk incurred by the materials due to inclement weather. On the first floor, the Museo Egizio occupied 8 rooms, while the Antiquarium, from rooms 9 to 20, contained the Etruscan sculptures, the collection of Etruscan, Greek and Roman bronzes, the room dedicated to the *Idolino* in addition to the *Torso* from Livorno, the protome of the horse that had belonged to Lorenzo il Magnifico and other priceless small Greek and Roman bronzes including the *Bacchus*, the *Zeus*, and the Polyclitus-type *Amazon*, and the Numismatic Cabinet. Minto himself organized the second floor once the Gallery of Tapestries had been transferred, setting up there the two rooms of Italic comparisons, and a third room with some Hellenistic statuettes and the Vagnonville collection. Nine rooms, from 7 to 14, followed along the Via della Colonna side with a chronological arrangement of the pottery collection while the Etruscan terra cottas were on display in room 15. This display remained more or less intact until 1986 when these rooms were dismantled during the renovation work of the former Museo Topografico. Even though there was a chronic lack of space, eleven rooms on the second floor of the building, from XVII to XXVII, were set aside to exhibit the copies of the frescoes of the paintings in the region under the Sovrintendenza's protection and the most important Etruscan paintings in Latium, the work of the draftsman Gatti. Some plaster casts were placed temporarily in the corridor. These were meant to prefigure the collection of plaster cast reproductions of the most important Etruscan monuments that had been planned in 1880 but which never did materialize. In establishing the International Institute of Etruscan and Italic Studies, Antonio Minto probably meant it to be an integral part of the museum, a kind of permanent scientific laboratory that would include a great variety of disciplines and be open to scholars from the whole world so that it would stimulate interest in the museum collections through direct contact with the latest trends in archaeological studies and the research programs in the territory. The Institute first started as the Permanent Committee for Etruria in 1926, but in 1928 it received a new stimulus with the celebration of the first important scientific event in the field of Etruscology represented by the first International Etruscan Congress. The duties that Minto assigned to the Institute, which were also representative of his own principles and the organization of his research, consisted primarily in the coordination of the historical, archaeological, religious, linguistic, epigraphic and naturalistic studies, together with the publication of catalogues, synthetic works on Etruscan civilization, and monographs on the cities and necropolises of Etruria. The work of the International Institute of Etruscan and Italic Studies would turn Florence, the capital of the region of Tuscany, into the centre of studies for ancient Etruria, and the Museo Archeologico of Florence into a vital structure in the production of culture. Between 1920 and 1930, particularly fertile years for research in the field of Etruscology, Florence and the Institute, as Massimo Pallottino acknowledged, really did become reference points for many Italian and foreign scholars who made important contributions to the study of Etruscan Civilization.

In the years between 1929 and 1940, nine rooms were built along the garden for the Museo Topografico: it was another important step in the renovation plan of the museum that included the entrance on Piazza Santissima Annunziata, the utilization of the rooms of the building of the Innocenti for the collection of classical sculptures, and the transfer of the Museo Egizio to the Via Laura rooms which then, as now, were occupied by the Law School.

In a report published in 1945, Minto underlined the scientific criteria at the basis of the organization of the Museo Topografico: after a "small representation of antiquities from the Etruscan centers of Latium, the collection proceeds topographically through the centers and territories of the Tyrrhenian coast and the interior ones of Etruria with the most representative documents from the Iron Age civilization to the late Roman period." The entrance hall to the Museum on Piazza Santissima Annunziata was to be decorated with Roman statues placed inside the wall niches and a Greek lion in Parian marble next to the stairway, according to the project designed by the architect Bartoli that remained unfinished until the Fifties.

It is important to point out that at the end of the 1940s Minto had already used many sculptures as decorative elements on the library stairs, in the rooms of the Institute of Etruscan Studies, on the garden paths, in the Numismatic Cabinet and on the museum stairs where most of them remained until the drastic dismantling of the 1980s.

In an essay that appeared in 1950 in the *Atti della Società Colombaria*, on the occasion of the public opening of the Museo Topografico and the museum entrance on Via Capponi, Antonio Minto indicated that the loss of jurisdiction over the Etruscan excavations of Latium was the reason why the Central Museum of Etruscan Civilization had never been established. In speaking about the Antiquarium, Minto did point out sagaciously that the arrangement of the Etruscan sculptures, the small Greek and Etruscan bronzes, and the Etruscan objects was not definitive inasmuch as this could only be achieved when the Museo Egizio was transferred. The large Etruscan bronzes and the *Idolino* required a special room and a more fitting display. The amphorae with inscriptions were exhibited in the first, rather short section of the "Medici" corridor alongside Via Laura whereas the Etruscan inscriptions were placed in the longer section in topographical order according to their origin. The Latin epigraphs were divided into two groups and affixed to the wall outside the corridor above the terrace: one group consisted of the epigraphs from the Uffizi Galleries referring for the most part to the suburban territory of Rome; the other was part of the old Strozzi di Montughi collection, while a small series of Greek epigraphs had been placed on the walls at the far ends of the terrace.

The Museo Topografico contained 52 rooms and, as Minto pointed out, its very nature as a museum made it subject to substitutions and additions. Each room was equipped with an archaeological map of the territory on a 1:100,000 scale and the rooms followed one another, to use Minto's words, as in a treatise on the "Historico-Archaeological Topography" of Etruria. At the entrance there was a plaque commemorating Milani, a general map of ancient Etruria which served for orientation, and a cast of the remains of the so-called "Throne of Claudius" which had been found in the Roman theatre of Cerveteri. All of this justified the decision, following the example of Milani and in the wake of Bormann's essay, of giving the rooms the names of the XII *populi Etruriae* as related by the ancient historiography of the Julio-Claudian era; the intention also being to underline the importance of the territory.

The opening of the new Museo Topografico seemed to have taken place in a minor key. There is no documentation whatsoever in the archives that mentions the participation of the authorities in the event. And perhaps it was not surprising that some years earlier, Minto himself, when his term as president of the Institute of Etruscan and Italic Studies came to an end, had expressed his bitterness in ascertaining how disinterested the city of Florence and the government itself were in the Museo Archeologico and the Institute. His words regarding the city are par-

ticularly relevant today: "the city of Florence is conscious of the fascination of its most recent history, its Middle Ages and its glorious Renaissance, but not the more ancient one of the Italic and Etruscan Civilization that constitutes its first title of nobility."
In 1950, the Ministry of Education provided substantial funds for the renovation and enlargement of the exhibition space of the Museum of Villa Giulia which was reopened to the public in 1955, while there was an increase in the number of interventions in Tuscany, for example at Fiesole, Populonia and Talamone, which augmented the collections on display in the Museo Topografico. The museum was becoming more and more of a "museum-storage" for the Sovrintendenza's excavations until it was completely destroyed by the terrible flood that hit Florence in 1966.
In the meantime some of the research projects that Minto as president of the Institute of Etruscan Studies had hoped for and planned were undertaken, among which the exploration of the city of Roselle which started in 1958. However, an archaeological map of the ancient mines, based on the latest modern criteria that included the gathering of testimonies that also referred to the modern era, had been interrupted at the outbreak of World War II, causing irreparable damage for the protection and study of man's long activity in the mountains around Campiglia and on the island of Elba.
The Soprintendenza Archeologica exerted tremendous efforts in the decades following the catastrophe of 1966 both in terms of finance and human resources in order to restore the mass of materials, the majority of which had never even been inventoried. From the time of Minto to the present day there has been a decentralization of authority and local agencies have been made responsible for the management and exploitation of their cultural heritage. The widespread and diligent work of protection that the Soprintendenza has carried out in the past twenty years, almost always in concordance with the region and its municipalities, and the interventions of systematic research it has undertaken with Tuscan and foreign university institutes, in addition to the so-called "fortuitous" discoveries, have enormously increased the archaeological patrimony, amplifying and in some cases innovating our knowledge not only of the history of Etruscan Civilization but also of the history and culture of Tuscany from the Roman era to the present, and rendering the problem of a new Museo Topografico more and more complicated.
Whereas the initiative of the "Year of the Etruscans" undertaken by the Region of Tuscany in 1985, gave rise to the Tuscan museum network, it is also true that it constituted a missing opportunity for reopening the discussion regarding the destiny of the Museo Topografico of Florence and the concept of a Central Museum. Today, numerous "historical" units of the former Museo Topografico, for example the Circolo degli Avori of Marsiliana d'Albenga, the Circolo delle Pellicce of Vetulonia and the Talamone pediment have been deposited in the Museum of Grosseto or the antiquarium of Orbetello as they await a new installation in the Florence museum, while many local communities, like those of Vetulonia, Piombino, Cortona and Chianciano, thanks to strong political policies that rightfully view archaeology as a possible or sure source of income and growth, have created and are creating small or large museum structures with the aim of (re)consigning the objects to their own historical environments. Precious documents for the study of the history of Etruscan Civilization are conserved in the storerooms of the Museo Archeologico of Florence; they are the fruit of new discoveries or testimonies of a history written more than half a century ago and then destroyed by a natural calamity. They are at the disposition of scholars and important manifestations such as this one organized by Palazzo Grassi, but they are still waiting to be consigned to a larger public, one that also includes young people who wish to take up Etruscological studies. In order to create a new Museo Etrusco in Florence, using only a part of the materials that are today located in the Antiquarium, but without interfering with the creation of other museums in the territory, considerable human resources and funds are necessary: this can only be made possible by extending the discussion to the entire archaeological community and by engaging political support. The words that Massimo Pallottino wrote in 1955 regarding the Museo di Villa Giulia and the Museo Archeologico of Florence come to mind, and still provide food for thought: "what occurs in institutes of that level does not have to do with one person or a few people, or a circle, administration or even a nation; it interests and concerns all men of culture."

Lanzi 1782; *Istituzione del Museo etrusco in Firenze* 1871; Gamurrini 1873; Milani 1898; Milani 1912; Minto 1921; Minto 1928, pp. 755–72; Levi 1935; Minto 1938, pp. 3–8; Minto 1939, pp. 3–26; Minto 1945, pp. 387–402; Bartoli 1945, p. 402; Minto 1948–49, pp. 361–63; Minto 1950, pp. 3–54; Pallottino 1955, pp. 91–101; Fiumi 1957, pp. 463 ff.; Romanelli 1957, pp. 15–32; Cristofani, 1969b; Garin 1976; Cristofani 1979c, pp. 1087–90; Cristofani 1981a, pp. 11 ff.; Bocci Pacini 1982, pp. 43–46; Borsi 1982; Cristofani 1982, pp. 78–81; *Luigi Adriano Milani* 1982, pp. 33–177; Martelli 1982, pp. 65–73; Tondo 1982, pp. 72–77; Bocci Pacini 1983, pp. 93–106 (with an appendix by L. Garella, pp. 106–08); Cristofani 1983c, pp. 355–66; Cristofani 1983d; Gregori 1983, pp. 367–93; Colonna 1984a, pp. 375–79; Pallottino 1984; Sassatelli 1984a, pp. 365–70; Maresca 1985, pp. 53–54; Magnanimi 1985, pp.121–29; Sforzini 1985, pp. 528–34; *L'archeologia italiana nel Mediterraneo* 1986; Maggiani 1987, pp. 189–93; Romualdi 1987, pp. 83–88; Zamarchi Grassi 1987, pp. 13–19; *Il Museo di Taranto* 1988; Donati 1989; Micheli 1989, pp. 115–32; Capecchi 1989–90, pp.199–230; Cygielmann 1990; Del Francia 1990, pp. 159–90; Meloni Trkulja 1990, pp. 101 ff.; Romualdi 1990, pp. 143 ff.; Tondo 1990, pp. 1–30; Barnabei, Delpino 1991; Delpino 1992, pp. 340–47; Romualdi 1992a, pp. 7–16; Esposito, De Tommaso 1993; Guzzo 1993a; Nicosia 1994–95, pp. 11–13; Bruni 1995, p. 39 ff.; Cygielman 1995, pp. 59–78; Delpino 1995, pp. 110–12; Romualdi 1995, pp. 151–69; Marzi 1996, pp. 35–53; Corsi 1997, pp. 21 ff.; Marzi, Bocci Pacini 1997, pp. 347–77; Sgubini Moretti 1997, pp. 9–17; Baglione, De Lucia Brolli 1998, pp. 117 ff.; Pacciani 1998; Cagianelli 1999b, p. 64 ff.; Rastrelli, Romualdi 1999; Sisi 1999, pp. 6–7; Celuzza 2000, pp. 7–10; Romualdi 2000, pp.14–24; Spini, Casali 2000, p. 279 ff.

COELIVS
EXQVILINVS
NECROPOLI DELL' AGRO FALISCO

The Museo Nazionale Etrusco di Villa Giulia

Anna Maria Moretti Sgubini

From its foundations to the early 1900s

Divided into two distinct sections, the Museo Nazionale Romano was founded by Royal Decree no. 5958 on 7 February, 1889. The section in the Thermae of Diocletian housed the antiquities found in Rome while the other, in the sixteenth-century Villa of Pope Julius III on Via Flaminia, contained relics discovered outside the city of Rome. Felice Barnabei, who was responsible for the museum's opening, was a brilliant and knowledgeable official of the Direzione Centrale degli Scavi e dei Musei, later renamed Direzione Generale delle Antichità e Belle Arti, created in 1875 by Ruggero Bonghi. Between 1897 and 1900 Barnabei himself was appointed to head this institution. The museum's founding was a milestone that marked not only the history of Roman museology but also the toilsome developmental process that came to characterize the history of the law that protects Italy's archaeological patrimony.

Opened to the public on 14 March, 1889—but officially inaugurated one year later—, the museum's collection initially included relics found in the area of Falerii Veteres. These discoveries were the result of the great endeavor involved in compiling the *Carta Archeologica*. The eminent archaeologists Adolfo Cozza, Gian Francesco Gamurrini and Angiolo Pasqui, later aided by Raniero Mengarelli, began working on the map in 1881. Villa Giulia thus came to represent the model and "testimonial of the kind of protection championed by the administration and its modern planning capabilities" in managing a territory that was still prey to occasional excavators who were merely interested in making a profit.

While Felice Barnabei's determination led to a project of immense cultural worth, the very scopes and developmental projects defined by the Royal Decree of 28 February, 1889 soon led to serious obstacles. The regulation of 1889 conferred upon the new museum the right over "objects excavated in the area surrounding Rome, on the side opposite to the territory of Corneto Tarquinia and Viterbo." Configured as a topographic museum, and its exhibits illustrating the cultures of civilizations that had flourished in the pre-Roman period, Villa Giulia spurred Luigi Adriano Milani's jealousy. Milani, who was the authoritative director of the Museo Etrusco Centrale, founded in Florence in 1870, governed an area that extended throughout the entire territory of the seventh Augustan region. In fact, a true and proper conflict of jurisdictions developed, giving rise to the "battle of Etruria," which raged on until 1912. On 2 August of that year, the territories of Corneto Tarquinia and Viterbo were entrusted to the Soprintendenza sugli Scavi e Musei of Rome. Villa Giulia was under the jurisdiction of this institute, established in 1907, which, in 1908, had also been assigned the territories belonging to the provinces of Aquila and Perugia, to the left of the Tiber River. In 1909, the territories subjected to the Soprintendenza had increased with the establishment of a managerial board, with offices in Villa Giulia to control excavations in the districts of Civitavecchia and Tolfa.

As a result of a common interest in protohistory, the developmental process marked by the regulations that came into existence with the creation of the new museum dedicated to "extra-urban" antiquities came into conflict with the dynamic activities of Luigi Pigorini and "his" Museo Preistorico-Etnografico. Founded in 1875 on the initiative of Minister Bonghi, along with the Museo Italico and the Museo Lapidario, this institute, unlike the other two, had grown thanks to Pigorini's own endeavors. He had progressively consolidated its functions and had extended the museum's original specific topics of interest to include vaster and more recent chronological themes. To this end, the vicissitudes relative to the Manios *fibula* are particularly significant. Donated to Barnabei by the antiquarian Francesco Martinetti and later purchased for the Villa Giulia collection, where it was included as of 1889, this relic had long been sought after by Pigorini. Finally, in 1901, urged by Wolfgang Helbig's and Giorgio Karo's conviction that the relic had originally been part to the grave goods of the Bernardini Tomb, Pigorini was finally able to acquire the *fibula* for the Museo Preistorico, where it is still kept today, unusually torn away from the coeval Orientalizing contexts of Praeneste, which were eventually reunited—at different time periods—in the collections of the Museo Etrusco.

Other difficulties clouded not only the future of Villa Giulia but that of Barnabei himself. His tenacious activity aimed at defending the nation's archaeological patrimony interfered with the interests of unscrupulous merchants, collectors and antiquarians.

Nonetheless, the effects of the activities resulting from the museum's additions in the years immediately following its founding proved to be profitable and intense. In 1890, the initial core of Faliscan antiquities grew, thanks to the acquisition of materials and burial goods from Etruria, Umbria and Latium. Meanwhile, between 1890 and 1891, Adolfo Cozza reconstructed a life-size "Etruscan" temple in the museum's garden, modeling it after the temple that he had excavated in Alatri. His work gave way to architectural solutions, which, adopted and adapted from the German tradition, were later imitated in Florence by Milani, who reconstructed Etruscan tombs in the garden of the Palazzo della Crocetta. A new and decisive addition to the collection was made in 1892, when the findings from Narce and other centers of the Faliscan Agro were exposed in the hemicycle of the little sixteenth-century palace. These findings were conducted by private researchers under the guidance of Count Cozza, and they were published in 1894 in the monographic volume *Monumenti Antichi dell'Accademia dei Lincei*. The Sarcophagus of the Married Couple was purchased the following year. It is an extraordinary monument, which Barnabei remembers recognizing among "a heap of clay scraps" that had been accumulated in a warehouse at the Castle of Cerveteri, where he had been visiting with Helbig. With great prudence and sagacity he was then able to secure it for the state.

While Villa Giulia's collection continued to increase thanks to the findings

pagine 522
Rome, Museo di Villa Giulia, Antiquarium of Falerii Veteres, central room on the ground floor in the nineteenth century

Rome, Museo di Villa Giulia, Antiquarium of sculpture, second room of the southern wing in the setting of the 1910s

resulting from the excavations on the territory, it soon became evident that the available expository space was insufficient; therefore, in 1893, construction was begun on a new building at the far south-east end of the sixteenth-century portico. This building was left incomplete for a long while.
At the turn of the century, however, the hostility stirred by Barnabei's activities flowed into what came to be known as the "scandal of Villa Giulia." In 1898, Helbig made serious public insinuations concerning the museum's arrangement, the authenticity of the collections, the scientific reliability of the funerary complexes of Narce and the methods used in conducting the archaeological research. Barnabei vividly recalled these events in his memoirs, which arouse an international resonance. In March of 1900, he resigned from his position as Managing Direttore Generale delle Antichità e Belle Arti. Though the Ministerial Inquiry Council—specifically created in 1899 and comprised of Adeodato Bonasi, president, Luigi Pigorini, chairman, and Gherardo Ghiradini—was not able to substantially verify the accusations or bring about changes in the collection's arrangement, the issue had devastating consequences on the museum's existence and development, so much so, in fact, that there was talk of the museum's closure. The late 1800s and early 1900s were, therefore, very difficult years, marked by a progressive impoverishment of the museum's collections in favor of other institutes, such as the Museo Preistorico. In addition to obtaining the Manios *fibula*, the Museo Preistorico also received relics from Falerii. Other important relics found their way to the Museo delle Terme, including the grave goods found in Vetralla in 1887 and immediately purchased by Augusto Castellani. Since he had then ceded them to the State on the insistence of Barnabei, they had been included in the Villa Giulia collection from the onset.
Antonio Sogliano, who was director of the museum for a short while, incessantly opposed the state of decadence and abandonment to which the museum was subjected for many years. In 1904 he created an organic renovation project of the collection according to topographic criteria, so that by 1906 the negative situation began to reverse. Corrado Ricci's directorship marked a new phase for the Head Office of Antiquities and Fine Arts's administrative structure. Aided by capable archaeologists such as Ettore Gabrici, Alessandro Della Seta, Lucia Morpurgo and Giulio Quirino Giglioli, in 1907 Giuseppe Angelo Colini took over directorship of the museum, which was by then managed autonomously. They were involved in a territory that was becoming increasingly vaster and more defined, and they were contributing to the museum's preparations for growth, as Colini opportunely specified, confronting the interminable polemics raised by Milani and the powerful Pigorini. Hence, as worthwhile restorations were being made on the sixteenth-century structure, the archaeological collection, was restructured and reorganized as Sogliano had already required. At the same time, new additions enriched the collections as a result of both the excavations conducted in centers like Satricum, Cerveteri, Veio, Capena or settlements around Viterbo and in Umbria, and the progressive acquisition of important collections. In fact, in 1908 the museum acquired the Barberini Collection while the Barsanti bronzes became part of the collection in 1912. A year later, in 1913, the museum was enriched by an important and dense group of materials from the dispersed Museo Kircheriano, comprising the core of the Antiquarium, which contained, among other artifacts, the Ficoroni cist. In the same year, the relics from the Nemi temple, transported to the Museo delle Terme in 1902, were returned, and the splendid Chigi *olpe* was added to the museum's collection. Instead, Colini's attempts to acquire the collection of Torlonia vases proved fruitless. A few years later, in two separate time periods—1923 and 1930—Augusto Castellani's collection, which had been relinquished to the State in 1919, was included in the Villa Giulia collection.
Given the mutated situation, the completion of the west wing in 1912 provided a temporary solution to the

Rome, Museo di Villa Giulia, Antiquarium of Veio, second room of the northern wing in the setting of the 1930s. On the background, the statue of the Capestrano Warrior moved here on December 1945

needs of the renewed exhibit, while a larger project, designed by Pietro Guidi in 1913, permitted additional expansion opportunities through the construction of new buildings both east and north of the existing structures. This construction project was made possible through the acquisition of areas that had been made available concurrently with the urban restructuring, which had directly involved Villa Giulia on the occasion of the Fine Arts Exhibition of 1911.
In 1918, Colini resigned from his position, leaving behind a museum, which, rearranged according to scientific criteria, had assumed a very distinct topographic connotation and a prominent role in the exposition of Etruscan and Italic culture, as evidenced by Della Seta's precious guide. Nonetheless, it was not until the 1920s that the new north wing was completed. Though it was principally employed as a warehouse, a single room was used to house the temporary installation of the extraordinary artifacts that Giulio Quirini Giglioli had found near the Portonaccio temple in Veio in 1916. A new building was then added to this extension, on the east side. Between 1929 and 1930 this new expository space contained Augusto Castellani's collection, which, arranged in four rooms, was open to the public.
Throughout the 1930s, the abundance of materials resulting from excavations conducted in the territory once again posed a pressing problem of space. Hence, three rooms were added to the north wing in 1938, two dedicated to Veio and the third to Vulci. In 1939 the creation of the new Soprintendenza alle Antichità dell'Etruria Meridionale marked Villa Giulia's autonomous state and its definite detachment from the Museo delle Terme. That same year, taking up an idea that had been presented by Guidi in 1913, Minister Bottai—on the occasion of the presentation of the new findings in Veio—was proposed the possibility of creating a new building in correspondence with the complex's posterior facade. The subsequent vicissitudes of World War II, however, put an end to this initiative. In the years following the war, the museum's north wing underwent numerous modifications. Here, in addition to the Capestrano Warrior, which was transferred to Villa Giulia from the Museo delle Terme in 1945, were housed materials from the necropolis of Terni. These alterations, however, were merely modest interventions, makeshift solutions, which, rather than strengthen the expository space, weighed it down. By then arranged in thirty rooms, the exhibit appeared to be completely inorganic, continuing to exclude fundamentally important artifacts such as, for example, those uncovered in Caere.

From the renewal of the 1950s to the end of the century

Since the collection's growth was so disadvantaged, the idea of transferring the museum to the Eur was proposed as a solution to the problem in 1950. Though this resolution had been employed for the Museo Preistorico Pigorini, it was fortunately dismissed for Villa Giulia, thanks to Renato Bartoccini's determination. Called to direct the Soprintendenza in 1950, and supported by a group of talented archaeologists such as Roberto Vighi, Mario Moretti, Goffredo Ricci and Giuseppe Foti, Bartoccini was able to have the proposal of a transfer put aside. He obtained approval for a different project, designed by Franco Minissi, which radically altered the arrangement and the physiognomy of the Museo Etrusco, still nineteenth-century in spirit. Work was begun and completed exceptionally fast. At the same time, important and highly-discussed restoration work was also made on some famous pieces such as the Sarcophagus of the Married Couple and some of the Veio statues. So, in 1955, the north wing and the Antiquarium, located in the new gallery of the north wing, were reopened to the public. Artifacts from Vulci, Bisenzio, Veio and Cerveteri were contained in the former. In 1959, the vases of the Castellani Collection were exposed in the hemicycle of the sixteenth-century building. Finally, in 1960, the expository space was completed with the reopening of the southern wing, newly dedicated to the overcrowded testimonials of the Falerii-

Rome, Museo di Villa Giulia, the Emiciclo room in the setting of 1959 with the vases of the Castellani Collection

Capena territory, the artifacts from the centers of Latium *vetus*, the antiquities of Praeneste (enriched that very year by the Bernardini Tomb, which was finally transferred from the Museo Pigorini), and Umbrian relics.

The bold solutions used in the restructuring did not go unnoticed, however, and so once again Villa Giulia found itself at the center of an ardent dispute, this time between authoritative archaeologists who were scandalized by the "futuristic" air of the new installations, and equally authoritative architects who were openly in favor of the new expository space. So the expository solutions of the Museo di Villa Giulia gave rise to a longstanding and lively debate that saw museologists, museographers, archaeologists, and architects pitted against each other. It was a debate that calmed down after a while, however, because the ancient relics' superiority over the installations could not be denied.

Beyond the now distant polemics and the architectural solutions adopted, it must be observed that the project of the "new" Museo di Villa Giulia, essentially aimed at resolving the historic problem of space, was successful in meeting its objective thanks to the creation of modern galleries, which, making use of the high ceilings of the rooms in the twentieth-century wings, were able to increase the expository space by about two-thirds. Furthermore, other appreciable elements are evident in the adopted solutions relative not only to the size of the expositional spaces but also to the continuity conferred onto the museum's course, the creation of room-deposits communicating with the museum open to scholars, and the addition of accurate didactic-illustrative apparatuses whose expression is perhaps best evidenced in the Caeretan Tomb II of the Maroi tumulus, which continues to impress visitors as much as the Alatri temple.

Nonetheless, there remained many unresolved issues and the incomplete exhibit continued to penalize the museum's true potential. The Veio installation was decidedly provisional, the Castellani Collection was limited to the ceramics, inland Etruria was not well represented, and new expository problems arose relative to exceptional discoveries in Pyrgi or other Etrurian centers. While for the immediate future it was still possible to rely on the rooms located on the Villa's ground floor and main floor, new and continuous discoveries from the territory made it imperative to determine long-term solutions. These were necessary not only for a programmed and organic growth of the museum, but also to suitably preserve the archaeological materials.

These issues strongly involved the presuppositions of a policy that was bound to the territory, the result of a decision that today continues to be one of the brightest taken during the second half of the twentieth century by the Soprintendenza, which was directed by Mario Moretti between 1961 and 1977. Beginning in the mid-1960s and within a ten-year period, southern Etruria experienced a proliferation of museums, which, for the most part, involved employing strategically-dislocated monumental structures in the more important centers of southern Etruria, with intelligent "recycling" solutions, leading to a sort of decentralized culture that proved profitable in terms of both utilization and archaeological tutelage. The creation of what were then termed "satellite" museums in centers such as Cerveteri, Pyrgi, Vulci, Civita Castellana, and Civitavecchia, to which were then integrated the more modest but by no means no less worthy communal Antiquaria of Trevignano, Tolfa, Ischia di Castro, and Barbarano Romano, assured in a determining manner a more organic distribution and preservation of the archaeological materials, which were thus rightly returned to their place of origin, simultaneously conferring new potentials on the Museo Nazionale Etrusco and its overcrowded deposits. While the decisions taken in those years proved to be determinant even for the resumption and the development of archaeological research in the territory, other changes were in store for the museum, whose hopes for expansion, so indispensable for the worth and consistency of the collections, had been concretized in the proposal to purchase Villa Poniatowski and the annexed Riganti tanneries. The proposal for the purchase had been advanced by the Soprintendenza in 1972. Hence the dynamic framework that was thus being delineated had concrete repercussions on the museum's existence. In fact, work on the installations of the rooms on the Villa's main floor was reinitiated with the aim of completing an expository course, which, following a standstill in the 1950s, had been expanded in 1965 in view of the need for a space in which to expose the Pyrgi findings. Such a space was made available in the room to the left of the atrium. In the early 1970s, instead, the rooms containing the topographic sections of Vulci and Bisenzio were partially restructured. In July of 1975, more than fifteen years after the installation of the ceramics section, with a solemnity intended to also celebrate the founding of the new Ministero per i Beni Culturali, the expository space for the Castellani Collection was completed. Instalments included new sections for the bronzes, terra-cotta artifacts and, most important, the famous jewellery, both ancient and modern. The solutions employed in presenting the gold artifacts to the public were particularly spectacular. On the same occasion, the recently acquired Cima Pesciotti Collection was also presented. Though in the long history of the Museo di Villa Giulia the 1970s represent a phase of positive growth—echoed in other initiatives that were undertaken within the territory (at the time proposals were made for initiating the founding of the new museums of Lucus Feroniae, of Tuscania, of the Rocca Albornoz in Viterbo, while the scientific rearrangement of the historic collections of the Tarquinia Museum were getting under way)—the complex procedures for the purchase of Villa Poniatowski soon fell prey to stalling and slowdowns. In fact, the Soprintendenza's proposal for the purchase met with great opposition from the private owners. This led to a long and complex dispute that was not resolved until December of 1988, year in which the Villa and its large properties were handed over to the state, thanks to the tenacity of Paola Pelagatti, who headed the Soprintendenza between 1979 and 1990.

In the 1980s, substantial resources were allocated to the restoration of the decorative program of Villa Giulia, and, at the same time, the museum hosted temporary exhibits that offered an equally profitable opportunity to delve deeper into the problems arising from its collections. Meanwhile, the first sections of the Tuscania Museum and of the Rocca Albornoz in Viterbo were being opened to the public, and the reorganization of the Tarquinia Museum was proceeding positively.

The situation altered in the early 1990s when new, delicate events marked the museum's existence. In the early 1990s the expository course began to contract until in 1995 it was reduced to 50% of its original size. Similar problems afflicted the monumental sixteenth-century complex, while the functional and safety systems proved to be completely inadequate. Given actual needs, financing for the restructuring of Villa Poniatowski, which seemed to be irrevocably abandoned to dilapidation, were also inadequate.

The Polo Museale Etrusco of Villa Giulia-Villa Poniatowski

Between 1995 and 1996 the museum experienced a rebirth. On that occasion, in collaboration with Francesca Boitani, I set up a specific scientific project, which, aimed at creating the Polo Museale Etrusco, was centered on four principal objectives: restructuring the collections according to a scientific matrix, giving full priority to the sections that had been closed for some time; restoring and adjusting the sixteenth-century complex; statically strengthening and restoring Villa Poniatowski's architectural structure and the annexed Riganti tanneries; and activating the connection between the two strong points of the Polo Museale by recuperating the boulevard and the green spaces at the edge of the park of Villa Strohl-Fern.

In 1997, as a result of this program and thanks to specific funding, the antiquities of Pyrgi were once again presented to the public in the Sala di Venere. In June of the following year the conspicuous testimonials of the centers of the Falerii-Capena territory were reopened. They were located in the renovated gallery of the south wing, where another two large rooms on the ground floor were dedicated to the relics of the great sanctuaries of Falerii Veteres. Finally, in December of 1999, the museum's course was completed with the new exhibition of the great historical collections, which, like other renovated sections of the museum, were the result of an accurate intervention that involved cataloguing and rearranging the materials. These more recent exhibits primarily involved the Augusto Castellani Collection, the Cima Pesciotti Collection, and various parts of the Antiquarium, with special emphasis placed on the relics of the seventeenth-century Museo Kircheriano, which hosted the famous Ficoroni cist, previously included in the collection of artifacts from Praeneste.

Now equipped with bilingual didactic and illustrative apparatuses arranged on five levels, the museum's course has also been enriched by three new sections, created by adopting a more rational use of space. These sections are dedicated to Etruscan epigraphy, the museum's toiled history and its collections, and the vicissitudes of Pope Julius III's Villa, whose complex layout has become more functional, thanks in part to the opening of a pathway that makes it possible to visit the underground chambers and the remains of a part of the Roman Acqua Vergine aqueduct.

A fourth section of the museum is due to open in 2001. It will be dedicated to Tarquinia, a center, which though it has been excluded from the exhibition to date, will find its symbolic significance in one of the most famous testimonials of Etruscan painting: the Tomb of the Funerary Bed.

Between 1998 and 1999 the architectural restoration of the sixteenth-century complex was completed, as was the rest of the museum's compendium. Such work also involved organic interventions aimed at adapting the functional and safety systems so as to bring them up to date with the norms in vigor. In addition, the museum has been equipped with an access for the disabled, essential public services, a communication and didactic activities center, as well as a second ticket counter reserved for groups and schools. This area opens onto Piazza Torwaldsen, high-

lighting the relationship that binds the Museo Etrusco to the museums that are dislocated in the Valle dei Musei.
The project completed between 1997 and 1999 represents the first phase of the larger project for the Polo Etrusco of Rome, which will be brought to term as soon as the current restoration work on Villa Poniatowski and the adjacent Riganti tanneries will be completed. Already connected to Villa Giulia via a picturesque road that unfolds at the foot of the cliff of Villa Strohl-Fern, Villa Poniatowski has been restored to its original splendor thanks to a philological restoration—which also permitted the Villa's refined decorative program to be recaptured—directed by Francesco Scoppola. Villa Poniatowski will house antiquities from Praeneste and the artifacts from Latium *vetus* and Umbria, which to date have been exhibited in four outdated exposition rooms in Villa Giulia. These four rooms are better suited to their new contents, the antiquities of Veio, which will finally be exposed after having been mortifyingly confined in the warehouses for fifty years. These artifacts will be inserted organically within a museum structure, which, arranged according to distinct topographic modules, already presents the flexibility it has lacked to date. The character of this expositional course, also made possible by opening up new access routes, makes it possible to recapture the direct relationship between the architectural complex and its extraordinary environmental frame, a binding rapport that had been created from the onset.
As part of the project, the topographic sections of the museum's north wing have been undergoing a scientific renovation. In this area, the semi-interred spaces, which were once used as warehouses, will be used as expository spaces for the artifacts from Bisenzio and other important centers of inland Etruria, making it possible to remodulate the Caere section, which will be brought further forward, adjacent to the reconstructed Maroi Tomb. On the one hand, this solution will make it feasible to eliminate the chronological hiatus that characterizes the current expository sequence of the Sarcophagus of the Married Couple, while on the other it will enable the public to

Rome, Museo di Villa Giulia, the Castellani jewellery in the setting of 1999

view the important findings that have been uncovered in more recent excavations in the city's ancient district. Finally, a suitable space will be made available for the artifacts of Pyrgi, now exposed in the Sala di Venere, which the project sees better suited to the materials belonging to the Berman Collection, the most recent of the great antiquities collections ceded to Villa Giulia. If, as we expect, all of these plans will be realized, then Villa Giulia will fully regain its position as an important international museum. Over one hundred years after its founding, and despite all the disputes between men and the injuries suffered over time, it will regain its well-deserved notoriety. It deserves this role of eminence because of the richness, the variety and the extraordinary historical importance of its collections.

The bibliography for the Museo di Villa Giulia and its collections is very vast; therefore, the bibliography included here is limited to the guides, catalogues of the various sections, and specific information that makes it possible to gain a deeper understanding of the museum's history.

Guides: Della Seta 1918; Stefani 1934; Stefani 1948; Vighi, Minissi 1955; Moretti 1962; Helbig 1969, pp. 467–862; Helbig 1972; Moretti 1973; Proietti 1980; Boitani 1983; Moretti Sgubini 1999. *Catalogues*: Bartoccini, d'Agostino 1961; Moretti 1966; Falconi Amorelli 1968; *Nuove scoperte e acquisizioni* 1975; Fugazzola Delpino 1984; Caruso 1985; Caruso 1988; Colonna 1996; De Lucia Brolli, Carlucci, 1998; Moretti Sgubini 1999; Moretti Sgubini forthcoming. *Museum history*: Sforzini 1985, pp. 528–34; Barnabei, Delpino 1991; Moretti Sgubini 1997, pp. 9–17; Moretti Sgubini 2000.

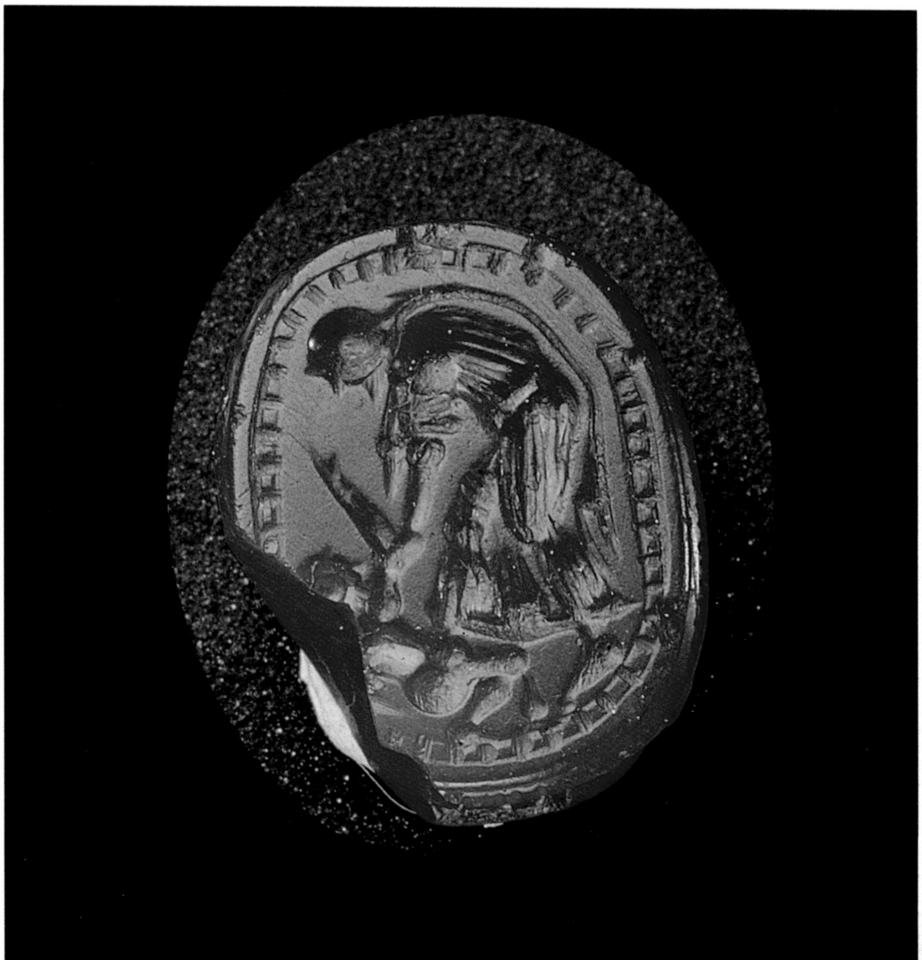

Gem with Tages.
Rome, Museo di Villa Giulia, Castellani Collection
cat. 325

Catalogue of Works

1. Stela of Lemnos
late seventh–early sixth
century B.C.
stone
Athens, Archaeological Museum
from Caminia, Lemnos Island

The Making

From the Bronze Age to the Iron Age

There were various ancient traditions about the origins of Etruscan civilization. Some saw it as the product of peoples who had come to the region between the Tyrrhenian Sea and the rivers Arno and Tiber shortly before historical times. Some, like Herodotus, said these people came from the world on the margins of Asiatic Greek civilization. Meanwhile, a completely contrasting tradition, reported by Dionysius of Halicarnassus, affirmed that Etruscan civilization was autochthonous. Modern research has for a long time held that the cultural processes that led to the birth of the Etruscan world began as early as the twelfth century B.C., when the territory which was to be the historical site of Etruria seems to have undergone a period of radical change, which ended around the end of the tenth century B.C., with the concentration of settlements on the sites of the future cities.

The whole region presents a broad cultural homogeneity, in which alongside some aspects which seem linked with manifestations of the previous period several aspects emerge which will find a wide echo in later centuries, so that the term "proto-Villanovan" has entered archaeological usage to describe the phenomenon of the Late Bronze Age in Tuscany and upper Latium north of the Tiber, thus implicitly underlining the prodromic features of Etruscan civilization.

From the middle of the second millennium B.C. in some localities both in the southern area (Luni sul Mignone, Norchia) and in the northern area (Pisa) there is evidence of a continuity of stable forms of settlement. Between the twelfth and the tenth centuries, however, in the so-called Final Bronze Age, there is a widespread occupation of the territory, with the development of forms of population distributed over small or tiny communities, which seem to be dominated, both because of their larger size and because of the presence of large artificial buildings, by certain centers which may have had a pre-eminent role in the area, forming the pole of reference for the development of common activities, which were probably of a ceremonial or political nature. The inhabited zones, which occupy a limited area, usually smaller than five hectares—though there are some larger centers (Elceto and Sorgenti della Nova in the Fiora Valley)—are generally situated on high ground or an isolated tufaceous plateau at the confluence of two watercourses. However, all the potential of the favorable environmental position are exploited and the settlement system also comprises centers on the plain (for example, Scarceta) or in caves (for example the shelter at Le Bagnare di Canino), or on the shores of lakes, like the settlement of Gran Carro on Lake Bolsena, or of the sea, such as the center of Torre Valdaliga near Civitavecchia, or actually on lakes, as at Pisa.

Although our knowledge is far from offering wide margins of certainty and no settlement has been investigated in its entirety, the internal organization of these centers seems to develop according to a non-organic plan with the structures, which in this period are exclusively huts, arranged on a rather loose- and irregular-meshed fabric with large empty spaces interspersed between the various dwellings. The huts vary in architectural type not only from one district to another but also within the individual districts. Some have an elliptical plan, some a round one, some a quadrilateral one; sometimes they have internal subdivisions and a little entrance porch. In some centers, Luni sul Mignone and Scarceta in the central Fiora Valley, it is possible to distinguish hierarchies within the settlement; these are indicated by the presence of a hut of markedly larger size, round which, in the case of Scarceta, smaller contemporary structures cluster. At Luni sul Mignone the structure also differs from the others in architectural form, with a base dug into the rock and the superstructure built with little dry-stone walls, load-bearing poles and a thatched roof. This situation is probably an echo on the town-planning level of a hierarchic organization within the social structure of the settlement: these buildings must have been the dwellings of the "chiefs" of the community to which they belong; a less likely hypothesis is that they had a political or cult function common to all inhabitants of the settlement.

The size of the individual communities seems to vary between a few dozen and a hundred individuals, with a tendency for the population size to increase in the Final Bronze Age. However, the phenomenon must be seen in the context of the overall picture of the occupation of the territory, and the progressive demographic growth is probably one of the causes of the changes which occur in the region between the twelfth and the tenth centuries B.C., both at the level of the settlement system and at the level of the social structures. Although the available evidence is very meager and recommends salutary caution, the examination of the necropolises makes it possible to follow some of these processes in detail. In the earliest phase the graves, almost all of which concern cremated individuals, are housed in modest tomb structures which comprise the biconical ossuary covered by an upturned dish and occasionally some rare objects of personal ornament. Then in the eleventh century B.C. we see a progressive emergence of a social differentiation, which shows, especially in the area of the Monti della Tolfa and Sasso di Furbara, in the differentiation of some graves by the erection of a small tumulus above the grave and the deposition of large *fibulae*, which will be supplemented in the tenth century by varied grave goods consisting of miniature vases, according to a custom also known in the area of Latium.

The economic basis of these communities is in the first place linked with the agricultural exploitation of the soil and the raising of livestock, as well as hunting, in a substantially closed system where every community produces what is necessary for its own requirements. The artisan activities seem to take place for the most part within the domestic environment; this is especially true of the production of wooden or ceramic articles, which are handmade according to a repertory which is strictly functional and still not very standardized. The activities connected with spinning and the making of woolen or vegetable-fibber fabrics also take place in the domestic environment; they may have been assigned to the female members of the individual families.

In this picture considerable importance and prominence attaches to the specialized activity of metalwork, which is devoted to the making of objects of personal ornament, weapons, tools of work and high-prestige tableware. Although, especially in the earliest period, it is difficult to distinguish strictly local types and morphologies, metal objects linked with the productions of Etruria are known over a wide area which includes Umbria, the Marches, Abruzzo and to a lesser extent Latium too. They are probably an archaeological trace of the mobility of the craftsman, who carried with them objects and technical and typological notions. This phenomenon is certainly connected with the important metalliferous deposits of the region, which gradually, but with increasing definition, inserts the mining districts in a network of medium- and long-distance trade by both land and sea routes. This trade is documented by the presence of ambers, glass pastes, and bronze objects, whose typologies lead to Greece, Cyprus, Campania, Sicily and Sardinia, as well as the Veneto area and in general the whole of northern Italy. The progressive growth of production is accompanied by the gradual insertion of metal-working craftsman in the communities and consequently by an acceleration of the process of community control over production, which makes, on the one hand, prestige and luxury objects intended to underline the higher echelons of the social structure, as in the case of the hoard of Coste del Marano the cups of embossed *lamina* and the great *fibulae*, and on the other hand the tools and utensils for specialized activities, whether artisan, subsistence or military, like the scythes, chisels, spearheads and swords of the hoard of Limone near Livorno or the harpoons of the hoard of Pariana in the northern part of the Versilia district.

At least from the twelfth century B.C. it is possible to see in the centers of southern Etruria organized forms of exchange managed by the communities, into which is inserted the growing interest of the Mycenaean world of Sicily, the Aeolian Islands and the islands of the Gulf of Naples, as is attested by the Late Mycenaean and sub-Mycenaean pottery of Luni sul Mignone, San Giovenale and Monte Rovello.

At the end of the tenth century the dynamic development of these processes registers a brusque and sudden interruption, the causes of which must be sought in that series of events which have left a trace in the signs of violent destruction of many of the settlements and in their consequent abandonment. The settlement system, and with it the socio-economic forms, radically changes its physiognomy with the concentration of the settlements round what will be the future cities which the ancient tradition remembered as the "twelve peoples of Etruria." [S.B.]

2. Hoard of bronzes from Massa Carrara La Tecchiarella, Pariana
tenth century B.C.
bronze, *lamina* and solid casting
Viareggio, Museo Civico, inv. 88148–88159

The deposit was found in 1918. Of the seventeen pieces found, five were put aside as a reward for the finding on behalf of the cav. Lazzoni, all trace of which has been lost. Presently are conserved in Florence:
• *1. Harpoon with five heads with grip handle sleeve*, inv. 88148
• *2. Sickle with grip handle*, inv. 88149
• *3. Sickle with grip handle*, inv.88150
• *4. Sickle with grip handle*, inv. 88159
• *5. Triangular-section ribbon armlet with incised and dotted decoration*, inv. 88152
• *6. Triangular-section ribbon armlet with incised and dotted decoration*, inv. 88153
• *7. Triangular-section ribbon armlet*, inv. 88154
• *8. Triangular-section ribbon armlet with incised decoration*, inv. 88151
• *9. Wedge with leaf blade*, inv. 88156
• *10. Scalpel with shank with leaf blade*, inv. 88158
• *11. Scalpel with pyramidal shank sleeve separate from the handle*, inv. 88155
• *12. Hatchet with tabs with indistinct tang*, inv. 88157

Cateni 1984, pp. 19–29; Cateni 1985, pp. 316 ff.; *Civiltà degli Etruschi* 1985, pp. 41–42, n. 1.17.
[C.Z.]

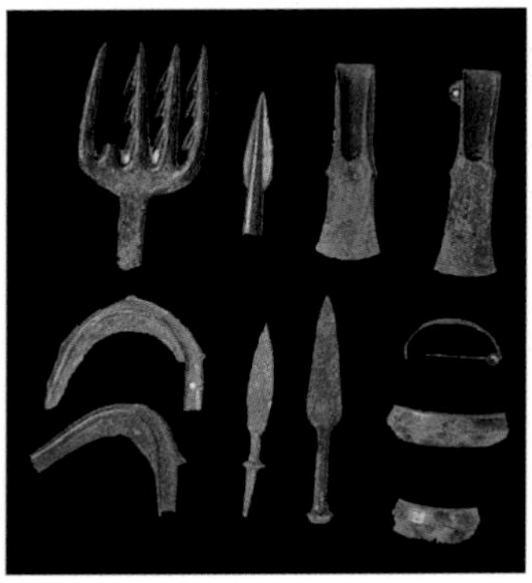

3. Hoard of bronzes from Monte La Poggia, farm of Limone, present locality Limoncino
late tenth–early ninth century B.C.
bronze, *lamina* and solid casting
Livorno, Museo Civico F. Fattori, invv. 1726–1829

The material of the trove, a random find, belonged to the collection of G. Chiellini, then donated in 1883. Presently a *fibula* with wavy bow, six other *fibulae*, a fragment of an armlet, two knife blades are missing. At the moment the following finds are conserved:
• *1–5. Hatchet with tabs*, invv. 1729; 1727; 1730;1726; 1728
• *6–9. Fragments of hatchet with tabs*, invv. 1737; 1738; 1749; 1740
• *10–14. Fragments of hatchet*, invv. 1741; 1742; 1743; 1744;1749;
• *15–20. Fragments of hatchet with tabs*, invv. 1733; 1734; 1736; 1735; 1731; 1732;
• *21–22. Sickles with grip handle*, invv. 1745;1746
• *23–24. Fragments of sickles with grip handle*, invv. 1742/1; 1742/2
• *25. Fragment of small knife-razor*, inv. 1777
• *26. Small knife with pin shank*, inv. 1799
• *27–28. Fragments of knife with pin shank*, invv. 1748/1; 1748/2
• *29. Fragment of knife with shank*, inv.1801
• *30. Fragment of brooch with biconical head*, inv. 1790
• *31. Fragment of brooch with flattened and perforated head*, inv.1789
• *32. Fragment of brooch with biconical head*, inv. 1809
• *33. Fragment of brooch with globular head*, inv. 1791
• *34. Tweezers with spirally handle*, inv.1827
• *35–36. Tips of spear with cannon*, invv. 1761; 1762/1–2
• *37. Ribbon armlet*, inv. 1760
• *38–40. Fragments of ribbon armlets*, invv.1725; 1766; 1767
• *41–42. Scalpels with shank*, invv. 1751; 1752
• *43. Fragment of scalpel*, inv. 1753
• *44. Fragment of staff*, inv. 1754
• *45–46. Fragments of scalpels*, invv. 1755; 1758
• *47–48. Punches*, invv. 1756; 1757
• *49. Fragment of staff*, inv. 1759
• *50. Scalpel with quadrangular cannon*, inv. 1750
• *51. Two fragments of embossed* lamina, inv. 1798
• *52. Element of horse bit*, inv. 1774
• *53–54. Fragments of fibula with wavy bow*, inv. 1778/a–b
• *55. Fragment of fibula with wavy bow*, inv. 1779
• *56. Fragment of fibula*, inv. 1780
• *57–58. Fragments of fibula with wavy bow*, invv. 1781; 1782
• *59. Fragment of fibula*, inv. 1783
• *60. Round-section pin*, inv. 1828
• *61. Scalpel with shank*, inv. 1763
• *62–64. Three fragments of* lamina, invv. 1803/a–c
• *65–71. Seven fragments of thick* lamina, invv.1802/a-g
• *72. Fragment perhaps belonging to a knife*, inv. 1803
• *73–76. Fibul*ae *with plain bow*, inv. 1769; 1827; 1770; 1771
• *77–78. Fragments of small spirally pin*, inv. 1775; 1793
• *79. Two fragments of round-section wire*, inv. 1794
• *80. Two fragments of rectangular-section wire*, inv. 1795
• *81. Fragment of round-section pin*, inv. 1787
• *82. Fragment of fibula*, inv. 1788
• *83. Fibula with plain bow*, inv. 1786
• *84–85. Fibulae with wavy bow*, inv. 1776; 1773
• *86. Biconvex-section sword tip*, inv. 1764
• *87. Fragment of lamina*, inv. 1806
• *88. Fibula with plain bow*, inv. 1768
• *89. Fragment of fibula with plain bow*, inv. 1785
• *90. Small pin*, inv. 1792
• *91. Pin of fibula with plain bow*, inv. 1797

Cateni 1977, pp. 3–37; Cateni 1997, pp. 206 ff.
[C.Z.]

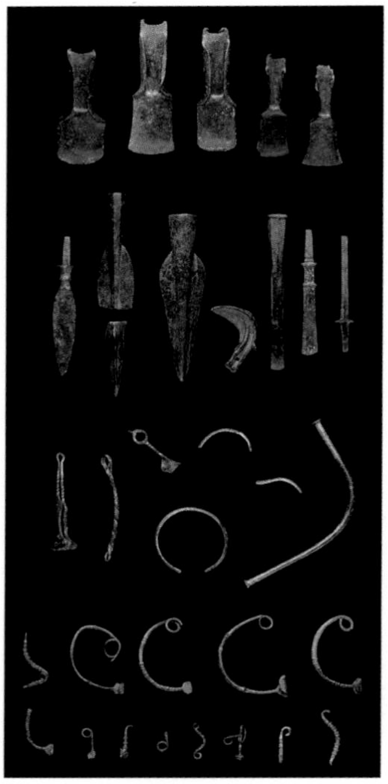

4. Hoard of bronzes at Coste del Marano
late eleventh–early tenth century B.C.
Rome, Museo Preistorico-Etnografico L. Pigorini

• *1. Bronze fibula*
l 27.5 cm
inv. 62624
Leaf violin bow. Embossed and chiseled decoration.
• *2. Bronze capeduncula*
h 15 cm
inv. 62755.
Semi-spherical vessel with embossed decoration with bands of large pods and dotted lines. Overhanging ribbon-handle, ending in an animal protome with long curved horns.

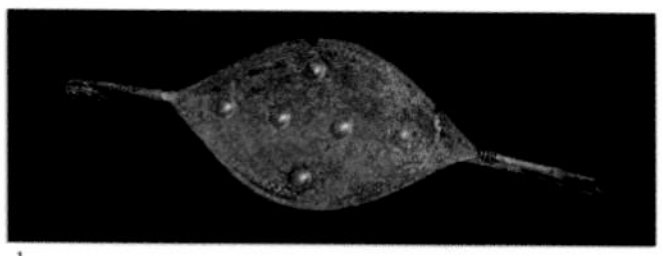
1

2

Civiltà degli Etruschi 1985, p. 39 n. 1.15.2; Torelli 2000, p. 93, fig. 7.
[C.Z.]

6. Tomb 25/1994 of Poggio della Pozza, Allumiere
Final Bronze Age
Allumiere, Palazzo Camerale, SAEM reserve

Cremation tomb in stone coffin. Remains of an individual, possibly female, died at the age of 20–40 years.
• *1. Biconical urn*
impasto not thrown on the wheel, reconstructed
h 24 cm; diam. of rim 18 cm
inv. 118360
With handle perforated horizontally, decorated with grooved geometric motifs.
• *2. Lid*
impasto not thrown on the wheel, reconstructed, crest missing
h 12 cm; diam. of base 23 cm
inv. 118361
Symbolic conical helmet lid, bell-knobbed, decorated with grooved geometric motifs.
• *3. Cup*
impasto not thrown on the wheel, reconstructed
h 6 cm; diam. of rim 8 cm
inv. 118364
With distinct neck with handle with vertical perforation, decorated with grooved geometric motifs.
• *4. Askos*
impasto not thrown on the wheel, neck and part of handle missing, reconstructed
h of handle 9 cm
inv. 118363
With stick-handle, decorated with grooved geometric motifs.
• *5. Three-legged stand*
impasto not thrown on the

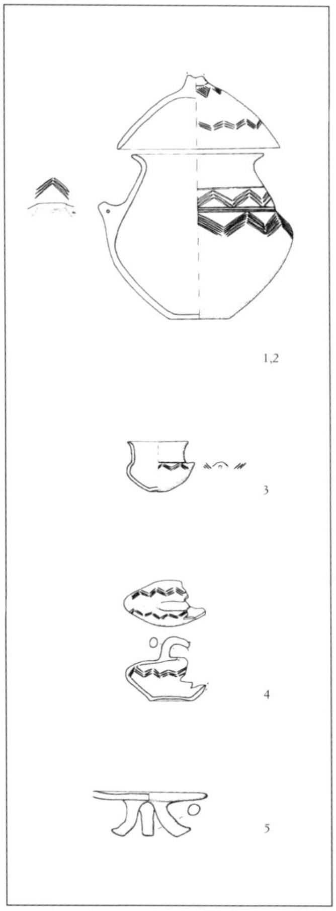

wheel, reconstructed
h 5 cm; diam. of rim 14.5 cm
inv. 118362
• *5. Ring*
bronze, fragmentary
diam. 2 cm
inv. 118365.
[F.T.]

5. Tomb 13/1994 of Poggio della Pozza, Allumiere
Final Bronze Age
Allumiere, Museo Civico
A. Klitsche de la Grange

Cremation tomb in stone coffin. Remains of an individual died at the age of 0–6 years.

• *1. Biconical urn*
impasto not thrown on the wheel, reconstructed
h 20 cm; diam. of rim 14 cm
Without handles, decorated with grooved geometric motifs.
• *2. Lid*
impasto not thrown on the wheel, reconstructed
h 13 cm; diam. of base 20 cm
Symbolic conical helmet lid, crested; decorated with grooved geometric motifs.
• *3. Zoomorphic vase*
impasto not thrown on the wheel, bronze; reconstructed
h 7 cm; l 10 cm
On four small feet and upper ovate hole with pair of passing holes on the sides for attaching the bronze plated lid.
• *4. Fibula*
bronze, complete
l 4 cm
With bow with three small knots, decorated with ring incisions and short symmetrical pin.
• *5. Two rings*
bronze, complete
diam. 2.7 cm
[F.T.]

1,2

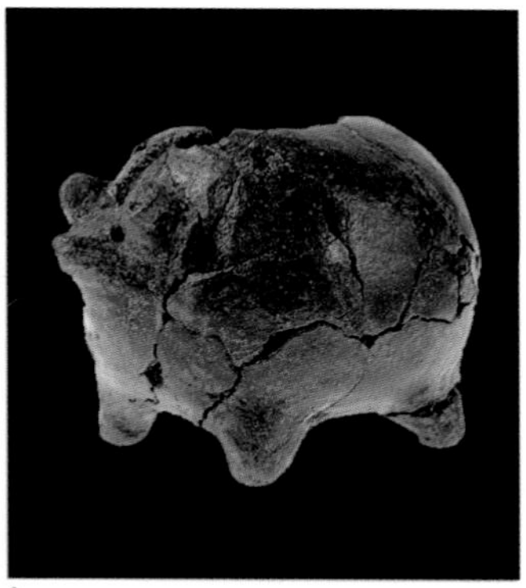
3

7. Tomb 21/1994 of Poggio della Pozza, Allumiere
Final Bronze Age
Allumiere, Museo Civico
A. Klitsche de la Grange

Cremation tomb in stone coffin. Remains of an individual, probably female, died at the age of 30–40 years.
• *1. Biconical urn*
impasto not thrown on the wheel, reconstructed
h 26 cm; diam. of rim 14 cm
With trapezoidal saddle-handle, not decorated.
• *2. Bowl-lid*
impasto not thrown on the wheel, reconstructed
h 11 cm; diam. of 18.5 cm
Grooved bowl-lid with rounded

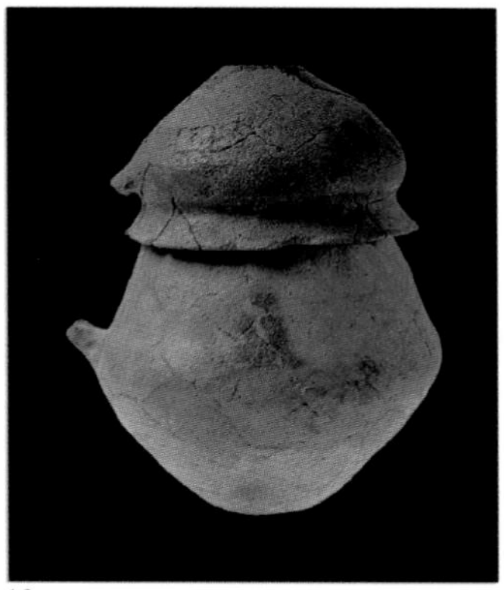
1,2

vessel with trapezoidal saddle-handle, not decorated.
• *3. Tankard*
impasto not thrown on the

wheel, complete
h 7,2 cm; diam. of rim 9 cm
With row of stamped decorations under the rim and ribbed handle with plaque attachment.
• *4. Fibula*
bronze, pin incomplete
15 cm
With wavy bow with several eyelets and wire disc stirrup.
• *5. Fragments, not reconstructible, of a small open form*
impasto not thrown on the wheel, not on exhibit
[F.T.]

3

8. Urn
Final Bronze Age
(ninth century B.C.)
impasto not thrown on the wheel, reconstructed from fragments, the top of the walls and the roof missing, door reconstructed and pin complete
diam. 28 cm; conserved h15 cm
necropolis of Cerveteri, reserves from Cerveteri, Monte Tosto Alto necropolis, Tomb 1/1997

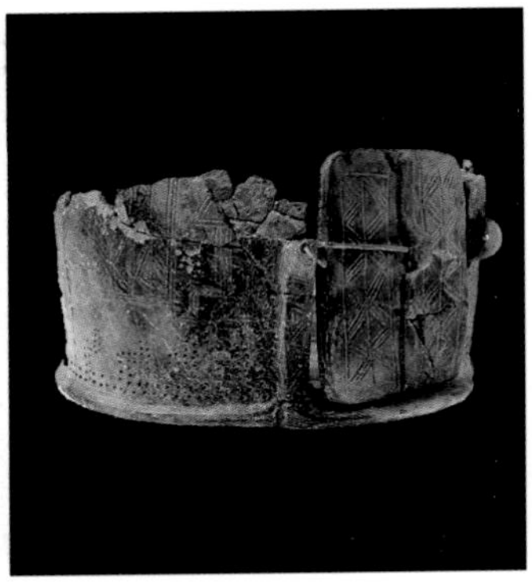

Cremation tomb in tufa cylinder. Remains of an individual of undetermined sex dead at the age of 20–40 years. Hut-shaped round-layout urn with grooved and cupped geometric, linear and metopal, and figured decoration, conserving the door with bronze pin with bent head with small ring inserted in the loop.

Trucco, Mieli, Vargiu 1999, pp. 103 ff., p. 106 fig. 1.1.
[F.T.]

The Villanovan Civilization

The transition from the Bronze Age to the Iron Age, which corresponds to the period between the tenth and the ninth centuries B.C., is the time which for the Etruscans themselves marked the birth of the *nomen etruscum*.
There are many elements which underline a substantial continuity with the preceding period, such as the persistence of the practice of cremation and the use of the biconical urn as a receptacle for cremated bones, a practice accompanied in some centers by the use of hut-shaped urns for some particular graves, or in the repertory of the metal objects and many ceramic objects. Nevertheless, the significant demographic growth and the different methods of exploiting the land, as well as the different system of population, are distinctive features of this new period, which is conventionally called "Villanovan" from the name of the village of Villanova di Castenaso near Bologna where the first archaeological remains of this culture were found in the mid-nineteenth century. This culture characterizes, with particular and peculiar accents that vary from district to district, a vast territory which includes the present Tuscany between the Arno and the Albenga, the part of Latium north of the Tiber, the valleys of the Tiber and the Chiana, the area of central Emilia delimited by the courses of the Panaro, the Po and the Santerno, the Marecchia basin in eastern Romagna, and in Campania the areas of Capua and the Salernitano (Sala Colinsilina, Pontecagnano, Capodifiume and Arenosola). A Villanovan nucleus is also attested at Fermo in the Marches. However, while this last case seems to end with the Iron Age, the others affect those areas which would see the continuous development of the later urban phase of Etruscan civilization.
Although they belong to a common cultural matrix, the various areas have individual features, and not only in a geo-morphological sense. An element common to the whole region seems to be the tendency of the population to concentrate in the places recognized as best suited to the various activities that characterize these communities and near natural routes of communication, according to a design which reveals a sort of planning of the territory. The settlements now occupy sizable areas usually situated on hill plateaus at the confluence of minor watercourses and the various groups of huts are separated by free spaces used for primary production. The rare evidence that is archaeologically documented at Veio, Torre Valdaliga and the Mattonara on the southern coast of Tarquinia, at Tarquinia itself, at the Gran Carro on Lake Bolsena, at Chiusi and in the area of Siena, shows a considerable variety of solutions for the types of houses. Most huts have a prevalently curvilinear plan, but some have a rectangular one, and it is not possible to make a chronological distinction between the various typologies, in significant analogy with the images of similar structures shown by the hut-shaped urns of the ninth and eighth centuries from the necropolises of Veio, Cerveteri, Tarquinia, Bisenzio, Vulci, Vetulonia, and perhaps Populonia. The cemeteries are located in clearly distinct and separate areas close to the natural trade routes which irradiate from the settlement area over the territory, and they present, in the cases where the evidence makes it possible to follow their development, a picture of a coherent use of space with the earliest graves dug at the top of the hills and the others occupying the area in regular progression, as can be seen in the case of the necropolis of Quattro Fontanili at Veio or in that of the eastern mounds of Tarquinia.
Agricultural activities form the main basis of the economy of these communities, though some centers, especially in the north Tyrrhenian area, combined farming with the exploitation of the local mineral resources, an activity which fostered the insertion of the whole area in a huge network of trade and exchange which extended far beyond the regional limits and which become over the decades one of the factors which determined the development of the Villanovan world in economic and other ways.
Important evidence for the study of the structures which underlie and support this situation comes from the analysis of the cemeteries and the grave goods, whose composition is the result of an intentional selection carried out by the members of the community in order to underline clear distinctions of image and function. The great centers of the Tyrrhenian area, Veio and Tarquinia in the southern area, and Ve-

tulonia and Populonia in the northern area, are the ones that offer the richest and most homogeneous evidence which makes it possible to follow, albeit only in outline, the cultural and social development of these communities.

The grave goods of the first half of the ninth century B.C. are meager and broadly uniform. They comprise, besides the ossuary, which is usually covered with an upturned dish, a few objects of personal use connected with custom. There is a clear and marked distinction between male graves and female graves, which reflects a difference of function: in the female graves we find instruments connected with the activity of spinning, such as reels and shuttles, while in the male grave goods we sometimes find a razor, a tool connected with the cutting of meat, an activity which the Greek world, too, reserved for men. In exceptional cases the ossuary consists of a hut-urn and in some male graves the lid of the biconical urn is shaped like a helmet, underlining the military function of the personage buried there.

With the second half of the ninth century B.C. the picture seems more varied and complex. Some graves now emerge in which the ideology connected with war is further emphasized by the deposition of spears and swords, with a differentiation between grave goods with spear and grave goods with spear, sword and helmet-lid, which probably reflects a hierarchical organization possibly linked with age-groups; in the female graves the number of *fibulae* and personal objects increases. We also find the appearance of accompanying vase grave goods, consisting of a small number of vessels.

The transition to the eighth century B.C. coincides with a radical change in the socio-economic structure of the region which will become increasingly evident in the course of the century. In the female burials some grave goods are notable for the multiplication of the objects of personal ornament, which now also include items made of precious metal; in the male ones some warrior figures acquire exceptional prominence, with grave goods which emphasize on the one hand the ideology of war with varied bronze panoplies comprising monumental parade helmets, engraved spears and swords, and on the other hand the ritual function. The number of vases, too, tends to increase progressively, forming increasingly complete services. The presence of objects produced in other regions characterizes some grave goods from the mid-ninth century B.C., constituting a testimony on the material level to the exchange and trade not only among the various Villanovan communities but also with distant environments, such as Sardinia, Sicily and the world of the southern part of the peninsula. From the beginning of the eighth century it is possible to identify traces of relations with the Greek world, through the presence of pottery of the middle geometric type in some graves of the southern Tyrrhenian area, which seems to have a mediating role between the external world and the rest of Etruria. This role is consolidated and reinforced in mid-century, when, after the first settlement on the Island of Ischia in about 770 B.C., the Greek presence in the Tyrrhenian is stabilized with the foundation of a colony at Cuma, which significantly was the northernmost of the *apioikiai* of the first Greek colonization that was attracted by the rich mineral deposits in the Tolfa area and the mining district of Vetulonia and Populonia. This increasingly intense contact with the Greek element, which came to flank the trade that the Phoenician world had carried on with the Villanovan world since the second half of the ninth century, contributed in some areas of Campania to a complete destructuring of the Villanovan communities; in Tyrrhenian Etruria, however, it led to the maturing of the processes of hierarchical structuring of the social fabric of the various communities and the development of the economy and the technologies of these centers. On the technological level the contact with the Greek world and the transfer of specialized workers to the centers of southern Etruria involved the introduction into the local artisan world of more advanced tools and techniques, like those connected with the working of the precious metals, which was inspired by the goldsmiths of the colonies of the Gulf of Naples, or in the field of pottery production the appearance of the rapid potter's wheel and consequently of vases made of well-purified clay of the Greek type, which come to merge with the imports and the traditional production of vases in more or less purified impasto. However, it is on the ideological level that the relations with the Greek element have their strongest influence, with the adoption of customs, like that of the "Greek-style" consumption of wine (see the section of the exhibition on Hellenization), which were used to mark the emergence of particular individuals within the community.

From the second half of the eighth century B.C. we find clearer signs of the structuring of a type society of the aristocratic type—a phenomenon which will become far more marked in the succeeding period—closely linked with the forms of land ownership. Evidence of great importance for an understanding of the ideology of these nascent aristocracies is provided by the cinerary urn of Tomb XXII of the necropolis of the Olmo Bello at Bisenzio and the ceremonial chariot of Tomb II from the same cemetery. Both are prestigious objects with a strongly evocative nature which emphasize the complete dominion of certain individuals over a rapidly growing socio-economic reality, the cinerary urn through the plastic representation of a collective ritual and the chariot through the exaltation of the virtues of the clan.

[S.B.]

9. Tomb 179 at Poggio Selciatello, Tarquinia
first half of ninth century B.C.
Florence, Museo Archeologico

Cremation burial in a cylindrical tufa casket.

Its belonging to a male individual, a warrior, leaves no doubt due to the presence, as lid of the ossuary, of an earthenware knobbed-bell helmet with a rich incised and applied decoration of metal plates and bronze knobs, a Terni-style moon-shaped razor, a *fibula* with wavy bow and disk pin.

In burial goods of Tarquinia Villanovan the presence of the illustrated *askos*, with little legs and long horns, is unusual.

• 1. *Biconical ossuary*
impasto; surface smoothed with a rod; small integration
h 33 cm; diam. of mouth 19.2 cm
inv. 83681 a
Single-handled, decorated with incised geometric motifs.

• 2. *Earthenware knobbed-bell helmet*
impasto; surface smoothed with a rod
h 15 cm; diam. 23.4 cm
inv. 83681 b
Decoration with incised, stamped and applied geometric motifs (lead plates and bronze knobs); the lead plates are missing; bronze knobs re-applied.

• 3. *Small dish*
impasto; surface smoothed with

a rod; light scratches
h 5 cm; diam. 14 cm
inv. 83681 c 1
• 4. *Small dish on tall foot*
impasto; surface smoothed with a rod; light splinters and scratches
h 8.2 cm; diam. 12 cm
inv. 83681 c 1
• 5. *Askos*
impasto; surface smoothed with a rod
lacunose (only one small foot left), reconstructed and integrated
h 15.7 cm; max. w 18 cm
inv. 83681 d
Bull-shaped; white glazed decoration.

• 6. *Terni-type moon-shaped razor*
bronze; cast in bi-valve mold
surface corroded
l 15 cm
inv. 83681 e
Incised decoration.
• 7. *Fibula*
bronze; cast, wire and *lamina*
surface corroded, small lacunas, bone bead in pieces
l 14 cm; diam. of disc 6.6 cm
inv. 83681 f
With wavy bow and disc pin; incised decoration, bone bead.

Pernier 1907, p. 258; Hencken 1968, p. 81, fig. 65; Bianco Peroni 1979, p. 91, pl. 45; Guidi 1980, pp. 24, 37. [A.M.E.]

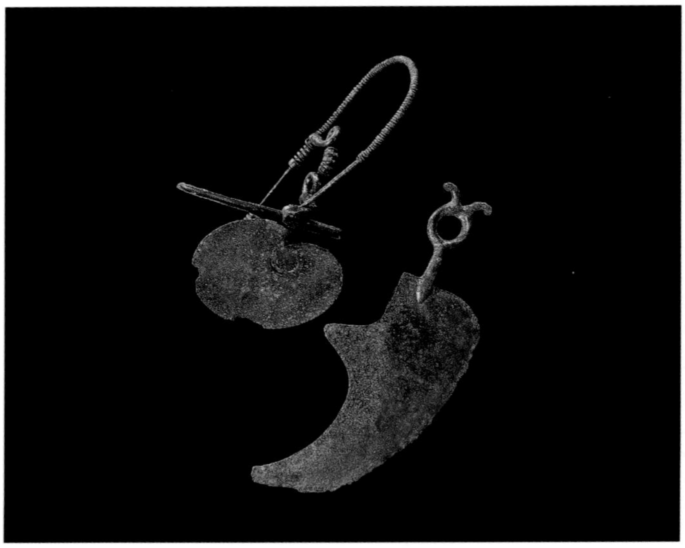

---

10. Tomb 59 at Poggio Selciatello, Tarquinia
first half of ninth century B.C.
Florence, Museo Archeologico

The grave, a cremation well-tomb, is certified as female by the presence in the grave goods of at least 29 impasto spools and a whorl. The grave goods, bare in the elements constituting it, is typical of the burials of the oldest Villanovan period at Tarquinia. Of some relevance the decoration of the ossuary, with composite geometric motifs, made with multiple-teeth combs, and the *fibulae*, including one with a wavy bow with a bent recess, two loops and a short pin, that seems to recall exemplars of the Sicilian Pantelica II area.

• 1. *Biconical single-handle ossuary*
impasto; surface smoothed with a rod; lacunose
h 9 cm; max. diam. 27.6 cm
inv. 83533 a
Decoration with incised and stamped geometric motifs.
• 2. *Single-handle bowl serving as lid*
impasto; surface smoothed with a rod; handle missing; splintering
h 9 cm; diam. of mouth 19 cm
inv. 83533 b
• 3. *Twenty-nine spools*
impasto
l 4.2–5.2 cm
inv. 83533 c 1/29
• 4. *Biconical whorl*
impasto
diam. 3.7 cm
inv. 83533 c 30
• 5. *Fibula with wavy bow*
bronze; slightly corroded
l 3,8 cm
inv. 83533 d 1
• 6. *Fibula with twisted-rope bow*
bronze; slightly corroded
l 3.3 cm
inv. 83533 d 2
• 7. *Fibula*
bronze and glass paste; reconstructed; small lacunas
l 3.5 cm
inv. 83533 d 3

1,2

With plain bow and faced with small discs and glass paste beads.
Pernier 1907, p. 334, n. 59; Hencken 1968, p. 42, fig. 31; Guidi 1980, pp. 29, 33. [A.M.E.]

3

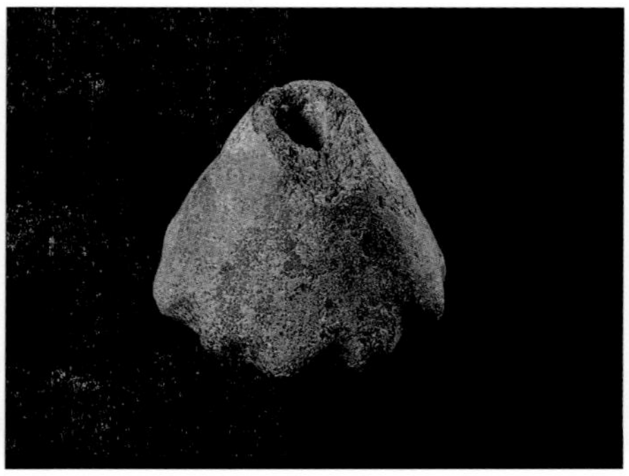

4

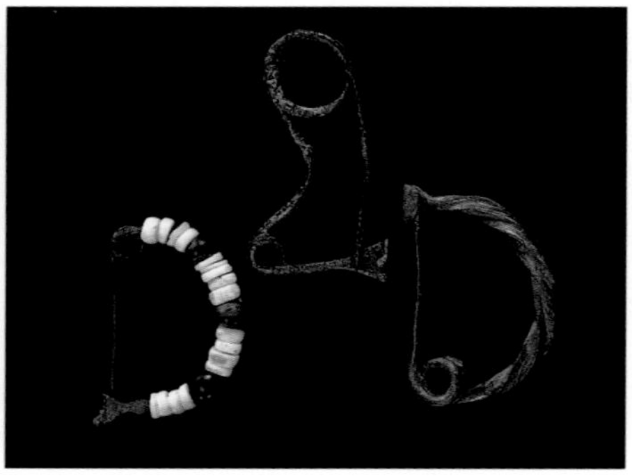

5,6,7

11. Hut-shaped cinerary urn
first half of eighth century B.C.
cast plated bronze
h 28.5 cm; l 40.5 cm; w 35.7 cm
Rome, Museo di Villa Giulia, inv. 84900/01
from Vulci, Osteria necropolis, tomb with stone cist

A cinerary urn shaped like a hut with an oval layout, with minute rendering of the structural details of a real house. It consists of parts assembled with beaten nails and is decorated with punch-stamped or incised geometric motifs, on the body and the roof from the edge of which hang small chains and rings. The rectangular door can open. On the master beam, with openings on both sides preceded by a bird-shaped acroterial element, there are six pairs of small crossed staff beams also with bird-shaped ends and decorated with small rings. The repeated bird representation, that returns also on the wall of the hut in the context of the symbolic motif of the "sun boat," specifically refers to the religious and funerary ideology. Produced by a Vulci workshop.
Inside the urn there was a lead tile of uncertain destination.

Bartoloni, Buranelli, D'Atri et al. 1987, pp. 53 ff., n. 67, with bibl.; Fugazzola Delpino [1990–91] 1993, p. 26, n. 13; Moretti Sgubini 1999, p. 22, fig. 13.
[L.R.]

12. Tomb of the Warrior of Poggio alle Croci, Volterra
last quarter of eighth century B.C.
Volterra, Museo Guarnacci

• 1. *Helmet*
bronze
h 34.6 cm; max. w 29 cm; diam. of base 23.8 cm
inv. SAT 215080
The helmet consists of a slightly elliptical cap with the lower edge curving outward and a pointed summit. The two sheets are overlayed, coinciding with the greater diameter of the cap and held in place by a rectangular plaque with four beaten nails. From the center of the plaque extend three cylindrical elements arranged vertically between the rivets placed at its four corners. The main axis of the cap is topped by a tall crest with a triangular tip. The crest is decorated with a triple row of embossed knobs, surrounded by rows of dots. At the base of the cap the decoration, symmetrical on each of the two laminae, consists of a triple row of embossed knobs, each one being placed in a rectangle made by a punch. Above, two pairs of stylized swans executed with a punch, symmetrical and connected by a T-shaped motif.
• 2. *Double flask*
bronze
h 32 cm; h with handle 37 cm; max. diam. 24 cm; w 15.5 cm
Inv. SAT 215081
The item consists of the juxtaposition of two fore-parts of the usual small flasks in laminated bronze that form a single container with a double spout, for the conservation of two different types of liquid. The decoration, identical on both parts of the body, features concentric circular bands decorated internally with small cups made with a punch. In the middle part a large band consisting of five rays of three vertical bands decorated internally with cups in relief that frame reserved squares in which are introduced, alternately, stylized horses and large cups with double concentric circular cords in relief. The central part features another cup with concentric circular cords.
• 3. *Two-handled patera*
bronze
h. cm. 6,2; max. diam. cm. 23,5.
inv. SAT 215082
One handle missing; the one left is fragmentary.
• 4. *Small semi-spherical bowl*
bronze
h bowl 3.8 cm; with handle 5.6 cm; max. diam. 9 cm
inv. SAT 215083
Flat rim, slightly receding, semi-spherical bowl, convex bottom with omphalos. Straight ribbon handle placed under the inner rim and on the outer part of the bowl held by two pairs of rivets.
• 5. *Sword blade*
bronze
remaining l 35.5 cm; max. w 3.2 cm
inv. SAT 215084
Parallel edges, decorated with four vertical ribbings along the back of the blade converging in the lower part toward the point (missing).
• 6. *Spear tip*
bronze
remaining h 40.5 cm; max. w 11.3 cm
point and part of cannon missing
inv. SAT n. 215085
Cannon with orthogonal faceting, leaf-shaped blade elongated with double cutting edge. Decorated with uneven slanting incisions between the blade and the cannon. The latter still bears traces of the shaft.

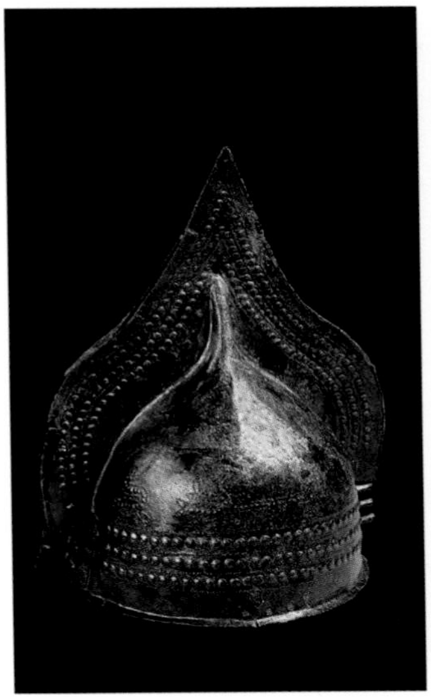
1

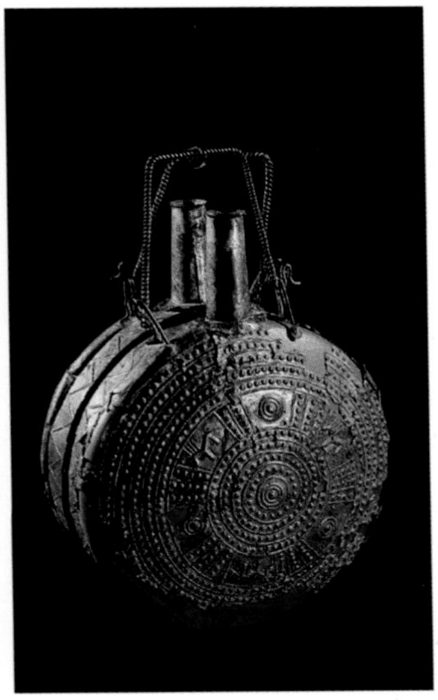
2

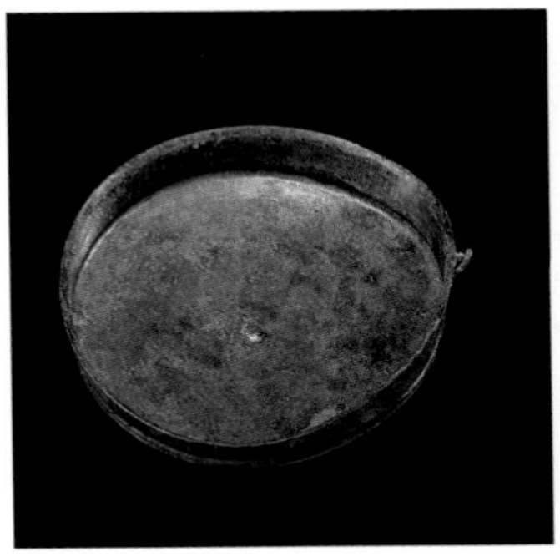
3

4

• *7. Javelin tip*
bronze
h 17 cm; max. width 3 cm; diam. cannon at base 2.5 cm
inv. SAT 215086.
Conical cannon with reinforced base and double passing hole for holding the staff, lanceolate-shaped blade, narrow and elongated, rhomboidal form.
• *8. Horse bit*
bronze
max. l 24 cm; h side 9.2 cm
inv. SAT 215087
Spiraled curb, sides in the shape of a horse carrying a smaller horse on its back, while a third one is placed under the belly next to the figure of a bird. Only one of the two sides is complete. Two-thirds of the other are missing.
• *9. Leech-type fibula*
bronze
max. w 3.2 cm
part of pin, tongue and spring missing
inv. SAT 215088
Hollow bow decorated with meshed squares bordered by bands of circular lines.
• *10. Bracelet*
bronze
max. diam. 8.7 cm
inv. SAT 215089
Round form consisting in a twisted rope-like band with overlapping heads and smooth end. Hinge clasp.
• *11. Wheel pendant*
bronze
diam. 5.5 cm
inv. SAT 215090
• *12. Wheel pendant*
bronze
diam. 6 cm
inv. SAT 215091
• *13. Knob*
bronze
remaining diam. 3.8 cm
inv.SAT 215092
• *14. Fragment of band*
bronze
remaining h 4 cm
inv.SAT 215093
• *15. Small chain*
bronze
inv. SAT 215094
• *16. Spiral*
bronze
remaining h 3.3 cm
inv. SAT 215095
• *17 Group of spirals*
bronze
inv. SAT 215096

Cateni 1998, p. 17-33; Cateni 1998–99, pp. 28–35.
[G.C.]

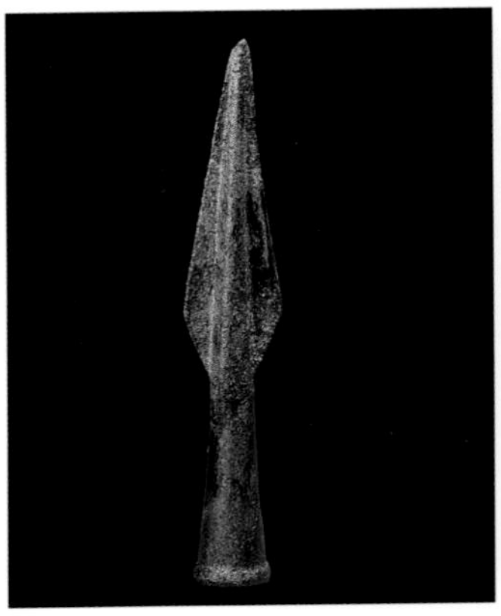
6

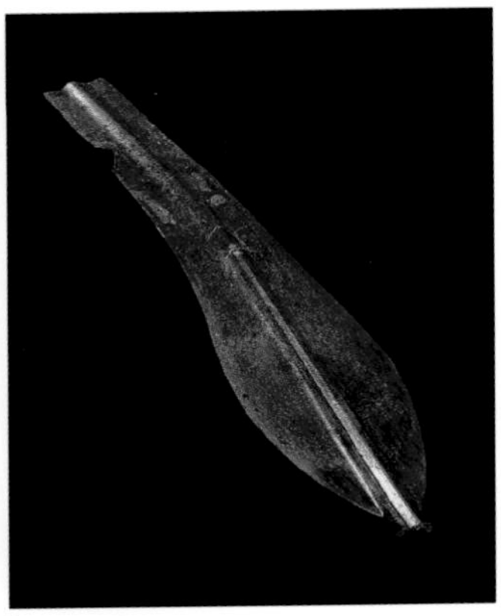
7

8

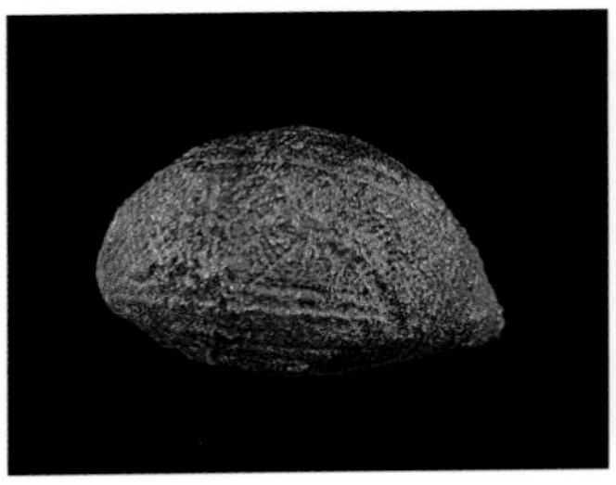
9

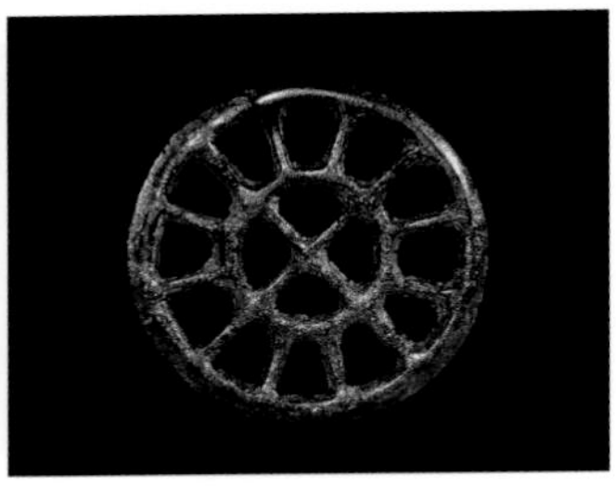
11

13. Badia Tomb, Volterra
last quarter of eighth century B.C.
Volterra, Museo Guarnacci

Tomb with stone *cistus*, unearthed at a depth of 70 cm during farm work at the former Badia dei Camaldolesi, north-west of the city in 1895
The parallelepipedal casket, consisting of six slabs of gypseous marl, with a base measuring 85 x 85 cm and a height of 100 cm, contained the impasto *dolium* (*ziro*), that was found completely shattered. Inside the *ziro*, aside from the ossuary with the bowl lid, were deposited the burial goods of the deceased.
• *1. Six slabs of stone cist*
gypsum *marna*
• *2. Dolium (ziro)*
non purified light brown impasto pottery
inv. MG 4198.
Broken into tiny fragments; nearly entirely reconstituted in plaster; pieces missing.
• *3. Two-handled biconical ossuary*
impasto pottery with bowl lid
h 0.41; diam. of mouth 0.16 cm; bowl: h 0.20 cm
inv.MG 4199
• *4. Hollow leech-type fibula*
bronze
l 0.10 cm
inv. MG 4200.
Tongue missing; few lacunas
• *5. Bronze incense-boat fibula*
l 0.095 cm
inv. MG 4201

1,2,3

• *6. Bronze incense-boat fibula*
l 0.77 cm
inv. MG 4202
• *7. Fragment of bronze incense-boat fibula*
l 0.063 cm
inv. MG 4203
• *8. Fragment of bronze incense-boat fibula*
l 0.065 cm
inv. MG 4204
• *9. Fragment of bronze incense-boat fibula*
l 0.042 cm
inv. MG 4205
• *10. Fragment of bow-spring of bronze incense-boat fibula*
l 0.035 cm
inv. MG 4206
• *11. Bronze incense-boat fibula*
l 0.04 cm
inv. MG 4207
• *12. Bronze incense-boat fibula*
l 0.038 cm
inv. MG 4208
• *13. Fibula with overlaid bow*
bronze
l 0.075 cm
inv. MG 4209
• *14. Fibula with overlaid bow*
bronze
l 0.075 cm
inv. MG 4210
• *15. Fibula with overlaid bow*
bronze
l 0.052 cm
inv. MG 4211
• *16. Fibula with overlaid bow*
bronze
l 0.023 cm
inv. MG 4212
• *17. Spindle*
bronze
l 0.22 cm; diam. of head 0.05 cm
inv. MG 4215
• *18.* Skewer
bronze
l 0.62 cm
inv. MG 4216
• *19. Spiral*
bronze
max. l 0.075 cm, diam. 0.04 cm
inv. MG 4217
There are three fragments left out of a total of twenty-two coils, plus countless separate fragments, deformed by the casting.
• *20. Flask*
bronze
diam. of discs 0.24 cm; diam. of mouth 0.028 cm; h of neck 0.095 cm
inv. MG 4218
Round laminated body consisting of two *laminae*, tall cylindrical neck with short splayed lip formed by a folded-over *lamina*. There also remains the *lamina* forming the side, and on the bottom a small folded-over *lamina* serving as a sort of pedestal. In three reconstituted fragments, pieces missing.
• *21. Thirteen nails*
bronze
diam. of head 0.017–0.043 cm; l 0.03–0.038 cm
inv. MG 4219
• *22. Ten small knobs*
bronze
diam. 0.003–0.012 cm
inv. MG 4220
• *23. Necklace*
bronze
diam. of beads 0.018 cm; diam. of pendants 0.016 cm

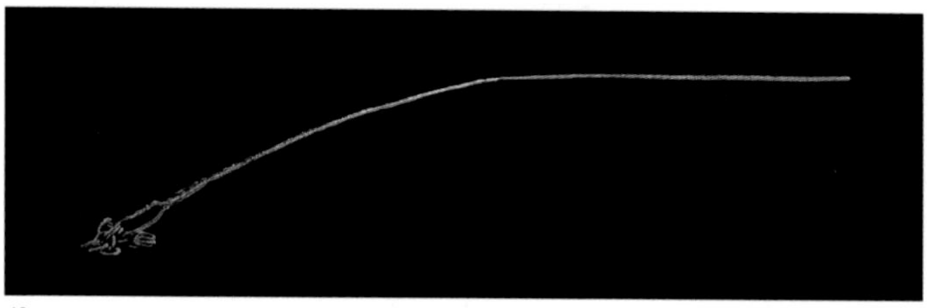
18

21

inv. MG 4221
Consisting of four globular beads crushed near the holes and of two spherical pendants ending in round eyelets.
• *24. Horse bit*
iron
l 0.10 cm
inv. MG 4223
In two fragments, oxidized, deformed by casting.
• *25. Gold leaf*
max. l 0.06 cm
inv. MG 4228
In seventeen deformed fragments, traces of contact with bronze and iron items.

Cateni 1998, pp. 40–47.
[G.C.]

---

14. Ceremonial chariot
second half of eighth century B.C.
cast bronze
h 29.5 cm; diam. of support 18 cm
Rome, Museo di Villa Giulia, inv. 57022/2
from Bisenzio, Olmo Bello necropolis, Tomb II

In the outer sections, archers and hunters with spear and leashed dog, ploughman with oxen, group composed of an armed man with helmet and spear, armed boy, with belt and shield and woman with a vase on her head, couple formed by an armed man with helmet, shield and spear and woman with a vase on her head and another in her right hand; inside, on the small wheel in front of the group of hunters, scene of a duel between two warriors armed with swords and knobbed shields; along the stanchion axes, birds and monkeys; on the inside of the support, ibexes, stags, dogs, one of them attacking a stag, and two wolves.

Menichetti 2000, pp. 228–29.
[I.B.]

15. Bronze cinerary urn
730–700 B.C.
bronze; *lamina*
h 32. 5 cm.
Rome, Museo di Villa Giulia, inv. 57066.
from Bisenzio, Olmo Bello necropolis, Tomb 22

Low cylindrical neck, broad shoulder, upside-down truncoconical body, high flared foot, stick-handles, bent at a straight angle, placed horizontally. On the shoulder, on a herring-bone stripe, nine ityphallic figures, with polos headgear, round shield and spear, presently lost, are dancing a pyrrhic. On the convex, herringbone motif lid, seven ityphallic figures dancing around a monstrous figure, that should be identified with a non-anthropomorphic underground divinity.

Helbig 1969, p. 518 n. 2542; Calvetti 1987, pp. 111; Torelli 1997, p. 36, fig; 25.
[C.Z.]

The Apogee

The economy of the Etruscan world was based on two main activities: agricultural production and the mining of mineral deposits accompanied by an intense activity of transformation. These two nuclei were linked with other activities connected with the artisan production dependent on these two sectors, with the possibility of having an agricultural surplus to exchange with other products, and with the distribution, sometimes over long distances, of the highly sought-after handicraft products—such as bronze artefacts—which earned the Etruscans their reputation as *philotechnoi*. These mechanisms of exchange are highly significant both for their organization and for the social groups involved. A purely aristocratic form of exchange in which the ideology of the gift plays a major part gives way to the phase of the emporia with navigators and merchants who operate under the protection of a deity, and finally the space of exchange is incorporated within the city structure.
Another factor which plays an important role in the Etruscan economic structure is war. As well as stimulating a specialized and prestigious kind of production, that of weapons, warfare is, from the Villanovan period onward, a privileged instrument for acquiring a basic element of wealth, namely land. The same is true of piracy, whose boundaries with respect to mercantile activity seem blurred and permeable, as in the whole of the contemporary Mediterranean world.
The quantity and quality of the whole range of productive activities is destined to change over the course of time, especially in the light of the transition from the archaic *tryphe* to the world of the city in the sixth and fifth centuries B.C. The opulence proper to the Etruscan aristocracies of the archaic phase, based on the accumulation and circulation of prestige goods made of precious material, gives way to productions which may be described as standardized and which reflect the structuring of the urban form, where there is a wider community which tends, in varying measure, to reject the more extreme manifestations of aristocratic luxury. And it is the urban reality which now stimulates new specialistic artisan skills, as in the case of the public works and, at the highest level, of the erection of the temple buildings with their complex decorative systems.

Most of the economic activity of the Etruscan world, from farming upward, involves a work force which may be generically termed servile. This bond of *servitus* acts in a manner which is in many respects analogous to that of Roman clientship, where the *gens* of the archaic period links under the bonds of *fides* the blood relatives of the *familia* and other individuals or groups of external provenance who have decided to renounce their own Lares to recognize those of the clan chief from whom they seek protection. It is the *clientes*, literally those who listen to obey, who form the human reservoir for the productive and military activities of the kin group. In fact, in their discussions of the Etruscan world the Greek and Latin sources seem to distinguish the domestic *servi* or *therapontes*, characterized partly by the luxury of their dress, from those who live in the countryside, whose condition is best known to us from a celebrated passage of Dionysius of Halicarnassus (IX, 5, 4): "Leading the army to the neighborhood of Veii (the consuls Gn. Manlius and M. Fabius) pitched camp on two hills not far from one another. The enemy troops, which were also numerous and strong, had similarly camped before the city. For the most powerful figures (*dynatotatoi*) in all Tyrrhenia had come together, bringing with them their subjects (*penestas*), and the Tyrrhenian army was a good deal larger than the Roman one." The contrast between *dynatotatoi* and *penestai* recurs in a broadly analogous form in other sources (Poseidonius in Diodorus Siculus, V 40; Zonara, VIII, 7, 4 ff; *Gromatici Veteres* 348–50 L), including the accounts of the powerful Aretine family of the Cilnii, the victims of an armed revolt by the *plebs* which was put down by the intervention of the Roman dictator M. Valerius Maximus (Livy, III, 3, 2 and X, 5, 13, which are connected with a passage of the *elogia Tarquiniensia*).
Dionysius's Greek terminology allows us to see the *penestai* as men tied to the land, subjected to the lord and virtually reduced to slavery, but juridically free, liable to harsh punishments but not to the death penalty or exile. We therefore find a less guaranteed condition than that of Roman clientship, which causes violent conflicts, like the one at Arezzo mentioned above or the one which will lead to the conquest of Volsinii by Rome in 264 B.C.
[M.M.]

Agriculture

Etruscan agriculture means in the first place the cultivation of the cereals which provide the staple diet completed by legumes, meat, especially pork, and fruit. Palaeobotanic analysis shows that the most common crop was *triticum dicoccum*, a species suited to damp soil; when roasted and ground it produces spelt, which Pliny the Elder (*Naturalis historia,* XVIII, 11) describes as the basis of the Roman diet. The importance of agriculture already emerges in the earliest iconographic tradition, as we see in the scene of a ploughman on a well-known bronze cinerary urn from Bisenzio dating from the second half of the eighth century B.C., while the cycle of the spelt crop is the basis of the oldest Roman calendar. The acquisition of land necessary for growing the crop is the main impulse behind the colonization of new territories, from the Villanovan age to the great wave of colonization in the Po Valley in the sixth century B.C.
The ancient sources, Greek and Roman, often praise the fertility of the Etruscan fields, as in the case of Diodorus Siculus (V, 40, 3, 5): "They (i.e. the Tyrrhenians) occupy a land which produces every kind of crop, and because they work it intensively they have fruit in great abundance, which is not only sufficient for sustenance but guarantees full enjoyment and luxury [...] for, since they occupy a territory which produces every kind of crop and which has a very good soil, they are able to store away a large quantity of every kind of fruit. For generally Tyrrhenia, where the soil is extremely fertile, possesses extensive plains and is scattered with cultivable hills; it receives a moderate amount of rain, which falls not only in the winter but also in the summer". The carefully cultivated lands with their rich harvests attract the menacing interest of the bordering peoples. Livy tells us (V, 36, 3): "Not even they (i.e. the Gauls) rejected the peace which they offered, provided that the people of Clusium, who possessed a larger territory than they cultivated, would give up part of their territory to the Gauls, who needed it." And later (IX, 36, 11), apropos of a Roman of uncertain identity, he writes: "The next day, at daybreak, he occupied the peaks of the Ciminian Mount; from here, after contemplating the rich countryside of Etruria, he sent his soldiers there to pillage".
Dionysius of Halicarnassus (II, 34, 2-5; IV, 12–16; 25, 2; 52, 5–8) mentions the supplies of Etruscan grain in Rome in the fifth century B.C., while Livy (XXVIII, 45) states that the Etruscan cities of Caere, Roselle, Volterra, Chiusi, Perugia and Arezzo supplied Scipio's army on its journey to Africa in 205 B.C. during the Second Punic War. Varro (*De re*

rustica, I, 9) speaks of a production of cereals that in some areas produces yields of fifteen times the amount of seed sown, as against an average rate in the archaic period that cannot have been much over five. Chiusi and Arezzo are mentioned as producing a prime quality corn which produces a fine bread (Pliny, *Naturalis historia,* XVIII, 87).
The seventh century B.C., in the context of the strong drive to accumulate wealth on the part of the aristocracies, saw a crucial development in the form of extensive crops, based on the practice of fallow farming, letting the fields lie uncultivated every other year, which was to remain the dominant practice until the classical period and the formation of the great urban centers. Now the previous palace and settlement structures on the aristocratic model which had been scattered round the territory disappeared, to be replaced by a largely uninhabited countryside which was cultivated as far as the eye could see.
Pliny the Elder (*Naturalis historia,* XVIII, 20) stresses the need for the ground to be ploughed nine times before the sowing, using a plough pulled by oxen; originally the plough had no yoke but later it acquired one, as can be seen from the Ploughman of Arezzo exhibited here. Ploughing had to be followed by hoeing and the uprooting of weeds, then by the reaping and gathering of the corn, activities which necessitated tools such as pitchforks, hoes, and sickles, like the one from Camaiore exhibited here. The fertility of the Etruscan countryside was enhanced by reclamation work involving complex hydraulic operations. In southern Etruria in particular, a network of *cuniculi* criss-crossed the countryside to improve the drainage of the water. The earthenware and fired pottery from Roselle shown in the exhibition is connected with the preservation, transformation and cooking of food.
From the seventh century onward, the extensive cultivation of corn was accompanied by the intensive cultivation of the vine and olive. Both of the latter were productions of a prestigious kind, which required a more specialized workforce than the cereal crops and a wait of several years before the first harvest could be made. Vine- and olive-growing certainly developed in connection with the world of the *tryphe* of the *principes*, who emphasize their social superiority through their use of a particular and prestigious drink—wine—and of scented ointments based on oil, elements characteristic of an exotic and prestigious lifestyle deriving from contacts with the Greek and oriental world, even though a much older type of wine is also known. The amphoras displayed here show that, alongside the extensive cultivation of corn, the intensive cultivation of the vine is functional to the production of a surplus distributed through the channels of trade.
The ancient sources indicate that livestock farming was of secondary importance, though references to herds of pigs, flocks of sheep, and cattle (Polybius, XII, 4; Licophrones, *Alexandra*, 1241; Livy, X, 4; Pliny the Younger, *Epistulae*, VIII, 20) undoubtedly indicate an important sector of the domestic economy which is also linked with the production of milk, cheese and wool. The working of wool by the women frequently appears in Etruscan iconography, while Pliny the Elder (*Nauralis historia*, XI, 241) and Martial (XIII, 30) praise the cheese of Luni.
The same sources attest to the importance and extent of the woods and forests which produced the wood for the needs of craftsmen and for larger-scale construction projects, as in the case of the birch wood sent from the cities of Roselle, Volterra, Perugia and Chiusi to Rome for the building of Scipio's fleet.
The agrarian landscape of Etruria is characterized by a rigorous and clearly perceptible subdivision of fields marked by recognizable boundaries: there was even a myth (Columella, X, 346) which named Tarchon, the founder of Tarquinia, as the first man to fence in his own fields, while the prophecy of Vegoia attributes this innovation to Tinia-Jupiter himself. The division of the fields, which are the basis of private property, seems homologous to a heavenly order reflected in the ritual division of heaven and earth by the Etruscan discipline. Indeed, the name of the standard tool of land-measurement, the *groma*, is a Greek term which entered Latin through Etruscan, a clear sign of the influence exerted by the experience of the western Greek colonists on the techniques of land division. The sacral and juridical force of the boundaries is clearly indicated by the importance attached to the boundary cippi, such as those of Bettona and Cortona exhibited here, which expound in great detail the controversies and laws of property.
A significant change in the structure of agricultural production can be noticed, especially in the southern Etruscan area, in the fourth century B.C., when the countryside is again occupied by settlements. The phenomenon can be clearly seen at Tarquinia, but is also evident at Caere, Vulci and Volsinii. It was probably an attempted response to the serious social conflicts which had developed during the oligarchic regime which lasted throughout the fifth century B.C. This new occupation involved old and new aristocratic families but also classes which had been previously excluded from the ownership of land and the enjoyment of political and civil rights, in line with wider historical and social developments, as we learn from the case of the laws of Licinius and Sextus passed in Rome in 367 B.C.
[M.M.]

16. Group of the Ploughman
400 B.C.
bronze
h 10 cm; l 19 cm
Rome, Museo di Villa Giulia, inv. 24562
from Arezzo

Consisting of a peasant driving a plough of the kind with share, handle and shaft to which is attached a double yoke and with a pair of oxen with inaccurate features.

La Civiltà degli Etruschi 1985, p. 44; Paturzo 1997, pp. 187 ff., figs 77–78.
[P.A.]

17. Sickle with handle grip
Final Bronze Age 3
bronze
h 10 cm; w 14 cm
Viareggio, Civici Musei di Villa Paolina, inv. 101381
from Camaiore, locality Colle Le Banche

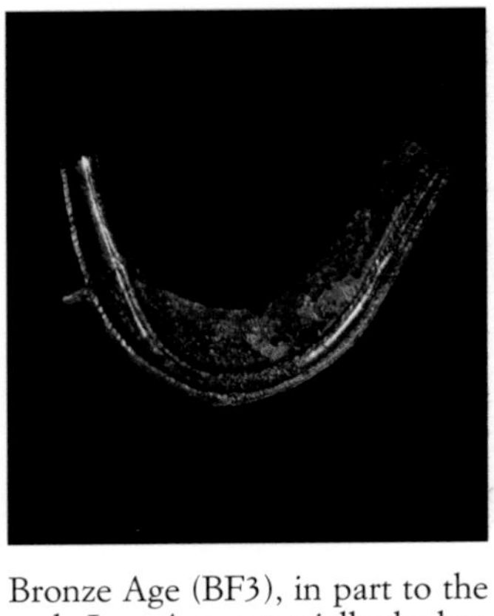

Two parallel ribbings with slanting notches along the handle grip and the back of the blade; a triangular protuberance and traces of another one on the back, a hole in the blade. The piece belongs to a deposit featuring items for the most part fragmentary (spears, hatchets, scalpels, sickles, fibulae, bracelets and other articles of adornment), referable in part to a terminal stage of the Bronze Age (BF3), in part to the early Iron Age, especially the late stage (I Fe2).

Cocchi Genick 1985, pp. 324–60
[D.C.G.]

18. Commercial amphora
last quarter of seventh–first half of sixth century B.C.
nut-colored clay with numerous coarse particles
h 56.3 cm; diam. of rim 16.5 cm
Cortona, Museo dell'Accademia Etrusca, inv. 2465

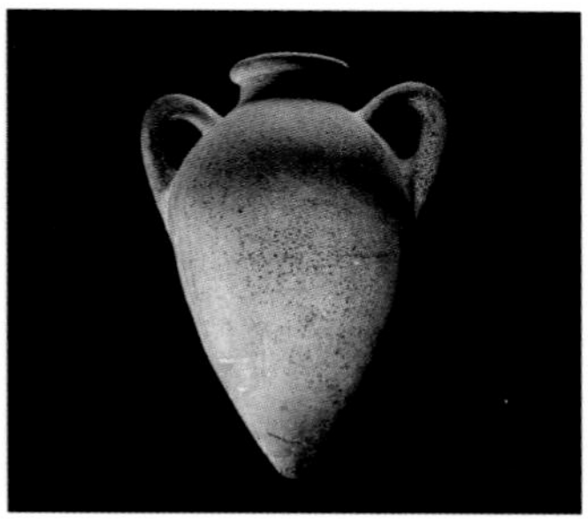

Amphora with oblong pyriform body, with short neck, cord-like brim, two passing stick-handles on the shoulder and the body. It is a container used for the transport of wine, produced in the countryside around the principal centers of southern and inland Etruria: like exemplars come from the Vulci territory, whence the typology spread to Orvieto and Clusian ambits, finally reaching the upper Tyrrhenian coast; numerous exemplars have been recently been identified in contexts of southern France, datable to the last quarter of the seventh century B.C.

Bocci Pacini, Maetzke 1992, p. 105; Giulierini 1998, pp. 44 ff., n. 32. [P.B.]

19. Etruscan wine amphora
late sixth–early fifth century B.C.
pinkish-beige clay with micaceous particles
h 52 cm; diam. mouth 18 cm
Florence, Museo Archeologico, inv. 100519.
from Castiglion della Pescaia (Grosseto), Isola dello Sparviero, random find in 1972

Large mouth, globular body tapering downward and ending in a conical appendage. Stick-handles placed vertically. Referable to the Py 4 type.

Nardi, Pandolfini 1985, p. 61. [C.Z.]

20. Pithos
end of seventh century B.C.
orange-red impasto; stamped decoration
h 73.9 cm; diam. of mouth 34.5 cm; h of frieze 5.6 cm
Florence, Museo Archeologico, inv. 96501
from Caere

The *pithos* belongs to a specifically Caeretan category, whose production lasted about a century: from the last quarter of the seventh century to just after the mid-sixth century B.C. The shoulder is decorated with a series of twenty-seven horses gradient left: the decoration, on separate metopes made with a flat stamp, instead of being a continuos cylinder-printed frieze, puts this exemplar among the oldest of the series. The dating is confirmed by the typology of the horses, of obvious Corinthian style, and by the use of the "dot in a circle" rosette, also Corinthian in origin, more precisely transitional, attested in Etruria by the last decades of the seventh century B.C.

Civiltà degli Etruschi 1985, p. 143, n. 6.8.4. [G.C.C.]

21. Roselle, House of the Impluvium
Grosseto, Museo Archeologico

• *1. Well-curb*
late sixth century B.C.
beige impasto
h 56.5 cm; diam. of mouth 78.5 cm; diam. of base 86 cm
inv. 163481
Out-turned lip, low, grooved neck, bell-shaped body, lower part cut, with four slits narrowing toward the inside; four big ribbon handles between the lip and shoulder; carved rope-decoration on the shoulder.
• *2. Olla*
late seventh century B.C.
reddish impasto
h 17 cm; diam. 16.5 cm

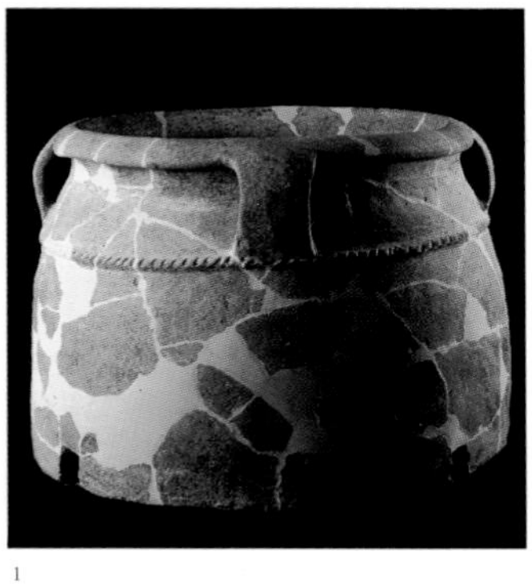

1

inv. 227450
from level V, well E
Tilted lip, ovate body, rope-like decoration, flat bottom.
• *3. Small oven*
seventh century B.C.
orange impasto
h 16.5 cm; diam. 25.5 cm
inv. 163482
from well E
Rounded edge with grooves, cylinder-shaped body, with three supports inside; on the back horizontal stick-handle.
• *4. Olla*
late seventh century B.C.
reddish impasto
h 31 cm; diam. 33 cm
inv. 123965 (old inventory)
from level IV
Out-turned lip, ovate body, rope-like decoration, flat bottom.

Donati 1994, pp. 23–26, ns. 75, 90, 101, 115; pls. VI, XXI, XXIV; figs. 10, 11, 13, 15. [C.Z.]

2,3

4

22. Boundary cippus
late third–early second century B.C.
sandstone
h 90 cm, w at base 30 cm
Bettona, Museo Civico

The cippus, that bears on the front a right-to-left inscription "tular larna," belongs to the series of inscriptions on stone with the word *tular* (Latin *fines*). The name Larna, attested in Orvieto and with variants in Perugia is also known at Bettona itself, thus confirming the presence of individuals from Volsinii, who moved to the Perusian an Clusine areas after the fall of Orvieto.

Buschetti in *Civiltà degli Etruschi*, 1985, cat. 61. [M.Sc.]

23. Boundary cippus
first half of the second century B.C.
gray-blue stone
91 x 38 x 9–10 cm
Cortona (Arezzo), Palazzo Comunale
from Cortona, Viale Passerini 170, presently property of the Ordine delle Suore Riparatrici

Cippus processed in the upper part, on view, and rough in the lower part, to be set in the ground, with three lines of inscription: "luϑcval / canϑiśa / l."

Torelli, Agostiniani, forthcoming, pp. 115–24.
[F.C.]

The Mines

The hoard from Coste del Marano which appears at the beginning of the exhibition indicates how in the course of the Bronze Age the territory which later corresponded to Etruria was affected by a significant circulation of metal, the basic element in the accumulation of wealth.
The situation at Pithecoussai (Island of Ischia) in the eighth century B.C., which is archaeologically perceptible to us as a settlement halfway between the oldest trading stations used by Levantine and Greek navigators and the model of the Greek colonies, reveals a great interest in the search for and the working of metals in the context of these ancient contacts. Phoenicians or Levantines, Greeks, Etruscans and native peoples seem to settle in one and the same place where a rich metallurgical activity flourishes which the literary sources link with *chryseia* (Strabo, V, 4, 9), goldsmiths' workshops, and which are archaeologically attested by ferrous slag whose archaeometric analysis proves a provenance from the Island of Elba. During the same period the nuraghic bronze statuettes found in Etruria are evidence of contacts with Sardinia, an area of intense metallurgical activity probably involving Cypriot craftsmen. Another series of elements points to the central-European and Carpatho-Danubian area, showing the diverse influences and stimuli which led to the rise of Etruscan metal-working.
Evidence of the intense mining activity is provided by large areas covered with slag which have been found near Campiglia, near Gherardesca and above all in the region of Populonia, which until the early decades of the twentieth century was covered by a thick layer of ferrous slag, up to 20 meters deep. Slag used as building material has been found in the village of Accesa near Massa Marittima and on Elba. The ancient literary sources insist exclusively on the mineral deposits of Elba. Thus Diodorus Siculus writes (V, 13, 1-2): "Off the city of Tyrrhenia called Populonia is an island known as Aethalia. This island, which lies about 100 stades from the coast, took its name from the smoke (*aithalos*) which is very dense in that area. For the island has many ferrous rocks which the inhabitants dig to smelt them and obtain iron, a metal which they possess in great abundance. The men engaged in this work beat the rock with hammers and burn the stones that they extract in cunningly devised furnaces, where they liquefy them through the action of an intense fire, thus extracting pieces of modest size which look like large sponges." Another source (Pseudo Aristotle, *De mirabilibus auscultationibus*, XCIII) mentions deposits of copper on Elba. For Virgil (*Aeneid*, X, 174) and his commentator Servius (*ad loc.*) the Elban cultivations take on fabulous dimensions and characteristics, which are also evoked by Rutilius Namatianus (vv. 351–56) in 416 A.D. during his journey from Rome to Gaul. Only Strabo (V, 2, 6) mentions some disused mines near Populonia in connection with the disembarking of the Argonauts—a myth linked with the search for metal in Colchis—near the port that takes its name from their ship, Argo, near Portoferraio.
The archaeological evidence shows that iron, copper, lead, tin, silver, and allum constitute the principal mineral wealth of Etruria and that these metals come mainly from works on the Island of Elba, the area of Populonia and Campiglia, in the Apuan Alps, on the Metalliferus district, on the Monti Rognosi in the district of Arezzo, and on the Monti della Tufa, near Volterra; silver, as well as ochre and cinnabar, which were used as colorants, comes from Monte Amiata.
The exploitation of the mineral deposits is carried out in Etruria by the identifying of surface veins or by the sinking of rows of narrow, shallow shafts, sometimes faced with drystone walls; the shafts were about ten meters apart. The working conditions can be gathered from Pliny the Elder's account of gold mines in the ancient world (*Naturalis historia*, XXXIII, 70): "With galleries stretching over long distances the mountains are excavated by lamplight; the lamps also serve as measures of the working shifts, because for many months no one sees the light of day. [...] Moreover, there are sudden landslips which crush the workers [...] and they encounter blocks of rock which are shattered by fire and vinegar, but more often, since this procedure makes the galleries suffocating with steam and smoke, they prefer to break the rocks with mallets loaded with 150 libras of iron. They carry away the pieces of rock on their shoulders, day and night, each man passing them to his neighbor in the darkness."
The main operations of the mining process must have consisted in the detachment of the masses with the aid of fire and vinegar, the shattering and the selection of the mineral, and finally the washing of the mineral. The operations are carried out by lamplight by the miner with the aid of picks, shovels, hammers, mallets and chisels. The workers were chiefly slaves or condemned prisoners, while there must have been specialized staff in charge of the operations of smelting the metal. Working the metal on the spot, as can be deduced from the remains of mining work in the area of Massa and Campiglia, avoids transport costs but is dependent on the availability of water and wood—Pliny the Elder recommends pine but we also know of charcoal remains of oak, turkey oak and service -tree wood—which were necessary for the smelting furnaces.
The mineral is loaded in alternate

layers with coal and inserted from above. For iron an optimal smelting temperature is about 1200–1250 degrees, at which the slag produces a residue of about 40 per cent of the mineral. The liquid slag passes out below through a conduit, while the pure mineral is deposited on the bottom; its extraction requires the destruction of the furnace, which is usually made of brittle stone.
The exploitation of the mineral deposits, though operative since the earliest times, becomes intensive from the seventh century B.C., with the great demand for metal weapons and objects among the Tyrrhenian aristocracy. All this is reflected, for example, in the birth and development of the mining village of the Accesa from the end of the eighth century to the sixth century B.C. or in the formation of the industrial area of Populonia, outside the city walls, from the second half of the sixth century B.C.. The oldest slag contains a smaller mineral residue, a sign that industrial activity as we see it at Populonia brings with it an increase in thoroughness.
It is possible to identify certain particular traditions of Etruscan metallurgy, linked to different areas of demand. Certainly the demand for agricultural implements from the earliest times influenced the development and organization of the metal-working sector, as can be inferred from the ploughshares from Gravisca shown in the exhibition. A second important impulse came from the lifestyle of the archaic aristocracies, led by warrior princes, who especially from the second half of the eighth century B.C. made insistent requests for wrought metal weapons, swords, shields, spears, greaves, daggers, and razors, as well as *fibulae* and belts, of which some examples are exhibited here. Moreover the ceremonial models linked with the consumption of wine and meat inspired by Greek and oriental models demand an appropriate display of *tryphe*, of wealth, which is translated above all into the accumulation of metal vases, especially bronze ones, and huge, extraordinary goldsmithery products. The urban phase, finally, multiplies the demand for metal votive gifts of small or large size for the sanctuaries, a practice which had already begun in the preceding phase. To have an idea of the dimensions of the phenomenon one only has to bear in mind the accounts of the conquest of Orvieto-Volsinii by the Romans in 264 B.C. with the consequent transference to Rome of 2,000 bronze statues or, in another context, the tribute paid by Corneto (Tarquinia) to the Pope in 1546, which comprised 6,000 libras of metal melted down from ancient works, to produce the bronze cladding of the columns of the basilica of San Giovanni in the Lateran. [M.M.]

24. Snares
590–580 B.C.
copper, with high percentage of iron, cast
diam. 45–55 cm; weight 40 kg
Florence, Museo Archeologico, inventory numbers:
from the Island del Giglio, rada di Campese, shipwreck

Four disc-shaped copper snares.

Bound 1991a, p. 190, fig. 14; Bound 1991c, p. 26; Cristofani 1999, p. 216.
[C.Z.]

25. Lingots
590–580 B.C.
cast lead
l 40–53 cm; w 11.5– 20 cm;
weight 8.40–11.70 kg
Florence, Museo Archeologico, from the Island of Giglio,
rada di Campese, shipwreck

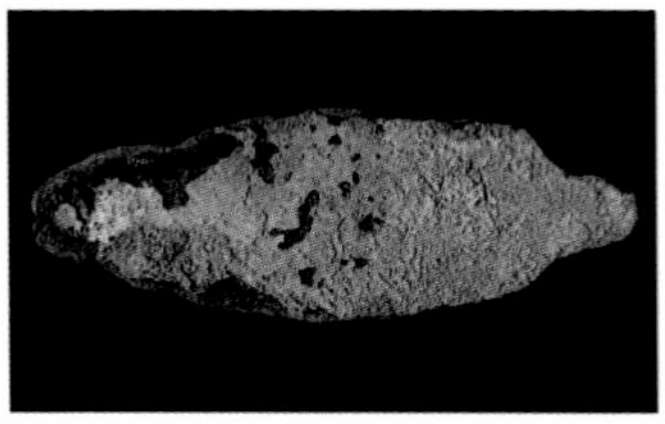

Nine lead lingots, three of which, flat and oblong, are the same length and marked with the same letter of the alphabet, an *ypsilon*, one that is combined with another lingot in the sequence *tau alfa*. Another exemplar, instead, presents the left-to-right sequence EYM.

Bound 1991a, p. 196, nn. 30–31; Bound 1991c, p. 26; Cristofani 1999, p. 217.
[C.Z.]

26. Bronze belt
Villanovan II b
Bronze
l 42 cm; max. h 13.5 cm
Florence, Museo Archeologico, inv. 82323
from Marradi (Florence)

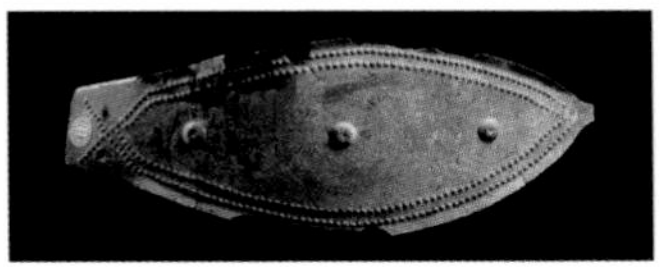

Bronze-plated belt in the shape of an oblong ellipse, with one wider end, with slightly convex edge and two passing holes, one narrower and bent backward to form a loop; slightly raised edge, emphasized by two rows of pods that intersect at the wider end; in the middle a large incised rose, with ringed edge alternating with two rows of dots, then a band with triangles on a background of dashes, then a series of dots and central medallion with large embossed bead, with central dot, from which bands of lines radiate; on each side of the central rose, two vertical bands incised with meanders on a background of dashes, smaller roses with ring edges and rows of dots, background triangles and central pod; at the ends background lozenge with triangular appendages at the summits.
[F.C.]

27. Fibulae from Poggio Gallinaro Tomb 9
Florence, Museo Archeologico
from Tarquinia,

The grave, found quite near tomb 8, belonging to a woman (see n. 128), made in a plain pit in the ground faced with *nenfro* slabs, should be connected with a male figure, that the presence of a sword and an iron spear connote as a warrior. Just like the female tomb, Tomb 9, ca. 700 B.C., represents one of the richest graves of the scene offered by the necropolis of Poggio Gallinaro during the old Orientalizing period. The burial goods include rich banquet furnishings, that, aside from two impasto ollas with feet and a painted pottery semi-spherical bowl, consists of at least seven bowls, a basin with beaded rim and a small bronze flask, as well as a great number of objects of personal adornment, including at least twenty-six *fibulae*, of which the ones on display offer a significant sample. If the exceptional wealth of the ornamental *parure* can, on the one hand, be explained by the style of dress that had changed since the previous period, when even the contexts of a certain wealth never presented more than about ten *fibulae*, on the other, it would seem quite obvious that the use of a great number of *fibulae*, both for women and for men, even belonging to various types of local fashion tra-

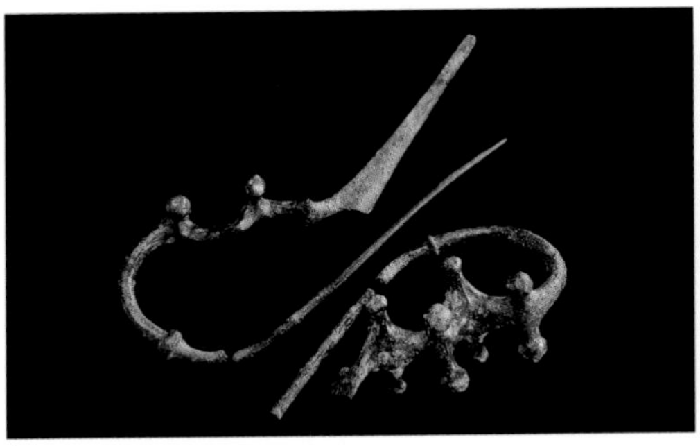
1

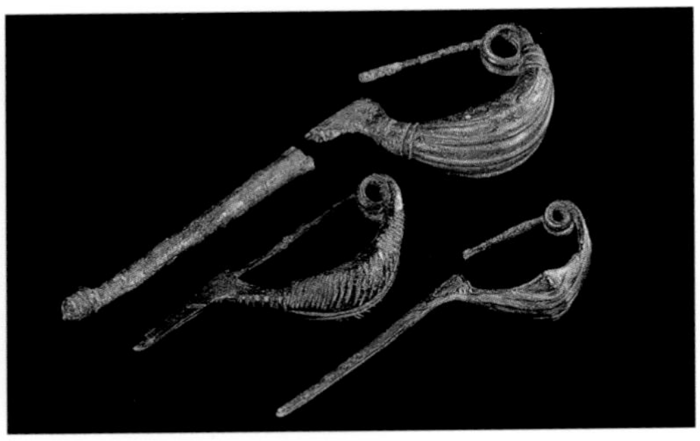
2

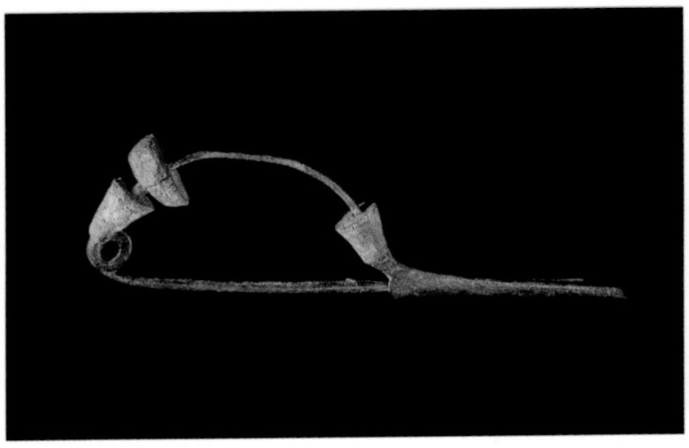
3

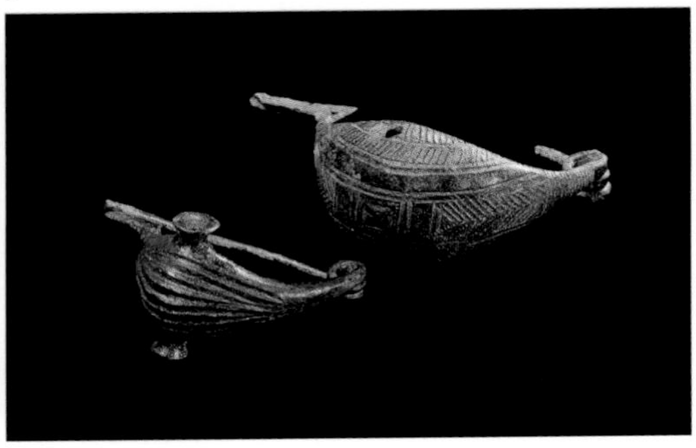
4

ditions, recall Hellenizing manners and life-styles connected with the world of the "Homeric" aristocracy, which we see in the mention, among the pretenders' gifts to Penelope, of a very handsome peplum with twelve *fibulae* (Homer, *Odissey*, XVIII, 292–93). At the time an object for offering and for long-distance exchanges, as documented in tomb 9 by the presence of at least three double leech-type *fibulae* (Hencken 1968, p. 350, fig. 349, f-g) in all likelihood made in Bologna (cf. *La necropoli villanoviana* 1979, fig. 73 n. 7), some types appear to be reserved to men, such as for instance dragon *fibulae*, whereas the leech-type and the incense-boat models appear equally in male and female burial goods, as is confirmed by the evidence of several exemplars exceptionally bearing inscriptions (cf. Cristofani 1984, p. 322).

• *1. Two dragon fibulae*
a) l 15.4 cm
inv. 21209
Pin and tongue lacunose. Wavy bow decorated with eight apophyses ending in little balls, arranged in opposite pairs on the elbows; flexible tongue, with small disk to hold the pleats at the connection with the needle; long pin.
Type Sundwall H.III.α.aa
Pernier 1907, p. 342, fig. 70; Hencken 1968, p. 350, fig. 349.d
b) l 9.4 cm
inv. 21210
Part of tongue missing. Wavy bow with two pairs of apophyses ending in little balls arranged in opposite pairs on the elbows, alternating with two pairs of pointed apophyses; flexible tongue, with small disk to hold the pleats at the connection with the needle; long pin.
Type Sundwall H.III.α.aa
Pernier 1907, p. 342, fig. 70; Hencken 1968, p. 350, fig. 349.h

• *2. Three incense-boat fibulae*
a) max. l left 9.2 cm
inv. 21189
Part of tongue missing, incense-boat bow, decorated on the back with two long smooth bands, that delimit a band with three quadrangular areas adorned, the outside ones in a herring-bone pattern and the central one with a row of dots following the perimeter of a central square; on the sides herring-bone bands; transversal incisions at the base of the bow, with two coils near the spring, and elongated at the fastening with the pin.
Type Sundwall F.I.a
Pernier 1907, p. 342, fig. 70; Hencken 1968, p. 350, fig. 350.h
b) max. l left 6.7 cm
inv. 21194
Tips of pin and of tongue missing. Incense-boat fibula with rather hollow rhomboidal body, decorated with deep longitudinal grooves and two lateral buttons; elongated pin; spring with two coils. Type Sundwall G.III. .a
Pernier 1907, p. 342, fig. 70; Hencken 1968, p. 350, fig. 350.g
c) l 5.9 cm
inv. 21198
Fragmentary tongue. Incense-boat bow with rhomboidal body, decorated on the back with deep longitudinal grooves; long pin; spring with two coils.
Type Sundwall G.III. .a
Pernier 1907, p. 342, fig. 70; Hencken 1968, p. 350.

• *3. Overlaid bow fibula*
l 7.7. cm
inv. 21206
Most of the overlaying on the bow missing. Bow formed by a quadrangular-section rod with bone overlaying and amber inlays; long pin; spring with two coils.
Type Sundwall G.I. .b
Pernier 1907, p. 342, fig. 70; Hencken 1968, p. 350, fig. 349.c; Guzzo 1981, p. 59.

• *4. Two leech-type fibulae*
a) l 5 cm
inv. 21200
Complete. Leech-type bow, decorated on the back: in the middle two longitudinal lines spread laterally into two series of thin transversal lines, delimited at the base of the bow, level with the fastening of the pin and that of the spring, by a series of transversal incisions. Oblong pin; spring with two coils.
Type Sundwall G.I. α.a
Pernier 1907, p. 342; Hencken 1968, p. 350, fig. 350.d.
b) max. l left 7.2 cm
inv. 21195
Tongue missing. Leech-type bow decorated with a series of deep longitudinal grooves, delimited at the fastening of the pin and that of the spring by two pairs of raised transversal bands; long pin; spring with two coils.
Type Sundwall G.I. .a
Pernier 1907, p. 342; Hencken 1968, p. 350.
[S.B.]

---

28. Plough push-rods
sixth century B.C.
iron
l 28.5 cm; w 19 cm
Tarquinia, Museo Archeologico, inv. II / 16180, II / 26047
From the sanctuary of Gravisca

Plough rod with chamfer, elongated conical, hollow, with dulled point and triangular opening. Inside, near the base, three rivets for attaching it to the wooden plough-stock.

Torelli 1977, pp. 411, 438, note 61; Torelli 1978, p. 401.
[F.C.]

Piracy and Trade

In the tenth and the ninth centuries B.C., after the end of the Mycenaean navigations, the Mediterranean sea routes are once again frequented by navigators of various origins, Phoenician, Levantine, Greek, but also Etruscan, as seems to be indicated by reports of an ancient thalassocracy of the Etruscans. Gradually, in the ninth and eighth centuries B.C., we see the reappearance of a Greek presence, with visits from Euboea and the Cyclades linked with the spread of late geometrical pottery, notably chevroned cups.
The settlement of Pithecoussai (on the island of Ischia) which was founded about 770 B.C., and organized by the Greeks of Euboea, marks the extreme limit of the northward expansion of western Greek civilization into the Tyrrhenian area. The decision to site it on an island, opposite the mainland, closely resembles a practice typical of Phoenician trade aimed at guaranteeing a secure relationship with the indigenous populations. The Italic horizon which opens up before the traders who come to Pithecoussai comprises the indigenous tribes of Campania later absorbed by Greek culture in the case of the Ausoni, the Etruscan areas, especially those gravitating round Pontecagnano, and, further north, the Latin world and Etruria. Alongside the Euboean, Phoenician and Levantine merchants, there were also groups of native peoples and also Etruscans operating at Pithecoussai. In the case of the Etruscans we must also suspect marriage exchanges, for these are indicated by the graves of Etruscan women on the island. Trade with the Etruscan world seems to be crucial in the choice of Pithecoussai as the site of the colony: the Tyrrhenian aristocracies, which have already formed at this time, require the precious goods typical of the eastern world, the supply of which is guaranteed by the varied provenance of the navigators of Pithecoussai. Conversely, the Etruscan chiefs can offer various things in exchange, especially metals, iron in particular, but also slaves and other goods. At the same time flows of trade seem already to be under way between Etruria and the Sardinian area, and here too they include marriage relationships between the two areas. Phoenicians, Greeks, Sardinians and Etruscans thus weave a dense network of trade on the sea routes: the oldest Villanovan colonization in Campania is attested at important trading points, and the sculptures of boats found in the Villanovan tombs indicate the importance of the relationship between these peoples and the sea, which also becomes a metaphor for the passage to the afterlife.
This ancient phase of contacts and exchanges seems to be organized in the first place by aristocratic chiefs both on the Etruscan and on the Greek side: this is what has been called the aristocratic *prexis idie,* to which there are references in Homer and Hesiod. This trade is essentially projected on the sea and organized by the owners of the ships, callled *basileis* (kings) in Greek terminology, who draw the basis of their wealth from the possession of land. This basic structure conditions all the phases and modalities of the exchange relationships. For the *prexis idie* is inherently bound up with the rhythms of agricultural production and permits the exchange of surpluses produced on the lord's estates. Furthermore, the crew of the ship is made up of individuals linked to the lord's family, and the itineraries and the ports of call are determined by the personal friendly relations which the aristocratic chief has been able to maintain with his peers in other *ethne*. The goods that are transported are of many kinds, ranging from agricultural surpluses, hides and animals to raw and wrought metals, ceramic containers and slaves. This trade is however mainly aimed at the acquisition of prestige goods such as gold weapons, bronze tripods and *lebetes*, perfumes, products of the goldsmith's art, silver vases, ivory, and objects and furniture made of fine wood. This kind of relationship and exchange on most of the shores of the Mediterranean activates and develops the growth and structuring of dominant groups within the indigenous societies which regard the exotic and precious materials as a certain legitimization of their power in that it recalls the lifestyle of the oriental sovereigns and the heroes of Homeric epic. The extreme commonness in Pithecoussai of the working of metals, which includes some goldsmiths' workshops (*chryseia*), is explained by this situation. Moreover, the high demand for these materials also stimulates the transformation of the *prexis idie* to include an intermediate kind of trade, whereby the surpluses and products of the lord's estate are supplemented by goods acquired during the itinerary.
This whole world corresponds to the story of the Corinthian Demaratus, an aristocratic member of the *genos* of the Bacchiades, a shipowner who, together with his crew, maintains a whole network of commercial exchanges and personal relations so that, when he has to leave his home city on the seizure of power by the tyrant Cypselus, he is able to take refuge in Tarquinia, where he can count on firm friendships. Here he marries a woman of high rank who guarantees him more or less complete integration in the community, until one of his sons emigrates to Rome and becomes king under the name of Tarquinius Priscus.
It was mentioned earlier that the goods included slaves, the trade in whom is well attested in Homeric epic. This fact leads us to the consideration that trade by sea finds a counterpart in the activity of piracy. In Homeric epic the traveler who arrives by sea is asked if he practices the trade *prexis* or piracy (Homerus, *Odissey*, III, 72–74; IX, 253–55). These two activities seem closely connected, as is indicated by accounts of the earliest appearances of the Euboeans in the West, apropos of which Thucydides (VI, 4,5; also Pausanias 23,7) explicitly mentions the founding of Zancle by pirates from Cuma, and piracy is also mentioned by the classical sources in connection with the Phoceans (Iustinus, XLIII, 3, 5–6; Herodotus, I, 166,1; VI, 17). But a well-known passage of Ephorus quoted by Strabo (VI, 267) says the same of the Etruscans: "Ephorus affirms that these two cities (sc. Naxos and Megara Iblaea) were the first Greek colonies founded in Sicily in the tenth generation after the Trojan war; previously people were terrified of the piracy of the Etruscans and of the primitive nature of the barbarians of those areas, so much so that no one wanted to travel there even for the purpose of trade". As can be seen, both the Greeks and the Etruscans seem greatly interested in the control of the sea routes which can guarantee the best ports of call and the richest points of exchange. In this context Etruscan piracy emerges more clearly, even becoming proverbial (Hesychius, s.v. *Tyrrhenoi desmoi*), because the reports that we have are written from a Greek point of view; thus we have the story of the Tyrrhenian pirates who kidnap the god Dionysus in the Homeric Hymn to Dionysus, and the reputation for cruelty attached to the Etruscan pirates, who are even accused of cannibalism (Hyginus, *Fabulae*, 274,20) or of tying their prisoners to a corpse (Aristotle, *Protreptic*, fr. 60 Rose; Virgil, *Aeneid*, VIII 478–88).
The bitter struggle for the control of the Lower Tyrrhenian emerges clearly in connection with Lipari, a Greek colony founded by the Rhodians and Cnidians in 580 B.C. Diodorus Siculus (V, 9, 4) mentions the division of the colonists into farmers and those responsible for defense against pirates, that is to say a practice of counter-piracy directed against the Etruscans (Diodorus Siculus, V, 9, 4–5; Strabo, VI, 275; Pausanias, X, 11, 3–4 and X, 16, 7). The violence of these clashes is reflected in the alternation of fortunes in what was probably an Etruscan occupation of Lipari, accompanied by a human sacrifice and the dedication of a tripod at Delphi, followed by a successful counter-attack by the Liparese with the consequent dedication of a votive offering at Delphi in the second quarter of the fifth century B.C.; this is referred to on the cast of the Delphi base exhibited here.
The complexity of the picture is accentuated by the intervention of the Punics, especially those of Carthage, and the Athenians. The Etrusco-Punic alliance against the cities of Magna Graecia leads to the battle of the Sardinian Sea about 540 B.C. and that of Cumae

in 474 B.C., after which the victor Hieron of Syracuse, as well as dedicating two Etruscan helmets at Delphi, occupied Pithecoussai in order to reduce the extent of the Etruscan navigations. The long rivalry continues with the Syracusan sack of Elba in 453 B.C. and the sack of Pyrgi by Dionysius of Syracuse in 384 B.C. On the other front, the Athenian expedition against Syracuse in 415 B.C., which ended in defeat, had the explicit support of the Etrusco-Punic alliance, which took concrete shape in the sending by Tarquinia of an expeditionary force to help the Athenians. It should, however, be remembered that an Athenian decree of 325–324 B.C. records the establishment of a colony in the Adriatic area against the Tyrrhenian pirates to defend the city's trade. The earliest phase of what might be termed the Demaratean trade, which was controlled and organized by high-ranking figures who were leaders of their communities, *reges*, and characterized by the pre-eminent role played by Graeco-Euboean mediation, ends in the third quarter of the seventh century B.C. From this time pottery of Corinthian and Greek-oriental production predominate in Etruria, in accord with the predominant new carriers in the trade channels of Samian, Milesian and Phocean origin. Corinthian pottery appears in Etruria already at the turn of the eighth century B.C., and intensifies until the middle of the seventh century, when there arrives in Etruria the so-called Chigi olpe, an extraordinary example of the kind of iconography that Corinthian pottery introduces to Etruria, and which leads in the second half of the century to the foundation of local Etrusco-Corinthian workshops. Graeco-Oriental pottery appears from the first half of the seventh century and increases in the second half with productions of the so-called "Style of the Wild Goat" and with pieces of extremely high quality like the Levy oinochoe. But it is above all between the end of the seventh and the middle of the following century that Graeco-oriental pottery reaches its widest diffusion, especially owing to the various kinds of container for perfumes and ointments—such as *alabastra*, balsam-holders, Samian *lekythoi*, marbled *lydia*, glazed or faience vases—which find wide acceptance as symbols of a lifestyle influenced by oriental *tryphe* and the world of the symposium. The Hellenizing fashion of the heavy coverings of buildings, which becomes widespread from the middle of the seventh century B.C., is now accompanied by the earthenware *pinakes* used for the decoration of the interiors and the cast technique which makes possible the spread of architectural terra cottas in relief. In the second half of the sixth century a final Graeco-Oriental wave comes with the black-figure pottery, whose models lead to the creation of workshops such as that of the Ceretan *hydriai* or of the Campana *dinoi* and the training of the painters of Tarquinian funerary art. This is also the phase when trade routes are activated between Etruria and the markets of the Italic world, mainly along the rivers, while others, attested by the wrecks of ships, are established leading to the markets of southern Gaul, where there are thriving rich Celtic aristocracies which see the buccheri, vases, bronze instruments and amphoras containing Etruscan wine and oil the as the most effective means of displaying their rank.

Etruria now seems to be part of a trading circuit which touches the Asiatic coasts, and especially the area of Lydia, the Greek emporium of Naucratis which is active on the Nile, the two ports of Corinth through which goods of every provenance pass, enabling the city to keep its dominant role at least until about 560 B.C., when it is the turn of Athens to flood the markets with her products. The ports of Pyrgi (Caere), Gravisca (Tarquinia), Regisvilla (Vulci), the Tiber port of Rome in the forum Boarium, Populonia, and Pisa, the last of which has now emerged thanks to recent excavations, are so many terminals in this network of exchange which extended all over the Mediterranean. The almost simultaneous activation of Massalia (Marseilles) and Gravisca at the beginning of the sixth century B.C. is a sign of the prominent part played by the Phocaean merchants, as reported by Herodotus (I, 163). That these trading stations were known and regularly visited by navigators is proved by the dedications of ex-votos at Gravisca which include the names of dedicants also known at Naucratis. A celebrated case is that of Sostratus, the son of Laodamas of Aegina, who dedicates an anchor block to Apollo Aeginetes at Gravisca and who is mentioned by Herodotus (IV, 152) as an immensely wealthy merchant "with whom nobody can compete".

The phase that begins in the last decades of the seventh century B.C. is remarkable not only for the predominant part played by the Graeco-Oriental merchants but especially for the novelties that affect the very modalities of exchange. This is now described as an emporium phase which involves profound changes both in the activation and organization of maritime trade and in the organization of the final destinations of this trade. In the former case it is no longer the people of regal and aristocratic rank who personally control a trade linked to their land possessions; now their place is taken by a class of professional navigators, of a different social extraction, which may be described as lower-middle class, for whom maritime and trading activity is a means to social promotion. In the latter case, with the end of the age of personal relations between high-ranking figures in the manner of Demaratus, the developing urban communities, as in the case of the Etruscan cities mentioned above—though there the aristocratic presence continues to be strong even though they have to come to terms with the incipient political structures—create specially marked-out and controlled places for the activity of trade. The first guarantor of the relationship between the community and the foreigners who come to exchange their goods is the deity, as is attested by the statuettes and dedications from Gravisca exhibited here. This cult leads to the development of three particular practices: that of offering to the gods a tenth of the sale of the goods, an archaic form of taxation and of storing resources under divine protection; that of *hierodulia*, which served the same end through the sacred prostitution of women who are "slaves of the deity", whose income goes to the sanctuary itself; and that of the institution of *asylia*, which guarantees the salvation and protection of anyone who appeals to the deity.

This phase corresponds to a period of extraordinary expansion in the Tyrrhenian world. All the processes that had begun in the previous period now seem to be multiplied and intensified in the context of a predominant Hellenization, which introduces artisan technologies and methods, skilled labor, lifestyles, and goods that are no longer aimed solely at the upper levels of aristocratic luxury, cultural models, and forms of knowledge including the familiarization and spread of Greek myth.

The picture described above implies, as we have seen, a massive flow into the Tyrrhenian area, especially into the southern coastal cities, of navigators, merchants, and craftsmen of foreign origin who in different ways are welcomed and integrated into the local communities. There is a great social mobility which is open both in the horizontal and in the vertical direction. The ties of hospitality which are established between *gentes* of different ethnic groups are attested by the ivory tesserae which serve as passports, like that of Arath Spuriana Silqetenas found in the Forum Boarium which probably concerns a Tarquinian personage linked to some *gentes* in Rome, or that found at Carthage in which a person gives his name in Etruscan: "mi Puinel Karthazie" (I am the Carthaginian Punic). At the same time craftsmen such as carpenters, bronze-workers, potters, painters, and architects are brought in to meet the need for skilled labor and for the technical knowledge necessary to the rapid social and monumental development of the city and the urbanized aristocracies. Literary traditions such as those relating to Tarquinius Priscus, son of the foreigner Demaratus and a Tarquinian woman, or Servius Tullius, son of a slave girl, also reflect the possibility of a rapid social climb. The onomastic data of the necropolis of Crocefisso del Tufo in Orvieto attest to the presence of Etruscan names as well as Latin, Umbrian, Sabine and Celtic ones, as we also find in the cases of Tarquinia, Caere and Veii. The picture described above mainly concerns the southern and coastal area of

Etruria. From the second half of the sixth century, new factors arise to modify significantly the areas of exchange, thanks to the emergence of the Po Valley area. Here the Etruscan presence seems strong and structured from the Villanovan phase onward, as is illustrated by the history of Felsina-Bologna. In the second half of the sixth century B.C. the Po Valley is involved in a second wave of colonization which, as well as including groups which had already settled here previously, seems strongly stimulated by the cities of inland northern Etruria such as Perugia, Chiusi and Volsinii-Orvieto. If it seems plausible to link this second colonization with a demographic drive mainly originating from inland Etruria, another crucial element is the new importance of the Adriatic coast, where we see the rise in the space of a few decades first of the Aeginetan colony of Adria, then of the port-emporium of Spina which is closely linked to Felsina. Although the development of this new and important trade route may have been influenced by the difficulties encountered by Tyrrhenian Etruscan trade in the aftermath of the battle of the Sardinian Sea, a decisive factor must have been Athens and her search for new markets partly, but not exclusively, linked to the supply of cereals. The amazing quantity of Athenian pottery imported to the Po Valley, mainly by Aeginetan merchants, who from about 530 B.C. prevail over the previous Graeco-Oriental carriers in the southern emporia as well, is a significant indication of this. The Po Valley therefore finds itself at the center of busy trade routes linking areas of the Greek world, inland and coastal Etruria and the transalpine world. In addition to the distribution of cereals, wine, oil, metals, wood, and slaves, the Po Valley, the setting for the myths of Phaeton and the Insulae Electrides, is also one of the crucial points in the distribution of the amber which flows from eastern central Europe into the Po Valley markets and onward, especially to the Italic world and Greece. The wealth of Spina may be illustrated by the report (Strabo, VIII, 6, 16) of the dedication of a *thesauros* at Delphi, a report which includes this dedication among those which were made as a result of the tithe taken from the war booty; this is probably another allusion to piracy.

As has already been mentioned, in connection with the prevalence of Aeginetan merchants in the Tyrrhenian and Adriatic trading areas from about 530 B.C. we now also find an absolute dominance of Athenian products, which strengthens from 560 A.D. to the end of the century. The Etruscan area is clearly attracted by all the main Athenian workshops, which produce first in the black-figure technique, then in the red-figure, passing through an intermediate mixed technique. The importance of the Etruscan markets in Athenian eyes is attested by productions which from about 530 B.C. appear to be made to order, so that vases are produced in the Athenian style with a shape borrowed from the Etruscan repertory, especially that of the buccheri and the metal vases. This is the case, for example, with the Nikosthenic amphoras, which were made in the workshop of Nikosthenes but are modeled on the Caeretan bucchero. On the Attic pottery of this period the mark *SOS* or *SO* indicates that the same Sostratus mentioned earlier imports to Etruria huge quantities of specially produced pottery. The great wave of Athenian products ceases with the first quarter of the fifth century in the southern Etruscan area, and in mid-century in the northern area, probably under the influence of a flow of trade linked with the Po Valley, where the importation of Athenian products lasts until the beginning of the fourth century B.C.

The whole world of the archaic *emporia* begins to decline at the end of the sixth century B.C., when the urban communities take definite shape. While it is true that the Graeco-Oriental commercial carriers which had been prevalent until that time falter as a result of the Persian advance toward the Greek cities of Asiatic Ionia, even more important was the fact that within the cities there was a radical change in the destination of wealth. As is shown by the exemplary cases of the disappearance or drastic reduction of the grave goods in the necropolises of Latium and the new broadly egalitarian structuring of the necropolises of Volsinii and Cerveteri, the aristocratic *tryphe* now seems to be significantly diminished. The city embraces within itself the points of exchange, which pass from the control of the deities to that of the public magistrates, from the emporium sanctuary to the public square. A consequence of all this is a new and more restrictive law on exchange, which seems to be regulated by real international treaties, as in the celebrated case of the Romano-Carthaginian treaty struck in 509 B.C. or that of the Etrusco-Carthaginian treaty which, according to Aristotle, specified the respective areas of influence. Moreover, the demand for skilled labor and technical knowledge activated by the previous expansion now collapsed, and all those processes of integration and social mobility that had been initiated in the past were brusquely interrupted. For the merchants who come to these new public points of exchange, norms were drawn up limiting their stay to the time necessary for making sacrifices and taking on supplies of water. The same process is noticeable at Gravisca with the restrictions on foreign merchants perceptible at the beginning of the fifth century B.C.

But the situation of the southern Etruscan cities seems to be aggravated still further by defeat off Cumae in 474 B.C. at the hands of the Syracusans, who occupy Pithecoussai and move on to control the sea routes of central-southern Etruria. It is certain, however, that the Upper Tyrrhenian between the sixth and the third centuries B.C. remains firmly in Etruscan hands, as is shown by the control exercised by Aleria on the Corsican front and by Populonia, Pisa and also Genoa—which had a large community of Etruscan-speaking inhabitants—along the north Etruscan coast, especially toward Massalia and the Celtic world.

A final observation must be made concerning the use and introduction of coinage. Bronze was an ancient vehicle of value and wealth linked with concrete objects, as we see in hoards from the Bronze Age onward or in the desposition of bronze artifacts in sanctuaries and tombs. The presence of *aes rude* (raw bronze) in funerary depositions is also connected with the concrete value of the metal. A well-known passage of Pliny the Elder gives us a glimpse of the beginning of a different situation (*Naturalis historia*, XXXIII, 43): "The king Servius Tullius was the first to stamp bronze. Timaeus tells that in the previous age at Rome raw bronze was used." Indeed from the middle of the sixth century we have archaeological knowledge of bronze ingots with the stamp known as that of the "ramo secco" which probably facilitated the subdivision of the piece into definite measures. The stamp indicates the evolution of the idea that an authority guarantees the value of the metal, evidently in response to the requirements of the long-distance emporium trade which certainly required more extensive forms of guarantee of exchange than those of the previous phase.

The contact with the Greek world, especially in the southern and coastal Etruscan area, must have introduced the concept of coinage, though coins seem to have had a very limited circulation in the Tyrrhenian points of exchange. Between the sixth and the fifth centuries B.C. we see the appearance of coin issues which are related chiefly to two areas: the Metalliferous district and Vulci. The significance of these issues, which show marked variations in weight and figurative symbols, is uncertain, but we cannot rule out the possibility that they may have been coinages linked to kin groups which attempt by this means to mediate the novelties now emerging in the enlarged urban communities and in the wider dimension of trade.

The beginning of a regular coinage in silver is attributable to Populonia in the second half or the middle of the fifth century B.C., and includes a unique coin type with the Gorgon and the value sign X. The official mint which strikes coins for the town of Populonia places itself on the same level as the ongoing process with respect to the control to which the various towns subject the spaces and agents of the trade networks. Like the places of exchange, which are now incorporated and regulated within the town walls, the town regulates the measure of value by introducing the abstract instrument of coinage. [M.M.]

29. Three small bronzes
second half of ninth century B.C.
Rome, Museo di Villa Giulia
from Vulci, Cavalupo necropolis, Tomb of the Small Sardinian Bronzes

Found in Cavalupo, in a well-tomb with stone box, the grave goods belong to a high-ranking woman and contained, along with the three small bronzes imported from Sardinia, rich personal adornments featuring, aside from a lozenged belt and many *fibulae*, items in gold and bronze.

1

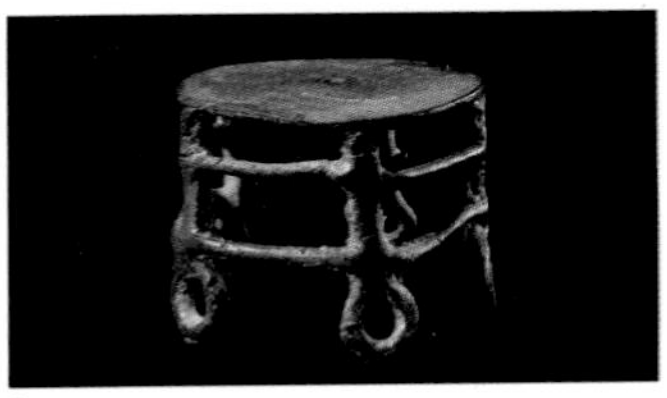
2

• *1. Human figure statuette*
bronze, solid cast
h 13.5 cm
inv. 59917
The figure, perhaps female, is wearing a conical headgear, out of which appear two thick braids, a long vest, the back of which is pointed, and sandals with thick soles. From her right forearm, wrapped in a sheath, hangs a globular element, on her left there is a folded elliptical element, perhaps made of leather.
• *2. Ritual "stool"*
bronze, solid cast
h 3 cm
inv. 55918
Maybe identifiable as such, it consists of a round table with central hole resting on five legs ending with loops, connected by round-section cross-bars
• *3. Miniature basket*
bronze, solid cast
h 3.3 cm

3

inv. 55919
Inspired by wickerwork models, it is complete with cover, platter and inside shutter, that was attached to the basket by strings (?) passing through the respective handles,

Fugazzola Delpino 1985, pp. 64–65, 2.5.2,4-6
[A.M.M.S.]

30. Bowl of Phoenician make
ca. 675 B.C.
gilt silver, reconstructed
h 3.1 cm; diam. 18.7 cm
Vatican City, Museo Gregoriano Etrusco, inv. 20364
from Cerveteri, necropolis of Sorbo, Regolini-Galassi Tomb

The bowl belongs to a group of precious vessels typical of the burial goods of the aristocratic tombs of Cerveteri, Palestrina and Pontecagnano of the Orientalizing period. Identification of the area of production of the silver bowls found in Italy is still under discussion, several theories locating it diversely between Cyprus, Syria and Phoenicia. During a recent restoration, the modern copper support was removed, revealing an unknown inscription, faintly incised on the outer wall of the bowl under the edge of the rim: larϑia velϑurus, that appears to have been done at a later time than that of the making of the vase. The first element of the inscription is an individual name, no longer undisputably identified as a male pronoun with the morpheme -ia of the Archaic genitive. The second part of the inscription constitutes an absolute novelty owing to the fact that, for the first time, we have a binomial onomastic formula, with the second element declined in the genitive, consisting of the male name Velϑur. The most linear interpretation could identify in Velϑurus a patronym. Yet we cannot neglect the conjecture that the individual name, the patronym, might have been turned into a gentilitial, in the manner of other Caeretan inscriptions that by the first quarter of the seventh century B.C. document the introduction of a bimembral formula. So in this new inscription we could see the beginning of the use of the *nomen* at an embrionic stage, in an aristocratic milieu undergoing deep transformations, and up to now seeming to tend to be refractory to an innovation that would mainly be asserted during the second half of the seventh century B.C.

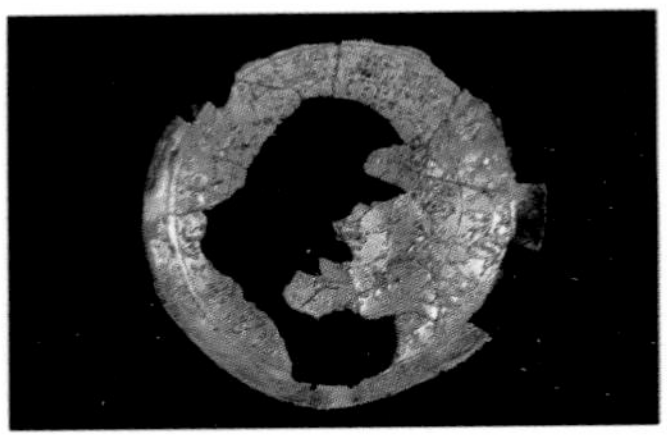

Pareti 1947, pp. 313–14, n. 322, tav. XLIII; Strøm 1971, pp. 124 ff.; Woytowitsch 1978, p. 85, n. 220; Hölbl 1979 I 308, fig. 11; II, 38, n 117, pl. 169 a–b; Canciani 1979, pp. 3 ff.; Rathje 1980, p 10, B9, fig 16; Culican 1982, pp. 23 ff.; Cristofani, Martelli 1983, p. 102, fig. 39, p. 264, n. 39; Markoe 1985, p. 197, fig. A, pp. 296–97; Hermary 1987, pp. 179–94, p. 185, n. 12; Buranelli, Sannibale 1998, pp. 424–26, n. 235, figs. 262–63; Buranelli, Sannibale forthcoming. [F.B., M.S.]

31. Bowl with incised decoration
ca. 630–620 B.C.
bronze; two small lacunas,one in the middle, the other below the animal frieze. The one handle, that was fastened by three holes visible on the edge of the bowl, is lost
h 4.4 cm; diam. 24 cm
Beaulieu-sur-Mer., Villa Kérylos

This bowl, often mentioned in studies devoted to the Orientalizing period, belonged to the collection of Count Tyszkiewicz. But until very recently its only reference was a drawing in Fröhner 1892 (pl. XV). Sold with the collection in 1898 without any further mention, the bowl was just recently rediscovered among the objects conserved at Villa Kérylos. The chiseled decoration is composed of a prevailingly ornamental central motif and an animal frieze passing to the left, in the area near the rim of the bowl.The center features a rose with six petals, whose circumference adjoins six matching petals, the intervals being filled with dots. The outer edge of the medalion is surrounded by a frieze of small uneven tongues, from which issue six protomes of griffins, with open beak and darting tongue. Between two rows of double dots arranged above and below the frieze, ten pairs of animals or fabulous monsters are striding to the left: two sphinxes, two deers, two panthers, two wild goats, two lions. These motifs and this imagery have been endlessly discussed. Their mixed style led some to propose a Corinthian origin (H. Payne and E. Kunze), whereas others (A. Furtwängler, F. Villard) describe the bowl as a production from Eastern Greece, in the spirit of the "wild goats" style. Yet a third interpretation, defended as of 1963 by Fr. Hiller, presents the work as a creation of Etruscan art, in which the co-existence of the two previous styles is easily explained. In fact the central motif, the sequence of the figures of the frieze, where certain details (the face of the sphinxes, the lions' heads) cannot be described in purely Greek terms, the incision technique, the place where the bowl was found, Sovana, argue in favor of that last suggestion. The bowl belong to the production of workshops influenced by Greek pottery. The decorations and the technique remind us of bucchero vases. The difference between a Greek work made for an Etruscan clientele and an Etruscan work formed under the strong influence of the Greek manner is very slight.

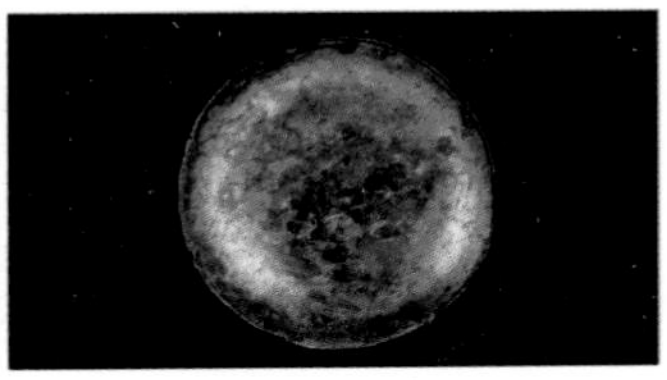

Hiller 1963, p. 27-37 Pasquier forthcoming. [A.PO.]

32. Handle of flabellum
ivory with incised decoration
conserved h 17 cm
Florence, Museo Archeologico, inv. 89274
from Populonia, Tomb of the Flabelli

Today the traces of polychromy are no longer visible, while, owing to the flood, the fragments of applied goldleaf have disappeared as well. Lacunose, heavily damaged surface. Hardly anything is left of the chiseled decoration : the upper edge of the chiton with a band with ovuli and lace, the belt tight at the waist that presents like motifs and the sleeve of the vest on the right arm outstretched along the side holding a hem. On the back you can still clearly see lines of the braided hair, rendered with thin incisions. The type of the vest, the rendering of the decoration, might relate the statuette to a workshop located in eastern Greece at Samos or Rhodes, whose production in the second half of the seventh century B.C. is well-known. But the state of conservation makes a more thorough interpretation of the piece difficult.

Minto, 1932 c. 321.; Huls 1957, n. 53 p. 60.
[A.Ro.]

33. Small New Year's flask
Saitic period
light green faïence
h 18 cm
Rome, Palazzo dei Conservatori, Musei Capitolini, inv. 544
provenance unknown, former Castellani Collection

Out-turned lip, cylindrical neck, passing handle decorated with ibex head with short beard. On the shoulder and the two sides, a wreath consisting of six rows of necklace beads, the first and the last in the shape of willow leaves, the fourth in spirals, separated by five rows of three lines each. Incised inscriptions colored dark-blue: "W3djt nbt nfrwB3stt wpj nfrt nb.s" (I swallow the lady of beauty and Bastet a happy new year to their patron); "Imn (') Pth wpj rnptnfrt n nb.s" (Amun and Ptah a happy new year to their patron).

Von Bissing 1931, pp. 531, ns. 6–8, pls. XXVII, 5; Bosticco 1952, pp. 37 ff. n. 544; Höbl 1979, pp. 20, ns. 70, pls. 8.
[C.Z.]

34. Alabastron with relief decoration
seventh–sixth century B.C.
faïence; white impasto; light blue glaze
h 10.8 cm; diam. 6.6 cm
Hannover, Kestner-Museum, inv. 1931
Cerveteri

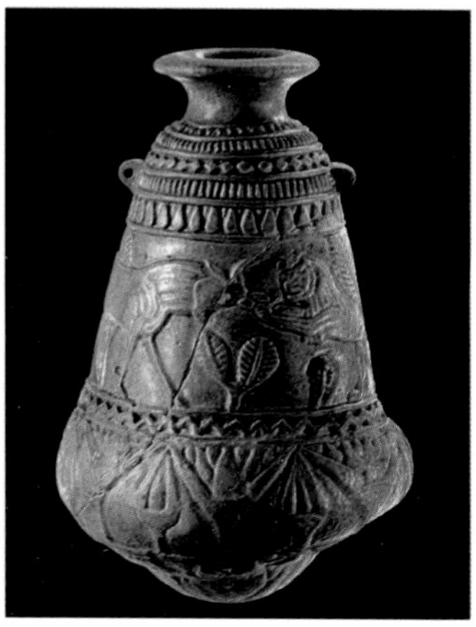

By its technique, style, decoration and color it belongs to a late-Egyptian context, as well as the execution and the theme of the fight between lions and bulls, while the gazelles are a typical motif of Middle Eastern art. It is conceivably a vessel by Eastern Greek craftsmen (Rhodes?).

Hölbl 1981, pp. 46–48; Busz, Gercke 1999, pp. 359–60, n. 191.
[A.S.V.]

35. Scarab
first half of eighth century B.C.
grey stone
16.5 x 13 mm
Rome, Museo di Villa Giulia, inv. 3121.
from Falerii, necropolis of Montarano, Tomb 17

Monstrous two-headed creature with hooked tail between two leafy plant elements with herringbone stalk. Between the two heads a vertical element with trident tip. The exergue decorated with dashes. Attributed to the Lyre-player Group.

Boardman, Buchner 1966, p. 25 n. 43, figs. 30, 43, 33.
[C.Z.]

36. Pseudo-scarab
first quarter of seventh century B.C.
l 1.5 cm; w 1 cm; h 0.5 cm; surface splintered, greenish-crème colored talc paste
Florence, Museo Archeologico, inv. 116826
from Populonia, Poggio della Porcareccia, pit tomb with circle of rough stones, 1930

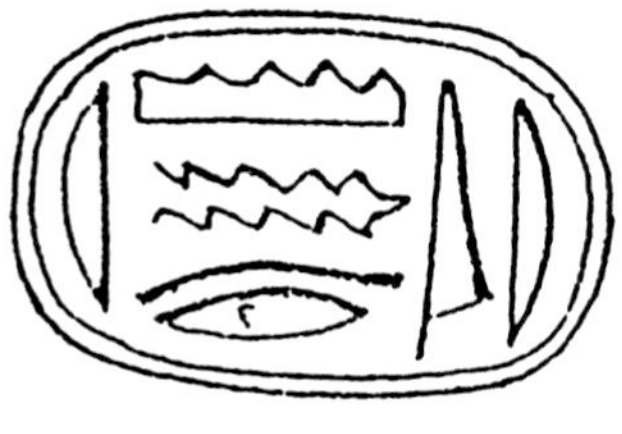

Pseudo-scarab with longitudinal passing-hole. On the base, inside a linear frame, cartouche.

Minto 1932, c. 378, fig. 44;
Bissing 1940, 1940, p. 381, tav. XXXIV, 76.
[S.B.]

37. Geometric bowl
ca. mid-eighth century B.C.
fine-grained brownish-red clay, crème slip; brown glaze, reddish in certain places owing to poor firing
reconstituted from fragments and integrated
h 6.9 cm; diam. of rim 11.8 cm; diam. bottom 6.1 cm
Florence, Museo Archeologico
from Tarquinia

The bowl, decorated in the space between the handles with a metope with two meander elements in sets on hatched ground delimited by two groups of vertical lines, has been attributed, on the grounds of the technical features of the clay and the glaze as well as of the decorative morphology and syntax, to a Euboean workshop of the Late-Geometric period. Its chronology around mid-eighth century B.C. or just after can back up to a certain degree the referring of the bowl to the burial goods of tomb 140 of Selciatello di Sopra, that contained within rich banquet furnishings another like bowl, now lost (Bartoloni 1986, p. 45. For the tomb see Hencken 1968, p. 138 f.; *L'etruria mineraria* 1985, p. 57 s.); nonetheless the provenance from a precise context remains uncertain. Aside from that question, the bowl belongs to the small number of imported Greek vases recovered from the centers of southern coastal Etruria during the evolved stage of the Villanovan period, whose circulation in the mid-Tyrrhenian area is part of the picture of the contacts and exchanges the Greek world, and especially Euboea, entertained during the eighth century B.C. with the wealthy centers of southern Etruria.

Civiltà degli etruschi 1985, p. 75 n. 2.9.1; Paoletti 1986, pp. 407 ff., figs. 1–2; Bartoloni 1986, p. 45; d'Agostino 1988, pp. 45 ff.
[S.B.]

38. Tessera hospitalis
ca. mid-sixth century B.C.
ivory
h 4 cm
Rome, Antiquarium Comunale, inv. 28776
from Rome, sacred area of Sant'Omobono

Small ivory sheet in the shape of a crouching lion; in the back part, flat, is incised the right-to-left inscription: "araz silqetanas spurianas," that can be interpreted as "Araz Silketena of Spuriana."

Messineo 1983, pp. 3–4, figs. 1-2; *Civiltà degli Etruschi* 1985, p. 129 n. 5.4; CIE II, 2, n. 8602.
[C.Z.]

39. Nuraghic incense-boat
late seventh century B.C.
bronze
h 9.3 cm; l 21 cm
Tarquinia, Museo Archeologico, temporary inv. II / 4
from the sanctuary of Gravisca

Oil-lamp shaped like a small oblong, flat-bottomed boat, with tall relief band along the edge; on the prow schematic bovine protome, with narrow muzzle, long horns curved backward, semispherical ears; nearly at the middle of the length two small bow rods attached to the edge, that connect with and end in a vertical rod with a suspension ring, on which is placed a bird facing the stern.

Torelli, Boitani, Lilliu et al. 1971, pp. 289 ff., fig. 2; Torelli 1971, pp. 44–67; Gras 1985, p. 138; Tronchetti 1988, p. 72.
[F.C.]

40. Statuette of armed Aphrodite
580–570 B.C.
solid cast bronze; cold-processing
h 9 cm
Tarquinia, Museo Archeologico, inv. 72/10674
from the sanctuary of Gravisca, edifice "gamma"

Upper part of standing Aphrodite, with Corinthian helmet, out of which six braids fall down her back and four on her chest, where they follow the shape of her breasts; long short-sleeved vest held tight at the waist by a belt; right arm raised, probably to brandish a spear, left arm lacunose.

Torelli 1977, p. 433; Torelli 1981, pp.180–84; *Civiltà degli Etruschi* 1985, p. 184, n.7; Bonghi Jovino 1986, p. 252, G2, fig. 247; Flemberg 1991, p. 43; Camporeale 1992, p. 121. [F.C.]

41. Statuette of armed Aphrodite
580–560 B.C.
solid cast bronze; cold-processing
Tarquinia, Museo Archeologico, inv. 75/18896
from the sanctuary of Gravisca, edifice "gamma"

Standing Aphrodite, with Corinthian helmet, out of which six braids fall down her back and four on her chest, where they follow the shape of her breasts; long vest held tight at the waist by a belt, with short sleeves with relief hem and a relief band along her hips ; right arm raised, probably to brandish a spear, the left folded in front of her chest, to hold the shield, lost.

Torelli 1977, p. 433; Torelli 1981, pp. 180–84; Bonghi Jovino 1986, p. 252, G2, fig. 247; Flemberg 1991, p. 43; Camporeale 1992, p. 121, fig. 58.
[F.C.]

42. Fragment of Ionian bowl
550–530 B.C.
clay; black glaze
Tarquinia, Museo Archeologico, inv. 72/10697
from Gravisca, edifice "gamma"

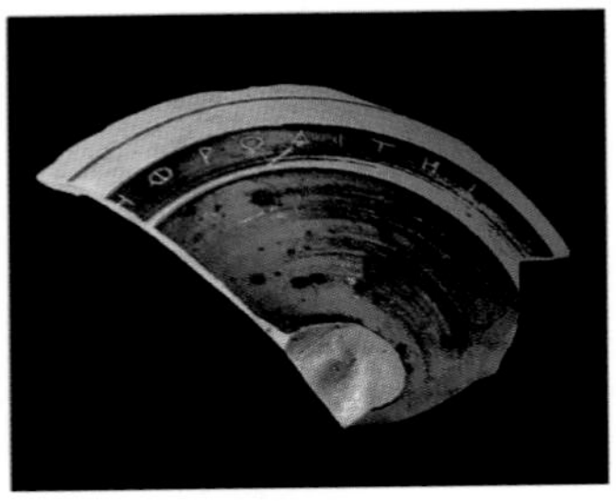

Foot of a type-B3 Ionian bowl, with dedicatory inscription in Greek to Aphrodite: [T] ηφποαιτηι.

Torelli 1982, p. 310, n. 34; *Civiltà degli Etruschi* 1985, p. 181 n. 7.1.1.1; *Gli Etruschi e l'Europa* 1992, p. 121, n. 59.
[C.Z.]

43. Fragment of black-figure Attic bowl
530–500 B.C.
orange clay; black glaze
Tarquinia, Museo Archeologico, inv. 73/25311.
from Gravisca, edifice "beta"

Foot and bottom of black-figured Attic bowl; on the lower surface of the foot inscription in Greek to Demeter: "ΔΗΜΗΤΡΟΣ."

Torelli 1982, p. 311 n. 41; *Civiltà degli Etruschi* 1985, p. 181 n. 7.1.1.3; *Gli Etruschi e l'Europa* 1992, p. 121 n. 61.
[C.Z.]

44. Fragment of Attic bowl
550–530 B.C.
orange clay; black glaze
h 2.8 cm; w 11.5 cm
Tarquinia, Museo Archeologico, inv. 74/8387.
from Gravisca, edifice "gamma"

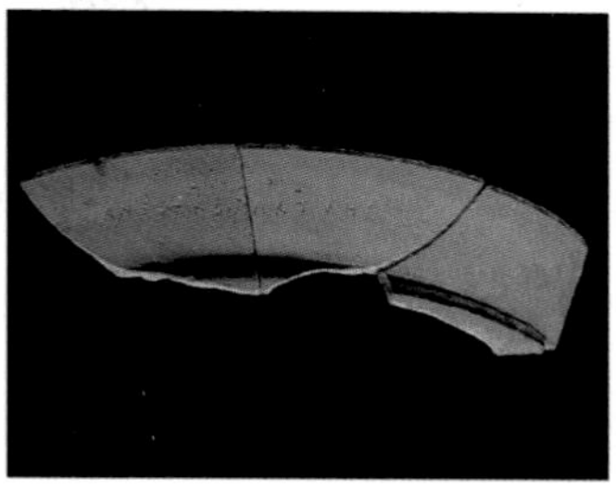

Fragments of lip of *Lip-cup*, with dedicatory inscription from Pakytes to Hera: "ΗΡΗΙ ΑΝΕΘΗΚΕ ΠΑΚΤΥΗΣ."

Torelli 1982, p. 310 n. 25; *Civiltà degli Etruschi* 1985, p. 181 n. 7.1.1.2; *Gli Etruschi e l'Europa* 1992, p. 121 n. 60.
[C.Z.]

45. Fragment of Laconian krater
third quarter of sixth century B.C.
light-brown clay; crème-colored slip; black glaze
h 3.2 cm
Tarquinia, Museo Archeologico, inv. 72/23122
from Gravisca, edifice "gamma," east of room I

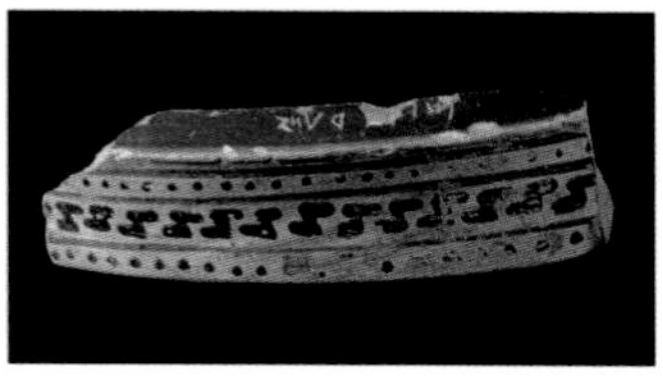

Vertical lip. Frieze with *sigma* between two lines, included between three rows of dots. On the horizontal rim incised inscription: "mi [tu]runs."

Boitani 1990, p. 47 n. 48; figs. 84, 85; *Gli Etruschi e l'Europa* 1992, p. 122 n. 63.
[C.Z.]

46. Black-figure Laconian bowl
550–540 B.C.
light-brown clay; crème-colored slip; black glaze; purple-red glaze in the overpaintings
h of the vessel 6.5 cm; reconstructed diam. 17.6 cm
Tarquinia, Museo Archeologico, inv. II/7762
from Gravisca, edifice "alpha," room A

Distinct lip, semi-spherical bowl, stick-handles placed horizontally. On the outside, reserved lip; beside the handles palmettes with red center and crown of incised parallel lines; on the vessel red band amid sets of black lines, rows of rays, two purple bands, each one between sets of black lines, rows of pomegranates alternating with dots. Inside, lip painted black; in the vessel Cadmus battling the dragon in front of a temple. Attributed to the Painter of the Horsemen.

Boitani 1990, pp. 35–37 n.18; figs. 33–35; *Gli Etruschi e l'Europa* 1992, p. 120 n. 52.
[C.Z.]

47. Two aurei worth twenty-five
second half of fifth century B.C.
gold
weight 1.41 grs.
Florence, Museo Archeologico, inv. 36246
provenance unknown

Lion head on right; behind it mark of value; reverse blank. Attributed to Populonia.

Tondo, *La monetazione*, in Maggiani 1985, pp. 168 ff., n. 225; Catalli 1990, p. 43.
[F.C.]

48. Small coin treasure
Florence, Museo Archeologico, inv. 34144–34446
from Populonia, locality Porcareccia, 1939

The most outstanding of the small treasures of Etruscan coins found in the course of the activity for the reuse of the iron dross left over by Etruscan processing. A first group (565 pieces), probably coming from a black glazed vase might constitute the original, authentic nucleus, to which another 70 pieces were added, in all probability belonging to other finds. The finding of the vase underneath the iron dross, and the estimation of the conclusion of the activity of the Etruscan industrial district that had brought about the accumulation of the dross, would allow us to date the burial of the treasure to a period not preceding the second quarter of the third century B.C.

Scamuzzi 1941, pp. 141 ff.; Petrillo 1976–77, pp. 69 ff. [F.Ca.]

49. Small boat vase
Villanovan II B
reddish-brown clay.
h 7.5 cm; l 22 cm; w 8.6 cm
Tarquinia, Museo Archeologico, inv. RC 249
from Tarquinia, Monterozzi, well tomb with knobbed-bell helmet and candelabra

Indistinct rim; prow with bird's head appendage, to which must have been applied bronze eyes; flat bottom.

Hencken 1968, p. 331, fig 329 c.
[C.Z.]

50. Oinochoe with ships and fishes
Italo-Geometric, 700–675 B.C.
polished clay, with numerous black and micaceous particles; dark red, opaque glaze. On the wheel
h 348 cm, diam. 21 cm
Museum of Art and Archaeology, University of Missouri-Columbia, 71.114
provenance unknown

The *oinochoe* has an oval body on a small flared, ringed foot, a high cylindrical neck and trilobate mouth, a ribbon-handle with central rope-like decoration from the mouth to the shoulder. The decoration on the body is arranged in three bands: the lower band has three wide wavy lines; in the middle band five ships are represented, separated by pendant rays, a tiny fish between the two ships to the right of the handle and a ray rising from the bottom. On the shoulder three roughly-drawn fish, but with a detailed scale motif on the body, swimming toward the right. Four rays come downward separating the fish, while one climbs on the right of the handle. A latticed motif with neat stripes adorns the neck below and above. The mouth of the vase is painted in full color on the outside and on the upper part of the inside. Thin vertical stripes adorn the handle. The ships, with curved rudders and hulls, are sailing from right to left with unfurled sails, some have rams on the prow, three on the stern have railings surrounding the raised platform for the helmsman, typical of Greek and Italian ships. On one ship, above the railing, perhaps the grip of the rudder with its tiller is figured. The ropes are schematically drawn and the sails do not look like real sails : the painter is more interested in a pleasing design than in a realistic representation of the ships (some of which without masts). The artist was called the Painter of the Palms, and two other vases by his hand have been found in Tarquinia. A fourth vase, certainly his, is conserved in the National Maritime Museum, Haifa, Israel.

Muse, Annual of the Museum of Art and Archaeology 1972, 6, 5; CVA *Tarquinia*, pl. 11.4; Biers, Humphreys 1977, pp. 153–56; Overby 1982, p. 32, n. 77; Hagy 1986, 15, p. 227, fig. 16; Dik 1981, 43 (n.s. 8), p. 73; Cristofani 1983, p. 23, fig. 9; Cristofani 1987, p. 43, pl. 111,1; Martelli 1987, pp. 79, 253, n. 24; Bruni 1994, p. 324, n. 4.
[J.B.]

51. Stamnoid olla
ca. mid-seventh century B.C.
scarcely purified yellowish-brown clay, pale yellow slip; dark brown glaze decoration
a restored handle; glaze damaged in many places
h 35.8 cm; dia. rim 18.2 cm; diam. foot 14.3 cm
Brussels, Musées Royaux d'Art et d'Histoire inv. A.3949
provenance unknown

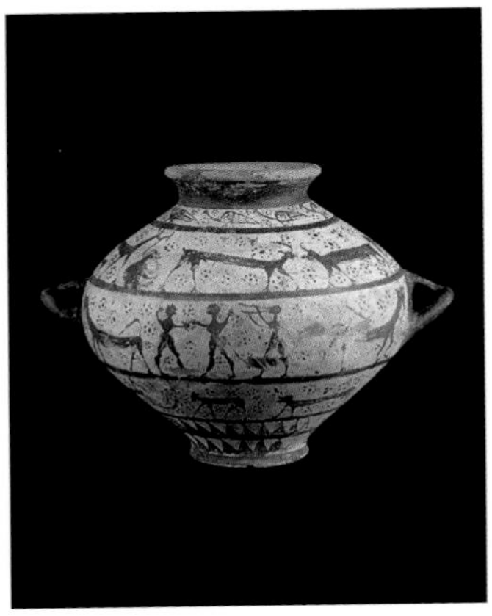

Stamnoid olla with big globular body tending to the biconical, tall flared lip and small trunco-conical foot, stick-handles with semicircular grip, placed at the widest part of the body and fastened to the base of the shouilder by an arched stick. Lip, foot and handle entirely glazed. On the body four friezes of uneven heights separated by a short horizontal band with a thick overpainted purple line in the middle, on the base two series, one on top of the other, of vertical rays. Right under the lip, eight birds gradient left. On the shoulder, two goats and two stags opposed separated by a deer and by a deer feeding a fawn followed by a seated figure with a theriomorphic head, with arms and legs extended forward and holding something (?), his neck attached by a rope to a vertical element hanging from above. In the area between the handles, two opposing pugilists followed by an aulete facing them, placed between two gradient panthers facing the handles and on the other side, a grazing goat between two gradient panthers also facing the handles. Below a long serpent-shaped monster is assailing a ship on whose sides are represented three gradient birds follwed by a procession of animals. Reserved spaces filled with dotted rosettes.
The olla has been convincingly attributed to the Painter of Civitavecchia, an apparently isolated decorator, active in the last thirty years of the seventh century B..C. perhaps in the area of Cerveteri, who seems to have a preference for themes and subject close to the Etruscan world and characterized by a formal language, not indifferent to subgeometric influences, who clearly stands out from the prevailingly Hellenizing and late-Orientalizing matrix of the ceramography of his time (on the painter cfr. Martelli 1987, p. 20, p. 268 n. 45; Szilágyi 1993, pp. 42 ff.). The Brussels olla offers a clear illustration of these features with the insertion of the traditional animal friezes or particular motifs, like the boxing scene or the chained daimon, in all likelihood a non-anthropomorphic underground divinity that revisits a subject and an iconography already known in the third quarter of the eight century B.C. on the lid of the cinerary urn of the tomb XXII of the Olmo Bello of Bisenzio (here n. 15. Cf. Torelli 1997, p. 36, n. 97) and that fits perfectly within the thematic legacy of the painter, who seems to prefer motifs of the funerary ambit (Martelli 1987, p. 268; Szilágyi 1993, p. 51).
The scene on the lower register must also refer to a local saga, the poor state of conservation making it so very difficult to interpret that a scholar of the standing of J.G. Szilágyi, who published the vase, merely mentioned the birds in front of the sea monster's jaws. Even with these reservations, we might be able to identify in the remaining traces the silhouette of a ship (for Etruscan ships see Bonino 1985; Hagy 1986; Höckmann 1997) assailed at the stern by the monster according to a design that also goes back to a renowned Caeretan dish from tomb 65 of Acqua Acetosa Laurentina around the middle of the seventh century B.C. (*Florence* 1985, p. 227 n. 8.2 [with prev. bibl.]; Leach 1987, p. 22 n. 1; Martelli 1987, p. 263, n.39).

Szilágyi 1993, pp. 39 ff., figs. 1–4
[S.B.]

52. Hydria
520–510 B.C.
wheel-thrown, slip decorated earthenware with incised details
ht. to top of handles 52.1 cm; h. to rim 45.7 cm; diam. with handles 35.4 cm, diam. of rim 21.6 cm; diam. of foot 15.5 cm; max. diam. of body 29.6 cm
The Toledo Museum of Art; purchased with funds from the Libbey Endowment, gift of Edward Drummond Libbey; inv. 1892.134
from Karl Haug, Switzerland

On the neck, two nude youths. On the shoulder, a triton swims, holding a dolphin in one hand and a fish in the other. On the body, six man-dolphins dive into the sea; to the left curls a vine tendril; the image represents the final episode in the myth of the abduction of Dionysos, as told in the seventh *Homeric Hymn*. Pirates from the Thyrrhenian Sea kidnapped the young god. Aboard the ship, the bonds that held him magically fell from his hands and feet, wine flowed throughout the vessel, and vines grew around mast and oars. Dionysos, transformed into a lion, sprang at the captain. In fear, the pirates divided into the sea, and in mid-air were transformed into dolphins. It is this moment of metamorphosis that is depicted. One of the rare illustrations of this myth, this vase is the only Etruscan example and reflects the influence—in style and subject matter—of Ionian vase painters probably working in Vulci.

Boulter, Luckner 1984, fasc. 2 (ed. Toledo), fasc. 20 (ed. Mainz) tav. 90, pp. 14–6; Martelli 1987, n. 130, pp. 38, 311; Spivey, Rasmussen 1986, figs. 3–6; *Les Etrusques et l'Europe* 1992, n. 77, p. 124, repr. P. 53; Bonfante L. 1993, pp. 226–27, fig. 22; Boardman 1994, fig. 7.12, pp. 242, 243 n. 47; *Toledo treasures* 1995, 42; *LIMC*, VIII, pt. 1, p. 155, repr. vol. VIII, pt. 2, p. 115.
[P.J.W.]

53. Basins
late seventh–early sixth century B.C.
bronze
Soprintendenza Archeologica per la Toscana, Centro di Restauro
from the waters between Enfola and Capo Vite (Elba Island, Livorno); random find 1989

• 1. *Basin with beaded rim*
h 4.7 cm; diam. 29.5 cm
inv. 222501
Basin in cold-hammered bronze *lamina*. Bowl with a tronco-conical profile and slightly curved walls. Rim with separate lip with embossed decoration with a double row of small ashlar or "beads," bottom with plain *omphalos*. Chips on the lip; the metal is oxidized and corroded in several places. Belongs to a group of twenty-five exemplars drawn up in a net for trawl-net fishing; among them, twenty-four (invv. 222479/222497; 222499/222503), completely homogeneous in size and typology, are referable to a single form (form A).
• 2. *Basin with beaded rim*
h. 6 cm; diam. 35 cm
inv. 222498
Basin in cold-hammered bronze *lamina*. Bowl with a tronco-conical profile and slightly curved walls. Rim with separate lip with embossed decoration with a double row of small ashlar or "beads," bottom with *omphalos* inscribed in a round crown. Very lacunose and corroded, it is cracked and dented too.
By the shape and the decoration of the lip it is typologically close to the rest of the group, of which it constitutes a variant by the larger size and the structure of the *omphalos* on two levels (form B).

Corsi, Firmati 1998, pp. 148–54
[S.D.S.R.]

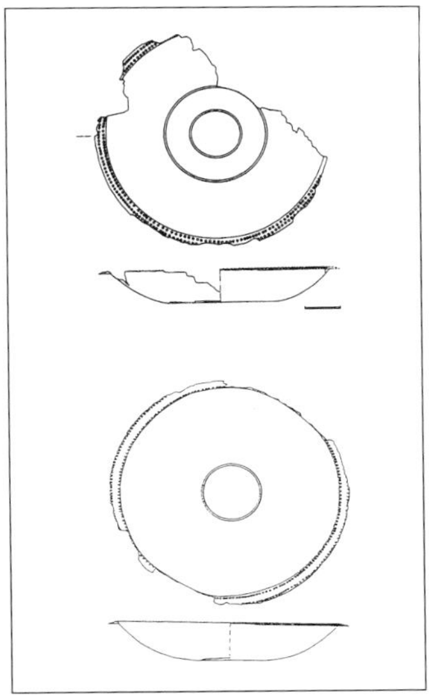

54. Tripod
cast bronze
h 62 cm
Le Cap d'Agde, Musée de l'Éphèbe, ME. 1171
from Le Cap dAgde, underwater excavations, deposit n. 28

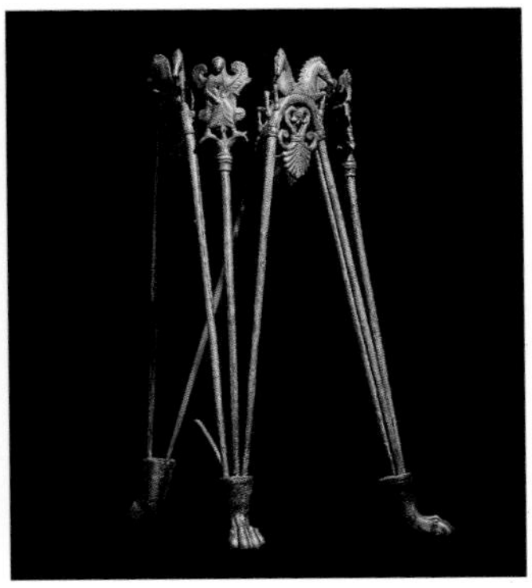

Tripod in cast bronze consisting of decorative elements connected by legs converging in three lion's claw feet.
The upper part is adorned with *appliques* formed by two alternating groups on the legs and the arches. The first is an archaic-style winged female figure, moving left above an open lotus flower. With her right hand she is raising her chiton, showing the tunic underneath. Above the arch, the other subject is a double horse protome. Below, on the intrados of the arch, an arabesque crowns an overturned palm frond. The elements have holes originally intended for rivets of a circle insuring cohesion and stability to the item. On the back of one of the subjects an incised letter might correspond to the ninth letter of the Etruscan alphabet.

Fonquerle 1986, pp. 111–19; Torelli 1986, pp. 120–21; Pomet 1987–88, p. 47; Berard 1989, pp. 37–38, 126; Berard n.d, p. 40
[O.B.-A.]

55. Dedication of the Tyrrhenians to Apollo
inscribed pedestal, perhaps base of a tripod
late sixth–early fifth century B.C.
gray calcareous stone
h 975 cm; l 408–455 cm; thickness 49–52 cm
Delphi, sanctuary of Apollo, between the Temple and the base of Gelo, MD1560

The pedestal, in the shape of a cippus, bears the inscription–on the upper frontal part-of a dedicatory epigram:
IV: aneqeka
V: opollo
VI: Turranoi
Those are the last words of an epigram that, in accordance with the formula of public dedications at Delphi, recalls the name of the persons who made the offering. The beginning of the verse is missing, where the gift should have been described. It has been assumed that the first missing words might have named a single donor: so it remains uncertain whether it was a private monument or a public dedication.
The Tyrrhenians adopted the Delphian alphabet; the shape of the letters and the punctuation allow us to date it to late sixth century–early fifth century. In the third century, under the original Archaic epigram and on the two other high sides of the cippus, an inscription was added bearing the list of the winners of the "Soteria," the music contest.
The rough surface of the right side and the presence of a peephole suggest it was in contact with a block below. Owing to this processing the Tyrrhenians' dedication can be reconstituted with two slabs (MD 4047, h 32 cm, l 107 cm, thick. 52 cm) placed on the sides of the cippus. On the top of the cippus there are one round hole and one for a rectangular pin: they were to hold the offering, in all probability a tripod. P. Almandry has suggested a reconstitution of a tripod of clear Etruscan style, very different from Attic and Boeotian ones, that would have been given by the Tyrrhenians to Delphi in the early fifth century B.C. Items displayed

on tripods, like candelabras for instance, are very common in Etruscan art. The inscribed Delphi cippus might have held a like offering, but the state of its conservation does not allow us to express a more explicit hypothesis.

Jaquemin, 1999, 335; Nachtergael, 1977, 479, 64-68; Flacelière, FD III 4, 124, 199, fig. 2, pl. XXII 1; Amandry, BCH 1987, 126.
[E.C.P.]

Warfare

Warfare, alongside agriculture and metalwork, is one of the great activities of the Etruscan world which are of major economic importance, as in the greater part of the ancient world. The Villanovan expansion, the second colonization of the Po Valley, the endemic warfare and raiding constantly carried out by the Etruscan princes and generals, the clashes between towns for the control of the territory, and maritime piracy, are so many examples of how military activity is part of the normal and common modes of acquisition of goods, men and land.
Moreover, warfare performs another important function, that of marking the rank and power of particular individuals. From the Villanovan phase the helmet-shaped earthenware and metal lids of cinerary urns, as well as the swords of various sizes, the spear points, the plates worn on the chest (hence their name, *kardiophylax*, "heartguard"), and the shields deposited among the grave goods, immediately indicate the military prowess of the dead man, which is linked with the economic function mentioned above in connection with the acquisition of wealth. These are bronze weapons which allude to hand-to-hand combat, the heroic duel.
As is typical of the ancient mentality, especially in these very early phases, warfare appears to be intimately linked with the general values of society which interweaves religious, economic, social and political values into a single strand. The archaic calendar of Rome gives us a picture not very dissimilar from what must have been the reality of Etruscan communities too, though allowance must be made for the differences between the various areas which persisted throughout Etruscan history. In effect warfare is part of a complex system which from March to October, i.e. in the summer months propitious to the most ancient kinds of warfare, places on the same level and on parallel paths the ritual certification of the growth of the young men, the times of human and natural reproduction, and the ceremonies of the purification of weapons before and after the military campaigns. The cycle of human activities reproduced by the relief groups of a well-known bronze cinerary urn from Bisenzio accords with this picture. What we know of the most ancient religion of the college of the Salii in Rome tells us once again of the bond that existed in the earliest phase between war, the initiation of the young, dances and rhythmic movements, and ritual combats. It is in this area, too, that we should look for the roots of the ceremony of the triumph, which will be fixed by the dynasty of the Etruscan kings at Rome in the sixth century B.C.
An important aspect of warfare, as has been mentioned, was defeating men and taking them prisoner, as is shown by the bronze cinerary urn from Bisenzio adorned with reliefs showing a row of warriors leading a man tied by the wrists. The fate of prisoners of war is determined by mechanisms and practices closely connected with the aristocratic ethic and the formation of social groups wider than the original families, the *gentes*. While in the context of existing relations between *aristoi*, based on the exchange of gifts and reciprocal ceremonies, the practice of ransoming could be activated in the case of high-ranking figures, as is attested by Homeric epic, in other cases the prisoners are sacrificed on the tomb of the *princeps* as a demonstration of the exalted rank of the dead man, on the heroic model of Patroclus, on whose tomb the Trojan prisoners were sacrificed. Another possibility is for a captured enemy to enter as slaves or *clientes* into the household of the lord after making the *deditio in fidem*, the request for protection from the lord according to the ties of *fides* in exchange for submission, work and the acceptance of the Lares of the new family, thus recognizing as his own the ancestors of the new *gens*.
The age of the full development of the Tyrrhenian aristocracies between the second half of the eighth and the sixth centuries B.C. sees a further enhancement of the signs relating to the military *virtus* of the lord, which is expressed in various directions. First of all, in the tombs of the aristocratic chiefs we find panoplies of weapons made of precious worked metal, often with more than one copy of each weapon, which at the same time form part of the display of a *tryphe* inspired by the Homeric models and the oriental world. Alongside this we see a process which is perceptible at various levels, and which may be described as the transition from a more specifically military significance of weapons to another which, while including the aspect of warfare, accentuates the symbolic dimension of the high rank held by those who possess the weapons. This process has been noted, for example, in the significance that the *hasta* acquires in the culture of Latium in the eighth century B.C., where it becomes the symbol of the rank and prerogatives proper to the *pater familias*; and in the multiplication of shields in a single deposition—which are therefore of no military use, not least because they are often represented in earthenware copies—and their exhibition or sculptural reproduction on the inner walls of the tomb, as an obvious status symbol. An analogous picture emerges in the use of one of the most spectacular prerogatives of aristocratic rank, the chariot, as can be seen from the examples from Castel San Mariano and Monteleone di Spoleto included in the exhibition. At present we know of about two hundred examples of chariots from funerary depositions between the middle of the eighth and the middle of the fifth century B.C. in the areas of Etruscan Latium, Picenum and Capena, as

well as harnesses of horses which allude to the chariot itself and numerous relief and pictorial figurations. While the woman usually uses the *carpentum*, a sort of gig on which one travels sitting down, the aristocratic warrior lord travels standing up in the *currus*, the two- or three- horse chariot (the four-horse variety is also attested, especially in figured scenes) driven by a charioteer. In contrast what is known of the Orient and the Celtic area, but in accord with the evidence from epic and from protohistorical Italy, the *princeps* does not fight in the chariot but gets into it followed and surrounded by his personal army, as attested by abundant iconographical evidence, then gets off at the place of battle while the charioteer remains in waiting. Thus the chariot has a largely ceremonial, parade significance: the lord gets into the chariot fully armed, at the moment of the *profectio*—echoing scenes featuring the Greek heroes such as the departure of Achilles—which will be followed by the victorious *reditus*. This assimilation to the heroic world is frequently expressed even more clearly by the reliefs that adorn the chariot itself, which show scenes of the feats of Achilles—as in the case of the Monteleone chariot shown here— or Theseus or Heracles, as paradigms of the initiatic and heroic achievement which leads to kingship. All this takes on clear triumphal aspects which are linked on the one hand with the funerary sphere, so that *profectio* and *reditus* allude respectively to the journey to the afterlife and the heroicization of the dead man, and on the other hand with the definitive canonization of the triumphal ceremony under the Tarquin dynasty at Rome, where the four-horse chariot becomes the chief attibute of Jupiter Capitolinus and the triumphant general who for a single day is identified with the god of the triumph. It has also been noted that the ivory *sella curulis* derived from a chariot seat, the prerogative of the republican magistrates of Rome, explains the description of the magistrates as *curules,* because they *curru vehebantur*, i.e. rode in a chariot (Festus, 43 L.), a final metamorphosis of the status linked with the chariot of the archaic *principes*.

Mention has already been made of the recurrence in Etruscan art of the image of the warrior *princeps* who gets into his chariot surrounded by foot soldiers and followed by a horseman or another person on the chariot, the last two figures being possibly identifiable as the successor of the chief. This kind of iconography raises a problem concerning the introduction into the Etruscan world and the significance there of the hoplite tactic which had been developed in the Greek area. As is well known, the phalanx of the hoplites armed with helmet, cuirass, graves, spear, sword, and a shield carried in such a way as to protect the comrade at one's side, presupposes a tactic which excludes the heroic duel and exploits the sheer driving force of the hoplites drawn up side by side several ranks deep. So in the Greek world the hoplite tactic seems to be connected with the formation of broadly democratic regimes which put the emphasis on the citizen-soldier who fights united with his comrades. In the Etruscan world Greek hoplite armor makes its appearance in the mid-seventh century B.C., while the ancient sources (Diodorus Siculus, XXIII, 2, 1; Inedita Vaticana, ch. 3; Athenaeus, VI, 273) state that the Romans learned the hoplite tactic from the Etruscans. Now the weapons broadly correspond to the models drawn from the Greek repertory, as in the case of the typical Corinthian helmets, and in particular they being to be made of iron, abandoning the bronze of which heroic arms were typically made. During the course of the sixth century B.C. the technique of cavalry warfare also develops, so we also see representations of hoplites on horseback.
The Etruscan iconographical evidence for the warrior who gets into his chariot followed by foot soldiers equipped with arms similar to those of hoplites suggests that this manner of fighting imported from the Greek world was indeed adopted by the Tyrrhenian *principes* and adapted to the requirements of personal armies dependent on the lord and chiefly made up of *clientes*. The existence of these personal armies is also known to us from another set of literary and archaeological evidence. In connection with Servius Tullius the sources, especially Tacitus (*Annales*, XI, 23 ff., to which should be added the text *Inscriptiones Latinae Selecatae*, 212 relating the emperor Claudius's speech reproduced on the Lyon tablet), describe Mastarna as being legate to his comrade Caelius Vibenna, the leader of an army which operates in Etruria until, for various reasons, he has to take refuge in Rome, occupying the hill which is named Caelius after the Etruscan general. On arriving in Rome with this army, Mastarna changes his name to Servius Tullius and becomes king. Similar conclusions can be drawn from the traditions concerning the settlement in Rome of the *princeps* Atta Clauso followed by his *gens* (Plutarch, *Poplicola*, 21), or the fateful episode of 478 B.C. when the Roman *gens* of the Fabii led its personal army against the Etruscans of Clusium and was annihilated. From the archaeological point of view, the inscription on the celebrated *lapis Satricanus* probably indicates the existence of *sodales* linked to a chief and a common cult.
The social drives which originated within the urban structures in the sixth and seventh centuries B.C., and which we see reflected, for example, in the egalitarian organization and the absence of *tryphe* in the Volsinii and Cerveteri necropolises of this period, certainly give a further impulse to the spread of hoplite tactics and armaments, a process clearly visible in the tomb of the Warrior from Vulci, the grave goods of which, dating from the last quarter of the sixth century B.C., are shown here in the exhibition. The scene of Achilles lying in ambush for Troilus on the plates in the grave goods alludes to a theme dear to the aristocratic ethic—that of human sacrifice—which is now reused by a wider class of citizens free of the original kin structures. The later reorganization which is noticeable in various cities in the 4th century B.C. and which aims at a widening of the civic bodies, though with obvious differences between the various regions of the Etruscan world, underlies the spread of the hoplite iconography, which we now see emerge even in standardized products such as cippi, urns and candelabra.
In this phase we can also distinguish two other elements which come to modify the characteristics of warfare in the Etruscan world. The archaeological evidence tells us that alongside the signs of the warrior there is an intensification of those related to athletic activity, a feature of the oldest aristocratic ethic of the Greek world which is now introduced via the channels that have been opened to Magna Graecia. Secondly, there is also an increase in the phenomenon of mercenary service, which involves individuals from the Etrusco-Latin area and in particular from the Italic world, and which is a response to the age-old economic differentiation between the developed and the marginal areas of ancient Italy. [M.M.]

56. Helmet
first half of the eighth century B.C.
bronze
l 42 cm
Florence, Museo Archeologico, inv. 83379 a, g 1-2, p.
from Tarquinia, Poggio dell'Impiccato, Tomb 1

Helmet formed by joining two embossed *laminae*, with high peak and pointed crest; plaques with the imitation nails punchings of concentric rings.

Pernier 1907, p. 80; Müller-Karpe 1959, pl. 28,14; Hencken 1968, p. 115 ff.; Bianco Peroni 1970, p. 85, n. 209; *Civiltà degli Etruschi* 1985 p. 57 nn. 2.4.10.7-10-27; *Les Etrusques et l'Europe*, p. 115, n. 30–33–34.
[F.C.].

57. "Pontecagnano type" sword and sheath
first half of eighth century B.C.
bronze
h of spear 36 cm; l of sheath 32.5 cm
Florence, Museo Archeologico, inv. 83379 a, g 1-2, p.
from Tarquinia, Poggio dell'Impiccato, Tomb 1

Sword with half-moon knob, soaring handle grip, wider in the middle; large arched shoulder. Bronze sheath with wooden inside, decorated with incisions outlining five areas, the three upper ones with a small figure of a spear-bearing man and rows of four-footed animals; a small leaf near the point; flattened globular terminal knob; remains of upper layer of bone plaques decorated with incised concentric rings.

Pernier 1907, p. 80; Müller-Karpe 1959, tav. 28,14; Hencken 1968, p. 115 sgg.; Bianco Peroni 1970, p. 85, n. 209.
[F.C.]

58. Head and tip of spear
first half of eighth century B.C.
bronze
l of head 20.5 cm; l of tip 16.5 cm
Florence, Museo Archeologico, inv. 83379 a, g 1-2, p.
from Tarquinia, Poggio dell'Impiccato, Tomb 1

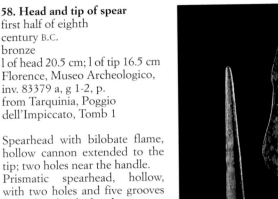

Spearhead with bilobate flame, hollow cannon extended to the tip; two holes near the handle. Prismatic spearhead, hollow, with two holes and five grooves incised under the head.

Pernier 1907, p. 80; Müller-Karpe 1959, pls. 28, 14; Hencken 1968, pp. 115 ff.; Bianco Peroni 1970, p. 85, n. 209. [F.C.]

59. Kardiophylax
late eighth–early seventh century B.C.
plaque of bronze *lamina*
max. dimensions: 16.8 x 14.5/12.1 cm
Carmignano, SAT, inv. 164159
from Artimino, Prato Rosello necropolis, well tomb of tumulus B, 1991 excavations

The *kardiophylax* belongs to the grave goods of a well tomb The grave goods, consisting in clay items and metal ones, was placed around a large impasto *dolium* covered with a round stone slab, containing the remains of the cremation (*fibulae*, silver clasps, gold bow and spiral) inside a bronze-plated biconical. The Artimino breastplate, characterized by the lateral hollows and the passing holes coinciding with the edges, for the time being is the most northern attestation of *kardiophilakes* and attests that the deceased belonged to the ruling class.

Poggesi 1999. [G.Po.]

60. Round shield
last quarter of eighth century B.C.
embossed bronze sheet; oxidations and corrosions; light green patina. Faint cracks repaired during restoration
diam. 73.5 cm
Venice, Centro Studi Ricerche Ligabue, inv. 42B

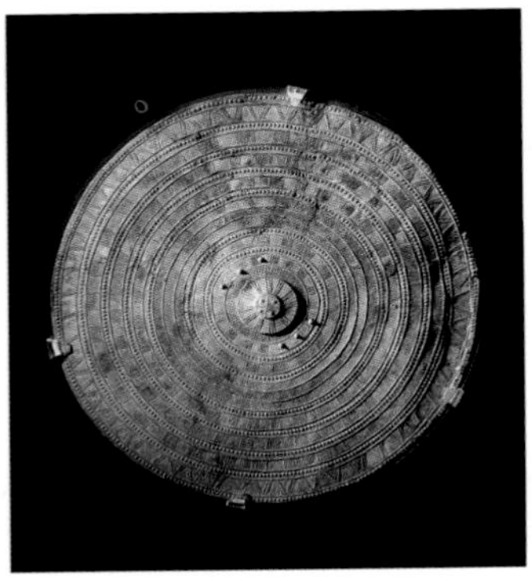

It is part of a set of late Villanovan burial goods and belongs to a group of shields with a geometric decoration, produced in Etruria from the late second half of the eighth century B.C. up to the Orientalizing period, diffused also in the bordering Latium territory, in Campania, in the Umbrian and Picene area and, further north, all the way to Verucchio. A formal item, present in the rich depositions of high-ranking persons and reproduced on the walls of monumental tombs as well.
[M.d.M.]

61–66. Armor from the Tomb of the Warrior of Vulci
ca. 520 B.C.
cast plated bronze; iron arms
Rome, Museo di Villa Giulia
from Vulci, Osteria necropolis, Tomb 47, Mengarelli excavations 1931

The armor belonged to the Etruscan "hoplite" buried in a small single-chamber tomb giving onto the same entrance (with access *dromos*) with three other graves. The burial goods feature Attic vases and bronze table vessels that show, together with the armor, the high level of the Vulci bronze production.

Ricciardi 1989, p. 33, nn. 38, 40, with bibl. [L.R.]

61. Helmet
ca. 520 B.C.
cast plated bronze
h 24 cm; w 25 cm
inv. 63579

Semi-spherical cap with high edge separated by a groove. On the edge incised decoration of lines and circles. On the sides, over the groove, two appliques, respectively with protome of Acheloos and protome of Typhon. On the top two round appliques with Bellerophon and Pegasus that also serve to support the *lophos*.

Le Monde Étrusque 1977–78, p. 92, n. 11; Proietti 1980, figs. 49–51; Sgubini Moretti 1981, p. 67, fig. 43.
[L.R.]

62. Pair of embossed plaques
ca. 520 B.C.
plated bronze
15 cm x 11.1 cm and
15 cm x 11.7 cm
inv. 63588

Profiled and embossed plaques, consisting of a rectangular part with the figured scene and an oval-shaped part decorated with palmettes with spirals on the sides and *gorgoneion* in the middle. The figured scene relates to the myth of Troilus, shown left next to two horses, while a servant precedes him and is taking water in a vase from a fountain in the shape of a lion's body, behind which Achilles is crouching, with knobbed-bell helmet, shield and sword, to take him by surprise. On one of the two plaques you can distinguish another person beside the horses. The two plaques are believed to be either the cheek guards of the helmet or belonging to the shield strap.

Le Monde Étrusque 1977–78, p. 93, n. 25 with bibl.; Proietti 1980, figs. 4–46; Sgubini Moretti 1981, p. 67, fig. 44.
[L.R.]

63. Parade shield
ca. 520 B.C.
plated bronze
diam. 95 cm
inv. 63555

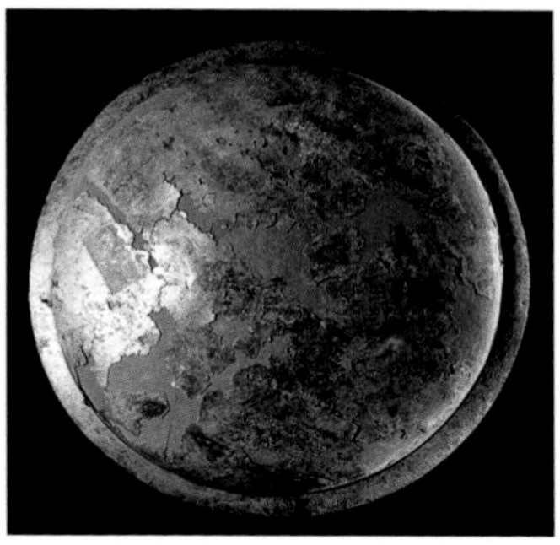

Round, flattened semi-spherical shield, with wide flat edge. In the inside ribbon grip attached by rivets.

Le Monde Étrusque 1977–78, p. 92, n. 12; Proietti 1980, fig. 47.
[L.R.]

64. Pair of greaves
ca. 520 B.C.
plated bronze
h 47 cm; max. w 14 cm
inv. 63575

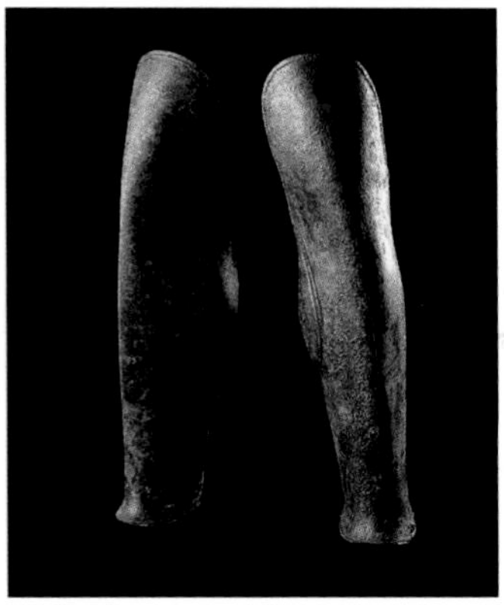

Anatomical greaves and with rendering of the calf muscles by grooves. Profiled edge that, above and below, present small passing holes for the laces.

Le Monde Étrusque 1977–78, p. 93, n. 13; Proietti 1980, fig. 48.
[L.R.]

65. Four spear tips
ca. 520 B.C.
iron and wood
l 27 cm and w 3 cm;
l 27 cm and w 3 cm;
l 22 cm and w 6.3 cm;
l 23 cm and w 6 cm
inv. 63578

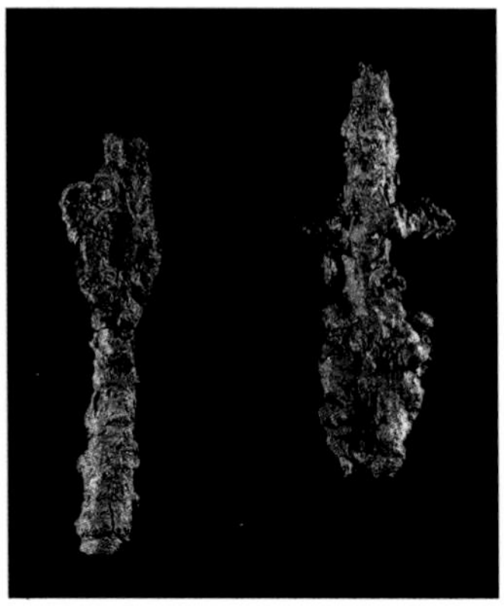

Spear tips, with leaf-shaped blade and tracing in the middle, with round cannon holder for inserting the wooden staff, partly conserved in two exemplars.

Le Monde Étrusque 1977–78, p. 94, ns. 28–29.
[L.R.]

66. Blade of sword
or of large knife
ca. 520 B.C.
iron
l 32 cm, w 3.5 cm; detached
fragment: 5 cm x 3.5 cm
inv. 63581

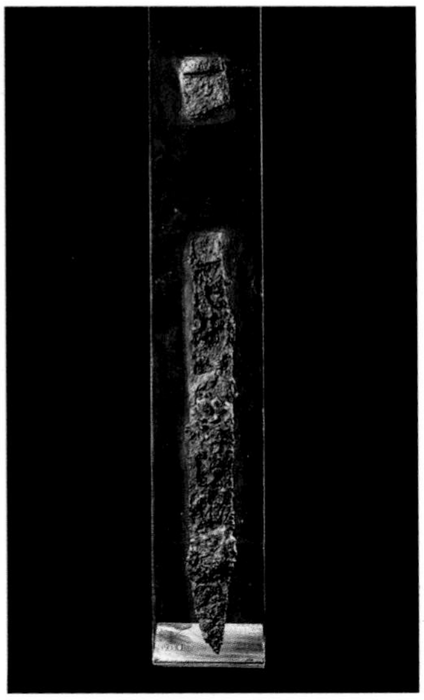

Long flat blade with asymmetrical tip.

Le Monde Étrusque 1977–78, p. 94, n. 30 (knife).
[L.R.]

67. Helmet
first half of sixth century B.C.
bronze
h 20.2 cm; diam. 26 cm
Siena, Museo Archeologico,
inv. Fi. 89664
from Murlo, Poggio Civitate,
random find

Tall cap, with splayed bottom part; four disc knobs with relief palmettes; on the edge a series of holes, some of which conserve their semi-spherical head, and on each side a larger hole.

Gregory Warden 1985, p. 107, n. 199.
[F.C.]

68. Helmet
second quarter of fifth century B.C.
laminated, cast bronze
h 30 cm
Florence, Museo Archeologico, inv. 239876
from the waters of the Golfo di Baratti

The helmet, only consigned to the Administration in 1998, is a further example of the "Vetulonia type" of a category of helmets, commonly known as the "Negau type," wide-spread in the fifth century B.C. mainly in central Italy (Egg 1988, pp. 247 ff.). Although still hidden by sea encrustations, the cap and the outer edge of the visor appear to be decorated with motifs not easy to interpret before cleaning but that might have a match in an exemplar found at Casola Valsenio in Romagna : this one presents a series of palmettes connected at the base of the cap and a braid motif between rows of notches on the edge of the visor. On the top of the cap, on each side of the crest, you can presently see the marks left by the two small rectangular plaques that must have held statuettes representing lions or boars, as we know by other known exemplars, and that enhanced the preciousness of the helmet. In the front part, at the base of the cap, you can clearly see the mark of the attachment of the perforated small plaque, today conserved separately, having already been entirely cleaned and restored at the time it was consigned. It figures on the left Herakles running to the right, his head viewed frontally and the lion skin knotted on his chest, brandishing his club with his right arm raised ; on the right a female figure dressed in chiton and cloak, wearing headgear shaped like a goatskin and winged shoes, is represented in left profile while she is launching an attack against the enemy, holding in her left hand the shield for defense and wielding in her upraised right hand a broadsword, its sheath slung at her side. The two figures are on a support formed by the head of a silenus from which are extended two excessively long arms that enclose nearly as to protect the two figures. The silenus head in turn rests on a palmette.
The small plaque, coming from a Vulci workshop, has an exact match in an exemplar in the Louvre Museum, in which the female figure has been identified as the war goddess Iuno Sospita, coinciding with the Greek goddess Hera. The scene was originally referred to a silenomachia, that is, to the myth of Hera assailed by sileni and defended by Herakles, according to a version of the myth that in all probability goes back to Stesichorus, and that is attested in the first half of the sixth century B.C. in the metopes of the temple in the sanctuary of Hera at the mouth of the river Sele (Torelli-Masseria 1996, pp. 215 ff.). In the iconographical design adopted by Vulci toreutic artists during the first half of the fifth century B.C., the two figures have lost their original relationship and are now fighting side by side against the savage enemy that was attacking the goddess, at this point recalled merely by the silenus protome (Zancani Montuoro 1946–48; see also Camporeale 1986).
Since these helmets were present in the equipment on board transport ships (Cavazzuti 1997), the recovery of another exemplar of the same type in the waters in front of the necropolis of the Buche delle Fate, now conserved at the Centro di Documentazione del Parco del Circeo (Gianfrotta 1997, p. 52), in the same area as the one the finder said to be that of our helmet too, permits us to connect these finds with the

events that, relative to Syracusan politics, had the area of the upper Tyrrhenian near the island of Elba playing an important role around the middle of the fifth century B.C., with the two expeditions of Phayllos and of Apelles in 453 B.C. (Colonna 1979, pp. 445 ff.).
[A.Ro.]

69. Helmet with eyes
sixth century B.C.
plated bronze
h 20.1 cm; l 23.7 cm; w 20.2 cm
Berlin, Staatliche Museen, Antikensammlung, inv. 30018a
from a Lombard tomb

Entirely cast; the top is the only added-on element. The upper part of the cap is slightly raised, and on the front half the rim is decorated with small knobs that, just like the Doric frieze at the base, are placed under the front edge of the cap, and chisel-processed. The front, rather like a tympanon on the forehead, as in Etruscan-Chalcedonian helmets, has the appearance of a face. Under the arched eyebrows, large eyes with mounted pupils, originally blue glass; each element is fastened with nails; the eyelashes around the eyes are incised. Between the eyes, the protome of a daimon.

Schröder 1912, pp. 244 ff., figs. 109–10; Schröder 1914, p. 13, n. 10, fig. 9; Nogara 1933, p. 78, fig. 37; Giglioli 1935, p. 57, fig. 305, 1.2; Egg, *Italische Helme*, 62.
[H.P.]

70. Helmets
early fifth century B.C.
bronze; plate
max. h 21 cm
Florence, Museo Archeologico, inv. 8797-8822
from Vetulonia, deposit near the walls of the Arce, year 1905

One hundred and twenty five helmets with high cap faired longitudinally with banded edge, separated by a groove, referable to the Negau type. On the lower edge is written the gentilitial *haspnas*.

Pernier 1905, pp. 13–15; Egg 1988, pp. 247–50; Maggiani 1990, pp. 48–49.
[C.Z.]

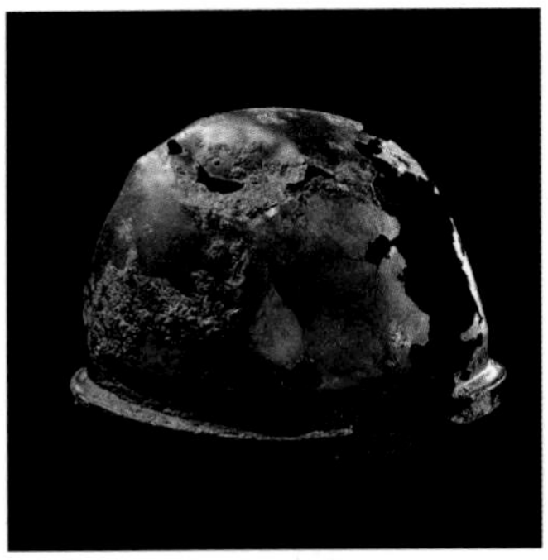

71–74. Golini Tomb I of Poggio del Roccolo
second half of fourth century B.C.
Orvieto, Museo Archeologico, previously Florence, Museo Archeologico, acquisition 1868
from Porano, Settecamini, locality Poggio del Roccolo

The following items come from a tomb found at Porano, near Orvieto, contrada Settecamini, loc. Poggio del Roccolo, in the course of digs executed after the two Golini painted tombs were found in the same locality. The panoply belonged to a deceased buried in a "gilt wooden coffin," probably deposited on the death couch of "one of the minor graves" (Conestabile 1865, pp. 120 ff.).

71. Helmet
bronze
h 0.19 cm; diam. 0.178–0.225 cm
inv. 70517

Bronze helmet with semi-spherical cap, ending with a button on the top, hollow inside, decorated with a relief rosette; the brim is adorned with tongues over which are incised two pairs of parallel lines; the back has a short neck-guard. The cheek-guards, attached with hinges, are formed by two overlapping plates, the outer one (conserved only on the left) is decorated with three embossed beads forming a triangle. It belongs to type B, differentiated in the Italic series by Coarelli, datable to the third quarter of the fourth century B.C. The area of diffusion of that type leads to assume that Etruria was one of the main centers of production.

Brunn 1863, p. 53; Conestabile 1865, pp. 125 ff., pl. XII; *Mostra dell'arte* 1955, p. 133, n. 453, pl. CIX; Coarelli 1976, p. 165, n. 27, p. 166 n. 29.
[A.E.F.]

72. Cuirass
bronze
h 0.43 cm; w at thorax 0.23 cm; w at back 0.32 cm
inv. 70518

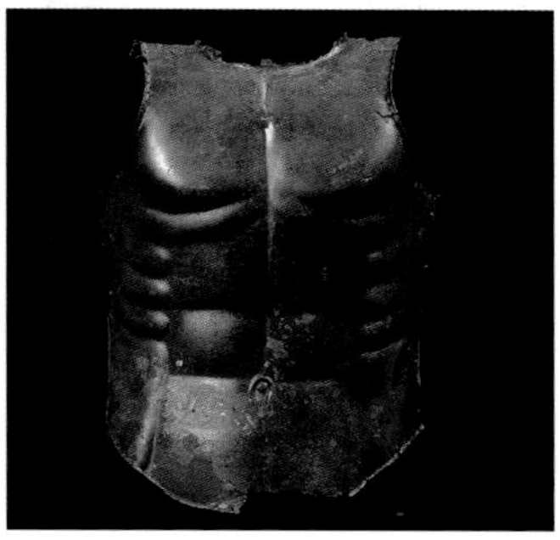

Bronze cuirass consisting of two valves, connected by hinges, along the hips and the sides of the neck opening; the raised edges feature a series of little holes, used for attaching the inside padding. It is the type of an anatomical cuirass, attested in Etruria by the middle of the fourth century B.C. The known Etruscan exemplars are not numerous but are frequently represented especially in wall paintings, for instance in the Tomb François at Vulci and the Tomb Gilioli at Tarquinia.

Brunn 1863, p. 53; Conestabile 1865, pp. 121 ff., pl. XII; *Mostra dell'arte e della civiltà etrusca*, 1955, p. 133, n. 453, pl. CIX; Adembri 1982, pp. 77 ff., n. 2 (with previous bibl.) [A.E.F.]

73. Pair of greaves
bronze
h right greave 0.406 cm; left greave 0.40 cm
inv. 70519

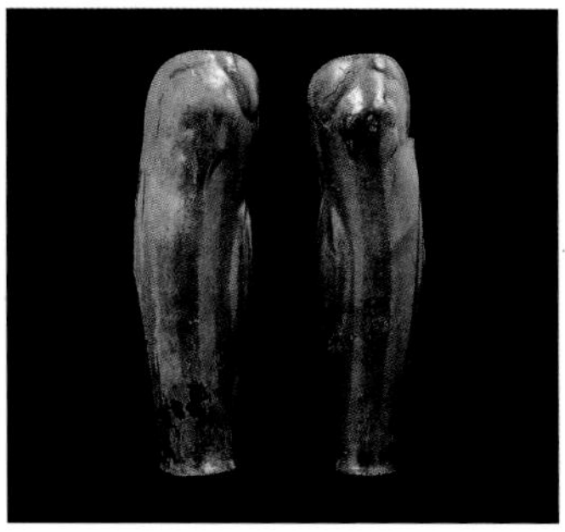

Pair of greaves of the anatomical type, bronze plated, reproducing the modeling of the leg; in the back they are fashioned to allow knee and ankle movements. Along the edges three parallel lines are incised.
Greaves of this type are quite wide-spread by the fourth century and during the third century B.C. in Etruria and Southern Italy and often documented in both wall and pottery painting.

Brunn 1863, p. 53; Conestabile 1865, pp. 124 ff., pl. XII; *Mostra dell'arte e della civiltà etrusca*, 1955, p. 133, n. 453, pl. CIX; Adembri 1982, pp. 78 ff., n. 3 (with previous bibl.)
[A.E.F.]

74. Round shield
bronze
diam. 0.90 cm
inv. 70520

Bronze-plated convex, round shield, with edge decorated with a double embossed guilloche with relief dots on the inside, held between two thin splines, also in relief.
The type is common in Greece and in Etruria already by the Archaic period and up to right after the middle of the fourth century B.C. It is often represented in wall painting in both Etruria (Tomb François at Vulci, Tomb Gilioli at Tarquinia) and southern Italy.

Brunn 1863, p. 53; Conestabile 1865, pp. 124 ff., pl. XII; Furtwängler 1890, p. 165; *Mostra dell'arte e della civiltà etrusca*, 1955, p. 133, n. 453, pl. CIX; Coarelli 1976, p. 166, note 29; Adembri 1982, pp. 78 ff., n. 4 (with previous bibl.)
[A.E.F.]

75. Biga
530–520 B.C.
oak wood; plated bronze; iron
reconstructed h 1.18 m.;
w 1.40 m
Viterbo, Museo Archeologico
from Ischia di Castro,
necropolis Poggio di Castro,
Tomb of the Biga

The vehicle consists of a box with arched bottom and high rounded front board and sides equipped with large semi-circular supporting handles, and a U-shaped chassis, to which the axle and the shaft were attached.
On the spindles of the axle the iron-circled wheels were mounted with nine spokes and hubs in a single piece conspicuously protruding on the sides in two cylindrical tubes. The wooden structure of the box and the hubs of the wheels was garnished with bronze plates held by little bronze nails. On the sides of the box the facing, applied also on the handles, bear an embossed figuration, along the edges contiguous to the front board, of two *kouroi*; above them there is an embossed round pod and two others at the ends of the plate coinciding with the bottom of the box. On the front board, the curvilinear edge and a band below are faced with flat plates that, on the central line of the board, have two large embossed opposing palmettes.

Civiltà degli Etruschi 1985, pp. 250 ff., n. 9.11; *Carri* 1988, pp. 203–06, p. 320, n. 1000.
[C.Z.]

76. Stela
before the mid-sixth century B.C.
gray sandstone (*pietra serena*)
mostly complete; surfaces damaged by many deep grooves and scratches
h 138 cm; w 41.5 cm; thick. 9 cm (top), 19 cm (base)
Florence, Casa Buonarroti, inv. 54
from the area around Fiesole

The stela, found before 1723 near Fiesole, having an oblong rectangular shape with ribbed upper edge and smooth sides, is decorated in low relief on one of the larger sides with a figure of a warrior, standing facing left. Along the right margin, behind the thigh of the figure, there is the vertical inscription "larthia ninie," bearing the morphem of the archaic possessive case, the given name and the gentilitial of the person represented. Wearing a loincloth, he displays both insignias of his rank that, beyond the obvious reference to the military and warrior context, constitute the symbols of political and religious auctoritas: in fact, if the spear represents both in Greece and in the mid-Tyrrhenian ambit the attribute of the *imperium*, the hatchet seems to refer concurrently to the central role played by Larth Ninie within the sphere of sacrificial ritual. The stela belongs to the series of funerary monuments from the area surrounding the basin of the middle Arno, and from the stylistic point of view appears at this point detached from the tradition of the oldest "Fiesole" school, apparent in the cippus from Barberino di Mugello, and seems full of Ionian stylems, that we can see in the forms of the relief as well as in the rendering of several details; however, the antiquarian aspects and the epigraphical characteristics of the inscription seem to allow us to date it still to before the mid-sixth century B.C.

Bruni 1997, pp. 38 ff. (with previous bibl.)
[S.B.]

77. Front side of small cinerary urn
pietra fetida
h 37 cm; l 41 cm
Pisa, Ottavio Simoneschi Collection, inv. 34
probably from Chianciano

Front of a rectangular-casket urn, resting on two quadrangular supports. In the middle, inside a frame carved in the slab, a relief scene: two horsemen leading their horses by the reins. The first is naked, the second is wearing a large cloak that he is upholding with his right hand, raised, thrust backward. Between the two figures a big bird in flight.
The fragment, regularized for antique-trade reasons, belongs to the collection that first Giuseppe Simoneschi, and then his son Ottavio, formed between the late nineteenth century and the first thirty years of the following century with material found in their properties of Chianciano (*Chianciano* 1989, p. 33 e nt. 3; Paolucci 1988, pp. 72 ff., ns. 88–108), and belongs to an exemplar of the series of small cinerary urns decorated in low relief that were widely popular in the Chiusi area during the sixth century B.C. (Paribeni 1938, pp. 64 ff.; Jannot 1984, pp. 211 ff.). Compared to the repertory of the series, that after the elaborate figurations of the oldest exemplars, by the middle of the century seemed to mostly favor convivial or prothesis scenes, the theme of the Simoneschi urn appears more directly linked with escatological beliefs, since we might be able to identify the two persons as the Dioscuri, as seems confirmed by the presence of the bird in flight, in all likelihood associated with Zeus (see Milonas 1945–46, pp. 203 ff.). The diffusion of the subject, that appears occasionally even in the more complex repertory of cippi (see Jannot 1984, p. 146, n. D.I.7, fig. 505), should be associated with the assertion in the funerary context of the worship of the divine Twins, attested at the end of the sixth century B.C. by a well-known dedication on a bowl by Oltos from Tarquinia (Cristofani 1988–89. On

the cult of the Dioscuri, see Strazzulla 1994; Colonna 1996; Scala 1997), as well as by the heroic ideals and the role played by cavalry in the late sixth-century B.C. ideology of the aristocracy.

[S.B.]

78. Statuette of horseman
second century B.C.
solid cast bronze
overall h 12.0 cm; h base 3.5 cm
Munich, Staatliche Antikensamlungen, SL 28 (formerly James Loeb Collection)

On a profiled stand, the horse is rearing. Its partly closed mouth, dilated nostrils, upright ears, as the tail is also, suggest excitement. The horseman, slightly turned right, is riding with an air of composure, keeping his arms close to his body and holding the reins firmly with both hands. The face is broad and spacious. The hair is close-set to the skull.

Sieveking 1913, p. 70, pl. 29; Pfister1940, p. 231.

79. Statuette of Ajax killing himself
480–460 B.C.
bronze
h 24 cm
Florence, Museo Archeologico, inv. 12193
from Populonia

Ajax, naked, bearded, with crested helmet with raised cheekguards, in the act of throwing himself on his sword stuck in the ground, grasped with his left hand by the base of the blade.

Davies 1971, pp. 148–60; Davies 1985, pp. 85–117; Haynes 1985, p. 290, n. 121.
[F.C.]

80. Earthenware acroteria
mid-sixth century B.C.
reddish clay with many bits of quartz and augite.
Traces of color: black, brown and red
Maximum h 26 cm; max. w 11 cm
Paris, Musée du Louvre; inventory n.: Cp
From Tuscania

• *1. Acroterion*
reddish clay with many bits of quartz and augite.
Traces of color: black, brown and red.
max. h 29.5 cm; max. w 17.5 cm
inv. Cp 5158
Male figure, partly conserved, with straight long hair close to the head. Receding forehead, large almond-shaped eyes, closed mouth. On the top of the head series of small holes in which perhaps a diadem was inserted, attached with iron clips, two of which remain. Wearing a chiton and a *himation*, that covers the left shoulder, leaving bare the chest and right shoulder.

• *2. Acroterion*
max. h 26 cm; max. w 11 cm
inv. Cp 5161
Male figure, partly conserved, with straight long hair close to the head. Receding forehead, large almond-shaped eyes, closed mouth. Below, on the back, part of a convex surface upon which the figure appears to be seated, maybe to be interpreted as a horse's back. The figure should probably be identified as a horseman.

Gaultier 1990, pp. 271–76; pls. 50, 1, 2, 3, 4; 51, 1–4.
[C.Z.]

The Ideal Forms

Our name for the Etruscans derives from the ethnic term used in the Latin and Italic languages, *Tursci / Tusci*, corresponding to the Greek *Tyrsenoi/Tyrrhenoi*. Dionysius of Halicarnassus (I, 30, 3) tells us that the Etruscans called themselves Rasenna (*rasna*), which probably means "those belonging to a community." In reality the available evidence makes it possible to affirm that the names current in Etruria were connected with the various *populi*, that is to say with the names derived from the main cities, such as Veientes, Caerites, Tarquinienses, and Volsinienses. All this very clearly reflects the fact that Etruria was never a single nation but comprised a group of communities and territories differing in their political, geographic and economic conditions, often at war with one another and free to choose their own foreign policies according to their own interests.

Despite these peculiarities and differences, we must certainly not forget the existence in the Etruscan world of forms of cooperation and political alliance, of a common recognition of religious and cultural values, and of the persistence of material and ideal structures capable of projecting a unitary image of the Etruscan nation, at least with respect to some great themes already absorbed by ancient historiography. One first image that may be mentioned in this connection is that of the link which the ancients made between the Etruscans and Lydia, the land of the legendary Croesus and Midas, chiefly because of the proverbial wealth of the Etruscan people. There must have been many other traditions linking the Etruscans with the arrival in the Tyrrhenian area of heroes traceable to Trojan epic such as Odysseus-Nanos or Dardanus. Herodotus knows about and confirms this oriental provenance of the Etruscans, to which archaeology can add the similarity of materials and writing perceptible in the North Aegean area, especially on the well-known Lemnos stela. Dionysius of Halicarnassus, in the Augustan period, disputes the oriental origin of the Etruscans—a characteristic which he reserves for the Romans-Trojans—and claims that they were autochthonous. It is clear that behind the reconstruction of origins we must imagine a bitter propagandistic struggle to justify, as the circumstances might require, relations, alliances, and tensions.

Wealth, as was mentioned earlier, is another of the constant characterizations of the Etruscans. Indeed the Etruscan aristocracies between the second half of the eighth and the sixth century B.C., encouraged by foreign influences, used the ostentation of *tryphe* as a means of legitimizing their own pre-eminent social role. The goldsmiths' artifacts, the bronzes and the lifestyle of the Etruscan *principes* were observed by the contemporary aristocracies of Latium, by the emerging classes of the Italic world, and by sectors of the Greek world. Pherecrates and Critias, two Attic writers of comedies and tragedies respectively, who wrote in the second half of the fifth century, mention how Greek houses were adorned with Etruscan bronzes and candelabra (Athenaeus, *Deipnosophistai* XV, 60, 700c; I 50, 286), objects clearly identified as symbols of the lifestyle of the upper classes of Etruria. The other face of the enormous wealth accumulated by the aristocratic classes is the recurrent characterization of Etruscan society as being made up of *principes* and *penestai* and permeated by continual social tensions which led many of the ruling classes of Etruria to resort to Rome for a guarantee of the continuity of their privileges.

Closely connected with the transmission of property and social rank is the attention paid to emphasizing the continuity of one's lineage, a field in which women have a special role. The grand funerary tumuli of the Orientalizing phase are the most striking sign of the affirmation of the kin groups which are based on the cult of their common ancestors, just as the spread of the two-part nomenclature, comprising a forename and a family name, indicates that for the designation of an individual the reference to his *gens* is now significant. In this context there also arises the right, reserved for the aristocratic groups, to possess the images of their ancestors, a true certification of social rank. This original nucleus also generates the great rituals of archaic power, such as the triumph, suitably adapted to the growing complexity of the urban structure.

Another image which we must associate with the Etruscan world is that of long and profound Hellenization. Contact with the Greek world may be said have started with the earliest phases and must be considered in its subsequent manifestations on the basis of the developments proper to the Greek world and the corresponding Tyrrhen-

ian world. In the latter case it must be borne in mind that the acceptance of elements originating from outside is not unanimous and univocal but obeys a selection and adaptation which the receiving society determines on the basis of the general levels of its own development and the viewpoint of the groups interested in the contact.
The structure of the earliest Greek settlements in southern Italy, in direct contact with the Tyrrhenian area, multiplied relations and trade between the different areas, the fruits of which can be seen, for example, in the way in which the Greeks transmitted to Etruria and Latium the writing technology based on a Chalcidian alphabet, a lifestyle which may be described as Homeric which includes the practices of the banquet, the use of wine according to the Greek models, the making with a potter's wheel of high-quality decorated ceramics, and funerary rituals aimed at heroizing the dead person.
But the most important contribution made by the Greek world to the Tyrrhenian area is certainly the idea of the city, the *polis*, in which the previous power of the few is conditioned and mitigated by the power proper to the political community of the citizens. In this case, too, it would be wrong to imagine a mechanical transposition of the Greek models—which anyway varied greatly from one another according to the various areas—to the Etruscan world, indeed the ongoing scholarly debate includes some views which deny the existence of an Etruscan *polis*. What is certain is that despite the specificity of the Tyrrhenian world and in the face of the long and profound influence of the aristocratic structures in the context of urban society, the Greek city proved essential as a point of reference for monumental building programs and for the management of the interests and relations between the different social groups.
The Etruscan city is structured in this way, with its public monuments, its sanctuaries, its artisan districts and points of exchange, the surrounding territory over which it exercises control, with its festivals, rituals of power and of the gods, with the crucial part played by the augural discipline which is able to interpret the signs of the gods and which inaugurates the city as a transposition of heaven on to earth, as in the founding of the Etrusco-Italic temple.
The development of the temple is, indeed, exemplary. Founded on the rules of the augural discipline proper to the Etruscan and Italic world, whose symbol is the lituus, it is structured in the sixth and fifth centuries B.C. according to the logic of the Greek model, starting from the idea of the temple as the house of the god and the concept of the anthropomorphic representation of the deity. All this opens the way to the identification of the indigenous divine figures with the more prestigious ones of the Greek pantheon. The temple as the house of the god built round the public space of the city departs from the previous arrangement, where the places of the sacred were contained within the aristocratic residences, as clear an image as there could possibly be of the uncontested dominion of the *principes*.
It is the *principes* themselves who seem to have been primarily responsible for the reception in the Tyrrhenian area of the mythological sagas of the Greek world which were destined to have a long and lasting fortune and to obliterate almost completely the older mythologies of the indigenous world. The exemplary stories of the heroes of Greek myth, such as Theseus against the Minotaur, Achilles against Troilus, Odysseus against Polyphemus or the monster Scylla, and Heracles against Geryon or the Nemean lion or the Cretan bull, seem in the eyes of the *principes* to be paradigmatic models of the attainment of kingship through one's own victorious enterprises. This process finally blends with what we have seen concerning the structuring of the temple: from the end of the sixth century B.C. the representation of myth is the exclusive apanage of the house of the god and no longer of the aristocratic residences, a clear sign of the growing force of the *polis*, which is now able to appropriate one of the classic instruments of the *principes*' propaganda.
Another image which was destined to characterize the Etruscan world and which emerges definitively in the fifth century B.C. is that of the League of twelve Etruscan peoples—the citizens of Caere, Tarquinia, Vulci, Roselle, Vetulonia, Veii (later replaced by Populonia), Volsinii, Chiusi, Perugia, Cortona, Arezzo and Volterra—united in a confederation, probably also inspired by Greek models, ruled by a *sacerdos Etruriae* and having as its central seat the *fanum Voltumnae* near Orvieto-Volsinii. The Etruscans of Campania and the Po area are also thought to have adopted a common organization into a dodecapolis.
The importance of the political organisms also emerges very clearly in funerary paintings starting in the 4th century B.C., when for the first time the rank of the dead person no longer depends solely on the signs of his wealth and lifestyle but mainly on the indication of the offices that he held in the administration of the *polis*.
[M.M.]

Opulence

"Twice a day they (sc. the Tyrrheni) prepare sumptuous tables and all the other things suited to excessive luxury, making beds with linen and colored embroidery, and silver cups of every kind, and they have ready and available a considerable number of slaves to serve them, some of whom are extremely beautiful, while others are adorned with more sumptuous clothes than is appropriate to their condition of slavery. Not only the magistrates but most men of free condition have special houses of various kinds" (Diodorus Siculus, V, 40,3–4). This passage from Diodorus Siculus, probably deriving from Poseidonius, illustrates very well the persistence of a view of the Etruscans that is widespread in the Greek and Latin sources and which often compares them to other peoples famous for their wealth and opulence, like the Lydians or Sybarites, or describes them as typified by *tryphe* (luxurious leisure) and *habrotes* (effeminacy). The great season of Etruscan opulence corresponds to the age of the full and undisputed social dominion of the Tyrrhenian *principes*, from the end of the eighth century to the sixth century B.C., when we perceive, especially in the archaeological evidence, what has been described as the "social comedy" of luxury. In order to understand all the historical implications of the process, well known in most ancient and modern societies, which leads to the ostentation of wealth by some restricted groups within the communities, we must first set all moral value judgements aside and concentrate instead on the real function of this behavior in the context of the relationships and social ties of which they are part. If we do this we can recognize various levels of interpretation and meaning connected with the stories in the literary sources and the extraordinary archaeological evidence of Etruscan opulence.
On examining the relevant part of the exhibition, one immediately notices a fact which might be described as the minimal level of interpretation: the widespread presence of objects produced by the working of precious materials such as gold, silver, bronze, iron, various kinds of wood, impasto pottery—sometimes in the local manner but often made in Greece or imitated from Greek models, and decorated in an attractive and costly style -, glass, materials of exotic origin such as the *tridacna*, ivory and the ostrich egg, containers of precious perfumes such as *alabastra* and *aryballoi*, metal *fibulae* which suggest refined cloths and sumptuous garments. The value of the objects derives from the type of material used and the craftsmanship which adds form and deco-

ration to it. Moreover, as one can see from the example of the grave goods exhibited here from the tomb of the Bronze Chariot at Vulci, the ostentation of wealth also includes the idea of accumulation, so that there may be several copies of the same object, magnifying the basic value of the pieces out of all proportion. The possibility of the use and accumulation of wealth by the *principes* is of course connected with the economic bases which they control, notably land and the management of trade.

All this leads to the consideration of a second level of meaning attached to this kind of evidence. The possibility of showing off such large quantities of such precious and exotic materials and objects is directly linked with the insertion of the owners in the channels of production and circulation of goods. In other words, a further added value visible in the precious objects lies in the fact that they attest that the *principes* are inserted in a context of exclusive relations with their peers, even at an international level, relations based on various mechanisms: trade in the manner of *prexis idie*, the booty gained from the exercise of warlike *virtus*, the tribute imposed on the defeated, the gift which initiates relations of friendship and familiarity between members of the same rank and which must necessarily be returned. In the context of these wide-ranging relations there seem to be two main models according to which the lifestyle of the Tyrrhenian princes forms and organizes itself: oriental kingship, especially that of Assyria, which was brought primarily by the Phoenician navigations, and where the demonstration of luxury is connatural to the sovereign's closeness to the divine sphere; and Homeric kingship, which was brought primarily by the contact with the Greek world which was intensified by the opening of the colonial channels, and which exemplifies the heroic lifestyle based on the *thalamos* full of wrought metal objects and containers of wine and oil, on the banquet where meat and wine are consumed and the bard introduces music and song, on the palaces, on the ties of hospitality, on the warrior ethic, and on the celebration of the "beautiful death" of the hero.

We may now touch on a third and last level of interpretation by considering the fact that the each of the different types of material that form part of the contexts demonstrative of Etruscan *tryphe* alludes to a specific aspect of the *principes*' lifestyle. The grave goods exhibited here include a bronze chariot, the greatest expression of *tryphe* and of the aristocratic chiefs' military ideology. Alongside the war chariot (*currus*), another type of chariot, resembling a gig, is attested in Etruria; this is the *carpentum*, used especially for women but also for men, as when Livy (I, 34, 8) describes how the future Tarquinius Priscus leaves Tarquinia on a *carpentum* together with his bride, taking his immense wealth with him. This type of carriage is closely connected with the travels of the lord, especially in the countryside where his estates are situated, so it alludes to one of the main sources of wealth, just as the *currus* alludes to the military conquest of men, goods and territories. A large group of iconographies, moreover, puts the figure of the horseman in the foreground, so the possession of a horse and the art of horsemanship are another aspect of the aristocratic lifestyle.

The archaeological evidence for Etruscan *tryphe* mainly derives from the grave goods, but it must not be forgotten that before they were deposited in the tombs these objects had a use and a circulation within the aristocratic channels, not least in the luxurious residences which had already taken shape in the seventh century, as is shown by the first phases of the palaces of Murlo and Acquarossa, or the now well-known case of Casale Marittimo. The Virgilian description (*Aeneid*, VII, 170–91) of the palace of Picus and Latinus at Laurentum still conveys the awesome, magnificent appearance of these houses: "The palace, august and spacious, supported on a hundred columns,/ was in the highest part of the city, the palace of Laurentine Picus,/ and the woods and the cult of the fathers wreathed it in holy awe./ Here it was auspicious for kings to receive the scepter/ and raise the first fasces of office; here was the temple for them, and the senate-house,/ and a site for banquets; here, after sacrificing a ram, / the fathers would sit at an unbroken row of sacred tables./ And the statues of the earliest ancestors/ [...] stood in line in the vestibule, and the other kings of early times,/ who had suffered war wounds fighting for their homeland./ Moreover, hanging from the sacred portals are numerous/ weapons and captured chariots and axes with curved blades,/ and crests of helmets, and mighty bolts of doors and spear-heads and shields and beaks torn from ships./ Picus himself, trainer of horses, with the quirinal/ lituus, sat wrapped in the short toga/ holding in his left hand a holy shield."

This passage, with its antiquarian tone, presents a lively and complete picture of a king's dwelling in the archaic age, in which political, religious and economic values are all combined. First we encounter the architectural skill and the wide, solemn spaces of the halls decorated by the weapons seized from the enemy and the portraits of the ancestors, a symbol of the continuity of the family line. We may, moreover, imagine the interiors as being decorated by terra-cotta *pinakes* or by wall paintings such as we see in the tombs; we may imagine the ceramic tableware and the vessels of precious metal for the solemn banquets where the participants drank wine and ate meat boiled in the great *lebetes*, in the Oriental manner, as we see for example in the friezes of the *regia* of Murlo; we may imagine the women of the house busy at their spinning, adorned with rings, bracelets, *fibulae* and precious garments. This, the interior of the palace, is the site of the sacrifices and the ceremonies in honor of the gods (as yet there is no public temple), and the meetings of the curia, i.e. of the people assembled under arms to receive orders from the king; and here the kings themselves receive the symbols of their power, such as the scepter, the fasces, and the lituus. Note also the stress laid on the fact that the king is seated—as we see for example in the statues of the tomb of Ceri, which dates from the first half of the seventh century B.C.— a symbol of authority and regality.

Alongside the *regiae*, in the countryside, stood the great funerary tumuli which signal from afar the princely dominion over the cultivable land and the *tryphe* involved in the building of the tumuli themselves. But the ostentation of luxury and wealth continues in the ceremonies of the laying-out, carrying-forth and interment of the dead man, which were accompanied by *ludi*, and in the deposition, once and for all, in the tomb of that huge wealth of materials described above, which would now be permanently withdrawn from circulation so that it could serve the otherwordly needs of the dead man.

The whole world of the *principes* begins to decline, with differences between the various areas, in the sixth century B.C., unequivocal signs being the reduction of funerary luxury which at various levels pervades Etruria and Latium in the sixth and fifth centuries B.C., a probable consequence of sumptuary laws and regulations adopted by the *poleis*, and the appearance of public temples which take the sphere of the sacred out of the control of the aristocratic chiefs. In both cases wealth is restricted and taken away from the private sphere to be channeled into the civic structures, as also happens in the case of the temples which house the deities of the community and the myths which tell of the origins. We should not, however, think of it as a univocal and linear transition. The structures of the ancient aristocratic *gentes* continue to be important within the city, too, and the recurrent reports of conflicts between the "powerful" and the "poor" in the urban Etruscan societies indicate that the reputation for princely *tryphe* was well deserved and never entirely disappeared.

[M.M.]

81. Tomb of the Bronze Chariot, Vulci

In 1965 at Vulci, in the northern necropolis of the Osteria, the Tomb of the Bronze Chariot was unearthed. The monument, found intact, brought to light an exceptional context. Dated, thanks to the presence of few imported items, around 680–670 B.C., it constitutes a fundamental testimony for the knowledge of the old Orientalizing period of Vulci and of all Etruria.
The ensemble, that right after the discovery was presented to the public at Turin in 1967 on the occasion of the exhibition *Arte e civiltà degli Etruschi* and in the early seventies was exhibited in the second room of Villa Giulia, despite its importance has not yet been the object of a thorough publication. If presently we do not avail of the documentation of the digs, carried out with great care and expertise, nonetheless the fortunate recovery of the precious, detailed photographic campaign executed at the time of the discovery (that makes up, although only in part, for the loss, we hope temporary, of the digs diary and the graphic documentation as well as the analyses performed on the "residues of food substances" gathered during the digs), has enabled us to begin the study of the ensemble and to present here a suggestion for a reconstruction.
The tomb, immediately reburied after the discovery and whose exact location is unknown, consisted of a small funerary chamber, which was reached through a *dromos* with steps, which was sided by "a small oven niche" where "the few remains of the bones of a dog were found."
The inside of the hypogeum, found intact, contained, aside from the remains of at least three cremated individuals gathered in bronze vases, to which we perhaps should add a fourth, very rich grave goods. Pottery, impasto, bronze, iron materials were crowded together, mostly placed on the paving and sometimes with copious traces of the offerings that in the past had been put in the tomb, offerings that, from the analyses performed at the time of the excavation or again recently on the few remains left, we know related to beef and lamb meat and fruit such as figs, apples and nuts, the latter still conserved. In our present state of knowledge, it is difficult to identify the exact location of these elements, maybe in the case of the fruit conserved in perishable containers, the existence of which we can assume, by the photographs of the digs, at least coinciding with the identifiable dark marks on the benches, in spaces that were not empty by chance.
A role of great importance was conferred on the parade chariot with its bronze-plated box that, placed in the left part of the funerary chamber, at first rested on the back-wall bench. The recognition of the layout of a whole series of functional elements has allowed a suggested reconstruction of the vehicle, executed for the present exhibition; similarly the attentive examination of the photographic documentation has also clarified the precise location of a group of bronze items such as the spherical element upon a neck, the two pairs of hands and some personal adornments, one of which with amber inlays, belonging to artifacts that, offering a schematic representation of the human figure, might seem to anticipate more elaborate, later formal experiences, known for instance at Marsiliana d'Albegna and even in Vulci. Furthermore, the layouts of these elements prove their close connection with the chariot, and suggest a unitary interpretation of the ensemble, according to an iconographic model that, attested for instance in the pottery decoration, the ivories and, especially the later architectural terra cottas, would now seem to be attested inside the tomb: a departure scene, filled with allegorical implications, that shows the *parabates*, that is, the lord, near the chariot driven by the charioteer.
Beyond any suggestive reconstruction, nonetheless there seems to be a certain emphasis, in a hierarchical connotation, on the role of the figure placed by the back wall, to whom appear to belong the bronze "head", constituted by the spherical element on a neck, the smaller pair of hands and the austere personal adornments.
In connection with the presence

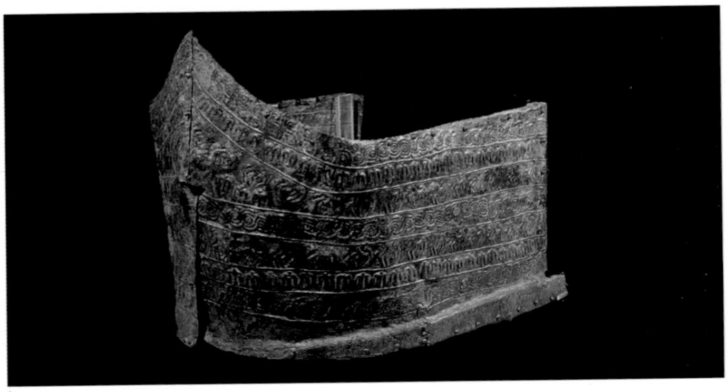

1

of the chariot, an element in itself characteristic of the aristocracy in the Orientalizing period, the rank of the ancient owners of the tomb is also underlined by the luxury of the grave goods, where arms are significantly missing. It should especially be observed that the grave goods, that however feature utterly rare, refined import items and offer a vast collection of locally-made pottery, are especially characterized by the number and quality of the bronze items, mostly from Vulci workshops, wherein the embossed ones are particularly outstanding. Special importance is given to vases and items relative to the banquet ceremony, confirming the essential role it played in the aristocratic class of the time, more and more receptive to the cultural inspirations coming from the Greek world.

• 1. *Facing of the box*
embossed plated bronze
h 60.5 cm; l 47.5 cm
inv. 84877
• 2. *Group of fragments of the wooden chassis*
elm wood and stake, leather, cast bronze
l biggest fragment 24 cm;
l smallest fragment 8.2 cm;
l railing 46 cm
inv. 84984, 84895
fragments of the wooden chassis and the wooden railing, with remains of leather held by bronze nails.
• 3. *Wooden "forcella" (forked stick)*
pear/apple wood
h 21.6 cm
inv. 84896
• 4. *Three iron nails*
l 12.3; 5.2, 4.7 cm
inv. 84891, 84892, 84893
Iron nails with curved head with remains of wood and leather cast iron, wood and leather.
• 5. *Two structural iron elements belonging to the box*
cast iron
l 22.5; 26 cm
inv. 84889, 84890
• 6. *Pair of rings*
cast iron
diam. c. 5.5 cm
inv. 84884, 84885
• 7. *Fragments of iron wheels with remains of wood*
cast iron; wood
l biggest fragment 42.5 cm; l smallest fragment ca.19 cm;
reconstructed diam. 52 cm
inv. 84879, 84880
• 8. *Pair of iron linchpins*
cast iron
l 12.5 cm
inv. 84882, 84883
• 9. *Iron wheel-hub ring*
cast iron
diam. 10.5 cm
inv. 84881
• 10. *Bronze "fermagavello" (?) with wood remains*
cast bronze, elm wood
l 3 cm; w 2.3 cm
inv. 84878
• 11. *Round bronze element belonging to the shaft (?)*
plated bronze
diam. 9 cm
inv. 84870
• 12 *Quadrangular-section iron element with flattened ends*
cast iron
l 15 cm
inv. 84888
• 13 *Biconical vase with M-shaped handles and lid with lotus-flower pommel*
plated bronze
max. h 50 cm, diam. of mouth 11.7 cm
inv. 8485
• 14. *Biconical vase with M-shaped handles and lid with lotus-flower pommel*
plated bronze
max. h 46.2 cm, diam. of mouth

11.3 cm
inv. 84854
• 15. *Biconical vase*
embossed bronze plate
inv. 84852
• *16. Cauldron*
plated bronze
h 27 cm, diam. 47.2 cm
inv. 84855
• *17. Spherical element on cylindrical neck*
plated bronze
h 19 cm; diam. 13.8 cm
inv. 84875
• *18. Pair of hands*
incised plated bronze
h 20 cm; diam. wrist 4.9 cm
inv. 84865, 84866
• *19. Pair of bracelets with rectangular bow*
plated and embossed bronze
h 5.5 cm; l 15.2 cm
h 5.5 cm; l 15.4 cm
inv. 84863, 84864
• *20. Bronze-wire ring decorated with twelve amber beads*
diam. 6.7 cm
inv. 84869
• *21. Small curvy ribbon band embossed plated bronze*
h 1.2 cm; diam. 9.4 cm
inv. 84870
• *22. Pair of hands*
incised plated bronze
h 23.5 cm; diam. wrists 5.5 and 4.8 cm
inv. 84867, 84868
• *23. Proto-Corinthian kylix decorated with rays*
refined clay
h 3.7 cm; diam. mouth 8.5 cm
inv. 84851
• *24. Achromatous Rhodian-Cretan aryballos*
refined clay
h 6.1 cm; diam. mouth 3 cm
inv. 84850
• *25. Achromatous Rhodian-Cretan aryballos*
refined clay
h 4.7 cm; diam. mouth 2.9 cm
• *26. Kotyle*
impasto, incised decoration
h 7.2 cm; diam. mouth 7.6 cm
inv. 84848
• *27. Kantharos*
brown impasto, ribbed vessel, decorated with metallic leaves
max. h 6.9 cm; diam. mouth 7.2 cm
inv. 84846
• *28. Kantharos*
brown impasto, ribbed vessel, decorated with metal leaves
max. h 6.9 cm; diam. mouth 7.2 cm
inv. 84847

13

14

15

16

18

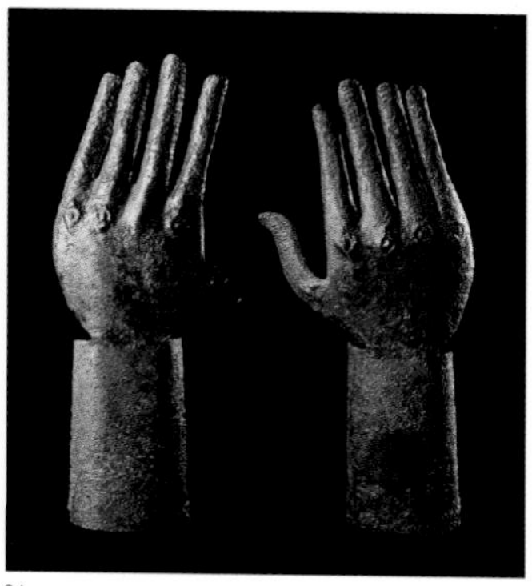
24

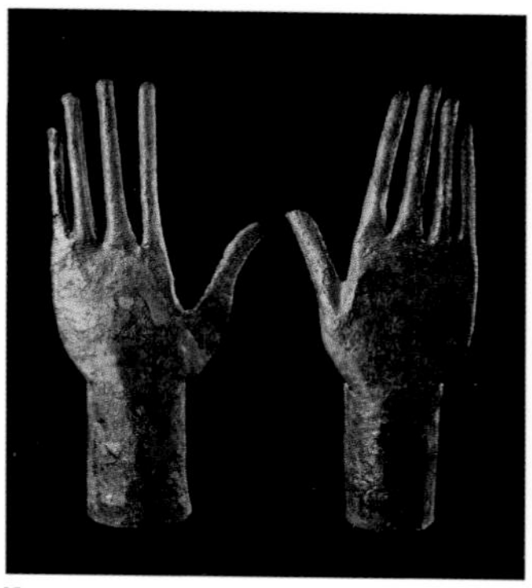
25

29

30

33

35

36

• *29. Chalice*
brown impasto, ribbed vessel
h 11.9 cm; diam. mouth 13.9 cm
inv. 84843
• *30. Chalice*
brown impasto, ribbed vessel
h 12 cm; diam. mouth 13.6 cm
inv. 84844
• *31. Chalice*
brown impasto, ribbed vessel
h 12 cm; diam. mouth 15.4 cm
inv. 84845
• *32. Large cup with single handle*
brown impasto, ribbed vessel, decorated with metal leaves
h 22.3 cm; diam. mouth 32.3 cm
inv. 84842
• *33. Two-handled globular olla*
brown impasto

h 30.5 cm; diam. mouth 19.4 cm
inv. 84839
• *34. Olla*
brown impasto
h 46.8 cm; diam. mouth 24.8 cm
inv. 84840
With foot, complete with lid and decorated with sets of ribbings
• *35. Olla*
brown impasto
h 44.5 cm; diam. mouth 25 cm
inv. 84841
With foot, complete with lid and decorated with sets of ribbings.
• *36. Olla*
impasto
h 56.8 cm; diam. mouth 24.3 cm
inv. 84837
Decorated with bands of triangles alternately on white background.
• *37. Olla*
impasto
h 58 cm; diam. mouth 24.5 cm
inv. 84838
Decorated with bands of triangles alternately on white background.
• *38. Large kantharos*
embossed plated bronze
max. h 32.8 cm; diam. mouth 32.9 cm
inv. 84856
On trumpet foot, with M-shaped handles, restored in the past.
• *39. Tripod*
embossed plated bronze
h 36.5 cm; diam. body 24 cm
inv. 84862
Cylindrical-body tripod, with upturned-ribbon supports.
• *40. Tripod-bowl*
incised plated bronze
h 32.2 cm; diam. 27.7 cm
inv. 84861
• *41. Bottle-shaped askos*
embossed plated bronze
h 10.5 cm; l 24.7 cm
inv. 84860
• *42. Patera with ribbed vessel*
plated bronze
h 5.5 cm; diam. 21 cm
inv. 84857
• *43. Patera with ribbed vessel*
plated bronze
h 5.9 cm; diam. 21 cm
inv. 84858
• *44. Patera with ribbed vessel*
plated bronze
h 6 cm; diam. 22 cm
inv. 84859
• *45. Support for candelabra*
cast and plated bronze
h 64.5 cm
inv. 84874
• *46. Support for loom*
cast and plated bronze
max. h 74.1 cm; w 95.5 cm
inv. 84873
• *47. Pair of skewers with wavy tips*
cast bronze
l 92 cm
inv. 84871, 84872
• *48. Knife with handle grip with raised edges and traces of wooden sleeve*
cast iron
l 21.4 cm
inv. 84886
• *49. Cannon hatchet with quadrangular joint and remains of wooden sleeve*
cast iron
l 9.2 cm; w 4.7 cm
inv. 84887
Sgubini Moretti 1999 pp. 139–45.
[A.M.M.S.]

37

38

38

39

39

40

41

41

---

82. Kotyle
675–650 B.C.
gold
h 7.8 cm; diam. 9 cm; h with sphinxes 13.2 cm
Rome, Museo di Villa Giulia, inv. 61544
from Palestrina, Bernardini Tomb

The form recalls early and middle proto-Corinthian exemplars. The vessel and the foot are made out of a hammered plate, the handles, plated also, are soldered separately and each one decorated with the figure of a sphinx, stamped and finished with granulation.

Rizzo 1985, p. 257, n. 19, fig. p. 89, with previous bibl.
[M.A.D.L.B.]

83. Lebes with snake protomes
675–650 B.C.
gilt silver, embossed, chiseled decoration
h 13.5 cm; diam. 16 cm
Rome, Museo di Villa Giulia, inv. 61566
from Palestrina, Bernardini Tomb

The decoration displays from top: sequence of geese; warriors on foot, on horseback and on chariot, stag pursued by a lion; similar procession of armed men, interrupted by duelists, and chariot with female figures; last, scenes of various types framed by palm trees (cows and calf, hunter, grazing horses, peasant at work, archer on horseback, two lions biting a bull, man struggling with a lion). In the medallion a fallen man overcome by a lion; above a soaring falcon. The figured fields include palms and birds.
The snake protomes were added at a later time.

Rizzo 1985, p. 256, n. 16, fig. p. 85, with previous bibl.
[M.A.D.L.B.]

84. Basin with mobile handles
Seventh century B.C.
bronze
Paris, Musée du Louvre, Département des Antiquités grecques, étrusques et romaines, inv. Br 4351
from Tarquinia

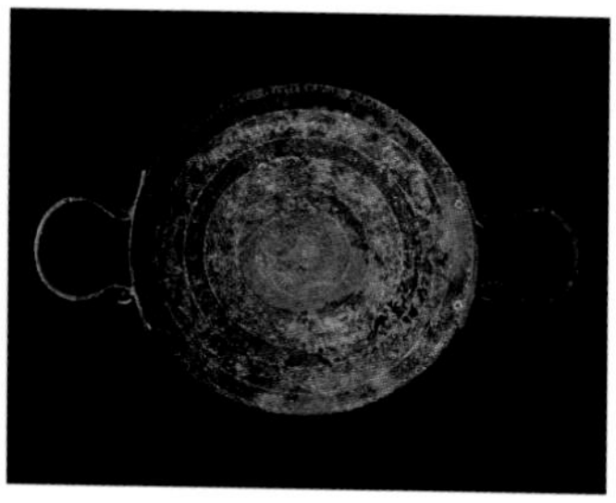

Convex basin with mobile handles inserted in two attachments placed beneath the rim, adorned with tiny tongues. In the middle of the vessel small rosette between palmettes and lotus flowers. In the first band a phytoid motif, in the second a hare-hunt scene with a dog and a naked man about to throw a javelin, followed by eleven figures of birds.

Villard 1956, pp. 25 ff., pl. IV; Camporeale 1984, p. 64, pl. XXIa
[G.P.]

85. Ribbed jug
plated silver; lacunose, bottom missing, deformed
max. h 13.8 cm; h to lip 11.4 cm; diam. of mouth 8.6 cm
Firenze, Museo Archeologico

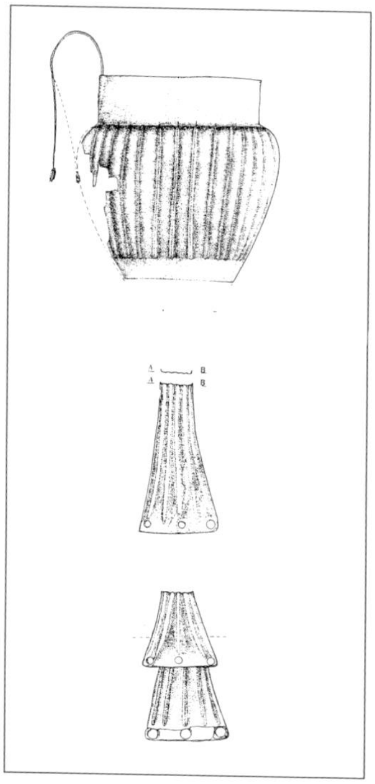

Heart-shaped vessel, strigilated, directly connected with a high, nearly vertical lip. Ribbon handle, decorated with longitudinal grooves, fan-shaped at the level of the attachments; the upper one is placed inside the neck. In both cases, there are three small nails in the same number of holes. The exemplar does not seem to belong to the metal tableware production of Greek origin (Mallwitz, Schiering 1964; Weber 1983); most analogies instead can be found in a well-defined category of smoothed black impasto attingitoi, widely attested in sevnth-century grave goods, and characterized by the high lip rim and a suggestion of podding on the upper part of the body (Mengarelli 1985; Bartoloni 1972), regarding which it has already been assumed they derived from metal prototypes (Pellegrini 1989).

[E.S.]

86. Spoon
480–470 B.C.
bronze
l 14.4 cm; w 4.3 cm
Florence, Museo Archeologico, inv. 97802
from Chiusi, Tomb of the Boncia (1881)

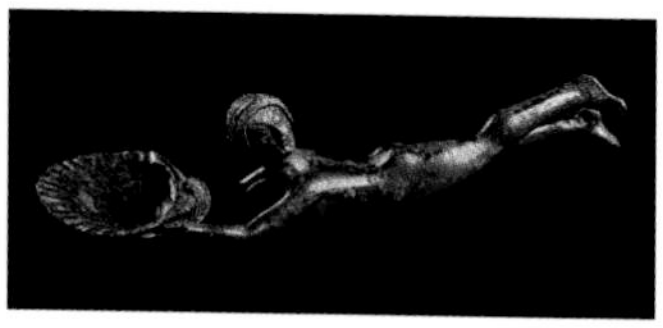

The spoon, modeled in the form of a naked female figure holding a shell, belonged to the grave goods of a chamber-tomb containing rich bronze furnishings (including a round brazier decorated with figures of satyrs, a quadrangular one with feet shaped like winged genii, a *thimiaterion* with the figure of an athlete, and a *stamnos*) and Attic and Etruscan painted pottery. References for this item, as for the other bronze items in the grave goods, are to be sought in the local bronze production of the late Archaic period.

Nardi Dei 1881, p. 243; Milani 1882, pp. 51, 232; Bianchi Bandinelli 1925, c. 251 ff.; Ducati 1927, p. 289, fig. 310; Rastrelli 1997 p. 75; Rastrelli 2000, p. 148, fig. 174.
[A.R.]

87. Dragon-shaped fibula
second quarter of seventh century B.C.
cast silver, laminated gold; decoration in the round and granulated
l 15.5 cm
Florence, Museo Archeologico, inv. 20982
from Marsiliana d'Albegna, Banditella necropolis, Circolo della Fibula

All the surfaces are decorated with granulation in geometric motifs; on the bow, pairs of little ducks, opposing two lions; on the stirrup, series of ten little ducks. This fibula is one of the most precious items of personal adornment belonging to the rich owner of this tomb, whose grave goods also featured bronze arms, ivory articles and tableware. This is an item of south-Etrurian make, probably Caeretan, the same to which some of the most gorgeous goldsmith work of the tombs of Palestrina and Cerveteri itself belong.

Milani 1912, pp. 315 ff.; Minto 1921, pp. 83 ff., 196 ff., pl. XI, 2; *L'Oro degli Etruschi 1983*, p. 266, n. 50 with ref.
[G.C.C.]

88. Fibula
end of seventh century B.C.
gold
l 8.9 cm
New York, The Metropolitan Museum of Art, inv. 95.15.198, acquired by subscription, 1895
from Roselle (?)

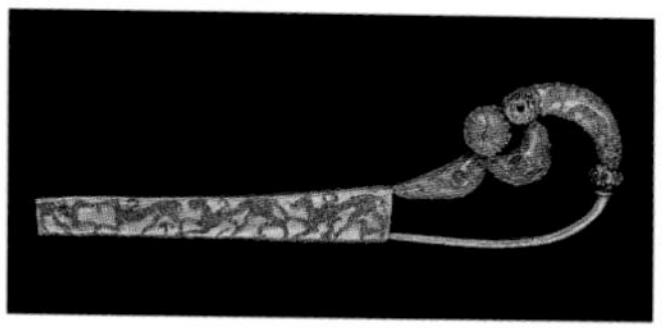

Snake fibula, with richly ornamented bow. Both the bow and the pin are decorated with very fine granulation, arranged to form figurines. On each side of the pin there are two rows of animals, while on the bow as well as animals there is a human figure. This type of very fine granulation (*pulviscolo*) is mainly known owing to the items from very rich tombs in the Vetulonia area, and that is why it is assumed this type of jewel was made in Vetulonia.

Alexander, 1928, 39 n. 90; Richter, 1940, p. 9, figs. 27, 29; Brown, 1960, p. 45, n. 9; Hackens, 1976, p. 31 b; Llewellyn Brown, 1960, p. 45, n. 9; Cristofani, Martelli, 1983, p. 282 n. 107, ill. p. 142-143; Duval, 1989, p. 29 n. 28.
[C.S.L.]

89. Disc fibula
650–625 B.C.
goldleaf
h 19.2 cm
Munich, Staatliche Antikensammlungen, NI 2331 WAF
from Vulci, necropolis of Ponte Sodo

The body of the fibula is arched with a rim and incised granulation; standing full triangles, in the upper part eight figures of ducks in the round. Over that shield-shaped piece two horizontal stirrups, also with granulation, in the middle of which a pair of lions is seated. Over the stirrups a disk in gold leaf slightly flattened toward the bottom. In the figured field, an incised image: above two lions turned toward a cross, above them a water-fowl in flight. Under the two parts of a triangle a pair of warriors fighting, behind the figures here also a flying water-fowl.

Kunst und Leben der Etrusker 1955, n. 382; Cristofani 1983, p. 281, n.100. [F.W.H.]

90. Fibula with plastic decoration
525–500 B.C.
gold (processed, chiseled, granulated, filigreed)
h 8.5 cm
Schaffhausen, Museum zu Allerheiligen, Ebnöther Collection, inv. 22170
from Vulci (?)

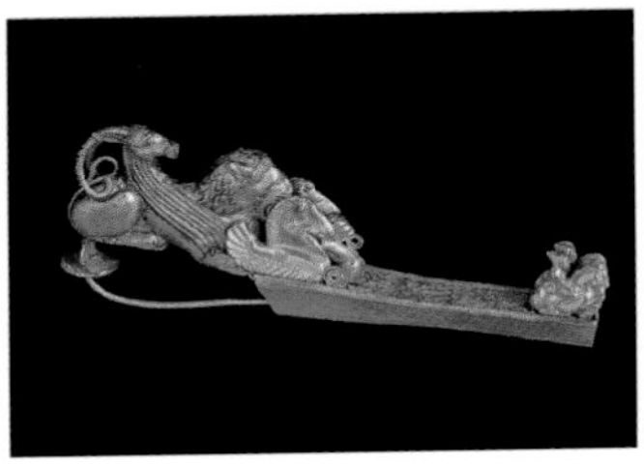

Reference to the myth of the Corinthian hero Bellerophon, who flies to Lycia on his winged horse Pegasus, to slay the Chimaera, represented here as a lion whose wings join to form a goat head. In front of the animal appears a duplicate winged Pegasus, in the middle a small lion, in front probably the spiral-shaped springs that gush when he stamps his hooves. The three Amazons on the front edge of the fibula refer to another of the hero's feats. [G.S.]

91–92. Pair of "bauletto" earrings
middle decades of the first half of the sixth century B.C.
gold leaf; one exemplar has small lacunas
w 0.19 cm; diam. 0.21 cm
Florence, Museo Archeologico; inv. 89262–89263
from Populonia, necropolis of Poggio della Porcareccia, Tomb of the Flabelli

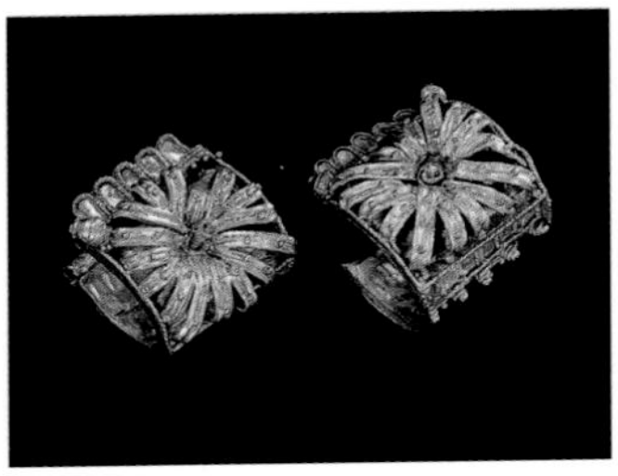

Made of a curved rectangular leaf open at the ends, the smaller sides being attached by a wire that passed through the lobe of the ear. In the visible part, inside a space topped by a band with five knurled petals and small balls at the corners, inflorescence formed by sixteen relief petals, in goldleaf, each of which is decorated with three tiny balls. On the back, four decorated transversal bands.
One of the styles of earrings that was the most popular during the Archaic period in Etruria is that of the production of these earrings "a bauletto," which are assumed to derive from well-known types within the gold production of the Orientalizing period generally attributed to Vetulonia. Widespread throughout Tyrrhenian central Italy and, perhaps, even in Magna Graecia, between mid-sixth century B.C. and the first thirty years of the following century, this type of jewel was made by countless ateliers located in various centers, among which the ones in Vulci must have had an eminent role (on the type now see Trümpler 1988). The pair being examined, probably referable to a Vulci workshop and connected with later depositions in the tomb, is one of the oldest examples of the entire group, chronologically situated around the middle decades of the first half of the sixth century B.C.

Minto 1932, c. 295, pl. II.7; Minto 1943, p. 140, pl. XXX.11; *Schätze der Etrusker* 1986, p. 202 n. 15; *Etrusker in der Toskana* 1987, pp. 222 ff., n. 8
[S.B.]

93. "Bauletto" earring
ca. 570–560 B.C.
w 0.17 cm; diam. 0.20 cm
goldleaf, complete
Florence, Museo Archeologico; inv. 89264
from Populonia, necropolis of Poggio della Porcareccia, Tomb of the Flabelli

The form is like the ones above. In the visible part, within a filigreed space, inflorescence formed by four lanceolate petals placed diagonally, alternating with the same number of ovate petals, around a central ring. On the back two raised longitudinal rope motifs. The decorative motif of the visible part is one of the most common of the repertory of the group. An exact match can be found in the earring from tomb N of the tumulus of Molinello di Asciano (*Schätze der Etrusker* 1986, p. 252 n. 7.2), that confirms the datation to the years around 570–560 B.C.

Minto 1932, c. 295, pl. II.9; Minto 1943, p. 140, pl. XXX.9; *Schätze der Etrusker* 1986, p. 202 n. 16; *Etrusker in der Toskana* 1987, p. 223 n. 9
[S.B.]

94. Chain with brooch
third quarter of seventh century B.C.
cast gold, laminated, decorated with filigree and granulation
l 0.52; l of brooch 0.067
Volterra, Museo Guarnacci, inv. MG 4314
gift of the Bishop Gaetano Incontri (1839)
from Volterra, Gesseri di Berignone

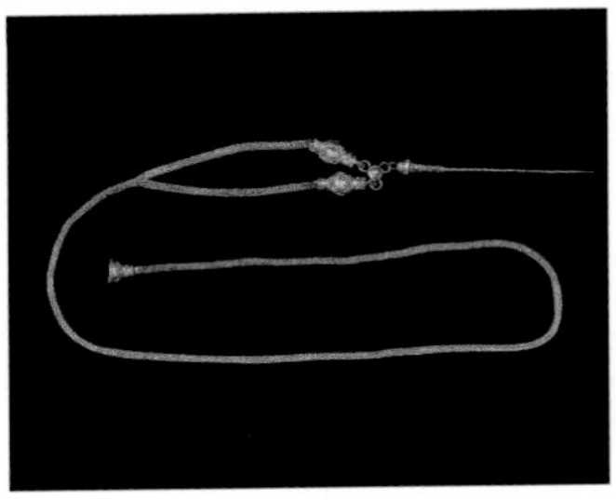

Chain of extremely fine gold links forking off at one end. The two segments end in as many small balls topped by little cylinders joined to a spheroidal element squeezed between two of the three loops it is equipped with. On the third loop hangs a brooch with a bulging head under which there is a decoration with nodules and filigree. Lacunose at one end. Part of a small ball is missing. There remains part of another small ball with cylinder at the other end.

Oro degli Etruschi 1985, p. 273, n. 68 [G.C.]

95. Necklace
third quarter of fourth century B.C.
laminated gold, embossed decoration
max. h pendants 2 cm
Florence, Museo Archeologico, inv. 15951
formerly Cinci Collection; from Volterra, Portone necropolis

The necklace consists of sixteen gold-leaf pendants decorated alternately with heads of sileni and of maenads, the two ends being two rams' heads. This exemplar, as well as two like necklaces, also from Volterra, belongs to a type, also figured on the earthenware statues of Lavinius, representing the Etruscan version of models widespread in Taranto goldsmith workshops; in particular, the Silenus head has many matches in Volterra circles not just in the goldsmith workshops, but in the black-glaze vases from the Malacena workshop as well.

Fiumi 1957, p. 481, fig. 6; *L'Oro degli Etruschi 1983,* p. 316, n. 265, with bibl.; *Gioielli e Ornamenti,* n. 78, p. 146. [G.C.C.]

96. Ring
first half of fourth century B.C.
cast gold; embossed decoration
diam. 2.3 cm; bezel 2 x 1.2 cm
Florence, Museo Archeologico, inv. 80882
from Populonia

Ring with almond-shaped bezel that figures a warrior, with helmet, cuirass and shield, and a standing woman, embracing: it is probably a farewell scene, recalling models often treated in Etruscan toreutics, especially on mirrors, yet whose figures cannot be identified, owing to the lack of specific attributes. The ring belongs to a series of typical Etruscan make, the so-called "Fortnum Group," already known by the end of the fifth century B.C., but more particularly asserted during the next century.

Boardman 1966, p. 12, n. XIX, pl. V, with previous bibl.; *Gioielli e Ornamenti dagli Egizi all'alto Medioevo* 1988, n. 75, p. 146. [G.C.C.]

97. Ring with scarab
third quarter of fourth century B.C.
gold and sardonyx; complete diameter 0.29 cm; scarab 0,93 x 0,65 x 0,65 cm
Florence, Museo Archeologico; inv. 84464
from Populonia, acquisition Vitalini (B.C. n. 1433 del 2.II.1910)

Ring with a plain band with a sardonyx scarab, fastened to the band by a braided gold wire. On the flat base, within a frame of dashes, is incised a frontal female head, wearing a necklace.

From the last third of the sixth century B.C. until the end of the Hellenistic age in Etruria, the use of rings with a revolving scarab gem inserted in a gold band was wide-spread (Boardman-Vollenweider 1978, pp. 48 ff.; Martelli 1983, p. 57). The stones, owed in the early stage to stone cutters from Eastern Greece, present for the most part figurations drawn from the repertory of Greek mythology and sagas, probably connected with the genealogical mythopoeisis of the Etruscan aristocracy (cf. Krauskopf 1995; Krauskopf 1996, pp. 405 ff.), influencing in the late classical age and early Hellenism also the Roman-Latium ambit, where at the time a workshop was active that produced in Archaizing style a series of scarabs with subjects not attested in Etruria (Moret 1995, pp. 51 ff.). The formal characteristics of the cutting of the Populonia scarab place it among the exemplars of the late "free style," also called "transition," allowing to date it to the third quarter of the fourth century B.C.

Zazoff 1968, p. 178 n. 937. [S.B.]

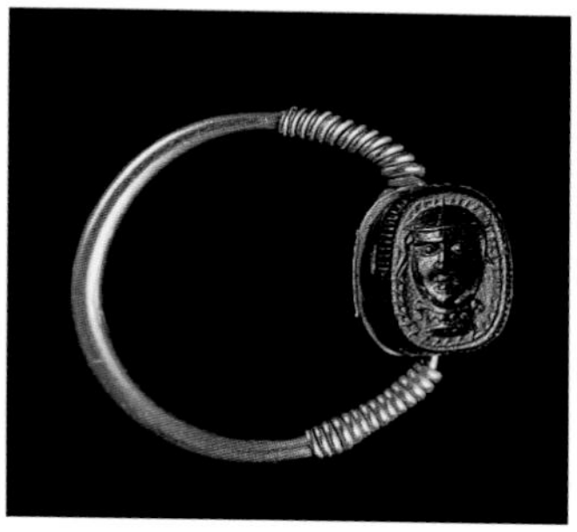

98. Pod
ca. 480 B.C.
gold-plated; quartz
h 3 cm; w 3.5 cm
Rome, Museo di Villa Giulia, inv. 44009
from Vignanello, necropolis of the Cupa, Tomb VII

It consists of a semi-circular plate, surrounded by small pods, decorated with a granulated palmette-motif; at the base the plate is completed by a semi-circular bezel with notched edges, in which a quartz-stone is set. The field is embossed with the image of a banqueting satyr, whose hairiness is rendered by an accurate hatched chiseling. The partly reclining figure is resting the upper part of its body on a series of double spirals, and the close-set granulation of the background produces a precious coloring effect. At top there is a rosette with lanceolate petals.

Rizzo 1985, p. 301, n. 195, fig. p. 192, with previous bibl. [M.A.D.L.B.]

99. Disc earring
last thirty years of the sixth century B.C.
gold; edges and disk slightly deformed, one of the knurled wires partly detached
diam. 3.10 cm; h small tube 0.70 cm; diam. 0.30 cm
Florence, Museo Archeologico; inv. 15950
from Pescia Romana, excavations L. Malducca 1879, acquisition 1880

Goldleaf disc filigreed and embossed on the outside with concentric motifs. From the outer edge, within smooth spaces, series of filigree rings, series of filigree *peltae*, series of rosettes with four diagonal petals in embossed goldleaf; in the middle six flowers in overlaid goldleaf with central pistil formed by a tiny ball. The outer edge presents a beaded knurled wire. In the inside part, small perpendicular tube attached to a goldleaf rosette.
In the past mistakenly thought to be a pod for fastening clothes on the shoulder (Marshall 1911, p. 137), this type of earring, whose way of being used is evidenced by

many attestations in the Etruscan figurative repertory of the second half of the sixth century B.C., belongs to styles in the Minor-Asiatic area (cfr. Brein 1982). Compared to other exemplars, that present, as a device for fastening the jewel to the person, a small cylindrical pin with a hole at the end placed vertically to the disk, the earring from Pescia Romana has on the back a small transversal tube which probably should be identified as serving the same purpose. The decoration, in its individual motifs, has likenesses with other exemplars of the series, some of which come from the same workshop (see for instance British Museum inv. BM-CJ 1420), as well as with other types of jewelry usually ascribed to Vulci production (cf. *Gioielli ed ornamenti* 1988, p. 141). Last thirty years of the sixth century B.C.

Gioielli ed ornamenti 1988, p. 141 n. 56 [S. Bruni]; *Ori e argenti nelle collezioni del Museo Archeologico* 1990, p. 28.
[S.B.]

100. Tube earring
second half fourth– early third century B.C.
laminated gold, embossed and granulated decoration.
diam. ring 3 cm; diam. pendant 1 cm
Florence, Museo Archeologico, inv. 15765
formerly Currie Collection; provenance unknown

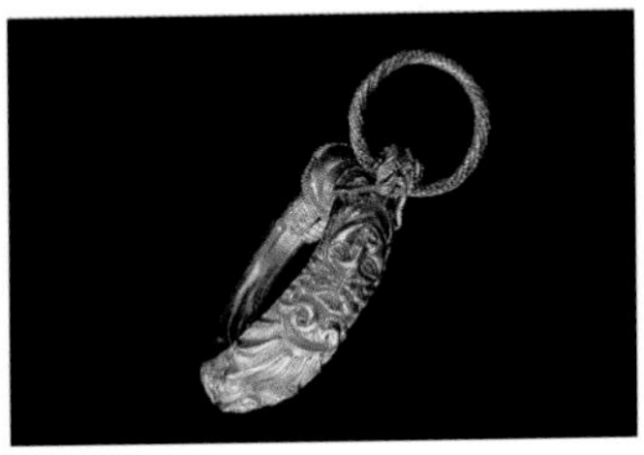

This earring is a variant of the "simple tube" type. That type, already recorded at Aleria in the second quarter of the fifth century B.C., became widespread, mainly in northern Etruscan circles, during the fourth-third centuries B.C., evolving into more and more complicated, elaborate forms. Yet lacking the provenance, and therefore the referential chronological elements, we can only suggest a generical dating between the second half of the fourth and the early third century B.C.

Gioielli ed Ornamenti 1988, n. 88, p. 149.
[G.C.C.]

101. Diadem
late fourth century B.C.
laminated gold; embossed, stamped and applied decoration
Florence, Museo Archeologico, inv. 94396
from Populonia, Piano delle Granate necropolis, known as "Buca di Spoglio"

On the small lateral plaques there is a Scylla viewed frontally with a dolphin held aloft in each hand and with snakelike lower extremities coiled in spirals and ending in a bearded dog protome. These pieces seem to belong to a single context, whose exceptional character in the Populonia context is obvious: in the first place because of its great wealth, having yielded at least three diadems, and in the second place because of the unusual presence of a helmet. Both circumstances are clearly significant, even if in Etruria we do know of other depositions with two or more crowns, sometimes associated with helmets.

De Agostino 1961, pp. 97 ff., figs. 34–35; Cianferoni 1992, pp. 25 ff., figs. 35–36. [G.C.C.]

102. Diadem
end of the fourth century B.C.
laminated gold; embossed, stamped and applied decoration
h 19.1 cm; l 33 cm
Florence, Museo Archeologico, inv. 84339
from Perugia, locality Sperandio

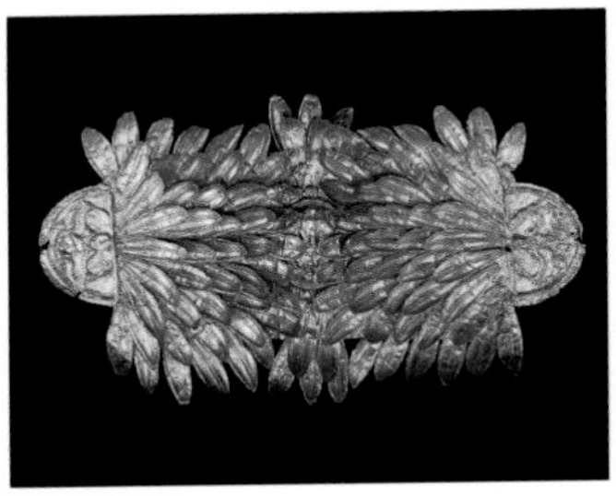

The diadem consists of a rectangular lamina bearing at the extremities small semi-circular plaques, on which is represented a Typhon, seen frontally, raising aloft a dolphin in each hand. On the band is applied a close-set series of laurel leaves, arranged in rays on five rows turned on each side toward the center, where an elliptical pod is mounted. On the pod there is a winged female figure holding a mirror in her right hand and an unguent jar in the left. This diadem, on the basis of the context, and also considering the figuration on the central pod, referring to feminine toiletries, appears to belong to a woman.

[G.C.C.]

103. Necklace
ca. 630 B.C.
gold, bronze, glass paste
length reconstructed 11 cm
Chianciano Terme, Museo Civico Archeologico, inv. 149
from Marsiliana d'Albegna

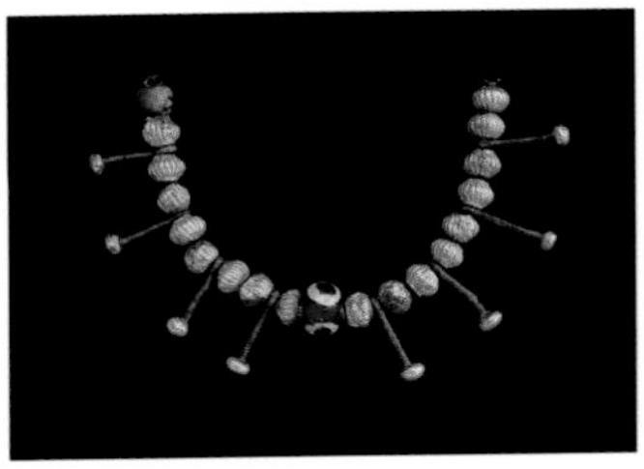

Necklace formed of eighteen goldleaf beads, adorned with thin pods, joined in pairs and alternating with eight cylindrical bronze elements, ending in a small flattened button; in the middle is placed a blue glass paste bead, decorated with three yellow circles.

De Tommaso, Nicosia 1991, p. 96.
[G.P.]

104. Two brooch heads
third quarter of seventh century B.C.
gold
diam. 1.3 cm
Chianciano Terme, Museo Civico Archeologico, inv. 148

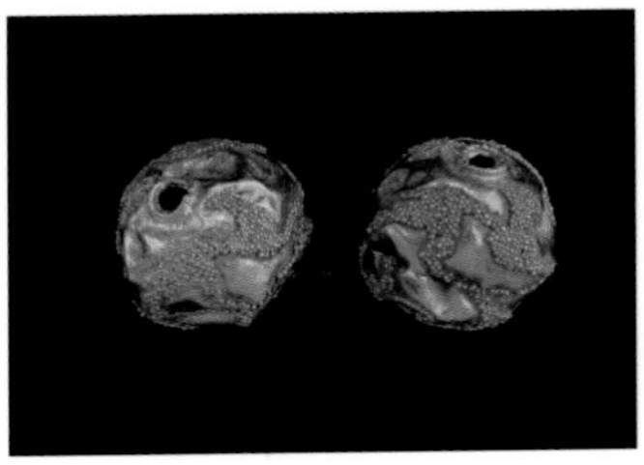

Heads formed by half-spheres connected in the middle section, plated with a thin gold dust wire upon which are arrayed figures of gradient right felines in a specular opposition.

De Tommaso, Nicosia 1991, p. 97.
[G.P.]

105. Brooch
third quarter of seventh century B.C.
gold
l 16.5 cm; diam. 1 cm
Chianciano Terme, Museo Civico Archeologico; inv. 147

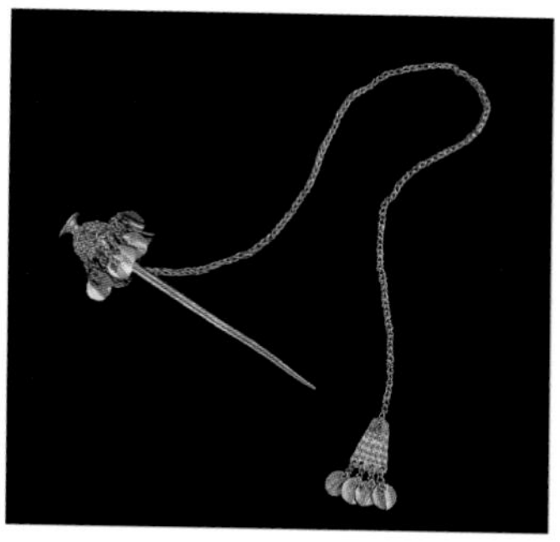

Sphere-shaped head, adorned in fine gold dust exclusively in the upper part and bearing on the median line several short fine chains ending in little round lamina leaves, with a central ribbing. Needle with upper tip holding a small disc with a fine rope-like chain attached, made of interwoven double threads forming a herringbone decorative motif. The chain carries a triangular pendant with rounded angles equipped with holes to which are attached four tiny leaves.

De Tommaso, Nicosia 1991, p. 99.
[G.P.]

106. Pair of armlets
seventh century B.C.
gold
diam. 8 cm
Chianciano Terme, Museo Civico Archeologico; inv. 152

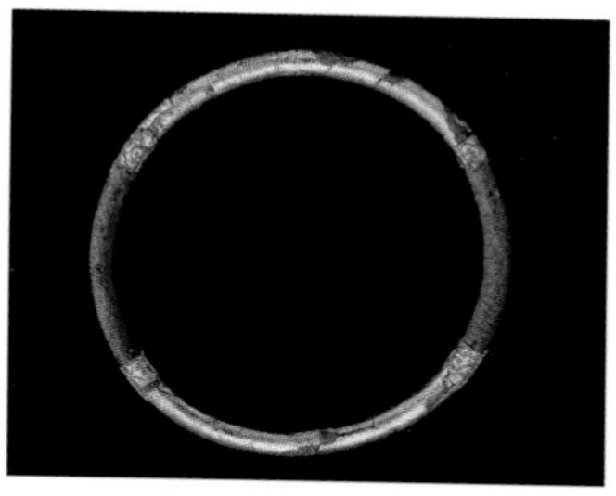

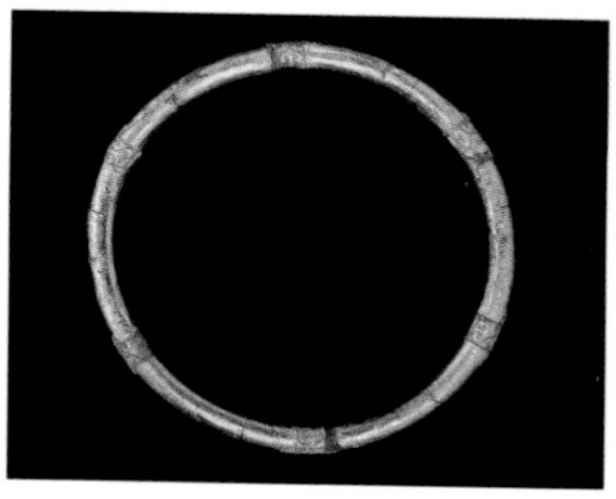

Circular round-section bronze armlets plated with goldleaf adorned with small rectangular bands (six in one exemplar, four in the other) decorated with granulation in a motif of two pairs of double spirals over two palmettes adorning the back of the bracelets.

De Tommaso, Nicosia 1991, p. 99.
[G.P.]

107. Pair of loop earrings
first quarter of sixth century B.C.
gold
diam. 0.8 cm
Chianciano Terme, Museo Civico Archeologico, inv. 140
from Pescia Romana

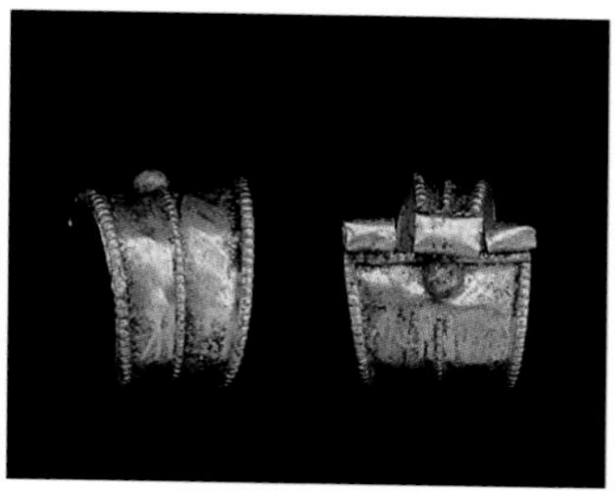

Trapezoidal gold leaf with two small rings on the ends for holding the clasp of the fastener hinge. On the edges and lengthwise in the middle part of the lamina narrow motif in coiled filigree, small semispherical granule placed at the center of the wider end

Paolucci 1991, p. 102.
[G.P.]

108. Pair of "bauletto" earrings
540–510 B.C.
gold
diam. 1.8 cm
Chianciano Terme, Museo Civico Archeologico, inv. 138
from Pescia Romana

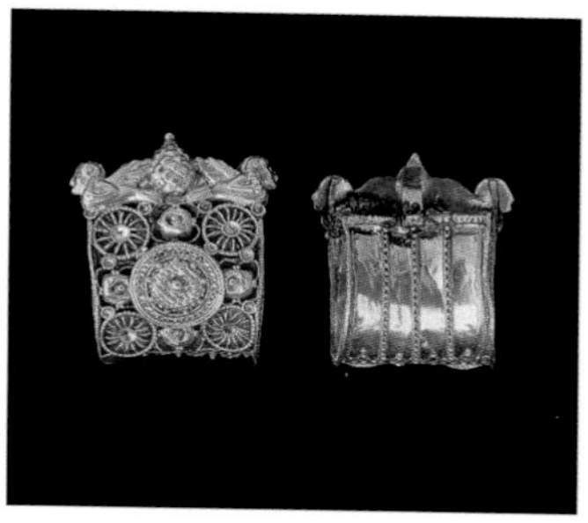

Curved rectangular lamina decorated on the upper extremity with two facing sphinxes with their heads in profile and a pinecone in between. In the median part element with a round ornamentation with nine small *repoussé* spheres along the circonference and one in the center surrounded by a braid and two gold threads. At the corners phytomorph motifs with rings radiating around a hollow pistil and in the reserved spaces four corollas formed by four goldleaf petals. On the back three lengthwise lines and four lanceolate petals. On the sides filigree braid.

Paolucci 1991, p. 104.
[G.P.]

109. Fibula
second half of the sixth century B.C.
gold
length cm 3; h cm 1.8
Chianciano Terme, Museo Civico Archeologico, inv. 137
from Vulci

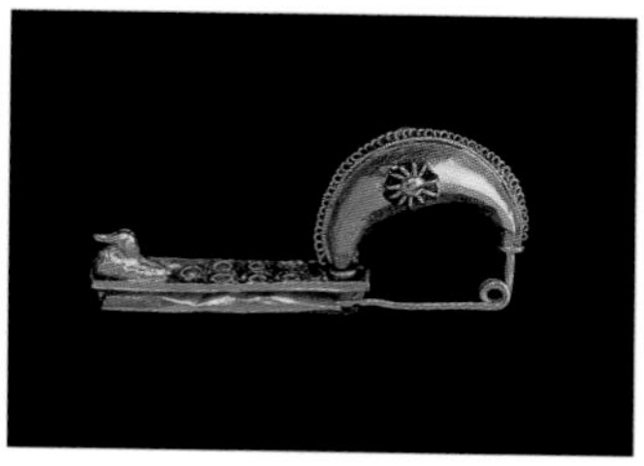

Bow formed by two soldered leaves, adorned lengthwise with a filigree braid motif; on the convex part a flower with six petals with vertical rings placed around a semispherical pistil. Short catchplate with slightly upturned edges, decorated with seven lamina flower corollas with small ball pistil arranged in pairs save the last one. At the tip, tiny figure of a duck

Paolucci 1991, p. 103.
[G.P.]

110. Tubular element (fragment of candelabra?)
late seventh century B.C.
glass paste
h 13 cm
Trevignano Romano (Rome), Museo Civico, inv. 70160
from Trevignano Romano, Olivetello necropolis, Annesi Piacentini Tomb

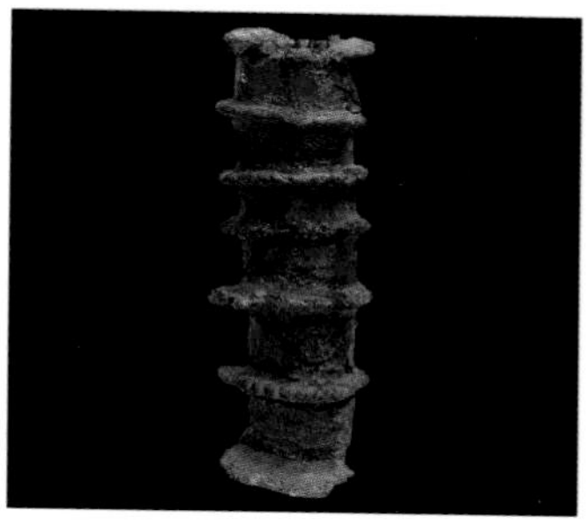

Tubular element with moldings made of fused glass. The tips are very lacunose and do not allow to accurately establish the typology of the fragment, that might belong to a candelabra or to a distaff. The glass paste processing technique is very interesting, and can be compared with coeval materials found in Cerveteri, Marsiliana and Campovalano. This technique should be associated with the production of the "bristly balsam" vessels found in Etruscan grave goods between the middle of the eighth century to the first thirty years of the sixth century B.C.

Martelli 1994, p. 76. [I.C.]

111–112. Oinochoai
late seventh century B.C.
blue glass with friable nucleus
h 3 cm
Florence, Museo Archeologico,
inv. 94080–94981
from Vetulonia, tumulus of
Castelvecchio

Two *oinochoai* with trilobate mouth, low neck, broad shoulder, trunco-conical body, large disk foot, ribbon handle.

Camporeale, Uggeri, Banti 1966, p. 30, ns. 13–14.
[F.C.]

113. Necklace
late seventh century B.C.
amber; blue glass
l of the beads 2.7 cm
Florence, Museo Archeologico,
inv. 94225
from Vetulonia, tumulus
of Castelvecchio

Necklace of amber and glass beads, roundish and cylindrical, alternating with four pendant beads, with a blue glass pendant bead in the middle.

Camporeale, Uggeri, Banti 1966, p. 41, n. 161.
[F.C.]

114. Tridacna
sixth century B.C.
shell
max. h 9.5; w 7 cm
Paris, Musée du Louvre;
inv. AO 7680
acquisition 1921

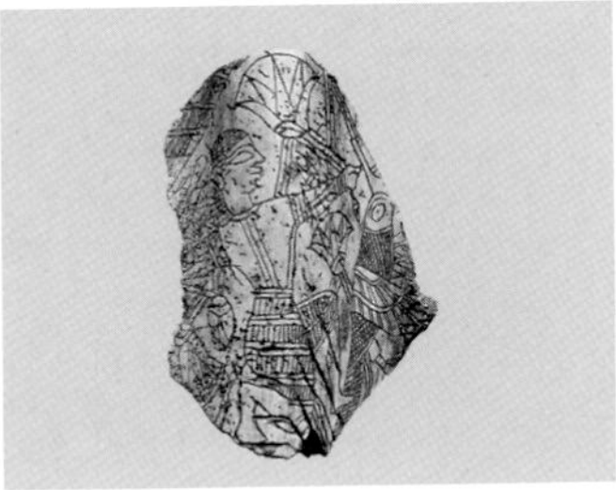

Fragment of *tridacna*, decorated on both the outer and inner surfaces. On the outside kneeling male figure facing right, with wig and short-sleeved vest with beaded skirt; facing, a large bird; in the field lotus buds. On the inside three registers: from top to bottom, kneeling figure facing left, with short-sleeved vest with beaded skirt facing a composite vegetable element, with palmetta in the middle; in the field, buds; series of triangles on latticed background alternating with other smaller, empty ones; chain of upside-down buds.

Blinkenberg 1931, cc. 176–78, figs. 22–23.
[C.Z.]

115. Antropomorphic alabastron
600–550 B.C.
plaster
h 24.5 cm
Florence, Museo Archeologico,
inv. 89293 b
from Populonia, Porcareccia,
Tomb of the Flabelli

Mouth with out-turned lip; upper part of the body figuring a female head, with long hair in parallel locks falling on her shoulders; long cylindrical body, with convex bottom.

Schätze der Etrusker 1986, p. 205, n. 29; Romualdi 1987, pp. 227 ff., n. 22.
[F.C.]

116. Aryballos
early sixth century B.C.
orange clay; black glaze; purple glaze
conserved h 4.5 cm
Florence, Museo Archeologico,
inv. 4205

Distinct cylindrical neck, black glazed; body shaped like a bivalve shell, with wavy, alternated black and purple lines. Eastern Greek make (Rhodes?)

Martelli 1978, p. 212, n. 122, fig. 90.
[F.C.]

117. Two halves of an ostrich egg
seventh century B.C.
ostrich egg; traces of color
max. h 6.7 and 5.5 cm; diam. 12.8 and 13.3 cm
Florence, Museo Archeologico, inv. 8792.
from Vetulonia, Circolo del Monile d'Argento

Twenty fragments belonging to about half of an egg, cut in two in the shape of a bowl. Inside remains of red colouring. On the outside surface traces of colour. Traces of emptying hole (?) about 30 mm wide. Near the old rim three incised parallel lines, combined with some oblique dashes and, practically in the middle, a small triangle on hatched background.
Nineteen fragments forming about half the rim of an egg, cut in two in the shape of a bowl.
The presence of a third egg seems hinted at by a series of twenty-one fragments, forming most of a half cap, decorated with three parallel bands of hatched wolves' teeth and two concentric equilateral triangles, probably decorated with blanks and hatching, next to three long lines. Six other fragments, instead, are difficult to identify.

Falchi, Pernier 1913, p. 427; Torelli 1965, pp. 335 ff. n. 5; Camporeale 1969, p. 102.
[C.Z.]

118. Ostrich egg
Mid-seventh century B.C.
ocher colored glaze
h 16.9 cm; diam. 12.1 cm
Tarquinia, Museo Archeologico, inv. 3987
confiscated at Montalto di Castro, 1961

Decoration of geometric motifs, interspersed with a procession of birds and a frieze of lotus buds and flowers in the upper half and a frieze with human figures dancing together in the lower half. Three holes, pierced before the painting, two coinciding with the caps and one in between the two other ones.

Torelli 1965, pp. 329–65; *Gli Etruschi e l'Europa* 1992, p. 126 n. 87.
[C.Z.]

119. Small rectangular plaque
640–630 B.C.
ivory carved in relief
h 10 cm; w 8.1 cm; thickness at rim 0.5 cm
Florence, Museo Archeologico, inv. 194662.
from Comeana, tumulus of Montefortini, from the *dromos* of the *tholos* tomb

Reconstituted from a number of fragments; splits, scratches and cracks are visible on the carved side as well as the unadorned back side. Remaining are the left edge, the lower one with lacunas, the left part of the upper one, the lower part of the right one. Because of a large lacuna in the right upper part, are lost: the head, part of the bust and the left arm of the person placed on the right, as well as the extremity of the upper left limb of the three-headed person on the left; also missing on this one, because they continued on the adjoining plaque, now lost, the part of the right upper limb from before the elbow and the part of the right lower limb from before the knee. The adjoining plaque to the left had been attached to this one by two precious iron pins in the upper part and an ivory pin inserted like a mortise in the lower lateral edge. Above on the left and below on the right there are the tips of two ivory pins, orthogonal to the plane of the plaque, meant for fastening it to the surface of the "furniture" to be adorned with ivory plaques: their surface extremity is part of in the decoration.
It belonged to a chest, or an important chair, or even—less probably—to an element of a parade chariot: the circumstances of the excavation seem to attest that, right after the earthquake that made the *tholos* tomb unfit for use or else unsafe, the most valuable elements present in the tomb were opportunely recovered, elements that were probably put aside while waiting for the construction of the rectangular chamber-tomb, that presumibly received the containers of the ashes of the deceased and the most prestigious objects; it well may be that the "furniture" had been broken or else part of it left in the *dromos*, and part thrown away; the items recovered in the successive tomb, with the rectangular *cella*, were subjected to various spoliations and various upheavals that occurred in the centuries between Antiquity and Modern times, for plunder.
The height of the plaque being examined coincides with that of the upper part of another plaque of the group (inv. 194659: *Principi Etruschi* 2000, p. 248,n. 292), that is conserved complete, with decoration on two registers and upon which is represented in relief a person holding onto the hide of a four-footed animal, according to an iconographical pattern analogous to the one used by Odysseus escaping from the Cyclop's cavern. Although, in its present state, I cannot suggest an identification of such a scene, it seems out of the question that the other plaque might represent Odysseus' Homeric flight from Polyphemus' cavern: the animal has high, nervous legs, like those of a stag, rather than of a ram; besides, on this one's back there is a long, branching antler; last, this possible stag seems to be yoked. The lower part of the same plaque (where we see a stag with a dog on its back and that is grazed by arrows) might coincide with the level of another plaque (inv. 194655: *Principi Etruschi* 2000, p. 248, n. 293) figuring a warrior and a fallen man. The upper edge of the scene of our plaque consists of a plain braid between two tores, whereas the lower edge here is not indicated by a horizontal frieze, perhaps because the braid was there to crown the top of a plaque underneath it.
On the left part of the plaque there is a monstrous three-headed person, whose *three heads* rise from a single bust, shown frontally, from which issue just *two* upper limbs: the left one, extended in back slanting upward, ended in the upper right part of the plaque, missing because of a break; the right limb, interrupted by the left edge of the plaque, is extended slanting upward. We cannot say whether these limbs ended in hands or in claws: actually, of the lower limbs the only one conserved, the left, ends in a clawed foot with five nails, while all that is left of the right one is

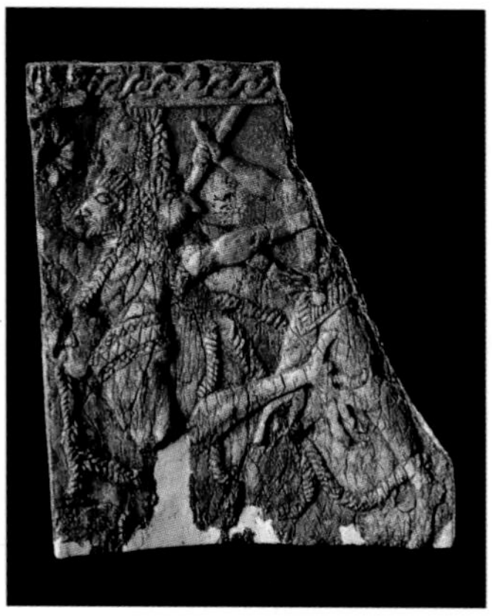

the initial part of the thigh. The positions of the limbs (the upper ones widely outstretched, the lower ones outstretched the same way, in a "cleft" position, toward the left) might suggest a position "in flight" of the person, or instead, in mid-air because of a leap (in fact there are no indications of wings). The pubic-buttucks area is somehow wrapped in a loincloth composed of three bands one on top of another, the two upper ones decorated with zigzags, the third with a lattice of lozenges. The nails of the only remaining clawed foot, arranged like the fingers of a hand (an upper nail opposed to four lower ones) are extended along the thigh and the left leg of the other person. Of the three heads (with beard and moustache) arranged in a pyramid, the top one is facing left, one of the lower ones is looking forward and the other backward. Into the latter one, or be-

side it, we can clearly see a rapier penetrating from above and coming out level with the left pectoral. The rapier is held in the antagonist's raised right hand (featuring a huge thumb). The latter, striding left with his right leg forward and the left on tiptoes, is wearing a loincloth with a pointed lower edge, in the middle of which you can see a round bead; the rest of the costume is decorated with thick pendent lines. Of the left hand two fingers remain, visible on the handle of a sword. The three-headed monster has a hairstyle in which you discern several very long "ramified" elements rendered either by "string-decoration" with slanting dashes, or by stems placed obliquely beside elements like small leaves. The elements of these long locks that start from the sides of the three heads and fall in waves to the ground, branching out in various points, remind us of long plant shoots (see the corded shoots on another plaque of the same series with a goat rampant, probably Amalthea: inv. n. 194658 [*Principi Etruschi* 2000, p. 249 n. 296]), the extremity of one of which appears to be wrapped around the antagonist's left ankle. The monstrous person seems to be running away, chased, caught and struck by the one on the right, armed with rapier and sword, held level with the waist and pointed against the backward-looking face of the three-headed figure. The particular treatment of the "locks" might indicate a close relationship of the monstrous person with the plant world. In the upper left corner is also conserved the tip of a floral or palmette-shaped element (you can see at least six uneven petals), whose origin, probably through a calyx, certainly arose from a plant element of the adjoining plaque. A quite like element is present in the Amalthea plaque mentioned above; another, rather similar, although a bit more closed, is placed behind the tail of the centaur represented in the plaque inv. n. 240155 (*Principi Etruschi* 2000, p. 249 n. 294). It seems quite natural to identify in the scene represented on our plaque the killing of Geryon by Herakles: yet such an identification seems contradicted by not only the Greek iconographical tradition on the myth (d'Agostino 1991), but by a number of Mediterranean iconographies as well (see Brize). Several elements are extraneous to the canons of the consolidated Greek iconography:
the mere three heads instead of the presence of three bodies juxtaposed and connected in a manner recalling the modern concept of "Siamese twins";
the absence of hoplitic armor found in the representations of Geryon since the Samos plaque, that Brize correctly dates to the last quarter of the seventh century B.C. (Brize, p. 187 n. 1), that is, before the Clusine *pyxis*;
the presence of at least one claw instead of a human limb;
the weird aspect of the hair-style, whose long ramified "locks" look like nearly "obedient" plant elements.
We should mention here that the Geryon of Hesiod's Theogonia (vv. 287–294) is not the source behind the traditional Greek iconography, that instead probably derives from the Geryonid of the *homerikotatos* Stesichorus, that tragedies follow: in the latter indeed, for all we know, Geryon is always *trisomatos* and protected by hoplitic armor, in some cases has wings and always walks on human legs, of which in late-Orientalizing representations known up to now there are two, whereas in Archaism the iconography with six legs and three distinct torsoes is asserted. A recurrent detail in Archaic iconography is the backward-looking third head, pierced by Herakles with a spear or an arrow: such a position seems persistent in the myth, and therefore appears in the Stesichoran tradition as well as in the preceding one, clearly abbreviated in Hesiod's text. In that tradition, Geryon might represent a strange person owner of his herd and lord of a wooded area, assailed by Herakles' violence: the Clusine figuration to which B.D'Agostino drew our attention might be marked by that tradition. On the subject, however, A.M. Adam's contribution (Adam 1985) remains essential. Due to the loss of the two plaques to the left and to the right of ours, we cannot determine the location of the herd and therefore its plotted or actual stealing by Herakles; the three-headed figure's position in mid-air recalls that of flight, but there are no wings, that furthermore a Classical source and Archaic iconographies attributed to Geryon.
The attribution of this plaque, like that of the others of the same context and the same area (northern Etruria hinterland), to specific "hands" and "masters and pupils" is still at an early stage, also because several events of the existence of the Montefortini tumulus and the Euboean necropolises in general remain to be clarified, or we still have but scarce indications about them (Nicosia 1966; Nicosia 1997a, pp. 25 ff.; Nicosia 1997b, pp. 49 ff.).
It has recently been suggested that the *athyrmata*, like the furniture to which decoration ours and other plaques belonged, had been produced by a workshop located in the northern Etruria hinterland, that is, in the territory that included the middle course of the Arno with its affluents Elsa, Pesa, Ombrone Pistoiese, Bisenzio, Mugnone, Sieve and the upper course of the Ombrone. Such a workshop usually produced *athyrmata*, that is, valuable items for display made of precious raw materials (ivory, ostrich egg, glass, faïence, silver and maybe gold) or else enhanced by the use of special techniques (buccheros and other high-quality earthenware (cfr. Tuck forthcoming; Nicosia 1983, pp. 15 ff.), embossed bronzes, bone, semi-precious stones). Among the first productions of this workshop we might count the ivory *pyxis* of Marsiliana and the embossed silver casket of the Tomb of the Duce of Vetulonia. Considering the need for raw materials imported from the "Phoenician" Orient and for personal technologies possessed by high-quality craftsmen, we might assume that the founder of such a workshop could have appeared on the scene after passing through a hitherto not identified stop-over in Po Valley Etruria, acquiring there other technological experiences and eventual clients: the hypothesis would allow to avoid ordering various finished Oriental items for various burial goods. The followers of such a workshop, at the time the urban formation of Chiusi was being stabilized, might have set up their businesses in that city (cfr. Nicosia, in *Principi Etruschi* 2000, pp. 246 ff.).
[F.N.]

120. Small plaques of a little chest
540–520 B.C.
ivory
h 6.5 cm; l 11.6–10.6 cm
Paris, Musée du Louvre, Département des Antiquités grecques, étrusques et romaines, inv. S 2028

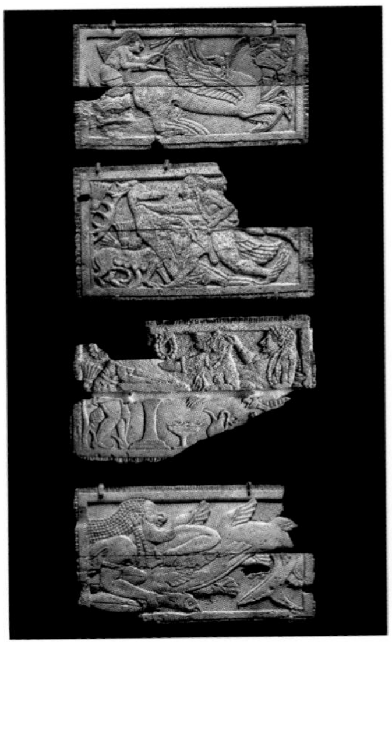

The plaques adorned a chest in perishable material, and are decorated with a biga drawn by winged horses; stag-hunt scene amid plant elements; couple in a banquet, with a servant, *oinochoe* and a dish; a sea monster.

Hus 1957, pp. 66–68; pls. XXXII–XXXIII; Martelli 1985, p. 208, figs. 1–4. [G.P.]

121. Comb
Final Bronze Age
horn, bone
l 9 cm; h 6 cm; lacunose
Rovigo, Museo Civico, IG 17438
from Frattesina di Fratta Polesine, hoard

Semi-circular comb, with a hole in the extremity, profiled with two pairs of triangles, and semi-circular hollows on the sides with the set of teeth. Decorated with small rings and central dot.

Bellintani, Peretto 1972, p. 37, n. 12 a; Bellato, Bellintani 1975, pp. 15–42, p. 31.
[F.C.]

122. Comb
mid-fifth century B.C.
wood
h 10.1 cm; w 8.6 cm
Ferrara, Museo Archeologico, inv. 20495
from Spina, Valle Pega, Tomb 34 D

Comb with double set of teeth, with slightly concave sides; on each side sets of incised horizontal lines.

Mostra dell'Etruriapadana e della città di Spina 1960, p. 354, n. 1152; Desantis 1993, p. 73, n. 4.
[F.C.]

123. Parasol
fourth–third century B.C.
bone
l handle 10.5 cm; l ribs 7.6–19 cm
Tarquinia, Museo Archeologico, inv. RC 6952

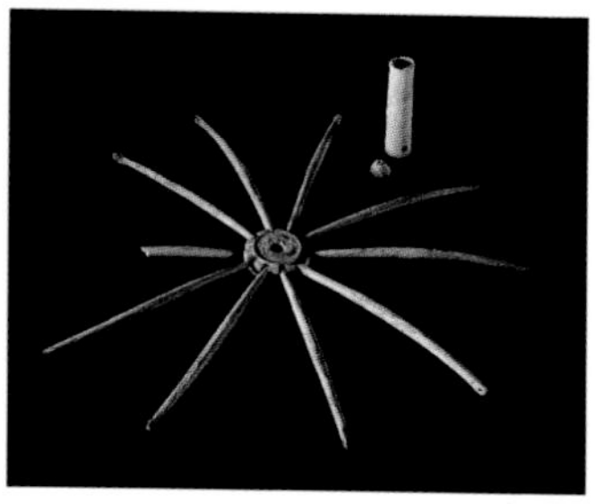

Disk wheel, with central hole and crown of teeth with horizontal holes, among which was inserted and held, with a rope or a metal wire, the end of the slightly curved ribs, with flattened and perforated tips; element of the cylindrical, hollow handle, with relief rings on the tips and at about mid-height; a hole near one end.
[F.C.]

124. Alabastron
650–550 B.C.
egyptian faïence (quartz powder) with decorations in yellow, and glaze only partially colored
h 10.9 cm; max. diam. 4.9 cm
Würzburg, Martin von Wagner Museum der Universität Würzburg, inv. H 5030
from Vulci

Three small feet separated by three holes, three decorated cords at the mouth, a crown of lotus leaves at the base, at centre two zoomorphic friezes, with three horses facing right amid papyrus plants and small stylized trees. The technique, the style and the use of yellow impasto suggest an eastern Greek provenance, probably Rhodian.

Scheunert 1999, p. 360, n. 192.
[I.W.]

125. Laconian aryballos
600–550 B.C.
purplish-brown clay; black glaze; purple and white color
h 6.1 cm
Florence, Museo Archeologico, inv. 89396
from Populonia, Porcareccia, Tomb of the Flabelli

Disk lip; low cylindrical body; globular body; vertical ribbon handle; wide purple band on lip; black-glazed body, with purple band between white lines and dots.

Martelli 1985, p. 414; Romualdi 1987, p. 260, n. 64.
[F.C.]

126. Bucchero aryballos
second half-late seventh century B.C.
bucchero; inscription to Turan
h 7 cm; max. diam. 4.4 cm; h of letters from 2.5 mm to 6 mm
Rome, Museo di Villa Giulia, temporary inv. S11/VI
from Cerveteri (?)

Pyriform *aryballos*. Form of proto-Corinthian inspiration. The continuous inscription of at least 174 Etruscan letters, incised after the firing and filled with white paste only in the residuous part, with rare punctuation marks, goes in a spiral and left to right from the shoulder to about the middle of the body, disposed on four or five lines. The recognition, among the few identifiable words in the text, of three groups of letters including Turan, the Etruscan name for Aphrodite, has led to assume it could be an amatory inscription or simply a votive one.

Torelli 1967, pp. 12 ff., n. 1a, fig. 1a; Bagnasco Gianni 1996, pp. 118 ff., n. 97, fig. 22, with bibl.; Moretti Sgubini 1999, p. 40, fig. 33. [L.R.]

The Role of Women

From the earliest phases of Etruscan history, the Villanovan necropolises constantly mark the difference in sex of the dead persons: the man is characterized by weapons, the woman by the tools of wool-making, such as distaffs, spools and fusaroles, and by personal ornaments.The reputation for licentiousness which is attached to the behavior of Etruscan women in the ancient sources, especially the Greek ones, which compare them to the women of Sparta and Locris, belongs to a later phase and is part of the Etruscan *tryphe* characteristic of the world of the Tyrrhenian *principes*. For we find Orientalizing tombs, as in the case of the Regolini-Galassi tomb at Caere, which was built for a woman who possesses *keimelia* equal to the ones found in male depositions; women of high rank are endowed with prestigious symbols such as the throne and the light chariot (*carpentum*) drawn by mules (there are also some cases of war chariots associated with women); the personal adornments include extraordinary golden ceremonial jewellery; *flabella*, also ceremonial and often carried by slave-girls, again emphasize the female rank. The world of women is also the target of much of the production of perfume and ointment containers which the sources criticize harshly, together with nudity, as a sign of excessive attention to the care of the body. Another feature of the Etruscan woman that was considered excessive and scandalous is her appearance on occasions when wine was consumed, such as banquets and symposiums, behavior also attested by the iconographic evidence, which the Greek sources can only interpret as comparable to the role of the *hetairae* in the symposiums of the Greek world.

All these points which struck the ancient writers and which have led the moderns to imagine an Etruscan matriarchy which never really existed are in fact perfectly explicable in the context of the markedly oligarchic nature of Etruscan society. The class of *principes* which places itself at the head of the community and controls most of the resources feels the need to guarantee the heriditary passage of wealth and power, and in this context the woman assumes the role of depositary of blood ties and vehicle of the transmission of the family rank. Moreover, the relatively limited number of the *principes* risks causing the dispersal of the inheritances and jeopardizing the closed, oligarchic nature of the ruling groups: the greater visibility of the woman serves to guarantee the functioning of these oligarchic societies by ensuring the total reproduction, both material and symbolic, of the group. Another important point is that a woman in this sort of society is a fundamental instrument in alliances and relations between aristocratic groups, owing to the practice of marriage exchange.

In fact the Etruscan woman belonging to the upper social classes becomes a Roman *domina* or *matrona*, celebrated for her virtues as a wife and her capacity to bear children, an attribute connected with the concern for family continuity mentioned above. Once she has passed from her father's power to that of her husband, the woman supervises the organizatory activities of the household and finds herself at the pinnacle of its chief domestic activity, the spinning and weaving of wool. This activity may be summed up as being a movement from the outermost to the innermost part of the home, where the rank of the people involved gradually increases: from the shearing of the sheep done outside by the servants to the winding of the wool in the inner courtyard by the serving-women or daughters of the *domina*, to the spinning and weaving supervised by the lady of the house. This ideology of the woman becomes permanently fixed in the context of the urban structures, and we find it documented by the married couple that appears in so many of the standardized productions of later periods. Around this basic nucleus other models of female figures which serve the needs of the evolution of society are grafted on in the course of time. We may recall in this connection the model of archaic kingship which was widespread in the seventh and sixth centuries B.C. and which may be described as that of the "goddess who gives the kingdom." This is an ancient motif of oriental provenance, but one that has been filtered through the Greek world; it justifies the a hero's ascent to the throne through the accomplishment of an extraordinary feat, and his subsequent sacred union with a goddess corresponding or similar to Aphrodite. The cult of Adonis reconstructed at Gravisca, or the story of Thefarie Velianas which is known from the gold tablets of Pyrgi, are just two of the most well-known examples. This motif, which is similar to that of Heracles reaching Olympus accompanied by Athena, lent itself very well to the function of signalling a new tyrannical power which was partly or wholly freed of the family dynasty, as in the case of Servius Tullius who becomes king of Rome despite being the son of a slave-girl. From the fourth century onward, in particular, we see a re-emergence in the representation of the woman of attention to the care of the body, under the influence of Hellenistic Greek and Greek-colonial models: alongside the mirror which had already been a symbol of feminine beauty in the past we find scenes of women naked beside a fountain engaged in the care of their bodies or hair, and we notice the spread of wedding gifts such as metal cistae for holding the combs, spatulas and cosmetics that may enhance the woman's power of seduction, a power exemplified, in the mythological scenes often associated with female objects, by the celebrated episode of the judgement of Paris. [M.M.]

127. Carpentum from Castel San Mariano near Corciano (Perugia)

Undoubtedly, one of the most significant ensembles of Archaic Italy is the one found in April 1812 on the slope of Colle di Castel San Mariano near Corciano, along the way connecting Chiusi and Val di Chiana with Perugia. The find belongs to a princely tomb, whose burial goods featured, among other things, two parade chariots, a carpentum, a good number of bronze furnishings (including thymiateria [cfr. n. 234], braziers, hearths on wheels, andirons, pateras, cauldrons, *oenochoai*, an *infundibulum*), a helmet and a series of bronze and silver laminas meant to panel the wooden part of furniture and furnishings, as well as black figure pottery (on the overall find see Vermiglioli 1813; Inghirami 1825, pp. 305 ff.; Höckmann 1982; *Carri da guerra 1997*, pp. 207 ff.). After complicated antiquarian vicissitudes, the items were dispersed between the museums of Perugia, Munich, Berlin, Paris, London and Copenhagen, a situation that weighed and continues to weigh negatively on the overall evaluation of the ensemble and the possibility of reconstituting the various pieces.

Already at the end of the nineteenth century several attempts had been made by E. Petersen (Petersen 1894), who had identified several panels pertaining to one of the two *curri* (*currus* II) and, corroborated by the comparison with an image on the front of a small Vulci cinerary urn (Micali 1833, pl. 57, 1–5), he had suggested a bizarre reconstitution of the *carpentum* that combined part of the panels of that chariot with those of the other *currus* (*currus* I) and with parts of the other furnishings (Petersen 1894, pp. 256 ff., pl. 1). If the appearance of this last *currus* has been convincingly reconstituted by A. Emiliozzi, only recently on the occasion of the exhibition "Carri da guerra e principi etruschi" held in Viterbo in 1997 (*Carri da guerra* 1997, pp. 210 ff., pls. 1–5), that of the female chariot, whose panels are for the most part split between the museums of Munich and Perugia, has been the object of a reconstitution by U. Höckmann, who, inspired by the same comparison behind Petersen's attempt, has suggested the image of a chariot with a quadrangular box on four wheels, to which two mules were yoked (Höckmann 1982, pp. 26 ff., fig. 12). However, this reconstitution presents several very questionable aspects, as regards both the structural and the decorative characteristics of the vehicle; nonetheless, Höckmann's effort offers quite pointed comments, that mark an essential stage in the knowledge of the complex of San Mariano and, more generally speaking, of Etr-

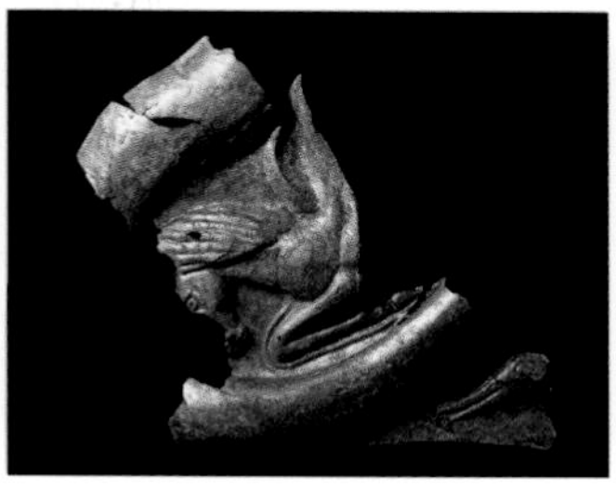

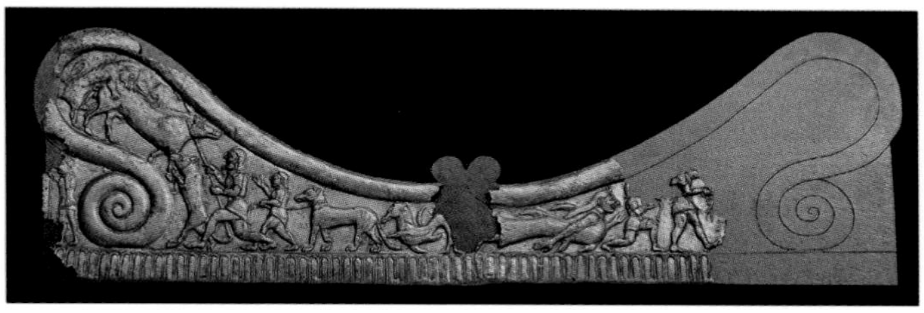

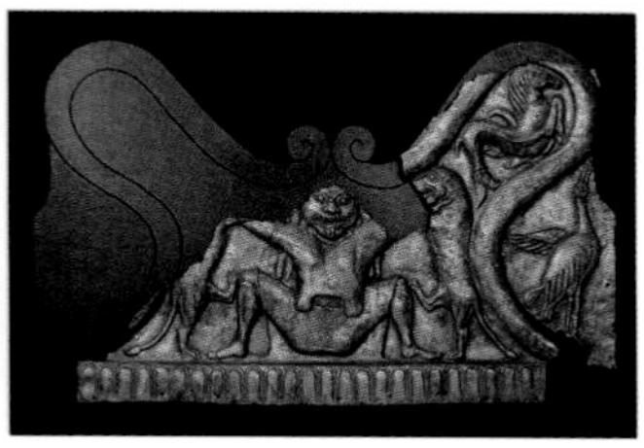

uscan and Archaic bronzework.
A fresh examination of the remaining elements has led to a new proposal, presented for the first time on the occasion of the Venice exhibition with a life-size model executed with galvanoplastic copies of each piece, the originals of which are nonetheless present in the exhibition.
Compared to the reconstitution suggested by Höckmann, the chariot has quite a different appearance. The following notes only touch on a few essential points, referring elsewhere for a broader and more detailed discussion (Bruni forthcoming).
In view of the dimensions and in the wake of concurrent or slightly posterior documentation (in particular see the chariot on the bezel of the ring I the Louvre Bj 1071), in all likelihood the chariot is a *carpentum*, that is, a two-wheeled vehicle, instead of a *pilentum* (four-wheeled chariot), with its box balanced on the axle around which the two wheels rotate. We do not have any elements for the reconstitution of the latter items, that hypothetically, based on the proportions of the frame and the examination of documentation offered by recent excavations, are assumed to have a diameter of about 80 cm. The frame is rectangular, as we had gathered from the various remaining elements of the bronze paneling of the sides and back; despite not having any element for the reconstitution of the shaft, on the model of real examples (for instance the Sirolo calash), it is likely that it consisted of two properly stripped branches placed on the sides along the baseboard, of which they formed the lateral frame, and that, sticking out from the baseboard, the arms of the frame probably contained a footrest suspended in front of the driver's seat. On the frame a box was placed, open in front, to which probably belonged—also considering the length of the remaining part of the panel—the paneling laminas with animal friezes framed above by an elaborate guilloche and below by high relief beading. On the corners of this box there must have been end pieces serving to mask the joining of the panel laminas, which we assume to be identified in four three- dimensional figures of winged divinities (Turan?: Höckmann 1982, pp. 73 ff. n. 30, pls. 40,4; 41, 1–4. Cf. also LIMC II, *voce* "Aphrodite-Turan," p. 170 n. 7 [R.Bloch]), up to now believed to belong to a small casket, and dispersed between Perugia and Munich, and that contribute to enhance the decorative profusion of the chariot adornment.
So, slightly to the rear of the walls of the box, the lateral and back sides rise, fashioned as opposing scrolls, that, according to a design that is also found, for instance, along the sides of the concurrent chariot of Monteleone di Spoleto (*Carri da guerra* 1997, pp. 179 ff.), display mythological scenes on one side and animal hunts on the other. The throne must have been placed in the middle of the box, as we gather from the concurrent representations of like-structured *carpenta*, of which perhaps a few elements of bronze paneling remain.
The chariot, to which two animals were yoked, not necessarily mules as we see from the example of the *carpentum* from Tomb XI of Colle del Forno which was drawn by two horses (*Carri da guerra* 1997, p. 300), can be dated to around the years 570 B.C., on the basis of the stylistic characteristics of its gorgeously chiseled reliefs, and the iconographies of each single motif, that can be compared, among others, to the repertory of Etrusco-Corinthian pottery of the so-called "third-generation Vulci" earthenware, and apparently should be attributed to a craftsman active in the Etrurian hinterland, whose characteristics concur with the overall scene of the artistic craftsmanship of Clusine circles even more than Orvietan ones.
[S.B.]

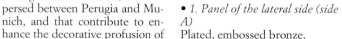

• *1. Panel of the lateral side (side A)*
Plated, embossed bronze, fragmentary
h 43.3 cm; l 110 cm
a - Munich, Staatliche Antikensammlungen, inv. 720 P WAF
Baseboard consisting of a beaded frieze; above it there is a solid relief rope decoration that is wound in spirals at the extremities. On the left a hunting scene: two dogs have pointed a boar; from the right a hunter drives his spear into the animal's neck; he is followed by a youth with the hounds, behind which a hippopotamus. On the right: a man lunges toward a centaur, stabbing it; behind, kneeling, an archer; followed by a triton.
b - Perugia, Museo Archeologico inv. B 1407
The right upper section of long side A. Two fragments that can be joined but only connect exactly on one cm, coinciding with the centaur's tail. Under the beading and above on the right, part of the original edge of the lamina is left, with a few holes for nails. The base of the largest fragment consists of a beaded frieze; above there is a relief rope winding in spirals. On the coil of the rope, figures in relief a centaur. The upper part of the equine body is covered with a coat with shiny tufts, while the belly is decorated with dots. The centaur is carrying on its back a stylized branch, visible above and parallel to the rump. Behind its tail, slightly raised, between the back hooves, you can see a person walking in the opposite direction, wearing a chiton adorned with incised vertical lines, of which only the lower part remains; in front of the person you can see a big bird's wing, the body of which is not conserved: the top of the wing is decorated with feathers overlayed nearly as if scaled, while the end part consists of long feathers, decorated with a herring-bone pattern: it has been assumed to be a Geranomachia.

• *2. Panel of lateral side (side B)*
plated and embossed bronze
a - Perugia, Museo Archeologico inv. B 1404
max. w 38 cm
The two sections coincide with the two ends, right and left. The section coinciding with the upper left end, is delimited by a smooth rope, with a stag attacked by lions. A smooth relief rope forms a spiral below, thus delimiting the edge of the chariot laterally and above. In the space of the rope there is a stag descending the spiraled rope and attacked from behind by a lion biting its rump. The body of the lion, whose head is seen frontally, is

covered with a shiny, tufted coat; the back of the stag is covered with a tufted coat, while the body is decorated with round spots and decorated with dots on the belly. In front of the stag traces remain of another animal, probably a lioness, attacking it. The lioness' body is covered with shiny tufts; under the belly you can perceive the udders.
b - Perugia, Museo Archeologico inv. B 1404
max. h of the three pieces side by side 0.275 cm; max. h of the fourth fragment 0,105 cm
Three fragments of the right upper end that can be joined with a very small connection between the two fragments of the relief; a fourth fragment is detached.
The base consists of a cornice with stylized pods. Above there is a relief rope wound in spirals. Above the base there is a gradient panther with a cub crouching under her, sucking milk from her udders. The panther's head, in what appears an unnatural movement, grasps by the throat an animal whose body is decorated with incised dashes, maybe a gazelle, whose dangling paws are visible, with hooves. The spotted coat of the panther is rendered with even concentric circles, with a dotted area inside; even the cub's hide is decorated with round elements. Above the rope there belongs another fragment with animal legs, detached from the preceding one.
• *3. Panel of the back side (side C)*
plated and embossed bronze
a - Munich, Staatliche Antikensammlungen, inv. 720 R WAF
h 42.5 cm; l 59.5 cm
Base consisting of a beaded frieze; above it there is a solid relief rope decoration that is wound in spirals at the extremities. In the middle a Gorgon seated on the ground, with legs bent and apart. With arms outstretched, it is holding onto some lions with all its might. On top right, in the curve of the arabesque, there is a hippocampus. At bottom right, outside the field of the arabesque, a crane.
b - Perugia, Museo Archeologico inv. n. B 1404
max. w 0.20 cm
This belongs to the upper left extremity. Fragmentary: on the left the original edge of the lamina remains and you can see a hole for the nail; on the right also a small piece of the original edge remains. In the space of a relief rope there is a hippocampus with front leg bent and with abundant curly mane; the body is scaled, whereas the fins are decorated with incised herring-bone lines. Outside of the rope you can see the head of a stork, whose entire body is missing. The representation is specular to the one of the upper right end, conserved in Munich. [A.E.F.]

Höckmann 1982, vol. I, ns. 1, 3, pp. 10 ff., figs. 7–8, 10–12, pls. 1–9, 11–13, with bibl.

128. Spindle and distaff
late eighth–early seventh century B.C.
bronze; bone
spindle: l 11.8 cm; distaff 4 cm; 4.6 cm
Florence, Museo Archeologico; inv. 83474
t 4, t 2
from Tarquinia, Poggio Gallinaro, pit Tomb 8
Spindle: square-section staff, swollen at the ends, onwhich are inlaid small bone disks; distaff: two flared extremities, hollow; on the outside relief disk with central button.

Pernier 1907, p. 338; Hencken 1968, p. 346, fig. 347, b; Donati 1985, p. 76, ns. 264–65.
[F.C.]

129. Spools and whorls from Tomb 1 of San Cerbone (Populonia)
• *1. Twenty-four spools*
seventh–sixth century B.C.
brown impasto
l 5.2–6.3 cm; 1.3–2.7 cm those with missing parts
Florence, Museo Archeologico, inv. 163029–163043, 163047–163057
Cylindrical spools, with flared tips and convex heads or, less frequently, and piatte or concave heads. Different kind of decorations.
• *2. Sixteen whorls*
seventh century B.C.
brown impasto
h 2.2–3.4 cm
Florence, Museo Archeologico, inv. 163016–163028,

1

2

163044–163046
Whorls with different shapes and decoration.

Minto 1934, p. 360. [F.C.]

130. Fragment of fabric
linen; fragmentary
max. h left 10.6 cm; max. l left 9.4 cm
Montopoli in Valdarno, Antiquarium Comunale
from Vetulonia, locality Poggio al Bello, Tomb del Duce

Found inside the *larnax* (cf. n. 134) containing the remains of the body of the person buried in the so-called Tomb del Duce, it was used to envelop the incinerated remains according to a ritual described in the Iliad for the funerary rites in honor of Hector (Homer, *Iliad*, XXIV, 790 ff.) and of Patrocles (Homer, *Iliad*, XXIII, 250 ff.), and attested in quite a few princely contexts of the mid-

Tyrrhenian area between the second half of the eighth century B.C. and the third quarter of the next.

Falchi 1887, pp. 503 ff.; Camporeale 1994, pp. 240 ff.
[S.B.]

131. Throne
mid-seventh century B.C.
plated bronze
h 93 cm
Paris, Musée du Louvre, Département des Antiquités grecques, étrusques et romaines, inv. MND 2302

All that remains of the base is fragments applied onto a modern support. Curved, stamp-decorated *lamina* back.

Jurgeit 1990, pp. 4, 24, 28, pl. 8.
[G.P.]

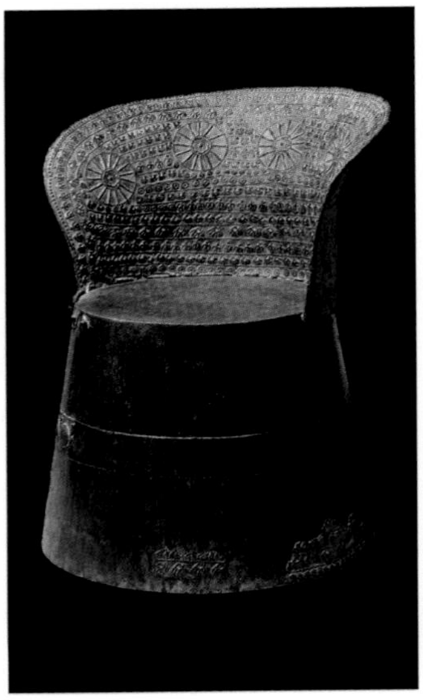

132. Tomb of Sarteano
Sarteano, Museo Civico Archeologico
from Sarteano, necropolis of Macchiapiana, unearthed in 1953

• *1. Male canopic vase*
late seventh–early sixth century B.C.
brownish-orange impasto
h of ossuary 28 cm; diam. 8.4 cm; h of head 20 cm
inv. 236963–4
Head with oval face set on a wide neck with two lateral holes. The almond-shaped eyes with hollow pupil are rendered by incision, as are the arched eyebrows; the nose is triangular and the lips thin, whereas the chin is rounded and the ears protruding. The hair forms heavy bangs on the forehead ending in shaped curls on the neck too, whereas on the top it is rendered by thin parallel incisions. Ossuary with separate cylindrical neck, ovate body, splayed base, vertical ribbon handles in which is inserted a mobile forearm with closed hand.
• *2. Female canopic vase on throne*
ca. 630–620 B.C.
brownish-orange impasto; throne in limestone; silver earrings
h ossuary 38 cm; diam. 10 cm; h of head 22 cm; h of throne 26 cm; w of base 45 cm; depth 37 cm
inv. 236965–6–7
Head, perforated on top, with triangular face with distinct features: clear-cut superciliary arch, almond-shaped eyes rendered by incision with hollow pupil, thin nose and lips, high, rounded cheeks, shapely ears with pierced lobes for inserting earrings. Hair rendered by thin parallel incisions. Wide neck, with two holes on the sides, that rests on the opening of the ossuary, also perforated, with an oblong ovate body, splayed base, vertical ribbon handles in which are attached two mobile forearms with closed hands. Throne without a base with semi-circular back.
• *3. Small clay model of two-edged hatchet*
last thirty years of seventh century B.C.
brownish-orange impasto
l 10 cm
inv. 236980
Miniature two-edged hatchet in terra cotta, more than half of which remains. Features a broad blade and concave sides with a cylinder in the middle for holding the handle; the latter, in relief and fluted, is elongated toward the bottom, and pierced with a hole for inserting the handle (lost).

Maetzke 1993, pp. 139–40 n. 2, pls. Va–b, VI–VII, XIb, XIIIa; Minetti 1997, pp. 48–52, fig. 31, 34, 37. [A.M.]

3

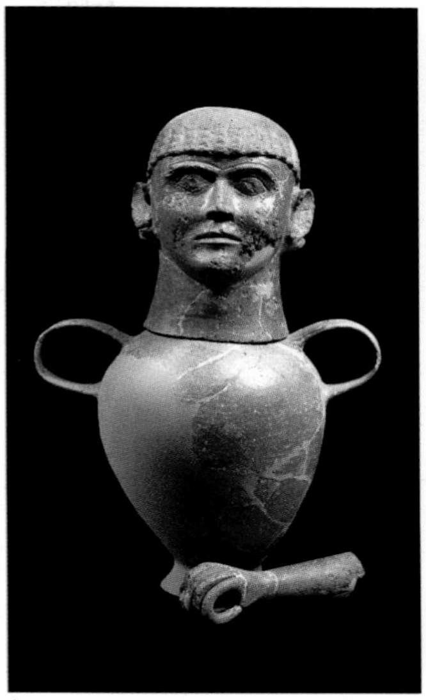
1

2

133. Clusine funerary cippus
490–480 B.C.
pietra fetida
h 49 cm; w 40 cm.
Rome, Museo Barracco, inv. 201
from Chiusi, formerly Scalambrini Collection

Parallelopipidal, with low relief decoration on all four sides, included between profiled frames with tongued frieze; at the corners stylized branches. Side A: scene of *prothesis*; scene of side B: gynaceum; side C: four advencing men holding sticks; side D: scene of funeral lament.

Jannot 1984, pp. 90–92 n. 3; figs. 317–21; *Civiltà degli Etruschi* 1985, p. 292 n. 11.5. [C.Z.]

The Cult of the Ancestors and the Continuity of the Clan

The hut urns of the Latin and Villanovan tradition, like other relics of Villanovan culture such as the helmet tips shaped like hut roofs, the tomb symbols of similar form or the representation of a hut on a stele from Felsina, are the clearest evidence of the formation of a system of values which finds its essential nucleus in the structure and symbology of the house. All this seems to be intimately linked with contemporary economic and social developments in Etruscan society, which sees the establishment of private ownership of land and the restricted family, the emergence of individuals who are essentially defined as warriors capable of seizing land and resources for themselves, the evolution of emergent social groups which may be summed up in the transition from the *oikos* to the *gens*, with the consequent creation of ideal, symbolic and material structures which become increasingly permanent, complex and refined, centring on the figure of the *pater familias* and the cult of the ancestors as the supreme guarantors of the continuity of the family line, and consequently of the transmission of social rank and inherited wealth within the kin group.
This original nucleus is destined to change and may broaden or narrow, but it remains in the background throughout the whole history of the Etruscan world, as is shown by the chronologies of the materials exhibited in this section. This implies an emphasis on the central role of the house, the model for the basic form of funerary architecture; a stress on marriage and the married couple as the founding nucleus of the kin group; and the celebration of the long genealogies of ancestors as a justification and legitimization of present fortune.
In order to reconstruct the various aspects of this system of values we must remember in the first place the importance that was attached from the very earliest phases to the couple, which includes the male figure of the *pater familias*, originally defined as a warrior. On to the couple is grafted a series of innovations concerning, for example, princely culture and the symbols of *tryphe*; the transformations of funerary ideology, which, under the Hellenizing influence of the Dionysiac religion, highlights the role of the symposium and the symposiasts; and the demands of the urban structures, which will lead to the emergence of the function of the magistratures as a new status symbol. The role of woman, as is shown by the relevant section of the exhibition, is charged with further elements, for example an original function connected with the management and storage of resources is interwoven with the value consisting in the ability to procreate, which was thought to be re-

lated to the cycle of natural reproduction. It is not surprising that this system of values should enjoy an extraordinary popularity and amplification during the period of the greatest expansion of the Tyrrhenian aristocracies. A first spectacular sign in this direction is the spread, from the end of the eighth century B.C. and with chronological differences in the different areas, of the great funerary tumuli containing several chamber tombs, as a demonstration of the common descendance of the family groups and a *tryphe* which was a symbol of the prestigious social rank that was their prerogative. A significance exactly equivalent to that of the tumulus lies in the spread of onomastic formulas consisting of two elements, the forename and the family name.
The ceremonies of the interment of the dead person and the subsequent recurrences of the funerary rituals are occasions when the clan assembles and strengthens its ties of solidarity, which are also underlined by appropriate strategies of a symbolic nature.
One example of this is the appropriation of the right to the ownership of images on the part of the aristocrats. As can be seen from the materials exhibited, the canopic urn, consisting of a cinerarium placed on a throne with the upper part modeled in anthropomorphic form and fitted with masks, constitutes an important stage in the structuring of a right to representation which typifies the aristocratic state, for it renders in a living and immediate form the presence of the dead person and the ancestors; this recalls the exposition of the *imagines maiorum* in the atrium of the Etrusco-Roman house which surround the *pater familias*, or the performing of Roman funerals as described by Polybius (VI, 53), where the closest relatives wear the masks of their ancestors during the celebration in the forum of the virtues of the dead person. One of the clearest examples of the *principes*' concern for continuity and for relations of solidarity between the living and the dead in the context of a clan structure is the Tomb of the Five Chairs, where, at the end of the entrance *dromos*, there are two rooms, one on the right and one on the left, the chamber at the end being intended for the two dead people. The room on the left contains an altar with three cavities in the top for sacrifices involving liquids, two empty thrones, two *trapezai* near which five seats are arranged, each with a statuette on it. This room communicates with the chamber of the dead, who are imagined as occupying the two empty thrones and, after the completion of the rites of domestic religion symbolized by the altar, joining their ancestors in a banquet. Another very clear example of the importance and persistence of these elements is the Tomb of the Reliefs, reconstructed here in the exhibition, which shows how this tomb, belonging to the family of the *Matunas*, is set in an area devoid of emergent tombs but in reference to the great Tumulus I of Caere, showing the evident intention of harking back to the great princely aristocracies of the archaic age. This whole world and system of values find their higest expression in a monumental complex like that found at Murlo, near Siena. This is a particularly important example of the princely *regiae* which we find scattered round the Etrusco-Latin area in the seventh and sixth centuries B.C., and it includes, in the phase datable to about 580 B.C., a large square inner courtyard on to which rooms used for entertainment, service, storage and stables open along the sides. A small structure visible inside the courtyard and offset toward the north-west side indicates that this was where the rites and ceremonies in honor of the gods and ancestors of the kin group were held and where the lord's family, slaves and domestic staff, and the *clientes* scattered round the countryside and subject to the dominion of the *princeps* gathered. Along the sides of the courtyard, at a certain height, there were figured friezes containing four motifs relating to fundamental aspects of the princely lifestyle. In the first place there is a race between young horseman for a prize of a large *lebes*, and the bridal procession of the woman sitting on the *carpentum* and attended by servants and domestics who carry the objects of her trousseau. These stages in the male and female apprenticeship conclude with a scene of banqueters which shows two *klinai* on each of which sits a couple consisting of a man and a woman, a symbol of the founding nucleus of the clan, attended by servants and surrounded by splendid furnishings; the presence of a dog under each *kline* probably alludes to another of the great symbols of aristocratic life, namely hunting. Finally, the fourth motif of the reliefs is an assembly of deities of heaven and the underworld, a proof of the familiarity between the gods and the lord's family and of the control that the princely residence can boast over the whole divine cosmos housed within it. The last decorative complex of the *regia* consists of the statues—about twenty in number—which stand on the roof of the building; in the exhibition we see examples of the types. These are *imagines maiorum* of almost natural size, interspersed with real and fantastic animals which allude to the world of the afterlife. The grand assembly of the ancestors, similar to that of the gods inside the building, indicates the power of the kin group and the protection accorded it by the heroicized ancestors who stand as guarantors of the fortunes of their descendants.
In the context of a profound Hellenization which leads to the anthropomorphization of the divine figures, to a reinterpretation in a Greek key of the original deities and to the introduction to the Tyrrehenian area of Greek mythology, the beliefs and symbologies relating to the cult of the ancestors also borrow from the Greek world new conceptions and ideas which serve the needs created by the evolution of Etruscan society. The arrival of this new Hellenizing wave in the sixth and fifth centuries B.C. is superimposed, in the field of Etruscan funerary religion, on the ancient conception of death as a dangerous journey undertaken on horseback in a landscape peopled by animals and monsters. Salvation and the success of the journey depend on the rites which the whole group performs for the dead person, comprising funeral games, ritual dances, ceremonies and sacrifices at predetermined intervals, and on furnishing the tomb like a house in which everything necessary for the material needs of the dead person is deposited, right down to the altars for the domestic sacrifices which the dead person is imagined as performing in honor of his ancestors. In this conception the tomb takes on the function of a place of passage to the door of the underworld depicted at the back, of transition toward the great journey which, later and under Greek influence, acquires the features of a journey by sea, across the ocean.
The religious beliefs of the Greek world come to modify profoundly these ancient local conceptions, especially through two strands which variously intertwine and overlap—the religion of the Dioscuri and that of Dionysus. In the former case, recent research has brought to light a widespread presence in Etruscan tombs from the seventh century to the middle of the fifth century B.C. of objects and symbols traceable to the Dioscuri and their cult, for example the *dokanon* or *dokana*, originally a representation of a door loom and later transformed into cult altars like those present in the Campana Tomb of Veii, the Tomb of the Monkey at Chiusi or in the well-known Regolini-Galassi Tomb in Caere. In the Tomb of the Funeral Bed in Tarquinia we find in the middle of the symposium a *kline* on which is depicted a head-covering symbolic of the Dioscuri, the *pileus*, also known to the Latin tradition as *tutulus* or *stroppus-struppus*. The presence of the Dioscuri in the funerary sphere is closely connected with the theme we are discussing. For their reputation as rescuers and helpers, especially on sea voyages, might make them dear to the Etruscan imagination, which, as we have seen, associated the theme of death with that of the voyage. But the crucial element is the mythical story of the twins to whom the father of the gods grants, on the request of one of them, the ability to share life and death alternately. In this way the assimilation of the dead person to the Dioscuri guaranteed the hope of a life after death, while the ancestors might be imagined as gathered together in the ceremony of the *Theoxeia*, the ritual banquet held in honor of the Dioscuri, as they wait to receive and welcome the dead man-Dioscurus.
From the second half of the sixth century B.C., both in funerary painting and in productions of wider circulation such as the cippi of Chiusi, there appear symbols of the Dionysiac religion, in the form of satyrs, sileni, and above all the

joyous ceremony of the *komos*. Simultaneously, in a development clearly visible in the funerary painting, the theme of the banquet and the symposium abandons the position of the tympanum in the funerary architecture of the tombs, a sacralizing place connected with the afterlife, and takes its place on the rear wall, invading the side walls and mingling with the representation of the *komos*, while the themes of the games and the hunt remain confined to the entrance area of the tomb. In other words, while in the past the tomb was felt to be a place of transit and the rites protective of the journey had to extend to the door of the underworld, now the tomb itself begins to be regarded as the final goal of the journey, the afterlife, where the ancestors assembled in a banquet welcome the dead person who, having already been initiated to the mysteries of Dionysus in his lifetime through the *komos* depicted on the lateral walls—which in the Dionysiac practices is the moment when the symposiasts move from one house to another—joins his ancestors. This process seems to be concluded and stabilized in the fourth century B.C., so from this time onward the tombs, containing rows of sarcophagi and urns, are intended to allude to the long generations of the kin group that are now in the Elysian Fields. The grand rock tombs of the late period, too, end up obeying this conception through a sacralizing architectural facade, often resembling that of a temple building, inside which two chambers are created, a lower one for the interment of the dead and an upper one in which the cippi and the benches allude to the happy banquet enjoyed by the dead together with their ancestors. The transformations which modify the archaic conceptions relating to the cult of the ancestors and the continuity of the clan imply the persistence of social groups with a strong interest in maintaining and adapting those conceptions in the face of the incumbent social changes. On the other hand the Hellenizing novelties that we have see being introduced also imply a profound revision of the world of the *principes*' archaic *tryphe,* which had fixed the strongest and clearest signs of family continuity. One only has to think of the popularity enjoyed by Dionysiac religion, which was able to meet the expectations of wider classes by granting access to the symbolic values of wine and the conviviality of the symposium to social groups which did not coincide exclusively with the aristocratic structures. The *senatusconsultum* passed by Rome in 189 B.C. prohibiting the ceremonies connected with the Dionysiac religion on the grounds that they caused disorder throws a little light on the various means by which the age-old recurring social conflicts could emerge in the Etruria of the "powerful" and the "poor." [M.M.]

134. Cinerary urn
650–630 B.C.
silver-plated bronze
h 42 cm; l 63 cm; w 37 cm
Florence, Museo Archeologico, inv. 7095
from Vetulonia, Circolo del Duce, group V

Silver-plated chest, with on the frame four bronze bands bent at a right angle, that also form the feet; lid with two bronze slopes, with bronze-plated tympans; entirely plated with embossed and chiseled silver leaf. Decoration in registers, framed by chains of small interwoven arcs and palmettes. Side A, upper register: lion, horseman, ibex, lion, lion; lower register: sphinx-griffin, bull, lion with front head, sphinx; slope A: upper register: winged lion, other composite animals and palmettes; lower register: facing griffins beside a palmette, lion, vegetable elements; side B, upper register: you distinguish lion's paws, horse's hooves and tail, wing, griffin, chimera; lower register: lion's head, winged lion's body, rear part of like animal with snake tail, vegetable motifs; slope B: upper register: you distinguish lion's rear paws and mane, a horse's hoof, opposing griffins, palmettes; lower register: fragments of wings and vegetable motifs; short side C: you distinguish a winged animal, part of a lion, a wing and palmettes; short side D: tympan with little ducks beside a palmette; upper register: remains of part of a wing; lower register: remains of vegetable motifs. Feet: group with standing male figure between two lions rampant, repeated several times on the two registers.

Camporeale 1967, pp. 141 ff.; Torelli 1986, n. 38.
[F.C.]

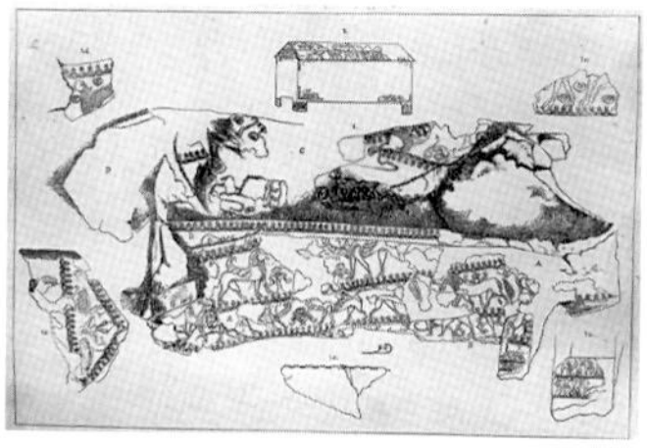

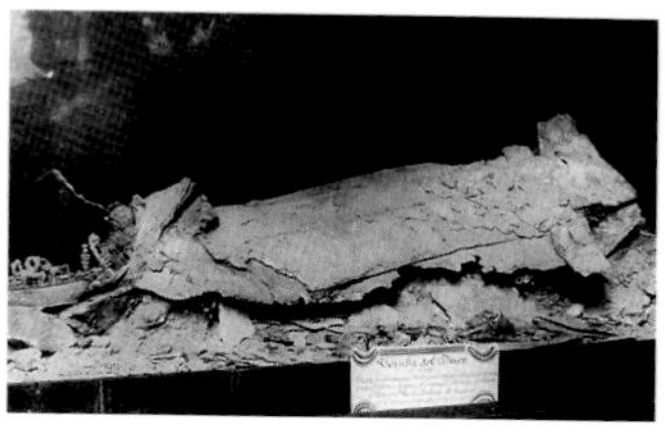

135. Grave goods from Fontecucchiaia
seventh century B.C.
Copenhagen, The National Museum of Denmark, Collection of Classical and Middle-Eastern antiquities
from Fontecucchiaia, Chiusi, "ziro" tomb closed by a slab of stone

• *1. Canopic urn on a throne*
red clay with gray-yellow slip
max. h 45 cm; h of head 14 cm; urn 33 cm; throne 37.6 cm
inv. 2074
The throne, the urn and the head were made on the wheel; several elements were modeled separately and then added. The head has protruding ears and nose. On the urn the arms are modeled with pointed shoulders, bent elbows and long separated fingers. There is a bracelet on each forearm. The throne presents round protuberances on the front and three engraved rosettes on the back.
• *2 Two small globular ollas with lid*
brown and red clay
h 4.6 cm; diam. 10.8 cm
inv. 2276, 2076
On the handles there are remains of two ornamental protuberances, perhaps griffin heads, now missing. The red lid fits the vase perfectly, but its lighter color indicates that it could have belonged to another vase, now lost.
• *3. Bowl*
red clay

h 4.6 cm; diam. 10.8 cm
inv. 2077.
Bowl with faired sides and low ring on the base.
• *4. Figure on a biga*
gray-yellow terra cotta with traces of black-brown paint
overall h 14.8 cm, l 15.9 cm
inv. 2078
The small earthenware group was modeled by hand. The man, with a narrow, long bust, head and arms, is standing with his arms bent forward. There are no traces of hair or clothing. The closed fists show that at one time he was holding the horses' reins. The biga is open at the back and has two bronze rings on each side, to which the wheels are attached. In the horses' mane there is a hole to which a chain of bronze rings used to be attached, now lost.
• *5. Mask*
bronze with brown and green patina
h 16.7 cm, w 12.2 cm
inv. 2079
The mask is made of a single bronze lamina. It has a low forehead, the line of the eyebrows is continuous, and the irises of the round, bulging eyes are indicated by dots.
The nose is triangular, the lips flat and straight. Around the edges, eight holes for attaching the mask over the face. The first accounts of the finding of the piece report that the mask was attached to a bronze urn, lost because too damaged.
• *6. Fire tongs*
bronze
le 14.8 cm
inv. 2080
Made out of a flattened bronze rod, bent in the middle to form an open curve in which a ring is inserted.
• *7. Two spits*
bronze
83.7 cm; 80.9 cm
inv 2081, 2082
Two spits: the first is round-sectioned, made out of a bronze rod, one end being spiraled and the other bent.
The second one, again round-sectioned, has one flat end to which a small spiraled, flat-section rod ending in a coil is held with two bronze nails.

Randall, MacIver 1924, 240; Steingräber 1979, 305, n. 558; CVA, Copenhagen pl. 209,5-7; Brijder 1990, p. 81, n. 69; Lund, Rasmussen 1995, p. 124
[B.B.R.]

136. Bronze bust
bronze *lamina*, lacunose
h 45 cm
Florence, Museo Archeologico
from Marsiliana d'Albegna, Banditella necropolis, Tomb XLI, Circolo della Fibula

The reconstitution of the monument, found inside the pit where it had been deposited is owed to M. Crostofani who, out of the stock of a series of anthropoid bronze lids from the Vulci area (cf. recent Cristofani 1985, p. 288 n. 107), joined to the bust the *lamina* globe, until then held to be a globular vase. Yet, if the reference to anthropoid lids of cinerary urns is feasible considering the strictly geometric volumetry of the head, the ideology that can be assumed to lie behind this creation would appear to be different. A few technical details, such as the underlining of the shoulder blades on the back or the fashioning of the remaining arm, confirm that is was conceived and executed by a toreut used to making armor, following a procedure that has also been supposed (Neumann) to be at the origin of the *sphyrelata* of the Hellenic world. It would seem to be more difficult to grasp its meaning in the economy of the rituals evidenced by the ensemble of the Circolo della Fibula, within which, off-center with respect to the pit intended for burial, there was also a large paved rectangular area, upon which bronze and impasto vases, as well as four iron spears, were found. If this last structure seems intended for ceremonies connected with forms of the funerary ritual, like the large pit of the Circolo del Tridente di Vetulonia (cf. Bruni 1998, p. 109; Bruni forthcoming), the bust does not seem to have had the function of a *cholossos,* that is, a substitutive image of the deceased, as it had been assumed up to now (Cristofani 1985, p. 288), but, just like the ivory statuette of a female divinity originally overlaid in goldleaf, present in the pit (*principi Etruschi* 2000, p. 132 n. 88, with previous bibiography), was perhaps to render the image of a divinity according to ritual forms that we find later on at the end of the century in the so-called Tomb d'Iside of Vulci (on which Roncalli 1998. Cf. also the related part in the article about sculpture in this same catalogue).

Minto 1921, p. 87, pl. XLIII, p. 89, pl. XXXVII,1; Cristofani 1985a, pp. 288 ff., n. 109; Bruni 1998a, p. 109.
[S.B.]

137. Wooden male head
second half of seventh century B.C.
wood with traces of golf leaf
h 21.3 cm; w 13.7 cm; depth 15.2 cm
Milan, Civiche Raccolte Archeologiche e Numismatiche, inv. A987.01.01
from Vulci (?)

Originally the head was probably placed on a support of a different material with a mortise joint held by two pegs with orthogonal pins of which the passing channels remain. The surface was plated with goldleaf, at least on the flesh areas, of which only a few fragments are left, fixed by an adhesive; traces of the said adhesive appear on the upper part of the head to hold a probable headgear. The eyes, whose contour is deeply outlined, were mounted in enamel or ivory, standing out on the gold background in any case. The symmetrical volute-shaped ears have two holes in the lobes to hang pendant earrings. The brow, high and square, is marked by a horizontal cut, the lower edge of the probable headgear. The piece had previously been defined as a ìcanopic headî, whereas more recent observations, confirmed by the analytical study on it still under way, suggest its identification as part of a statue or a cippus with a human head from the Vulci area.
[A.S.]

138. Bearded head (Group of the "Ancestors")
580–570 B.C.
terra cotta, reconstructed from four fragments and integrated
h 42.5 cm; w 18.5 cm
Murlo, Antiquarium of Poggio Civitate, inv. FI 110463
Murlo, Poggio Civitate

It belongs to one of the many exemplars of acroterial statues of a seated male with a wide-brimmed hat, that characterize the decoration of the roof of the Archaic Etruscan palace of Poggio Civitate. The features of the face are simply modelled on the same frontal plan: the big round eyes beneath the eyebrows, that continue the contour of the triangular nose. The protruding mouth is modelled by hand, and the surface of the face goes down to form the beard, that becomes flat and rectangular on the chest. The fragments belonging to the acroterial figures, that recent studies esteem as being nearly 200 exemplars, were found all over the plain of Poggio Civitate, from both destruction layers and dumping pits, backing the assumption of the intentional destruction of the site and the ritual spreading and burying of the architectural terra cottas.

Phillips 1968a; Phillips 1969b; Poggio Civitate 1970, n. 3; Siena, CP 1985, 104 n. 259, fig. 3, 259; Edlund-Berry 1992, pp. 43–44, figs. 41–42. [S.G.]

139. Acroterial statue of a seated woman, lower half (Group of the "Ancestors")
580–570 B.C.
terra cotta, reconstructed from many fragments and integrated
h 71 cm
Murlo, Antiquarium of Poggio Civitate, inv. FI 111187
Murlo, Poggio Civitate

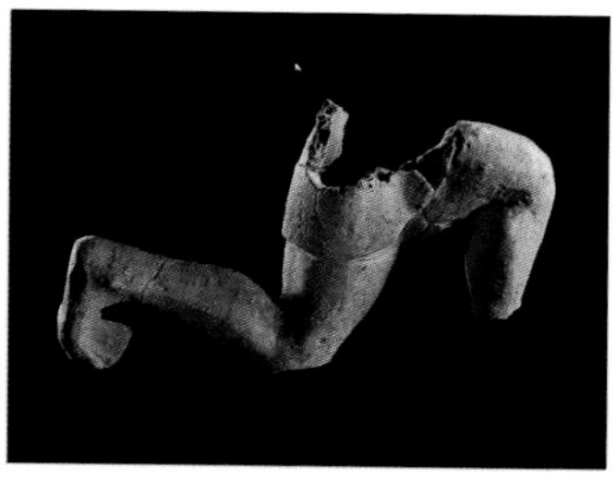

The figure is conserved from the hem of the vest to the middle of the torso, including part of the left arm. The hands, fists closed in a vertical position, were holding, in all probability, a symbolic object, a flower or fruit. At the centre of the chest a round pod represents a pendant, or a pointed necklace. The female acroterial statues are definitely smaller than the male ones, but have the same stylistic and technical characteristics.

Poggio Civitate 1970, n. 3; Siena, CP 1985, 106, n. 266; Edlund-Berry 1992, pp. 71–73, figs. 61–68.
[S.G.]

140. Helmeted head (Group of the "Ancestors")
580–570 B.C.
terra cotta, reconstructed from many fragments and integrated. Portions of the right upper and back part are conserved
h 23 cm
Murlo, Antiquarium of Poggio Civitate, inv. FI 111690
Murlo, Poggio Civitate

The right side of the head still has part of the eye, the lateral surface of the face, the well-shaped ear and a smooth mass of hair falling behind the ear. It is wearing a smooth cap helmet, topped by a short cylindrical crest, in the central hole of which was probably inserted a feather.

Poggio Civitate 1970, n. 6; Siena, CP 1985, 107, n. 276, figs. 3, 276; Edlund-Berry 1992, pp. 44–45, figs. 43–46 [S.G.]

141. Bust of sphinx (Group of the "Ancestors")
580–570 B.C.
terra cotta, reconstructed from many fragments and integrated
h 33 cm
Murlo, Antiquarium of Poggio Civitate, inv. FI 110464
Murlo, Poggio Civitate

At the top of the head the hair is parted in two straight bands that fall along the two sides of the head and behind the ears in long braids that outline the bulging chest. The face is finger-modelled, in the same manner as the big statues of human figures and presents the typical prominent nose, bulging eyes and slightly protruding mouth. Beside the large male and female seated figures, from Poggio Civitate also come fragments of other figures: animals, either fantastic, like the sphinx, or real, like horses, bulls, lions, boars, rams. *Disjecta membra* (scattered members) of the fabulous bestiary that adorned the roof of the great Archaic edifices of the palace of Murlo. [S.G.]

142. Cinerary urn with married couple
second half of sixth century B.C.
yellowish impasto with reddish traces
h 60 cm; w 26.5 cm
Cerveteri; Museo Cerite "Claudia Ruspoli," inv.??
from Cerveteri, Banditaccia necropolis, chest tomb

Cinerary urn shaped like a *kline*, with a double spiraled element on the front supports; above, on a mattress slightly furled at the ends, a married couple, partly reclining on their left side, represented during the banquet; the man has his right arm on the shoulders of the woman who is wearing a long chiton, *tutulus* and *calcei repandi*, while presumably holding in his left hand a drinking glass (*kylix?*)

Proietti 1986, p. 156, n. 63.
[I.B.]

143. Cinerary urn-statue known as Pluto
ca. 550–530 B.C.
tufa and shell limestone, red and black highlights
h 135 cm
Palermo, Museo Archeologico, inv. ??
from Chiusi, formerly Casuccini Collection

Male figure, bearded and with short hair like a cap, colored black, seated on a throne with a cylindrical base and curved back. Both forearms are stretched forward: the right hand, closed in a fist, was holding onto a lost item; the left hand is outstretched. The bust and the lower part of the statue were made in two separate parts; the head and the forearms were made separately.

Mingazzini 1935, pp. 61–66; pls. VII-IX; Cristofani 1975, p. 49.
[C.Z.]

144. Semi-recumbent youth-cinerary urn statue
early fourth century B.C.
bronze
h 42 cm, base 69.5 x 23.5 cm
Hermitage, Saitn Petersburg, B.485
found at Perugia in 1843. At the Hermitage in 1862 with the Campana Collection

A young man is reclining on a platform. His left elbow is resting on the pillows and his open left hand used to hold a goblet. In the past the eyes had been mounted. On each side of the base a wave patten is incised. The corners of the base by the youth's feet are decorated with floral elements, while at the other corners there only remain the supporting pins for identical flowers. The gold decoration (diadem and bulla) and the bronze sheet with the figure of a sphinx are now in the Louvre. The ashes had been placed inside the figure.

Kunze, Kastner 1988, pp. 216–18, n. 1010; Roncalli 1990, n. 8.1, pp. 391–96, 402; Pallottino 1992, cat. 533, p. 232; Karabelnik 1993, cat. 106, pp. 204–05. [N.G.]

145. Mater Matuta
third quarter of fifth century B.C.
pietra fetida
90 x 58 x 50 cm
Florence, Museo Archeologico, inv. 73694
from Chianciano Terme, Pedata necropolis (1846–47)

The *Mater Matuta* was discovered inside a chamber tomb dug in the rock, two lions decorating the entrance. Inside the statue, aside from the ashes of the deceased, were found a small Attic *oinochoe* with a female head, a gold brooch with the gold-dust adorned bezel, a gold ring with the figure of a warrior and an Etruscan inscription, and two spiral earrings. This monument, one of the most significant of the Clusine production of foetid stone cinerary statues, in which the remains of the deceased were conserved in a hollow in the top of the bust, that was closed by the separately-made head, belongs to a group of female figures seated on an Oriental-style throne with armrests shaped like sphinxes, that copy the mid-Archaic pattern of the seated male figure with an honorary function; this is the one instance in which the woman is holding a babe; rather than divine or divinized images, these could be women represented in their opulent mater familias luxury. In this statue, as in the urn lid from the same necropolis, the utter receptivity to Attic classicism is obvious, mediated in all probability by the Greek cities of southern Italy.

Cristofani 1975, pp. 17, 29 ff., 3 with bibl.; Bartoloni, Sprenger 1983, pls. 182–83, p. 135, with bibl; Maggiani 1993, pp. 157 ff., pl. V with bibl.; LIMC VI, *voce* "Mater Matuta," p. 381; Rastrelli 1999, p. 33.
[A.R.]

The Rituals of Archaic Power

Ancient societies, like modern literate ones, evolve particular strategies to construct and preserve their identities, their cultural memories. Ancient societies, however, are generally typified by the rarity of a knowledge of writing and reading, so that they have to resort to various instruments for the recording or the *a posteriori* reconstruction of the past from their origins onward. The oral memory, which is often entrusted to the guardianship of elders or specialized figures such as priests, bards, fortune-tellers, or shamans, is one of these instruments. Moreover, the cultural memory of the group, the element which guards most of the forms of behavior and the beliefs in which the community recognizes itself, is so to speak engraved in the very folds of experience, in the space and time of human beings. The calendar is a sort of great diachronic and synchronic recorder of the history of the social group which recognizes itself therein: it is possible to see in it additions and transformations due to changing historical conditions, and their insertion in the framework of an annual cycle which involves and regulates the chief material and symbolic activities of the community. The festivals, the rituals in honor of gods, heroes and ancestors, the treatment of death, the practices aimed at increasing the fertility of the fields and human reproductivity, the sacralization of spaces and places where a divine being has manifested itself or a prodigious event has taken place, are examples of how the cultural memory of ancient societies can function. The Etruscan world is no exception in this sense. Most of the rituals known to us in the Etruscan world developed at a very early stage, during the long process of the development of the urban structures, and, as one would expect, they were profoundly influenced by the culture and the interests of the *principes*. In this sense the rituals of archaic power usually act in contexts which seem to us to lie halfway between the public and the private: the initiative starts from regal and princely figures, who were originally the leaders of kin groups, but who later extend their influence to wider social structures, such as *curiae* or *populi*, in line with the growing complexity of the urban forms and with the consequent need felt by the aristocratic chiefs to transfer their long-held prerogatives of power and status to an urban context.
A first great ritual which we may note in the Etruscan world is that of the taking of the auspices, a ritual also known in the Italic context which goes back to very ancient times. The Etruscans' reputation as a people who are careful and scrupulous in their observation of religious laws is perfectly reflected in this complex ritual,

according to which one carries out the foundation of a city or a temple only after a positive judgement communicated by the gods to men. The person who is authorized and able to interpret the signs of the gods is a priest, the augur—some iconographic representations of whom are shown in the exhibition—and the whole operation of the taking of the auspices is like a transfer of a portion of heaven to earth, a process equivalent to a divine investiture. The augur cannot perceive the signs of the gods' will except on certain conditions and in a specific place. The whole ceremony actually corresponds to the traditional story of the foundation of Rome, whereby Romulus and Remus subject themselves to a trial to decide who is to have the right and duty to found the city. The trial consists in observing the number of birds in the sky and the direction they are coming from, the birds being regarded as the truthful witnesses of the gods who dwell in the vault of heaven. The etymology of the word auspice fully reflects these points, for it derives from *avis* (bird) and *spicere* (observe). Romulus supposedly saw twice as many birds as his brother, and saw them coming from the right part of the sky. The story of the origins of Rome takes us back to a very early phase when the king himself, Romulus, holds the two functions, later separated, of the person who takes the auspices, who asks to know the response of the gods, and the augur, the priest who directs the rite. The architectural slab from Cisterna exhibited here also signals the association of the lituus with military *imperium*, a high prerogative of the archaic kings.
The augur acts through the *lituus*, the curved staff certifying his ability to mediate with the gods: he delimits in the sky a rectangular portion which is symbolically transferred to the earth, traced on the ground and denominated *templum*, as can be seen in the reconstruction shown here. This space, which is perfectly orientated to the cardinal points, is then delimited by posts and a fence and takes the name of *auguratorium*, the place free from negative influences from which the augur can observe the sky and the relevant divine signs, seated in the middle of the west side looking eastward. The person who is taking the auspices positions himself in the middle of the *auguratorium*, but looking southward. As soon as a flight of birds appears, the augur judges the direction they are coming from by reference to a deity, as can be seen in the *templum* traced on the ground. For here are placed a number of cippi indicating the various directions, each of which corresponds to a deity and to the prediction connected with that deity, as is shown by the archaeological evidence of the *auguratorium* of Banzi. The most favorable deities are those to the east, the most negative ones to the north; the others recommend that one should suspend, postpone or repeat the operation of taking the auspices. Only after this prior authorization may the subsequent rites of foundation be carried out, so a city is said to have been "inaugurated" in the sense that the augur has freed the relevant space from every negative influence. This operation, however, constitutes not only a negative action—a removal—but also the fixing of an *omen*, of a destiny of wealth and power indicated by the Latin verb *augere* (to increase with force), which is related to the term augur.
"Ritual is the adjective used for the Etruscan books which prescribe the rites of foundation of the city, temples and altars, the religious practices for the building of city walls, the sacred laws of the gates, the manner of subdividing tribes, *curiae* and centuries, of organizing the army, and all the other operations of this kind pertaining to peace and war" (Festus 358 L.). During the late republic and the early empire the greater part of the corpus of writings of the *Etrusca disciplina* was formed; this corpus, which was supposed to have been revealed to the child Tagetes in ancient times, was divided into *libri haruspicini*, *fulgurales*, and *rituales*. In fact writings of this kind known as *libri lintei* had been circulating for a long time, at least since the fifth century B.C.; a celebrated example is the Zagreb mummy. Cicero (*de legibus*, II, 9, 21) gives us some vital information: "Let the *prodigia* and the *portenta* be subjected, when the senate so decides, to the Etruscan haruspices, and let Etruria teach the *principes* discipline." This latter affirmation reveals to us one of the great, fundamental tools in the hands of the archaic aristocracies of the Tyrrhenian world, namely their exclusive control, which continued down to Roman times, over the procedures, rites, and norms concerning the "Etruscan discipline" which provides access to the will of the gods. In the tomb of the Reliefs at Cerveteri belonging to the family *Matunas*, a reconstruction of which is shown in the exhibition, a *liber linteus* is seen folded back on the *scrinium* of the *pater familias*, i.e. on the archive where the *tabulae* attesting the estates and the rank of the kin group are kept.
The augur and the taking of the auspices described above are only part of the *Etrusca disciplina* aimed at uncovering the hidden will of the gods and its effect on the destinies of peoples, cities and individuals. The haruspex, a series of representations of whom are shown in the exhibition, succeeds in identifying the signs of the divine will in the entrails of animals, as in the case of the bronze liver of Piacenza exhibited here, or in thunderbolts, falling stars and comets, in luminous phenomena of various kinds, in earthquakes, and in the changes in the human, animal and plant world. The *libri fatales* reveal the *fatum*, i.e. the individual and collective destiny, as in the case of the ten *saecula* of the Etruscan people, which was destined to disappear at the end of the appointed time. Hunting is another activity which expresses the prestige and power of the *principes* of the archaic period, as we can see from the presence of this theme in monuments of the highest level, such as the Villanovan razor or the reproduction of the tympanum of the first back wall of the tomb of Hunting and Fishing at Tarquinia, which are both on show here. The relation between hunting, initiatic practices and regal power is a very old motif of the oriental tradition which finds its greatest expression in the lion hunt, which was reserved for the sovereign, for he alone had the right to kill "the king of the animals," as the Babylonian texts say. Subsequently Alexander the Great and the Hellenistic courts adopt this theme because of its significance for the legitimization of absolute power. It is significant that in the second half of the seventh century B.C. the motif of the lion hunt disappears from the repertory of Greek pottery, while it remains in the pottery produced in the Etruscan area, as is shown by the case presented here of a *hydria* from Cerveteri. The persistence of this theme in the Tyrrhenian world indicates the deep roots of princely power, which cloaks itself in symbologies some of which are borrowed from the repertory of oriental kingship, in contrast to the Greek world of the same period, where a more marked development of urban structures and political institutions acts as a filter to the penetration of themes dear to the princely and regal ethic.
The hunt for hares, boars and goats is the most recurrent theme in Etruscan iconography, as is confirmed by another *hydria* from Cerveteri shown here. Hunting is presented as a distinctive feature of the aristocratic lifestyle for reasons which are worth analyzing. In the first place it implies leisure time free from the immediate occupations linked to subsistence, so that it becomes a symbol of princely *tryphe* which is reinforced by the fact that the lord flaunts his arms, horse and hounds and leads the hunt over lands subject to his dominion. Moreover, in an interpretation dear to the Greek world, the hunt represents the initiatic moment which reveals how well trained the young nobleman is and certifies his skill, a skill which must be able to apply a particular quality which the Greeks call *metis*, a cunning intelligence which can make use of the ambush and the snare, and which is an essential prerequisite to the training of a warrior. In the tympanum of the tomb of Hunting and Fishing, with its scene of the return from a hare hunt, we can probably see another element dear to Greek culture, the relationship between hunt and eros, including homosexual love, so that the relationship between lover (*erastes*) and beloved (*eromenos*) is identified with the chase or with the hunter's catch-

ing of the prey. The festival is an interruption of the normal course of time; it is quite literally a different time, often the time of early Etruscan history or of an extraordinary event whose consequences extend into the present. The forms of behavior displayed by human society on this kind of occasion also show a difference which involves in the first place an interruption of everyday activities. Certain festivals are attested, for example, by the olla of the Bucacce and by the black-figure amphora exhibited here. Certainly a very important stimulus to festivals comes from the temples dedicated to the gods and from the various days and ceremonies linked with them. Processions, sacrifices, cult acts, and banquets regularly animate the area allotted to the house of the gods, a house which was founded according to the procedures of the augural discipline and the essential part of which is the altar and the *templum* raised on a podium because it stands in a place free from evil influences and is therefore raised above the human space.

Before the founding of the public temples, the religious ceremonies in honor of the gods were under the control of the noble houses interested in establishing a privileged relationship with the divine world, as we have already seen in the case of the palace of Murlo. The slabs from Velletri shown here come from a similar aristocratic residence and again show us a picture of the grandeur and magnificence of the ceremonies and the festivals connected with the celebration of princely rank. Horse races, like those of Murlo, allude to the apprenticeship of the young nobles, just as the three- and two-horse chariot races are a symbol of the *tryphe* and military prowess of the *principes* which we have already encountered. We also find the sumptuous banquets held in the hall of the *regia* with the participants reclining on *klinai* according to the Greek custom. The slabs showing a procession and the scene of an assembly of deities are directly linked with the rituals of archaic power and also includes some significant novelties with respect to the situation that we find at Murlo. There, as we have seen, the power of the *princeps* derives from his familiarity with the gods and from the protection provided by the long genealogy of his ancestors. Now, however, as we see from the Velletri slabs, there are other references that can legitimize princely power, a clear sign of the need to reinforce and adapt the language of power in the face of the novelties created by the formation of the urban communities. In the case of the scenes with procession, based on real ceremonies that took place in connection with the palace residences, we find a reference to hierogamy, that is to say to the holy union between a hero and a goddess which guarantees access to power, a concept deriving from the rituals of oriental kingship based on the union between the king and Ishtar-Aphrodite. On the slab with the assembly of deities we find a variation on the same theme: in front of the assembly of seated gods Heracles makes his entrance to Olympus accompanied by Athena, a motif based on the aforementioned oriental model. All this indicates that the power of the *princeps* is no longer automatic and guaranteed by the father-son descendance but must also count on a personal *virtus* which enables him to perform heroic feats leading to union with the goddess or ascent to Olympus, again accompanied by a goddess. Heracles, indeed, cannot boast an illustrious lineage and therefore becomes the symbol dearest to the hearts of those who aspire to a tyrannical power, such as Servius Tullius, the slave-girl's son.

To trace another important sector related to the rituals of archaic power we must now turn to the treatment of death. As is well known, the rituals connected with death usually have the function of reviving the meaning and continuity of life in the face of a break in the everyday flux and the chaos produced by the loss and absence of our dear ones. On top of this basic nucleus every society and social group imparts to its funerary rituals some signs of its own which may obey various logics and interests. In the Etruscan world from the Villanovan phase some of these signs intervene to mark an further level of meanings linked with death: the reference to the home or to the possession of arms, for example, signify a privileged state of the dead person which continues into the ulteraterrestrial world. This view is destined to have a wide and long-lasting influence and becomes one of the keystones of the legitimization of power by the emerging hereditary aristocracies of the Tyrrhenian world. In other words, the role and the rank which the dead person held in his lifetime guarantee a different state in the context of death, which is ultimately transformed into heroicization: conversely, the demonstration, through ceremonial and symbolic displays, of survival beyond the passage of death legitimizes the role of social pre-eminence. All this explains the pomp with which the aristocratic groups underlined some aspects of the funerary rite and the various symbologies connected with it, as in the case of the cult of the ancestors and the stress on the continuity of the kin group that we have already noted.

In the eighth and seventh centuries B.C. the adoption in Etruria of heroic rituals of the Homeric type significantly coincides with the rise of the Tyrrhenian aristocracies. Although the dead person's passage through fire had long been a symbol of rank, as is shown by the Villanovan urns and cineraria, the ritual of cremation now assumes the features of the "beautiful death" reserved for the Homeric heroes: the bones of Achilles, collected after burning on the pyre, are wrapped in a cloth and deposited in a precious urn together with those of Patroclus. With some variations from one area to another, rituals of this kind are well attested in Etruria and respond to the requirements of the heroicization of the *principes*.

If on the occasion of the preparation and execution of the funeral rites the clan concerned could meet together and perform the appropriate religious acts, the great centre of the funeral ceremonies becomes the tumulus tomb, the final point in the journey of the dead person which began from the kin group's home. The materials shown in the exhibition such as the bowl from Pitigliano, the Campana slabs, the cippus from Chiusi and the slab of the "weeping women" from Camucia illustrate various stages in the aristocratic funeral ritual, which combines elements drawn from the Greek world with others native to the local tradition. In the first place the holding of the funeral may be described as a festive occasion in the sense that the whole group dependent on the princely house is involved in the accompanying ceremonies. The first act is that of *prothesis*, the laying-out of the dead person in his own home surrounded by his family and by the weeping women, as we also see from the iconography known from the Greek world. Then a solemn procession (*ekphora*), made up of carriages, horsemen, and participants on foot, moves from the residence to the burial place, round which a long and complex series of ceremonial acts is carried out.

These acts, as recent research has established, take place in a space specially marked out for the purpose, which is either in front of the entrance *dromos* of the tomb or includes part of it, and which is in many cases provided with tiers of steps and benches for the participants of the funeral rites, with a capacity sometimes exceeding a hundred people. At this point it is will be appropriate to quote a well-known passage from the Greek historian Polybius (VI 53), who came to Rome as a hostage in 168 B.C. and was struck by the Roman funeral ritual, which was completely different from the Greek practice: " When the funeral of a distinguished citizen is celebrated in Rome, the body is carried with great pomp into the forum near the rostra [...] In the presence of the whole people a son who has reached the age of majority [...] or else his closest relative, gets up on to the tribune and speaks of the virtue of the dead man and the achievements which he performed during his lifetime [...] After the burial and the ritual ceremonies, the image of the dead man is placed in the most prominent place in the house, in a sacrarium of wood. The image is a wax mask very similar to the dead person in features and complexion. In honor of the public sacrifices the Romans exhibit these images and honor them solemnly; when another distinguished figure of the family dies, they make the masks

participate in the funeral, by having them worn by people who resemble the dead man in stature and in physical form [...] All these people advance on carriages preceded by fasces, axes and other honorific insignia according to the honors which each man has deserved in his life for his public activities."The passage from Polybius provides us with an updated version, in accordance with the innovations that had been made in the Late Republican period, of the oldest Etrusco-Roman funeral rites. The solemn procession of family members, instead of heading for the forum, as the city now requires, goes, as we have seen, to the space prepared in front of the princely tomb. The honorific insignia carried by the family members in the passage from Polybius significantly correspond to the archaeological and iconographical evidence of the archaic period, confirming the reports of the ancient sources on the transmission of the insignia of power from the Etruscan world to the Roman. The relatives themselves wear the masks of the ancestors, which are usually kept in the atrium of the house, as has also been mentioned in the section on the cult of the ancestors, and once they have arrived and taken their places on the terraces, the dead man's closest relative pronounces his *elogium*. Then begin the rites of accompaniment of the dead man in the area in front of the tomb entrance and against the background of the door, a metaphor for the passage to the underworld and the long journey toward the afterlife according to the most ancient notions. The dangerous journey toward the other world must be protected and guaranteed by the rites which the relatives perform; these include funeral dances, as is shown by the pyxis of the Pania exhibited here, games including boxing and wrestling, the game of Phersu, and sacrifices. When the rites and the treatment of the dead person's body are completed, the corpse makes its entry through the *dromos* into a space resembling a new house which, as we have seen in the section on the cult of the ancestors, takes on various meanings over the course of time. After some other sacrifices have been performed, the dead man is deposited in the chamber allotted to him. There he is surrounded by his grave goods, by a sort of religious tableau, as in the case of the tomb of the Five Chairs with the ancestors banqueting and waiting for the dead men, and in some cases by the funerary paintings which help to clarify, as we have seen, aspects of the conception of death and which allude ambiguously either to aspects of the ritual or to exemplary moments in the life of the aristocratic class. The subject of the rituals of death leads inevitably to the idea handed down by the ancient sources of the *funus triumpho simillimum*, the funeral which resembles a triumph. In other words, in the funeral rites and in the symbologies connected with them we find the basic idea of the archaic triumph linked with the surpassing of the limits proper to man. The sarcophagus of the Sperandio and the pyxis of the Pania exhibited here reflect this notion. The triumph is the greatest celebration of military victory, through which a king, a prince, or an aristocratic chief celebrates the acquisition of wealth and the subjection of the defeated enemy. The rituals connected with death, comprising the eulogy of the dead man, the celebration of his achievements, the demonstration of his wealth and rank, and the surpassing of human limits thanks to the practices which guarantee access to the heroic world, thus come to correspond to a triumph. On the pyxis of the Pania the top frieze but one, showing the departure of the warrior, is accompanied by a *threnos*, a funeral dance which alludes to the heroic "beautiful death" of the warrior chief thanks to the protection of the funeral rites. The same concept is portrayed in the top frieze, where the mythical episodes of Odysseus facing the monster Scylla or fleeing with his companions from the cave of Polyphemus under the rams' fleeces allude, respectively, to the victorious achievements of the hero and his triumph over death. The roots of the archaic triumph also emerge from the evidence concerning the most ancient Roman religion of the Salii connected with the training of the young for war. This group of elements is developed and canonized during the sixth century B.C. under the Etruscan dynasty of the kings of Rome. At this stage there takes shape one of the great ceremonies of archaic power—which, significantly, will often be revived by the victorious generals of the late Republic and the emperors—including the *reditus*, the victorious return of the leader, who, as in the case of Rome, lays down his arms together with his troops at the sacred boundary of the city, the *pomoerium*, and then parades through the city, passing via the forum, showing off his defeated enemy in chains and the wealth that he has taken from them, while the army can hurl banter and jokes at the commanders. The triumphal procession thus reaches the temple of Jupiter Capitolinus, the god of the triumph with whom the person holding the triumph comes to be identified, though only for that day, thus surpassing his own human limits. In this connection it should be added that the term *triumphus* derives from *thriambos*, the distinctive song of the Dionysiac processions, so the triumph also seems to be linked to the sphere of Dionysus, whose drink—wine—throws open to man the doors to another, different dimension, to a surpassing of his own limits, a process which we see developed to the highest degree in the world of the symposium.
[M.M.]

THE AUSPICE

146. Statuette of augur
ca. 550 B.C.
bronze, solid lost wax casting
h 7.5 cm
Rome, Museo del Foro, inv. 885
from Rome, Stipe del Lapis Niger

Standing male figure with short hair rendered by incised lines. Legs joined, arms bent forward. Holding horizontally in both hands a lituus. Triangular loincloth on the hips.

Gjerstadt 1960, fig. 155, 8; *Civiltà degli Etruschi 1985* p. 276 n. 10.18 c 1.
[C.Z.]

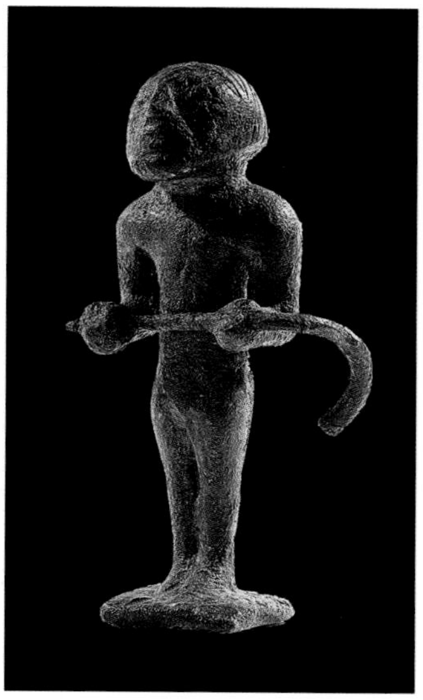

147. Slab with procession of warriors
last quarter of the sixth century B.C.
terra cotta
70 x 130 cm
Oxford, Ashmolean Museum of Art and Archaeology
from Cisterna di Latina (?)

Procession with two chariots to the right. A helmeted warrior holds a whip and the reins of two horses. Beyond the horses walks a man with a staff on the shoulder and a spear in his hand. Before them is a *triga* with winged horses; a warrior steps on the chariot and holds a whip in his left hand. First in the procession is a helmeted warrior holding a spear and a curved trumpet.

[F.P.]

148. Cippus
gray sandstone (so-called *pietra serena*)
max. reconstituted h 60.5 cm; base 37.5 x 36 x 38,5 x 35,5 cm
the crown and base shank are missing; regularized; surfaces mostly complete, except for scratches and splinterings, as well as indications of washing away of the surfaces.
Florence, Museo Archeologico inv. 13263
from Florence, recovered in 1891 during demolishing work in the center, near the Church of San Tommaso

The parallelopiped-shaped cippus, slightly tapering toward the top, is one of the most relevant examples of the series of "Fiesole stones," displaying on one side, topped by a tongued cornice decorating all four sides, the figure of an augur, coinciding on the other side with a griffin and on the two other sides with a lion. The augur, who in all likelihood should be identified with the titulary of the tomb the cippus belongs to, is—despite the lacunas and the scratches disfiguring the image— shown dressed and shoed with *calcei repandi*, whereas the presence of headgear is rather uncertain; in his right hand, extended forward, he is holding vertically a lituus. A like subject is also shown on the so-called Inghirami cippus from the vicinity of Florence (Heres 1988, p. 211 n. B 9.5) and on the stela from Frascole (Nicosia 1970, p. 17, n. 12, pl. VI, with bibl.) as well as stelae from the Volterra area, in particular the one from Lajatico (Bruni 1995, pp. 144 ff., pl. II.b) and the one of Larth Tharnie from Pomarance (Bruni 1995, p. 144, nt. 60), with the display of the *signa* of religious power connoting the person as the bearer of omens and augur himself, and seems to refer to a social structure where the role of the person in charge of the *nuntiatio* of divine signs is not yet separated from the role as the holder of political power (on the issue see Torelli 1997, p. 100 and note 47, with bibl.; for Fiesole cf. Bruni forthcoming).

De Marinis 1996, pp. 150 ff., with previous bibl.
[S.B.]

149. Fragment of lituus
sixth century B.C.
laminated bronze
h 11.3 cm; w 8.6 cm; thick. 0.2 cm
Reggio Emilia, Museo Gaetano Chierici, inv. 15492
from Reggio Emilia, Sant'Ilario d'Enza

In the fragment we can identify part of a *lituus*. The spiral-shaped top remains, whereas the stem is nearly entirely gone. In the upper part the spiral widens into a sort of protuberance, that conceivably was on the axis of the stem. It could serve for sight and for alignments, allowing to direct the field of vision toward a fixed point. One can also imagine a royal use of the lituus in the exercise of the *limitatio*.

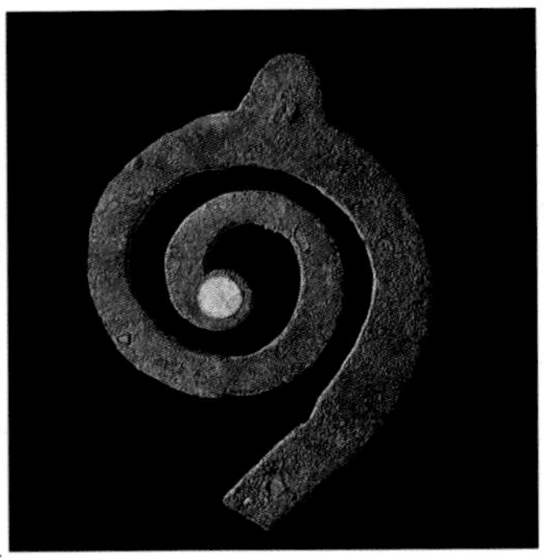

Macellari 1994, pp. 209–12; Malnati 1993, p. 163, fig. 137. [R.M.]

HARUSPICY

150. Schnabelkanne handle
late fifth century B.C.
cast bronze
h 18.6 cm; w of the lower plaque 0.8 cm
Arezzo, Museo Archeologico C. Cilnio Mecenate, inv. 11151

Handle ending above in a ram's head and below in a small quadrangular plaque. The middle is decorated with a relief line, that forks at the top and at the bottom ends in a palmette with spirals. On the small plaque a bearded naked man, with a cloak around his right leg, seated on a block construction. His head, on which he is wearing a tight headgear, is turned upward to the left, and he is resting his chin on his right hand.

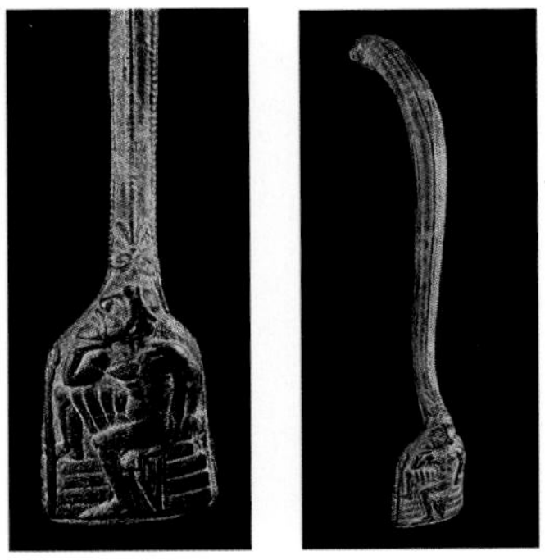

[C.Z.]

151. Small bronze plaque with haruspex
400–375 B.C.
bronze
l of handle 19.5 cm; weight of handle 210 gr; h of panel 4.2 cm; w of panel 3.1 cm
Allard Pierson Museum, Amsterdam, 1481

The plaque on the handle of the *Schnabelkanne* shows a bearded haruspex, leaning forward, holding a liver (probably of an ox) in his left hand; the scene is in low relief with incised details. The soothsayer's left leg is raised and resting on a rock, the figure is naked but has a cloak wrapped around his hips. His right hand is above the liver, and you can glimpse a staff under his left arm. The interpretation of the liver is performed on an altar that looks like a basin, supported by a pillar with a wide, round base.

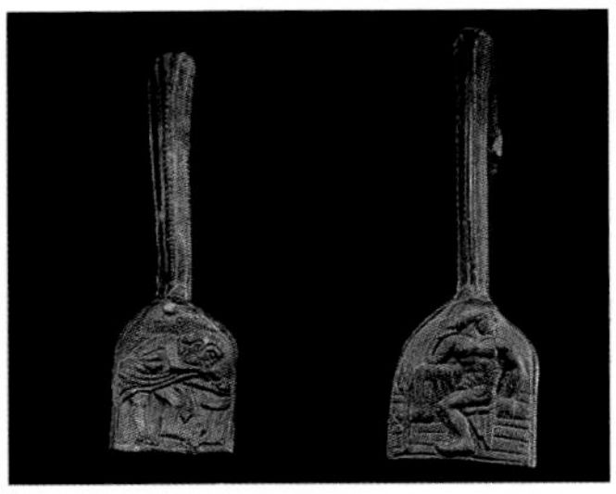

Van der Meer 1979, p. 51, n. 2, figs. 8–9; Cristofani 1985b, p. 144 with figs.; Van der Meer 1990, pp. 161–62, fig. 150. [H.A.G.B.]

152–155. Statuettes of haruspices
late third–second century B.C.
h 13.5 cm–11.5 cm
bronze; slightly lacunose and oxidized
Goettingen, inv. M 12, M 13, M 14, M 15
from an unspecified sanctuary in the territory of Siena

152. Standing haruspex, with conical leather headgear with chinstrap and disk-shaped protuberance under the pointed top, tunic and mantle fastened on the chest; in the right hand a hole for inserting an attribute; inscriptions *temres' alpan* and perhaps *tina*

Koerte 1917, pp. 7 ff.; Giglioli 1952–53, pp. 49–67.

153. Another like one with a more bulbous hat and inscription *temre*.

Koerte 1917, pp. 7 ff.; Giglioli 1952–53, pp. 49–67.

154–155. Others similar to the previous one.

Koerte 1917, pp. 7 ff.; Giglioli 1952–53, pp. 49–67.
[F.C.]

152

153

154

155

156. Scarab with haruspex
fourth century B.C.
cornelian
1.53 x 1.18 x 0.94 cm
Berlino, Staatliche Museen, Antikensammlung, inv. FG 374

On the stone is shown a bearded haruspex wearing a himation striding leaning on a cane. The head appears to be covered by a round hat. He is holding in his right hand a large liver he points at with his left hand. The bulge underneath is the gall bladder. The exceptional dimensions of the organ mean good omens. Behind the haruspex, from top to bottom, appears the inscription NATIΣ."

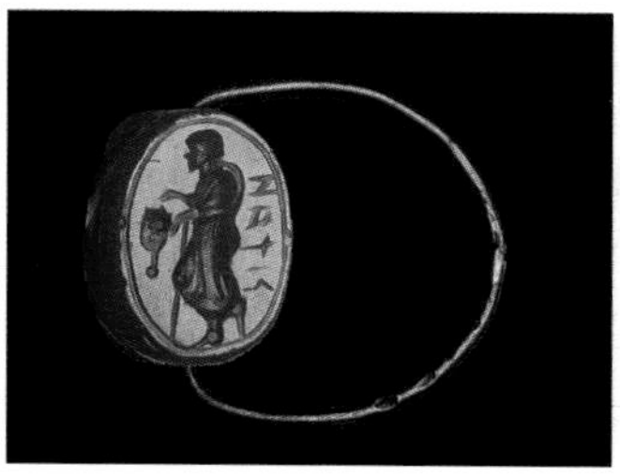

[E.Z.D.]

157. Lid of cinerary urn
late second century B.C.
alabaster
h 0.53 cm, l 0.80 x 0.26 cm
Volterra, Museo Guarnacci, inv. MG 136
from Volterra

Recumbent male figure, veiled and crowned, wearing a tunic and cloak. The right arm (partly missing) was probably outstretched along the body. The left arm, bent, is resting on two cushions and in the corresponding hand the person is holding an animal liver. On the base an Etruscan inscription: "au. lecu. l. ril. xxviii."

Corpus Urne Volterrane II, 1, n.192; for the inscription, *CIE 92* with corrections in reading *REE* 1977, p. 35 [A. Maggiani].
[G.C.]

158. Pottery fragment
ca. 15 B.C.
terra cotta, red glaze
workshop of Rasinius
h 6.8 cm; w 5.5 cm
Tübingen, Sammlung des Instituts für Klassische Archäologie, inv. 1873
from Arezzo

The haruspex, a bearded, bareheaded figure with his hair adorned with bands, is examining the large liver with his left hand. With the index of his right hand he seems to be pointing to the *pyramidion*. As seen in a fragment from Berlin representing a like scene, his short-sleeved tunic just barely reaches his knees, whereas his left shoulder and the lower part of his body are covered by the cloak.

Dragendorff, Watzinger 1948, n. 402, pl. 28; Pfiffig 1975, pp. 118–20, fig. 48. [B.F.L.]

159. Painted column-krater
ca. mid-fifth century B.C.
fine-grained clay; yellowish paintings
h ca. 38 cm.; diam. 29.5 cm
Chiusi, Museo Archeologico, inv. 63128
from Chiusi, Tomb of the Paccianese (excavations 1985)

The krater, belonging to the burial goods of a chamber-tomb dug in the limestone, nearly entirely destroyed by the agricultural activity, is attributed to the Painter Bargagli of the Vagnonville Group, a Clusine workshop of followers of the Vulci pottery-maker Praxia. It is painted with religious scenes that are difficult to interpret: the one with an old man with a long cane bent over an altar, while a youth threatens him with a stone, represents perhaps a sooth-sayer forced with violence to respond; the other represents a cloaked figure seated on a throne in front of a box with a building in the background.

Rastrelli 1993, p. 125; Bruni 1993, pp. 282 ff., pl. IX.
[A.R.]

160. Model of sheep's liver
late second–early first century B.C.
bronze, solid lost wax casting
max. h 6 cm ; max. l 12, 6 cm;
max. w 7,6 cm.
Piacenza, Museo Civico,
inv. 1101
from Settima (Piacenza)

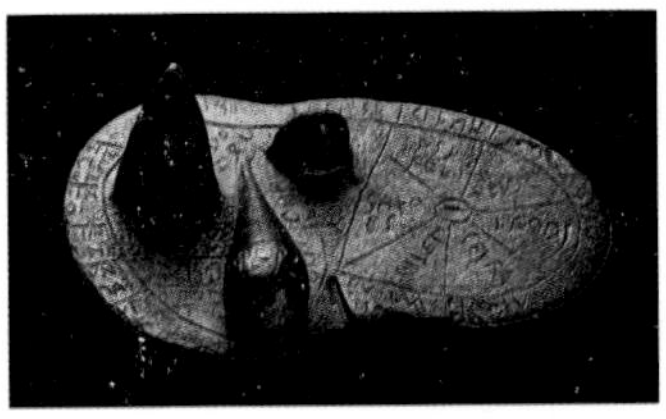

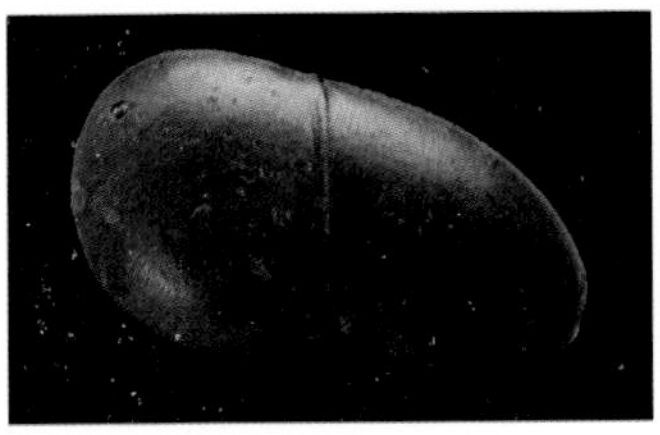

The convex part is divided, by an incision, in two lobes, of which the right is dedicated to *Usil* and the left to *Tivr*. The flat part is divided in forty compartments, where the names of divinities are written. Along the edge sixteen compartments, coinciding with the sixteen compartments in which the sky is divided, according to Etruscan beliefs..

Maggiani 1982, pp. 53–88; Van Der Meer 1987.
[C.Z.]

HUNTING

161. Razor
ninth century B.C.
cast and laminated bronze
h 8 cm; l 14.8 cm
Grosseto, Museo Archeologico e d'Arte della Maremma, inv. 1348
from Vetulonia, necropolis of Colle Baroncio (Guidi Collection)

Crescent-shaped razor of the Tarquinia type; cast handle with close-set grooves and suspension ring topped by two appendages. Both sides of the blade are decorated. Along the back and the spur are incised wolves' teeth framed by tiny lines. On one side in incised a hunting scene: a huntsman wielding a bow casts an arrow toward an antlered deer; in front are three smaller animals without antlers, perhaps two females and a little one. On the other side is incised a swastika on a background of tiny lines.

Mazzolai 1963, pp. 62–63, fig. p. 61; Bianco Peroni 1979, pp. 69–70, n. 363; Camporeale 1984, p. 21, n. 2, pl. Ib, fig. 4.
[M.C.]

162. Caeretan Hydria by the Eagle Painter
520–510 B.C.
h 44.5 cm; max. diam. of body of the vase 33.3 cm; diam. with handles 38.5 cm; h of neck 12.3 cm; diam. of foot 20.4 cm
Allard Pierson Museum, Amsterdam, 1346

The vase has been restored: many missing pieces have been replaced by plaster; in a number of places the black paint is oxidized, taking on a reddish-brown hue. On side A of the main frieze a kneeling youth is taming two frisky horses, the scene is contained between two large handles with palmettes. On the other side a youth is hunting a goat.

Pfuhl 1923, p. 183; *CVA* 1927, III F, pls. 1, 3–4; Lunsingh Scheurleer 1936, pl. 25; Hemelrijk 1984a, pp. 28–29, fig. 13; Hemelrijik 1984b, pp. 34–36, figs. 24, 52, 61, 74, 79, pls. 10, 16, 77–79, 132, 136, 152, 160, 166; Brijder 1990, pp. 150, 155, fig. 145.
[H.A.G.B.]

163. Black figure Caeretan Hydria
540–530 B.C.
clay
Paris, Musée du Louvre, Départment des Antiquités grecques, étrusques et romaines, inv. E698
from Cerveteri

On the Hydria are figured a scene of a lion hunt and two eagles in flight as they fall upon a hare. Attributed to the Eagle Painter.

THE PARTY

164. Two-colored Italo-Geometric olla with foot
early seventh century B.C.
beige clay, creme-colored slip; red and black glaze
h 34.8 cm; max. diam. 31.5 cm; diam. of rim 21 cm
Florence, Museo Archeologico, inv. 85629
from Bisenzio, Bucacce necropolis, Tomb 3

Out-turned rim, upside-down trunco-conical neck, flattened globular body, tall splayed foot. On the body five friezes, framed by horizontal red bands. From top to bottom, wolf teeth on black background, losanges on latticed background, alternately red and black, series of metopes in red, separated by narrow vertical rectangles, decorated with a black herring-bone pattern; inside each metope a red square with lattice background, alternately in red and black, and surrounded by S-shaped motifs; lozenges on latticed background, alternately red and black; row of 48 small human figures, alternately red and black, dancing holding hands. In the lower part of the body four radial bands in red. On the foot three red horizontal bands. Attributed to a worshop of Visentii.

Prima Italia 1981, p. 74 n. 33; Martelli 1987, p. 250 n. 18.
[C.Z.]

165. Black figure amphora
ca. 470 B.C.
beige clay, brown glaze, white and brown-red highlights
h 49.5 cm; diam. 31 cm
Berlin, Staatliche Museen, Antikensammlung, inv. 2154
from Vulci

Amphora with small echinus base, large ribbon-handles. Side A: a scene of the judgement of Paris. On the right Hermes with winged shoes. Behind him, three goddesses, one of whom is presenting a fruit to another. In front of Hermes, a youth—maybe Paris—with stick and *alabastron*. Upper part: race of bigas drawn by three horses; one is driven by a youth. Side B: Four persons, on the outside two women, on the inside a youth (Dionysius?), on the right a woman holding a panther on a leash. Upper part: race of bigas like the one on side A. The third biga, driven by a youth, is overturned, one horse fallen on its knees and another on the ground.

Kästner 1988. [U.K.]

166–169. Velletri Slabs
Naples, Museo Archeologico
from Velletri, church of the Santissime Stimmate

The four slabs belong to a larger group of eartheware wall-facings, antefixes and other elements in Ionian-type style, referrable to the monumental period of the Archaic temple found in 1784 under the chapel of the Santissime Stimmate.

Fortunati 1988, pp. 3–11; Fortunati 1990, pp. 199–204 with bibl. [M.M.]

166. Slab with banqueting scene
ca. 530 B.C.
terra cotta, stamped
h 36.8 cm; l 71.8 cm; thick. 7 cm
inv. 21600

The slab, delimited on top by a row of concave pods and a convex scaled moulding, figures a banquet scene: the pair of banqueters half-reclining on the couch on the right—the female figure is identified by her tall *tutulus*—is assisted by a standing, naked young servant, while in the middle of the scene, between the two couches there is a female double-flute player and a small serf in the background.
[M.B.]

167. Slab with chariot race
ca. 530 B.C.
terra cotta, stamped
h 37.2 cm; l 70.7 cm; thick. 6.8 cm
inv. 21608

The slab, figuring a chariot race facing right, is delimited on top by a double continuous meander with swans and stars and by a frame of concave pods. Faint traces of the original polychromy: dark blue, red, yellow .
[M.B.]

168. Slab with procession
ca. 530 B.C.
terra cotta, stamped
h 29 cm; l 70 cm; thick. 6.5 cm
inv. 20606

The frieze figures a procession of coaches facing right: a herald with large hat and caduceus precedes a coach pulled by three horses, while the chariot behind it is pulled by a pair of horses with large curved wings. Standing in each coach, the charioteer and another person. The slab is adorned with a series of concave pods.
[M.B.]

169. Slab with horsemen
ca. 530 B.C.
terra cotta, stamped
h 21 cm; l 64.5 cm; thick. 74.5 cm
inv. 21595.

The slab, frameless and partly lacunose, figures a battle scene. Three pairs of horses are galloping leftward. Their riders are armed with axes and shields. In the foreground, three figures wearing helmets.
[M.B.]

170. Pyxis
third quarter of seventh century B.C.
ivory
h 19 cm; upper diam. 14.6 cm; lower 15.9 cm
Florence, Museo Archeologico, inv. 73846
from Chiusi, Tomb of the Pania (1873)

The *pyxis*, one of the most significant articles of Clusine artistic craftsmanship of the late Orientalizing period, presumably belonged to the grave goods of a female inhumation grave found in the partition-tomb of the Pania. It is decorated on four illustrated registers, delimited by bands with phytomorphic motifs: on the first are represented two episodes of the myth of Ulysses (Scylla and the flight from the cave of Polyphemus), separated by a figure of a sphinx, on the second the departure of a warrior amid ritual dances, on the third a horseman with two centaurs and some wild animals, on the last, the most lacunose, some real and imaginary animals amid trophies of Phoenician palmettes. If some scholars interpret the scene on the second register as a military departure, while the mythical scenes on the first might evoke the hardships of the journey, and the figures of the third initiation rites, others believe the figurative programme of the pyxis refers to the journey of the deceased in the world beyond the grave, anyway akin to the initiatory one.

Minetti 1998, pp. 47 ff. with bibl.
[A.R.]

171. Sarcophagus
late sixth–early fifth century B.C.
pietra fetida; abundant traces of color, in particular red
h of coffin with lid 62 cm ; h coffin 52 cm; l of coffin 191 cm; w of coffin 64 cm
Perugia, Museo Archeologico, inv. 195 (formerly 61 and 340)
from Perugia, necropolis of the Sperandio, 1843

Coffin resting on four feet, the two front ones lion paws; sloping lid, with passing holes, evenly placed. Relief decoration on the short sides: three persons at a banquet on two *klinai* and small naked cup-bearer. On the front of the coffin, between the cornice with pods and smooth spline, a procession facing right is represented. In front a beardless man, with tunic and cloak and a long stick held upright in his right hand: a thick rope around his neck attaches him to three bearded men following him, probably captives: two of them are holding on their shoulders with their right hand a bag or a wineskin or an animal (?), the first also a little bundle and the last also a situla in his left hand; the one in the middle is not carrying anything. Two women come behind, wearing double tunics, cloaks over their heads, the first turns backward while the second leans on a stick. Behind comes a man with a stick (or a spear?) on his shoulder, beside a dog with a collar. The procession also features two loaded donkeys, led by two drivers looking backward. The representation on the main side of the sarcophagus, that contained the remains of a warrior, whose burial-goods included arms, has been diversely interpreted: a *ver sacrum*; the migration of a gentilitial group from Chiusi to Perugia, probably datable to the era of Porsenna; the return from a foray; the departure of a leader and his suite toward the Po Valley; the representation of a procession in which are blended triumphal return and apotheosis. The typology and the style of the monument seem closely connected with the Clusine cippi and sarcophaghi produced in the late sixth century and the early fifth, even if the scene appears to be a *unicum*.

Bull. Inst. 1844, pp. 42, 143; Giglioli 1952, pp. 81–87, tavv. XXIII–XXIV (with previous bibl.); Jannot 1984, pp. 42-44, p. 384, figs. 155–59 (with previous bibl.); Feruglio 1985, pp. 253–54 (with previous bibl.); Torelli 1992, pp. 264 ff.; Cherici 1993, pp.13 ff.; Stopponi 1996, p. 333 (with previous bibl.).
[A.E.F.]

172. Fresco
ca. 520 B.C.
max. l remaining 322 cm; max. h remaining 59 cm
lacunose, especially in the right half
Florence, Museo Archeologico, inv. 82085
from Tarquinia, Monterozzi necropolis, locality Villa Tarantola, Tomb Tarantola

The fragment of a fresco, detached in the early years of the twentieth century and sold to the Museum of Florence in 1905 by a certain A. Perrini, belongs to the back wall of a hypogea chamber-tomb and conserves the decoration of the tympanum and part of the frieze consisting originally of thirteen running black, red, pink, gray bands alternating with light-colored reserved bands. On the tympanum banquet scene with four male figures reclining on a single matress and wearing light-colored chitons and red or blue himatia, the second person from the left is holding in his left hand a large kylix, turning toward the third commensal, the last person on the right is shown asleep. In the far part of the right semi-tympanum, there are an oinochoe, an amphora and crowns, in the left one a panther gradient right.
Although it entirely fits in the scene of Tarquinia painting of the last decades of the sixth century B.C., characterized by a language strongly marked by the Ionian style of Minor-Oriental Greekness, the decoration of the tomb differs from the other concurrent ones by the subject, not the symposium of the aristocratic couple glorifying the *oikos* and the values underlying it, but the celebration of wine-drinking as socializing function within a political association of equals responding to that Hellenizing-style ideology embodied in more accomplished forms, also thanks to the contribution of the inscriptions, in the just slightly more recent Tomb of the Inscriptions.

Steingräber 1984, p. 349 n. 114 (with previous bibl.); d'Agostino 1983, pp. 7 ff.; Weber Lehmann 1985; d'Agostino, Cerchiai 1999, p. 24 (with some misunderstanding with the contemporary Tomb Stefani, also known as Tomb of the Fondo Tarantola [see Steingräber 1984, p. 348 n. 112; with previous bibl.])
[S.B.]

173. Lebes with plastic decoration
second half of seventh century B.C.
reddish-brown impasto
h 14 cm; h of figures 7.8–9.7 cm; diam. of rim 38.5 cm
Florence, Museo Archeologico, reserve, inv. 89852.
from Pitigliano (Grosseto), locality Valle Rodeta, chamber tomb found in 1939

Among the many pottery items, of various typologies, found inside the small funeral chamber, this *lebes* stands out by its morphological features. The little figures decorating the top of the rim of the vase, three horsemen alternating with three weeping women, recall a particular local production that belongs to the late-Villanovan formal tradition, attested in the ossuary of Montescudiao and the Gualandi-type Clusine cinerary urns. In the choice of subjects and their representation, the reference to the funerary ideology and the aristocratic rank it reflects is obvious

Scamuzzi 1940, pp. 19–29; Adembri 1985, p. 291, n. 11.2; Torelli 1997, pp. 28 ff; Maggiani 1999 p. 61. [A.P.]

174. Campana slabs
third quarter of sixth century B.C.
painted terra cotta
h 125 cm; w 59–33 cm
Paris, Musée du Louvre, Département des Antiquités grecques, étrusques et romaines, inv. Cp 6624-6628
Cerveteri, Banditaccia necropolis

Each one of the figured scenes is delimited above by a beaded cornice, painted in turn red, black, white. Below there is a horizontal line and broad vertical red and white bands.

Roncalli 1965, pp. 16-22, tpls. I–V; Briguet 1988, pp. 73–74, figs. 73–74. [G.P.]

175. Death bed
second half of sixth century B.C.
tuff
h 57 cm; l 92 cm; 96 cm; 79 cm; w 32 cm; 38 cm; 15 cm
Castello (Florence), Villa Corsini, inv. 9781
from Camucia (Arezzo), "Melone", Tomb A

The bed consists of three combined blocks decorated in low relief; on the sides, profiled legs and above, the spline, showing the level of the bed. On the front side eight kneeling female figures, identified as mourners, wearing the Ionian chiton, held at the waist by a belt, are beating their breasts, except the two central ones who are clawing their cheeks.

Prayon 1975, p. 57, pls. 67, 2; Neppi Modona 1977, pp. 70–71; *Cortona dei principes* 1992 p. 49 n. 40. [C.Z.]

176. Fragment of a cippus
490-480 B. C.
pietra fetida, carved, fragmentary
h 38 cm; l 55 cm
Paris, Musée du Louvre, Département des Antiquités grecques, étrusques et romaines inv. MA 3602
Chiusi

Prothesis scene: an entirely draped woman is lying on a funeral couch. Two opposed female figures are holding alabasters, at the foot of the couch is figured another woman with flay and a backward-looking man. Under the couch there are a dog and a goose.

Jannot 1984, p. 92 n. 4, fig. 322. [G.P.]

Hellenization

The penetration of Mycenaean navigators to Italy is now well attested, especially in the south, but it also reaches the Tyrrhenian area. After the fall of the Mycenaean kingdoms, navigators of Phoenician and oriental origin reactivate the Mediterranean routes, and are soon joined by Greek navigators from Boeotia and the Cyclades. The earliest Villanovan phase begins in this context, and the Greek presence gradually strengthens until it culminates in the foundation of permanent colonies in the eighth century B.C. From the earliest phases of Etruscan history there is therefore evidence of a series of contacts with the Greek world, which were to have a lasting effect, and this suggests at least two considerations. The first it that this situation completely nullifies the scholarly debate, especially in the first half of the twentieth century, which tended to see Etruscan—and Roman—art and civilization as having originally been completely independent from the models proposed by the Greek world. We must therefore start from the consideration that influences, including some of crucial ones, of external origin are present in the Tyrrhenian area from the formative phase of Etruscan and Latin civilization. In the second place, all this does not exclude the possibility that there was periodically, according to the changing influences and relationships, a national response, so to speak, to the external models, tending to accept what was compatible internal needs and to reject what seemed incompatible. Thus we see over the whole course of Etruscan history the arrival and the acceptance of every kind of fashion, idea, craft tradition, religious and funerary conception of Greek origin, which systematically become filtered, adapted and flanked by elements originating from the local tradition or, at least, already active at an earlier stage. The process of the Hellenization of Etruria and of ancient Italy in general is perceptible to us especially through the circulation of manufactures, techniques and styles, but it must be borne in mind that all this means at the same time a circulation of ideas, mentalities, customs and forms of behavior which have a deep impact on Etruscan society.

In the history of the forms and modalities of the Hellenization of Etruria, a first great vehicle of transmission of the Hellenic way of life was the consumption of wine. We do now know of an Italic wine (*temetum*) which went back at least to the last phases of the Bronze Age, which requires the appropriate forms of pottery for its consumption, which were actually the origin of some forms in the repertory of Attic pottery, as can be seen in the section of the exhibition devoted to "original wine." In the eighth century B.C.,

the consumption of wine seems already to have been widespread, together with the use of Greek, or imitation Greek, pottery, as can be seen from the section of the exhibition concerning "acquired wine." The drink in question was probably a strongly spiced wine, which was originally produced in the Levant and circulated by Phoenician navigations, but later taken over by the Greeks too. About the middle of the seventh century B.C. Etruria adopted the main ceremony connected with wine consumption, the symposium (see the relevant section of the exhibition), which was destined to have a profound influence on the lifestyle of the aristocracies. In this sense the contact with the Greek colonial world must have been fundamental, though one should not forget the arrival in the Tyrrhenian world of an iconographical repertory linked with Corinthian pottery which may illustrate the development and characteristics of this ceremony. Although in the Etruscan world the distinction between banquet and symposium does not often seem so well defined, the gathering of the Etruscan symposiasts follows in outline the forms known in the Greek world, with the exception of the the presence, already noted on several occasions, of women of high social status. The archaeological contexts give us an idea of the wide diffusion of the symposium, for it is attested by countless finds of types of pottery and instruments necessary to the ceremony of wine-drinking, such as the candelabrum, one example of which is present in the exhibition. The wine is poured from the *oinochoe* into the most important vase, the crater, and mixed with a varying amount of water according to its strength and aroma. The mixture thus obtained may be cooled or heated through the insertion into the middle of the vase of the *psykter* containing snow or ice or cold or hot water. The symposiarch who directs operations, after a libation, initiates the drinking phase by giving the order to fill and circulate the cups. The occasion is accompanied by recitations and songs, such as the *carmina convivalia* known from the Latin tradition, and by games and shows. We must not forget the importance that the symposium assumed as an opportunity for meetings between aristocratic groups to make agreements and alliances. Moreover we have already seen the role that the symposium acquired in the funerary ideology.
In the seventh and the sixth centuries a profound Hellenization also affected the religious sphere, leading to the representation of the divine figures in human form; the interpretation in a Greek sense of the local divinities, which is illustrated in the bronze statues of gods present in the exhibition; and finally, the adoption by the Etruscans of the forms of worship of the gods, culminating in the temple. The adoption of forms and customs of Greek religion cannot be separated from the parallel penetration into the Tyrrhenian world of the Greek mythological repertory, a process fostered by the circulation of Homeric epic in the Tyrrhenian area, as is shown by the well-known cup of Nestor from Pithecoussai. Greek myth arrives in Etruria and Latium drawn by the interest of the Tyrrhenian *principes*, who see the great, superhuman stories of Theseus, Heracles, Odysseus, and Achilles as exemplary models of the acquisition of kingship. Greek myth immediately becomes part of a language of power which had been developed much earlier by the Tyrrhenian aristocracies and which now superimposes an older language, a language centered on the rite though not foreign to local mythologies, on a newer and more prestigious one which makes it possible to assimilate the military achievements of the warrior princes to the deeds of the heroes. Round these basic motifs the representations of Greek myth which come to Etruria are periodically imbued with other meanings thanks to the polysemy of these images, as can be seen from the materials exhibited here. On the so-called crater of the Hunchbacks the deeds of Heracles which were dear to the Tyrrhenian princes also convey a *paideia* of the just sacrifice, represented on the neck of the vase, in opposition to the human sacrifice which appears among the scenes of the main body. On the *oinochoe* of Tragliatella, the dance of the *geranos* performed by the Athenian boys and girls rescued from the Cretan monster is adapted to an armed male dance according to the perspective of the warrior aristocracies of Etruria. Furthermore, the double sexual union alludes to the ancient oriental motif of hierogamy with the goddess which we have met earlier. The Etrusco-Corinthian *oinochoe* with the scene of the destruction of Troy probably alludes to the various traditions that circulated about the provenance and the ethnic origins of the Tyrrhenian peoples, an element which can also be traced on the *olpe* of bucchero with Medea, where there is a strong allusion to Lemnus and therefore to the possible oriental connections of the Etruscans' origins. Initially an exclusively aristocratic apanage, myth moves to the urban spaces, as is shown for example by the groups of Apollo and Latona from Veii and that of Eos and Kephalos from Cerveteri exhibited here. Later it dominates the temple decorations from the late sixth century onward, proof that the ideology of the *principes* had been dimished in favor of the communitarian structures of the city. The channels of exchange which affected the Tyrrhenian world brought to the territories of the Etruscan and Latin cities not only goods but also and especially craftsmen who, since they possessed specialized techniques, found plentiful opportunities for commissions and stimulated the start of local imitation production first in the context of the archaic *tryphe* on the aristocratic pattern and then in the context of the wider social structures of the city. The crucial contribution of these men of foreign origin in possession of advanced techniques is matched by a low social status similar to that of the metics, and is confirmed in the ancient sources by the frequent application to them of the epithet *Graeculi*. The materials on display exemplify the contribution of craftsmanship of a Greek kind in Etruscan territory; during the course of the sixth century B.C. it came to cover virtually every sector. The diffusion of this craftwork through wider production aimed at a larger urban public, like the Hellenization of the forms of worship and mythology and of agricultural techniques and production, the diffusion of hoplitism after its original insertion in the structures of the aristocratic chiefs, and the perception of the influences, at different times and in different ways, of the achievements of Greek art, make the land of the Etruscans a province of the wider Greek world. Writing, too, is an important Greek contribution. The materials on display illustrate various levels of the circulation of writing, from the model alphabets connected with forms of exercise and the learning of writing technology, to the Tile of Capua, the copy of the gold *laminae* from Pyrgi, and the letter of Pech-Maho concerning commercial transactions. Certainly the introduction of writing technology closely affects the highest social groups, as is shown by the bronze stylus found in the Sodo II Tumulus at Cortona and shown here. An example of its possible use is the writing of the *tabulae* preserved in the archive of the kin group where the main deeds attesting to the family estate are recorded. The *libri lintei* which emerge later in the available evidence also indicate a use of writing in the exclusive aristocratic channels which were in charge of the *Etrusca disciplina*. The process of Hellenization continues through a period of time which embraces practically every phase of the history of Etruscan civilization and it actually conceals some extremely varied aspects and modalities. For the arrival of manufactures and cultural influences from the Greek world takes on a wide variety of forms if we consider the earliest navigations and the most ancient colonial contacts which were later to intensify, the Orientalizing fashion, the effects of the structure, political institutions and culture of the *polis* of the classical age, and the models of the Hellenistic world based on the dynastic courts. Moreover, the intensity of the Greek influences and fashions which reach the Tyrrhenian world changes appreciably over the centuries, so that it is possible to perceive both long-term, slow-filtering processes and peaks and troughs that last only a few decades. All this is directly linked with the social groups within the Etruscan world which were responsible at various times for the activation of contacts with the Greek world and for the degree of acceptance and selection of the relevant material and cultural models which reach the Tyrrhenian area. [F.C.]

WINE

176 bis. Impasto capeduncula
first half of eighth century B.C.
brown impasto
h 7 cm; diam. 10.2 cm
Florence, Museo Archeologico,
inv. 83652 c
from Tarquinia, Selciatello di Sopra, well tomb 135

Thinned, out-turned rim; large low vessel, faired, with slightly convex bottom; overhanging ribbon-handle, placed on the shoulder and the rim.

Milani, inNSc 1907, p. 253; H. Hencken, *Tarquinia, Villanovans and EarlyEtruscans*, I, Cambridge (Mass.) 1968, p. 137, fig. 124 e. [F.C.]

177. Single-handle semi-spherical bowl
Villanovan IIB
plated bronze
h 11 cm; diam. 16.5 cm
Tarquinia, Museo Archeologico ,
inv. RC 4218
From Tarquinia, necropolis of Monterozzi, *dolium* tomb M7

Out-turned distinct lip; semi-spherical bowl with *omphalos*, overhanging vertical ribbon handle, held below by a small plate with rivets and decorated with two vertical lines of dots between bands of slanting dashes.

Hencken 1968, p. 194, fig. 175 e.
[C.Z.]

178. Kyathos
sixth century B.C.
black bucchero with stamped decoration
h 8.6 cm; diam. 6.5 cm
Florence, Museo archeologico
inv. 2924
Clusine production

Deep vessel, with slanted walls, separated from the flat bottom by a protrusion; ribbon-handle placed vertically on the rim and the bottom, with a small trapezoidal plaque decorated with palmettes at the top of the inner side of the handle.

179. Attic black-figure Lydos kyathos
560–540 B.C.
painted earthenware
h 15 cm; h at rim 7.3 cm; diam. 11.5 cm
Rome, Museo di Villa Giulia,
inv. 84466
from Vulci, Necropolis of the Osteria (Hercle excavations 1963), Tomb 145

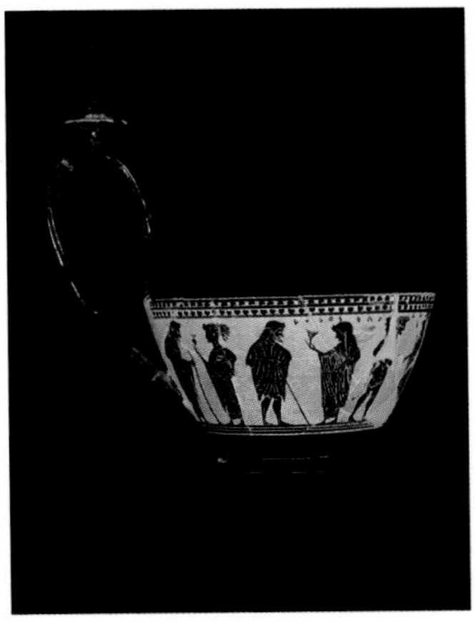

Curved, trunco-conical vessel, foot with flared spline, high ribbon handle topped by an acorn and bearing on the side toward the container a ribbing ending in a little upturned leaf. Colored background inside, on the handle and the bottom of the vessel with the foot. Under the rim two short horizontal rows of heart-shaped leaves between lines, underneath which is the painted inscription: "Lydos egraphsen ho dolo...".
On the vessel, above a group of three bottom lines, are figured six pairs of opposing divinities, in reference to the *Antesterie* celebrations: Zeus (?) with sceptre and female person carrying a flower (pair repeated twice), Hercules and Athena, Dionysus and Hermes, Poseidon and a female figure holding a flower, another pair of persons, one of whom bearded. The form of the *kyathos* is typical of Vulci, which indicates that the vase as made in Greece purposely for the Etruscan market.

Rizzo 1985, p. 523 with bibl.; Rizzo 1988, p. 88, n. 47, fig. 155, with some bibliographical references.
[L.R.]

180. Small impasto amphora
first half of eighth century B.C.
brown impasto
h 12 cm
Florence, Museo Archeologico,
inv. 83557 e
from Tarquinia, Selciatello di Sopra, Tomb 20

Out-turned rim; low trunco-conical neck; flattened globular body; flat bottom; ribbon-handles placed on the shoulder and rim; two small knobs in the widest part.

Pernier 1907, p. 80; Hencken 1968, pp. 126 ff.
[F.C.]

181. Small amphora with spirals
third quarter of seventh century B.C.
brown impasto.
h 12.6 cm
Florence, Museo Archeologico, inv. 89390
from Populonia, Porcareccia, Tomb of the Flabelli

Out-turned lip; concave trunco-conical neck; globular body, with faired shoulder; low ringed foot; vertical ribbon handles; on body incised double spiral and herring-bone pattern amid vertical bands with four incisions; under the handles two bands with triple incisions, converging toward their lower attachment; on the handles four incised vertical lines.

Martelli 1985, p. 404; Bruni 1987, p. 252, n. 54.
[F.C.]

182. Amphora
end of seventh century B.C.
black bucchero; scratched and stamped decoration
h 18 cm; max. diam. 33 cm; diam. of mouth 18 cm
Florence, Museo Archeologico, inv. 81526
from Veio, Monte Michele necropolis, Tomb E

Flared rim, trunco-conical neck, globular body, splayed foot; four ribbon-handles decorated with two stamped metopes figuring a horse. On the widest part of the body appears a frieze with a series of scratched birds in flight, below which there is a series of twenty partly-closed little dotted fans, arranged horizontally. The exemplar, probably of Caeretan make, although recalling the so-called Nicosthenes amphoras, has a most peculiar shape, especially owing to the presence of four handles, which has only a single match, in bucchero, in an exemplar at the Louvre Museum.

Cristofani 1969, p. 37, n. 1, fig. 16, pl. XVIII, 1.
[G.C.C.]

183. Nikosthenic amphora
ca. 530 B.C.
nut-brown clay, black glaze
h 31 cm; diam. 17.6 cm
Rome, Museo Archeologico di Villa Giulia, inv. 50558
formerly Castellani Collection

On the rim of the lip, chain of palmettes and lotus flowers joined and opposing at the base. The scenes on the body are separated by a chain of palmettes. Below the lower scene tall black band and sunburst. On the handles chain of open lotus flowers alternating with palmettes that continue on the shoulder. On the shoulder: side A monomachia between hoplite and amazons; in the field an inscription; side B, monomachia around a fallen man. On the body, sides A and B *komos*.

Mingazzini 1930, n. 462 , pls. LIX, 1–4; *ABV*, 221, 37; Caruso 1985, p. 23 n. 18.
[C.Z.]

184. Attic amphora SOS
675–625 B.C.
compact orange clay; brown-red/black glaze
h 71.5 cm; diam. 46.5 cm; outside of mouth 21 cm; diam. of foot 12 cm
Cerveteri, Museo Archeologico, inv. 87944
from Cerveteri, Monte Abatone necropolis, Tomb 4

Ovate body, hanging shoulder, tall, slightly trunco-conical foot, cylindrical neck with small collar at the joining with the lip, lip decorated with echinus, rather narrow stick-handles, placed between the middle of the neck and the shoulder. On the neck is painted the motif SOS of the type Sc Oa Sc. Graffiti marks on the handles and on their lower attachments.

Rizzo, 1990, p. 51 [P.A.]

185. Workshop of Polychromy
Tarquinia, Museo Archeologico
from Tarquinia

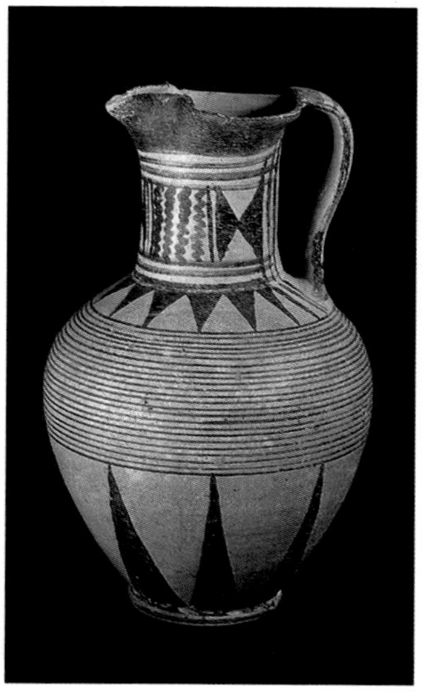

1

• *1. Italo-Geometric oinochoe*
first quarter of seventh century B.C.
pink clay; yellowish slip; opaque black and reddish glaze
h 26.8 cm
inv. RC 7208
Trilobate mouth; tall cylindrical neck; thin, elongated ovate body; low trunco-conical foot; vertical double stick-handle; mouth glazed black; on the body horizontal lines alternately red and black; on the shoulder triangles on latticed background alternating stars and swastikas; on the lower part of the body two wide bands alternating with red and black lines; on the shoulder horizontal lines.

• *2. Italo-Geometric kotyle*
early seventh century B.C.
pink clay; yellowish slip; pinkish-brown glaze
h 10.2 cm
inv. RC 1921
Indistinct rim, slightly tilted inward; ovate vessel, wide and deep; low ringed foot; horizontal stick-handles, slightly slanting on top. On the rim horizontal lines; level with the handles, band with row of sigmas framed by two groups of vertical lines; on the body horizontal lines; lower part glazed; reserved foot, with horizontal line; inside glazed; on the handles horizontal line.

2

Bibl.: *CVA Tarquinia III*, p. 47, tav. 35,1.
Gabrici 1911, p. 93, fig. 37; *CVA Tarquinia III*, pp. 20, 47, pls. 14, 6–7; Tanci, Tortoioli forthcoming n. 81.
[F.C.]

186. Small-column krater
reconstructed from fragments and partly reintegrated
h 40 cm; upper diam. 34.2 cm
Rome, Sinopoli Collection

Accessory decoration: on the top of the rim, sunburst; on the handle plaques on one side a crouching panther in left profile, on the other a crouching lion also in left profile, lacking the rear part that did not fit on the plaque. Purple bands and overpainted thin white lines frame the friezes and the bands on the body.
Side A: at center winged, bearded male figure, shown running toward the right between two seated, opposing sphinxes. Side S: two gradient, opposing horsemen with in the center a siren looking backward. Frieze with procession of animals: a gradient ram in left profile, a gradient lion inright profile, an ibex in left profile, a gradient lion in right profile, an ibex in left profile, a lion in left profile and a grazing ibex in left profile. The krater, by its shape, with quite developed neck and body tending to the ovate, and very broad shoulder, belongs to Bakir's group III, dated between 590 and 575 B.C. The presence of the sunburst on the rim and especially the figured frieze still contained in panels, with the area below the handles devoid of decoration, seem to point to a rather ancient phase of Middle Corinthian.

Romualdi 1995, n.49, pp.182–91. [A.R.]

187. Laconian krater
second half of sixth century B.C.
bronze
h 41.8 cm; diam. 45.2 cm
Santa Maria Capua Vetere, Museo Archeologico dell'Antica Capua, inv. T.1426
from Santa Maria Capua Vetere, locality Fornaci, north-west necropolis

The Laconian-style krater was found in 1973 in a tufa cube-tomb, in the inner cavity of which it was placed to contain the cremated bones, wrapped in a piece of cloth, and covered by a bronze cauldron. It is made of curved plate, with the rim hidden by the applied *kymation*; cast separately and applied with bolts and mastic, there are also the foot and the spiralled handles with ropes ending in snake heads, chiselled at the top, separated by hands of which four fingers can be seen. The comparison with other exemplars, in Syracuse, Munich (from Campania), Trebenischte and Vix, had led the finder, W. Johannowsky, to identify a Lucanian provenance.

Johannowsky 1974, pp. 3–20. [V.S.]

188. Black figure column-krater
orange clay, black figure decoration with white and purple highlights
h 43.6 cm
reconstituted from fragments and integrated
Rome, Giuseppe Sinopoli Collection

A krater of a rather ancient form derived from Middle-Corinthian models, with short rim and neck, entirely glazed. On the lip a series of parallel lines and bearded male heads on the attachment plaques. On the shoulder, frieze of black and purple tongues, on the ground wide horizontal band and sunburst; the foot entirely glazed with the edge emphasized by an over-painted purple band. On side A: centauromachia scene. A Lapith faces two centaurs who are throwing stones, followed by a second Lapith who is striking with his spear a fleeing centaur, who is looking back. Both Lapiths are wearing helmet, cuirass and holding a big Boeotian-style shield. On side B: two opposing bulls, a palmette rising between two scrolls above and a lotus flower below between the two animals' heads. In the space beneath the attachment of the handles, a swan with an outspread wing. R.Guy attributed the krater to Lydos, one of the leading figures working in the pottery center (Cerameicus) of Athens in the middle decades of the sixth century B.C. Actually, if the form of the vase seems similar to the British Museum krater 1948.10–15, the still rather limited use of the graffito, the layout of the decoration on the edge of the lip, would appear to date this vase at a time when this master's production was just beginning, making it comparable to works like the Louvre hydria E 804 and the Louvre amphora C 10634, or else to a krater previously on the Swiss antique market, that Beazley considered to be a school-work, by a different hand, in between the Vatican Painter 309 and the Louvre Painter F 6. (*Munzen und Medaillen,* Basel, Auktion 40, 13.XII.1969, n. 61).

Glimpses of Excellence. A Selection of Greek Vases and Bronzes from the Elie Borowski Collection 1985, n. 4 (R. Guy); *Meisterwerke griechischer Keramik. Die Sammlung Giuseppe Sinopoli* 2000, n. 34 (S. Bruni). [S.B.]

189. Attic red figure krater
520–510 B.C.
clay, glaze, on the wheel; reconstituted from fragments with lacunas
h 44.8 cm; diam. of rim 55 cm
Paris, Musée du Louvre, Département des Antiquités grecques, étrusques et romaines, inv. Cp 748
from Cerveteri

Side A: Herakles naked in close combat with the giant Anteus, both shown with their own names. On the sides three women fleeing in fright. Side B: A youth about to mount on a podium is holding an aulos in his left hand. On the sides three youths with bare torsos are seated, leaning on long canes. On the podium there is the inscription *Melaskalos* or *Hylaskalos* (?); in the field there are four other names: *Leagroskalos; Policlès; Kephisodoros; Hylas* (?). Attributed to Euphronios.

Denoyelle, *Capolavori*, pp. 82–85 [G.P.]

190. Red-figure amphora
510–500 B.C.
clay, glaze, on the wheel; reconstituted from fragments with lacunas
conserved h 47 cm; diam. of rim 20.1 cm
Paris, Musée du Louvre, Département des Antiquités grecques, étrusques et romaines
inv.G 30
Vulci

Side A: youth banqueting with a crown on his head, frontal bust, bent legs, who is about to perform with a goblet, held with his right hand forefinger, the casting of the kottabos. In the field there is the inscription *pais Leagros kalos*.
Side B: youth banqueting with a crown on his head, reclining, with bent legs. With his right hand he is playing the lyre he is holding in his left. Near the mouth there is the inscription *mamekapoteo*, the first words of a poem by Sappho, and in the field the epigraph *Leagroskalos*.
Attributed to Euphronios

Denoyelle, *Capolavori*, pp. 138–39.
[G.P.]

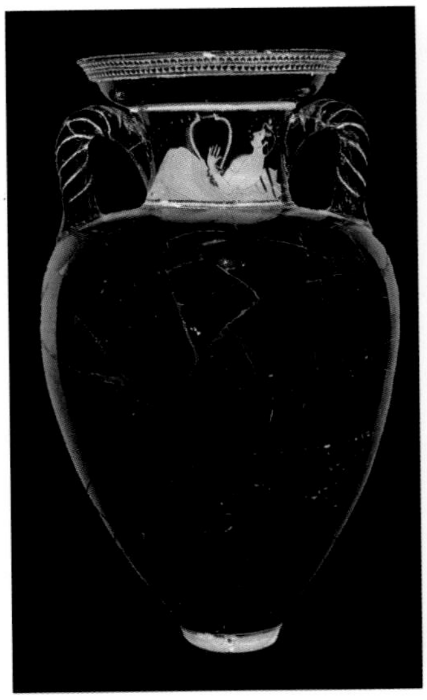

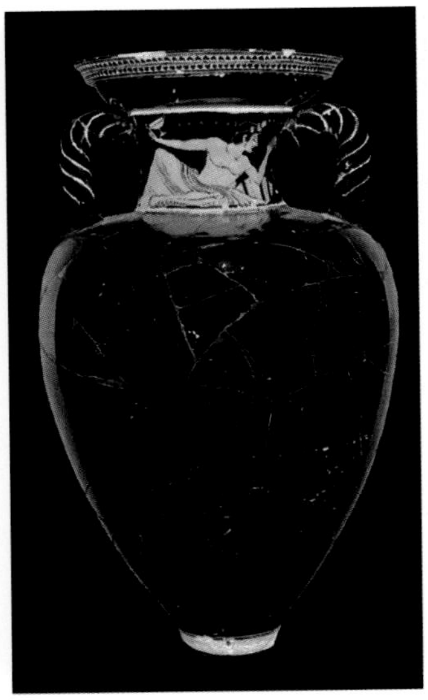

191. Silvered pottery panoply for symposium
second half fourth century B.C.
Florence, Museo Archeologico

• 1. *Chalice krater*
beige clay; orange slip; silver-grey coating
h 52 cm
inv. 87528
High flared lip, with relief vine-shoots, with hanging rim decorated with ovoli and lancets; faired semispherical vessel, ending in a profiled element that is connected, by a bayonet base, to a tall stem with upper part with tongues, relief ring at mid-height and strigilated in the lower part; profiled foot on plinth; horizontal handles curved upward, placed on the fairing, strigilated, and attachment with heads with "melon" hairdress and leaf crown on the neck amid scrolls.

• 2. *Patera*
pinkish-beige clay; silver-grey coating
diam. 24 cm
inv. 77648
from Poggio Sala, chamber tomb
Vertical rim, emphasized by an incised line; ample vessel; concave cylindrical foot; inside relief vine-shoots around a medalion with female figure seated on a rock, with a cloak over her legs and upper part naked, facing Hercules, seated on a rock; between the two a naked winged female figure, offering something to Hercules.

1

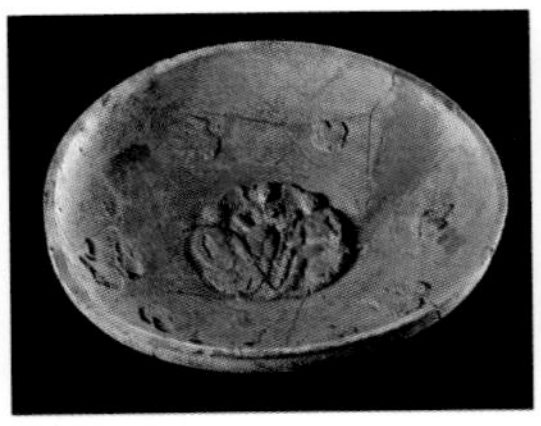

2

3

5

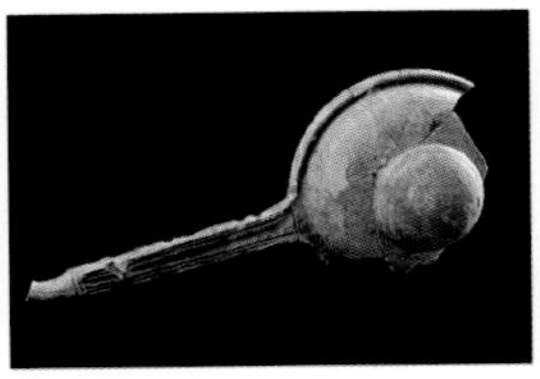

4

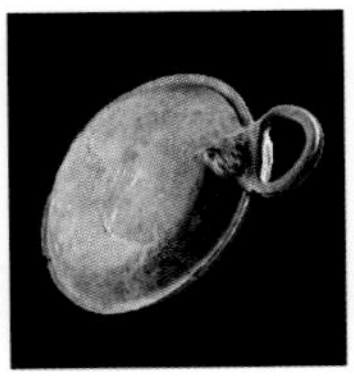

6

7

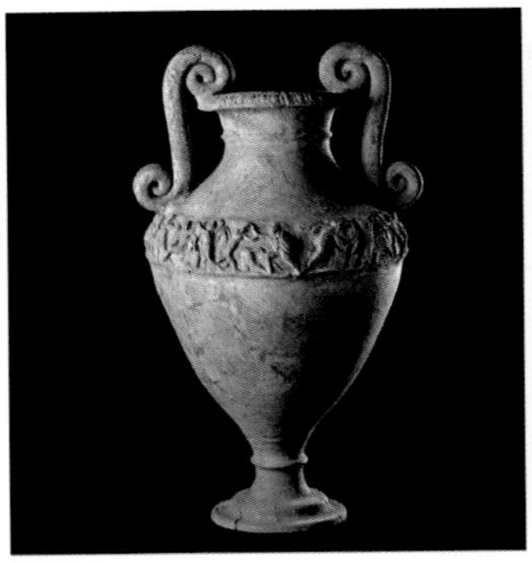

8

9

10

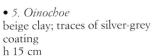

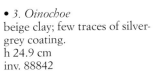

• 3. *Oinochoe*
beige clay; few traces of silver-grey coating.
h 24.9 cm
inv. 88842
Long spout; narrow trunco-conical neck; cylindrical, slightly concave body, with faired sharp-edged shoulder; flat bottom; vertical handle with triple ribbing, with unidentifiable protome on top and plaque with winged figure on the lower attachment.

• 4. *Colum*
pinkish-beige clay; traces of slip and silver-grey coating
l 23 cm
inv. 77651
from Poggio Sala, chamber tomb
Small brimmed lip with hanging rim; low vessel with semispherical, non-perforated *omphalos*; flat ribbon handle, adorned with two rope-decoration lines and ending in a lacunose protome.

• 5. *Oinochoe*
beige clay; traces of silver-grey coating
h 15 cm
inv. 77660
from Poggio Sala, chamber tomb
Trilobate mouth; low, narrow neck; ample body, with rounded shoulder, tapering downward;

low ringed foot; vertical ribbon handle, lacunose, with three ribbings, with heart-shaped lower attachment.

• *6. Patera with handle*
beige clay; greenish-orange slip; traces of silver-grey coating
h 4.8 cm; diam. 35 cm
inv. 88868
Out-turned lip; large, low vessel with slightly convex bottom; horizontal ribbon handle with triple ribbing; under the handle small heart-shaped plaque attachment with palmette.

• *7. Three kyathoi*
beige clay; slip and coating lost
h 6.1 cm; 6.3 cm; 5.6 cm
inv. 88873
Small out-turned lip; very low neck; concave cylindrical body; flat bottom; vertical handle, nearly entirely missing.

• *8. Amphora*
light orange clay; traces of silver-grey coating.
h 48 cm
inv. 4661
Reversed out-turned lip, with ovoli and lancets; low cylindrical neck; ovate body, with faired shoulder, tapering downward; stem with relief ring; disk foot; vertical double stick-handles, ending in large spirals above and below; on the shoulder relief frieze with Amazonomachia.

• *9. Amphora*
beige clay; greenish-orange slip; traces of silver-grey coating
h 42.3 cm
inv. 88837
Distinct profiled lip; low concave neck, with relief spline on the base; ovate body; concave stem; disk foot; twisted vertical handles, with two pairs of small acanthus leaves on the lower attachment.

• *10. Situla*
orange-beige clay; reddish slip; orange-grey coating
h 29.5 cm
Florence, Museo Archeologico, inv. 4658
Rim emphasized by three grooves and a series of stamped dots; ovate body, tapering downward; ringed and grooved near the foot; flat bottom; on the rim two facing small plaques, with overhanging upper part, with youthful male head crowned with leaves between two spirals, and lower part with ivy leaves.

Milani 1896, p. 390, ns. 9–12, 14–15; De Chiara 1960, pp. 12, 14, 133–134, ns. 25, 43, 50.
[F.C.]

192. Candelabrum
450 B.C.
bronze; ivory
h 100.5 cm
Ferrara, Museo Archeologico, inv. 2290
from Spina, Valle Trebba, T omb 614

Three-footed base with lions' paws resting on globular elements; octogonal-section stem, with profiled base and upper extremity; four crossed arms, curved upward and each ending in a lotus flower; in the middle a ivory group with a youth holding a maiden dressed in chiton and *himation*.

Aurigemma 1960, pp. 73 ff.; Hostetter 1986, pp. 89 ff., n. 56.
[F.C.]

193. Ossuary
last quarter of seventh century B.C.
clay, on the wheel, reconstituted from fragments with some small lacunas
h 36 cm; diam. rim 15 cm
Chianciano Terme, Museo Civico Chianciano Terme, locality Tolle, Tomb 13

Ossuary: slanting lip, convex body, flat bottom, vertical stick-handles. Cap-like cover bearing on top a reclining male figure wearing a light, white cloak.

Chianciano Terme 1997, p. 96, fig. 90.
[G.P.]

194. Cinerary urn
first half of fourth century B.C.
painted alabaster
h 88 cm; l 123 cm; w 38 cm
Florence, Museo Archeologico, inv. 73577
from Città della Pieve (Perugia), locality Bottarone

The Bottarone urn, one of the latest items of the great Clusine funerary statuary, is perhaps the first (if not the only) exemplar in which the female figure seated at the foot of the deceased and shown drawing aside the veil covering her head, is certainly the wife and not a daimon from the Afterlife. The figure of the deceased, a reclining banqueter holding an "umbilical" patera in his left hand, his right resting on his wife's shoulder, has been completed with the head, that some scholars consider fake. Even if the heads of the two figures were made separately, the monument is a cinerary urn, consisting of a lid and a casket with two cavities for a double grave. Both the two figures' clothes and the kline casket are decorated with bright polychromy. In this monument we see used for the first time the alabaster marble that during the Hellenistic period in Chiusi would replace *pietra fetida*.

Cristofani 1975, n. 19, p. 44; Maggiani 1993, pp. 160 ff.; Rastrelli 1999, p. 35.
[A.R.]

THE GODS

195. Tinia
ca. 480 B.C.
bronze
h 17.2 cm
Los Angeles, J. Paul Getty Museum, inv. 55.AB.12
from Populonia

The solid cast statuette may represent Tinia, wearing a tebenna and holding in his left hand a staff or a torch. The lower part of the left arm, the calves and the left side of the apparel are missing. The hair is carefully combed, held by a ribbon, and was fashioned with a comb instrument, just as the minute details of the beard and moustache.

Lamb 1929, p. 88, tav. XXVIII c; *Accessions of American and Canadian Museum* 1955, p. 403, *sv. Ionic-Etruscan*; *The J. Paul Getty Museum Guidebook* 1956, pp. 14–15, n. 11 (ill.); Stothart, Herbert 1965, p. 11, tpl. 2; Getty 1965, p. 49 (ill.); Del Chiaro 1967, p. 39, n. 42; Mitten, Doeringer 1967, p. 166; Teitz 1967, pp. 55–56, 58–59, n. 44, ill. p. 152; Mansueli 1968, p. 82; Jucker, Hans 1970, pp. 212–13; Sprenger 1972, pp. 52–53, pl. 24: 1; Frederickson, Burton 1975, pp. 18, 33; Sams, Kenneth 1976, n. 50 (ill.); Sprenger, Bartoloni 1977, p. 129; Brendel 1978, pp. 249–50, p. 464 n. 12, p. 469 n. 26, fig. 174; Cristofani 1979, pp. 88–89, pl. 25; Richardson 1983, vol. I, p. 235 n. 3, 11, figs. 533–35; Sprenger, Bartoloni 1983, p. 115, pl. 129; Adam 1984, pp. 157–58, cf. n. 232; *Civiltà degli Etruschi* 1985, pp. 186, 277, n. 81 (ill.); Haynes 1985, cfr. n. 96, p. 281; Maule, 1986, pp. 61–74, pls. 62, 65, 70, ill. pl. XXIV b, cat. n. II, 11; Kozloff, Mitten 1988, pp. 219–23, cat. n. 39 (ill.); Fernandez 1990, pp. 48–56, pl. 51; Scott, Podany 1990, p. 45, pl. 3; Ortiz 1990, pp. 262–64, figs. 8a-d; *The J. Paul Getty Museum. Handbook of the Collections* 1997, p. 30; Camporeale 1997, p. 409, n. 103, pl. 266.
[K.W.]

196. Laran
ca. 450–440 B.C.
bronze; solid lost wax casting
max. h 33 cm
Florence, Museo Archeologico, inv. 586

Armed male figure with left leg forward of the right. Right arm, bent at the elbow, raised holding a sword; left arm, held in front of the chest and holding a round shield decorated, from outside to inside, with a latticed band, two bands of small rings, one band of rings with a dot in the middle and, at centre, a motif with curved rays, inscribed in a circle. Wearing a helmet with a tall crest, raised neck-guard and cheek-guards. On the frontal, decorated on the edge with small knobs, palmette and scrolls. On each side a spiral motif. Knobs on the neck-guard. The crest is decorated with a chequered pattern, with some squares decorated with series of parallel lines. Short pleated vest, with series of rings along the edge, leaving the phallus bare; over it a cuirass with scaled bodice and fringed skirt. On the back, fringe coinciding with the shoulder-blade. Shoulder-straps crossed on the chest, with border adorned with knobs, decorated with a rectangular pattern, on a latticed background. Wearing greaves, adorned with a pair of S-shaped racemes, with a series of small knobs along the edge. Bare feet. North Etruscan make. For Maule it is the eponymous work of the Master of Florence Warrior 586.

Richardson 1983, pp. 180–81, n. 2, pl. 121, fig. 413; Cristofani 1985a, p. 279, n. 87, fig. 87; Torelli 1985, p. 134, fig. 89; *Santuari d'Etruria* 1985, p. 28, n. 1.2, fig. 1.2; Maule 1991, pp. 55–57, pl. XV, a-b.
[C.Z.]

197. Fufluns
ca. 480 B.C.
bronze
h 17.2 cm; w 5.9 cm
Modena, Museo Estense, inv. 12505/523 P, Collection of the Dukes of Este

Fufluns (Dionysus) is wearing on his head a crown with three rosettes that holds his long hair falling on his shoulders, incised with close-set wavy lines. He has a beard and is wearing a chiton (tunic) and a himation (cloak). His right arm is missing: he was probably holding a pottery vase, maybe a kantharos. The statuette of the god, shown walking with his left leg forward, is missing also the lower part of the legs and the feet. It is referrable to the production of a north-Etruscan workshop and comparable to a bronze statuette representing a walking female figure found in the votive deposit of Monte Falterona (*Les Etrusques et l'Europe* 1993, p. 405, n. 510).

Corradini 1985, p. 284, n. 10.29; Corradini 1992, p. 142, n. 72.
[E.C.]

198. Menerva
first quarter of fifth century B.C.
bronze
h 21.5 cm; w 12 cm
Modena, Museo Estense, inv. 12016/14 P, Collection of the Dukes of Este

The goddess is shown in a posture of assault, typical of Greek statuettes representing Minerva Promachos: her right arm is raised to brandish her spear, missing, and her left extended forward to hold her shield, also missing. She is wearing on her head an Attic helmet with a high lophos, of which the upper part is missing, and mobile cheek-guards, one of which is missing. It should be identified as a votive image that, referrable to a Vulci production, borrows motifs and solutions typical of late archaism, associated with modules already belonging to the "Severe" style.

Corradini 1985, pp. 283–84, n. 10.28
[E.C.]

199. Statuette of Turms
ca. 480 B.C.
lost wax bronze
h 17 cm
Paris, Musée du Louvre, Département des Antiquités grecques, étrusques et romaines, inv. MNE 948

The divinity, characterized by the *petasus*, the winged boots and the lost caduceus, is wearing a short-sleeved chiton gathered in tight folds in the lower part, whereas one fold covers the left elbow. Both forearms are stretched forward, with the hands closed in fists.The face has detailed, delicately modeled features.
Gaultier 1990, fasc. 1, pp. 1–6.
[G.P.]

200. Culsans
first half of third century B.C.
cast bronze with file and burin retouches, dark green patina
h 30 cm
Cortona, Museo dell'Accademia Etrusca, inv. 1278
from Cortona, Piazzale del Mercato, near the Porta Bifora; unearthed in 1847

Naked male bifrons statuette, standing, with right arm extended forward, perhaps to hold an attribute, and the left resting on his hip; his head is covered with a wild animal's skin. He is wearing a *torques* around his neck and *endromides* on his feet. On the left thigh is written the dedicatory inscription "v . cvinti . arnt/iaś . culśanśl / alpan . turce" (CIE 437 = TLE 640). The figure of the divinity can be compared to that of Janus, to whom the care of doors was entrusted. The style of the small bronze, and especially the pose and the sinuousness of the body recall the first half of the third century B.C., the period when the influence of the post-Polycletian models can still be felt. Its being found near one of the main entrance gates to the city of Cortona indicates the presence of a sacred place, whose characteristics however are not known.

Cagianelli 1992, pp. 30 ff., 68 ff., n. 53; Bocci Pacini 1992, pp. 95 ff.; Bruschetti, Gori Sassoli, Guidotti, Zamarchi Grassi 1996, p. 29. [P.B.]

201. Selvans
first half of third century B.C.
cast bronze with file and burin retouches, dark green patina
h 30 cm
Cortona, Museo dell'Accademia Etrusca, inv. 1279
from Cortona, piazzale del Mercato, near the Porta bifora; unearthed in 1847

Standing naked male statuette, his head covered with a panther skin; he is wearing a torque around his neck and endromides on his feet. His left arm is extended forward and his right rests on his hip. His pose is like the one of Culsans, found with it. On the right hip is written the dedicatory inscription "v . cvinti . arn/tiaś . śelan/śl . tez . alpan / turce" (CIE 438 = TLE 641). The figure can be identified as Selans, a divinity that in the Roman world is known as Silvanus, in charge of the care of woods, but also of boundaries: that aspect justifies its presence in a sacred area near a town gate, as well as the association with the other small bronze found with it. The style is not remote from that of Culsans, so it is conceivable it was the same craftsman who made both works.

Cagianelli 1992, pp. 30 ff., 70 ff., n. 54; Bocci Pacini, Maetzke 1992, pp. 96; Bruschetti, Gori Sassoli, Guidotti, Zamarchi Grassi 1996, p. 29.
[P.B.]

202. Turms
480 B.C.
bronze
h 22 cm
Oxford, Ashmolean Museum of Art and Archaeology, inv. 1943.38
from Uffington, Oxfordshire

Cast bronze statuette. It dresses an earl example of toga and wears winged shoes, which identify him as Turms, the Etruscan Hermes. It is related to the statuettes found at Montegurazza, on the route from Etruria to Bologna. There is no certainty that it reached England in antiquity, though it was found there.

Brown 1980, pp. 62–64. [F.P.]

203. Iuno Sospita
ca. 500–480 B.C.
bronze; solid lost wax casting
max. h 12.5 cm
Florence, Museo Archeologico, inv. 8

Head turned to the left and three-quarter bust and legs. Left leg bent forward; right leg slightly bent with heel raised. Barefoot. Left arm extended forward; right arm raised above; the right arm must have held the shield, and the left an offensive weapon. Hair with two long, narrow tresses and thick bangs. Wearing disc earrings. The eyes are hollow and filled with another material. Wearing a goatskin, that covers her head and is tied in front, short-sleeved vest, decorated on the hem, over which a cloak is buttoned on her right shoulder, leaving the left arm bare. Southern Etruscan make. For Riis it can be attributed to the London Group.

Richardson 1983, p. 361, n. 1, pl. 261, figs. 864–65; Cristofani 1985a, p. 198, p. 281, n. 93, fig. 93; La Rocca 1990, p. 821, n. 29; Riis 1997, pp. 88, 119, 128. [C.Z.]

204. Heracles
fifth century B.C.
bronze
h 16.8 cm
Fiesole, Museo Civico Archeologico, inv. 484, given by Elena Edlmann-Martini (1898), municipal property
from Fiesole, locality Sant'Apollinare

Small votive bronze representing Hercules in his youth (the "Heracles of Cyprus" type) nearly entirely covered, from his head to his calves, by the lion skin that clings to his limbs. The *leonte* is closed on his breast by the knotted forepaws; small clasp at the height of the navel. Under the skin you can glimpse a pleated fabric garment, perhaps a chiton. The hero's left hand is extended along his hip, his right—now lost—brandished his spear or his club. His bare feet stand on a thin, rectangular bronze base, originally nailed at the corners onto a support of another material. The small bronze is broken in two places under the armpits; pieces missing from the hand and part of the right forearm; dents and scratches to be found especially on the face but also over the whole body.

Galli 1914, p. 114, figs. 100a, 100b; De Agostino 1949, p. 40, fig. 34; De Agostino 1973, p. 53, fig. 44; De Marco 1981, p. 28, fig. 26. [M.d.Ma.]

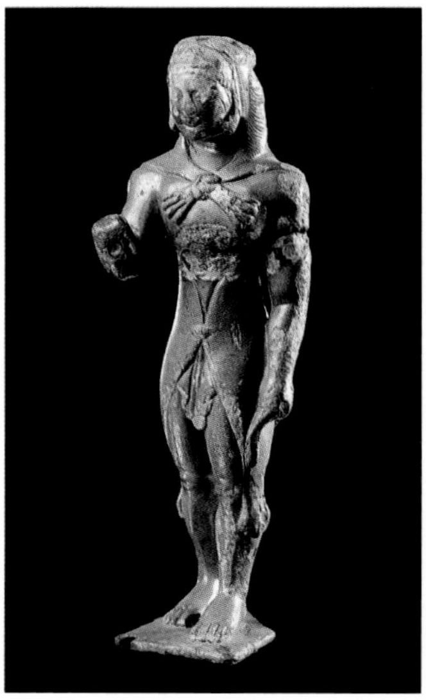

205. Heracles
ca. 400 B.C.
bronze, solid cast
h 27.9 cm
Bologna, SAER, inv. 41409
from Bologna, sanctuary of Villa Cassarini

The naked hero is brandishing a knotty club and holding the five apples of the Hesperides. His face, slightly turned and with *appliqué* eyes, lost, appears out of the lion skin.
The little bronze, of Etruscan make but inspired by fifth-century Greek sculpture, shows an excellent stylistic quality in the anatomical rendering and in the care to details, often highlighted with the burin.

Gualandi 1974, pp. 54–56, pls. X–XI; Gualandi 1978, pp. 291–309; Colonna 1985, 4.11 B 1, pp. 92–94; Cristofani 1985a, pp. 120121, 260; Romualdi 1987, pp. 90–91, fig. 55. [J.O.]

206. Male offerer
first quarter of fifth century B.C.
cast bronze
h 22 cm
Paris, Musée du Louvre, Département des Antiquités grecques, étrusques et romaines, inv. Br.218
from Mount Falterona

Naked male figure with bouffant hair falling on his shoulders and in a braid on each side of his chest. His right arm must have held an attribute, now lost, whereas the left one is bent at his side.

Richardson 1983, p. 229 n. 5; Cristofani 1985a, p. 254 n. 4.1. [G.P.]

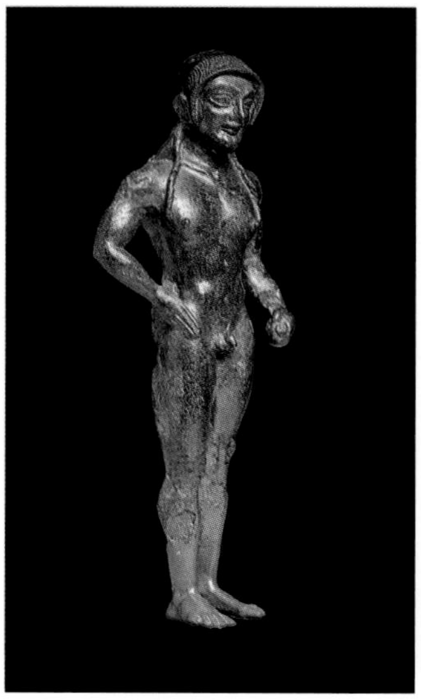

THE MYTH

207. Black-figure amphora
ca. 670 B.C.
clay, ivory color coating, dark brown and red glaze partly damaged
h 46.5 cm; max. diam. 32.3 cm
Würzburg, Martin von Wagner Museum der Universität Würzburg, inv. ZA 66
loan from Takuhito Fujita, Tokyo

Eponymous work of the Painter of the Heptachord, active in a workshop of Caere in the second quarter of the seventh century B.C. and faithful to eastern Greek models. The amphora is adorned with a passing frieze figuring five persons involved in an acrobatic war dance, an armed cithara player identified by E. Simon as Orpheus, and a bird of prey represented in front view. Again E. Simon recognizes in the scene the epic legend of the Argonauts. On neck a lion with gaping jaws.

Martelli 1987, n. 38; Martelli 1988, pp. 285–96; Simon 1995a, pp. 483–87; Simon 1995b, pp. 28–33.
[I.W.]

208. Oinochoe of the Caeretan Polychrome Group
630–600 B.C.
beige clay; brown glaze
h 24 cm
Rome, Musei Capitolini, Palazzo dei Conservatori, inv. 358 Mob
from Tragliatella, excavations 1877–78, formerly G. Tittoni Collection

Trilobate lip; low trunco-conical neck with relief ring at the base; ovate body; low ringed foot; vertical ribbon-handle. On the neck, band with goat a male figure is holding by a bridle, two opposed birds, opposed female and male figures, ship and goat placed vertically. On the body, band with vertical line, female figure in front of two objects (thrones), female figure with round object in front of smaller-sized male and female figures, flanked by inscriptions; next comes a series of seven warriors with round shield with boar, a naked male figure with staff, two horsemen with round shields with bird; next a picture of a labyrinth and two erotic groups separated by a horizontal line.

Szilàgyi 1992, p. 82, n. 3; Menichetti 1992, pp. 7–30. [F.C.]

209. Etrusco-Corinthian oinochoe
ca. 600 B.C.
clay, glaze, on the wheel
h 26.5 cm
Paris, Bibliothèque Nationale de France, inv. 179

On the shoulder, figure of a horse out of which emerge four men wearing just a cuirass and holding spears, swords and helmets. Facing them are two hoplites, a man on the chariot and a horseman blowing the horn. Three figures hidden behind the walls, of whom we can just see the heads, while in the opposite direction two other persons are approaching. It has been suggested this scene could be identified with the representation of the Ilioupersis, with the Trojan horse, the battle between the Greeks and the Trojans and Aeneas' escape, but that assumption is not widely shared. Attributed to the Group of the Dotted Rosettes.

Szilágyi 1992, p. 122 n.102, p. 125. [G.P.]

210. Etrusco-Corinthian small-column krater
570–560 B.C.
light nut-colored clay
h 43 cm; diam. 31.5 cm
Cerveteri, Museo Archeologico, inv. 19539
Cerveteri, Banditaccia necropolis, zone A "del Vecchio Recinto", Tumulus 1, Tomb 2

Etrusco-Corinthian krater, also known as "the Hunchback krater." Low cylindrical neck and globular body tapering at the base. Rim and neck decorated with beaded motif and false meander. Handles adorned with zoomorphic and anthropomorphic molding. On the shoulders, side A: Hercules and Eurystheus; sie B: zoomorphic motifs. On the body, side A: mythical scene with Hercules and Eurystheus; side B: other Hercules' feats. Bell-shaped foot with dark-brown red glaze.

Proietti 1986, p. 116 [P.A.]

211. Amphora of the Painter of Amsterdam
600–640 B.C.
clay
h ca. 45.3 cm;
max. diam. 23.5 cm
Amsterdam, Allard Pierson Museum, inv. 10.188

The vase is made of coarse brownish clay. An oily, beige-colored slip coats the outside of the vase all the way into the neck. On the surface of the slip the glaze was applied with light brushstrokes.
The color of the glaze is reddish-brown verging on dark brown. The figurative frieze consists of two representations: a struggle of a serpent-shaped three-headed monster and a human figure (perhaps Medea and the dragon), and a serpent facing right whose head tops the neck of another serpent facing left.

Dik, Donker 1980, pp. 2–10, figs. 1–5, 10; Dik 1981, pp. 45–74, figs. 1a-b, 8, p. 67, figs. 1–4, 72, fig. 32; Brijder 1984a, pp. 105–06, fig. 89; Martelli 1984, pp. 193–97, figs. 2a-c; Christiansen 1984, p. 11, fig. 10; Martelli 1987, p. 20, p. 94 fig. 41, p. 265 n. 41; LIMC VI (1992), *voce* "Medeia," p. 388, n. 2; Brijder 1990, pp. 63, 85, figs. 72–73; *The Art of the Italic Peoples* 1993, p. 229; Simon 1998, p. 16, fig. 2. [H.A.G.B.]

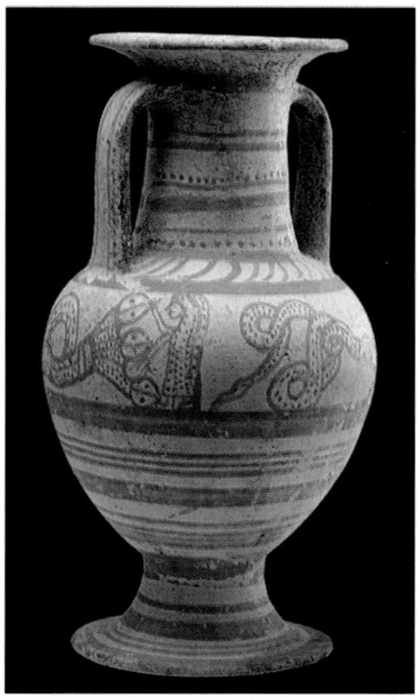

212. Bucchero olpe
ca. 630 B.C.
black bucchero
max. h 15.2 cm; diam. 13.1 cm; diam. of foot 5.2 cm
Rome, Museo di Villa Giulia, inv. 110976
from Cerveteri, San Paolo, Tomb 2

Ovate body, trunco-conical foot. Relief and incision decoration. Frieze figured on two registers, delimited by relief horizontal ropes with slanting dashes, separated by a band of incised beads. Around the foot incised multiple-sign halo. In the upper register, at center, plant trophy, beside which is a lion; next come two panthers, symmetrically arranged on the sides of the lost handle, with a human leg in their mouths; spirals and rosettes fillings. In the lower register, at center, beside an altar (?), Medea, called "Metaia" in the inscription, and a youth whose upper part emerges from a cauldron. To their right six naked youths, moving left, are carrying a long piece of cloth designated with the inscription "kanna." Behind the last one, a quadrangular element which we can perhaps identify as a casket. On the left of the first group, instead, two pugilists and a naked, winged person next to whom is incised the name "Taitale;" facing him a casket for the cloth; rosette and star filling.

Rizzo, Martelli 1993, pp. 7–56; Massa-Pairault 1994, pp. 437–68; Menichetti 1995, pp. 273–83. [C.Z.]

213. Caeretan hydria of the Busiris Painter
ca. 510 B.C.
black figure pottery, highlighted with white, red and yellow
h 45 cm, diam. 42.7 cm
Vienna, Kunsthistorisches Museum, Antikensammlung, inv. IV 3576
from Cerveteri, Calabresi excavations

Ascribed, within Greek pottery, in a category of some of the most typologically original vessels, and defined as Caeretan owing to the place it comes from, the city of Caere. The lower circular frieze shows a boar hunt, while the upper register shows, in a blaze of colors, the Greek national hero, Herakles, who, soon after coming into the world, presses hard on the Egyptian king Busiris, who was used to capturing and killing every enemy crossing his country.

Hemelrijk 1984b, pp. 50 ff., n. 34, pls. 3, 18, 118–25, 140, 145, 154; Miller 2000, pp. 417 ff., ill. 16, 1. [A.B.W.]

214. Amphora of the La Tolfa Group
ca. 530 B.C.
refined light brown clay (Munsell 7,5 YR 6/4)
reconstructed from several fragments, with pieces missing and entirely reconstructed base
h 31.8 cm (reconstituted); diam. of mouth 15.5 cm; max. diam. 22.9 cm
Vatican City, Museo Gregoriano Etrusco, inv. 35708
previously Astarita Collection n. 742

Amphora with separate neck, black glaze with metope squares. On the neck: daimon with wings on its head on both sides of the vase. On the body: a) Achilles behind the fountain; b) Troilus on horseback.
The amphora, attributed to the La Tolfa Group, is one of the few vases of the group to be decorated with a mythological subject. This being Achilles' trap for Troilus, that is, an event featuring several persons and located in the wood of the sanctuary of Apollo Timbreus, next to a monumental fountain, our painter divided the cartoon between the two metopes, interrupting the episode and losing the sequence and the dramatic intensity of the moment, as well as the very close connection between the two figures who, each in his own metope, becomes the single subject of the representation.
The exaggerated proportions of the figures, due to a lack of plan in the drawing, and the introduction of special elements of the Etruscan world, like the little spirit with a wolf-head, placed above the fountain, symbolising death, document how in the Etruscan artistic production and more particularly in late-Archaic pottery, subjects of Greek mythology are received and re-elaborated. The representation on the one hand magnifies the warrior's cunning and on the other recalls the sphere of sacrifice of which young Troilus is the victim.

Brommer 1960, pp. 359, 363; Schavenburg 1970, pp. 71 ff., figs. 38 a-b; Schmidt 1971, pp. 118 ff.; Simon 1973, pp. 39 ff.; Prayon 1977, p. 184, n. 18, p. 192, n. 55, pl. 98/1-2; Zilverberg 1986, p. 59, n. 13; *Gli Etruschi di Tarquinia* 1986, p. 273, n. 706; *Rasenna* 1986, fig. 544; Gaultier 1987, p. 218, n. 16, pl. 63, ns. 22-23; Harari 1987, p. 289; Krauskopf 1987, pp. 20 ff., pl. 1c; Rizzo 1988 p. 102, figs. 198–99. [F.B.]

215. Etruscan black-figure amphora
clay, glaze, on the wheel; reconstituted from fragments with large lacunas
h 26 cm
Paris, Musée du Louvre, Département des Antiquités grecques, étrusques et romaines, inv. 11069

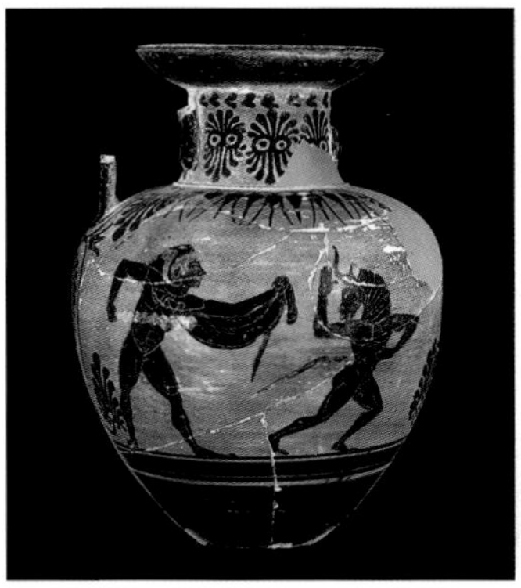

Side A: Heracles with his club in his left hand, wearing the *leonte*, pursueing the backward-looking Minotaur. Side B: battle between two opposed warriors, in the middle there is another one fallen to the ground. Attributed to the Painter of the Dancing Satyrs.

Spivey Oxford 1987, p. 45. [G.P.]

216. Etruscan black-figure hydria
last quarter of sixth century B.C.
thin refined impasto, hard, pinkish-beige with suede color surface, granulose black glaze, opaque, barely covering, scratched in many places, with marks of the wheel and paintbrush
max. h 52.5cm; h to lip 45–45.5 cm; max. w 35 cm; diam. at foot 16 cm
Florence, Ceccanti Collection

Reconstructed and integrated in several places. Ovate body, slightly tapering, rounded shoulder, vertical double stick-handle. Crown of ivy leaves on the lip; chain of alternating lotus buds and flowers at the base of the neck. The vase can be attributed to a period of the Painter of Micali between Spivey's Early II and Middle I.

Spivey 1987, pp. 9 ff.; Cherici 1988a, p. 103, figs. 202–03; Cherici 1988b, pp. 155 ff., pls. LXXIX c, LXXX a-b. [L.L.]

217. Black-figure Etruscan stamnos
ca. 500 B.C.
light brown pottery clay, orange-red slip; brownish black glaze
h 29 cm
Florence, Museo Archeologico, inv. 96780

Out-turned rim, convex cylindrical neck, ovate body, disc foot, stick-handles placed horizontally. On side A: a craftsman, whom we can identify with the mythical craftsman Epeios who built the Trojan Horse, busy finishing a horse protome; in the background work tools and rear end of a horse. Around the figure the painted inscription: "επω[χ]ώς καλό." On side B: a citharist, wrapped in a long vest, seated on a chair; around the figure the painted inscription: καλός ὁ κι [---]ς". Attributed to the Group of the Lotus Buds.

Civiltà degli Etruschi 1985, p. 148, n. 6.19; Bocci Pacini, Maggiani 1985, pp. 49–54; *Gli Etruschi e l'Europa* 1992, p. 135 n. 140.
[C.Z.]

218. Acroterion with Eos and Tythonos
last quarter of sixth century B.C.
red clay with black and brick particles, polychromy
h 84.3 cm; w 90 cm; depth 27 cm
Berlin, Staatliche Museen, Antikensammlung, inv. TC 6681.1
from Caere

The acroterion consists of a fish-tailed arch with six symmetrically-grouped scrolls. Above arises in an Archaic pattern a female figure with winged shoes and wings on her back, advancing toward the left holding a naked child in her arms. The piece was an acroterial element of a temple and the female figure has been identified as Eos (Thesan), goddess of Dawn. The child might be Tythonos (Tinthun), the son of a Trojan king. Eos was worshipped by the Etruscans with votive offerings.

V. Kästner 1988. [V.K.]

219. Group of Latona and Apollo
caa. 510–500 B.C.
pinkish clay, with traces of polychromy
h 166 cm.
Rome,Museo di Villa Giulia
from Veio, sanctuary of the Portonaccio

Latone striding, wearing a chiton and *himation*, and carrying the infant Apollo, of which only the lower part of the trunk and of the legs is conserved. It served as an acroterion in the Temple of Apollo together with the statues of Apollo, Herakles with the Ceryneian hind and Hermes.

Pallottino 1945. [C.Z.]

220. Statuette of Perseus
first half of fourth century B.C.
bronze, solid cast
h 13.7 cm
Hamburg, Museum für Kunst und Gewerbe, inv. 1929.22

Perseus brings to the king Polydectes the head of the Medusa, whose gaze has the power to turn to stone all those it looks upon. The statuette shows the hero triumphant. Perseus, wearing Hades' winged helmet that makes its wearer invisible, holds his weapon, the billhook, in his right hand, and in his left brandishes aloft the macabre trophy. The hero's head seems slightly turned aside, to avoid the enemy's deadly gaze. The piece belongs to a sculpture typology that will be used again about two thousand years later in the famous *Perseus* by Benvenuto Cellini.

Hornbostel 1981, pp. 91–92. [F.P.]

ARTISANSHIP

221. Statuette of diver
450–425 B.C.
solid cast bronze
h 14.5 cm; w at shoulders 4.6 cm
Munich, Staatliche Antikensammlungen, NI 10 WAF (formerly Dodwell Collection)
from Perugia

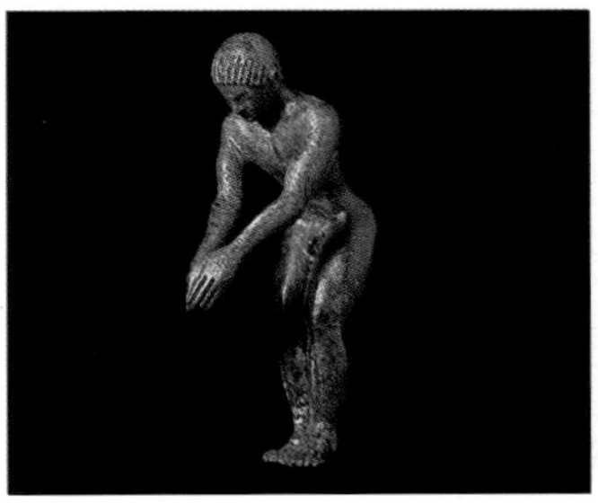

The youth, shown in the act of diving, has his legs joined and arms extended forward. The athletic body appears tensed and at the same time balanced. In the simple, roughly modeled face the vivacious eyes and the small mouth are rendered by incised lines. Sportsmanlike simplicity also characterizes the hair style, consisting of parallel locks falling on the shoulders and the forehead, short hair close-set to the skull on the top of the head.

Die Etrusker 1977, pl. 143; Höckmann 1982, vol. I, n. 50, pls. 52, 1–2; Richardson 1983, III 6 "Divers No.1." [F.W.H.]

222. Chalice on tall foot
first quarter of fourth century B.C.
laminated bronze
h 26.5 cm; diam. rim 29.5 cm
Florence, Museo Archeologico, inv. 85115
from Cerveteri, Banditaccia necropolis, Tomb "delle Olive"

The chalice, found in a pair with another of the same type, comes from a chamber tomb of the necropolis of the Bandaccia, known for having yielded an important group of bronzes, in all probability from a same workshop between 570 and 540 B.C. (see Cristofani 1979, pp. 25 ff., that more specifically dates the chalices to the first thirty years of the sixth century B.C.). Typologically similar to this item we have the so-called Castellani vase, more elaborate, with supports shaped like caryatids, also coming from Cerveteri.

Cristofani 1979, p. 7, n. 13, figs. 2, 4, 5; Cianferoni 1991, p. 109, n. 10 with other bibl. [G.C.C.]

223. Kantharos
635–600 B.C.
bronze
h without handles: 13–13.6 cm; h with handles: 19.8–21.2 cm; diam. of rim 22–22.5 cm; h of foot: 3 cm; diam. of foot: 9.3 cm
Allard Pierson Museum, Amsterdam, 10.859

The *kantharos* is made of delicately hammered bronze, about 1 cm thick, not weighing over 200 grams. It is in four parts held together by rivets: foot, faired body and two strip-handles. The foot is shaped like a small overturned bowl. The body has a high rim and a deep, curved vessel. A distinct, slanting rope-like decoration marks the transition between the neck and the vessel; the handles are high and very protruding, and have on the central part two flat bands between reliefs caused by the bushhammering of three parallel grooves on the back surface.

Brijder 1984a, pp. 106–07, fig. 89B; Brijder 1984b, pp. 1–5, figs. 1-2; Brijder 1988, pp. 103–14, figs. 1–4; Brijder 1990, pp. 91, 93, fig. 78. [H.A.G.B.]

224. Barrel
plated, soldered bronze, hammered, cold-chiselled
h 23.3 cm; l 29.7 cm; diam. 17.2 cm; vol. ca. 6 dm³; reconstituted, lacunose
Policoro, Museo Archeologico, inv. 210593
from Chiaromonte, locality Sotto La Croce, Tomb 76

The body is a cylinder formed by a curved *lamina*, with a base made of two discs decorated with an embossed motif forming a corolla (17 and 19 petals) around an *omphalos* recalling the bottom of podded *phialai* of the same period. On the edges, traces of the related solderings are hidden by the application of a band adorned with large relief "beads," to which are attached the ends of the horizontal handle (ribbon-type molded in parallel listels) and upon which are set two protomes in the round that, by a small spout placed above, now lost, served for pouring. These are formed by the fastening, without nails, of two laminas, according to the same *sphyrelaton* technique adopted for instance in the male statue of Dreros (Cellini 1980); the joining coincides with the lateral edge of the face, on the vertical of the ear, and with the separation between the forehead and the cranial cap.
The hypothesis of a direct derivation from an item of common use is confirmed in Caeretan finds: the Bufolareccia 170 burial goods contain in fact a small cylindrical barrel with curved bases and pairs of spouts (*Civiltà degli Etruschi* 1985, pp. 195 ff.), whereas tomb 425 of the Banditaccia (*MonAnt* 62,1955, col. 978, n.50, fig. 238) contains a clay version of it; yet several details, such as the presence of a single, bigger spout, analogous to that of certain globular-bodied *askoi* (Rasmussen 1986, n. 259), leads to imagine a prototype made of a different material. Besides, a like item is represented on the Ficoroni cist: a detail that (Rouveret 1994) suggested considering part of additions made by Preneste. Judging mainly from some evidence from Vallo di Diano (La Geniere 1968, pls.15,6c; 41,9f), the form seems to have somewhat influenced the Oenotrian Subgeometric production, perhaps already inspired by clay versions. Both faces of the protomes display a solid three-dimensional structure giving them a nearly swollen appearance. The profile is defined by an oval cut at the hairline, marked by a relief that coincides with the soldering of the laminas. The large, oblong eyes are enhanced with a round pupil; instead the mouth is small and narrow, with narrow, protruding lips; a hollow separates them from the chin. The long, thin protruding nose is prolonged by the large arched eyebrows. The hairdo, in the old Oriental style, figures a mass of hair, with close-set parallel grooves starting from a part in the middle, first flattened like a half-cap and thus in horizontal waves, leaving the ears bare, falling on the neck and widening downward. Lacunas prevent understanding how it was defined at the base: comparison with small bronzes like the armed offerer of Leiden (Cristofani 1985, n. 15) allows us to imagine however that it ended without "hathoric" curls (cf. Mallowan 1966, II, pp. 530, 535, n. 449). The overall structure of the faces derives from a late-Daedalian matrix (recalling for instance the first Selinunte temple plastics) that, in the Tyrrhenian ambit, is recurrent in the oldest monumental testimonies, beginning with the Vetulonia head of the Pietrera, marked by the same hairdo: (Hus 1961, pp. 110 ff.), as in the first architectural terra cottas of the Campania area (Riis 1981, pl. I, type F2); in more schematic forms it is also often found in small castbronzes like the offerer from Montalcino, at Leiden, too (Cristofani 1985, n. 14). Keeping to plated items, we can further note that these protomes on the one hand present a greater fluidity and "roundness" compared to the bust of the "Tomb of Isis" of Vulci (Riis 1997, pp. 15 ff.), and on the other differ even more distinctly from the triangular faces, both of the discussed Capuan *infundibulum* in the form of a male head, conserved prevailingly in Copenhagen (Hoeckmann 1982, pl. 63,2. *contra* the attribution to Italiot bronze production in Canciani, review in *ArchCl* 35, 1984, pp. 408 ff.), and of the caryatids (consisting of the sole front lamina) at the base of the Castellani goblet, probably Caeretan (Colonna 1982). The finishing of the eyelashes and eyebrows, with hatched or herring-bone bands, is on the other hand completely analogous with the one used in the faces—Ionicizing—of the two standing *sphyrelaton* figures of the Castel San Mariano ensemble (Hoeckmann 1982, ns. 24 ff., figs. 43 ff., pl. 34,3; cf. also cat. 127); in more simplified forms it also is recurrent in small cast bronzes, like the offerer of the Brolio deposit (Romualdi 1981 pp. 10 ff., fig. 17d). So in conclusion it seems possible to suggest for this singular container a Tyrrhenian origin and a datation around 600 B.C., keeping in mind the significant existence—between late seventh and middle sixth century B.C.—of a certain number of bronze containers, in more or less usual styles, that present figured elements in vari-

ous ways (see also the Siren-shaped container of the British Museum: Haynes 1985, n. 23), and considering, on the other hand, that in this "Italic" context, the presence of metal items produced in Etruria proper as well as in the Campania area constitutes a reality thoroughly documented by a great number of finds, first of all precisely in Oenotria.
Yet it is more difficult to suggest a reply to the question regarding its function; the lack of a central mouth in any case excludes its containing anything but a liquid able to pass by a spout, having the second function of letting out air. So first of all there are oil and honey, the two products that an ancient tradition attributed to Aristaios (Bruni 1995). On the subject we are struck by the fact that a bivalve *askos* in bronze lamina(cf. *Piceni* 2000, p. 248, n. 420), not so very remote in form and size, found in tomb A of Casale Marittimo, contained a piece of honeycomb (Esposito 1999, pp. 56, 80 ff.): just think of the *melikreton* (milk and honey) mentioned in *Odissey*, 11 24 ff., together with wine, water and flour like those offered to the deceased, and the *nephalios* sacrifice—without wine—made with water, milk and honey in honor of the chtonian divinities.
On the other hand, the exceptional burial goods of possessions (Bottini 1999) has restituted, aside from the ones having multiple uses such as barrels, several metal items that pertain to various liquids and fluids: in fact wine is recalled by a "Rhodian" *oinochoe* and a *colum*, oil and other unguents by an *exaleiptron* and an *aryballos*, while an extremely rare *phiale mesomphalos* with an animal frieze might suggest a libation praxis to which could be linked a jar with a single handle, yet quite suited for drinking. In short everything concurs to lead us to conclude that this "barrel" completed a "set" allowing to celebrate ceremonies focusing on conviviality as well as cultual acts with respect to the deceased.

MonAnt, 62, 1955, col. 978, n. 50, fig. 238; Bottini 1999; Bruni 1995; Canciani, review in *ArchCl* 35, 1984, pp. 408 ff.; Cellini in Papadopulos 1980; *Civiltà degli Etruschi* 1985, pp. 195 ff.; Colonna 1982; Cristofani 1985, ns. 14, 15; Esposito 1999, pp. 56, 80 ff.; *Greci, Enotri* 1996, pp. 141 ff., 144, n. 2. 10. 37; Haynes 1985, n. 23; Hoeckmann 1982, n. 24 ff., fig. 43 ff., pls. 34, 3 and 63, 2; Hus 1961, pp. 110 ff.; La Geniere 1968, pls. 15, 6c; 41, 9f; Mallowan 1966, II, pp. 530, 535, n. 449; *Piceni* 2000, p. 248, n. 420; Rasmussen 1986, n. 259; Riis 1981, pl. I, type F2; Riis 1997, p.15 ff.; Romualdi 1981, p. 10 ff., fig. 17d; Rouveret 1994.
[A.B.]

225. Grater
wood and bronze lamina, lacunose
Florence, Museo Archeologico, inv. 89330
from Populonia, Tomb of the Flabelli

Rectangular lamina with folded-over edges. Wooden handle in the shape of a crouching fawn, very lacunose, of which the back part is left; along the edges holes for attaching the lamina.
The first attested custom of depositing bronze graters in grave goods goes back to ninth-century B.C. Greece: in fact three were found inside three depositions belonging to warriors in the Toumba necropolis at Lefkandis in Euboea. During the seventh century B.C. they are also documented in the princely grave goods of Campania, Latium and Etruria : here they also appear in the rich Orientalizing tombs of the northern mining district at Vetulonia and Populonia. The grater, as Homer tells us (*Iliad*, XI, vv. 628–43), was used to prepare a special beverage, the *kykeion*, made of wine, white flour and goat cheese, that was even said to cure wounds. It has been assumed that the Etruscan princes had learned the use of this "heroic" beverage following contacts with the Euboeans who sought their supplies of minerals in northern Etruria. Bronze graters were also offered as ex-votos in sanctuaries as well, as is evidenced by finds in the Samos Heraion.

Minto 1932, cc. 341–42, pl. X,2,6,8; Ridgway 1997, ns. 14–16, pp. 334–35; for *Samo*: Brize, 1989–90, p. 323, fig. 3.
[A.Ro.]

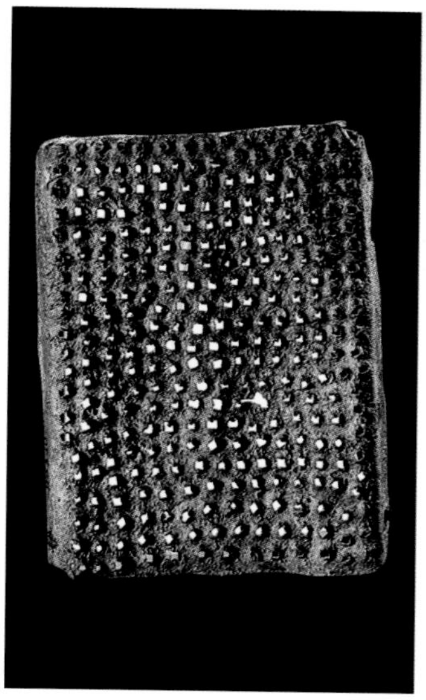

226. Oinochoe with trilobate mouth
600–550 B.C.
bronze
h 25
Florence, Museo Archeologico, inv. 89366
from Populonia, Porcareccia, Tomb of the Flabelli

Trilobate mouth, with out-turned rim; low cylindrical neck, with relief ring at mid-height; ovate body; disc foot; vertical ribbon handle, with close-set ribbings; upper wheel attachment with rosette and palmette plaquette on spiralled scrolls, lower attachment with palmette and spirals.

Shefton 1979, p. 79, pls. 6, 1–2; Romualdi 1987, p. 242, n. 40.
[F.C.]

227. Antropomorphic oinochoe
350–325 B.C.
bronze
h 22.5 cm; diam. of base 9.9 cm
Munich, Staatliche Antikensammlungen, NI 3169

Highly idealized head of a youth, with slightly curved forehead and eyebrows, incised, slightly upturned irises and pupils. The part-closed mouth shows the teeth. Under the temples, hints of a beard. The forehead is bare, the cap covers a mass of spiral-shaped curls of various lengths, either in relief or flat.

Hayes 1965, p. 524 pl. 125 b.
[F.W.H.]

228–230. Grave goods: bronze vessels and furnishings for the symposium
second half of fifth century B.C.
bronze
Florence, Museo Archeologico, from Populonia, San Cerbone necropolis, Tomb 13
(1908 excavation)

The tomb is one of the few Populonia contexts of the second half of the fifth century B.C. to have come down to us complete. The grave goods, probably belonging to a youth, judging by the presence of many elements connected with the sphere of games and gymnastics, has an exact match in the tombs found in Po Valley Etruria at Spina and Felsina, and features, as well as the candelabrum for lighting the symposium, the tableware for ritual libations, consisting of the characteristic Beazley VI type *oinochoe* and combined basin, the container vase for the wine and the pitcher for water, that is, the cylindrical situla and the round-mouthed olpe. The colander was used to purify and filter the wine that was then poured in the goblets, while the simpulas, that differed by the sizes of the vessels and the number of the ends of the handles, were used by the cup-bearers as measures in pairs and side by side to concurrently draw the water and the wine.
The red figure Attic *kylixes* found in the grave goods were most certainly the precious goblets used for drinking in the symposium.

228. Candelabrum
inv. 11809

229. Bronze vessels
• *1. Olpe, type Beazley 9*
inv. 11810
• *2. Oinochoe, type Beazley VI*
inv. 11811
• *3–4. Pair of simpulas*
inv. 11812–11813
• *5. Cylindrical situla*
inv. 11814-a-c
• *6 Patera or basin*
inv. 11815
• *7. Colum or colander*
inv. 11816

230. Strigil
inv. 11817

Minto 1943, n. 29b, I group, p. 231; Fedeli 1983, n. 145, p. 261; Donati 1998, pp. 165–66, pl. XLI,5; Romualdi 1998; Romualdi forthcoming.
[A.Ro.]

228

229.2

229.6

229.7

229.5

229.1

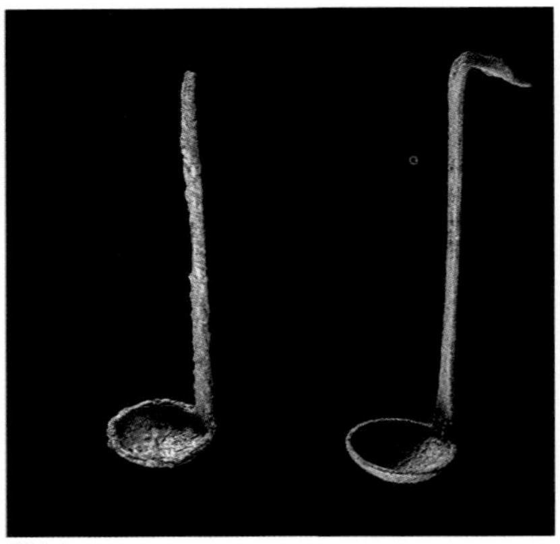
229.3–4

230

231. Candelabrum with dancer
ca. 500 B.C.
bronze
35.6 x 19 x 17 cm
Karlsruhe, Badisches Landesmuseum, inv. 62/93
from Vulci

A naked youth with elegant footwear and bracelets is dancing on a base equipped with three lion claw feet and figures of ducks. He is balancing on his head an incense-boat of which the only part left is the soaring stem. The base and stem were processed separately and only later fixed onto the main body of the item. The motif of dancing suggests celebrative occasions, to the panoply of which such censers belong.

During such festivities, obviously, one of the pastimes was dancing, performed also on the tables.

Riederer 1999, n. 819
[M. Ma.]

232. Candelabrum
510–480 B.C.
solid cast bronze
h 50.3 cm
Munich, Staatliche Antikensammlungen, NI 55 WAF (formerly Dodwell Collection)
from Vulci

Tall, round, decorated base. The youth is shown striding, with knees slightly bent. The left hand rests on the hip, the right is holding with an elegant, nearly affected, gesture, a pomegranate. The outlines appear graceful, even idealized. The face is attractive, with determined eyes and a small, prettified mouth. The hair style consists of locks rendered with incised wavy lines.

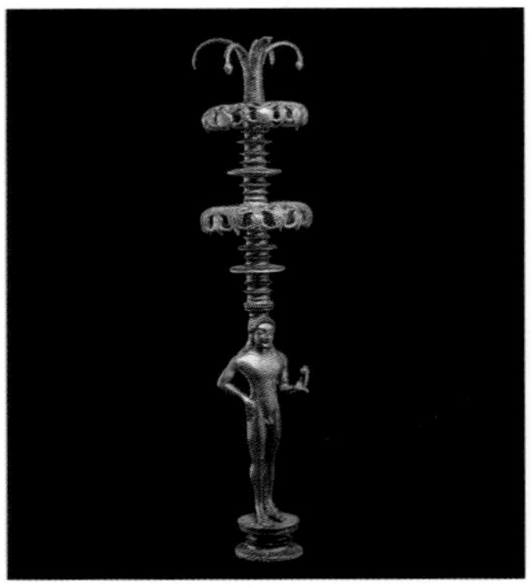

Above rises the stem, broken by garlands of flowers and gems, crowned by a centrepiece of leaves.

Brendel 1978, p. 468; Hus 1975, p. 89. [F.W.H.]

233. Bronze tripod
500–480 B.C.
bronze
h 51 cm
Ferrara, Museo Archeologico,
inv. 2899
from Spina, Valle Trebba,
Tomb 128

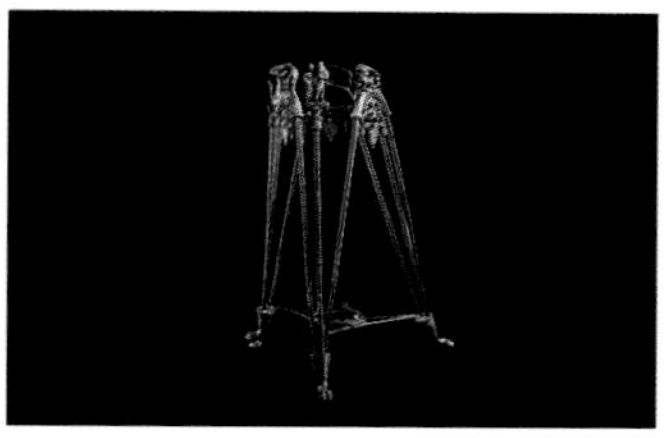

Flat round band, attached to three supports ending in animal paws, each formed by three rods: the straight, one in the middle ends on top in a modeled group (Heracles and woman; bearded man grasping a woman by the wrist; beardless man grasping a woman by the wrist); the side ones are attached to those of the adjoining support forming a half-circle, upon which there is a modeled group (panther attacking a bull, twice a panther biting a goat); under the half circles openwork scrolls ending in three pendent palmettes; the animal paws are connected by horizontal staffs, that are joined in the middle in a round band topped by three ducks.

Patitucci 1967, p. 149, n. 412; Hostetter 1986, pp. 16 ff., n. 1.
[F. C.]

234. Base of thymaterion
520–500 B.C.
bronze
h 28 cm; h of figures 18 cm
Munich, Staatliche
Antikensammlungen,
NI 720 g WAF (formerly
Dodwell Collection)
from Perugia

Triangular base, formerly attached to three lions' paws. In the two illustrated fields from Munich, a striding figure, framed by connecting elements: a)Heracles facing left, with short chiton and *leonte* and sword; b) Iuno Sospita, with *leonte* over her vest and covering her head. In her left hand, large oval shield, profusely decorated. The details of the lion's skin and of the adornments are rendered by elegant incisions.

Höckmann 1982, vol. I, n. 26, pls. 35, 1–2; 36, 2, figs. 45–47.
[F.W.H.]

235. Lid of pyxis
mid-eighth century B.C.
bucchero
diam. 19.5 cm
Rome, Museo di Villa Giulia,
temporary inv. S10/V2
from Cerveteri, sporadic find

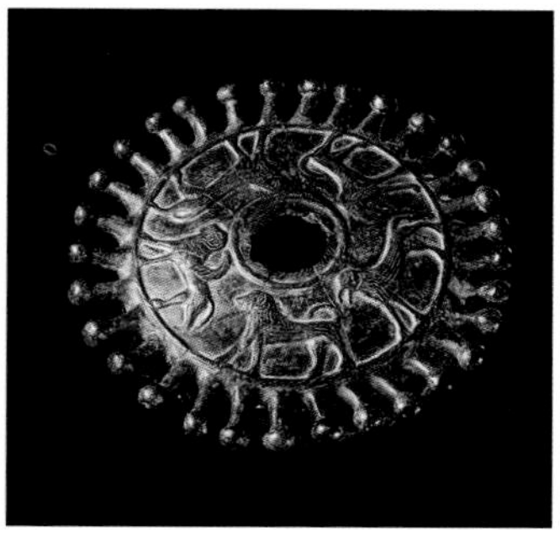

Trunco-conical shape. On the upper edge crown of carved rays, protruding outward, ending in tiny spheres. On the flat surface zoomorphic relief frieze, consisting of five lions, one of which winged, moving toward the left. Its prototypes should almost certainly be sought in models of Oriental provenance.

Proietti 1986, p. 101.

236. Hydria
early sixth century B.C.
brown bucchero after
defective firing
h 55 cm
Florence, Museo Archeologico,
inv. 3389

Pendent out-turned rim, with grooves; concave neck; ovate body; trunco-conical foot with passing hole, made separately; vertical ribbon handle; horizontal stick-handles with beads and rope-decoration incisions; on both sides applied small vertical discs; decoration with facing rows separated by grooves; on the lower part of the neck opposing lions crouching or with raised paw; on the shoulder sphinxes facing left, separated by small sticks; at the level of the handles crouching lions and tongues; below the handles grazing stags facing right; on the small discs of the rim *gorgoneia*; on the vertical handle spear-bearing hoplite.
[F.C.]

237. Kyathos
first quarter of sixth century B.C.
black bucchero
h 17 cm; diam. 13.6 cm
Florence, Museo Archeologico,
inv. 2892

Indistinct rim; deep vessel, with slanting wall, separated from the slightly convex bottom by a diamond-point edge; trumpet foot with stem; vertical very overhanging ribbon handle, with outer stanchion projecting onto the inside, with diamond point at the top. On the wall cylinder-band, framed above and below with grooves, with series of figures repeated five times: naked male figure, gradient left, between two horse-headed chimeras he is holding by the reins; among the figures phytomorphic elements; on the outer stanchion of the handle groups of longitudinal and transversal lines, on the inner one intersecting transversal and oblique lines.
Clusine make.
[F.C.]

238. Chalice
first half of sixth century B.C.
black bucchero
h 15 cm; diam. 15.5 cm
Florence, Museo Archeologico,
inv. 2897

Indistinct rim; deep vessel, with slanting wall, separated from the slightly convex bottom by an edge; spline between vessel and foot; trumpet foot with tall stem, with splines at mid-height. On the wall cylinder-band framed by grooves, with motif repeated five times: from the left, standing female figure facing right with arms raised, enthroned bearded figure facing left, with arms raised, two female figures, the first holding a crown in her right hand, two gradient spear-bearing warriors facing left, enthroned bearded figure facing left, with arms raised and crown in the right hand, spear-bearing warrior, female figure with crown in her right hand, two gradient spear-bearing warriors facing right. On the bottom of the vessel three grooves.
Clusine make.

Scalia 1968, p. 368, n. 57.
[F.C.]

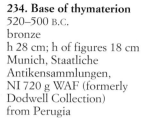

239. Olpe
third quarter of sixth century B.C.
black bucchero
h 17 cm; diam. 10 cm
Florence, Museo Archeologico, inv. 94574

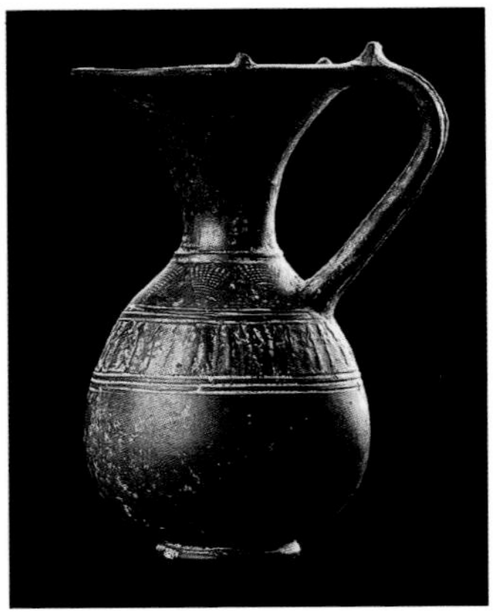

Large trunco-conical lip, with out-turned rim; spline at the base of the neck; ovate body; low ringed foot; vertical double stick-handle; on the lip three semi-elliptic apophyses. On the shoulder small vertical fans; on the body cylinder-band framed above and below by grooves, with thrice-repeated motif: three spear-bearing warriors, female figure with vessel, bird, five female figures, two female figures.
Clusine make.

Scalia 1968, p. 400, n. 281.
[F.C.]

240. Amphora
sixth century B.C.
grey bucchero
h 48 cm; diam. of rim 15.8 cm
Florence, Museo Archeologico, inv. 2996

Rimmed lip, with thick, profiled rim; tall trunco-conical neck; broad shoulder; ovate body tapering downward; trunco-conical foot; double stick-handle, placed on the shoulder and neck. Relief splines in the middle and at the base of the neck; on the shoulder two cylinder-bands, with motif repeated five and seven times: enthroned male figure facing right, with bird under the throne; gradient spear-bearing warrior; two female figures; warrior; figure on stool facing right, two female figures, male figure gradient left with bow.
Clusine make.

Scalia 1968, p. 368, n. 47.
[F.C.]

241. Kylix
first half of sixth century B.C.
black bucchero
h 12 cm; diam. 17 cm
Florence, Museo Archeologico, inv. 77509
from Orvieto; acquisition Neri 1897

Straight rim tilted outward; ample, low vessel, with rounded shoulder, tapering downward; disc foot with flared stem; horizontal stick-handles, slightly curved upward; on the shoulder cylinder-relief band, framed by dashes and a procession of eight animals facing right (winged lion, grazing stag, bull, boar, grazing stag) repeated four times (frieze XI Camporeale type)

Camporeale 1972, p. 46, n. 1.
[F.C.]

242. Oinochoe
first half of sixth century B.C.
black bucchero
h 41.5 cm; diam. of body 19 cm
Florence, Museo Archeologico, inv. 3190, gift of the Società Colombaria
from Chiusi, Fonte Rotella necropolis, Società Colombaria excavations

Upper part figuring the head of a bull, a small trilobate mouth opening on its nape; on the nape two incised lion heads; trunco-conical neck, separated by series of relief splines, with incised rosettes; on the distinct shoulder a series of relief splines, with lion heads alternating with relief tongues; ovate body, with relief frieze repeated five times, with male figure holding a bull by the horns and front leg; trunco-conical foot; vertical handle with triple ribbing, with braid on the edges and two small wheels on the upper attachment.

Batignani 1965, p. 306, n. 192; Rastrelli 1980, pp. 143 ff, n. 80. [F.C.]

243. Kantharos
first half of sixth century B.C.
black bucchero
h 16.1 cm; diam. 14 cm
Florence, Museo Archeologico, inv. 2891

Indistinct rim; deep vessel, with slanting wall, separated from the slightly convex bottom by a notched edge; trumpet base with tall stem; very overhanging ribbon handles, placed on the rim and at the base of the wall; on the wall cylinder-band with series of front male figures, framed above and below by incised lines.
Clusine make.

Scalia 1968, p. 400, n. 280.
[F.C.]

244. Skyphos
first half of sixth century B.C.
black bucchero
h 11.5 cm
Florence, Museo Archeologico, inv. 2923

Straight lip, slanting outward; deep ovate vessel; small trunco-conical foot; handle with schematic bull protome; on the rim cylinder-band, framed above and below by grooves, with gradient animals facing right (winged lion, horse, lion).
[F.C.]

245. Lid of cinerary urn
first quarter of fifth century B.C.
terra cotta; traces of polychrome decoration
l 90 cm
Cerveteri, Museo Claudia Ruspoli, inv. 67157
from Cerveteri, Banditaccia necropolis

Male figure, partly reclining on his left side, with the same arm on a folded cushion; crossed legs, face crowned with curls, hair on his back held in a hairnet, held by a ribbon on the top of his head.

Proietti 1986, p. 166, n. 69.
[I.B.]

246. Terra-cotta head of a warrior
first quarter of fifth century B.C.
pink clay; black and red color
h 23 cm
Rome, Museo di Villa Giulia, inv. 39749
from Veio, Portonaccio sanctuary

Fragment of a head with the upper part of a warrior's bust, with a helmet with big cheekguards leaving most of the face visible, with big almond-shaped eyes, moustache with upturned tips, pointed beard, mouth suggesting the "Archaic smile."

Torelli 1967, p. 108, n. 318; Sprenger 1972, pp. 29 ff., n. 1.
[F.C.]

247. Female head
late sixth–early fifth century B.C.
pinkish clay
h 26 cm
Rome, Museo di Villa Giulia
from Veio, votive deposit of Campetti

Female head with *tutulus*. Bouffant bangs on the forehead and two locks falling on each side of the neck. The back surface is flat.

Vagnetti 1971, p. 32 A IV; pl. VIII; *Civiltà degli Etruschi* 1985, p. 279 n. 10.23. 1.
[F.C.]

248. Male head
mid-fifth century B.C.
pinkish clay
h 29 cm
Rome,Museo di Villa Giulia
from Veio, votive deposit of Campetti.

Bearded male head. Hair forming a compact mass crowned by a *stephane*.

Vagnetti 1971, p. 54 D1; pl. XXIII; *Civiltà degli Etruschi* 1985, p. 279 n. 10.23. 6.
[F.C.]

249. Stela of the warrior Avile Tite
mid-sixth century B.C.
local limestone
h 1.70 cm; w 70 cm; thick. 30 cm
Volterra. Museo Guarnacci, inv. MG 4295
from Volterra, Portone necropolis (?)

The monument consists of a squared slab in the shape of an oblong rectangle, curved at the top, that has a raised border with a flat band on the left side onto which is deeply carved an Etruscan inscription (from bottom up and right to left): "mi aviles tite[s...] uxsie mulenike." (I [am] of Avile Tite [...] who gave me). In the middle of the square a male figure in relief, in profile, upright, moving toward the left, holding a spear in his right hand in front of himself. The person has a beard and long wavy hair in horizontal layers. It is legitimate to imagine the figure was wearing a tunic (as the marks on his neck and left arm allow to suppose) with over it a lorica with shoulder straps, probably rendered with painted details.

Cateni 1988, p. 36.
[G.C.]

WRITING

250. Alphabet
second half of seventh century B.C.
terra cotta
h 10.3 cm; w 5.3 cm
New York, The Metropolitan Museum of Art, inv. 24.97.21a-b
from Viterbo (?)

Small bucchero vase diversly interpreted as a toy, a small jug or an inkstand. It was certainly used as a container, the head serving as a cork, while the small ring on the back shows that it was either suspended or carriedabout. The tail of the cockerel is missing, it was probably curved downward to form a third foot. Aside from the decoration incised on the head

and body, on the belly the twenty-six letters of the Etruscan alphabet were inscribed.

Alexander 1925, pp. 269–70, fig.1; Richter 1940, p. 13, figs. 46–48; Bonfante 1983, pp. 108–09, figs. 13 a-b; Pandolfini, Prosdocimi 1990, pp. 22–23, pl. IV; Pallottino 1992, p. 148, n. 204, ill. pp. 86, 87; Jucker 1991, p. 200 n. 262.
[C.S.L.]

251. Spindle
first quarter of sixth century B.C.
polished brown impasto
h 1. 4 cm; max. diam. 1.9 cm
Rome, F. P. Bongiovì Collection, inv. 159
from Vulci, Osteria necropolis, chamber tomb 21

Trunco-conical form. Incision of the letters "a e v z h," constituting the beginning of an alphabet altered on the basis of northern spelling norms.

Pandolfini, Prosdocimi 1990, p. 38 n. II.3; tav. XVIII.
[F.C.]

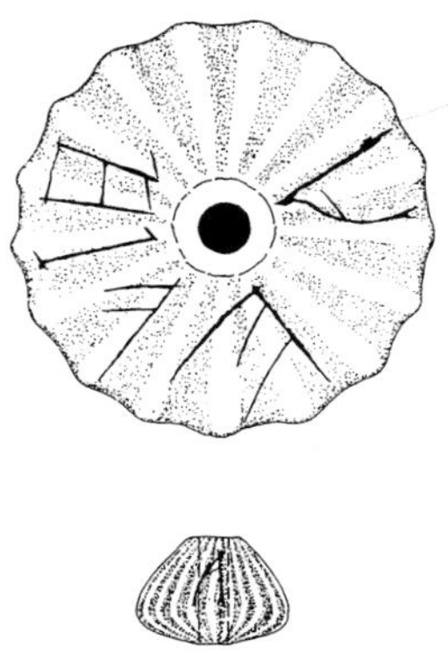

252. Three fragments of an oinochoe
second quarter of sixth century B.C.
thin black bucchero
5.5 x 5 cm; 4, 3.5 cm
Tarquinia, Museo Archeologico, inv. S II/3.
from Gravisca

The fragments, two of which joined, belong to the belly of an *oinochoe.* Placed between three grooves you can read the following scratched right-to-left alphabetical sequence: "a [c? e v z] h ϑ i k lm n [p ś q? s] t u φ χ."

Torelli 1967, pp. 522–24, pl. CVI-c; CIE III, 1, n. 10232; Pandolfini, Prosdocimi 1990, p. 40 n. II.5. [C.Z.]

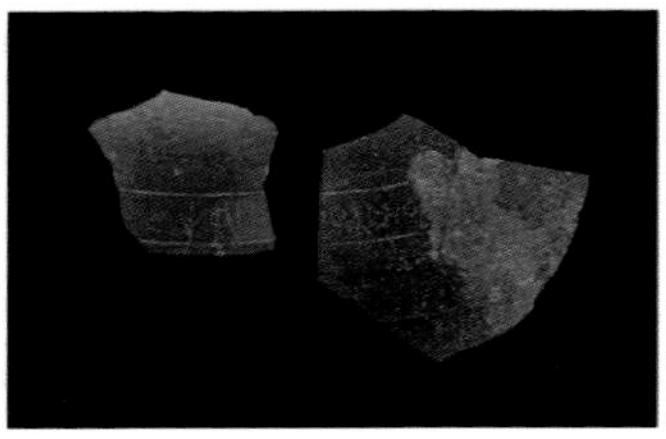

253. Writing stylus
480–460 B.C.
cast bronze
h 13 cm; h of figure 5.6 cm
Museo dell'Accademia Etrusca di Cortona, inv. 202575
from Sodo di Cortona, tumulus II, Tomb 2 (found in 1992)

Conical stem with wavy grooves and a smooth bottom tip, ending at the top with a figure representing Heracles with late-Archaic stylistic features, to be interpreted in this case as the civilizing hero. The function of the article can be established by comparing it to several other fifth-century exemplars, in particular one from Orvieto, probably of Vulci make, conserved in Berlin, on which precisely the figure of a

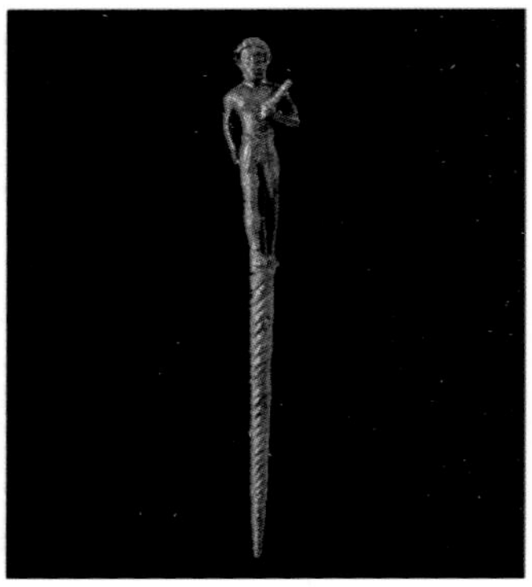

scribe appears (Szilágyi 1980).

Szilágyi 1980, pp.13–27; Zamarchi, 1996 figs. on pp. 103, 105*; Gli amici per Orlando* forthcoming. [P.Z.G.]

254. Small amphora
last quarter of seventh century B.C.
thin bucchero
h 17 cm; diam. of mouth 8 cm, diam. of foot 5 cm
Rome, Museo di Villa Giulia, inv. 22678
from Monte Acuto, Formello

Rasmussen 1dform with zigzag motif incised in the lower part of the neck and two pairs of parallel horizontal lines on the body. On the neck, alphabet followed by a series of letters whose meaning is uncertain "a b c d v e z h q i k l m n s o p s' q r s t u s f c;" on the body another alphabet inserted between letters with no meaning "a b c d e v z h q i k l m n s o p s' q r s t u s f c." Underneath the lat-

ter on two lines the left-to-right inscription *mi atianaia acapri alice venelisi velqur zinace* ("I [am] from Atianai;" Achapri [?] gave to Venel; Velthur made"), followed by other letters not in syllabic nexus.

Civiltà degli Etruschi 1985, p. 87 n. 3.8; Pandolfini, Prosdocimi 1990, pp. 24-26 n. I.4; tavv. V–VI. [F.C.]

255. Pyrgi Laminae
fifth century B.C.
gold
19 x 9 cm; 19 x 9 cm; 13 x 9 cm
Rome, Museo di Villa Giulia
from the enclosure of area C of Pyrgi (Santa Severa)

The tablets formed a triptych, consisting of the "bilingual" pair with the short Etruscan inscription. The first two commemorate the dedication to the goddess Astarte (Etruscan Uni), of a holy place (Tmia) with the cult statue. The author of the dedication is Thefarie Velianas, king over Caere (Caisra) in the third year of his reign. The short inscription specifies the ritual of the cult, on the occasion of its commemoration.

Colonna 1985b, pp. 127–34.
[R.C.]

256. Capuan Tabula
second quarter of fifth century B.C.
brown clay
max. h 62 cm; w 48 cm; thick. 3.5 cm
Berlin, Staatliche Museen, Antikensammlung, inv. 30892
from locality Quattordici Ponti near Santa Maria Capua Vetere

Tile with humped back edged by a rectangular-section frame, except for the upper part where it is broken. Two holes pierced before firing in the lower corners and two level with the tenth line. The text, divided in ten sections of nine lines incised before firing, and contains prescriptions pertaining to religious rites.

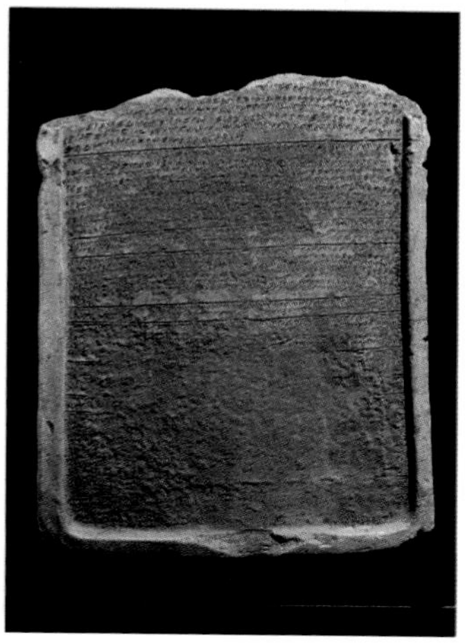

Cristofani 1955.
[F.C.]

257. Pech Maho Plaque
Iron Age (fifth century B.C.)
lead
l 11.5 cm; w 5 cm; h of letters 0.3–4 cm (Greek text), 0.4–0.8 cm (Etruscan text)
Sigean, Aude, Musée des Corbières, inv. 86.01.195
from Sigean (Languedoc), *oppidum* of Pech Maho

The plaque was found in a layer dated to the fifth century B.C. Both the outside and the inside bear inscriptions. On the former is incised the Etruscan text, not translated, that features the toponym "Venelus," the Greek name for Orvieto. On the latter the Ionian Greek text appears, of which one line, with the name "Kuprios," was added onto the outer side. The text, translated, is the report, written by a Greek intermediary, of a commercial transaction between some inhabitants of Ampurias and an inhabitant of Pech Maho.

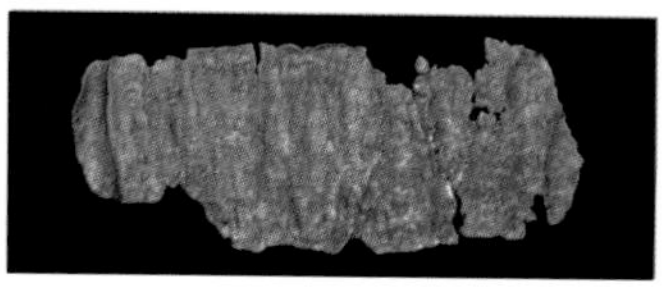

Les Ibères 1997. [F.S.]

The Urban Political Forms

In the second half of the seventh century and in the sixth century B.C., with obvious variations according to the different levels of social and economic development of the different communities, there takes place in Etruria a crystallization of the processes of transformation which have their roots in the early Villanovan period with the complete emergence of the urban forms in a close unity of political and institutional elements founded on the juridico-economic link between the citizen and ownership of the land. The phenomenon, which is common to Latium and the Greek world of southern Italy, is in fact one of the most distinctive features of Etruria in comparison to the other areas of the peninsula. With its cities and the individual *populi* with which the Etruscans themselves identify, Etruria provides a contrast with the villages of the rest of the indigenous world of pre-Roman Italy.
The emergence of a unitary entity on the political and religious level, which delimits and contains the power of the aristocratic elites, is fostered by the growth of a well-to-do class which does not identify with the *principes*—though it imitates their lifestyle—and which derives its wealth mainly from production and trade.
Despite the laconicism of the literary sources about this development, significant evidence clarifying the extent of the phenomenon can be elicited from a study of the necropolises. The most emblematic cases are Cerveteri and Volsinii. At Cerveteri, which in the course of the seventh century B.C. saw the erection of large and small tumuli, in the sixth century the panorama of the necropolises is characterized, with very rare exceptions, by numerous cube and facade tombs organized according to systematic town-planning criteria which reflect the strong isonomic tension and the normative action of a supra-clan entity. At Volsinii we find a grandiose arrangement of the cemetery, also on town-planning principles, with the construction of a series of cube tombs along the sides of necropolar roads arranged in an orthogonal scheme, all the tombs being broadly similar in both plan and size; the only distinctive element is the inscription engraved on the architrave of the entrance, which records the name of the family to which the tomb belongs. These inscriptions, which concern more than ninety families, confirm the existence of a wide social base to some extent comparable with the Greek *demos*, into which were probably integrated people of external origin, from the Umbro-Sabine and Latino-Faliscan area or to a lesser extent from the Greek world or from the Celtic and Illyrian worlds.
Since our knowledge of the urban structures of the Etruscan cities is extremely limited, the most clearly perceptible signs of political development are the symbolic representations of the context of decisions which were either shared—an illustration of which is the repertory of some cippi from Chiusi (see n. 260)—or projected into the dimension of myth or the heroic sagas, as in the case of the decoration engraved on the of a famous gem which shows the episode of the council of the heroes of the Theban expedition (n. 259).
As in the Greek world, though with important differences and nuances, the ideology of the city is expressed in the figure of the hoplite, that is, the armed citizen organized with his peers in the ranks of the city. Significantly the ceremonial chariots which were linked with the emergence of particular individuals and which were the heritage of now out-of-date social structures, are known exclusively from non-urban centers.
Important information on the changes that affected the various cities of Etruria comes from the tradition of the insignia, which are known to us in the undoubtedly privileged case of Rome, but which nevertheless may be taken as example of Etruscan practice too, since the ancient authors stress that the insignia were transmitted to Rome, either from Tarquinia in the time of the Etruscan kings (Strabo) or from Vetulonia at an unspecified period (Silius Italicus).
The insignia, which derive from the signs of power of an earlier age, concern in the first place the sphere of clan prestige, underlining various roles—the military (the spear), the priestly (the *lituus*), or the regal (the scepter)—before later becoming the symbols of public authority at the end of the archaic period. The old instruments of power, such as the military and sacrificial axe (cf. n. 264–265), the *toga* with purple border and the foldable stool (cf. n. 266) now become the insignia of the magistrates, as we learn, for example, from the paintings in the Tomb of the Jugglers at Tarquinia, where the dead man is portrayed in his magistrate's dignity as judge of the games that are being held in his honor. A good example of this process is that of the regal insignia, which are known at the archaeological level in Etruria in the great Orientalizing tombs and which in the high archaic age are transferred as attributes to the divinities: in Rome they adorn the statue of Jupiter Optimus Maximus, who only gives them up to allow the celebration of a triumph, symbolically conferring them on the victorious commander, who thus rides along on a four-horse chariot, dressed in the *tunica palmata* and the *toga picta*, wearing a golden crown of oak leaves on his head and a golden bulla on his chest, and holding the ivory scepter in his hand. In Rome, and probably also in Etruria, this process of sacralization of the symbols of

power was related to the new role attributed to the divinity, who now becomes the guarantor of the organization and the laws of the city. The clearest sign of the urban political context is the refounding of the divine cults, with the development of the great sacred building in the public areas of the *arx* or the *agora*; this process goes hand in hand with a loss in importance, or at least a radical reduction, of the clan cults connected with devotional practices in honor of the ancestors which usually took place around the *sepulcrum*. If the simulacrum of the divinity only now, in the context of an open Hellenization, takes on an anthropomorphic aspect, appropriating the iconic elements which had characterized the *imagines maiorum* on the ridges of the roofs of princely residences (cf, for example, the *regia* of Murlo or that of Tuscania) or in the *dromoi* of the tombs (see the statues of the tomb of Ceri near Cerveteri), the temple—the house of the god—now acquires a specific architectural typology, characterized by the great podium on which stands the sacred building adorned with a front porch and ornate clay decoration on the roof. The increasing importance assumed by the divinity in Etruscan society brings toward this context that set of objects which had previously been the gifts circulating between the *principes*, imparting a totally new substance and wealth to the votive depositions.

A central role in this picture is played by the priests, who have a prestige of their own and a strong authority, as is confirmed by the case of the augur Attus Navius, who opposed Tarquinius Priscus's attempt to double the equestrian centuries bearing the name of the early tribes of Rome (Tities, Ramnes and Luceres). Their action, too, probably led to the spread of the use of writing outside the strictly aristocratic circles, with the creation of schools of scribes, as is attested, for example, by the complex of dedicatory inscriptions recovered from the sanctuary of Portonaccio at Veio, which, incidentally, show a broad homogeneity of scriptorial methods. With time the artisans of writing gain an increasingly important role in the social context of the Etruscan cities, assisting the magistrates as secretaries and drafting with sometimes complex techniques the public documents, usually engraved on bronze, as in the case of the inscription from Tarquinia (n. 262) and in the recently discovered inscription from Cortona (n. 263), both of which are included in the exhibition.
[S.B.]

THE SIGNS OF POLITICS

258. Small cinerary urn
second century B.C.
pietra fetida
container: 33 x 51.5 x 34.5 cm;
lid: 10.5; x 54.5 x 38 cm; overall
h 43.5 cm
Florence, Museo Archeologico,
inv. 5539.
from Chiusi (?)

Decorated in very low relief in the form of a one-storey edifice with loggia: the short sides figure an arched door between two pillars with Aeolian chapters, upon which are placed two vases; on the long sides, between two tall pillars there is a sort of aedicule resting on small columns, inside which various wall decorations are reproduced. The comparison with monuments like the Porta Marzia of Perugia and the Ildebranda Tomb of Sovana suggests a dating at the end of the Hellenistic period.

Bartoloni, Sprenger, 1983, p. 274, pp. 159–60; *Rasenna* 1986, fig. 163; Rastrelli 1999, p. 37. [A.R.]

259. Gem
500–480 B.C.
cornelian
1.66 x 1.22 x 0.52 cm
Berlin, Staatliche Museen,
Antikensammlung, inv. FG 194
from Perugia

On the stone five characters of the myth of the Seven Against Thebes are represented. The group is gathered around the oracle who is predicting the death of Amphiaraos. In the foreground, bareheaded, are seated Parthenopaios, Amphiaraos and Polynices; standing behind are Adrastus and Tydeus with helmet and arms. The surface of the stone is incised with thefive names of the persons shown.

Zwierlein-Diehl 1969, vol. II, pp. 103–04, n. 237. [E.Z.-D.]

260. Base of cippus
450–430 B.C.
limestone, fragmentary
h 60 cm; width50 cm;
depth 50 cm
Munich, Glyptothek,
NI 2012 WAF
probably from Chiusi

Upper and lower edges with flat, arched cyma decorated with leaves. Four reliefs: a)prothesis: on the klinè the defunct, wrapped in bands and a sheet. At one end of the couch wife and son (remains of a head); b)parting of two young horsemen. On the left a woman with upraised hands, waving. c) two bearded persons seated in conversation. In the background three youths are vivaciously taking part. D) Two women seated in conversation. In the background three women wearing long chitons, head and shoulders hidden by a veil, are also clearly taking part in what is going on.

Giglioli 1935, pl. 146. [F.W.H.]

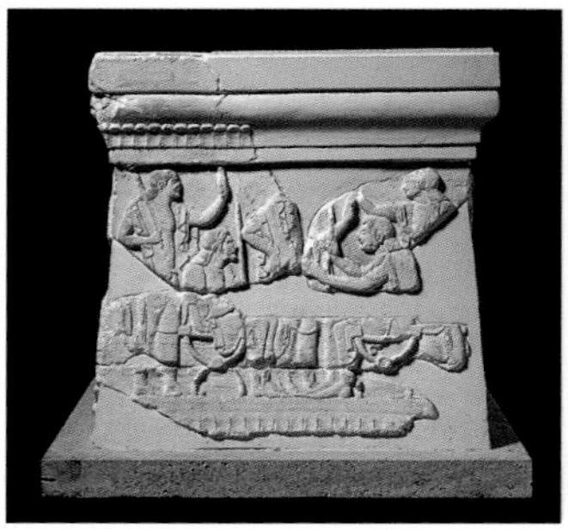

261. Clusine funerary cippus
480–470 B.C.
pietra fetida
h 39.5 cm; w 68 cm
Palermo, Museo Archeologico, inv. 8385.
from Chiusi, formerly Casuccini Collection

The low relief decoration is placed inside two hatched frames with small tongue frieze; in the corner a stylized branch is left. Side A: cloaked man going left and with a cane; to his left remains of another male person; side B: on the left, on a large wooden tribune, are seated two competition judges and a scribe; a third judge, on the left, indicates the six wineskins in the foreground as being the prizes; on the right, a hoplite, a crotala-player, a flute-player, a nude athlete and a fourth judge; side C: triga race toward the right.

Jannot 1984, pp. 48–49 n. 8; figs. 171–73; *Civiltà degli Etruschi* 1985, p. 252 n. 9.15.
[C.Z.]

262. Inscribed tablet
late third–early second century B.C.
bronze *lamina*
h 13 cm; w 15 cm; thick. 0.2 cm
Tarquinia, Museo Archeologico, inv. 86580
from Tarquinia, near the sacred area of the Ara della Regina (random find of 1981)

Rectangular tablet, only the right part remaining. On the right there are the holes for attaching it and the beginning of the text, that starts with a clause of datation and is arranged in nine lines in the following manner: "zilci: ceisiniesi ˙ v ˙ ..../ esic˙ v ˙v ˙ clevsinas....../ teis ˙ q ˙ rutzss ˙ u ....../ umis ipa ˙ ilqcv ....../ ine˙ésis ˙ svaleni ˙ t ....../ ar ˙ ilqcvav ˙ tenaqa......./ se ˙ fateltre ˙ lua ˙ ei ˙ ....../ icamsanquni˙ am ...." On the fourth line a large blank space, probably to be interpreted as a separation pause in the text.

Civiltà degli Etruschi 1985, pp. 258 ff., n. 9.26; Pallottino 1983, pp. 611–14.
[C.Z.]

263. Tabula Cortonensis
end of third–first half of second century B.C.
cast bronze
28.5 x 45.8 cm (50 cm with the handle)
Florence, Museo Archeologico, inv. 234918
from Cortona (consigned 14.10.1992 to the Camucia Stazione di Carabinieri by G. Ghiottini)

Rectangular bronze tablet, in the past intentionally broken into eight parts, one of which is missing; at top centre, handle grip with semi-spherical knob on an overturned lotus flower-base, attached to the tablet by a small plaque folded over on each side and pierced with two holes with copper rivets. On both sides text in Etruscan.

Agostiniani, Nicosia 2000.
[F.C.]

THE INSIGNIA

264. Ax
seventh century B.C.
bronze
l 30 cm; h 21 cm
Florence, Museo Archeologico,
inv. 84507
from Trestina, Città di Castello
(acquisition G. Nicosi,
2.02.1910)

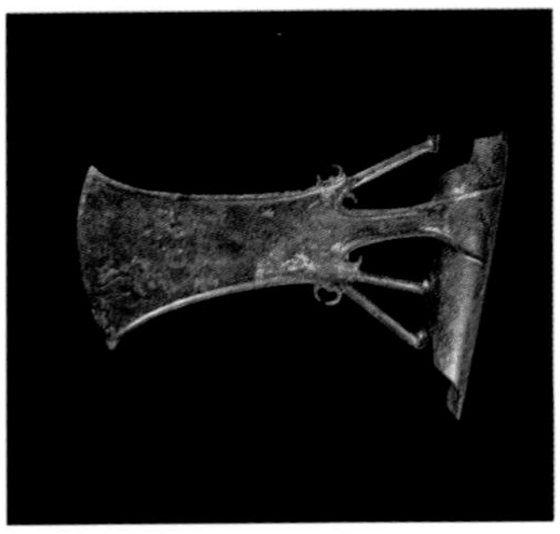

Long cannon handle grip, tapering toward the bottom, with upper edge having a relief band and triple ribbing on the back; curved blade, with raised edges, attached to the cannon by three rod elements and one larger one with a band with raised edges ending in spirals; double spiral also on the upper and lower edges of the blade, next to the socket.

NSc 1880, p. 4, nn. 1–2; Milani 1912, pl. CXIX; *Kunst und Kultur Sardiniens* 1980, p. 131, fig. 95 b. [F.C.]

265. Ax
second century B.C.
iron
l 88 cm
Chianciano Terme, Museo
Civico Archeologico, inv. 174307
from Chianciano Terme, locality
Fucoli, sacred area

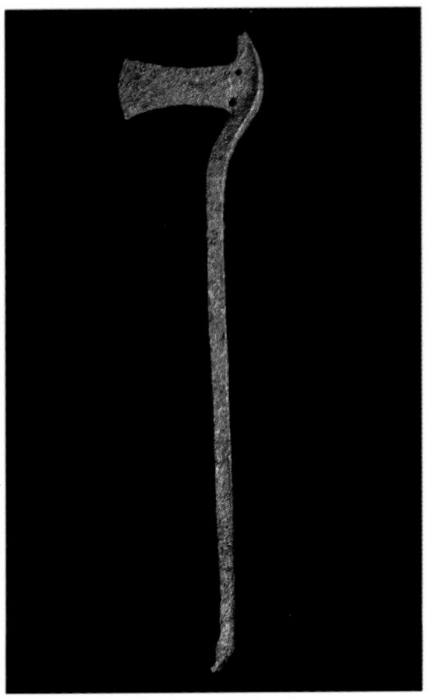

Trapezoidal blade equipped at the top with two holes and inlaid with a thin copper leaf in the shape of a knife; long convex-profiled handle coinciding with the blade and ending at the tip in the shape of a stylized ram's head.

Rastrelli 1993, p. 475, pl. XXIVa; Eadem 1993a, pp. 352–53, fig. 2; *Chianciano Terme* 1997, pp. 79–80, fig. 67. [G.P.]

266. Diphros leg
last quarter of seventh
century B.C.
ivory, iron
l 22.5 cm
Florence, Museo Archeologico,
inv. 110422
from Quinto Fiorentino
(Florence), Montagnola Tomb

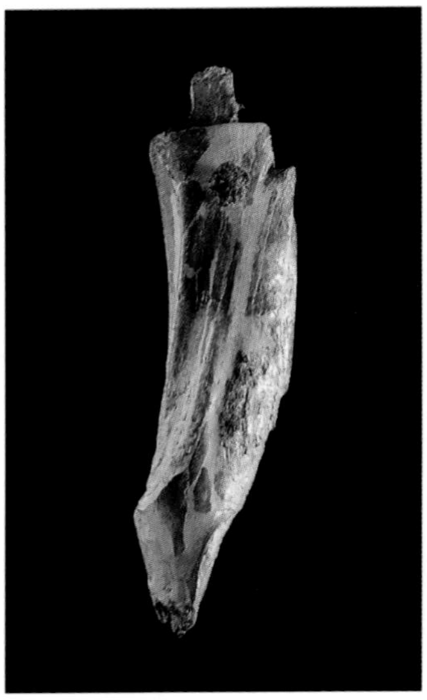

Diphros (stool) leg figuring an animal paw, with long iron articulation pin.

Caputo 1969, p. 57, n.1; Nicosia 1984, p. 149, n. 118; Nicosia 1986, p. 273, n. 1.
[F.C.]

TEMPLI, DECORATIONS AND VOTIVE GIFTS

267. Terra-cotta fragment of votive model of a temple
fifth century B.C.
beige clay, white, black and red
glaze
10 x 15 x 13 cm
Florence, Museo Archeologico,
inv. 68570
from Orvieto, Vigna Grande

There remains part of a slope of a two-sloped roof, with projecting spline and slanting projecting band, as well as part of the wall underneath. The slope retains rows of flat tiles and one of bowls with rosette antefixes. The spline is decorated with braid; the band is decorated with beading above, rope in the middle and on the *anthemion*, narrowing at the edge, below; the part coinciding with the tympan is painted red; the frieze is decorated with a black band above and below, a meander in the middle.

Melis 1984, pp. 367–74, pl. III; *Civiltà degli Etruschi* 1985, p. 156, n. 6.28.1.
[C.Z.]

268. Spiraled acroterion
490–480 B.C.
terra cotta
max. h reconstructed 63 cm;
max. w reconstructed 74 cm
Perugia, Museo
Archeologicodell'Umbria,
inv. 80560, 83595, 770
from Orvieto, sanctuary
of Cannicella

The central acroterion, referrable to the back pediment of the temple of the Cannicella sanctuary and proof of the high qualitative level of the Volsinii art of modelling in the first decades of the fifth century B.C., presents between two sharp-edged spirals, painted in red and blue bands (some traces of color are left on the black background), a square figured by a very well-conserved polychromy, with a relief on the front and on the back painted only. Typologically close to analogous late-Archaic monuments, it is in particular comparable to the Faliscan exemplar with monomachia from Sassi Caduti. The remaining fragments of the scene show a young warrior with chlamys and cuirass with shoulder-straps and fringe hurling himself on a woman falling backward, her left knee on the ground, and with her right arm pushing away the assailant's arm that seems to be holding her by the hair. The woman's red costume with black dots has its sleeves unlaced, showing her left breast. The composition and the details of the group closely recall Etruscan mirrors with legends indicating it as Oreste's matricide, thus offering a probable exegesis of the scene of the acroterion. The detail of the bare breast could also refer to Polyxena, that classical tradition recalls baring her breast to show her throat to Neoptolemus who is sacrificing her on the altar of his father Achilles.

Stopponi 1991a, pp. 261–63, 6.1; Stopponi 1991b, pp. 1103–161; Stopponi 1993, p. 160, fig. 10; Stopponi 1996, p. 137, fig. 195, color pl.; Haynes 1998, pp. 236–38, pls. LXVI–LXVII.
[S.S.]

269. Earthenware pediment
470–460 B.C.
terra cotta, fragment
52 x 58.5 cm; 53 x 60 cm;
59 x 58.5 cm; 45 x 59 cm; h 16 cm
Arezzo, Museo Cilnio Mecenate
from Arezzo, Piazza San Jacopo

Three clay slabs of pedimental cyma. Lower *torus*, painted in scales, on which there is a smooth band, a smaller *torus*, a large *torus* covered with small interwoven leaves; on the lower *torus* high relief figures: a) a naked warrior striking an adversary; b) two warriors with cuirass; c) galloping horseman, with cuirass. A perforated curtain, that formed the crowning of the former, to which it was attached with bronze pins and a special container. Interwoven, connected scrolls, white with red outline, with crowning of palmettes alternating with rhombs, in red and white. Youthful head of Hermes with "curlicue" curls, large almond eyes, hat with small brim and fastening of a little wing. Probably belongs to an acroterion.

Maetzke 1949, pp. 251–53; *Il Museo Archeologico Nazionale G.C. Mecenate* 1987, pp. 52.
[F.C.]

270. Pinax
530–520 B.C.
red clay and red, yellow, white and black paint
fragment A: 9.5 x 9.5 cm
fragment B: 13.3 x 10.9 cm
Berlin, Staatliche Museen, Antikensammlung, inv. TC 6681.22
from Caere

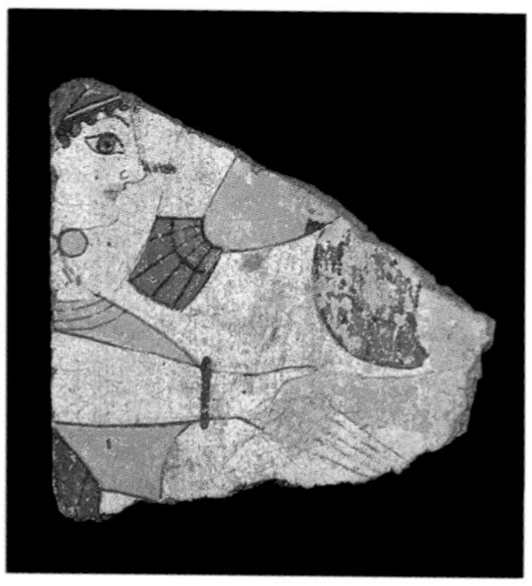

Pair of fragments, originally not tallying, of a same polychrome slab. Fragment A presents on a white ground a yellow arm, coming out of a dark red vest; fragment B instead allows to recognize the upper end part of two horses' heads with one ear each. The stylization of the red manes coincides with the visible band on fragment A.

V. Kästner 1988.
[V.K.]

271. Female head antefix
ca. 540 B.C.
red clay with black and red particles
h 15.3 cm; max. w 19.2 cm
Berlin, Staatliche Museen, Antikensammlung, inv. TC 6681.4
from Caere

Sub-Daedalian antefix in the shape of a female head with a triangular face, black eyes and eyebrows and little smiling mouth. The black hair is parted on the forehead in two curls that fall down in a horse-shoe shape behind the ears and are highlighted by wavy lines painted white. The head belongs to a series of like East- antefixes, and straddles the older generation still influenced by Daedalian models and the more lively and bejeweled female heads of the second half of the sixth century B.C.

V. Kästner 1988.
[V.K.]

272. Statuette of warrior
ca. 550 B.C.
bronze; solid lost wax casting
h 36.2 cm
Florence, Museo Archeologico, inv. 562
from Brolio (Arezzo), farm of Montecchio, votive deposit

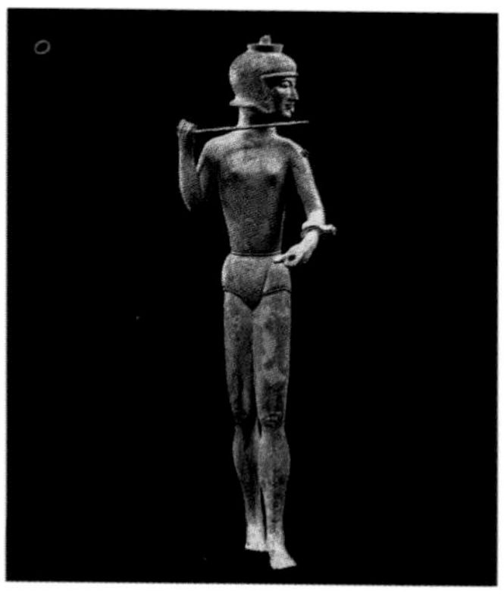

Gradient warrior, with front body and head in right profile. Left arm, not touching the body, bent forward with on the forearm remains of the shield strap, that rested on the shoulder. Right arm bent upward holding a spear that reaches the chin. On the hips loincloth with relief hems and triangular appliqué. On the head a cap helmet with cheek-guards, topped by an upside-down trunco-conical element, flattened on top, with broken central pin. Attributed to Clusine production.

For bibl., see cat. 274. [C.Z.]

273. Statuette of warrior
ca. 550 B.C.
bronze; solid lost wax casting
h 35.7 cm
Florence, Museo Archeologico, inv. 563
from Brolio (Arezzo), farm of Montecchio, votive deposit

Gradient warrior, with front body and head in right profile. Left arm bent forward with on the forearm remains of the shield strap, that rested on the shoulder. Of the hand there only remains a cylindrical pin. Right arm bent upward holding a spear of which only the first part remains. On the hips loincloth with relief hems and triangular *appliqué*. On the head a cap helmet with cheek-guards, topped by an upside-down trunco-conical element. Attributed to Clusine production.

For bibl., see cat. 274. [C.Z.]

274. Statuette of warrior
ca. 550 B.C.
bronze; solid lost wax casting
h 36 cm
Florence, Museo Archeologico, inv. 564
from Brolio (Arezzo), farm of Montecchio, votive deposit

Gradient warrior, with front body and head in right profile. Left arm bent forward with on the forearm remains of the shield strap, that rested on the shoulder. Holding a spear with tip bent inward. Right arm bent upward holding a spear of which only the first part remains. On the hips loincloth with relief hems and triangular *appliqué*. On the head a cap helmet with cheek-guards, topped by an upside-down trunco-conical element. Attributed to Clusine production.

Romualdi 1981, pp. 8–11, ns. 14–16; *Santuari d'Etruria* 1985, p. 164, n. 9.2.8; Cristofani 1985a, p. 248 n. 2.3-5; *Cortona dei principes* 1992, pp. 203–04, ns. 14–16. [C.Z.]

275. Female statuette
ca. 550 B.C.
bronze, solid lost wax casting
h 36.1 cm
Florence, Museo Archeologico, inv. 561
from Brolio (Arezzo), farm of Montecchio, votive deposit

Standing female figure with long, short-sleeved vest, fastened at the waist with a high belt; hairdo formed by a smooth cap upturned at the bottom with bangs on the forehead, two braids on the chest and eight in the back; around the neck a necklace formed by twelve round pendants; arms, bent at the elbows, outstretched forward with hands closed in fists with raised thumb. Attributed to Clusine production.

Romualdi 1981, pp. 10–11; 26–29 n. 17; Cristofani 1985, p. 248 n. 2.6; *Cortona dei principes* 1992, p. 205 n. 17. [F.C.]

276. Head of kouros
ca. 500 B.C.
white marble of Cycladic provenance
max. h 17.2 cm; h occiput-chin 16.8 cm; h forehead-chin 11.2 cm; w of face 10 cm
Marzabotto, Museo Etrusco Pompeo Aria, inv. 702
from Marzabotto, *regio* IV, *insula* I, on *plateia* A, in front of house 2 (1952)

Head belonging to a small-sized statue, probably standing. Hair dressed with tight semi-circular curls, arranged evenly in parallel rows, according to a nearly geometric motif; full round face; bulging eyes with almond contour, without details; high, rounded cheeks; straight, closed lips, with rather marked lateral dimples. Extensive chipping on the left occipital area, other minor ones on the eyebrows, nose, right cheek and chin.

Sassatelli 1985, cat. 7.11, p. 219, with previous bibl.
[E.L.]

277. Head of statue
375–350 B.C.
bronze
h 21.5 cm
London, British Museum, inv. GR 1824 4-70.6
found on an island of the Lake of Bolsena in 1771

Head of a youth, in hollow cast bronze, probably part of a votive statue. The long face, with strongly-marked features, is crowned with short, thick hair, combed in tight braids. The irises of the eyes are rendered by incised circles and the beard by thin lines. Despite the influence of late fifth-century Greek models, the clearly-marked features and the ornamental treatment of the hair are distinctively Etruscan.

Haynes 1985, pp. 211, 300, n.150; Cristofani 1985a, pp. 293–94. [J.S.]

278. Statuette of kore
480 B.C.
bronze, with shiny dark green patina
25 cm (including the support under the feet 1.2 cm)
Copenhagen, Nationalmuseet, inv. 4203
from Covignano (Rimini), Villa Ruffi

The *kore* was found with two other statuettes now conserved at Villa Giulia, and two marble statuettes, perhaps made in Magna Graecia and now at the Ny Carlsberg Glyptotek of Copenhagen. It follows the tradition of Athenian *korai* and has been compared to the *korai* of north-eastern Etruria, although the style recalls southern Sicilian examples; maybe it was made in Magna Graecia and brought from the south to the Rimini area, an assumption that may also be true for the marble statuettes.

Riis 1941, p. 129, pl. 22.3; Giglioli 1954, p. 19, fig.; Riis 1957, p. 13; Moltesen 1982, p. 36, fig. 11; Richarson 1982, p. 279, pl. 192.651; Cristofani 1985a, n. 32, p. 265. [B.B.R.]

279. Male head
ca. 500 B.C.
lost wax cast bronze
h 31 cm (base included), w 15 cm, depth 16 cm
Copenhagen, Ny Carlsberg Glyptotek, I.N. 1624
presumibly from Ariccia

The head, slightly smaller than life, was removed from a statue. It has been assumed that the head might have belonged to a religious image of Diana Nemorensis, forming part of a group of three like figures, connected to one another by a rod at the back of the head: that typology is known by coins of the late-republican period. Instead others suppose it to be the head of a votive statue. The only Archaic bronze piece to represent the sculpture school of southern Etruria.

Riis 1966, pp. 65–67; Cristofani 1985a, p. 290, n. 113; Colonna 1985b, 261, 10.3; *La grande Roma dei Tarquini*, 1990, p. 144, n. 6.9, pl. XIV; Moltesen 1997, p. 128. [J.C.]

280. Head so-called "Malavolta"
430–420 B.C.
pinkish clay
h 18 cm
Rome, Museo di Villa Giulia, inv. 53217
from Veio, Portonaccio sanctuary

Head of male youth belonging to a statue. Hair style with modeled locks; large eyes and pronounced mouth.

Sprenger 1972, pp. 35 ff.
[C.Z.]

281. Foot of tripod
480–460 B.C.
bronze; hollow lost wax casting
h 27.5 cm
Florence, Museo Archeologico,
inv. 710

on's paw support, on which rests a shelf decorated with ovoli, palmettes and lotus flowers; on the flat surface of the shelf Perseus, wearing a short vest and cloak, in the act of killing with the *harpe* Medusa, who is wearing a chiton with tight, narrow pleats, tucked up at the waist, and *himation*, kneeling and with her left arm grasped by the hero's right arm. Attributed to North Etrurian production.

Rocchetti 1961, pp. 119–23; pls. LIX–LXI, 1; *Civiltà degli Etruschi* 1985, p. 289, n. 10.37.1. [C.Z.]

282. Red-figure Attic kylix
550–490 B.C.
clay, glaze, overpainting and graffiti
h 18.8 cm; diam. 46.5 cm
Rome, Museo di Villa Giulia,
inv. 121110
Cerveteri, area of the sanctuary of Hercules

Signed by Euphronios as the ceramist (remains of an inscription on the outer part of the foot), it is the biggest type C exemplar yet known. The decoration, attributed to Onesimos, offers episodes of the war and the capture of Troy. The story, filled with figures, unfolds on the two friezes on the outside and the inside, and ends with the dramatic picture, inscribed in

the central circle, where is shown the killing of Priam in the presence of Polyxene, by the hand of Neoptolemus who is holding by the feet little Astyanax. Under the foot a right-to-left inscription on two lines and perhaps incised at different times bears, in the Caeretan Etruscan alphabet, a dedication to Hercle: "Euphronios epoiesen."

Moretti Sgubini 1999. [A.M.M.S.]

The Renewed Society of the Fourth Century

In the late fifth and early fourth century, after a period of considerable politico- and economico-social difficulties which the historiographical tradition identifies by the conventional term "the crisis of the fifth century," the oligarchy which characterizes the entire Etruscan social system, though marked by different features in the north and south of the region, lays the basis for the creation of a new *polis* characterized by a different relationship between city and countryside. Although the available evidence is not homogeneous and consistent for the whole of Etruria, it appears to be no coincidence that the phenomenon shows a certain completeness in the case of Tarquinia, a city which between the end of the fifth century and the middle of the fourth seems to have a leading role within the Etruscan nation, as is attested by the inscriptions of the *elogia* which in the first century A.D. the descendants of the Spurinna family transcribed in Latin on marble and placed near the temple of the Ara della Regina. The city now organizes the territory with the foundation, either ex novo or on the site of settlements destroyed a century earlier, of a large number of *oppida* and *castella* equipped with defensive structures, from Tuscania to Ferento, from Norchia to Castel d'Asso, from the Castellina to Luni sul Mignone and San Giovenale, with the evident aim of establishing permanent defensive garrisons on the margins of the territory and intensifying the agricultural exploitation of the land. This constitutes a kind of "internal colonization," which sanctions the end of oligarchic control over the vast stretches of public land, which were now assigned to cadet branches, such as the Curunas or the Tarquinese Spurinas who moved to Tuscania, or to *gentes* of lower rank, who thus come to swell the numbers of a new class of an intermediate type, which is granted allotments of land, as well as civil rights in more or less partial forms.
The complex stratification of the social tissue emerges in all its clarity from the picture of the urban necropolis. Here we can follow the development of the new aristocracy through an analysis of the clan hypogeums, which are rare in the first half of the fourth century B.C. and then gradually increase in number until in the third century and the first half of the second there are about thirty of them. We can also observe the organization of the social structure in the only portion of the cemetery that has been completely excavated (the so-called "fondo Scataglini"), where the great clearing, on which the family Tomb of the Aninas is situated, is surrounded by dozens and dozens of tombs of small or medium size which are crammed together to exploit all the available space and which give us a picture of the social stratification of the fourth century B.C. and the Hellenistic Age, which centered on the emergence of the *gentes* who were a point of reference for the whole community. Connected with the changes that take place at the level of the rituals, the tomb now takes on a more markedly scenographic appearance, which probably has some connection with the theatrical performances which must have been an integral part of the funeral ceremonies, as seems to be indicated by the deposition from the late fourth century onward in the grave goods of Tarquinia—and then through the influence of this city at Vulci too—of models of theatrical masks of the Greek type as replacements for real ceremonies (cf. n. 296). The tombs of the new classes seem complexes of a "medium" level characterized by grave goods inspired by those of the aristocratic class, imitating in some ways its ideological forms, albeit only in their external appearance.
Central to the ideology of the *gentes* is the exaltation of the family line and of the public role of its individual members, which is recalled by the representation of the symbols and attributes of power conferred by the city, as is illustrated already in the second half of the fourth century B.C. by the images of the tomb of the Velcha family at Tarquinia better known as the Tomb of the Shields, where the banquet of Larth Velcha escorted by lictors, a symbol of the magistratural powers that he had in his lifetime, according to a scheme which will later be fairly widespread both on the sarcophagi and in the funerary painting of the high Hellenistic Age. In this climate this aristocracy soon develops a tendency to become closed within the ranks of endogamic matrimonial practices, in a network of family relationships which involves almost the whole *nobilitas* of the entire region, revealing the broadly oligarchic matrix of this class. This phenomenon, together with the concentration of magistratural offices in the hands of a few *gentes,* an aspect confirmed by the inscriptions, will lead over the course of the following centuries to the crisis of the intermediate class, which is literally crushed by the internal tensions between *domini* and *servi* on the one hand, and by the conflict with Rome on the other.
At the same time there is also a revival of great public commissions, chiefly concerned with the building of new, imposing temples or with the renovation and restoration of existing constructions, such as Temple A in the Pyrgi complex near one of the ports of Cerveteri. Some particularly fine examples, at the stylistic level, are provided by the new temples of Volsinii; the exhibition includes some examples of the decoration of the Temple of Via San Leonardo (ns. 283–284) and of the slightly later sanctuary of

the Belvedere (n. 285), which lead to the birth of a flourishing coroplastic tradition, which from the years around 400 B.C. onward spreads, probably partly as a result of the prestige gained by Volsinii in the league of the twelve *populi*, to many centers of Etruria, including those in the maritime area (Tarquinia, Vulci, Talamone, Roselle, Pisa, Arezzo, Chiusi, and Perugia) with the circulation not only of models and matrices, but presumably also of craftsmen, as the case of Vulci seems to confirm. At the same time we find, especially in the area of Volsinii and in northern Etruria, great votary offerings in the sanctuaries, such as natural-size or smaller bronze statues, and offerings with a political significance, exemplified in the exhibition by the bronze weight probably offered by the two magistrates Larce Penthe and Vel Lape in the sanctuary of Hercle at Cerveteri (n. 287). These are accompanied by the ex votos of the middle classes, which express themselves in the fertility and healing cults with the deposition of offerings consisting of heads, images of infants and anatomical parts made of terra cotta, making an increasingly wide use of molds and matrices (cf. ns. 290–291). The practice of depositing anatomical ex votos begins in the fifth century B.C. at Veio and Falerii, in connection with a precise Hellenic influence and the growing prestige of the medical cult of Asclepius; later it spreads to Tarquinia, Cerveteri and the areas of Vulci and Volsinii and is particularly popular in the Latin environment in close connection with the Romano-Latin colonization of the fourth and third centuries B.C. If we exclude the rare examples of the northern canton, where significantly clay anatomical ex votos are only recorded at Populonia, whose composite social structure may in part explain their presence, the spread of this phenomenon marks the limits of the model of the social transformation of southern Etruria. In the northern district the social conservatism is also reflected in the panorama of the votive offerings, which prefer the tradition of the archaic age of depositing at the cult places little bronze statues of the offerers and divinities; these are illustrated in the exhibition by the two statuettes ns. 288–289, which imitate the aristocratic custom of votive offerings made of precious metal. [S.B.]

283. Male torso
early fourth century B.C.
painted terra cotta
h 31 cm, w 22
Orvieto, Museo C. Faina,
inv. 143
from Orvieto, Temple of Via
San Leonardo

Standing male figure, with bust slightly leaning to the left; the right arm, lost, was upraised, while the left is stretched along the hip, with the forearm extended forward holding an edge of the vest falling from behind; on the arm an armlet with round *bullae*. The bare torso displays a detailed anatomical rendering, also emphasised by the use of colour. In the back there are remains of the attachment to the pediment, to which the statue belonged. The person has beenapproximated to the figure of Veltune.

Andrén 1940, p. 161, I:5, pl. 61,198; Bruschetti 1985, p. 270, 10.15.1 (with previous bibl.); Massa-Pairault 1992, pp. 144 ff. [P.B.]

284. Fragmentary male head
early fourth century B.C.
terra cotta
h 14 cm
Orvieto, Museo C. Faina
from Orvieto, Temple of Via
San Leonardo

Face with regular features and correct rendering of the modeling; beard formed by long, orderly, and well-defined curls; hair rendered with long wavy locks, parted in the middle of the forehead. Big, open eyes, with pupils rendered with color. Together with the more refined head of the supposed Tinia, it belongs to a series of works influenced by the Athenian school of Phidias. The head belonged to a figure that adorned the temple pediment.

Andrén 1940, p.160, I:2, pl. 61,197; Roncalli 1991, pp. 271 ff. (with previous bibl.); Massa-Pairault 1992, pp.144 ff. [P.B.]

285. Pediment of the Belvedere Temple
late fifth–early fourth century B.C.
terra cotta
Orvieto, Museo C. Faina
from Orvieto, Belvedere Temple

• 1. *Male figure with chlamys*
h 82 cm; w 31 cm.
inv. 2005
Standing bearded figure, naked except for the chlamys laced on the chest and covering the back of the body. The left arm rests on the hip, the right hangs along the body, maybe holding a spear, lost with the hand. The anatomy of the torso is correctly rendered; the head, tilted to left and raised, with big eyes looking upward; the hair, parted in two on the forehead, is formed by small ribbed curls, like the beard. There still remains part of the base and rear support of the statue, that was placed on the left side of the pediment, toward the middle, attached with nails of which the holes remain.
[P.B.]

• 2. *Male figure*
h 87 cm, l of base 27 cm
inv. 1377
Youthful-looking male figure, naked, with chlamys and footwear, facing right. Presently the head is missing. Traces of the original polychromy are visible, as well as the holes for holding the relief in place.The edge of the slab is straight on the left side and slanting on the right side, so it very probably occupied the lateral edge of one of the *mutuli*. The find, unearthed during the accidental digs in 1828, belonged to the rear pediment of the temple.
[G.M.D.F.]

• 3. *Fragmentary figure of a warrior*
h 80 cm
inv. 2009
Several fragments, that cannot be reconstructed, of a figure of a standing warrior, with right leg bent and resting on a rock; the right arm is bent and the hand is resting on the knee, the left hanging along the body and the hand, lost, was holding the hilt of the sword slipped in the sheath. The warrior is wearing a short tunic and over it a cuirass held by shoulder-straps; the head, slightly tilted to the right, is covered with a helmet of which most is lost, from out of which little curls appear on the forehead. There still remains part of the base and back of the statue, that was placed on the pediment of the temple, attached with nails of which the holes can be seen.
[P.B.]

• 4. *Pedimental high relief*
h 52 cm
inv. 2117
Figure of a youthful-looking warrior, standing, wearing a short tunic and an anatomical cuirass. The head and part of the trunk are missing, only part of the legs remain. The arm that was not lost

is resting on the corresponding hip. There are traces of the original polychromy.
The find, unearthed in the digs performed by Luigi Pernier between 1920 and 1923, belonged to the front pediment of the temple and, based on the digger's explanations, probably to the left-side *mutulus* or to the *columen*.
[G.M.D.F.]

• *5. Fragmentary figure of a warrior*
h 43 cm; w 28 cm
inv. 2006
Fragmentary figure of a standing warrior, with left leg slightly forward; wearing a short tunic and a cuirass with plates forming horizontal bands and a single series of *pteryges*; over it a cloak draped on the shoulders and held by the left arm bent at the elbow and outstretched forward; the right arm is lost, but was probably grasping a spear. In the back part there remains a fragment of the attachment to the pediment to which the statue belonged, and where a hole for the nail can be seen
[P.B.]

• *6. Head of a youth*
h 13 cm
The head, found near the north corner of the temple, could have belonged to one of the statues of warriors that adorned the pediment; it is slightly tilted toward the left, with wide-open eyes and closed mouth; the hair is rendered with unruly little curls, parted in the middle of the forehead.
The bright polychromy emphasizes the details of the face and hair. The executive technique and the rendition of details is analogous to that of the other pedimental statues of the temple of the Belvedere.
[P.B.]

• *7. Bearded head*
h cm. 16
inv. 1348
Head of bald and bearded old man, the features of the face rendered with remarkable care and realism. The right hand is holding the point of the thick beard, emphasizing the attitude of concentration and reflection of the person represented, who has been diversely identified. Traces of the original polychromy are very visible. The find, unearthed during the accidental digs of 1879, belonged to the rear pediment of the temple.
[G.M.D.F.]

1

2

5

3

6

7

8

9

• *8. Figure with drapery*
h 46 cm
inv. 1378
What remains is the lower part of a female figure, dressed with the chiton and himation and characterized by wearing also a deerskin. She in wearing sandals. Traces of the original polychromy are clear. The lateral edge of the slab is slanting. The figure is usually identified with Artemis. The find, unearthed during the accidental digs of 1879, belonged to the rear pediment of the temple.
[G.M.D.F.]

• *9. Sitting figure*
h 48 cm
inv. 1379
Female figure with head and feet missing, seated on a rock and facing left, with chiton and *vittae*. Clear traces of the original polychromy. According to one theory (Strazzulla 1985 and 1989), there had been a similar, specular figure opposing her in the same pedimental space. Holes for holding it in place are visible on the person's hip and the lower part of the rock. The remaining edge of the slab is straight so it must have occupied the lateral edge of one of the *mutuli*.
The find, unearthed during the accidental digs of 1879, belonged to the rear pediment of the temple.
[G.M.D.F.]

Andrén 1940, pp. 172–178, II:1–II:6, II:9–II:10, II:24, pls. 64, 209–18 (with previous bibl.); Cristofani 1985b, pp. 9–12; Massa-Pairault 1985, pp. 41 ff.; Stopponi 1985, pp. 80 ff.; Strazzulla 1985, pp. 376–77; Strazzulla 1989, pp. 971–82; Massa-Pairault 1992, pp. 44 ff.; Della Fina 1998, pp. 41–54.

286. Head of youth with diadem
ca. 375–350 B.C.
bronze
Etruscan workshop
(for most scholars Falerian)
h 22 cm; l 15 cm
Ancona, Museo Archeologico,
inv. 27797
from Cagli, locality Coltone

The diadem on the brow has such an exact match in the gold one from tomb 136/A of Valle Pega at Spina, belonging to a male type specific to that center, that its attribution to the same Po Valley production center should not be entirely ruled out. The late-Phidian inspiration of the hairstyle and certain details appearing regularly in votive bronzes and pottery especially from Falerii, with which they also share certain convergent stylistic assonances (Colonna 1992, 111), suggest a date around the beginning of the second quarter of the fourth century B.C.

Bendinelli 1920, pp. 239–42 and *passim*; Dohrn 1982, pp. 61 ff.; Baldelli 1991 (with several other references); Coen 1999, pp. 48 ff., 150 and 166. [G.B.]

287. Aequipondium
third century B.C.
cast bronze and lead
h 10 cm; max. diam. 6 cm; diam. of the suspension ring 2.40 cm; weight 750 gr
Rome, Museo di Villa Giulia,
inv. 121561
from Cerveteri, locality
Sant'Antonio

Ovate-shaped weight. Soldered onto the upper extremity a round-section suspension ring, inside which is inserted another mobile stick-ring. Dedicatory inscription, cold-incised, horizontally on ten lines that follow the curving surface: "raqs turmsal/ velus xrcmsal/ qusti quimeqlmq/ mu[..]s[....]xmse / macuni hercles/ alpan teceII/ eVIIa CC/ lc.penqe.vel/ lape.zilci.laq/alpnu laqes." The weight, belonging to Turms, but formerly the property of Vel of Archmsi, would have been dedicated by Larce Penthe and Vel Lape in the sanctuary of Hercle, in the course of the exercise of the magistrature of *zilc*.

Cristofani 1996, pp. 39–54.
[C.Z.]

288. Statuette of offerer
second half of second
century B.C.
bronze; solid lost wax casting.
max. h 22.5 cm
Florence, Museo Archeologico,
inv. 158

Male figure with cloak that leaves the right shoulder and chest bare, and is wrapped around the left forearm. Hair with wavy locks, parted in the middle, adorned with a crown of leaves. Left leg slightly bent forward with raised heel. Right arm extended forward, holding a patera with *ombelos*, decorated inside with a set of concentric rays. Left arm, bent at the elbow, outstretched in front holding a *pyxis* with a lid decorated with concentric rays. Production of inland Etruria.

Bentz 1992, p. 120, n. 32.2.4, pl. XLII, figs. 238–39 (with wrong caption). [C.Z.]

289. Male statuette
third century B.C.
bronze; plate; solid lost wax
casting
max. h 6.3 cm
Florence, Museo Archeologico,
inv. 135

Male figure with short cloak, partly covering the buttocks and leaving the genitals bare. Long hair, adorned with a crown of leaves, with bangs on the forehead. Right arm alongside the body, but not touching it, with the hand laid on the hip; left arm bent at the elbow with hand on hip, with the palm toward the buttock. Attributed to Arretine production.

Romualdi 1984, p. 470, pl. II, c-d; Bentz 1992, p. 109, n. 25.2, 4, pl. XXXIV, fig. 189.
[C.Z.]

290. Female votive head
third century B.C.
pinkish-yellow clay
h 26.5 cm
Florence, Museo Archeologico,
inv. 4770
from Nemi, sanctuary of Diana

Veiled female head. Loose hair, parted in the middle, falling along the sides of the face, divided in three separate curly locks on each side. Close-set eyes with incised pupils, small nose, fleshy lips. On the nape of the neck a hairnet. Back part convex.

Bartoloni 1970, p. 259 n. 3; pl. XIX c; Cristofani 1982, p. 79, fig. 1.
[C.Z.]

291. Male votive head
third century B.C.
pinkish-yellow clay
h 24 cm
Florence, Museo Archeologico,
inv. 4768
from Nemi, sanctuary of Diana

Veiled and bearded votive head. Short hair parted in the middle. Far-set, narrow eyes, narrow nose showing nostrils, part-closed mouth. Smooth moustache with twisted tips; beard formed by thick, short curls. Back part convex.

Bartoloni 1970, p. 258 n. 2; pl. XIX b; Cristofani 1982, p. 79, fig. 1.
[C.Z.]

292. Gem
late fourth century B.C.
sardonyx
13 x 17 mm
Florence, Museo Archeologico,
inv. 14400

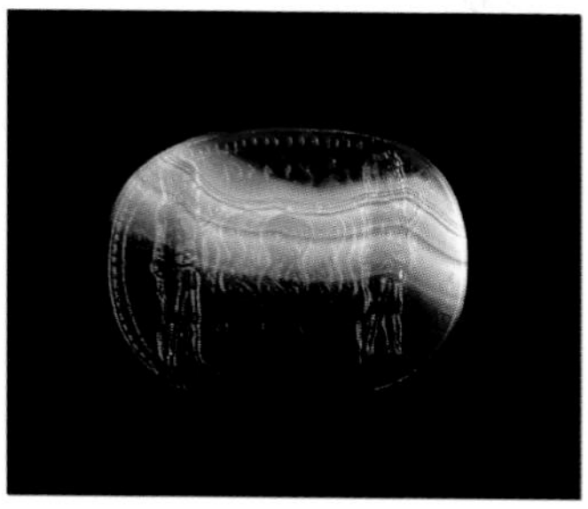

Incised oval gem. Edge with incised lines. Base line a series of triangles on background of dashes. Two Salians, bearded and *capite* velato, wearing short tunics, over which a short cloak in one case adorned with a triton, in the other with a figure of a capricorn, carrying toward the left six *ancilia*, decorated with spirals, hanging from a perch. On top the inscription "Appius," below "alce," both right to left (TLE 777).

Richter 1971, p. 16 n. 16 bis; Torelli 1999, pp. 227–55.
[C.Z.]

293. Lid of the so-called "Sarcophagus of the Priest"
360–350 B.C.
Paros marble
l 215 cm; w 68 cm; thick. 33 cm
Tarquinia, Museo Archeologico,
inv. RC 9871
from Tarquinia, Tomb of the Partunus

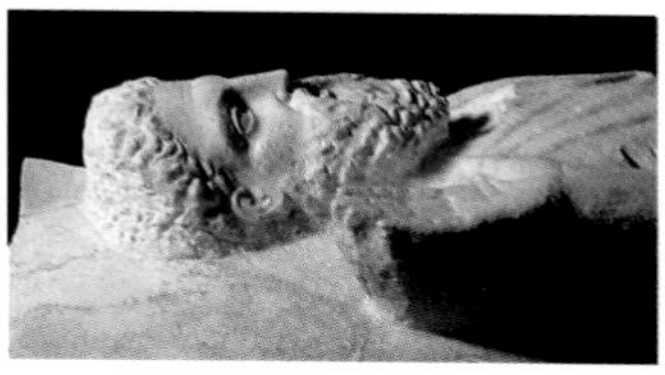

Lid with sloping roof, with three small acroterions at the corners and the top of the pediment. The deceased is reclining while performing a religious act. Hair with wavy locks, curly beard; wearing a long vest with sleeves and fringed shawl on his left shoulder, sandals on his feet resting on a curved support. His right arm is bent upward with palm extended; in his left hand he is holding a pyxis.
The lid was placed on a coffin, on which is painted the myth of the killing of the Trojan captives on the Patrocles' tomb.
Attributed to a Sicilian production for a high-ranking Punic commissioner.

Blanck 1982, pp. 11–28; *Sarcofagi* 1988; Torelli 1994, p. 306, pl. XIV, 1. [C.Z.]

294. So-called "Sarcophagus of the Magnate"
third quarter of fourth century B.C.
white limestone; traces of green, yellow, red and brown color
h 120 cm; l 220 cm; w 80 cm
Tarquinia, Museo Archeologico,
inv. 9873
from Tarquinia, Tomb of the Partunus

On the lid the deceased is reclining, resting on his left side, hiships and legs covered by a cloak. The left arm, bent, supports the head; the patera is in the right hand. At the ends,the lid is decorated with acroterions: on the left two seated sphinxes and in between a mask of Acheloos, on the right two crouching lions and in the middle female bust. On the front of the coffin the inscription: "velϑur partunus larisaliśa clan ramϑas cuclnial zilχ ceχaneri tenϑas avils svalϑas LXXXII" (TLE 126).

Herbig 1952, pp. 53 ff., n. 98; *Gli Etruschi di Tarquinia*, p. 340 n. 885; *Sarcofagi* 1988.
[C.Z.]

295. Sarcophagus
third century B.C.
nenfro stone
casket: l 205 cm, h 65 cm,
w 55 cm; lid: l 169 cm, h 85 cm,
w 65 cm
Rome, Museo di Villa Giulia
from Tarquinia, Cavalluccio necropolis, chamber tomb of the Camna family

Casket: on the front, procession with three lictors preceding a Vanth with overturned torch and the two-horse chariot of the deceased. Behind the horses Charun with hammer and snake, turned toward the deceased; behind the chariot a horn player.
Lid: recumbent deceased with bare bust, plant wreath around his neck and pad with ribbon on his head.

Moretti 1967, p. 126, n. 358.
[F.C.]

296. Terra-cotta models of masks
late fourth–early third century B.C.
Tarquinia; Museo Archeologico
from Tarquinia

• *1. Mask of Papposilenus*
light beige clay
h 14.2 cm; w 8.8 cm
inv. 1365a
Bald head, adorned with a small crown of berries and leaves, and a taenia falling down in front of his animal ears. Little eyes, snub nose, hollowed mouth. Wavy beard separated in two separate locks.
• *2. Mask of satyr*
light beige clay; traces of red color
h 11.9 cm; w 11 cm
inv. 2311
On its head a cap with brim raised, on which the horn and the point of its animal ears rest. Open mouth, inside which the teeth can be glimpsed.
• *3. Mask of Dionysus*
pinkish clay
h 12.7 cm; w 9.1 cm
inv. RC 2339.
Long oval face; mouth closed. On his head smooth cap and *taenia*, attached to the sides of his face with two daisies, framed in little bunches of grapes that cover his ears.

Stefani 1984, p. 75 n. 195, p. 79 n. 211, p. 81 n. 211; pls. XLIV, a, XLV, a, XLV, e; *Civiltà degli Etruschi* 1985, p. 389 n. 17.3.1, 17.3.3, 17.3.4. [C.Z.]

The Decline

The decline of the hegemony of the Etruscan aristocracy is slow and inexorable. In the Campanian area the admission of Samnite peoples into the *societas urbis agrorumque* of Capua in 424 B.C. marks the beginning of the rapid Etruscan collapse and the emergence of Samnite culture in this region. In the Po Valley the strong Syracusan presence in the area of the upper Adriatic which will lead in the early decades of the fourth century B.C. to the foundation of colonies and fortresses along the coast from Adria to Ancona, and the progressive expansion of the Celtic populations, which in the mid-fourth century occupy the whole region north of the Apennines, caused the complete destruction of the Etruscan societies of the Po Valley area. In 388 B.C. the Celts reached Rome and sacked the territory of Chiusi.
Meanwhile Etruria proper began to feel the serious consequences of the confrontation with the nascent Roman hegemony in Italy. Although in 388 B.C., during Brennus's siege of Rome, Cerveteri gave shelter to the priests, vestals and sacred symbols of Rome, soon afterward, in 396 B.C., Veii was taken by the Romans, who annexed the territory of that town and settled it with plebeian colonists, who are responsible for the clay ex votos and the Latin dedications recovered from the Veii sanctuaries and included in this exhibition (ns. 297–298). In their choice of strongly evocative themes, such as the group of Aeneas carrying Anchises on his shoulders on the fatal night of the burning of Troy, these ex votos are an integral part of the Roman political choices, in the context of the disputes about the rebuilding of the city after its burning by the Gauls.
In 358 B.C. there was an attempt to restore the Etruscan hegemony in the mid-Tyrrhenian area with the war declared on Rome by Tarquinia, supported by her allies the Falisci and by the Caerites. According to the not always clear accounts of events by the Roman sources, the theatre of operations first occupied Faliscan territory, and the Romans lost their fortresses of Sutri and Nepi, after which the Etruscans advanced in 356 B.C. as far as the salt-flats at the mouth of the Tiber. Then in 354 B.C. the Roman counter-offensive induced Cerveteri to abandon the field and in 351 B.C. the war, which had dragged wearily on without any significant events, ended with the making of a fourty-year truce. The results for the Etruscan side, however, were rather meagre, if we exclude the probable echo in Rome of the outcome of this conflict in the assumption of consular posts by plebeian and patrician members of families which had strong links with Etruria, such as the Fabii and the Manlii. In the changed situation of the peninsula, during the years of the truce the presence of Rome became increasingly incisive in central and southern Italy, first through the dissolution of the Latin League and then through expansion into Campania and Apulia, as well as the making of an important treaty between Rome and Carthage. And the confrontation with Rome becomes central even in the ideological world of the Etruscan aristocracies, as is attested by the paintings of the so-called François Tomb of Vulci, the great hypogeum of the *gens* of the Saties, in which the Etruscan version of the saga of Servius Tullius, the slayer of Tarquinius Priscus, and of the national heroes the Vibenna brothers, is presented in forms that are symmetrical and analogous to the killing of the Trojan prisoners on Patroclus's pyre by Achilles, in the context of a conception that is strongly allusive to contemporary reality. In 311 B.C. another war is waged by the Etruscans against Rome. The initiative in the offensive is taken this time by the cities of the central and northern area, which were the object of Roman offensives that threatened Perugia. The war concluded in 307 B.C. with a separate truce with Tarquinia and an Etruscan defeat, owing partly no doubt to the general disunity of the Etruscans, a fact confirmed by the separate truce with Tarquinia and Arezzo's initial abstention from the war. The repercussions in Etruria of the outcome of the war must have been serious, even at the level of internal tensions, as is shown by the episode of the dictator M. Valerius Corvus, who in 302 B.C. intervened to put down the slaves of Arezzo. The resumption of hostilities between the Samnites and the Romans was the occasion for a renewed Etruscan attempt to oppose Rome by participating in the anti-Roman coalition which brought together Samnites, Sabines, Umbrians, Gauls and Etruscans, probably those of the cities of the inland area of the central and northern district. The definitive victory of Rome at Sentinum in 295 B.C. marks the beginning of the end for the Etruscans. Between 294 B.C., the year of the fall of Roselle, and 273 B.C., when the Romans finally overcame Cerveteri, the whole region effectively came within the orbit of Rome.
The consequent Roman policy toward Etruria is not homogeneous, but shows a variety of aspects, which probably reflect the diversity of the economico-social structure of the southern area and the central-northern one. In the north the Roman victory was compensated with large payments of money imposed by the truce of 307 B.C. on Volsinii, Perugia and Arezzo, contributing to the reinforcement of the dominant oligarchies, as is confirmed by the episode of M. Valerius Corvus at Arezzo. In the southern and coastal areas, on the other hand, Rome imposed concessions of large portions of territory, where the victor founded colonies: in 273 B.C. Cosa in the territory of Vulci, and between 264 and 245 B.C. the four maritime colonies of Pyrgi, Castrum Novum, Alsium and Fregenae in the district of Cerveteri.
The final erasure of Etruria from the political and historical map of Italy coincides with the siege of Volsinii in 265 B.C. and the consequent destruction of the city, with the *evocatio*, that is, the "summoning to Rome," of Vertumna-Vertumnus, the great tutelary divinity of the confederation of the Peoples of Etruria, which was thus dissolved, to re-emerge later in a quite different context and with a different meaning at the time of the antiquarian restorations of the period of the Julio-Claudian dynasty.
The repercussions of the historical situation on the internal affairs of the individual centers soon make themselves felt at the level of archaeological evidence. Although the aristocracies make alliances with Rome, the recession consequent on the defeat causes the rapid impoverishment of the intermediate classes, who now find alternative ways of making a living, notably the military profession, a choice which has precedents at the end of the fourth century B.C., when there was a strong component of Etruscan mercenaries in the armies of Agathocles and the Carthaginians, and which is confirmed for the years of the Second Punic War by an obscure Tarquinian funerary text concerning a personage of the middle class who died at the grand old age of 106, a text where mention is made of Capua and Hannibal (TLE^2, n. 890). The crisis of this intermediate class probably causes migrations to distant lands in search of a better future, as is attested by the late Etruscan cippi in Tunisia or the case of the *Liber Linteus* of Zagreb, which somehow ended up in Egypt, where it was used to wrap a mummy.
The integration in the Roman world of the Etruscan aristocracies continues into the Roman empire, when it is emblematically represented by figures of the first rank in the Augustan circle such as Maecenas (a scion of the Aretine *gens* of the Cilnii), Virgil, and Propertius. At the level of the economic structures this integration brought with it the wholesale introduction of forms of money, with the minting of bronze issues of coins based on Roman measures at Tarquinia, Volterra and in the inland area (the series of the wheel: Chiusi?). At the more strictly ideological level it sees the adoption of forms proper to the central-Italian world and widely observed in Rome, such as the adoption of statues which may be votive or celebrative in function (the two are difficult to divide) of "Roman" appearance; these are illustrated in the exhibition by the well-known *Arringatore* from the Florence museum (n. 306) and by the Fiesole head from the Louvre (n. 303).
The resumption of large-scale public commissions saw at the end of the third century and in the first half of the second century B.C. the flourishing, especially in the northern centers, of a vigorous coroplastic tradition, which created the fronton reliefs and the other roof decorations of the sanctuaries at Populonia, Talamone, Sovana, Vulci, Fiesole, Volterra, Arezzo, and Chianciano. The themes represented—though most of the evidence allows us to see them only extremely hypothetical and conjectural forms—seem to allude to the universal values of *concordia ordinum*, as in the case from Talamone that is shown in the exhibition (n. 307). [S.B.]

297. Offerings from the Portonaccio sanctuary at Veio
Rome, Museo di Villa Giulia

• *1. Statuette of offerer*
fourth century B.C.
bronze; solid lost wax cast
h 11 cm, inv. C 307
Standing female figure, wearing chiton and *himation*, and with piglet against her bosom.
• *2. Small pitcher*
second half of fourth century B.C.
pinkish clay
h 7.5 cm
Lip rounded at the rim; trunco-conical body; ovate body; disc foot; overhanging flattened ribbon handle. On the shoulder the inscription: "L. Tolonio[s] ded[et] Menerva."

Santangelo 1952, pp. 46–54; *Santuari d'Etruria* 1985, p. 107. [F.C.]

298. Offerings from the Campetti sanctuary at Veio
Rome, Museo di Villa Giulia

• *1. Statuette of Aeneas and Anchises*
first half of fifth century B.C.
h 20.5 cm.
inv. 40272
Group representing Aeneas, with Attic helmet, greaves and round shield, carrying on his left shoulder Anchises, bald and bearded, partly cloaked, who is hanging onto his son's neck.
• *2. Small pitcher*
second half of fourth century B.C.
yellowish clay
h 10 cm
Rounded rim, trunco-conical neck; ovate body, disk foot. Handle missing. On the neck, incised before firing, the inscription: "Crere L. Tolonio d."

Vagnetti 1971, pp. 88, 176–77, n. 1; pl. XLVIII; *Civiltà degli Etruschi* 1985, p. 316, n. 13.1.2.3–6; *Roma* 2000, p. 197. [C.Z.]

299. Scenes with Vel Saties and mythical-historical events from the François Tomb
ca. 340 B.C.
frescoes; colors: red, brown, black, blue, yellow, white
Roma, Villa Albani
from Vulci, Ponte Rotto necropolis François Tomb

Anteroom. Back wall on right and right wall: below, red running base; above, frieze in perspective with running meander in red, brown, black, yellow, white. Battle scena between Etruscans. Beside a round shield, decorated with a large rose motif, Caile Vipinas (Caelius Vibenna), naked and bearded, is facing right toward Macstrna (Mastarna), he also naked and bearded, wearing two shoulder-belts, setting him free by cutting the ropes binding his wrists; Larth Ulthes, bearded, wearing a short, light-colored chiton with a red trim, stabs with his sword Laris Papathnas of Volsinii, whose light-colored cloak falls from his shoulders onto the ground; Pesna Arcmnsnas of Sovana, his head covered by the light-colored cloak, is stabbed by Rasce, naked and bearded; Venthi Caules (?) from Falerii (?), with brown armor, fallen to his knees beside his own shield, is stabbed from behind by Aule Vipinas (Aulus Vibenna), naked and bearded, wearing a shoulder-belt. The scene continues on the adjacent wall of the anteroom. Atrium. Back wall: below, red running base; above, animal frieze. Battle scene: Marce Camitlnas, naked, bearded, stabs Cneve Tarchunies Rumach, bearded and dressed, crouched close to the ground. Left wall: below, red running base; above, animal frieze.
To the left of the door, placed in the middle of the wall, the figure of Vel Saties, wearing a crown, and a dark red toga picta, decorated with figures of a dancer and a pyrrhic dancer, and trimmed with a motif of plant scrolls, facing right; in front of them, kneeling on the ground, young Arnza, dressed in a light-colored tunic trimmed in red, holding in his raised left hand a bird attached to a string. Left of the door it would seem that Arnza is represented again with a male figure.

Mingazzini 1935, pp. 61–66; *Civiltà degli Etruschi* 1985, pp. 310–12; Cristofani 1985; Steingräber 1985, pp. 380–83 n. 178; *La tomba François di Vulci* 1987; Torelli 1991, pp. 355–67. [C.Z.]

300. Helmet with inscription
second half of third century B.C.
cast and hammered bronze (cap); laminated bronze (chin-guard)
h 25 cm; max. w 26 cm; chin-guard 16 x 14 cm
Cremona, Museo Civico Ala Ponzone, inv. St. 11055
from Pizzighettone (Cremona)

Montefortino A-type helmet with conical cap with button decorated with ova, around which the iron piece for holding the crest remains. The base of the cap, which widens to form a neck-guard, presents a cord-like decoration with slanting grooves interrupted by beading on the frontal part. One anatomical chin-guard is preserved. On the lower rim is incised the inscription "M(ARCO). PATOLCIO. AR. L. P. VIII" referring to the name and perhaps the rank of the owner, as well as the weight of the helmet.

Pontiroli 1974, p. 211, n. 317, pl. CLXI; Coarelli 1976, pp. 157–79; Galli 1998, p. 275, cat. II.20. [M.V.]

301. Pedestal of offerer with inscription
264 B.C.
h 26 cm; original l of each block 116.5 cm; thick. 24.5 cm
Rome, Musei Capitolini
from Rome, sacred area of Sant'Omobono

Five fragments belonging to two twin inscriptions that adorned two pedestals of offerers, with numerous stamps and pins for fastening bronze votive statues. The texts are the following:
M. Folv[io(s) Q. f. cos]ol // d(edet) Volsi[nio cap]to.
[M. Fo]lvio(s) [Q. f. cosol] // [d(edet) Volsinio capto].

Torelli 1968, pp. 71–75; Torelli 1973, pp. 103 ff., n. 89; Coarelli 1988, pp. 213 ff. [F.C.]

302. Head of bronze statue of a youth
first half of third century B.C.
bronze; hollow lost wax casting
max. h 23 cm
Florence, Museo Archeologico, inv. 548

Youthful male head. Short hair, arranged in locks on several rows, parting from the center. Short bangs on the forehead and a lock in front of each ear. On the nape the hair is bouffant. Part-closed mouth. Hollow irises, that must have been in another material. Eyebrows executed with a braided motif.

Cristofani 1985a, p. 297, n. 122, fig. 122; Torelli 1985, p. 184, fig. 131; Haynes 1985, p. 318, n. 190, pl. 112, fig. 190; Strazzulla 1997, pp. 9–10, fig. 6.
[C.Z.]

303. Portrait head
late fourth century B.C.
lost wax bronze
h 30 cm
Paris, Musée du Louvre, Département des Antiquités grecques, étrusques et romaines, inv. Br. 19
from Fiesole

The head must have belonged to a life-size statue, and is characterized by long facial surfaces emphasized by grooves below the cheeks and near the nose.

Cristofani 1985a, p. 297 n.123
[G.P.]

304. Painted terra cotta male portrait
first quarter of first century B.C.
refined nut-colored clay
h 32 cm
Rome, Museo di Villa Giulia, inv. 56513
from Cerveteri, sanctuary of the Manganello

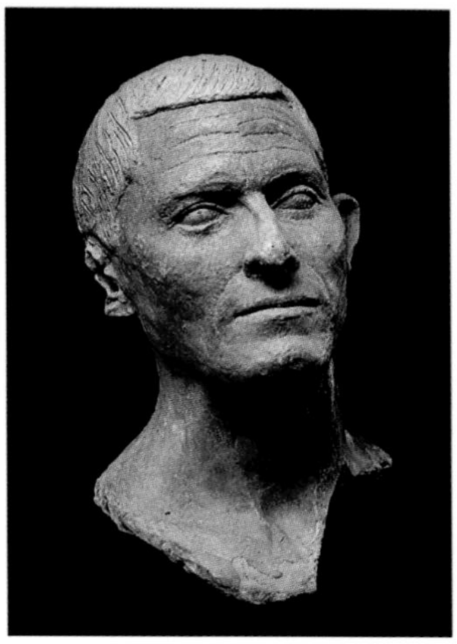

Portrait of a mature person, very accurately modeled with studied physiognomic details.

Arte e Civiltà degli Etruschi 1967, p. 132, n. 373.
[P.A.]

305. Votive terra-cotta male head
first half of second century B.C.
light-colored clay with many inclusions; greenish slip; traces of red color
h 24 cm
Tarquinia, Museo Archeologico, inv. 3733
from Tarquinia, votive hoard near the Ara della Regina

Short hair, divided in locks, broad forehead, marked by three incised wrinkles, eyes with raised eyelids, partly open lips, square jaw. On the right cheek traces of red coloring.

Comella 1982, p. 48 B IV, pl. 8b; *Civiltà degli Etruschi* 1985, p. 388, n. 17.2 .3.1.
[C.Z.]

306. Statue of the so-called "Arringatore"
late second–early first century B.C.
bronze; solid and hollow lost wax casting
h 180 cm
Florence, Museo Archeologico, inv. 2
from Cortona (Arezzo),Valle di Sanguineto, near Lake Trasimeno

Mature male figure with *exigua praetexta* toga leaving the right shoulder bare, and tunic with an *angustus clavus*. On the tails of the toga an inscription incised on three lines in apical characters: "aulesi metelis ve(lus) vesial clensi/ cenfleres tece sansl tenine/ tuqines cisvlics" (TLE[2] 651). High Roman-style footwear with laces. The head slightly turned to the right. Short hair with locks barely outlined. Wrinkles on forehead and on the sides of the mouth and the eyes, hollow, that must have been filled with another material. Right arm raised and extended forward, with the palm of the hand open; left arm lowered, under the toga, along the body with partly closed hand. On the left-hand ring finger a ring with oval bezel. Left leg slightly bent forward. Attributed to Aretine production.

Dhorn 1968; Cristofani 1985a, p. 300, n. 129; Torelli 1985, p. 233, fig. 157; *Civiltà degli Etruschi* 1985, pp. 394–95, n. 19.1, fig. 19.1; Haynes 1985, pp. 322–23, n. 200, figs. 200–200a; Colonna 1990, pp. 219–26, pls. 38, 39, 1; *Gli Etruschi e l'Europa* 1992, p. 155, n. 240.
[C.Z.]

307. Pedimental high relief
mid-first century B.C.
polychrome terra cotta, partly reconstructed and integrated
h 147 cm; w 882 cm (reconstructible)
Florence, Museo Archeologico
Orbetello (Grosseto), Talamone, hill of Talamonaccio, Temple B

It is with Oedipus' great deed that the tragedy of the accursed family of Labdacus ends : the blind king sees the fulfilling of his fate with the eyes of his soul, aware of the reciprocal fratricides of his sons Eteocles and Polynices and the cruel deathof the seven heroes in the assault of the citythat had once welcomed him asits saviour. In von Vacano's definitive, unquestionable reconstruction, the group of Oedipus and his sons' lifeless bodies occupies the central position in the layout of the pedimental relief (crowned by the futile attempt of Capaneus, whom Zeus will cast from the walls) and constitutes its thrust and at the same time the focus toward which the entire composition is directed. The two chariots, that of Amphiaraüs on the right, about to be swallowed by the Underground, and that of Adrastus—the only surviving hero of the seven against Thebes—on the left, that the divine steed Arion is carrying away to safety, occupy the main spaces of the pedimental decoration in a design of exceptional technical mastery, inspired perhaps more by pictorial models than by contemporary carving. The obvious relationship with the reliefs of small Clusine, Perugian and Volterran urns, beginning by the mid-second century B.C., confirm the chronology of the pediment, that Milani situated instead at the so-called battle of Talamone in 225 B.C., where the Gauls were defeated by the army of Rome with its confederates' forces, united for the first time in a common objective. It is much more probable that around 150 B.C. the temple of Talamonaccio, going back to the second half of the fourth century B.C., underwent a complex process of renovation, involving the entire ensemble of architectural sculptures, including naturally the two pediments, closed and entirely decorated (a rare examplar in Etruscan templar modelling), among which furthermore the one with the myth of the Seven against Thebes occupied the back elevation of the temple, looking north, toward the bay of Talamone. Of the front pediment, on the south side, few fragments are left, that might have to do with a mythological theme closely related to the sea (parts of sea monsters and dolphins, a fragment of a "trident" cutwater), with clear referral to the portuary nature of the ancient Telamon and the great seafaring tradition of the Etruscan nation.
The question of the commission is still open and, consequently, of the political significance of the choice of the "Seven against Thebes" theme, that has been diversely interpreted in the complex framework of the Romanization of this part of the Etruscan territory. In any case the iconographical choice remains closely bound to Etruscan tradition and to those elements of the spirit of Greek tragedy that largely nurtured Hellenistic culture.

Milani 1898, pp. 95, 158 ff., notes 118 ff.; Milani 1912, pp. 67 ff., pls. 104–06; von Vacano, von Freytag Löringhoff 1982; Massa-Pairault 1985, pp. 119–21; von Freytag Löringhoff 1986; von Vacano 1992, pp. 57–68, pls. I–V; von Freytag Löringhoff 1992, pp. 69–76. [P.G.]

The Servants

The destructuring of the aristocratic system of production, chiefly based on the presence of an extensive social class, which the ancient Latin sources describe as servants and the Etruscans by the term *lautni*, and which was made up of people who occupied an intermediate position between the slave and the free man, led to the heightening of latent tensions within the various communities from the fourth century B.C. onward. Although the sources are fairly laconic about the revolt which was put down in 302 B.C. at Arezzo by the intervention of the Roman dictator M. Valerius Corvus and there are uncertainties even about the chronology of the attempt at a plebeian revolution known to have taken place in Volterra, the revolutionary processes which had as their object the society of Volsinii in the early decades of the third decade B.C. show how the process of freeing the servants and integrating them in the civic body came about by degrees starting with access to land ownership and the consequent assurance of military service passing through the right of intermarriage with members of the higher class, the acquisition of the *ius honorum* and entry to the senate, and culminating in attainment of the magistratures and the attempted subversions of civic order in 265 B.C., which ended in a bloodbath owing to the intervention of Rome, which in 264 B.C. took Volsinii by siege, destroying it as a punishment and rebuilding it later close to the modern Bolsena, after killing or restoring to their old masters the former *servi*. Despite the Roman intervention, the tensions were only mitigated, not completely removed, as is confirmed by the servile revolt of 196 B.C. and the tumults of the Bacchanalia of 186

B.C. and again at the time of the agrarian reforms of M. Lucius Drusus of 91 B.C. by the text of the "Vegoia prophecy" with the description of apocalyptic scenarios if the traditional structures of property were overturned. It is not easy to find archaeological evidence for this servile class. In the second half of the fourth century B.C. in the central-southern part of Etruria there appear some figures identified by an onomastic formula that adds the name of the master to that of the individual. While on the one hand this form of nomenclature still underlines the relationship of dependence between the servant and the *dominus*, on the other it presupposes processes of adoption into the circle of the *gens* and the achievement of the state of freedom. The slave uprising which in 196 B.C. put Etruria to fire and the sword and which was bloodily suppressed by the intervention of the Roman legion commanded by the praetor Acilius Glabrio, and the later attempted revolt in connection with particular Dionysiac rites of an interclassist nature which ended in 186 B.C. with the well-known episode of the Bacchanalia, are probably the causes that led to the liberation of the numerous servants and the consequent emergence of an extensive agrarian "lower-middle" class in the area of Chiusi and Perugia, with the corresponding phenomenon of a massive spread in the population. The servile extraction of this society is evident from the very data of personal nomenclature, in which the family names are identical to the old individual names or similar to the first names. We know little or nothing about the urban servile classes and their ideology: the little evidence that comes from the sanctuaries, such as the inscribed ex voto from Tarquinia included in the exhibition (n. 308), show how the former *lautni* of southern Etruria tend to blend in with the intermediate well-to-do class, while the different degree of freedom and the different structures of the societies in the northern area foster higher aspirations, as is clearly shown by the Tomb of Arnth Cae Cutu Celusa of Perguia, whose sarcophagus, also included in the exhibition (n. 309), came from the same atelier which produced the urns of the Volumnii, the noblest family in the city. Similarly in the countryside the new class of the former servants tends to merge with the ideology of the middle class, with tombs of a family type, where the various depositions in modest terra-cotta urns are accompanied by grave goods of a lower-middle kind with a very small number of objects which are rarely made of metal. Highly significant of the ideal forms of these personages are the reliefs which decorate the front of the urns, for they are standardized in the adoption of two mythological themes, one taken from the Hellenic repertory, the reciprocal killing of Eteocles and Polynices, and the other drawn from the local heritage, the battle of the hero with the plough (n. 310). [S.B.]

---

308. Anatomical leg-shaped ex voto
second century B.C.
brick-colored clay
h 10 cm
Tarquinia, Museo Archeologico, inv. 4291
from Tarquinia, votive hoard near the Ara della Regina

Fragment of left leg, ending just above the knee. Inscription incised before firing: "vel: tiples."

Comella 1982, p. 115, D9, Fr.1; pl. 77, c; *Civiltà degli Etruschi* 1985, p. 388 n. 17.2 3. 7.
[C.Z.]

---

309. Cinerary urn of arnϑ cai cutu
third century B.C.
travertine; painted plaster
casket: h 57 cm; l 75 cm; depth 52.5 cm
Perugia, Museo Archeologico, inv. 99982
from Perugia, locality Monteluce, Madonna del Riccio; hypogeum of the cai cutu (1983)

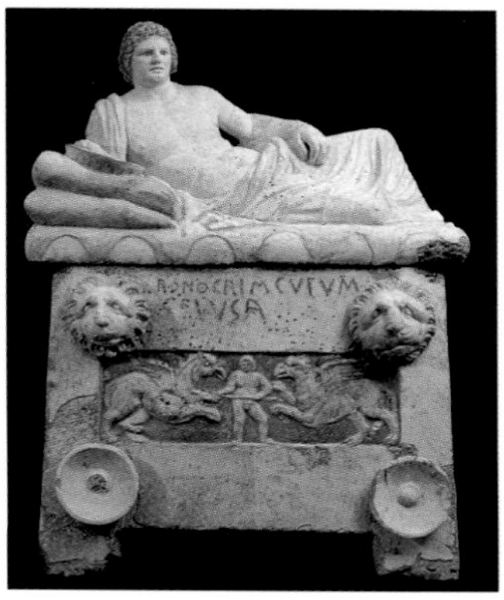

Urn resting on four feet. On the front two *ombelos* pateras next to the two lower corners and two lions' heads near the upper ones, made separately. In the middle of the front, inside a slightly hollowed rectangular field, is figured a standing naked youth, bearing a spear, who is defending himself from two griffins attacking him, one to his right, one to his left.

Cristofani 1984, pp. 78 ff.; Feruglio 1993, pp. 49 ff. [A.E.F.]

---

310. Small earthenware cinerary urn
second–third quarter of second century B.C.
terra cotta
33 x l 56 x 27 cm
Florence, Museo Archeologico, inv. 5686
from Chiusi (?)

This small urn belongs to the late Clusine production of molded earthenware cinerary urns, that is, made in series with moulds and painted in bright colours. Their relatively low cost and the symbolic value insure a mass production addressed to a class with limited means. The container figures a part-naked hero fighting with a plough shaft, formerly identified as the hero Echetlo, who fought at Marathon, whereas recently it has been suggested seeing in it a local myth relative to the social conflicts upsetting Etruria during the second century.

Brunn, Körte 1916, p. 10, type B.
[A.R.]

---

311. Small earthenware cinerary urn
second half of third century B.C.
terra cotta
14 x 27 x 12 cm
Florence, Museo Archeologico, inv. 5544
from Chiusi (?)

The small urn, that belongs to the commonest production of Clusine earthenware cinerary urns, figures a door, whose leaves are divided in three parts by a cornice adorned with pods and equipped with door-knockers, connected with two cypresses by wreathes strung with taenias. The door, rather than to the entrance to the realm of the Underground, seems to refer to the grave. On the upper edge an illegible inscription is painted. On the lid, veiled lying figure.

Brunn, Körte 1916, p. 121, CI,2.
[A.R.]

312. Small earthenware cinerary urn
second century B.C.
terra cotta
20 x 30 x 15 cm
Florence, Museo Archeologico, inv. 5566
from Chiusi (?)

This small urn belongs to the group figuring scenes of funeral leave-taking, a subject that on Clusine earthenware cinerary urns, although documented by a greater number of variants, in replicated in a lesser number of exemplars than mythological ones. A married couple parts in front of Hades' door, equipped with lion-head door-knockers, between two underground daemons, Charun wielding a hammer on the left and a female winged genii holding a sword on the right; the scene is framed between two columns. On the upper edge is painted the inscription "larthi.cainei.laucanesa."

CIE 1894; Brunn, Körte 1916, p. 67, LVII, 7; Rix 1991, p. 213, Cl 1.1382; LIMC III, *voce* "Charun," p. 230, 59a.
[A.R.]

313. Bell-shaped cinerary olla
second half of second century B.C.
fine-grained clay; white slip; black, red and blue glazed decoration
h 22 cm; diam. of mouth 19 cm
Florence, Museo Archeologico, inv. 5632
from Chiusi (?)

The olla belongs to a group of Clusine cinerary urns of the late Hellenistic period in the shape of a bell, a cylinder or a small bottle, mostly with motifs of wreathes or garlands (but also branches of laurel or vine-leaves) interwoven with taenias hanging from nails, inspired by funerary painting: in fact the wreath motif is found in the painted Clusine tomb of the Tassinaie, in which an olla of the same style was deposited. In our exemplar little blue bells hang from the wreathes. On the relief edge is painted the inscription "thana:cusnei:curvesa."

CIE 2061; Rix 1991, p. 218, Cl 1.1560. [A.R.]

The Anguish of the Decline

The tensions which characterize Etruscan society from the end of the fourth century onward are also reflected in the mental forms relating to the afterlife and more generally to the funerary world of the aristocracies and the lower classes, which tend, as we have seen, to fall into line with this ideology.
The proud aggregation of the old and recent elites in the ideology of the *gens* and its continuity implies a different conception of the tomb, which is now seen as the pole of aggregation of the group, but above all as the final home, whose tablinum were the site of a symposium of the dead who were represented on the lids of the sarcophagi and urns as recumbent banqueting figures. However, unlike in the archaic world, where the eternalization of the feast and the banquet exalts the *dies festus* which sanctions the social role of the dead person and perpetuates it without a break in continuity, the banquet of the late-classical and Hellenistic age is transferred to Hades, and is peopled with cruel, inexorable demons. Thus there is a stress on the opposition between earthly existence and the afterlife and on the duality of the two worlds, two notions which characterize the new conceptions, which are the origin of the dramatic sense of the detachment of death and the anguish of the afterlife which are evident in the scenes of the journey to the Underworld which appear on many Hellenistic urns (cf. n. 316) or those of the farewell at the gates of Hades in the presence of the funerary demons Charun, Tuchulcha, Vanth and the numerous *Lase* of monstrous and terrifying aspect. Even the magistratural processions, ideal referents of the role and prestige conferred on the dead person in his lifetime by the city community, and depicted in frescoes on the walls of the tombs, as in the case of the sepulchre of the Apunas of Tarquinia (n. 315) or reproduced in bas-relief on the front of the coffins and urns, contain or are framed by demons and monstrous figures which emphasize their supreme, metahistorical nature.
The phenomenon also characterizes in increasingly marked forms the whole Hellenistic age, and from the second century B.C. the same figurative culture, now renewed by the arrival of influences and craftsmen from the Asiatic Greek world, bends its language to pathetic ciphers with strong chiaroscuro tensions intended to produce dramatic effects, as in the high reliefs of the temple of the Catona which is present in the exhibition (n. 318), selecting themes also congenial to representations charged with symbolic messages of references to the present, as in the case of the fronton of Talamon, shown in another part of the exhibition (n. 307), which participates, albeit in more provincial forms, in the same formal language, and whose subject is related to the exaltation of the safeguarding of the *concordia ordinum*, an indispensable precondition for the prosperity of the country, which must have still had vivid memories of the dramatic events that culminated in the clash with the Gauls in 225 B.C. [S.B.]

314. Cinerary urn
120 B.C.
calcarenite
61.5 x 23 x 40 cm
Florence, Museo Archeologico, inv. 5800

Chest of small cinerary urn, with profiled frame; on the front relief with two magistrates wearing togas, one of them kneeling, assailed from behind by two cutthroats wearing tunic, cloak and pileus; to the left assistants with scale and hatchet, to the right musicians. Volterran make.

Brunn, Körte 1890, p. 258, pl. CXV,1; Massa-Pairault 1985, pp. 224 ff., n. 74, fig. 132; Massa-Pairault 1992, pp. 243 ff; *Civiltà degli Etruschi* 1985, p. 392, n. 18.2. [F.C.]

315. Bruschi Tomb, back wall
late third–early second century B.C.
fresco
w 700 cm
Tarquinia, Museo Archeologico from Tarquinia, Monterozzi necropolis

Below, continuous frieze with waves and leaping dolphins; at the ends and in the center of the wall, palmettes. From left to right, two standing cloaked men; winged daemon with short tunic, three men gradient right, wrapped in light cloaks, among whom the one on the right stands out by his much larger proportions; seven men in light cloaks, going toward the right, some with *litui* and horns; a boy and six (?) men gradient left; daemon wearing a tunic, leading a horseman toward the left. Numerous inscriptions on several lines that allow to attribute the tomb to the Ap(u)na family.

Steingräber 1985, p. 296 n. 48. [C.Z.]

316. Chest for cinerary urn
end of third century B.C.
alabaster
0.41 cm; 0.78 x 0.26 cm
Volterra, Museo Guarnacci, inv. MG 114
from Volterra

Parallelopipidal chest on feet joined by a listel with relief. On the front, in bas relief scene of a journey to the Underground. At center a horseman going toward the left followed by a wingèd daimon holding a short-handled hammer (Charun). In front of the horseman another female wingèd daimon with a torch in her left hand clasping the shoulders of a cloaked female figure. At the left end female daimon with little wings on her temples holding in her right hand an unsheathed sword and in her left a torch.

Corpus Urne Volterrane II, 1, n. 177.
[G.C.]

317. Cinerary urn
second half of second century B.C.
calcarenite
58.5 x 36.5 x 17 cm
Florence, Museo Archeologico, inv. 5522

Chest of snall cinerary urn; on the front relief of leavetaking between a man and a woman in front of an arched two-leaf door, closed; on right, behind the woman, Charun; on left, behind the man, group of figures, in the foreground a row of three children, in back three men and a veiled woman. Volterran make.

Brunn, Körte 1916, p. 59, pl. L, 12.
[F.C.]

318. Two heads from La Catona
first quarter of the second century B.C.
Arezzo, Museo Cilnio Mecenate, from Arezzo, locality La Catona, Porta San Clemente, Pernier excavations 1919

• 1. *Female head*
grey clay; traces of white color
h 18 cm
inv. 87674
Woman's three-quarters head (probably an Amazon), tilted toward the left shoulder, with Phrygian cap; oval face, with wrinkled brow, open mouth and pathetic expression. It was part of the sculpted decoration of a pediment.

Grassi Zamarchi 1980, pp. 219 ff., n. 143; Cristofani 1985, pp. 381 ff., 16.6.4; Ducci 1987–88, pp. 131–52, p. 140, n. 3.
[F.C.]

• 2. *Male head*
grey clay
h 20 cm
inv. 87667
Head of youth with Phrygian cap, beardless, with long wavy locks framing his face.

Cristofani 1985, pp. 381 ff, 16.6.10; Ducci 1987–88, pp. 131–52, p. 140, n. 2.
[F.C.]

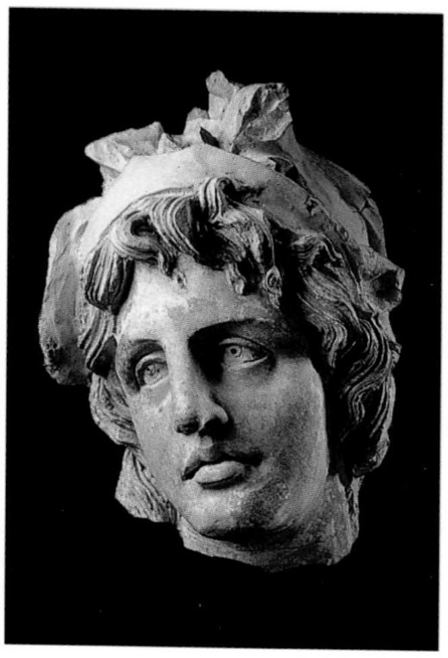

The Role of the Past and of the Esoteric Doctrines

From the fourth century onward, and with increasing intensity in the dramatic moments of the conflict with Rome, the culture of the new classes which rule the various Etruscan areas tends to turn back on itself and exalt the past. Nor could it have been otherwise considering the importance that the renewed aristocracies attributed to the exaltation of the continuity of the family line. The accent, shifted from the dimension of myth to that of antiquity, from which both the legendary element and the aspect of prestige are recovered, is thus placed not only on the past as such, but also on those who had been leading figures in that past, throwing the echoes of their prestige on to their present-day descendants.
There thus spread, also at the level of the iconography of classes of objects destined for the aristocratic elites, such as mirrors or gems, myths which exalt sagas and legends proper to the *nomen etruscum*. The same tradition of the origin of the Etruscan nation is recalled by the myth of the handing down of the art of the haruspex from Tages, the mysterious earth-born boy, to Tarchon, the founder of Tarquinia and Pisa and therefore of the whole nation, which is illustrated in the exhibition by a well-known mirror from Tuscania (n. 319), while local sagas are recalled by the representation of a combat between Laran and the son of Cel on a mirror from Populonia or the evocation of a monstrous being emerging from a well which characterizes the front of some urns of the northern region, or the myth of the adoption of Hercle by Uni through the symbolic gesture of the offering of the breast, an episode illustrated in the exhibition by a mirror from Volterra (n. 310). Though the predilection for subjects taken from the local mythological repertory is counterbalanced by the recourse, in many other cases, to legends and myths of the Hellenic heritage, there are also choices in the direction of the heroic deeds of Etruscan national history. The frescoes of the François Tomb of Vulci, as we have seen in another part of the exhibition, project in allusive forms, thanks to a series of intersecting references in the sphere of myth, the saga of Macstarna and the Vibenna brothers, which an inscription from Veio of the first part of the sixth century B.C., included in the exhibition (n. 299), shows us in its full historical reality. A mirror from Bolsena, preserved in the British Museum and included in the exhibition (n. 321), documents the elaboration of a saga connected with the deeds of the two brothers, whose fame is confirmed for the fifth century B.C. by the inscription painted on a red-figure Etruscan cup, also exhibited here (n. 323). Although it is not always possible to identify the subject and the dynamics of the episodes that are represented, the scene on the mirror seems linked with the Vibenna brothers' attempt to capture the bard Cacu, an Etruscan parallel of the Greek saga of the capture of the soothsayer Helenus, son of Priam, by Ulysses and Diomedes.
While these subjects characterize the products destined for members of the aristocratic group, the imagery of those destined for the middle class is characterized by the choice of standardized subjects, featuring now a Lasa, handmaiden of the female toilet and Moira of the woman, now the Dioscuri, a subject which interweaves the theme of the origins of the Etruscan people linked with the highly popular sanctuary of Samothrace with religious themes of a salvific type exalted by the figures of the divine twins (cf. mirror n. 324 in the exhibition).
Intimately connected with the feelings of anguish illustrated in the previous section of the exhibition and with the tendency to take refuge in the national past that has just been summarily described is also the exaltation of the tradition of the art of the haruspex. This extremely ancient tradition was now boldly and repeatedly flaunted with the displaying of the signs of native religiosity and the representation of the *libri lintei*, volumes written on linen cloth, and of the sacred texts on scrolls presented sometimes rolled, sometimes unrolled, by personages invested with priestly rank, an exclusive apanage of the aristocratic group, which through this underlines its own international prestige and at the same time its detachment from the rest of the community thanks to its control of a religious heritage which imprints itself on the very deepest layers of the nation.
A wide popularity was enjoyed, especially in the lower levels, by forms of religiosity connected with the salvific aspects of Dionysianism and the cult of Fufluns Pachies. This was a widespread form of religion, which influenced even some groups of the aristocracies of Tarquinia and Volterra, as is shown by some sarcophagi of Tarquinia and in Volterra by the iconographic choices of the decoration of a series of cineraria, which significantly reproduce the morphology of a crater, the vase par excellence for the consumption of wine. However, the interclassist characteristics of this religion, which was sometimes practiced in buildings of the domestic type, as is attested by the clay throne found at Bolsena (n. 328), fostered its wide diffusion in the lower classes, and even after the repression of 186 B.C. these cults continued to be widely practiced, as seems to be indicated from the early years of the second century B.C. by the presence in many grave goods, especially in the countryside, of *lagynoi*, a type of vase which characterizes the ritual of interclassist Dionysiac feasts which were founded in Alexandria by Ptolemy IV and which soon spread widely in Greece, southern Italy and Etruria. [S.B.]

319. Mirror
mid-fourth century B.C.
cast bronze; incised decoration
diam. 12.3 cm; max. l 25 cm
Florence, Museo Archeologico, inv. 77759
from Tuscania, Falaschi acquisition

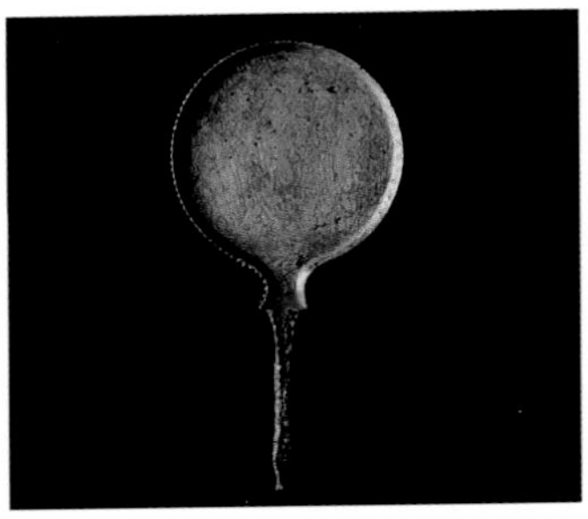

Haruspicy scene. In the center Pava Tarchies (Tages?), examining the liver of a victim; on his right a couple of persons, intent on his revelations, another haruspex named Aul(e) Tarchunus (Tarchun?) and a woman, Ucernei. The scene has been interpreted as the transmission of the art of haruspicy by Tages to Tarchun, the founder of Tarquinia. But in the romanced tale shown here, Aule son of Tarchun could also want to glorify the dynasty of the Tarquinis, since the scene is also attended by a woman, Ucernei, whose Etruscan name transcribes the Latin Ocresia, the mother of Servius Tullius.

Civiltà degli Etruschi 1985, pp. 353–54, n. 15.1.72. [G.C.C.]

320. Mirror
third quarter of fourth century B.C.
cast bronze; incised decoration
diam. 19 cm; max. l 31 cm
Florence, Museo Archeologico, inv. 72740
from Volterra, Pacini 1884 acquisition

Scene of breast-feeding of Hercle (Heracles) by Uni (Hera). In the middle Uni is breast-feeding Hercle. In the background Apollo and two female figures, one identified as Aphrodite. Behind Uni, there is Tinia (Zeus), with a sceptre, holding in his right hand a quadrangular tablet with an inscription running on five lines: "eca:sren:tva: ichnac: hercle:unial:clan:thra:sce." The scene is explained by the inscription, highly complicated and that probably leads to suppose it was a copy of a large painting: we know of but few representations of this Greek myth, that is only attested on two older mirrors.

Prima Italia 1980, p. 190, n. 120 [G.C.C.]

321. Mirror
fourth–third century B.C.
bronze
h 30.8 cm
London, British Museum,
inv. GR 1873 8-20.105/ Walters *BMBronzes 1692*
from Bolsena, Castellani Collection

Bronze mirror, with the Etruscan legend of Cacus engraved on the back;; the incised names belong to Roman tradition. The seer Cacus is playing the lyre, while at his side Artile is reading a diptych; Artile (little Arnth) could perhaps be identifiedwith Arruns, the son of Lars Porsenna. From each side the Vibenna brothers, Caelius and Aulus Vipinas, come forward, either to eavesdrop or to set a trap for the two. A satyr is peering from behind. The border is decorated with wine-shoots, the handle ends in a ramís head, the flat extension features an Eros with a strigil or a curved racket.

De Grummond 1982, ill. 103, pp. 71, 77, 84, 101, 104, 109, 127–28, 160; Small 1982. [J.S.]

322. Foot with stem
mid-sixth century B.C.
black bucchero
max. h 17 cm; diam. of stem 5 cm
Rome, Museo di Villa Giulia
from Veio, Portonaccio sanctuary

Splayed foot with tall cylindrical rope-decorated stem. Incised in the middle part, with syllabic interpunctuation, the right-to-left inscription: "mini muluv[an]ece avile vipiennas" (Avile Vipiennas gave me)

Civiltà degli Etruschi 1985, p. 277 n. 10.19. 2; *Gli Etruschi e l'Europa* 1992, p. 133 n. 122.
[F.C.]

323. Bowl of Aulus Vibenna
fourth century B.C.
yellowish clay, red figures, the bowl was reconstructed from fragments and there are pieces missing; the base belongs to another vase
h 9 cm; diam. 23.2 cm
Paris, Musée Rodin, inv. Co. 1387
from Pouilles (?)

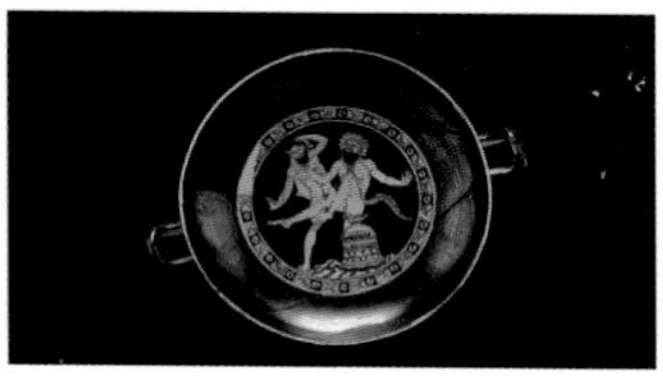

On the medallion, two satyrs: the one on the left is carrying a wineskin, while the one on the right is seated on an overturned krater. On the left is painted in red: "AVLES V[I]PINAS NAPLAN." On the other side, two *komos* scenes with three satyrs are separated on each side by two groups of palmettes placed below the handles. The decoration on the back is a simplified copy of an Attic bowl of the school of Douris, executed around 470 B.C., now at the Vatican (ARV 451, I). In more recent publications, the dating has been shifted to the late fifth or perhaps early fourth century B.C. (Fischer-Graf 1980 and ff.).

Plaoutine 1937, pp. 22–27, pls. II–III; Boardman 1994, p. 266, 7.42 a, b, pp. 268, 345. [B.G.]

324. Mirror
330–320 B.C.
bronze
diam. 18 cm; h 27 cm;
weight 1250 gr
Florence, Museo Archeologico, inv. 604

Convex disk, with raised edge decorated with *ovoli*; rectangular plate with horizontal summits; flat shank, to be inserted in the handle made of perishable material.
Reflecting side with palmette among pairs of spirals on three acanthus leaves; back side with Meleager seated, Menelaus standing behind him, the Dioscures on each side; in the background Tuscan pillars supporting an architrave and a gored roof; inscriptions: "menle, melakre, pultuke, kastur"; on the plate "parapetasma" and an acanthus leaf. Northern Etruria make.

Maggiani 1985, pp. 168 ff, n. 225. [F.C.]

325. Scarab
fourth–third century B.C.
chalcedony-cornelian; "globule" technique
h 1.50 cm x 1.10 cm x 0.82 cm
Rome, Museo di Villa Giulia, inv. 53217
from the Castellani glyptics Collection

Etruscan-Italic workshop. On the base within an imitation rope-decoration frame is represented a male figure bent toward the child, Tages, shown as he is coming up out of the ground.

Zazoff 1968, p. 241, pl. 46.
[R.C.]

328. Throne of the "Panthers"
Hellenistic Age
terra cotta
base 77 x 77 cm; h ca. 100 cm
Bolsena (Viterbo), Museo Civico Rocca Monaldeschi della Cervara, inv. 2081
from Bolsena, Poggio Moscini, *domus* II or "delle pitture"

The throne consists of a square base that supports the plane of the seat, and of a semi-circular back with zoomorphic and plant decoration, in the round or *appliqué*. On each side of the base there is a panther in a watch-guard posture, whose fierce attitude is nuanced by a cupid playfully pulling the animal's ears. A third cupid, winged, is on the outside of the back, between garlands of wreathes. The inner part of the throne figures a satiny fabric. On the seat there was an object, maybe a cist. The artifact is to be connected with the Dionysian cult.

Massa-Pairault 1979; Pailler 1979. [A.T.]

The Diaspora and Nostalgia

At the time of the fall of the Roman republic and the final loss of their national identity, the Etruscans desperately underline the signs of their millennial culture with the continuity of religious practices of a strongly ritual nature entrusted to the direction of the *haruspices*, who will have a very important role in the imperial age. Decimated by the events of the civil wars which characterized the first century B.C., the Etruscan oligarchy—or what was left of it—entered with full rights into the ranks of the senate of the Augustan principate.
In the climate of the antiquarian restoration favored by the *Princeps*, in which the local Etruscan traditions find a privileged position, the ancient league of the Peoples of Etruria is reconstructed at the Fanum Voltumnae, with the holding of games and feasts, and the *praetores* and the *aediles Etruriae* are appointed, purely honorary posts which enrich the titles of personages of senatorial and equestrian rank. At the same time in Tarquinia the local glories are celebrated by the erection of a statue of the mythical founder, Tarchon, the compilation at the behest of the Caesennii of the list of the *summi haruspices,* and the erection of honorary statues with a eulogy of the deeds of ancient members of the Spurinna family, by one of their descendants, who was to be twice consul, T. Vestricius Spurinna. Now integrated into the Roman aristocracy, the Etruscan nobles emphasize their own tradition, exalting the lineage of their ancestry and recalling more or less genuine royal descendances. The case of Maecenas, a member of the *gens* of the Cilnii of Arezzo, apostrophized by Horace as the heir of kings, is paralleled at the archaeological level by that of the Plautii Laterani, the family destroyed in the Pisonian conspiracy in the time of Nero, or rather of a member of this family, Urgulania, who descended from a *rex* of Cerveteri of the fourth century B.C. It is to Urgulania, and to the exaltation of her stock, that we must attribute the marble copy of an Etruscan regal throne of the fifth century B.C. found in the villa of Plautius Lateranus on the Via Tusculana, fortunately handed down to us and included in the exhibition (n. 330). Exhibited in the middle of the *imagines maiorum* in the tablinum of the house in the climate of genealogical self-glorification of the new patriciate fostered by the Augustan restoration, the throne must have underlined with clear immediacy to those visiting the villa that the ancestry of the *gens* went back to ancient *principes* of the most prestigious civilization in pre-Roman Italy.
[S.B.]

329. Pesaro bilingual inscription
mid-first century B.C.
limestone
172 x 70 cm
Pesaro, Musei Oliveriani, inv. 378
found in reuse within the late-classical walls of Pisaurum, together with a large amount of material coming from a Roman necropolis

On the slab we find side by side the two onomastic formulas of a person of Etruscan birth. After acquiring Roman citizenship in 90 B.C., for about three generations the Etruscans continued to use traditional names next to the official ones of Roman citizens. A series of North-Etruscan funerary inscriptions, known as ìbilingualî, bear both of the deceasedís names; with the exception of some rare older cases, withobvious interferences of the Etruscan epigraphical tradition even in the Latin part, these inscriptions belong for the most part to the second half of the first century B.C. and can be attributed to groups of ruling families connected to one another. The Pesaro bilingual, as well, belongs to this revival of pre-Roman traditions, not extraneous to the Augustan Italicist ideology; it is the only one found outside Etruria, owed probably to the origin of the person, a priest specialized in traditionally Etruscan forms of soothsaying.

Exceptional is the use of a sign to express the sound /o/, lacking in the Etruscan alphabet, and thus derived from the Venetic, clearly proving that the text was conceived in the upper Adriatic area.

Corpus Inscriptionum Latinarum I2, 2127; *Corpus Inscriptionum Latinarum*, Berolini XI, 6363; Dessau 1982–1916, 4958; Conway, Whatmough, Johnson 1933, 346; Degrassi 1965, p. 791; Pallottini 1968, p. 697; Rix 1991, Um 1.7; Rix 1956, p. 155; Benelli 1994, pp. 13–15.
[E.B.]

330. Corsini Throne
ca. 40 B.C.
marble
h 82. 5 cm; diam. 49. 5 cm
Rome, Palazzo Corsini, inv. 666
from Rome, Basilica of San Giovanni in Laterano, below the Corsini Chapel

Throne with cylindrical base and curved back. On the back two figured areas one on top of another, framed above and on the sides by a strand of ivy, while below the frame is a running wave motif. From top to bottom you see a procession of hoplites and horsemen and a hunting scene. The top of the base presents a strand of ivy with curved strands and corymbs with running waves; underneath there is a scene of sacrifice with a procession and a wrestling scene on a frieze with palmettes and hanging ivy leaves. Roman copy of a fifth-century B.C. Etruscan throne, made to celebrate the regal quality of the *gens* of Urguliana, of Etruscan stock, the wife of M. Plautius Silvanus.

Civiltà degli Etruschi, p. 397 n. 19.6; Torelli 1987, pp. 355–67; fig. 1.
[C.Z.]

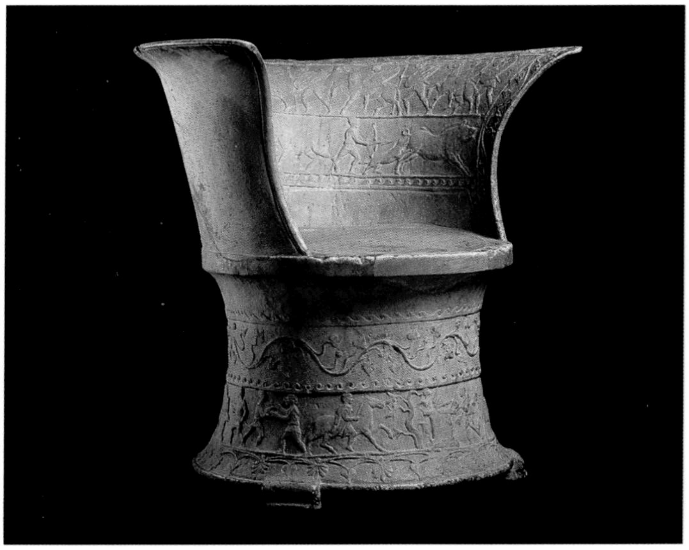

Authors of the Catalogue of Works

A.B.	*Angelo Bottini*
A.B.-W.	*Alfred Bernhard-Walker*
A.E.F.	*Anna Eugenia Feruglio*
A.F.B.	*Anita Feldman Bennet*
A.M.	*Alessandra Minetti*
A.M.E.	*Anna Maria Esposito*
A.M.M.S.	*Anna Maria Moretti Sgubini*
A.P.	*Anna Patera*
A.Pa.	*Alain Pasquier*
A.R .	*Anna Rastrelli*
A.Ro.	*Antonella Romualdi*
A.S.	*Andrea Sartori*
A.T.	*Angelo Timperi*
A.V.S.	*Anne Viola Siebert*
B.B.R.	*Bodil Bundgaard Rasmussen*
B.G.	*Bénédicte Garnier*
B.v.F.L.	*Bettina von Freytag Loringhoff*
C.S.L.	*Christopher S. Lightfoot*
C.Z.	*Cristiana Zaccagnino*
D.C.G.	*Daniela Cocchi Genick*
E.B.	*Enrico Benelli*
E.C.	*Elena Corradini*
E.C.P.	*Elena C. Partida*
E.F.	*Elisabeth Fontan*
E.K.-D.	*Erika Zwierlein-Diehl*
E.L.	*Enzo Lippolis*
E.S.	*Elisabetta Setari*
F.B	*Francesco Buranelli*
F.C.	*Fabio Colivicchi*
F.Ca.	*Fiorenzo Catalli*
F.N.	*Francesco Nicosia*
F.P.	*Federica Pascotto*
F.S.	*Françoise Sarret*
F.T.	*Flavia Tucco*
F.W.H.	*Friedrich Wilhelm Hamdorf*
G.B.	*Gabriele Baldelli*
G.C.	*Gabriele Cateni*
G.C.C.	*Giuseppina Carlotta Cianferoni*
G.M.D.F.	*Giuseppe M. Della Fina*
G.P.	*Giulio Paolucci*
G.Po.	*Gabriella Poggesi*
G.Po.	*Gabriella Poggesi*
G.S.	*Gérard Seiterle*
H.A.G.B.	*H.A.G. Brijder*
H.P.	*Hermann Pflug*
I.B.	*Irene Berlingò*
I.C.	*Ida Caruso*
I.M.	*Inka Mejer*
I.W.	*Irma Wehgartner*
J.B.	*Jane Biers*
J.C.	*Jette Christiansen*
J.O.	*Jacopo Ortalli*
J.S.	*Judith Swadding*
L.L.	*Lucia Lepore*
L.R.	*Laura Ricciardi*
M.A.D.L.B.	*Maria Anna De Lucia Brolli*
M.B.	*Mariarosaria Borriello*
M.C.	*Mariagrazia Celuzza*
M.d.M.	*Maurizia de Min*
M.d.Ma.	*Marco de Marco*
M.M.	*Mauro Menichetti*
M.Ma.	*Michael Maaß*
M.S.	*Maurizio Sannibale*
M.Sc.	*Marisa Scarpignato*
M.T.	*Marcello Tagliente*
M.V.	*Marina Volonté*
N.G.	*N. Gulyaeva*
O.B.-A.	*Odile Berard-Azouz*
P.A.	*Patrizia Aureli*
P.B.	*Paolo Bruschetti*
P.G .	*Pamela Gambogi*
P.I.O.	*Peter Im Obersteg*
P.J.W.	*Patricia J. Whithsides*
P.Z.G.	*Paola Zamarchi Grassi*
R.C.	*Rita Cosentino*
R.M.	*Roberto Macellari*
R.v.B.	*René von Beek*
S.B.	*Stefano Bruni*
S.Bo.	*S. Boriskovskaja*
S.D.S.R.	*Silvia Ducci Sanna Randaccio*
S.G.	*Silvia Goggioli*
S.S.	*Simonetta Stopponi*
U.K.	*Ursula Kästner*
V.K.	*Volker Kästner*
V.S.	*Valeria Sampaolo*

Appendix

Bronze Chimera from Arezzo
late fifth century B.C.
Florence, Museo Archeologico

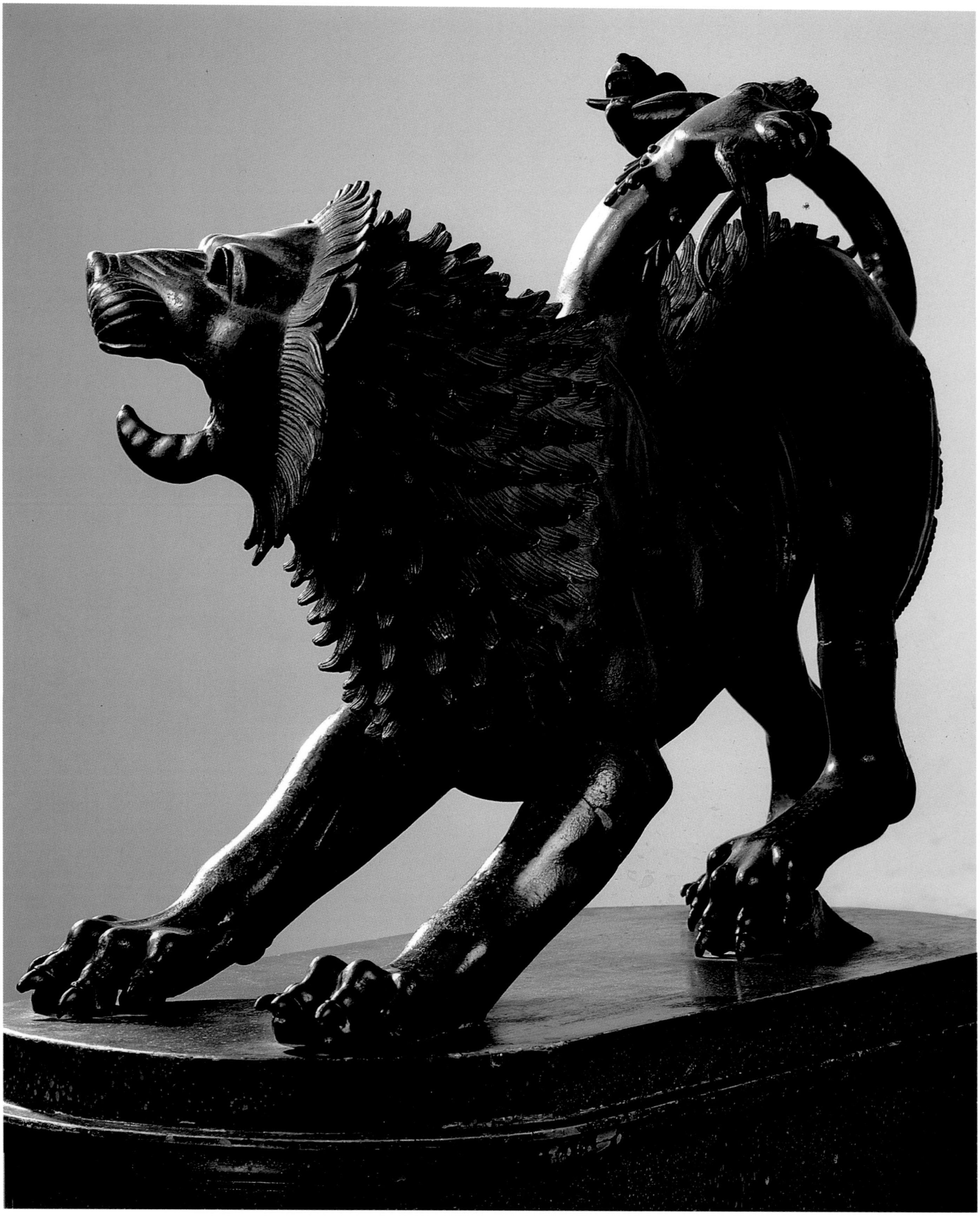

Chronology

by Mauro Menichetti

all dates are approximate and before Christ

Etruscans

Late Bronze Age (1350–1200)

History

- Late Apennine civilization.
- Greatest Mycenaean contacts with the Tyrrhenian and south Italy coasts (Mycenaean III A-B).

Culture

- Sub-Apennine pottery.
- Long distance trading with the Aegean and Central Europe.

Final Bronze Age (1200–1000)

History

- Proto-Villanovan civilization.
- Cessation of Mycenaean contacts.

Culture

- Elaboration of funerary rituals and development of a metallurgical production typical of the mid-Tyrrhenian area.

Beginning of the Iron Age (1000)

History

- Process of private appropriation of land.
- Formation of urban communities: villages abandoned in favor of large inhabited areas of 100–150 hectares.

Culture

- Archaeological evidence of the formation and differentiation of diverse populations in ancient Italy.

Greeks

Mycenaean Age (1600–1200 ca.)

History

- The fortified palaces: Mycenae, Tirinto (Tiryns ?), Pylos.
- Traditional date of the Trojan War (ca. 1200).

Culture

- Construction of the monumental *tholos* tombs.

Geometric Age (1100–750)

History

- Dorian invasion and the destruction of the Mycenaean fortresses.
- So-called Hellenic Middle Ages.
- Formation of the first city-states. Birth of the *polis*.
- The aristocratic city.
- Greek expansion in Asia Minor. Beginning of colonization in the West (ca. 775).
- First evidence of the diffusion of writing.

Culture

- Proto-Geometric and Geometric pottery.
- Construction of the first temple buildings: Thermos, sacellum at the mouth of the Sele River.
- First Olympic Games (776).
- Epic poetry: Homer.

Romans

Middle Bronze Age (1600–1350)

History

- Apennine civilization.
- Settlements on the left bank of the Tiber River and the Capitoline Hill.

Culture

- Apennine pottery.

Late Bronze Age (1350–1200)

History

- Late Apennine civilization.
- Mycenaean contacts.

Culture

- Sub-Apennine pottery.
- Mid-Tyrrhenian area part of a network of long-distance exchanges.

Final Bronze Age (1200–1000)

History

- Sub-Apennine civilization.
- Expansion of the villages into the valley and onto the heights overlooking the Tiber.

Culture

- Formative elements of the legends regarding the formation of Rome: Alba Longa and the kingdom of Picus, Faunus, and Latinus.

Beginning of the Iron Age (1000)

History

- Process of private appropriation of land.
- Evolution of the process of urban formation in line with the development of inhabited areas throughout the mid-Tyrrhenian territory.

Culture

- Differentiation of the peoples of ancient Italy which is settled definitively by Indo-European speaking communities.

I Latial Period (1000–900)

History

- Constitution of the league of the Latin *populi* (peoples) at the federal sanctuary of Iuppiter Latialis on the Alban Hill.

Culture

- Funerary rites including cremation of the deceased and the miniaturisation of his weapons.
- Development of agriculture and the working and circulation of metals.

Etruscans

HISTORY | CULTURE

Villanovan Period
I (900–820)
Intermediate (820–770)
II (770–720)

History
- Formation of Etruscan cities.
- Etruscan colonization in Campania and in Emilia Romagna.
- Phoenician and Euboean navigation begins again.
- Beginnings of Etruscan thalassocracy.
- Foundation of Carthage (814).
- Trading post established at Pithekoussai by Euboeans, Easterners and Etruscans (ca. 775).

Culture
- Process of strong social differentiation evidenced in the necropolises (Veii, Tarquinia).
- Beginnings of a pottery production influenced by the Greek Geometric style.
- Development of agriculture, mining and metalworking.

Orientalizing Period
Ancient (720–670)
Middle (720–670)
Late (630–580)

History
- Phoenician trading posts in Spain, Sardinia and Sicily.
- Beginning of Greek colonization in the West (Cuma, 720).
- Arrival of Demaratus at Tarquinia. His son Tarquinius Priscus becomes King of Rome (615–578).
- Foundation of Marseille by Phocaea (600).
- Flourishing of trading posts (end of seventh century).
- First Celtic incursions in northern Italy (early sixth century).

Culture
- Adoption of the Chalcidian alphabet.
- Diffusion of tumulus graves and palatial buildings (*regiae*).
- Cultivation of the olive and the vine according to Greek methods.
- Adoption of the forms of the Greek symposium.
- Diffusion of construction using durable materials.
- Etrusco-Corinthian and bucchero pottery. Jewellery.
- First examples of painting and large-scale sculpture.
- Introduction of the myths and divinities of the Greek world.

Archaic Age
(580–480)

History
- Second Etruscan colonization of Emilia Romagna and Campania.

Culture
- Palace of Murlo. Architectonic plaques of the so-called I stage.

Greeks

HISTORY | CULTURE

Orientalizing Period
(725–610)

History
- The age of the great tyrannies: Polycrates di Samos, Periander of Corinth.
- Legislation of Draco (ca. 625).
- Introduction of money and the development of a mercantile class.
- Crisis of the *polis*.

Culture
- Proto-Corinthian pottery, proto-Attic pottery.
- Construction of monumental temples: Heraion of Samos, Artemision of Ephesus, Didymaion of Miletus.
- Dedalic style in sculpture.
- The development of epic poetry: Hesiod.

Archaic Age
(610–450)

History
- Reform of Solon (594).
- Tyranny of Pisistratus and Hippias (546–510).

Culture
- Lyric poetry: Alcaeus, Sappho.
- Corinthian style pottery (615–550).

Romans

HISTORY | CULTURE

II Latial Period
A (900–830)
B (830–770)

History
- Proto-urban phase probably corresponding to the inhabited area of the *Septimontium*.

Culture
- Demographic increase.
- Reorganisation and elaboration of cults and rituals.

III Latial Period
A (770–750)
B (750–725)

History
- Boundary of the inhabited area of the *Septimontium* and the construction of a wall circling the Palatine Hill probably corresponding to an earlier urban foundation of the time of Romulus (kingdom of Romulus according to traditional chronology: 753–716).
- Foundation of Rome according to Varro (754–753).

Culture
- Introduction of pottery produced in Greece and the establishment of workshops in which Greek or local artisans imitate the Greek production.

IV Latial Period
A (725–625)
B (625–580)

History
- Construction of a second ring of walls substituting the previous one (700–675).
- Institution of the principal poliadic cults.
- The city expands from the Palatine Hill: the area of the Roman Forum becomes the new political and religious centre after the draining of the swamps in the valley near the Velabro.
- First stages of the *Comitium*, *Regia* and *Atrium Vestae*.
- Reigns of Numa Pompilius (715–672), Tullius Hostilius (672–640), Ancus Marcius (640–616), Tarquinius Priscus (616–578) according to traditional chronology.

Culture
- Strong social differentiation underway.
- An important trading area is set up at the Forum Boarium.
- King Numa Pompilius is attributed with important religious reforms among which the oldest calendar conserved, the so-called Numan calendar.
- Introduction of Grecian manners and ideas such as the symposium, the myth, and the Hellenic divinities, which are reinterpreted according to the indigenous divinities.
- Territorial expansion of Rome into Latium.

Period of the kings or the Etruscan dynasty
(580–509)

History
- The reign of Tarquinius Priscus followed by those of

Culture
- Strengthening of Rome's position in the Tyrrhenian world.

Etruscans

HISTORY

- Development of Spina and Adria and opening to East Greek trade.
- Exploits of Mastarna and the Vibenna brothers.
- Reigns of Servius Tullius (578–534) and Tarquinius Superbus (534–509) in Rome.
- Foundation of Alalia (565) and Velia by the Phoceans (535).
- Battle of the Sardinian Sea (540).
- First battle of Cuma (524).
- Expulsion of the Etruscan kings from Rome (509).
- Exploits of Porsenna.
- Victory of Aristodemos of Cuma and the Latins over the Etruscans, Umbrians and Daunii (battle di Aricia, 504).
- Thefarie Velianas at Caere.

CULTURE

- Urban planning of Etruscan cities and the diffusion of temple buildings.
- Vulca of Veii works on the Temple of Jupiter Capitolinus in Rome.
- Importation of Eastern pottery and subsequently that of Athenian manufacture with red and black figures.
- Establishment of local workshops.
- Tarquinian painted tombs.
- Development and exportation of Etruscan bronzeware.
- Production of Clusine reliefs in stinkstone.

Classical Age
(480–320)

HISTORY

- War Rome-Veii and the slaughter of the Fabii (477).
- Second battle of Cuma and the victory of Syracuse over the Etruscans (474).
- Syracusan incursions in northern Etruria mining territory (453).
- Expansion of Etruria into the Po Valley and inland into the Tiber Valley.
- War Rome-Veii (428).
- Samnite occupation of Capua and end of the Etruscan dominion of Campania (423).
- Etruscan participation in the Athenian expedition against Syracuse (414–413).
- Destruction of Veii by Rome (396).
- Sack of Pyrgi by Syracuse (384).
- War Rome-Tarquinia (358–351).
- Social restructure of the southern Etruscan cities (second half of fourth century).

CULTURE

- Production of bronze candelabra and mirrors.
- Coroplastic production reflects the Greek classical models.
- Clusine cinerary statue.
- End of great pottery production and its revival at Vulci and Volsinii (late fifth century).
- Tomb painting at Tarquinia (Tombs of the Black Sow and Orcus I and II), Vulci (François Tomb) and Volsinii (Golini Tombs I and II).
- Production of marble (Caere, Vulci, Tarquinia) *nenfro* sarcophaghi (Tarquinia).
- Pottery produced in local workshops at Falerii, Caere, Tarquinia, Volsinii, Chiusi and Volterra (fourth–third century).
- Bronze artifacts produced at Volsinii and Arezzo.

Greeks

HISTORY

- Cleisthenes and the democratic reform (509–507).
- First Persian War (490).
- Second Persian War (480–479).

CULTURE

- Beginning of the production of Attic black-figure pottery (610): Kleitias, Amasis, Exekias.
- Beginning of the production of Attic red-figure pottery (530): Oltos, the Kleophrades Painter, Euphronios.
- Severe Style in sculpture.

Classical Age
(450–323)

HISTORY

- The Athens of Pericles and the development of the democratic state (443–429).
- Peloponnesian War (431–404).
- Spartan hegemony (404–378).
- Theban hegemony (377–371).
- The Macedonian apogee: the age of Philip (356–336).
- The age of Alexander the Great (336–323).

CULTURE

- The great constructions of the Acropolis. The Parthenon and the propylaeum: Phidias, Ictinus.
- The great tragedies: Aeschylus, Sophocles, Euripides.
- Historiography: Herodotus, Thucydides.
- Comedy: Aristophanes.
- Polygnotus of Thasos conquers space pictorially.
- Sculpture studies rhythm and movement: Myron, Polyclitus, Praxiteles, Scopas.
- Rhetoric: Lysias, Isocrates, Demosthenes.
- Philosophy: Socrates, Plato, Aristotle.

Romans

HISTORY

Servius Tullius (578–534) and Tarquinius Superbus (534–509) according to trad. chronology.
- Civil reforms attributed to Servius Tullius.
- Expulsion of Tarquinius Superbus (509).

CULTURE

- Re-elaboration and establishment of rituals relative to regality, among which the triumphal ceremony.
- Emergence of social groups connected to commerce, exchange, and crafts.

Early Republican Period
(509–366)

HISTORY

- Foundation of the Republic (509).
- First treaty Rome-Carthage (509).
- Battle of Cuma (504).
- Succession of the *plebs*, tribunate (493).
- Treaty Rome-Latins (493).
- Slaughter of the Fabii (477).
- Decemvirs and Laws of Twelve Tables (451–450).
- Government of *tribuni militum* (444–366).
- War Rome-Veii (428).
- Roman conquest of Fidene (426).
- Conquest of Veii (405–396).
- Conquest of Falerii (394).
- Sack of Rome by the Gauls (390).
- Conquest of Praeneste (380).
- Licinio-Sextian Laws (366).

CULTURE

- Completion of the temple of Jupiter Capitolinus.
- Temple of Saturn (497).
- The Greek artisans Damofilus e Gorgasus work on the Temple of Ceres, Liber e Libera (496–494).
- Temple of the Dioscuri (484).
- Temple of Semo Sancus Divus Fidius (466)
- Execution of the Capitoline Shewolf.
- End of the intensive trading and artisan production of the preceding period.
- Stasis of temple dedications and the so-called fifth century B.C. crisis.
- Revival of dedications with the Temple of Apollo Medicus (431).
- Dedication of the first honorary statues

Middle Republican Period
(366–201)

HISTORY

- War Rome-Tarquinia (358–351).
- Rome dissolves the Latin League (338).
- Roman victory over the Etruscans, Gauls, Umbrians and Samnites at Sentino (295).
- Second Roman-Carthaginian treaty (279).
- War against Tarantum (282–272).
- Roman victory over Pyrrhus in the battle of Beneventum (275).
- Foundation of Cosa and Paestum (273).
- First Punic War (264–241).

CULTURE

- Construction of the Appian Way (312).
- Development of a mid-Italic *koine* following the Roman expansion.
- Organization of the area of the Roman Forum by Gaius Menius (318).
- Paintings with military scenes from a tomb on the Esquiline.
- Paintings in the Temple of Salus by Fabius Pictor (303).
- Elaboration of the *tabulae triumphales*.
- Tomb of the Scipios (280).

Etruscans

Hellenistic Age
(320–27)

HISTORY

• Roman intervention in support of the aristocratic faction of Arezzo (302). Roman victory at Sentino over the Etruscans, Gauls, Umbrians and Samnites (295).
• Roman victory over Roselle (292). Roman triumph over Vulci and Volsinii (280).
• Foundation of the Latin colony of Cosa by Rome in Etruscan territory (273).
• Roman conquest of Volsinii (264).
• Roman conquest of Falerii (241).
• Contribution of the Etruscan cities to the Roman expedition against Scipio (205).
• The Social War and the granting of Roman citizenship to the Italians south of the Po River (90–88).
• Sulla's expeditions against the Etruscan cities (83–82).
• War of Perugia and the end of the Etruscan nation (41–40).
• Etruria becomes part of the *Regio* VII in the Augustan division of Italy (27).

CULTURE

• Production of terra-cotta and bronze votive offerings in the shape of heads and body parts.
• Coroplastic production for temples adopts the full pediment.
• Production of earthenware sarcophagi at Tuscania and Clusium.
• Workshops producing funerary urns at Clusium, Volterra and Perugia.
• Tarquinian painted tombs.
• Production of bronzes in Arezzo (*Arringatore*).

Greeks

Hellenistic Age
(323–31)

HISTORY

• The great Hellenistic kingdoms arise from the ashes of Alexander's empire.
• Struggle for power among the Diadochi (323–280).
• End of the struggle and the formation of three great monarchies: Macedon, Antigonids; Asia Minor, Seleucids; Egypt, Ptolemies.
• Beginning of the Roman expansion in the East.
• Macedonian Wars. First interventions of Rome in Greece (215–168).
• Destruction of Corinth by Rome. Greece becomes a Roman province (146).
• Attalus III bequeaths the kingdom of Pergamum to Rome (133).
• Fall of the last Hellenistic kingdoms. Rome commands the entire Mediterranean.
• Pompey conquers the kingdom of the Seleucides (70–65).
• Battle of Actium. Egypt becomes a Roman province (31).

CULTURE

• Development of Greek (*koine*) which becomes the principal language of the entire Mediterranean.
• The great libraries of Alexandria, Pergamum and Antioch.
• Pottery of Paestum and Campania.
• New Comedy: Menander.
• The search for drama in sculpture: Leochares and Lysippus.
• The mosaics at Pella.
• Construction of the Lighthouse of Alexandria (ca. 280).
• Beginning of the baroque and alexandrine styles in sculpture (265).
• Pottery of Kales (250).
• Celebratory poetry: Callimachus.
• Pastoral poetry: Theocritus.
• The new epic: Apollonius of Rhodes.
• Development of the sciences: Archimedes and Eratosthenes.
• The Pergamene school of sculpture.
• Altar of Pergamum.
• Neo-Attic sculpture.

Romans

HISTORY

• Repeated campaigns against the Gauls and Insubres: Roman occupation of Mediolanum (222).
• First Macedonian War (215–205).
• Second Punic War (218–201).

CULTURE

• Development of the so-called Italic portraiture (Brutus Capitolinus).
• Conquest of Syracuse (212) and decisive opening to Grecian world.

Late Republican Period
(201–31)

HISTORY

• Second Macedonian War (200–196) and victory of Flamininus at Cynoscephalae (197).
• Repeated campaigns in Spain (198–178).
• The Syrian War (192–189) and peace of Apamea (188).
• Third Macedonian War(172–167)and defeat of Perseus at Pydna by Lucius Aemilius Paullus (167).
• Third Punic War (149–146).
• Kingdom of Pergamum bequeathed to Rome (133).
• Agrarian Laws of Tiberius Sempronius Gracchus (133).
• Beginning of Jugurtha's anti-Roman campaign in Africa (112).
• Mario's triumph over Jugurtha (104).
• Social War (91–89).
• First Mithridatic War (88–85). Sullan reforms (88).
• Civil War between Marius and Sulla (87).
• Death of Marius (86).
• Second Mithridatic War (83–82).
• Dictatorship of Sulla (82–81).
• Third Mithridatic War (73–63).
• Conspiracy of Catiline (63).
• First triumvirate (60).
• Caesar in Gaul (58–51).
• Death of Crassus (53)
• Caesar crosses the Rubicon (49).
• Victory of Caesar against Pompey (48).
• Murder of Caesar; second triumvirate (43).
• Battle of Actium (31).

CULTURE

• Introduction of artistic and architectonic forms inspired by Hellenistic models.
• Success of Italic merchants in the East.
• Diffusion of great wealth that senatorial sources brand as *luxuria Asiatica.*
• Stimulus for the urbanisation of Roman Italy.
• Economy based on slave labor: construction of the great villas.
• System of building construction ranging from *opus incertum* to *opus reticulatum* entrusted to slave labour.
• Diffusion of "Achilleae" statues celebrating the *virtus* of generals and commanders.
• Diffusion of a standardised craft production.
• The- Roman house imitates the luxurious Hellenistic models.
• I and II Style painting.
• Struggle for power and propaganda based on the models of the Hellenistic dynasties.
• Urban transformation of Rome according to the projects of Pompey and Caesar.
• Augustan reorganisation of political, social and religious life of the Roman Empire.

A

Adam A.M., Briquel D., Massa-Pairault F.-H. • 1977 "Marzabotto. Recherches sur l'insula," in *Mélanges de l'Ecole Française de Rome*, V, 3; **Adam R., Briquel D., Gran-Aymerich K. et al.** • 1992 *I rapporti transalpini*, in G. Camporeale (ed. by), *Gli Etruschi e l'Europa*, ex. cat., Paris-Berlin, Milano; **Adembri B.** • 1990 *La più antica produzione di ceramica falisca a figure rosse. Inquadramento stilistico e cronologico*, in *La civiltà dei Falisci*, proceeding of the XVConvegno di studi etruschi e italici, Civita Castellana 1987, Firenze; **Agostiniani L.** • 1982 *Le iscrizioni parlanti dell'Italia antica*, Firenze • 1984 "La sequenza eiminipicapi e la negazione in etrusco," in *Archivio Glottologico Italiano*, 69 • 1986 "Sull'etrusco della Stele di Lemno e su alcuni aspetti del consonantismo etrusco," in *Archivio Glottologico Italiano*, 71 • 1992 "Contribution à l'étude de l'épigraphie et de la linguistique Étrusques," in *Lalies*, 11 • 1993 "La considerazione tipologica nello studio dell'etrusco," in *Incontri Linguistici*, 16 • 1995a "Sui numerali etruschi e la loro rappresentazione grafica," in *Annali di Studi del Mondo Antico*, L, 17 • 1995b *Genere grammaticale, genere naturale e il trattamento di alcuni prestiti lessicali in etrusco*, in *Studi linguistici per i 50 anni del Circolo Linguistico Fiorentino*, Firenze • 2000 *Il vino degli Etruschi: la lingua*, in D.Tommasi, C.Cremonesi (ed. by), *L'avventura del vino nel bacino del Mediterraneo. Itinerari storici e archeologici prima e dopo Roma*, proceeding of the international symposium, Conegliano Veneto 1998, Treviso; **Agostiniani L., Nicosia F.** • 2000 "Tabula Cortonensis," in *Studia Archaeologica*, 105; **Aigner Foresti L.** • 1980 *Der Ostalpenraum und Italien: ihre kulturellen Beziehungen im Spiegel der anthropomorphen Kleinplastik aus Bronze des 7. Jh.s v. Chr.*, Firenze • 1992a *Gli Etruschi e la loro autocoscienza*, in "Autocoscienza e rappresentazione dei popoli nell'antichità," in *Contributi dell'Istituto di Storia Antica*, 18 • 1992b *Relazioni protostoriche tra Italia ed Europa centrale*, in G. Camporeale (ed. by), *Gli Etruschi e l'Europa*, ex. cat., Paris-Berlin, Milano; **Akerstrom** E. • 1943 "Der geometrische Stil in Italien," in *Acta Instituti Romani Suedici*, IX, Lund; **Albanese Procelli M. R.** • 1985 *Considerazioni sulla distribuzione dei bacini bronzei in area tirrenica e in Sicilia*, in *Il commercio etrusco arcaico*, proceeding of the meeting, Roma 5–7 december 1983, C.N.R., Roma; **Albizzati C.** • 1922-1942 *Vasi antichi dipinti del Vaticano*, Città del Vaticano; **Almagro Gorbea M. et al.** • 1990 "Cancho Roano. Un palacio orientalizante en la Península Ibérica," in *Madrider Mitteilungen*, 31; **Amadasi M.G** • 1991 "Coppe 'orientali' nel Mediterraneo occidentale: qualche nota," in *Scienze dell'Antichità*, V; **Ampolo C.** • 1994 *Tra empória e emporía: note sul commercio greco in età arcaica e classica*, in "Apoikia. Scritti in onore di G. Buchner," in *Annali dell'Istituto universitario orientale di Napoli. Sezione di archeologia e storia antica* • 1980a "Le condizioni materiali della produzione. Agricoltura e paesaggio agrario," in *Dialoghi di Archeologia*, n.s. 2 • 1980b *La città antica. Guida storica e critica*, Roma-Bari • 1981 "Il gruppo acroteriale di Sant'Omobono," in *La Parola del Passato* • 1984 "Il lusso funerario e la città antica," in *Annali dell'Istituto universitario orientale di Napoli. Sezione di archeologia e storia antica*, VI; **Andren A.** • 1939 *Architectural Terracottas from Etrusco-Italic Temples,* Lund-Leipzig; **Annali** • 1981 *Annali della Facoltà di Lettere e Filosofia dell'Università di Siena*, II; **Architettura etrusca** • 1986 *Architettura etrusca nel Viterbese*, Roma; **Arietti F., Martellotta B., Ghini G.** • 1987 "Recupero di una tomba orientalizzante presso Rocca di Papa," in *Archeologia Laziale*, VIII, Roma; **Arrigoni G.** • 1985 *Le donne in Grecia*, Bari; **Artigianato artistico** • 1985 *Artigianato artistico. L'Etruria settentrionale interna in età ellenistica,* ex. cat., Volterra-Chiusi, Milano; **Asheri D.** • 1975 "Osservazioni sulle origini dell'urbanistica ippodamea," in *Rivista Storica Italiana*, 77; **Aspetti delle aristocrazie** • 1984 "Aspetti delle aristocrazie fra VIII e VII secolo a.C.," in *Opus*, III, 2; **Aubet M.E.** • 1971 *Los marfiles orientalizantes de Praeneste*, Barcelona;

B

Baglione M.P., De Lucia Brolli M.A. • 1998 "Documenti inediti nell'Archivio storico del Museo di villa Giulia. Contributi all'archeologia di Narce," in *Archeologia Classica*, 50; **Bagnasco Gianni G.** • 1996a "Imprestiti greci nell'Etruria del VII secolo a.C.: osservazioni archeologiche sul nome dei vasi," in A. Aloni, L. Delfinis (ed. by), *Dall'Indo a Thule: i Greci, i Romani, gli altri*, proceeding of the international meeting, Trento • 1996b *Oggetti iscritti di epoca orientalizzante in Etruria*, Firenze • 1999a La ceramica depurata 'acroma' e 'a bande'," in Chr. Chiaramonte Treré (ed. by) *Tarquinia. Scavi sistematici nell'abitato. Campagne 1982-1988. I materiali 1*, Roma; **Bagnasco Gianni G., Cordano F.** • 1999 *Scritture mediterranee tra il IX e il VII secolo a.C.,* Milano; **Bailo Modesti G.** • 1998 "Coppe a semicerchi penduli nella necropoli di Pontecagnano," in M. Bats, B. d'Agostino (ed. by), *Euboica. L'Eubea e la presenza euboica in Calcidica e in Occidente*, Napoli; **Baldelli G.** • 1996 "Fermo preromana: regesto e bibliografia dei rinvenimenti," in E. Catani (ed. by), *I beni culturali di Fermo e territorio,* Fermo • 1998 "Fermo. Necropoli villanoviane," in E. Percossi (ed. by), *Museo archeologico nazionale delle Marche: Sezione protostorica*, Falconara; **Barbieri G.** • 1987 *L'alimentazione nel mondo antico. Gli Etruschi*, ex. cat., Roma; **Barnabei M., Delpino F.** • 1991 *Le "Memorie di un Archeologo" di Felice Barnabei*, Roma; **Barocchi P., Gallo D.** • 1985 *L'Accademia etrusca*, ex. cat., Cortona, Firenze-Milano; **Bartoccini R., De Agostino A.** • 1961 *Museo di Villa Giulia. Antiquarium e collezione dei vasi Castellani*, Milano; **Bartoli L.** • 1945 "Progetto di massima per la sistemazione dell'ala ovest del fabbricato destinato al nuovo ingresso del Museo archeologico ed a sede dell'Istituto internazionale di studi etruschi ed italici," in *Studi etruschi*, 18; **Bartoloni G.** • 1984 "Riti funerari dell'aristocrazia in Etruria e nel Lazio. L'esempio di Veio," in *Opus*, III, 1 • 1986 "La storia del popolamento nell'Etruria meridionale protostorica. Aspetti e problemi," in *Analecta romana Instituti danici*, 15 • 1987 "Esibizione di ricchezza a Roma nel VI e V secolo. Doni votivi e corredi funerari," in *Scienze dell'Antichità*, I • 1989 *La cultura villanoviana. All'inizio della storia etrusca*, Roma • 1991 "Populonium etruscorum quodam hoc tantum in litore: aspetti e carattere di una comunità costiera nella prima età del ferro. Studi in onore di M. Pallottino," in *Archeologia Classica*, XLIII • forthcoming "Le strutture a tholos della prima età del ferro, in L'architettura funeraria a Populonia tra IX e VIII secolo a.C.," in *Quaderni del Dipartimento di Archeologia e Storia delle Arti, Sezione Archeologica*, Università di Siena, Populonia 1997; **Bartoloni G., Baglione M.P.** • 1987 "Elementi scultorei decorativi nelle tombe tarquiniesi del primo Ellenismo," in *Tarquinia: ricerche, scavi e prospettive*, proceeding of the meeting, Milano 1986, Milano; **Bartoloni G., Berardinetti A., De Santis A., Drago L.** • 1997 "Le necropoli villanoviane di Veio. Parallelismi e differenze," in *Le necropoli arcaiche di Veio*, symposium devoted to the memory of Massimo Pallottino, Roma; **Bartoloni G., Buranelli F., D'Atri V.** • 1987 *Le urne a capanna rinvenute in Italia*, Roma; **Bartoloni G., Cataldi Dini M., Zevi F.** • 1982 "Aspetti dell'ideologia funeraria nella necropoli di Castel di Decima," in G. Gnoli, J.-P. Vernant (ed. by), *La mort, les morts dans les sociétés anciennes*, Cambridge-Paris; **Bartoloni G., De Santis A.** • 1995 "La deposizione di scudi nelle tombe di VIII e VII secolo a.C. nell'Italia centrale tirrenica," in N. Negroni Catacchio (ed. by), *Preistoria e protostoria in Etruria. Tipologia delle necropoli e rituali di deposizione. Ricerche e scavi*, proceeding of the Farnese meeting 1993, Milano; **Bartoloni G., Delpino F.** • 1979 *Veio I. Introduzione allo studio delle necropoli arcaiche di Veio. Il sepolcreto di Valle la Fata*, Roma; **Bats M.** • 1988 *Vaisselle et alimentation à Olbia de Provence. Modèles culturels et catégories céramiques*, Paris • 1998a *Euboica. L'Eubea e la presenza euboica in Calcidica e in Occidente*, proceeding of the international meeting, Napoli 1996, Napoli • 1998b "Marseille archaïque. Etrusques et Phocéens en Méditerranée nord-occidentale," in *Mélanges de l'Ecole francaise de Rome. Antiquité*, 110; **Baurain Cl., Bonnet C., Krings V.** • 1991 *Phoinikeia Grammata, Lire et écrire en Méditerranée*, Namur; **Bayet J.** • 1929 *Herclé. Étude critique sur les principaux monuments relatifs à l'Hercule étrusque*, Paris; **Bearzley J.D., Magi F.** • 1939 *La raccolta Benedetto Guglielmi nel Museo Gregoriano Etrusco. I. Ceramica*, Città del Vaticano; **Beazley J.D.** • 1947 *Etruscan Vase-Painting*, Oxford; **Becatti G.** • 1955 *Oreficerie antiche dalle minoiche alle barbariche*, Roma; **Bedini A.** • 1984 "Struttura ed organizzazione delle tombe 'principesche' nel Lazio. Acqua Acetosa Laurentina: un esempio," in *Opus*, III, 2, • 1985 "Tre corredi protostorici dal Torrino. Osservazioni sull'affermarsi e la funzione delle aristocrazie terriere nell'VIII secolo a.C. nel Lazio," in *Archeologia Laziale*, VII, Roma; **Bedini A., Cordano F.** • 1977 "L'ottavo secolo nel Lazio e l'inizio dell'Orientalizzante Antico alla luce delle recenti scoperte di Decima," in *La Parola del Passato*; **Beijer A. J.** • 1978 "Proposta per una suddivisione delle anfore a spirali," in *Mededelingen van het Nederlands Instituut te Rome*, XL; **Benelli E.** • 1996 "'Sui cosiddetti penesti etruschi," in *La Parola del Passato*, LI; **Bentz M.** • 1992 *Etruskische Votivbronzen des Hellenismus,* Firenze; **Berardinetti Insam A.** • 1990 "La fase iniziale della necropoli villanoviana di Quattro Fontanili. Rapporti con le comunità limitrofe," in *Dialoghi di Archeologia*, I; **Bergamini M.** • 1991 *Gli Etruschi maestri di idraulica*, Perugia; **Bermond Montanari G.** • 1987 *La formazione della città in Emilia Romagna. Prime esperienze urbane attraverso le nuove scoperte archeologiche*, ex. cat., Bologna; **Berti F.** • 1985 *Spina: l'abitato alla luce degli ultimi scavi*, in *La Romagna tra VI e IV sec. a.C. nel quadro della protostoria dell'Italia centrale*, Imola; **Berti F., Bonomi S., Landolfi M.** • 1996 *Classico e Anticlassico. Vasi alto-adriatici tra Piceno Spina e Adria*, ex. cat., Comacchio, San Giovanni in Persiceto; **Berti F., Guzzo P.** • 1993 *Spina. Storia di una città tra Greci ed Etruschi*, ex. cat., Ferrara; **Beschi L.** • 1996 "Atitas," in *La Parola del Passato*, CCLXXXVII • 1998a "Arte e cultura di Lemnos arcaica," in *La Parola del Passato*, CCXCVIII • 1998b "Nuove iscrizioni da Efestia," in *Annuario della Scuola Archeologica di Atene e delle Missioni Italiane in Oriente*, LXX–LXXI; **Bettelli M.** • 1997 *Roma. La città prima di una città:*

i tempi di una nascita, Roma; **Bettini M.C.** • 2000 "L'età del Ferro," in A. Rastrelli (ed. by), *Chiusi etrusca*, Chiusi; **Bianchi Bandinelli R.** • 1973 *Storicità dell'Arte Classica*, Bari; **Bickerman E.J.** • 1985 "Religions and Politics in the Hellenistic and Roman Periods," (*Origines gentium*, in *Classical Philology*, 47, 1952), Como; **Bieg G.** • 1995 *Studien zu griechischen und etruskischen Bronzekesseln und Stabdreifüssen archaischer Zeit*, Tübingen; **Bietti Sestieri A.M.** • 1981 *Produzione e scambio nell'italia protostorica*, in *L'Etruria mineraria*, proceeding of the XII Convegno di studi etruschi e italici, Firenze • 1998 "L'Italia in Europa nella prima età del Ferro: una proposta di ricostruzione storica," in *Archeologia Classica*, L; **Bizzarri M.** • 1966 "La necropoli di Crocifisso del tufo," in *Studi etruschi*, 34; **Bizzarri M., Costa A.** • 1962 "La necropoli di Crocifisso del tufo in Orvieto. Appendice 1-2," in *Studi etruschi*, 30; **Bloch R.** • 1970 "Urbanisme et religion chez les Etrusques. Explication d'un passage fameux de Servius," in *Annales. Economies, Sociétés, Civilisations*, 25 • 1976 *Prodigi e divinazione nel mondo antico*, Milano; **Blumhofer M.** • 1993 *Die etruskische Cippi. Untersuchungen am Beispiel von Cerveteri*, Koln-Weimar; **Boardman J.** • 1968 *Archaic Greek Gems. Schools and Artists in the Sixth and Early Fifth Centuries BC*, London • 1970 *Greek Gems and Finger Rings, Early Bronze Age to Late Classical*, London • 1975 *Intaglios and Rings Greek, Etruscan and Eastern from a Private Collection*, London; **Bocci Pacini P.** • 1982 *Dal Museo archeologico nazionale del Pigorini al Museo topografico del Milani*, in "Luigi Adriano Milani: origini e sviluppo del Complesso Museale archeologico di Firenze," in *Studi e Materiali*, vol. 5 (n. s.) • 1983 "Considerazioni sulla storia del Museo archeologico di Firenze," in *Bollettino di Archeologia*, with appendix by L. Garella; **Boethius A.** • 1964 "The Old Etruscan Towns. A Scetch," in *Classical, mediaeval and Renaissance studies in honor of B.L. Ullman* , Roma; **Boëthius A., Ward Perkins J.B.** • 1978 *Etruscan and Early Roman Architecture*, Harmondsworth; **Boitani F.** • 1983a *Museo di villa Giulia*, Roma • 1983b "Veio: la tomba 'principesca' della necropoli di Monte Michele," in *Studi etruschi*, LI, • 1998 *Il carro di Castro dalla tomba della Biga*, in *Carri da guerra e principi etruschi*, ex. cat., Viterbo; **Boitani F., Cataldi, M. et al.** • 1978 *Le città etrusche*, III ed., Verona; **Boldrini S.** • 1994 *Gravisca. Scavi nel santuario greco : le ceramiche ioniche*, Bari; **Bonamente G., Coarelli F.** • 1996 *Assisi e gli Umbri nell'antichità*, proceeding of the meeting, Assisi; **Bonamici M.** • 1974 *I buccheri con figurazioni graffite*, Firenze • 1985a "L'uso del marmo nell'Etruria settentrionale. Le statue funerarie," in *Artigianato artistico. L'Etruria settentrionale interna in età ellenistica*, ex. cat., Volterra-Chiusi, Milano • 1985b *La plastica votiva*, in *Artigianato artistico. L'Etruria settentrionale interna in età ellenistica*, ex. cat., Volterra-Chiusi, Milano • 1991 "Contributo alla bronzistica etrusca tardo-classica," in *Prospettiva*, 62 • 1996a "Apo dè Antiou.... Contributo alle rotte arcaiche nell'alto Tirreno," in *Studi etruschi*, LXI • 1996b "La Proserpina del Catajo ritrovata," in *Prospettiva*, 81; **Bonfante L.** • 1994 "Etruscan Women," in *Women in the Classical World*, New York-Oxford; **Bonghi Jovino M.** • 1986a *Gli Etruschi di Tarquinia*, ex. cat., Milano, Modena • 1986b *Gli Etruschi e la Magna Grecia*, in *Rasenna. Storia e civiltà degli Etruschi*, Milano • 1993 *Produzione artigianale nel mondo antico. Il bucchero etrusco*, Milano; **Bonghi Jovino M., Chiaromonte Treré C.** • 1997 *Tarquinia. Testimonanze Archeologiche e ricostruzione storica. Scavi sistematici nell'abitato. Campagne 1982-1988*, Roma; **Bonomi Ponzi L.** • 1997 *La necropoli plestina di Colfiorito di Foligno*, Perugia; **Bordenache Battaglia G., Emiliozzi A.** • 1986–90 *Le ciste prenestine. Corpus*, Roma; **Borsi F.** • 1982 *La città degli Uffizi*, ex. cat., Firenze; **Borsi G.F.** • 1985 *Fortuna degli Etruschi*, ex. cat., Firenze, Firenze-Milano; **Bottini A.** • 1996 "Il vasellame metallico," in *Greci, Enotri, Lucani nella Basilicata meridionale*, ex. cat., Policoro, Napoli • 1999 "Principi e re dell'Italia meridionale arcaica," in *Les princes de la protohistoire et l'émergence de l'état, Actes de la table ronde internationale*, Napoli-Roma • forthcoming "Gli Etruschi fuori d'Etruria. La Lucania," in G. Camporeale (ed. by); **Bottini A., Setari E.** • 1996 "Il mondo enotrio fra Greci ed Etruschi," in *Greci, Enotri, Lucani nella Basilicata meridionale*, ex. cat., Policoro, Napoli; **Bottini A., Tagliente M.** • 1994 "Osservazioni sulle importazioni etrusche in area lucana," in *Magna Grecia Etruschi Fenici*, proceeding of the XXIII Convegno sulla Magna Grecia, Taranto 1993, Napoli; **Botto M.** • 1993 "Anfore fenicie dai contesti indigeni del Latium Vetus nel periodo orientalizzante," supplement to *Rivista di Studi Fenici*, 21 • 1995 "I commerci fenici nel Tirreno centrale: conoscenze, problemi e prospettive," in *I Fenici: ieri, oggi domani. Ricerche, scoperte, progetti*, Roma • forthcoming "Tripodi siriani e tripodi fenici dal Latium Vetus e dall'Etruria meridionale," in *La ceramica fenicia di Sardegna*, proceeding of the I Congresso internazionale sulcitano; **Bouke van der Meer L.** • 1986 "Le jeu de Truia. Le programme iconographique de l'oenochoé de Tragliatella," in *Ktema*, XI; **Bouloumié B.** • 1973 *Les oenochoés de bronze du type "Schnabelkanne" en Italie*, Roma • 1985 "Les vases de bronze etrusques et leur diffusion hors d'Italie," in *Il commercio etrusco arcaico*, proceeding of the meeting, Roma 5–7 december 1983, C.N.R., Roma • 1986 "A propos des fortifications d'Etrurie," in *La fortification dans l'histoire du monde grec*, Paris • 1989 "L'Etrurie et les ressources de la Gaule," in *Atti del II Congresso Internazionale Etrusco*, Firenze 1985, Roma; **Bound M.** • 1991 *The Giglio Wreck*, Atene; **Braccesi L.** • 1998 "Erodoto e l'origine degli Etruschi," in *Hesperia*, 9; **Braun E.** • 1837 "Museo Gregoriano d'etruschi monumenti," in *Bull.Ist.*, pp. 1–10; **Brendel O.J.** • 1978 *Etruscan Art*, Harmondsworth; **Briguet M.F.** • 1989 *Le Sarcofage des Epoux de Cerveteri du Musée du Louvre*, Firenze; **Briquel D.** • 1984 *Les Pélasges en Italie, recherches sur l'histoire de la légende* (Bibliothèque des Écoles Françaises d'Athènes et de Rome, 252), Roma • 1986 "Visions étrusques de l'autochtonie," in *Dialogues d'Histoire Ancienne*, 12 • 1991 *L'origine lydienne des Étrusques, histoire du thème dans la littérature antique*, (Collection de l'École Française de Rome, 139), Roma • 1993a *Les Étrusques peuple de la différence*, Paris • 1993b *Les Tyrrhènes, peuple des tours, l'autochtonie des Étrusques chez Denys d'Halicarnasse*, (Collection de l'École Française de Rome, 178) Roma; **Briquel D., Gaultier F.** • 1997 *Les Étrusques, les plus religieux des hommes*, Paris; **Brize Ph.** • 1991 "Archäische Bronzevotive aus dem Heraion von Samos," in *Scienze dell'Antichità*, 3–4; **Brocato P.** • 1995 "Sull'origine e lo sviluppo delle prime tombe a dado etrusche. Diffusione di un tipo architettonico da Cerveteri a San Giuliano," in *Studi etruschi*, 61; **Broise H., Jolivet, V.** • 1986 "Musarna," in *Studi etruschi*, 54 • 1997 *Une colonie étrusque en territoire tarquinien*, in *Académie des incriptions et belles lettres. Comptes rendus des séances de l'année 1960*; **Brown W.L.** • 1960 *The Etruscan Lion*, Oxford; **Bruni S.** • 1986a "Chianciano, via Tagliamento: Tombe A e A[1]," in A.Rastrelli (ed. by), *Le necropoli etrusche di Cianciano Terme*, Cianciano Terme • 1986b *I lastroni a scala*, (Materiali del Museo archeologico nazionale di Tarquinia, 9), Roma • 1989a "Attorno alla Tomba del Bronzetto d'offerente di Populonia," in *Römische Mitteilungen*, 96 • 1989b "Note su un gruppo di oinochóai di bucchero con decorazione a stampo di produzione tarquiniese," in *Annali dell'Istituto universitario orientale di Napoli. Sezione di archeologia e storia antica*, XI • 1991 "Materiali tarquiniesi del Museo Archeologico di Firenze: i lastroni a scala," in *Studi e Materiali*, VI • 1993 "Ceramiche sovradipinte del V sec. a.C. dal territorio chiusino: il Gruppo Vagnonville. Una proposta di definizione," in *La civiltà di Chiusi e del suo territorio*, proceeding of the XVII Convegno di studi etruschi ed italici, Chianciano Terme 1989, Firenze • 1994 "L'altare arcaico del tempio di Fiesole e la tradizione delle 'pietre fiesolane'," in *Archeologia Classica*, XLVI • 1995 "Dai '2 Trattenimenti popolari sulla storia della Maremma' a 'Vetulonia e la sua necropoli antichissima': appunti per una biografia di Isidoro Falchi," in S. Bruni (ed. by), *Isidoro Falchi un medico al servizio dell'archeologia. Un protagonista della ricerca italiana di fine Ottocento*, Pontedera • 1996 "Appunti su alcune sculture populoniesi di età ellenistica," in *Studi etruschi*, LXII • 1997 *La Valdera e le Colline Pisane Inferiori: appunti per la storia del popolamento*, in *Aspetti della cultura di Volterra etrusca fra l'Età del Ferro e l'Età Ellenistica*, proceeding of the XIX Convegno di studi etruschi e italici, Volterra 15–19 october 1995, Firenze • 1998a *Pisa etrusca. Anatomia di una città scomparsa*, Milano • 1998b "Una 'pietra scema'. Contributo allo studio della statuaria etrusca di età arcaica dell'Etruria settentrionale," in *In memoria di Enrico Paribeni*, Roma • 1999 "I confini del territorio della polis pisana in età arcaica. Una proposta," in *Athenaeum*; **Buranelli F.** • 1983 *La necropoli villanoviana "Le Rose" di Tarquinia*, Roma • 1985 *L'urna Calabresi di Cerveteri*, Roma • 1987 *Testa di Eracle*, in *La tomba François di Vulci*, ex. cat., Città del Vaticano • 1988 *Divagazioni vulcenti*, in *La coroplastica templare etrusca fra il IV e il II secolo a.C.*, proceeding of the XVI Convegno di studi etruschi e italici, Orbetello • 1989 *La raccolta Giacinto Guglielmi*, ex. cat., Roma; • 1991a "Si sarebbe potuta chiamare "vulcente" la cultura villanoviana," in *Bollettino dei Musei e Gallerie Pontificie*, 11; • 1991b *Gli scavi a Vulci della Società Vincenzo Campanari - Governo Pontificio (1835-1837)*, Roma • 1997 F. Buranelli (ed. by) *La raccolta Giacinto Guglielmi, I, La ceramica* (Museo Gregoriano Etrusco, Cataloghi, 4.1), Città del Vaticano; **Buranelli F. Sannibale M.** • 1998 "Reparto di antichità etrusco italiche (1984-1996)," in *BmonMusPont*, 18, pp. 136–44; **Burkert W.** • 1992 *The Orientalizing Revolution. Near Eastern Influence in the Early Archaic Age*, Cambridge (Mass.) • 1999 *Da Omero ai Magi. La tradizione orientale nella cultura greca*, Padova;

C

Cagianelli C. • 1999 *Bronzi a figura umana* (Museo Gregoriano Etrusco, Cataloghi, 5), Città del Vaticano; • forthcoming "La stipe di Mandoleto (Perugia). Nuovi-vecchi dati per lo studio dei culti del Trasimeno," in *Depositi votivi e culti dell'Italia antica dall'età arcaica a quella tardo-repubblicana*, proceeding of the meeting, Perugia 2000 • 1995–96 "Il tempio etrusco di Fiesole: due secoli di indagini," in *Annuario Accademia Etrusca di Cortona*, XXVII • 1999a *Bronzi a figura umana* (Museo Gregoriano Etrusco, Cataloghi, 5), Città del Vaticano • 1999b *Monumenti Musei e Gallerie Pontificie. Bronzi a figura umana*, Roma; **CAMBITOGEON A.** • 1995 "Lucani, vasi," in *Enciclopedia dell'arte antica*, II supplement, III, Roma; **CAMPANELLI A., FAUSTOFERRI A.** • 1997 *I luoghi degli dei. Sacro e natura nell'Abruzzo italico*, ex. cat., Pescara; **CAMPOREALE G.** • 1958 "Sull'organizzazione statuale degli Etruschi," in *La Parola del Passato*, LVIII • 1972a *Buccheri a cilindretto di fabbrica orvietana*, Firenze • 1972b "Buccheri a cilindretto di fabbrica tarquiniese," in *Studi etruschi*, XL • 1973–74 "Vasi plastici di bucchero pesante," in *Archeologia Classica*, XXV–XXVI • 1985a Introduction to G. Camporeale (ed. by), *L'Etruria mineraria*, ex. cat., Portoferraio-Massa Marittima-Populonia, Milano • 1985b in *L'Etruria mineraria*, Milano • 1991 *La collezione C.A. Impasti e buccheri*, Roma • 1992 *Gli Etruschi e l'Europa*, ex. cat., Paris-Berlin, Milano • 1995 "Un ceramista ceretano a Massa Marittima nel tardo orientalizzante," in *Studi etruschi*, LX • 1997 *L'abitato etrusco dell'Accesa. Il quartiere B*, Roma; **CANCIANI F.** • 1974 *Corpus Vasorum Antiquorum, Tarquinia*, 3; **CANCIANI F., VON HASE F.-W.** • 1979 *La tomba Bernardini di Palestrina*, Roma; **CAPDEVILLE G.** • 1993 "Riflessi del mito cretese in Etruria," in *Studi e Materali di storia della Religione*, LIX, n.s. XVII, 2; **CAPECCHI G.** • 1989–90 "Un catalogo mai edito, un disegno archiviato. Vittorio Poggi e la nascita del Museo archeologico di Firenze," in *Annali della Facoltà di Lettere di Perugia*; **CAPECCHI G., GUNNELLA A.** • 1975 "Calici di bucchero a sostegni figurati," in *Atti e Memorie dell'Accademia Toscana La Colombaria*, XL; **CAPOGROSSI BOLOGNESI L.** • 1994 *Proprietà e signoria in Roma antica*, I, Roma; **CAPOZZA M.** • 1965 *Movimenti servili nel mondo romano in età repubblicana*, Roma; **CAPUIS L.** • 1992 "Il Veneto nel quadro dei rapporti etrusco-italici ed europei dalla fine dell'età del bronzo alla romanizzazione," in *Etrusker nordlich von Etrurien*, proceedings of the symposiums, Wien • 1993 *I Veneti. Società e cultura di un popolo dell'Italia preromana*, Milano • 1999 "Altino tra Veneto euganeo e Veneto orientale," in *Preistoria e protostoria del 'Venetorum angulus'*, proceeding of the XX Convegno di studi etruschi e italici, Roma, Pisa; **CAPUIS L., GAMBACURTA G.** • forthcoming "I materiali preromani del santuario in località Fornace: osservazioni preliminari," in *Orizzonti del sacro. Culti e santuari antichi in Altino e nel Veneto orientale*, proceeding of the meeting, Venezia 1999; **CARAFA P.** • 1998 *Il Comizio di Roma dalle origini all'età di Augusto*, Roma; **CARANDINI A.** • 1997 *La nascita di Roma. Dei, Lari, eroi e uomini all'alba di una civiltà*, Torino; **CARANDINI A., CAPPELLI R.**, • 2000 *Roma, Romolo, Remo e la fondazione della città*, ex. cat., Roma; **CARUSO I.** • 1985 *Collezione Castellani. Le ceramiche*, Roma • 1988 *Collezione Castellani. Le oreficerie*, Roma; **CASE E PALAZZI D'ETRURIA** • 1985 *Case e palazzi d'Etruria*, ex. cat., Siena; **CASSIO A.C.** • 1994 *KEINOS KALLISTEFANOS e la circolazione dell'epica in area euboica*, in B. d'Agostino, D. Ridgway (ed. by), "Apoikia. I piú antichi insediamenti greci in Occidente: funzioni e modi dell'organizzazione politica e sociale," in *Annali dell'Istituto universitario orientale di Napoli. Sezione di archeologia e storia antica*, n.s. I; **CASTAGNOLI F.** • 1966–67 "Sul tempio italico," in *Römische Mitteilungen*, 73–74 • 1956 *Ippodamo di Mileto e l'urbanistica a pianta ortogonale*, Roma • 1963 "Recenti ricerche sull'urbanistica ippodamea," in *Archeologia Classica*, 15 • 1971 *Orthogonal Town Planning in Antiquity*, Cambridge (Mass.) • 1981 "Aspetti urbanistici di Roma e del Lazio in età arcaica," in *150 Jahre Deutsches Archäologisches Institut*, Mainz; **CATALANO P.** • 1966 *Contributi allo studio del diritto augurale*, Torino; **CATALDI M.** • 1988 *Museo archeologico Nazionale di Tarquinia. I sarcofagi etruschi delle famiglie Camna, Partunu e Pulena*, Roma; **CATALLI F.** • 1998 *Monete etrusche*, Roma; **CATANI E., PACI G.** • 2000 *La Salaria in età antica*, proceeding of the meeting, Roma; **CATENI G.** • 1998 *Volterra, La tomba del Guerriero di Poggio alle Croci*, Firenze • 1999 *Ombre della Sera*, Pontedera; **CATENI G., MAGGIANI A.** • 1997 "Volterra dalla prima età del Ferro al V secolo a.C. Appunti di topografia urbana," in *Aspetti della cultura di Volterra etrusca fra l'età del ferro e l'età ellenistica*, proceeding of the XIX Convegno di studi etruschi e italici, Firenze; **CAVAGNARO VANONI L., SERRA RIDGWAY F.R.** • 1989 *Vasi etruschi a figure rosse. Dagli scavi della Fondazione Lerici nella necropoli dei Monterozzi a Tarquinia*, Roma; **CELUZZA M.G.** • 2000 "Un museo a Grosseto, una mostra a Bologna," in *Vulci e il suo territorio nelle collezioni del Museo archeologico e d'arte della Maremma*, Milano; **CERCHIAI L.** • 1984 "Geras thanonton: note sul concetto di 'belle mort'," in *Annali dell'Istituto universitario orientale di Napoli. Sezione di archeologia e storia antica*, VI • 1985 "Una tomba principesca del periodo orientalizzante antico a Pontecagnano," in *Studi etruschi*, LIII • 1988 "Le stele villanoviane," in *Annali dell'Istituto universitario orientale di Napoli. Sezione di archeologia e storia antica*, X • 1995 *I Campani*, Milano • 1996 "Le scimmie, i Giganti e Tifeo: appunti sui nomi di Ischia," in L. Breglia Pulci Doria (ed. by), *L'incidenza dell'Antico. II. Studi in memoria di E. Lepore*, Napoli; **CHEVILLON J.A.** • 1999 "Populonia: un "tritartémorion" gréco-étrusque inédit à la tete féminine à gauche, avec perruque étagée," in *Bulletin de la Société Française de Numismatique*, Paris; **CHIARAMONTE TRERÉ C.** • 1999 *Tarquinia. Scavi sistematici nell'abitato. Campagne 1982-1988. I materiali 1*, Roma; **CIAMPOLTRINI G.** • 1992 "Le monete etrusche del Romito di Pozzuolo (Lucca)," in *Rivista Italiana di Numismatica*, 94; **CIANCIO A.** • 1995 "Un gruppo di vasi apuli a figure nere del V secolo a.C.," in *Bollettino d'Arte*, 93–94; **CIANFERONI G.C.** • 1985 *I bronzi. Il vasellame*, in *Artigianato artistico in Etruria. L'Etruria settentrionale interna in età ellenistica*, ex. cat., Volterra-Chiusi, Milano; **CIPRIANI G.** • 1980 *Il mito etrusco nel Rinascimento fiorentino*, Firenze; **CLEMEN C.** • 1936 *Die Religion der Etrusker*, Bonn; **COARELLI F.** • 1983 *Il Foro Romano*, Roma • 1988 *Il Foro Boario. Dalle origini alla fine della Repubblica*, Roma • 1993 *Note sui ludi Saeculares*, in *Spectacles sportifs et scéniques dans le monde étrusco-italiques*, proceeding of the round table, Roma 1991, Roma • 1995 "Vino e ideologia nella Roma arcaica," in O. Murray, M. Tecusan (ed. by), *In vino veritas*, Roma • 1998 "Comitium e Comitia: l'assemblea e il voto a Roma in età repubblicana," in *Venticinque secoli dopo l'invenzione della democrazia*, proceeding of the meeting, Paestum 1994, Paestum; **COCHE DE LA FERTÉ E.** • 1956 *Les bijoux antiques*, Paris; **COHEN A.** • 1991 *Complessi tombali di Cerveteri con urne cinerarie tardo-orientalizzanti*, Firenze • 1998 "Bulle auree dal Piceno nel Museo archeologico nazionale delle Marche," in *Prospettiva*, 89–90, • 1999 *Corona etrusca*, Viterbo; **COLONNA DI PAOLO E.** • 1978 *Necropoli rupestri del Viterbese*, Novara; **COLONNA G.** • 1967 "L'Etruria meridionale interna dal villanoviano alle tombe rupestri," in *Studi etruschi*, 35, • 1970a "Pyrgi. Scavi nel santuario etrusco (1959-1967)," in *Notiziario degli scavi di antichità*, II supplement • 1970b "Una nuova iscrizione etrusca del VII secolo e appunti sull'epigrafia ceretana dell'epoca," in *Mélanges de l'Ecole Française de Rome*, 82 • 1973 "Ricerche sull'Etruria interna volsiniese," in *Studi etruschi*, 41, • 1973–74 "Nomi etruschi di vasi," in *Archeologia Classica*, 25–26 • 1974 "La cultura dell'Etruria meridionale interna con particolare riguardo alle necropoli rupestri," in *Aspetti e problemi dell'Etruria interna*, Firenze • 1975 "Firme arcaiche di artefici nell'Italia centrale," in *Römische Mitteilungen*, 82 • 1976a "Basi conoscitive per una storia economica dell'Etruria," in *Annali. Istituto italiano di numismatica*, 22, supplement • 1976b "Il sistema alfabetico," in *L'etrusco arcaico*, proceeding of the meeting, Firenze 1974, Firenze • 1976–77 "La dea etrusca Cel e i santuari del Trasimeno," in *Rivista storica dell'antichità*, VI–VII • 1977a "Nome gentilizio e società," in *Studi etruschi*, 45 • 1977b "Un aspetto oscuro del Lazio antico: le tombe del VI–V secolo," in *La Parola del Passato* • 1978 "Archeologia dell'età romantica in Etruria," in *Studi etruschi*, 46, pp. 88–92 • 1980–81 "La Sicilia e il Tirreno nel V e IV secolo," in *Kokalos*, XVII–XVII • 1981a "La Dea di Pyrgi: bilancio aggiornato dei dati archeologici (1978)," in *Die Göttin von Pyrgi. Archäologische, linguistiche und religionsgeschichtliche aspekte*, proceeding of the meeting, Tübingen 16–17 january 1979, Firenze • 1981b "Presenza greca ed etrusco-meridionale nell'Etruria mineraria," in *L'Etruria Mineraria*, proceeding of the XII Convegno di studi etruschi e italici, Firenze • 1981c "Tarquinio Prisco e il tempio di Giove Capitolino," in *La Parola del Passato*, XXXVI • 1982 "Di Augusto Castellani e del cosiddetto calice a cariatidi prenestino," in H. Blanck, S. Steingräber (ed. by), *Miscellanea archaeologica Tobias Dohrn dedicata*, Roma • 1983 "Identità come appartenenza nelle iscrizioni di possesso dell'Italia preromana," in *Epigraphica*, 45 • 1984a "Le copie ottocentesche delle pitture etrusche e l'opera di Carlo Ruspi," in C. Morigi Govi, G. Sassatelli (ed. by), *Dalla stanza delle Antichità al Museo civico. Storia della formazione del museo civico archeologico di Bologna*, Bologna • 1984b "Etruschi nell'ager Gallicus," in *Picus*, IV • 1984c "Etrusco dapna: latino damnum," in *Opus*, 3, 2 • 1985a "Società e cultura a Volsinii," in *Annali della Fondazione per il Museo Claudio Faina*, II • 1985b *Santuari d'Etruria*, Milano • 1985c "Le forme ideologiche della città," in M. Cristofani (ed. by), *Civiltà degli Etruschi*, ex. cat., Firenze, Milano • 1986 "Urbanistica e architettura," in G. Pugliese Carratelli (ed. by), *Rasenna. Storia e civiltà degli Etruschi*, Milano • 1987a "Etruria e Lazio nell'età dei Tarquini," in *Etruria e Lazio arcaico*, proceeding of the meeting, Roma 1986, Roma • 1987c "I culti del santuario della Cannicella," in *Annali della Fondazione per il Museo Claudio Faina*, III • 1987b "Il Maestro dell'Ercole e della Minerva," in *Opuscola romana*, XVI • 1988 "Il lessico istituzionale etrusco e la formazione della città (specialmente in Emilia Romagna)," in *La formazione della città in Emilia Romagna*, proceeding of the meeting, Bologna, Marzabotto 1985, Bologna • 1989a "Gli Etruschi e l'"invenzione" della pittura," in *Pittura etrusca al Museo di villa Giulia*, Roma • 1989b "Riflessi dell'epos greco nell'arte degli Etruschi," in *L'epos greco in Occidente*, proceeding of the XIX Convegno di studi sulla Magna Grecia, Taranto 1979, Taranto • 1989c "Nuove prospettive sulla storia etrusca tra Alalia e Cuma," in *Atti del II Congresso Interna-*

zionale Etrusco, Firenze 1985, Roma • 1989–90 "Il posto dell'Arringatore nell'arte etrusca di età ellenistica," in *Studi etruschi*, LVI • 1991a "Gli scudi bilobati dell'Italia centrale e l''ancile' dei Salii," in *Archeologia Classica*, XLIII • 1991b "Riflessioni sul dionisismo in Etruria," in *Dionysos Mito e Mistero,* proceeding of the meeting, Comacchio 1989, Comacchio • 1992a "Apporti etruschi all'orientalizzante 'piceno': il caso della statuaria," in *La civiltà picena nelle Marche,* proceeding of the meeting, Ancona 1988, Ripatransone • 1992b "Praeneste arcaica ed il mondo etrusco-italico," in B. Coari (ed. by), *La necropoli di Praeneste. Periodi orientalizzante e medio-repubblicano*, proceeding of the meeting, Palestrina 1990, Palestrina • 1993a "Ceramisti e donne padrone di bottega nell'Etruria arcaica," in *Indogermanica et Italica, Festschrift für Helmut Rix zum 65. Geburstag*, Innsbruck • 1993b "Doni di Etruschi e di altri barbari occidentali nei santuari panellenici," in A. Mastrocinque (ed. by), *I grandi santuari della Grecia e l'Occidente*, Trento • 1993c "I sarcofagi chiusini di età ellenistica," in *La civiltà di Chiusi e del suo territorio,* proceeding of the XVII Convegno di studi etruschi e italici, Cianciano Terme 1989, Firenze • 1993d "Strutture teatriformi in Etruria," in *Spectacles sportifs et scéniques dans le monde étrusco-italiques*, proceeding of the round table, Roma 1991, Roma • 1994 "Etrusca Arte: Urbanistica e Architettura," in *Enciclopedia dell'arte antica*, II supplement, II, Roma • 1995 "Etruschi a Pitecusa nell'Orientalizzante antico," in A. Storchi Marino (ed. by), *L'incidenza dell'antico. Studi in memoria di Ettore Lepore*, I, Napoli • 1996 *L'altorilievo di Pyrgi. Dei ed eroi greci in Etruria,* Roma • 1999a *I Piceni. Popolo d'Europa*, ex. cat., Roma • 1999b "L'iscrizione del biconico di Uppsala: un documento del paleoumbro," in *Incontro di studi in memoria di Massimo Pallottino*, Pisa • 2000a "Tyrrhenus Lipari frater," in *Scritti dedicati a P. Pelagatti*, Roma • 2000b "La scultura in pietra," in *Piceni popolo d'Europa*, ex. cat., Frankfurt; **Colonna G., Di Paolo E.** • 1997 "Il letto vuoto, la distribuzione del corredo e la "finestra" della Tomba Regolini Galassi," in G. Nardi, M. Pandolfini, L. Drago, A. Berardinetti (ed. by), *Etrusca et Italica. Scritti in ricordo di M. Pallottino*, Pisa, Roma; **Colonna G., von Hase F.W.** • 1984 "Alle origini della statuaria etrusca: la tomba delle Statue presso Ceri," in *Studi etruschi*, LII; **Comella A.M.** • 1982 *Il deposito votivo presso l'Ara della Regina,* Roma • 1993 *Le terrecotte architettoniche del santuario dello Scasato a Falerii*, Perugia • 1978 *Il materiale votivo tardo di Gravisca*, Roma; **Comella A.M., Stefani G.** • 1990 *Materiali votivi del santuario di Campetti a Veio*, Roma; **Confini e frontiera** • 1997 *Confini e frontiera nella grecità d'Occidente*, proceeding of the XXXVII convegno di studi sulla Magna Grecia, Taranto; **Contributi introduttivi** • 1976 "Contributi introduttivi allo studio della monetazione etrusca," proceeding of the V Congresso del Centro internazionale di studi numismatici, in *Annali dell'Istituto italiano di numismatica*, 22, supplement; **Cordano F.** • 1986 *Antiche fondazioni greche*, Palermo; **Corsi S.** • 1997 *Casa Buonarroti. La collezione archeologica*, Sesto San Giovanni; **Crise et transformation** • 1990 *Crise et transformation des sociétés archaiques de l'Italie antique au V siècle av. J.-C.*, proceeding of the round table, Roma; **Cristofani M.** • 1973–74 "Appunti di epigrafia etrusco arcaica-III," in *Archeologia Classica*, XXV–XXVI • 1966 "Sulla paleografia delle iscrizioni etrusche di Pyrgi," in *Archeologia Classica*, XVIII • 1967 "Ricerche sulle pitture della tomba Francois di Vulci. I fregi decorativi," in *Dialoghi di Archeologia*, I, 2 • 1969a "Appunti di epigrafia etrusca arcaica," in *Atti della Scuola Normale Superiore di Pisa*, II, 38 • 1969b *Le tombe da Monte Michele*, Firenze • 1971a "Per una nuova lettura della Pisside della Pania," in *Studi etruschi*, 39, • 1971b "Sul più antico gruppo di canopi chiusini," in *Archeologia Classica*, XXIII • 1975a "I "dono" nell'Etruria arcaica," in *La Parola del Passato*, 30 • 1975b "Società e istituzioni nell'Italia preromana," in *Popoli e civiltà dell'Italia antica*, VII, Roma • 1975c *Statue-cinerario chiusine di età classica,* Roma 1975 • 1977a "Appunti di epigrafia etrusco arcaica-III," in *Studi etruschi*, 45 • 1977b "Artisti etruschi a Roma nell'ultimo trentennio del VI secolo a.C.," in *Prospettiva*, 9 • 1977c "Strutture insediative e modi di produzione," in *Caratteri dell'ellenismo nelle urne etrusche*, Firenze • 1978 "L'attività edilizia nei centri urbani," in *L'arte degli Etruschi*, Torino • 1979a *L'arte degli Etruschi. Produzione e consumo*, Torino • 1979b "La 'Testa Lorenzini' e la scultura tardoarcaica in Etruria settentrionale," in *Studi etruschi*, XLVII • 1979c "La collezione di sculture classiche," in *Gli Uffizi. Catalogo generale*, Firenze • 1981a "*Il cratere François nella storia dell'archeologia "romantica"*, in "Materiali per servire alla storia del vaso François," in *Bollettino d'Archeologia*, 62 • 1981b "Varietà linguistica e contesti sociali di pertinenza nell'antroponimia etrusca," in *Annali Istituto Orientale di Napoli. Sezione linguistica* • 1982 "Per una storia del collezionismo archeologico nella Toscana granducale. IV. Gli ex-voto di Nemi," in *Prospettiva*, 29 • 1983b *Gli Etruschi del mare*, Milano • 1983a *Gli Etruschi. Una nuova immagine*, Firenze • 1983a "Il quadro ambientale e l'urbanesimo," in *Gli Etruschi. Una nuova immagine*, Firenze • 1983c *La scoperta degli Etruschi. Archeologia e antiquaria nel '700*, Roma • 1983d "Luigi Lanzi antiquario," in P. Barocchi, G. Ragionieri (ed. by), *Gli Uffizi quattro secoli di una galleria*, proceeding of the international meeting, Firenze 1982, Firenze • 1984 "Iscrizioni e beni suntuari," in *Opus*, 3, 2 • 1985a *Civiltà degli Etruschi*, ex. cat., Firenze, Milano • 1985b *Contributi alla ceramica etrusca tardo-classica*, proceeding of the seminar, Roma 1984, Roma • 1985c *I bronzi degli Etruschi,* Novara • 1986a "Economia e società," in *Rasenna. Storia e civiltà degli Etruschi*, Milano • 1986c "Nuovi dati per la storia urbana di Caere," in *Bollettino di archeologia*, 71 • 1986b "Sul rinvenimento dell'Arringatore," in *Prospettiva*, 45 • 1987a "I santuari: tradizioni decorative," in *Quaderni del centro di Studio per l'Archeologia Etrusco italica*, 15, Roma • 1987b "Il banchetto in Etruria," in G. Barbieri (ed. by), *L'alimentazione nel mondo antico. Gli Etruschi*, ex. cat., Roma • 1987c "La 'Venere' della Cannicella," in *Annali della Fondazione per il Museo Claudio Faina*, III • 1987d "La ceramica a figure rosse," in M. Martelli (ed. by), *La ceramica degli Etruschi*, Novara • 1987e "La cultura artistica a Vulci fra età classica ed ellenismo," in *La tomba François di Vulci*, ex. cat., Città del Vaticano 1987, Roma • 1987f "La formazione della scrittura," in *Saggi di storia etrusca arcaica*, Roma • 1987g "Nuovi spunti sul tema della talassocrazia," in *Saggi di storia etrusca arcaica*, Roma • 1990a "Arte ufficiale e arte privata nell'Etruria del primo Ellenismo," in *Akten des XIII. Internationalen Kongress für klassische Archäologie Berlin 1988*, Mainz • 1990b *La Grande Roma dei Tarquini*, ex. cat., Roma • 1991a "Chimereide," in *Prospettiva*, 61 • 1991b *Introduzione allo studio dell'etrusco*, Firenze • 1992 "La ceramografia etrusca fra età tardo-classica ed ellenismo," in *Studi etruschi*, LVIII, • 1993 "Il testo di Pech Maho, Aléria e i traffici del V secolo a.C." in *Mélanges de l'Ecole Française de Rome* • 1995a "talica, arte," in *Enciclopedia dell'arte antica*, II supplement, III, Roma • 1995b "La terza Regia. Problemi decorativi," in *Archeologia Laziale*, 12, Roma • 1995c Tabula Capuana. *Un calendario festivo di età arcaica*, Firenze • 1996a *Etruschi e altre genti nell'Italia preromana. Mobilità in età arcaica*, Roma • 1996b "Paideia, arete e metis: a proposito delle pissidi della Pania," in *Prospettiva*, 83–84, • 1996c "Un naukleros greco-orientale nel Tirreno," in *Etruschi e altre genti nell'Italia preromana*, Roma • 1997a "Alcune questioni di lessico istituzionale etrusco," in *Quaderni del centro di Studio per l'Archeologia Etrusco italica*, 26, Roma • 1997b "I 'principi' adriatici: appunti per un capitolo di storia italica," in *Etrusca et Italica*, Pisa • 1998 "Un naukleros greco-orientale nel Tirreno. Per un'interpretazione del relitto del Giglio," in *Annuario della Scuola archeologica di Atene*, LXX–LXXI; **Cristofani M. et al.** • 1992 *Caere 3.1. Lo scarico arcaico della Vigna Parrocchiale* , Roma; **Cristofani M., Martelli M.** • 1977 *Caratteri dell'ellenismo nelle urne etrusche*, proceeding of the meeting, Firenze; **Cristofani M., Boitani F., Moscati P. et al.** • 1985 *Strade degli Etruschi. Vie e mezzi di comunicazione nell'antica Etruria*, Milano; **Cristofani M., Martelli M.** • 1977 *Caratteri dell'ellenismo nelle urne etrusche*, proceeding of the meeting, Firenze • 1983 *L'oro degli Etruschi*, Novara • 1994 "Lo stile del potere e i beni di prestigio," in J. Guilaine, S. Settis (ed. by), *Storia d'Europa II. 2 Preistoria e antichità*, Torino; **Cristofani Martelli M., Cristofani M., Bonamici M.** • 1972 "Contributi alla classificazione del più antico bucchero decorato a rilievo," in *Studi etruschi*, XL; **Cultrera G.** • 1921 "Frammenti di rilievi etruschi nel Museo Nazionale Tarquiniese," in *Ausonia*, X; **Curty O.** • 1995 "Les parentés légendaires entre cités grecques," in *Hautes Études du Monde Gréco-Romain*, 20, Paris-Genève; **Cygielmann M.** • 1988 "Su alcune terrecotte architettoniche da Vetulonia," in *La coroplastica templare etrusca fra il IV e il II secolo a.C.,* procceding of the XVI Convegno di studi etruschi e italici, Orbetello • 1990 *Ori e Argenti nelle collezioni del Museo archeologico di Firenze*, Firenze • 1993 "Casa privata e decorazione coroplastica: un ciclo mitologico da Vetulonia," in *Ostraka* II, 2 • 1994 "Note preliminari per una periodizzazione del villanoviano di Vetulonia," in *La presenza etrusca nella Campania Meridionale*, proceeding of the meeting, Salerno-Pontecagnano, Firenze • 1995 "Isidoro Falchi e Vetulonia: storia e scoperte," in S. Bruni (ed. by), *Isidoro Falchi un medico al servizio dell'archeologia. Un protagonista della ricerca italiana di fine Ottocento*, Pontedera;

D

D'Agostino B. • 1977 "Tombe 'principesche' dell'Orientalizzante antico da Pontecagnano," in *Monumenti antichi pubblicati dall'Accademia dei Lincei*, misc.II • 1982 "L'ideologia funeraria nell'età del ferro in Campania: Pontecagnano. Nascita di un potere di funzione stabile," in G. Gnoli, J.P. Vernant, *La mort, les morts dans les sociétés anciennes*, Napoli • 1988 "L'immagine e la società," in *Annali dell'Istituto universitario orientale di Napoli. Sezione di archeologia e storia antica*, X • 1990 "Military organisation and social structure in archaic Etruria," in O. Murray, S. Price (ed. by), *The greek city from Homer to Alexander*, Oxford • 1993 "La donna in Etruria," in M. Bettini (ed. by), *Maschile / Femminile. Genere e ruoli nel-*

le culture antiche, Roma, Bari • 1995a "Considerazioni sugli inizi del processo di formazione della città in Etruria," in A. Storchi Marino (ed. by), *L'incidenza dell'Antico. I. Studi in memoria di E. Lepore*, proceeding of the meeting, Anacapri 1991, Napoli • 1995b "Eracle e Gerione. La struttura del mito e la storia," in *Annali dell'Istituto universitario orientale di Napoli. Sezione di archeologia e storia antica*, n.s. 2, • 1996 "L'incontro dei coloni greci con le genti anelleniche della Lucania," in *I Greci in Occidente*, Venezia • 1998 "La non-polis degli Etruschi," in *Venticinque secoli dopo l'invenzione della democrazia*, proceeding of the meeting, Paestum 1994, Paestum • 1999a "Dal palazzo alla tomba. Percorsi della 'imagerie' etrusca arcaica," in B. d'Agostino, L. Cerchiai, *Il mare, la morte, l'amore. Gli Etruschi, i Greci e l'immagine*, Roma • 1999b "I principi dell'Etruria tirrenica in epoca orientalizzante," in *Les princes de la protohistoire et l'émergence de l'état*, proceeding of the international round table, Napoli-Roma; **D'Agostino B., Cerchiai L.** • 1999 *Il mare, la morte, l'amore*, Roma; **D'Agostino B., Gastaldi P.** • 1988 *Pontecagnano* II. *La necropoli del Picentino. 1. Le tombe della prima età del ferro*, Napoli; **D'Ambrosio R.** • 1956 *Alle origini della città. Le prime esperienze urbane*, Napoli; **D'Ercole V., Cairoli R.** • 1998 *Archeologia in Abruzzo*, Tarquinia; **D'Ercole V., Trucco F.** • 1992 "Canino (Viterbo), località Bandinella. Un luogo di culto all'aperto presso Vulci," in *Bollettino di Archeologia*, 13–15; **Damgaard Andersen H.** • 1997 "The archaeological evidence for the origin and development of the Etruscan city in the 7th to 6th centuries B.C.," in *Acta hyperborea. Danish studies in classical archaeology*, 7; **De Juliis E.M.** • 1994 *Importazioni e influenze etrusche in Puglia*, proceeding of the XXXIII Convegno di studi sulla Magna Grecia, Taranto 1993, Taranto; **De La Genière J.** • 1968 *Recherches sur l'âge du fer en Italie méridionale*, Napoli; **De Lucia Brolli M.A., Carlucci C.** • 1998 *Le antichità dei Falisci al Museo di Villa Giulia*, Roma; **De Marinis G., Salvini M.** • 1999 "Le testimonianze villanoviane," in *Lunga memoria della piana. L'area fiorentina dalla preistoria alla romanizzazione*, Firenze; **De Marinis R.** • 1986 *Gli Etruschi a Nord del Po*, ex. cat., Mantova, • 1986 "L'abitato etrusco del Forcello di Bagnolo San Vito," in *Gli Etruschi a nord del Po*, ex. cat., I, Mantova; **De Min M.** • 1984 "Frattesina di Fratta Polesine (Ro). L'abitato e la necropoli protovillanoviani," in *Il Veneto nell'antichità. Preistoria e protostoria*, Verona; **De Min M., Gerhardinger E.** • 1986 "Frattesina di Fratta Polesine. L'abitato protostorico," in *L'antico Polesine. Testimonianze archeologiche e paleoambientali*, Padova; **De Natale** • 1988 *Pontecagnano II. La necropoli di Sant'Antonio: propr. ECI.1. Le tombe della prima età del Ferro*, Napoli • 1996 "Un elmo d'impasto con decorazione figurata da Pontecagnano," in *Ostraka*, V; **De Puma R.D., Small J.P.** • 1994 "Murlo and the Etruscans. Art and Society" in *Ancient Etruria*, Madison; **De Ruyt F.** • 1934 *Charun, Démon étrusque de la mort*, Roma; **De Santis A.** • 1995 "Contatti fra Etruria e Lazio antico alla fine dell'VIII secolo a.C.: la tomba di Guerriero di Osteria dell'Osa," in N. Christie (ed. by), *Settlement and Economy in Italy 1500 BC-AD 1500, Papers of the Fifth Conference of Italian Archaeology*, Oxford; **De Sensi Sestito G.** • 1987 "La Calabria in età arcaica e classica: storia, economia società," in S. Settis (ed. by), *Storia della Calabria antica*, Reggio Calabria; **De Simone C.** • 1968 *Die griechischen Entlehnungen im Etruskischen*, I, Wiesbaden • 1970 *Die griechischen Entlehnungen im Etruskischen, II: Untersuchung*, Wiesbaden • 1978 "Un nuovo gentilizio etrusco da Orvieto (Katacina) e la cronologia della penetrazione celtica (gallica) in Italia," in *La Parola del Passato*, 33 • 1986 "La stele di Lemnos," in *Rasenna*, Milano • 1992 *Le iscrizioni etrusche dei cippi di Rubiera*, Reggio Emilia • 1995 "I Tirreni a Lemnos: L'alfabeto," in *Studi etruschi*, LX • 1996a "Il problema storico-linguistico," in *Magna Grecia Etruschi e Fenici*, proceeding of the XXXIII Convegno di studi sulla Magna Grecia, Taranto 1993, Napoli • 1996b *I Tirreni a Lemnos. Evidenza linguistica e tradizioni storiche*, Firenze • 1997 "I Tirreni a Lemnos: Paralipomena metodologici (nonché teorici)," in *Ostraka*, VI, 1 • 1998 "Etrusco e 'Tirreno' di Lemnos: 'Urverwandschaft'?", in *Rivista di Filologia e di Istruzione Classica*, 126, 4; **De Waele J.A.K.E.** • 1996 'The Lapis Satricanus and the chronology of the temples of Mater Matuta,' in *Ostraka*, V, 2; **Decourt J.-Cl.** • 1999 'Le plomb de Pech Maho. Etat de la recherche 1999," in *Archéologie en Languedoc*, 23; **Del Chiaro M.A.** • 1957 *The Genucilia Group: a Class of Etruscan Red-Figured Plates*, Berkeley-Los Angeles • 1974a *The Etruscan Funnel Group: a Tarquinian Red-Figured Fabric*, Firenze • 1974b *Etruscan Red-Figured Vase-Painting at Caere*, Berkeley-Los Angeles-London; **Del Francia P.R.** • 1990 "I Lorena e la nascita del Museo egizio fiorentino," in *L'Egitto fuori dall'Egitto. Dalla riscoperta all'egittologia*, proceeding of the meeting, Bologna; **Della Fina G.M.** • 1983 *Le antichità a Chiusi. Un caso di "arredo urbano"*, Roma; **Della Seta A.** • 1918 *Museo di villa Giulia*, Roma • 1937 "Iscrizioni tirreniche di Lemnos," in *Scritti in onore di B. Nogara*, Roma; **Delpino F.** • 1977a "La prima età del ferro a Bisenzio. Aspetti della cultura villanoviana nell'Etruria meridionale interna," in *Memorie dell'Accademia nazionale dei Lincei*, XXI • 1977b "Elementi antropomorfi in corredi villanoviani," in *La civiltà arcaica di Vulci e la sua espansione*, proceeding of the X Convegno di studi etruschi e italici, Grosseto-Roselle-Vulci, Firenze • 1984 "Sulla presenza di oggetti "enotri" in Etruria: la tomba di Poggio Impiccato 6 di Tarquinia," in *Studi di antichità in onore di G. Maetzke*, II, Roma • 1987 "Bisenzio," in G. Bartoloni (ed. by), *Le urne a capanna rinvenute in Italia*, Roma • 1992 "L'età del positivismo,"in *Gli Etruschi e l'Europa*, Paris-Milano • 1995 "Vetulonia e il problema delle origini etrusche nelle indagini e nelle riflessioni di Isidoro Falchi," in S. Bruni (ed. by), *Isidoro Falchi un medico al servizio dell'archeologia. Un protagonista della ricerca italiana di fine Ottocento*, Pontedera • 1998 "Tra omogeneità e diversità. Il trattamento della morte a Tarquinia villanoviana," in N. Negroni Catacchio (ed. by), *Preistoria e protostoria in Etruria*, proceeding of the meeting, Manciano Farnese 1995, Firenze; **Dennis G.** • 1907 *The cities and Cemeteries of Etruria*, London, pp. 427–59; **Denoyelle M.** • 1994 *La ceramica protoitaliota: alcune testimonianze delle relazioni tra Magna Grecia ed Etruria*, in *Magna Grecia Etruschi Fenici*, proceeding of the XXXIII Convegno internazionale sulla Magna Grecia, Taranto 1993, Napoli; **D'Ercole V., Trucco F.** • 1995a "Canino (Viterbo). Località Banditella. Un luogo di culto all'aperto presso Vulci," in *Bollettino d'Archeologia*, 13–15 • 1995b "Nuove acquisizioni sulla protostoria dell'Etruria meridionale," in N. Christie (ed. by), *Settlement and Economy in Italy 1500 BC-AD 1500. Papers of the Fifth Conference of Italian Archaeology*, Oxford; **Dewes R.** • 1992 "Herodotus, I, 94, the Draught of 1200 B.C. and the Origins of the Etruscans," in *Historia*, 41; **Di Gennaro F.** • 1986 *Forme di insediamento tra Tevere e Fiora dal bronzo finale al principio dell'età del Ferro*, Firenze • 1996 "Protovillanoviano," in *Enciclopedia dell'arte antica*, II supplement, IV, Roma; **Di Vita A.** • 1985 "L'urbanistica," in G. Pugliese Carratelli (ed. by), *Sikanie. Storia e civiltà della Sicilia greca*, Milano • 1996 "Urbanistica della Sicilia greca," in *I Greci in Occidente*, ex. cat., Venezia, Milano; **Die Göttin von Pyrgi** • 1981 *Die Göttin von Pyrgi*, proceeding of the meeting, Tübingen 1979, Firenze; **Die Welt der Etrusker** • 1988 *Die Welt der Etrusker, Archäologische Denkmäler aus Museen der sozialistischen Länder*, Berlin; **Dohrn T.** • 1937 *Die schwarzfigurigen etruskischen Vasen der zweiten Hälfte des sechsten Jahrhunderts*, Berlin • 1982 *Die etruskische Kunst im Zeitalter der griechischen Kunst. Die Interimsperiode*, Mainz; **Donati F.** • 1989 "Aspetti della policromia sui monumenti antichi: il caso delle urne etrusche," in *Ricerche di Storia dell'arte*, 38; **Donati L.** • 1967 "Buccheri decorati con teste plastiche umane. Zona di Vulci," in *Studi etruschi*, XXXV • 1968 "Vasi di bucchero decorati con teste plastiche umane. Zona di Chiusi," in *Studi etruschi*, XXXVI • 1969 "Vasi di bucchero decorati con teste plastiche umane. Zona di Orvieto," in *Studi etruschi*, XXXVII • 1977 "Skyphoi chiusini di bucchero con anse piatte," in *Studi etruschi*, XLV • 1984 "Un nuovo tipo di coperchio antropoide a Saturnia," in *Studi di antichità in onore di G.Maetzke*, Roma • 1989 *Le tombe di Saturnia nel Museo archeologico di Firenze*, Firenze • 1991 "L'atelier delle rosette," in *Studi e Materiali. Scienza dell'Antichità in Toscana*, VI • 1994 *La Casa dell'Impluvium. Architettura etrusca a Roselle*, Roma; **Drago Troccoli L.** • 1999 "Il villanoviano di Fermo," in *I Piceni. Popolo d'Europa*, Roma; **Drews R.** • 1981 "The coming of the city to Central Italy," in *American Journal of Ancient History*, 6; **Ducati P.** • 1911 "Le pietre funerarie felsinee," in *Monumenti antichi pubblicati dall'Accademia dei Lincei*, XX, c. 357 • 1943 "Nuove stele funerarie felsinee," in *Monumenti antichi pubblicati dall'Accademia dei Lincei*, XXXIX; **Ducci E.** • 1987–88 "Le terrecotte architettoniche della Catona," in *Studi etruschi*, LV; **Durante M.** • 1969 "Le sibilanti dell'etrusco," in *Studi in onore di Vittore Pisani*, Brescia;

E

Edlund Berry I.E.M. • 1992 *The seated and Standing Akroteria from Poggio Civitate (Murlo)*, Roma; **Egg M.** • 1991 "Ein neuer Kesselwagen aus Etrurien," in *Jahrbuch des Römisch-germanischen Zentralmuseums Mainz*, 38 • 1996 "Das hallstattzeitliche Fürstengrab von Strettweg bei Judenburg in der Obersteiermak," *Jahrbuch des Römisch-germanischen Zentralmuseums Mainz Monographien*, 37; **Emiliozzi A.** • 1991 "Leoni funerari da Ferento," in *Archeologia Classica*, XLIII • 1997 *Carri da guerra e principi etruschi*, ex. cat., Roma; **Esposito A.M.** • 1985 "La coroplastica. Le terrecotte architettoniche," in *Artigianato artistico in Etruria. L'Etruria settentrionale interna in età ellenistica*, ex. cat., Volterra-Chiusi, Milano • 1999 *Principi guerrieri. La necropoli etrusca di Casale Marittimo* ex. cat., Cecina 1999, Milano; **Esposito A.M., De Tommaso G.** • 1993 *Museo archeologico nazionale di Firenze. Antiquarium. I vasi attici*, Firenze;

F

Falconi Amorelli M.T. • 1968 *La Collezione Massimo*, (Quaderni di Villa Giulia, 2), Milano; **Fauth W.** • 1974 "Der Schlund des Orcus. Zu einer Eigentümlichkeit der römisch-etruskischen Unterweltvorstellung," in *Numen*, XXI; **Feruglio A.E.** • 1998 "Il carro I da Castel San Mariano di Corciano," in *Carri da guerra e principi etruschi*, ex. cat. Viterbo; **Feruglio A.E., Bonomi Ponzi L., Manconi D.** • 1991 *Mevania: da centro umbro a municipio romano*, ex. cat., Perugia; **Fiumi E.** • 1957 "Materiali volterrani nel Museo archeologico di Firenze: la collezione Cinci," in *Studi etruschi*, 25; **Fogolari G., Prosdocimi A.L.** • 1988 *I Veneti antichi. Lingua e cultura*, Padova; **Fontaine P.** • 1994 "Tarquinia. L'enceinte et la porte nord. Contribution à l'architecture militaire étrusque," in *Archäeologischer Anzeiger* • 1997 "Pour une carte archéologique des fortifications étrusques," in *Revue Belge de Philosophie et d'Histoire*, 75; **Forme di contatto** • 1983 *Forme di contatto e processi di trasformazione nelle società antiche,* proceeding of the meeting, Cortona 1981, Pisa-Roma; **Forni G.** • 1989 "Questioni di storia agraria preromana: le quattro fasi dell'agricoltura etrusca," in *Atti del II Congresso Internazionale Etrusco*, Roma, III; **Forte M.** • 1988-1989 "Problemi storici e urbanistici nella necropoli orvietana di Crocifisso del Tufo," in *Bollettino storico di Orvieto*, 44–45; **Frankfort Th.** • 1959 "Les classes serviles en Etrurie," in *Latomus*, XVIII; **Freytag von B.** • 1986 *Das Giebelrelief von Telamon*, Mainz; **Fugazzola Delpino M.A.** • 1984 *La civilta villanoviana. Guida ai materiali della prima età del Ferro nel Museo di villa Giulia*, Roma; **Furtwängler A.** • 1900 *Die antiken Gemmen, Geschichte der Steinschneidekunst*, III, Berlin;

G

Gallini C. • 1973 "Che cosa intendere per ellenizzazione. Problemi di metodo," in *Documenti di archeologia*, VII; **Gamurrini G.** • 1873 *Relazione storica del R. Museo egizio ed etrusco in Firenze*, Firenze; **Garbini G.** • 1996 *Fenici e Cartaginesi nel Tirreno*, in *Magna Grecia, Etruschi, Fenici*, proceeding of the XXXIII Convegno di studi sulla Magna Grecia, Taranto 1993, Napoli; **Garin E.** • 1976 *La cultura italiana tra '800 e '900*, Bari; **Gasperini L.** • 1989 "La dignità della donna nel mondo etrusco e il suo lontano riflesso nell'onomastica personale romana," in A. Rallo (ed. by), *Le donne in Etruria*, Roma; **Gaultier F.** • 1987 in *Mélanges de l'Ecole Française de Rome*, 99–1 • 1990 "A propos de quelques elements de decor architectural archaiques en terre cuite conservés au Musée du Louvre," in H. Heres, H. Kunze (ed. by), *Die Welt der Etrusker*, proceeding of the meeting, Berlin 1988, Berlin • 1995 *Corpus Vasorum Antiquorum, Paris, Louvre*, 24; **Gaultier F., Briquel D.** • 1989 "L'iscrizione arcaica di Lucio Mezenzio," in *Miscellanea ceretana*, I; **Gempeler R.D.**, • 1974 *Die etruskischen Kanopen;* **Gentili D.** • 1984 "L'Etruria meridionale interna nel settore delle necropoli rupestri," in *Romana gens. Bollettino dell'Associazione archeologica romana*, 1; **Gentili G.V.** • 1985 "Il villanoviano verucchiese nella Romagna orientale ed il sepolcreto Moroni," in *Studi e Documenti di Archeologia,* I • 1987a "Il villanoviano della Romagna orientale con epicentro Verucchio," in *Romagna Protostorica*, proceeding of the meeting, San Giovanni in Galilea 1985, Viserba di Rimini • 1987b "Verucchio," in *La formazione della città in Emilia Romagna. Prime esperienze urbane attraverso le nuove scoperte archeologiche,* ex. cat., Bologna; **Gentili G.V., Mansuelli G.A.** • 1974 "Problemi dell'urbanistica dell'Etruria interna," in *Aspetti e problemi dell'Etruria interna*, Firenze; **Gentili G.V., Mansuelli G.A., Gualandi G. et al.** • 1970 "Problemi e testimionianze della città etrusca di Marzabotto," in *Studi etruschi*, 38; **Gentili M.D.** • 1994 *I sarcofagi etruschi in terracotta di età ellenistica*, Roma; **Gerhard E.** • 1837 "Etruskisches Museum des Vaticano," in *Archäol. Intelligenblatt*, 2, c.; **Gerhard E.** • 1840-1897 *Etruskische Spiegel*, Berlin; **Gill D.W.J.** • 1987 "METRU.MENECE: an Etruscan painted inscription on a mid-5th-century BC red-figure cup from Populonia," in *Antiquity*, LXI, 231; **Gilotta F.** • 1986 "Appunti sulla più antica ceramica etrusca a figure rosse," in *Prospettiva*, XLV • 1989 "Il sarcofago del "magistrato ceretano" del Museo Gregoriano Etrusco," in *Rivista dell'Istituto nazionale di archeologia e storia dell'arte*, s. III, XII • 1995 "Nota di plastica spinetica," in *Prospettiva*, 77 • 1997 "Nikosthenes a Cerveteri," in M. Cristofani (ed. by), *Miscellanea etrusco-italica*, II vol.; **Ginge B.** • 1988–89 in *Annali Perugia*, n.s. 12 • 1987 *Ceramiche etrusche a figure nere* (Archeologica, 72), Roma; **Girardon S.P.** • 1992 "Una testa fittile da altorievo nel British Museum," in *La coroplastica templare etrusca fra il IV e il II secolo a.C.*, proceeding of the XVI Convegno di studi etruschi e italici, Orbetello 1988, Firenze; **Giuliano A.** • 1966 *Urbanistica delle città greche*, Milano; **Godelier M.** • 1977 *Antropologia e marxismo*, Roma • 1999 "Chefferies et états, une approche anthropologique," in P. Ruby (ed. by), *Les princes de la protohistoire et l'émergeance de l'état*, proceeding of the round table, Napoli 1994, Roma; **Gran Aymerich J.M.J.** • 1972 "Situles orientalisantes du VIIe siècle en Étrurie," in *Mélanges de l'Ecole Française de Rome*, LXXXIV • 1973 "Un conjunto de vasos de bucchero inciso. Ensayo de formalización," in *Trabajos de Prehistoria*, XXX • 1982 *Corpus Vasorum Antiquorum, Louvre, 20*, Paris • 1992 *Corpus Vasorum Antiquorum, Louvre, 23*, Paris; **Gras M.** • 1985a "Il commercio etrusco arcaico," proceeding of the meeting, in *Quaderni del Centro di Studio per l'Archeologia Etrusco-Italica*, 9, Roma • 1985b *Trafics tyrrhéniens archaïques*, Roma • 1997 *Il Mediterraneo nell'età arcaica*, Fondazione Paestum • 2000 "Les Etrusques et la Gaule méditerranéenne," in *Mailhac et le premier âge du fer en Europe occidentale*, Carcassonne 1997 • forthcoming-a *La battaglia del mare sardonio. Appunti e ricordi*, round table, Oristano 1998 • forthcoming-b "Gli scambi fra Oriente e Occidente," in *Magna Grecia e Oriente mediterraneo prima dell'età ellenistica*, Taranto 1999; **Greco E.** • 1996 "La città e il territorio," in *I Greci in Occidente*, ex. cat., Venezia, Milano; **Greco E., Sommella P.** • 1997 "Urbanistica," in *Enciclopedia dell'arte antica*, II supplement, V, Roma; **Greco E., Torelli M.** • 1983 *Storia dell'urbanistica. Il mondo greco*, Roma-Bari; **Greco G., Pontrandolfo A.** • 1990 *Fratte. Un insediamento etrusco-campano*, Salerno; **Gregori M.** • 1983 "Luigi Lanzi e il riordinamento della Galleria," in P. Barocchi, G. Ragionieri (ed. by), *Gli Uffizi quattro secoli di una galleria*, proceeding of the international meeting, Firenze 1982, Firenze; **Gros P.** • 1981 *Bolsena, Guida agli scavi*, Roma; **Gros P., Torelli M.** • 1988 *Storia dell'urbanistica. Il mondo romano*, Bari; **Guerrero V.M.** • 1991 "El palacio-santuario de Cancho-Roano (Badajoz) y la commercializacion de ànforas fenicias indigenas," in *Rivista di Studi Fenici*, 19, 1; **Guggisberg M.** • 1996 "Eine Reise von Knossos nach Strettweg. Tiergefässe und Kesselwagen als Ausdruck religiöser Kontakte zwischen der Égais und Mitteleuropa im frühen 1. Jahrtausend v. Chr.," in *Archäeologischer Anzeiger*; **Guida alla città etrusca** • 1982 *Guida alla città etrusca e al museo di Marzabotto,* Bologna; **Guidi A.** • 2000 *Preistoria della complessità sociale*, Roma-Bari; **Guldlager Bilde P.** • 1994 "Ritual and Power: The Fan as a Sign of Rank in Central Italian Society," in *Analecta romana Instituti danici*, 22; **Gullini G.** • 1983 "Urbanistica e architettura," in G. Pugliese Carratelli (ed. by), *Megale Hellas*, Milano; **Guzzo P.G.** • 1987 "Taranto a Vulci?," in *Taras*, VI, 1–2, • 1993a *Antico e archeologia. scienza e politica delle diverse antichità*, Bologna • 1993b *Oreficerie della Magna Grecia*, Taranto; **Guzzo P.G., Moscati S., Susini G.** • 1994 *Antiche genti d'Italia*, ex. cat., Rimini, Roma;

H

Hampe E., Simon E. • 1964 *Griechische Sagen in der frühen etruskischen Kunst*, Mainz; **Harari M.** • 1980 *Il "Gruppo Clusium" della ceramografia etrusca*, Roma • 1988 "Les gardiens du Paradis. Iconographie funéraire et allégorie mythologique dans la céramique étrusque à figures rouges tardive," in *Numismatica e antichità classiche. Quaderni ticinesi*, XVII, • 1990 "Il Pittore dell'Aja a Leida e il problema del Gruppo 'Funnel'," in *OudheidKendige mededelingen uit het Rijksmumeum van Oudhen te Leiden*, LXX • 1996 "Ceramica etrusca e falisca a figure rosse e a suddipintura," in *La Collezione Casuccini*, II, *Ceramica attica, etrusca e falisca*, Roma • 1997 "Di nuovo sul cratere guarnacciano del Pittore di Montebradoni: questioni di sintassi e di semantica," in *Aspetti della cultura di Volterra etrusca fra l'età del Ferro e l'età ellenistica*, proceeding of the XIX Convegno di studi etruschi e italici, Volterra 1995, Firenze; **Harris W.V.** • 1971 *Rome in Etruria and Umbria*, Oxford; **Hase von F.-W.** • 1989 "Der etruskische Bucchero aus Karthago," in *Jahrbuch des Römisch-Germanischen Zentralmuseums Mainz*, XXXIX • 1995a "The ceremonial Jewellery from the Regolini Galassi Tomb at Cerveteri. Some Ideas concerning the Workshop," 1952 in G. Morteani, J.P. Northover (ed. by), *Prehistoric Gold in Europe. Mines, Metallurgy and Manifacture*, Dordrecht, Boston, London • 1995b "Ägäische, griechische und vorderorientalische Einflüsse auf das tyrrhenische Mittelitalien," in *Römisch-germanischen Zentralmuseums Mainz Monographien*, 35, Bonn; **Haynes S.** • 1965 *Etruscan Bronze Utensils*, London • 1985 *Etruscan Bronzes,* London-New York • 1989 "Muliebris certaminis laus: bronze documents of a changing ethos," in *Atti del II Congresso Internazionale Etrusco*, Firenze 1985, Roma; **Helbig W.** • 1963 *Führer durch die [...]*, I, Roma, pp. 469–716• 1969 *Führer durch die [...]*, III, Tübingen • 1972 *Führer durch die [...]*, IV, Tübingen; **Hemelrijk J.M.** • 1984 *Caeretan Hydriae* (Kerameus, vol. 5), Mayence; **Hencken H.** • 1968 *Tarquinia, Villanovans and Early Etruscans*, Cambridge (Mass.) • 1971 *The Earliest European Helmets*, Cambridge; **Herbig G.** • 1922 "Religion und Kultus der Etrusker," in *Mitteilungen des Schlesingen Gesellschafts für Volkskunde*, XXXIII; **Herbig R.** • 1952 *Die jungeretruskische Steinsarkophage*, Berlin • 1957 "Zur Religion und Religiosität der Etrusker," in *Historia*, VI • 1965 *Götter und Dämonen der Etrusker*, Mainz; **Hermansen G. M.** • 1940 *Studien über den italischen und den römischen Mars*, Copenhagen; **Herring E., Whitehouse R., Wilkins J.** • 1991 *The Archaeology of Power. Papers of the Fourth Conference of Italian Archaeology,* 1–2, London; **Herrmann H.-V.** • 1984 "Altitalisches und Etruskisches in Olympia. Neue Funde und Forschungen," in *Annuario della Scuola archeologica di Atene e delle Missioni italiane in Oriente*, 61, 1983; **Hérubel Fl.** • 2000 "Mobilier étrusque en Languedoc occidental (VIème-Vème s. av. J.-C.)," in *Documents d'archéologie mé-*

ridionale, 23; HEURGON J. • 1957 "L'état etrusque," in *Historia*, VI, 1, • 1959 "Les Pénestes étrusques chez Denys d'Halicarnasse," in *Latomus*, 18, • 1961a *La vie quotidienne chez les Étrusques*, Paris • 1961b "Valeurs feminines et masculines dans la civilisation étrusque," in *Mélanges de l'Ecole Française de Rome*, LXXIII • 1969 "Le problème des origines étrusques," in *Rome et la Méditerranée occidentale jusqu'aux guerres puniques*, Paris • 1970 *Classes et ordres chez les étrusques*, in *Recherches sur les structures sociales dans l'Antiquité classique*, proceeding of the meeting, Caen 1969, Paris; HIGGINS R • 1980 *Greek and Roman Jewellery*, Berkeley-Los Angeles; HILLER F. • 1966 "Beiträge zur figürlich geritzen Buccherokeramik," in *Marburger Winckelmann-Programm*; HILLGRUBER H. • 1994 "Ein etruskischer Votivkopf," in *Hefte des archäologischen Seminars der Universität Bern*, 15; HIRSCHLAND RAMAGE N. • 1970 "Studies in Early Etruscan Bucchero," in *Papers of the British School at Rome*, XXXVIII; HOFTER M.R. • 1985 *Untersuchungen zu Stil und Chronologie der mittelitalischen Terrakotta-Votivkoepfe*, Bonn; HOSTETTER E. • 1986 *Bronzes from Spina*, I, Mainz; HOWES SMITH B.G.G. • 1984 "Bronze Ribbed Bowls from Central Italy and Etruria," in *Bulletin antieke beschaving. Annual Papers on Classical Archaeology*, 59, 2; HUDSON M. • 1992 "Did the Phoenicians introduce the Idea of interest to Greece and Italy- and if so, when?" in G. Kopcke, I. Tokumaru (ed. by), *Greece between East and West: 10th-8th Centuries BC*, Mainz am Rhein; HULS Y. • 1957 *Ivoires d'Etrurie*, Bruxelles-Rome; HUS A. • 1961 *Recherches sur la statuaire en pierre étrusque archaique*, Paris • 1966 "Réflexions sur la statuaire en pierre de Vulci après l'époque archaique (400-100 environ avant notre ère)," in *Mélanges d'archéologie et d'histoire offerts à A. Piganiol*, Paris • 1975 *Les bronzes étrusques*, Bruxelles • 1977 "La statuaire en pierre archaique de Vulci (travaux et découvertes de 1961 à 1975)," in *La civiltà arcaica di Vulci e la sua espansione*, proceeding of the X Convegno di studi etruschi e italici, Grosseto-Roselle-Vulci 1975, Firenze • 1980 *Les Etrusques et leur destin*, Paris;

I

I NUOVI SCAVI DELL'UNIVERSITÀ DI BOLOGNA • 1990 *I nuovi scavi dell'Università di Bologna nella città etrusca di Marzabotto*, photography ex. cat., Bologna; IL COMMERCIO ETRUSCO ARCAICO • 1985 *Il commercio etrusco arcaico*, proceeding of the meeting, Roma 1983, Roma; IL MUSEO DI TARANTO • 1988 *Il Museo di Taranto. Cento anni di archeologia*, Taranto; INTERACTIONS IN THE IRON AGE • 1996 "Interactions in the Iron Age: Phoenicians, Greeks and the indigenous Peoples of the western Mediterranean. Akten des internationalen Kolloquiums," in *Hamburger Beiträge zur Archäologie*, 19–20; IOZZO M. • 1997 "Attività della Soprintendenza Archeologica della Toscana nel territorio comunale di Volterra: 1990-1995," in *Aspetti della cultura di Volterra etrusca fra l'Età del Ferro e l'Età Ellenistica,* proceeding of the XIX Convegno di studi etruschi e italici, Volterra 1995, Firenze; ISLER H.P. • 1983, in *Numismatica e antichità classiche. Quaderni ticinesi*, 12; ISLER KERÉNYI C. • 1976 "Stamnoi e stamnoidi," in *Numismatica e Antichità Classiche*, V; ISTITUZIONE DEL MUSEO ETRUSCO • 1871 *Istituzione del Museo etrusco in Firenze cui si aggiungono i R.R. Decreti per la tutela dei Monumenti di Etruria*, Firenze; IZZET V. • 1996 "Engraving the boundaries. Exploring space and surface in Etruscan funerary architecture," in *Approaches to the study of ritual. Italy and the ancient Mediterranean,* London;

J

JANNOT J.R. • 1984 *Les reliefs archaiques de Chiusi*, Roma • 1982 "Images humaines, images divine. A propos des statues cinéraires étrusques," in *Ktema*, 7 • 1997 "Charu(n) et Vanth, divinités plurielles?," in *Les plus religieux des hommesgg. Etat de la recherche sur la religion étrusque*, proceeding of the meeting, Paris 1992, Paris; JIMÉNEZ ÁVILA J. • 1998 "El lecho funerario de época orientalizante de "El Torrejón de Abajo" (Càceres)," in *Madrider Mitteilungen*, 39; JOHANNOWSKY W. • 1983 *Materiali di età arcaica dalla Campania*, Napoli • 1996 "Aggiornamenti sulla prima fase di Capua," in *Annali dell'Istituto Orientale di Napoli. Archeologia e Storia Antica*, 3; JOHANSEN F. • 1971 *Reliefs en bronze d'Etrurie*, Copenhagen; JOLIVET V. • 1982 *Recherches sur la céramique étrusque à figures rouges tardive du Musée du Louvre*, Paris; JONES R.E., VAGNETTI L. • 1992 "Traders and craftsmen in the central Mediterranean. Archaeological evidence and archaeometric research. An addendum," in *The Annual of the British School at Athens*, 87; JUDSON S., HEMPHILL P. • 1981 "Sizes of Settlements in Southern Etruria, 6th - 5th Centuries B.C.," in *Studi etruschi*, 49;

K

KAHANE A. • 1963 *Underground Drainageways in Southern Etruria and in Northern Latium*, in "Papers of the British School at Rome", 31; KILIAN K. • 1970 *Früheisenzeitliche Funde aus der Südostnekropole von Sala Consilina (provinz Salerno),* Heidelberg; KLAKOWICZ B. • 1972 *La necropoli anulare di Orvieto*, 1, Roma; KOCH C. • 1939 *Gestirnverehrung im alten Italien,* Frankfurt a. M; KRANZ P. • 1998 "Zu den Anfängen der Vasenmalerei in Caere," in *Numismatica e Antichità classiche. Quaderni ticinesi*, 27; KRAUSKOPF I. • 1987 *Todesdämonen und Todesgötter im vorhellenistischen Etrurien. Kontinuität und Wandel*, Firenze • 1995 *Heroen, Götter und Dämonen auf etruskischen Skarabäen*, Mannheim; KUNZE E. • 1951 "Etruskische Bronzen in Griechenland," in *Studies Presented to D.M. Robinson*, I, St. Louis;

L

L'ALBUM • 1839 *L'album* vol. I, Roma, pp. 17–20, 97–99, 321–22 (now in *Descrizione dei nuovi Musei Gregoriani Etrusco ed Egizio aggiunti al Vaticano*, Roma 1939); L'ARCHEOLOGIA ITALIANA • 1986 *L'archeologia italiana nel Mediterraneo fino alla seconda guerra mondiale*, proceeding of the meeting, Catania; LA CIVILTÀ PICENA NELLA MARCHE • 1992 *La civiltà picena nella Marche*, proceeding of the meeting, Ripatransone; LA DIVINATION • 1985 "La divination dans le monde étrusco-italique," in *Caesarodunum. Bulletin de l'Institut d'Etudes Latines et du Centre de recherches A. Piganiol*, suppl. 52, Tours; LA FORMAZIONE DELLA CITTÀ PREROMANA • 1988 *La formazione della città preromana in Emilia-Romagna*, proceeding of the meeting, Bologna 1987, Imola; LAMBRECHTS R. • 1959 *Essai sur les magistratures des républiques étrusques*, Bruxelles, Roma • 1970 *Les inscriptions avec le mot 'Tular' et le bornage étrusque*, Firenze; LANZI L. • 1982 *La Reale Galleria di Firenze accresciuta e riordinata per comando di S.A.R. l'Arciduca Granduca di Toscana*, Firenze 1782, reprint; LE BUCCHERO NERO ET SA DIFFUSION • 1979 *Le* bucchero nero *et sa diffusion en Gaule Méridionale*, Bruxelles; LE CITTÀ DI FONDAZIONE • 1978 *Le città di fondazione*, preceeding of the II Convegno internazionale di storia urbanistica, Lucca 1977, Venezia; LEACH S. • 1986 in *Italian Iron Age Artefacts*; L'EMPORION • 1993 *L'Emporion textes réunis par A. Bresson et P. Rouillard*, Paris; LEPORE E. • 1975 "La tradizione antica sui Lucani e le origini dell'entità regionale," in *Antiche civiltà lucane*, proceeding of the meeting, Oppido Lucano 1970, Galatina; L'ETÀ DEL BRONZO FINALE IN ITALIA • 1979 *L'età del bronzo finale in Italia,* proceeding of the XXI Riunione scientifica, Istituto italiano di Preistoria e Protostoria, Firenze; LEVI D. • 1935 *Il Museo civico di Chiusi*, Roma; LEVI, M.A. • 1989 *La città antica. Morfologia e biografia dell'aggregazione urbana nell'antichità,* Roma; LO SCHIAVO F., RIDGWAY D. • 1987 "La Sardegna e il Mediterraneo occidentale allo scorcio del II millennio," in *La Sardegna nel Mediterraneo tra il secondo e il primo millennio a.C.*, aproceeding of the II Convegno di studi, Cagliari; LOMBARDO M. • 1997 "L'organizzazione militare degli Italioti," in Pugliese Caratelli G. (ed. by), *Magna Grecia. Lo sviluppo politico, sociale e economico*, Milano; LUGLI G. • 1957 *La tecnica edilizia romana*, Roma; LUIGI ADRIANO MILANI • 1982 "Luigi Adriano Milani: origini e sviluppo del Complesso Museale archeologico di Firenze," in *Studi e Materiali*, n.s. 5; LULOF P.S. • 1991 *Monumental Terracotta Statues from Satricuma Late Archaic Group of Gods and Giants*, Amsterdam • 1996 *Ridge-Pole Statues from the Late Archaic Temple at Satricum*, Amsterdam • 1997 "Myths from Greece. The Representation of Power on the Roofs of Satricum," in *Mededelungen van het Nederlandsch historisch Intituut te Rome*, LVI;

MACINTOSH J. • 1974 "Etruscan Bucchero Pottery Imports in Korinth," in *Hesperia*, XLIII; MAETZKE G. • 1993 "Tre canopi inediti da Sarteano," in *La civiltà di Chiusi e del suo territorio,* proceeding of the XVII Convegno di studi etruschi e italici, Cianciano Terme 1989, Firenze; MAGGIANI A. • 1982a "Le iscrizioni di Asciano e il problema del cosiddetto 'M cortonese'," in *Studi etruschi*, L • 1982b "Qualche osservazione sul fegato di Piacenza," in *Studi etruschi*, L • 1987 "Le copie Gatti del Museo archeologico di Firenze," in F. Buranelli (ed. by), *La tomba François di Vulci*, Roma • 1988 "Terrecotte architettoniche da Sovana," in *La coroplastica templare etrusca fra il IV e il II secolo a.C.,* proceeding of the XVI Convegno di studi etruschi e italici, Orbetello • 1989a "Immagini di aruspici," in *Atti del II Congresso Internazionale Etrusco*, Firenze 1985, Roma • 1989b "Un artista itinerante: il Maestro di Enomao," in *Atti del II Congresso Internazionale Etrusco*, Firenze 1985, Roma • 1990a "Alfabeti etruschi di età ellenistica," in *Annali della Fondazione per il Museo Claudio Faina*, IV, 1988 • 1990b "La situazione archeologica nell'Etruria settentrionale nel V sec.a.C.," in *Crise et transformation des sociétés archaïques del l'Italia antique au Ve siècle av.J.-C.*, proceeding of the round table, Ecole Française de Rome e Unité de recherches étrusco-italiques associée au CNRS, Roma 1987, Roma • 1991 "Un nuovo bronzetto del tipo 'Swordsman' da Volterra," in *Archeologia Classica*, XLIII • 1993a "Concessioni della "isopoliteia" nelle città etrusche. Un indizio per l'età ellenistica," in *Miscellanea etrusco-italica*, I, Roma • 1993b "Problemi della scultura funeraria a Chiusi," in *La civiltà di Chiusi e del suo territorio,* proceeding of the XVII Convegno di studi etruschi e italici, Cianciano Terme 1989, Firenze • 1995 "Sulla cronologia dei sarcofagi etruschi in terracotta di età ellenistica. A proposito di una recente monografia," in *Rivista di Archeologia*, XIX • 1997a "Agoni funebri 'hellenikois nomois' per Vel Kaiknas," in *OCNUS*, 5 • 1997b "Modello etico o antenato eroico? Sul motivo di Aiace suicida nelle stele felsinee," in *Studi etruschi*, LVII • 1997c "Volterra dalla prima età del Ferro al V sec. a.C. Appunti di topografia urbana. II. Dal Villanoviano II all'età tardo arcaica," in *Aspetti della cultura di Volterra etrusca fra l'Età del Ferro e l'Età Ellenistica,* proceeding of the XIX Convegno di studi etruschi e italici, Volterra 1995, Firenze • 1998 "Appunti sulle magistrature etrusche," in *Studi etruschi*, 62 • 1999 "Nuovi etnici e toponimi etruschi," in *Incontro di studi in memoria di Massimo Pallottino*, Pisa • forthcoming-a "Aspetti della organizzazione statuale degli Etruschi," in *La maturazione politica del mondo italico*, proceeding of the international meeting, Napoli 2000 • forthcoming-b "Magistrature cittadine, magistrature federali," in *La lega etrusca dalla dodecapoli ai quindecim populi*, proceeding of the meeting, Chiusi 1999;

M

Maggiani A., Simon E. • 1983 "Il pensiero scientifico e religioso," in M. Cristofani (ed. by) *Gli Etruschi. Una nuova immagine*, Firenze; **Magi F.** • 1940 in J.D. Beazley, F. Magi, *La raccolta Benedetto Guglielmi nel Museo Gregoriano Etrusco*, II, Città del Vaticano • 1941 *La raccolta Benedetto Guglielmi nel Museo Gregoriano Etrusco. II. Bronzi e oggetti vari*, Città del Vaticano • 1963 "Il Museo Gregoriano Etrusco nella storia degli scavi e degli studi etruschi," in *Etudes Etrusco-Italiques*, Louvain, pp. 119–30; **Magi F., Josi E., Speier E.** • 1957–59 "Monumenti, Musei e Gallerie pontificie nel quinquennio 1954-1958. Relazione generale," in *Rendiconti della Pontificia Accademia Romana di Archeologia*, 30–31, pp. 250–57; **Magnanimi G.** • 1985 "Tommaso Corsini archeologo e collezionista, in F. Borsi (ed. by), *La fortuna degli Etruschi*," ex. cat., Firenze; **Malnati L.** • 1993 "Le istituzioni politiche e religiose a Spina e nell'Etruria padana," in *Spina. Storia di una città tra Greci ed Etruschi*, ex. cat., Ferrara; **Malnati L., Violante A.** • 1995 "Il sistema urbano di IV e III secolo in Emilia-Romagna tra Etruschi e Celti," in *Europe celtique du Ve au IIIe siècle avant J.C. Contacts, échanges et mouvements de populations. Actes du Deuxième symposion internat. d'Hautvillers*, 8–10 october 1992, Sceaux Cedex; **Malzahn M.** • 1999 "Das lemnische Alphabet: eine eigenständige Entwicklung," in *Studi etruschi*, LXIII; **Mandolesi** • 1999 *La "prima" Tarquinia. L'insediamento protostorico sulla Civita e nel territorio circostante,* Firenze; **Mangani E.** • 1989–90 "Asciano. Le sculture tardoorientalizzanti del tumulo del Molinello," in *Studi etruschi*, LVI • 1985a "Le fabbriche di specchi nell'Etruria settentrionale," in *Bollettino di Archeologia*, 70 • 1985b "Gli specchi," in *Artigianato artistico in Etruria. L'Etruria settentrionale interna in età ellenistica*, ex. cat., Volterra-Chiusi, Milano • 1992 "Le fabbriche a figure rosse di Chiusi e Volterra," in *Studi etruschi*, LVIII • 1995 Review to "Corpus Speculorum Etruscorum. Great Britain 2; Italia 2; Italia 3; Città del Vaticano 1," in *Archeologia Classica*, 47; **Mansuelli G.A.** • 1962 "La città etrusca di Misano (Marzabotto)," in *Arte antica e moderna*, 17 • 1963 "La casa etrusca di Marzabotto," in *Mitteilungen des Deutschen Archäologischen Instituts, Römische Abteilung*, 70 • 1965 "Contributo allo studio dell'urbanistica di Marzabotto," in *La Parola del Passato* • 1967 "Problemi e prospettive di studio sull'urbanistica antica. La città etrusca," in *Studi storici*, 8 • 1970a "La necropoli orvietana di Crocifisso del Tufo. Un documento di urbanistica etrusca," in *Studi etruschi*, 38 • 1970b *Architettura e città. Problemi del mondo classico*, Bologna • 1972 "Marzabotto. Dix années de fouilles et de recherches," in *Mélanges de l'Ecole Française de Rome*, 84 • 1974 "La civiltà urbana degli Etruschi," in *Popoli e civiltà dell'Italia antica*, III, Roma • 1979 "The Etruscan City," in *Italy before the Romans*, London • 1984 "Tyrrhenoi philotechnoi. Opinioni di antichi sull'arte etrusca," in *Studi di antichità in onore di G. Maetzke*, II, Roma • 1989 "Urbanistica ed architettura etruscoitalica. Prospettive di ricerca," in *Atti del II Congresso Internazionale Etrusco*, Firenze 1985, Roma, I; **Mantino L.** • 1986 *Architettura etrusca in relazione col mondo mediterraneo e transalpino*, Torino; **Maresca M.P.** • 1985 "Palazzo Bucelli," in F. Borsi (ed. by), *La fortuna degli Etruschi,* ex. cat., Firenze; **Markoe G.M.** • 1985 *Phoenician Bronze and Silver Bowls from Cyprus and the Mediterranean*, Berkeley-Los Angeles-London • 1996 "In Pursuit of Silver: Phoenicians in central Italy," in *Hamburger Beiträge zur Archäologie*, 19–20, 1992–93; **Martelli M.** • 1971 "Testa femminile fittile di provenienza templare nel Museo di Volterra," in *Archeologia Classica*, XXIII • 1976 "Il ripostiglio di Volterra," in *Contributi introduttivi allo studio della monetazione etrusca*, supplement to *Annali dell'Istituto Italiano di Numismatica*, 22, Roma • 1979 "Osservazioni sulle 'stele' di Populonia," in *Studi per E. Fiumi,* Pisa • 1980 "Gruppo bronzeo," in *Palazzo Vecchio: committenza e collezionismo medicei*, ex. cat., Firenze • 1982 "La necropoli di Settecamini: lettura dei materiali di scavo ottocentesco nel Museo archeologico di Firenze," in *Pittura etrusca ad Orvieto. Le tombe di Settecamini e degli Hescanas ad un secolo dalla scoperta. Documenti e materiali*, Roma • 1983 "Il 'Marte' di Ravenna," in XENIA, 6 • 1985a "Bologna," in *Bibliografia topografica della colonizzazione greca in Italia e nelle isole tirreniche*, IV, Pisa-Roma • 1985b "Gli avori tardo-arcaici: botteghe e aree di diffusione," in *Il commercio etrusco arcaico*, proceeding of the meeting, Roma 1983, Roma • 1987 *La ceramica etrusca*, Novara • 1988 "La cultura artistica di Vulci arcaica," in *Un artista etrusco e il suo mondo. Il Pittore di Micali*, ex. cat., Roma • 1991a "I Fenici e la questione orientalizzante in Italia," in *Atti del II Congresso Internazionale di Studi Fenici e Punici*, Roma • 1991b Rview to A. Rallo (ed. by), *Le donne in Etruria*, Roma 1989, in *Rivista di Filologia Classica*, 119 • 1994a "Il prestigio del Levante," in J. Guilaine, S. Settis (ed. by), *Storia d'Europa II. 2. Preistoria e antichità*, Torino • 1994b "Sulla produzione di vetri orientalizzanti," in M. Martelli (ed. by), *Tyrrhenoi philotechnoi*, procceding of the meeting, Roma • 1995 "Circolazione dei beni suntuari e stile del potere nell'orientalizzante," in B.M. Giannattasio (ed. by), *Viaggi e commerci nell'antichità*, Genova • 1996 "Bronzi ciprioti dall'Etruria" (M.G. Picozzi, F. Carinci, *Studi in memoria di Lucia Guerrini*), in *Studi miscellanei. Seminario di archeologia e storia dell'arte greca e romana dell'Università di Roma*, 30, Roma; **Martin P.M.** • 1973 "Contribution de Denys d'Halicarnasse à la connaissance du ver sacrum," in *Latomus*, XXXII; **Martinez Pinna J.** • 1994 "L'oenochoé de Tragliatella: considerations sur la société étrusque archaique," in *Studi etruschi*, LX; **Martini W.** • 1971 *Die etruskische Ringsteinglyptik*, Heidelberg; **Marunti M. G.** • 1959 "Lebeti etruschi," in *Studi etruschi*, 27; **Marzi M.G.** • 1996 "Le oreficerie," in *Le collezioni di antichità nella cultura antiquaria europea*, international meeting, Warsav; **Marzi M.G., Bocci Pacini P.** • 1997 "La collezione Galluzzi di Volterra, I-II. I bronzetti e le urne," in *Aspetti della cultura di Volterra etrusca fra l'età del Ferro e l'età ellenistica e contributi della ricerca antropologica alla conoscenza del popolo etrusco*, proceeding of the XIX Convegno di studi etruschi e italici, Volterra 1995; **Massa Pairault F.-H.** • 1997 "Religion étrusque et culture grecque. Quelques problèmes," in *Les plus religieux des hommes - état de la recherche sur la religion étrusque*, proceeding of the meeting, Paris 1992, Paris • 1990 "Crise et transformation des sociétés archaïques de l'Italie antique au Ve siècle av. J.-C.," in *Mélanges de l'Ecole Française de Rome*, CXXXVII, Roma • 1992 *Iconologia e politica nell'Italia antica. Roma, Lazio, Etruria dal VII al I secolo a.C.*, Milano • 1996 *La cité des étrusques*, Paris; **Mastrocinque A.** • 1998 "Servitus pubblica e Roma e nella società etrusca," in *Studi etruschi*, LXII; **Matthiae P.** • 1996 *L'arte degli Assiri*, Roma-Bari; **Maxwell-Hyslop K.R.** • 1965 "Urartian Bronzes in Etruscan Tombs," in *Iraq*, 18; **Mazzarino S.** • 1945 *Dalla monarchia allo stato repubblicano*, Catania • 1957 "Sociologia del mondo etrusco e problemi della tarda etruscitas," in *Historia*, 76, • 1970 "Intorno alla tradizione su Felsina princeps Etruriae," in *Studi sulla città antica*, proceeding of the meeting on the Etruscan and the pre-Roman Italic city, Bologna • 1992 *Dalla monarchia allo stato repubblicano* (I ed. Catania 1945), Milano; **Mele A.** • 1979 "Il commercio greco arcaico Prexis ed Emporié," in *Cahiers du Centre J.Bérard*, 4, Napoli • 1991 "Le popolazioni italiche," in *Storia del Mezzogiorno. I. 1. Il Mezzogiorno antico*, Napoli • 2000 "Viticoltura nella Campania antica," in D. Tommasi, C. Cremonesi (ed. by), *L'avventura del vino nel bacino del Mediterraneo. Itinerari storici e archeologici prime e dopo Roma*, proceeding of the international symposium, Conegliano Veneto 1998, Treviso; **Meloni Trkulja S.** • 1990 "La trasformazione dei Cenacoli in Musei," in C. Acidini Luchinat, R.C. Proto Pisani (ed. by), *La tradizione fiorentina dei Cenacoli*, Firenze; **Menichetti M.** • 1988 "Le aristocrazie tirreniche: aspetti iconografici," in A. Momigliano, A. Schiavone (ed. by), *Storia di Roma. I. Roma in Italia*, Torino • 1992 "L'oinochoe di Tragliatella: mito e rito tra Grecia ed Etruria," in *Ostraka*, I, 1, • 1994 *Archeologia del potere. Re, immagini e miti a Roma e in Etruria in età arcaica*, Milano • 1998 "La pyrriche degli eroi: a proposito di un'anfora del pittore dell'Eptacordo," in *Ostraka*, VII, 1–2 • 2000 "Il vino dei "principes": aspetti iconografici," in *Ostraka*, IX, • forthcoming "Il vino dei 'principes': aspetti iconografici,' in *Ostraka*; **Mertens D.** • 1994 "Elementi di origine etrusco-campana nell'architettura della Magna Grecia," in *Magna Grecia Etruschi Fenici*, procceing of the XXXIII Convegno sulla Magna Grecia, Taranto 1993, Napoli; **Mertens D., Greco E.**, • 1996 "Urbanistica della Magna Grecia," in *I Greci in Occidente*, ex. cat., Venezia, Milano; **Mertens Horn M.** • 1995 "Corinto e l'Occidente nelle immagini. La nascita di Pegaso e la nascita di Afrodite," in *Corinto e l'Occidente,* proceeding of the XXXIV Convegno sulla Magna Grecia, Taranto 7–11 october 1994, Taranto; **Messerschmidt F.** • 1929 "Griechische und etruskische Religion," in *Studi e materiali di storia delle religioni*, V; **Messineo G.** • 1983 "Tesserae hospitales?," in *Xenia*, 5 • 1997 "Gli scavi di Efestia a Lemno. Tradizione micenea nella civiltà tirrenica," in *Studi Micenei ed Egeo Anatolici*, 39, 2; **Meyer J.W.** • 1985 "Zur Herkunft der etruskischen Lebermodelle," in *Phoenicia and its neighbours*, Leuven; **Micheli M.E.** • 1986 "Su una testa di guerriero del Museo Gregoriano Etrusco," in *Prospettiva,* 44 • 1989 "Storia delle collezioni," in A. Giuliano, *I cammei dalla collezione medicea del Museo archeologico di Firenze*, Roma; **Micozzi M.**

• 1993 "Il giovane "egineta" di Caere e il suo contesto," in *Prospettiva*, 71 • 1994 *"White-on-Red", una produzione vascolare dell'orientalizzante etrusco*, Roma • 1996 "Il sarcofago dei Leoni dal Procoio di Ceri," in *Prospettiva*, 82; **Milani L.A.** • 1898 *Museo Topografico dell'Etruria*, Firenze-Roma • 1912 *Il R. Museo archeologico di Firenze*, Firenze; **Miller M.** • 1995 *Befestigungsanlagen in Italien vom 8. bis 3. Jh. v. Chr.*, Hamburg; **Minetti A.** • 1998 "La tomba della Pania: corredo e rituale funerario," in *Annali dell'Istituto universitario orientale di Napoli. Sezione di archeologia e storia antica*, 5 • 2000 "Le necropoli chiusine del periodo orientalizzante," in A. Rastrelli (ed. by), *Chiusi etrusca*, Chiusi; **Mingazzini P.** • 1930 *Vasi della collezione Castellani*, I, Roma; **Minoja M.** • 2000 *Il bucchero del Museo provinciale campano*, Pisa-Roma; **Minto A.** • 1948-1949 "Commiato," in *Studi etruschi*, 20 • 1921 *Marsiliana d'Albegna*, Firenze • 1922 *Populonia*, Firenze • 1928 "Il Regio Museo archeologico di Firenze," in *Studi etruschi*, 2 • 1938 "Attività della Commissione per la Carta Archeologica sulle antiche coltivazioni minerarie," in *Studi etruschi*, 12 • 1939 "Le ricerche archeologiche in Etruria," in *Archivio Storico Italiano* • 1945 "Il Museo centrale dell'Etruria e l'Istituto internazionale di studi etruschi ed italici," in *Studi etruschi*, 18 • 1950 "Il Museo archeologico dell'Etruria e l'Istituto di studi etruschi ed italici," in *Atti dell'Accademia fiorentina di scienze morali La Colombaria*, 8; **Momigliano A.** • 1975 *Alien Wisdom. The Limits of Hellenization*, Cambridge; **Momigliano A. Schiavone A.** • 1988 *Storia di Roma*, I, Torino; **Monumenti** • 1842 *Monumenti del Museo Etrusco Vaticano*, ed.B, Roma **Montagna Pasquinucci M.** • 1968 *Le kelebai volterrane*, Firenze; **Morel J.P.** • 1981 "Le commerce étrusque en France, en Espagne et en Afrique," in *L'Etruria mineraria*, Firenze 1979, Firenze; **Moretti M.** • 1962 *Il Museo nazionale di Villa Giulia*, Roma • 1966 "Tomba Martini Marescotti," in *Quaderni di Villa Giulia*, 1, Milano • 1973 *Il Museo di Villa Giulia*, Roma; **Moretti Sgubini A.M.** • 1999a Euphronios epoiesen: *un dono d'eccezione ad Ercole Cerite*, ex. cat., Roma • 1999b *Il Museo nazionale etrusco di Villa Giulia. Guida breve*, Roma • 2000 *Villa Giulia dalle origini al 2000. Guida breve*, Roma • forthcoming *La Collezione Augusto Castellani*; **Morigi Govi C. Sassatelli G.** • 1993 "Il sepolcreto etrusco del Polisportivo di Bologna: nuove stele felsinee," in *OCNUS* • 1996 "Felsina etrusca," in *Bologna I. Da Felsina a Bononia: dalle origini al* XII *secolo* (Atlante della Città Italiane, Emilia Romagna), Bologna; **Morigi Govi C., Tovoli S., Vitali D. et al.** • 1979 *Villanova, Cà dell'Orbo a Villanova di Castenaso. Probemi di popolamento dal* IX *al* VI *secolo a.C.*, Bologna; **Moroni G.** • 1847 "Museo Gregoriano Etrusco," in *Dizionario di erudizione storico-ecclesiastica*, vol. XLVII, Venezia, pp. 109–21; **Morris I.** • 1999 "Iron Age Greece and the meanings of 'princely tombs'," in P. Ruby (ed. by), *Les princes de la Protohistoire et l'émergence de l'état*, proceeding of the round table, Napoli 1994, Roma; **Morselli C., Tortorici E.** • 1981 "Regisvilla porto di Vulci in loc. Le Murelle: note topografiche e saggi di scavo," in *Quaderni di topografia antica*, 9; **Moscati P.** • 1985 "Studi su Falerii Veteres. 1. L'abitato," in *Atti dell'Accademia nazionale dei Lincei. Classe di scienze morali, storiche e filologiche. Rendiconti*, 40; **Moscati S.** • 1988 "Le coppe metalliche," in S. Moscati (ed. by), *I Fenici*, ex. cat., Venezia 1988, Milano; **Moustaka A.** • 1985 "Spätarchaische Weihgaben aus Etrurien in Olympia," in *Archäologischer Anzeiger*; **Müller K.O., Deecke W.** • 1877 *Die Etrusker*, II, Stuttgart; **Murray O.** • 1994 *Nestor's Cup and the Origins of the Greek symposion*, in B. d'Agostino, D. Ridgway (ed. by), "Apoikia. I più antichi insediamenti greci in Occidente: funzioni e modi dell'organizzazione politica e sociale," in *Annali dell'Istituto universitario orientale di Napoli. Sezione di archeologia e storia antica*, n.s. I; **Musei Etrusci** • 1842 *Musei Etrusci* Roma; **Musti D.** • 1963 "Sull'idea di "suggéneia" in iscrizioni greche," in *Annali della Scuola Normale Superiore di Pisa*, 32 • 1970 "Tendenze nella storiografia romana e greca su Roma arcaica, studi su Livio e Dionigi di Alicarnasso," in *Quaderni Urbinati di Cultura Classica*, 10, Roma • 1987 *Etruria e Lazio arcaico nella tradizione. Demarato, Tarquinio, Mezenzio*, in *Etruria e Lazio arcaico*, proceeding of the meeting, Roma 1986, Roma • 1989 "L'immagine degli Etruschi nella storiografia antica," in *Atti del II Congresso Internazionale Etrusco*, Firenze 1985, Roma;

N

Nagy H. • 1988 *Votive Terracottas from the "Vignaccia", Cerveteri in the Lowie Museum of Anthropology*, Roma; **Naso A.** • 1995 "Alle origini della pittura etrusca: decorazione parietale e architettura funeraria in Etruria meridionale nel VII secolo a.C.", in *Jahrbuch Römisch-germanischen Zentralmuseums Mainz*, 37, 1990 • 1996a *Architetture dipinte. Decorazioni parietali non figurate nelle tombe a camera dell'Etruria meridionale (*VII-V *secolo a.C.)*, Roma • 1996b "Osservazioni sull'origine dei tumuli monumentali nell'Italia centrale," in *Opuscola romana*, 20 • 1998 "I tumuli monumentali in Etruria meridionale: caratteri propri e possibili ascendenze orientali," in *Archaeologische Untersuchungen zu den Beziehungen zwischen Altitalien und der Zone Nordwaerts der Alpen waehrend der fruehen Eisenzeit Alteuropas*, proceeding of the meeting, Regensburg 1994, Regensburg • 2000 *I Piceni*, Milano; **Negroni Catacchio N.** • 1988 *Il Museo di preistoria e protostoria della valle del fiume Fiora*, Manciano • 1995 *Sorgenti della Nova. L'abitato del Bronzo Finale*, Firenze • 1999 "Produzione e commercio dei vaghi d'ambra tipo Tirinto e tipo Allumiere alla luce delle recenti scoperte," in *Protostoria e Storia del "Venetorum Angulus"*, proceeding of the XX Convegno di studi etruschi e italici, Pisa-Roma; **Neugebauer K.A.** • 1943 "Archaische Vulcenten Bronzen," in *Jahrbuch des Deutschen Archäologischen Instituts*; **Nicosia F.** • 1994–95 "Antonio Minto, l'archeologo di Populonia," in *Rassegna di Archeologia*, 12 • 1967 "Schedario topografico dell'agro fiorentino e zone limitrofe," in *Studi etruschi*, XXXV; **Nielsen M.** • 1990 "Sacerdotesse e associazioni culturali femminili in Etruria: testimonianze epigrafiche ed iconografiche," in *Acta Romana Instituti Danici*, XIX • 1998 "Etruscan Women: a cross-cultural Perspective," in *Proceedings of the First Nordic Symposium on Women's Lives in Antiquity*, Göteborg 1997; **Nogara B.** • 1915 "Cenni intorno alla formazione del Museo Gregoriano Etrusco," in G. Pinza, *Materiali per l'etnologia antica toscana e laziale*, Milano, pp. 3–8 • 1933 *Guide du Musée Etrusco-Gregorien du Vatican*, Città del Vaticano 1933 *Guide du Musée Etrusco-Gregorien du Vatican*, Città del Vaticano; **Nuove scoperte e acquisizioni** • 1975 *Nuove scoperte e acquisizioni in Etruria Meridionale*, Roma;

O

Oleson J. P. • 1982 *The Sources of Innovation of later Etruscan Tomb Design*, Roma; **Olzscha K.** • 1939 *Interpretation der Agramer Mumienbinden*, Leipzig • 1955 "Göterformeln und Monatdaten in der grossen etruskischen Inschrift von Capua," in *Glotta*, XXXIV • 1964 "Aus einem etruskischen Priesterbuch," in *Glotta*, XLII; **Orlandini P.** • 1983 "Le arti figurative" in *Megale Hellas*, Milano; **Östenberg C.E.** • 1974 " problemi dei centri minori dell'Etruria meridionale interna alla luce delle scoperte di San Giovenale e di Acquarossa," in *Aspetti e problemi dell'Etruria interna*, Firenze • 1975 *Case etrusche di Acquarossa*, Roma; **Özgen I., Öztürk J.** • 1996 *Heritage recovered. The Lydian Treasure*, Istanbul;

P

Pacciani B. • 1998 *Il Museo archeologico nazionale di Firenze. Dieci anni di lavori (1983-1993)*, Firenze; **Pacciarelli M.** • 1997 *Acque, grotte e dei. 3000 anni di culti preromani in Romagna, Marche e Abruzzo*, ex. cat., Fusignano; **Paci G.** • 1999 *Cupra Marittima e il suo territorio in età antica*, proceeding of the meeting, Tivoli 1993, Roma; **Pailler J.-M.** • 1988 *Baccanalia. La répression de 186 av. J.-C. à Rome et en Italie*, Roma; **Paisi Presicce C.** • 2000 *La Lupa capitolina*, Roma; **Paleani M.T.** • 1993 *Le lucerne paleocristiane* (Museo Gregoriano Etrusco, Cataloghi, Antiquarium romano), Roma; **Pallottino M.** • 1945 *La scuola di Vulca*, Roma [now in *Saggi di Antichità*, Roma 1979, pp. 1003 ff.] • 1950 "Il grande acroterio femminile di Veio," in *Archeologia Classica*, II [now in *Saggi di Antichità*, Roma 1979, pp. 1037 ff.] • 1955 "Intorno alla sistemazione del Museo nazionale di villa Giulia," in *Archeologia Classica*, 7 • 1968 *Testimonia Linguae Etruscae*, Firenze • 1970–71 "La città etrusco-italica come premessa alla città romana. Varietà di sostrati formativi e tendenze di sviluppo unitario," in *Atti. Centro ricerche e documentazione sull'antichità classica*, 3 • 1978 *Thesaurus Linguae Etruscae*. I. *Indice Lessicale*, Roma • 1981 *Annio da Viterbo. Documenti e ricerche*. I, Roma • 1984 *Etruscologia* (I ed. 1942), Milano • 1986 "I documenti scritti e la lingua," in *Rasenna. Storia e civiltà degli Etruschi*, Milano • 1989 "Prospettive attuali del problema delle origini etrusche," in *Atti del* II *Congresso Internazionale Etrusco*, Firenze 1985, Roma, I • 1992 *Les Étrusques et l'Europe*, Paris-Milan; **Pandolfini M., Prosdocimi A.L.** • 1990 *Alfabetari e insegnamento della scrittura nell'Italia antica*, Firenze; **Paolucci G.** • 1998 "La diffusione dei tumuli nell'area chiusina e l'errata provenienza della seconda pisside della Pania," in *Annali dell'Istituto universitario orientale di Napoli. Sezione di archeologia e storia antica*, n.s. 5 • forthcoming "Prime considerazioni sulla necropoli di Tolle," in *Annali della Fondazione per il Museo Claudio Faina*, 7; **Pareti L.** • 1947 *La tomba Regolini Galassi nel Museo Gregoriano Etrusco e la civiltà dell'Italia centrale nel* VII *secolo a.C.*, Roma; **Paribeni E.** • 1974 in *Aspetti e problemi dell'Etruria interna*, Firenze • 1980 "Incontri e contatti tra la plastica della Magna Grecia e l'Etruria," in *Annali della Fondazione per il Museo Claudio Faina*, I; **Parise N.F.** • 1985 "La prima monetazione etrusca. Fondamenti metrologici e funzioni," in *Il commercio etrusco arcaico*, Roma; **Pautasso A.** • 1994 *Il deposito votivo presso la Porta Nord a Vulci*, Roma; **Payne** • 1931 *Necrocorinthia*, Oxford; **Pebarthe C. Delrieux F.** • 1999 "La transaction du plomb de Pech Maho," in *Zeitschrift für Papyrologie und Epigraphik*, 126; **Penny Small J.** • 1982 *Cacus and Marsyas in Etrusco-Roman Legend*, Princeton; **Perali P.** • 1948 "Il Museo Gregoriano Etrusco," in *Gregorio* XVI *miscellanea commemorativa*, Roma; **Peroni R.** • 1969 "Per uno studio dell'economia di scambio in Italia nel quadro dell'ambiente culturale dei secoli intorno al Mille a.C.," in *La*

Parola del Passato, XXIV • 1989 *Protostoria dell'Italia continentale. La penisola italiana nell'età del Bronzo e del Ferro* (Popoli e civiltà dell'Italia antica, 9), Roma • 1993 in *Armi. Gli strumenti della guerra in Lucania*, ex. cat., Melfi, Bari • 1996 *L'Italia alle soglie della storia*, Roma, Bari; **Peruzzi E.** • 1973–76 *Origini di Roma*, I–II, Bologna • 1998 *Civiltà greca nel Lazio preromano*, Firenze; **Pfiffig A.J.** • 1963 *Studien zu den Agramer Mumienbinden*, Wien • 1968 *Ein Opfergelubde an etruskischen Minerva*, Wien • 1969 *Die etruskische Sprache, Akademische Druck- u. Verlagsanstalt*, Graz • 1975 *Religio Etrusca*, Graz; **Phillips Jr. K.M.** • 1993 *In the Hills of Tuscany. Recent Excavations at the Etruscan Site of Poggio Civitate (Murlo, Siena)*, Philadelphia; **Pianu G.** • 1980 *Materiali del Museo archeologico nazionale di Tarquinia. Ceramiche etrusche a figure rosse*, Roma • 1982 *Materiali del Museo archeologico nazionale di Tarquinia. Ceramiche etrusche sovradipinte*, Roma • 1985 "I luoghi della cultura figurativa," in Torelli M., *L'arte degli Etruschi*, Roma-Bari • 1989 "La standardizzazione," in *Atti* del *II Congresso Internazionale Etrusco*, Firenze 1985, Roma, II; **Pietrangeli C.** • 1985 *I Musei Vaticani. Cinque secoli di storia*, Roma, pp. 156–61 • 1986 "L'appartamento del cardinal Zelada in Vaticano," in *BmonMusPont*, VI, pp. 152–98; **Piganiol A.** • 1953 "Les Étrusques, peuple d'Orient," in *Cahiers d'histoire mondiale*, 1; **Pincelli R., Morigi Govi C.** • 1975 *La necropoli villanoviana di San Vitale*, Bologna; **Pohl I.** • 1972 *The Iron Age Necropolis of Sorbo at Cerveteri*, Stockhölm • 1985 "Nuovi contributi alla storia dell'abitato etrusco di San Giovenale nel periodo fra il 500 e il 200 a.C.," in *La Parola del Passato*, 40; **Polany** • 1963 "Port of trade in Early Societies," in *The Journal of Economic History*, 23; **Pomeroy S.** • 1984 "Selected Bibliography of Women in Classical Antiquity," in *Women in the Ancient World. The Arethusa Papers*, Albany; **Pomey P.** • 1997 "Un exemple de l'évolution des techniques de construction navale antique: de l'assemblage par ligatures à l'assemblage par tenons et mortaises," in *Techniques et économie antiques et médiévales: le temps de l'innovation*, Aix-en-Provence 1996, Paris; **Pontrandolfo A., Rouveret A.** • 1992 *Le tombe dipinte di Paestum*, Modena; **Potter T.W.** • 1979 *The Changing Landscape of South Etruria*, London • 1991 "Towns and territories in southern Etruria," in *City and country in the ancient world*, London; **Poupé J.** • 1963 "Les aryballes de bucchero imitant des modèles protocorinthiens," in *Études Étrusco-italiques*, Louvain; **Prag A.J.N.W.** • 1985 *The Oresteia. Iconographic and Narrative Tradition*, Warminster - Chicago; **Prayon F.** • 1975a *Fruehetruskische Grab-und Hausarchitektur*, Heidelberg • 1975b "Zur Datierung der drei frühetruskischen Sitzstatuetten aus Cerveteri," in *Mitteilungen des Deutschen Archäologischen Instituts, Römische Abteilung*, 82 • 1986 "Architecture," in L. Bonfante (ed. by), *Etruscan Life and Afterlife*, Detroit • 1989 "L'architettura funeraria etrusca. La situazione attuale delle ricerche e dei problemi aperti," in *Atti del II Congresso Internazionale Etrusco*, Firenze 1985, Roma, I • 1994 "L'architettura etrusca ed il problema degli influssi (magno-)greci," in *Magna Grecia Etruschi Fenici*, proceeding of the XXXIII Convegno sulla Magna Grecia, Taranto 1993, Napoli • 1995 "Ostmediterrane Einflusse auf den Beginn der Monumentalarchitektur in Etrurien?," in *Jahrbuch des Römisc-Germanischen Zentralmuseums*, XXXVII, 2 • 1998a "Die Anfänge grossformatiger Plastik in Etrurien," in *Archäologische Untersuchungen zu den Beziehungen zwischen Altitalien und der Zone nordwärts der Alpen während der frühe Eisenzeit Alteuropas*, proceeding of the meeting, Bonn • 1998b "Phöniker und Etrusker. Zur Goldlaminierung in der frühetruskischen Kunst," in R. Rolle, K. Schmidt (ed. by), *Archäologische Studien in Kontaktzonen der antiken Welt*, Göttingen; **Proietti G.** • 1980 *Il Museo nazionale etrusco di Villa Giulia*, Roma; **Prosdocimi A.L.** • 1989 "Le religioni degli Italici," in *Italia omnium terrarum parens*, Milano; **Pugliese Carratelli G.** • 1986 *Rasenna, Storia e civiltà degli Etruschi*, Milano; **Putz U.** • 1998 "Gesellschaftlicher Wandel in Mittelitalien im Spiegel villanovazeitlicher Prunkgräber," in *Archäologische Untersuchungen zu den Beziehungen zwischen Altitalien und der Zone nordwärts der Alpen während der frühe Eisenzeit Alteuropas*, proceeding of the meeting, Bonn; **Py F. e M.** • 1974 "Les amphores étrusques de Vaunage et de Villevieille (Gard)," in *Mélanges de l'Ecole Française de Rome*; **Py M.** • 1995 "Les Etrusques, les Grecs et la fondation de Lattes," in *Sur les pas des Grecs en Occident, Etudes massaliètes*, 4 • 1996 "Pyrgi" in *Enciclopedia dell'arte antica*, II supplement, IV, Roma;

Q

Quilici L. • 1989 "Le antiche vie d'Etruria," in *Atti del II Congresso Internaz. Etrusco*, Firenze 1985, Roma, I;

R

Radke G. • 1979 *Die Götter Altitaliens*, Münster; **Rallo A.** • 1989 *Le donne in Etruria*, Roma; **Randsborg K.** • 1996 *Absolute Chronology-Archaeological Europe, 2500-500 B.C.*, supplement to *Acta Archaeologica*, Copenhagen; **Rasmussen T.B.** • 1979 *Bucchero Pottery from Southern Etruria*, Cambridge; **Rastrelli A.** • 1985 "La produzione in terracotta a Chiusi," in *Artigianato artistico in Etruria. L'Etruria settentrionale interna in età ellenistica*, ex. cat., Volterra-Chiusi, Milano • 1993 "La decorazione fittile dell'edificio sacro in loc. I Fucoli presso Chianciano Terme," in *Ostraka*, II, 2; **Rastrelli A., Romualdi A.** • 1999 *Bronzi greci e romani dalle collezioni del Museo archeologico nazionale di Firenze*, ex. cat., Firenze; **Rathje A.** • 1979 "Oriental Imports in Etruria in the Eight and Seventh Centuries B.C.: Their Origin and Implications," in D. e F.R. Ridgway (ed. by), *Italy Before the Romans. The Iron Age, Orientalizing and Etruscan Periods*, London, New York, San Francisco • 1984 "I *keimelia* orientali," in *Opus*, 3 • 1986 "Five ostrich eggs from Vulci," in J. Swaddling (ed. by), *Italian Iron Age Artefacts in the British Museum. Papers of the Sixth British Museum Classical Colloquium*, London • 1990 "The Adoption of the Homeric Banquet in Central Italy in the Orientalizing Period," in O. Murray (ed. by), *Sympotica. A Symposium on the Symposion*, Oxford • 1991 "An exotic Piece from Vulci: the Egyptian Blue Pyxis in Berlin," in *Stips votiva. Papers presented to C.M. Stibbe*, Amsterdam • 1995 "Il banchetto in Italia centrale: quale stile di vita?," in O. Murray, M. Tecusan (ed. by), *In vino veritas*, Roma; **Rebecchi F.** • 1998 *Spina e il delta padano*; **Regter W.** • 1988 "Fascinating Fans," in J. Christiansen, T. Melander (ed. by), *Ancient Greek and Related Pottery. Proceedings of the 3rd Symposium on Ancient Greek and Related Pottery*, Copenhagen; **Rendeli M.** • 1991 "Sulla nascita delle comunità urbane in Etruria meridionale," *Annali. Sezione di archeologia e storia antica. Istituto universitario orientale*, 13 • 1993 *Città aperte. Ambiente e paesaggio rurale nell'Etruria meridionale costiera durante l'età orientalizzante ed arcaica*, Roma; **Ridgway D.** • 1990 "The First Western Greeks and their Neighbours, 1935 - 1985," in *Greek Colonists and Native Populations. Proceedings of the First Australian Congress of Classical Archaeology*, Sydney 1985, Oxford • 1996 "Relazioni di Cipro con l'Occidente in età precoloniale," in G. Pugliese Carratelli (ed. by), *I Greci in Occidente*, ex. cat., Venezia 1996, Milano • 1997 "Nestor's Cup and the Etruscans," in *Oxford Journal of Archaeology*, XVI, 3; **Riis P.J.** • 1938 "Rod-Tripods," in *Acta Archaeologica*, 10 • 1941 *Tyrrenikà. An Archaeological Study of Etruscan Sculpture in the Archaic and Classical Period*, Copenhagen • 1981 *Etruscan Types of Headsgg. A Revised Chronology of the Archaic and Classical Terracottas of Etruscan Campania an Central Italy*, Copenhagen • 1997 *Vulcentia vetustiora. A Study of Archaic Vulcian Bronzes*, Copenhagen; **Rix H.** • 1963 *Das Etruskische Cognomen*, Wiesbaden • 1977 "L'apporto dell'onomastica personale alla conoscenza della storia sociale," in M. Cristofani, M. Martelli (ed. by), *Caratteri dell'Ellenismo nelle urne etrusche*, proceeding of the meeting, Firenze • 1983 "La scrittura e la lingua," in M. Cristofani (ed. by) *Gli Etruschi. Una nuova immagine*, Firenze • 1984 "Etrusco mechl rasnal = lat. Res publica," in *Studi in onore di G. Maetzke*, Roma • 1985 "Descrizioni di rituali in etrusco e in italico," in *L'etrusco e le altre lingue dell'Italia antica*, proceeding of the meeting of the Società italiana di glottologia, Pisa 1984, Pisa • 1991 "Etrusco un, une, unu 'te, tibi, vos' e le preghiere dei rituali paralleli nel *liber Linteus*," in *Miscellanea etrusco-italica in onore di M. Pallottino*. I, in *Archeologia Classica*, XLIII, Roma; **Rix H. et al.** • 1991 *Etruskische Texte. Editio minor*, I, *Einleitung, Konkordanz, Indices*, II, *Texte*, Tübingen; **Rizzo M.A.** • 1990 *Le anfore di trasporto e il commercio etrusco arcaico*, Roma; **Rocco G.** • 1999 *Avori e ossi dal Piceno*, Roma; **Rohde E.** • 1990 "Bildhauerarbeiten der orientalisierenden Periode aus etruskischen Gräbern," in *Die Welt der Etrusker*, proceeding of the international meeting, Berlino 1988, Berlin; **Roncalli F.** • 1984 "Il reparto di antichità etrusco italiche," in *BmonMusPont*, I, 3, pp. 227–78; **Romanelli P.** • 1957 "La cerimonia in onore di Antonio Minto," in *Studi etruschi*, 25, • 1986 *Necropoli dell'Etruria rupestre. Architettura*, Viterbo; **Romualdi A.** • 1987 "Ritratti romani di epoca repubblicana e giulio-claudia del Museo archeologico di Firenze," in *Mitteilungen des Deutschen Archäologischen Instituts, Abteilung Rom*, 94 • 1988 "Terrecotte da Populonia," in *La coroplastica templare etrusca fra il IV e il II secolo a.C.*, proceeding of the XVI Convegno di studi etruschi e italici, Orbetello • 1990 "La stipe di Bibbona nel Museo archeologico di Firenze," in *Die Welt der Etrusker*, proceeding of the international meeting, 1988, Berlin • 1992a "I bronzi di Lorenzo il Magnifico: alle origini di una tradizione collezionistica," in G. De Marinis, A. Romualdi (ed. by), *Itinerario Laurenziano nel Museo archeologico di Firenze*, Firenze • 1992b *Populonia in età ellenistica. I materiali dalle necropoli*, proceeding of the seminar, Firenze 1986, Firenze • 1993 "La polis nel periodo arcaico e l'attività di lavorazione del ferro," in *Populonia e il suo territorio. Profilo storico-archeologico*, Firenze • 1995 "Isidoro Falchi e la scoperta della necropoli di S. Cerbone a Populonia," in S. Bruni *Isidoro Falchi un medico al servizio dell'archeologia. Un protagonista della ricerca italiana di fine Ottocento*, Pontedera • 1998 "Il kouros di Selvanera, in In memoria di Enrico Paribeni," Roma • 2000 *Il giardino della Crocetta ed il Museo archeologico di Firenze*, in

Guida al Giardino del Museo archeologico di Firenze, Firenze; **Roncalli F.** • 1973 "Il 'Marte' di Todi. Bronzistica etrusca ed ispirazione classica," in *Memorie Atti della Pontificia accademia romana di archeologia*, s. III, 11. 2 • 1985 *Scrivere etrusco,* ex. cat., Perugia, Milano • 1988 *Gens antiquissima Italiae*, ex. cat., Perugia • 1998 "Una immagine femminile di culto dalla 'tomba d'Iside' di Vulci," in *Annali della Fondazione per il Museo Claudio Faina*, V; **Rose H.J.** • 1928 "On the Relations between Etruscan and Roman Religions," in *Studi e materiali di storia delle religioni*, IV; **Roselle, gli scavi** • 1975 *Roselle, gli scavi e la mostra*, Pisa; **Rosemberg A.** • 1913 *Der Staat der alten Italiker*, Berlin; **Ruby P.** • 1995 *Le crépuscole des marges. Le premier âge du fer à Sala Consilina*, Roma-Napoli; **Ruiz A.** • 1996 "Los príncipes iberos: procesos ecònómicos y sociales," in *Los Iberos, príncipes de Occidente*, international meeting, Madrid • 1999 "Origén y desarrollo de la aristocracía en época ibérica, en el alto Valle del Guadalquivir," in *Les princes de la protohistoire et l'émergence de l'état*, proceeding of the international round table, Napoli-Roma; **Rystedt E., Wikander C., Wikander O.** • 1993 *Deliciae fictiles. Proceedings of the First International Conference on Central Italic Architectural Terracottas at the Swedish Institute in Rome*, Roma 1990, Stockhölm;

S

Saeflund G. • 1986 "'Hieros Gamos'. Motive in der etruskischen Sepulcralkunst," in J. Swaddling (ed. by), *Italian Iron Age Artefacts in the British Museum. Papers of the Sixth British Museum Classical Colloquium*, London; **Salomon N.** • 1997 *Le cleruchie di Atene. Caratteri e funzione*, Pisa; **Salvini M.** • 1996 "L'età del Ferro a Firenze: le tombe del Gambrinus," in *Alle origini di Firenze dalla preistoria all'età romana,* Firenze; **Sannibale M.** • 1994 *Le urne cinerarie di età ellenistica, Museo Gregoriano Etrusco,* Roma; **Santuari d'Etruria** • 1985 *Santuari d'Etruria*, ex. cat., Arezzo, Milano; **Sassatelli G.** • 1983 *Bologna e Marzabotto. Storia di un problema, in Studi sulla città antica. L'Emilia Romagna*, Roma • 1984a "La Galleria della pittura etrusca nel salone X," in *Dalla stanza delle Antichità al Museo civico. Storia della formazione del Museo civico archeologico di Bologna*, Bologna • 1984b "Una nuova stele felsinea," in *Culture figurative e materiali tra Emilia e Marche. Studi in memoria di M. Zuffa,* Rimini • 1986 "Bologna etrusca: nuovi dati e recenti acquisizioni," in *Atti e Memorie della Deputazione di Storia Patria per le Province di Romagna*, n.s., XXXV, • 1987 "Topografia e 'sistemazione monumentale' delle necropoli felsinee," in *La formazione della città in Emilia Romagna*, proceeding of the meeting, Imola • 1989 *La città etrusca di Marzabotto*, Casalecchio di Reno • 1989 "Problemi cronologici delle stele felsinee alla luce dei rispettivi corredi tombali," in *Atti del II Congresso Internazionale Etrusco*, Firenze 1985, Roma • 1990 "La situazione in Etruria Padana," in *Crise et transformations des Sociétés archaiques de l'Italie Antique au Vème siècle av. J.C.*, proceeding of the round table, Roma 1987, Roma • 1991 "Nuovi dati epigrafici da Marzabotto e il ruolo delle comunità locali nella 'fondazione' della città," in *Archeologia Classica*, XLIII • 1993 "La funzione economica e produttiva: merci, scambi, artigianato," in *Spina. Storia di una città tra Greci ed Etruschi*, ex. cat., Ferrara • 1994a *Iscrizioni e graffiti della città etrusca di Marzabotto*, Bologna • 1994b "Problemi del popolamento nell'Etruria Padana con particolare riguardo a Bologna," in *La presenza etrusca nella Campania meridionale*, proceeding of the meeting, Salerno Pontecagnano 1990, Firenze • 1999a "Nuovi dati epigrafici e il ruolo degli Etruschi nei rapporti con l'Italia nord-orientale," in *Protostoria e Storia del Venetorum Angulus*, proceeding of the XX Convegno di studi etruschi e italici, Portogruaro, Quarto d'Altino, Este, Adria, 1996, Pisa, Roma • 1999b "Spina e gli Etruschi Padani," in *La Dalmazia e l'altra sponda. Problemi di archaiologhia adriatica*, proceeding of the meeting, Venezia, Firenze; **Sassatelli G. Govi E.** • 1992 "Testimonianze di età preromana. Strade e monumentalizzazione," in *Tecnica stradale romana*, Roma; **Scarano Ussani V.** • 1996 "Il significato simbolico dell'hasta nel III periodo della cultura laziale," in *Ostraka*, V, 2; **Scarpignato M.** • 1985 *Oreficerie etrusche arcaiche* (Museo Gregoriano Etrusco, Cataloghi, 1), Roma; **Scarpignato M., Di Gennaro F.** • 1988 "L'età del bronzo e della prima età del ferro a Orvieto," in *Antichità dell'Umbria in Vaticano,* Perugia; **Schmiedt G.** • 1970a *Atlante aerofotografico delle sedi umane in Italia II. Le sedi antiche scomparse*, Firenze • 1970b "Contributo della fotografia aerea alla ricostruzione dell'urbanistica della città italica ed etrusca preromana," in *Studi sulla città antica*, Bologna; **Schnapp A.** • 1999 "Les voies du commerce grec en Occidente," in *La colonisation grecque en Méditerranée occidentale*, proceeding of the meeting, Roma-Napoli 1995, Roma; **Schwarz S.J.** • 1984, in *Mitteilungen des Deutschen Archäologischen Instituts*, 91; **Sforzini C.** • 1985 "Nota bibliografica sulla storia del Museo di villa Giulia," in *Studi etruschi*, 51; **Sgubini Moretti A.M.** • 1991 "Nuovi dati della necropoli rupestre di Pian di Mola di Tuscania," in *Bollettino di Archeologia*, 7 • 1997 "Massimo Pallottino e il Museo di villa Giulia," in G. Bartoloni (ed. by), *Le necropoli arcaiche di Veio. Giornata di studio in memoria di Massimo Pallottino*, Roma; **Shefton B.B.** • 1967 "Attisches Meisterwerk und etruskische Kopie," in *Wissenschaftliche Zeitchrift der Universität Rostok*, XVI • 1989 "The Paradise Flower, a 'Court Style' Phoenician Ornament: its History in Cyprus and the Central and Western Mediterranean," in V. Tatton Brown (ed. by), *Cyprus and the East Mediterranean in the Iron Age. Papers of 7th BM Classical Colloquium*, London; **Schmitt Pantel P.** • 1990 *Storia delle donne in Occidente. L'Antichità*, Bari; **Sisi C.** • 1999 *Palazzo Pitti. Galleria d'arte moderna*, Firenze; **Snodgrass A.M.** • 1993 'The Hoplite Reform Revisited,' in *Dialogues d'histoire ancienne*, XIX; **Sommella P.** • 1988 *Italia antica. L'urbanistica romana*, Roma; **Sordi M.** • 1995 "La donna etrusca," in M. Sordi, *Prospettive di storia etrusca*, Como; **Spadea G.** • 1980 "Cippe iconique de Arnth Paipnas," in *Prima Italia. Arts italiques du premier millénaire avant J.-C.*, ex. cat., Bruxelles; **Spini G., Casali A.** *Storia delle città italiane*; **Spivey N.** • 1987 *The Micali Painter and his Followers*, Oxford • 1992 "Ajax in Etruria," in *Omaggio a Paola Zancani Montuoro*, proceeding of the meeting, in *Atti e memorie della Società Magna Grecia*, 3 s., 1 • 1997 *Etruscan Art*, London - New York; **Sprenger M.** • 1972 *Die etruskische Plastik des V: Jahrhunderts v: Chr. Und ihr Verhältnis zur griechischen Kunst*, Roma; **Staccioli R.A.** • 1968 *Modelli di edifici etrusco-italici*, Firenze • 1968 "Urbanistica etrusca," in *Archeologia Classica*, 20 • 1976 "Considerazioni sui complessi monumentali di Murlo e di Acquarossa," in *Mélanges offerts à J. Heurgon*, Roma; **Stary P.F.** • 1981 *Zur eisenzeitlichen Bewaffnung und Kampwesen in Mittelitalien*, Mainz a.R.; **Stary-Rimpau J.** • 1981 "Fremdeinflüsse in Bologneser Stelen," in *Die Aufnahme fremder Kultureinflüsse in Etrurien und das Problem des Retardierens in der etruskischen Kunst*, proceeding of the meeting, Mannheim; **Stefani E.** • 1934 *Il Museo nazionale di Villa Giulia*, Roma • 1948 *Il Museo nazionale di villa Giulia*, Roma; **Steingräber S.** • 1979 *Etruskische Möbel*, Roma • 1981 *Etrurien. Städte, Heiligtümer, Nekropolen*, München • 1985 "Felsgrabarchitektur in Etrurien," in *Antike Welt. Zeitschrift für Archäologie und Kulturgeschichte*, 16, 2 • 1992 "Neue Grabungen in der Felsgräbernekropole von San Giuliano bei Barbarano Romano (VT)," in *Antike Welt. Zeitschrift für Archäologie und Kulturgeschichte*, 23 • 1996 "New Discoveries and Research in Southern Etruscan Rock Tombs," in *Etruscan Studies*, 3; **Stella L.A.** • 1930 *Italia antica sul mare*, Milano; **Stenico A.** • 1958 "Un nuovo cratere protofalisco," in *Archeologia Classica*, X; **Stopponi S.** • 1985 *Case e Palazzi d'Etruria*, ex. cat., Siena, Milano • 1987 "Note sulla topografia della necropoli," in *Annali della Fondazione per il Museo Claudio Faina*, 3 • 1990a "Acroterio," in *Antichità dall'Umbria a Leningrado,* ex. cat., Leningrado • 1990b "Iscrizioni etrusche su ceramiche attiche," in *Annali della Fondazione per il Museo Claudio Faina*, IV, 1988 • 1991 "Un acroterio dal santuario di Cannicella ad Orvieto," in *Archeologia Classica*, XLIII; **Strandberg Olofsson M.** • 1989 "On the reconstruction of the monumental area at Acquarossa," in *Opuscola romana*, 17; **Strøm I.** • 1992 "Evidence from the Sanctuaries," in G. Kopcke, I. Tokumaru (ed. by), *Greece between East and West: 10th-8th Centuries BC*, Mainz am Rhein • 1997 "Conclusioni," in G. Bartoloni (ed. by), *Le necropoli arcaiche di Veio. Atti della giornata di studio in memoria di M. Pallottino*, Roma; **Studi sulla città antica** • 1970 *Studi sulla città antica*, proceeding of the meeting on the Etruscan and the pre-Roman Italic city, Bologna 1966, Bologna; **Studi sulla città antica** • 1983 *Studi sulla città antica. L'Emilia Romagna*, Roma; **Szilagyi J.G.** • 1992-1998 *Ceramica etrusco-corinzia figurata*, 2 vol., Roma • 1989 in *Atti II Congresso Internazionale etrusco*, Firenze 1985, Roma • 1993 "Polyclitus Etrusca?," in H. Beck, P.C. Bol (ed. by), *Polykletforschungen,* Berlin;

T

Taglione C. • 1999 *L'abitato etrusco di Bologna,* Imola; **Tamburini Müller M.** • 1987 "Dati preliminari sulla composizione dei corredi di IX secolo da Verucchio," in *Romagna Protostorica,* proceeding of the meeting, San Giovanni in Galilea 1985, Viserba di Rimini; **Tamburini P.** • 1997 *Un abitato villanoviano perilacustre. Il Gran Carro sul lago di Bolsena (1959-1985)*, Roma; **Tarditi C.** • 1996 *Vasi di bronzo in area apula. Produzioni greche ed italiche di età arcaica e classica*, Galatina; **Taylor L.R.** • 1923 *Local Cults in Etruria*, Roma; **Testa A.** • 1989 *Candelabri e Tymiateria* (Museo Gregoriano etrusco, Cataloghi, 2), Roma; **Thuillier J.-P.** • 1993 *Spectacles sportifs et scéniques dans le monde étrusco-italique*, Roma; **Thulin C.** • 1909 *Die etruskische Disziplin,* Göteborg; **Todisco L.** • 1994-1995 "Nuovi dati e osservazioni sulla 'tomba delle danzatrici' di Ruvo," in *Atti e Memorie della Società Magna Grecia*, III; • 1999 "La tombe delle danzatrici di Ruvo di Puglia," in *Le mythe grec dans l'Italie antique. Fonction et image, proceeding of the meeting,* Roma 1996, Roma; **Toms J.** • 1986 "The relative chronology of the villanovan cemetery of Quattro Fontanili at Veii," in *Annali dell'Istituto Orientale di Napoli-Archeologia e Storia Antica*, VIII; **Tondo L.** • 1982 "Il Milani numismatico: studi e metodo, in Luigi

Adriano Milani: origini e sviluppo del Complesso museale archeologico di Firenze," in *Studi e Materiali*, vol. 5 n.s. • 1990 "I cammei," in L. Tondo, F.M. Vanni, *Le gemme dei Medici e dei Lorena nel Museo archeologico di Firenze*, Firenze; **Torelli M.** • 1965 "Un nuovo alfabetario etrusco da Vulci,"in *Archeologia Classica*, 17 • 1975a *Elogia tarquiniensia*, Firenze • 1975b "Tre studi di storia etrusca," in *Dialoghi di Archeologia*, VIII • 1976 "Glosse etrusche. Qualche problema di trasmissione," in *Mélanges offerts à J. Heurgon*, Roma • 1977 "L'ellenismo fuori del mondo ellenistico," in R. Bianchi Bandinelli (ed. by), *Storia e civiltà dei Greci*, 10, Milano, • 1980 *Etruria*, Bari • 1981b "Il commercio greco in Etruria fra VIII e VI sec. a.C.," in M. Mello (ed. by), *Il commercio greco nel Tirreno in età arcaica. Studi in memoria di M. Napoli*, Salerno • 1981a *Storia degli Etruschi*, Bari • 1982 "Per la definizione del commercio greco-orientale: il caso di Gravisca," in *La Parola del Passato* • 1983 "Polis e 'Palazzo'. Architettura, ideologia e artigianato greco in Etruria tra VII e VI secolo a.C.," in *Architecture et société de l'archaisme grec à la fin de la République Romaine*, proceeding of the meeting, Roma 1980, Paris-Roma • 1984 *Lavinio e Roma. Riti iniziatici e matrimonio tra archeologia e storia*, Roma • 1985a "Introduzione," in S. Stopponi (ed. by), *Case e palazzi d'Etruria*, ex. cat., Siena, Milano • 1985b *L'arte degli Etruschi*, Roma-Bari • 1986a "La storia," in *Rasenna*, Milano • 1986b "La religione," in G. Pugliese Carratelli (ed. by), *Rasenna*, Milano • 1987a *La società etrusca* (Studi Nuova Italia Scientifica, Archeologia, 5), Roma • 1987b "Il commercio greco in Etruria tra l'VIII e il VI secolo a.C.," in *La società etrusca. L'età arcaica, l'età classica*, Roma • 1987c *Per una storia dello schiavismo in Etruria*, in *La società etrusca. L'età arcaica, l'età classica*, Roma • 1987d "Terre e forme di dipendenza: Roma ed Etruria in età arcaica," in *La società etrusca. L'età arcaica, l'età classica*, Roma • 1988a "Etruria principes disciplinam doceto". Il mito normativo dello specchio di Tuscania, in *Studia Tarquiniensia*, Roma • 1988b "Le popolazioni dell'Italia antica: società e forme del potere," in A. Momigliano, A. Schiavone (ed. by), *Storia di Roma. I. Roma in Italia*, Torino • 1989 "Topografia sacra di una città latina. Praeneste," in *Urbanistica e architettura dell'antica Praeneste*, Palestrina • 1990a "Riti di passaggio maschili di Roma arcaica," in *Mélanges de l'Ecole Française de Rome*, CII, 1, • 1990b *Storia degli Etruschi*, Bari • 1991a "Alle radici della nostalgia augustea," in M. Pani (ed. by), *Continuità e trasformazioni fra repubblica e principato. Istituzioni, politica, società*, Bari • 1991b "L'acqua degli Etruschi: dalle forme ideologiche alle pratiche sociali," in *Gli Etruschi maestri d'idraulica*, proceeding of the meeting, Perugia 1991, Perugia • 1991c *La création étrusque*, in *La sculpture. Le prestige de l'antiquité du VIIIe siècle avant J.C. au Ve siècle après J.C.*, Genève • 1992 "I fregi figurati delle regiae latine ed etrusche. Immaginario del potere arcaico," in *Ostraka*, I, 2 • 1993 "Fictiles fabulae. Rappresentazione e romanizzazione nei cicli figurativi fittili repubblicani," in *Ostraka*, II, 2 • 1994 "L'immaginario greco dell'Oltremare. La lekythos eponima del pittore della Megera, Pausania I, 23, 5-6 e Pitecusa," in B. d'Agostino, D. Ridgway (ed. by), "Apoikia. I più antichi insediamenti greci in Occidente: funzioni e modi dell'organizzazione politica e sociale," in *Annali dell'Istituto universitario orientale di Napoli. Sezione di archeologia e storia antica*, n.s. I • 1996 "Riflessi in Etruria del mondo fenicio e greco d'Occidente," in *Magna Grecia Etruschi Fenici*, proceeding of the del XXXIII Convegno di studi sulla Magna Grecia, Taranto 1993, Taranto • 1997a "'Domiseda, lanifica, univira'. Il trono di Verucchio e il ruolo e l'immagine della donna tra arcaismo e repubblica," in *Il rango, il rito e l'immagine. Alle origini della rappresentazione storica romana,* Milano • 1997b "'Secespita, praefericulum'. Archeologia di due strumenti sacrificali romani," in *"Etrusca et Italica". Scritti in ricordo di Massimo Pallottino*, Roma • 1997c "I fregi figurati delle "regiae" latine ed etrusche. Immaginario del potere arcaico," in *Il rango, il rito e l'immagine. Alle origini della rappresentazione storica romana*, Milano • 1997d *Il rango il rito e l'immagine. Alle origini della rappresentazione storica romana*, Milano • 1997e "Les Adonies de Gravisca. Archéologie d'une fête," in F. Gaultier, D. Briquel (ed. by), *Les Etrusques. Les plus religieux des hommes. Etat de la recherche sur la religion étrusque*, proceeding of the meeting, Paris 1992, Paris • 1999a "Appius Alce. La gemma fiorentina con rito saliare e la presenza dei Claudii in Etruria," in *Studi etruschi*, s. III, LXIII • 1999b "I Principi guerrieri di Cecina. Qualche osservazione di un visitatore curioso," in *Ostraka*, VIII, 1 • 2000 "Primi appunti per un'antropologia del vino degli Etruschi," in D. Tommasi, C. Cremonesi (ed. by), *L'avventura del vino nel Mediterraneo. Itinerari storici prima e dopo Roma,* international symposium, Conegliano 1998, Treviso • forthcoming-a "I Greci nel Tirreno: un bilancio," in *Atti dell'incontro per l'inaugurazione dell'esposizione del frontone di Pyrgi*, Roma • forthcoming-b "'Principi guerrieri' di Cecina: qualche osservazione di un visitatore curioso," in *Ostraka*; **Torelli M., Menichetti M.** • 1997 "Attorno a Demarato," in *Corinto e l'Occidente*, proceeding of the XXXIV Convegno di studi sulla Magna Grecia, Taranto 1994, Taranto; **Tovoli S.** • 1989 *Il sepolcreto villanoviano Benacci Caprara di Bologna*, Bologna; **Trendall A.D.** • 1953-1955 *Vasi italioti ed etruschi a figure rosse*, I-II, *Vasi antichi dipinti del Vaticano;* **Trendall A.D.** • 1976 *Vasi Italioti ed etruschi a figure rosse e di età ellenistica, La collezione Astarita nel Museo Gregoriano Etrusco*, part III, *Vasi antichi dipinti del Vaticano*, Città del Vaticano; **Tripponi A., Manino L., Schiffone C. et al.** • 1971 "Problemi e testimonianze della città etrusca di Marzabotto," in *Studi etruschi*, 39; **Trucco F.** • forthcoming in *Bollettino di Archeologia*; **Tuerr E.S.** • 1969 *Spaetetruskische Tonsarkophage*, Giessen; **Tundall A.D.** • 1967 *The red-figured Vases of Lucania Campania and Sicily*, Oxford • 1989 *The red-figured Vases of South Italy and Sicily. A Handbook*, London;

U

Un artista e il suo mondo • 1988 *Un artista e il suo mondo, il Pittore di Micali*, Roma;

V

Vagnetti L. • 1971 *Il deposito votivo di Campetti a Veio. Materiale degli scavi 1937-1938,* Firenze • 1985 "I contatti precoloniali fra le genti indigene e i paesi mediterranei," in G. Pugliese Carratelli (ed. by), *Magna Grecia. Prolegomeni*, Milano • 1993 "Mycenaean Pottery in Italy. Fifty Years of Study," in *Wace and Blegen. Pottery as Evidence for Trade in the Aegean Bronze Age, 1939-1989. Proceedings of the International Conference Held at the American School of Classic Studies at Athens*, 1989, Amsterdam; **Valvo A.** • 1988 *La "Profezia di Vegoia". Proprietà fondiaria e aruspicina in Etruria nel I secolo a.C.*, Roma; **Van der Meer L.B** • 1979 "*Iecur Placentinum* and the Orientation of the Etruscan Haruspex," in *Bulletin antieke beschaving. Annual Papers on Classical Archaeology*, LIV • 1987 *The bronze liver of Piacenza. Analysis of a polytheistic structure*, Amsterdam; **Van Essen C.C.** • 1927 *Did Orphic Influences on Etruscan Tornb Painting Exist?*, Amsterdam; **Verger S., Kermorvant A.** • 1994 "Nouvelles données et hypothèses sur la topographie de la ville étrusque de Marzabotto," in *Mélanges de l'Ecole Française de Rome*, 106; **Verzár M.** • 1973 "Eine Gruppe etruskischer Bandhenkelamphoren. Die Entwicklung von der Spiralamphora zur nikosthenischen Form," in *Antike Kunst*, XVI • 1980 "Pyrgi e l'Afrodite di Cipro. Considerazioni sul programma decorativo del tempio B," in *Mélanges de l'Ecole Française de Rome*, XCII; **Vighi R., Minissi F.** • 1955 *Il nuovo Museo di villa Giulia*, Roma; **Visonà P.** • 1989 "Monete etrusche e di imitazione massaliota nel Museo civico di Bassano del Grappa," in *Rassegna dal Chiostro Maggiore*, Milano; **Vitali D.** • 1992 *Tombe e necropoli galliche di Bologna e territorio*, Bologna;

W

Waldbaum J.C. • 1994 "Early Greek Contacts with the Southern Levant, ca. 1000-600 B.C. The Eastern Perspective," in *Bulletin of the American Schools of Oriental Research*, 29–3; **Warden P.G., Thomas M.L., Galloway J.** • 1999 "The Etruscan settlement of Poggio Colla. 1995-98 excavations," in *JRA*, 12; **Ward-Perkins J.** • 1961 "Veii. The Historical Topography of the Ancient City", in *Papers of the British School at Rome*, 29; **Wells P.S.** • 1980 *Culture Contact and Culture Change. Early Iron Age Central Europe and the Mediterranean World*, Cambridge; **Wikander C., Wikander Ö** • 1990 "The early monumental complex at Acquarossa. A preliminary report," in *Opuscola romana*, 18; **Will E.** • 1973 *La Grande-Grèce, milieu d'échanges - Réflexions méthodologiques*, in *Economia e società nella Magna Grecia*, proceeding of the XII Convegno internazionale Magna Grecia, Taranto 1972, Napoli; **Williams D.** • 1986 in *Italian Iron Age Artefacts*; **Winther H.C.** • 1997 "Princely Tombs of the Orientalizing Period in Etruria and Latium Vetus" in *Acta Hyperborea*, 7, Copenhagen;

Z

Zamarchi Grassi P. • 1987 "La formazione del Museo e le collezioni," in *Il Museo archeologico G.C. Mecenate in Arezzo*, Arezzo • 1992 in *Cortona dei principes*, ex. cat., Cortona; **Zanker P.** • 1976 *Hellenismus in Mittelitalien*, proceeding of the meeting, I–II, Göttingen 1974, Göttingen; **Zapicchi B.** • 1993 *Cerveteri. Le necropoli della Banditaccia*, Cerveteri; **Zazoff P.** • 1968 *Etruskische Skarabäen*, Mainz • 1983 *Die antiken Gemmen,* München • 1990 "Archaische Werkstätten in Etrurien," in *Die Welt der Etrusker*, proceeding of the meeting, Berlin 1988, Berlin; **Zifferero A.** • 1991 "Forme di possesso della terra e tumuli orientalizzanti nell'Italia centrale tirrenica," in E. Herring, R. Whitehouse, J. Wilkins (ed. by), *The Archaeology of Power. 1. Papers of the Fourth Conference of Italian Archaeology*, London • 1995a "Economia, divinità e frontiera: sul ruolo di alcuni santuari di confine in Etruria meridionale," in *Ostraka*, IV, 2 • 1995b "Rituale funerario e formazione delle aristocrazie nell'Etruria protostorica: osservazioni sui corredi femminili e infantili di Tarquinia," in N. Negroni Catacchio (ed. by), *Preistoria e protostoria in Etruria. Tipologia delle necropoli e rituali di deposizione. Ricerche e scavi*, proceeding of the meeting, Farnese 1993, Milano; **Zimmermann J.-L.** • 1989 *Les chevaux de bronze dans l'art géométrique grec*, Mayence.

A

Accessions • 1955 "Accessions of American and Canadian Museums," in *Art Quarterly*, 18; **Adam A.M.** • 1984 *Bronzes etrusques et italiques*, Paris; • 1985 "Monstres et divinités tricéphales dans l'Italie primitive," in *Mélanges de l'Ecole Française de Rome*, 97, pp. 577 ff.; **Adembri B.** • 1982 in *Pittura etrusca a Orvieto*, Roma, p. 77, n. 2; p. 79, n. 4; • 1985 in *Civiltà degli Etruschi*, p. 291, n. 11.2, Firenze; **Agostiniani L., Nicosia F.** • 2000 *Tabula Cortonensis*, Roma; **Alexander C.** • 1925 "Classical Inscriptions: Recent Accessions," in *MMA Bulletin*, 20–11; 1928 *Jewelry. The Art of Goldsmith in Classical Times*, New York; **Ancient Copper Studies** • 1990 *Ancient Copper Studies of Greek and Roman Alloys: Some Metallurgical and Technological Studies of Greek and Roman Bronzes*; **Andrén C.** • 1940 *Architectural Terracottas from Etrusco-Italic Temples*, Lund Leipzig, pp.160–61, p.172, II:1, pls. 64, 66, 209, 215; **Arte e Civiltà degli Etruschi** • 1967 *Arte e Civiltà degli Etruschi*, ex. cat., Torino, Torino; **Aurigemma S.** • 1960 *Scavi di Spina, Valle Trebba* I, Roma, pp. 73 ff.;

B

Bagnasco Gianni G. • 1996 *Oggetti iscritti di epoca orientalizzante in Etruria*, Firenze; **Baldelli G.** • 1991 *Testa giovanile con diadema*, in *Gens antiquissima Italiae. Antichità dall'Umbria a New York*, Perugia, pp. 329–31; **Bartoloni G.** • 1970 *Alcune terrecotte votive delle Collezioni Medicee ora al Museo Archeologico di Firenze*, in *Studi etruschi*, XXXVIII; • 1972 *Le tombe da Poggio Buco nel Museo Archeologico di Firenze*, Firenze; • 1983 in M. Sprengher, G. Bartoloni, M. Hirmer (ed. by) *Etruschi. L'arte*, Milano; • 1986 "Le comunità dell'Italia tirrenica e la colonizzazione greca in Campania," in *Etruria e Lazio arcaico*, proceeding of the meeting, Roma, Roma 1987, pp. 37 ff.; **Bartoloni G., Buranelli F., D'Atri V., De Santis A.** • 1987 *Le urne a capanna rinvenute in Italia*, Roma; **Bartoloni G., Sprenger M.** • 1983 *Etruschi, l'arte*, Milano, pp. 135, 159–60, 274; pls. 182–83; **Batignani G.** • 1965 "Le oinochoai di bucchero pesante di tipo chiusino," in *Studi etruschi*, 33, p. 306, n. 192; **Beazley J.D.** • 1947 *Etruscan vase-painting*, Oxford; • 1956 *Attic Black-figure Vase-painter*, Oxford; **Bellato F., Bellintani G.F.** • 1975 "Dati per uno studio della tecnologia e tipologia dei manufatti in corno ed osso nell'abitato protostorico di Frattesina di Fratta Polesine," in *Padusa*, 11, pp. 15–42, 31; **Bellintani G.F., Peretto R.** • 1972 "Il ripostiglio di Frattesina ed altri manufatti enei raccolti in superficie. Notizie preliminari," in *Padusa*, 8, p. 37, n. 12 a; **Bendinelli G.** • 1920 "Bronzi votivi italici del Museo Nazionale di Villa Giulia," in *Monumenti antichi Lincei*, 26; **Benelli E.** • 1994 *Le iscrizioni bilingui etrusco-latine*, Firenze; **Bentz M.** • 1992 *Etruskische Votiv Bronzen des Hellenismus*, Firenze; **Berard O.** s.d. *Les bronzes antiques du musée de l'Éphèbe*; • 1989 *Regard sur l'Art Étrusque*, ex. cat., Le Cap d'Agde; **Bianchi Bandinelli R.** • 1925 "Clusium," in "*Monumenti antichi Lincei*, XXX; **Bianco Peroni V.** • 1970 "Le spade nell'Italia continentale," *Praehistorische Bronze Funde*, IV, 1, München p. 85, n. 209; • 1979 "I rasoi dell'Italia continentale," in *Praehistorische Bronze Funde*, VIII, 2, München; **Biers C.J., Humphreys S.** • 1977 "Eleven ships form Etruria," in *International Journal of Nautical Archaeology*, 6; **Bissing Fr.W., von** • 1931" Materiali archeologici orientali ed egiziani scoperti nelle necropoli dell'antico territorio etrusco," in *Studi etruschi*, 5; **Blanck H.** • 1982 "Die Malereien des sogenannten Priester-Sarcophage in Tarquinia," in *Miscellanea Archaelogica T. Dohrn dedicata*, Roma; **Blinkenberg Ch.** • 1931 *Lindos, Fouilles de l'Acropole, 1902-1914, I, Les petits objects*, Berlin; **Boardman J.** • 1994 *The diffusion of Classical Art and Antiquity*, Princeton; **Boardman J. Buchner G.** • 1966 "Seals from Ischia and the Lyre-player Group," in *JdI*, 81; **Boardman J.D.** • 1966 in *BRS*, XXXIV; **Bocci Pacini P., Maetzke A.M.** • 1992 *Il Museo dell'Accademia Etrusca di Cortona*, Firenze; **Bocci Pacini P., Maggiani A.** • 1985 "Una particolare hydria a figure nere del Museo Archeologico di Firenze," in *Bollettino d'Archeologia*, 3; **Boitani F.** • 1990 "Le ceramiche laconiche a Gravisca" (P. Pelagatti, C.M. Stibbe, ed. by, *Lakonikà I, Ricerche e nuovi materiali di ceramica laconica*), in *Bollettino d'Archeologia*, 64, supplement; **Bonfante L., Bonfante G.** • 1983 *The Etruscan Language*, Manchester; • 1986 *Etruscan Life and Afterlife: A Handbook of Etruscan Studies*, Detroit; • 1993 "Funfluns Pacha: the Etruscan Dionysus," in T.H. Carpenter (ed. by), *Masks of Dionysus*, Ithaca, (NY); **Bonghi Jovino** • 1986 *Gli Etruschi di Tarquinia*, Milano; **Bonino M.** • 1989 "Imbarcazioni arcaiche in Italia: il problema delle navi usate dagli Etruschi," in *Atti del II Congresso Internazionale Etrusco*, Firenze 1985, Roma, pp. 1517 ff.; **Bosticco S.** • 1952 *Musei Capitolini III. I monumenti egizi ed egittizzanti*, Roma; **Bottini A.** • 1999 "I manufatti metallici arcaici: osservazioni sull'uso, la produzione e la circolazione nella mesogaia," in *Koina. Miscellanea di studi archeologici in on. di P. Orlandini*, Milano, pp. 235–43; **Boulter C.G., Luckner K.T.** • 1984 in *Corpus Vasorum Antiquorum*, The Toledo Museum of Art, Toledo, USA; **Bound M.** • 1991 b "The Giglio wreck, A wreck of the archaic period (c. 600 B.C.) of the Tuscan Island of Giglio. An account of its discovery and excavation. A review of the main finds," in *Enalia*" 1, supplement; • 1991 a "The pre-classical wreck at Campese Bay. First season report," in *Studi e Materiali*, VI; **Brein F.** • 1982 "Ear Studs for Greek Ladies," in *Anat.St.*, XXXII, pp. 89 ff.; **Brendel O.J.** • 1978 *Etruscan Art*, Harmondsworth, p. 468; **Brijder H.A.G.** • 1984 b "Een Etrusckische bronzen kantharos," in *Medelingenblad Amsterdam*, 32; • 1984 a *Griekse, Etruskische en Romeinse kunst, Allard Pierson Museum Amsterdam*, Amsterdam; • 1988 "The Shapes of Etruscan Bonze Kantharoi from the Seventh Century and the Earliest Attic Black-Figure Kantharoi," in *BABesch*, 63; • 1990 *De Etrusken*, ex. cat., Amsterdam, Den Haag; **Brize Ph.** • 1989-1990 Archaische Bronzevotive aus dem "Heraion von Samos," in "Scienze dell'Antichità", 3–4, p. 323, fig. 3; **Brommer F.** • 1960 *Vasenlisten zur griechischen Heldensagen*, Marburg; **Brown A.C.** • 1980 *Ancient Italy before the Romans*, Oxford; **Brown W.L.** • 1960 *The Etruscan lion*, Oxford; **Bruni S.** • 1987 in *Etrusker in der Toskana, Etruskische Gräber der Frühzeit*, ex. cat., Amburgo, Firenze, p. 252, n. 54; • 1993 "Ceramiche sovradipinte del V secolo nel territorio. Una proposta di definizione," in *La civiltà di Chiusi e del suo territorio*, proceeding of the XVII Convegno di studi etruschi e italici, Chianciano Terme 1989, Firenze, pp. 282 ff. pl. IX; • 1994 "Prima di Demarato. Nuovi dati sulla presenza di ceramiche greche e di tipo greco a Tarquinia durante la prima età orientalizzante," in *La presenza etrusca nella Campania meridionale*, proceeding of the meeting, Salerno-Pontecagnano 1990, Firenze, pp. 293 ff.; • 1995 "Orthia, Aristaios e il Pittore della caccia," in *Ostraka*, 4, 2, pp. 213–28; • 1997 a "Stele," in S. Corsi (ed. by), *Casa Buonarroti. La collezione archeologica*, Milano, pp. 38 ff.; • 1998 *Pisa etrusca. Anatomia di una città scomparsa*, Milano; • 1997 b "La Valdera e le Colline Pisane Inferiori: appunti per la storia del popolamento," in *Aspetti della cultura di Volterra etrusca fra l'Età del Ferro e l'Età Ellenistica*, proceeding of the XIX Convegno di studi etruschi e italici, Volterra 1995, Firenze, pp. 129 ff.;• forthcoming "Il carpentum del complesso di Castel San Mariano: una proposta di ricostruzione," in *Science and Technology for Cultural Heritage*, 9, 2000; • forthcoming a "L'architettura tombale dell'area costiera dell'estrema Etruria settentrionale. Appunti per l'Orientalizzante antico e medio," in *L'architettura tombale a Populonia tra IX e VI secolo a.C.*, proceeding of the meeting, Populonia 1997, Firenze; • forthcoming. b "La Valle dell'Arno: i casi di Fiesole e Pisa," in *Città e territorio in Etruria. Per una definizione di città nell'Etruria settentrionale*, proceeding of the meeting, Colle di Val d'Elsa 1999; **Brunn E., Körte G.** • 1916 *I rilievi delle urne etrusche*, pp. 10 tipo B, 59, 67, 121, 258, pls. L,12; LVII,7; CI, 2; CXV,1; **Brunn H.** • 1863 in "Bull. Inst."; **Bruschetti P.** • 1985 in *Civiltà degli Etruschi*, ex. cat., Firenze, Milano, p. 270, 10.15.1; **Bruschetti P., Gori Sassoli M. et al.** • 1996 *Il Museo dell'Accademia Etrusca di Cortona. Catalogo delle collezioni*, Cortona; **Bull. Inst.** • 1844 *Bull. Inst.* pp. 42, 143; **Buranelli F., Sannibale M.** • 1998 "Reparto Antichità Etrusco-Italiche (1984-1996)," in *Bollettino Monumenti Musei e Gallerie Pontificie*, 18; • forthcoming "Non più solo Larthia. Un documento inedito dalla tomba Regolini Galassi di Caere," in *Prospettiva*; **Burresi M.G., Paolucci G.** • 1989 *Tra Ottocento e Novecento. La collezione di Ottavio Simoneschi*, ex. cat., Chianciano Terme; **Busz R., Gercke P.** • 1999 *Türkis und Azur. Quarzkeramik im Orient und Okzident*, ex. cat., Kassel;

C

Cagianelli C. • 1992 "Bronzetti etruschi, italici e romani del Museo dell'Accademia Etrusca," in *Annuario dell'Accademia Etrusca*, XXV, Cortona; **Calvetti A.** • 1987 "Rappresentazioni "saliari" nella decorazione plastica di un vaso bronzeo a Bisenzio (VIII sec. a.C.)," in *StudRom*, XXXV; **Camporeale G.** • 1967 *La tomba del duce*, Firenze pp. 141 ff.; • 1969 "I commerci di Vetulonia in età orientalizzante," in *AcI*, supplement VII, Firenze; • 1972 *Buccheri a cilindretto di fabbrica orvietana*, Firenze, p. 46, n. 1; • 1984 *La caccia in Etruria*, Roma; • 1992 *Gli Etruschi e l'Europa*, ex. cat., Milano; • 1994 "Frammento di lino," in S. Bruni (ed. by), *Isidoro Falchi: un medico al servizio dell'archeologia. Un protagonista della ricerca italiana di fine Ottocento*, Montopoli in Valdarno, pp. 240 ff.; • 1997 *Zeus/Tinia* in *Lexicon Iconographicum Mythologiae Classicae*, VIII, Zurich; **Camporeale G., Uggeri G., Banti L.** • 1966 "Vetulonia. Esplorazione di una tomba a tumulo e di una fossa in località Castelvecchio," in *Notizie degli scavi*; **Canciani F.** • 1979 "Coppe 'fenicie' in Italia," in *Archäologischen Anzeigen*; **Caputo G.** • 1969 in *La tomba della Montagnola*, ex. cat., Sesto Fiorentino, p. 57, n.1; **Carri** • 1998 *Carri da guerra e principi etruschi*, ex. cat., Viterbo, Roma.; **Caruso I.** • 1985 *Collezione Castellani, Le ceramiche*, Roma; **Catalli F.** • 1990 *Monete etrusche* Roma; **Cateni G.** • 1977 "Il ripostiglio di Limone (Livorno)," in *Studi etruschi*, XLV; • 1984 "Il ripostiglio di Pariana," in *Studi in onore di G. Maetzke*, vol. II, Roma; • 1985 "Pariana," in *L'età dei metalli nella Toscana nordoccidentale*, ex. cat., Viareggio; • 1988 *Il Museo Guarnacci di Volterra*, Pisa; • 1997 *Limone, dal bronzo* *al ferro. Il* II *millennio nella toscana centroccidentale*, ex. cat., Livorno; • 1998 in *The Shadow of the Night: Etruscan Splendors from Volterra in Tuscany*, ex. cat. New York-London 1998–99; • 1998 *Volterra. La Tomba del Guerriero di Poggio alle Croci*, Firenze; **Cavazzuti L.** • 1997 "Nuovi rinvenimenti sottomarini per lo studio della pirateria," in *Archeologia subacquea. Studi, ricerche e documenti*, II , pp. 197 ff.; **Cherici A.** • 1988 "Nuovi vasi del Pittore di Micali della Collezione Poggiali di Firenze," Appendix I in *Un Artista Etrusco e il suo mondo, Il Pittore di Micali*, in *Studi di Archeologia*, 5, Roma, p. 103, figs. 202–03; • 1993 "Per una lettura del sarcofago dello Sperandio," in *Xenia Antiqua*, II, pp. 13 ff.; **Chianciano Terme** • 1997 *Il Museo Civico Archeologico di Chianciano Terme,* Siena; **Chieco Bianchi A.M., Capuis L.** • 1985 *Este* I. "Le necropoli Casa di Ricovero, Casa Muletti prosdocime e Casa Alfonsi," in *Mon.Ant.Linc.*, LI, s.m. II, Roma; **Chierici A.** • 1988 *Ceramica etrusca della Collezione Poggiali di Firenze*, Roma n. 124, p. 155 ff., pls. LXXIX c, LXXX a-b.; **Christiansen J.** • 1984 "A Pair of Amphorae from Caere," in *Analecta Romana Instituti Danici*, XIII; **Cianferoni G.C.** • 1992 in *Populonia in età ellenistica. I materiali dalle necropoli*, proceeding of the seminar, Firenze; **Civiltà degli Etruschi** • 1985 *Civiltà degli Etruschi*, ex. cat., Firenze, Milano, pp. 381 ff., nn. 16.6.4; 18.2; **Coarelli F.** • 1976 "Un elmo con iscrizione latina arcaica al Museo di Cremona," in *L'Italie préromaine et la Rome républicaine. Mélanges offerts à Jacques Heurgon*, Roma; • 1988 *Il Foro Boario*, Roma, pp. 213 ff.; **Cocchi Genick D.** • 1985 "Colle Le Blanche (com. di Camaiore, prov. di Lucca)," in D. Cocchi Genick, R. Grifoni Cremonesi (ed. by), *L'età dei metalli nella Toscana nord-occidentale*, ex. cat., Pisa; **Coen A.** • 1999 *Corona etrusca*, Viterbo; **Colonna G.** • 1981 "Presenza greca ed etrusco-meridionale nell'Etruria mineraria," in *L'Etruria mineraria,* proceeding of the XII Convegno di studi etruschi e italici, Firenze-Populonia-Piombino 1979, Firenze, pp. 443 ff.; • 1982 "Di Augusto Castellani e del cosiddetto calice a cariatidi prenestino," in *Miscellanea archaeologica T. Dohrn dedicata*, Roma, pp. 33 ff.; • 1984 "Apollon, les Etrusques et Lipara," in *Mélanges de l'Ecole française de Rome*, 96; • 1985 b "Il santuario di Leucotea - Ilizia a Pyrgi," in *Santuari d'Etruria*, Milano, pp. 127–34; • 1985 a *Le forme ideologiche della città*, in *Civiltà degli Etruschi*, Milano; • 1990 "Il posto dell'Arringatore nell'arte etrusca di età ellenistica," in *Die Welt der Etrusker*, proceeding of the meeting, Berlin 1988, Berlin; • 1992 *La coroplastica templare etrusca fra il* IV *e il* II *secolo a. C.*, proceeding of the XVI Convegno di studi etruschi e italici, Orbetello 1988, Firenze, pp. 109–26, pls. I–XXV; • 1996 "Il dokanon, il culto dei Dioscuri e gli aspetti ellenizzanti della religione dei morti nell'Etruria tardo-arcaica," in *Studi in memoria di S. Stucchi*, Roma, pp. 177 ff.; **Comella A.** • 1982 "Il deposito votivo presso l'Ara della Regina," in *Materiali del Museo Archeologico di Tarquinia*, IV, Roma; **Conestabile G.C.** • 1865 *Pitture murali a fresco,* Firenze; **Conway R.D., Whatmough J., Johnson S.E.** • 1933 *The Prae-Italic Dialects of Italy*, London; **Corradini E.** • 1985 in *Civiltà degli Etruschi*, Milano; • 1992 in *Dyonisos. Mito e mistero*, Bologna; **Corsi L., Firmati M.** • 1998 "Il relitto di Capo Enfola all'Elba," in *Memorie sommerse. Archeologia subacquea in Toscana*, ex. cat., Porto Santo Stefano; **Cristofani M.** • 1969 *La tomba del Tifone. Cultura e società a Tarquinia in età tardoetrusca*, Roma; • 1975 *Statue cinerario chiusine di età classica*, Roma pp 17, 29 ff., 39, 63; • 1979 "La 'Testa Lorenzini' e la scultura tardoarcaica in Etruria settentrionale," in *Studi etruschi*, XLVII; • 1982 "Per una storia del collezionismo archeologico nella Toscana granducale. IV. Gli ex voto di Nemi," in *Prospettiva* 29; • 1983 *Gli Etruschi del mare*, Milano; • 1984 "Iscrizioni e beni suntuari," in *Opus*, III, pp. 319 ff.; • 1984 "Siamo scesi nella tomba dei Cai Cutu," in *Atlante*, april, pp. 78 ff.; • 1985 b *Die Etrusker*, Stuttgart-Zürich; • 1985 c "Faone, la testa di Orfeo e l'immaginario femminile," in *Prospettiva*, 42, pp. 9 ff.; • 1985 a *I bronzi degli Etruschi*, Novara; • 1987 "Nuovi spunti sul tema della talassocrazia," in *Xenia*, 8, 1984, pp. 3–5, *Saggi di storia etrusca arcaica,* Roma; • 1988–89 "Dedica ai Dioscuri," in *Prospettiva*, 53–56, pp. 14 ff.; • 1995 *Tabula Capuana. Un calendario festivo di età arcaica*, Firenze; • 1996 *Due testi dell'Italia preromana*, Roma; • 1998 "Un naukleros greco-orientale nel Tirreno per un'interpretazione del relitto del Giglio," in *ASAtene*, LXX–LXXI; **Culican W.** • 1982 "Casnola bowl 4555 and other Phoenician bowls," in *Rivista di Studi Fenici* 10;

D

D'Agostino B. • 1981 "Noterelle iconografiche a proposito di Eracle nell'Etruria arcaica," in *Annali dell'Istituto Universitario Orientale di Napoli. Sezione di Archeologia e Storia antica*, 1991, pp. 125 ff.; • 1983 "L'immagine, la pittura e la tomba nell'Etruria arcaica, in Prospettiva," 32, pp. 2 ff.; • 1988 "Ceramica greca e di tipo greco," in B. D'Agostino, P. Gastaldi (ed. by), *Pontecagnano*, II, *La necropoli del Picentino*. 1. *Le tombe della prima Età del Ferro*, Napoli, pp. 44 ff.; **D'Agostino B., Cerchiai L.** • 1999 *Il mare, la morte, l'amore. Gli Etruschi, i Greci e l'immagine,* Roma; **D'Agostino B., Garbini G.** • 1977 "La patera da Pontecagnano riesaminata," in *Studi etruschi*, XLV, pp. 51 ff.; **Davies M.I.** • 1971 "The Suicide of Ajax: a Bronze Etruscan Statuette from the Käppeli Collection," in *AntK*, 14; • 1985 "Ajax at the Bourne of Life," in *Eidolopoiia, Actes du Colloque sur les problèmes de l'image dans le monde méditerranéen classique*, Château de Lourmarin en Provence 1982, Roma; **De Agostino A.** • 1961 *Fiesole. La zona archeologica e il Museo*, Roma; • 1961 in *Notizie degli scavi*; • 1973 *Fiesole. La zona archeologica e il Museo*, Roma; **De Chiara I.** • 1960 a *Guida alla ceramica volsiniese del Museo di Firenze*, Firenze; • 1960 b "La ceramica volsiniese," in *Studi etruschi*, 18, p. 134, n. 50; **De Grummond N.T.** • 1982 *A Guide to Etruscan Mirrors*, Tallahassee, Florida; **De La Geniere J.** • 1968 *Recherches sur l'age du Fer dans l'Italie méridionale*, Napoli; **De Marco M.** • **1981** *Fiesole, Museo archeologico. Scavi*, Firenze; **De Marinis G.** • 1996 "Due "pietre fiesolane'," in *Alle origini di Firenze. Dalla preistoria alla città romana,* ex. cat., Firenze, pp. 150 ff.; **De Tommaso Nicosia** • 1991 in G. Paolucci (ed. by), *La collezione Terrosi nel Museo Civico Archeologico di Chianciano Terme*, Chianciano Terme; **Degrassi A.** • 1965 *Inscriptiones Latinae liberae rei publicae*, 2, Firenze; **Del Chiaro M.** • 1967 *Etruscan Art from West Coast Collections*, Santa Barbara (CA); **Deliciae fictiles II** • 1997 *Deliciae fictiles II. Proceedings of the Second International Conference on Archaic Architectural Terracottas from Italy hed at the Netherlands Institute in Rome*, 1996, Amsterdam; **Della Fina G.M.** • 1998 "Elementi per una nuova interpretazione dei frontoni del tempio di Belvedere in Orvieto," in *Annali della Fondazione per il Museo C. Faina*, V, pp. 41 ff.; **Desantis P.** • 1993 in *Due donne dell'Italia antica. Corredi da Spina e da Forentum*, ex. cat., Comacchio, Padova, p. 73, n. 4; **Dessau H.** • 1892–16 *Inscriptiones Latinae selectae, Berolini*; **Die Etrusker** • 1977 *Die Etrusker*, pl. 143; **Die Welt der Etrusker** • 1988 *Die Welt der Etrusker, Archaeologische Denkmaler aus Museen der sozialistischen Länder*, Berlin; **Dik R.** • 1981 "Un'anfora orientalizzante etrusca nel museo Allard Pierson," in *BABesch*, 56; • 1981 "Un oinochóe ceretana con decorazione di pesci; implicazioni culturali," in *Mededelingen van het Nederlands Historisch Instituut te Rome*, 43; **Dik R., Donker C.E.** • 1980 "Een Etruskische amfoor in het Allard Pierson Museum," in *Mededelingenblad Amsterdam*, 21; **Dohan E.H.** • 1942 *Italic Tomb-Groups in the University Museum, Philadelphia,* Philadelphia; **Dohm T.** • 1968 "Der Arringatore. Bronzestatue im Museo Archeologico von Florenz," in *Monumenta artis romanae*, 8, Berlin; **Dohrn T.** • 1982 *Die etruskische Kunst im Zeitalter der griechischen Klassik. Die Interimsperiode*, Mainz; **Donati L.** • 1985 *Tarquinia, Poggio Gallinaro: tomba 8,* in *L'Etruria mineraria,* ex. cat. Portoferraio-Populonia-Massa Marittima, pp. 76 ff., nn. 264–265; ; • 1994 *La casa dell'Impluvium. Architettura etrusca a Roselle*, Roma; • 1998 "Sul simposio etrusco: osservazioni in margine al restauro di un rilievo chiusino," in *In memoria di Enrico Paribeni*, Roma, pp.165–66, pl. XLI,5; **Dragendorff H., Watzinger C.** • 1948 *Arretinische Reliefkeramik*, Tübingen; **Ducati P.** • 1927 *Storia dell'arte etrusca*, Firenze; **Ducci E.** • 1987–88 "Le terrecotte architettoniche della Catona" in *Studi etruschi*, 55, pp. 131–52, 140, n. 3; **Duval C.** • 1989 *Infinite Riches: Jewelry Through the Centuries,* St. Petersburg;

E

Edlund- Berry I.E.M. • 1992 *The Seated and Standing Statue Acroteria from Poggio Civitate (Murlo)*, Roma • 1992; **Egg M.** • 1988 "Italische Helme mit Krempe," in *Antike Helme*, Mainz, pp. 247 ff.; **Esposito** • 1999 *Principi guerrieri – la necropoli etrusca di Casale Marittimo*, Milano; **Etrusker in der Toskana** • 1987 *Etrusker in der Toskana. Etruskische Gräber der Frühzeit*, ex. cat., Hamburg; **Euphronios epoiesen** • 1999 *Euphronios epoiesen: un dono d'eccezione ad Ercole Cerite*, ex. cat., Roma;

F

Falchi I. • 1887 "Scavi di Vetulonia. Terza relazione," in *Notizie degli Scavi*, pp. 471 ff.; **Falchi Pernier L.** • 1913 "Vetulonia. Il Circolo del Monile d'Argento e il Circolo dei Lebeti di Bronzo," in *Notizie degli Scavi*; **Fedeli F.** • 1983 *Populonia. Storia e territorio*, Firenze, n. 145, p. 261; **Fernandez I.G.** • 1990 "J. Paul Getty Museum," in *Revista de Arqueologia*, 115; **Feruglio A.E.** • 1985 in *Civiltà degli etruschi*, Firenze, pp. 253–54; • 1993 "La città e il territorio in età ellenistica" in *Perugia*, I, Milano in R. Rossi (ed. by) *Storia illustrata delle città dell'Umbria*, pp. 49 ff.; **Fiumi E.** • 1957 "Materiali volterrani nel Museo archeologico di Firenze: la collezione Cinci," in *Studi etruschi*, XXV; **Flemberg J.** • 1991 *Venus Armata. Studien zur bewaffneten Aphrodite in der griechisch-römischen Kunst*, Stockhölm; **Fonquerle D.** • 1986 "Le trépied étrusque et le mobilier d'accompagnement dans le gisement sous-marin de 'La tour du Castellas'," in *Dial. d'Hist. Anc.*, 12, pp. 111–19; **Fortunati F.R.** • 1988 "Ipotesi ricostruttiva della decorazione del tempio di Velletri," in *Prospettiva*, 47, pp. 3–11; • 1990 "Velitrae," in *La grande Roma dei Tarquini*, Roma, pp.199–204; **Fracelière R.** • 1954 *Fouilles de Delphes*, III, 4, Paris; **Frederickson B.** • 1975 *The J. Paul Getty Museum*, Malibu; **Fugazzola**

Delpino M.A. • 1985 in *Civiltà degli Etruschi*, ex. cat., Firenze, Milano; • 1993 in *La Civiltà degli Etruschi. Scavi e studi recenti*. ex. cat. Osaka-Nagoya-Fukuoka, Tokyo 1990–91, Roma; **Furtwängler A.** • 1890 *Olympia IV, Die Bronzen und die übrigen kleineren Funde von Olympia*, Berlin;

G

Gabrici E. • 1911 "Cenni sull'origine dello stile geometrico di Cuma e sulla propagazione sua in Italia," in *Memorie della Reale Accademia di Archeologia, Lettere e Belle Arti*, Napoli, p. 93, fig. 37; • 1913 "Cuma. Parte prima: dalle origini ai principi del VI secolo a.C.," in *Mon.Ant.Linc.*, XXII, c. 5 ff.; **Galli E.** • 1914 *Fiesole. Gli scavi, il Museo Civico*, Milano s.d. (1914); **Galli G.** • 1998 in *Tesori della Postumia. Archeologia e storia intorno a una grande strada romana alle radici dell'Europa*, ex. cat., Cremona, Milano; **Gaultier F.** • 1987 "Dal Gruppo della Tolfa alla Tomba dei Tori: tra ceramica e pittura parietale," in *Tarquinia: ricerche, scavi e prospettive*, proceeding of the meeting, Milano; • 1990 "A propos de quelques élémets de décor architectural archaïques en terre cuite consevés au Musée du Louvre," in in *Die Welt der Etrusker*, proceeding of the meeting, Berlin 1988, Berlin; • 1990 in *La Revue du Louvre*, fasc. 1, pp. 1–6; **Gempeler R.D.** • 1974 *Die etruskischen Kanopen, Herstellung, Typologie, Entwicklungsgeschichte*; **Getty J.P.** • 1965 *The Joys of Collecting*, New York; **Gianfrotta P.** • 1997 "La piraterie," in P. Pomey (ed. by), *La navigation dans l'Antiquité*, Aix-en-Provence, pp. 46 ff.; **Giglioli C.Q.** • 1935 *L'Arte Etrusca*, pl. 146; • 1952 "Il sarcofago dello Sperandio del Museo Archeologico di Perugia," in *Archeologia Classica*, IV, 1, pp. 81–87, pls. XXIII–XXIV; • 1952–53 "Su alcuni bronzetti etruschi," in *Studi etruschi*, 22, pp. 49–67; **Giglioli G.Q.** • 1935 *L'arte etrusca*, p. 57, fig. 305, 1.2; **Giglioli Q.** • 1954 in *Studi etruschi*, XXIII; **Gilotta F.** • 1987 *La tomba François di Vulci*, ex. cat., Roma; **Gioielli e Ornamenti** • 1988 *Gioielli e Ornamenti dagli Egizi all'alto Medioevo*, ex. cat., Arezzo, Firenze; **Gjerstadt E.** • 1960 *Early Rome III*, in *ActaInstRomSue*, XVIII, 3; **Gli amici per Orlanda** • forthcoming *Gli amici per Orlanda. Studi in onore di Orlanda Pancrazi*, Pisa; **Gli Etruschi di Tarquinia** • 1986 *Gli Etruschi di Tarquinia* , ex. cat., Modena; **Gli Etruschi e l'Europa** • 1992 *Gli Etruschi e l'Europa*, ex. cat., Paris, Berlin 1993, Milano; **Glimpses of Excellence** • 1985 *Glimpses of Excellence* n. 4 (R.Guy); **Gras M.** • 1985 *Trafics thyrréniens archaïques*, Roma; **Grassi Zamarchi P.** • 1980 in *Prima Italia. Arts italiques du premier millénaire avant J.C*, ex. cat., Bruxelles • 1980–81, Bruxelles; **Greci, Enotri** • 1996 *Greci, Enotri, Lucani nella Basilicata meridionale*, ex. cat., Policoro, Napoli; **Gregory Warden P.** • 1985 *The Metal Finds from Poggio Civitate (Murlo) 1966-1978*, Roma; **Gualandi G.** • 1974 "Santuari e stipi votive dell'Etruria padana," in *Studi etruschi*, XLII; • 1978 "L'Ercole bronzeo di Villa Cassarini," in *Il Carrobbio*, IV; **Guidi A.** • 1980 *Studi sulla decorazione metopale nella ceramica villanoviana*, Firenze; **Guzzo P.G.** • 1981 *Pisa*, p. 59;

H

Hackens T. • 1976 *Catalogue of the Classical Collection. Classical Jewelry*, Providence; **Hagy J.W.** • 1986 "800 years of Etruscan ships," in *International Journal of Nautical Archaeology*, XV, p. 217 ff.; **Harari M.** • 1987 *Dibattito, in Tarquinia: ricerche, scavi e prospettive*, proceeding of the meeting, Milano; **Haynes S.** • 1965, in *Studi etruschi*, 33, p. 524, ill. 125 b; • 1985 *Etruscan Bronzes*, London; • 1998 "The Workshop of the Bronze Tripod-Feet in Florence, Museo Archeologico inv. Nos. 710 e 711," in G. Capecchi e altri (ed. by), *In memoria di Enrico Paribeni*, Roma, pp. 236–38, pls. LXVI–LXVII; **Helbig H.** • 1969 *Führer durch die öffentlichen Sammlungen Klassischer Altertümer in Rom*, III, Tübingen; **Hemelrijk J.M.** • 1984 a in Brijder H.A.G. (ed. by), *Griekse, Etruskische en Romeinse kunst, Allard Pierson Museum Amsterdam*, Amsterdam; • 1984 b *Ceretan Hydriae, Kerameus*, vol. 5, Mainz; **Hencken H.** • 1968 *Tarquinia, Villanovans and Early Etruscans*, I, Cambridge (Mass.), pp. 115, 346, figs. 124 e, 347 b; **Herbig R.** • 1952 *Die jüngereetruskische Steinsarkophage*, Berlin; **Heres H.** • 1988 "Pfeilerförmiger Cippus," in *Die Welt der Etrusker. Archäogische Denkmäler aus Museen der sozialistischen Länder*, ex. cat., Berlin, p. 211; **Hermary A.** • 1987 "La coupe en argent du British Museum," in R. Laffineur e altri, *Amathonte* III. *L'orfèvrerie*, Paris; **Hölbl G.** • 1979 *Beziehungen der Ägyptischen Kultur zu Altitalien*, Études Préliminaires aux Religions Orientales dans l'Empire Romain, Leiden; **Höckmann O.** • 1997 "Schiffahrt der Etrusker," in *Der Orient und Etruria*, proceeding of the meeting, Tübingen, Pisa-Roma 2000, pp. 77 ff.; **Höckmann U.** • 1982 *Die Bronzen aus dem Fürstengrab von Castel San Mariano bei Perugia, Staatliche Antikensammlungen München, Katalog der Bronzen*, München, vol. I, p. 71 ff.; nn. 29, pl. 39, 1-5; 30, pl. 41, 1-4; 3, pls. 11–13, fig. 12, app. 2; 50, pl. 52, 1-2; 26, pl. 35, 1-2; 36, 2, figs. 45–47; 1, pls. 1–7, app. 1; **Hölbl G.** • 1981 "Zur kunsthistorischen Stellung der ägyptischen Alabastra aus Fayence," in Dorothea Arnold (ed. by), *Studien zur altägyptischen Keramik*, Mainz; **Hornbostel W.** • 1981 in *Kunst der Etrusker*, Hamburg; **Hostetter E.** • 1986 *Bronzes from Spina*, I, Mainz am Rhein, pp. 16 ff., nn. 1 e 56; **Huls Y.** • 1957 *Ivoires d'Etrurie*, Bruxelles-Roma, n. 53 p. 60; **Hus A.** • 1961 *Recherches sur la statuaire en pierre étrusque archaique*, Paris; • 1975 *Les bronces étrusques* (Collection Latomus, n. 139), p. 89;

I

Il Museo Archeologico • 1987 *Il Museo Archeologico Nazionale G.C. Mecenate in Arezzo*, Firenze, pp. 52; **Inghirami F.** • 1835 *Monumenti etruschi o di etrusco nome*, vol. III, Fiesole;

J

Jannot J.R. • 1984 *Les reliefs archaïques de Chiusi*, Roma, pp. 42–44, p. 384, figs. 155–59; **Johannowsky W.** • 1974 *Un corredo tombale con vasi di bronzo laconici da Capua*, in "Rend.Acc.Archeol.Lett. e Belle Arti," XLIX, pp. 3–20; **Jucker H.** • 1970 "Etruscan Votive Bronzes of Populonia," in *Art and Technology*; **Jucker I.** • 1991 *Italy of the Etruscans*, Jerusalem-Mainz; **Jurgeit F.** • 1990 "Fragmente eines etruskischen Rundthron in Karlsruhe," in *R*, 97;

K

Karabelnik M. • 1993 *Aus den Schatzkammern Eurasiens. Meisterwerke antiker Kunst*, Zürich; **Kästner V.** • 1988 in *Die Welt der Etrusker*, october–december, Berlin; **Koerte G.** • 1917 "Figuren aus einem unbekannten etruskischen Heiligtum," in *Abhandlung der K. Gesellschaft der Wissenschaft. zu Göttingen, Phil.-Hist.-Klasse*, NF 16, p. 7 ff.; **Kozloff A.P., Mitten D.G.** • 1988 *The Gods Delight. The Human Figure in Classical Bronze*, ex. cat., Cleveland; **Krauskopf I.** • 1987 *Todesdämoner und Totengötter* in *Vorhellenistischen Etruria. Kontinuität und Wandel*, Firenze; **Krauskopf J.** • 1995 *Heroen, Götter und Dämonen auf etruskischen Skarabäen*, Mannheim; • 1996 "Interesse privato nel mito. Il caso degli scarabei etruschi," in *Le mythe grec dans l'Italie antique. Fonction et image*, proceeding of the meeting, Roma, Roma 1999, pp. 405 ff.; **Kunst und Kultur Sardiniens** • 1980 *Kunst und Kultur Sardiniens vom Neolitikum bis zum Ende der Nuraghenzeit*, ex. cat., Karlsruhe - Berlin, Karlsruhe, p. 131, fig. 95 b; **Kunst und Leben der Etrusker** • 1955 *Kunst und Leben der Etrusker*, ex. cat., Zürich, n. 382; **Kunze M.** • 1988 in *Die Welt der Etrusker*, proceeding of the meeting, Berlin;

L

L'Etruria mineraria • 1985 *L'Etruria mineraria*, ex. cat., Portoferraio-Populonia-Massa Marittima; **L'oro degli Etruschi** • 1983 *L'oro degli Etruschi*, Novara; **La Civiltà degli Etruschi** • 1993 *La Civiltà degli Etruschi. Scavi e studi recenti*, ex. cat., Osaka-Nagoya-Fukuoka, Tokyo 1990–91, Roma; **La Cortona dei Principes** • 1992 *La Cortona dei Principes*, ex. cat., Cortona; **La grande Roma dei Tarquini** • 1990 *La grande Roma dei Tarquini*, Roma; **La necropoli villanoviana** • 1979 *La necropoli villanoviana di Ca' dell'Orbo a Villanova di Castenaso. Problemi del popolamento dal IX al VI secolo a.C.*, ex. cat., Bologna; **La Rocca E.** • 1990 "Iuno," in *LIMC*, V; **La tomba François di Vulci** • 1987 *La tomba François di Vulci*, ex. cat., Città del Vaticano; **Lamb W.** • 1929 *Greek and Roman Bronzes*, New York; **Lambrechts R.** • 1963 "'C.I.I., S.I., 254' nunc ubi sit comperi," in *Études étrusco-italiques. Mélanges pour le XXVe anniversaire de la Chaire d'Étruscologie à l'Université de Louvain*, Louvain; • 1970 *Les inscriptions avec le mot "tular" et le bornage étrusques*, Firenze; **Le Monde Étrusque** • 1977 *Le Monde Étrusque*, ex. cat., Marseilles 1977–78; **Leach S.S.** • 1987 *Subgeometric Pottery from Southern Etruria*, Göteborg; **Les Etrusques et l'Europe** • 1992 *Les Etrusques et l' Europe*, ex. cat., Paris, Milano; **Les Ibères** • 1997 *Les Ibères*, ex. cat., Paris-Barcelone-Bonn 1997–98; **Llewellyn Brown W.** • 1960 *The Etruscan Lion*, Oxford; **Lund J. Rasmussen B.B.** • 1995 *Greeks, Etruscans, Romans, The Collection of Near Eastern and Classical Antiquities, The National Museum of Denmark*, Copenhagen; **Lunsingh Scheurleer C.W.** • 1936 *Grieksche Ceramiek*, Rotterdam;

M

Macellari R. • 1994 "Lituo in bronzo nel Museo 'Gaetano Chierici' di Paletnologia a Reggio Emilia," in *Quaderni del Museo Archeologico Etnologico di Modena, I. Studi di Preistoria e Protostoria*; **Maetzke G.** • 1949 "Terrecotte architettoniche etrusche scoperte ad Arezzo," in *Bollettino di Archeologia*, pp. 251–53; • 1993 "Tre canopi inediti da Sarteano," in *La civiltà di Chiusi e del suo territorio*, proceeding of the XVII Convegno di studi etruschi e italici, 1989; **Maggiani A.** • 1977 in *REE*, p. 35, reading corection of *CIE*, 92; • 1982 "Qualche osservazione sul fegato di Piacenza," in *Studi etruschi*, 50; • 1985 *Artigianato artistico. L'Etruria settentrionale interna in età ellenistica*, Milano, pp. 168 ff., n. 225; • 1990 "La situazione archeologica dell'Etruria settentrionale nel V sec. a.C.," in *Crise et transformation des sociétés archaïques de l'Italie antique au Ve siècle av.J.C.*, proceeding of the round table, Roma 1987, Roma; • 1993 *Problemi di scultura funeraria a Chiusi*, proceeding of the XVIII Convegno di studi etruschi, Chianciano 1989, pp. 157 ff., pl. V; • 1999 "Pitigliano," in E.

Pellegrini (ed. by), *Insediamenti preistorici e città etrusche nella media valle del Fiume Fiora*, Pitigliano, p. 61; **Mallowan M.E.L.** • 1966 *Nimrud and its Remains*, London; **Mallwitz A., Schiering W.** • 1964 in *Olympische Forschungen*, 5, Berlin; **Malnati L.** • 1993 "Le istituzioni politiche e religiose a Spina e nell'Etruria padana," in *Spina. Storia di una città tra Greci ed Etruschi*, ex. cat., Ferrara; **Mansueli G.A.** • 1968 "La recezione dello stile severo e del classicismo nella scultura etrusca (Note problematiche)," in *Revue Archeologique*, n.s. XI; **Markoe G.E.** • 1985 "Phoenician Bronze and Silver Bowls from Cyprus and the Mediterranean," in *Classical Studies*, 26, University of California Publications, Berkeley-Los Angeles-London; **Marshall F.H.** • 1911 *Catalogue of the Finger-Rings in the British Museum*, London; **Martelli M.** • 1978 "La ceramica greco-orientale in Etruria," in *Les céramiques de la Grèce de l'Est et leur diffusion en Occident*, proceeding of the meeting, Napoli 1976, Paris; • 1983 *L'arcaismo*, in *L'oro degli Etruschi*, Novara; • 1984 "Prima di Aristonothos," in *Prospettiva*, 33; • 1985 "Gli avori tardoarcaici: botteghe e aree di diffusione," in *Il commercio etrusco arcaico*, proceeding of the meeting, Roma 1983, Roma; • 1985 in *L'Etruria mineraria*, ex. cat., Portoferraio, Massa Marittima, Populonia, Firenze p.404; • 1987 *La ceramica degli Etruschi. La pittura vascolare*, Novara; • 1994 "Sulla produzione di vetri orientalizzanti," in *Tyrrhenoi Philotechnoi*, proceeding of the meeting, Viterbo 1990, Roma; **Massa-Pairault F.-H.** • 1985 in A. Carandini (ed. by), *La romanizzazione dell'Etruria: il territorio di Vulci*, ex. cat., Milano; • 1985 *Recherches sur l'art et l'artisanat étrusco-italiques à l'époque hellénistique*, Roma, pp. 41, 224 ff., n. 74, fig. 132; • 1992 *Iconologia e politica nell'Italia antica*, Milano, pp. 144 ff.; • 1994 "Lemnos, Corinthe et l'Étrurie. Iconographie et Iconologie a propos d'une olpè de Cerveteri (VII siècle AV. N. È)," in *La Parola del Passato*, XLIX; **Massa-Pairault F.-H., Pailler J.-M.** • 1979 *Bolsena, V, I. La Maison aux Salles Souterraines. Les Terres cuites sous le peristyle*, Roma; **Mater Matuta**, *voce* in *LIMC* VI, p. 381; **Maule Q.** • 1986 "The Montaguragazza Style," in *Studi etruschi*, 54; • 1991 "The Master of Florence Warrior 586," in *Studi etruschi*, 57; **Mazzolai A.** • 1963 "Inediti del Museo Archeologico di Grosseto," in *Bollettino della Società Storica Maremmana*; **Meisterwerke griechischer Keramik** •2000 *Meisterwerke griechischer Keramik. Die Sammlung Giuseppe Sinopoli*, Mainz, n. 34; **Melis F.** • 1984 *Frammenti di modelli architettonici fittili*, in *Studi in onore di G. Maetzke*, vol. II, Roma; **Mengarelli R.** • 1955 "Caere," in *Monumenti antichi del Lincei*, LXII; **Menichetti M.** • 1992 "L'oinochoe di Tragliatella: mito e rito tra Grecia ed Etruria," in *Ostraka*, 1, pp. 7–30; • 1995 "Giasone e il fuoco di Lemno su un'olpe etrusca in bucchero di epoca orientalizzante," in *Ostraka*, 2; •2000 in A. Carandini, R. Cappelli (ed. by), *Roma. Romolo, Remo e la fondazione della città*, ex. cat., Milano; **Messineo G.** • 1983 "Tesserae hospitales?," in *Xenia*, 5; **Micali G.** • 1833 *Monumenti per servire alla Storia degli antichi popoli italiani*, Firenze; **Milani L.** • 1882 in *Notizie degli scavi*; • 1896 "Tomba con vasi argentati a Poggio Sala," in *Notizie degli scavi*, p. 390, n. 14; • 1898 *Museo Topografico dell'Etruria*, Firenze-Roma; • 1907 in *Notizie degli scavi*, p. 253; • 1912 in *Rend-Linc*, XXI; • 1912 *Il Real Museo Archeologico di Firenze*, II, Firenze, tav. CXIX; **Miller M.C.** •2000 "The Myth of Bousiris: Ethnicity and Art," in *Not the classical ideal*, Leiden; **Minetti A.** • 1997 *Museo Civico Archeologico di Sarteano*, Siena; • 1998 "La tomba della Pania: corredo e rituale funerario," in *Annali dell'Istituto Universitario Orientale di Napoli. Sezione di Archeologia e Storia antica*, 5 n.s., p. 47 ff. with bibliography; **Mingazzini P.** • 1930 *Catalogo dei Vasi della Collezione Augusto Castellani I*, Roma; • 1935 "Una statua cineraria inedita della Collezione Casuccini a Palermo," in *Studi etruschi*, IX, pp. 61–66; **Minto A.** • 1921 *Marsiliana d'Albegna. Le scoperte archeologiche del principe Don Tommaso Corsini*, Firenze; • 1932 "Le ultime scoperte archeologiche a Populonia (1927-1931)," in *Mon.Ant.Linc.*, XXXIV, c. 289 pp.;• 1934 in *Notizie degli scavi* ; • 1943 *Populonia*, Firenze, n. 29b I group, p. .231; **Mitten D.G., Doeringer S.F.** • 1967 *Master Bronzes from the Classical World*, Mainz; **Moltesen M.** • 1982 *Membra collecta, Analecta Romana Instituti Danici*, XI; • 1997 *In the Sacred Grove of Diana. Finds from a Sanctuary at Nemi*, Ny Carlsberg Glyptotek; **Moret J.M.** • 1995 "Un groupe de scarabés italiques," in *Journal des Savants*, p. 51 ff.; **Moretti M.** • 1967 in *Arte e civiltà degli Etruschi*, ex. cat., Torino, Torino, p. 126, n. 358; **Moretti Sgubini A.M.** • 1999 *Il Museo Nazionale Etrusco di Villa Giulia. Guida breve*, Roma; **Mostra dell'arte e della civiltà etrusca** • 1955 *Mostra dell'arte e della civiltà etrusca*, Milano, p. 52, nn. 187–89; p. 53, nn. 192–95 pl. XXIII; **Mostra dell'Etruria padana e della città di Spina** • 1960 *Mostra dell'Etruria padana e della città di Spina*, ex. cat., Bologna, Bologna, p. 354, n. 1152; **Müller-Karpe H.** • 1959 *Beiträge zur Chronologie der Urnenfelderzeit nördlich und südlich der Alpen*, Berlin, pl. 28,14; **Muse** • 1972 *Muse, Annual of the Museum of Art and Archaeology*, 6, 5; **Mylonas G.E.** • 1945–46 "The Eagle of Zeus," in *Classical Journal*, 41, pp. 203 ff.;

N

Nardi Dei • 1881 in *Notizie degli Scavi*; **Nardi G., Pandolfini M.** • 1985 "La diffusione delle anfore etrusche nell'Etruria Settentrionale," in *Il commercio etrusco arcaico*, proceeding of the meeting, Roma 1983, Roma; **Neppi Modona A.** • 1977 *Cortona etrusca e romana nella storia e nell'arte*, Firenze; **Neugebauer K.A.** • 1936 "Kohlenbecken aus Clusium und Verwandtes," in *Mitteilungen des Deutschen Archaologischen Instituts, Römische Abteilung*, 51; **Nicosia F.** • 1966 *Il tumulo di Montefortini e la tomba dei Boschetti a Comeana*, Firenze; • 1970 *Reperti archeologici del territorio di Dicomano*, Firenze; • 1983 in *Fonologia etrusca, fonetica toscana. Il problema del sostrato*, Firenze, pp. 15 ff.; • 1984 in *Cento preziosi etruschi*, ex. cat., Arezzo, Firenze, p. 149, n. 118; • 1986 in *Schätze der Etrusker*, ex. cat., Saarbrücken, Firenze, p. 273, n. 1; • 1997 a "La ricerca archeologica su Artimino," in M.C. Bettini, F. Nicosia, G. Poggesi, *Il Parco archeologico di Carmignano*, Firenze, pp. 25 ff.; • 1997 b "La necropoli monumentale di Comeana," in M.C. Bettini, F. Nicosia, G. Poggesi, *Il Parco archeologico di Carmignano*, Firenze, pp. 49 ff.; **Nogara B.** • 1933 *Gli Etruschi e la loro civiltà*, p. 78, fig. 37; **Notizie degli scavi** • 1880 *Notizie degli scavi* , p. 4, nn. 1–2;

O

Ori e argenti • 1990 Cygielmann M. (ed. by), *Ori e argenti nelle collezioni del Museo Archeologico di Firenze*, Firenze; **Ortiz G.** • 1990 "Coinnoisseurship and Antiquity," in *Small Bronze Sculpture from the Ancient World*, Malibu; **Overby O.** • 1982 *Illustrated Museum Handbook, A guide to the Collections in the Museum of Art and Archaeology*, University of Missouri-Columbia;

P

Pallottino M. • 1945 *La scuola di Vulca*, Roma [now in *Saggi di Antichità*, Roma 1979, pp. 1003 ff.]; • 1968 *Testimonia linguae Etruscae*, 2, Firenze; • 1985 "Presentazione di due iscrizioni etrusche," in *Studi etruschi*, 51; • 1992 in *Les Etrusques et l' Europe*, ex. cat., Paris, Milano; **Pandolfini M., Prosdocimi A.L.** • 1990 *Alfabetari e insegnamento della scrittura in Etruschi e nell'Italia antica*, Firenze; **Paoletti O.** • 1986 "Una coppa geometrica euboica da Tarquinia," in *Arch.Anz.*, p. 407 ff.; **Paolucci G.** • 1988 *Il territorio di Chianciano Terme dalla preistoria al medioevo*, Roma; • 1991 *La collezione Terrosi nel Museo Civico Archeologico di Chianciano Terme*, Chianciano Terme; **Papadopulos J.** • 1980 *Xoana e sphyrelata. Testimonianza delle fonti scritte*, Roma; **Pareti L.** • 1947 *La tomba Regolini-Galassi nel Museo Gregoriano Etrusco*, Città del Vaticano; **Pariben E.** • 1938 "I rilievi chiusini arcaici," in *Studi etruschi*, XII, pp. 57 ff.; **Patitucci S.** • 1967 in *Arte e civiltà degli Etruschi*, ex. cat., Torino, Torino, p. 149, n. 412; **Paturzo F.** • 1997 *Arezzo antica. La città dalla preistoria alla fine del mondo romano*, Cortona, p. 187 ff.; **Pellegrini E.** • 1989 *La necropoli di Poggio Buco. Nuovi dati per lo studio di un centro dell'Etruria interna nei periodi orientalizzante e arcaico*, Firenze; **Pernier L.** • 1907 "Corneto, Tarquinia. Nuove scoperte nel territorio tarquiniese," in *Notizie degli Scavi*, pp. 80, 321, 338, 342 ff.; • 1919 "Ricordi di una storia etrusca e di arte greca nella città di Vetulonia," in *Ausonia*, IX; **Peroni R.** • 1961 "Ripostigli nel grossetano," in *Inventaria Archeologica*, Italia 2. 5, Firenze; **Petersen E.** • 1894 "Bronzen aus Perugia," in *RM*, 9, pp. 253 ff.; **Petrillo Serafin P.** • 1976–77 "Nota in margine al 'tesoro di monete antiche rinvenuto in Populonia'," in *Annali dell'Istituto Italiano di Numismatica*, 23–24, Roma, pp. 69 ff.; **Pfiffig A.** • 1975 *Religio Etrusca*, Graz; **Pfister K.** • 1940 *Die Etrusker*, p. 231; **Pfuhl E.** • 1923 *Malerei und Zeichnung der Griechen*, I, München; **Pflug H.** • 1988 in *Antike Helme*, Mainz; **Phillips K.M. Jr** • 1968 a "Bryn Mawr College Excavations in Tuscany, 1967," in *AJA*, pp. 72, 121–24, figs. 45–52; • 1968 b "Poggio Civitate," in *Archeology*, 21,4, pp. 252–61; **Piceni** •2000 *Piceni popolo d'Europa*, ex. cat., Roma; **Plaoutine N.** • 1937 "An Etruscan imitation of an Attic cup," in *The Journal of Hellenic Studies*, LVII; **Poggesi G.** • 1999 *Artimino: il Guerriero di Prato Rosello*, Firenze; **Poggio Civitate** • 1970 *Poggio Civitate, Murlo, Siena: il Santuario arcaico*, ex. cat., Firenze-Siena, Firenze; **Pomet P.** • 1987–88 *Recherches sous marines*, Hérault, Agde, Gallia Informations; **Pontiroli G.** • 1974 *Catalogo della sezione archeologica del Museo Civico "Ala Ponzone" di Cremona*, Milano; **Prayon F.** • 1975 "Frühetruskische Grab- und Hausarchitektur," in *RomMitt*, 22; • 1977 "Todesdämoner und die Troilossage in der frühetruskischen Kunst," in *RomMitt*, 84; **Prima Italia** • 1980 *Prima Italia. Ars italiques du premier millénaire avant J.C*, ex. cat., Bruxelles, p. 190, n. 120; **Principi etruschi** •2000 *Principi etruschi tra Mediterraneo ed Europa*, ex. cat., Bologna; **Proietti G.** • 1980 *Il Museo Nazionale Etrusco di Villa Giulia*, Roma; • 1986 *Cerveteri*, Roma, pp. 101, 116, 156 n. 63, p. 166 n. 69;

R

Rasenna • 1986 *Rasenna. Storia e civiltà degli Etruschi*, Milano, fig. 163; **Randall-MacIver R.** • 1924 *Villanovans and Early Etruscans*; **Rasmussen T.** • 1986 "Campanian Bucchero Pottery," in *Italian Iron Age Artefacts in the British Museum. Papers of the*

Sixth BM Class. Colloqium, London, pp. 273–81; **Rastrelli A.** • 1980 in *Prima Italia. Arts italiques du premier millénaire avant J.C*, ex. cat., Bruxelles, pp. 143 ff., n. 80; • 1993 b "La decorazione fittile dell'edificio sacro in loc. I Fucoli presso Chianciano Terme," in *Ostraka*, II, 2; **Rastrelli A.** • 1993 a "Le scoperte a Chiusi negli ultimi decenni," in *La civiltà di Chiusi e del suo territorio*, proceeding of the XVII Convegno di studi etruschi e italici, Chianciano Terme 1989, Firenze, p. 125; • 1993 b "Scavi e scoperte nel territorio di Chianciano Terme: l'edificio sacro dei Fucoli," in *La civiltà di Chiusi e del suo territorio*, a proceeding of the XVII Convegno di studi etruschi e italici, Chianciano Terme 1989, Firenze; • 1997 in A. Minetti (ed. by), *Etruschi e Romani ad Acquaviva*, Grotte di Castro; • 1999 in A.M. Esposito, M.C. Guidotti (ed. by), *Museo Archeologico di Firenze*, Firenze, pp. 33, 37; **Rathje A.** • 1980 "Silver Relief Bowls from Italy," in *Analecta Rom*, 9; **Ricciardi L.** • 1989 "La necropoli settentrionale di Vulci. Resoconto di un'indagine bibliografica e d'archivio," in *Bollettino d'Arte*, 58; **Richardson E.** • 1983 *Etruscan Votive Bronzes, Geometric, Orientalizing, Archaic*, Mainz am Rhein; **Richter G.M.A.** • 1940 *MMA Handbook of the Etruscan collection,* New York; • 1971 *The Engraved Gems of the Greeks Etruscans and Romans* II, London; **Ridgway D.** • 1997 "Nestor's cup and the Etruscans," in *Oxford Journal of Archaeology*, 16, 3 nn.14–16, pp. 334–35; **Riederer J.** • 1999 in *Die etruskischen und italischen Bronzen sowie Gegenstände aus Eisen, Blei und Leder im Badischen Landesmuseum Karlsruhe*, 2 voll., Pisa-Roma, n. 819; **Riis P.J.** • 1941 *Tyrrhenika*, Copenhagen; • 1957 *Studi etruschi*, 30; • 1966 in *Acta Archaeologica*, 37; • 1981 *Etruscan Types of Heads*, Copenhagen; • 1997 "Vulcentia Vetustiora. A Stydy of Archaic Vulcian Bronzes," in *Historisk-filosofiske Skrifter*, 19, Copenhagen; **Rix H.** • 1956 *Die Personennamen in den etruskisch-lateinischen Bilinguen, Beiträge zur Namenforschung*, 7, pp. 147–72; • 1991 *Etruskische Texte*, Tubingen, p. 213, Cl 1.1382; p. 218, Cl 1.1560; **Rizzo M.A.** • 1983 in *L'Oro degli Etruschi*, Novara; • 1985 Appendix to P. Pelagatti, "Il Museo di Villa Giulia e gli altri Musei dell'Etruria Meridionale," in *Studi etruschi*, LI, MCMLXXXIII, p. 523; • 1985 in *Un artista etrusco e il suo mondo: il Pittore di Micali* (Studi di Archeologia pubblicati dalla Soprintendenza Archeologica per l'Etruria Meridionale, 5), Roma 1988, p. 88, n. 47, fig. 155; • 1988 "La ceramografia etrusca tardoarcaica," in *Un artista etrusco e il suo mondo. Il pittore di Micali*, ex. cat., Roma; • 1990 *Le anfore da trasporto e il commercio etrusco arcaico*, Roma, p. 51; • 1983 in *L'Oro degli Etruschi*, Novara; **Rizzo M.A., Martelli M.** • 1993 "Un incunabolo greco in Etruria," in *ASAtene*, LXVI–LXVII; **Rocchetti L.** • 1961 "Due bronzetti del Museo Archeologico di Firenze," in *ArchCl*, XIII; **Roma** •2000 A. Carandini, R.Cappelli (ed. by), *Roma, Romolo, Remo e la fondazione della città*, ex. cat., Milano; **Romualdi A.** • 1981 *Catalogo del deposito di Brolio in Val di Chiana*, Roma; • 1984 "Una serie di statuette di offerenti al Museo Archeologico di Arezzo," in *Studi in onore di G. Maetzke*, vol. II, Roma; • 1986 "La tomba delle hydrie di Meidias," c.s. in *Ostraka*; • 1987 in *Etrusker in der Toskana, Etruskische Gräber der Frühzeit*, ex. cat., Amburgo, Firenze, p. 242, n. 40; • 1987 in G. Bermond Montanari (ed. by), *La formazione della città in Emilia Romagna*, Bologna; • 1995 *Aristaios . La collezione Giuseppe Sinopoli*, Venezia, n. 49, pp. 182–91; • 1998 *Una donna di rango a Populonia*, ex. cat., Firenze; **Roncalli F.** • 1965 *Le lastre dipinte da Cerveteri*, Firenze; • 1990 *Gens antiquissima Italia. Antichità dell'Umbria a Leningrado,* Perugia; • 1998 "Una immagine femminile di culto dalla 'tomba d'Iside' di Vulci," in *Annali della Fondazione per il Museo C. Faina*, V, pp. 15 ff.; **Rouveret A.** • 1994 "La ciste Ficoroni et la culture romaine du IV s. av. J.-C.," in *BantiFr*, pp. 225–42;

S

Sams G.K. • 1976 *Small Sculptures in Bronze from the Classical World*, ex. cat., Chapel Hill (NC); **Santuari d'Etruria** • 1985 *Santuari d'Etruria*, ex. cat., Arezzo, Milano; **Sarcofagi** • 1988 *Sarcofagi etruschi delle famiglie Partunu, Camna e Pulena*; **Sassatelli G.** • 1985 in *Civiltà degli Etruschi*, Milano; **Scala N.** • 1997 "La tomba del Letto Funebre di Tarquinia: un tentativo di interpretazione," in *Prospettiva*, 85, pp. 46 ff.; **Scalia F.** • 1968 "I cilindretti di tipo chiusino con figure umane. Contributo allo studio dei buccheri neri a cilindretto," in *Studi etruschi*, 36, p. 400, n. 280; **Scamuzzi E.** • 1940 "Pitigliano," *voce*, in *Nsc*, pp. 19–29; • 1941 "Tesoretto di monete antiche rinvenuto a Populonia," in *Studi etruschi*, XV, Firenze, pp. 141 ff.; **Schätze der Etrusker** • 1986 *Schätze der Etrusker,* ex. cat., Saarbrücken, Firenze; **Schavenburg K.** • 1970 "Zur griechischen Mythen in der etruskischen Kunst," in *JdI*, 85; **Scheunert V.** • 1999 in R. Busz, P. Gercke (ed. by), *Türkis und Azur, Quarzkeramik in Orient und Okzident*, ex. cat., Kassel; **Schmidt M.** • 1971 "Ein Ägyptische Damon in Etrurien," in *ZAS*, 97; **Schröder B.** • 1912 in *Amtliche Berichte aus den königlichen Kunstsammlungen Berlin*, 33, p. 244 ff., figs. 109–10; • 1914 in *74. Berliner Winkelmanns Programm*, p. 13, n. 10, fig. 9; **Scott D.A., Podany J.** • 1990 *Ancient World*, Malibu; **Sgubini Moretti A.M.** • 1981 in *Gli Etruschi in Maremma. Popolamento e attività produttive*, Milano; • 1997 *Il carro di Vulci dalla necropoli dell'Osteria*, in *Carri da guerra e principi etruschi*, ex. cat., Viterbo 1997–98, Roma; **Shefton B.B.** • 1979 *Die "rhodischen" Bronzekannen*, Mainz, p. 79, pl. 6, 1-2; **Sieveking J.** • 1913 *Die Bronzen der Sammlung Loeb*, p. 70, pl. 29; **Simon E.** • 1973 "Die Tomba dei Tori und der etruskische Apollon Kull," in *JdI*, 88; • 1995 b "Argonauten beim Waffentanz," in *"Telemanniana et alia Musicologica", Festschrift Günter Fleischhauer;* • 1998 in A. Kämmerer, M. Schuchard, A. Speck (ed. by), *Medeas Wandlungen*, Heidelberg; **Small J.P.** • 1982 *Cacu and Marsyas in Etrusco-Roman Legend* (Princeton Monographs in Art and Archaeology, 45), Princeton; **Spivey N.J.** • 1987 *The Micali Painter and his followers*, Oxfor, pp. 9, 45 ff.; **Spivey N.J., Rasmussen T.** • 1986 "Dioniso e i pirati nel Toledo Museum of Art," in *Prospettiva*, 44; **Sprenger M.** • 1972 "Die etruskische Plastik des V. Jahrhunderts v. Chr. Und ihr Verhältnis zur griechischen Kunst," in *Studia archaeologica*, XIV, pp. 29 ff.; **Sprenger M., Bartoloni G.** • 1977 *Die Etrusker: Kunst und Geschichte*, München; • 1983 *The Etruscans: Their History, Art and Architecture*, New York; **Stefani G.** • 1984 *Terrecotte figurate, Materiali del Museo Archeologico Nazionale di Tarquinia* VII, Roma; **Steingräber S.** • 1979 "Etruskische Möbel," in *Archaeologica*, 9, 305, n. 558; • 1984 *Catalogo ragionato della pittura etrusca,* Milano; **Stopponi S.** • 1983 *La Tomba della "Scrofa Nera"*, Roma; • 1985 in *Santuari d'Etruria*, ex. cat. Arezzo, Milano, pp. 80 ff.; • 1991 "Acroterio," in F. Roncalli, L. Bonfante (ed. by), *Antichità dall'Umbria a New York*, ex. cat., Perugia pp. 261–63, 6.1; • 1991 "Un acroterio dal santuario di Cannicella ad Orvieto. Miscellanea etrusca e italica in onore di Massimo Pallottino," in *Archeologia Classica*, XLIII, pp. 1103–161; • 1993 "Terrecotte architettoniche da Orvieto: alcune novità," in *Deliciae fictiles. "Acta Sueciae"*, L, p. 160, fig. 10; • 1996 "Orvieto," *voce*, in *Enciclopedia dell'Arte Antica*, II suppl., IV, Roma, p. 137, fig.195; • 1996 "Perugia," *voce*, in *Enciclopedia dell'Arte Antica*, II suppl., IV, Roma, p. 333; **Stothart H.** • 1965 *Handbook of Sculpture in the J. Paul Getty Museum*, Malibu; **Strazzulla M.J.** • 1985 a "La decorazione frontonale del tempio di Belvedere di Orvieto," in *Atti del II Convegno Internazionale di Studi Etruschi*, Firenze; • 1985 b "La decorazione architettonica," in *Civiltà degli Etruschi*, ex. cat., Firenze; • 1994 *Attestazioni figurative dei Dioscuri nel mondo etrusco*, in *Castores. L'immagine dei Dioscuri a Roma*, ex. cat., Roma, pp. 38 ff.; • 1997 "La testa in bronzo di personaggio virile da S. Giovanni Lipioni," in *I luoghi degli dei, sacro e natura nell'Abruzzo italico*, Pescara; **Strøm** • 1971 *Problems Concerning the Origin and Early Development of the Etruscan Orientalizing Style*, Odense; **Szilàgyi J.G.** • 1980 "Un style etrusque en bronze," in *Bulletin du Musèe hongrois des Beaux- Arts*, 54, Budapest; • 1992 *Ceramica etrusco-corinzia figurata*, I, Firenze, p. 82, n. 3; • 1993 "'Da buon etrusco'. Il Pittore di Civitavecchia," in *Bulletin des Musées Royaux d'Art et d'Histoire,* 64, pp. 39 ff.;

T

Tanci S., Tortoioli S. • forthcoming *La ceramica italo-geometrica*, in *Materiali del Museo Archeologico Nazionale di Tarquinia*, Roma, n. 81; **Teitz R.S.** • 1967 *Masterpieces of Etruscan Art*, ex. cat., Worcester (Mass.); **The Art of the Italic Peoples** • 1993 *The Art of the Italic Peoples from 3000 to 300* BC *- Swiss Collections*, ex. cat., Génève-Paris 1993-1994, Génève; **The J. Paul Getty Museum** • 1956 *The J. Paul Getty Museum Guidebook*, Los Angeles; • 1997 *The J. Paul Getty Museum. Handbook of the Collections*, Los Angeles; **Toledo treasures** • 1995 *The Toledo Museum of Art. Toledo treasures*, Toledo-New York; **Tondo L.** • 1985 "La monetazione," in A. Maggiani (ed. by) *Artigianato artistico. L'Etruria settentrionale interna in età ellenistica*, Milano; **Torelli M.** • 1965 "Un uovo di struzzo dipinto, conservato nel Museo di Tarquinia," in *Studi etruschi*, XXXIII; • 1967 in *Arte e Civiltà degli Etruschi*, ex. cat., Torino, Torino, p. 108, n. 318; • 1967 "REE, Ager Tarquiniensis: Graviscae," in *Studi etruschi*, XXV; • 1968 "Il donario di M. Fulvio Flacco nell'area di S. Omobono. Studi di topografia romana," in *Quaderni dell'Istituto di Topografia Antica dell'Università di Roma*, V, Roma, pp. 71–75; • 1971 "Il santuario greco di Hera a Gravisca," in *La Parola del Passato*, 26; • 1973 in *Roma medio repubblicana*, ex. cat., Roma, p. 103 ff., n. 89; • 1977 "Il santuario greco di Gravisca," in *La Parola del Passato*, 32; • 1978 "Il santuario greco di Gravisca," in *Quaderni de La Ricerca Scientifica del CNR*, 100, 2; • 1981 "Precisazioni su Gravisca," in *La Parola del Passato*, 36; • 1982 "Per la definizione del commercio greco-orientale: il caso di Gravisca," in *La Parola del Passato*, XXXVII; • 1985 *L'Arte degli Etruschi*, Bari; • 1986 "Dialogue sur le trépied étrusque," in *Dial. d'Hist. Anc.*, 12, pp. 120–21; • 1986 in M. Torelli, R. Bianchi Bandinelli, *L'arte nell'antichità classica. Etruria - Roma*, Torino n. 38; • 1991 "La 'Sedia Corsini', monumento della genealogia etrusca dei Plautii,' in *Mélanges P. Lévêque, 5., Anthropologie et société*, Besançon, pp. 355–67; • 1992 "I fregi figurati delle 'regiae' latine ed etrusche. Immaginario del potere arcaico, in *Ostraka*, I, 2, pp. 264 ff.; • 1994 "Riflessi in Etruria del mondo fenicio e greco d'Occidente," in *Magna Grecia Etruschi e Fenici*, proceeding of the XXXIII Convegno di studi sulla Magna Grecia, Taranto 1993, Taranto; • 1997 *Il rango, il rito e l'immagine, Alle origini della rappresentazione storica romana*, Milano; • 1999 "Appius Alce, La gemma fiorentina con rito saliare e la presenza dei Claudii in Etruria," in *Studi etruschi*, LXIII - MCMXCVII; • 2000 "Primi appunti per un'antropologia del vino degli etruschi," in D. Tomasi, C. Cremonesi (ed. by), *L'avventura del vino nel bacino del Mediterraneo, Itinerari storici ed archeologici prima e dopo Roma*, international symposium, Conegliano 1998, Treviso; **Torelli M., Masseria C.** • 1999 "Il mito all'alba di una colonia greca. Il programma figurativo delle metope dell'Heraion alla Foce del Sele," in *Le mythe grec dans l'Italie antique. Fonction et image,* proceeding of the meeting, Roma 1996, Roma, pp. 205 ff.; **Torelli M., Agostiniani L.** • forthcoming "Un cippo confinario etrusco da Cortona," in *Dieci anni di archeologia cortonese*; **Torelli M., Boitani F., Lilliu G. et al.** • 1971 "Gravisca (Tarquinia). Scavi nella città etrusco-romana. Campagne di scavo 1969 e 1970," in *Notizie degli scavi*; **Tronchetti C.** • 1988 "La Sardegna e gli Etruschi," in *MedA*, 1; **Trucco F.** • 1999 "I primi scavi nella necropoli di Monte Tosto Alto," in *Ferrante Rittatore von Willer e la Maremma. Paesaggi naturali, umani, archeologici*, Ischia di Castro, pp. 103 ff.; **Trümpler C.** • 1990 "Die etruskischen Körbchenohrringe," in *Die Welt der Etrusker,* proceeding of the meeting, Berlin 24-26 october 1988, Berlin, pp. 291 ff.; **Tuck A.** • forthcoming *Orientalizing period wing – handle cups from Poggio Civitate: ceramique tradition and regional production in Inland Etruria*, forthcoming;

V

Vagnetti M. • 1971 *Il deposito votivo di Campetti a Veio: materiale delgi scavi 1937-1938*, Firenze; **Van Der Meer L.B.** • 1979 "Iecur Placentinum and the Orientation of the Etruscan Haruspex," in *BABesch*, 54, pp. 51, n. 2, figs. 8–9; • 1987 *The Bronze Liver of Piacenza. Analysis of a Polytheistic Structure*, Amsterdam; • 1990 in H.A.G. Brijder (ed. by), *Die Etrusken*, ex. cat., Amsterdam 1989–90, Den Haag; **Vatin C.** • 1991 *Monuments votifs de Delphes*, Roma; **Vermiglioli G.B.** • 1813 *Saggio di bronzi etruschi trovati nell'agro perugino*, Perugia; **Villard F.** • 1956 "Vases de bronze grecs dans une tombe étrusque du VII siècle," in *MonPiot*, 48, 2; **von Freytag Löringhoff B.** • 1986 *Das Giebelrelief von Telamon und seine Stellung innerhalb der Ikonographie der Sieben gegen Theben*, Mainz; • 1992 "Annotazioni al frontone dei Sette a Tebe," in *La coroplastica templare etrusca fra il IV e il II secolo a. C.*, proceeding of the XVI Convegno di studi etruschi e italici, Orbetello 1988, Firenze; **von Vacano O.W.** • 1992 "Osservazioni riguardanti la storia edilizia del tempio di Talamonaccio," in *La coroplastica templare etrusca fra il IV e il II secolo a. C.*, proceeding of the XVI Convegno di studi etruschi e italici, Orbetello 1988, Firenze; **von Vacano O.W., von Freytag Löringhoff B.** • 1982 *Il frontone di Talamone e il mito dei "Sette a Tebe"*, ex. cat., Firenze; **Vostchinina A.I.** "Statua-cinerario in bronzo di arte etrusca nelle collezioni dell'Ermitage," in *Studi etruschi*, XXXVIII;

W

Weber Lehmann C. • 1985 "Spätarchaische Gelagebilder in Tarquinia," in *RM*, 92, pp. 19 ff.; **Weber T.** • 1983 *Brozekannen*, Frankfurt a.M. Bern; **Woytwitsch E.** • 1978 "Die Wagen der Bronze- und frühen Eisenzeit in Italien," in *Praehistorische Bronze Funde*, XVII, 1;

Z

Zamarchi P. • 1996 *Il Museo dell' Accademia Etrusca di Cortona*, Cortona; **Zancani Montuoro P.** • 1946–48 "Un mito italiota in Etruria," in *ASAA*, XXIV–XXVI, pp. 85 ff.; **Zazoff P.** • 1968 *Etruskische Skarabaen*, Mainz am Rhein, p. 241, pl. 46; **Zilverberg M.** • 1986 "The La Tolfa Painter. Fat or thin?" in *Enthousiasmos, Essays on Greek and related Pottery presented to J.M. Hemelrijk*, Amsterdam; **Zwierlein-Diehl E.** • 1969 in *Antike Gemmen in deutschen Sammlungen*, München vol. II, pp. 110, n. 247; 103–04, n. 237.

Agde
• Musée de l'Éphèbe:
Tripod
from underwater excavations at Le Cap d'Agde
p. 108; cat. 54

Allumiere
• Museo Civico:
Askos
from Poggio della Pozza, Tomb 25/1994
cat. 6.4
Biconical urn
from Poggio della Pozza, Tomb 13/1994
cat. 5.1
Biconical urn
from Poggio della Pozza, Tomb 25/1994
cat. 6.1
Biconical urn
from Poggio della Pozza, Tomb 21/1994
cat. 7.1
Bowl-lid
from Poggio della Pozza, Tomb 21/1994
cat. 7.2
Cup
from Poggio della Pozza, Tomb 25/1994
cat. 6.3
Fibula
from Poggio della Pozza, Tomb 21/1994
cat. 7.4
Fibula
from Poggio della Pozza, Tomb 13/1994
cat. 5.4
Fragments, not reconstructible, of a small open form
from Poggio della Pozza, Tomb 21/1994
cat. 7.5
Lid
from Poggio della Pozza, Tomb 13/1994
cat. 5.2
Lid
from Poggio della Pozza, Tomb 25/1994
cat. 6.2
Ring
from Poggio della Pozza, Tomb 25/1994
cat. 6.6
Tankard
from Poggio della Pozza, Tomb 21/1994
cat. 7.3
Three-legged stand
from Poggio della Pozza, Tomb 25/1994
cat. 6.5
Two rings
from Poggio della Pozza, Tomb 13/1994
cat. 5.5
Zoomorphic vase
from Poggio della Pozza, Tomb 13/1994
cat. 5.3

Amsterdam
• Allard Pierson Museum:
Amphora, Amsterdam Painter
p. 420; cat. 211
Caeretan hydria and support of a dinos, Eagle Painter
p. 428; cat. 162
Kantharos
p. 394; cat. 223
Small plaque with haruspex
p. 280; cat. 151

Ancona
• Museo Archeologico Nazionale delle Marche:
Head of youth with diadem
from Cagli, locality Coltone
cat. 286

Arezzo
• Museo C. Cilnio Mecenate:
Earthenware pediment
from Arezzo, Piazza San Jacopo
cat. 269
Small plaque of a Schnabelkanne
p. 280; cat. 150
Sors cleromantica
from Arezzo
p. 482
Terra-cotta head
from Arezzo, Catona
p. 388; cat. 318.1
Terra-cotta head
from Arezzo, Catona
p. 388; cat. 318.2

Athens
•Archaeological Museum:
Stela of Lemnos
pp. 47, 500; cat. 1

Bassano del Grappa
• Museo Civico:
Genucilia-type plate
p. 453

Beaulieu-sur-Mer
• Villa Kérylos:
Bowl with incised decoration
cat. 31

Berlin
• Staatliche Museen, Antikensammlung:
Acroterion with Eos and Tythonos
from Cerveteri
cat. 218
Black-figure amphora
p. 72; cat. 165
Capuan Tabula
from Santa Maria Capua Vetere, locality Quattordici Ponti
cat. 256
Female head antefix
from Cerveteri
cat. 271
Helmet with "eyes" decoration
p. 86; cat. 69
Scarab "Gemma von Stosch"
from Perugia
p. 459; cat. 259
Scarab with haruspex
from Volterra
p. 455; cat. 156
Slab with female figure (fragment)
from Cerveteri
p. 346; cat. 270

Bettona
• Museo Civico:
Boundary cippus
p. 294; cat. 22

Blera (Viterbo)
Cube tomb at the necropolis,
p. 339
Aerial view of the necropolis,
p. 33

Bloomington
• Indiana University Art Museum:
Mirror depicting Paris Judgement
p. 136

Bologna
• Museo Civico Archeologico:
Stela from Felsina
p. 178
Tintinnabulum
from Bologna, Arsenale necropolis, Ori Tomb
p. 134
• Soprintendenza per i Beni Archeologici dell'Emilia Romagna:
Heracles
from Bologna, sanctuary of Villa Cassarini
p. 177; cat. 205

Bolsena
• Museo Rocca Monaldeschi della Cervara
Trone of the "Panthers"
from Bolsena, Poggio Moscini, domus II or "delle pitture"
cat. 328

Bruxelles
• Musées Royaux d'Art et d'Histoire:
Olla with boxing scene, Civitavecchia Painter
p. 425; cat. 51

Carmignano (Prato)
• Deposits of the Soprintendenza ai Beni Archeologici della Toscana:
Kardiophylax
from Artimino, necropolis of Prato Rosello
p. 393; cat. 59

Castello
• Villa Corsini:
Death bed
from Arezzo, Camucia, "Melone"
cat. 175

Cerveteri
• Museo Archeologico Nazionale Cerite:
Attic amphora
from Cerveteri
p. 99; cat. 184
Bucchero amphora
from Casaletti di Ceri, Tomb 2
p. 410
Cinerary urn with married couple
from Cerveteri, Banditaccia necropolis
cat. 142
Etrusco-Corinthian column krater
from Cerveteri, Banditaccia necropolis
p. 432; cat. 210
Lid of cinerary urn
from Cerveteri, Banditaccia necropolis
cat. 245
Plate
from Casaletti di Ceri, Tomb 2
p. 482
Tomb of the Five Chairs, interior,
p. 342
Views and plan of the Banditaccia necropolis,
pp. 128, 212, 213, 334, 335, 336
View of Cerveteri necropolis,
p. 40

Chianciano Terme
• Museo Civico Archeologico delle Acque:
Ax
from Chianciano Terme, sacred area at Fucoli
p. 250; cat. 265
Gold brooch
p. 466, cat. 105
Leech-type fibula
from Vulci
p. 467; cat. 109
Necklace
from Marsiliana d'Albegna
p. 464; cat. 103
Ossuary
from Chianciano Terme, locality Tolle
cat. 193
Pair of armille
p. 465; cat. 106
Pair of "bauletto" earrings
from Pescia Romana
p. 470; cat. 108
Two brooch heads
p. 466, cat. 104
Pair of loop earrings
from Pescia Romana
cat. 107

Chiusi
• Museo Archeologico Nazionale:
Cippus with battle scenes
from Chiusi
p. 227
Krater with scene of divination, Bargagli Painter
from Chiusi, Paccianese Tomb
p. 441; cat. 159
Lid of cinerary urn
from Chiusi
p. 408

Columbia
• University of Missoury Museum of Art and Archeology:
Oinochoe with ships and fishes
p. 96; cat. 50

Copenhagen
• The National Museum of Denmark:
Canopic urn on a throne
from Chiusi, Fontecucchiaia

p. 31; cat.135.1
Bowl
from Chiusi, Fontecucchiaia
p. 31; cat.135.3
Figure on a biga
from Chiusi, Fontecucchiaia
p. 31; cat.135.4
Fire tongs
from Chiusi, Fontecucchiaia
p. 31; cat.135.6
Grave goods
from Chiusi, Fontecucchiaia
p. 31; cat.135
Kore
from Rimini, Covignano
p. 170; cat. 278
Mask
from Chiusi, Fontecucchiaia
p. 31; cat.135.5
Two small globular ollas with lid
from Chiusi, Fontecucchiaia
p. 31; cat.135.2
Two spits
from Chiusi, Fontecucchiaia
p. 31; cat.135.7
• Ny Carlsberg Glyptotek:
Male head
from Ariccia (?)
cat. 279
Smaller-than-life-size head of a statue
from Ariccia, locus Dianus
p. 376; cat. 279

Cortona
• Museo dell'Accademia Etrusca:
Etruscan amphora
p. 82; cat. 18
Statuette of Culsans
from Cortona
p. 286; cat. 200
Statuette of Selvans
from Cortona
p. 286; cat. 201
Writing stylus
from Sodo di Cortona
cat. 253
• Palazzo Comunale:
Boundary cippus
from Cortona, Viale Passerini 170
cat. 23
Aerial view,
p. 292
Tumulus II of Melone del Sodo,
monumental staircase to the altar,
p. 368

Cremona
• Museo Civico Ala Ponzone
Helmet with inscription
cat. 300

Delphi
• Apollo Sanctuary:
Pedestal with the dedication of the Tyrrhenians
p. 141; cat. 55

Este
• Museo Nazionale:
Benvenuti situla
from the Benvenuti Tomb 126
p. 194, 195
Statuette of a warrior
from Lozzo
p. 190

Ferrara
• Museo Archeologico Nazionale:
Candelabrum
from Spina, Valle Trebba,
Tomb 614
p. 176; cat. 192
Comb
from Spina, Valle Trebba
p. 474; cat. 122
Tripod from Vulci
from Spina, Valle Trebbia,
Tomb 128
p. 398; cat. 233
Oinochoe with "Xanthippos" graffito
from Spina, Valle Trebba,
Tomb 709
p. 260

Fiesole
• Museo Civico Archeologico:
Statuette of Heracles
from Fiesole
p. 289; cat. 204

Florence
• Biblioteca Nazionale Centrale:
Thomas Dempster, *De Etruria regali*
p. 507
• Casa Buonarroti:
Stela of Larth Ninie
from Fiesole
p. 251; cat. 76
• Ceccanti Collection:
Hydria a figure nere
cat. 216
• Museo Archelogico Nazionale:
Entrance to the Museo Archeologico
from Piazza Santissima Annunziata,
p. 519
View of the ground floor great room
of the Spedale degli Innocenti,
p. 514
Amber and glass necklace
from Vetulonia, tumulus
of Castelvecchio
p. 112; cat. 133
Amphora
p. 153; cat. 191.8
Amphora
p. 153; cat. 191.9
Antropomorphic alabastron
from Populonia, Porcareccia,
Tomb of the Flabelli
cat. 115
Aryballos
cat. 116
Ax
from Città di Castello, Trestina
cat. 264
Battle scene fron the Sarcophagus of the Amazons
p. 344
"Bauletto" earring
from Populonia, Poggio
della Porcareccia
p. 470; cat. 91
"Bauletto" earring
from Populonia, Poggio
della Porcareccia
p. 470; cat. 92
"Bauletto" earring
from Populonia, Poggio
della Porcareccia
p. 470; cat. 93
Bell-shaped cinerary urn
from Chiusi
cat. 313
Biconical ossuary
from Tarquinia, Poggio
Selciatello, Tomb 179
cat. 9.1
Biconical whorl
from Tarquinia, Poggio
Selciatello, Tomb 59
cat. 10.4
Black-figure stamnos
pp. 436, 437; cat. 217
Bronze belt
from Marradi
cat. 26
Bronze coin
from the hoard of Populonia
p. 92; cat. 48
Bronze coins
from Vetulonia
p. 94
Bronze statuette of discophoros
p. 382
Bucchero amphora
p. 417; cat. 240
Bucchero chalice
p. 416; cat. 238
Bucchero drinking glass
p. 415; cat. 244
Bucchero hydria
p. 419; cat. 236
Bucchero kánthtaros
p. 413; cat. 243
Bucchero kyathos
p. 415; cat. 237
Bucchero oinochoe
p. 412; cat. 242
Bucchero olpe
p. 419; cat. 239
Bull-shaped askos
from Tarquinia, Poggio Selciatello
di Sopra
p. 407; cat. 9.5
Burial goods
from Tarquinia, Poggio Selciatello,
Tomb 179
p. 61; cat. 9
Bust
from Marsiliana d'Albegna,
Banditella necropolis
cat. 136
Candelabrum
from Populonia, San
Cerbone necropolis
cat. 228
Capeduncula
from Tarquinia, Selciatello
di Sopra
p. 146; cat. 176
Chalice
from Cerveteri
p. 395; cat. 222
Chalice krater
p. 153; cat. 191.1
Chimera
from Arezzo
p. 641
Cinerary statue
from Chianciano, Pedata
necropolis
pp. 378, 379; cat. 145bis
Cinerary statue "Mater Matuta"
from Chianciano, Pedata
necropolis
p. 377; cat. 145
Cinerary urn
cat. 314
Cinerary urn
p. 257; cat. 317
Cinerary urn
from Perugia, Città della Pieve
cat. 194
Cinerary urn
from Vetulonia, Circolo
del Duce, group V
cat. 134
Cippus
from Firenze, near the church
of San Tommaso
cat. 148
Coins, silver series
from the hoard of Populonia
pp. 88, 89, 90, 91; cat. 48
Colum
cat. 191.4
Colum
from Populonia, Tomb 13/1908
p. 401; cat. 229.7
Crested helmet
from Tarquinia, Poggio
dell'Impiccato, Tomb I
p. 26; cat. 56
Diadem
from Perugia, locality Sperandio
cat. 102*Single-handle bowl*
from Tarquinia, Poggio
di Selciatello,
Tomb 59
cat. 10.2
Diadem
from Populonia, Piano delle
Granate necropolis
cat. 101
Diphros leg
from Quinto Fiorentino, Tomb
della Montagnola
cat. 266
Disc earring
from Pescia Romana
p. 470; cat.99
Euboean bowl
from Tarquinia
p. 103; cat. 37
Feet of tripode
p. 399; cat. 281
Female head and bust
from Vetulonia, Pietrera tumulus
p. 364
Female statuette
from Brolio (Arezzo)
cat. 275
Fibula
from Tarquinia, Poggio Selciatello,
Tomba 59
cat. 10.7
Fibula
from Tarquinia, Poggio Selciatello,
Tomb 179
p. 61; cat. 9.8
Fibula "Corsini"
from Marsiliana d'Albegna
p. 467; cat. 87
Fibula wiht bow
from Tarquinia, Poggio Gallinaro,
Tomb 9
p. 78; cat. 27.3
Fibula with twisted-rope bow
from Tarquinia, Poggio Selciatello,
Tomb 59
cat. 10.6

Fibulae
from Tarquinia, Poggio Selciatello, Tomb 59
p. 60; cat. 10.5
Fresco
from Tarquinia, Monterozzi necropolis, Tomb Tarantola
cat. 172
Furniture decoration
from Vetulonia
p. 68
Gem
cat. 292
Grater
from Populonia, Tomb of the Flabelli
cat. 225
Handle of flabellum
from Populonia, Tomb of the Flabelli
cat. 32
Head of a youth
cat. 302
Helmet
from the waters of the Golfo di Baratti
cat. 68
Helmet with the inscription "haspnas"
from Vetulonia
p. 262; cat. 70
Hut cinerary urn
from Vetulonia
p. 312
Knobbed-bell helmet
from Tarquinia, Poggio Selciatello di Sopra
p. 407; cat. 9.2
Krater with conversation scene, Argonauts Painter
from Chiusi
p. 445
Krater with episode of geranomachy, Florence Painter 4035
from Volterra
p. 438
Kyathoi
p. 154; cat. 191.7
Kyathos
from Vetulonia, Poggio al Bello, Tomb of the Duce
p. 483
Kyathos
cat. 178
Kylix
from Orvieto
cat. 241
Laconian aryballos
from Populonia, Porcareccia necropolis
p. 149; cat. 125
Lebes with weeping figures and horse men
from Pitigliano (Grosseto), Valle Rodeta
p. 404; cat. 173
Lingots
from the Island of Giglio
cat. 25
Male statuette
p. 235; cat. 289
Mirror with haruspicy scenes
from Tuscania
p. 272; cat. 319
Mirror with the breast-feading of Heracles
p. 288; cat. 320
Mirror with the Dioscures
p.25; cat. 324
Moon-shaped razor
from Tarquinia, Poggio Selciatello, Tomb 179
p. 61; cat. 9.7
Necklace
p. 454; cat. 95
Necklace
from Volterra, Portone necropolis
p. 454; cat. 95
Oinochoai
from Vetulonia, tumulus of Castelvecchio
p. 112; cats. 111–112
Oinochoe
from Populonia, Tomb 13/1908
p. 400; cat. 229.2
Oinochoe
from Vetulonia, tumulus of Castelvecchio
p. 112; cat. 111
Oinochoe
from Vetulonia, tumulus of Castelvecchio
p. 112; cat. 112
Oinochoe
p. 154; cat. 191.3
Oinochoe
p. 154; cat. 191.5
Oinochoe with trilobate mouth
from Populonia, Poggio della Porcareccia, Tomb of the Flabelli
p. 392; cat. 226
Olla
from Bisenzio
p. 219; cat. 164
Olpe
from Populonia, Tomb 13/1908
p. 400; cat. 229.1
Pair of simpulas
from Populonia, San Cerbone necropolis
cat. 229.3; 229.4
Patera
from Populonia, Tomb 13/1908
p. 401; cat. 229.6
Patera
p. 152; cat. 191.2
Patera with handle
cat. 191.6
Pediment of the Talamone temple (fragments)
pp. 264, 266–269; cat. 307
Pithos
from Cerveteri
p. 83; cat. 20
Pseudo-scarab
from Populonia, Poggio della Porcareccia, pit tomb with circle of rough stones
cat. 36
Pyxis
from Chiusi, Pania Tomb
p. 216; cat. 170
Ribbed jug
cat. 85
Ring with a warrior and a female figure
from Populonia
p. 471; cat. 96
Ring with scarab
from Populonia
cat. 97
Sarcophagus of Larthia Seianti
from Chiusi, Marcianella necropolis
p. 390
Scarab
p. 461; cat. 36
Signature of the Greek artisan Metru
from Populonia
p. 260
Single-handled biconical ossuary
from Tarquinia, Poggio Selciatello, Tomb 59
p. 60; cat. 10.1
Situla
from Populonia, Tomb 13/1908
p. 400; cat. 229.5
Situla
p. 153; cat. 191.10
Small amphora with spirals
from Populonia, Porcareccia
cat. 181
Small bronze
from Vetulonia, Costiaccia Bambagini
p. 52
Small dish
from Poggio di Selciatello, Tomb 179
cat. 9.3
Small dish on tall foot
from Poggio di Selciatello, Tomb 179
cat. 9.4
Small earthenware cinerary urn
from Chiusi
cat. 310
Small earthenware cinerary urn
from Chiusi
cat. 311
Small earthenware cinerary urn
from Chiusi
cat. 312
Small cinerary urn
from Chiusi
cat. 258
Small Nikosthenic amphora
from Veio, Monte Michele
p. 147; cat. 182
Small plaque with Geryon
from Comeana, tumulus of Montefortini
p. 474; cat. 119
Small two-handled amphora
from Tarquinia, Selciatello di Sopra
p. 146; cat. 180
Snares
from the Island of Giglio
cat. 24
Spear-head and ferrule
from Tarquinia, Poggio dell'Impiccato, Tomb I
p. 61; cat. 58
Spindle and distaff
from Tarquinia, Poggio Gallinaro, pit tomb 8
cat. 128
Spools
from Populonia, Tomb 1 of San Cerbone
cat. 129.1
Spools
from Tarquinia, Poggio Selciatello, Tomb 59
p. 60; cat. 10.3
Spools and whorls
from Populonia, Tomb I
p. 135; cat. 129
Spoon
from Chiusi, Tomb of the Boncia
p. 403; cat. 86
Statue of Aule Meteli
from Perugia, Pila (?)
p. 385; cat. 306
Statuette of Ajax killing himself
from Populonia
p. 245; cat. 79
Statuette of an armed man
p. 244; cat. 196
Statuette of Iuno Sospita
p. 36; cat. 203
Statuette of offerer
p. 235; cat. 288
Statuette of warrior
from Brolio (Arezzo)
p. 244; cat. 272
Statuette of warrior
from Brolio (Arezzo)
cat. 273
Statuette of warrior
from Brolio (Arezzo)
cat. 274
Stela
from Antella (Florence)
p. 366
Strigil
from Populonia, San Cerbone necropolis
cat. 230
Sword with sheath
from Tarquinia, Poggio dell'Impiccato, Tomb I
p. 69; cat. 57
Tablet with incised alphabet
from Marsiliana d'Albegna, Banditella Circolo degli Avori
p. 480
Tabula Cortonensis
pp. 492, 493, 494; cat. 263
Three navicella fibulae
from Tarquinia, Poggio Gallinaro, Tomb 9
p. 78; cat. 27.2
Tripod (fragment)
from Vetulonia, Poggio la Guardia
p. 56
Two aurei
from Populonia (?)
p. 90; cat. 47
Two fibulae
from Tarquinia, Poggio Gallinaro, Tomb 9
p. 78; cat. 27.1
Two leech fibulae
from Tarquinia, Poggio Gallinaro, Tomb 9
p. 78; cat. 27.4
Votive female head
from Nemi, sanctuary of Diana
p. 239; cat. 290
Votive male head
from Nemi, sanctuary of Diana
p. 238; cat. 291
Votive model of temple
from Orvieto
p. 331, cat. 267
Whorls
from Populonia, Tomb 1 of San Cerbone

cat. 129.2
Wine amphora
from Castiglione della Pescaia, Isola dello Sparviero
cat. 19
• Soprintendenza Archeologica per la Toscana
Basins
from the Elba Island
cat. 53
Limestone statue
from Casale Marittimo (Pisa), necropolis of Casa Nocera
p. 367
Plan and section of the Montagnola Tomb near Florence,
p. 337
View of the room dedicated to Tarquinia in the Museo Topografico dell'Etruria before 1966,
p. 516

Göttingen
• Archäologisches Institut der Universität:
Statuette of haruspex
p. 278; cat. 154
Statuette of haruspex
p. 279; cat. 152
Statuette of haruspex
p. 279; cat. 153
Statuette of haruspex
p. 279; cat. 155

Gravisca (port of Tarquinia)
Aerial view of site,
p. 105

Grosseto
• Museo Archeologico e d'Arte della Maremma:
Olla
from Roselle, House of the Impluvium
cat. 21.2
Olla
from Roselle, House of the Impluvium
cat. 21.4
Razor
from Vetulonia, Colle Baroncio necropolis
cat. 161
Small oven
from Roselle, House of the Impluvium
cat. 21.3
Well-curb
from Roselle, House of the Impluvium
cat. 21.1

Hamburg
• Museum für Kunst und Gewerbe:
Statuette of Perseus
cat. 220

Hannover
• Kestner-Museum
Alabastron with relief decoration
from Cerveteri
cat. 34
Rhodian (?) alabastron
from Cerveteri
p. 106; cat. 3

Karlsruhe
• Badisches Landesmuseum:
Candelabrum with dancer
from Vulci
p. 198; cat. 231

Lemnos
• Myrina Museum:
Mermaid
from Lemnos
p. 504

Livorno
• Museo Civico G. Fattori, Chiellini Collection:
Hoard of bronzes
from Monte La Poggia, fattoria di Limone
cat. 3

London
• British Museum:
Head of statue
found on an island of the Lake of Bolsena
cat. 277
Helmet with dedication to Zeus
from the Olimpia sanctuary
p. 50
Mirror
from Bolsena, Castellani Collection
cat. 321
Sarcophagus lid
from Tarquinia
p. 138

Los Angeles
• J. Paul Getty Museum:
Tinia
from Populonia
p. 373; cat. 195

Marzabotto (Bologna)
• Museo Archeologico Nazionale Pompeo Aria:
Kouros head
from Marzabotto, Cycladic provenance
p. 142; cat. 276
Aerial view,
p. 168, 301
View of the acropolis,
p. 173
View of the necropolis,
p. 172

Massa Marittima
Remains of houses at Accesa,
p. 299
View of Lake Accesa,
p. 298

Milan
• Civiche Raccolte Archeologiche e Numismatiche:
Male head
from Vulci (?)
p. 222, 223; cat. 137

Modena
• Galleria Estense:
Statuette of Fufluns
cat. 197
Statuette of Menerva
p. 372; cat. 198

Montalcino
Walls of the Poggio Civitella fortress,
p. 315

Monterenzi
The settlement at Monte Bibele, near Monterenzi,
p. 303

Montopoli in Valdarno
• Antiquarium Comunale:
Fragment of fabric
from Vetulonia, Poggio al Bello, Tomb of the Duce
cat. 130

Munich
• Staatliche Antikensammlungen und Glyptothek:
Fragments of a cippus
from Chiusi (?)
pp. 230, 231; cat. 260
Antropomorphic oinochoe
cat. 227
Base of candelabrum
from Vulci
p. 32; cat. 232
Base of thymaterion
from Castel San Mariano (Perugia)
p. 397; cat. 234
Disc fibula
from Vulci, Ponte Sodo
p. 463; cat. 89
Panel of the back side of the carpentum from Castel San Mariano
cat. 127.3
Panel of the lateral side of the carpentum from Castel San Mariano
cat. 127.1
Panel of the lateral side of the carpentum from Castel San Mariano
cat. 127.2
Scarab with haruspex
cat. 156
Statuette of diver
from Perugia
cat. 221
Statuette of horseman
cat. 78

Murlo
• Antiquarium:
Architectonic slabs
from Murlo, Poggio Civitate
p. 127
Acroterial statue of a seated woman, lower half
from Murlo, Poggio Civitate
cat. 139
Bearded head
from Murlo, Poggio Civitate
p. 206; cat. 138
Bust of sphinx
from Murlo, Poggio Civitate
cat. 141
Helmeted head
from Murlo, Poggio Civitate
p. 206; cat. 140
Seal
from Murlo, Poggio Civitate
p. 456

Neaples
• Museo Archeologico Nazionale:
Wall-facing slab
from Velletri
pp. 204, 208; cat. 168
Wall-facing slab
from Velletri
p. 208; cat. 167
Wall-facing slab
from Velletri
p. 209; cat. 166
Wall-facing slab
from Velletri
p. 209; cat. 169

New York
• Metropolitam Museum of Art:
Cockerel-shaped vase
from Viterbo
p. 476; cat. 250
Fibula
from Roselle (?)
cat. 88

Norchia
View of necropolis,
p. 41

Orvieto
• Museo Archeologico C. Faina:
Acroterion with Ajax
from Orvieto, sanctuary of Cannicella
p. 242; cat. 268
Bearded head
from Orvieto, Belvedere Temple
p. 39; cat. 285.7
Cuirass
from Porano, Settecamini, Poggio del Roccolo
cat. 72
Figure with drapery
from Orvieto, Belvedere Temple
cat. 285.8
Fragmentary figure of a warrior
from Orvieto, Belvedere Temple
cat. 285.3
Fragmentary figure of a warrior
from Orvieto, Belvedere Temple
p. 381; cat. 285.5
Fragment of male head
from Orvieto, temple in Via San Leonardo
p. 247; cat. 283
Head of a youth
from Orvieto, Belvedere Temple
cat. 285.6
Helmet
from Porano, Settecamini, Poggio del Roccolo
cat. 71
Male figure
from Orvieto, Belvedere Temple
cat. 285.2
Male figure with chlamys
from Orvieto, Belvedere Temple
cat. 285.1
Male torso
from Orvieto, temple in Via San Leonardo
p. 246; cat. 283
Pair of greaves
from Porano, Settecamini, Poggio del Roccolo
cat. 73

Pedimental high relief
from Orvieto, Belvedere Temple
cat. 285.4
Shield
from Porano, Settecamini, Poggio del Roccolo
p. 402; cat. 74
Sitting figure
from Orvieto, Belvedere Temple
cat. 285.9
Plan of the Crocifisso del Tufo necropolis,
p. 259
Young serf
from Orvieto, Golini Tomb I
p. 254

Oxford
• Ashmolean Museum:
Bronze statuette of Turms
from Uffingham (Berkshire)
p. 372; cat. 202
Slab with procession of warriors
from Cisterna di Latina (?)
cat. 147

Padua
• Museo Civico:
Funerary stela
from Camin
p. 192

Paestum
Tomb of the Diver,
p. 196, 201

Palermo
• Museo Archeologico Regionale A. Salinas:
Cinerary urn-statue known as Pluto
from Chiusi
cat. 143
Clusine funerary cippus
from Chiusi
cat. 261

Paris
• Bibliothèque Nationale:
G. B. Passeri, *Picturae Etruscorum in vasculis*
p. 508
Oinochoe with Ilioupersis, Bearded Sphinx Painter
p. 427; cat. 209
• Cabinet des Médailles:
Krater with Alcesti, Alcestis Painter
from Vulci
p. 452
Scarab with Glaukos, Pasiphae, Minos and Polyeidos
p. 460
• Musée du Louvre:
Attic krater
from Cerveteri
p. 151; cat. 189
Attic kylix
from Cerveteri
p. 151
Black-figure amphora
p. 435; cat. 215
Black figure Caeretan hydria
from Cerveteri
cat. 163
Campana slabs
from Cerveteri, Banditaccia necropolis
cat. 174
Chalice
p. 483
Duck-shaped askos, Montediano Painter
p. 449
Earthenware acroteria
from Tuscania
cat. 80
Eurytios krater
p. 81
Head of statue
from Fiesole
p. 383; cat. 303
Fragment of cippus
from Chiusi
cat. 176
Patera with movable handles
from Gravisca
p. 100; cat. 84
Red figure amphora
from Vulci
p. 140, 150; cat. 190
Sarcophagus of the Married Couple
from Cerveteri
p. 130, 131
Small plaques of a little chest
cat. 120
Stamnos with frieze, The Hague Painter
from Vulci
p. 451
Statuette of Hermes
p. 289; cat. 199
Statuette of offerer
from Mount Falterona
p. 234; cat. 206
Throne
cat. 131
Tridacna
cat. 114
• Musée du Petit Palais:
Satyr-head-shaped jug, Montediano Painter or Montebrandoni Painter
p. 447
• Musée Rodin:
Vibenna kylix, Rodin Painter
from Vulci (?)
p. 444; cat. 323

Perugia
• Museo Archeologico Nazionale:
Cinerary urn of arnϑ cai cutu
from Perugia
cat. 309
Sarcophagus
from Perugia, necropolis of the Sperandio
cat. 171

Pesaro
• Museo Archeologico Oliveriano:
Inscription in Etruscan and Latin
from Pesaro
p. 186; cat. 329

Piacenza
• Museo Civico Archeologico:
Model of a sheep's leaver
from Settima (Piacenza)
p. 277; cat. 160

Policoro
• Museo Archeologico Nazionale della Sirtide:
Barrel with protomes
from Chiaromonte
p. 199; cat. 224

Pisa
• Museo Nazionale di Palazzo Reale, Ottavio Simoneschi Collection
Front side of small cinerary urn
from Chianciano (?)
cat. 77

Pyrgi (port of Caere)
Aerial view of Pyrgi archaelogical site,
p. 104
View of the sanctuary of Pyrgi,
p. 300, 332

Reggio Emilia
• Musei Civici:
Fragment of lituus
from Reggio Emilia, Sant'Ilario d'Enza
p. 274; cat. 149

Rome
• Antiquarium Comunale:
Tessera hospitalis
from Roma, sacred area of Sant'Omobono
cat. 38
• Eredi Torlonia
Tomba François, frescoes
pp. 8–9; cat. 299
• Galleria Nazionale d'Arte Antica, Palazzo Corsini:
Corsini Throne
from Rome, San Giovanni in Laterano
p. 184,185; cat. 330
• Museo Barracco:
Funerary cippus
from Chiusi
cat. 133
• Musei Capitolini:
Female head
from Veio, votive deposit of Campetti
cat. 247
Male head
from Veio, votive deposit of Campetti
cat. 248
Oinochoe
from Tragliatella
cat. 208
Pedestal of offerer
from Sant'Omobono sacred area
cat. 301
Small new Year's flask
cat. 33
Tessera hospitalis
from Rome, sacred area of Sant'Omobono
p. 188; cat. 38
• Museo del Foro:
Small statue of an augur
from Rome, votive hoard of Lapis Niger
p. 180; cat. 146
• Museo Archeologico Nazionale di Villa Giulia:
Antiquarium of Falerii Veteres,
p. 522
Antiquarium of sculture,
p. 525
Antiquarium of Veio,
p. 525
The Castellani jewellery,
p. 528
The Emiciclo room,
p. 526
Aequipondium
from Cerveteri, Sant'Antonio
p. 497; cat. 287
Apollo, acroterial statue
from Veio, Portonaccio Temple
p. 35
Aryballos with dedicatory inscription to Turan
from Cerveteri (?)
p. 484; cat. 126
Attic black-figure Lydos kyathos
from Vulci, Osteria necropolis
cat. 179
Biconical vase
from Vulci, Tomb of the Bronze Chariot
p. 118; cat. 81.13
Blade of sward or of large knife
from Vulci, Osteria necropolis, Tomb of the Warrior
cat. 66
Boss
from Vignanello, Cupa necropolis
p. 470; cat. 98
"Botticella" askos
from Vulci, Tomb of the Bronze Chariot
p. 116; cat. 81.18
Bowl of the Pharaoh
from Palestrina, Bernardini Tomb
p. 217
Bucchero kotyle
from Cerveteri
p. 411
Bucchero olpe
from Cerveteri, San Paolo
p. 224; cat. 212
Cart
from Bisenzio, Olmo Bello necropolis
p. 210; cat. 14
Cart
from Bolsena
p. 76
Chalice with caryatids
from Palestrina, Barberini Tomb
p. 473
Chalices
from Vulci, Tomb of the Bronze Chariot
p. 121; cat. 81.37
Cinerary urn
from Bisenzio, Olmo Bello necropolis
p. 211; cat. 15
Couple of bracelets
from Vulci, Tomb of the Bronze Chariot
p. 120; cat. 81.29
Couples of hands
from Vulci, Tomb of the Bronze Chariot
p. 125; cat. 81.24
Couples of hands
from Vulci, Tomb of the Bronze Chariot
p. 125; cat. 81.25
Drinking bowl
from Palestrina, Bernardini Tomb

p. 110
Drinking bowl
from Palestrina, Bernardini Tomb
p. 126
Foot with Aule Vipienna's inscription
from Veio, Portonaccio sanctuary
p. 478; cat. 32.2
Gem with Tages
Castellani Collection
p. 529; cat. 325
Golden Kotyle
from Palestrina, Bernardini Tomb
pp. 42, 44; cat. 82
Group of the Ploughman
from Arezzo
p. 74; cat. 16
Handles of flabelli
from Palestrina, Barberini Tomb
p. 472
Head and part of the bust of a warrior
from Veio, Portonaccio sanctuary
p. 370; cat. 246
Head so-called "Malavolta"
from Veio, Portonaccio sanctuary
cat. 280
Hermes, acroterial statue
from Veio, Portonaccio Temple
p. 34
Helmet
from Vulci, Osteria necropolis,
Tomb of the Warrior
p. 228; cat. 61
Human figure statuette
from Vulci, Cavalupo necropolis
cat. 29.1
Kantharoi
from Vulci, Tomb of the Bronze
Chariot
p. 124; cat. 81.38
Kantharos
from Vulci, Tomb of the Bronze
Chariot
p. 118; cat. 81.14
Kotyle
from Vulci, Tomb of the Bronze
Chariot
p. 118; cat. 81.39
Laminae with inscriptionsi
from Pyrgi, near Santa Severa
p. 489; cat. 255
Lebes with snake protomes
from Palestrina, Bernardini Tomb
p. 44; cat. 83
Lid of pyxis
from Cerveteri
p. 418; cat. 235
Miniature basket
from Vulci, Cavalupo necropolis
cat. 29.3
Oenotrian-Geometric jug
from Vulci, Osteria necropolis
p. 67
Olla
from Vulci, Tomb of the Bronze
Chariot
p. 119; cat. 81.33
Olla
from Vulci, Tomb of the Bronze
Chariot
p. 119; cat. 81.35
Male portrait
from Cerveteri, Manganello
sanctuary
p. 49; cat. 304
Nikosthenic amphora
p. 148; cat. 183
Pair of greaves
from Vulci, Osteria necropolis,
Tomb of the Warrior
cat. 64
Pair of plaques
from Vulci, Osteria necropolis,
Tomb of the Warrior
p. 229; cat. 62
Parade shield
from Vulci, Osteria necropolis,
Tomb of the Warrior
cat. 63
Poculum with inscription
from Veio, sanctuary of Campetti
p. 252; cat. 297.2
Proto-Corinthian kylix
from Vulci, Tomb of the Bronze
Chariot
p. 119; cat. 81.40
Red-figure Attic kylix
from Cerveteri, area of the sanctuary
of Hercules
cat. 282
Rhodian aryballoi
from Vulci, Tomb of the Bronze
Chariot
p. 120; cat. 81.41
Ribbed cup
from Vulci, Tomb of the Bronze
Chariot
p. 121; cat. 81.36
Ring
from Vulci, Tomb of the Bronze
Chariot
p. 123; cat. 81.30
Ritual "stool"
from Vulci, Cavalupo necropolis
cat. 29.2
Sarcophagus
from Tarquinia, Cavalluccio
necropolis
cat. 295
Sarcophagus of the Married Couple
from Cerveteri
p. 24
Scarab
from Falerii, Montarano
necropolis,
Tomba 17
cat. 35
Small amphora
from Monte Acuto, Formello
cat. 254
Small jug with dedicatory inscription
from Veio, sanctuary of
Portonaccio
p. 252; cat. 298.2
Spear tips
from Vulci, Osteria necropolis,
Tomb of the Warrior
cat. 65
Spools
from Veio, Casale del Fosso
necropolis, Tomb 870
p. 478
Statue of Latona with Apollo
from Veio, Portonaccio Temple
p. 371; cat. 219
Statuette of Aeneas and Anchises
from Veio, Campetti sanctuary
cat. 298.1
Statuette of offerer
from Veio, Portonaccio sanctuary
p. 236; cat. 297.1
Tripod
from Vulci, Tomb of the Bronze
Chariot
p. 117; cat. 81.15
Tripod
from Vulci, Tomb of the Bronze
Chariot
p. 117; cat. 81.16
Two-headed kantharos with Heracles and Onphale
from Cerveteri (?)
p. 448
Votive model of temple
from Vulci
p. 333
• Museo Nazionale Romano:
Female bust
from Ariccia
p. 203
Female figure
from Ariccia
p. 202
• Museo Preistorico ed Etnografico
L. Pigorini:
Capeduncula
from the hoard of Coste
del Marano
p. 20; cat. 4.2
Fibula
from Coste del Marano, hoard
cat. 4.1
• Sinopoli Collection:
Black-figure column-krater
cat. 188
Small-column krater
cat. 186
•Private Collection:
Spindle
from Vulci, Osteria necropolis
cat. 251
The Foro Romano area,
p. 319

Rovigo
• Museo Civico:
Comb
from Frattesina di Fratta Polesine,
hoard
cat. 121

San Giovenale (Viterbo)
Remains of houses in the Borgo,
p. 297, 318

Saint Petersburg
• The State Hermitage Museum:
Cinerary statue of young man
from Perugia
pp. 16, 19; cat. 144

Santa Maria Capua Vetere
• Museo Archeologico Nazionale
dell'Antica Capua:
Biconical olla
from Santa Maria Capua Vetere,
Tomb N.M.1/86
p. 159
Bowl
from Santa Maria Capua Vetere,
Fornaci Tomb 722
p. 160
Fibula
from Santa Maria Capua Vetere,
Fornaci Tomb 363
p. 161
Fibula
from Santa Maria Capua Vetere,
Fornaci Tomb 365
p. 161
Gorgon-head antefix
from Santa Maria Capua Vetere
p. 156
Laconian krater
from Santa Maria Capua Vetere,
Tomb 1526
p. 165; cat. 187
Pottery grave goods
from Santa Maria Capua Vetere,
Fornaci Tomb 312
p. 162

Sarteano
• Museo Civico Archeologico:
Female canopic vase
from Sarteano, Macchiapiana
necropolis
cat. 132.2
Male canopic vase
from Sarteano, Macchiapiana
necropolis
cat. 132.1
Small clay model of two-edged hatchet
from Sarteano, Macchiapiana
necropolis
cat. 132.2

Schaffhausen
• Museum zu Allerheiligen,
Sammlung Ebnöther:
Fibula with plastic decoration
from Vulci (?)
p. 468; cat. 90

Siena
• Museo Archeologico Nazionale:
Helmet
from Murlo, Poggio Civitate
cat. 67

Sigean
• Musée des Corbières:
Slab
from the oppidum of Pech Maho
p. 486; cat. 257

Sovana (Grosseto)
View of the cavone,
p. 310
Views of the Ildebranda Tomb,
pp. 340, 341

• Sydney
Nicholson Museum:
Bowl with female head,
Florence Painter 4035
p. 449

Tarquinia
• Museo Archeologico Nazionale:
Black-figure Laconian bowl
from Gravisca
cat. 46
Bocchoris necklace
from Tarquinia
p. 114
Bocchoris situla
from Tarquinia
p. 115
Bowl with dedicatory inscription to
Aphrodite (fragment)

from the sanctuary of Gravisca
p. 107; cat. 42
Bowl with dedicatory inscription to Demetra (fragment)
from the sanctuary of Gravisca
p. 107; cat. 43
Bowl with dedicatory inscription to Hera (fragment)
from the sanctuary of Gravisca
p. 107; cat. 44
Bruschi Tomb, fresco
from Tarquinia, Monterozzi necropolis
cat. 315
Cart
from Tarquinia, Monterozzi necropolis
p. 55
Fragment of Laconian krater
from Gravisca
cat. 45
Fragments of oinochoe
from Gravisca
cat. 252
Glazed ostrich egg
from Montalto di Castro (?)
p. 348; cat. 118
Italo-Geometric kotyle
from Tarquinia
p. 144; cat. 185.2
Italo-Geometric oinochoe
p. 144; cat. 185
Leg-shaped balsam
from Tarquinia
p. 412
Leg-shaped votive offering
p. 490; cat. 308
Mask of a satyr
from Tarquinia
p. 241; cat. 296.2
Mask of Dionysius
from Tarquinia
p. 240; cat. 296.3
Mask of Silenus
from Tarquinia
p. 240; cat. 296.1
Nuragic incense-boat
from the sanctuary of Gravisca
p. 97; cat. 39
Oinochoe from the Group of the Phantom
from Tarquinia
p. 453
Sarcophagus of Laris Pulena
from Tarquinia, Monterozzi
p. 481, 488
Sarcophagus of the "Magnate"
from Tarquinia, Partunus Tomb
pp. 248, 249; cat. 294
Sarcophagus of the Priest
p. 233; cat. 293
Semispherical bowl
from Tarquinia, Monterozzi, dolium Tomb M7
p. 394; cat. 177
Statuette of Aphrodite
from Gravisca
p. 101; cat. 40
Statuette of Aphrodite
from the sanctuary of Gravisca
p. 101; cat. 41
Tablet with inscriptions
p. 496; cat. 262
Tomb of the Triclinium
from Tarquinia; interior, left wall (*lyre player*) and right wall (*dancer*)
pp. 360, 361
Two halves of an ostrich egg
from Vetulonia, Circolo del Monile d'Argento
cat. 117
Votive terra-cotta male head
from Tarquinia, Ara della Regina sanctuary
p. 387; cat. 305
Tomb of Orcus I
Velia Spurinai
p. 137
Tomb of the Augurs
Detail with priest
p. 226
Rear wall,
p. 356
Tomb of the Bulls, rear wall of the eastern chamber
The ambush of Troilus by Achille
p. 352
Tomb of the Hunting and Fishing
Real wall of the second chambers,
pp. 358, 359
The diver
p. 200
Tomb of the Jugglers, real wall,
p. 357
Tomb of the Lionesses, real wall
Female dancer and dancers
pp. 354, 355
Tomb of the Shields
*Symposium scene*s
pp. 132, 133, 263
Tomb of the Ship, left wall,
p. 362
View of the Anina Tomb,
p. 270

Toledo
• Museum of Art:
Hydria
p. 434; cat. 52

Trevignano Romano
• Museo Civico:
Tubular element (fragment of candelabra?)
from Trevignano Romano, Olivetello necropolis, Annesi Piacentini Tomb
cat. 110

Tübingen
• Institut für Klassische Archäologie des Eberhard-Karls-Universität:
Pitcher
from the Falerii area
p. 409
Pottery fragment
from Rasinius' workshop
p. 276; cat. 158

Tuscania
View,
pp. 28, 29

Vatican City
• Museo Gregoriano Etrusco:
Room of the Bronzes and Room of the Italiot Vases,
p. 512
Amphora of the La Tolfa Group
cat. 214
Bowl of Phoenician make
dalla tomba Regolini Galassi
cat. 30
Disc fibula
from the Regolini Galassi Tomb
p. 513
Exekias' amphora
pp. 510, 511
Gold bracelets
from the Regolini Galassi Tomb
p. 513
Sarcophagus of magistrate
from Tuscania
p. 227
Statue dedicated by Ahal Trutilis
from Todi, Monte Santo
p. 380

Veio
Altar on the area of the Portonaccio Temple,
p. 300

Venice
• Centro Studi e Ricerche Ligabue
Scudo circolare
cat. 60

Verucchio
• Museo Archeologico:
Handle of flabellum
from Verucchio, Tomb 89
p. 472
Wooden throne
from Verucchio, Tomb 89
p. 174

Viareggio
• Civici Musei di Villa Paolina:
Sickle with handle grip
from Camaiore, Colle Le Banche
cat. 17

Vienna
• Kunsthistorisches Museum:
Hydria with Heracles and Busiris, Busiris Painter
p. 431; cat. 213

Viterbo
• Museo Archeologico:
Biga
from Ischia di Castro, Poggi di Castro necropolis
cat. 75
Mosaic of Musarna
p. 305
• Palazzo Comunale, Sala Regia
Noah Showing to His Sons the Twelve Colonies
p. 506
Walls of Santa Maria di Falerii,
p. 290

Volterra
• Museo Guarnacci:
Bracelet
from Volterra, Poggio alle Croci, Tomb of the Warrior
cat. 12.10
Chain with brooch
from Volterra, Gesseri di Berignone
cat. 94
Chest for cinerary urn
from Volterra
cat. 316
Dolium
from Volterra, Badia dei Camaldolesi
cat. 13.2
Double flask
from Volterra, Poggio alle Croci, Tomb of the Warrior
p. 64; cat. 12.2
Fibula with overlaid bowl
from Volterra, Badia dei Camaldolesi
cat. 13.13
Fibula awith overlaid bowl
from Volterra, Badia dei Camaldolesi
cat. 13.14
Fibula awith overlaid bowl
from Volterra, Badia dei Camaldolesi
cat. 13.15
Fibula with overlaid bowl
from Volterra, Badia dei Camaldolesi
cat. 13.16
Flask
from Volterra, Badia dei Camaldolesi
cat. 13.20
Fragment of band
from Volterra, Poggio alle Croci, Tomb of the Warrior
cat. 12.14
Fragment of bow-spring of incense-boat fibula
from Volterra, Badia dei Camaldolesi
cat. 13.10
Fragment of bronze incense-boat fibula
from Volterra, Badia dei Camaldolesi
cat. 13.8
Fragmeni of bronze incense-boat fibula
from Volterra, Badia dei Camaldolesi
cat. 13.9
Gold leaf
from Volterra, Badia dei Camaldolesi
cat. 13.25
Group of spirals
from Volterra, Poggio alle Croci, Tomb of the Warrior
cat. 12.17
Helmet
from Volterra, Poggio alle Croci, Tomb of the Warrior
p. 65; cat. 12.1
Hemispheric bowl
from Volterra, Poggio alle Croci, Tomb of the Warrior
p. 65; cat. 12.4
Hollow leech-type fibula
from Volterra, Badia dei Camaldolesi
cat. 13.4
Horse bit
from Volterra, Badia dei Camaldolesi
cat. 13.24
Horse bit